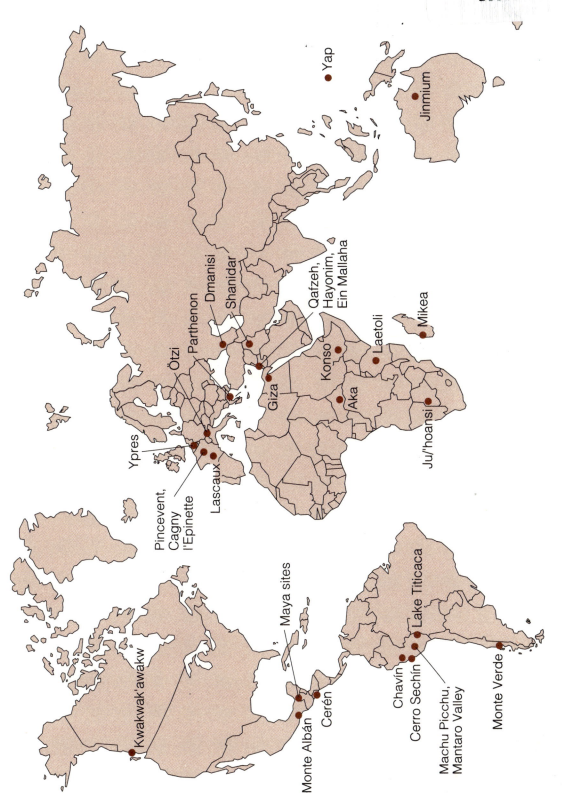

Yap

Jinmium

Dmanisi

Parthenon

Shanidar

Ötzi

Qafzeh,
Hayonim,
Ein Mallaha

Mikea

Laetoli

Konso

Giza

Aka

Ju/'hoansi

Ypres

Pincevent,
Cagny
l'Epinette

Lascaux

Maya sites

Lake Titicaca

Kwakwak'awakw

Monte Albán

Cerén

Chavín

Cerro Sechín

Machu Picchu,
Mantaro Valley

Monte Verde

www.wadsworth.com

www.wadsworth.com is the World Wide Web site for Thomson Wadsworth and is your direct source to dozens of online resources.

At *www.wadsworth.com* you can find out about supplements, demonstration software, and student resources. You can also send email to many of our authors and preview new publications and exciting new technologies.

www.wadsworth.com
Changing the way the world learns®

THOMSON
WADSWORTH
™

Anthropology Editor: Lin Marshall
Development Editor: Sherry Symington
Assistant Editor: Nicole Root
Editorial Assistant: Kelly McMahon
Technology Project Manager: Dee Dee Zobian
Marketing Manager: Wendy Gordon
Marketing Assistant: Annabelle Yang
Advertising Project Manager: Linda Yip
Project Manager, Editorial Production: Catherine Morris
Art Director: Maria Epes
Print Buyer: Barbara Britton
Permissions Editor: Sarah Harkrader

Production Service: Melanie Field, Strawberry Field Publishing
Text and Cover Designer: Gopa
Photo Researcher: Terri Wright
Copy Editor: Carol Lombardi
Illustrators: Network Graphics, Dennis O'Brien, Diana
Compositor: Stratford Publishing Services
Salles, and Nicholas Amorosi
Cover Image: Peabody Museum, Harvard University
Cover Printer: Coral Graphic Services, Inc.
Interior Printer: Quebecor World/Versailles

For more information about our products, contact us at
Thomson Learning Academic Resource Center
1-800-423-0563

For permission to use material from this text or product, submit a request online at **http://www.thomsonrights.com**. Any additional questions about permissions can be submitted by email to **thomsonrights@thomson.com**.

Library of Congress Control Number: 2004112365

ISBN 0-15-505899-1

Thomson Higher Education
10 Davis Drive
Belmont, CA 94002-3098
USA

Asia (including India)
Thomson Learning
5 Shenton Way #01-01
UIC Building
Singapore 068808

Australia/New Zealand
Thomson Learning
102 Dodds Street
Southbank, Victoria 3006
Australia

Canada
Nelson
1120 Birchmount Road
Toronto, Ontario M1K 5G4
Canada

Europe/Middle East/Africa
Thomson Learning
High Holborn House
50/51 Bedford Row
London WC1R 4LR
United Kingdom

Latin America
Thomson Learning
Seneca, 53
Colonia Polanco
11560 Mexico D.F.
Mexico

Spain/Portugal
Paraninfo
Calle Magallanes, 25
28015 Madrid, Spain

Archaeology

FOURTH EDITION

David Hurst Thomas
American Museum of Natural History

Robert L. Kelly
University of Wyoming

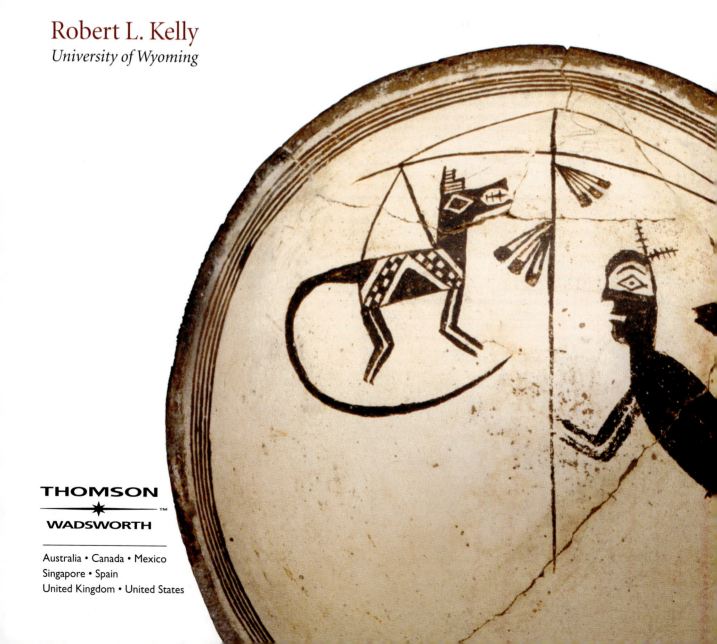

THOMSON

WADSWORTH

Australia • Canada • Mexico
Singapore • Spain
United Kingdom • United States

Brief Contents

Contents

CHAPTER 9   THE DIMENSIONS OF ARCHAEOLOGY: TIME, SPACE, AND FORM   206

CHAPTER 10   TAPHONOMY, EXPERIMENTAL ARCHAEOLOGY, AND ETHNOARCHAEOLOGY   233

CHAPTER 11   PEOPLE, PLANTS, AND ANIMALS IN THE PAST   265

CHAPTER 16   HISTORICAL ARCHAEOLOGY: INSIGHTS ON AMERICAN HISTORY   408

Preface

ARCHAEOLOGY, Fourth Edition, is a user-friendly introduction to archaeology: what it is, who does it, and why we should care about it. This text addresses archaeological methods and theory and yet it departs, in some important ways, from the standard introductory textbook.

Students tell us that they sometimes don't bother reading the introductory textbooks they've purchased—whether the books are about archaeology, chemistry, or whatever. We've heard several reasons for this paradox: The instructor covers exactly the same material, using the same examples as the text—so why bother reading what you can get condensed in a lecture? Or their textbooks are deadly dull, written in arcane academic jargon that nobody (including the professor) really understands. Still others tell us that they take an archaeology course just because it sounds like a fun way to fulfill a distribution requirement—but the text actually has nothing to say to them.

We want students to know that we've heard them.

PERSONAL EXAMPLES, HIGH-INTEREST TOPICS

In most archaeology texts, the approach is fairly encyclopedic and dispassionate. But we can't do it that way. To be sure, modern archaeology is a specialized and complicated academic discipline, with plenty of concepts, several bodies of theory, and a huge array of analytical methods—all things we'd like students to learn about. But we think that the best way for students to begin to understand archaeology (or any subject, for that matter) is through a few well-chosen, extended, personalized examples—stories that show how archaeologists have worked through actual problems in the field and in the lab. So that's the approach we take here.

Writing an introductory textbook is not easy. We must provide a solid foundation for students who intend to become professional archaeologists. This requires a thorough review of the discipline, including all its major concepts and jargon. But we must also write for the many students who will *not* become professional archaeologists. Accordingly, we picked many of the book's topics with the non-professional in mind.

As it turns out, these are the very subjects that the budding career archaeologist should know. Almost all the chapters, for instance, include sidebars titled "Archaeological Ethics," which touch upon sensitive subjects that influence both the professional archaeologist and the public (who pays for most of the archaeological research in the United States). Many archaeological texts avoid these sensitive issues, such as the excavation of the dead, repatriation of artifacts, and working with descendant communities. But we think that these are precisely the issues that matter most to students and to instructors, and so we've not backed away from them.

In fact, instructors tell us they have used previous editions of this text precisely because their students will actually *read* it.

ABOUT THIS EDITION

The first edition of *Archaeology* was published back in 1979, and each succeeding edition focused on retaining the coverage and writing style that users praised and ensuring that the book reflected up-to-the-minute changes in the discipline.

Confronted with the present revision, David Thomas decided one person just couldn't adequately cover the field anymore, and he invited Robert Kelly to join in the project. These two first met more than 30 years ago, when Thomas was excavating Gatecliff Shelter in Nevada and Kelly was a gangly, enthusiastic high school kid. They continued to work together for several years, after which their careers diverged. When the time came to expand the authorship, Thomas turned to Kelly as the obvious choice for a co-author.

This new partnership means that this fourth edition is more than a polishing and updating of the old. The better parts of the third edition have survived here, and a newer, fresher perspective has emerged.

Aids to Learning, Old and New

Archaeological Ethics We are especially proud of this new series of sidebars (in Chapters 2 through 17), which address critical issues of archaeological ethics, such as the relationship between industrial development and archaeology (should Peru build a cable car to Machu Picchu?), the selling of artifacts in electronic auction houses, the excavation of human skeletons, and the ownership of sacred sites. We think that students will find these topics thought provoking (and these essays could easily form the basis of writing assignments or group discussions). Reviewers were enthusiastically unanimous in their support for this new feature. "Keep them at all costs," wrote one.

Looking Closer A popular feature from the third edition, "Looking Closer" sidebars cover ancillary topics in each chapter. In the chapter on federal archaeological legislation, a Looking Closer sidebar explores an ARPA violations case that led to the arrest of a looter who was later charged with conspiracy to commit murder; in Chapter 17 (which explores preserving America's heritage), a sidebar discusses the protection of archaeological sites in Iraq before the recent war. We've carried over some sidebars from the third edition, but many are new. Some tell students what sort of equipment they need for survey and excavation, what courses they might take, or how they can help catch looters. Others look at the lighter side of archaeology, such as how sites get their names, or they give personal glimpses into fieldwork—what it's like to do survey or ethnoarchaeology. Others discuss origin and usage of terms such as "Eskimo" and "Bushmen."

Profile of an Archaeologist In Chapter 1, "In His/Her Own Words" biographies recount the history of archaeology in the United States. But, concerned that these historical sketches did not address the full range of contemporary archaeology, we added five "Profile of an Archaeologist" sidebars to emphasize the diversity of today's working archaeologists and to illustrate the varied ways in which archaeologists can make a living.

The above features combine with the following learning aids to help students master this complex, fascinating discipline:

- Chapter Outlines at the beginning of each chapter.
- Bulleted Chapter Summaries at the end of each chapter.
- Running glossaries in each chapter (with glossary terms defined at the bottom of the page on which the term is introduced) plus an alphabetized Glossary at the end of the text.
- Photographs and figures that were carefully chosen or created to give students a visual sense of a case study and to act as integrated pedagogical aids to the text.
- Additional Readings at the end of each chapter, including articles and books that will be comprehensible to students taking an introductory course.
- Online Resources at the end of each chapter to remind students of resources available—including practice quizzes and exercises—on the text's Web site.
- A chapter-by-chapter Bibliography that provides an easy way to find references and additional reading on each chapter's subjects. We have eschewed placing in-text citations, but students will still be able to locate material discussed in the text, as well as additional readings, in a chapter's bibliography. Page references for the few longer quotes that appear are noted in the relevant bibliographic entry.

A Distinctive Approach

The following strategies all contribute to a fuller, more up-to-date exploration of the field:

Discussions of archaeological objects in context You'll notice that there is no chapter on "archaeological objects"—stone tools, ceramics, metals, architecture, and so forth (and what archaeologists can do with them). We've never found this encyclopedic approach especially useful in teaching, because it tends to encourage students to simply memorize a laundry list of techniques without context. Instead, we've embedded and contextualized discussions of things like stone tools and ceramics in other substantive examples. For example, we talk about pottery—its manufacture and basic constituents—in Chapter 13, which deals with using petrographic analysis to track down trade networks. This presentation ensures that students learn about these basic archaeological objects in ways that carry significance for them—so that they see why, for instance, it might be useful to know where a sherd's temper comes from.

Expanded coverage of key methods/technologies topics We've expanded coverage to reflect the growing importance of certain methods and technologies. For instance, geographic information systems (GIS) technology, which appeared in a sidebar in the third edition, has its own section in Chapter 5. And Chapter 8's discussion of dating techniques gives more space to trapped-charge dating methods, such as optically stimulated luminescence. We've also completely rewritten the material on stratigraphy to emphasize geoarchaeology and site formation processes (Chapter 7). Chapter 10 updates explanations of taphonomy, experimental archaeology, and ethnoarchaeology with new examples and a discussion of the difference between analogy and middle-range theory.

New focus of chapter on neo-evolutionary approaches Chapter 15 now focuses on the ways in which different archaeological paradigms can help us achieve a more complete understanding of two key transitions in world prehistory: the origins of agriculture and the origins of the state. We did this for two reasons. First, given that this introductory course may very well be the only archaeology class that a student ever takes, we need to communicate at least some appreciation for world prehistory (even if the course focuses on methods). Second, we want students to know that different paradigms are not simply different stories about the past, but are different perspectives that contribute to our understanding of the past. Too often, students see debates about different theoretical paradigms as an academic Super Bowl—winner takes all, and the loser goes home with its tail between its legs. We prefer to emphasize the compatibility of various paradigms—even if they sometimes appear to conflict.

Streamlined presentation We reduced the number of chapters from 22 to 18, making the text more amenable to semesters and quarters. Cutting chapters meant condensing some topics, relocating vital discussions, and removing other material. For example, we moved a discussion of site seasonality into the chapter on zooarchaeology and paleoethnobotany. So, if you think we've left something out from the third edition, look around first: It may be in a different chapter.

Balanced Coverage: Depth, Breadth, Theory

The text is not encyclopedic, but it does cover the field in a comprehensive manner. Given the background knowledge that a first- or second-year college student brings to an introductory course, this text strikes a first-rate balance among the different directions that archaeologists can take. We do believe that this text is the most readable one available and also the most "intellectual": We know of no other textbook that provides extended discussions of theoretical paradigms, the nature of science (what it can and cannot do) and of the humanities, and the intellectual process of learning about the past. Students will learn a bit about the Enlightenment, the origins of postmodern perspectives, and evolutionary thinking in these pages. And students can apply the topics in this textbook—especially those in the first three chapters—to virtually any area of study.

Expanded Geographic Coverage

Many of the examples used in this text are drawn from the archaeology of western North America. Between us, we've spent seven decades working there and, frankly, it's what we know best. But we've expanded the geographic coverage as well, drawing upon work in the eastern United States, Central and South America, Egypt and the Near East, Madagascar, France, Australia, Micronesia, and other places. Although the text is focused, it is not provincial—and should thereby inspire classroom discussions of research projects from around the world.

All in all, we think you'll find this text is one that both instructors and students will appreciate.

ORGANIZATION OF THE TEXT

We constructed this text so that various ideas build upon one another. We know that each archaeologist teaches his or her introductory course differently, but you should know that many chapters cross-reference material discussed in other chapters. We note each instance within the text.

Chapter 1 begins with a discussion of the Kennewick Man case—a purposeful selection, because this textbook makes an explicit point of discussing the ethical matters that confront modern archaeology. We thus use the Kennewick controversy to set the tone (and we return to that subject in Chapters 17 and 18). The remainder of Chapter 1 addresses the history of American archaeology, with an emphasis on several individual archaeologists who have defined the field.

In Chapters 2 and 3, we relate archaeology to the rest of anthropology and wrestle with the diversity of theoretical paradigms evident in contemporary archaeology. We've introduced this diversity not as the interbraided stream that it really is—with all its side channels, backwaters, eddies, and periodic flash floods—but rather in terms of simple dichotomies: Science and humanism, adaptive and ideational approaches, processual and postprocessual archaeology. We hope that our discussion of paradigms and of low-, middle-, and high-range theory in Chapter 3 will help organize the rest of your course. This somewhat simplified presentation provides an easy entry into the diversity of contemporary archaeology. And rather than come down on the side of processual or postprocessual archaeology, we take a centrist position that we believe characterizes the majority of working archaeologists today: There is something to be gained from looking at prehistory through both of these paradigms—each of which is well suited for answering a particular kind of question.

Chapters 4 through 6 provide the nuts and bolts of archaeology, explaining how archaeologists go about doing surface survey, using remote sensing equipment, and excavating sites. We give students some sense of how much fun fieldwork can be, but we also deal with issues such as sampling bias, how a survey's on-the-ground procedures can bias results, the cost of dating methods, and the utility of GIS to a postprocessual perspective.

In Chapter 7 we discuss the field of geoarchaeology, with a decided emphasis upon site formation processes. We believe that this subject is more important than its usual treatment suggests and that it deserves a good chunk of a chapter. This chapter also covers archaeological stratigraphy, beginning with the Law of Superposition, and shows students how a site's stratigraphy can be "read" to provide a context to the artifacts contained there.

Chapter 8 covers dating methods used in prehistoric and historic archaeology. The range of dating technology seems to increase annually, and we had to make some tough choices about what to include. The major purpose of this chapter is not to write an encyclopedia of available methods, but instead to provide enough information about key techniques so that students can relate dating technology to ancient human behavior.

Chapter 9 discusses various archaeological concepts—types, cultures, and phases—that help construct large-scale patterns in space and time. Our goal is to help the student see the world as an archaeologist views it, as an ever-changing spatial and temporal mosaic of material culture.

The next chapters consider how archaeologists go about breathing some anthropological life into this spatial and temporal mosaic—how they actually use material remains to infer something about past human behavior.

Chapter 10 is about middle-range theory—how it is different from standard analogy and how archaeologists construct it through taphonomic, experimental, and ethnoarchaeological research. Our goal here is to convince students that archaeologists don't just make stuff up, but instead give plenty of thought to how they infer ancient behavior from material objects and their contexts.

Chapter 11 recounts how archaeologists reconstruct diet from faunal and floral remains and how they infer hunting strategies and symbolic meanings attributed to the natural world.

Chapter 12 considers what we can learn—about diet, disease, and workload—from human skeletal remains and explores the relatively new field of molecular archaeology.

Chapter 13 shows how archaeologists can reconstruct social and political systems of the past and looks at gender, kinship, and social hierarchies.

Chapter 14 presents how archaeologists address the symbolic meanings once attached to the material remains; here, we look at the nature of symbols and what archaeologists can realistically hope to learn about them.

After describing (and rejecting) unilineal thinking about evolution, Chapter 15 addresses two major evolutionary transitions in human history: the origins of agriculture and the origins of the state.

Chapter 16 explores historical archaeology, especially those aspects that set the field apart from prehistoric archaeology—the ability to uncover "hidden history," the ability to provide a near-forensic analysis of historical events, and the ability to present alternative perspectives on American history.

Chapter 17 examines the legal structure of modern archaeology, emphasizing the field of cultural resource management (how it came to be and the critical role it plays in archaeology today). This chapter also covers the subjects of reburial and repatriation in some detail.

Chapter 18 looks at the future of archaeology, especially the ways in which archaeologists apply their knowledge to contemporary problems. We conclude by discussing the increased involvement of indigenous peoples in the archaeology of themselves and asking whether we are on the brink of another revolution—one that might produce a newer "new" archaeology?

Supplemental Materials

This text also comes with a strong supplements program to help instructors use their class time most effectively and to aid students in mastering the material. (Each item is followed by its ISBN number.)

Online Instructor's Manual with Test Bank (0155059084): The instructor's manual offers chapter outlines, learning objectives, key terms and concepts, and lecture suggestions. The test bank consists of 40–60 test questions per chapter, including multiple-choice, true/false, and essay questions.

Doing Fieldwork: Archaeological Demonstrations CD-ROM (0155059297): Granted that students can learn field techniques only from actually participating, this CD shows professional archaeologists involved in various digs (many of which are referenced in the text), illustrates field techniques, gives students perspective about what they're learning, reinforces concepts and techniques via live examples, and encourages students to participate in a dig themselves. The presentation is organized by the main techniques that one uses on a dig. Users are taken through each step automatically or can navigate to any point via the navigation bar. Students review illustrations and video clips of each technique. After reviewing a step in the dig process, students are taken to "Check points," which are concept questions about each step of the dig. Students can see the answers, receive their score, and e-mail the score to the instructor.

Archaeology Modules: New class-enhancement modules will be available to bundle with your text.

JoinIn on TurningPoint® (0495004030): Instructors can transform their lectures into an interactive student experience with JoinIn. Combined with a choice of keypad systems, JoinIn turns your PowerPoint® application into audience response software. With a click on a hand-held device, students can respond to multiple-choice questions, short polls, interactive exercises, and peer review questions. Instructors can also take attendance, check student comprehension of concepts, collect student demographics to better assess student needs, and even administer quizzes. In addition, instructors receive interactive text-specific slide sets that they can modify and merge with any PowerPoint lecture slides. This tool is available to qualified adopters. More information is available at http://turningpoint.thomson learningconnections.com.

ExamView Computerized Test Bank (0155059459): Create, deliver, and customize tests and study guides (both print and online) in minutes with this easy-to-use assessment and tutorial system. *ExamView* offers both a Quick Test Wizard and an Online Test Wizard that guide instructors step-by-step through the process of creating tests, and its unique WYSIWYG capability allows you to see the test you are creating on the screen exactly as it will print or display on-line. You can build tests of up to 250 questions using up to 12 question types. Using *ExamView*'s complete word processing capabilities, you can enter an unlimited number of new questions or edit existing questions.

Companion Website (015505959): The companion website includes the following for each chapter of the text: tutorial practice quizzes that can be scored and e-mailed to the instructor, Internet links and exercises, flashcards of the text's glossary, crossword puzzles, essay questions, learning objectives, and much more. From this site, students can link to the Wadsworth exclusive "Earthwatch Journal," "Applying Anthropology," and "The Latest Dirt" websites.

Who Helped Out?

Despite the personal flavor of these pages, this text was created by more than four hands. Many people helped out, and we'd like to thank them here.

The overall presentation was vastly improved by a contingent of top-notch colleagues and friends who provided advice and critical reviews of the manuscript. We are particularly grateful to Jack Broughton (University of Utah), Robert Gargett (San Jose State University),

Kevin Johnston (Ohio State University), Janet Levy (University of North Carolina, Charlotte), Heather McInnis (University of Oregon), Robert Preucel (University of Pennsylvania), Ralph Rowlett (University of Missouri), and Mary Vermillion (University of Illinois, Chicago), each of whom slogged through the revised manuscript and contributed immeasurably to the final product. We are most grateful for their advice and suggestions.

Many others commented on portions of chapters or entire chapters, answered questions, provided photographs or text for sidebars, and checked facts for us. We gratefully acknowledge timely and sometimes-detailed assistance on this and previous editions from

David Anderson (University of Tennessee)
Roger Anyon (Pima County, Arizona)
Bettina Arnold (University of Wisconsin, Milwaukee)
George Bagwell (Colorado Mountain College)
Doug Bamforth (University of Colorado)
Pat Barker (Bureau of Land Management, Nevada)
Ofer Bar-Yosef (Harvard University)
Mary C. Beaudry (Boston University)
Jeffrey Behm (University of Wisconsin, Oshkosh)
Lewis Binford (Truman State University)
Michael Blakey (College of William and Mary)
Colonel Matthew Bogdanos (U.S. Marine Corps)
Charles A. Bollong (University of Arizona)
Rob Bonnichsen (Center for the Study of the First Americans, Texas A&M University)
Bruce Bradley (Exeter University, UK)
Steven Brandt (University of Florida)
Robert Brooks (Oklahoma State Archaeologist)
Peter Brosius (University of Georgia)
Margaret Sabom Bruchz (Blinn College)
Jane Buikstra (University of New Mexico)
Richard Burger (Yale University)
Virginia Butler (Portland State University)
Catherine Cameron (University of Colorado)
Robert Carneiro (American Museum of Natural History)
Philip J. Carr (University of South Alabama)
Beverly Chiarulli (Indiana University of Pennsylvania)
Cheryl Claassen (Appalachian State University)
C. William Clewlow (Ancient Enterprises)
Margaret Conkey (University of California, Berkeley)
John Cornelison (National Park Service)
The late Don Crabtree
George Crothers (University of Kentucky)
Jay Custer (University of Delaware)
Hester Davis (formerly Arkansas State Archaeologist)
William Davis (formerly University of California, Davis)
Kathleen Deagan (Florida State Museum of Natural History)
Jeffrey Dean (University of Arizona)

Rob DeSalle (American Museum of Natural History)
Christophe Desantes (University of Missouri)
Phil DiBlasi (University of Louisville)
William Dickinson (University of Arizona)
Tom Dillehay (Vanderbilt University)
Diana DiZerega-Wall (City College of New York)
William Doelle (Desert Archaeology, Inc.)
Kurt Dongoske (Zuni Cultural Resource Enterprises)
Sam Drucker (Bureau of Land Management, Wyoming)
Jeffrey Eighmy (Colorado State University)
Robert Elston (formerly Intermountain Research)
James Enloe (University of Iowa)
Clark Erickson (University of Pennsylvania)
George Esber (Miami University)
T. J. Ferguson (Anthropological Research, Tucson)
Terry Fifield (U.S. Forest Service, Alaska)
Ben Fitzhugh (University of Washington)
Kent V. Flannery (University of Michigan)
Don Fowler (University of Nevada, Reno)
Anne Fox (University of Texas, San Antonio)
Richard Fox (University of South Dakota)
Julie Francis (Wyoming Department of Transportation)
George Frison (University of Wyoming)
Ervan Garrison (University of Georgia)
Joan Gero (American University)
Diane Gifford-Gonzalez (University of California, Santa Cruz)
Dean Goodman (University of Miami, Japan Division)
Martha Graham (National Park Service)
Donald K. Grayson (University of Washington)
David Grimaldi (American Museum of Natural History)
Donny Hamilton (Texas A&M University)
The late Marvin Harris
Charles Hastings (Central Michigan University)
Christine Hastorf (University of California, Berkeley)
William Haviland (University of Vermont)
Brian Hayden (Simon Fraser University)
Michelle Hegmon (Arizona State University)
Kim Hill (University of New Mexico)

Matthew G. Hill (Iowa State University)
Robert Hitchcock (University of Nebraska)
Richard Holmer (Idaho State University)
Andrea A. Hunter (Northern Arizona University)
Tony Hynes (Danville Area Community College)
The late Cynthia Irwin-Williams
Steve Jackson (University of Wyoming)
Gregory Johnson (Hunter College of CUNY)
Rosemary Joyce (University of California, Berkeley)
John Kantner (Georgia State University)
Barry D. Kass (Orange County Community College, SUNY)
William Kelso (Jamestown Rediscovery Archaeological Project)
Thomas King (National Park Service)
Keith Kintigh (Arizona State University)
Vernon James Knight, Jr. (University of Alabama)
Clea Koff (independent scholar)
Stephen Kowalewski (University of Georgia)
Steve Kuhn (University of Arizona)
Chapurukha Kusimba (Field Museum)
The late Charles Lange
Clark Spencer Larsen (Ohio State University)
Robert Leonard (University of New Mexico)
Mark Leone (University of Maryland)
Barry Lewis (University of Illinois, Champaign-Urbana)
David Lewis-Williams (University of Witwatersrand)
William Lipe (Washington State University)
Dorothy Lippert (Smithsonian Institution)
Sharon Long (Wyoming State Historic Preservation Office)
Diana Loren (Peabody Museum, Harvard)
The late Scotty MacNeish
David B. Madsen (formerly Utah State Archaeologist)
Joyce Marcus (University of Michigan)
Alexander Marshack (Harvard University)
Fiona Marshall (Washington University)
Patrick E. Martin (Michigan Technological University)
Patricia McAnany (Boston University)
Randall McGuire (State University of New York, Binghamton)
Heather McKillop (Louisiana State University)
Frank McManamon (National Park Service)
Shannon McPherron (Max Planck Institute, Germany)
George Miller (California State University, Hayward)
Barbara Mills (University of Arizona)
Paul Minnis (University of Oklahoma)
Paula Molloy (National Park Service)

Craig Morris (American Museum of Natural History)
Juliet E. Morrow (Arkansas State University)
Cheryl Munson (Indiana University)
Fraser Neiman (Monticello Archaeology Program)
Margaret Nelson (University of Arizona)
Michael J. O'Brien (University of Missouri)
James O'Connell (University of Utah)
John Olsen (University of Arizona)
Tim Pauketat (University of Illinois)
Christopher Peebles (University of Indiana)
Stephen Plog (University of Virginia)
William Rathje (Stanford University)
Elizabeth Reitz (University of Georgia)
David Rhode (Desert Research Institute)
John Rick (Stanford University)
Anibal Rodriguez (American Museum of Natural History)
Nan Rothschild (Columbia University)
Irwin Rovner (North Carolina State University)
Ken Sassaman (University of Florida)
Nicholas Saunders (University College, London)
Verne Scarborough (University of Cincinnati)
Michael Schiffer (University of Arizona)
Enid Schildkrout (American Museum of Natural History)
Lynne Sebastian (SRI Foundation)
Payson Sheets (University of Colorado)
Stephen Silliman (University of Massachusetts, Boston)
Steve Simms (Utah State University)
Theresa Singleton (Syracuse University)
Jeff Sommer (University of Michigan)
Stanley South (University of South Carolina)
Janet Spector (formerly University of Minnesota)
Charles Spencer (American Museum of Natural History)
Charles Stanish (University of California, Los Angeles)
Amy Steffian (Alutiiq Museum)
Vin Steponaitis (University of North Carolina)
Simon Stoddart (Cambridge University)
Elizabeth Stone (State University of New York, Stonybrook)
The late William Tallbull
Ian Tattersall (American Museum of Natural History)
Anya Taylor (John Jay College of CUNY)
Mark Taylor (Manhattan College)
The late W. W. Taylor
Lawrence Todd (Colorado State University)
Bruce Trigger (McGill University)
Ruth Tringham (University of California, Berkeley)
Bram Tucker (Ohio State University)

Donald Tuohy (formerly Nevada State Museum)
Christy Turner (Arizona State University)
Danny Walker (Wyoming State Archaeologist Office)
Mike Waters (Texas A&M University)
Patty Jo Watson (Washington University)
Gloria Cranmer Webster (U'mista Cultural Center)
Kathryn Weedman (University of Florida)
Konstance Wescott (Argonne National Laboratory)
John Weymouth (University of Nebraska)

The late Joe Ben Wheat
Mary Whelan (University of Iowa)
Nancy Wilkie (Carleton University)
Chip Wills (University of New Mexico)
Al Woods (Florida Museum of Natural History)
James Woods (College of Southern Idaho)
John Yellen (National Science Foundation)
Amy Young (University of Southern Mississippi)

Each contributed worthwhile suggestions, which we often followed. We alone, however, are responsible for any errors of commission or omission.

Thomas also wishes to thank others in the American Museum of Natural History, especially Lorann S. A. Pendleton, Matt Sanger, and Molly Trauten, each of whom cheerfully helped out with dozens of details.

Kelly is grateful to his colleagues at the University of Wyoming, many of whom supplied photographs, answered innumerable questions about archaeological and anthropological trivia, and generally provided support. He is especially grateful to Lin Poyer, who, once again, has shown her unbounded patience and thoughtfulness.

We are also grateful to the crew at Wadsworth—Anthropology Editor Lin Marshall, Development Editor Sherry Symington, Production Project Manager Catherine Morris, Technology Project Manager Dee Dee Zobian, Assistant Editor Nicole Root, Editorial Assistant Kelly McMahon, Permissions Editor Sarah Harkrader, and Marketing Manager Matthew Wright. We thank the production team: production manager Melanie Field (Strawberry Field Publishing), copy editor Carol Lombardi, and photo researcher Terri Wright. We also gratefully acknowledge Dennis O'Brien, who created many of the illustrations used in this edition, as well as the contributions of the illustrators Diana Salles and the late Nicholas Amorosi, both of the American Museum of Natural History.

KEEPING IN TOUCH WITH YOUR AUTHORS

We see this textbook as an opportunity to become more available to both instructors and students. With e-mail, we can all have casual conversations with people around the globe, in more or less real time. We want to know what you think about this text and about archaeology—what you like and what you don't care for—so we can improve future editions. And so we encourage you to write us at the e-mail addresses below. Provided that we're not off on some remote dig somewhere, we'll get back to you right away. Drop us a line—we'd enjoy hearing from you.

D. H. T.
New York, New York
thomasd@amnh.org
October 2004

R.L.K.
Laramie, Wyoming
RLKELLY@uwyo.edu

A Note about Human Remains

In several instances, this book discusses important new frontiers of bioarchaeological research. But we also recognize the need to deal with human remains in a respectful and sensitive manner. Several Native American elders have requested that we refrain from publishing photographs or other depictions of American Indian human remains. Although we know that not all Native Americans feel this way, no images of Native American skeletal remains appear in this book. Should other groups express similar concerns, their requests will be addressed in succeeding editions as appropriate.

About the Petroglyphs

Sidebars used throughout this text are highlighted with several rock art symbols. To the best of our knowledge, they do not infringe on anyone's intellectual property rights. They are not intended to suggest a cultural or religious connotation.

About the Authors

DAVID THOMAS has served since 1972 as Curator of Anthropology at the American Museum of Natural History in New York City. A specialist in Native American archaeology, Thomas discovered both Gatecliff Shelter (Nevada) and the lost 16th/17th century Franciscan mission Santa Catalina de Guale on St. Catherines Island, Georgia. Since 1998, he has led the excavation of Mission San Marcos near Santa Fe, New Mexico. A founding trustee of the National Museum of the American Indian at the Smithsonian since 1989, he has published extensively, including 100 papers and 30 books—most recently, the best-selling *Skull Wars: Kennewick Man, Archaeology, and the Battle for Native American Identity.* As an archaeologist, Thomas likes "old stuff," including his 1961 Corvette, his 120-year-old house, and the Oakland Raiders.

ROBERT KELLY began collecting arrowheads in farmers' fields when he was 10 years old and has participated in archaeological research since 1973 when he was a high school sophomore. He has worked on excavations in North and South America and conducted ethnographic research in Madagascar. He is currently conducting research into the Paleoindian archaeology of Wyoming's Bighorn Mountains. A former president of the Society for American Archaeology and a past secretary of the Archaeology Division of the American Anthropological Association, Kelly has published nearly 100 articles and books, including the 1996 *Choice* Magazine Outstanding Academic Book *The Foraging Spectrum: Diversity in Hunting and Gathering Societies.* Dr. Kelly has been a professor of Anthropology at the University of Wyoming since 1997.

1 Meet Some Real Archaeologists

OUTLINE

Alfred Kidder (right) and Jesse Nusbaum conducting an archaeological survey at Mesa Verde, Colorado, in 1907.

Preview

THIS BOOK IS ABOUT what archaeologists want to learn, how they go about learning it, and what they do with what they have learned. These tasks require archaeologists to piece together a picture of the past from scraps of bone, rock, pottery, architecture, and other remains that are hundreds, thousands, or tens of thousands of years old. And, as we will see, the very nature of archaeology carries with it some serious ethical dilemmas.

In this book, we will look at some of the perspectives that characterize today's archaeology: scientific and humanistic, objective and subjective, ecological and ideational. Sometimes these approaches coexist, sometimes they clash. As we discuss these various archaeological perspectives, you should keep a couple of things in mind: First, no archaeologist fits perfectly into any of these named categories, and second, there is more than one way to do good archaeology.

This chapter looks at how archaeology has evolved. Archaeology is a relatively young discipline, still going through some growing pains. To raise some key issues that define the way modern archaeologists practice their craft, we begin with an example that illustrates some of the ethical dilemmas that archaeologists face today.

INTRODUCTION

July, 1996: The two college students never intended to make a federal case out of the day's fun. They never meant to rock the ethical foundations of American archaeology, either. All they wanted was to see hydroplane boat races for free.

The month of July in the city of Kennewick (Washington) is a month of festivals topped off by hydroplane races on the Columbia River. To avoid paying admission to the races, two young men snuck through a brushy area of riverbank. There, they could get a good view, even if it meant getting wet. Trudging along the river's edge, they spied a smooth white rock. One of them picked it up and jokingly pronounced it a skull. Imagine his surprise when he saw two dark eye sockets staring back at him. It *was* a skull.

After the races, the students reported their find to police, who called in the coroner to see if the remains were those of a murder victim. The coroner eventually called in archaeologist James Chatters. Although there

was no evidence of a burial pit, the skull's near-pristine condition suggested that it had eroded from the riverside only days earlier; in fact, Chatters eventually found much of the skeleton in the shallow water.

Who Was "Kennewick Man"?

Chatters's preliminary analysis showed that the individual was male and roughly 45 years old when he died. He stood about 5 feet 8 inches high. Subsequent laboratory analysis showed that two-thirds of his protein probably came from fish and that he ate limited amounts of starchy foods. In his time, the man might have been considered healthy, but today we would call him a "survivor." He suffered from severe disease or malnutrition when he was about 5 years old. He had minor arthritis in his knees, elbows, lower back, and neck from a lifetime of daily, intense physical activity. As a young adult, he had damaged the nerves to his left arm. He'd also suffered a serious chest injury, a blow to the head, and an injury to his right shoulder and left elbow. And, as if that weren't enough, he had a stone spear point embedded in his hip. He had survived this injury, too—although it left him in constant pain.

Chatters knew spear points like the one in the skeleton's hip were manufactured thousands of years ago, but he was still surprised when a radiocarbon date indicated that the man had died 9400 years ago. So-called "Kennewick Man" was one of the oldest human skeletons ever found in the Americas.

Even more intriguing was that the skull did not look like other Native American skulls; some even thought it might be European! It's not, but that suggestion titillated the media, who created sensationalist stories of how Europeans, rather than the ancestors of American Indians, first colonized the Americas. One group, the Asatru Folk Assembly, which says it practices an ancient Celtic religion, even claimed that Kennewick Man was their ancestor. (See "Looking Closer: American Indian or Native American?")

Who Controls Human Remains?

Many federal and state laws govern archaeology in the United States (we'll examine some of these in Chapter 17). One such law, the 1990 Native American Graves Protection and Repatriation Act (NAGPRA) provides for the repatriation of Native American human remains to their culturally affiliated tribes. Several tribes from the Kennewick area claimed the new find to be their ancestor and requested that the remains be turned over to them under this law. Kennewick Man had been discovered on lands administered by the U.S. Army Corps of Engineers, and that agency quickly agreed to halt all scientific studies and return the skeleton to the tribes.

But then a group of eight archaeologists and biological anthropologists filed a lawsuit, arguing that handing over the bones would actually violate NAGPRA—not only because the skeleton was not affiliated with the modern tribes, but also because it might not even be Native American. The scientists also claimed that their First Amendment rights would be violated if the government kept them from studying the remains.

The Corps turned to the U.S. Department of Interior for guidance, which commissioned a set of studies. Relying heavily on oral history from the tribes, Bruce Babbit, then Secretary of the Interior, declared that Kennewick Man was indeed culturally affiliated with the tribes and should be returned to them.

In protest, the eight plaintiffs reopened their suit, and the case was heard by the Ninth District Circuit Court (in Oregon). The judge faced uncharted legal waters: Was this 9400-year-old man a Native American or not? And, if so, was he culturally affiliated with the five modern tribes who claimed him as an ancestor? These are tough questions, both legally and scientifically. And the answers could potentially change forever the direction of American archaeology.

Five years after the boys found the skull, the judge ruled that Kennewick Man was not Native American. And even if he were, the judge ruled, the bones could not be culturally affiliated with the consortium of five tribes. The judge also granted the plaintiffs the right to study the remains. The tribes, along with the Department of Interior, appealed the ruling. And, in February of 2004, the appeals court upheld the district court's ruling: Kennewick is not Native American. The tribes have promised to try and strengthen NAGPRA by amending the law.

Kennewick and American Archaeology

The Kennewick decision is a landmark, and it raises important questions that we will address throughout this book. How did archaeologists know that the bones are 9400 years old? How did Chatters know that the spear point was ancient? How do we know that he ate a lot of fish? Can he really *not* be Native American? Answering questions like this is what archaeologists do: They reconstruct the human past from the crumbling remains that survive.

But Kennewick also raises some difficult ethical questions: What gives archaeologists the right to poke into the past, the right to study the dead? Who owns the past, anyway? And who gets to decide? This is also what archaeologists do: They make difficult ethical and moral decisions about the past (and the present).

The discipline of archaeology is presently experiencing some growing pains. With more than 7000 practicing archaeologists in the United States alone, the discipline harbors a host of diverse and sometimes conflicting perspectives. Some believe that archaeology is a science, pure and simple; others argue that archaeology must be responsive to humanistic concerns.

Looking Closer
American Indian or Native American?

Some years ago, as Thomas was telling his son's third grade class what it's like to be an archaeologist, a small (but adamant) voice of protest came from the back of the room.

"How come you keep saying 'Indians'? Don't you know they want to be called 'Native Americans'?" a girl asked.

She had a good point. Many people are confused about these terms. In fact, our Native American colleagues tell us that people often correct them when they say "Indian," as if the term has become a dirty word.

Names are important because they are power; the people who names things are generally the people who control them. Throughout this text, therefore, we discuss the names we use, because a discussion of names is also a discussion of people's rights.

The word "Indian," of course, is a legacy from fifteenth-century European sailors, who mistakenly believed they'd landed in India. "Native American" arose among Indians in the 1960s and 1970s, during the civil rights movement. But many Indians point out the ambiguity in this term. Although your authors are not American Indians, we are native Americans (because we were born in the United States).

Most indigenous people of North America today simply accept the imprecision of today's terms and use American Indian, Canadian Native, First Nations, Native American (or Native Hawaiian), Indian, and Native interchangeably; we follow this lead.

Of greater concern to most Indian people is the tribal name. Many Navajo people, for instance, wish to be known as Diné (a traditional name meaning "The People"). When discussing particular tribes, whenever possible we will use the term preferred by the particular tribe in question.

We will argue that both statements are true. Scientists insist on high standards of evidence, and they also continually examine their methods of making inferences from evidence. Science in this sense is self-correcting, making the approach essential to most inquiry (including archaeology). But even scientific inquiry is susceptible to cultural biases. Alternatively, humanistic approaches downplay scientific standards of evidence to explore new ideas and perspectives and to examine the biases and larger agenda of science. The ongoing dialogue about the ethics of archaeology will ultimately benefit scientific perspectives by pinpointing some biases that may hold us back from achieving a more complete understanding of humanity's shared past.

Archaeologists often say that we study the past in order to avoid repeating it and that understanding where humanity has been helps us to chart the future. But the Kennewick case points up the dilemma buried in both aphorisms. By claiming the skeletal remains as their own, the Indian tribes asserted that no scientific studies should be conducted. The tribes believed that they already understood their own past and resented attempts by non-Indian scientists to probe the remains of their ancestors. Although not all Native Americans agree with this position, many do, and this dispute underscores the important point that archaeology is not just about the dead; it is also about the living. How can we justify "studying the past to create a better tomorrow" if the very act of conducting research offends the living descendants of the ancient people being studied? Our position will be that archaeologists must work closely with indigenous peoples and descendant communities to achieve the goals of a scientific archaeology (as in Figure 1-1, which shows a working example of this compromise).

Rather than sweep the ethical dilemmas that confront modern archaeology under the rug, we will highlight them in the "Archaeological Ethics" boxes that appear in Chapters 2 through 17. And, after we learn something more about the practice of archaeology, we

Figure 1-1 Americanist archaeology today confronts both scientific and ethical challenges. Yet, there are many signs that archaeology need not be antagonistic to indigenous peoples. Here, Bryceson Pinnecoose (Hopi/Cheyenne, on right) and Kevin Woolridge are mapping buried structures at Mission San Marcos, New Mexico.

will return to the case of Kennewick Man to explore its implications for the future of the past in Chapter 18.

We now turn to a brief history of archaeology. This will help set the stage for an understanding of modern archaeological approaches explored in Chapters 2 and 3.

THE WESTERN WORLD DISCOVERS ITS PAST

Most historians ascribe the honor of "first archaeologist" to Nabonidus (who died in 538 BC), the last king of the neo-Babylonian Empire (see "Looking Closer: AD/BC/BP...Archaeology's Alphabet Soup"). A pious man, Nabonidus's zealous worship of his gods compelled him to rebuild the ruined temples of ancient Babylon and to search among their foundations for the inscriptions of earlier kings. We are indebted to the research of Nabonidus's scribes and the excavations by his subjects for much of our modern picture of the Babylonian Empire. Though nobody would call Nabonidus an "archaeologist" in the modern sense of the term, he remains an important figure for one simple reason: *Nabonidus looked to the physical residues of antiquity to answer questions about the past.* This may seem like a simple step, but it contrasted sharply with the beliefs of

his contemporaries, who regarded tradition, legend, and myth as the only admissible clues to the past.

For archaeology to become an intellectual field, scholars first had to recognize the idea of "the past." A major contribution of the Renaissance (circa AD 1300 to 1700), particularly in Italy, was the distinction between the present and the past. Classical Greeks and Romans recognized only a remote past, which they reified through myth and legend. Because Europeans of the Middle Ages likewise failed to distinguish between themselves and ancient populations, it fell to Renaissance scholars to point up the differences between classical and medieval times.

Petrarch (1304–1374), perhaps the most influential individual of the early Renaissance, defined an intellectual tradition that continues to be important in today's archaeology. Beyond his considerable talents as poet and linguist, Petrarch also provided strong impetus for archaeological research. To him, the remote past was an ideal of perfection, and he looked to antiquity for moral philosophy. Of course, to imitate classical antiquity, one must first study it. In a real sense, Petrarch's approach led to a rediscovery of the past by those in the Western European intellectual tradition. Petrarch's influence can best be seen in the work of his close friend Boccaccio, who wrote extensive essays on classical mythology, and also in that of Giovanni Dondi, who is generally credited with the first systematic observations on archaeological monuments.

But it remained for the fifteenth-century Italian scholar Ciriaco de' Pizzicolli (1391–1455) to establish the modern discipline of archaeology. After translating the Latin inscription on the triumphal arch of Trajan in Ancona, Italy, he was inspired to devote the remainder of his life to studying ancient monuments, copying inscriptions, and promoting the study of the past. His travels took him into Syria and Egypt, throughout the islands of the Aegean, and finally to Athens. When asked his business, Ciriaco is said to have replied, "Restoring the dead to life"—which today remains a fair definition of the everyday business of archaeology.

Archaeology and Society

From the beginning of Renaissance Europe's interest in the past, however, it was clear that not everyone wanted the dead to be restored to life. In 1572 Matthew Parker, Queen Elizabeth's archbishop of Canterbury, formed

Looking Closer
AD/BC/BP ... Archaeology's Alphabet Soup

In anything written by archaeologists, you'll encounter a blizzard of acronyms that refer to age. Let's clear the air with some concise definitions of the most common abbreviations:

BC ("before Christ"): For instance, 3200 BC; note that the letters follow the date.

AD (*anno Domini*, meaning "in the year of the Lord") indicates a year that falls within the Christian era (that is, after the birth of Christ). Given the English translation of the phrase, archaeologists place the "AD" prior to the numerical age—we say the Norman Invasion occurred in "AD 1066" rather than "1066 AD." The earliest AD date is AD 1; there is no AD 0 because this year is denoted by 0 BC, and double numbering is not allowed.

AC ("after Christ"): Basically the same as AD, except that it's written AC 1066 (with the abbreviation written before the number). This usage is confusing, and hardly anybody uses it anymore. Neither do we.

BP ("before present"): Many archaeologists feel more comfortable avoiding the AD/BC split altogether, substituting the single "before present" age estimate (with AD 1950 arbitrarily selected as the zero point; we'll explain why in Chapter 8). By this convention, an artifact from the Hastings battlefield would be dated 884 BP (1950−1066 = 884).

Note that all the abbreviations used so far are capital letters. Just in case you're not confused enough, you may also run into a date written in lowercase, such as 3200 b.c. This convention denotes that a date was derived by radiocarbon methods and reflects radiocarbon years rather than calendar years (we'll explain the difference in Chapter 8). So the term "3200 b.c." would be read "3200 radiocarbon years before Christ." We find this usage confusing and won't employ it here.

---

the Society of Antiquaries, devoted to the study of Anglo-Saxon law and writings.

At the same time, Parliament upheld English Common Law, said to have been granted by William the Conqueror upon his conquest of England in 1066. English Common Law was based on the laws and customs of the Anglo-Saxons. Unfortunately, British kings had persistently claimed that their authority to rule—the "divine right of kings"—originated in their descent from the legendary King Arthur (who probably lived about AD 500, but no one really knows). King James therefore asserted that Common Law did not apply to the Anglican Church or the King, because it originated with William rather than with Arthur. But the Society of Antiquaries used ancient documents to demonstrate that William the Conqueror did not actually create

English Common Law—instead he had simply allowed it to stand and to be fused with his own ideas of justice. This was a problem for King James, for in English Common Law the people had the right to rebel against an unlawful and unjust king. King James saw that meddling with this particular piece of the past had too much potential to start riots in the streets, and so he ordered the dissolution of the Society of Antiquaries. The study of the past will often be controversial.

But the die was cast, and the Society for Antiquaries was only the first of many British scholarly societies interested in the past. Of course, many private collectors were concerned only with filling their curio cabinets with *objets d'art*, but the overall goal of British antiquarianism was to map, record, and preserve national treasures. By the late eighteenth century, members of Europe's leisure classes considered an interest in classical antiquities to be an important ingredient in the "cultivation of taste," hence the non-scientific bent implied in the term "**antiquarian**."

The Discovery of Deep Time

Archaeological research until the eighteenth century proceeded mostly within the tradition of Petrarch—that is, concerned primarily with clarifying the picture of classical civilizations. This lore was readily digested by the eighteenth- and early-nineteenth-century mind, because nothing in it challenged the Bible as an authoritative account of the origin of the world and humanity.

A problem arose, however, when very crude stone tools like that shown in Figure 1-2 were discovered in England and continental Europe. About 1836, a French customs official and naturalist, Jacques Boucher de Crèvecoeur de Perthes (1788–1868), found ancient axe heads in the gravels of the Somme River. Along with those tools, he also found the bones of long-extinct mammals. To Boucher de Perthes (as he is more commonly known), the implication was obvious: "In spite of their imperfection, these rude stones prove the existence of [very ancient] man as surely as a whole Louvre would have done."

But few contemporaries believed him, in part because prevailing religious thought held that human beings had been on earth for only 6000 years. Why? Some 200 years before Boucher de Perthes' discoveries, several scholars had calculated the age of the earth as no more than about 6000 years. Perhaps the most meticulous of these calculations was that of James Ussher (1581–1656), Archbishop of Armagh, Primate of All Ireland, and Vice-Chancellor of Trinity College in Dublin. Using Biblical genealogies and correlations of Mediterranean and Middle Eastern histories, Ussher concluded in 1650 that Creation began at sunset on Saturday, October 22, 4004 BC. His effort was so convincing that the date 4004 BC appeared as a marginal note in most Bibles published after 1700.

This reckoning, of course, allowed no chance of an extensive human antiquity; there simply wasn't enough time. Therefore, the thinking went, Boucher de Perthes must be mistaken—his rude implements must be something other than human handiwork. Some suggested that the "tools" were really meteorites; others said they were produced by lightning, elves, or fairies.

One seventeenth-century scholar suggested that the chipped flints were "generated in the sky by a fulgurous exhalation conglobed in a cloud by the circumposed humour," whatever that means.

But customs officials have never been known for their reserve, and Boucher de Perthes stuck to his guns. More finds were made in the French gravel pits at St. Acheul (near Abbeville), and similar discoveries turned up across the Channel in southern England. The issue was finally resolved when the respected British paleontologist Hugh Falconer visited Abbeville to examine the disputed evidence. A procession of esteemed scholars followed Falconer's lead and declared their support in 1859; the idea that humans had lived with now-extinct animals in the far distant past was finally enshrined in Charles Lyell's 1865 book *The Geological Evidences of the Antiquity of Man*.

The year 1859 turned out to be a banner year in the history of human thought: Not only was the remote antiquity of humankind accepted by the scientific establishment, but Charles Darwin published his influential *On the Origin of Species*. Although Darwin mentioned humans only once in that book (on nearly the last page he wrote, "Much light will be thrown on the origin of man and his history...."), he had suggested the process by which modern people could have risen from ancient primate ancestors. In the beginning, though, Darwin's theory (which had to do with the

Figure 1-2
Boucher de Perthes found Paleolithic handaxes like this in the Somme River gravels.

© American Museum of Natural History

antiquarian Originally, someone who studied antiquities (that is, ancient objects) largely for the sake of the objects themselves—not to understand the people or culture that produced them.

transformation of species) was unconnected to the antiquity of humanity (which was a simple question of age). We'll come back to Darwin's contributions in Chapter 15.

Nonetheless, the discovery of deep time—the recognition that life was far more ancient than Biblical scholars argued and that human culture had evolved over time—opened the floodgates. British archaeology soon billowed out across two rather divergent courses. One direction became involved with the problems of remote geological time and the demonstration of long-term human evolution. Others continued the tradition of Petrarch and focused on classical studies, particularly the archaeology of ancient Greece and Rome, a field now known as **classical archaeology**. This philosophical split has continued into modern times, although some signs hint that these fields are coming back together.

Archaeology and Native Americans

Across the Atlantic, American archaeology faced its own vexing issues of time and cultural development. How, nineteenth-century scholars wondered, could regions such as the Valley of Mexico and Peru have hosted the civilizations of the Aztecs and the Inkas while people in many other places—such as the North American West—seemed impoverished, even primitive? When did people first arrive in the New World? Where had these migrants come from, and how did they get here?

Speculation arose immediately. One idea held that Native Americans were one of the Lost Tribes of Israel. Another suggested that Indians came from Atlantis. Others said they were voyaging Egyptians, Vikings, Chinese, or Phoenicians.

Gradually, investigators came to realize the considerable continuities that existed between the unknown prehistoric past and the Native American population of the historic period. As such knowledge progressed, profound differences between European and American

classical archaeology The branch of archaeology that studies the "classical" civilizations of the Mediterranean, such as Greece and Rome, and the Near East.

ethnology That branch of anthropology dealing chiefly with the comparative study of cultures.

Americanist archaeology The brand of archaeology that evolved in close association with anthropology in the Americas; it is practiced throughout the world.

archaeology became more apparent. While Europeans wrestled with their ancient flints—without apparent modern correlates—American scholars saw that living Native Americans were relevant to the interpretation of archaeological remains. In the crass terms of the time, many Europeans saw Native Americans as "living fossils," relics of times long past.

New World archaeology thus became inextricably wed to the study of living Native American people. Whereas Old World archaeologists began from a baseline of geological time or classical antiquity, their American counterparts developed an anthropological understanding of Native America. The **ethnology** of American Indians became an important domain of Western scholarship in its own right, and Americanist archaeology became linked with anthropology through their mutual interest in Native American culture.

Let us stress an important point here: As Europeans refined the archaeology of Europe, they were studying their own ancestors (Anglo-Saxons, Celts, Slavs, Franks, and so forth). But New World archaeology was a matter of Euro-Americans digging up somebody else's ancestors. This fundamental difference explains the following elements peculiar to New World archaeology:

- The racist, anti–American Indian theories that dominated the thinking of early nineteenth-century American scholars,
- The form of antiquity legislation in North America, and
- The fact that many contemporary Native Americans still do not trust conventional Western scholarship to interpret their past.

We'll return to these issues in later chapters.

FOUNDERS OF AMERICANIST ARCHAEOLOGY

We are now prepared to look more closely at how Americanist archaeology is currently practiced. Although many other terms—such as "scientific archaeology," or "anthropological archaeology"—are used, we prefer Robert Dunnell's phrase **Americanist archaeology** because it is descriptive, yet it contains the many perspectives that constitute American archaeology today. Let us also emphasize that archaeologists working in the Americanist tradition practice their craft around the world, and not only in North America.

The history of Americanist archaeology (all history, really) is a commingling of tradition and change—illustrated here by a few individuals whose lives and careers typify archaeology of their time. These individuals were by no means the only ones practicing archaeology over the last 150 years. However, their stories demonstrate stages in the growth of Americanist archaeology and show how goals and perspectives have changed.

C. B. Moore: A Genteel Antiquarian

Clarence Bloomfield Moore (1852–1936), pictured in Figure 1-3, was born into an affluent family of Philadelphia socialites. After receiving his BA degree from Harvard University in 1873, Moore followed the social circuit, rambling through Europe and joining safaris into exotic Africa. By 1892, however, Moore found the well-to-do socialite lifestyle to be shallow and boring. Somewhere along the line, Moore was introduced to American archaeology and, at age 40, he transformed himself from gentleman socialite into gentleman archaeologist.

Smitten by his new pastime, he purchased a specially equipped flat-bottomed steamboat, which he christened the *Gopher*. Moore set off to explore the seemingly endless waterways of America's Southeast, excavating the major archaeological sites he encountered. Particularly drawn to ancient cemeteries, Moore enlisted the services of Dr. Milo G. Miller as secretary, physician, and colleague.

From the outset, Moore's annual archaeological campaigns were models of organization and efficiency. Aboard *Gopher*, Moore and Miller conducted preliminary investigations so likely sites could be located and arrangements could be made with landowners; actual excavations began in the spring. Moore hired and supervised the workers and kept the field notes. As human skeletons were located, Dr. Miller examined the bones to determine sex, age, probable cause of death, and any unusual pathologies. They spent the summers cleaning and repairing the finds and then photographing and analyzing the collection. Moore prepared detailed excavation reports for publication and distributed the more unusual **artifacts** to major archaeological institutions.

Moore's first investigations concentrated on the shell **middens** and the sand burial mounds sprinkled along

Figure 1-3
C. B. Moore, an antiquarian who explored southeastern archaeological sites in the nineteenth century.

the Gulf Coast of Florida. Year after year, Moore worked his way around to Florida's eastern shore and eventually to the Sea Islands of coastal Georgia and South Carolina. In 1899, Moore returned to the Gulf Coast, traveled up the Alabama River, and examined the coast of northwest Florida. He excavated dozens of archaeological sites on each expedition.

Finally, in 1905, Moore paused on the Black Warrior River, Alabama, to excavate the ruins known as Moundville (we'll return to this site in Chapter 13). Working with several trained assistants and a crew numbering 10 to 15, Moore explored the large temple mounds to examine the human burials and unearth spectacular pieces of pre-Columbian art. Moore concluded that Moundville had been a prominent regional center. He further surmised from the varied art forms that the ancient people of Moundville worshiped the sun, and that motifs such as the plumed serpent and eagle suggested strong ties with contemporaneous Mexican civilizations.

By 1916, Moore concluded that the *Gopher* had explored every southeastern river then navigable by steamer. In fact, once a sandbar was removed, Moore promptly piloted the *Gopher* up the newly navigable Chocktawatchee River in northern Florida. He had truly exhausted the resources available for riverboat

artifact Any movable object that has been used, modified, or manufactured by humans; artifacts include stone, bone, and metal tools; beads and other ornaments; pottery; artwork; religious and sacred items.

midden Refuse deposit resulting from human activities, generally consisting of sediment; food remains such as charred seeds, animal bone, and shell; and discarded artifacts.

archaeology. Of course, archaeological techniques have improved markedly since Moore's time, and many a contemporary archaeologist wishes that Moore had been somewhat less thorough.

Moore typifies archaeology's roots because he was an antiquarian, more interested in the objects of the past than in reconstructing the lives of the people who produced them or in explaining the past. We should not hold this against Moore's generation because, frankly, you can't move to understanding the past until you have some idea of what that past was like. Antiquarians like Moore helped to lay the groundwork for the archaeology that was to follow.

Nels Nelson: America's First-Generation "Working" Archaeologist

Whereas C. B. Moore was born into a wealthy family, Nels Nelson (1875–1964), shown in Figure 1-4, grew up on a poor farm in Jutland, Denmark. Although first a farmhand and a student only in his spare time, he stumbled onto James Fenimore Cooper novels—*The Last of the Mohicans* and *The Deerslayer*—while still quite young and became fascinated with the lore of Native Americans. Several of his relatives had already emigrated to America and, in 1892, Nelson's aunt in Minnesota sent him a steerage ticket to New York. On his way westward, he worked at a number of jobs (including driving a six-mule team and butchering hogs) and finally saved enough money to enroll in Stanford University, where he studied philosophy by day and took odd jobs at night to pay his expenses.

Quite by accident, someone invited Nelson to attend an archaeological excavation in Ukiah, north of San Francisco. He was immediately hooked. The dig apparently rekindled the same fascination with Indian lore he had first experienced while reading the pages of Cooper. Nelson immediately enrolled in all the archaeology courses available at the University of California.

Nelson's MA thesis was an archaeological survey of the shell middens surrounding San Francisco Bay. He walked more than 3,000 miles during his reconnaissance and recorded 425 prehistoric shell mounds. His report discussed the location of these sites relative to available natural resources, listed the animal bones

© American Museum of Natural History

Figure 1-4 Nels Nelson, one of the first professional archaeologists, on the stone steps leading to Acoma Pueblo, New Mexico.

found in the shell heaps, and pondered the ecological adaptation implied by such a bayside lifeway. Urban sprawl has today destroyed all but a handful of these sites, and Nelson's map, originally published in 1909, remains an irreplaceable resource to modern archaeologists interested in central California prehistory.

Then, in 1912, the American Museum of Natural History in New York City launched an archaeological campaign in the American Southwest, and Nelson was engaged to oversee this influential research program. Nelson's stratigraphic excavations in New Mexico were a breakthrough in archaeological technique (we will discuss **stratigraphy** in more detail in Chapters 6 and 7). By looking at the kinds of artifacts found in different, superimposed layers of earth at a site, Nelson could document culture change over time. In the next few years, Nelson broadened his experience by excavating shell mounds in Florida and caves in Kentucky and Missouri. In 1925, Nelson accompanied an American Museum of Natural History expedition to Central Asia; his North American and European fieldwork continued until his retirement in 1943.

stratigraphy A site's physical structure produced by the deposition of geological and/or cultural sediments into layers, or strata.

Nels Nelson typifies the state of Americanist archaeology during the first quarter of the twentieth century. Although receiving better archaeological training than did his predecessors, such as C. B. Moore, Nelson nevertheless learned largely by firsthand experience. Archaeology was still in a pioneering stage, and no matter where Nelson turned, he was often the first archaeologist on the scene. Like others of his generation, his first responsibility was to record what he saw, then to conduct a preliminary excavation where warranted, and finally to proffer tentative inferences to be tested and embellished by subsequent investigators. Nelson also typified the new breed of early twentieth-century museum-based archaeologists, who strongly believed that the message of archaeology should be brought to the public in books, popular magazine articles, and, most of all, interpretive displays of archaeological materials.

Today, archaeologists acknowledge Nelson's 1912 excavations in New Mexico's Galisteo Basin as the first significant stratigraphic archaeology in the Americas. At that time, the cultural chronology of the American Southwest was utterly unknown, and Nelson's painstaking excavations and analysis of the pottery recovered provided the first solid chronological framework.

A. V. "Ted" Kidder: Founder of Anthropological Archaeology

Although he was born in Michigan, the life and career of Alfred V. Kidder (1886–1963), shown in Figure 1-5, revolved about the academic community of Cambridge, Massachusetts. Kidder's father, a mining engineer, saw to it that his son received the best education available. First enrolled in a private school in Cambridge, Kidder then attended the prestigious La Villa, in Ouchy, Switzerland, after which he registered at Harvard. Kidder soon joined an archaeological expedition to northeastern Arizona, exploring territory then largely unknown to the Anglo world. The southwestern adventure sealed his fate.

When Kidder returned to Harvard, he enrolled in the anthropology program and in 1914 was awarded the sixth American PhD specializing in archaeology—and the first with a focus on North America. Kidder's dissertation examined prehistoric Southwestern ceramics, assessing their value in reconstructing culture history. Relying on scientific procedures, Kidder demonstrated ways of deciphering meaning from one of archaeology's most ubiquitous items, the **potsherd** (a fragment

© Faith Kidder Fuller

Figure 1-5
A. V. Kidder, an archaeologist of the American Southwest and the Maya region, advocated multidisciplinary field research.

of pottery). Urging accurate description of ceramic decoration, he explained how such apparent minutiae could help determine cultural relationships among various prehistoric groups. Kidder argued that only through controlled excavation and analysis could inferences be drawn about such anthropological subjects as acculturation, social organizations, and prehistoric religious customs (see "In His Own Words: The Pan-Scientific Approach to Archaeology" by A. V. Kidder).

In 1915, the Department of Archaeology at the Phillips Academy in Andover, Massachusetts, was seeking a site of sufficient size and scientific interest to merit a multiyear archaeological project. Largely because of his anthropological training, Kidder was selected to direct the excavations. After evaluating the possibilities, he decided on Pecos Pueblo, a massive prehistoric and historic period ruin located southeast of Santa Fe, New Mexico. Kidder was impressed by the great diversity of potsherds scattered about the ruins and felt certain that Pecos contained enough stratified debris to span several centuries. Kidder excavated at Pecos for ten summers.

The excavations at Pecos were consequential for several reasons. Kidder modified Nelson's stratigraphic method of digging to construct a cultural chronology of the southwest. He went beyond the pottery to make sense of the artifact and architectural styles preserved at Pecos. His intensive artifact analysis, done before the advent of radiocarbon dating or tree-ring chronology (methods that we discuss in Chapter 8), established the framework of Southwestern prehistory, which remains intact today.

potsherd Fragment of pottery.

In His Own Words
The Pan-Scientific Approach to Archaeology

by A. V. Kidder

Teamwork is a requirement of all modern archaeology. Kidder fully anticipated this modern trend with his "pan-scientific" approach at Chichén Itzá (Yucatán, Mexico) in the 1920s:

   In this investigation the archaeologist would supply the Prehistoric background; the historian would work on the documentary record of the Conquest, the Colonial, and the Mexican periods; the sociologist would consider the structure of modern life. At the same time studies would be made upon the botany, zoology, and climate of the region and upon the agriculture, economic system, and health conditions of the urban and rural, European mixed and native populations. It seems probable that there would result definite conclusions of far-reaching interest, that there would be developed new methods applicable to many problems of race and culture contacts, and that there would be gained by the individuals taking part in the work a first-hand acquaintance with the aims of allied disciplines which would be of great value to themselves, and through them to far larger groups of research workers.

Kidder then joined the Carnegie Institution of Washington, DC as director of the Division of Historical Research. He launched an ambitious archaeological program to probe the Maya ruins of Central America. Kidder directed the Carnegie's Maya campaigns for two decades, arguing that a true understanding of Maya culture would require a broad plan of action with many interrelated areas of research. Relegating himself to the role of administrator, Kidder amassed a staff of qualified scientists with the broadest possible scope of interests. His plan was a landmark in archaeological research, stressing an enlargement of traditional archaeological objectives to embrace the wider realms of anthropology and allied disciplines. Under Kidder's direction, the Carnegie program supported research by ethnographers, botanists, geographers, physical anthropologists, geologists, meteorologists, and, of course, archaeologists.

Kidder even proved the potential of aerial reconnaissance by convincing Charles Lindbergh, already an international figure, to participate in the Carnegie's Maya program. Early in 1929, Lindbergh flew Kidder throughout British Honduras, the Yucatán peninsula, and the Petén jungle of Guatemala. Beyond discovering new ruins, the Lindbergh flights also generated a wealth of previously unavailable ecological data, such as the boundaries of various types of vegetation. Today, the interdisciplinary complexion of archaeology is a fact of life. But when Kidder proposed the concept in the 1920s, it was revolutionary.

In addition to his substantive Maya and Southwestern discourses, Kidder helped shift Americanist archaeology toward more properly anthropological purposes. Unlike many of his contemporaries, Kidder maintained that archaeology should be viewed as "that branch of anthropology which deals with prehistoric peoples," a doctrine that has become firmly embedded and expanded in today's Americanist archaeology. To Kidder, the archaeologist was merely a "mouldier variety of anthropologist." Although archaeologists continue to immerse themselves in the nuances of potsherd detail and architectural specifics, the ultimate objective of archaeology remains the statement of anthropological universals about *people.*

James A. Ford: A Master of Time

Born in Water Valley, Mississippi, James A. Ford's (1911–1968) major research interest centered on the archaeology of the American Southeast. While Ford (shown in Figure 1-6) was attending Columbia, Nels Nelson retired from the Department of Anthropology at the American Museum of Natural History, and Ford was chosen as the new assistant curator of North American archaeology.

Ford came of age during the Great Depression, part of an archaeological generation literally trained on the job. As the Roosevelt administration created jobs to alleviate the grim economic conditions, crews of workmen were assigned labor-intensive tasks, including building roads and bridges and general heavy construction. One obvious make-work project was archaeology, and thousands of the unemployed were set to work excavating major archaeological sites. This program was, of course, an important boost to Americanist archaeology, and data from government-sponsored, Depression-era excavations are still being analyzed and published.

Ford worked at Poverty Point, a Louisiana site explored 40 years earlier by C. B. Moore. Poverty Point is a large, 400-acre site that dates to the first and second millennia BC. It contains a number of large earthen mounds, one in the shape of a bird that is 70 feet high and 700 feet wide. Lying before this mound, like a gigantic amphitheater, is a set of concentric 1½ meter-high earthen semi-circles, three-quarters of a mile in diameter. We still don't fully understand their purpose. After mapping these and the site's other mounds, Ford launched a series of stratigraphic excavations, using Nelson's principles, designed to define the prehistoric sequence.

Ford's objective was to learn what Poverty Point had to say about the people and culture who lived there, a considerably more ambitious goal than that of C. B. Moore, who dug primarily to unearth outstanding examples of artwork. Ford continually asked, what does archaeology tell us about the people? As he excavated the mounds, he tried to recreate the social and political networks responsible for this colossal enterprise. In this regard, his approach typified the overarching anthropological objectives of mid-twentieth-century Americanist archaeology (see "In His Own Words: The Goals of Archaeology" by James A. Ford).

The unprecedented accumulation of raw data during the 1930s was a boon for archaeology, but it also created

© American Museum of Natural History and Junius Bird

Figure 1-6
James A. Ford helped develop the technique of seriation to sort out cultural changes over time.

a crisis of sorts: What was to be done with all these facts? Ford and his contemporaries were beset by the need to synthesize and classify and by the necessity to determine regional sequences of culture chronology. Unlike Kidder and the others working in the American Southwest, Ford did not have access to deep, well-preserved refuse heaps; southeastern sites were more commonly shallow, short-term occupations. To create a temporal order, Ford relied on an integrated scheme of surface collection and classification.

Ford refined techniques to place the various stages of pottery development in sequential order, a process known as seriation (which we discuss further in Chapter 8). The central idea is simple: By assuming that cultural styles tend to change gradually, archaeologists can chart the relative popularity of a style, such as pottery decoration, through time and across space. By fitting the various short-term assemblages into master curves, Ford developed a series of regional ceramic chronologies. Although sometimes overly simplistic, Ford's seriation technique was sufficient to establish the baseline prehistoric chronology still used in the American Southeast.

Ford then synthesized his ceramic chronologies into patterns of regional history. When C. B. Moore was excavating the hundreds of prehistoric mounds throughout the Southeast, he lacked a system for adequately dating his finds. Using seriation along with other methods, Ford helped bring temporal order to his excavations, and he rapidly moved to synthesize these local sequences across the greater Southeast. He proposed the basic division between the earlier Burial

In His Own Words
The Goals of Archaeology

by James A. Ford

The study of archaeology has changed considerably from a rather esthetic beginning as an activity devoted to collecting curios and guarding them in cabinets to be admired for their rarity, beauty, or simple wonder. Students are no longer satisfied with the delights of the collector and are now primarily interested in reconstructing culture history. In recent years methods and techniques have progressed rapidly, and there are indications which suggest that some phases of the study may develop into a truly scientific concern with general principles. This trend seems to be due more to the kinds of evidence that past human history offers than to any planned development. For centuries the perspective of the study of history was narrowed to a listing of battles, kings, political situations, and escapades of great men, an activity which is analogous to collecting curios and arranging them in cabinets. Such collections are fascinating to those who have developed a taste for them, but they contribute little towards the discovery of processes which are always the foremost interest of a science. The evidence that survives in archaeological situations has made it impossible to study prehistory in terms of individual men, or even in terms of man as an acculturated animal. When the archaeologist progresses beyond the single specimen, he is studying the phenomena of culture.

I join a number of contemporaries in believing that archaeology is moving in the direction of its establishment as a more important segment of the developing science of culture than it has been in the past. This does not mean that such objectives as discovering chronological sequences and more complete and vivid historical reconstructions will be abandoned; rather these present aims will become necessary steps in the process of arriving at the new goal.

Mound Period and the subsequent Temple Mound Period, a distinction that remains in use today.

Americanist Archaeology at Mid-Twentieth Century

The biographies of these forebears provide a sense of how Americanist archaeology developed during the first half of the twentieth century. You have no doubt noted that none of them are women. Nonetheless, women such as Madeline Kneberg (1903–1996), Frederica de Laguna (1906–), H. Marie Wormington (1914–1994; see Figure 1-7), and Florence Hawley Ellis (1906–1991) were, in fact, contributing—but because they were commonly excluded from traditional communication networks, their contributions are more difficult to find. Today, this is no longer true—in fact, half of all American archaeologists are women.

American archaeology began as a pastime of the genteel rich such as C. B. Moore, but through the years, it developed into a professional scientific discipline. As trained practitioners, most archaeologists after Moore's time have been affiliated with major museums and universities; others have joined the private sector, working to protect and conserve America's cultural heritage. This institutional support not only encouraged a sense of professionalism and fostered public funding, but also mandated that public repositories would care for the archaeological artifacts recovered. The twentieth-century Americanist archaeologist is not a collector of personal treasure: All finds belong in the public domain, available for exhibit and study.

We can also see a distinct progression toward specialization in our target archaeologists. Scholars knew virtually nothing about American prehistory in the early nineteenth century. But by the end of that century, so

Figure 1-7 Marie Wormington, a female pioneer in American archaeology.

much archaeological information had already accumulated that no single scholar could know everything relevant to Americanist archaeology. Although C. B. Moore became the leading authority on Southeastern archaeology, he knew little about the finds being made by his contemporaries in Peru, Central America, and the American Southwest. By the mid-twentieth century, archaeologists like Ford were forced to specialize in specific localities within limited cultural areas. Today, it is rare to find archaeologists with extensive experience in more than a couple of specialized fields.

Possibly the greatest change, however, has been the quality of archaeologists' training. Although Harvard-educated, Moore was untrained in archaeology; his fieldwork methods were based on personal trial and error. Nelson and Kidder were members of the first generation of professionally trained Americanist archaeologists, and they studied under America's most prominent anthropologists. From then on, Americanist archaeologists were, almost without exception, well versed in anthropology.

Although archaeologists by mid-century wished to transcend mere cultural chronology, in truth classifying artifacts and sorting out their patterns in space and time left little time for more anthropological objectives, such as reconstructing society. Most archaeologists by mid-century were involved in what is called **culture history**. Their main goal was to track the migrations and development of particular prehistoric cultures by documenting how material culture changed over time and space. Differences in artifact frequencies between sites were attributed to the presence of different cultures; changes in artifact frequencies over time, such as the types of pottery found in different layers of earth at a site, were attributed to the diffusion of ideas from other cultures or the replacement of one culture by another. Archaeologists tried to explain changes by relating them to climatic change, for example, or to some vague ideas about cultural development. But for the most part, artifact changes were "explained" by the diffusion of ideas or the influx of a new people.

However, by the 1950s, the basic prehistory of North America was sufficiently well understood that some archaeologists were ready to move beyond simple documentation to more in-depth reconstructions of prehistory and even to efforts at explaining prehistory.

REVOLUTION IN ARCHAEOLOGY: AN ADVANCING SCIENCE

Beginning in the 1940s, a succession of scholars challenged orthodox archaeological thinking, urging explosive change and demanding instantaneous results. Two such crusaders were particularly influential in shaping modern archaeological thought.

Walter W. Taylor: Moses in the Wilderness

Educated first at Yale and then at Harvard, Walter W. Taylor (1913–1997), shown in Figure 1-8, completed his doctoral dissertation late in 1942. After returning from overseas military service, he published in 1948 an expanded version of his dissertation as *A Study of Archeology*. It was a bombshell. Greeted with alarm and consternation by the archaeological community, the book was no less than a public call for revolution. Taylor blasted the archaeological establishment of the day. Few liked Taylor's book, but everybody read it.

> **culture history** The kind of archaeology practiced mainly in the early to mid-twentieth century; it "explains" differences or changes over time in artifact frequencies by positing the diffusion of ideas between neighboring cultures or the migration of a people who had different mental templates for artifact styles.

Figure 1-8
Walter W. Taylor in Coahuila, Mexico in 1937; Taylor advocated that archaeologists focus less on grand temples and more on the lives of common people.

Courtesy of Walter W. Taylor

Taylor launched a frontal attack on the elders of Americanist archaeology. This assault was particularly plucky, as Taylor was himself a wet-behind-the-ears newcomer, having published little to establish his credentials as an archaeologist, much less a critic.

A Study of Archeology blasted A. V. Kidder, among others. Kidder repeatedly maintained that he was an anthropologist who had specialized in archaeology. But Taylor probed Kidder's publications to determine how well his deeds conformed to his stated anthropological objectives and boldly concluded that they did not. He could find in Kidder's research no cultural synthesis, no picture of life at any site, no consideration of cultural processes, no derivation of cultural laws—no anthropology at all, in Taylor's opinion.

These were serious charges, considered blasphemous by most archaeologists of the time. But Taylor supported his case with a line-by-line dissection of Kidder's published record. Kidder's research at Pecos and elsewhere in the American Southwest was said to be full of "apparent contradictions," merely "description for its own sake." Taylor claimed that Kidder was incapable of preparing a proper site report (a charge that was a bit

trait list A simple listing of a culture's material and behavioral characteristics, for example, house and pottery styles, foods, degree of nomadism, particular rituals, or ornaments. Trait lists were used primarily to trace the movement of cultures across a landscape and through time.

conjunctive approach As defined by Walter W. Taylor, using functional interpretations of artifacts and their contexts to reconstruct daily life of the past.

over the top), much less of writing the anthropology of the prehistoric Southwest.

Taylor turned to Kidder's prestigious research into the archaeology of the Maya and, once again, accused him of failing to live up to his own goals. Granting that Kidder began his investigations with anthropology in mind, Taylor concluded that "the road to Hell and the field of Maya archeology are paved with good intentions." Taylor deduced that the Carnegie Institution, under Kidder's direction, "has sought and found the hierarchical, the grandiose. It has neglected the common, the everyday." Kidder, Taylor declared, had been blinded by the "pomp and circumstance" of Classic Maya archaeology, the grand temples and ceremonial centers. According to Taylor, Kidder merely skimmed off the sensational, the spectacular, the grandiose—and forgot all about the Maya people themselves: How did they live? What did they do? What did they believe?

In 1948, Taylor was indeed archaeology's angriest young man. Kidder and other luminaries were accused of compiling **trait lists**, an account of the presence or absence of particular kinds of artifacts at different sites to no real purpose; of classifying artifacts and describing them, but for the mere sake of classification and description. Taylor pointed out that whereas Kidder and his generation claimed to be anthropologists, they failed to do anthropology (at least according to Taylor). Though careful not to deny the initial usefulness of their strategies, Taylor urged archaeologists to get on with the proper business of anthropology: finding out something about ancient people. Chronology, to Taylor, was merely a stepping-stone, a foundation for more anthropologically relevant studies of human behavior and cultural dynamics.

Taylor's prescription was his so-called **conjunctive approach** to archaeology. By this, Taylor meant combining ("conjoining") a variety of lines of evidence to create a picture of what the past was like and to discuss the functions of artifacts, features, and sites. From his critique, we can see that Taylor would have scrutinized the artifacts and features of a single Maya center, inferred their functions, and then written a comprehensive description of the people who once lived there. Taylor urged archaeologists to forsake the temples for the garbage dumps, for it was there that the lives of everyday people were recorded.

Taylor proposed that archaeologists quantify their data, rather than merely create trait lists, and that they test hypotheses that would progressively refine their impressions (too often, Taylor asserted, initial observations were taken as gospel). He also argued that archaeologists must excavate less extensively and more intensively (too many sites were just "tested" then compared with other remote "tests" with no effort to detect patterning *within* sites). Archaeologists must recover and decode the meaning of unremarkable food remains (the bones, seed hulls, and rubbish heaps were too often simply shoveled out) and embrace specialties in the analysis of finds (zoological, botanical, and petrographic identifications were too often made in the field and never verified). Taylor also argued that we should write more effective and detailed site reports (too often only the glamorous finds were illustrated, with precise proveniences omitted).

In perusing Taylor's propositions nearly six decades after he wrote them, we are struck by how unremarkable they now seem. Where is the revolution? Today's archaeologists do quantify their results; they do test hypotheses; they do excavate intensively; they do save food remains; they do involve specialists in analysis; and they do write detailed site reports.

But archaeologists did not do these things routinely in 1940, and this is what Taylor was sputtering about. Oddly, though, Taylor himself never carried through and actually implemented the conjunctive approach. Maybe the time just wasn't right. Nonetheless, Taylor's suggestions of 1948 embody few surprises for today's student—testimony to just how far archaeological doctrine and execution have matured since Taylor wrote *A Study of Archeology*.

Lewis R. Binford: Visionary with a Message

Americanist archaeology's second angry young man is Lewis R. Binford (1930–) (Figure 1-9). After a period of military service, Binford enrolled in 1954 at the University of North Carolina, wanting to become an ethnographer. By the time he moved on for graduate education at the University of Michigan, however, Binford was a confirmed archaeologist.

As a young professional, Binford was a man on the move—literally. He taught a year at the University of Michigan, then moved on to the University of Chicago, to the University of California at Santa Barbara, down the coast to UCLA, on to the University of New Mexico, and then to Southern Methodist University (in Dallas).

Figure 1-9 Lewis R. Binford (right) at Tulugak Lake in Alaska in 1999 with a Nunamiut friend, Johnny Rulland. Binford helped develop the "new archaeology" of the 1960s.

The mid-1960s was a hectic time for archaeology. Baby-boom demographics and the GI Bill inflated university enrollments. Campuses were the focal point of waves of social and political confrontation that rolled across the nation. Clashing opinions over the war in Vietnam and civil rights created a revolutionary atmosphere.

Archaeology was firmly embedded in this intellectual climate. Everyone, including archaeologists, was primed for change.

Binford fit into this cultural climate. He could lecture, sometimes for hours, with the force and enthusiasm of an old-time southern preacher, and he rapidly assumed the role of archaeological messiah. His students became disciples, spreading the word throughout the land: as the study of cultural change, archaeology has obvious relevance to modern problems. To fulfill this role, archaeology must transcend potsherds to address larger issues, such as cultural evolution, ecology, and social organization. Archaeology must take full advantage of modern technology by using scientific methods and sophisticated, quantitative techniques. Archaeology must be concerned with the few remaining preindustrial peoples in order to scrutinize firsthand the operation of disappearing cultural adaptations. And archaeology must be concerned with the methods we use to reconstruct the past. In the 1960s, this became known as the **new archaeology** (see "In His Own Words: The Challenge of Archaeology" by Lewis R. Binford).

new archaeology An approach to archaeology that arose in the 1960s emphasizing the understanding of underlying cultural processes and the use of the scientific method; today's version of the "new archaeology" is sometimes called processual archaeology.

In His Own Words
The Challenge of Archaeology

by Lewis R. Binford

As I was riding on the bus not long ago, an elderly gentleman asked me what I did. I told him I was an archaeologist. He replied: "That must be wonderful, for the only thing you have to be to succeed is lucky." It took some time to convince him that his view of archaeology was not quite mine. He had the idea that the archaeologist "digs up the past," that the successful archaeologist is one who discovers something not seen before, that all archaeologists spend their lives running about trying to make discoveries of this kind. This is a conception of science perhaps appropriate to the nineteenth century, but, at least in the terms which I myself view archaeology, it does not describe the nature of archaeology as it is practiced today. I believe archaeologists are more than simply discoverers. . . .

Archaeology cannot grow without striking a balance between theoretical and practical concerns.

Archaeologists need to be continuously self-critical: that is why the field is such a lively one and why archaeologists are forever arguing among themselves about who is right on certain issues. Self-criticism leads to change, but is itself a challenge—one which archaeology perhaps shares only with palaeontology and a few other fields whose ultimate concern is making inferences about the past on the basis of contemporary things. So archaeology is not a field that can study the past directly, nor can it be one that merely involves discovery, as the man on the bus suggested. On the contrary, it is a field wholly dependent upon inference to the past from things found in the contemporary world. Archaeological data, unfortunately, do not carry self-evident meanings. How much easier our work would be if they did!

The new archaeology (an odd term, since it is now quite old to all of us—and especially to today's student) became associated with a new way of studying the past and doing archaeology. The plan for it was set forth in a series of articles published through the 1960s and early 1970s, many by Binford and his students.

Binford asked why archaeology had contributed so little to general anthropological theory. His answer was that, in past studies, material culture had been simplistically interpreted. Too much attention had been lavished on artifacts as passive traits that "blend," "influence," or "stimulate" one another. Echoing Taylor, Binford proposed that artifacts be examined in terms of their cultural contexts and interpreted in their roles as reflections of technology, society, and belief systems.

Binford also underscored the importance of precise, unambiguous scientific methods. Archaeologists, he argued, should stop waiting for artifacts to speak up. They must formulate hypotheses and test these on the remains of the past. Binford argued that, because archaeologists always work from samples, they should acquire data that make the samples more representative of the populations from which they were drawn. He urged archaeologists to stretch their horizons beyond the individual site to the scale of the region; in this way, an entire cultural system could be reconstructed (as we discuss in Chapter 4). Such regional samples must be generated from research designs based on the principles of probability sampling. Random sampling is commonplace in other social sciences, and Binford insisted that archaeologists apply these scientific procedures to their own research problems.

Binford's mostly methodological contributions were gradually amplified by projects designed to demonstrate how the approach fosters the comprehension of cultural processes. Intricate statistical techniques were applied to a variety of subjects, from the nature of Mousterian (some 150,000 years old) campsites to the patterning of African Acheulian (500,000 years old) assemblages. He proposed new ideas, rooted in the field of human ecology, to explain the origins of plant domestication. These investigations were critical because they embroiled Binford in factual, substantive debate. Not only did he advocate different goals and new methods, but he also gained credibility among field archaeologists through these substantive controversies—he argued about specifics, not just theory. And Binford conducted his own ethnographic fieldwork among the Nunamiut Eskimo, the Navajo, and the Australian aborigines, testing the utility of archaeological concepts and methods on the trash of living peoples.

In Taylor-like fashion, Binford lambasted archaeology's principals, accusing them of retarding progress in the discipline. And yet his reception was quite different from Taylor's. Whereas *A Study of Archeology* languished on the shelf, Binford was hailed as "the father of the new archaeology." Taylor was the unwelcome harbinger of impending change, but Binford was the architect.

Binford and his students set off a firestorm that quickly spread throughout the archaeological community. A 1970s generation of graduate students and young professionals was greeted with the inquisition, "Are you a new archaeologist, an old archaeologist, or what? Make up your mind!"

Today, the new archaeology of the 1960s has transformed into what is termed processual archaeology. In subsequent chapters, we explore the tenets of this position and also examine how yet another wave of archaeological criticism—postprocessual archaeology—finds fault with Binford's approach and suggests some alternative directions.

ARCHAEOLOGY IN THE TWENTY-FIRST CENTURY

So, what about today? Who is a mover and shaker of the twenty-first century?

Perhaps in another 50 years or so, hindsight will suggest one person who truly captures the spirit of these times. But right now, we do not detect a single, defining trend that dominates Americanist archaeology; instead, the discipline has several branches, each growing and intersecting in interesting ways. Many of these diverse approaches result from new techniques and perspectives; others arise from the nature of employment in archaeology. Some archaeologists still work in muse-

ums and universities, but many more are employed in federal agencies and private archaeology firms (companies that arose as a response to federal legislation passed in the 1960s designed to protect the nation's archaeological resources—more about these in Chapter 17).

Prior to the 1970s, most American archaeologists were white and male. Today, the archaeological profession comprises equal numbers of men and women, and more minorities, including Native Americans, are actively involved in the field. Throughout these pages, we will meet some archaeologists who exemplify those trends (in boxes labeled "Profile of an Archaeologist"). For now, we wish to present one more archaeologist as a way to introduce modern archaeology.

Kathleen A. Deagan: Archaeology Comes of Age

Born the year that Walter Taylor published his harangue of American archaeology, Kathleen Deagan (1948–) represents in many ways the fulfillment of Taylor's call. Pictured in Figure 1-10, Deagan received her doctorate in anthropology from the University of Florida in 1974. Former chair and currently a curator at the Florida Museum of Natural History, she specializes in Spanish colonial studies. She is pushing the frontiers of historical archaeology (see Chapter 16), pioneering the archaeological investigation of disenfranchised groups and actively involved in bringing archaeology to the public. She is concerned with the people and culture behind the artifact and with explaining the social and cultural behaviors that she reconstructs from archaeology. Taylor would have approved of all this (but so would have Kidder).

Deagan is perhaps best known for her long-term excavations at St. Augustine (Florida), continuously occupied since its founding by Pedro Menéndez in 1565. St. Augustine is the oldest European enclave in the United States (complete with the "oldest pharmacy," "oldest house," "oldest church," and so on). Deagan's research here dates back to her graduate student days, her doctoral dissertation neatly encompassing the traditionally separate studies of historical archaeology, ethnohistory, and anthropology (see "In Her Own Words: The Potential of Historical Archaeology" by Kathleen Deagan).

Deagan addressed the processes and results of Spanish–Indian intermarriage and descent, a topic dear to the hearts of many anthropologists and

Figure 1-10 Kathleen Deagan, a contemporary archaeologist, excavating at St. Augustine, Florida.

ethnohistorians. The fact that people of such mixed descent (**mestizos**) constitute nearly the entire population of Latin America brought this issue to the forefront long ago. Similar processes took place in Spanish Florida, but the Hispanic occupation left no apparent mestizo population in La Florida, what Deagan calls "America's first melting pot." Accordingly, when she began her doctoral research, we knew virtually nothing about such early race relations in North America.

Deagan hypothesized how the mestizo population fit into this colonial setting. Given the nature of the unfortunate interactions that characterized eighteenth-century Florida, she expected the burdens of acculturation to have fallen most heavily on the Indian women living in Spanish or mestizo households. Because no mestizo people survive here, the tests for her hypothesis were necessarily archaeological. If her hypothesis is true, then acculturation should affect mostly the Native American women's activities visible in archaeological sites (food preparation techniques, equipment, household activities, basic food resources, child-related activities, and primarily female crafts such as pottery manufacture). Moreover, male-related activities (house construction technology and design, military and political affairs, and hunting weapons) should show less evidence of Indian infusion.

To explore these processes, Deagan began in 1973 a series of archaeological field schools at St. Augustine. This long-term, diversified enterprise excavated sites whose inhabitants represented a broad range of incomes,

occupations, and ethnic affiliations. Hundreds of students have learned their first archaeology at St. Augustine, where a saloon long sported an aging placard celebrating the years of "Digging With Deagan."

It was not long before her explorations into Hispanic–Native American interactions led Deagan to the Caribbean, where she headed interdisciplinary excavations at Puerto Real, the fourth-oldest European New World city (established in 1503). As she steadily moved back in time, Deagan's research eventually led her literally to the doorstep of Christopher Columbus.

In northern Haiti, Deagan discovered La Navidad, the earliest well-documented point of contact between Spanish and Native American people. On Christmas Eve, 1492—following two nights of partying with local Taino Arawak Indians—Columbus's flagship *Santa Maria* ran aground. He abandoned ship, moved to the *Nina,* and appealed to the local Native Americans for help. This disaster left the explorers one boat short. When Columbus sailed home with his world-shattering news, he left 39 unfortunate compatriots behind, protected by a small stockade built from the timbers of the wrecked *Santa Maria.* Returning a year later, Columbus found the settlement burned, his men killed and mutilated.

Columbus soon established the more permanent settlements of La Isabela and Puerto Real—sites of the first sustained contact between Europeans and Native Americans—and Deagan has also conducted important field excavations there. Having a population of nearly 1500 people, La Isabela was home to soldiers, priests, stonecutters, masons, carpenters, nobles, and warriors. Although this first Columbian town lasted only four years, several critical events took place here: the first intentional introduction of European plants and animals; the first expedition into the interior; and the first Hispanic installation of urban necessities, such as canals, mills, streets, gardens, plazas, ports, ramparts, roads, and hospitals.

The biological effects of the Columbian exchange soon overtook La Isabela. European and Native American alike suffered from dietary deficiencies, an excessive workload, and contagious disease. Influenza struck during the first week, affecting one-third of the population. When Columbus ordered the settlement abandoned in 1496, fewer than 300 inhabitants were left. Deagan extended her research to investigate daily life in the initial colonial period, including the ways in which European colonists coped with their new and largely unknown New World environment.

mestizos Spanish term referring to people of mixed European and Native American ancestry.

In Her Own Words

The Potential of Historical Archaeology

by Kathleen Deagan

From its emergence as a recognized area of research in the 1930s, historical archaeology has advanced from providing supplemental data for other disciplines, through an anthropological tool for the reconstruction of past lifeways, to a means of discovering predictable relationships between human adaptive strategies, ideology, and patterned variability in the archaeological record.

Because it can compare written accounts about what people said they did, what observers said people did, and what the archaeological record said people did, historical archaeology can make contributions not possible through any other discipline. Inconsistencies and inaccuracies in the written records may be detected and ultimately predicted. Insights into conditions provided by such written sources may be compared to the more objective archaeological record of actual conditions in the past in order to provide insight into cognitive processes.

The simultaneous access to varied sources of information allows the historical archaeologist to match the archaeological patterning of a given site against the documented social, economic, and ideological attributes of the same site to arrive at a better understanding of how the archaeological record reflects human behavior.

The unique potential of historical archaeology lies not only in its ability to answer questions of archaeological and anthropological interest, but also in its ability to provide historical data not available through documentation or any other source. Correcting the inadequate treatment of disenfranchised groups in America's past, excluded from historical sources because of race, religion, isolation, or poverty, is an important function of contemporary historical archaeology and one that cannot be ignored.

Beyond new directions in historical archaeology, Deagan's research demonstrates the degree to which contemporary Americanist archaeology is played out in the public arena; she creates headlines wherever she works. Newspapers around the world chronicle her success, and her research was featured in consecutive years in the pages of *National Geographic* magazine. Most recently, she published, with Venezuelan archaeologist José María Cruxent, two books on La Isabela, one a data-laden professional monograph, the other a readable volume for the public.

Deagan shows skill and patience with the onslaught of well-meaning reporters because she knows that archaeologists cannot afford to isolate themselves in ivory towers or archaeology labs. One way or another—whether through federal grants, state-supported projects, tax laws, or private benefaction—archaeology depends on public support for its livelihood, and consequently it owes something back to that public.

Decades ago, Margaret Mead, one of the nation's first anthropologists, recognized the importance of taking the work of anthropologists to the public, and she spent considerable effort keeping anthropology alive in the print and electronic media. Today, archaeology enjoys unprecedented press coverage, and archaeologists like Deagan know that without such publicity, Americanist archaeology has no future.

Deagan's research and publications have also helped establish historical archaeology as an anthropologically relevant specialty of archaeology. Although awash in time-specific details and artifacts, she is ultimately addressing the general processes behind the particulars: the sexual and social consequences of Spanish–Indian intermarriage, the demographic collapse and biological imbalance resulting from Old World/New World interchange, and the processes behind the disintegration of traditional cultural patterns. Although her data are documentary and archaeological, Deagan is confronting issues of anthropological relevance.

Conclusion: Archaeology's Future

Archaeology has a vibrant, lively future. The field enjoys enormous public interest, as shown by the popularity of places such as Mesa Verde National Park, television programming, and related college courses. This level of public support suggests that more, not less, archaeology will be needed in the future.

Americanist archaeology has evolved from a pastime of the wealthy to an established scientific discipline. But with these changes have come the realization that studying the human past raises numerous ethical issues. Nobody can practice archaeology in a political or cultural vacuum. As we learn more about how archaeologists go about studying the past, we will also confront, in each of the following chapters, some of the ethical issues facing archaeology today.

Summary

- Archaeology today is a lively field that contributes enormously to an understanding of the human condition and confronts serious ethical dilemmas.

- The beginnings of an interest in the past can be traced back to the sixth century BC Babylonian king Nabonidus, who looked at the physical residues of antiquity to answer questions about the past.

- In North America, archaeology began as the pastime of antiquarians, the curious and the wealthy, who lacked formal training.

- Archaeology as a formal discipline dates to the late nineteenth century and was characterized by a scientific approach and rigorous methods of excavation and data collection.

- Early on, archaeology was necessarily concerned with description and with culture history, constructing chronologies of material culture and relating these to the diffusion of ideas and the movements of cultures; but it also drew upon a variety of fields, especially the natural sciences, to help recover and reconstruct the past.

- By the 1950s, archaeology began to move beyond description and chronology to more focus on the reconstruction of past lifeways.

- This trend continued in the 1960s, with the addition of efforts to employ a scientific approach aimed at discovering universal laws and to develop theories to explain the human history uncovered by archaeology.

- Today, archaeology is a diverse field that covers both prehistoric and historic archaeology. The number of archaeologists has grown dramatically since the 1960s, and the field today is diverse, representing many different theoretical perspectives and acknowledging the need to communicate results to the public.

Additional Reading

Chatters, James C. 2001. *Ancient Encounters: Kennewick Man and the First Americans.* New York: Simon and Schuster.

Daniel, Glyn, and Colin Renfrew. 1988. *The Idea of Prehistory.* Edinburgh: University of Edinburgh Press.

Patterson, Thomas. 1995. *Toward a Social History of Archaeology in the United States.* Fort Worth: Harcourt Brace.

Thomas, David Hurst. 2000. *Skull Wars: Kennewick Man, Archaeology, and the Battle for Native American Identity.* New York: Basic Books.

Trigger, Bruce. 1999. *A History of Archaeological Thought.* 2d ed. Cambridge, England: Cambridge University Press.

Willey, Gordon R., and Jeremy A. Sabloff. 1993. *A History of American Archaeology.* 3d ed. New York: Freeman.

For court documents on the Kennewick case, visit the Society for American Archaeology's Web site, www. saa.org, and click on government affairs.

Online Resources

COMPANION WEB SITE
Visit **http://anthropology.wadsworth.com** and click on the Student Companion Web Site for Thomas/Kelly *Archaeology*, 4th edition, to access a wide range of material to help you succeed in your introductory archaeology course. These include flashcards, Internet exercises, Web links, and practice quizzes.

RESEARCH ONLINE WITH INFOTRAC COLLEGE EDITION
From the Student Companion Web Site, you can access the InfoTrac College Edition database, which offers thousands of full-length articles for your research.

2

Archaeology, Anthropology, Science, and the Humanities

Outline

Courtesy of the Southeast Archaeological Center, National Park Service, photo by David G. Anderson

Preview

IN THIS CHAPTER we consider how archaeologists relate to the broader approaches of anthropology, science, and the humanities. The concept of culture has long been critical in anthropology and, as you will see, the anthropological use of the term takes on quite a different meaning from its everyday use. We will also explore the adaptive and ideational perspectives, two rather different ways of studying culture.

These contrasting perspectives also condition the contrast between scientific and humanistic approaches. These opposing, yet complementary, research strategies are each important to understanding diversity and universals among humanity.

INTRODUCTION

Some 50 years ago, archaeologist Philip Phillips declared, "Archaeology is anthropology or it is nothing." Today, Americanist archaeology remains a subfield of anthropology. Both of us have earned multiple degrees in anthropology, and we both work in departments of anthropology.

A diversity of perspectives and goals characterizes archaeology in the twenty-first century. In fact, there are few U.S. departments of archaeology (the most prominent is at Boston University). Outside the United States, however, archaeology is often more closely aligned with the humanities, such as history, classics, or art history (and it sometimes appears in these departments in U.S. universities). But the boundaries between these various archaeologies and their former affiliations are crumbling. Many classical archaeologists, for instance,

are turning to anthropology as a source of ideas. And although many American archaeologists remain committed to a scientific approach, others look to the humanities for insight. Americanist archaeology is surely changing, but we believe that it will always remain closely aligned with anthropological thinking.

In this chapter, we examine the broader anthropological context of archaeology. We will also explore how scientific and humanistic perspectives condition archaeological approaches to the past. Although we draw a dichotomy between science and humanism, you should know that most archaeologists are a bit of both; many archaeologists, for example, receive funding for their research from the National Science Foundation and the National Endowment for the Humanities.

Excavation of a 500-year-old Mississippian Mound at Shiloh National Military Park.

So, What's an Anthropological Approach?

Everyone thinks they know what anthropologists do: They study native people and fossils and chimpanzees. They grin from the pages of *National Geographic* magazine, make chit-chat on late-night talk shows, and show up on the Discovery Channel. They are Richard Leakey, Jane Goodall, and Don Johanson. Some people think that the late Stephen Jay Gould was an anthropologist (actually, he was a paleontologist and a brilliant historian of science).

But this is a limited vision of anthropology. The truth is that few people seem to know what anthropologists actually do, what anthropologists share, what makes them anthropologists at all. **Anthropology** is tough to pin down because anthropologists do so many different things.

So, what makes an anthropologist an anthropologist?

The answer is surprisingly simple: All anthropologists believe that the best understanding of the human condition arises from a global, comparative, and holistic approach. It is not enough to look at a single group of Americans, Chinese, or Bushmen to find the keys to human existence. Neither is it enough to look at just one part of the human condition, as do economists, historians, political scientists, and psychologists. Looking at part of the picture only gives you just that—part of the picture.

What holds anthropology together is its dogmatic insistence that every aspect of every human society, extant or extinct, counts. For a century, anthropologists have tried to arrive at the fullest possible understanding of human similarities and diversity. Because of this broad-brush approach, anthropology is uniquely qualified to understand what makes humankind distinct from the rest of the animal world. This is not to say that all anthropologists study everything: Margaret Mead never excavated an archaeological site, and Richard Leakey never interviewed a native Lakota speaker. The

Renaissance anthropologist—the individual who does everything—has passed into folklore. Today, nobody can hope to do everything well.

So anthropologists specialize, and archaeologists are anthropologists who specialize in the deceased. But archaeologists still draw upon each of the other subfields of anthropology (not to mention several other sciences). Before examining how modern archaeology articulates with the rest of anthropology, we first must see just how anthropologists have carved up the pie of human existence.

Kinds of Anthropologists

The basic divisions within anthropology reflect the very nature of human existence. Anthropology embraces four primary fields of study: biological anthropology, cultural anthropology, linguistic anthropology, and archaeology (all shown in Figure 2-1). Although these are not wholly independent divisions, they do divide the discipline into manageable domains of study.

Biological Anthropology

Biological anthropologists (also known as physical anthropologists) study humans as biological organisms. One major concern is the biological evolution of humans. How did *Homo sapiens* come into being? To answer this question, biological anthropologists have pieced together an intricate family tree over the past century, working largely from fossil evidence and observation of living primates.

A second focus of modern physical anthropology is the study of human biological variability. No two human beings are identical, even though we all are members of a single species. The study of inherited differences has become a strategic domain of scientific investigation and also a matter of practical concern for educators, politicians, and community leaders.

Yet a third area of biological anthropology is bioarchaeology, the study of the human biological component of the ancient past. Archaeology overlaps with biological anthropology in that archaeologists often encounter human skeletal remains and work with biological anthropologists in their recovery and analysis. (We devote Chapter 12 to bioarchaeological inquiry.)

Each year, roughly 12 percent of the 250–300 anthropology PhD degrees granted in the United States are awarded in biological anthropology. This healthy per-

anthropology The study of all aspects of humankind—biological, cultural, and linguistic; extant and extinct—employing an all-encompassing holistic approach.

biological anthropology A subdiscipline of anthropology that views humans as biological organisms; also known as physical anthropology.

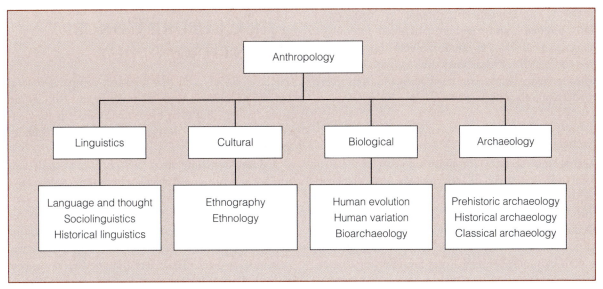

Figure 2-1 The four subfields of anthropology and their areas of study.

centage indicates that, although biological anthropology remains a fairly small subfield of anthropology, it has a remarkable ability to adapt to changing technologies and an increasingly diverse academic environment. Spectacular recent fossil finds, the progress in studying human DNA, the expansion into forensic and medical studies, and advances in evolutionary anthropology have all given biological anthropology a very visible academic and public profile.

Cultural Anthropology

Cultural anthropologists describe and analyze the culture of human groups in the present and relatively recent past. Cultural anthropologists commonly employ the method of **participant observation,** gathering data by personally questioning and observing people while living in their society. Anthropologists study rituals, kinship, religion, politics, art, oral histories, medical practices—anything and everything that people in contemporary societies do, say, or think.

Conventionally, cultural anthropologists who describe present-day cultures on a firsthand basis are termed **ethnographers**, and their descriptions are called **ethnographies** (we mentioned in Chapter 1 that the comparative study of cultures is termed ethnology). About 60 percent of the PhDs in anthropology are awarded to cultural anthropologists. Archaeology overlaps with cultural anthropology in that some archaeologists conduct research with living peoples to

understand the relationships between behavior and material remains (see Chapter 10), and all archaeologists look to ethnographic research for ideas about how to interpret the things they find in sites.

Linguistic Anthropology

Anthropological linguists evaluate linguistic behavior in detail: how sounds are made, how sounds create languages, the relationship between language and thought, how linguistic systems change through time, the basic structure of language, and the role of language in the development of culture. Anthropological linguists also use language to chart historical relationships and track ancient migrations between now-separate, but linguistically related, populations. Today, many linguists study the process whereby people acquire second languages and work with native peoples to revive dying languages.

cultural anthropology A subdiscipline of anthropology that emphasizes nonbiological aspects: the learned social, linguistic, technological, and familial behaviors of humans.

participant observation The primary strategy of cultural anthropology in which data are gathered by questioning and observing people while the observer lives in their society.

ethnographers Anthropologists who study one culture and write detailed descriptions of that culture's traditions, customs, religion, social and political organization, and so on.

ethnographies The descriptions of cultures written by ethnographers.

The field of linguistic anthropology is shrinking; in 2001 **linguistic anthropology** accounted for only 1 percent of all PhDs in anthropology (down from 7 percent in 1970). Archaeology overlaps with linguistics when language helps reconstruct when and from where modern populations migrated.

Archaeology

Archaeology accounts for about a quarter of the doctoral degrees awarded in anthropology. Most archaeologists also attempt to understand human culture, but their technology and field methods differ radically from those of ethnologists and linguists. Because archaeologists commonly study extinct cultures, they work at some disadvantage. Lacking living, breathing informants, archaeologists have formulated a powerful array of techniques for gleaning relevant information from the material remains of the past. As we will see, these methods sometimes give archaeologists information that living, breathing informants probably never would (or could) have told them.

The future of archaeology is bright indeed. Archaeology is a strong element of many graduate programs in anthropology, and undergraduates often find archaeology to be the most lively and exciting program within anthropology. This excitement is due, in part, to the dazzling assortment of new ways to explore the past that we discuss in this text.

Archaeology is also the subfield of anthropology most capable of delivering jobs to undergraduates. Americanist archaeology is expanding, especially in such areas as historical archaeology, heritage programs, and cultural resource management programs. Look for archaeology to continue making significant contributions to the overall mission of anthropology.

linguistic anthropology A subdiscipline of anthropology that focuses on human language: its diversity in grammar, syntax, and lexicon; its historical development; and its relation to a culture's perception of the world.

archaeology The study of the past through the systematic recovery and analysis of material remains.

culture An integrated system of beliefs, traditions, and customs that govern or influence a person's behavior. Culture is learned, shared by members of a group, and based on the ability to think in terms of symbols.

THE CULTURE CONCEPT IN ANTHROPOLOGY

We have already said that a global, comparative, and holistic perspective tends to unite the diversity within anthropology. But even more than that, it is the concept of **culture** that brings together the subfields of anthropology.

A dozen academic disciplines purport to study culture (or at least cultural behavior): economics, sociology, linguistics, political science, history, cultural geography, psychology, and so forth. "Classical" historians, for instance, might investigate Greek, Roman, or Byzantine culture; their interest centers on the cultural characteristics of each particular society. But one does not expect to find classical historians discoursing on the general nature of culture; if they did, they would cease to be classical historians and would become anthropologists. This overarching conception and investigation of culture traditionally forms the central theme melding so many diversified (and sometimes conflicting) concerns into the anthropological perspective.

What Is Culture?

Nearly 50 years ago, Alfred Kroeber and Clyde Kluckhohn compiled more than 200 distinct definitions of culture. Since that time, the number of definitions of culture must have tripled.

Do these definitions have anything in common? Absolutely.

Suppose we begin with the classic definition offered by Sir Edward Burnett Tylor (the person considered by many to be the founder of modern anthropology). Tylor's (1871) definition of culture appeared in 1871 on the first page of anthropology's first textbook and remains one of the clearest:

> Culture…taken in its wide ethnographic sense is that complex whole which includes knowledge, belief, art, morals, law, custom, and any other capabilities and habits acquired by man as a member of society.

Culture in Tylor's sense is *learned*—from parents, peers, teachers, leaders, and others. Note that culture is not biological or genetic; any person can acquire any culture. And under the anthropological definition, all peoples have the same amount of culture. Someone who can recite Shakespeare and who listens to Beethoven's

Moonlight Sonata is no more (or less) cultural than someone who reads *Reader's Digest* and prefers Flatt and Scruggs' *Foggy Mountain Breakdown*. If a baby born to European parents in Europe were raised in China, that individual's appearance would come from its genes (as moderated by environmental factors), but he or she would speak Chinese and act and think as other Chinese do.

Culture creates very different conceptions of life, of what is proper and what is not. Tribal people in New Guinea think it laughable that American women wear earrings, but they think it normal to wear bone or shell nose ornaments for ceremonies. Cultures change over time in part by changes in **enculturation**, the process whereby an individual learns their culture as a child. Material factors (such as nutrition) and historical factors (such as contact with other peoples) affect this process. Given that archaeology is concerned with how cultures change over time, the concept of learned culture is essential to archaeology.

Culture is also *shared*. By this, we mean that although each person is an individual with their own particular values and understandings, human groups share some basic ideas about the world and their place in it. Shared ideas, rather than individual variations on them, are the traditional focus of anthropology.

Many Euroamerican homes, for instance, are divided into multiple rooms, including a living room, a smallish kitchen, family room, and bedrooms. The main entry often opens directly into the living room. This pattern is considered normal and comfortable by most Euroamericans.

But, according to George Esber (Miami University), when Apache people were given the chance to design their own homes, they preferred a single large living area that included the kitchen, with only the bedrooms and baths separate. These large living areas could accommodate large social gatherings. In order to cook for so many people, Apaches also preferred kitchens with an almost industrial capacity, including large cabinets to accommodate large cooking pots. In this case, different ideas about life result in different social behaviors that result in different material remains. By delving into material remains, then, archaeology investigates and expands anthropology's concept of culture.

Finally, culture is *symbolic*. Consider the symbolism involved in language: There is no reason that the word "dog" in English means "a household pet," anymore than do "chien," "perro," or "alika" (French, Spanish,

and Malagasy). And there is no reason that dogs are necessarily pets. Indeed, in many places in the world, such as Micronesia and Southeast Asia, dogs are feast foods. Many Americans consider this disgusting, and some Vietnamese immigrants in California have wound up in court over it. But neither the idea of "pet" nor "food" is inherent in a dog—they are symbolic meanings that cultures give to dogs (the same is true for guinea pigs, which are eaten in highland Peru). Symbolic meanings such as these affect which bones wind up in ancient middens.

Virtually all human behavior is symbolic to some degree, and this symbolism can create considerable misunderstanding. When North Americans talk, for example, they tend to stay about an arm's length away from each other. Latin Americans stand much closer, often touching one another. As a result, Latin Americans sometimes see North Americans as cold and distant, whereas North Americans often feel their southern neighbors are too intimate or aggressive. Such symbolic meanings of behavior condition what we do, which in turn affects the material traces of those behaviors (such as the structure of houses and public places). Again, archaeology studies the concept of culture by studying these material traces.

So, culture is learned, shared, and symbolic; it provides you with a way to interpret human behavior and the world around you; and it plays a key role in structuring the material record of human behavior—which archaeologists recover.

How Do Anthropologists Study Culture?

To oversimplify a bit, anthropologists study culture in two basic ways. An **ideational perspective** focuses on ideas, symbols, and mental structures as driving forces in shaping human behavior. Alternatively, an **adaptive perspective** isolates technology, ecology, demography, and economics as the key factors defining human behavior. Let's examine each perspective.

enculturation The process whereby individuals learn their culture.

ideational perspective The research perspective that defines ideas, symbols, and mental structures as driving forces in shaping human behavior.

adaptive perspective A research perspective that emphasizes technology, ecology, demography, and economics in the definition of human behavior.

Culture as Ideas

According to anthropologist Roger Keesing (1935–1993), the basic theme of the ideational perspective in anthropology is that culture is a complex set of conceptual designs and shared understandings that underlie the way people act. Culture, in this sense, is principally what humans learn, not what they do or make. This perspective emphasizes ideas, thoughts, and shared knowledge and sees symbols and their meanings as crucial to shaping human behavior. It encompasses material culture insofar as material things manifest symbolic ideas.

The ideational theorist insists on "getting inside a person's head" to seek out the shared meanings of a society. According to the ideational view of culture, one cannot comprehend human behavior without understanding the symbolic code for that behavior. Moreover, according to this view, our interpretation and, in fact, the symbolic meaning(s) that we give to things heavily influence our perception of the world around us.

Culture as Adaptation

An adaptive perspective is primarily concerned with "culture as a system." Social and cultural differences are viewed not as reflections of symbolic meanings, but rather as responses to the material parameters of life, such as food, shelter, and reproduction. Human behaviors are seen as linked together systemically, such that change in one area, say technology, will result in change in another area, such as social organization. Leslie White (1900–1975) pioneered the investigation of cultural systems, and archaeologists have reworked White's reasoning to suit the study of extinct cultural systems. Following White's lead, Lewis Binford (discussed on page 17) defined the cultural system as a set of repetitive articulations among the social, technological, and ideological aspects of culture. These three facets are, in White's terminology, "extrasomatic," meaning "outside the body" or "learned," as noted above. And it is the cultural system—technology, modes of economic organization, settlement patterns, forms of social grouping, and political institutions—that articulates the material needs of human communities with their ecological settings.

potlatch Among nineteenth-century Northwest Coast Native Americans, a ceremony involving the giving away or destruction of property in order to acquire prestige.

trade language A language that develops among speakers of different languages to permit economic exchanges.

In the adaptive perspective, culture keeps societies in equilibrium with their ecosystems. Adaptive prime movers are those elements of technology, subsistence economy, and social or political organization most closely tied to life's material needs: food, reproduction, and shelter. Archaeologists working with the adaptive perspective link cultural behaviors largely to the environment, demography, subsistence, or technology. They see ideational systems as secondary.

Let's look at an example of how these two perspectives produce different but complementary understandings of cultural behavior.

An Example: The Kwakwak'awakw Potlatch

The Kwakwak'awakw (see "Looking Closer: Who Are We?" by Gloria Cranmer Webster) are a Native American tribe that lives on the coast of British Columbia. Prior to extensive European contact, they were hunter-fishers, living primarily by fishing for salmon and halibut, hunting sea mammals, and gathering shellfish. Importantly, they were quite dependent on a few large salmon runs in the fall to provide them with nearly all their food for the long winter. They once lived in villages that consisted of many large decorated houses built of cedar plants and that often housed several related families. They had a social hierarchy in which some families could claim a higher rank (and perhaps a greater share of resources) than other families. Slaves were occasionally taken in raids between villages. Many modern Kwakwak'awakw still live in their original territory and, although many are commercial fishermen, others are carpenters, computer programmers, lawyers, and teachers.

The element of Kwakwak'awakw life that has most fascinated anthropology for the last century is the **potlatch** (Figure 2-2 shows a contemporary artist's rendering). The potlatch is an example of competitive feasts, a social custom found in many societies. The term comes from Chinook, a Northwest Coast **trade language**, and means "to give." Potlatches varied in size, from small affairs between families to huge feasts between villages—the kind the Kwakwak'awakw called "doing a great thing."

The potlatch existed when James Cook explored the northwest coast of North America in 1778. Taking some American sea otter pelts with him across the Pacific, Cook discovered that the Chinese valued them highly. A lively transpacific trade began: the Europeans supplying blankets, beads, metal pots, and axes to the

Figure 2-2 Artist's rendering of a late-nineteenth-century Kwak-wak'awakw (Kwakiutl) potlatch ceremony (painting by Will Taylor).

involved ambitious, status-hungry men who battled one another for social approval by hosting massive, opulent feasts. These feasts proceeded according to culturally dictated rules. One chief functioned in the role of host, inviting neighbors to his village for the festivities. The host parceled out gifts of varying value: boxes of candle-fish oil, baskets of berries, stacks of blankets, animal skins. As the chief presented each gift, the guests responded with a great degree of (culturally prescribed) dissatis-faction, for they could not insinuate that their host was generous.

There were bonfires, magic tricks, and singing at pot-latches, and ranking families displayed valuable family heirlooms such as carved dishes. There were elaborate dances (such as the cannibal dance, in which members of the audience might be bitten) and others where birds and whales were portrayed by wooden masks whose hinged mouths would dramatically open wide to reveal a human face peering up from the throat.

And there was food, lots and lots of food. Men drank fish oil from shovel-sized spoons, spilling it all over themselves. Guests would "eat themselves under the table" and crawl groaning into the forest, only to vomit and return for more. The more food one gave away, the greater one's prestige.

The feasting extended beyond simple gluttony. A high-ranking member of the host village would give away blankets, slaves, canoes, food, and other things to a high-ranking man from a rival village. One particularly impor-tant item was "coppers"—hammered, shield-like sheets of European copper, often with designs embossed or painted on their surfaces. These copper sheets had

Native Americans in exchange for pelts to be taken to China and elsewhere. The influx of so many European goods increased the size and significance of potlatches. One in 1921 included motorboats, sewing machines, gramophones, musical instruments—even a pool table!

Potlatches accompanied high-ranking marriages be-tween villages (like those between Europe's royal houses), funerals, and the raising of totem poles. And all of them

Looking Closer
Who Are We?

We are not the Kwakiutl, as the white people have called us since they first came to our territory. The only Kwaki-utl...are the people of Fort Rupert. Each of our village groups has its own name....The language we speak is Kwakwala. The name Kwak-wak'awakw refers to Kwakwala speakers and accu-rately describes who we are. To call all of us who live in a specific cultural area "Kwakiutl" is like call-ing all indigenous people of the Americas "Indians." No longer is either acceptable.

by Gloria Cranmer Webster (Kwakwak'awakw), a historian and former director of the U'mista Cultural Centre (Alert Bay, British Columbia)

names, such as "Killer Whale," "Beaver Face," and "All Other Coppers Are Ashamed to Look at It." Late nineteenth-century potlatching sometimes culminated in the outright destruction of property—hosts threw coppers into the sea and burned food, clothing, money, and canoes.

The logic behind this conspicuous consumption was this: The more goods given away or destroyed, the greater the host's prestige. The guest chief would belittle the host's efforts, but he knew that to regain prestige he would eventually have to give an even grander feast.

So, what was this all about?

The Potlatch as Ideational Message

What was the symbolic message of the feasts? What did the participants think was happening?

For the person giving the feast, the objective was prestige. Hosts obtained the dispersed goods through hard work, but also by giving smaller potlatches within their own villages. Traditionally, the value of goods given in those potlatches had to eventually be returned (not the exact same gifts, but their equivalents) plus a little bit more. It was investment banking.

By giving away all the collected goods to a visitor or by destroying them, a host insulted his guests by symbolically saying "This is how powerful I am. I can give all this away and it does me no harm. You can't do this." And through association with this man, village members also gained prestige. For them, a successful potlatch truly was "doing a great thing."

To the non-Kwakwak'awakw, the images of killer whales, huge spoons, bears, and boxes of candlefish oil seemed bizarre and chaotic. Indeed, the Canadian government found potlatches to be barbaric and wasteful and banned them in 1885 (a ban that was not lifted until 1951). This is because white Canadians did not share in Kwakwak'awakw culture. They did not know the stories and legends that "made sense" of the masks and symbols—stories and legends that every Kwakwak'awakw child knew. White Canadians saw no good purpose to potlatching; instead, they saw only a material chaos and waste that stood in the way of converting the Kwakwak'awakw to Christianity and a system of western values.

But imagine if we could bring a nineteenth-century Kwakwak'awakw man to an American football game. Costumed men smash into one another below. The observers in the stands scream, some literally calling for blood; many have their faces (and bodies) painted in garish colors, wear horned masks, and wave giant point-

ing puppet hands in the air. Observers drink to excess, and fights may break out in the bleachers. A streaker dashes down the visiting team's side of the field. Based on who wins the contest, supporters celebrate far into the night and enjoy increased status—until the next game.

Would the Kwakwak'awakw have understood? Or would he have thought he was in the presence of madness?

There was even more to the potlatch than the search for prestige. Many cultures contain rituals or festivals in which prohibited behaviors are demonstrated by symbolically indulging in them, by temporarily inverting the social order. During Halloween, for example, American children are allowed to dress (and act) like ghouls and make demands of adults—behavior that is normally banned. The potlatch involved the excessive consumption of food among a people where table manners were normally as precise and rigorous as those at a Victorian banquet or a Japanese tea ceremony. Stanley Walens argues that the potlatch was a way of enforcing such behavior by demonstrating what happens when people do *not* control their hunger: they turn into cannibals and become like killer whales that swallow people whole.

The Potlatch as Adaptive Strategy

A different interpretation of the potlatch arises when we look at the potlatch from the adaptive perspective. How did the loss of so much personal property serve useful ecological, technological, or economic purposes?

Recall that the Kwakwak'awakw depended on salmon for their winter food supply. Some villages were located on streams with large, reliable salmon runs; others were on streams of smaller, less reliable runs. These less-fortunate villages tried to ally themselves with the larger, more fortunate villages—villages they could count on for assistance in years of poor salmon runs. Through alliances cemented by potlatching, the large villages also alleviated the possibility that smaller villages might, under desperate conditions, try to attack them. They therefore fought wars of "property" in addition to (or instead of) wars of "blood." Through the potlatch system, the less fortunate villages were invited to potlatches hosted by their more prosperous neighbors. Although visitors were required to endure seemingly endless barbs and slights, they departed with full bellies—and, more important, with a powerful ally.

And what if some villages sustained a continued subsistence catastrophe? Some research suggests that the potlatch helped shift population from less productive to more productive villages: economically prosperous villages could boast of (and demonstrate) their affluence at the potlatch ceremonies, thereby inducing guests to leave their impoverished situations and join the wealthier, more ecologically stable village. More people meant more laborers and bigger, more elaborate feasts that would allow a chief to outcompete his rivals. In other words, the drive for individual prestige held a material significance for the rank-and-file villagers.

Potlatches also allowed villagers to judge the leadership capacity of a man vying for prestige. If he gave a poor potlatch, then it was apparent that he did not have much backing or clout and therefore was not capable of establishing intervillage ties—social ties that were critical in times of poor salmon runs, storms, harsh winters, or warfare. If people wanted to have a better chance of "making it" through bad times, then they should want to be part of a village that had ties to neighbors who could, and would, help in times of need.

Which Perspective Is Better?

In a word, neither. The differences between these two perspectives on culture are a lot like the differences between any two cultures themselves, such as Kwakwak'awakw and European culture. Each perspective looks at the world in a different way, highlighting some aspects and downplaying others; each makes mistaken interpretations here and finds insights there. The adaptive perspective recognizes that humans must respond to the material conditions of their environments, and the ideational perspective shows how they do this through particular symbolic behaviors. The adaptive perspective cannot account for the particular way in which the potlatch was conducted, and the ideational perspective cannot account for why the potlatch occurred where and when it did or what goods were given away. Hence, we need both adaptive and ideational perspectives to understand human diversity and history.

SCIENTIFIC AND HUMANISTIC APPROACHES IN ARCHAEOLOGY

Anthropologists also distinguish between scientific and humanistic approaches. This struggle is between two incompatible views of the world (culture again!) and consequently is a disagreement about which tools are best for any particular task. This difference is critical to understanding the two major flavors of modern archaeology (which we will discuss in Chapter 3).

What's a Scientific Approach?

Science (from the Latin "to know") refers, in its broadest sense, to a systematic body of knowledge about any field. Although the era of modern science is generally considered to have begun in the Renaissance, the origins of scientific thought extend far back in human history. The **archaeological record**—the documentation of artifacts and their contexts recovered from archaeological sites—has preserved examples of early scientific reasoning: astronomical observations, treatment of disease, calendrical systems, recipes for food and drink. Cave paintings and carvings in bone or stone are often cited as early instances of systematizing knowledge.

Science as a distinct intellectual endeavor began in the seventeenth century with work in mathematics, astronomy, and physics by such luminaries as Galileo, Newton, Kepler, Pascal, and Descartes. Sir Francis Bacon codified the scientific method in his book *Novum Organum* (1620). Darwin's nineteenth-century consideration of evolution added a biological component to the scientific picture.

Today, pure science is divided into the physical sciences (including physics, chemistry, and geology), the biological sciences (such as botany and zoology), and interdisciplinary sciences, such as biochemistry (which understands life processes in terms of chemical substances and reactions) and anthropology (which aims to understand humans as biological and social beings).

So, what exactly is science? A good definition is hard to pin down; perhaps it is easiest to simply list some key characteristics. Lawrence Kuznar (Indiana-Purdue University at Fort Wayne) provides several:

- **Science is empirical, or objective.** Science is concerned with the observable, measurable world and has nothing to say about the non-material world. Questions are scientific (a) if they are concerned with the detectable properties of things and (b) if the result of observations designed to answer a question cannot be predetermined by the biases of the observer.
- **Science is systematic and explicit.** Scientists try to gather information in such a way that they

science The search for universals by means of established scientific methods of inquiry.

archaeological record The documentation of artifacts and other material remains, along with their contexts recovered from archaeological sites.

collect all data that are relevant to a problem, and they aim to do this in such a way that any trained observer under the same conditions would make the same observations.

■ **Science is logical.** It works not only with data, but with ideas that link data with interpretations and with ideas that link other ideas themselves together. These linkages must be based on previously demonstrated principles, otherwise an argument is a house of cards.

■ **Science is explanatory and, consequently, predictive.** Science is concerned with causes. It seeks theories—explanatory statements that allow one to not only predict what will happen under a specified set of conditions, but also explain why it will happen. The goal of science is to develop theories that can be criticized, evaluated, and eventually modified or replaced by other theories that explain the data better.

■ **Science is self-critical and based on testing.** Many people think that science requires white lab coats, supercomputers, and complex equations. Although science might entail these things, it is really about honesty. Scientists propose hypotheses, tentative ideas about the world or explanations of previous observations. Then they say, "Here is my idea, here is the evidence that will prove it wrong, and here is my attempt to collect that evidence." Scientists acquire understanding not by proving that an idea is right, but by showing that competing ideas are wrong. Consequently, scientists always ask themselves: How do I know that I know something? They are professional skeptics, always looking for biases in their data, always testing their methods and prevailing ideas against competing ones.

■ **Science is public.** A scientist's method and observations and the arguments linking observations with conclusions are explicit and available for scrutiny by the public. The source or political implications of ideas are unimportant; what matters in science is that the ideas can be tested by objective methods. Taken together, these characteristics of science combine to produce the scientific method, an elegant and powerful way to understand the workings of the material world—and to conduct archaeology.

Archaeologists have been doing scientific research for a long time. Consider, for example, how scientific methods were used to solve the "mystery" of the Moundbuilders.

How Science Explains Things: The Moundbuilder Myth

When Europeans arrived on the North American continent in the sixteenth century, they of course met Indians. And in so doing, they confronted a serious issue: Who were these people? This was an important question, for in its answer lay the answer to another question: Did Europeans have the right to take the land?

Later, as colonial Americans began to expand westward through Indian lands, they discovered thousands of mounds and earthworks, especially in the Ohio River and Mississippi River valleys. Some of these mounds were modest, a meter or so high and a few meters in diameter. Others were enormous: Monk's Mound at the site of Cahokia, in Illinois, just across the Mississippi River from St. Louis, stands nearly 70 feet high and covers as many acres as the largest pyramid in Egypt. Some were conically shaped; others were truncated pyramids. Some were "effigy mounds," fashioned in the shape of animals such as serpents and birds (Figure 2-3 shows an example); still others were precise geometric embankments that enclosed many acres.

Colonial farmers leveled the mounds with plows, and the curious dug into them. Many contained human skeletal remains, but it was the remarkable artifacts that really caught the eye: copper and antler headdresses; stone pipes beautifully carved into birds, frogs, bears, and other animals; sheets of mica, intricately cut into hands and talons; carved shells; massive log tombs; beautiful spear points; incised pottery; copper ornaments; and polished stone disks (Figure 2-4 shows an etched disk from Alabama). We now know that mounds were constructed as early as 3500 BC in the southern Mississippi River valley and that the practice was fairly widespread in the eastern United States by 1000 BC. In the early sixteenth century, the Spanish explorer Hernando de Soto and other explorers saw mounds being made and used as burial grounds and as foundations for priestly temples in the southeastern United States, but elsewhere the practice had ceased hundreds of years earlier.

But the colonists knew nothing about de Soto's observations, and so they devised a variety of hypotheses to account for the mounds. Some argued that the Moundbuilders were the ancestors of living Indians,

© Ohio Historical Society

Figure 2-3 Aerial photo of Serpent Mound, an effigy mound in Ohio.

but the "race" had degenerated. Others believed that the Moundbuilders had migrated to Mexico, where they became the Toltecs and Aztecs.

But the favored interpretation was that the Moundbuilders were a superior race that had been wiped out by the Indians. Some scholars claimed that this earlier race was Viking; others said Moundbuilders were actually Egyptians, Israelites, Chinese, Greeks, Polynesians, Phoenicians, Norwegians, Belgians, Tartars, Saxons, Hindus, Africans, Welsh, and Atlanteans from the lost continent of Atlantis. A nineteenth-century Ohio reverend suggested that God had created the Serpent Mound in southern Ohio to mark the site of Eden.

Anyone, it seemed, could have been the Moundbuilders—except the ancestors of American Indians. Instead, scholars saw the Indians as late-coming marauders, destroyers of what was obviously a magnificent civilization. The human bones in the mounds were evidence of great battles fought on the monuments. In various mounds, stones allegedly incised with Hebrew, Chinese, Celtic, Runic, Phoenician, or other languages were proffered as evidence that the Moundbuilders were, in fact, Europeans—or at least not Indians. And thus, the myth of a Moundbuilder civilization arose.

This was a handy idea, because it gave colonists a sense of superiority and the right to avenge the Moundbuilders by dispossessing Native Americans of their land. Handy, but was it true?

A President's Attention

From its beginning, the Moundbuilder myth attracted scrutiny at the highest levels of American society. One of the most notable was Thomas Jefferson (1743–1826), author of the Declaration of Independence,

© Peabody Museum, Harvard University

Figure 2-4 An etched slate from Moundville, Alabama. Artifacts such as these convinced nineteenth-century scholars that the Moundbuilders were a superior culture.

third president of the United States—and the first scientific archaeologist in America.

Jefferson was described by a contemporary as "an expert musician (the violin being his favorite instrument), a good dancer, a dashing rider, and proficient in all manly exercises." He was an inventor, an avid player of chess (avoiding cards), an accomplished horticulturalist, scientist, distinguished architect, and a connoisseur of French cooking.

Jefferson was also curious about the origins of Native Americans. Fascinated by Indian lore since boyhood and trained in classical linguistics, Jefferson believed that Native American languages held valuable clues to the origins of the people. Jefferson collected linguistic data from more than 40 tribes and wrote a treatise on the subject. From his linguistic studies, Jefferson sensed an Asiatic origin for Native Americans (a conclusion that few scholars would argue with today).

Jefferson's contribution to Americanist archaeology was presented in his only book, a response to a number of questions sent to him by French scholars. It appeared as a limited French edition in 1784 and as a widely distributed American edition in 1787. *Notes on the State of Virginia* dealt, in part, with the aborigines of Virginia, their origin, and the question of the mounds. Jefferson listed the various Virginian tribes, relating their histories since the settlement of Jamestown in 1607 and incorporating a census of Virginia's current Native American population. In it, Jefferson argued that Native Americans were in no way mentally or physically inferior to the white race and rejected all current racist doctrines used to explain Indians' origins. (He later argued for intermarriage between Europeans and Native Americans, a practice he did not support between Europeans and Africans, although he probably fathered children with one of his slaves.) He reasoned that Native Americans were wholly capable of having constructed the prehistoric earthworks of the United States.

Then Jefferson took a critical step: He proceeded to excavate a burial mound located on his property. Today, such a step seems obvious, but Jefferson's contemporaries would have rummaged through libraries and archives rather than dirty their hands with bones, stones, and dirt to answer intellectual issues. This is why Jefferson is often said to be the founder of American archae-

ology (some paleontologists claim Jefferson to be the founder of their field as well).

Jefferson's account described his method of excavation, the different layers of earth, and the artifacts and the human bones that he encountered. He then tested the **hypothesis** that the bones resulted from warfare. Noting the absence of traumatic wounds (such as those made by arrows) and the interments of children, Jefferson rejected the idea that the bones were those of soldiers who had fallen in battle. Noting that some remains were scattered, he surmised that the burials had accumulated through repeated use. And he saw no reason to doubt that the ancestors of Native Americans had constructed the mounds.

Although many years later another future president, William Harrison, would argue that the mounds were built for defensive purposes, few archaeologists today would modify Jefferson's conclusions: Some mounds might have been defensive, but the majority were not, and there is no reason to attribute them to someone other than the ancestors of Indians.

The Myth Gains Momentum

Nonetheless, Jefferson did not come out strongly on either side of the Moundbuilder debate and, in 1799 (as president of the American Philosophical Society), he distributed a pamphlet calling for the systematic collection of information on the mounds. Others were not so silent. Ignoring the fact that conquest, racism, forced movements, poverty, and disease had forever altered Native American communities, nineteenth-century scholars were convinced that Indians were not capable of building the mounds. In 1820, Caleb Atwater reasoned in *Antiquities Discovered in the Western States* that, because living Indians had not buried their dead in mounds, or constructed earthworks, or made artifacts of metal, they could not possibly be the descendants of the Moundbuilders. Instead, Atwater attributed the mounds to Hindus. Josiah Priest came to a similar conclusion in his 1833 best seller, *American Antiquities and Discoveries in the West.*

Some of these scholars actually did dig into mounds, but it was not until 1848 that the systematic compilation that Jefferson desired finally appeared.

The Surveyor and the Doctor

Ephraim Squier (1821–1888) was a Connecticut civil engineer, surveyor, journalist and, later in life, a politician intent on making a name for himself (he advocated the

---

hypothesis A proposition proposed as an explanation of some phenomena.

Archaeological Ethics
Does Archaeology Put Native Americans on Trial?

We've mentioned that many American Indians do not trust anthropologists, including archaeologists. This is especially odd because anthropologists have long been the champions of Native American legal and cultural rights; many anthropologists, for example, testified on behalf of tribes in the 1950s and 1960s when Indian land claims were decided in courts, and many work to maintain Indian rights and languages today.

One problem is that anthropologists often take a scientific perspective toward American Indian culture, while Native Americans more commonly express humanistic views. This is to be expected, given that most of us take a humanistic perspective when examining our own history. Few Euroamericans, for instance, would "explain" the American Revolution as a product of demography and economy; instead, they explain it as the search for freedom from tyranny.

Many Native Americans see a "scientific" approach to understanding their history as denigrating their own indigenous versions of history. This disconnect is particularly evident in the research regarding American Indian origins—one of the major questions in American archaeology (and a topic put in the public spotlight with the Kennewick discovery). As early as 1589, the Jesuit missionary José de Acosta wrote in *Historia Natural y Moral de las Indias* that Indians had walked to the New World via a land route that connected the New World with Asia. Acosta served among the Indians of Mexico and Peru and knew little, if anything, about the land to the north. Yet, he was prescient: biological and linguistic data today demonstrate without a doubt that the ancestors of Native Americans indeed migrated from Asia at least 13,500 years ago.

Such a position stands in stark contrast to most Native American origin stories. In many of these, the first people emerged from a hole in the earth, having traveled up from successive layers of worlds that lie below this one. Traditional Hopi beliefs, for example, hold that the modern world is but the fourth of many worlds.

None of the various religions of Native North Americans explicitly state that "people came from Asia," and many Native Americans consider this suggestion insulting, an affront to their religious beliefs (just as the idea of evolution is insulting to fundamentalist Christians). Some scholars agree, suggesting that archaeologists have no right to ask questions that put Native American religion on trial.

We disagree with this implied censorship; no one can deny another the right to ask questions. But more to the point, asking questions about Native American origins does not challenge American Indian (or any other) religion. Science evaluates claims about the *material* world, and religion is fundamentally about the *nonmaterial* world. But religions do sometimes make claims about the material world: How old is the earth? Where did people come from? What's the relationship between humans and animals? Because these are claims about the material world, we can subject them to scientific scrutiny.

So, what does it mean that scientific archaeology holds that the ancestors of Native American people came from Asia? Does this prove that Native American religions are wrong?

Absolutely not. We can neither prove nor disprove claims of the nonmaterial world using a method that evaluates claims about the material world. Archaeologists can only prove that a religious claim about the material world cannot be taken at face value. Some might think this means that the religion is false; but it might also mean that a religion's claim about the material world, even if unsubstantiated by science, holds deeper truths. From such a perspective, science encourages one to look deeper into religious beliefs, to find a significance that goes beyond mere space and time to something that is truly religious. In this way, scientific and humanistic perspectives are compatible.

radical idea of building a canal across Central America). Like many educated people of the time, his interests were wide ranging, but the Moundbuilders held a special fascination for him.

Edwin Davis (1811–1888) was an Ohio physician. He was intrigued by the mounds, especially those near his hometown of Chillicothe. Unlike Squier, he was content to live a calm life with his family near his hometown.

With Squier's ambition and Davis's money, the two gentlemen formed an alliance to study the mounds. Although the two came to dislike one another intensely, their names will forever be wed in American archaeology because of their 1848 monograph, *Ancient Monuments of the Mississippi Valley*—the first publication by the newly formed Smithsonian Institution.

Squier and Davis claimed that they did not seek to "sustain" any particular hypothesis, but only "to arrive at truth" and to avoid "speculation." True to this intent, the book devotes its first 300 pages to meticulous description. Squier and Davis defined six kinds of earthworks: defensive enclosures, sacred enclosures (including effigy mounds), altar mounds, burial mounds, temple mounds, and "anomalous mounds." They based this classification on others' reports, as well as on their own investigations of some 200 sites, primarily in the Ohio River Valley. The volume contains over 200 beautiful illustrations of artifacts, mound cross-sections and maps of earthworks (like that shown in Figure 2-5). Squier embellished some of the maps—completing earthen walls that had been destroyed by erosion or making his circular and rectangular earthworks a bit neater than reality. Still, his survey work recorded some remarkable features. And since most of the sites have now been obliterated by the plow or have disappeared beneath cities, *Ancient Monuments* is archaeology's only record of them.

Only in the final pages of their monograph did Squier and Davis allow themselves to speculate. The Moundbuilder population, they wrote, "was numerous and widely spread" as was "evident from the number and magnitude of the ancient monuments and the extensive range of their occurrence." It was also homogeneous in customs and habits, as was "sustained by the great uniformity which the ancient remains display." They described the Moundbuilders as agricultural peoples because agriculture, they assumed, was necessary to a "large population, to fixedness of institutions, and to any considerable advance in the economical or ennobling arts."

Although Squier and Davis claimed no commitment to the Moundbuilder hypothesis, they nonetheless

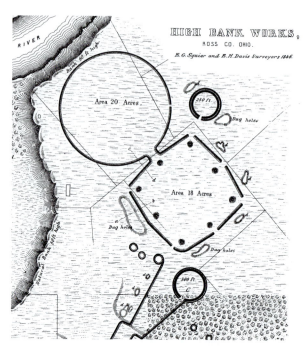

Figure 2-5 A portion of one of Squier and Davis's maps—showing a mound group in Ohio. *From Squier, E. G., and E. H. Davis. 1848. Ancient Monuments of the Mississippi Valley. Smithsonian Contributions to Knowledge, vol. 1. Washington, DC: page 51.*

pointed out the differences between the Moundbuilders and American Indians. The art in the mounds, they claimed, was "immeasurably beyond anything which the North American Indians are known to produce." They saw differences in burial practices, skull form, warfare, and defensive structures. They even argued for a difference in subsistence, the Moundbuilders being agriculturalists, the Indians only hunters (despite the fact that they taught maize horticulture to the colonists).

In the end, Squier and Davis suggested that the Moundbuilders were related to the "semi-civilized" nations of Mexico and Central America (such as the Aztecs), thus providing more fodder for supporters of the Moundbuilder hypothesis. By 1873, the president of the Chicago Academy of Sciences thought it "preposterous" that Indians could have built the mounds. And in his 1872 book, *Ancient America*, J. D. Baldwin considered any relationship between the Moundbuilders and Indians to be "absurd."

The Engineer and the Entomologist

During the Civil War, at the Battle of Shiloh, a young Union captain had raised his right arm to give an order to fire when a Confederate minie ball took it off at the elbow. A lesser man's career would have ended there, but John Wesley Powell (1834–1902) went on to explore the West, mount the first expedition down the Colorado River through the Grand Canyon, and hold several important posts in the federal government.

After the war, Powell's western explorations brought him into close personal contact with many Native Americans, an experience that many East Coast scholars could not claim. It is telling, then, that Powell held a different, and much higher, opinion of Indians.

Powell was intrigued by Native Americans and the evidence of their history. Before the Civil War, he had even tested a few mounds himself. (We wonder if those at Shiloh—one of which is pictured in the opening of this chapter—caught his eye.) He concluded that close ancestors of Native Americans had built the mounds, although he thought they had done so soon after European contact.

Powell found himself in a position to pursue the Moundbuilder issue when, in 1879, he became head of the newly formed Bureau of Ethnology (later the Bureau of American Ethnology, which was placed within the Smithsonian), as well as the U.S. Geological Survey. Because the Moundbuilder issue was of such public interest, Congress insisted that the Bureau of Ethnology spend $5000 a year—*one-fifth of the Bureau's budget*—on mound exploration. Powell looked for someone to head up the bureau's new division of mound studies and finally settled on Cyrus Thomas.

Born in Tennessee, Thomas (1825–1910) spent his early career as a lawyer and merchant, and then served as an entomologist for geographical surveys. He was Illinois state entomologist from 1874 to 1876 and a member of the U.S. Entomological Commission from 1874 to 1882. The study of insects may seem an odd background for an archaeologist but, as an educated man, Thomas was as qualified as any of his predecessors or contemporaries to do archaeology (recall that Nels Nelson, a member of the first trained generation of archaeologists, was born in 1875).

Through the Bureau of Ethnology, Thomas began his own program of survey and excavation. Over the next 12 years, and with the aid of local affiliates, he compiled data on some 2000 sites in 21 states, finally publishing a 700-page report in 1894. In the beginning, Thomas was a proponent of the Moundbuilder hypothesis. But unlike Squier and Davis, Thomas began with an explicit question: "Were the mounds built by the Indians?"

Thomas took each claim made previously as evidence of a separate Moundbuilder race and evaluated it. Did the Indians have the knowledge of moundbuild-

Figure 2-6 Mounds in use among southeastern Indians as illustrated in the account of Jacques Le Moyne, a sixteenth-century French explorer. © *Wiley, G., and J. Sabloff, 1980. A History of American Archaeology, 2nd ed. San Francisco: W. H. Freeman and Company.*

ing? Thomas pointed out that earlier scholars overlooked Spanish and French explorers' reports that described mound construction and use in the southeastern United States (see Figure 2-6).

Was the Moundbuilder culture older than Indian culture? Thomas made an error here when he discounted some earlier efforts to date the mounds—for example, by counting the rings of trees growing on their tops—and concluded that the mounds had been built after European arrival.

What about those tablets inscribed with Hebrew or other scripts? Thomas showed that the circumstances of the discovery of each of these tablets made them all suspect; indeed, even Squier and Davis had written the tablets off as hoaxes (as indeed they were). And what about the copper objects? Indians had no smelting technology, but Thomas's examination of the artifacts led him to conclude (correctly) that the copper was a raw metal that is not smelted and is found naturally in the Great Lakes region. Mining and shaping such native copper required little more than a stone hammer.

Thomas quietly but definitively concluded that "the author believes the theory which attributes these works [the mounds] to the Indians to be the correct one." There was no lost race of Moundbuilders. They had not been overrun by Native Americans. There was no justification for Europeans to seek revenge. The myth that had helped perpetuate a racist attitude toward Native Americans was simply that—a myth. Sadly, by 1894, the truth about the Moundbuilders had come too late. The Indian Wars were officially over, virtually all Native Americans were confined to reservations, and a change in racist attitudes toward Native Americans was still decades away.

The Scientific Method

The history of the Moundbuilder myth provides a simple example of some characteristics of the **scientific method**, which we can reduce to six simple steps:

1. Define a relevant problem.
2. Establish one or more hypotheses.
3. Determine the empirical implications of the hypotheses.
4. Collect appropriate data through observation and/or experimentation.
5. Test the hypothesis by comparing these data with the expected implications.
6. Reject, revise, and/or retest hypotheses as necessary.

We admit that this is an ideal process only, and, in hindsight, we can see that scientific research often does not proceed neatly through each of these steps, although that remains the goal of scientists today.

The Role of Inductive Reasoning

The first two tasks (Steps 1 and 2) are to define a relevant question and translate it into an appropriate hypothesis. The idea is to get beyond a simple description of the known facts and create a hypothesis to account for them. Such hypotheses are generated through **inductive reasoning,** or working from specific facts or observations to general conclusions. The facts as known serve as premises in this case; the hypothesis should not only account for the known facts but should also predict properties of as-yet unobserved phenomena.

Unfortunately, no rules exist for induction (just as there are no rules for thinking up good ideas). Some hypotheses are derived by enumerating the data, isolating common features, and generalizing to unobserved cases that share these features. At other times, archaeologists turn to analogies, relatively well-understood ethnographies that seem to have relevance to poorly understood archaeological cases. Judgment, imagination, past experience, and even guesswork all have their place in science. It does not matter where or how one derives the hypothesis. What matters is how well the hypothesis accounts for unobserved phenomena.

It is, of course, entirely possible that several hypotheses apply to the same data. Scientists work their way systematically through the various possibilities, testing them one at a time. This method of **multiple working hypotheses** has long been a feature of scientific methods. Most scientists assume that the simplest hypothesis is the most likely to be correct (an idea referred to as "Occam's Razor"). Thus, they begin with the simplest hypothesis and see how well it holds up against some new data. If it fails the test, scientists will then try the next least complicated hypothesis, and so on.

The Moundbuilder hypothesis was based in part on a set of facts and in part on cultural biases: Nineteenth-century scholars could not reconcile what they found in mounds with what they knew of Native American culture. Squier and Davis (as well as Jefferson) were scientists in the tradition of Francis Bacon. They believed that when a sufficiently large number of facts were collected—when 200 mound sites were mapped and probed for artifacts—the meaning of those facts would become apparent. This is why Jefferson called for a systematic collection of data; he knew that too little was known even for the kind of legitimate speculation that could advance scholars to Step 2 in the process. In a sense, this means that nineteenth-century scholars jumped from Step 1 to Step 4. But such data collection is only the beginning of the scientific process.

Jefferson, Squier, and Davis worked in the inductive phase (Steps 1 and 2) of Moundbuilder research. Because no one knew much about the mounds, the first order of business was to gather some facts: How many mounds were there? What sort of variability was present among the mounds? What exactly was in the different types of mounds? How old were they? What were they made of? From these data, Squier and Davis inductively derived a conclusion: The living Indians of the United States were not descendants of the Moundbuilders.

Science Is Self-Correcting

Squier and Davis, as it turned out, were completely wrong; but the beauty of the scientific method is that it

---

scientific method Accepted principles and procedures for the systematic pursuit of secure knowledge. Established scientific procedures involve the following steps: define a relevant problem; establish one or more hypotheses; determine the empirical implications of the hypotheses; collect appropriate data through observation and/or experimentation; compare these data with the expected implications; and revise and/or retest hypotheses as necessary.

inductive reasoning Working from specific observations to more general hypotheses.

multiple working hypotheses A set of hypotheses that are tested against the empirical record from the simplest to the most complex.

is self-correcting. Science insists that we always ask: Do we really know what we think we know? Squier and Davis thought they were at Step 6 in the process, but in hindsight we can see that they had only inductively formulated a hypothesis. It was left to others to test this idea, to take their conclusion and treat it as a hypothesis. This is how science sometimes proceeds, by backtracking and rethinking things that others thought was over and done with. And that was the case here. Even in Squier and Davis's day, other investigators found facts that contradicted their Moundbuilder hypothesis. John Wesley Powell was one; Cyrus Thomas was another. Although Thomas never used the rhetoric of science, he was indeed testing Squier and Davis's hypothesis that Indians were not the descendants of the Moundbuilders.

How does one accomplish Steps 4 and 5—that is, test a hypothesis? Once a hypothesis is defined, the scientific method requires its translation into testable form. Hypotheses *can never be tested directly* because they are abstract statements. The key to verifying a hypothesis is simple: you don't. What you verify are the logical material consequences of hypotheses (the empirical implications established in Step 3).

Deductive reasoning is required to uncover these logical outcomes. A deductive argument is one for which the conclusions must be true, given that the premises are true. Such deductive arguments generally take the form of "if…then" statements: *If* the hypothesis is true, *then* we will expect to observe the following outcomes. Bridging the gap from *if* to *then* is a tricky step.

In the "harder" sciences, these bridging arguments derive directly from known mathematical or physical properties. In astronomy, for instance, the position of "unknown" stars can be predicted using a chain of mathematical arguments grounded in physics. The classic deductive method begins with an untested hypothesis and converts the generalities into specific predictions based on established mathematical and/or physical theory. These are sometimes called **bridging arguments**.

But how do archaeologists bridge this gap? Where is the well-established body of theory that allows us to transform abstract hypotheses into observable predictions?

Although Thomas was never explicit about this, we can see in his reasoning the simple bridging arguments he employed for his version of Step 5. For example, *if* American Indians did not know about mound building, *then* there should be no explorer accounts of mound building by Indians (or evidence should be found that those people whom explorers observed building mounds were *not* Indians). Or, *if* the mounds were built by a long-vanished race, *then* they should be considerably older than the known age of Indian culture. And, *if* the metal artifacts in mounds were signs of a "superior" Moundbuilder culture, *then* the manufacturing technology associated with them should have been absent from later Indian culture. In doing this, Thomas laid out the criteria whereby he could claim the Moundbuilder hypothesis to be false. (We will return to a discussion of these bridging arguments in archaeology when we discuss middle-range research in Chapters 3 and 10.)

For Thomas, "testing" meant collecting data, analyzing it, publishing it, and openly evaluating it against the competing hypotheses. The **testability** of a hypothesis is critical. An idea is testable if the hypothesis' implications can be measured in some fashion *with the same results by different observers*. That is, the observation has to be independent of whoever is doing the observing. We have to know that you would make the same observations that we would make.

Science Is Reiterative

The process we have sketched out, commonly called the scientific method, is really more of a cycle because it is repetitive, as shown in Figure 2-7. Step 6 (testing, rejecting, or revising the hypothesis) normally leads back to Step 1 (redefining the problem at hand). Figure 2-7 shows the same process with more emphasis on the kinds of reasoning that researchers use to move through the steps.

Scientific cycles commence in the world of facts—in the Moundbuilder example, the amassed data from hundreds of excavations and maps plus contemporary accounts plus bogus artifacts. Through the process of induction, these facts are probed, and hypotheses are devised to account for what is already known. But because hypotheses are general declarations, they cannot be tested against further facts until they are translated

deductive reasoning Reasoning from theory to account for specific observational or experimental results.

bridging arguments Logical statements linking observations on the static archaeological record to the dynamic behavior or natural processes that produced it.

testability The degree to which one's observations and experiments can be reproduced.

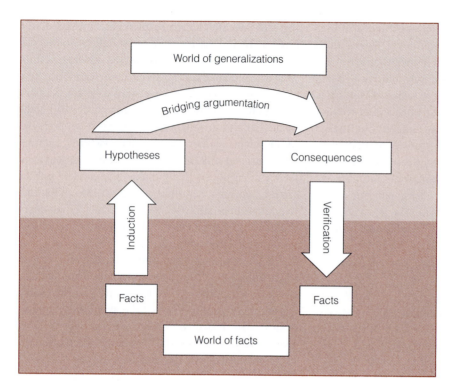

Figure 2-7 The scientific cycle. *After Kemeny (1959:86).*

into their logical consequences, through the judicious use of bridging arguments.

The scientific cycle thus begins and ends with facts. But these newly discovered facts themselves will suggest new hypotheses, and, once again, inductive reasoning will lead from the world of facts to the world of abstraction, initiating a new cycle of investigation. As a method, science implies a continual spiral in knowledge.

Scientific thinking applies at many different levels, from "small" questions such as "What's this red stain in the soil?" or "What was this stone tool used for?" to "big" questions such as "Why did humans switch from hunting and gathering to agriculture?" or "What is human nature?" Sometimes the cycle is played out over the course of a day, sometimes over the course of many lifetimes (as it did in the Moundbuilder controversy).

The scientific process is often not explicit. And since science is a human venture, it is subject to false starts, dead ends, preconceived notions, and cultural biases. A scientific approach does not always deliver the right answer on the first try or even the second or third. It tends to make halting, stumbling progress, often by taking two steps forward and one step back. Sometimes we can see what we have learned only in hindsight. But we

generally find, in the end, that we have learned something. And that is what science is all about.

Science Is Not Infallible

Although philosophers of science rarely agree on many points, they do generally agree that (1) there is no single right way to do science and (2) a scientific approach cannot guarantee truth.

It is clear, for instance, that the Moundbuilder hypothesis was not drawn directly and inductively from sterile archaeological facts. This idea was widespread well before anyone knew much about the mounds because the myth facilitated and justified what colonists wanted all along—seizure of Indian land. Science is unavoidably embedded in the scientist's culture and hardly free of cultural biases. The social, cultural, and political context of archaeology influences its theories.

Because of these biases, some archaeologists reject scientific methods in archaeology. The argument often goes like this: Because archaeology is not precise in the same sense as are the physical sciences, then the methods of science are inappropriate (or even harmful) when applied to the study of humans. Although these claims contain some truth, most blatant attacks on the scientific methods are directed at exaggerated caricatures that depict science as claiming infallibility (a claim rejected by even the most "scientific" of archaeologists).

Science offers no ironclad assurance that application of its methods will *necessarily* result in the absolute, final truth about anything; rather, scientists claim only that scientific methods provide a means to determine, more or less, whether the evidence favors the validity of a hypothesis. And, as we saw in the Moundbuilder example, careful, honest, scientific analysis can help reveal and shatter cultural biases and, indeed, arrive at the truth. Nonetheless, these observations about the nature of science lead some archaeologists to another approach.

What's a Humanistic Approach?

In general, **humanism** tends to emphasize the dignity and worth of the individual. Humanistic-style inquiry begins with the premise that all people possess a capacity for self-realization through reason. Unlike the purely scientific approach, which stresses objectivity and independent testing, humanists believe that their scholarship should proceed in precisely the opposite direction: By stressing the intuitive and subjective, humanists seek strength and understanding in the very biases that science seeks to circumvent.

Virtually all modern archaeologists, whether "humanist" or "scientific," subscribe to the basics of science. All of us believe in careful scholarship, in generalizations backed by firm data, in honesty, and in giving full consideration to "negative" evidence (data that run contrary to a hypothesis' predictions).

But archaeologists are not emotionally or politically neutral data-gathering machines. Archaeologists will always make moral or ethical judgments about the past (and particularly about its use in the present). This occurs because archaeologists are "historically situated," meaning simply that archaeologists are products of the times in which they live. This is why many archaeologists bring a humanistic perspective to their understanding of the past and, in this section, we will see why most archaeologists are both scientists and humanists.

The primary distinction between scientific and humanistic approaches occurs over the issue of **objectivity**. If you believe that archaeology is "mostly objective," then you probably lean more toward the scientific side. You probably see a clear-cut separation between the observer and what is observed—the "facts" of archae-

ology. And you probably search for an inherent regularity to cultural behavior (which you might term "laws"). You probably believe that the world out there can be known in a manner more or less independent of your ability to perceive and engage it. Finally, you likely are more inclined to take an adaptive perspective on human cultural behavior, looking for explanations in factors that are "outside" the culture—that is, in the environment, in biology, in technology, or in demography.

But if you think that archaeology is "mostly subjective," then you are likely more comfortable with humanistic perspectives, which emphasize that the observer and the observed can never really be separated, that our knowledge of the past mostly depends on who is doing the observing. You probably mistrust conventional science and feel more comfortable with an ideational perspective. You may be more interested in empathetic approaches, more connected with what people think rather than with what they do. You are probably more intrigued by human languages, cultural values, and artistic achievements of other cultures.

Humanistic Archaeology at a Dakota Village

We can explore the basics of humanistic perspectives in archaeology by looking at Janet Spector's study of a Dakota site in Minnesota.

Spector (retired, formerly a professor of anthropology at the University of Minnesota) is a specialist in the archaeology and ethnohistory of the Great Lakes region. Spector was interested in excavating a site that would allow her to examine the activities of men and women and that also would reveal the nature of early contacts between the Dakota and Europeans. Eventually, she encountered the Little Rapids site in Minnesota, which had been occupied by the Eastern Dakota (or "Sioux"; see "Looking Closer: Sioux or Dakota?") sometime in the early to middle 1800s. Spector decided to work there because a number of documentary sources that depicted life at sites like Little Rapids (shown in Figure 2-8) could help with interpretation of the site; likewise,

humanism A doctrine, attitude, or way of life that focuses on human interests and values. In general, a humanistic approach tends to reject a search for universals and stress instead the importance of the individual's lived experience.

objectivity The attempt to observe things as they actually are, without prejudging or falsifying observations in light of some preconceived view of the world—reducing subjective factors to a minimum.

© American Museum of Natural History

Figure 2-8 Dakota village (engraving by Seth Eastman, 1853).

the site could supplement the information contained in the historical documents.

Involving Dakota People in Dakota Archaeology

The work at the Little Rapids site was done according to standard archaeological procedures: In her excavation and analysis, Spector was a scientist. But as she wrote her site report, she felt something was lacking. She came to realize that, as a relatively privileged non-Indian university professor, she was in danger of doing something that had bothered her for years: Inadvertently, she was excluding exactly the people she wished to learn about.

Once she recognized the problem, Spector began talking to Dakota people. Initially, she encountered some resentment toward the "anthros," as the Indians called them; throughout Indian Country, many Native American people question whether archaeologists can really be trusted. But after months of discussion and site visits, Spector enlisted several Dakota people to help her understand the archaeology of their ancestral site. Excavations began again at Little Rapids, this time with the hands-on participation of members of the Wahpeton Dakota community.

Tribal members helped by providing Dakota names for various plants and animals, and some crew members learned the rudiments of the Dakota language as they dug. During lunchtime, Dakota people led discussions about their culture and history. On Fridays, the project historian helped the groups work through the strengths and limitations of the available documentary evidence. "For the first time in my archaeological career," Spector wrote, "a project felt right. We worked as an interdisciplinary, multicultural team."

The dig proceeded in a standard scientific fashion, and the crew fell into the rhythm typical of all digs. Arrive early, split into small teams, dig, write notes. Get together at lunch and talk about the finds. Work all afternoon digging or doing labwork, then finally knock off for the day.

But Spector came to see archaeology in a different light. Although she continued to dig according to standard scientific procedures, the style of her archaeology changed. Spector found herself trying to transcend the detail of the archaeological and written records. "I sometimes imagine being transported into the past by a bilingual, bicultural, bi-temporal guide—a Dakota per-

Looking Closer
Sioux or Dakota?

The term "Sioux" (pronounced "sue") is French pronunciation of a fragment of the Ojibwa word "nadoweisiw-eg." This name is a derogatory term, meaning "little snakes," and implies "enemy." The Chippewa used it to refer to their western "Sioux" neighbors (and to distinguish them from the Iroquois, who were the "true snakes," or major enemy). Although "Sioux" remains in common use, many contemporary tribal members resent its use and prefer the more specific, indigenous terms "Dakota," "Nakota," and "Lakota," which refer to three mutually intelligible dialects of the "Dakota Sioux" language.

son willing and able to explain to me his or her view of the area's politics, tensions, and interactions." She encouraged students to speculate about what had taken place on this or that part of the site, why artifacts had been left where they were found, how the nineteenth-century Dakota people felt living there: "Did they watch the darkening skies some days as we did, hoping to finish our work before a thunderstorm struck? Was their community life, like ours, punctuated by summer romances and interpersonal tensions, or were such relationships a product of our particular time and place only?"

Eventually, Spector located a part of the site that she had interpreted as a dance area. After some excavation there, Spector's team applied for permission from the Minnesota Intertribal Board for further testing in the suspected dance area. A non-Dakota Indian board member objected strongly. Spector found that "to them, a dance area—even a suspected one—was sacred and, like a burial place, should not be disturbed." Respecting these views, Spector shifted the excavation. More and more, archaeologists are conflicted by episodes like this. Spector noted: "Do I wish we might have had a chance to follow these tantalizing leads? Yes. Would I knowingly dig in sacred areas? No."

Archaeology in the Active Voice

When it came time to publish the results, Spector wrestled with the meaning of what she had found. Although conducted according to standard scientific procedures, the Little Rapids project had also been strongly conditioned by Spector's changing perceptions of archaeology. The dig itself was part of the story, and so was the world around it.

In the fall of 1991, as Spector was writing up the Little Rapids materials, the Atlanta Braves baseball team made it to the World Series. Three months later, professional football's Washington Redskins played in the Super Bowl. That year, Indian people across the country protested the use of Indian images as sport mascots, highlighting tensions between themselves and the dominant Euroamerican community. To Spector, this was a repetition—150 years later—of the initial confrontation between Indians and Europeans evident in the archaeological record at Little Rapids.

Maybe if the American public knew more about Indian cultural roots and sensibilities, she thought, they would better understand why being considered a sport mascot is so offensive to Indian people, why so many

Figure 2-9
The awl from Little Rapids.

Native Americans object to the way movies, television, and pop culture portrays them.

Spector felt a growing need to communicate with others what she had learned about this abandoned Dakota site. She wanted to highlight women's activities and the relationship between men and women, but she also wanted to draw Dakota voices and perspectives into her story.

One particular find captured her imagination: the deer antler handle of an awl, and its iron tip found nearby (shown reassembled in Figure 2-9). From her ethnohistoric research, Spector knew that nineteenth-century Dakota women used such awls for working hides into moccasins, bags, and clothing. Although buried for more than a century, this particular awl was remarkably well preserved, with traces of red pigment still evident in the decorations along the edge. Because it was not broken or worn out, Spector felt that someone must have lost it, rather than deliberately thrown it away. She became intrigued with the woman who once had owned it.

This simple yet elegant artifact symbolized for Spector what she was learning by doing archaeology at Little Rapids. She was concerned that the strictly scientific, "lifeless" format of the standard archaeological report failed to communicate much about the *people* who had lived at Little Rapids, and she sought another way to convey what she had learned from the site.

The answer came in describing the awl.

From her archival reading, Spector learned that Dakota women kept count of their accomplishments

In Her Own Words
What This Awl Means

by Janet Spector

The women and children of Inyan Ceyaka Atonwan (Little Rapids) had been working at the maple sugar camps since Istawicayazan wi (the Moon of Sore Eyes, or March). At the same time, most of the men had been far from the village trapping muskrats. When Wozupi wi (the Moon for Planting, or May) came, fifteen households eagerly reunited in their bark lodges near the river....

One day some villagers brought their tanned furs and maple sugar to the lodge of Jean Baptiste Faribault. He lived among them a few months each year with his Dakota wife, Pelagie. In exchange for furs and maple sugar, Faribault gave them glass beads, silver ornaments, tin kettles, and iron knives, awl tips, axes, hatchets, and hoes for their summer work....

Mazomani (Iron Walker) and Hazawin (Blueberry Woman) were proud of their daughter, Mazaokiyewin (Woman Who Talks to Iron). The day after visiting Faribault, they had given her some glass beads and a new iron awl tip. The tip was the right size to fit into the small antler handle that Hazawin had given Mazaokiyewin when she went to dwell alone at the time of her first menses. Mazaokiyewin used the sharp-pointed awl for punching holes in pieces of leather before stitching them together with deer sinew. Though young, she had already established a reputation among the people at Inyan Ceyaka Atonwan for creativity and excellence in quillwork and beadwork.

Mazaokiyewin's mother and grandmothers had taught her to keep a careful record of her accomplishments, so whenever she finished quilling or beading moccasins, she remembered to impress a small dot on the fine awl handle that Hazawin had made for her. When Mazaokiyewin completed more complicated work, such as sewing and decorating a buckskin dress or pipe bag, she formed diamond-shaped clusters of four small dots which symbolized the powers of the four directions that influenced her life in many ways. She liked to expose the handle of this small tool as she carried it in its beaded case so that others could see she was doing her best to ensure the well-being of their community.

When she engraved the dots into her awl handle, she carefully marked each one with red pigment, made by boiling sumac berries with a small root found in the ground near the village. Dakota people associated the color red with women and their life forces. Red also represented the east, where the sun rose to give knowledge, wisdom, and understanding. Red symbolized Mazaokiyewin's aspirations to these qualities.

When the designated day in Wasuton wi arrived, Mazomani led the people in the medicine dance near the burial place of their ancestors. Members of the medicine lodge danced within an enclosed oval area, separated from the audience by a low, hide-covered fence....

One hot day following the dance, Mazaokiyewin gathered together all of the leatherwork she had finished since returning to Inyan Ceyaka Atonwan after the spring hunting and sugaring seasons.... Now, Mazaokiyewin eagerly anticipated the quilling contest and feast called

on their implements in the way that men kept war records. In their ambition to excel, women recorded the number of robes and tipis they completed by incising dots along the handles of their elk antler tools. For Spector, such a realization "provided a kind of access to the people at Little Rapids that [she] had never before imagined possible," and this had an effect on how she finally decided to describe the awl.

Archaeologists, of course, describe things all the time. Using the standard archaeological typologies and language, such awls would be grouped into a series of carefully defined, objective categories according to size, material, shape, and so on. Spector had done such classifications many times. But she gradually realized that bland, impersonal typologies did not describe Native American life in the way that she wanted to, for

by a woman of a neighboring household to honor a family member. Mazaokiyewin knew she had produced more beaded and quilled articles than most of the community's young women, and she looked forward to bringing recognition to her parents and grandparents....

She started uphill carrying the miniapahatapi (skin water bags) carefully, but near the quilling-contest lodge she slipped on the muddy path where water had pooled in the driving rain. As she struggled to regain her footing without dropping the bags, the leather strap holding her awl in its case broke, and the small awl dropped to the ground. It fell close to one of the cooking fires outside the lodge entrance.

Mazaokiyewin did not miss her awl that day, because as soon as she entered the lodge with the water, the host of the contest took her hand and escorted her to the center of the crowd. The host had already counted each woman's pieces and distributed a stick for each. Mazaokiyewin had accumulated more sticks than all but three older women. The host then led the four to the place of honor in the lodge and gave them their food first to honor their accomplishments. Later, the results of this contest would be recorded for all to see on the hides lining the walls of the lodge. This pleased Hazawin and Mazomani.

The heavy rain that day had scattered debris over the village, and on the day after the quilling contest and medicine dance, people joined together to clean up the encampment. Using old hides and baskets, they carried off loads of fallen branches, wet fire ash and charcoal, and the remains of the feast to the community dump above the slough. Somehow, Mazaokiyewin's small awl was swept up and carried off with other garbage from the quilling contest. It disappeared in the dump as the villagers emptied one basketload after another on top of it.

Later, the loss of the awl saddened Mazaokiyewin and Hazawin, but they knew the handle was nearly worn out, and both realized it was more a girl's tool than a woman's. Mazaokiyewin was almost a woman ready to establish her own household, no longer a child of her mother's lodge. It was time to put aside her girl-tools, she knew, but she had intended to keep this awl. Its finely incised dots and engraved lines showed how well she had learned adult tasks, and she took as much pleasure in displaying it as her mother did in watching others admire it....

The following day, they packed the equipment that the family would need over the next several months. As they assembled their hide-working tools, they spoke again of Mazaokiyewin's missing awl. They realized that their feeling of loss was not simply about that one small tool. Instead, as fall approached and they prepared to leave Inyan Ceyaka Atonwan, they had troubling premonitions about the future.

Source: Janet D. Spector, *What This Awl Means: Feminist Archaeology at a Wahpeton Dakota Village* (St. Paul: Minnesota Historical Society Press, 1993), 19–29. Used with permission.

they minimized the role of actual living, breathing people.

So Spector took a different approach. She wrote an imaginative reconstruction of Mazaokiyewin, the young Dakota woman who Spector envisioned as the owner of the awl—which was lost in a rainstorm and later swept up and discarded in the dump (see "In Her Own Words: What This Awl Means" by Janet Spector).

Although Spector made up the specific circumstances about the awl, Mazaokiyewin was a real person (a grandmother of one of the Dakota women who worked on the excavation). Such narratives, though uncommon, are one way of injecting more humanistic perspectives into archaeology, of trying to see things in a different light—specifically, from that of the Dakota, rather than the Euroamerican perspective.

CONCLUSION: SCIENTIST OR HUMANIST?

So, should Americanist archaeology declare a preference for scientific or humanistic perspective? Archaeologist Steve Lekson (University of Colorado) sees it this way: "I divide scientific and humanistic approaches by method: scientific approaches build knowledge that is external and cumulative while humanist approaches seek knowledge that is internal and historical. The former depersonalizes, the latter is highly personal. The two are compatible and co-exist in each of us—think of Leonardo da Vinci, artist and scientist."

When archaeologists wish to seek and understand patterns and regularities in prehistoric cultures, they are scientists. When they wish to understand the history and culture of particular past societies, they are humanists. When archaeologists wish to test their ideas about the past, they are scientists. When they wish to present their results in a way that will be meaningful to the public, they are humanists. So archaeologists will be more one than the other, at different times, depending on their objective.

But there is more. We noted earlier that cultures have their own unique views of the world. We also pointed out that a hallmark of science is its ability to correct itself, to ask if the current "view" of the world is correct. Where do we get new ideas, new thoughts, new insights? One place is through other cultures: By taking humanistic approaches that ask us to step into another culture's shoes and see the world differently, we discover new ideas, new insights, and new ways of understanding the past. This is why a humanistic approach is critical to a scientific approach.

But at the same time, the scientific method is critical for checking whether the conclusions derived from humanistic approaches are correct. A humanistic approach is good at generating ideas, but it is less useful for testing those ideas; that's where science comes in. Good archaeologists know that they need a humanist in their hearts, and a scientist in their hands.

Summary

- Anthropologists believe that a true understanding of humankind can arise only from a comparative and holistic perspective.

- Biological anthropology views people as biological organisms, focusing on human evolution and diversity in human biology.

- Cultural anthropology is interested in understanding variation in traditions, customs, religion, kinship—the non-biologically-driven components of human behavior.

- Linguistic anthropology focuses on variation in the specific cultural behavior of language, looking at the historical development of language, the relationship between language and thought, and the evolution of sound systems.

- Archaeology can be thought of as a branch of cultural anthropology, but it is primarily concerned with using past societies to further document the range of human cultural behavior and with understanding how human societies change over time.

- Culture unifies these diverse fields. Culture is a learned, shared, and symbolically based system of knowledge that includes traditions, kinship, language, religion, customs, and beliefs.

- Two major strategies of research characterize contemporary anthropological thinking: The ideational perspective deals with mentalistic, symbolic, cognitive culture; it sees culture as primarily an instrument to create meaning and order in one's world. The adaptive perspective emphasizes those aspects of culture that most closely articulate with the environment, technology, and economics, and sees culture as the way that humans adapt to their natural and social environment.

- Archaeologists draw upon both ideational and adaptive perspectives, and no single anthropological school dominates contemporary archaeology.

- For more than a century, archaeology has been firmly grounded in a scientific perspective, which provides an elegant and powerful way of allowing people to understand the workings of the visible world. The goal of science is to develop ideas that can be criticized, evaluated, and eventually modified or replaced by ideas that explain the archaeological data better.

■ Scientific ideas must be testable; hypotheses must predict consequences that are measurable in the material world.

■ All archaeologists believe in certain scientific fundamentals: in honest and careful scholarship, in generalizations backed by firm data, and in full disclosure

and consideration of evidence that runs contrary to a hypothesis.

■ Many archaeologists also believe in humanistic approaches—those that incline archaeologists to look for holistic syntheses of the cultural patterns of the past, for the role of the individual, for the feelings and thoughts of the long dead.

■ For decades, archaeologists have prided themselves on their ability to straddle the fence between scientific and humanistic perspectives.

Additional Reading

Harris, Marvin. 1968. *The Rise of Anthropological Theory.* New York: Thomas Y. Crowell.

Horgan, John. 1996. *The End of Science: Facing the Limits of Knowledge in the Twilight of the Scientific Age.* Reading, MA: Addison-Wesley.

Kuznar, Lawrence. 1997. *Reclaiming a Scientific Anthropology.* Walnut Creek, CA: Altamira.

Mcgee, R. Jon, and Richard L. Williams. 2004. *Anthropological Theory: An Introductory History.* 3d ed. New York: McGraw Hill.

Watson, Patty Jo. 1995. Archaeology, anthropology, and the culture concept. *American Anthropologist* 97: 683–694.

Online Resources

COMPANION WEB SITE
Visit **http://anthropology.wadsworth.com** and click on the Student Companion Web Site for Thomas/Kelly *Archaeology*, 4th edition, to access a wide range of material to help you succeed in your introductory archaeology course. These include flashcards, Internet exercises, Web links, and practice quizzes.

RESEARCH ONLINE WITH INFOTRAC COLLEGE EDITION
From the Student Companion Web Site, you can access the InfoTrac College Edition database, which offers thousands of full-length articles for your research.

3

The Structure of Archaeological Inquiry

OUTLINE

© Ofer Bar-Yosef

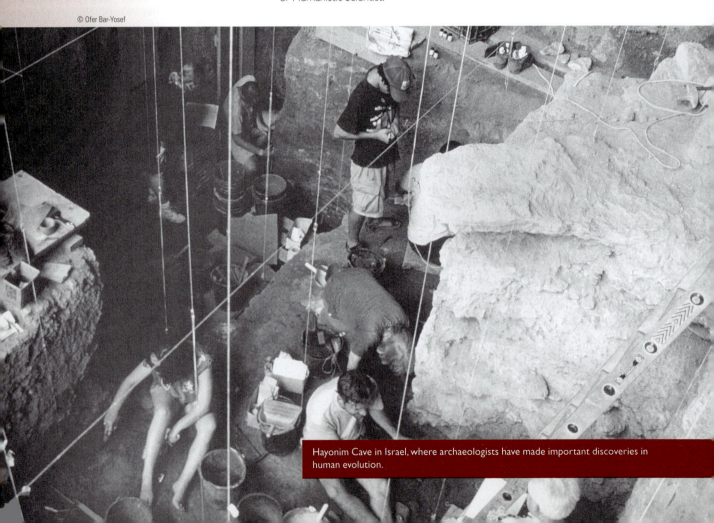

Hayonim Cave in Israel, where archaeologists have made important discoveries in human evolution.

Preview

THIS CHAPTER SETS OUT the theoretical baseline for the rest of the book, as follows:

- Low-level theory is required in order to make relevant observations about the archaeological record. This is how archaeologists get their "data," their "facts."
- Theory at the middle level is what links these archaeological data to human behavior. Sometimes archaeologists generate these links by conducting controlled experiments, sometimes by observing living peoples to see how behavior is translated into the archaeological record.
- High-level (or "general") theory aims to answer larger "why" questions.
- Paradigms provide the overarching frameworks for understanding the human condition.

We conclude the chapter by showing how these various concepts fit together into a model of archaeological inquiry.

Paradigms apply to all intellectual inquiry about human beings; it is not restricted to archaeology. We will concentrate on two kinds of paradigms—cultural materialism and postmodernism—to see how these paradigms translate into research strategies that archaeologists pursue. We understand that many students are put off by obscure discussions of various "-ologies" and "-isms," but it's important that you understand these basic theoretical points. We'll try to minimize the jargon; in the coming chapters, we think you'll recognize the importance of understanding these basic theoretical concepts.

INTRODUCTION

We all use the term "**theory**" in a number of different ways. In the more casual, popular usage, a theory is simply an idea. Sometimes theory is a put-down, referring to an untested explanation that the speaker believes to be clearly false. For example, some might speak of Erich Von Dähniken's goofy *Chariots of the Gods* "theory," in which he argues that major accomplishments in prehistory, such as construction of the pyramids, were performed or directed by extraterrestrial beings.

A theory may also be a set of untested principles or propositions—in other words, theory as opposed to practice. Thus a new invention to harness solar energy might work "in theory" (that is, on paper), but would require extensive field testing before one could decide whether it was a successful design. If the solar device functioned as expected, the theory would be valid; if the device failed, scientists would consider the theory behind it invalid.

Although both usages are common, neither has much to do with scientific theories, which are statements that purport to explain observed, empirical phenomena. Theories are answers to "why" questions. These questions occur at different levels; we will call them low-level, middle-level, and high-level. We distinguish the different levels not by complexity or difficulty, but by their functions in the process of archaeological inquiry.

Low-level theories help make the observations that emerge from hands-on archaeological fieldwork. Although

---

theory An explanation for observed, empirical phenomena. It is empirical and seeks to explain the relationships between variables; it is an answer to a "why" question.

low-level theories The observations and interpretations that emerge from hands-on archaeological field and lab work.

you may be accustomed to thinking of such observations as self-evident data or facts, we will see why even the baseline facts of archaeology are themselves really the results of theories.

Middle-level theory (or, more commonly, "middle-range theory") links archaeological data with the relevant aspects of human behavior or natural processes (for example, the actions of water or animals) that produced them. This is the unique realm of archaeology because it moves from the archaeologically observable (the "facts") to the archaeologically invisible (human behavior, cultural beliefs, or natural processes of the past). Here the archaeologist answers questions such as "*Why* do we think that this stone tool was used for scraping wood (and not hides)?" or "*Why* do we know that these bones came from an animal hunted and butchered by humans, and not killed and eaten by lions?"

Then there is **high-level (or general) theory**, which seeks answers to larger "why" questions, such as *why* did hunter-gatherers become agriculturalists? *Why* do some societies fight whereas others cooperate? *Why* did some societies evolve stratified social and political systems whereas others remained egalitarian? These are the sorts of questions that we really wish to answer; they are the reason that we do archaeology. Low-level and middle-level theories are steps toward the creation of high-level theory.

We also need the concept of **paradigm**, which provides the overarching framework for understanding some research problem (in our case, the human condition). Paradigms are not specific to archaeology, but apply to intellectual inquiry in general. A paradigm is a lot like "culture" because (as we explained in Chapter 2) just as culture provides you with some idea about what is (or is not) acceptable behavior, a paradigm also

---

guides a researcher's path of inquiry. Your paradigm defines what will or will not be an interesting question. Paradigms also define what will (or will not) be acceptable data by drawing our attention to some facts and blinding us to others. In so doing, paradigms not only define questions, they also direct a researcher to particular answers. In this chapter, we will introduce two major research paradigms in Americanist archaeology.

LEVELS OF THEORY

Before we can explore these different levels of theory and paradigms in more detail, we must first address the concept of data. Although many may think of data as a straightforward concept—scientists collect data and then explain them—data are actually much more complex. Data do not lie out there waiting for us to pick them up like Easter eggs on the lawn (as James Ford—introduced in Chapter 1—used to say). In fact, data are as dependent on theory as theory is on data.

What Are Data?

Low-level archaeological theory defines what constitutes archaeological data. But what, exactly, are archaeological data? To answer this question, we will introduce an archaeological site that crops up later in this text.

Gatecliff Shelter is a prehistoric **rockshelter** in Nevada where people camped now and again beneath a shallow overhang over a period of some 7000 years (Figure 3-1). Thomas found Gatecliff in 1970, and he worked there with an interdisciplinary team that, throughout the 1970s, excavated the deposits in the shelter.

Gatecliff was discovered by old-fashioned, dogged fieldwork (see Chapter 4 to find out how). The excavation was "vertical"—in some places nearly 40 feet deep, with cultural deposits stacked up within a floor area of about 300 square feet. Buried within Gatecliff Shelter were thousands of cultural objects—that is, artifacts: projectile points made of chipped stone, bone awls, basketry made of willow splints, grinding stones, small pieces of slate incised with enigmatic geometric designs, woven sagebrush bark mats, stone scrapers, shells and turquoise used as ornaments. Gatecliff also contained objects not made by humans—**ecofacts**—which are items relating to the natural environment, such as bighorn sheep bones, charcoal, piñon nut hulls, and pollen. We also encountered **features**—pits, hearths, rodent burrows—which are cultural and non-cultural

---

middle-level (or middle-range) theory Hypothesis that links archaeological observations with the human behavior or natural processes that produced them.

high-level (or general) theory Theory that seeks to answer large "why" questions.

paradigm The overarching framework, often unstated, for understanding a research problem. It is a researcher's "culture."

rockshelter A common type of archaeological site, consisting of a rock overhang that is deep enough to provide shelter but not deep enough to be called a cave (technically speaking, a cave must have an area of perpetual darkness).

ecofact Plant or animal remains found in an archaeological site.

feature The nonportable evidence of technology; usually fire hearths, architectural elements, artifact clusters, garbage pits, soil stains, and so on.

Figure 3-1 Gatecliff Shelter, late in the excavation: removing deposits through a bucket brigade method.

things that archaeologists measure, draw, photograph, and sample, but that they cannot take home in a bag.

The point here is simple but important: After nearly a decade of excavating at Gatecliff, Thomas excavated no data at all. Why would any right-thinking archaeologist waste a decade digging holes that produce no archaeological data?

Thomas found no data at Gatecliff because archaeologists do not excavate data. Rather, they excavate objects. **Data** are *observations made on those objects*. Those observations are critical to making *interpretations* of the objects. Observations answer one or more questions that will permit the archaeologists to make interpretations: Is this grubby little black thing a piece of pottery? To answer that question, we need to ask if it contains the characteristics of pottery: Does it contain clay and temper (material added to the clay to give it strength)? Does it look as though it had been fired (heated)? If the answers are yes, then we "interpret" the grubby little black thing to be a piece of pottery.

Cleaning this piece of pottery off, we might observe

that the convex surface (the pot's outer surface) is covered with white paint, with remnants of a black design on top of the white paint. This observation might allow us to further "interpret" the piece as belonging to a particular kind of pottery, perhaps one called Chupadero Black-on-white (a kind of pottery found in the American Southwest).

Likewise, we might look at a small black circle of earth that we've just uncovered, make observations on its properties (its diameter, depth, and fill), and interpret it, depending on the exact observations, as nothing more than a filled-in rodent burrow or, alternatively, as an ancient posthole, filled with the decayed remains of a post.

Data, therefore, are observations that allow us to make interpretations. They tell us *why* something is what we think it is. And this means that the observations we make on objects, as well as the interpretations of those observations, *are all theory-driven*. This is why it is important to understand the different levels of theory in archaeology.

Low-Level Theory

Low-level theory begins with archaeological objects; it then generates some relevant facts or data about those objects. Some data consist of physical observations. For example, "Artifact 20.2/4683 is (a) made of obsidian, (b) 21.5 mm long, and (c) weighs 2.1 grams." This statement contains three pieces of data—observations made on an archaeological object (the number 20.2/4683 is the item's unique catalog number for identification—more on that in a later chapter). Other observations might be contextual: "Artifact 20.2/4683 was found in unit B-5, 56 cm below the surface." Why are these

data Relevant observations made on objects that then serve as the basis for study and discussion.

theoretical statements? Because each of them is actually based on a "why" question: Why do we know that something is obsidian? Because the stone has certain characteristics that fit a definition of obsidian (a dark volcanic glass) and that clearly differentiate it from other stone types, such as chert or quartzite. Why do we know the length, weight, and provenience? Because these measurements were made using digital instruments whose ability to measure things reliably is based on theories from the field of electronics.

Another example: While excavating, a student comes upon a curving red band in the sediment. On the concave side of the red band are some black flecks that turn out to be charcoal. The student calls to her crew chief, "I've got a hearth over here!" How did she know it was a hearth? The charcoal was a clue, but archaeological sites often contain scattered charcoal.

This student apparently knows that sufficient heat has a predictable effect on sediments with high iron content: The iron is oxidized (bonded with oxygen) and turns red. She may be unaware of the theory that accounts for the oxidation and color change, just as someone making measurements may be unaware of the theory of electronics that permits them to measure a projectile point's length with a digital caliper. But both of these observations are nonetheless based on theories. Likewise, the ability to identify an animal bone as bison rather than deer, or as a femur rather than a humerus, is based on evolutionary theory.

We refer to this area of archaeology as "low-level" theory, not because it is simple or unimportant (indeed, evolutionary theory is anything but simple and is incredibly important to many fields), but because archaeologists normally give little thought to the theories that stand behind basic observations such as those we've described here. We record that we found something—a hearth or bison femur—without presenting the geochemical or evolutionary theory that gives us the ability to identify something as a hearth or a bison bone.

We can make an infinite number of observations on any single archaeological object. Many of these are made on the object itself: length, width, thickness, weight, angle measurements, material, color, curvature, chemical composition, manufacturing techniques, and so forth. Others might be observations on the object's context, that is, where it was found in a site. Overall, the important dimensions of low-level theory are the classical ones in archaeology: form and context.

Low-level theory is critical because it allows archaeologists to know that their data are comparable. How-

ever, these basic observations can become the focus of scrutiny if, for instance, archaeologists try to determine when humans began to use fire intentionally (perhaps some hundreds of thousands of years ago). In this case, what constitutes an *intentional* hearth becomes of more than passing interest. The same is true when archaeologists try to determine whether some chipped stones are tools or simply rocks that Mother Nature has broken in fortuitous ways (more than one archaeologist has been fooled). When archaeologists give this sort of attention to inferences made from observations, they move into the realm of middle-level theory.

Middle-Level Theory

Archaeological theory at the middle level links some specific set of archaeological data with the relevant aspects of human behavior or natural processes that produced them. At this middle level, we make a critical transition by moving from the archaeologically observable (the low-level theoretical facts) to the archaeologically invisible (relevant human behaviors or natural processes of the past). How, you might wonder, does this transition actually take place?

First, remember that the archaeological record is the *contemporary* evidence left by people of the past. Strictly speaking, the archaeological record is composed only of static objects—the artifacts, ecofacts, and features that have survived the passage of time. Those objects are the products of two things: human behavior and natural processes. Our job is to infer the long-gone behavior and processes from the static results—the objects we recover from archaeological sites. For example, Figure 3-2 shows a large scatter of bison bone at a site in Wyoming. All that the archaeologist can record is the kind of bones that are present and their arrangement. But how does the archaeologist infer from these observations whether people killed these bison? (You may think the answer is straightforward but, in Chapter 10, we will show you that it is not.)

Archaeologists conducting research at the middle level seek situations in which they can observe (1) ongoing human behavior or natural processes and (2) the material results of that behavior or those processes. This requires that archaeologists step out of their excavation trenches and turn to experimental archaeology, ethnoarchaeology, or taphonomy. We'll discuss these fields in much more detail in Chapter 10. For now, we will briefly introduce them, so that you can see how they

© University of Wyoming, Frison Institute

Figure 3-2 The Horner site in Wyoming. The bones are those of dozens of bison: How would we know if these animals had been hunted?

contribute to the goal of inferring behavior and natural processes from archaeological remains.

In **experimental archaeology**, we use controlled experiments to determine the effect of one archaeologically invisible variable on an archaeologically observable one. For example, archaeologists sometimes conduct controlled experiments in which they manufacture their own stone tools. In doing so, they study specific stoneworking techniques (which are obviously not directly visible archaeologically) to learn how different tool manufacturing methods are translated into archaeologically observable evidence (such as flaking scars, breakage patterns, and by-products). For similar reasons, archaeologists conduct intensive studies of pottery manufacture, house-construction methods, ancient agricultural technologies, and hunting and gathering techniques, to name but a few areas.

Some archaeologists conduct middle-level research as **ethnoarchaeology**, in which they observe ongoing, present-day societies (as shown in Figure 3-3) to see how behavior translates into the archaeological record. Research with living hunter-gatherers, for instance, shows that people butcher animals in different ways depending on several variables, such as the size of the animal, the distance from the kill site back to the camp, the number of people available to carry the meat, and so forth. Under some conditions, hunter-gatherers may

bring the entire carcass back to camp. Under other conditions, they may leave some of the less-useful portions behind; and sometimes they return with only the meat, leaving all the bones behind. Such behaviors result in distinctly different arrangements and assortments of bones left at the kill sites and at the residential camps. Such patterns give archaeologists tools with which to interpret the animal remains in archaeological sites.

Taphonomy studies the role that natural processes play in the formation of an archaeological site. This includes the effects of climate, rivers, soil formation, plants, and animals on archaeological sites. The aim is to distinguish the patterns caused by natural processes from those produced by human behavior. Humans butcher animals that they kill, for instance, but carnivores also kill animals; other animals die of old age and are eaten by scavengers, or simply decay. To tell the difference between bones resulting from these different processes, we need to understand not only how hunter-gatherers butcher game, but also how carnivores consume a carcass, how carcasses decompose, and how natural factors, a river for example, affect a carcass.

High-Level Theory

High-level (or general) theory is archaeology's ultimate objective; low- and middle-level research are necessary steps to attain this goal. High-level theory goes beyond the archaeological specifics to address the "big questions" of concern to many social and historical sciences. High-level theory applies to all intellectual inquiry about the human condition, raising questions such as: Why did we humans become cultural animals? Why did hunter-gatherers become agriculturalists? Why did social stratification arise? Why did human history take the particular course it did in the New World as opposed to the Old World? Why did aboriginal hunter-gatherers in California not take up agriculture? Why did large civilizations develop in some parts of the world and not in others?

experimental archaeology Experiments designed to determine the archaeological correlates of ancient behavior; may overlap with both ethnoarchaeology and taphonomy.

ethnoarchaeology The study of contemporary peoples to determine how human behavior is translated into the archaeological record.

taphonomy The study of how organisms become part of the fossil record; in archaeology it primarily refers to the study of how natural processes produce patterning in archaeological data.

Figure 3-3 Kelly (in middle) conducting ethnoarchaeological research in Madagascar.

Some general theories stress environmental adaptation, some emphasize biological factors, and some involve only cultural causality; others try to combine these. In Chapter 15, we will look at some of the general theories that archaeologists have offered as answers to some big questions.

Paradigms

Paradigms provide the overarching framework for understanding "how the world works" that each researcher brings to a particular question or problem. This is the most abstract and yet the most important of our concepts.

As we said above, paradigms are a lot like culture—both are learned, shared, and symbolic. Archaeologists

processual paradigm The paradigm that explains social, economic, and cultural change as primarily the result of adaptation to material conditions; external conditions (for example, the environment) are assumed to take causal priority over ideational factors in explaining change.

postprocessual paradigm A paradigm that focuses on humanistic approaches and rejects scientific objectivity; it sees archaeology as inherently political and is more concerned with interpreting the past than with testing hypotheses. It sees change as arising largely from interactions between individuals operating within a symbolic and/or competitive system.

sharing the same paradigm can converse with one another and leave a lot unstated; an archaeologist following another paradigm might have to ask many questions, seeking definitions of basic concepts and terms. Like culture, your paradigm influences how you view humanity, how you frame your questions about the present and the past, and how you interpret the answers that you receive to these questions. It consists of some *a priori* notions of which variables are relevant and which are not. And, like culture, a paradigm can give you both correct and incorrect answers. Paradigms are not open to direct empirical verification or rejection; they simply turn out to be useful or not.

Just as all humans participate in a culture, all archaeologists operate within a paradigm, whether they are aware of it or not. Without a paradigm, nothing would make sense. So, although a paradigm can give you an inaccurate bias, our goal cannot be to free ourselves of any paradigm. Instead, we simply must be aware of the paradigm we are using.

The central message of anthropology is that there is value in other ways of being human and in other cultures. Extrapolating that lesson to paradigms, you should not ask, "Which paradigm is best?" but rather "Which paradigm will be most useful for the kind of theory I am trying to construct or for the problem I am trying to solve?"

Paradigms in Archaeology

We are going to characterize Americanist archaeology in terms of two paradigms—the **processual** and the **postprocessual**—which define what modern Americanist archaeology is all about. However, our presentation of these paradigms is necessarily abstract and a simplification of the field of archaeology. No archaeologist falls neatly into either category; some, in fact, achieve the difficult posture of straddling the two.

Paradigms are sometimes categorically opposed to one another, in other cases they overlap, and most are embedded in still more-abstract frameworks of thinking. Processual archaeology is embedded within **cultural materialism,** and postprocessual archaeology is embedded within **postmodernism**. We will present the basics of cultural materialism and sketch its importance to archaeology's processual paradigm. We then look at the premises of postmodernism to see how it gave rise to archaeology's postprocessual paradigm.

Cultural Materialism

Although its roots extend back at least a century, modern cultural materialism is largely associated with the late Marvin Harris (1927–2001), a cultural anthropologist, who gave it its name.

Harris argued that anthropology is a science, and its knowledge should therefore be acquired through public, replicable, empirical, and objective methods. Armed with such methods, the cultural materialist aims to formulate theories to scientifically explain the evolution of differences and similarities in human societies. Rival theories are judged by the same criteria, based on their power to predict outcomes and to admit independent testing. Cultural materialism posits that environmental, technological, and economic factors—the *material* conditions of existence—are the most powerful and pervasive determinants of human behavior. By explicitly (and exclusively) embracing a scientific framework to examine the effects of material factors on human societies, cultural materialists reject humanist, ideational approaches and advocate the adaptive view of culture discussed in Chapter 2.

Cultural materialism focuses on behavioral events, which must be distinguished from mental events because they are observed in different ways. Modern human behavior is available to the scientific community in a form that can be observed, measured, photographed, and objectively described. We observe human thought, the events of the mind, only indirectly. Although distinct relationships exist between behavior and thought, we must demonstrate these associations, not assume them. This is obviously true for archaeology—given that the people who left the objects behind are long dead—and it is also true for cultural anthropology, because we must still infer ideas from speech and other behaviors.

Although behavior is symbolic—actions carry meaning to the one doing the action and to those observing it—cultural materialists concentrate on the observable outcomes. Within these guidelines, cultural materialist research covers an array of topics, among them: warfare, marriage, dietary patterns and food taboos, settlement and demographic trends, and the origin and evolution of gender roles. It contains within it a wide variety of sub-paradigms—some that take an explicitly evolutionary approach and others that are more ecological.

Cultural materialists use three fundamental concepts in their approach: infrastructure, structure, and superstructure. **Infrastructure** denotes those elements considered most important to satisfying basic human needs: food, shelter, reproduction, and health. These demographic, technological, economic, and ecological processes are assumed to lie at the causal heart of every sociocultural system. The infrastructure mediates a culture's interactions with the natural and social environment through the following two mechanisms:

- Mode of production refers to the technology, practices, and social relations employed in basic subsistence production (especially food and other energy production), given the specific technology used.
- Mode of reproduction concerns the technology, practices, and social relations employed for expanding, limiting, and maintaining population size (specifically, demography, mating patterns, fertility, natality, mortality, nurturing of infants, medical controls, contraception, abortion, infanticide).

cultural materialism A research paradigm that takes a scientific approach and that emphasizes the importance of material factors—such as environment, population density, subsistence, and technology—in understanding change and diversity in human societies.

postmodernism A paradigm that rejects grand historical schemes in favor of humanistic approaches that appreciate the multiple voices of history. It seeks to see how colonialism created our vision of the world we occupy today; it eschews science and argues against the existence of objective truth.

infrastructure In cultural materialism, the elements most important to satisfying basic human survival and well-being—food, shelter, reproduction, health—which are assumed to lie at the causal heart of every sociocultural system.

At the next level, the sociocultural system's **structure** is made up of those interpersonal relationships that emerge as behavior. It includes the **domestic economy**, which is the organization of reproduction and basic production, exchange, and consumption within camps, houses, apartments, or other domestic settings. This entails information on family structure, division of labor, enculturation, age and sex roles, hierarchies, and sanctions.

A society's structure also includes the **political economy,** which is the organization of reproduction, production, exchange, and consumption within and between bands, villages, chiefdoms, states, and empires. It includes political organizations, factions, clubs, associations, corporations, division of labor, taxation, tribute, political socialization and education, social divisions and hierarchies, discipline, police/military control, and warfare.

Finally, **superstructure** refers to a society's values, aesthetics, rules, beliefs, religions, and symbols, which can be behaviorally manifested as art, music, dance, literature, advertising, religious rituals, sports, games, hobbies, and even science.

The Principle of Infrastructural Determinism

Distinguishing cultural materialism from other approaches is the **principle of infrastructural determinism.** This principle has two tenets: (1) human society strives to meet those needs most important to the survival and well-being of human individuals (primarily sex, sleep, nutrition, and shelter); responses to these needs occur directly in the realm of infrastructure; and (2) the infrastructure determines the rest of the sociocultural system. To cultural materialists, *change in the sociocultural system is largely a product of change in the infrastructure.*

Though clearly interrelated, the infrastructure, structure, and superstructure influence one another differentially, and cultural materialists assign causal priority to the modes of production and reproduction (as indicated by the size of the arrows in Figure 3-4). Technological, demographic, ecological, and economic processes become the independent variables, and the structure and superstructure become second- and third-level responses. Cultural materialists argue that different modes of production and reproduction foster quite distinctive ideological systems. Hunter-gatherers think differently than farmers, who in turn view the world differently than industrialists. *To cultural materialism, infrastructure is the key to understanding the growth and development of all cultures.*

Cultural materialists see such causality as probabilistic, however: Not all hunting and gathering societies have precisely the same sociocultural structure or superstructure. Some sociocultural traits in a given society arise from arbitrary, historically contingent events. And feedback flows among the three components (as shown by the smaller arrows in Figure 3-4). However, as scientists, cultural materialists look past arbitrary or historical events to seek overarching generalities that we can test.

Stating that structure and superstructure are causally dependent on infrastructure does not mean that determinations are transmitted in a single direction; as anthropologist Leslie White put it, the influences are *reciprocal* but not necessarily *equal.* No component is a passive recipient. Without input from domestic, political, and ideological subsystems, the observable modes of production and reproduction would have evolved differently. However, the important point is that *significant* changes in human society result from those factors that directly influence the infrastructure—subsistence and the extraction of energy from the environment.

Cultural materialists argue that their paradigm is better than alternatives in conforming to the canons of acceptable scientific explanation. One can therefore discredit their strategic principles only by providing alternative principles that produce better and more scientifically acceptable theories.

structure The behavior that supports choices made at the level of the infrastructure, including the organization of reproduction, production, exchange, family structure, division of labor, age and sex roles, political units, social organization, and warfare.

domestic economy The organization of reproduction and basic production, exchange, and consumption within camps, houses, apartments, or other domestic settings.

political economy The organization of reproduction, production, exchange, and consumption within and between bands, villages, chiefdoms, states, and empires.

superstructure A group's values, aesthetics, rules, beliefs, religions, and symbols, which can be behaviorally manifested as art, music, dance, literature, advertising, religious rituals, sports, games, hobbies, and even science.

principle of infrastructural determinism Argument that the infrastructure lies at the causal heart of every sociocultural system, that human society responds to factors that directly affect survival and well-being, and that such responses determine the rest of the sociocultural system.

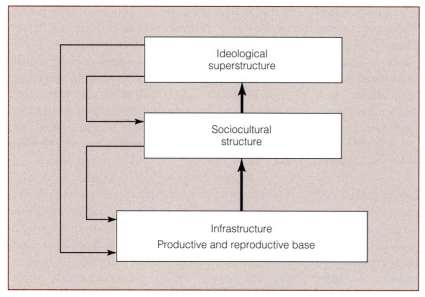

Figure 3-4 How the cultural materialist views causality.

Processual Archaeology: Materialism at Work in Archaeology

The processual paradigm is cultural materialism applied to the study of the past. It includes the new archaeology of Lewis Binford and others, and it also extends to brands of evolutionary archaeologies practiced by a large segment of Americanist archaeologists today. For now, it is only important that you understand the basics of the processual paradigm and how they differ from those of postprocessual archaeology (these differences are summarized in Table 3-1).

If you recall our discussion of Walter Taylor and Lewis Binford in Chapter 1, you will see how processual archaeology grew out of dissatisfaction with the increasingly sterile cultural-historical and largely descriptive archaeology of the 1950s. Processual archaeologists correctly noted that culture history, as a paradigm, was inadequate for the description of ancient lives, as well as for the explanation of how cultures operated in the past. The "new archaeologists" of the 1960s retained the chronology-building tools perfected in cultural-historical archaeology, but they rejected the rest in favor of the processual paradigm.

The processual paradigm has several key characteristics:

1. *Processual archaeology emphasizes evolutionary generalizations, not historical specifics, and it downplays the*

importance of the individual. In the early days of the processual paradigm, archaeologists viewed history as the opposite of science, as description rather than explanation. But the processual paradigm is scientific, not historical. It focuses on regularities and correlations. An interest in developing cultural (as opposed to biological) evolutionary theory directed the processual paradigm away from ideology and history and toward environmental change, population growth, food production, trade, and conflict over limited resources as the forces driving cultural evolution.

In its early days, processual archaeology was interested in particular historical sequences, but primarily as data sets that would allow them to test or develop ideas about cultural evolutionary theory. Put another way, processual archaeologists saw particular historical sequences as individual "experiments" from which one could construct theory and law-like generalizations. Early processual archaeologists did not consider culture history by itself to be important.

TABLE 3-1 Some Contrasts between Processual and Postprocessual Archaeology	
PROCESSUAL ARCHAEOLOGY	**POSTPROCESSUAL ARCHAEOLOGY**
Emphasizes evolutionary generalizations and regularities, not historical specifics; it downplays the importance of the individual.	Rejects the search for universal laws and regularities.
Views culture from a systemic perspective and defines culture as adaptation.	Rejects the systemic view of culture and focuses on an ideational view of humanity's extrasomatic means of culture.
Explanation is explicitly scientific and objective.	Rejects scientific methods and objectivity.
Attempts to remain ethically neutral; claims to be explicitly non political.	Argues that all archaeology is unavoidably political.

As part of the processual paradigm's focus on historical regularities and correlations, Binford and others rejected "great man" explanations of history—these are explanations that attribute major changes in economy or social or political organization to a single person who had a "great idea." For example, archaeologists once thought that the origin of agriculture was a product of one of these great ideas, a hypothesis that has been disproven.

2. *Processual archaeology views culture from a systemic perspective and defines culture as humanity's extrasomatic means of adaptation.* Because culture provides the nonbiological system through which people adapt to their environment, processual archaeology could (and briefly, did) tap into a much larger body of established external theory, often called **general systems theory**. The theoretical premise here is that various complex entities—thermostats, computers, glaciers, living organisms, and even human societies—are most profitably viewed as systems composed of multiple parts that interact in a limited number of predictable ways. Depending on the application, the general rules governing all systems (such as positive feedback, negative feedback, and equilibrium) could explain the behavior of the major parts of any system—regardless of the specifics of that system. (Although many processual archaeologists today still look at the interconnections between things, they no longer seek to explain human societies in the sterile terms of general systems theory.)

Processual archaeology focuses attention on technology, ecology, and economy and takes an adaptive rather than ideational perspective on culture. Processual archaeology tends to focus on behavior rather than on the cultural ideas, values, and beliefs that stand behind that behavior. Religion and ideology are seen as "epiphenomena"—cultural add-ons with little long-term explanatory value. Thus, the processual paradigm agrees with the principle of infrastructural determinism.

3. *Explanation in processual archaeology is explicitly scientific.* Procedures in processual archaeology depended on deductive models grounded in the hard sciences (math, chemistry, physics) and emphasized the importance of being objective. By objective, we mean

that processual archaeologists believed that they could see the world "as it really is," and not through a filter that colored their perception of the world.

Initially, the processual paradigm championed the view that predicting events (even those in the past) is equivalent to explaining them. More recent approaches, however, stress the interplay between induction and deduction, the *relative* objectivity of observations, and the probabilistic nature of explanation in the social sciences.

4. *Processual archaeology attempts to remain ethically neutral and claims to be explicitly non-political.* Processual archaeology tries to provide evidence about the past that is deliberately disconnected from the present. Politics of the present, processual archaeologists argue, should have nothing to do with the study of the ancient past. Archaeology should avoid subjectivity, and its conclusions should not be influenced by modern politics. Processual archaeology is not interested in passing moral judgments on people of the past.

However, processual archaeology does wish to be relevant to the modern world and to provide an understanding of cultural evolution that is useful in directing the world's future. Archaeology should influence politics, but politics is not to influence archaeology.

Roughly half of Americanist archaeologists today pursue the processual paradigm in one form or another (although many of these agree with some tenets of the postprocessual paradigm, as discussed below). Why does the paradigm of cultural materialism hold such appeal to archaeologists? One reason is that cultural materialism emphasizes technology, economy, environment, and demography—those aspects of human existence that leave the clearest traces in the archaeological record. But cultural materialism may also be popular because it suggests that the world and cultural change result from orderly processes—an idea that the postmodern paradigm challenges.

Postmodernism

Postmodernism is a world apart from cultural materialism. Although "postmodernism" is more often used to describe literary and artistic styles, it helped structure the late twentieth-century format of the social sciences as well. Just as cultural materialism informs processual archaeology, postmodernism underlies the postprocessual paradigm of Americanist archaeology.

Most new paradigms, whether in the sciences or the arts, are responses to the perceived excesses or failures

general systems theory An effort to describe the properties by which all systems, including human societies, allegedly operated. Popular in processual archaeology of the late 1960s and 1970s.

Archaeological Ethics
Excavating the Dead of World War I

Most people think that archaeologists study only very ancient sites, like Egypt's pyramids. But archaeologists also study the more recent past, including the two world wars. A prominent element of this archaeology is the remains of the soldiers lost on battlefields.

As you might imagine, the looting and plundering of human burials is a problem the world over, but so is their professional excavation. We see both of these issues in the excavation of World War I's dead.

The "Great War," the "War to End All Wars," was truly a horror. Mechanized and chemical warfare brought death on a scale that was horrendous even to soldiers accustomed to cavalry charges into cannons. Tens of thousands of men died in the trenches along the western front in France and Belgium. Their bodies were often lost in seas of mud churned by shellfire; even if found, they were frequently buried in shallow, hastily dug graves.

The war ended in 1918, but its horrors continue as relic hunters plunder the buried trenches and bunkers in search of war memorabilia and jewelry. Looting is especially prevalent in Belgium, where some 50,000 British and untold numbers of French, German, African, Australian, Canadian, and Native American soldiers were lost (Choctaws served as codetalkers in World War I, just as Navajo did in the Pacific theater in World War II).

In Ypres, a town in Flanders, collectors gather each month at a pub to buy and sell war memorabilia and swap stories. A British television program in 2000 showed looters brazenly bragging of what they had robbed from the dead: "This is something I've got which is very nice. It's a British officer's ring. Gold with a diamond. I always told my wife one day I'd come home with gold."

Many of the sites are patrolled by police, but they are few and they can hardly stop the looting that occurs under cover of darkness. Military memorabilia, stolen by those who did not fight in the war, is increasingly valuable on an international market. "It's not human, it's just greed," said one veteran.

To help stop the looting, in 1992 Ypres authorized a group of avocational archaeologists, who call themselves The Diggers, to remove burials from the trenches for proper burial. In two years they unearthed more than 100 burials, and their work continues. The Diggers are sanctioned by the Belgian government and are licensed by professional archaeologists. All remains and artifacts are turned over to the Commonwealth War Graves Commission for burial in military cemeteries.

Some veterans support The Diggers; others believe that their comrades should remain where they fell. But this option is not always possible. For example, The Diggers have worked at Boezinge, near the town of Ieper, where in 1915 the German army launched its initial gas attack. This land is now being developed, and the choice is to bulldoze the bodies, preserve the battlefield as a memorial, or professionally excavate and rebury the remains.

How should we treat these remains? Bulldozing them seems disrespectful, and preservation may not be feasible in a small, crowded nation. Professional excavation seems the logical solution. But the dead come from different nationalities and religions with different opinions and customs on treatment of the dead. Do we bulldoze, preserve in place, or excavate? How should the dead of recent wars be treated?

of a previous paradigm. To understand postmodernism, therefore, you need to understand how it was a response to a set of European philosophical, political, and ethical ideas that reigned from the seventeenth through nineteenth centuries—an exciting period known as the **Enlightenment**.

Enlightenment A Western philosophy that advocated ideas of linear progress, absolute truth, science, rational planning of ideal social orders, and the standardization of knowledge. It held that rational thought was the key to progress; that science and technology would free people from the oppression of historical traditions of myth, religion, and superstition; and that the control of nature through technology would permit the development of moral and spiritual virtues.

What Was the Enlightenment?

The Enlightenment, or "Age of Reason," was a shift in Western thought in the seventeenth and eighteenth centuries when thinkers tried to develop objective sciences and universal standards for morality and law. The Enlightenment worldview held that rational (not religious) thought was the key to progress, and that technology, governed by rational thought, would free people from the control of nature and permit the development of moral and spiritual virtues.

Enlightenment thought saw the world as knowable through science. Scholars argued that scientific thought would always produce truth, and truth was always right (and good). This was a period of great optimism, when scholars threw off the fetters of religious dogma and made scientific discoveries that helped humanity control the perversities of nature.

To liberate humans from the perceived oppression of myth, religion, and superstition, Enlightenment thinkers appealed to the ideas of linear progress, absolute truth, planning of ideal social orders, and the standardization of knowledge. They searched for order and believed that order in the physical and social world was natural and good. The period was characterized by great thinkers who saw world history as unfolding according to a great, orderly plan that involved and ensured continual improvement for humanity. John Locke (1632–1704) was an Enlightenment scholar; so were Immanuel Kant (1724–1804) and Thomas Jefferson (1743–1826). Sigmund Freud, Karl Marx, and Charles Darwin, all of whom saw society as improving (although for different reasons), were scholars of the late Enlightenment—a period that sociologists refer to as "modern." This gives us the "modern" in "postmodern."

What Is Postmodernism?

Serious cracks began to appear in this system of thought in the early twentieth century, especially after World War I. The "Great War" showed many people that science and rational thought, which promised to produce a better society, could also produce the horrors of tank and gas warfare. Many young intellectuals felt betrayed, for the world was not as they thought it was.

deconstruction Efforts to expose the assumptions behind the alleged objective and systematic search for knowledge. A primary tool of postmodernism.

The initial result was modernism, artistic and literary styles that shrugged off optimism, rationality, and ideals of progress (be careful not to confuse modernism with "modern," defined above). This artistic movement tried to see all perspectives simultaneously, as can be seen in the art style of cubism, best known through the work of Pablo Picasso. Novels and poetry by Gertrude Stein, Virginia Woolf, T. S. Eliot, Franz Kafka, and Ezra Pound eschewed straightforward narrative in favor of new literary techniques such as multiple narratives and stream-of-consciousness writing, as well as moral ambiguity.

Postmodernism arose from modernism in the latter half of the twentieth century, especially after the 1960s. Postmodernism takes some modernist themes to an extreme. Andy Warhol was a postmodern artist, and Jorge Luis Borges and Thomas Pynchon were postmodern writers. Although modernists saw the fragmentation of knowledge as a tragic loss, they believed that art and literature could help people find some moral unity and coherence in the world. But postmodernism sees no forward movement to history, no "grand narrative," and no promise of a brighter future made possible by science. Indeed, postmodernism argues that there really is no truth and no coherence *except* that all understanding and meaning is "historically situated."

By "historically situated," postmodernists mean that our understanding of the world is not really truth, but rather only a product of the time in which we live. For this reason, postmodernism often seeks to understand how colonialism, a major social force of the past several hundred years, constructed the Western world's understanding of humanity. Some postmodernists try to correct the previous worldview by documenting the multiple voices of history (especially those of colonized and oppressed peoples) and by showing how colonialism constructed our image of others. The idea is that each group has a right to speak for itself, in its own voice, and to have that voice accepted as authentic and legitimate. Such pluralism is an essential theme of postmodernism.

Deconstruction and the Maya

Just as science was the primary tool of the Enlightenment, **deconstruction** is the primary tool of postmodernism. Coined by French philosopher Jacques Derrida (1930–) in the 1960s, the term refers to efforts to expose the assumptions behind the allegedly scientific (objective and systematic) search for knowledge.

Here's an archaeological example. The Maya civilization flourished in portions of Central America and Mexico, reaching a zenith about AD 700. The Maya constructed magnificent centers with stone pyramids, surrounded by thousands of households. These complexes were the center of a rich ceremonial life, places where kings recorded their exploits in hieroglyphics on stone monuments called **stelae** (Figure 3-5). The society ran according to a set of complex calendars and supported its agriculture with water storage systems. By AD 900, however, Maya civilization had collapsed; people abandoned the centers, which were gradually consumed by the jungle. Why?

Processual archaeologists proposed many explanations for the collapse of Maya civilization (the Maya people never disappeared; they are still there today). These fell into three major areas: war, environmental degradation, and the abuse of power by political elites. Anthropologist Richard Wilk (Indiana University) showed that these three explanations waxed and waned in popularity, as indicated by articles published in professional journals, in relation to major U.S. political events. Warfare as an explanation began in 1962, the beginning of the Vietnam War, and grew in popularity until the end of that war. During the ecology movement of the mid-1970s, explanations that focused on environmental degradation became prominent. After 1976, in the aftermath of the Watergate fiasco and historic resignation of Richard Nixon, abuse of government power was the favored explanation.

Wilk argues that by deconstructing archaeological thinking about the Maya collapse, we can see the degree to which modern political events affected the views of archaeologists working on this problem. There is nothing new in suggesting that archaeologists are products of their own culture: People who consider themselves scientists (like Wilk) have always tried to discover biases, remove their effects, and move on. What is new in postmodernism is that deconstruction is often the *goal* of research.

Many contemporary ethnographers see their task as analyzing a culture the way a literary critic reads a book or poem. They reject the goal of discovering scientific truths in favor of composing elegant and convincing interpretations about the target culture. According to one postmodern critic, ethnography, or an archaeological report, is not an empirical account, it is instead a species of fiction. As part of this approach, many anthropologists adopted a *reflexive* viewpoint, focusing

Figure 3-5 Stela B at Copán, Honduras; erected AD 731 it depicts the ruler, 18-Rabbit.

more on what the anthropological endeavor says about the anthropological process and less on ethnographic descriptions of other cultures.

An extreme form of postmodernism even suggests that objectivity is impossible and that truth is subjective and relative (mediated by one's cultural identity and background and influenced by who is seeking the knowledge and for what purpose). If these premises are accepted, then science becomes merely one way of telling a story about the world around us, and there are no criteria for determining the validity of any competing story. Some critics argue that in postmodernism "anything goes," and hence that there are no real gains in knowledge. Most postmodernists, however, adhere to a weaker version of this thesis, seeing the effects of cultural biases as difficult, but not impossible, to remove.

stelae Stone monuments erected by Maya rulers to record their history in rich images and hieroglyphic symbols. These symbols can be read and dated.

Postprocessual Archaeology: Postmodernism at Work in Archaeology

Although it had forerunners in the United States and elsewhere, the formal postprocessual paradigm arose largely in Great Britain and Europe, nurtured by archaeologists such as Ian Hodder (formerly Cambridge, now Stanford University). Adherents today can be found on both sides of the Atlantic. We can perhaps best characterize postprocessual archaeology by contrasting it with processual archaeology. We will list some of these characteristics below, but we caution that postprocessual archaeologists, like their processual colleagues, have ameliorated the initial, extreme position in recent years.

1. *Postprocessual archaeology rejects the processual search for universal laws.* The postprocessual paradigm holds that universals of human behavior simply do not exist and that scientific explanations are inadequate because they downplay historical circumstances in their search for universals. Processual archaeology saw the particulars of history—such as cultural ideas about men and women or specific religious beliefs—as playing no significant role in the grand scheme of history. Postprocessual archaeologists see the grand scheme, if it exists at all, as uninteresting; instead, they see the trajectory of particular societies as heavily influenced by that society's particular cultural ideas. For some postprocessual archaeologists, archaeology should be more closely allied with history (as it is in Europe) than with anthropology (as it is in the United States).

In fact, postprocessual archaeology often emphasizes the role of the individual in human society. We do not mean that postprocessual archaeology aims to see particular individuals in archaeology, for example, to find the name of the person who made a particular pot. Instead, postprocessual archaeology argues that large social change results from individuals going about their daily lives. In this view, societies are not animated solely by change from the "outside" (such as environmental change). More specifically, postprocessual archaeology tends to see social tension—for example, competition between men and women, elites and non-elites, or regional groups—as especially important in generating social change. This has prompted some to observe that the postprocessual world is a sad one indeed, where individuals prosper only by exploiting one another and where cooperation is mere pretense.

2. *Postprocessual archaeology rejects the systemic view of culture and focuses on an ideational perspective.* Postprocessual archaeology discredits the systems approach as a "robotic view of humans." Postmodernism in general distrusts any deterministic perspective that reduces individual humans to the status of a historical droid, not significantly different from conditioned laboratory rats.

Postprocessualists argue that the systemic view of human society suggests a coordinated, uniform organism responding only to outside pressures, mainly the environment and demography. But, postprocessualists argue, a society is composed of conflicting individuals, groups, families, and classes, whose goals are not necessarily identical and whose interests and actions are often in conflict with the adaptive success and functional needs of the cultural system as a whole. How can we reconcile a vision of society as a well-oiled machine of checks and balances with the fact that specific individuals with interests that are maladaptive for others, such as dictators, often control a society?

Whereas processual archaeology is grounded in the adaptive perspective of culture, postprocessual archaeology follows the ideational perspective we discussed in Chapter 2. As a result, many postprocessual archaeologists pursue humanistic approaches, seeking explanations that consider human thoughts, emotions, and symbolic meanings. A culture's understanding of the environment, for instance, affects the way that the culture interacts with it—meaning that cultures could respond differently to similar environmental pressures. In Figure 3-4 (page 59), postprocessual archaeologists might reverse the size of the arrows. For example, during the Dust Bowl days of the 1930s, the federal government instituted livestock reduction programs as a way to drive prices up and move the nation out of the Depression. But in the American Southwest, Navajo sheepherders actually *increased* production as their land degraded. Why? The Navajo view the natural and cultural worlds as not only mechanically but also spiritually linked. To them, if land is not productive, then supernatural forces will punish them by degrading the land. Navajos, therefore, responded to Dust Bowl conditions by raising more, not fewer, sheep. Sheep can be very destructive to land, however, and so the Navajo response only exacerbated the conditions brought on by climate change. (And they were horrified when the federal government arrived to kill their sheep.) This example suggests that we cannot understand different cultural approaches to environmental change without understanding different cultures' ideas about the relationships between humans and land.

As a result, postprocessualists tend to look at artifacts differently than do processual archaeologists. Processual archaeologists tend to look at the things, such as the pot shown in Figure 3-6, in terms of functions: Was the pot used for cooking? Food or water storage? Is it a serving vessel? But postprocessual archaeologists remind us that things also carry symbolic meanings: Did this pot "stand for" women, or hospitality, or the Raven clan? Thus, postprocessualists argue that we cannot understand what artifacts mean simply by looking for their functions; we also must consider their symbolic meanings. Consider, for example, what a Dodge minivan versus a Porsche convertible tells you about your neighbor.

It is understandable, then, that postprocessual archaeology has become more firmly entrenched in historical rather than prehistoric archaeology, because historical documents provide us with some access to the symbolic meanings of objects.

3. *Postprocessual archaeology rejects objectivity and explicitly scientific methods.* Given the importance of the ideational perspective, many postprocessual archaeologists argue that objectivity is impossible. They argue that we all see the world through a cultural lens; we can never see the world "as it really is." Postprocessual archaeologists argue that we should therefore drop any pretense of objectivity, because our understanding of the past is merely a construction in the present. Knowledge is not absolute, postprocessualists argue, but only relative to the culture that produced it. This view argues that there are "many pasts" and no way to judge which is better. Today, many postprocessual archaeologists have backed away from this extreme position, although it still forms a major criticism of research conducted under the processual paradigm.

Having posited that objectivity is impossible, postprocessualists argue that the kind of science practiced by processual archaeology is impossible, because it required a strict separation of data and theory. Even though many processual archaeologists admit that the notion of science practiced early on in processual archaeology was limiting, many postprocessualists still distrust science in any form.

4. *Postprocessual archaeology argues that all archaeology is political.* Although processual archaeologists wished to be "relevant" to modern society, they considered themselves politically neutral. This was a derivative of their view of scientific objectivity: They believed they saw the world as it actually was, uncolored by any political or personal agenda.

© Stuart Rome, Drexel University

Figure 3-6 A Maya polychrome vessel (Tikal, Guatemala, AD 350–400); processual archaeology focuses on its function, postprocessual archaeology on its meaning.

But postprocessual archaeology argues that all research is inescapably political. The Moundbuilder researcher Ephraim Squier, for example, was a confirmed polygenist—that is, he believed that humankind included several "races," each having separate instances of creation and separate capacities for progress. In his opinion, demonstrating that someone other than the Indians built the mounds showed that the Indians did not originate in the same act of creation as did those of European ancestry. This belief probably clouded his interpretation of the evidence. Likewise, postprocessualism argues that a cultural evolutionary view of the past is based on Western notions of progress and hence is potentially (and some would say fundamentally) racist.

Postprocessual archaeologists place the political implications of their research front and center. For many, this means that the study of the *presentation* of the past, in museums, scientific publications, and popular media, is as critical as the study of the past itself, if not more so.

Is Postmodernism All That New?

Despite their claims of "newness," the basic concerns of processual and postprocessual archaeology have deep historical roots. In Chapter 2, we presented the process of understanding the mounds as an example of archaeology-as-science. Although it might have seemed a curious choice, we selected this example to make a simple point:

Though lacking in all the jargon, the process of figuring out who the Moundbuilders were employed all the fundamentals of scientific inquiry. Although we described the "new archaeology" as concerned with conducting archaeology as a science, the truth is that the canons of science were with us long before the new archaeology came along.

We make a similar point here: Some of the key ideas and concerns of postprocessual archaeology have been kicking around for a long time. To demonstrate that point, we turn to one (particularly colorful) nineteenth-century archaeologist—Adolph Bandelier (1840–1914).

Adolph Bandelier: Scientific Humanist or Humanistic Scientist?

Born in Switzerland, Adolph Francis Bandelier came to America at the age of 8 and grew up in Highland, Illinois. He worked in the family banking and mining businesses, but it was American Indians that fascinated him. In 1880, when he was 40 years old, the newly founded Archaeological Institute of America hired him to explore Ancestral Pueblo ruins in the Southwest (see "Looking Closer: Anasazi or Ancestral Pueblo?"). An intrepid explorer, he traveled thousands of miles, often unarmed and ill-equipped, on foot and horseback, working under the most adverse conditions. At one point, Bandelier was erroneously reported dead at the

hands of Geronimo and his Apache warriors in southern Arizona.

But when he arrived at Pecos Pueblo (where Alfred Kidder would later excavate) in 1880, he wrote, "I am dirty, ragged, and sunburnt, but of good cheer. My life's work has at last begun." Most archaeologists today understand just how he felt.

The Scientific Bandelier

Bandelier knew the basics of Pecos history from documentary research. Founded in the distant past, Pecos Pueblo had grown to 2000 inhabitants by the time the Spanish explorer Coronado passed through in 1540. It was a flourishing trade center, straddling the border between the farming Pueblo world to the west and the buffalo hunters of the high plains. Out of Pueblo country came turquoise, pottery, maize, cotton blankets, and marine shells (imported from the Pacific Coast). From the plains to the east came hunters, such as the Comanche, bringing bison meat, fat, and tanned hides; flint cores for tool making; and wood for bows. A Franciscan mission was established, but the native population began dying out, and by 1838, the site was deserted.

From this sketchy background, Bandelier concluded that the lengthy archaeological record at Pecos could provide an important baseline to long-term cultural development in the American Southwest. He mapped

Looking Closer
Anasazi or Ancestral Pueblo?

For more than 60 years, archaeologists have used the word "Anasazi" to denote the last prehistoric (ca. AD 200–1600) culture centered on the Four Corners area of northwestern New Mexico, northern Arizona, southwestern Colorado, and southern Utah. Generally, archaeologists consider the Anasazi to be ancestors of modern Pueblo groups in New Mexico and the Hopi people of northwestern Arizona.

But over the past several years, some Pueblo people have expressed concern over use of this term. "Anasazi" comes from a Navajo word meaning "ancient enemy." Why, Puebloan peoples ask, should their ancestors be known by a non-Puebloan term, especially one that means "enemy"? (Recall that this is very similar to the problem that the Lakota/Dakota people face, discussed on page 44.) Although archaeologists have offered a number of substitutes, many today prefer the term "ancestral Pueblo" to "Anasazi."

the ruins, measured wall thickness and room dimensions, collected samples of artifacts and building materials, and photographed the site.

Bandelier also conducted ethnography, working first at Santo Domingo Pueblo, on the banks of the Rio Grande, but later switching to Cochiti Pueblo. Here he recorded details about Pueblo customs and beliefs, religious ceremonies, and daily life. Though he had no formal training in such things, he even recorded the Keresan language as well as myths, legends, and origin tales.

Bandelier spent the next decade of his life exploring and describing nearly 400 major archaeological ruins throughout the American Southwest and northern Mexico. His *Final Report* describing this fieldwork is an 800-page monument to his focus on detail and accuracy; it is still a source of baseline information about the archaeology of the American Southwest. So great were his contributions that, two years after his death in 1914, President Woodrow Wilson designated the

archaeological site of Tyuonyi (near Santa Fe) and the surrounding region "Bandelier National Monument," one of the nation's first national monuments, shown in Figure 3-7.

The Postmodern Bandelier

Bandelier was a scientist, but he was also deeply concerned about popular perceptions of the American Indian. He was annoyed with the success of James Fenimore Cooper (the author who had piqued Nels Nelson's interest), whose five-volume *Leatherstocking Tales* (1823–1841) celebrated both the American wilderness and the basic frontier life that played out there.

Many romantic authors of the nineteenth century, such as Cooper, rejected the Enlightenment's optimism and believed that science, art, and European social institutions corrupted humankind from its natural, or primitive state—which was seen as morally superior to the civilized state. He idealized the American Indian as a heroic yet sadly vanishing species, creating an image

© David H. Thomas

Figure 3-7 The circular ruin of Tyuonyi (New Mexico).

of Indians as the "noble savage," full of innate simplicity and virtue.

In truth, though, most of what Cooper knew about Indians was distorted or false. In *The Last of the Mohicans* (1826), for instance, Cooper appropriated the name "Uncas" for his title character. Although Uncas was a historical figure—a seventeenth-century chief of the Mohegan (Mohican) people—the fictionalized Uncas was transplanted and sanitized into a "good Indian," a noble and loyal friend of the colonist. And Cooper convinced generations of Americans that, with the death of the fictional Uncas, the Mohican people became extinct. In truth, the Mohegan people survive today, many still residing in Uncasville (in southeastern Connecticut).

Bandelier detested inaccuracy and romantic sentimentality. He ridiculed Cooper's superficial knowledge of American Indians and stewed about the impact the "cigar-store red man" was having on the American public. In the late 1880s, as Bandelier was preparing the manuscript describing his scientific explorations, he decided to write his own novel.

Originally published in German (as *Die Koshare*) in 1890, *The Delight Makers* was based on Bandelier's extensive knowledge of ethnography and history—what he called "the sober facts"—to create a rich description of Pueblo life projected back into the past. The book is a tale about the pre-contact (that is, before the arrival of Europeans) people living at Tyuonyi and, in the title role as "delight makers," Bandelier featured the **Koshare** (ko-*shar*-ee), individuals who are members of a powerful secret society whose functions include performing as a kind of clown.

The story begins on a sparkling June day at Tyuonyi in AD 1450. Okoya, an adolescent boy, is confronted by his younger brother, Shyuote, who complains about the older boy's cynical attitude toward the Koshares. This worries Okoya. He had confided these inner thoughts to his mother, and yet his father is a Koshare, and Shyuote is pledged to become one.

Okoya's doubt about Koshares escalates into accusations of witchcraft. The dissidents perform their own rituals, but little happens except that much-needed rain does not fall. Navajo intruders side with the anti-Koshare forces and threaten to murder Okoya's grandfather, a war chief. As the Koshare search for evidence of heresy, antagonism within Tyuonyi intensifies. When

Koshare An English rendering of a Keresan (one of the Pueblo Indian languages) word that refers to ritual clowns in Rio Grande Pueblo society.

the grandfather's scalped corpse is found, a revenge-driven blood feud breaks out with the neighboring Pueblo group (although it was Navajo interlopers who did the deed). As the Pueblo people fight it out, the Navajos destroy Tyuonyi. But thanks to heroism, many escape. The story ends when the Pueblo fugitives begin building a new village (see "Looking Closer: Bringing Tyuonyi's Past Alive" by Adolph Bandelier).

Why did Bandelier write this particular tale?

In the first place, he thought it a more accurate portrayal of Indians than any that existed at the time. Reacting against the sentimentality of Cooper, Bandelier drew on his years of experience in the Southwest to describe Puebloan society, ceremonies, and customs. But Bandelier also stepped out of his role as scientific observer. He adopted an *empathetic* approach to prehistory and attempted to describe ancient daily Pueblo life from the inside, from the perspective of the participants.

Bandelier interrupted his basic storyline with asides about nature, the human condition, or general characteristics of "The Indian" ("The reader will forgive a digression…," "This tradition was told me by…," and so forth). By jumping in—as first-person author—Bandelier shifted the narrative and made his own reflexive comments.

Ethnographer, literary critic, and professor of English Barbara Babcock (University of Arizona) highlights Bandelier's postmodern penchant for "deconstruct[ing] stereotypes of the savage, past and present." In *The Delight Makers*, Bandelier employed both the authoritative tone of the ethnographer and the insider view of the Cochiti Indian. In postmodern fashion, Bandelier struck up a dialogue between himself (Anglo-American ethnologist) and his Cochiti friends (the "informants"). To deconstruct Cooper's noble savage, Bandelier felt obliged to step out of his role as objective scientist and bring something of the complexity of real American Indian lifeways to the greater American public. He could not do this through pages of archaeological detail, but he could do it through a novel. Bandelier used his own intimate knowledge of the past and present to educate the public about the "true" nature of Native Americans to give a voice to a people who at that time were rarely heard in American society.

Bandelier: A Nineteenth-Century Scientist "in Full Ritual Undress"

But there is even more to *The Delight Makers*. Babcock suggests that Bandelier was motivated by a reflexive

In His Own Words
Bringing Tyuonyi's Past Alive

by Adolph Bandelier

Here are some excerpts from the first and last chapters of The Delight Makers:

The Keres of Cochiti declare that the tribe to which they belong, occupied, many centuries before the first coming of the Europeans to New Mexico, the cluster of cave-dwellings, visible at this day although abandoned and in ruins, in that romantic and picturesquely secluded gorge called in the Keres dialect Tyuonyi, and in Spanish "El Rito de los Frijoles" ["bean creek"].

These ruins, inside as well as outside the northern walls of the cañon of the Rito, bear testimony to the tradition still current among the Keres Indians of New Mexico that the Rito, or Tyuonyi, was once inhabited by people of their kind, nay, even of their own stock. But the time when those people wooed and wed, lived and died, in that secluded vale is past long, long ago. Centuries previous to the advent of the Spaniards, the Rito was already deserted. Nothing remains but the ruins of former abodes and the memory of their inhabitants among their descendants. These ancient people of the Rito are the actors in the story which is now to be told; the stage in the main is the Rito itself....

"Umo,—'grandfather!'"

"To ima satyumishe,—'come hither, my brother,'" another voice replied in the same dialect, adding, "see what a big fish I have caught."

It sounded as though this second voice had issued from the very waters of the streamlet.

Pine boughs rustled, branches bent, and leaves shook. A step scarcely audible was followed by a noiseless leap. On a boulder around which flowed streams of limpid water there alighted a young Indian....

After twenty-one long and it may be tedious chapters, no apology is required for a short one in conclusion. I cannot take leave of the reader, however, without having made in his company a brief excursion through a portion of New Mexico in the direction of the Rito de los Frijoles.

It is a bare, bleak spot, in the centre of the opening we see the fairly preserved ruins of an abandoned Indian pueblo....

Over and through the ruins are scattered the usual vestiges of primitive arts and industry,—pottery fragments and arrow-heads. Seldom do we meet with a stone hammer, whereas grinding slabs and grinders are frequent, though for the most part scattered and broken. We are on sacred ground in this crumbling enclosure. But who knows that we are not on magic ground also?

We might make an experiment. Let us suffer ourselves to be blindfolded, and then turn around three times from left to right. One, two, three! The bandage is removed. What can we see?

Nothing strange at first [but] a change has taken place in our immediate vicinity, a transformation on the spot where stood the ruin. The crumbling walls and heaps of rubbish are gone, and in their place newly built foundations are emerging from the ground; heaps of stone, partly broken, are scattered about; and where a moment ago we were the only living souls, now Indians move to and fro, busily engaging.

Some of them are breaking the stones into convenient size. The women are laying these in mortar made of the soil from the mesa, common adobe. We are witnessing the beginning of the construction of a small village. Farther down, on the edge of the timber, smoke arises; there the builders of this new pueblo dwell in huts while their house of stone is growing to completion. It is the month of May, and only the nights are cool.

These builders we easily recognize. They are the fugitives from the Rito.

And now we have, though in a trance, seen the further fate of those whose sad career has filled the pages of this story. We may be blindfolded again, turned about right to left; and when the bandage is taken from our eyes the landscape is as before, silent and grand. The ruins are in position again; an eagle soars on high.

Figure 3-8 Three Koshares at San Juan Pueblo (New Mexico).

concern with himself as observer, and, according to Babcock, *The Delight Makers* was his attempt to come to terms with something he saw at Cochiti that deeply disturbed him.

The Koshares entranced Bandelier. He described them as "hideous, often obscene clowns or jesters [who] endeavor to provoke merriment by performances which deserve decided reprobation." Bandelier and his contemporaries were clearly confused and conflicted over Koshares (shown in Figure 3-8). Year after year, Bandelier returned to Cochiti to observe what he once called those "disgusting creatures … in full ritual undress." In his diary he wrote:

> During [the dancing] the skirmishers kept acting around them. One of [the Koshares], who was particularly fond of rolling in the dust, was at last dragged about and through the lines [of dancers] by his companions till he was completely naked. There an exhibition of obscenity hard to describe took place. [Numerous sexual acts were] performed to greatest perfection…to the greatest delight of the spectators (certainly over a hundred), men, women, girls and boys.… I was terribly ashamed, but nobody seemed to take any concern about it.… The naked [Koshare] performed masturbation in or very near the center of the plaza, alternately with a black rug and with his hand. Everybody laughed. I went home.

Bandelier was both repulsed and intrigued by the lewd conduct of the Koshares. Even today, much of the public misunderstands the Koshare. But anthropologists understand them as an example of ritual clowns, who mediate between the spiritual and material worlds. Like cannibal dancers at a Kwakwak'awakw potlatch, they invert accepted ways of living and demonstrate how to live by showing how ludicrous an opposite way of living would be. But for Bandelier, these scandalous clowns destroyed the boundary between sacred and secular, between dignified and obscene, terror and delight.

Babcock suggests that Bandelier wrote *The Delight Makers* over a seven-year period in which he tried to come to terms with the Koshares. Bandelier remained precise and literal in his scientific writings. But in his novel, Bandelier could let his imagination run free, allowing him to confront another culture in a way denied him by sterile scientific reporting; this is why he can let Okoya doubt the Koshares. It was another approach to understanding, and it is perfectly valid because science does not care where ideas come from, only how they are evaluated.

ARCHAEOLOGY TODAY

At this point, you may be asking yourself if there is anything new about archaeology. If Cyrus Thomas was doing science long before Binford was born, and if Bandelier was writing postmodern novels more than a century ago, did archaeologists fool themselves into thinking that they had hit on something novel in processual and postprocessual archaeology?

Yes and no. Elements of scientific and postmodern thought can be found throughout the history of archaeology. But several things changed along the way. For one, we've learned a great deal about basic world prehistory. One hundred years ago, for example, we did not know when people first occupied the New World, when the first agricultural economies began, or how old humanity was. With a better understanding of the world's basic prehistory, archaeologists have moved on to investigate other topics, and this has led some archaeologists to new research paradigms.

Other changes have taken place as well. With more fieldwork came greater understanding of how archaeological sites form and a greater appreciation for how difficult it is to infer human behavior from archaeological remains. The initial optimism of processual archaeology—that everything about the past was knowable if we were just clever enough to figure out how to get at it—has given way to the more sobering realization that some aspects of the past may lie forever beyond our grasp.

The relationship between archaeologists and indigenous peoples has also changed as indigenous people gained a greater voice and archaeologists realized that they could not ignore other perspectives on the past. Perhaps as a result of these indigenous voices, archaeologists saw that their work, whether they liked it or not, existed within a political context that they simply could not ignore.

Processual-Plus

Considerable tension still exists between those who call themselves processualists and those who prefer the postprocessual label. But much intellectual change occurs through the process of "thesis–antithesis–synthesis." An analogy to a clock is useful here. One paradigm pulls the clock's pendulum far to one side. In response, another paradigm pulls it to the opposite side. And in the end, it comes to rest in the middle. In recent years, many (perhaps the majority) of Americanist archaeologists have listened to debates between hard-core processual and postprocessual archaeologists and found a middle road that Michelle Hegmon (Arizona State University) calls "processual-plus" (see "Profile of an Archaeologist: Michelle Hegmon").

Hegmon points out that archaeologists practice their craft in many different ways today. Many adhere to some form of scientific inquiry as a way to evaluate ideas about what happened in the past; few subscribe to the extreme postmodern idea that we cannot know anything true about the past. And many still feel that material factors such as technology, subsistence, and environment play critical roles in how human societies have changed. But few seek universals; instead, many seek generalities, patterns that point to how material factors may constrain or channel, but not determine, cultural change.

These same archaeologists also recognize the importance of other factors. All archaeologists know that artifacts carried symbolic meanings for people in the past and that humans respond to their situations in terms of cultural understandings of the world. Likewise, few see the details of history (and prehistory) as minor matters whose effects can easily be subtracted to discover the evolutionary processes behind them. History is a product of evolutionary processes, but it is also the result of myriad contingencies—environmental disasters, particular political decisions, cultural views, and so on—that are as integral to a culture's particular history as any evolutionary process. Archaeologists today are as interested in history as they are in cultural evolutionary theory.

And most archaeologists recognize that all of history is, indeed, the result of the actions of individuals and, in one way or another, an understanding of individual actions and motivations for those actions is critical to understanding the larger cultural evolutionary processes at work. Especially important has been a trend to look at gender, at the roles that men and women played in ancient societies (we'll return to this topic in Chapter 13).

Most archaeologists today recognize the links between politics and their research. Although few approach their research for purely political purposes, most archaeologists at least understand the political context of their research. The Archaeological Ethics boxes will discuss these issues, and we will return to this sensitive subject in Chapter 18.

THE STRUCTURE OF ARCHAEOLOGICAL INQUIRY

A century of archaeological practice has taught us a great deal about how archaeologists need to go about doing archaeology. So, what did we learn from this?

Figure 3-9 on page 74 presents a model of the process of archaeological inquiry. This synthesis is similar to the model of the scientific cycle (described in Chapter 2), but is presented in a format specific to archaeology.

Notice that the entire process of archaeological inquiry takes place within a box labeled "Social, Cultural, Political Context." This arrangement recognizes that no scientist can step outside his or her culture—should we try that, we would cease being human, and

Profile of an Archaeologist
Michelle Hegmon

A professor of anthropology at Arizona State University

Michelle Hegmon (left)

I work in the Mimbres region of New Mexico, a place that is famous for its pottery, but it was analysis rather than artifacts that originally drew me to archaeology. I don't remember my first piece of pottery, but I definitely remember the Introduction to Archaeology class in which Steve Plog described how ceramic designs could tell us about the social lives of people 1000 years ago. That's what caught my interest: solving puzzles and learning from artifacts.

I began graduate school in 1981 at the University of Michigan—renowned for its processual approach—and in 1982, postprocessualism appeared. Those were heady days for me and my fellow students (including Kelly). Born too late to be a real hippie, I tried to rebel intellectually. No ecology or evolution for me, I was going to be a real postprocessualist. I cringe when I think back on my young theoretical ego, passionately identifying with labels, and now appreciate the patience of my teachers (especially Henry Wright and Richard Ford). By the time I finished my dissertation, which returned me to my early interest in pottery design, I had developed much of what I now call processual-plus: a melding of postprocessual's interest in symbols and meaning with processual concerns regarding systematic generalizations.

At the conclusion of my PhD defense, my committee stood to congratulate me. I stood, and (I am only 5'3")

Two tenets are key to my brand of archaeology, processual-plus. The first is open-mindedness, a willingness to set theoretical egos aside, and the second is recognition of the power of theory, words and labels to shape our understanding of the past.

our ability to analyze and understand the world would disappear. Still, we cannot ignore how our cultural context affects our understanding of the past. By constantly checking ourselves, over time, we should be able to distinguish between what is cultural bias and what is actually true.

The dotted line surrounding the Paradigm box symbolizes this interplay between one's research agenda and cultural context. As emphasized above, both paradigm and culture provide (often vague) understandings

of the world, and each points the researcher toward a question's answers. These biases are not necessarily wrong. For example, Richard Wilk's analysis suggests that it was the Vietnam War that encouraged 1960s researchers to consider war the primary cause of the Maya civilization's collapse. Although Wilk's hypothesis was true, this does *not* mean that war was *not* the cause.

Paradigms provide specific guidelines for high-level theory—general statements such as "Agriculture occurs

literally looked up at the tall men surrounding me. Until then, I had paid little attention to gender. My mother, a physicist and feminist, had fought those battles for me; her generation made it possible for women in mine to move ahead with relative ease. For me, Southwest archaeology was a supportive environment. At a seminar on engendering Southwest archaeology, I joined a group of colleagues who pushed the intellectual envelope. As my mother's daughter, I assumed prehistoric women's domestic labor (such as corn-grinding) was drudgery, but others assumed it was highly respected. This disagreement made clear the importance of labels and of prior experience. Gender research—a key component of processual-plus—also taught me that feminism still has much to do.

I've done most of my professional research as part of the Eastern Mimbres Archaeological Project (EMAP), which Peggy Nelson and I began in 1993. The rich floodplain of the Mimbres River of southwest New Mexico is known for its Classic Mimbres villages, many of which were depopulated at a time of low rainfall around AD 1130. Unfortunately, looters have destroyed many of those sites, searching for pottery. In contrast, the eastern Mimbres region is drier but more remote. Landowners (including Ted Turner) have protected sites and supported our research. One of EMAP's most important conclusions is that the eastern area sustained a more continuous occupation than the Mimbres Valley. We documented a post-AD 1130 regional reorganization, when people changed their lifestyle and their pottery, but remained in their homeland.

EMAP is, above all, a collaboration, and becoming part of it is one of the best things I have ever done. Peggy Nelson's specialties include lithic technology and ecology, while mine are ceramic style and social theory, but rather than dividing these realms we have brought our perspectives together to delve into issues such as socio-ecology and the technology of style. Together we also have more fun. For many years we have run a large field project and school, in which we teach our students the importance of collaboration and the many skills—ranging from tire-changing to soils analysis—that are part of archaeological research. We also prepare a generation of young scholars to move ahead in a world of both women and men. Finally, our collaboration has taught me the importance of relinquishing some degree of control, trusting that Peggy or one of our students knows what they are doing.

This lesson is key to a new direction in our research. Together, with our colleagues at Arizona State University, we are embarking on several interdisciplinary projects, that, by their very nature, draw on data and theory more vast than any of us can master single-handedly. They must be collaborations in which we set our theoretical egos aside.

when a human population grows to the point where it exceeds the natural carrying capacity of the local environment." But paradigms can also generate more specific claims about a region's prehistory, such as "In the Mimbres Valley of southern New Mexico, there was a change in social organization as evidenced by a shift from pithouse to pueblo villages about AD 1000." Both statements are linked to the overarching paradigm by directing researchers to measure some variables (such as demography and changing social organization) and to set other variables (such as religion) aside. Propositions like this statement occur to archaeologists operating within a materialist paradigm.

In contrast, someone operating within a postprocessual paradigm might say, "Agriculture originated from the need to create goods to give away at competitive feasts" or "In the Mimbres Valley a new symbolic order appeared about AD 1000, as evidenced by an art style involving painted naturalistic designs on bowls that are ritually killed and placed in human burials."

Testing Ideas

In either case, the next step is to construct hypotheses designed to test the various propositions—to see if our ideas might actually be true. For each hypothesis, we would frame one (or more) if … then statements that build upon the research proposition and predict some presently unknown aspect of the archaeological record. This is how we test ideas. Figure 3-9 shows this as "Hypotheses" resulting from high-level theory.

Take, for example, the question relating population growth and agriculture. Suppose we already know that in our research area, an agricultural economy began by 2000 BC. We might hypothesize thus: If our proposition is true—that is, if population is the driving force behind agriculture—then signs of population growth and subsequent pressure on the food base should appear prior to 2000 BC.

This is where the Hypotheses lead to Middle-level theory (as shown in Figure 3-9). Testing the proposition requires some way of inferring population numbers from archaeological data. We can't measure population directly, of course—the people in question died a long time ago—so we need a bridging argument to infer changes in population over time from archaeo-

logical variables. To do so, we might have to survey existing ethnographic data or conduct our own ethnoarchaeological research to find correlates between population size and things that an archaeologist could record, for example, house or village size.

We also need a way to measure "stress" on the food base. Perhaps we can find ethnographic evidence demonstrating that people use certain types of foods only under conditions of stress (such as those foods that are more difficult to harvest or that are less nutritious). On the other hand, we may need to conduct experiments, such as gathering foods with aboriginal technologies and measuring the efficiency with which they are collected. Such research might tell us that very small seeds are less efficiently harvested than large seeds and therefore that their use might signal subsistence stress.

Once we have adequate middle-level theory, we can define what constitutes relevant archaeological data (shown at lower right in Figure 3-9). If we believe that house size is the best variable, we will need to measure a sufficient number of houses from sites that date to various time periods before and after 2000 BC—to see if there is evidence of population growth *before* the appearance of an agricultural economy. If we decide that decreasing seed size is a good way to show that an ancient population was approaching an environment's carrying capacity, then we must recover and measure seeds from the appropriate archaeological sites (in Chapter 11, we discuss how archaeologists do this).

This background work done, we can state the general hypothesis in a more specific way: If agriculture appears because population exceeds carrying capacity, then (1) house size should increase before 2000 BC, and (2) seeds found in trash associated with those houses should become smaller through time.

This brings us to the fun part, the archaeological fieldwork (shown in the center of Figure 3-9) to collect the data necessary to test our hypothe-

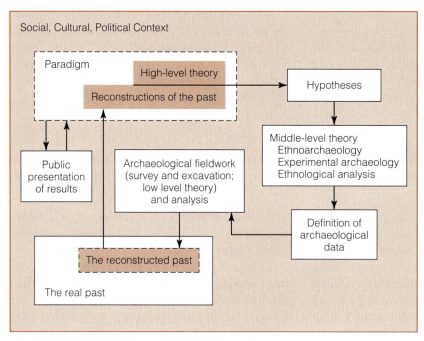

Figure 3-9 A model of archaeological inquiry.

sis. We must design such fieldwork to generate adequate samples of house floors and seeds from the right time periods. Low-level theory is required to identify house floors (through the presence of postholes, packed clay floors, hearths, and so forth) and to identify seeds (we'll discuss fieldwork much more in the following chapters).

Reconstructing the Past

Testing such hypotheses requires that we reconstruct the past, that we say something about what actually happened back in time (as shown at the lower left in Figure 3-9). Perhaps we will find that houses became larger over time (or maybe not); perhaps we learn that seeds became smaller through time (or maybe not). Notice that in Figure 3-9, the dotted line enclosing "The reconstructed past" is itself inside a larger box labeled the "The real past." We did this to emphasize, first, that we cannot hope to reconstruct the complete past. Although we are always improving our ability to recover and extract better information from material remains, a complete picture of the past will always elude us. There was, to be sure, a real past made up of real people who lived real lives and who died real deaths; but our reconstructed past will never be an exact duplicate.

As the postprocessual critique makes clear, our experiences in the present heavily colors our vision of the past. The particular hypothesis used here as an example looks to demography (rather than religion or social change) to explain a change in subsistence. The upshot of this hypothesis is that, to reconstruct the past, we will focus on some issues and downplay others. Had we hypothesized a religious cause to agricultural origins, we would have sought very different data during our fieldwork. For example, we might have looked for evidence of how plants were used in different rituals, and that might have led us to excavate religious structures rather than houses.

Now we return to our original propositions to see whether we confirmed or falsified them. Did the fieldwork and ensuing analyses find evidence of population growth and resource stress prior to 2000 BC, or did it not?

At this point, the archaeologist presents the results to a public audience. This presentation begins with scientific monographs or papers that other archaeologists will scrutinize. But modern archaeologists also know

that results need to be conveyed to a broader public through books or magazine articles written in lay terms, public lectures, television presentations, museum exhibitions, or even novels (like *The Delight Makers*). In this way, the public can learn from and comment upon the research. From all of this professional and public feedback, the archaeologist may revisit the research propositions and commence the process all over again. And, through this recursive process (shown at left in Figure 3-9), archaeologists may find such a lack of fit between their ideas and the empirical archaeological record that they may discard their paradigm for another.

In truth, few archaeologists can do every step in the process; instead, almost everyone specializes. Some focus their careers on middle-level theory, doing experimental or ethnoarchaeological research. Others concentrate on the public side, presenting their research and that of others to a broader audience. Others work mostly with theory, and still others spend most of their time doing fieldwork. It's even more important then, that archaeologists understand what role they are playing in the whole process.

CONCLUSION: PROCESSUALIST OR POSTPROCESSUALIST?

Although there will always be competing paradigms in archaeology, we believe that Americanist archaeology works best when it sees paradigms as tools, rather than dogmatic religions. If you look at the field that way, then archaeologists should be able to draw what is useful from each paradigm, rather than be forced to ally themselves unwaveringly with one way of viewing the world.

And indeed, one sees relatively few hard-core processualists or diehard postprocessualists these days. Most are processual-plus archaeologists, refusing to reduce the past to mechanical processes, but still believing in the power of scientifically tested ideas. Most contemporary archaeologists agree that multiple ways exist to learn about the past and that some aspects of the past will remain unknown. However, most would also agree that we can accept a certain amount of ambiguity and yet still learn something real about, and from, the past. And in the following chapters, we show you how archaeologists go about doing exactly that.

Summary

- Low-level theory involves the observations that emerge from archaeological fieldwork; this is how archaeologists get their "data," their "facts."

- Middle-level (middle-range) theory links archaeological data with human behavior or natural processes; it is produced through experimental archaeology, taphonomy (the study of natural processes on archaeological sites), and ethnoarchaeology (the study of living peoples to see links between behavior and material remains).

- High-level ("general") theory provides answers to larger "why" questions.

- Paradigms are frameworks for thinking that interrelate concepts and provide research strategies. They apply to intellectual inquiry in general and are not specific to archaeology.

- Two major paradigms in modern Americanist archaeology are processual and postprocessual archaeology; they are derived, respectively, from cultural materialism and postmodernism. The former takes a scientific approach and focuses on the material factors of life; the latter emphasizes humanistic perspectives and symbolic meaning.

- Processual and postprocessual approaches to prehistory have existed within archaeology for a long time. Individual archaeologists emphasize one more than the other, and some move back and forth between the two. They have different purposes and should not be confused.

- A model of archaeological inquiry shows how the different levels of theory, paradigms, and the public presentation of results help to ensure that our understanding of the past continually improves over time and overcomes the biases presented by the archaeologist's particular cultural context.

Additional Reading

Binford, Lewis R. 1983. *In Pursuit of the Past*. London: Thames and Hudson.

Harris, Marvin. 1979. *Cultural Materialism: The Struggle for a Science of Culture*. New York: Random House.

Hodder, Ian. 1999. *The Archaeological Process: An Introduction*. Oxford: Blackwell.

Hodder, Ian (Ed.). 2001. *Archaeological Theory Today*. Oxford: Blackwell.

Johnson, Matthew. 1999. *Archaeological Theory: An Introduction*. Oxford: Blackwell.

Online Resources

COMPANION WEB SITE
Visit **http://anthropology.wadsworth.com** and click on the Student Companion Web Site for Thomas/Kelly *Archaeology*, 4th edition, to access a wide range of material to help you succeed in your introductory archaeology course. These include flashcards, Internet exercises, Web links, and practice quizzes.

RESEARCH ONLINE WITH INFOTRAC COLLEGE EDITION
From the Student Companion Web Site, you can access the InfoTrac College Edition database, which offers thousands of full-length articles for your research.

4

Doing Fieldwork: Surveying for Archaeological Sites

OUTLINE

Chaco Canyon, in northwestern New Mexico, contains several massive pueblos that were occupied in the eleventh century, and many smaller sites that were revealed by surface survey.

Preview

NOW THE FUN BEGINS. In the next few chapters, you will get a glimpse of what it's like to actually do archaeology. For many in the discipline—ourselves included—fieldwork is why we became archaeologists in the first place. That said, we must begin this introduction to archaeological field techniques with two important warnings:

- There is no one "right" way to look for and excavate sites (but there are plenty of wrong ones).
- Nobody ever learned how to do proper archaeological fieldwork from a book (including this one).

Despite recent advances, archaeological fieldwork remains as much art as science. All we can do here is examine some common techniques, list some archaeological standards and principles, and give you a sense of what it feels like to participate in an archaeological exploration.

INTRODUCTION

Every archaeologist addressing a general audience is eventually asked the same question: "How do you know where to dig?"

There are many answers. We've known about some **archaeological sites,** such as Egypt's pyramids, for centuries—they were never lost. The locations of other sites have been handed down through the generations, preserved in oral and written traditions. For example, archaeologists identified the site of Tula in northern Mexico as the prehistoric Toltec capital by tracing and testing Aztec traditions. Sites are sometimes deliberately discovered in large-scale systematic surveys, during which large regions are scanned for the remains of previous habitation. And some of the most important archaeological sites in the world were found by accident, hard work, and luck.

GOOD OLD GUMSHOE SURVEY

In Chapter 3, we mentioned Gatecliff Shelter in Nevada, where both of us excavated in the 1970s. But before we could dig at Gatecliff, of course, the site had to be found. How did that happen?

Gatecliff was found by a fortunate combination of happenstance, hard work, and luck, a process that James O'Connell (University of Utah) calls old-fashioned "gumshoe survey."

In the summer of 1970, Thomas was in central Nevada's Reese River Valley conducting systematic archaeological survey (a technique we discuss later in this chapter). Basically, this fieldwork entails mapping and collecting archaeological stuff found on the

archaeological site Any place where material evidence exists about the human past. Usually, "site" refers to a concentration of such evidence.

ground. The survey went well, but it could not answer all the questions. Thomas needed to know, for example, something about prehistoric subsistence and the chronology of different artifact types. Such information can only come from buried sites, where food remains (bones and seeds) might be preserved and where artifacts can be dated. Rockshelters and caves often contain the necessary buried deposits but, despite the Reese River crew's best efforts, they could not locate one.

At the end of the first field session in Reese River, Thomas assembled the crew for steak dinners in the town of Austin, about an hour's dusty ride away. Austin is a pocket-sized Nevada mining town with fewer than 250 citizens, a picturesque little desert dive. Writer Oscar Lewis described it as "the town that died laughing," and William Least Heat Moon called it "a living ghost town: 40 percent living, 50 percent ghost and 10 percent not yet decided."

When two dozen grubby archaeologists come to such a town for steaks and beverages, word gets around quickly. Thomas soon found himself talking with the waitress' husband, Gale Peer, a mining geologist who had prospected central Nevada for 40 years. There are few places Gale Peer had not been, so Thomas asked if he knew of any caves or rockshelters.

Indeed, Mr. Peer did know of a cave—in Monitor Valley, about 20 kilometers east of Austin. He had not been there in years, but the details were fresh in his mind.

"You take the main dirt road south in Monitor Valley, then turn west, up one of the side canyons. I don't remember which one. As you drive along, oh, let's see, maybe 10 or 15 miles, there's a large black chert cliff. At the bottom of the cliff is a cave. Some time, a long time ago, the Indians painted the inside of the cave. There are pictures of people and animals, plus a lot of writing I don't understand. Top of the shelter's caved in. Maybe in an earthquake. There's not much of the cave left. Drive out there when you get a chance. I'd like to know what's in that cave." He sketched a map on his business card.

This is the essence of gumshoe survey—hanging out in coffee shops, bars, and gas stations, listening to those who know more about the landscape than you do.

Searching for Gatecliff

The next summer Thomas and his crew returned, hoping to find the cave that Mr. Peer had described. They knew that the rockshelter was several miles up a canyon, on the north side—but there were 15 such canyons.

Beginning at the southern end of Monitor Valley, the crew drove up and down each side canyon, working their way northward. They were hampered by spring snow and washed-out roads—typical fieldwork conditions in central Nevada.

Each of the canyons had potential. The crew would see something, stop the truck, and skitter up the hillside. But each time, the "something" turned out to be a shadow, an abandoned mine shaft, or just a jumble of boulders.

After a week, Thomas came to Mill Canyon, just the next one on the list, with no greater potential than the ten canyons they had already combed. The road was a little worse than most and, even in four-wheel drive, the truck lurched down a steep ridge into the rocky canyon. Finally, as the crew moved up the flat canyon bottom, a black cliff loomed ahead, riddled with small caves and rockshelters.

As had happened many times before, the shelters were empty, unless you count coyote scats and packrat nests. Finally, the crew spied a dim shadow where the black dolomite formation was swallowed up beneath the Mill Canyon bottomland.

The paintings were invisible until you stood right in the mouth of the shelter. But there they were, just as Mr. Peer had said: small human figures, painted in red and yellow. On the other wall were cryptic motifs in white and black. And, yes, the roof had caved in years before. One boulder dwarfed the pickup.

There was nothing "archaeological" on the surface, but a small test pit turned up telltale signs that people had once lived in the shelter: several pieces of broken bone, a few of them charred, and a dozen stone flakes (probably debris from resharpening stone knives or **projectile points**).

Across the campfire that night, the crew assayed the finds. The rock art was intriguing; only two similar sites were known in central Nevada. The stones and bones were suggestive, but the shelter seemed hardly the deep site they were seeking. Thomas named the site after the rock formation, Gatecliff, in which they found it (see "Looking Closer: How Do Archaeological Sites Get Their Names?").

On the strength of this meager evidence, they decided to dig some—a good decision, it turned out, because the deposits inside Gatecliff Shelter proved to

projectile points Arrowheads, dart points, or spear points.

Looking Closer
How Do Archaeological Sites Get Their Names?

It's an archaeologist's prerogative to name new sites. Many are named after a prominent topographic feature, for example, the canyon in which the site is located, or a nearby mountain, river, town—or a rock formation, in the case of Gatecliff Shelter.

Sites on private land are commonly named after the landowners; some become the namesake of the amateur archaeologists who find them. And sometimes the archaeologist can have fun with a site's name. Robert Bettinger (University of California, Davis) named one California cave site Gimme Shelter (after the Rolling Stones' tune).

Some names have stories attached to them. Danger Cave, on the edge of Utah's Great Salt Lake, for example, was originally called Hands and Knees Caves by locals, to describe how it was entered. But

during Elmer Smith's 1941 excavation a huge piece of the lip broke off and crashed into the excavation, narrowly missing several of the crew members and, according to legend, landing right where some had just finished lunch. This incident resulted in a permanent name change. During Jesse Jennings's excavations there in the 1950s, several students elected to change the name to Lamus Cave, after Blair Lamus, a superintendent of the potash plant in nearby Wendover, to recognize the help he had given to the project (which apparently included small amounts of dynamite to help speed the digging). Jennings apparently nixed the suggestion.

So sites acquire their names in many different ways. There is, in fact, only one cultural rule to follow: The archaeologist can *never* name a site after him- or herself.

be 12 meters deep, making it one of the deepest rockshelters in the Americas. And the strata were spectacularly layered, not jumbled up like most sites in the area. Flash floods had periodically inundated the shelter, the surging waters laying down thick layers of rock-hard silt. This flooding occurred at least a dozen times, separating the deposits into clean occupational "floors."

This meant that Gatecliff had what textbooks—including this one—describe as "layer-cake stratigraphy." Sandwiched between these sterile flash-flood deposits was a wonderful 7000-year record of human activity and environmental change in Monitor Valley. The University of California (Davis) began the research, followed by the American Museum of Natural History, which dispatched five major expeditions to Gatecliff Shelter. The National Geographic Society supported part of the fieldwork, shot an educational film, and wrote a book about the site. The *New York Times* and *The New Yorker* magazine published stories about Gatecliff. There was television and radio coverage. Even a United States congressman became involved in preserving the site.

Gatecliff Shelter was on the map—and all because a waitress' husband in Austin, Nevada remembered an interesting place from years before. In fact, many important sites have been found by ranchers, cowboys, sheepherders, farmers, geologists, and amateur archaeologists—anyone who spends a lot of time wandering about outdoors.

ARCHAEOLOGY IS MORE THAN JUST DIGGING SITES

Archaeologists feel lucky to find sites like Gatecliff Shelter, which was a marvelous place to dig. But as John Hyslop (1945–1993) worked his way up and down the Andes Mountains, he wasn't looking for a place to dig. Hyslop was surveying the ancient Inka road (Figure 4-1). Though they did not have wheeled vehicles, the extraordinary Inka civilization of the fourteenth and fifteenth centuries still created thousands of miles of roads connecting coastal and highland cities from Ecuador to northern Chile. Although excavation would

Figure 4-1 Inka road survey.

have been possible at many of the places he recorded, Hyslop knew that his Inka Road survey would, in itself, produce a huge quantity of valuable details about ancient road building and engineering, as well as about Inka economy. In fact, Hyslop wrote an important book, *The Inka Road System*, based strictly on his survey results—without ever digging at all.

This is an often forgotten point about archaeological reconnaissance. Sometimes archaeologists survey to find good places to dig (this is why Thomas was looking for Gatecliff Shelter). But other times, the archaeological survey itself is a way to generate archaeological data on a regional scale. In the following sections, we will examine a few ways developed by archaeologists to systematize the survey process. As you will see, archaeologists can learn plenty without ever lifting a shovel.

The Fallacy of the "Typical" Site

Survey is important because of the problem of representation. Suppose you spend 7 years digging a site like Gatecliff (which we did). You recover plenty of artifacts from the stratified and well-dated sediments. But what do all these ancient things mean in human terms?

The first thing to remember is that nobody lives in just one place—not now and certainly not millennia ago.

To understand the past, therefore, we need to examine the range of places in which ancient peoples lived their lives. This is why many archaeologists employ the **systematic regional survey** as a way of recording the full range of human settlements, rather than just seek out a "typical" site.

To see why this is so, take a look at the map of the **seasonal round** of the Western Shoshone people of the central Great Basin (Figure 4-2). Produced by ethnographer Julian Steward (1902–1972), this map charts the cultural landscape of the Shoshone, a people who survived by hunting antelope and bighorn sheep and by collecting various plant foods.

This ecological adaptation depended on a precise exploitation of Great Basin environments. The prehistoric Shoshone were nomadic hunter-gatherers and, because of their intimate relationship with the natural environment, they were able to work out a seasonal round that allowed them to travel from one habitat to another to harvest local wild foods as they became available.

Look closely at the map. The numbered triangles in the Toiyabe and Shoshone mountain ranges are winter villages, inhabited seasonally to hunt bighorn sheep and to exploit the piñon nuts that grow there. These nutritious nuts ripened in the late summer and early autumn and were stored for the winter, along with buffalo berries and currants available in the low foothills. Other kinds of sites (denoted by letters) occur at lower elevations and along the Reese River; the Shoshone lived there during the summer to gather ricegrass seeds and roots, catch rabbits, and hunt antelope. In upland areas they gathered berries, tubers, and hunted bighorn sheep. They did other things at other places on the landscape for ceremonial purposes or in pursuit of specific foods.

Steward based this reconstruction on what Shoshone people told him between 1925 and 1936. Because most of the mapped sites were abandoned sometime in the nineteenth century, Steward's native consultants were often recalling events of 50 years ago. Despite the fact that Steward's consultants most likely did not recall

systematic regional survey A set of strategies for arriving at accurate descriptions of the range of archaeological material across a landscape.

seasonal round Hunter-gatherers' pattern of movement between different places on the landscape timed to the seasonal availability of food and other resources.

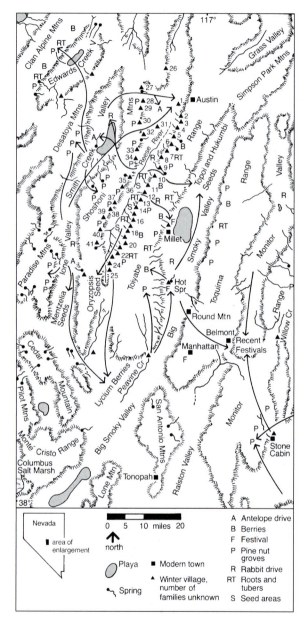

Figure 4-2 Julian Steward's reconstruction of the seasonal round of the Western Shoshone and Northern Paiute people (Nevada), projected for the mid-nineteenth-century period. *After Steward 1938, figure 8.*

ologists call a **settlement pattern**—the distribution of sites across a landscape—and a **settlement system,** which describes that movements and activities inferred from the sites that make up the settlement pattern (a seasonal round is one type of settlement system).

This map also illustrates the fallacy of the typical site. Suppose that an archaeologist had a chance to locate and excavate just one of Steward's Shoshone sites. Which one should he or she choose? Winter village sites are of interest because they represent the lengthiest occupation and probably contain remains of a great variety of activities. But winter village sites are almost always located on windswept ridges (where the wind blows the snow away), and all that is preserved are stone tools and ceramics.

Would it be better to seek out one of the small upland shelters where hunters briefly camped while pursuing bighorn sheep? The preservation in these shelters is often good, and the chances are excellent for finding remains of sandals, snares, pieces of bows, arrows, food bones, seeds, and fire-making apparatus. But these small shelters represent only a minor portion of the overall Shoshone pattern. Women were probably not included in such small hunting parties, and men conducted only a limited range of activities there. Perhaps one might choose to excavate a seed-gathering camp, an antelope drive, or a place where women gathered berries.

The difficulty is clear: No matter which site we select, we will miss a great deal, and the archaeologist will come away with a biased image. Let's suppose, for example, that you decided to excavate a piñon-gathering camp in the Toiyabe Range. You would probably conclude that the economy was based on harvesting piñon nuts, the camp contained between 12 to 24 people, and the men made lots of stone tools and repaired their weapons. You might also conclude that the women spent a great deal of time collecting piñon nuts and grinding them into meal, sewing hide clothing, and making basketry.

But now suppose that someone else decided to excavate the scene of a *fandango* (or festival site, denoted by "F" on Steward's map). The ensuing reconstruction would probably suggest a grouping of 200 to 300 people who subsisted on communal hunting of jackrabbit and antelope and who spent a great deal of time dancing and gambling.

In other words, you would have reconstructed a hardworking society composed of extended families, whereas your colleague would have seen a more exu-

everything, the map nonetheless demonstrates the native peoples' intricate and complex seasonal round. This seasonal round also provides examples of what archae-

settlement pattern The distribution of archaeological sites across a region.

settlement system The movements and activities reconstructed from a settlement pattern.

Looking Closer
The Surveyor's Toolkit

If you are thinking of doing archaeology, your first job will likely be survey. To prepare yourself, you'll need many of the following items in addition to the normal things you would carry on a long day hike (water, food bar, first aid kit, matches, rain gear/sunscreen, and so on):

- A GPS instrument (Garmin makes some good, inexpensive models.)
- A two-way radio (with at least a 2-mile capacity)
- A good but cheap watch (We've crushed several climbing over rocks.)
- A good compass (Brunton's pocket transit or Finland's Suunto)
- A K+E field notebook (College bookstores carry them.)

- Mechanical or regular pencils (Wrap them with duct tape; use the duct tape to protect blisters.)
- Ziploc bags (of different sizes): These can be purchased inexpensively on-line.
- A black Sharpie marker
- A trowel (for quick test pits)
- A tape measure (metric only!)
- Graph paper (for site maps). Crew chiefs often carry this and other paperwork in an aluminum clipboard box.
- A small flashlight (useful when investigating caves and rockshelters)
- In some places you may need a snake bite kit (although we have yet to use one), pepper spray in bear country (archaeologists in grizzly territory often carry guns), mosquito repellent, or shin guards to protect against snakes in more densely vegetated areas.

berant people living in large aggregations and particularly concerned with ritual and feasting.

In truth of course, the same people produced both sites throughout the course of a single year, as part of the Western Shoshone's seasonal round. Our point is simple: Neither site is typical.

This is not just a problem for archaeologists who study nomadic hunter-gatherers. Agricultural peoples also do not live their lives in one location. They create residences in one place, field houses near outlying crops, check dams in the arroyos, hunting camps in the mountains, and maybe ritual centers in yet another place. This holds true for your daily life as well. Trying to reconstruct your life from just one of the places you use would present a very biased view.

The goal of archaeological survey is not just to find deep sites full of interesting artifacts. Instead, survey can document the range of archaeological remains that occur across a landscape to avoid a biased image of the lives of ancient peoples.

We do this by looking at the distribution of sites across a region. Decades ago, archaeologists often ignored surface sites because they lacked the contextual relations necessary to establish solid cultural chronologies. But such sequences, although important, are only part of the puzzle. Surface sites provide unique data regarding past human–land relationships. In the next section, we consider the surface archaeology of the Carson Desert in western Nevada to illustrate how archaeologists implement this regional perspective (see "Looking Closer: The Surveyor's Toolkit").

SURFACE ARCHAEOLOGY IN THE CARSON DESERT

The Great Basin is best known for vast stretches of sagebrush and arid mountain ranges, but it also contains a number of substantial wetlands. Julian Steward's Depression-era research documented the lives of those

Figure 4-3 Students collecting a site found during survey in the Carson Desert.

Shoshone and Paiute people who lived in areas *without* wetlands. So, without much ethnographic data, archaeologists in the 1970s debated how the wetlands were incorporated into the seasonal round of the region's native peoples.

One hypothesis held that the wetlands provided a permanent, sedentary home for hunter-gatherers; an opposing one held that the wetlands served as but one element in a broader seasonal round. Both of these hypotheses were grounded in the materialist paradigm and focused on food. The first hypothesis argued that wetlands provide abundant, high-quality foods; it also assumed that people would become sedentary (that is, stay in one location year-round) wherever food was abundant. The latter hypothesis viewed wetland food resources as lower quality and more difficult to gather than others, such as piñon and large game. And in contrast it assumed that hunter-gatherers became sedentary when the lack of food elsewhere forced them to do so. Expressed as research questions, the hypotheses were: Did prehistoric peoples settle down and focus exclusively on the wetlands, or did they incorporate the mountains' resources into a more diversified seasonal round?

One of the Great Basin's largest wetlands lies in the Carson Desert, about 100 kilometers east of Reno, Nevada. A large basin filled with sand dunes and alkali flats (Figure 4-3), the Carson Desert is also the termi-

nus of several large rivers. These create a vast, slightly alkaline wetland. This wetland is host to many species of plants and animals that provided ancient peoples with food and various kinds of raw material for clothing, houses, and tools: cattail, bulrush and other plants, fish (especially tui chub), muskrats, and other small mammals. Piñon pine nuts grow in the piñon-juniper forest of the Stillwater Mountains that form the eastern edge of the Carson Desert, and foragers could find tubers, seeds, bighorn sheep, and other game there as well. Previous research suggested that people had lived in this region off and on for more than 9000 years.

In the late 1970s, we were excavating Hidden Cave, a site located at the south end of the Stillwater range, which overlooks the Carson Desert. The site was used primarily between 5000 and 1500 years ago as a place to cache hunting gear and as a cool escape from the desert's extreme summer heat (Figure 4-4). Hidden Cave is an intriguing site, but remember the "fallacy of the typical site": Because we knew that people had lived in the Carson Desert for at least 9000 years, we assumed that Hidden Cave documented only a portion of the region's prehistory. And furthermore, a specialized cache cave obviously gives us only limited insights about the lives of the people who had lived in this area—like trying to reconstruct someone's life by looking at only their safe deposit box or back porch. (We'll have more to say about Hidden Cave in Chapter 11.)

Figure 4-4 Archaeologists excavating inside Hidden Cave (Nevada). Without the 500-watt quartz-halogen landing lights (evident on the left), the excavation area would be pitch black. Note also the respirators and hard-hats—often required equipment for working inside such enclosed cave environments.

To understand ancient life in the Carson Desert, we therefore needed to explore the regional archaeological record: What kind of archaeological remains are found near the marsh, in the dunes, in the low foothills of the Stillwater Mountains, and, higher in the mountains, in the piñon-juniper forest? Put simply, we hypothesized that if the wetland was exploited by a sedentary population, then we should find evidence of large, year-round populations living near the marsh. There should be little evidence of use of the mountains, except perhaps by hunting parties seeking bighorn sheep. People should have made far less use of the dunes and alkali flats, because their economic potentials are low compared with that of the wetland.

But on the other hand, if the wetlands were just one stop on a broad-scale seasonal round, then we should find evidence of more transient use of the wetlands and a more intensive use of the mountains.

With this in mind, we generated some archaeological expectations for each hypothesis. Because we would rely strictly on surface archaeology, where organic remains are not preserved, we focused on stone tools (pottery is rare in this region) and the waste flakes from their manufacture and resharpening. We'll talk more about these kinds of artifacts in Chapter 10.

The point is this: Long before we took to the field, we had a good idea of what we should find *if* one hypothesis was correct and the other was incorrect. For example, if a sedentary population had used the wetlands, then we expected to find dense scatters of waste flakes and broken tools (the remains of villages occupied for years at a time) in the wetland. In the uplands, we expected to find only evidence of hunting activities, evidenced by small campsites containing broken projectile points.

But if the second hypothesis was correct, then we expected to find smaller, less-dense settlements on the valley floor and evidence of hunting, but also tuber, seed, and piñon gathering in the mountains, as shown by the **manos** and **metates** (grinding stones) used for processing seeds and nuts.

Some Sampling Considerations

So, you can see that the fieldwork needed to test our hypotheses required that we explore the character of archaeological evidence across the region. But what should that region be? And did we need to search every square inch of it? Given the practicalities of desert archaeology, it was obvious that we could not look everywhere. We must *sample*, but capricious and biased sampling methods can lead the archaeologist astray. What if we looked only in places where we thought sites would be located? Not being Great Basin hunter-gatherers, we would surely not see the landscape as past foragers did. We would undoubtedly overestimate the importance of some places and overlook others, generating a biased image of the region's archaeology.

The best way to ensure unbiased results is through judicious use of **statistical sampling**. We'll cover only

mano A fist-sized, round, flat, hand-held stone used with a metate for grinding foods.

metate A large, flat stone used as a stationary surface upon which seeds, tubers, and nuts are ground with a mano.

statistical sampling The principles that underlie sampling strategies that provide accurate measures of a statistical population.

the basic principles of this large and complex subject here. (But note that any student contemplating a career in archaeology will need to take several statistics courses, because statistical analysis is as indispensable to archaeologists as their trowels.)

To acquire a statistical sample, you must first define the **statistical population** that you wish to characterize. In biology, "population" refers to a group of organisms of a single species that is found in a circumscribed area at a given time. Cultural anthropologists also commonly use the term "cultural population" to denote a specific society, and archaeologists often speak of archaeological populations, such as "Ancestral Pueblo populations" or the "Shoshone-speaking population."

But statisticians use the term "population" to refer not to physical objects but to data, which are, as you will recall, *observations made on objects*. The difference is subtle yet important. A defined group of people, such as Shoshone Indians or American males, could make up a biological or sociocultural population, but they are not a statistical population. Only measurements made on variables—such as stature, daily caloric intake, or religious beliefs—could constitute a statistical population. A statistical population consists of a defined set of observations of interest.

The population of interest to us in our project was the observations we could make on the stone artifacts and waste flakes found in the archaeological sites of the

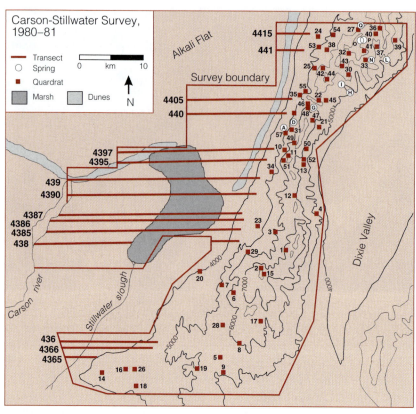

Figure 4-5 Map of the Carson Desert and Stillwater Mountains (Nevada), showing the locations of survey transects, quadrats, and spring surveys.   Robert Kelly, "Prehistory of the Carson Desert and Stillwater Mountains," University of Utah Anthropological Papers, No. 123, 2001. Used by permission.

wetlands and dunes of the Carson Desert and the piñon-juniper forests of the Stillwater Mountains.

Statistical sampling also requires that we define a relevant sample universe, the archaeological sites that will provide the sample population. Because the research question concerned the relationships between sites on the valley floor, in particular, those in the wetland and those in the mountains, our **sample universe** had to contain both of these regions.

The result was a sample universe—a survey area—of some 1700 square kilometers that looks like the head of a large, barking dog (shown in Figure 4-5). The size and shape of a survey area is a result of the research question and practical considerations. In this case, the survey area's odd shape was a product of the need to encompass the wetland, dune area, and alkali flats, as well as the northern Stillwater Mountains, where there is a piñon-juniper forest today, and the southern mountains, which are covered primarily by sagebrush. But we also needed to avoid (1) the town of Fallon, (2) a large wildlife refuge that lies in the dog's "mouth," and

statistical population A set of counts, measurements, or characteristics about which relevant inquiries are to be made. Scientists use the term "statistical population" in a specialized way (quite different from "population" in the ordinary sense).

sample universe The region that contains the statistical population and that will be sampled. Its size and shape are determined by the research question and practical considerations.

(3) up in front of the dog's ear, a large naval bombing range that contained unexploded ordinance. (Fallon is home to one of the U.S. Navy's elite fighter pilot schools. Watch the film *Top Gun*, and you'll catch some glimpses of the Carson Desert and Stillwater Mountains beneath the screaming F-14s.)

Because soil formation in deserts is often slow and vegetation is sparse, many archaeological remains still lie on the surface, where people dropped or discarded them hundreds or even thousands of years ago. Doing surface archaeology in such places means that you simply spot an artifact, plot its location in your field notes, pick it up, and label it—no digging!

But who could survey all 1700 square kilometers? That could take lifetimes! This is where statistical sampling theory helps out, providing a set of methods that allows us to characterize a population without having to record data on every item in that population. We draw upon the same set of methods and theory that pollsters use to take the nation's political pulse by interviewing only a thousand people.

You begin by randomly selecting those sites that will be included in the sample. The word "random" here is critical, for it specifically means that *each site has an equal chance of being selected for the sample.* If there were 100 sites, say, then each site must have a 1/100 = 1 percent chance of being included in the sample. If the sample is not selected in a random manner, then some sites may be overrepresented and others underrepresented in the sample. And that would bias the final results.

Random sampling provides the only way for archaeologists to collect meaningful negative evidence. This is important because, in addition to knowing what activities took place where, archaeologists want to know which activities did *not* occur in a particular area or biotic community. As you will see, the requirement for negative evidence imposes severe yet necessary requirements on survey fieldwork.

Randomly selecting the samples also permits us to analyze the results statistically. Because statistical analysis generally requires a random sample, archaeologists who use a biased sampling design will never know if their results are meaningful or not.

Getting the Sample

Once we had decided on the sample universe, the next task was to select the sample. The first step here is to decide on the **sample fraction**. What portion of the sample population would be included—1 percent of the sites? 5 percent, 10 percent, 50 percent? Archaeologists are somewhat hampered in this regard because the size of the sample depends on characteristics of the population being sampled. For example, if there is a lot of variation, say, in the number of projectile points in sites (some have a few, others have many), then we would want a larger sample than if there were only a small amount of variation. The problem is that archaeologists rarely know much about the populations they are sampling; this is especially true when undertaking survey in a new region.

One solution to this problem is to start with a small uniform sample across the region and then use the findings from that sample to decide whether some regions need more intensive sampling. And so, in 1980 we began with a 1 percent sample of the entire region and then increased the sample fraction in particular areas the following summer.

The second step is more pragmatic: How do you actually acquire the sample? Ideally, we would take all the sites in the sample universe, give each one a number, and then randomly select some portion of those numbers and examine those sites. But we don't know anything about the region—we don't know how many sites there are, let alone their locations. This means that we have to sample the landscape in order to sample the sites.

We could just go out and start walking across the land, but it would be hard to keep track of how much land we covered and hence difficult to compute the sample fraction. And we would almost certainly bias the sample by avoiding areas that were hard to reach or unpleasant to walk across.

We solved this problem by using randomly selected **sample units**. Sample units can be many different shapes, although squares, circles, and transects (long, narrow rectangles) are the most commonly used; all three were employed in this survey. The choice of which to use depends somewhat on the research questions, but also on practical considerations.

In the mountains, we used 500 × 500 meter squares (we called them quadrats) as the sample unit. Kelly

sample fraction The percentage of the sample universe that is surveyed. Areas with a lot of variability in archaeological remains require larger sample fractions than do areas of low variability.

sample units Survey units of a standard size and shape, determined by the research question and practical considerations, used to obtain the sample.

selected this size because Thomas's previous experience in other Nevada surveys showed that they were a manageable size, given the exigencies of survey in the desert mountains and the number of crew members he had.

We located these squares randomly using the **UTM grid** (Universal Transverse Mercator). What is the UTM grid? Simply put, mapmakers divide the world into a grid of 1×1 meter squares; each intersection in that grid has north and east coordinates. Look at a standard USGS topographic map, and you will see these coordinates written in small, black numbers along the map's margins. (And many maps today include 1×1 kilometer blocks of the UTM grid drawn in black lines.) These numbers provide a handy, pre-existing way to sample a landscape.

We randomly selected sets of north and east coordinates (by putting the UTM coordinates in a hat—nothing fancy here!). Each set of north and east coordinates defined the northwest corner of a 500×500 meter sample square; for example, the coordinates of Quadrat 36 were 4416000 North, 407500 East. We then located these squares on the appropriate topographic map and drew them in. We selected a number of units from predefined portions of the mountains to ensure that survey units were spread throughout the extent of the Stillwater Mountains.

We also drew 500-meter radius circles around all the active springs in the northern mountains. Water is obviously critical for hunter-gatherers living in a desert environment. In the Stillwater Mountains, water is mostly present as springs that create a small seep or a short creek. Only one "stream" exists in the Stillwaters; jokingly labeled "Mississippi Canyon" on USGS maps, it trickles only a few hundred meters before disappearing beneath rock and sand. In his Reese River Valley survey, Thomas found that sites tended to occur within about 450 meters of a water source, so we chose to survey a 500-meter radius around a sample of the springs. These 500-meter radius circles were then completely surveyed for sites.

On the valley floor (defined as all land below 1340 meters [4400 feet] in elevation), we used 100 meter-wide transects (instead of 500-meter squares) to sample the area. We chose this width because we had 10–12 stu-

dents working on the project, and this meant that they could be spaced about 10 meters apart—an interval that previous experience told us was the maximum distance surveyors should be apart to avoid missing small sites.

We located the first transect by randomly selecting a UTM north coordinate from near the north end of the valley survey and used that line to define the middle of the 100-meter transect width (that is, the transect extended 50 meters north and 50 meters south of the random UTM north coordinate). To increase the sample to the desired fraction, we then selected additional transects at 10 km intervals south of the first. Later, additional transects were selected by placing them between these existing ones. It may seem that these later transects were not randomly selected, but they actually were, given that their locations were predicated on that of the first—and it was randomly selected.

Why didn't we use our 500×500 quadrats on the valley floor? Quadrats are fairly easy to locate on the ground in areas with topographic relief. Plotted on the map, we could see that the southeast corner of Quadrat 36, for example, could be reached by walking up a particular canyon, then, where the canyon makes a turn to the south, going north up a small draw to the ridge top.

But the Carson Desert is flat, with only 1 to 2 meters of elevation over vast stretches. We could have spent hours just trying to locate the corner of a survey unit through triangulation with a compass (this was before GPS units were available—more on those under "GPS Technology and Modern Surveys" later in this chapter). We used transects because we could locate them on the ground where they crossed a road or two-track on the map (using the truck's mileage gauge from some known point, such as an irrigation canal or a permanent USGS marker). Once we found the transect, we spread out over the 100-meter width and walked due east or west with the help of a compass. We didn't use transects in the mountains because there are few roads and hence few entry points. This meant that surveyors might have had to walk many kilometers in straight lines across steep, rocky terrain before they could reach a point where a vehicle could pick them up. One long day on an experimental transect in the mountains showed us how impractical they were in that environment!

Doing the Work

We completed the Carson-Stillwater survey in two summers. As we've already said, in the first summer we

---

UTM Universal Transverse Mercator, a grid system whereby north and east coordinates provide a location anywhere in the world, precise to 1 meter.

took a 1 percent sample of the entire sample universe. This meant surveying a total of about 17 square kilometers—35 quadrats in the mountains (8.75 km²) and about 82 kilometers of transects (8.2 km²). We found that archaeological remains were most dense and variable in the piñon-juniper forest of the mountains and in the dune area (the dog's "nose") and southern portions of the valley floor (the dog's "chin"). Site density and variability was somewhat less in the wetland region of the valley floor and in the unforested portion of the mountains.

This is why, during the second summer, we pursued a **stratified random sample,** which takes the sample universe and stratifies it into sub-universes. We eventually divided the sample universe into five strata: the wetland, the dune area to the west of the wetland, the south valley, the northern Stillwater Mountains, and the southern Stillwater Mountains. As a result of the first summer's survey sample, we sampled some of these areas more intensively than the others.

As mentioned above, the first summer's survey team consisted of 10–12 student archaeologists and volunteers (see "Looking Closer: Archaeological Survey in the Carson Desert"). When surveying the transects, surveyors walked at 8–10 meter intervals, winding their way through the sagebrush and greasewood. A similar procedure was used on the quadrats but, because these units were 500 × 500 meters, we made five 100 meter-wide passes across them; we used the same procedure for the spring surveys, but with up to 10 such passes.

When someone found a site, each crew member marked his or her place on the line (so they'd know where to resume surveying) and then gathered together. We located the site on a sketch map of the quadrat and then sketched a map of the site itself. Most sites were unglamorous scatters of flakes, but occasionally we found rock art on scattered boulders and once a standing **wickiup** (a conical log structure) that had been built sometime in the early twentieth century, judging from the enamel pots hanging in a tree and the steel axe cuts on the logs.

For each site, we filled out a form that asked for a variety of information—the site's location and topographic setting; distance to water; the type and density of surrounding vegetation; evidence of disturbance by people or erosion; potential for buried deposits; estimates of site age and size; outcrops of stone suitable for making tools; structures or features such as hearths; slope; and general comments. We photographed each

site and collected a large sample of the stone tools and waste flakes.

We gave each site a field number, but eventually each site was assigned a permanent **Smithsonian number**—a cataloging system that most states use to keep track of their sites. (In most states, these numbers are given out by the state's historic preservation office—we'll talk about these more in Chapter 17.) For example, one site found in our survey acquired the number 26CH798: The 26 stands for Nevada, because it is the twenty-sixth state alphabetically (excluding Alaska and Hawaii, which acquired statehood after this system was in place; they are now 49 and 50). The CH stands for Churchill County, and 798 means it was the 798th site recorded in that county.

After two summers, we had surveyed 57 quadrats, 8 springs, and 260 kilometers of transects—about 47 square kilometers, or a sample fraction of the total survey universe of about 3 percent. But some strata were sampled more intensively than others; Table 4-1 shows how the sample was distributed across the five strata. We recorded 160 sites and collected some 10,400 stone tools and more than 70,000 manufacturing and resharpening waste flakes. We analyzed these over the next several years.

What We Learned

Recall that the original research question concerned two different hypotheses about the role of wetlands in the ancient hunter-gatherer seasonal round. The first hypothesis held that wetlands had been the focus of a sedentary settlement system, predicting that the highest site density should be in the wetland. But our survey found that the highest site densities are found in the dunes, the south valley region, and the northern forested portion of the mountains.

The first hypothesis also predicted that sites in the wetlands should contain evidence of long-term habitation.

stratified random sample A survey universe divided into several sub-universes that are then sampled at potentially different sample fractions.

wickiup A conical structure made of poles or logs laid against one another that served as fall and winter homes among the prehistoric Shoshone and Paiute.

Smithsonian number A unique catalog number given to sites; it consists of a number (the state's position alphabetically), a letter abbreviation of the county, and the site's sequential number within the county.

Looking Closer
Archaeological Survey in the Carson Desert

Part of the joy of fieldwork is living outdoors. In the Carson Desert, we camped at line cabins, in an abandoned one-room schoolhouse, at miners' camps, and alongside many dirt roads.

Our day began at 4 AM. Depending on who the cook was (we all took turns), breakfast might be eggs and bacon or just a bag of granola and carton of milk on the table. Someone else checked the vehicles' fluid levels and tires and made sure there was emergency food and water in the trucks.

When surveying the valley floor, we dropped a truck off in the afternoon where the transect we would survey the next day crossed a dirt road. We'd also leave a cooler full of water underneath the truck. The next morning, we left camp before sunup, parking at the opposite end of the transect. We spread out over the 100-meter width, sat down, and waited for the sun to come up. At sunrise we'd start our slow trek to the truck at the opposite end of the transect. We tried to finish the day's work by 2 PM, but sometimes we arrived at the truck closer to sundown, our packs full of labeled bags of artifacts. There's nothing like carrying a pack full of rocks across the desert to get you in shape.

Lunch was oranges, cookies, and peanut butter and jelly sandwiches—affectionately known as "death wads" (a survey tip: Put peanut butter on both halves so the jelly doesn't soak through). We often ate beneath a couple of bedsheets draped over greasewood for shade. The sun's reflection off the alkali flats sometimes burned the *bottom* of our chins, and we welcomed the chance to wade across an irrigation ditch or through a stretch of wetland. Occasionally a dust devil would blow up, and the crew would call out bets as to who would get hit!

In the mountains, we drove as close as we could to the day's quadrat—but even with a four-wheel drive this still meant walking many kilometers just to reach the survey area. Once we hiked until lunchtime to reach a unit high in the mountains. The crew was so tired that *everyone* fell asleep after eating—and did not wake up until 4 PM. We finished the job, but returned to camp that night about 10 PM—hiking by flashlight.

After finishing a unit in the mountains, we drove as close as possible to the next unit, camped by the truck, and then got up the next morning to start again.

Living in close quarters for weeks on end can create tensions, and crews solved this problem the same way small hunting and gathering bands do—through humor. It was not unusual to see someone jump on the hood of the truck and dance to Steppenwolf's *Born to be Wild* at 5 AM. Conversations along the survey line and at mealtimes were running jokes and embarrassing, but good-natured, stories. "Oranges are better than sex!" announced one crew member on an especially hot day at lunch. This began days of suggestions involving conjugal relations and fruit. Cow-chip fights and rock-throwing contests were also popular.

But the archaeological survey recovered stone tools and evidence of stone tool manufacturing techniques suggesting that wetland sites were short-term camps. This evidence is more in line with the second hypothesis, which argued that the wetland was but one stop on a complex seasonal round (and, in fact, the sites in the dune region contained tools and waste flakes that suggested even more transient stays than those in the wetland).

The second hypothesis, however, also suggested that the piñon forests should have been included in the seasonal round. But although we found evidence of hunting there, evidence for plant collecting, in the form of grinding stones, was almost nonexistent.

TABLE 4-1 Sampling Fractions of the Survey Strata and Predicted Site Densities, Carson Valley

REGION	SIZE (Km²)	QUADRATS	SPRINGS	TRANSECTS (Km)	SAMPLE FRACTION	SITES	SITE DENSITY (Sites/km²)
Piñon-juniper forest	150	23	5	–	6.5	41	4.2
Unforested mountains	820	34	3	–	1.3	12	1.1
Wetland	305	–	–	133	3.4	30	2.9
Dunes	243	–	–	93	3.8	57	6.1
South valley	53	–	–	34	6.4	20	5.9
Total	1571	57	8	260	2.7*	160	3.4*

SOURCE: Kelly 2001, table 6-1

Some areas of survey, such as the alluvial fans, are excluded from this table, and the areas covered by open water are excluded from the Wetland total.
(*indicates values calculated from entire survey region)

In sum, neither hypothesis seemed to provide an adequate reconstruction of ancient life in the Carson Desert and Stillwater Mountains. We have come full circle in the research cycle and are now back at the beginning, proposing new hypotheses that take into account what we learned.

But maybe the survey's conclusions are completely wrong. Maybe the site densities and contents that we recorded are unknowingly biased. Is there reason to think that survey tells us anything valid?

Does Sampling Actually Work? The Chaco Experiment

Samples are supposed to give us an accurate picture of what a population is like. Given that we didn't know—and still don't know—the actual population of sites in the Carson Desert, how do we know that the survey actually did what it was supposed to do?

To test the accuracy of survey methods, we need to do a sample survey in an area where archaeologists have already conducted a 100 percent survey—that is, where the population is already known. Few such surveys have been conducted: After all, why do a survey to approximate the population if the population is already known?

Sample surveys were one of the methodologies advocated by the new archaeology of the 1960s. Early on,

therefore, archaeologists asked themselves whether this method actually worked: Did a survey sample adequately characterize a region's surface archaeology? Concerned with this, James Judge (Fort Lewis College), Robert Hitchcock (University of Nebraska), and James Ebert (Ebert & Associates, Albuquerque) conducted a test of survey methods against the known archaeology of Chaco Culture National Historical Park, located in Chaco Canyon in northwestern New Mexico (shown in this chapter's opening photo).

Today, Chaco Canyon is smack in the middle of nowhere, but in the eleventh century, Chaco was the place to be in the American Southwest. Beginning about AD 700, early Ancestral Pueblo people began constructing their distinctive multiroom apartment complexes that would give their descendants, the Pueblo Indians of New Mexico, their popular name. By AD 1050, Chaco was the center of a complex, centralized social and political system based on maize horticulture. The canyon contains many sites; among them are nine large pueblos, known to archaeologists as "Great Houses," made of beautifully shaped and coursed stonework, which are virtually impossible to miss as one enters the canyon. Pueblo Bonito (Spanish for "beautiful town"), for example, contains more than 600 rooms and is four stories high in places (Figure 4-6). It holds more than 24 kivas (round semi-subterranean ceremonial structures), one more than 20 meters (60 feet) in diameter. America would not witness a larger apartment building until the nineteenth century and the Industrial Revolution.

© Charles A. Lindbergh, courtesy of the School of American Research

Figure 4-6 Pueblo Bonito, photo by Charles Lindbergh, 1929.

Chaco Canyon was the center of a vast sociopolitical system. Although the Ancestral Pueblo people used no wheeled vehicles or beasts of burden, roads radiate out from the canyon like spokes on a wheel (we'll return to these in Chapter 5). Some run for 50 kilometers (almost 30 miles). People brought massive pine trunks for roof beams from mountains 80 kilometers away. Turquoise, shell bracelets, copper, iron pyrite, conch shells, and macaws in the Great Houses point to a vast trade network.

Although the reasons are still unclear, by AD 1150 Chaco's power and population began to decline. People moved elsewhere and, by AD 1350, the canyon was all but abandoned.

Chaco became a national monument in 1907, and in the 1970s it was the focus of a long-term National Park Service–sponsored research project. For inventory purposes, this project conducted a 100 percent survey of the 50 km^2 monument with archaeological crews walking over every hot, dusty square inch. They found 1130 sites and, of these, 621 could be pigeonholed into a "cultural phase," a period of time based on architecture and pottery types (we'll talk about this term in Chapter 9). These phases were Archaic sites (sites that are older than 100 BC), Basketmaker II (100 BC–AD 400), Basketmaker III (AD 400–700), Pueblo I (AD 700–900), Pueblo II (AD 900–1100), Pueblo III (AD 1100–1300), Navajo sites (late, but the actually age is uncertain), and multicomponent sites (sites with evidence of occupation during two or more of the phases).

Later, in 1975, Judge, Ebert, and Hitchcock re-surveyed the monument, although this time from the comfort of an air-conditioned office. They used several different sampling strategies—regularly spaced and randomly spaced transects and quadrats, with both stratified and unstratified samples (using ecological zones as the strata). They selected a 20 percent sample in all the experiments, plotted the selected transects or quadrats on maps of the monument, and tallied which sites were "found."

Their experiment showed that archaeological survey sampling really does work. Table 4-2 shows the results of their regularly spaced transect sample. Notice that the frequency of sites generated by the survey sample mirror the actual frequency of sites. For example, using the sample alone, we could say that half the datable sites in Chaco Canyon are Navajo sites—and we would be right. The sample survey also would lead us to claim, correctly, that site density (and perhaps population as well) grew between Pueblo I and Pueblo II times and then declined during the Pueblo III period. The point is this: We can draw the same conclusions from the 20 percent survey as we can from the 100 percent sample—and it would have required only one-fifth the work!

Judge, Ebert, and Hitchcock found little difference between the systematic transect and random transect designs. Transects, in fact, appeared to be better indicators of site density and population attributes for the

TABLE 4-2 Actual and Predicted Site Frequencies from the Systematic Interval Transect Sample in Chaco Canyon National Monument

SITE TYPE	ACTUAL COUNT	ACTUAL FREQUENCY (%)	INTERVAL TRANSECT COUNT	INTERVAL TRANSECT FREQUENCY (%)
Archaic	5	0.8	–	–
Basketmaker II	3	0.5	1	0.8
Basketmaker III	67	10.8	12	9.0
Pueblo I	38	6.1	6	4.5
Pueblo II	53	8.5	12	9.0
Pueblo III	40	6.4	11	8.3
Navajo	317	51.0	69	51.9
Multicomponent	98	15.9	22	16.5
Total	621	100.0	133	100.0

Source: Judge, Hitchcock, and Ebert 1971

monument as a whole. The quadrat sample provided better indicators of population attributes within ecological zones, that is, when using a stratified sample. Judge and his colleagues urged archaeologists to take a small initial sample of an unknown region and use that as the basis for a second sampling strategy applying a stratified sample and different sample fractions in the strata. And that's just what we did in the Carson Desert survey.

But there is more. Although the Chaco experimental surveys were notable for what they found, they were also notable for what they *missed*—namely, most of the Great Houses. How could this be? Once in the valley, most archaeologists could find Pueblo Bonito blindfolded—if only by walking into one of its massive two- or three-story high walls. Missing Pueblo Bonito would be like walking across a college campus and not seeing the football stadium. What good is a survey that misses a 600-room pueblo?

Sample surveys are very good at recording the general character of a region, but they are less useful for finding unique or rare sites. In fact, even (relatively large) 20 percent surveys are likely to miss rare items, like Pueblo Bonito. Note in Table 4-2 that the transect sample also missed all the Archaic sites as well—because they are rare (only 5 in the survey area). Surveys are not designed to find rare sites—that takes common sense, open eyes, and some plain old gumshoe survey.

QUALITY CONTROL IN SURFACE SURVEY

The Chaco experiment demonstrates that survey sampling can be quite effective. But the quality of a survey is affected by factors other than the attention given to the sampling strategy. In fact, the on-the-ground implementation of survey itself affects what you recover.

Any archaeologist can tell you that crews are not as effective when working in a driving rainstorm or oppressive summer heat. In the Carson Desert, where afternoon temperatures could reach 110° Fahrenheit, we began work before sunrise, and we tried to complete the day's survey by 2 PM (although this wasn't always possible)—partly out of a concern for the crew's safety but also because we knew that the quality of data collection would be compromised.

The interval between surveyors is another variable whose effect on survey results is difficult to determine. In doing survey, especially in desert regions, archaeologists often record "sites" and "isolates"—sites are clusters of material; isolates are artifacts that occur by themselves. How do we separate isolates from sites? Is this one projectile point an isolate, even though a scraper and a potsherd lie 20 meters away? Or do the three items together constitute a site? The answer depends partly on understanding how surveyors actually go about doing survey.

As a surveyor is walking across the survey unit, he or she will find something—a flake or projectile point or pottery sherd. The surveyor will stop, flag the item, and then take a few steps around, looking a bit more intently than otherwise. If the surveyor finds nothing within a few seconds, he or she will collect, label, and map the item as an isolate. If the surveyor finds more cultural items, he or she will call out that they've found a site. The crew will then assemble on the location and complete the site form and collection.

One of the Chaco researchers, James Ebert, conducted an experiment to find out how this survey behavior affects the way archaeologists record surface archaeology. During a survey in southwestern Wyoming, he planted washers and nails in one survey unit. Some were painted buff (the same color as the surrounding sand), and others were painted black. Ebert mapped the locations of each washer and nail and then turned a survey crew loose on the unit.

The crew found only two-thirds of the "artifacts," and slightly more of the black- than buff-colored items. Of greater interest was the fact that the surveyors found washers and nails placed near one another at a much higher frequency (80 percent) than washers and nails planted by themselves (22 percent). Why? Surveyors look a bit more intensely after they find an item. If they find another, they'll look even more intensely until they decide that they have a site, at which point they and the entire crew really scour the surface. As a result, the artifact recovery rate goes up when artifacts occur near one another. But if a surveyor sees nothing within a few seconds' glance after finding an artifact, he or she will move ahead with the survey. As a result, artifacts that occur in less-dense scatters could be systematically underrepresented in a surface survey.

Two points arise from this observation. First, artifacts that were discarded or lost *individually* have a smaller chance of being discovered later. The implication is that surveys do not recover many isolated items, even though Ebert's surveyors walked at 5-meter intervals. We could lessen this problem by having surveyors walk at 1- or 2-meter intervals—although this would greatly increase the cost and time required for the survey.

So, What's a Site?

Ebert's experiment raised a second problem. Archaeologists speak all the time about sites, but many would be hard-pressed to define what "site" actually means. In

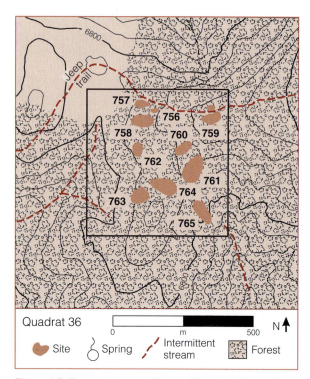

Figure 4-7 Topographic map of Quadrat 36 in the Stillwater Mountain survey. Sites are shown as numbered patches. Is there one site here, or ten? *Robert Kelly, "Prehistory of the Carson Desert and Stillwater Mountains," University of Utah Anthropological Papers, No. 123, 2001. Used by permission.*

the Carson Desert, we defined a site as five pieces of cultural material within approximately 50 square meters. Often geography places a boundary on a site's edges, for example, a riverbank or a steep slope. But sometimes, artifact scatters are more or less continuous, and the archaeologist has to make a judgment call. For example, Figure 4-7 is a map of Quadrat 36 in the Stillwater Mountains. We recorded ten sites in this quadrat; but it's possible that another archaeologist might have recorded eight sites, or five, or just one big one.

Figure 4-8 illustrates the problem with defining a site on the ground. All four boxes in this figure contain the same hypothetical scatter of artifacts, consisting of two artifact concentrations with a light scatter between and around them. In A, the dashed line indicates that an excruciatingly careful archaeologist has found everything and categorized it all as one site. In B, surveyors did not recover the isolated items at the same rate as clumped remains (as Ebert's experiment suggests might happen), and so the archaeologist decided that there were two sites. In C, another careful archaeologist found the same scatter that was recorded by A, but this

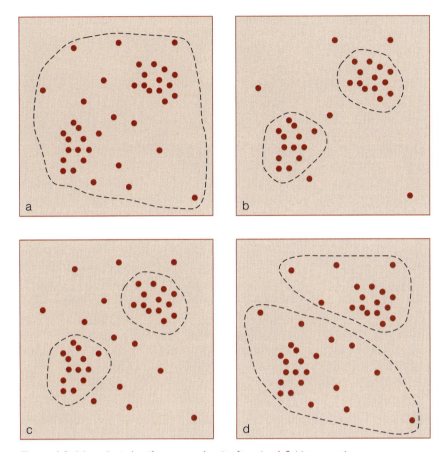

Figure 4-8 A hypothetical artifact scatter showing four site-definition scenarios.

Desert were, in fact, nothing more than such geologic aggregates of cultural material.

Finally, even if we could define sites "correctly," what would they be? We tend to think of sites as discrete behavioral entities. But sites, especially surface sites, are not necessarily the archaeological equivalent of the ethnographer's village, hamlet, or foraging camp (although sometimes they are). Sites can result from multiple occupations over decades, or even hundreds or thousands of years, and archaeologists have to be wary of all the natural processes that go into the formation of a site (we'll discuss more of these in Chapter 7).

Is There a Solution?

One way around this problem is to dispense with the notion of "site" altogether. Instead of using sites as our unit of data collection, current technology allows us to use the artifacts themselves. Some archaeologists have done this by intensively surveying their sample units and plotting every single item found using an electronic **total station**, also known as an electronic distance meter (EDM). This device uses a beam of infrared light to obtain *X,Y,Z* coordinates relative to a known point. Total stations can obtain accurate locational data over distances of a kilometer or more, and they make the precise mapping of large areas practical.

In essence, the archaeologist treats the entire survey unit as if it were one large site. He or she can then use a variety of statistical methods to look for patterns in which artifact types are physically associated—do

archaeologist felt that the two scatters were sufficiently distinct to call them two sites. In D, the same artifact distribution is recorded, but the archaeologist felt that all items had to be considered part of one site or the other.

The problem is even more complex when we factor in geology. In the Carson Desert, it was clear that many of the "sites" on the valley floor were actually conglomerates of unrelated material produced through **deflation,** the geologic process whereby fine sediment is blown away by the wind and larger items—mostly stone artifacts in this case—are left behind. This process results in archaeological remains—which originally might have been discarded at different times in the past throughout an accumulating dune—being eventually left together on the same surface after the sand was blown away. This process produces a dense scatter of debris that is not a site in the traditional sense of the term, but a number of isolated items brought together through a geologic process. Many of the sites we recorded in the Carson

deflation A geologic process whereby fine sediment is blown away by the wind and larger items—including artifacts—are lowered onto a common surface and thus become recognizable sites.

total station A device that uses a beam of light bounced off a prism to determine an artifact's provenience; it is accurate to +/− 3 millimeters.

projectile points occur near scrapers, or are potsherds found near hearths? Alternatively, the archaeologist could define clusters of artifacts—that is, sites—based on tightly mapped artifact distributions rather than on decisions possibly made by a hot, tired, and hungry surveyor in the field.

This approach, however, is not practical when dealing with very large regions. It would have been impractical, for example, to try to plot all artifacts within the 1700 km² Carson Desert survey area (even if the technology to do so were available in the early 1980s, which it was not). An alternative is known as **non-site archaeology,** which focuses not on the analysis of materials from within a batch of artifacts collected from a single site, but on *regional* patterns in artifacts—patterns manifested on a scale of kilometers or hectares.

In the Carson Desert, we never analyzed a single site. We never tried to reconstruct the daily activities that transpired at a site, because we began with the assumption that the sites in our sample were merely different-sized samples of a more or less continuous distribution of archaeological debris. Thus, we analyzed the data in terms of the five sample strata. For example, we compared what we found in the piñon-juniper forest *as a whole* to the other four strata. In this way, it did not matter if Quadrat 36, mentioned above, contained one or ten sites—we added the artifacts from this quadrat's sites to everything else found in the piñon-juniper zone for analysis. In this way, we looked for large-scale patterns in artifact distribution that were more meaningful, in terms of our research questions, and more reliable than a fine-grained interpretation of any single site.

Archaeologists will never completely dispense with the notion of "site" because the concept is critical from an administrative point of view. All state archaeological databases record archaeology in terms of sites, and researchers receive permits to work on particular sites. But all archaeologists today have a more realistic and sober understanding that, under many conditions, sites are *samples* and are rarely equivalent to something that might make immediate intuitive sense to us, such as a "village" or "camp."

WHAT ABOUT THINGS THAT LIE BELOW GROUND?

So far, the archaeological surveys that we have discussed recorded only evidence that is visible with a pedestrian survey. In places like the Carson Desert, important archaeological remains have lain on a stable desert surface for millennia. But in many other places, artifacts may be washed away or deeply buried (as at Gatecliff Shelter). In Grand Teton National Park in Wyoming, for example, you can walk over an area south of Jackson Lake known as "the potholes," a land surface that mammoths tread upon some 14,000 years ago. But 3 kilometers north, that same ancient land surface is buried beneath 30 to 40 meters of **glacial till** and outwash sediments. And at the south end of the park, that land surface doesn't exist at all—it was eroded away thousands of years ago.

This issue cropped up in the Carson Desert project after we finished our survey in 1981. Two years later, and about 300 kilometers away, torrential rains and heavy snows began falling across the headwaters of the Humboldt River, which eventually drains into the Carson Desert. The heavy precipitation kept up until the Carson Desert—that barren basin of sand dunes and alkali flats—had become a 40-mile-wide lake.

During the summer of 1986, the floodwaters began to recede. As they did, they stripped away the tops of dunes and exposed hundreds of human burials and archaeological sites containing shallow houses (Figure 4-9 shows an example), storage pits, bones, stone tools, beads, and grinding stones (we discuss these sites and burials in Chapters 11 and 12). When the U.S. Fish and Wildlife Service (the agency that manages the Carson Desert's wetland) plotted the newly exposed finds, their maps showed that our survey crews had literally walked right over some of these sites. We missed them because there was no surface indication of what lay buried below. However, the kinds of projectile points found in the wetland strata of the survey and in the newly exposed sites were the same: The survey had, in this regard, accurately characterized the wetland's archaeology.

Still, it is clear that surface archaeology documents only what lies on or near the ground surface. Surface

non-site archaeology Analysis of archaeological patterns manifested on a scale of kilometers or hectares, rather than of patterns within a single site.

glacial till The mixture of rock and earth pushed along the front and sides of a glacier.

Figure 4-9 An archaeological crew excavating a semi-subterranean house pit in the Stillwater Marsh (Nevada). Surface survey missed dozens of sites like this because they were not visible beneath sand and saltgrass.

and subsurface material often correlate, but you can never be absolutely certain about what lies below.

Shovel-Testing

Archaeologists working in the eastern United States, Europe, and elsewhere confront this problem all the time, because these areas witness considerable soil buildup, and artifacts rarely lie on the undisturbed ground surface. In agricultural regions, archaeologists do **plow-zone** archaeology, walking through plowed fields after spring tilling (and especially after a rain), because the plow will turn up shallowly buried archaeological remains.

In other areas, archaeologists use a procedure known as **shovel-testing**. Survey crews carry small shovels and sometimes a backpacked screen with them. As the crew moves across a survey unit, each member stops at a pre-determined interval, digs a shallow hole and screens the dirt back into the hole, looking for evidence of buried archaeological remains. It is slow going, and it obvi-

ously cannot locate remains that are more than a foot or two deep.

Looking for more deeply buried remains, some archaeologists use backhoe trenches or hand or mechanical soil augers, but the former can be very expensive (as well as destructive) and the latter very slow. We normally use them in areas that previous research suggests are good places to prospect for buried remains. In other cases, archaeologists use natural exposures, such as arroyos or riverbanks, that sometimes expose deeply buried deposits.

In Chapter 5, we will discuss some high-tech ways to "see" below ground. Here, we consider a way in which surface survey was combined with a subsurface

plow zone The upper portion of a soil profile that has been disturbed by repeated plowing or other agricultural activity.

shovel-testing A sample survey method used in regions where rapid soil buildup obscures buried archaeological remains; it entails digging shallow, systematic pits across the survey unit.

© Robert Kelly

sampling strategy to find Mission Santa Catalina, a Spanish Franciscan mission lost in Georgia's Sea Islands for more than 300 years.

How to Find a Lost Spanish Mission (Part I)

At its seventeenth-century zenith, Spanish Florida had three dozen Franciscan missions, each a satellite settlement heavily dependent on the colonial capital at St. Augustine. To the west lived the Timucuan, Apalachee, and Apalachicola Indians; to the north, toward St. Catherines Island, lay the province of Guale. Although a dozen sixteenth- and seventeenth-century missions once existed in the present state of Georgia, archaeologists and historians had not identified one such mission site when Thomas began his search for Santa Catalina.

Many historians and archaeologists felt that the lost mission of Santa Catalina lay along the western margin of St. Catherines Island, a 1400-acre tract 80 kilometers south of Savannah. Unlike the other so-called Golden Isles, St. Catherines Island has not been subdivided and suburbanized. The Georgia-based, not-for-profit St. Catherines Island Foundation owns the island and regulates a comprehensive program of research and conservation. This enlightened and progressive land management policy ensured that Mission Santa Catalina was not destroyed beneath the crush of condos and fast-food joints that typify the southern barrier islands.

The Survey: Stage One

In 1974, when we first visited St. Catherines Island, the combined French, English, and Spanish historic documentation supplied only vague geographic clues and, although several first-rate archaeologists had previously worked on the island, none had successfully located this important mission site.

Virtually uninhabited, St. Catherines Island is today blanketed with dense forest, briar patches, and almost impenetrable palmetto thicket. When we began our search for Santa Catalina, we were overwhelmed by the vastness of the area involved. We knew so little about the landscape that we could not overlook any portion of St. Catherines Island.

By its nature, archaeological fieldwork is slow and tedious—and nobody could (or should) excavate an entire island—so we began by random sampling. Taking the island's size into consideration, Thomas figured that 30 east-west transects, each 100 meters wide, would

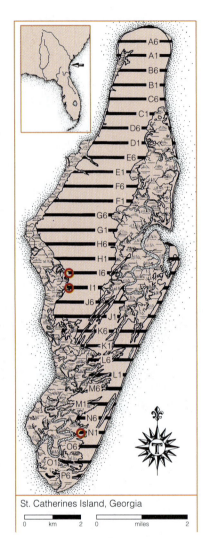

Figure 4-10
Systematic transect research design used to derive a 20 percent regional randomized sample on St. Catherines Island (Georgia). All surveyed transects (the darker stripes) have a letter + number designation. Occurrences of sixteenth- and seventeenth-century Spanish ceramics have been circled. *From the American Museum of Natural History.*

provide a 20 percent sample of the island (Figure 4-10). This sample would allow us to characterize the island's archaeology and help search for the lost mission of Santa Catalina de Guale. But recall that sampling, even with a relatively large 20 percent sample, is not always good at finding rare sites—and there was only one Santa Catalina de Guale.

In surveying, the idea is to walk in the straightest line possible, climbing over rocks and deadfalls, walking along the sides of steep ridges—looking even in places where you really don't expect to find anything. In Nevada's wide-open spaces, it is fairly easy to keep your bearing even if you don't have a compass: Just keep walking toward that peak, mesa, or other landmark in the distance. But on densely vegetated St. Catherines Island, it was impossible to see past the palmetto bush a

Archaeological Ethics
Professional and Avocational Archaeologists

There are many avocational archaeologists in the United States—individuals interested in archaeology but who have no academic credentials. Many of these collect artifacts on their own. Some professionals love them, others begrudgingly tolerate them, and others won't deal with them at all because they feel that any association with collectors condones looting (also known as pothunting). They are often important sources of information for gumshoe survey.

But most archaeologists differentiate between the weekend collector of surface artifacts and those who dig for profit. They condemn the looters, but find relationships with avocationals to be productive. George Frison, professor emeritus at the University of Wyoming, a member of the National Academy of Sciences, and past-president of the Society for American Archaeology, says, "I think you gain a hell of a lot more by cooperating with amateurs… than if you deride them and chase them underground. Then they'll really do you some damage." Should professionals work with avocational archaeologists? Hester Davis provides a few reasons why we should:

The term "avocational archaeologist" is often used synonymously with "amateur archaeologist," presumably to differentiate these people from "professional archaeologists," on the one hand, and "artifact dealers" and "grave robbers," on the other. And then there are "collectors" and "relic hunters": those who do not profess to be "archaeologists," but who are quick to point out that they do not destroy sites, as do grave robbers and vandals.

There is, perhaps, another way of looking at the semantics of this universe of people: there are archaeologists and there are nonarchaeologists, and the basic distinction is that of attitude toward the archaeological resources. Archaeologists consider sites and artifacts as sources of information; non-archaeologists consider sites as sources of artifacts.

The greatest potential for greater site protection is through statewide avocational groups. The secret weapon held by these organizations is their ability to influence their own members, politicians, landowners, teachers, schoolchildren, and even pothunters. By their very numbers and the fact of their organization, avocational archaeological societies should be the real advocates for site protection, in the most contemporary use of that term.

Avocational archaeological groups have the greatest potential for making a real difference in which sites and how many sites are protected in the future. All archaeologists, in my use of the term, must coordinate, communicate, organize nationally, and become pro-protection. Legislation protecting unmarked graves must hit hard on the looters and vandals; ordinances at the local level must become commonplace. The names and faces of archaeological organizations speaking for less wanton destruction must be on educational television and the evening news.

There are probably four or five times as many avocational archaeologists as there are professional ones. There are probably dozens more avocational archaeological organizations than there are professional ones. Since their interests are supposed to be the same, they must all become strong active advocates for site protection, from the individual site where the shopping center is going in, to the national historic landmarks still in private ownership.

by Hester A. Davis, retired state archaeologist, Archaeological Survey, Fayetteville, Arkansas

meter in front of you (Figure 4-11). The entire crew was experienced in desert survey and carried compasses, but even then, some veered off their paths as they wound their way through bushes and briars. Palm-sized orb spiders hung down from Spanish moss–draped oaks; an occasional scream told others that someone had taken one in the face. Fortunately, orb spiders are not dangerous. But the cottonmouths and canebrake

© American Museum of Natural History, photo by Dennis O'Brien

Figure 4-11 Systematic archaeological survey on St. Catherines Island (Georgia).

rattlesnakes are, and the crew quickly learned about tides and alligators.

In Nevada we could see sites on the ground—but on St. Catherines, most of the sites are buried. We searched for them partly by using probes—meter-long, sharpened steel rods. We would push the probe down into the ground every few steps and see if we hit something. This was effective because St. Catherines Island is one huge sand dune—there is no natural stone on the island. Eventually, we learned to tell the difference between the feel of a tree root and rock or shell—the last two suggesting a buried archaeological site. We recorded 135 sites, ranging from massive shell middens to isolated shell scatters. We investigated each site with several 1-meter square test units (see Chapter 5); we excavated more than 400 such test pits.

The Survey: Stage Two

The surface survey and testing told us that sixteenth- and seventeenth-century Spanish ceramics occurred only at 5 of the 135 archaeological sites, all but one along the western perimeter of the island. The ruins of Mission Santa Catalina almost certainly lay buried in a target area the size of 30 football fields along the southwestern margin of the island.

But 30 football fields is still a huge area to dig with dental pick and camel hair brush. Moreover, although our confidence was growing, we had to admit almost

complete ignorance of what we were looking for. Did Santa Catalina survive merely as heaps of sixteenth- and seventeenth-century garbage? Or could we realistically hope to find buried evidence of buildings as well? Clearly, it was time to scratch the surface.

Looking around for better ways to find the needle hidden in this haystack, Thomas learned from Kathleen Deagan about her successful search for sixteenth-century St. Augustine. She and her students used a gasoline-powered posthole digger and excavated hundreds of round holes on a grid system. Following her lead, we did the same on St. Catherines Island for the area that the survey had identified as most likely to contain the mission. With the noisy, nasty auger, two people could dig a 3-foot-deep hole in less than a minute. The power auger threw up a neat doughnut of dirt that was hand-sifted for artifacts. Hundreds of such holes were dug.

Once the field-testing was complete, we identified all materials recovered and plotted the distribution in a series of simple maps. Since then, a number of readily available computer programs have greatly assisted the data conversion process. But even using the hand-plotted maps, the power auger data allowed us to focus further field evaluation on a single 100 × 100 meter square in the overall sampling grid where diagnostic mission-period artifacts were found.

Although this area contained absolutely no surface evidence to distinguish it from the surroundings, judicious use of surface and subsurface sampling had narrowed the search from an entire island to a relatively small area. And this is indeed where we eventually discovered the remarkably well-preserved ruins of Mission Santa Catalina de Guale.

In Chapter 5, we complete the Santa Catalina story by showing how remote sensing technology helped find the invisible mission site. By using a combination of proton magnetometers, ground-penetrating radar, and soil resistivity techniques, we pinpointed actual buildings inside the mission complex—before we ever excavated them.

GPS TECHNOLOGY AND MODERN SURVEYS

Surveys today are also assisted by **global positioning system** (GPS) technology. This system did not exist when we surveyed St. Catherines Island and the Carson Desert, but we certainly wish that it did. We had to use triangulation, pacing, and topography to locate sites on maps—and all that took time. Additionally, we've since discovered that, in the heat of the day, a lot of mistakes can be made.

GPS technology has changed all that. The GPS consists of 27 satellites (24 active ones and 3 spares) that circle the earth in 12-hour evenly distributed orbits at an altitude of about 14,000 kilometers. These orbits repeat the same ground track (because the earth turns beneath them) twice each day. Each satellite carries a computer and very accurate atomic clocks.

Hand-held GPS units operate by picking up the continuously broadcast signals from at least four satellites. The GPS receiver triangulates a position fix using the interval between the transmission and reception of the satellite signal.

The global positioning system is funded and controlled by the U.S. Department of Defense. It was originated, and continues primarily, to provide continuous, worldwide position and navigation data to U.S. and allied military forces. But legitimate commercial and scientific applications were recognized early in the system's development, and it was decided to allow access to GPS signals within certain constraints. The satellite signals were originally coded (and used a practice called selective availability, because the coding function could be turned on and off by the military), so that real-time locational data were (often wildly) inaccurate. This was to prevent a hostile military power from using the GPS as a free, super-accurate, targeting computer.

In the 1980s, GPS units cost thousands of dollars, were bulky and heavy, and required a car battery for their power. And they were not terribly accurate. But today you can buy a cell phone–sized GPS unit at discount stores for about $150. And a few years ago, the military turned off selective availability, so now the field archaeologist can get 5-meter accuracy within seconds with an easily portable and affordable unit. Most units give locations using the UTM coordinates mentioned above (or latitude and longitude, but UTM coordinates are easy to use). Expensive devices can even give subcentimeter accuracy.

GPS technology has not only made fieldwork easier—calculating a location is as easy as pushing a button—but it also permits survey sample units to be odd shapes. We used squares, circles, and transects in the Carson Desert and on St. Catherines Island in large part because they are easier to locate on a map and on the ground. Hence, they make it possible to keep track of how much land we surveyed. But with a GPS, a surveyor's individual line of survey can be tracked. A crew could wander anywhere across the landscape and, at the end of the day, plot out the covered area. It would not matter if they walked a square, circle, or some shapeless blob. The archaeologist can calculate the area surveyed and keep a running sample fraction tally. No archaeologist would undertake fieldwork today without a GPS unit.

FULL-COVERAGE SURVEY

We have spent most of this chapter discussing and advocating survey sampling. But there are instances in which you may not want to sample a region at all, times when you really need to look at the whole thing. Research in southern Mexico's Valley of Oaxaca provides an example.

The Valley of Oaxaca Archaeological Survey

For more than a century, explorers and archaeologists have celebrated the monumental ruins at Monte Albán (*mon*-tay al-*bahn*), overlooking Oaxaca (wa-*ha*-kuh) City in the highlands of southern Mexico. Literally "white mountain," Monte Albán is an extraordinary concentration of pre-Columbian architecture atop an artificially flattened mountain summit (Figure 4-12).

Beginning in 1931, Alfonso Caso and several other Mexican archaeologists undertook 18 field seasons of excavation. They determined that Monte Albán was founded shortly after 500 BC, the mountaintop settlement reaching its maximum physical size around AD 700.

Along the edge of the plaza, which covered nearly four football fields, rose low masonry pyramids. Stepped

global positioning system Hand-held devices that use triangulation from radio waves received from satellites to determine your current position in terms of either the UTM grid or latitude and longitude.

© David H. Thomas

Figure 4-12 The central plaza at Monte Albán (Oaxaca, Mexico).

platforms at either end hid tombs and served as foundations for palaces and temples, a complex of buildings that housed the ruling families and provided formal spaces for these rulers to meet with high-ranking government officials and ambassadors from afar. Nearby was a ballcourt for ritual ball games, which were important throughout Mesoamerica. The main plaza served as the center of government for the city and the region.

Caso's Monte Albán project explored more than 170 tombs in the vicinity of the sprawling central plaza, the perimeter of which was decorated with carved stone monuments depicting sacrificial victims killed, and sometimes mutilated, by the rulers of Monte Albán.

The discoveries in Tomb 7 grabbed headlines around the world. Sometime during the decline of Monte Albán, a very powerful leader had been buried in a tomb constructed earlier. Inside was one of Mesoamerica's greatest treasures: gold, shell, turquoise, jet, crystal, and carved jaguar bones. This was one of the richest caches ever discovered in the New World.

Today, many tourists travel to Oaxaca to view firsthand the partially restored ruins of Monte Albán, and local Aeromexico flights sometimes circle the site, dipping wingtips so that the passengers can catch an aerial view of the fabled sacred city of the Zapotecs.

What's Outside Monte Albán?

But the potential of Oaxacan archaeology was hardly exhausted by the excavations at Monte Albán. Spectacular as it may be, Monte Albán is only a single site. In 1971, another team of archaeologists undertook a decade-long regional survey to determine how Monte Albán fit into the regional landscape of Oaxaca. They began with a complete mapping of Monte Albán, estimating a total population between 25,000 and 30,000. The archaeological reconnaissance project soon expanded into a systematic **full-coverage survey** of the hinterlands—covering the entire Valley of Oaxaca.

The main players—Richard Blanton (Purdue University), Gary Feinman (Field Museum), Laura Finsten (McMaster University), Linda Nicholas (Field Museum), and Stephen Kowalewski (University of Georgia)—selected this area for several good reasons. First, the cultural chronology for the Valley of Oaxaca was fairly well understood—a critical factor for anybody designing a regional survey. Second, the physical land conditions

full-coverage survey Performing 100 percent coverage of a large region; used where topography and archaeological remains make it feasible and where the relationships between specific sites (as opposed to types of sites) are the subject of interest.

were conducive to the regional surface survey: The land surface over the past 3000 years had been relatively stable (meaning that most sites remained visible from the surface), and vegetative ground cover was relatively thin and sparse. Third, settled villages were established in the Valley of Oaxaca beginning about 1500 BC, creating huge quantities of archaeological debris—readily datable remains that could be observed simply by walking along.

The Valley of Oaxaca Settlement Pattern Project established a set of systematic protocols to ensure that data were collected in standardized format. The survey crews consisted of three or four trained people, each familiar with the basic ceramic sequence of the area. They covered all terrain in the survey area by systematically walking 25 to 50 meters apart while searching for archaeological materials. Unlike some regional survey projects, the Valley of Oaxaca research design called for the surveyors to walk in a zigzag pattern, checking all suspicious features along either side of the survey line. Through geological studies, interpretation of aerial photographs, and field inspection of geological cuts, the researchers determined where soil erosion or buildup had occurred (thereby modifying the dimensions of the sites encountered).

The idea here was the same that was used when surveying a sample quadrat in the Carson Desert: Find *everything archaeological* by looking even in places where nothing is expected to be. As Stephen Kowalewski has learned from his experiences in Oaxaca and the red clay country of Georgia, this survey strategy also ensures an up-close appreciation of "alluviation, erosion, mesquite thickets, manzanillo thickets, palmetto thickets, copperheads, pine forests, precipices, cities and their dumps, salt marshes, mean dogs, and meaner land owners."

Sites were usually recognized from surface scatters of potsherds and/or building stones. Once found, sites were plotted on aerial photographs and mapped by the crew leader, while others took notes and made sherd collections. Time-diagnostic sherds were analyzed on-site, enabling the crew to map the distribution of each archaeological phase separately while still in the field.

In the course of 10 years, the archaeologists spent five field seasons on the Oaxaca survey. They searched about 2100 square kilometers completely, resulting in about 2700 places being recorded as containing archaeological remains. But these field-numbered sites were not very meaningful units, because they often lumped together numerous components (evidence of occupation at a site during a particular time period; we'll dis-

cuss this concept further in Chapter 9). These 6353 components, defined and mapped right in the field, became the basic units of analysis for the Valley of Oaxaca survey. For each such unit, the investigators recorded 97 substantive variables, such as environmental zone, soil characteristics, degree of erosion, predominant vegetation, current land status, present irrigation (if any), artifact types, and building materials. In addition, the survey teams located 2000 pyramidal mounds, 9000 residential terraces, and 124 tombs. Overall, the Valley of Oaxaca personnel feel satisfied that they found most occupations, even the small ones, in this huge area.

The massive database from the Oaxaca survey has enabled archaeologists to understand the nature of ancient Zapotec society. Using the number of size-specific components and the variable ceramic densities, for instance, it was possible to estimate human population sizes through time and develop a quantitative model of settlement location and land use. These models, in turn, helped archaeologists understand the dynamics behind the evolution of one of America's ancient civilizations.

The Case for Full-Coverage Survey

The Valley of Oaxaca survey employed the full-coverage technique, an alternative to the random sampling designs discussed earlier. This technique involves large-scale, 100 percent reconnaissance of an archaeological region. Many specific research designs exist for such surveys, but the single common denominator is the systematic examination of contiguous blocks of terrain, surveyed at a uniform level of intensity.

By "region," most archaeologists usually mean something ranging anywhere from a few dozen to several thousand square kilometers. This is not just a matter of semantics: Define too large a region, and a satisfactory survey becomes too expensive. Define too small a region, and you will end up with an incomplete view of the cultural system you are trying to understand.

The question of "How big?" depends on what the project is trying to find out. To answer this question correctly requires the ability to estimate—*before the survey starts*—the expected spatial limits of the system being studied, so that the overall scope of the survey region can be adequately defined as early as possible.

We would, of course, like to have 100 percent coverage of the Carson Desert and St. Catherines Island to ensure that rare items are included. But when can the expense and effort of full-coverage survey be justified?

The full-coverage approach seems most appropriate to areas (1) with a highly visible archaeological record and (2) where the topography is not too formidable. Arid or semiarid environments are ideal for both full-coverage and sample surveys because of the optimal surface visibility. When these conditions are not met, full-coverage survey can become too expensive.

For the same reason, full coverage of regions is most appropriate when the main objective is finding relatively large, dense concentrations of artifacts—that is, in places where the nature of ancient residential patterns is reasonably clear from the surface evidence. This will most frequently be true for ancient societies that built substantial houses and public buildings, had high population densities, and produced large amounts of nonperishable material culture (for example, pottery).

In such cases, a full-coverage survey can treat a region as if it were a single site. It can better examine the relationships between different settlements and settlement types because it will have a large sample of those relationships. And, perhaps most importantly, the full-coverage survey can talk about *specific relations between specific communities, rather than about types of relationships between types of communities.*

The Special Case of Cultural Resource Management

Full-coverage survey is becoming increasingly common in archaeology for several reasons. We will look at one of them here and consider yet another in Chapter 5.

As you will learn in Chapter 17, most archaeology done in the United States today is part of a field called "cultural resource management," whose archaeological surveys are conducted to clear the way for roads, pipelines, dams, and other projects so that the sites can be excavated before the bulldozers move in, or so that the project can be redirected and the sites avoided.

Two aspects of these projects are important. First, the survey area is defined by the construction project, not a research question. This can lead to some survey universes that have even odder shapes than a dog's head. A fiber optic cable survey area, for example, may be 50 meters wide and 500 kilometers long. It is often challenging, but archaeologists do try to devise research questions that can be addressed with such a sample.

Second, these areas are often surveyed in their entirety, 100 percent. The objective is not to sample, but to make sure that no significant site will be destroyed. Significant sites may be very rare, like Mission Santa Catalina. As you have seen, sample surveys are not very good at finding rare sites. If Thomas had not suspected that a Spanish mission lay on St. Catherines Island, the mission might still remain undiscovered. Instead, finding rare sites often requires a full-coverage survey.

As a result of these two factors, culture resource management surveys often have a different character than purely research-driven surveys, although, to be sure, the culture management surveys contribute enormous amounts of data that are useful to a range of research questions. At any rate, because most U.S. fieldwork is done through cultural resource management, many surveys undertaken today are full-coverage surveys.

CONCLUSION

We began this chapter with a discussion of "gumshoe survey," looking around for a good site to excavate by talking with lots of people, none of whom may be archaeologists. This is a good way to find rare or spectacular sites because those are the kinds of places that non-archaeologists will remember. Few would note, or even notice, small scatters of potsherds or stone flakes.

But archaeologists aren't just interested in the big, spectacular sites. They are interested in whole range of human settlement, in everything from big spectacular pueblos to the small scatter of a single broken pot. Sample surveys arose in the 1960s as a way not to find sites, but to adequately characterize a region's archaeology. Spectacular sites are always informative, but they are much more informative when we know something about their regional context. And sample survey provides that context.

Although a 100 percent sample is always preferable, because it alone can guarantee the discovery of rare sites, such surveys are usually too expensive, and, as we have shown here, most research questions can be addressed with a far smaller sample. In addition, even a 100 percent survey may miss sites that lie deeply buried. What archaeology needs is a way to see below ground, and, as you will see in Chapter 5, we have some ways to do precisely that.

Summary

- Archaeological sites are found in different ways, and there is no single formula. Luck and hard work are the major keys; other sites are found through systematic regional survey.

- Settlement pattern archaeology transcends the single site in order to determine the overarching relationships among the various contemporaneous sites used by societies. The regional approach precludes assuming single sites as typical of a given culture; instead, the emphasis is on variability among sites within the settlement pattern.

- In some places, archaeological remains have simply lain on stable ground surfaces rather than becoming buried by sand, silt, and gravel. We can sample such areas using one or more probability-based sampling designs to minimize bias in recovering settlement pattern data.

- Sometimes these archaeological surveys record the distribution of archaeological sites. In other cases, the concept of "site" is not used at all, particularly when archaeological artifacts are distributed across broad areas. The Carson Desert is an example of non-site archaeology.

- Experimental studies show that survey sampling does indeed work—it can accurately characterize a region's archaeology. But survey sampling is *not* good at finding those rare sites that so often play an important role in understanding a region's prehistory. These are found by gumshoe survey.

- Many factors enter into an archaeologist's understanding of just what the survey data mean. Both the survey and natural geologic processes act together to create sites. Where one or both of these are demonstrably significant factors, archaeologists should adopt the non-site approach.

- Judicious use of survey sampling can help locate a rare buried site whose existence, if not its exact location, is already known.

- Sometimes, the full-coverage technique—large-scale, 100 percent reconnaissance—is better than random sampling designs. These entail the systematic examination of contiguous blocks of terrain, surveyed at a uniform level of intensity. Full-coverage surveys are necessary when trying to ensure that no rare but significant site will be missed—for example, in surveys undertaken in advance of a construction project.

- Full-coverage survey is also useful (1) when the research question concerns complex settlement systems and seeks to explain their changes through time; (2) when a surface archaeological record is clearly visible; and (3) when addressing questions regarding specific relations between specific sites.

- Above all, remember that there is no one right way to do survey or to sample a region. The survey unit shape, the sampling fraction, and the collection policy all depend on the question the archaeologist seeks to answer, the time and resources available, the topography, and the specific character of the archaeology (for example, ephemeral surface scatters of stone flakes or deeply buried sites with no surface indications).

Additional Reading

Banning, E. B. 2002. *Archaeological Survey.* New York: Kluwer Academic/Plenum.

Drennan, Robert D. 1996. *Statistics for Archaeologists: A Commonsense Approach.* New York: Plenum Press.

Madrigal, Lorena. 1995. *Statistics for Anthropology.* Cambridge: Cambridge University Press.

Orton, Clive. 2000. *Sampling in Archaeology.* Cambridge: Cambridge University Press.

Thomas, David Hurst. 1986. *Refiguring Anthropology.* Prospect Heights, IL: Waveland Press.

Online Resources

COMPANION WEB SITE
Visit **http://anthropology.wadsworth.com** and click on the Student Companion Web Site for Thomas/Kelly *Archaeology*, 4th edition, to access a wide range of material to help you succeed in your introductory archaeology course. These include flashcards, Internet exercises, Web links, and practice quizzes.

RESEARCH ONLINE WITH INFOTRAC COLLEGE EDITION
From the Student Companion Web Site, you can access the InfoTrac College Edition database, which offers thousands of full-length articles for your research.

5

Doing Fieldwork: Remote Sensing and Geographic Information Systems

OUTLINE

David Hurst Thomas (right) and Lawrence Conyers (University of Denver) conduct a ground-penetrating radar survey on the site of a Spanish mission at San Marcos, a pueblo site in New Mexico.

Preview

GENERATIONS OF ARCHAEOLOGISTS have longed for some magical x-ray machine that would allow us to peer beneath the earth's surface without digging. Today, that dream has almost come true. Remote sensing technology comprises a battery of different geophysical methods that provide cost-effective ways of doing archaeology in a noninvasive, nondestructive manner. It's often possible to learn much about the extent and contents of a site before excavation; sometimes, these new techniques can even acquire the necessary information and obviate the need for any excavation at all.

Those same archaeologists who longed for ways to see below the earth's surface also wished to search for spatial patterns in their data quickly and reliably. They previously did so by laboriously compiling data on paper maps. Geographic information systems are a new way to compile and analyze spatial data at multiple scales of resolution—from that of a single site to an entire continent to, conceivably, the world. It allows more rapid input and analysis of locational data, and it permits entirely new perspectives on the archaeological record.

INTRODUCTION

Modern archaeology has much in common with modern medicine. It was not long ago that a slipped disk or blown-out knee—both common archaeological ailments—meant immediate and sometimes radical surgery. And surgery was often more painful than the injury itself. Although your knee joint bounced back pretty quickly after the cartilage was removed, the muscle tissues and nerves needed months to recover from the 10-inch-long incision required to access the injured area. Here was a classic case of the cure being almost worse than the disease.

Modern medical technology has changed all that. CAT scan and MRI technology today allow the physician to map afflicted areas in detail without any nasty exploratory surgery or damage to the patient. And when surgery is warranted, techniques like arthroscopy and laser microsurgery permit physicians to trim, cut, excise, and repair even gross damage with only the slightest incision. Today's noninvasive medicine minimizes tissue damage and surgical intervention.

Americanist archaeology has undergone a parallel revolution. In the good old days, archaeologists didn't have much choice but to dig in order to determine the extent of a site or to locate a buried structure. At Colonial Williamsburg, for example, the architectural historians who conducted the first excavations in the 1930s used an extraordinarily destructive method known as cross-trenching, which entails digging parallel trenches a shovel blade in width and throwing up the dirt on the unexcavated space between. The strategy was designed to disclose foundations for restoration, but the workers paid little attention to the artifacts and none whatsoever to their context. To archaeologists at mid-century, the greatest technological revolution was the advent of the backhoe as a tool of excavation.

Americanist archaeology today views its sites differently. A new conservation ethic suggests that we dig less and save more of our archaeological remains for the future. No ethical archaeologist would ever dig all of a site just because it's there. We always try to save something for future archaeologists, who will have new questions and technology that we cannot even imagine.

Augmenting this more ethical approach is an array of remote sensing techniques for doing relatively nondestructive archaeology. Using the archaeological equivalents of CAT scan and ultrasound, archaeologists can now map subsurface features in detail—without ever excavating them. And when it does become necessary to recover samples, we can execute pinpoint excavations, minimizing damage to the rest of the site.

REMOTE SENSING: DATA AT A DISTANCE

Remote sensing refers to an array of photographic and geophysical techniques that rely on some form of electromagnetic energy—it might be raw electricity, light, heat, or radio waves—to detect and measure some characteristics of an archaeological target. This greatly enhances our ability to see, quite literally, given that the human eye can detect less than 1 ten-millionth of the entire electromagnetic spectrum.

Most of these techniques were initially designed to measure geophysical features on the scale of hundreds of meters or even kilometers. Yet to be effective in archaeology, such measurements must be scaled down to the order of meters or even centimeters. As you will see, researchers have made this advance in several of these technologies.

High Altitude Imagery

The first aerial photograph was taken from a balloon suspended over Paris in 1858, and not too long afterward a few archaeologists were taking aerial photos of their sites, primarily with cameras attached to crewless balloons.

But it was World War I that opened up the possibilities of aerial photography for archaeology. Airplanes developed into a reliable technology during this war, and future British archaeologist O. G. S. Crawford (1886–1957) saw the potential in aerial photography when he analyzed aerial photographs of German military units. In fact, during the war itself, German military aviators photographed ruins in the Sinai from biplanes.

Taken with sunlight at an oblique angle, black and white photographs show shadows alongside slight undulations in the ground surface that point to shallowly buried walls not discernible on the ground. Soon after World War I, Crawford used aerial photography to locate networks of Roman settlements in Britain. And about the same time a French Jesuit priest, Père Antoine Poidebard (1878–1955), used aerial photography to find Roman-age settlements in the deserts of Syria. Since these early efforts, archaeologists have used everything from balloons and airplanes to the Space Shuttle and satellites to take aerial photographs and "sense their sites remotely."

In the western hemisphere, Charles Lindbergh (1902–1974), the famous American aviator-explorer, took some of the earliest archaeological aerial photographs. Two years after his 1927 nonstop transatlantic solo flight, Lindbergh undertook "goodwill tours" throughout Mexico, Central America, and the West Indies. Working closely with archaeologist A. V. Kidder, Lindbergh photographed important Maya archaeological ruins at Chichén Itzá (Mexico) and Tikal (Guatemala). He also did extensive photographic reconnaissance at Chaco Canyon, New Mexico. These photographic records have proven invaluable to archaeologists working in these areas today. Let's look at what they did for Chaco Canyon.

The Ancient Roads of Chaco Canyon

As mentioned in Chapter 4, Chaco was the center of a vast social and political network between AD 1050 and 1150. During this time, two distinct kinds of sites appeared in the region. Throughout the Four Corners area, numerous smaller pueblo sites dotted the landscape. But huge sites—the Great Houses such as Pueblo Bonito (pictured in Figure 4-6, page 92)—appeared in Chaco Canyon and a few other places on the Colorado Plateau. The Great Houses were centrally located amid a cluster of smaller sites, defining a "community." By AD 1100, the Great Houses had developed into large, formal ancestral Pueblo towns.

In 1970–1971, archaeologist R. Gwinn Vivian (Arizona State Museum) was mapping what he thought was a series of ancient canals in Chaco Canyon. As he began excavating, Vivian realized that the linear features were like no canals he'd ever seen. Instead of having a U-shaped cross-section, the Chaco "canal" appeared to

---

remote sensing The application of methods that employ some form of electromagnetic energy to detect and measure characteristics of an archaeological target.

be a deliberately flattened and carefully engineered *roadway*. Although some archaeologists working in Chaco had speculated about possible roads, they lacked the technology to trace these possibilities very far, and their ruminations were buried deep inside voluminous field notes, unavailable to Vivian.

Vivian described his curious find to Thomas Lyons, a geologist hired to experiment with remote sensing possibilities in Chaco Canyon. Together, Vivian and Lyons started looking at the available aerial photographs from the area. They compared one set taken in the 1960s with Lindbergh's 1930s series, which was taken before grazing was permitted at Chaco.

The more they looked, the more they saw unmistakable traces of a prehistoric road network. They commissioned new flights, and road segments were field-checked against the aerial photographs. By 1973, Gwinn and Lyons had identified more than 300 kilometers of prehistoric roads (diagrammed in Figure 5-1). Amazingly, Lindbergh's photographs actually showed the famous Chacoan roads. But nobody recognized them as such until 1971, when archaeologists had a clue of

what to look for (actually, Navajos living in Chaco Canyon had known about portions of the roads more than a century ago, although they, too, were unaware of their complete extent).

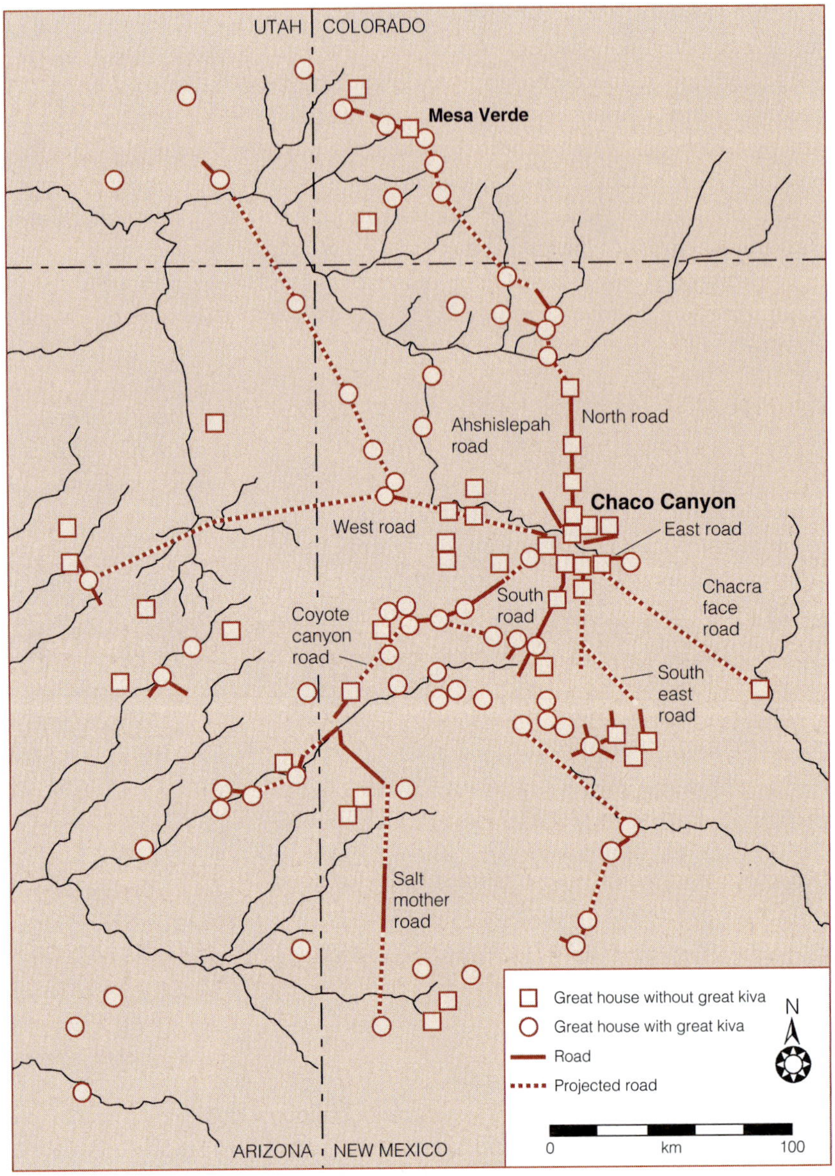

Figure 5-1 Schematic diagram of Chaco road system as it may have appeared by AD 1050.

thermal infrared multispectral scanner (TIMS) A remote sensing technique that uses equipment mounted in aircraft or satellite to measure infrared thermal radiation given off by the ground. Sensitive to differences as little as 0.1° centigrade, it can locate subsurface structures by tracking how they affect surface thermal radiation.

Aerial photography today is far more advanced than the simple black and white photographs obtained by hanging off the side of a biplane. Early photographic techniques were restricted to the visible portion of the electromagnetic spectrum, and cloud cover often hampered them. A variety of new photographic techniques allows film to capture portions of the electromagnetic spectrum that the naked eye cannot see and that are unaffected by cloud cover.

One technique that NASA used at Chaco in the 1980s was thermal infrared multispectral scanning, or **TIMS**.

Looking Closer
Remote Sensing Imagery: Other Ways of Seeing

These are just a few of the remote sensing approaches that are available to archaeology today.

Aerial Photography

These are black and white or color photographs taken from various elevations; the lower the elevation, the greater the resolution. Aerial photography can show features that are too indistinct or too large to discern from ground level. Photos taken over agricultural fields at different seasons are especially useful; plants growing over buried walls are browner because they are less vigorous due to the presence of buried stone or adobe walls. Likewise, buried trenches or houses contain looser, organic sediment and promote plant growth; these appear on the surface as greener plants. Taken at the right time of the year, aerial photos show buried walls and features as browner or greener circles, lines, and rectangles. Its drawback: It is limited to the visible light spectrum and is hampered by cloud cover or haze.

Color Infrared Film (CIR)

CIR detects wavelengths at and beyond the red end of the light spectrum. In this way, it can detect heat (and was used at night in World War II to locate camouflaged tanks and artillery that retained more daytime heat than did the surrounding land). CIR can record differences in vegetation, because plant cover affects the heat reflected from the ground; if differences in plant cover suggest buried features as

in standard aerial photography, then it can detect those buried features. But like aerial photography, CIR also needs light and cloudless skies.

Synthetic Aperture Radar (SAR)

SAR uses radar beams to locate buried features, working on the principle that hard buried surfaces reflect more energy than do softer surfaces, which absorb the energy. SAR works well when searching for linear and geometric features and when the background is dry, porous soils. In 1982, radar aboard the Space Shuttle penetrated the Saharan sands, revealing the presence of previously undiscovered ancient watercourses, along which ancient towns lie. Using airborne radar in Costa Rica (along with other methods), Payson Sheets found prehistoric footpaths, deeply buried by ash.

Landsat Multi-Spectral Scanner (MSS)

Used in the late 1970s, MSS images were taken from Landsat satellites and used the infrared spectrum (like TIMS) to construct false-color images that track infrared radiation. However, the resolution was only about 80 meters.

SPOT

SPOT is a French-based satellite imagery system that can simultaneously record one or more bands of the electromagnetic spectrum. Some of its images have a resolution of only 2.5 meters and can be produced as three-dimensional images; it is unaffected by cloud cover and shadows.

TIMS measures infrared thermal radiation given off by the ground; it is sensitive to differences as little as 0.1° centigrade. Although we've had the ability to make infrared photographs for some time—the Landsat Satellite was doing it in the 1970s—TIMS is an advance because of the quality of the photographs.

All photographs consist of pixels, and an instrument cannot record anything smaller than the size of a par-

ticular technique's pixel. In earlier satellite imagery (for example, Landsat photos) the pixels were 30 meters on a side, and so these techniques could not record anything smaller than about 900 square meters. Such photos were of limited use to archaeology. The resolution of TIMS images still depends on the altitude at which the photos are taken. This can vary since the TIMS instrument is flown in NASA aircraft (and will eventually be placed in satellites). At 3000 meters (10,000 feet), for example, the photos have a resolution of about 8 meters, but some projects have attained resolutions as small as 1–2 meters. These photographs can be quite useful to archaeology, and they are unaffected by cloud cover.

TIMS images are taken with a very complex kind of camera, and the data—the sensed infrared radiation—are transformed via a computer program into so-called "false-color" images. False-color images map the ground in terms of infrared radiation—rendering terrain in garish colors, such as red, blue, and purple. Because the Chacoan roads are more compacted than the surrounding soil (even if their compacted surface is buried), they should reflect more radiation than the surrounding sand.

And indeed they do. In false-color images, the roads appear as clear, tan lines against a backdrop of red sand. The Chaco experiment proved that TIMS can detect features such as buried road systems, even if they are invisible to an archaeologist standing on top of them.

Today, analysis of aerial and high-altitude photographs has revealed possibly as much as *600 kilometers* of ancient roadways around Chaco Canyon. These roads are only 5 to 10 centimeters deep and yet sometimes 7 to 10 meters wide. Often they turn suddenly in doglegs and are occasionally edged by low rock berms. Sometimes they are littered with potsherds. Sometimes they are cut into the earth, and sometimes they were made by clearing away the surface rock and vegetation.

The longest and best-defined roads, probably constructed between AD 1075 and 1140, extend some 50 kilometers outward from Chaco Canyon. Sometimes the roads are just short segments, and it is unclear if they were intended to be segments, if they were unfinished, or if portions of the road have disappeared through erosion. In places, the Chacoans constructed causeways, and elsewhere they cut stairways into sheer cliffs. The generally straight bearings suggest that the Ancestral Pueblo laid out the roads prior to construction, although archaeologists are unsure exactly how they did it.

Why did the Chaco people build these roads across the desert? This elaborate road system covered more than 250,000 square kilometers, and yet the Ancestral Pueblo had no wheeled vehicles or even beasts of burden. Why are the roads so wide and so straight? What were they used for?

Although we don't have answers to these questions yet (but we'll return to them below), it is clear that archaeologists had unknowingly walked over the remains of the Chaco road system for decades. Their discovery had to come from data that were sensed remotely. Today, a battery of different, highly sophisticated photographic techniques helps archaeologists find buried remains (see "Looking Closer: Remote Sensing Imagery: Other Ways of Seeing"). Other techniques, used on the ground rather than in airplanes or satellites, also help archaeologists see below the ground.

HOW TO FIND A LOST SPANISH MISSION (PART II)

You'll remember from Chapter 4 that we used transect survey and power auger testing to narrow down the location of Mission Santa Catalina to a 1-hectare (2.6-acre) area on St. Catherines Island, Georgia. One of the survey units in this area, Quad IV, was an undistinguished piece of real estate covered by scrub palmetto and live oak forest. The only evidence of human occupation was a little-used field road for island research vehicles. Although we could see aboriginal shell midden scatters here and there, Quad IV betrayed absolutely no surface clues as to what lay below.

At this point, we shifted our field strategy from preliminary subsurface testing to noninvasive, nondestructive remote sensing. Choosing the right method depends on what you expect to find. What, exactly, were we looking for? For more than a century, Santa Catalina had been the northernmost Spanish outpost on the eastern seaboard, and this historical fact implied considerable size and permanence. The seventeenth-century mission must have had a fortified church; some buildings to house soldiers and priests; plus enough granaries, storehouses, and dwellings for hundreds of Guale Indian neophytes.

We reasoned that the mission buildings were built by a wattle-and-daub technique (Figure 5-2). Freshly cut timbers were probably set vertically along the walls and reinforced with cane woven horizontally between the uprights. This sturdy wattlework was then plastered (daubed) with a mixture of marsh mud, sand, and plant fibers (probably Spanish moss). Roofs were thatched with palmetto.

So constructed, wattle-and-daub buildings are biodegradable. If the roof does not burn, the roof's thatch will eventually rot and blow away. And once directly exposed to the weather, mud and twig walls will simply

Figure 5-2 Artist's reconstruction of the wattle-and-daub technique used to build Mission Santa Catalina. The upright wattlework is being daubed (plastered) with a mixture of marsh mud and organic fibers.

wash away. Archaeologists seeking such a dissolved mission would soon be out of business.

But thatched roofs often burn, and if that happened at Santa Catalina, the heat would have fired and hardened the daub walls, like a pot baking in a kiln. Fired daub, nearly as indestructible as the ubiquitous potsherd, thus became a key in our search for the mission.

So, how do you find chunks of burned mud buried beneath a foot of sand without excavating thousands of square meters?

The Proton Magnetometer

It turns out that the marsh mud used in daub plaster contains microscopic iron particles. Normally, these are randomly oriented to all points of the compass. But when intensely heated, the particles orient toward magnetic north—like a million tiny compass needles. To pinpoint these magnetically anomalous orientations, we relied upon a **proton precession magnetometer**. The theory behind this device is complicated, but the principle is simple: Magnetometers measure the strength of

magnetism between the earth's magnetic core and a sensor controlled by the archaeologist. If hundreds of these readings are taken across a systematic grid, a computer plotter can generate a magnetic contour map reflecting both the shape and the intensity of magnetic anomalies beneath the ground surface.

Many subsurface anomalies are archaeologically irrelevant magnetic "noise"—interference from underlying rocks, AC power lines, or hidden iron debris. The earth's magnetic field fluctuates so wildly on some days that the readings are meaningless, and electrical storms can hopelessly scramble magnetometer readings. Even minor interference, such as the operator's wristwatch or eyeglasses, can drive a magnetometer crazy.

But when everything works just right, the magnetometer provides the equivalent of a CAT scan, telling archaeologists what is going on beneath the earth's surface. Many archaeological features have characteristic magnetic signatures—telltale clues that hint at the size, shape, depth, and composition of the archaeological objects hidden far below. Shallow graves, for instance, have a magnetic profile vastly different from, say, a buried fire pit or a wattle-and-daub wall.

We worked with Ervan Garrison (now with University of Georgia) and a magnetometer team from Texas A&M University (Figure 5-3). As they were packing up their field equipment to work up the data in their lab, they shared a couple of hunches, based strictly on their raw magnetometer readings: "If we were y'all, we'd dig in three places: here, over yonder, and especially right here." We took their advice, exploring each of the three magnetic anomalies in the few days remaining in our May field season. One anomaly—"especially right here"—turned out to be a large iron barrel ring. Excavating further, we came upon another ring, and more below that. At about 3 meters down, we hit the water table. Digging underwater, we encountered a well-preserved oak well casing.

Archaeologists love wells because, like privies, they can be magnificent artifact traps. After removing the bones of an unfortunate fawn (which had long ago drowned), we found an array of distinctive Hispanic and Guale Indian potsherds and a metal dinner plate

proton precession magnetometer A remote sensing technique that measures the strength of magnetism between the earth's magnetic core and a sensor controlled by the archaeologist. Magnetic anomalies can indicate the presence of buried walls or features.

Figure 5-3 Ervan Garrison and Deborah Mayer O'Brien looking for Mission Santa Catalina (on St. Catherines Island, Georgia) using a proton magnetometer. She is holding the sensor, and he is recording magnetometer readings.

dropped (or tossed) into the well. All artifacts were typical of the sixteenth and seventeenth centuries. We had indeed found Mission Santa Catalina, and we pressed on to see what else the magnetometer might have turned up.

Our second magnetic anomaly—the one "here"— was a small mound. We thought at first that it might be a grave or tomb. But after removing the overburden, we came across a burned daub wall that, as it fell, had crushed dozens of Spanish and Guale domestic artifacts: imported tin-enameled glazed cups, painted ceramic dishes, a kitchen knife, and at least two enormous pots for cooking or storage. Charred deer and chicken bones littered the floor, and dozens of tiny corncobs lay scattered about. This time, the magnetometer had led us to the kitchen (in Spanish, *cocina*) used by seventeenth-century Franciscan friars at Santa Catalina.

Finally, we began digging the "over yonder" anomaly, which proved to be a linear daub concentration more than 12 meters long—obviously the downed wall of yet another, much larger mission building. Here excava-

tions turned up none of the everyday implements and debris so common in the scorched *cocina*. Instead, we found human graves.

The search was over. We had discovered the church, the paramount house of worship at Santa Catalina de Guale. Our magnetometer survey had given us trustworthy directions to the buried daub walls and iron barrel hoops. Even without computer enhancement, the magnetometer had taken us to the very heart of Mission Santa Catalina.

Since the discovery of Santa Catalina, we have spent a decade excavating the church ruins. The lateral church walls were constructed of wattle and daub that, when encountered archaeologically, consisted of a densely packed linear rubble scatter; this is what the magnetometer "saw" in Quad IV. Beneath the nave and sanctuary of the church, we discovered the cemetery, where the Franciscans had interred 400 to 450 Christianized Guale Indians.

Soil Resistivity

Proton magnetometry was just one of the techniques used to locate and define Santa Catalina de Guale. **Soil resistivity survey** monitors the electrical resistance of soils in a restricted volume near the surface of an archaeological site. Perhaps partially because of its relatively low cost, soil resistivity survey has become a popular technique of geophysical prospecting over the past four decades.

The degree of soil resistivity depends on several factors, the most important of which is usually the amount of water retained in the soil—the less water, the greater the resistance to electrical currents. Compaction such as occurs in house floors, walls, paths, and roads tends to reduce pore sizes and hence the potential to retain water; this registers as high resistance. In effect, when electricity is sent through the soil, buried features can often be detected and defined by their differential resis-

soil resistivity survey A remote sensing technique that monitors the electrical resistance of soils in a restricted volume near the surface of an archaeological site; buried walls or features can be detected by changes in the amount of resistance registered by the resistivity meter.

tance to electrical charge (caused by their differential retention of groundwater).

The aggregation of fill in pits, ditches, and middens will also alter resistivity. Foundations or walls, particularly those in historic-period sites, generally have *greater* resistivity than surrounding soil, whereas the generation of humus by occupation activity increases the ion content of the soil, *reducing* resistivity.

After the initial discovery of the mission and a pilot resistivity survey, Mark Williams and the late Gary Shapiro returned to St. Catherines Island to conduct a more comprehensive study.

We measured soil resistance by setting four probes in line at 1-meter intervals, each probe inserted to a depth of 20 centimeters. We passed an electrical current between the probes and recorded the electrical conductivity between the two center probes.

We took readings on east-west grid lines at 1-meter intervals. The line was then advanced a meter north or south, and another set of readings were taken. This procedure resulted in a gridded array of resistance values, recorded in the field on graph paper and eventually transferred to a computer. We also charted the locations of trees, backdirt (the piles of dirt created by excavation), roads, and other features that might influence resistance.

We conducted one of the preliminary resistivity surveys in a 15 × 15 meter area that straddled a test excavation of Structure 2 at Santa Catalina, initially located by the proton magnetometer survey. From our test excavations, we suspected that this building was probably the kitchen, but we had no idea of the building's configuration. Figure 5-4 shows the resistivity diagram of this area, clearly identifying the margins of the unexcavated building. Later, excavations confirmed the accuracy of the soil resistivity diagram.

In some circumstances, archaeologists opt to use conductivity meters, which measure the inverse of what a resistivity meter measures—that is, how well sediment *conducts* electricity. A conductivity instrument, which looks like a 1- to 3-meter-long carpenter's level, is easy to use. The archeologist simply lays it on the ground along a grid line, pushes a button, and records the reading. Conductivity meters are useful when soil is completely dry, because resistivity meters require wet, but not saturated, soils. However, conductivity meters are expensive (about $17,000) and the data they generate are not as easily manipulated and analyzed as are resistivity data.

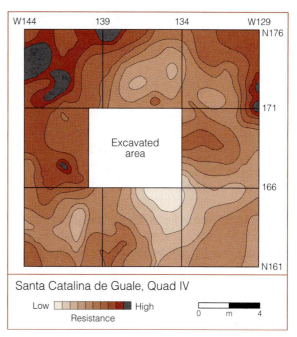

Figure 5-4 Soil resistivity contour map from Mission Santa Catalina (Georgia). The top of this map is oriented toward magnetic north; the buried kitchen building appears as a large square outline below right center, oriented at 45° off north. *Courtesy American Museum of Natural History.*

Ground-Penetrating Radar

Yet another method of geophysical prospecting is **ground-penetrating radar** (GPR). Although this method tends to be expensive, its cost is offset to some degree by its speed. But neither operating the radar equipment nor interpreting the results is simple, and the assistance of trained specialists is required.

GPR was first developed in 1910, but a significant peak in relevant articles coincided with the *Apollo 17* lunar sounding experiment in the early 1970s. Today, environmental engineering firms commonly employ GPR techniques to find buried rock or deep swamp deposits, or to search for caverns.

In GPR, radar pulses directed into the ground reflect back to the surface when they strike targets or interfaces within the ground (such as a change in the density of dirt, groundwater, buried objects, voids, or an interface

ground-penetrating radar A remote sensing technique in which radar pulses directed into the ground reflect back to the surface when they strike features or interfaces within the ground, showing the presence and depth of possible buried features.

between soil and rock). As these pulses are reflected, their speed to the target and the nature of their return are measured. The signal's reflection provides information about the depth and three-dimensional shape of buried objects.

With transducers (a device that converts electrical energy to electromagnetic waves) of various dimensions, a researcher applying GPR can direct the greatest degree of resolution to the depth of specific interest. A pulsating electric current is passed through an antenna, inducing electromagnetic waves that radiate toward the target and return in a fraction of a microsecond to be recorded. The dimensions of the transducer influence the depth and detail that are desired in any specific archaeological application. As the antenna is dragged across the ground surface, a continuous profile of subsurface electromagnetic conditions is printed on a graphic recorder. The location and depth of subsurface targets can be inferred from, and tested against, this graphic record.

Groundwater can pose a problem in GPR studies, because it changes the relative permeability of most sediments. Soils are good reflectors when they are associated with steep changes in water content, as occurs in coarse materials. Unsorted sediments, such as glacial till, will have a broad and varying capillary zone, and thus no clear reflection. GPR is generally ineffective over saltwater, in penetrating some clays, and at depths of more than about 30 meters below the surface. The maximum depth of penetration depends on the conductivity of the overlying deposit.

GPR works best when the soil resistivity is high, as in well-drained soils and those with low clay content. Subsurface wells, foundations, cellars, voids, cavities, and well-defined compacted zones, such as house floors, can provide clear radar echoes.

Why did we begin using GPR at Santa Catalina? Historical documents suggested that the Spanish had fortified the mission as a precaution against British attack, perhaps by building a stockade and moat complex to protect the buildings immediately adjacent to the central plaza. Yet, after 3 years of using magnetometer and resistivity surveys and limited test excavations, we had failed to locate any trace of defensive fortifications, such as palisades, bastions, or moats encircling the central mission zone. Given that these features might not have burned and because they could be as saturated with water as the surrounding sediment, they might have eluded the magnetometer and resistivity instruments. However, these features might have differed from the

background sediment in terms of their compaction, and that suggested to us that GPR might help locate them.

We used the existing grid system, having cleared brush and palmetto from the transect lines before our survey. Initially, a number of systematic north-south transects were run at 20-meter intervals, followed by a series of east-west transects. Obvious anomalies were hand-plotted on the grayscale computer output, and additional transects were run across these target areas. We located significant anomalies on the ground by means of pin flags. We then ran a third set of transects at a 45° angle, to intercept buried anomalies at a different angle.

So, what happened? Directed by the radar profiles, test excavations led directly to the discovery of the palisade and bastion complex encircling the central buildings and plaza at Santa Catalina. Although this defensive network could surely have been located by extensive test trenching, the radar approach proved to be considerably more cost-effective and less destructive than conventional archaeological exploration.

CERÉN: THE NEW WORLD POMPEII?

Remote sensing studies work best when we can calibrate instrumentation and imagery to local conditions and when field verification is possible. Such a situation existed at the site of Cerén, located in the Zapotitán Valley of El Salvador.

A bulldozer operator discovered the Cerén site in 1976 as he attempted to level a platform on which to build some grain storage silos. When he noticed that his bulldozer blade had uncovered the corner of a deeply buried building, the curious workman stepped down and looked around. When he found some old-looking pottery buried in the building, he stopped work and notified the National Museum in San Salvador. Unfortunately, when a representative of the museum arrived 3 days later, he dismissed the find as very recent construction and gave the heavy equipment operator his blessing to continue working. As an unfortunate result, several other ancient buildings were bulldozed.

Two years later, when Payson Sheets and his students from the University of Colorado arrived to conduct a survey of the Zapotitán Valley, townspeople told them of the unusual find and showed them where some of it remained. Sheets saw some adobe columns protruding from the disturbed area and expected to find bits of

© Payson Sheets

Figure 5-5 Adobe columns and flooring of Structure 1 at the Cerén site (El Salvador). This Maya house was buried instantaneously in about AD 590 by nearly 5 meters of volcanic ash from the nearby Loma Caldera. When archaeologist Payson Sheets and his crew excavated this house, they found all artifacts left in place. Even the thatched roof had been preserved.

plastic and newspaper eroding out of the ruined building. Even when he found some Maya polychrome pottery (that Sheets knew dated to about AD 500–800), he too thought that the building was modern—the thatch roof was almost perfectly preserved, even though it was buried beneath nearly 5 meters of volcanic ash (Figure 5-5).

But after a few hours of excavation, Sheets found lots of ancient Maya artifacts—without any sign of historic-period material. Sheets worried: What if he announced these well-preserved buildings were prehistoric and they turned out to be recent? The whole issue turned, of course, on dating. Sheets collected some of the buried roof thatch for radiocarbon analysis (we'll discuss dating methods in Chapter 8). When the results of the tests came back, he no longer worried about embarrassing himself—all the thatch samples (and therefore the buried houses as well) were 1400 years old.

Large volcanoes and cinder cones, many of which are active, surround the Zapotitán Valley. The Cerén site, as

it came to be known, was buried in about AD 590 by several meters of volcanic ash from the nearby Loma Caldera. Because the ash had cooled off considerably by the time it hit, nearly all the ancient agricultural features and cultural artifacts were miraculously preserved—crops still in the field, orchards, a central public plaza surrounded by adobe houses with artifacts left exactly as buried—even ancient Maya farmers' footprints!

But the ash that so preserved Cerén also completely obscured it. How could Sheets map a village buried beneath 5 meters of volcanic debris?

Sheets and his colleagues turned to GPR as a way to see what lay below the surface. The depositional conditions at Cerén were almost ideal for remote sensing. The overlying volcanic ash contained relatively little clay and there was only minimal soil formation. One of the radar antennas, using 300 MHz frequency radar energy, could penetrate 5 meters deep, and it could detect features as small as 45–50 centimeters (about

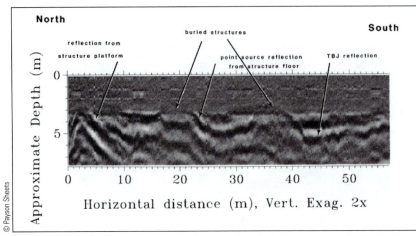

© Payson Sheets

Figure 5-6 Ground-penetrating radar profile across three buried structures at the Cerén site.

18–20 inches). The resulting readout is shown in Figure 5-6.

But radar antennas are unwieldy and difficult to pull over rocky terrain. And to make matters worse, much of the ground surface at Cerén was a functioning maize field. Sheets found an innovative solution that used local technology: They loaded their GPR system into the back of an oxcart. Although it was an incongruous sight—a wooden cart laden with hundreds of pounds of high-tech radar equipment, pulled by plodding oxen—it worked well.

Sheets mapped and reconstructed the entire ancient landscape at Cerén from the GPR results and then verified the reconstruction with test pits and broad excavations. By carefully working out the various radar signatures from the excavated houses, Sheets was able to map these unexcavated pre-Columbian houses precisely using remote sensing and associated computer modeling techniques. The population density of the buried zone

was surprisingly high. On the day it was buried, Cerén was a prosperous farming village with closely packed domestic, civic, and religious buildings constructed on elevated platforms, with all intervening space between them taken up by agricultural crops (Figure 5-7).

Because of its extraordinary Pompeii-like preservation, the Cerén site is one of the most important places in Central America for studying ancient land-use practices. And GPR mapping proved to be a cost-effective method for discovering buried houses—some of which were excavated; the rest preserved for the future.

THE POTENTIAL AND LIMITATIONS OF NONINVASIVE ARCHAEOLOGY

It is clear from these examples that remote sensing can help archaeology in very significant ways. One drawback has been that remote sensing techniques are expensive, but the cost has been going down as the machinery becomes more widely available. And remote sensing can pay for itself, given that the alternative—hand excavation—is also costly. By targeting excavation efforts, remote sensing could actually reduce a project's cost.

But remote sensing cannot work everywhere—at least not yet. The different geophysical devices work best under certain conditions. In places where there is a lot of background noise—such as a high groundwater table, lots of background rock, or natural subsurface features—it is often difficult to pick out which anomalies in the magnetometer, resistivity, or GPR readings are worth

© Payson Sheets

Figure 5-7 Artist's reconstruction of the buried structures at the Cerén site. The domicile (Structure 1) appears in the center, with the workshop on the right, and the storehouse on the left.

investigating. And high-altitude imagery has to be ground-truthed (that is, verified with physical observation) to determine what the images are recording. But with increasing refinements to the technology, remote sensing has become an indispensable excavation tool.

For years, archaeologists considered only artifacts that they could hold in their hands or features that they could see with their eyes as sources of data. Remote sensing changes that, provided that we can construct the requisite linkages between the larger things that archaeologists find—walls, structures, and features—and the way that they are remotely perceived by the sensors of geophysical machinery and remote imagery.

GEOGRAPHIC INFORMATION SYSTEMS

Archaeological data are inherently spatial, and archaeologists map things all the time. Maps show where things are, and, more importantly, how they relate to each other. Archaeologists use maps to plot the results of remote sensing, such as artifact distributions within a site and distributions of sites across a region, state, or even a continent.

But in their traditional form, maps are difficult to update with new information, and the resulting distributions are often unwieldy to analyze.

This all changed in the late 1980s with the advent of **geographic information systems (GIS),** computer programs designed to store, retrieve, analyze, and display cartographic data. GIS lets you view information—any geographically related information—visually. The most common programs in use today are ArcView and ArcInfo.

Every GIS consists of three primary components: a powerful computer graphics program used to draw a map, one or more external databases that are linked to the objects shown on the map, and a set of analytical tools that can graphically interpret or statistically analyze the stored data. Most U.S. states are in the process of putting all their site records into a GIS. Clearly, GIS is a basic skill that any student contemplating a career in archaeology should learn.

In true GIS format, the earth's various features are not depicted visually—as they would be on standard two-dimensional maps—but as digital information. Virtually every standard USGS topographic map is now available digitally (some high-end GPS units contain

them already). Data stored digitally, of course, can be manipulated and displayed in numerous ways.

In GIS, a database is composed of several themes, or layers. Envision a base topographic map—that's one theme. Now envision laying a clear sheet of Mylar plastic over that map (this is how we used to do it!). You will plot on the Mylar sheet all the archaeological sites you just found in a survey. This layer is another theme. Over the first Mylar sheet, we will lay another on which we will draw in all the water sources; this is a third theme. On yet another sheet, we will draw the distribution of different vegetation communities. On another, we will plot the results of high-altitude imagery. On still another, the region's different soils…you get the picture.

Mapping like this with physical sheets of paper or Mylar is unwieldy, and the resulting patterns are difficult to analyze statistically. However, by inputting all these different data digitally into a single **georeferenced** database, we can call up one or more of the layers and analyze the distributions. "Georeferenced" means that all the data are input using a common mapping reference, for example, the UTM grid system mentioned in Chapter 4. Because the data are digital, we can do spatial analyses in minutes that previously might have taken weeks or longer. Each of the data points are linked to a database, which can include complete information on that point. A site record, for example, might contain information on a site's artifacts—how many projectile points or potsherds were found there—plus other data such as its size, its slope, and the kind of architecture that was present.

We can ask myriad questions of this database. For example, we might ask, "How far away from water sources are pueblo sites found?" With a GIS database we can quickly *buffer* springs and streams at some standard distance, say 1-kilometer intervals. Think of this as drawing concentric circles around the springs with radii of 1 kilometer, 2 kilometers, 3 kilometers, and so on. Likewise, we would trace out land areas within 1, 2, and 3 kilometers from rivers and streams. We could then ask the program to tell us how many pueblo sites versus other kinds of sites are in the various buffers. We

geographic information system (GIS) A computer program for storing, retrieving, analyzing, and displaying cartographic data.

georeferenced Data that are input to a GIS database using a common mapping reference—for example, the UTM grid—so that all data can be spatially analyzed.

Archaeological Ethics
Remote Sensing the Sacred

Archaeologists today consistently face ethical dilemmas. A major one is that whereas the study of an object can give us knowledge—which most consider a good thing—the very act of studying it can be offensive to living peoples. Here is one example and how remote sensing helped to solve the dilemma.

Many Plains Indians groups once used, and continue to use, medicine bundles to store sacred objects important for various curing rituals. Individually owned and carefully guarded, these sacred bundles often have a definite set of rules, songs, and rituals associated with them. Most medicine bundles contain a smoking pipe and tobacco; they may also contain a wide variety of sacred items including animal bones and skin, unusually shaped rocks, bunches of sweetgrass, beads, bells, and so forth. In the hands of someone properly trained, medicine bundles seem capable of effecting some remarkable cures.

Tribal tradition and museums have on occasion clashed over the ownership of these culturally charged sacred objects. In recent years, some tribal elders have asked museums to return certain key bundles considered to be critical for the modern performance of Native American religion. Some museums have agreed to do this; others have refused.

Such interactions will always require sensitivity from all parties involved, but remote sensing technology has recently provided an intriguing solution to the issues of sacredness versus scholarship. Here, high-tech methods have offered a resolution satisfactory to all parties concerned.

In 1987, a Pawnee tribal member donated a family-owned medicine bundle to the Kansas State Historical Society with the request that it be cared for, studied, and exhibited. This particular bundle held great cultural significance for Pawnee people because, during a nineteenth-century battle at Massacre Canyon, a young Pawnee girl was sent out of the family lodge by her father with this sacred bundle tied to her back. It has remained in family hands ever since—until it was donated to the historical society.

Following standard curatorial procedures, the museum staff cleaned and conserved the bundle. The curator in charge was anxious to learn as much as possible about this well-documented and highly significant bundle. Although the donating Pawnee owner granted permission for it to be opened for study, other Indian people objected.

Recognizing the sensitivity of the situation (and also the likelihood that the bundle had not been opened within the last century), the museum staff proposed an alternative. Rather than opening it to inventory and identify the contents, why not use remote sensing techniques instead?

Everyone involved agreed and, employing a specialized technique known as computerized axial tomography, personnel of the Kansas State Historical Society x-rayed and precisely identified the bundle's contents: a woven grass mat, bundles of sticks or reeds, leather pouches, a raccoon penile bone, eight bird skulls with associated wing and leg bones, a large talon, 11 metal bells, a possible human scalp, and some glass beads. The bird bones could even be identified to species (merlin, Swainson's hawk, and harrier hawk).

This innovative and sensitive use of noninvasive remote sensing technology fostered cooperation and goodwill, balancing the sometimes-conflicting interests of Native American and scientific communities. At the request of the Pawnee donor, the bundle is currently on display at the Pawnee Indian Village Museum near Republic, Kansas.

And, significantly, the bundle has yet to be opened.

could also see if sites are more frequently associated with a particular kind of vegetation community or soil types—in fact, with any data set that has a spatial dimension to it.

In this fashion, GIS allows archaeologists to do many things that otherwise might be too time-consuming to tackle. GIS, for instance, can create a viewshed that shows what portion of a landscape is visible from a particular site. With such a capability, we could test the proposition that a site on a ridge top is a hunting stand or lookout. Obviously, the view from a hunting stand should encompass land where we would expect to find grazing animals or migrating herds of game.

The Predictive Capacity of GIS: The Aberdeen Proving Ground

GIS databases do require an *enormous* amount of time to construct. Although many archaeologists record their data digitally today and can download them to a GIS database, decades worth of archaeological data remain to be manually input. But the eventual time savings can be significant, because a GIS database can be used to predict site locations. This can be extremely cost-effective because it can help target surveys just as remote sensing techniques can help target excavations; it can also help prevent the needless destruction of archaeological sites. Konnie Wescott and James Kuiper (Argonne National Laboratory) developed such a predictive model for the Aberdeen Proving Ground in Maryland.

The Aberdeen Proving Ground consists of 39,000 acres of land on the north end of Chesapeake Bay. Only 1 percent of the entire area has seen a traditional archaeological survey. This area is especially difficult to survey, because much of it is marsh and the sites are mostly ephemeral shell middens and scatters of ceramics and stone flakes. And a traditional survey could be dangerous, because unexploded ordnance litters the military proving grounds. Still, the Army wished to develop a plan that would help them take cultural resources—archaeological sites—into account as the proving ground developed. A predictive model would help the Army know where they were likely to encounter sites and allow them to plan construction in areas of low expected site densities.

Wescott and Kuiper developed a predictive model by using characteristics of 572 archaeological sites *outside* the proving ground along the shores of Chesapeake Bay—sites that had been found by traditional archaeological surveys. They recorded many different variables that described the site locations—distance to water, topography, slope, soil type, and elevation.

A good predictive model will use the fewest number of variables possible so that noise is eliminated from the predictions. Wescott and Kuiper analyzed the data on the 572 sites to discover which variables were the best predictors of site locations. They found that a combination of type of nearest water (for example, bay shoreline, river shoreline, freshwater creek), elevation, topographic setting (for example, floodplain, hill slope, interior flat), and distance to water were sufficient to predict most of the known site locations.

They then went about creating a predictive model for the proving ground by creating several layers for the key variables. One layer created 1000-foot buffers around water of different types. Another drew buffers (at 100, 500, and 1000 feet) around water sources. A third blocked out the different kinds of topography. A fourth layer made use of a digital elevation model (DEM—a three-dimensional virtual model of a landscape) to block out elevations in 10-foot intervals. The layers are shown in Figure 5-8.

So far, all they had were some pretty maps (and they look even better in color). What they really needed, however, was a map that shows where sites might be found and where they probably will not be found. Wescott and Kuiper used their four identified best predictors (type of water, elevation, topography, and distance to water) in order to define areas in the proving ground of high, medium, and low potential to contain sites. For example, they found that most shell midden sites (those composed mostly of discarded shells from meals) were found within 500 feet of fresh or brackish water; below 20 feet in elevation; and on terraces, bluffs, floodplains, or flats. By digitally overlaying the layers, the GIS developed a new map showing areas where all these criteria were met. This map is shown at the bottom of Figure 5-8, with known site locations plotted. Although the sample of known sites is limited, the predictive model seemed to work fairly well, especially for shell midden sites. With this map in hand, the Army can locate their new facilities on land with the least potential for disturbing archaeological sites.

Landscape Archaeology

GIS is a tool that opens up new ways to analyze spatial data. Partly because of this new ability, archaeology developed a new approach called **landscape archaeology**. Although the word "landscape" has a colloquial meaning, Carole Crumley (University of North Carolina) defines landscape as "the material manifestation of the relation between humans and their environments." Landscape archaeology allows us to return to the difference between processual and postprocessual paradigms and see how we can think about a landscape in different but productive ways.

In a sense, landscape archaeology has been around since the 1940s, when Gordon Willey (1913–2002) conducted the first archaeological settlement pattern study in Peru's Virú Valley. In this regard, landscape archaeology is similar to the settlement pattern archaeology we discussed in Chapter 4, but it adds a concern with how people use and modify their environment. Landscapes from the perspective of the processual paradigm are made of places with different economic potential. Fertile bottomlands are good places to grow maize; the uplands are places to gather nuts; the mountains to the east contain trees for houses, but good clay for pots is found to the west; turquoise for trade is found at the base of a far-off butte. The Carson Desert study is an example of a processual perspective on a landscape, because it focused on the economic use of a region's resources.

But postprocessualism adds to this economic vision of a landscape the social and symbolic meanings of land as well. Places on the landscape are often laden with meaning, sometimes linked to a culture's origin myths. A mountain may be sacred because it is where a mythical hero destroyed monsters in "the time before people." Directions may be associated with particular sacred beings, supernatural powers, or human emotions. The site of the World Trade Center is now a symbolically powerful part of the American landscape; so is Dealey Plaza in Dallas, where President Kennedy was assassinated.

GIS is not limited to one of these perspectives on the landscape. It fact, the following examples show how it can be a very powerful tool for both.

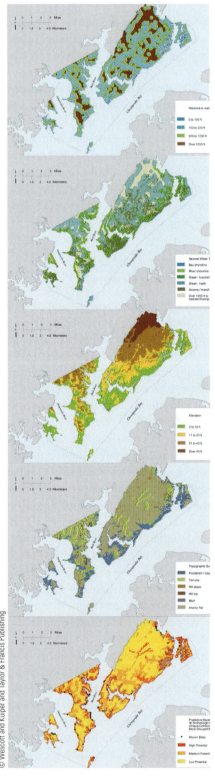

© Wescott and Kuiper and Taylor & Francis Publishing

Figure 5-8 Wescott and Kuiper's GIS maps showing distribution of water type, elevation, topographic setting, and distance to water. The bottom map shows the distribution of known sites and areas of predicted high and low site potential.

landscape archaeology   The study of ancient human modification of the environment.

Modeling an Economic Landscape: The Carson Desert Revisited

Following up on Kelly's Carson Desert research discussed in Chapter 4, David Zeanah (California State University, Sacramento) was interested in devising even better models for predicting the archaeology of the Carson Desert and Stillwater Mountains, and he turned to GIS models to do so. Specifically, Zeanah used ethnographic data to map out the territory of one Northern Paiute group, the Toedökadö, as it existed in the late nineteenth century. Their territory encompassed the Carson Desert, Stillwater Mountains, and some lands beyond. Zeanah divided the Toedökadö territory into 1-kilometer squares using the UTM system and then georeferenced this block of grid squares to the digitized topographic maps for the region.

Zeanah then developed a landscape model in which he defined 41 vegetation communities using modern range management data. Each of these vegetation communities was made up of varying percentages of different plants, some of which were important food sources for people, such as ricegrass (*Oryzopsis hymenoides*), and some of which were important sources of food for animals. Using wildlife management data, Zeanah then graded each vegetation community in terms of its potential for key animal species, such as bighorn sheep.

Soil type and topography largely control the distribution of particular vegetation communities across a landscape. Using soil maps—again, georeferenced to the topographic maps—Zeanah could characterize each 1-kilometer square in terms of its vegetation community and game productivity (Figure 5-9). In this way, he created baseline "economic potential" maps of a range of food plants and game animals for the Northern Paiute's ethnographically known territory.

But the baseline maps were only the beginning. We know that climate has changed over time in the Great Basin and that such climatic changes affect the abundance and distribution of plants and animals. Can the GIS be altered to take those climatic changes into account?

Changes in precipitation and temperature change effective moisture, and that, in turn, affects plant productivity and the abundance and distribution of animals. Range management data tell us that plant productivity responds in predictable ways to increases or decreases in effective moisture. Using what archaeologists already knew about changes in temperature and precipitation

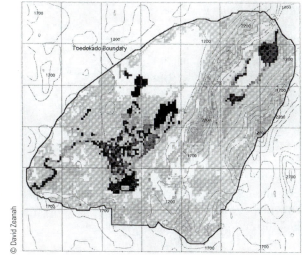

© David Zeanah

Figure 5-9 A map of Toedökadö territory showing the predicted productivity of ricegrass; the darker the square, the higher the productivitiy.

over time in the Great Basin, Zeanah altered the baseline model by increasing and decreasing a community's productivity by an appropriate percentage for each climatic period of the past. He could even shift the percentage of perennial or annual plants depending on whether the paleoclimatic data suggested a shift to summer precipitation (which favors annuals) or winter precipitation (which favors perennials). In addition, he could remove the piñon pine layer for the layers describing the landscape prior to 1500 years ago, because we know that piñon pine did not exist in the region before that date.

By massaging the data in this fashion, Zeanah modeled the changing effects of climate on the economic productivity of the region. His model thus predicts where we might expect to see archaeological evidence of prehistoric activities at different times in the past as a product of climatically induced changes in plant and animal abundance and distribution.

By making predictions based on an explicit model, archaeologists can evaluate the role of subsistence as opposed to some other factor in conditioning past human behavior. Such predictions could then be tested by one of the survey strategies we described in Chapter 4. In fact, Zeanah chose to use 1-kilometer squares as the basic unit of map construction so that they could provide easy sample units for future field research.

Zeanah used existing survey data (457 sites) to test the baseline model for 94 1 × 1 kilometer units. The baseline model ranked sample units in terms of how productive a unit was expected to be and thus how likely it was that archaeological remains would be found in that unit. Zeanah found that he could accurately predict the archaeological record of between 60 and 78 percent of the 94 sample units. The model worked best where sample units were predicted to offer very low or, alternatively, very high amounts of food to a mobile, hunting-and-gathering population. These are very good results, especially for a first-generation model.

GIS and the Chacoan Roads

Zeanah's research was undertaken entirely within the processual paradigm, and it looked on the Carson Desert landscape purely from an economic point of view. To show how GIS can assist with a view of the landscape as a set of symbolically laden places, let's return to the Chacoan roads

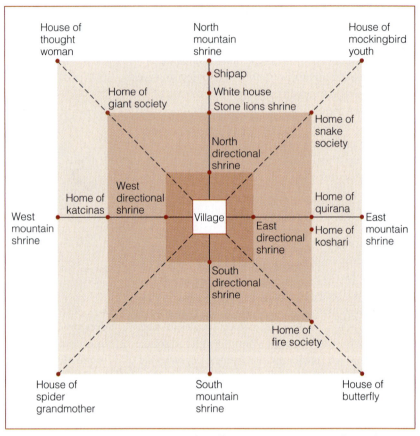

Figure 5-10 A schematic representation of the Keres symbolic landscape. *From J. Snead, and R. Preucel, "The Ideology of Settlement: Ancestral Keres Landscapes in the Northern Rio Grande." In W. Ashmore and A. B. Knapp (Eds.),* Archaelogies of Landscape: Contemporary Perspectives *(pp. 169–197). Oxford: Blackwell Publishers. Used by permission.*

that we mentioned above and the question, "If the Chacoans had no wheeled vehicles or beasts of burden, what were these roads for?"

One hypothesis is that the Chaco roads functioned as we believe the Inka roads (also discussed in Chapter 4) functioned, as a way to move foods and goods across the landscape. The roads radiate outward from Chaco Canyon, so perhaps they were a way to provision the inhabitants of the canyon's Great Houses with maize, timber, and other supplies.

But as we pointed out above, landscape carries symbolic meanings as well as economic potentials. Perhaps the roads were not economic at all, but instead served some ceremonial function with symbolic meanings. In fact, the roads' tendency to cut straight across hills, rather than skirt around their bases, and to make inexplicable sharp turns in the middle of desert have led many to favor a non-economic interpretation.

The likely descendants of the people who inhabited Chaco Canyon are the Keres, the Puebloan peoples who

live along the northern Rio Grande in New Mexico in the pueblos of Cochiti, San Felipe, Santa Ana, Santo Domingo, and Zia. In traditional Pueblo theology, the world consists of several nested layers, surrounded at the edges by four sacred mountains. As James Snead (George Mason University) and Robert Preucel (University of Pennsylvania) describe them, these nested layers center on a village, and different directions are associated with different powers, societies, and supernatural beings, as well as with maleness and femaleness (Figure 5-10). Direction is important in this view of the world (although the directions are not always the same, even for neighboring pueblos).

This symbolic landscape is physically manifested by different kinds of shrines. For example, the shrine on Mount Taylor, the west mountain shrine for Laguna Pueblo, is a shallow pit where people still come to pray. Directional shrines may be located closer to the villages and are often found in caves or near springs. One important directional shrine is two mountain lions carved from bedrock and surrounded by a circle of stones. Closer to the village are directional shrines that mark a village's boundaries. Located in the four cardinal directions, they are often keyhole-shaped stone structures with openings to the north or east. Other shrines are found within the village itself, especially in plazas where important dance rituals take place.

So, it is clear that in the Puebloan world, the landscape has economic and symbolic meanings. Direction, in particular, seems to hold special symbolic significance in Pueblo religion. Although the ancient Chacoans probably did not share the Keres worldview exactly, they may have had a similar one, or at least one in which shrines marked significant places and directions on the landscape.

Working in a region just south of Chaco Canyon, John Kantner (Georgia State University) used a GIS to test whether the roads were linked to the economic or symbolic aspects of the desert landscape. He reasoned that if the roads were for purely economic purposes, then they should follow the path of least resistance between Pueblo villages; if they did not, then perhaps the roads fulfilled a more religious purpose that was driven by the ancient peoples' symbolic interpretation of the landscape.

Using a digital elevation model, Kantner asked the GIS to do a straightforward task: Find the easiest walking route between settlements that are connected by roads. The easiest walking route would be the one where a person gained the least amount of elevation in walking from one village to another. Although it would take an archaeologist many days to walk out the possibilities in the field or even to trace them out on topographic maps, the GIS could quickly calculate the "path of least resistance" for someone walking from one settlement to another.

Interestingly, Kantner found that the GIS did *not* predict the locations of the roads. In fact, some of the roads cross terrain that is substantially different from that predicted by the GIS. The Chacoan roads do not follow the path of least resistance.

Kantner had assumed that anyone as familiar with their landscape as the Ancestral Pueblo people were would know the easiest way to walk from one settlement to another. But perhaps this assumption was wrong—perhaps people did *not* know or did *not* use the easiest paths between settlements. To test this hypothesis, Kantner asked whether there were any archaeological remains associated with the GIS-predicted paths.

In fact, he found that small stone shrines occur along the predicted footpaths; it appears that someone was using the predicted paths and probably on a regular basis. In addition, large circular stone shrines, ones that required more effort to construct, were almost always found with the roads, not the predicted footpaths.

From this, Kantner concluded that the roads did not serve simply as part of Chacoan economy. Although food and goods may have been moved along the roads, this does not appear to have been their primary purpose. People probably moved food and goods along trails that followed the paths of least resistance between villages, footpaths that are marked only by small shrines today. But the formal roads' association with large shrines suggests that they performed some other role. Perhaps they were religious paths; some, in fact, lead directly to places on the landscape that figure prominently in modern Puebloan religion. Or perhaps they helped to integrate the small far-flung pueblos with the Great Houses in Chaco Canyon. We still don't know the purpose of the roads for sure, but GIS clearly casts doubt on the "economic hypothesis."

CONCLUSION: THE FUTURE OF REMOTE SENSING AND GIS

Archaeology today is pervaded by a new conservation ethic. Because only a finite number of sites exist in the world, we excavate only what we must to answer a particular research question, saving portions of sites, or entire sites, for future researchers. Remote sensing will never (and should never) completely replace excavation. But by giving archaeologists a cost-effective means of making observations on objects and features that have not yet been excavated, it will obviate the need for excessive excavation and permit archaeologists to preserve more of a site for the future. And that is important to any ethical archaeologist.

GIS has likewise become an important tool. One of archaeology's strengths is its ability to use spatial patterns to test hypotheses about ancient cultural behavior. Although a high-powered, quantitative technique might seem to be most useful to processual archaeology, the examples we have cited here show that it can be useful to research conducted within the postprocessual paradigm as well. GIS is also extremely useful to federal and state agencies that must manage the archae-ological sites on their properties. For these reasons, it is likely that GIS will become as indispensable to archae-ologists as their Marshalltown trowels. However, these methods will never replace our trowels, or our need to excavate sites. And that realization brings us to the next chapter.

Summary

- In the days of C. B. Moore, archaeologists had no choice but to excavate large portions of sites to acquire data on the distribution of artifacts and features within site. Even in the 1970s, archaeologists had no choice but to excavate.

- Today, a new conservation ethic alters how we view archaeological sites: They are nonrenewable resources that we need to use carefully so that future generations can bring better techniques and new questions to them.

- Important to carrying out this task are a variety of methods for doing noninvasive, and hence relatively nondestructive, archaeology.

- Using a variety of methods that provide the archaeo-logical equivalents of CAT scans, archaeologists can often map subsurface features in detail without ever excavating them.

- When it does become necessary to recover samples, we can target excavations and hence minimize damage to the rest of the site.

- High-altitude imagery involves a series of techniques like take photos from hot air balloons, airplanes, the Space Shuttle, or satellites that can see the ground in the electromagnetic spectrum invisible to the human eye and that betray subsurface features.

- Various geophysical prospecting techniques, such as proton magnetometry, soil resistivity, and ground-penetrating radar, are just a few tools that permit archaeologists to see under the ground before they excavate.

- Geographic information systems, or GIS, allow archaeologists to construct georeferenced databases. These permit us to graphically portray and statisti-cally analyze spatial relationships between archaeo-logical and other kinds of data or to create powerful models to predict regional patterns in the spatial dis-tribution of archaeological data.

- Although high-tech, this new technology is not restricted to one paradigm; landscape archaeology, as an improvement of settlement archaeology or as a way to look at landscapes in more terms of rituals or symbols, are both enhanced by GIS.

Additional Reading

Aldenderfer, Mark, and Herbert Maschner (Eds.). 1996. *Anthropology, Space, and Geographic Information Systems.* New York: Oxford University Press.

Donoghue, D. N. M. 2001. Remote Sensing. In D. Brothwell and A. Pollard (Eds.), *Handbook of Archae-ological Sciences* (pp. 555–564). Chichester, England: John Wiley and Sons.

Wescott, Konnie L., and R. Joe Brandon (Eds.). 1999. *Practical Applications of GIS for Archaeologists: A Predic-tive Modeling Kit.* London: Taylor and Francis.

Wheatley, David, and Mark Gillings. 2002. *Spatial Tech-nology and Archaeology: The Archaeological Applications of GIS.* London: Taylor and Francis.

Online Resources

COMPANION WEB SITE

Visit **http://anthropology.wadsworth.com** and click on the Student Companion Web Site for Thomas/Kelly *Archaeology*, 4th edition, to access a wide range of material to help you succeed in your introductory archaeology course. These include flashcards, Internet exercises, Web links, and practice quizzes.

RESEARCH ONLINE WITH INFOTRAC COLLEGE EDITION

From the Student Companion Web Site, you can access the InfoTrac College Edition database, which offers thousands of full-length articles for your research.

6

Doing Fieldwork: Why Archaeologists Dig Square Holes

Outline

Preview

ASK MOST PEOPLE WHAT archaeologists do, and they'll tell you this: "They dig." And that's true. Despite what we have seen in the preceding two chapters about archaeological survey techniques and remote sensing technology, digging up old stuff remains at the heart of archaeology—and probably always will.

But excavation is a much more complex and sophisticated venture than throwing a shovel into a pickup and heading off for the mountains. Archaeologists are well aware of the fact that, as they gather data from a site they are also destroying that site, because once a site is excavated, it can never be excavated again. Therefore, it's essential that archaeologists record as much detail as possible, so that future archaeologists can reconstruct what earlier archaeologists did and use the records to answer new questions. This means that you dig slowly and take excruciatingly careful and detailed notes. Nonetheless, as Kent Flannery (University of Michigan) once said, "Archaeology is the most fun you can have with your pants on." And he's right, as anybody who has ever participated in a dig will tell you. Thomas joined his first archaeological expedition as a college junior; Kelly as a high school sophomore. We were both hooked from the start.

We warned earlier about the problems of learning archaeological field techniques from a book (even this one): You just can't do it. But in this chapter we describe common archaeological field methods, and we do hope to show you how fieldwork is done and what it really feels like.

INTRODUCTION

In Chapter 4, we talked about how archaeologists go about finding sites, such as Gatecliff Shelter. But locating sites is only the beginning, and actually excavating these sites can be far more time-consuming. Along with fields such as geology and paleontology, the science of archaeology destroys data as it is gathered—for once we excavate a site, nobody can ever dig it again. This is why archaeologists are compulsive about field notes—recording, drawing, and photographing everything we can about an artifact or a feature before removing it. This is also why we usually try to leave a portion of a site unexcavated for the future.

This chapter can be reduced to one simple point: An artifact's **provenience,** its location and context within a site, is the most important thing about that artifact; some might even say it is more important than the artifact itself. Here's one account that demonstrates that fundamental principle.

Excavations at the *convento* (friars' housing) at Mission Santa Catalina (Georgia). Archaeologists in the foreground are mapping finds within a horizontal grid system. Those in the mid-ground use the shovel-skimming technique (a technique used to remove sandy deposits that contain few artifacts; skimming the surface of the excavation unit, the excavator removes only a fraction of an inch each time). All dirt is screened in gasoline-powered sifters evident in the background.

provenience An artifact's location relative to a system of spatial data collection.

The Folsom Site and Humanity's Antiquity in North America

In Chapter 2, we discussed how eighteenth-century scholars were preoccupied with the question of where Native Americans came from. A closely related question was "How long have Native Americans been here?" As we saw in the Moundbuilder controversy, many scholars believed that American Indians arrived in the western hemisphere only shortly before European colonists. This matter was politically important because, if archaeology showed that American Indians were long-time inhabitants of the New World, then their claim to the land was strengthened. But if Indian people were only recent immigrants, their hold on the land could be minimized in favor of the Europeans.

And so, from the earliest colonial times, scholars debated the antiquity of humanity in the New World (and they still do). Some claimed that the discovery of apparently crude stone tools demonstrated that humans had been in the New World for thousands of years, since the last phase of the Ice Age, but others showed that these crude artifacts could be mere quarry rejects, unfinished pieces that the artisans deemed too flawed to complete. For some scholars (notably, most of them worked for the federal government), the lack of ancient tools similar to those that Boucher de Perthes had found in France (see Chapter 1) showed that Indians were recent arrivals in the New World.

Eventually, the argument over the antiquity of humanity in the New World came down to animals. Nineteenth- and early twentieth-century archaeologists had no way to date their sites absolutely. But they knew that the world had experienced a great Ice Age in the distant past. And they reasoned (quite accurately it turns out) that this Ice Age, more properly called the **Pleistocene**, had ended about 10,000 years ago. Scholars also knew that different kinds of animals lived in North America during the Pleistocene—mammoths, mastodons, a large species of bison, giant bears, ground sloths, horses, camels, and so on. Anybody who found artifacts in undisputed association with the bones of such extinct fauna would prove that humans had been in North America for at least 10,000 years. And thus, the quest relied heavily on context: seeking ancient artifacts in unquestionable association with the bones of extinct fauna.

In Chapter 4, we mentioned that some of the most important archaeological sites are found by non-archaeologists. A hard-rock miner found Gatecliff Shelter, and an ex-slave named George McJunkin (1851–1922) found the Folsom site—the place that proved the extent of human antiquity in the Americas (Figure 6-1).

The Black Cowboy

Born into slavery in 1851, McJunkin acquired his freedom at age 14. That year, he "borrowed" a mule that belonged to his former owner and left his home on a Texas plantation in search of work. By 1868, he was breaking horses for a Texas rancher and later held down a string of ranch jobs in Colorado and New Mexico. He became an expert cowboy and knew just about all there was to know about horses and cattle.

McJunkin also learned a lot about many other things. Although he never received a formal education, he taught himself to read and play the fiddle. He was curious about everything, especially natural history, and one of his prize possessions was a wooden box filled with rocks, bones, fossils, and arrowheads. McJunkin never married and lived most of his life as the only African-American in his community.

Early in the 1890s, McJunkin's talents were recognized by the owner of the Crowfoot Ranch, in northwestern New Mexico near the town of Folsom. Soon, McJunkin was ranch foreman and proved himself an able leader of men, as well as cowpuncher and wrangler.

One day in August of 1908, torrential rains fell on the Crowfoot Ranch, creating a flash flood that destroyed much of Folsom. (Many people were killed, but more would have died had not the local telephone operator, Sarah Rooke, remained at her post, calling people to warn them until the floodwaters claimed her life.) After helping to search for the dead, McJunkin began checking the Crowfoot's fences. Up Wild Horse Arroyo, he found a line that dangled across a now-deep, muddy gully. Pondering how to fix it, he spotted bones protruding from the walls of the arroyo, some 15 feet down the embankment.

McJunkin had seen plenty of cow bones in his day, and these were definitely not cow. The bones even seemed too large for bison. McJunkin returned to the site over the years to collect bones that he then stacked on his mantle at home. He would talk to anyone who

Pleistocene A geologic period from 2 million to 10 thousand years ago, which was characterized by multiple periods of extensive glaciation.

Figure 6-1 The Folsom site in 1997. Wild Horse Arroyo runs through the middle of the photo; site excavators David Meltzer and Lawrence Todd are at the lower left.

showed an interest in them and showed the site to several interested townsfolk.

A Spear Point between the Ribs

Eventually, the site was brought to the attention of Jesse Figgins, director of the Colorado Museum of Natural History (now the Denver Museum of Nature and Science), who was looking for skeletons of the extinct Pleistocene bison, *Bison antiquus*, for a museum display. Sadly, McJunkin had died a few years before Figgins's arrival and so he did not live to see the day that his site made archaeological history.

Some of the townsfolk who had visited the site with McJunkin had occasionally found an artifact or two among the bones (now identified as ancient bison), but they did not document their finds, meaning that the context of these artifacts was unknown. And in 1926, Figgins's crew also found a beautifully made spear point with a distinct central groove or channel (what we now call a "flute"). But, unfortunately, they could not tell whether the artifact was found with the bison skeletons

or had fallen from a later, higher level—meaning that the newest find still lacked the necessary context.

Figgins telegrammed the crew to leave any artifacts exactly where they were discovered, so that he could personally observe them in place. And so, when excavators located similar spear points the following summer, they left the artifacts **in situ** (in place), so that their context could be recorded. One of these points lay between the ribs of a bison (Figure 6-2). Figgins sent telegrams to prominent members of the archaeological community, including the skeptical A. V. Kidder, who was excavating at Pecos only 100 miles away.

After joining other archaeologists at the excavation site, Kidder solemnly pronounced that the association between the spear points and the extinct bison remains was solid. There was no evidence that rodents had burrowed into the deposit, carrying later artifacts from

in situ From Latin, meaning "in position"; the place where an artifact, ecofact, or feature was found during excavation or survey.

© Denver Museum of Nature and Science

Figure 6-2 A fluted Folsom spear point lying between the ribs of an extinct form of bison at the Folsom site.

higher in the ground down to the bison skeletons. There was no indication that streams had redeposited the artifacts on top of the remains. Everyone present saw undeniable evidence that the spear points had killed the extinct bison.

For the first time, the association between extinct fauna and human artifacts was confirmed: People had been in the Americas since at least the end of the Pleistocene, some 10,000 years ago. Today, we know McJunkin's site as the Folsom site, and the distinctive spear points found there are called Folsom points—both named after the nearby town that had been nearly destroyed by the deadly flood that first exposed the site.

As you can see, context was everything at the Folsom site. And this is true for any site. In fact, other than "When's lunch?", what you'll hear most frequently on any archaeological dig is "Show me exactly where that came from."

EXCAVATION: WHAT DETERMINES PRESERVATION?

The exact procedures in any excavation depend on several factors, beginning with the kind of materials

that have survived the passage of time. Some sites have wonderful preservation of organic materials, including basketry, leather, and wood; but in other sites, only ceramics, stones, and bones survive; and in the earliest archaeological sites, only the stone tools remain. Here are some examples that demonstrate the various conditions under which organic remains are preserved.

The Duck Decoys of Lovelock Cave

Lovelock Cave (Nevada) sits on a barren hillside, just north of the Carson Desert. But thousands of years ago, anybody sitting in the cave's mouth would have looked out upon a vast wetland, just a few kilometers away. Lovelock Cave was first excavated in 1912 (by Lewellyn Loud, a museum security guard at the University of California, who was sent by anthropologist Alfred Kroeber to gather museum specimens), and again in 1924, by Mark Harrington of New York's Museum of the American Indian. Like Hidden Cave (mentioned in Chapter 4), the dry and dusty interior of Lovelock Cave was used more for storage than habitation.

Loud and Harrington found several caches of gear. One that Harrington found, Pit 11, held a buried basket that contained 11 duck decoys. Cleverly crafted from tule reeds twisted to simulate the body and head of a duck, some had plain tule reed bodies and others were adorned with paint and feathers. As artifacts, the decoys are striking (Figure 6-3). Even *Sports Illustrated* extolled the creativity and craftsmanship of these prehistoric duck hunters.

Someone buried this basket of decoys in Pit 11 (in fact, they were interred beneath the pit's false bottom) intending, evidently, to use them on a later duck hunt. Although the person who buried the decoys never retrieved them, it was wise to cache them inside Lovelock Cave because they were perfectly preserved; they are usable even today. We now know from radiocarbon dating (discussed in Chapter 8) that these decoys were made about 2000 years ago.

Figure 6-3. A 2000-year-old duck decoy from Lovelock Cave, Nevada.

Figure 6-4 The archaeological site of Ozette on the coast of Washington.

The Houses of Ozette

Equally remarkable, yet strikingly different, preservation is seen at the site of Ozette on Washington's Olympic Peninsula (Figure 6-4). Ozette was a major beachside village once occupied by the ancestors of the Makah people. In fact, some Makahs remained at Ozette into the 1920s, and their oral traditions helped lead Richard Daugherty (then at Washington State University) to the site in the first place.

Ozette was once a lively village stretching for a mile along the Pacific Coast, home to perhaps 800 people who lived in massive split-plank cedar houses. They hunted; gathered berries in the forest; collected shellfish along the coast; and fished for halibut, salmon, and other fish. They even hunted killer whales.

Part of Ozette village lay along the bottom of a steep hill. Some 300 years ago, during an especially heavy rain (or possibly a tsunami), the hillside above the village became saturated and, with a roar, an enormous mudslide descended on the village, shearing the tops off five houses and burying their interiors. Some people escaped, but others were caught inside. Because the coast of Washington is so wet, the destroyed portion of Ozette remained waterlogged and was capped by a thick layer of clay by the mudslide.

The saturated dirt and the clay cap preserved entire houses with all their furnishings and gear. During the 1970s, Richard Daugherty excavated the houses, recovering some 42,000 artifacts, including baskets, mats, hats, halibut hooks, bowls, clubs, combs—even an entire cedar canoe. The archaeological team worked closely with the Makah people, and many of the artifacts from Ozette village are now on display at the Makah Cultural and Research Center in Neah Bay, Washington. These displays highlight the remarkable degree of preservation at this important waterlogged site.

The Ice Man of the Alps

Our third example demonstrates yet a different kind of archaeological preservation. In 1991, two skiers in the Alps came upon the body of a man lying in a pool of icy glacial water at 10,000 feet. The body was so well preserved that the authorities thought at first he was perhaps a mountaineer who had perished in a blizzard a few years earlier. But today, we know this man as Ötzi, the "Ice Man," who died some 5300 years ago. His body was remarkably well preserved—even tattoos are clearly visible on his skin—because he froze shortly after he died, and a small glacier then sealed his body in the shallow depression where it had come to rest. Here he freeze-dried and lay undisturbed until the warmth of recent decades caused the glacier to recede, exposing his remains (Figure 6-5).

Realizing the significance of the Ice Man, archaeologists scoured the site and recovered portions of his clothing—a belt to hold up a leather breechcloth and leggings, a coat of deerskin, a cape of woven grass, a leather fur-lined cap, and calfskin shoes, filled with grass. They also recovered tools, including a hafted copper axe, a bow and a quiver of arrows, bone points, extra bowstrings, a wooden pack frame, birchbark containers, a stone scraper, a hafted knife, and a net.

By analyzing the contents of the Ice Man's stomach and intestine, scientists determined that he had not eaten for at least 8 hours before his death and that his final meal had been barley, wheat, deer, and wild goat. Pollen analysis of the contents of his intestine suggests that he died in the spring.

Why did this 30-year-old man die at such a high elevation, far from any village or camp? An arrow point that penetrated past his shoulder blade suggests that he had been attacked shortly before his death. One of his hands also bears unhealed cuts, as though he warded off an assailant armed with a knife. One guess is that he was fleeing, stopped to rest in a depression away from the wind, and quietly passed away from his wounds.

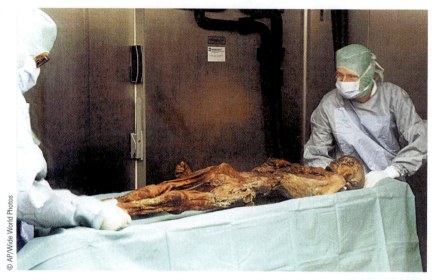

Figure 6-5 Ötzi, the "Ice Man" (above) and portions of some of his tools (below).

The Preservation Equation

So, why were the Lovelock duck decoys, the houses of Ozette, and the Ice Man so well preserved?

Decomposition is carried out by microorganisms that require warmth, oxygen, and water to survive. In each of the above cases, one of these was lacking: Lovelock Cave lacked moisture, the wet deposits beneath the clay cap at Ozette were anaerobic (oxygenless), and the Ice Man's glacial environment lacked warmth.

These different preservation conditions present the archaeologist with both opportunities and challenges. At Ozette, for example, the waterlogged archaeological deposits were a muddy gumbo that was almost impossible to trowel or shovel. And because the wooden artifacts were saturated with water, a misplaced shovel stroke could slice them like a knife through butter. To cope with these conditions, Daugherty assembled a complex system of pressurized hoses to wash the mud away. By adjusting the water pressure, they could use fire hoses to clean off the massive house posts and wall planks, switching to a fine misting spray when exposing delicate basketry.

Likewise, sites such as Lovelock Cave offer a wealth of artifacts not normally found, but such sites tend to be extremely complex. They are favorite places for rodents and carnivores, whose actions can move artifacts up and down, making it difficult to sort out what belongs with what. This means that they require especially slow excavation.

Looking Closer
The Excavator's Toolkit

In Chapter 4, we presented a list of equipment that the modern archaeological surveyor should carry. Here we list things that the well-equipped excavator should carry in his or her excavation toolbox:

- A 5- to 6-inch trowel (Marshalltown brand only, accept no substitute! Sharpen the edges and cut a V-notch in one of the back edges—it's useful for cutting roots. It's also useful to have both a pointed- and a square-ended kind—the latter is especially helpful when cleaning stratigraphic profiles.)
- A metal file (for sharpening that Marshalltown)
- A 2-meter and a 25-meter tape measure (metric only)
- Work gloves
- A builder's line level and string (nylon, yellow)
- A builder's angle finder (to take artifact inclinations)
- A compass (to take artifact orientations)
- Pencils (regular and mechanical), pencil sharpener, and Sharpie pens
- Spoon (a very useful excavation tool and handy at lunchtime)

- Jackknife (One with a serrated edge is useful against larger roots.)
- Nails (of various sizes, for example, to hold a level string for drawing a stratigraphy)
- Straight-edge 12-inch ruler with metric markings
- Torpedo level (to maintain good vertical profiles)
- Root clippers
- Small wire cutters (to cut root hairs to prepare a stratigraphic profile for photos)
- Empty film canisters (for various sorts of samples)
- A variety of small Ziploc bags (as in your survey kit)
- Toilet paper (for wrapping delicate artifacts)
- Dental tools (Dentists throw them out after a limited number of uses.)
- Brushes (whisk broom and 1- to 2-inch paint brushes)
- Bamboo slices (whittle the ends to a rounded tip; essential for excavating bone)
- Aluminum foil (for radiocarbon and other samples)
- Toothpicks (useful for temporarily marking artifact locations or strata in a profile)

And although the Ice Man contributed enormously to our knowledge of the past, his preservation now requires a sophisticated storage chamber (at Italy's South Tyrol Museum), where museum personnel control the temperature and humidity.

Preservation, of course, is only one factor conditioning how we excavate a site; other determinants include the site's depth, time and financial constraints, accessibility, and, perhaps most important, the research questions being pursued. We have excavated with backhoes, shovels, trowels, dental tools, and garden hoses (see "Looking Closer: The Excavator's Toolkit"). We even used a jackhammer once (to remove rooffall in Gatecliff Shelter).

Sometimes the archaeologist can rely on the latest technology; but other times, financial constraints or remote conditions require the use of less-elegant methods. Archaeologists excavate ancient Pueblo sites in New Mexico that contain well-defined room clusters very differently from high-altitude caves in Peru. Peeling off sequential levels of a Maya temple in Guatemala differs radically from excavating through seemingly homogeneous shell midden deposits in Georgia. Submerged sites, such as ancient shipwrecks, require their own special brand of archaeology.

There are many ways to excavate a site, and each is appropriate if it allows the archaeologist to achieve the project's research goals within the constraints of time, funding, and technology. The only important thing is that *the excavation techniques must record an artifact's context as precisely as possible.*

PRINCIPLES OF ARCHAEOLOGICAL EXCAVATION

The key to maintaining information about an artifact's context is to record its provenience. Provenience means an artifact's location, but location is both hierarchical and relative.

Location is hierarchical because an artifact's provenience is simultaneously a particular country, a particular state in that country, a particular county in that state, a particular site in that county, a particular excavation unit in that site, a particular vertical level in that unit, and a particular position and orientation in that level. Obviously, the last levels in this hierarchy are more useful than the first levels. Figgins's excavators found some spear points at the Folsom site, but it was not until they were found in situ, lying between the bison's ribs, that their provenience became meaningful to a particular question. Of course, we can make use of artifacts whose proveniences are imprecise to answer some types of research questions, but nonetheless *the excavator's first goal is to record context by recording provenience as accurately as possible.*

Location is relative because we measure an artifact's position relative to a spatial system. We could use the UTM grid (mentioned in Chapter 4), or we could use a site-specific format. The key is to find a procedure that will allow a future archaeologist to reconstruct, in great detail, where you found things in the site.

So, how do we go about excavating a site so that we recover an artifact's provenience? Let's return to Gatecliff Shelter to see how this is done.

Test Excavations

From day one, Thomas wanted to learn two things: how long people had used Gatecliff Shelter and whether the buried deposits could tell us about how human life had changed over time in this part of the Great Basin. The initial goal, then, was to decide if Gatecliff could help answer these questions. This meant that Thomas had to know what kind of historical record Gatecliff preserved. Was it a short or long record? Was it nicely stratified or a jumbled mess?

For this reason, the initial **test excavation** strategy was vertical, designed to supply, as expediently as possible, a stratified sequence of artifacts and ecofacts associated with potentially datable materials. Consequently, Thomas "tested" Gatecliff with two test pits (the French call them *sondages*, or "soundings"). Like most archaeologists, we dig metrically, typically in 1-meter squares for practical as well as scientific reasons: Squares much smaller would squeeze out the archaeologist, and larger units might not allow sufficient accuracy and would remove more of the site than necessary to answer the initial questions.

Test pits are quick and dirty because we must excavate them "blind"—that is, without knowing exactly what lies below. But even when digging test pits, archaeologists maintain three-dimensional control of the finds, recording the X and Y axes (the horizontal coordinates) and the Z axis (the vertical coordinate) for each one. This is one reason why archaeologists dig square holes. Provided the pit sidewalls are kept sufficiently straight and perpendicular, excavators can use the dirt itself to maintain horizontal control on the X and Y axes by measuring directly from the sidewalls. Here the horizontal provenience is relative to the sidewalls of the pit. (In some sites, this can become problematic if one is not careful: As test pits deepen, their sidewalls will slope inward, creating a "bathtub" effect that throws off the measurements.)

What about vertical control? At Gatecliff, Thomas dug the test pits in arbitrary, but consistent, 10-centimeter levels. Everything of interest—artifacts, ecofacts, soil samples, and so forth—was kept in separate level bags, one for each 10-centimeter level. The Z dimension for each level was usually designated according to distance below the ground surface: Level 1 (surface to 10 centimeters below), Level 2 (10 to 20 centimeters below), and so forth. This way, excavators measured vertical provenience relative to the ground surface. This also can be a problem, given that the ground surface can change over time and make it potentially difficult for future archaeologists to correlate their levels with those of a previous archaeologist. But every project requires trade-offs, and there is no point to investing much effort in a site before knowing if it will provide the necessary information. This is why test pits often record only minimal levels of provenience.

test excavation A small initial excavation to determine a site's potential for answering a research question.

Expanding the Test Excavation

At Gatecliff, the test pits told Thomas that the site warranted a closer look, and he returned the next year to do just that. He first divided the site into a 1-meter grid system, oriented along the long axis of the shelter. The exact compass orientation of this grid was recorded (many archaeologists today routinely orient their grids to magnetic or true north, but sometimes pragmatics dictate otherwise). He assigned consecutive letters to each north-south division and numbered the east-west division (see Figure 6-6). By this method, each excavation square could be designated by a unique alphanumeric name (just like Bingo—A-7, B-5, and the ever-popular K-9). Other archaeologists use different systems, some numbering each unit according to the X and Y coordinates of the units' southwest (or some other) corner. In this system, a unit with the designation North 34 East 45 (or N34 E45) means that its southwest corner is 34 meters north and 45 meters east of the site's N0 E0 point.

At Gatecliff, the east wall of the "7-trench" (so named because it contained units B-7 through I-7) defined a major profile that exposed the site's stratigraphy. Stratigraphy, you will recall from Chapter 1, is the structure produced by the deposition of geological and/or cultural sediments into layers, or strata. The stratigraphy is a vertical section against which the archaeologist plots all artifacts, features, soil and pollen samples, and radiocarbon dates. (Some archaeologists use the term "stratification" to refer to the physical layers in a site, reserving "stratigraphy" only for the analytical interpretation of the temporal and depositional evidence.)

A vertical datum was established at the rear of the shelter. For all on-site operations, this **datum point** was

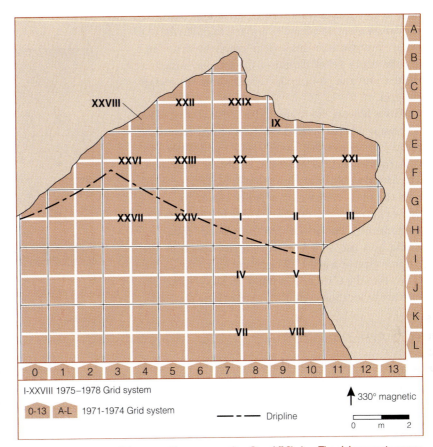

Figure 6-6 Plan view of the two grid systems used at Gatecliff Shelter. The alphanumeric system (consisting of letters and numbers) defined 1-meter excavation squares used in the first four seasons. Roman numerals designate the 2-meter squares used later, when large horizontal exposures were excavated. *After Thomas (1983b: figure 8). Courtesy American Museum of Natural History.*

arbitrarily assigned an elevation of zero. All site elevations from this point on were plotted as "x centimeters below datum," rather than below surface (given that the surface almost never has the same elevation across any given site). Using an altimeter and a U.S. Geological Survey topographic map, Thomas determined the elevation of this datum point to be 2319 meters (7607 feet) above sea level. All archaeological features—fire hearths, artifact concentrations, sleeping areas, and the like—were plotted on a master site map, and individual artifacts found in situ were plotted in three dimensions—their X and Y coordinates based on the map, and

datum point The zero point, a fixed reference used to keep control on a dig; usually controls both the vertical and horizontal dimensions of provenience.

their *Z* coordinates (that is, their elevation) based on the datum point. Incidentally, artifacts found in the test pit are brought into this system simply by determining the depth below datum of the ground surface at the test unit and plotting the test unit onto the master site grid.

This is how we did things in the 1970s. Today, however, we would have placed the datum many meters off the site in an area that would remain undisturbed by construction, natural processes, or future excavation. The datum would be an aluminum or brass cap marked with the site's Smithsonian or other identifying number, set in concrete or on top of a long piece of concrete reinforcement bar driven into the ground. Today, we would also use a GPS instrument to determine the datum's elevation and UTM location. Once the datum is tied into the UTM grid, a future archaeologist could recreate its location even if the marker were destroyed.

How Archaeologists Dig

Despite what action-hero characters like Indiana Jones or Lara Croft might lead you to believe, archaeologists do not dash in, grab the goodies, and then run for their lives. We don't even mindlessly shovel dirt into a bucket. Instead, we excavate within horizontal excavation units in **natural levels** and **arbitrary levels.** Natural levels are the site's **strata** (singular, "stratum"), which are more or less homogeneous or gradational material, visually separable from other levels by a change in the texture, color, rock or organic content, or by a sharp break in depositional character (or any combination of these).

Archaeologists prefer to excavate in natural levels wherever possible. Figure 6-7 shows the main reason for this practice. In this hypothetical profile are four natural strata—A, B, C, and D—each containing a particular kind of artifact (denoted by the different sym-

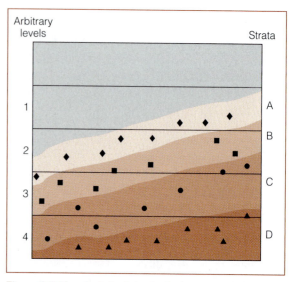

Figure 6-7 Hypothetical relationship between natural (A through D) and arbitrary (1 through 4) levels showing how arbitrary levels can potentially jumble together artifacts that come from different natural strata.

---

natural level A vertical subdivision of an excavation square that is based on natural breaks in the sediments (in terms of color, grain size, texture, hardness, or other characteristics).

arbitrary level The basic vertical subdivision of an excavation square; used only when easily recognizable "natural" strata are lacking and when natural strata are more than 10 centimeters thick.

strata (singular, "stratum") More or less homogeneous or gradational material, visually separable from other levels by a discrete change in the character of the material—texture, compactness, color, rock, organic content—and/or by a sharp break in the nature of deposition.

---

bols). If you imagine that each of these strata represents some unit of time, then you can see that there was a clear change in the kind of artifacts left behind at this site over the four time periods. But note that these strata slope. If we excavated them blindly using arbitrary levels—denoted by the solid lines and numbers 1, 2, 3, and 4—those levels would crosscut the various strata. Arbitrary Level 1 contains artifacts from only Stratum A; but Level 2 contains artifacts from three different time periods: Strata A, B, and C; Level 3 contains artifacts from all four strata; and Level 4, artifacts from Strata C and D. If we assumed that the arbitrary levels correlate to time, then the results of this method of excavation would suggest a very different—and erroneous—image of artifact change over time than that suggested by the natural strata.

Excavators at Gatecliff—most of them college students—excavated by natural levels wherever possible. Where these natural levels were thicker than 10 centimeters, they excavated in arbitrary levels no more than 10 centimeters in thickness within the natural levels. (Today, when many archaeologists excavate in arbitrary levels, they excavate ones only 5 centimeters deep to maintain even greater control over provenience.)

Excavators carefully troweled the deposit, then passed it outside the cave for screening (we'll have more to say about this later); artifacts and ecofacts found in the screen were bagged by level. Individual excavators kept field notes at this stage in bound, graph-paper note-books. Good field notes record everything, whether or not it seems important at the time. Remember, the excavator's goal is to capture the detail that will allow a future archaeologist to "see" what the excavator saw as he or she was digging. Today, field notes employ standardized forms (unique to each excavation) so that excavators record the same detailed information for each level (Figure 6-8). Depending on how much he or she finds, it might take the excavator a week to complete this one form (but usually it is less than a day). This information will include the date, the excavator's name, a map of the unit showing where artifacts and features were found, and a detailed description of the sediments ("rock hard clay, grading from brown to reddish-orange" or "loose, and dusty, with a lot of packrat feces and cactus spines"). A geologist's Munsell soil color chart is often used to record sediment colors.

The form will also include the level's beginning and ending elevations, observations on how this level was different from that above it ("there is more charcoal in this level"), whether any samples were taken (soil, carbon, plant materials), and so on. In addition, copious photographs (black and white, color slides, and digital) are taken of all unit profiles, all significant finds in situ, and all features. Nowadays, some archaeologists make a video recording of all excavation units at the end of each day or during the excavation of important features and finds.

Expanding Gatecliff's Excavation

The vertical excavation strategy at Gatecliff was a deliberately simplified scheme designed to clarify chronology. By the end of the fourth field season, Trench 7 had reached a depth of 9 meters below the ground surface. We had learned a good deal about the cultural sequence of Gatecliff Shelter, but our vertical excavation strategy had also left us with a series of extremely steep and hazardous sidewalls. Even though the excavation was stairstepped to minimize the height of these sidewalls (see the terraces in Figure 3-1 on page 53), they were still dangerous. Today, deep excavation trenches are heavily shored. Unshored walls higher than 4 feet are a violation of federal OSHA—Occupational Safety and Health Administration—regulations. And with good reason: More than one archaeologist has been nearly killed by collapsing profiles. Clearly, a change was in order for reasons of safety.

Change was required for conceptual reasons as well. The early excavations demonstrated that Gatecliff could contribute much more than mere chronology. The vertical excavation showed us that Gatecliff had witnessed something unique. Periodically, flash floods filled the shelter with thick beds of silt. Eventually, the shelter dried out, and people used it once again. The result was that layers of sterile silt neatly separated **living floors**, occupational surfaces, inside the overhang. This was a remarkable opportunity to study discrete living surfaces within a rockshelter environment.

Few archaeologists have such a chance, and so we shifted away from the initial chronological objectives to concentrate on recording the spatial distributions of artifacts and features on the living floors. The goal now was to reconstruct what activities took place in the shelter as indicated by the distribution of artifacts across the living floors sandwiched between the silt layers. With the stratigraphy suitably defined, extensive vertical sections were no longer necessary, and we concentrated on opening entire (horizontal) living surfaces.

We switched to 2 × 2 meter units, but excavated the living floors more slowly than in the previous vertical excavations, and excavators tried to recover and map all artifacts in situ. We excavated and screened features such as hearths separately, and soil samples were retained for laboratory processing. We plotted artifacts, scatters of waste flakes from stone tool manufacture, concentrations of bone—anything found in situ—on master living floor maps.

This horizontal strategy required significantly more control within contemporary layers. A single excavator carefully worked each 2-square-meter unit, attempting to find as many artifacts as possible in situ. All artifacts, features, and large ecofacts were plotted onto the large-scale living floor maps for each surface. The result was a set of living floor maps that are rare among rockshelter excavations in the world (Figure 6-9).

PRECISION EXCAVATION

This description of the Gatecliff excavation provides a general sense of what goes on at archaeological sites. But excavation has become an even more exact science

living floors A distinct buried surface on which people lived.

Juniper Cave (48BH3178) Excavation Form

Date: _____ / _____ /04

Excavators _____ Unit _____

Opening depths: SW _____ NW _____ NE _____ SE _____

Closing depths: SW _____ NW _____ NE _____ SE _____

Strata _____. Feature number (if any) _____. Describe level and sediment on back of form; show on map where excavated if less than entire unit; show rodent burrows, roots, rocks; note soil changes.

Total sediment weight (before screen) _____ kg After screen _____ kg

Screen size (circle):   1/4   1/8   1/16   Water screened?

Screen/piece plot total counts:

Debitage _____   Bone _____   Other (_____) _____

Samples taken (circle): C14 sediment (weight): _____) botanical other

Number of level bags: _____ Artifact catalog numbers: _____

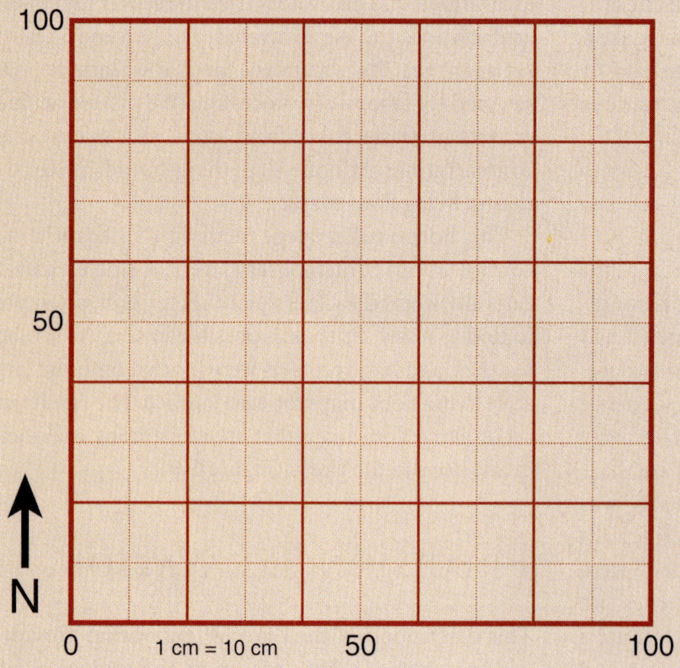

Crew chief form check: _____

Page _____ of _____

Figure 6-8 A typical excavation form.

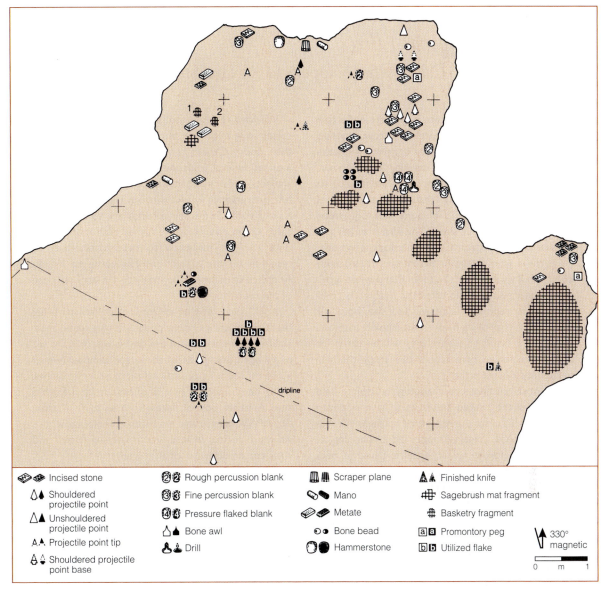

Figure 6-9 A living floor map showing the distribution of artifacts and hearths on Horizon 2 (deposited about AD 1300) at Gatecliff. *Courtesy American Museum of Natural History.*

since Thomas excavated Gatecliff in the 1970s. Given the importance of an artifact's context, archaeologists continue to devise ways to record provenience for more objects with greater precision.

For example, at Gatecliff we first used string line levels tied to the datum and tape measures to determine an artifact's vertical provenience (its depth below datum); we later switched to a more precise builder's level and measuring rod. We recorded horizontal provenience by measuring distances from two of a unit's sidewalls. But today, many archaeologists, ourselves included, use the

total stations (mentioned in Chapter 4) to record provenience. New instruments still cost a pricey $5000, but they are necessary for state-of-the-art excavation.

How do total stations work? The devices are set up on a tripod over the site's datum. After workers input the correct data, the total station "knows" where it is on the grid system and which direction it is pointing. When an artifact is found, a glass prism is held on the artifact's location, and the total station is turned and aimed at the prism. Push a button, and the station shoots a beam of infrared light at the prism. By measur-

Archaeological Ethics
The Curation Crisis: What Happens to All That Stuff after the Excavation?

Archaeologists are inveterate collectors of stuff. They hate to throw anything away, and many even consider it unethical to dispose of *anything* found on survey or during an excavation. But archaeologists personally keep nothing that they find during research—not one scrap of bone, not one stone point, not one ceramic sherd. The idea is to keep all the artifacts for posterity. You can't do that by keeping them in your garage or basement—they'd likely end up in a yard sale or the town dump when a relative inherited them. No, after the analysis is completed, the report is written, and the book or monograph is published, all those labeled bags and cataloged artifacts go where they will be cared for and where future researchers can study them in perpetuity. Where is this?

In most instances, archaeologists doing field research in the United States must have evidence that they will curate the recovered artifacts in a federally approved, taxpayer-supported archaeological repository before they can acquire a permit or a research grant. Most states have several such repositories; these are a continuing cost to the taxpayer, given that rent and utilities must be paid, and they must be staffed.

The curation issue became noticeable after the late 1960s, when Congress passed historic preservation laws requiring archaeological survey and excavation prior to construction (see Chapter 17). As a result, the amount of material that entered repositories rapidly escalated. No one knows for sure today how many objects are held in museums and other repositories, but a good estimate might be between 100 and 500 *million*.

We have reached the point where some repositories have filled up—and some have literally shut their doors. Others cannot afford to meet recommended federal guidelines, and so they house their artifacts under substandard conditions where artifact provenience is lost through neglect, mold, and leaking roofs. Some repositories are so strained to catch up on inventories that they cannot afford the time to loan materials to researchers, and so research on the collections has come to a halt. And that, of course, is contrary to the very purpose of the repositories.

It will cost tens of millions of dollars to bring these repositories up to code and to expand their abilities. Some wonder if the cost is worth it. Do we really need, some ask, all those soil samples (which some repositories already refuse to accept)? Do we really need another box of sherds from a Pueblo site? Another box of flakes from an early Archaic site in Wyoming? Have we reached the point where we must decide what is worth keeping *forever* and what can be disposed of after analysis?

For example, many archaeologists used to record observations on sherds and flakes and then dispose of them. But every archaeologist can tell you a story about how they wished that some past archaeologist had kept *all* the animal bones and not just the clearly identifiable ones, or all the charcoal, or all the stone waste flakes. We have to make a trade-off here—between the realistic abilities of our society to support archaeological repositories that cannot expand infinitely and the need to keep materials for future archaeologists with new questions and new techniques. Although the problem is clear, the answer is not.

---

ing the time it takes the light to bounce back, the total station calculates and records the artifact's X, Y, and Z coordinates—its provenience. This information is later downloaded to a database for mapping and analysis. Total stations take only a second or two to make measurements that are accurate to +/− 3 *millimeters*. And these instruments can be used at distances of hundreds of meters so that a site may need only one, rather than the several datums that other measurements systems may require (Figure 6-10).

Some archaeologists record the provenience of virtually every item found in situ (a practice sometimes called piece-plotting). Others set a cut-off, recording provenience on everything found in situ that is larger than, say, 3 centimeters (about an inch) in any dimension. As we said before, there are always trade-offs. Recording the provenience of every item found in situ provides the archaeologist with a very accurate record of where you found things, but it takes much more time—meaning that less gets excavated (this is a special problem if the site is threatened with destruction). How much you piece-plot depends on how much time you have for the excavation and the questions you need the data to answer.

Figure 6-10 Harold Dibble (center) and Shannon McPherron (right) record data on site while excavating Pech de L'Azé IV in France; the student at the far left is using a total station.

Is That All There Is to It?

No, there is more to recording provenience than simply location. Today, archaeologists sometimes record not only an artifact's *X, Y,* and *Z* coordinates, but also which side of the artifact was "up" when it was found (sometimes we mark the object's "up" side with a dot in permanent ink), the compass orientation of its long axis, and its slope or inclination (recorded with a builder's angle finder or clinometer). We would also note whether the artifact is burned, has calcium carbonate or a particular kind of sediment adhering to it, or possesses other characteristics. Although this can make excavation mind-numbing, we will see in Chapter 7 the resulting information is critical to understanding how a site was formed and consequently for inferring what people did at a site.

SIFTING THE EVIDENCE

Digging is just the beginning of excavation. No matter how carefully you excavate, it is impossible to see, map, and recover everything of archaeological interest; this is why we use sifters to find things that hand excavation

misses. This is also the second reason why we excavate in square units—sometimes only .5 × .5 meters in size. If the excavator misses something, the sifting process can at least tie its provenience down to a particular level in a particular unit—a very small area of the site.

At Gatecliff, excavators removed deposit with a trowel and whisk broom or paint brush, carefully sweeping it into a dustpan. When excavators found an artifact in situ, he or she recorded the artifact's provenience; sometimes it was photographed in place and a sketch drawn in the field notes before the artifact was placed in a separate bag and labeled with an identifying number.

The dustpan of dirt was then poured into a bucket and tagged with a label identifying the unit and level. When the bucket was full, the day's "gopher" took it to the screening area, outside the shelter in the hot sun (the gopher is the person whose daily assignment was to "go for" this and "go for" that). Here the bucket was poured onto a screen with ⅛-inch mesh (to give you some idea of the size, standard window screen is ¹⁄₁₆-inch mesh), where workers sifted and carefully checked for any artifacts missed by the excavators, including stone tool manufacturing waste flakes, fragments of bone, and anything else of importance.

Although archaeologists agree that Marshalltown makes the only trowel worth owning, there are many opinions on screens. Many archaeologists manufacture their own, and so the design and workmanship of screens varies from dig to dig (a few are shown in Figure 6-11). Some are suspended from tripods, some are mounted on rollers, and others are driven by gas engines to speed things up. When Thomas dug Alta Toquima, a village located at 12,000 feet in the mountains of central Nevada, he invented a "backpacker" design for the screens. At Gatecliff, we used the most common kind—a shaker screen mounted on two pivoting legs.

Exactly what kind of screen you use is far less important than the mesh. Many archaeologists prefer ⅛-inch hardware cloth, but the choice of mesh size varies with the circumstances. The important point is that *screen size affects what you recover and how fast you can recover it.* Use ¼-inch mesh and you can process dirt faster, but you will lose a surprising number of important objects. Use ¹⁄₁₆-inch mesh and the recovery rate goes up—but so does the time to process the dirt.

Thomas did an experiment some years ago to see how different screen sizes might affect the recovery of animal bones in archaeological sites. He built a three-decker screen with superimposed layers of ¼-inch over ⅛-inch over ¹⁄₁₆-inch mesh screens. He then ran a set of faunal remains recovered from a site through the screens.

As you might guess, he found that ¼-inch mesh was adequate for recovering bones of large animals such as bighorn or bison. But he also found that significant numbers of bones of medium-sized animals, such as rabbits and rodents, were lost. The ⅛-inch mesh screen was better for recovering the bones of these small mammals. But, in fact, significant amounts of small mammal bones are even lost through ⅛-inch screens! One needs ¹⁄₁₆-inch mesh (or flotation; see below) to recover the remains of animals the size of, say, pack rats, small birds, and especially fish.

Water-Screening and Matrix-Sorting

Archaeologists sometimes use **water-screening,** especially when the artifacts and ecofacts are expected to be very small. As the name suggests, water-screening requires that plenty of water be available. The dirt is simply poured onto a screen (usually ⅛- or ¹⁄₁₆-inch mesh) and sprayed with a garden hose until all the sediment is washed through. The screen will then be set aside and, once dry, searched. Kelly used water-screening at a site in the Stillwater Marsh in the Carson Desert (Figure 6-12). Because the site was located on a clay dune that contained no natural rock, he simply water-screened the deposits through ¹⁄₁₆-inch mesh, dried what was left, and bagged it all. He saved literally everything—flakes from the manufacture of stone tools, burned pieces of mud, fish and bird bones, and shell fragments—and sorted it later in the field camp.

You should always use the finest mesh screen possible. But using very fine mesh during the excavation can slow everything down to the point where you do not excavate a sufficient sample of the site to say anything worthwhile. Dense clay deposits, for example, can clog even a ¼-inch screen quickly. For this reason, many archaeologists use a larger screen mesh in the field, but take bulk sediment samples from each level. These samples are processed in the lab and provide a sample of those items missed by the ¼-inch screens. If the deposit has a low clay content, the sediment samples may simply be fine-screened. If they have a high clay content, they may be deflocculated (have the clay removed) by soaking the sediments in a solution of dishwasher detergent. After the clays are broken down, the slurry is poured through a fine screen (or often a set of screens), dried, and sorted by hand to separate stone from small stone tool waste flakes, shells, bits of ceramics, and bones. This is known as **matrix-sorting**, and, along with writing catalog numbers on artifacts, it is often one of the first tasks a novice may be assigned in a lab.

Ideally, as with piece-plotted artifacts, we wish to record data from the screening process that will allow us to reconstruct the site in the most detail possible. Running dirt through a screen, believe it or not, is *not* enough. In some sites, we also weigh it: We've recorded how much each bucket of deposit weighs, keeping a running tally on the level's excavation form. After screening a bucket, we return the material remaining in the screen to the bucket and weigh it again. (In most cases, the material that goes back into the bucket is unmodified rock.) By recording the before- and after-screening bucket weights, we record the frequency of rock in the deposits and determine the different densities of artifacts and ecofacts among a site's strata. These data help us understand how a site formed (more on

---

water-screening A sieving process in which deposit is placed in a screen and the matrix washed away with hoses; essential where artifacts are expected to be small and/or difficult to find without washing.

matrix-sorting The hand-sorting of processed bulk soil samples for minute artifacts and ecofacts.

Figure 6-11 A few of the innumerable sifter designs used by archaeologists.

that in Chapter 7) as well as changes in the intensity of site use over time.

Flotation

In some archaeological sites, like the upper parts of Gatecliff Shelter, the deposits are sufficiently protected from moisture that plant remains simply dry up and can be recovered by screening. But in other kinds of deposits, plant remains may be preserved only if they were burned and carbonized. These remains are often quite small and nearly impossible to collect by hand in the field.

The most common method of recovering such plant remains is **flotation,** a technique that is standard at most excavations.

Several procedures exist for floating archaeological samples, but all are based on the same principle: Dirt doesn't float, but carbonized plant (and some animal) remains do. By using water flotation, archaeologists can float most burned plant remains out of samples of archaeologically recovered dirt.

In one of the earliest applications, Stuart Struever (retired, former president of the Crow Canyon Archaeological Center) floated soil samples from 200 features attributable to the Middle Woodland component at the Apple Creek site, Illinois. The samples were hauled to nearby Apple Creek, where they were placed in mesh-bottomed buckets and then water-separated by students who worked midstream. Over 40,000 charred nutshell fragments, 2000 carbonized seeds, and some 15,000 identifiable fish bones were collected in this manner. Standard dry screening techniques would have missed most of these.

While excavating at Salts Cave in Kentucky, Patty Jo Watson (Washington University) and her associates were not blessed with a nearby stream, so they improvised (Figure 6-13). The sediments to be floated were

---

flotation The use of fluid suspension to recover tiny burned plant remains and bone fragments from archaeological sites.

© Robert Kelly

Figure 6-12 Wet-screening in the Stillwater Marsh, Nevada.

placed in double plastic bags and carried outside the cave. They first spread the samples (weighing a total of 1500 pounds) in the shade to dry. They then filled two 55-gallon drums with water, and placed the dry samples in metal buckets whose bottoms had been

© Patty Jo Watson

Figure 6-13 Patty Jo Watson (left) and Louise Robbins operating a flotation device constructed in a 55-gallon drum. Carbonized seeds and other plant remains are recovered as they float to the surface.

replaced with window screen. They submerged the buckets in the 55-gallon drums.

After a few seconds, the investigator skimmed off the charcoal and carbonized plant remains that had floated to the surface, using a small scoop made from a brass carburetor screen (cloth diapers work well, too). They spread the debris that floated to the top (called the light fraction) and the stuff that sank (the heavy fraction) on labeled newsprint to dry again. These flotation samples yielded carbonized remains of hickory nuts and acorns, seeds from berries, grains, sumpweed, chenopods, maygrass, and amaranth.

Today, flotation is not an expensive or even a particularly time-consuming process. Flotation techniques can (and should) be fitted to the local requirements. At Mission Santa Catalina, Thomas also used a converted 55-gallon drum, and one person could process dozens of samples each day. Some elaborate power-driven machines are equipped with aeration devices and use deflocculants or chemicals to remove sediment that might adhere to and sink carbonized plant remains. The technology is available to fit any budget.

But accuracy, not technology, is the issue. For a long time archaeologists saved only bone (and even then, just the large, identifiable pieces) but ignored plant remains. This frequently led archaeologists to overemphasize hunting and herding, thereby de-emphasizing the plant component of the economy. Now that flotation techniques have come into their own, we are discovering new things about the past. For example, from those seemingly innocuous burnt seeds of sumpweed, chenopods, maygrass, and amaranth that Patty Jo Watson and others collected through flotation, archaeologists made the important discovery that Native Americans had domesticated some indigenous plants of North America's eastern woodlands more than 4000 years ago—more than 1000 years before maize appeared on the scene. Those tiny bits of burnt plant material floating on the water turned out to be very important.

Cataloging the Finds

Excavating objects is just the beginning; in fact, excavation is only about 15 percent of a project—most of our time is spent in the lab analyzing the finds. And before the artifacts and field data can be analyzed, the objects must be cataloged. In many cases, the archaeologist assigns artifacts their catalog numbers in the field, as they are excavated. We do this by printing up sheets of sequential catalog numbers on peel-off return address forms (we've used the format 48BH3178/xxxx, where the 48BH3178 is the site's Smithsonian number and the xxxx is a sequential number, but others use more complex systems). When an artifact is found, it is piece-plotted and placed in a small Ziploc bag. The excavator peels a catalog number off the sheet (ensuring that there can be no duplicate numbers) and places it inside the bag (in case the label peels off, it will still be in the bag with the artifact). A crew member then records the number in the total station's data log.

Back in the lab, the archaeologist catalogs the artifacts. Most archaeologists are fanatical about cataloging their finds, because it's easy for one distracted lab worker to mess up an artifact's record of provenience. The catalogers work through the field bags, writing the catalog number onto the artifact itself with an archival pen, and sealing the number with clear fingernail polish; numbered tags are sometimes tied to some artifacts, such as small beads. Some archaeologists pre-print the catalog numbers on minute labels and glue them to artifacts with archivally stable glue. Even those items that were not found in situ or otherwise assigned a catalog number in the field will be given a number in the lab. The catalog number is what ties a particular artifact back to observations made in the field. Thus, although cataloging can often take hundreds of person-hours, it is necessary to ensure that an artifact's original provenience, and consequently its context, is never lost.

Lab workers then enter the cataloged artifacts' information into a computer database, usually including rudimentary observations (such as weight, condition, color), collection date, its provenience (for example, unit, level, *X,Y,Z* coordinates), and contextual data (for instance, stratum, inclination, orientation). A digital photo may be attached to the data record. Copies are then made of the database so that the artifacts' all-important contextual data will not be lost.

Conclusion: Archaeology's Conservation Ethic: Dig Only What You Must

Archaeologists have traditionally protected their excavations against vandals and pothunters. Excavation often draws unwanted attention, and vandals have been known to attack sites during field season even during the night. On Thomas's first job in archaeology, a 24-hour guard (armed, appropriately enough, with bow and arrow) was posted to protect the open excavation units from looters. At Gatecliff, we tediously backfilled the site by hand every year to protect the archaeology from the curious public, and the public from the dangers of open-pit archaeology.

On St. Catherines Island, the problem is somewhat different. The only visitors are scientists, who realize the research value of archaeological sites and leave the excavations untouched. It is thus possible to open a few test units on several sites, process the finds, and then

Profile of an Archaeologist
An African Archaeologist

by Chapurukha (Chap) M. Kusimba, Curator of African Archaeology and Ethnology at the Field Museum of Natural History (Chicago)

Chap Kusimba

I became interested in the natural history of East Africa when, as a youth, I learned of the discoveries of Louis and Mary Leakey in Olduvai Gorge in my native country of Kenya. I was intrigued by claims that East Africa was the cradle of humankind and fascinated by the idea that all humankind ultimately traced its beginnings to Africa. The fact that there was so much to discover in my own backyard shaped the way I viewed my heritage and encouraged my interest in becoming a scientist.

From 1986 to 1996, I focused my attention on understanding how foraging, fishing, pastoral, and agropastoral communities of the East African Coast developed into complex coastal chiefdoms and city states over the past 2000 years.

The study of social complexity has long been contentious in Africa. Assuming that Africans could not be innovative, previous scholars credited the origins of social complexity and "high culture" to immigrants from Southwest Asia. Today, African archaeologists have rejected diffusion as the initiator of cultural and technological transformations in Africa, and look instead to the specific processes of development.

My research focuses on the role of technology, economy, and interregional interaction in the development of chiefdoms and states in East Africa. In so doing, it evaluates the roles of Indian Ocean trade, iron working technology, and interregional interaction in the development of social complexity in East Africa. I have conducted regional archaeological surveys, defined settlement patterns, and augmented these with problem-oriented exca-

return next year to the more promising sites for more intensive excavation.

On strictly research projects—like our work at Mission Santa Catalina—the sites are not threatened by outside incursions, and one must adopt a conservative excavation strategy. Archaeologists never excavate more of a site than is needed to answer their research questions; extensive excavations are undertaken only in the case of sites threatened by development or erosion. Most archaeologists leave as much of a site intact as possible for later investigators, who undoubtedly will have different questions and better techniques. And, as we have seen, remote sensing technology and archaeological survey techniques sometimes provide archaeologists with low-impact ways of learning without digging at all.

Regardless of whether we use high-tech instruments or old-fashioned elbow grease, our personal responsi-

bility for site conservation remains unchanged and fundamental. Archaeology is a destructive science. We said it at the beginning of this chapter and it is worth repeating: Sites can be excavated only once, and so it is imperative we do things right. Sometimes those sites have remarkable preservation and many, many kinds of materials are preserved; other times, only stone artifacts are preserved. This affects what kind of excavation techniques are used and how quickly the excavation can proceed. But how much or how little is found in a site does not change the fact that we must take any step necessary to ensure that provenience for virtually every artifact, ecofact, and feature is acquired during the excavation and recorded. We excavate in controlled units, sometimes as small as .5 × .5 meter, using a systematic grid system; we excavate in natural levels where possible, and, even if natural strata are present, in levels no more than 10 or even 5 centimeters thick; we record every-

vations in key locales and sites in Southeastern Kenya. The results are published in a number of research articles and in my book, *The Rise and Fall of Swahili States*, a text on the archaeology of social complexity in Africa.

With a few exceptions, all thoroughly investigated sites on the Kenya coast are large urban centers with monumental structures composed of elite residences, chiefly courts, and mosques. The focus on large urban sites inevitably introduced significant biases in data collection and influenced the rendering of the regional history.

But African archaeologists cannot ignore the relationship between urban areas and their trading partners in the hinterlands. And so, beginning in 1998, Dr. Sibel Barut Kusimba (Northern Illinois University) and I began to examine the role of trade in shaping East Africa's diverse ethnic identities. We did this by surveying areas in the Tsavo National Park and surrounding area, 150 kilometers from Kenya's eastern coast. We described more than 200 sites, from the Early Stone Age into the historic era, including hunter-gatherer rockshelter camps and residences, pastoral, agropastoral, and agrarian villages and chiefdom-level settlements, fortified stockades, market centers, and iron production areas. So far, we have excavated twelve of these sites and conducted intensive interviews with local communities called the Wataita, Somali, and Waata.

An important pattern emerging from our research is the web of social interactions among peoples of diverse origins and languages practicing and inventing different ways of life. The Tsavo region was a mosaic of political and economic alliances, an example of regional systems that exist in many areas of the world but are not completely understood. Understanding the development of social complexity in Africa requires attention to such regional interactions. Indeed, the mosaic is important to us not just as grist for the archaeologist's mill, but as a reservoir for potentially understanding Africa's future, since Africa's modern dynamics of ethnicity, social, and political power are rooted in these earlier interactions.

thing we can about an item before we pull it from the ground; and we assign catalog numbers to everything found so that each item can be related back to information gathered on its context. Once we have this information in hand, we are prepared to move on to the next chore of archaeology: making sense of everything we have found.

Summary

- The guiding rule in all excavation is to record context, and this means recording provenience of the artifacts, features, and ecofacts. Diverse excavation strategies respond to different preservation conditions, constraints, and objectives.

- Preservation is enhanced in continuously dry, continuously wet, and/or very cold environments—any place where conditions prevent the existence of the microorganisms that promote decay.

- Initial tests of a site may employ a vertical strategy, designed largely for chronological control.

- In a horizontal strategy, designed to explore the conditions of past lifeways, the context of artifacts and ecofacts within excavation strata becomes critical; excavation proceeds with the goal of finding all artifacts in situ. When an excavator misses an artifact—and it turns up in the screen—a significant piece of information has been lost because that artifact can then be located only within the excavation square and level.

■ Archaeologists use screening, flotation, and bulk matrix processing to recover extremely small artifacts with some control on provenience.

■ All recovered materials are cataloged so that each item is permanently linked to its excavation record.

■ From test pit through full-scale excavation, archaeologists maintain exact records of the three-dimensional provenience of the objects being recovered and their context. The objective of archaeological records is to record the excavation in such a way that another archaeologist could "see" what the original excavator saw.

■ It's hard to overemphasize the importance of hands-on experience in archaeology. There is no substitute for personal field experience, and no textbook, computer simulation, or classroom exercise satisfactorily simulates the field situation.

Additional Reading

Collis, John. 2001. *Digging Up the Past: An Introduction to Archaeological Excavation.* Phoenix Mill, Stroud, UK: Sutton Publishing.

Roskams, Steve. 2001. *Excavation.* Cambridge: Cambridge University Press.

Online Resources

COMPANION WEB SITE
Visit **http://anthropology.wadsworth.com** and click on the Student Companion Web Site for Thomas/Kelly *Archaeology*, 4th edition, to access a wide range of material to help you succeed in your introductory archaeology course. These include flashcards, Internet exercises, Web links, and practice quizzes.

RESEARCH ONLINE WITH INFOTRAC COLLEGE EDITION
From the Student Companion Web Site, you can access the InfoTrac College Edition database, which offers thousands of full-length articles for your research.

7 Geoarchaeology and Site Formation Processes

Outline

Students expose a profile of a burial mound on St. Catherines Island, Georgia.

Preview

EVERY ARCHAEOLOGICAL SITE is unique. Some sites are remarkably well preserved; others are not. Some sites lie on the surface, some are deeply buried, and others lie underwater. Some are frozen; others are dry. Each site that we have personally worked on has presented new challenges. But they all had one thing in common: dirt.

Although Americanist archaeology is firmly embedded in anthropology, it has a foot securely in geology as well. In fact, we can't do archaeology without also doing geology. Archaeological sites are created by human activities, but they also build up through many natural processes, including those that are commonly studied by geologists (and, especially, geomorphologists). The study of the dirt in and around archaeological sites has become an important subfield of archaeology, known as geoarchaeology.

Geologists first pulled together the major principles of stratigraphy. This chapter introduces the important concept of superposition, the simple operating principle behind the interpretation of archaeological sediments. We then discuss how geoarchaeologists contribute to our understanding and interpretation of archaeological sites, focusing on natural and cultural site formation processes.

INTRODUCTION

Michael Waters (Texas A&M University) defines **geoarchaeology** as "the field of study that applies the concepts and methods of the geosciences to archaeological research." In his opinion, geoarchaeology has two objectives: The first is to place sites (and the artifacts found in them) in a "relative and absolute temporal context through the application of stratigraphic principles and absolute dating techniques." We'll focus on stratigraphic principles here (and discuss dating techniques in Chapter 8).

Waters's second objective of geoarchaeology is "to understand the natural processes of **site formation**," which includes all the human and natural actions that work together to create an archaeological site. In the past, many archaeologists worked with geologists to fulfill this need. But as important as these collaborations were, it became clear that archaeology needs geologists who are not only trained in **geomorphology**, the geological study of landforms and landscapes (rivers, sand dunes, deltas, marshes, glacial and coastal environments, and so on), but who also understand the special brand of geology that applies specifically to archaeological sites. Rockshelter sediments—like those that filled Gatecliff Shelter—are often foreign to traditionally trained geologists, as are the sediments that fill a collapsed pueblo room. Traditional geologists may also look at sediments on a broader temporal scale than is required for understanding the formation of archaeological sites.

Despite their different emphases, however, geological and geoarchaeological analyses share a common foundation, beginning with the law of superposition.

---

geoarchaeology The field of study that applies the concepts and methods of the geosciences to archaeological research.

site formation The human and natural actions that work together to create an archaeological site.

geomorphology The geological study of landforms and landscapes, for instance, soils, rivers, hills, sand dunes, deltas, glacial deposits, and marshes.

THE LAW OF SUPERPOSITION

Nicolaus Steno (1638–1686) is generally acknowledged as having formulated the **law of superposition,** which says that, in any pile of **sedimentary rocks** undisturbed by folding or overturning, the strata on the bottom were deposited first, those above them were deposited second, those above them third, and so on. This principle seems preposterously simple, but it was a critical observation in the seventeenth century. Why?

Steno was an anatomist (a curious background for one who would make a major contribution to geology). In dissecting a shark, he noticed that the teeth looked exactly like things that naturalists occasionally found in rocks, and that Steno's colleagues called "tongue stones." The tongue stones were, in fact, fossil shark teeth, but scholars of Steno's day commonly believed that fossils were stones that had fallen from the moon or had grown inside rocks; a contemporary of Steno attributed them to "lapidifying virtue diffused through the whole body of the geocosm," which isn't especially helpful.

But others, including Steno, held the then-radical notion that these odd "stones" were in fact ancient shark teeth. Left unsolved, however, was the perplexing question of how one solid, a shark's tooth, came to be inside another solid, a rock. In his *Preliminary Discourse to a Dissertation on a Solid Body Naturally Contained Within a Solid* (1669), Steno pondered this question. He concluded that at some point in time, one of them must not have been solid. But which one? Believing that all rock began as liquid, Steno postulated that rocks must have been laid down horizontally (a concept he termed the principle of original horizontality); any departure from the horizontal, Steno reasoned, must have resulted from later disturbance. He then argued that if a thing were already a solid when the liquid rock was laid down, it would force that liquid to mold itself around the existing solid. Thus, Steno argued that fossils came to be inside solid rock because the fossils were older, and because the rock was originally laid down as a liquid. Conversely, if a solid formed after the rock had hardened, it would conform to voids and fissures already in the rock (thus crystals and mineral-filled veins conform to voids in the rock that contains them).

Working from these observations, Steno postulated that if rock were originally deposited horizontally as a liquid, then the oldest layer should be the deepest and progressively younger layers should lie above it. Although formulated as an aside, Steno's law of superposition became the foundation of all stratigraphic interpretation—whether we are talking about the Grand Canyon or Kidder's excavations at Pecos Pueblo. Here's an example of how it helps to place things in time.

Fossil Footprints at Laetoli: The Law of Superposition in Action

Mary Leakey (1913–1996) was one of the world's most famous fossil finders. With her esteemed husband, Louis Leakey (1903–1972), she scoured East Africa, seeking archaeological evidence of the earliest human ancestors who once lived there. In 1959, the Leakeys electrified the world with finds that included the celebrated *Zinjanthropus* skull (now known as *Australopithecus boisei* or *Paranthropus boisei*) from Olduvai Gorge in northwestern Tanzania. To many, Mary Leakey's discovery of the "Zinj" cranium heralded a new age, the beginning of modern paleoanthropological research in East Africa.

But two decades later, as she stood staring at the ground in a place called Laetoli (lay-*toe*-lee, a Masai name for a red lily that grows throughout the area), it was Mary Leakey's turn to be shocked. Just below the surface of the Serengeti Plain, her research team found animal footprints—hundreds of them—as clear as if they had been cast in fresh concrete.

Why were the footprints preserved? At some time in the remote past, the nearby Sadiman volcano had erupted, blanketing the landscape around Laetoli with a lens of very fine volcanic ash. Then a light rain moistened the ash layer without washing it away, turning it into a thin slurry. Animals meandered across this wet surface, apparently on the way to a nearby water hole: spring hares, birds, buffaloes, pigs, a saber-tooth tiger, and baboons—each leaving dozens of footprints in the gooey ash. Fortuitously, the ash was a kind called

law of superposition The geological principle stating that, in any pile of sedimentary rocks that have not been disturbed by folding or overturning, each bed is older than the layers above and younger than the layers below; also known as Steno's law.

sedimentary rock Rock formed when the weathered products of pre-existing rocks have been transported by and deposited in water and are turned once again to stone.

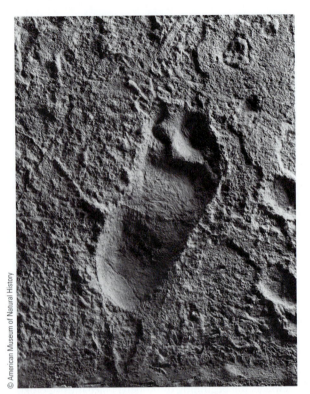

© American Museum of Natural History

Figure 7-1 The famous hominid footprints at Laetoli (Tanzania, Africa).

carbonatite, which quickly solidifies to a concrete-like hardness after being wet, and in this case it captured the footprints in an enduring land surface.

But not only birds and four-legged mammals had been there. At one point, at least two **hominids,** early human ancestors, also strolled across the ash (Figure 7-1). More than five dozen individual human footprints clearly demonstrate a human-like gait—fully bipedal with a stride and balance similar to our own. Across a distance of about 25 meters, two of our ancestors, one larger than the other, walked side-by-side, close enough to touch one another. The tracks of the smaller of the two suggest that he or she may have been burdened with extra weight on one hip—perhaps carrying an infant (Figure 7-2)? Some analyses of the tracks even suggest that a third, still smaller, individual followed close behind, in the footprints of the largest hominid.

Assuming that this evidence could be trusted—and assuming that the ancient age could be firmly estab-

hominids Members of the evolutionary line that contains humans and our early bipedal ancestors.

lished—Mary Leakey realized that these footprints could test a major hypothesis of paleoanthropology. For decades, specialists in human evolution had argued that bipedalism (walking upright on two feet), a preeminent human characteristic, must have arisen in response to tool use. After all, if you're going to make and use stone tools, having your hands free would certainly be advantageous. This hypothesis therefore predicted that stone tools are older than bipedalism. At the time, the world's oldest stone tools were about 1.3 million years old (today the earliest known stone tools, found in Ethiopia, are between 2.5 and 2.6 million years old).

Based on her knowledge of the region's geology, Leakey guessed that the age of the footprints was considerably older (more than a million years older) than 1.3 million years. If so, then the world's oldest human footprints implied that our human ancestors walked upright long before the appearance of the oldest stone tools in the area. And if that were true, then the hypothesis that tool use led to bipedalism was wrong.

The Geologic Background

The fossil footprints were contained in the upper portion of the so-called Laetolil Beds, within a geological subunit known as Tuff 7 ("tuff" refers to hardened volcanic ash). Leakey found the actual footprints near the bottom of the Tuff 7 formation in what she called, appropriately enough, the Footprint Tuff. However, to determine the age of the footprints, it was necessary to place this key geological stratum within its appropriate stratigraphic context.

Richard Hay (University of Illinois, Urbana-Champaign) spearheaded the geological investigation. Over a period of 6 years, Hay worked out the complicated geological sequence at Laetoli, which is summarized in Figure 7-3 on page 156 and in the following generalized stratigraphic descriptions (with, of course, the youngest layer on top):

Ngaloba Beds	sheetwash and mudflow sediments containing volcanic ash, pebbles, and cobbles
Olpiro Beds	volcanic tuff layers, maximum thickness about 6 meters
Naibadad Beds	volcanic tuff layers, generally 11–15 meters thick
Ogol Lavas	a series of distinctive lava flows and ash sediments; in places, 230 meters deep

© American Museum of Natural History

Figure 7-2 Reconstruction of the early humans (*Australopithecus afarensis*) who made the 3.5-million-year-old footprints at Laetoli. Although the fossil-based proportions are accurate, many of the details (such as hair density and distribution, sex, skin color, form of the nose and lips, and so on) are conjectural.

Footprint Tuff is evidence that this surface was gently rained upon—actual raindrop impressions occur along with the footprints. Then, toward the upper part, widespread erosion occurs, which Hay attributed to rainy season downpours.

Therefore, the research team concluded, the Footprint Tuff was deposited over a short span of time, probably only a few weeks, beginning near the end of the dry season and lasting into the rainy season. This is an amazingly detailed reconstruction, based strictly on the available geological evidence.

How Old Are the Footprints?

Because the footprints themselves cannot be dated, we have to rely on the geology. Here the law of superposition comes to our aid. Steno's law holds that, all else being equal, older layers lie at the base of the stratified geologic sequence.

So we work from the bottom up. The Laetolil Beds lie beneath the Ndolanya Beds: this is a geological fact. The law of superposition applied to this stratigraphic fact *suggests* that the Laetolil Beds *should be* older than the Ndolanya Beds: this is geological interpretation. Similarly, because the Ogol Lavas lie above both the Laetolil and Ndolanya beds, these lavas should be younger still. Because they lie uppermost in the stratigraphic column at Laetoli, the Ngaloba Beds should be the most recent of all. The law of superposition provides the interpretive key to unlock the *relative* stratigraphic sequence at Laetoli.

The potassium-argon dating technique pinned down the date of the Laetoli footprints. (Chapter 8 will describe how archaeologists use this technique to date strata and artifacts, so you will have to bear with us here.)

Leakey worked with geologists Robert Drake and Garness Curtis (then of the University of California, Berkeley), who processed a series of potassium-argon dates on samples from the major stratified layers recognized in the Laetoli area. The bottom of the upper Laetolil Beds dated to about 3.76 million years. The

| Ndolanya Beds | upper and lower units of sedimentary layers generally 19–23 meters thick; apparently windblown sediments |
| Laetolil Beds | the basal stratigraphic unit, consisting of a series of eight tuffs (divided into upper and lower beds) reflecting eight periods of major volcanic ash deposition, in places more than 150 meters thick |

(*Note:* The name of the site is spelled "Laetoli"; the basal formation is called the Laetolil Beds.)

These are the geological "facts," but what do they tell us about the footprints?

From evidence preserved on the surface of the Footprint Tuff, it was clear the ash buried the footprints rapidly, soon after they formed. This accounts for their extraordinary state of preservation. Geologists could also infer the season in which the hominids had taken their walk. There was no evidence of grasses at the base of the ash lens. This meant that the grass had been grazed off, suggesting that the eruptions took place during the dry season. But toward the middle of the

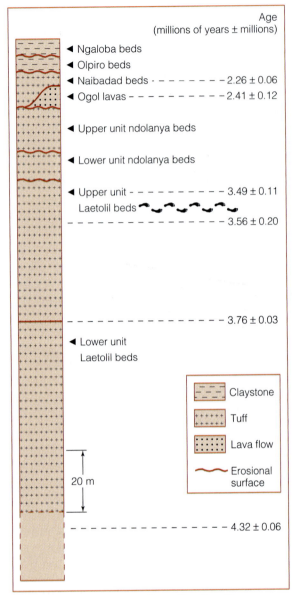

Figure 7-3 The major stratigraphic profile at Laetoli.

Naibadad stratum, lying near the top of the stratified layer, dated to 2.26 million years. Dates of intermediate age (between 3.56 and 2.41 million years) occur from tuffs sandwiched in the middle of the stratigraphic column. Note particularly how the suite of dates follows in stratigraphic order, from most ancient at the bottom to most recent at the top. In this case, absolute dating technology confirmed the relative stratigraphic sequence inferred from the law of superposition.

The base of the Footprint Tuff—recall that it was located near the bottom of Tuff 7—dated to about 3.56 million years; the base of the tuff above, Tuff 8, dated to

3.49 million years. Finally, we can answer the single most important question at Laetoli: *The fossil hominid footprints are between 3.49 and 3.56 million years old.* Given that the footprints are closer to the bottom of Tuff 7 than to its top, they are probably closer to 3.56 than 3.49 million years old in age (see "Looking Closer: What Happened to the Laetoli Footprints?").

With the dating of the Laetoli footprints, Leakey showed that humans were bipedal long before they made stone tools. Therefore, the hypothesis that stone tool use led to bipedalism must be incorrect (unless there are still older stone tools that we have not yet found).

READING GATECLIFF'S DIRT

The law of superposition gives us the first geoarchaeological tool for reading a site's stratigraphy. With it, we know that the story begins at the bottom, with succeeding "chapters" lying above. With a few more tools, we can fill in the story of a site's geologic history. Gatecliff Shelter, with a 40-foot stratigraphic profile covering more than 7000 years, again provides an example (Figure 7-4 on page 158).

The Gatecliff sediments, like those of all archaeological sites, resulted from both natural processes and human behavior. The first question we need to ask is, "What are all the possible ways in which the materials in Gatecliff—artifacts, bones, rock, and dirt—entered the shelter?"

The artifacts and a good portion of the animal bones entered Gatecliff through human behavior of course, but natural processes were also at work. Many of the bones are of animals that lived (and died) in the site, or whose bodies were brought in by carnivores, raptors, or human hunters. And, of course, there is a lot of rock and dirt. The geoarchaeologist must consider both human and natural factors in reading a stratigraphy.

Gatecliff's Stratigraphy

In Gatecliff's master stratigraphy, the thin dark levels (such as those numbered 9, 11, and 13) are living surfaces. Altogether there are 16 such surfaces, all of which resulted largely from human activities. These surfaces contain fire hearths, charcoal, broken stone tools, grinding slabs, flakes, food remains, and occasional fragments of basketry and cordage. (Although it was not true for Gatecliff, in many other sites people might

Looking Closer
What Happened to the Laetoli Footprints?

The Laetoli footprints were one of the world's most important archaeological discoveries. *Did the archaeologists just leave them there?*

When Leakey completed her work with the footprints, she did what most archaeologists do when they complete an excavation: She backfilled the site to preserve it. After putting about 2 feet of soil on top of the footprints, Leakey covered the site with large basalt boulders to prevent elephants from walking on the tracks.

Unfortunately, the soil was rich and loose, and the shade from the boulders helped this garden-like soil hold moisture. After a few years, acacia trees began to grow on the spot, and some archaeologists worried that the roots would destroy the footprints.

So, in 1995 (when Leakey was in her 80s), Fiona Marshall (Washington University), an archaeologist with years of experience in African archaeology, returned with a team from the Getty Conservation Institute. Marshall's team carefully excavated the site again, but this time the goal was to carefully unearth the trees' roots without disturbing the tracks. Fortunately, they discovered that the roots had not yet done significant damage.

Although various ideas were proposed as to how the footprints could be safely removed, the Getty team finally decided that the footprints were best preserved in the ground, for now, with periodic removal of the trees. In 100 years, the footprints will be uncovered again to check on their condition and (in case new technology permits) the footprints will be safely removed to a museum.

---

very well have built walls, houses, or floors; dug deep pits or wells; and in general contributed much more to a site's stratigraphic record.) At any rate, because the living surfaces are so vividly separated by the sterile flood layers, we can see clearly what was brought into the cave by (or during) human activity.

Most of the strata in Gatecliff Shelter are of purely geological origin—the rock, silt, and dirt entered the shelter via non-human processes. Thomas divided the Gatecliff profile into a sequence of 56 strata: layers of more or less homogeneous material, visually separated from adjacent layers by a distinct change in the character of the material deposited (see Table 7-1). Some strata, such as Stratum 8, consisted of coarser **alluvial** (water-carried) **sediments,** grading from gravels at the bottom to fine sand silts at the top. Apparently, an ephemeral stream that occasionally flows in front of Gatecliff Shelter today flooded several times in the past and ran through the shelter. The water of such flash floods would first deposit coarse sediments, such as pea-sized gravels. As the water's velocity diminished, its carrying capacity decreased, and smaller particles were

deposited. Finally, when the water slowed, the tiniest silt particles would cap the stream sediments. Such floods occurred several times throughout the 7000 years of deposition at Gatecliff and, each time, they buried the existing occupation surface. When the inhabitants returned to Gatecliff, they thus lived on a new "floor," separated from the previous one by nearly a meter of sterile alluvial or **eolian** (wind-blown) **sediments.** In some cases, such as Stratum 2, small ponds formed at the rear of the shelter after one of the flash flood episodes. The pond water acted as a trap for eolian dust particles. Dust blew into the shelter (as it did the whole time we excavated it), was caught in the pond, and then settled to its bottom as finely laminated silts.

---

alluvial sediments Sediments transported by flowing water.

eolian sediments Materials transported and accumulated by wind (for example, dunes).

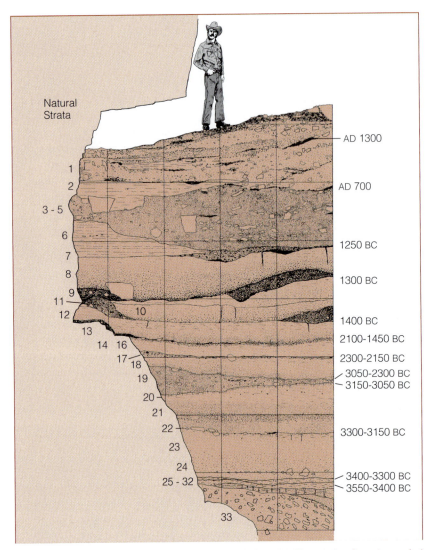

Natural
Strata

AD 1300

AD 700

1250 BC

1300 BC

1400 BC
2100-1450 BC
2300-2150 BC
3050-2300 BC
3150-3050 BC

3300-3150 BC

3400-3300 BC
3550-3400 BC

Figure 7-4 The master stratigraphic profile from Gatecliff Shelter. The standing figure is exactly 6 feet tall, and the grid system shows 1-meter squares. Only the upper 33 of the 56 stratigraphic units show in this particular profile. © *American Museum of Natural History; from Thomas 1983b, figure 22.*

Thomas described in detail each of the 56 such strata stacked up inside Gatecliff. Here is how he described one stratum near the bottom of the master stratigraphy, shown in Figure 7-5 on page 160:

Stratum 22, Rubble:
Angular limestone clasts, charcoal firepit, and baked area at top, somewhat churned into the underlying silty top of Stratum 23. Maximum thickness 50 cm. on the southwest pile and formed continuous layer up to 15 cm. thick in eastern parts of excavation, but was discontinuous elsewhere. Almost as voluminous as

Stratum 17, the top was ~4.85 m. [below datum] on the southwestern pile and ranged from ~5.50 to ~5.30 m. elsewhere, and its bottom was about ~5.30 m. in the south-west corner, ~5.35 m. in the Master Profile, and ~5.32 m. in the present excavation. . . . Stratum 22 was created by gradual accumulation of roof fall and talus [loose, broken rock] tumbling over the shelter lip between 5,250 and 5,100 years ago. Stratum 22 was called GU 6R-74 in the field and contained [living floor] 14.

Note first the detail of description. Exact depths are given relative to the site datum. When paired with the horizontal grid system, these arbitrary elevations document the exact configuration of each geological stratum.

Each geological term is sufficiently well defined so that geologists who have never visited Gatecliff can understand what Stratum 22 looked like. Note also how Thomas separated such descriptions from interpretation. This way, others can use his data to make their own assessments.

You can also see the dates we found for Stratum 22. Of the 47 radiocarbon dates (we'll describe these in Chapter 8) processed on materials from Gatecliff, 4 were available from this particular stratum. This information, combined with the added radiocarbon evidence from strata above and below Stratum 22, allowed us to estimate that the stratum was laid down between 5250 and 5100 years ago.

Marker Beds

Most of the strata in Gatecliff are unique to this site; they are found nowhere else. But sometimes, archaeologists encounter strata that are distinct and that are

TABLE 7-1 Part of the Physical Stratigraphy of Gatecliff Shelter

STRATUM	SOIL	NATURE OF SEDIMENT	FIELD DESIGNATION	AGE IN RADIOCARBON YEARS BEFORE PRESENT (C-14 yr BP)
1	S-1	Rubble	GU-14	0–1250 BP
2		Sand and silt	Upper GU 13	1250 BP
3	S-2	Rubble	Part of GU 12	1250–1350 BP
4		Sand and silt	GU 13 and GU 12 Silt	1350 BP
5	S-3	Rubble	Part of GU 12	1350–3200 BP
6		Sand and silt	GU 11	3200 BP
7		Rubble	GU 11 and GU 10R	3250–3200 BP
8		Sand and silt	GU 10	3250 BP
9		Rubble	GU 9R	3300–3250 BP
10		Sand and silt	GU 8 A and B	3300 BP
11		Rubble	GU 7R	3400–3300 BP
12		Sand and silt	GU 7	3400 BP
13		Rubble	6 Living Floor	4050–3400 BP
14		Sand and silt	GU 5 Silt	4050 BP
15		Rubble	Part of GU 5	4100–4050 BP
16		Sand and silt	Part of GU 5	4100 BP
17		Rubble	GU 4	4250–4100 BP
18		Silty sand	GU 3	4250 BP
19		Sand and rubble	GU 2	5000–4250 BP
20	S-4	Silt and clay	GU 1A	5100–5000 BP
21		Sand and silt	GU 1 and GU 7–74	5100 BP
22		Rubble	GU 6R–74	5250–5100 BP
23		Gravel, sand, and silt	GU 6–74 and GU 5–74	5250 BP
24		Rubble	GU 4R–74	5350–5250 BP
25		Silt	GU 4–74	5350 BP
26		Rubble	GU 3R–74	5500–5350 BP
27–29		Silts	GU 3A–74	5500 BP
30		Sand	GU 3B–74	5500 BP
31		Rubble	GU 2R–74	5700–5500 BP
32		Fine sand and silt	GU 2–74	
33		Fine sand and silt	GU 12–76, GU 1–78, and GU 1–74	
34		Silt and very fine sand	GU 2–78	
35		Rubble	GU 3R–78	
36		Silty medium sand	GU 3–78	

SOURCE: Thomas 1993b, table 3.

found in other sites in the same region. These are known as **marker beds,** and if they've been dated in other sites, they can provide clues to the age of sediments in a new site.

Gatecliff contained one of these marker beds. Stratum 55, near the very bottom of the site, contained an inch-thick lens of sand-sized volcanic ash, or tephra, which consisted of fragments of crystal, glass, and rock once ejected into the air by a volcanic eruption. Not discovered until the last week of the last field season, the tephra was indistinct, mixed with the cobbles and rubble of Stratum 55. In the laboratory, Jonathan Davis (1948–1990), a leading expert on the volcanic ashes of the American West, confirmed that this was

ash from the eruption of Mount Mazama. When this mountain (in the Oregon Cascades) blew up 6900 years ago, it spewed out 11 *cubic miles* of pumice and related materials, forming a caldera that contains Crater Lake. The Mount St. Helens eruption in 1980 was a firecracker in comparison. The prevailing winds, coupled with the force of the explosion itself, carried Mazama ash across eight western states and three Canadian provinces.

marker bed An easily identified geologic layer whose age has been independently confirmed at numerous locations and whose presence can therefore be used to date archaeological and geological sediments.

Figure 7-5 An exposure of the lower stratigraphy at Gatecliff Shelter. Stratum 23 is the thick dark layer capped by a layer of white silt just above the student's head; Stratum 22 (quite thin at this place in the shelter) is the layer of rocky debris that sits on top of the white silt. Incidentally, an exposure such as this today would be extensively shored.

Mazama ash appears—and it appears in many archaeological sites in the western United States—it tells the archaeologist that everything above the ash is less than 6900 years old, and everything below it is more than 6900 years old.

Gatecliff as a Geologic Deposit

What can we learn from Gatecliff's stratigraphic profile? For any archaeological site, the archaeologist must consider the ways in which that site formed *as a geologic deposit*.

In a rockshelter like Gatecliff, there are three primary ways that sediment enters the site (Figure 7-6). First, there are rocks that fall from the ceiling and the shelter's front lip (known as the dripline). As the front lip of the shelter erodes, the shelter's habitable space moves toward the back wall; this, incidentally, means that earlier habitations might be found outside the modern dripline. Large blocks falling from the roof may also reduce the habitable space. This happened at Gatecliff, when a pickup truck-sized piece of the roof broke off the ceiling about 1000 years ago, covering the eastern side of the shelter and reducing the amount of floor space by almost half. Such changes in a shelter's floor plan can alter the way people use it (or can cause them to abandon it altogether). Eventually, a shelter may erode back so far that it will be no more than a cliff face (and archaeologists may not even recognize it as a site).

Rocks also enter a shelter as **colluvial sediments** from the surrounding hillside. Colluvial sediments are rock and dirt that move downslope through gravity or during rainstorms or summer snowmelt. These sedi-

Wherever the ash settled, it created a marker bed—a geologic layer that geoarchaeologists can identify and whose age has been independently confirmed at numerous locations. Archaeologists can use it, therefore, as a check on age estimates. The Mazama ash is dated at numerous locations to 6900 years old. Wherever the

colluvial sediments Sediments deposited primarily through the action of gravity on geological material lying on hillsides.

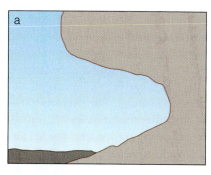
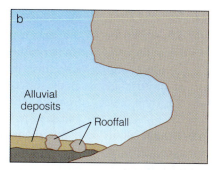
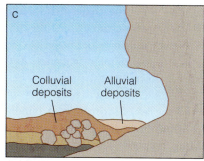
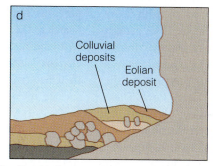

Figure 7-6 A hypothetical rockshelter, filling with colluvial and eolian sediments, as well as rooffall, over time.

ments fall over a shelter's dripline, or they may creep, roll, or wash in around the sides. As a result, rockshelters sometimes have a berm of earth at their fronts and one at either or both sides.

Fine eolian dust will blow into the shelter (sometimes from a source near the shelter, sometimes from distant sources), and alluvial sediments may accumulate if a stream runs into the shelter, carrying, depending on the stream's force, various-sized rocks into it, as well as silt and clay. A fast-moving stream, on the other hand, may remove sediments from a shelter.

With this information, what do the sediments at Gatecliff tell us about how this particular site formed? We can begin with Stratum 55, where Jonathan Davis found the Mazama ash marker bed. This stratum was composed of angular rubble, with bedding planes that conformed to the sloping surface of the site and no alluvial sediments. Davis argued that slow, downslope colluvial action and debris falling from the shelter's lip and ceiling created this stratum. He also suggested that this stratum tells us that precipitation fell primarily in the winter. Why did he say this?

Winter precipitation falls as snow, but during the day it melts and seeps into cracks in the shelter's ceiling. There it will freeze at night, expand, and break off chunks of the ceiling that fall to the shelter's floor (pro-

ducing that angular rubble in Stratum 55). In addition, winter snow normally melts slowly and does not produce the energy needed to move much sediment and rock downslope. Hence, it does not move much colluvium into the shelter (resulting in the bedding planes seen in Stratum 55).

This mode of deposition changed between 6500 and 4250 years ago. Strata of this age consist of thick beds of silt (giving the stratigraphy its layer-cake appearance) interspersed with thin layers of angular rock. Davis interpreted these sediments as indicating an increase in summer precipitation and perhaps overall drier conditions. Summer precipitation tends to fall as torrential thunderstorms and thus tends to produce mud and debris flows or flash floods that can rapidly (that is, in a single storm) contribute large amounts of silt and/or rock to the shelter. Moreover, with less overall precipitation, there was less vegetation to hold sediments back when downpours did occur.

Then, about 5100 years ago, a **soil** developed in the shelter's sediments. Why would this happen?

A Word about Soils

By definition, soils are not depositional units. They are developmental sequences—distinctive layers that develop in place. You've seen these as dark bands in road cuts or pipeline trenches. The **A horizon** is the topsoil—the dark, humus layer where organic material and rock undergo chemical and mechanical decomposition. The **B horizon** lies below this and is where clays

soil Sediments that have undergone in situ chemical and mechanical alteration.

A horizon The upper part of a soil, where active organic and mechanical decomposition of geological and organic material occurs.

B horizon A layer found below the A horizon, where clays accumulate that are transported downward by water.

accumulate as rainfall and snowmelt transport them downward from the A horizon. Still deeper lies the **C horizon,** a mineral horizon that consists of the sediment's parent material. Below the C horizon is bedrock. (This is only a basic soil description; soils are often more complex with subdivisions of each of these horizons.)

The fact that a soil developed inside Gatecliff tells us that about 5100 years ago, sediments accumulated more slowly; at this time, in fact, sediments primarily entered the shelter around its edges as colluvium, with lesser amounts of rooffall and eolian sediments. This pattern continued for the rest of the shelter's history. Most of the upper strata are the result of the slow accumulation of colluvium coming over the dripline and around the sides of the shelter, with a few minor debris flows. These sediments suggest fluctuations between wet and dry intervals, and winter and summer precipitation.

Thus, the dirt and rock at Gatecliff have as much of a story to tell about the shelter's history as do the artifacts themselves. In this case, the geoarchaeology provided important clues as to the nature of the changing environments to which the ancient hunter-gatherers who used Gatecliff had to adapt.

IS STRATIGRAPHY REALLY THAT EASY?

Unfortunately, no. Gatecliff has textbook stratigraphy precisely because it makes for nice photographs and is relatively easy to understand. Some sites are like this. For example, the site of Cerén in El Salvador (discussed in Chapter 5) was caught by volcanic activity and "frozen" in time, buried so deep that very little happened to it until its discovery.

But, frankly, many archaeological sites can be geological nightmares. Human and natural processes churn the sediments, moving things up or down. In Figure 7-7 you see a hypothetical scenario that makes this point. Hunter-gatherers first live in a temporary camp beside a stream at about 3000 BC, leaving behind some artifacts on the surface, along with a hearth and some postholes from a windbreak that they built. The river overflows and deposits layers of silt over the camp. So far, so good.

But about 1000 BC, people arrive who live in **pithouses**—semi-subterranean homes with log roofs covered with sod. To make these houses, they dig into the previous campsite and throw the charcoal from the hearth of the 3000 BC temporary camp up onto the current land surface—thereby moving older material (the charcoal) upward in the stratigraphic sequence. And their habitation has cut down into the previous living surface, introducing "young" artifacts to older layers of earth. You can see that the law of superposition, blindly applied, would lead us astray here.

But we're not done. Suppose that, in AD 800, the nearby river is diverted and cuts an arroyo next to the pithouse. The hillside slumps, pushing part of the pithouse and its contents into the arroyo. People build a pueblo, like those in Chaco Canyon. A new hearth is made outside the walls, as well as a trash pit. Again, later materials move downward in the stratigraphic sequence.

Many years pass. The pueblo is abandoned, its roofs and walls collapse, and the rooms accumulate eolian deposits. A nineteenth-century farmer scavenges posts from the now-abandoned pueblo and uses them to build a fence. He digs a canal through the buried pithouse and pueblo trash pit. The canal is later abandoned and left as a dry ditch. If an archaeologist were to walk through this ditch, he or she would see pithouse occupation debris on one side and, at the same elevation, pueblo trash on the other. The law of superposition might suggest that they were of the same age, yet clearly, they are not.

Most archaeological sites are similarly complex. Let's turn to an archaeological example that shows how the law of superposition can mislead us if we do not consider the human behavior that goes into the formation of a site.

C horizon A layer found below the B horizon that consists of the unaltered or slightly altered parent material; bedrock lies below the C horizon.

pithouse A semi-subterranean structure with a heavy log roof, covered with sod.

reverse stratigraphy The result when one sediment is unearthed by human or natural actions and moved elsewhere, whereby the latest material will be deposited on the bottom of the new sediment, and progressively earlier material will be deposited higher and higher in the stratigraphy.

Reverse Stratigraphy at Chetro Ketl

Florence Hawley Ellis (1906–1991) was a pioneer of Southwestern archaeology. Beginning in the 1920s, she embarked on a long-term research program in Chaco Canyon, focusing on the site of Chetro Ketl (*chee*-tro

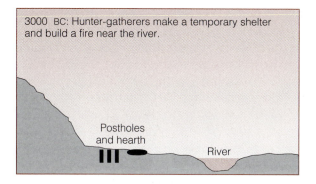

3000 BC: Hunter-gatherers make a temporary shelter and build a fire near the river.

Postholes and hearth

River

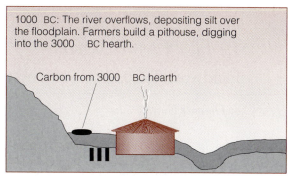

1000 BC: The river overflows, depositing silt over the floodplain. Farmers build a pithouse, digging into the 3000 BC hearth.

Carbon from 3000 BC hearth

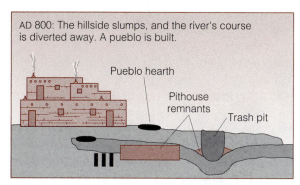

AD 800: The hillside slumps, and the river's course is diverted away. A pueblo is built.

Pueblo hearth

Pithouse remnants

Trash pit

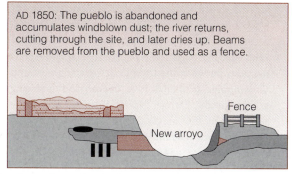

AD 1850: The pueblo is abandoned and accumulates windblown dust; the river returns, cutting through the site, and later dries up. Beams are removed from the pueblo and used as a fence.

Fence

New arroyo

Figure 7-7 The development of a hypothetical archaeological site over time, showing how cultural and natural processes affect a site's formation.

ket-tle), along the northern wall of the canyon. This three- to five-story pueblo contained more than 500 rooms, although it was located only about a quarter-mile from the equally large Pueblo Bonito. On the cliffs behind Chetro Ketl are near-vertical steps cut into the rock face that lead to one of the Chacoan roads. Excavating there in the 1920s, Hawley figured out that Chetro Ketl had been built in four major construction periods, beginning in AD 945 and continuing until AD 1116 (see "In Her Own Words: Fieldwork 1920s-Style at Chetro Ketl," by Florence Hawley Ellis).

But Hawley was less successful in creating a ceramic chronology, a record of how pottery styles had changed over time (more on this in Chapter 9). She returned to the site again and again, excavating the huge refuse heap to the east of Chetro Ketl—archaeological sediments that reached nearly 6 meters deep in places. (She later conducted field school sessions nearby, as shown in Figure 7-8.)

Hawley recognized that two kinds of strata were present. Beginning at the bottom, she defined Strata 1 and 3 as household debris: daily sweepings containing ash, charcoal, and potsherds heaped in small, overlapping mounds. After examining comparable dumps in mod-

ern pueblos, Hawley decided that these sediments must have accumulated basketful by basketful, as trash was thrown out of individual homes daily.

By contrast, Strata 2 and 4 consisted of a mass of refuse, with a generalized gray color signaling a mixing of ash and charcoal throughout. Although these strata also consisted of stone, ash, and charcoal debris, they lacked the laminations and outlines of small basketloads.

But the kind of pottery contained in these strata seemed wrong. What Hawley knew to be the more-recent pottery turned up near the base of the trash mound. This material seemed to have been removed in bulk from some abandoned section of the pueblo, perhaps to make way for a new building to be constructed on the site of a previous dumping area.

In other words, part of the dump appeared to be upside down. Hawley stewed about this interpretation: "The suggestion looked far fetched, however, for this would place *half the mound* as re-dumped material." But eventually, tree-ring dating (which we will discuss in Chapter 8) confirmed that yes, indeed—the lower sediments were *younger* than the upper sediments. The stratigraphy violated the law of superposition: It was reversed.

In Her Own Words
Fieldwork 1920s-Style at Chetro Ketl

by Florence Hawley Ellis

It was 1928. [Ellis was 22 years old.] At Chetro Ketl we were 60 miles from the railroad; mail came only when our truck went for provisions. If summer storms struck, everyone gathered along the steep-sided but usually dry Chaco arroyo to watch the return of the heavy vehicle through a tumbling torrent. Pushing might be necessary. Telephone connections between the little Chaco trading post and Crownpoint (administrative center and boarding school for the Eastern Navajo Reservation) finally were put in, the line being on the top wire of 40 miles of ranch fencing. When a cow leaned against that fence, the phone went out.

A canvas bag of water was delivered to each occupant of the two-party tents every morning. Those who could not scrub teeth, underwear, and their persons in the single gallon must carry their own water. On weekends we washed our hair and then our jeans in a scant bucket of well water and finally used what remained to settle the sand of the tent floor. Then, virtuously clean, we could drop in to the post to watch the trader dicker for rugs, still sold by the pound, from Navajo women who with equal care took out their credit in flour, lard, sugar, Arbuckle's coffee, sometimes a small bag of hard candy, and perhaps a payment on some item of pawn hung back in the closet. If we were hungry we could do as the Navajo did: Buy a can of tomatoes and a box of soda crackers. The trader opened the can and furnished the spoon; the consumer perched on the high counter to swing his heel and enjoy the treat.

Courtesy Museum of New Mexico

Figure 7-8 Florence Hawley Ellis (right) supervising University of New Mexico's 1964 field school at Chaco Canyon (New Mexico).

Why was it upside down? Decades later, archaeologist Steven Lekson (University of Colorado) and others found out that the midden Hawley excavated at Chetro Ketl was actually a deliberately constructed *architectural* feature. (Archaeologists have recognized these large earthen platforms at several of the major sites in Chaco Canyon, including at Pueblo Bonito.) The strata were layers of trash, deliberately hauled in for building purposes. When the ancient Chacoans looked around for easily excavated fill sediments, they turned to their own trash. Naturally, then, the first material they scooped up in baskets was the material on top of the trash mounds—material that had been thrown out the most recently. That recent material was the first to be placed down for the mound's base. As they dug deeper into the trash mound, they removed progressively older sediments and piled these on top of the younger trash.

In a way, the law of superposition was still correct—the material at the bottom had been deposited first, the material above that, second and so on. But because the ages of the artifacts in the layers of fill are in reverse order, archaeologists refer to this situation as **reverse stratigraphy.**

SITE FORMATION PROCESSES: HOW GOOD SITES GO BAD

The casual observer may think of the ground as stable and unchanging, and yet every archaeologist knows better. Sites are complex, and things can move around after they are buried. It's the job of the archaeologist to draw inferences about human behavior from sites, but to do that we have to know how a site formed over time.

To accomplish this important task, we must always bear in mind that *the archaeological record is only the contemporary evidence left over from past behavior.* Artifacts are the static remains of past dynamic behavior. However, because both natural and cultural factors impinge on these remains to such a degree, the archaeological record is rarely a *direct* reflection of past behavior.

The archaeological record is a contemporary phenomenon. Although the objects and their contexts might have existed for centuries or millennia, observations and knowledge about those objects and contexts are as contemporary as the archaeologists who do the observing. Archaeological strata are "leaky," and artifacts can move around quite a bit from where they were originally deposited.

To interpret the archaeological record more accurately, Michael Schiffer (University of Arizona) distinguishes between **archaeological** and **systemic contexts.** Artifacts, features, and residues were once part of an ongoing, dynamic behavioral system. Arrowheads were manufactured, used for specific tasks, broken, repaired, and then lost or deliberately discarded. Potsherds were once part of whole pots, which were manufactured and decorated according to prescribed cultural criteria. People used the pots for cooking or storage or ceremonial functions. The pots broke or were intentionally broken or discarded, perhaps as part of a ritual. Food

bones and plant remains are the organic residues of a succession of activities—hunting or gathering, butchering or processing, cooking, and eating. While these materials are being manufactured and used, they exist in their systemic context. These items are part of the living behavioral system.

By the time such materials reach the archaeologist's hands, though, they have long since ceased to participate in this behavioral system. The artifacts, features, and residues encountered by archaeologists are recovered from their archaeological context, where they may continue to be affected by human action, but where they are also affected by the natural environment.

Formation Processes in the Systemic Context

Using Schiffer's distinction between systemic and archaeological context, we can discuss **formation processes,** how artifacts enter the archaeological record and how they are modified once they are there (Table 7-2). For our purposes, we will distinguish among four distinctive processes in the systemic context that influence the creation of archaeological sites: cultural deposition, reclamation, disturbance, and reuse.

Cultural Depositional Processes

Cultural depositional processes constitute the dominant factor in forming the archaeological record. Following are the four primary ways in which artifacts enter the archaeological record:

Discard Tools, clothing, structures—everything eventually breaks or wears out and is discarded. When this happens, the object ceases to function in the behavioral system and becomes part of the archaeological context. This is one way that things enter the archaeological record.

Loss Other things are inadvertently lost, such as an arrow that misses its target or a necklace or pot

systemic context A living behavioral system wherein artifacts are part of the on-going system of manufacture, use, reuse, and discard.

archaeological context Once artifacts enter the ground, they are part of the archaeological context, where they can continue to be affected by human action, but where they also are affected by natural processes.

formation processes The ways in which human behaviors and natural actions operate to produce the archaeological record.

TABLE 7-2 Site Formation Process Summary

SYSTEMIC CONTEXT	ARCHAEOLOGICAL CONTEXT
Cultural Deposition	Floralturbation (plants)
Discard	Faunalturbation (animals)
Loss	Cryoturbation (freezing)
Caching	Argilliturbation (wet-dry cycles)
Ritual interment	Graviturbation (hillslopes)
Reclamation	
Cultural Disturbance	
Reuse	

left at an abandoned camp. In this case, the items are most likely small and still in usable condition.

Caching Still others are intentionally cached. The duck decoys we mentioned in Chapter 7 were intentionally buried in Lovelock Cave. They remained part of the archaeological record because the person who cached them never returned.

Ritual Interment Burials and their associated grave goods are the most obvious example of ritual interment, but other examples include offerings left at a shrine or, alternatively, deliberate destruction and burial of a shrine or religious site.

Reclamation Processes

Part of the archaeologist's job is to figure out whether the artifacts entered the archaeological record through discard, loss, caching, or ritual interment. This task is made difficult because artifacts can move back and forth between the systemic and archaeological contexts. For example, artifacts can be *reclaimed*. Archaeologists frequently find artifacts that were scavenged by later peoples. Pueblo peoples, for example, believed that ancient stone arrow and spear points contained power. If they happened to encounter a point while out working, they might keep it and later make a ritual offering

reclamation processes Human behaviors that result in artifacts moving from the archaeological context back to the systemic context, for example, scavenging beams from an abandoned structure to use them in a new one.

cultural disturbance processes Human behaviors that modify artifacts in their archaeological context, for instance, digging pits, hearths, canals, and houses.

reuse processes Human behaviors that recycle and reuse artifacts before the artifact enters an archaeological context.

of it. In this case, the arrowhead has moved from a context where it was (perhaps) unintentionally lost to one in which it was intentionally interred. It has also moved from the context of an earlier time period to one of a later time period, as well as from a context that records its original everyday function to one that records another culture's ritual.

Whenever a discarded projectile point is resharpened, a potsherd picked up and used to scrape hides, or an old brick reused in a new fireplace, reclamation has occurred. The farmer who used roof beams to build a fence in our hypothetical scenario above was reclaiming older materials.

Likewise, all archaeologists must cope with the fact that nonprofessionals (amateur archaeologists and looters) often collect artifacts from sites. If we ignore this fact, we run the risk of misinterpreting archaeological data. In the Carson Desert, for example, we knew that local people had collected projectile points from sites in the wetland for decades. One man had more than 25,000 points in his collection. The walls of his dining room were covered with picture frames full of points, and he lined his driveway with large stone mortars and metates. The fact that our survey recovered relatively few projectile points from sites in the marsh probably reflected this reclamation process—otherwise known as looting—and not necessarily a lack of hunting.

Cultural Disturbance Processes

Reclamation processes are the transfer of materials from the archaeological to the systemic context. But the archaeological record is also heavily conditioned by transformations *within* the archaeological contexts. Disturbance changes the contexts of materials within the archaeological site itself. Examples include such diverse cultural mechanisms as dam building; farming; and construction of houses, pits, hearths, and so on. In the hypothetical example above, the movement of charcoal from the early hunter-gatherer hearth upward in the stratigraphic sequence was an instance of cultural disturbance.

Reuse Processes

In reuse process, an object moves through a series of different behavioral settings before it enters the archaeological record. This can entail the recycling of some objects. Potsherds, for example, are sometimes ground up and used as temper in manufacturing new vessels. Broken arrowheads are sometimes re-chipped into drills and scrapers. Beams from one building are sometimes pulled out and reused in another. The point here is that an object can be created for one purpose, but it can be modified and deposited in an entirely different context than are similar objects that are not reused.

The difference between reuse and reclamation has to do with whether the archaeological context is involved. If beams are taken from a currently occupied building, it is an instance of reuse; if they are taken from a building long abandoned, then it is reclamation. The distinction seems trivial and yet it tells us something about the potential difference in the age of the items being reused. Items that are reclaimed are probably moving from an archaeological context considerably older than the systemic context they enter; reused items, on the other hand, are probably moving between systemic contexts that are much closer in age.

This review of cultural formation processes shows that archaeologists need to be aware that human activities frequently move things from their original depositional provenience to another. This can make archaeological sites very complicated and difficult to interpret. And natural processes can complicate matters even more.

Formation Processes in the Archaeological Context

Once an object enters an archaeological context, a host of natural as well as cultural formation processes takes place. These natural processes determine not only whether organic material will be preserved (as we discussed in Chapter 6) but also where objects will be found. In the hypothetical example above, a river and a landslide played major roles in creating the archaeological record. Following are a few major categories of natural site formation processes (Figure 7-9). This assortment of processes is only a brief introduction, and its purpose is to help you conceptualize just how complex an archaeological site can be. Additionally, this discussion shows that natural processes can both disrupt patterns that would otherwise tell us something about human behavior and, at the same time, create their own patterns, which could be misinterpreted as the result of human behavior. They warn us, then, that *there is no simple correspondence between the distribution of artifacts in a site and human behavior.* We'll give an example of how important an understanding of site formation processes can be, and we'll revisit this important aspect of archaeology in Chapter 10, as well.

Floralturbation

Anybody who has walked down a sidewalk knows what tree roots can do to concrete slabs. Roots do the same to buried ancient walls; and, by loosening soil, they also promote the downward movement of artifacts from their original stratigraphic context. But they can also move artifacts upward. When a large tree falls over, its roots pull up large amounts of sediment. We call this tree-throw and, after hundreds or thousands of years, it can churn a site's sediments, pulling ancient materials up to more recent surfaces and creating holes that then fill with material of various ages.

Faunalturbation

Rodents and other animals often dig into sites, producing two major effects: First, burrowing rodents can push artifacts that were originally deposited in lower layers up to the surface. This can place old artifacts in a younger stratigraphic context. Second, burrowing can size-sort artifacts vertically, moving larger artifacts downward and smaller artifacts upward. For example, pocket gophers dig their burrows around any object larger than about 5 centimeters; anything smaller than this they push out of their burrows to the surface. The larger artifacts and rocks left behind might eventually tumble to the bottom of the burrows. Repeat this process over hundreds or thousands of years (and burrows), and you end up with a site where all the small artifacts and stones are near its top, and the large artifacts and stones are near its bottom. Someone applying the law of superposition blindly might conclude that people changed from using large to small tools over time. But you would be wrong: The pattern only tells us about pocket gophers, not people.

Sometimes these burrows are filled with rock and earth washed or blown in from above, forming a feature called a **krotovina** (kro-toe-*vee*-na; the term comes to us from Russian soil science). If so, then archaeologists can excavate the burrow separately from the surrounding sediments. But if the burrows simply collapse, they can be difficult or impossible to see.

floralturbation A natural formation process in which trees and other plants affect the distribution of artifacts within an archaeological site.

faunalturbation A natural formation process in which animals, from large game to earthworms, affect the distribution of material within an archaeological site.

krotovina A filled-in animal burrow.

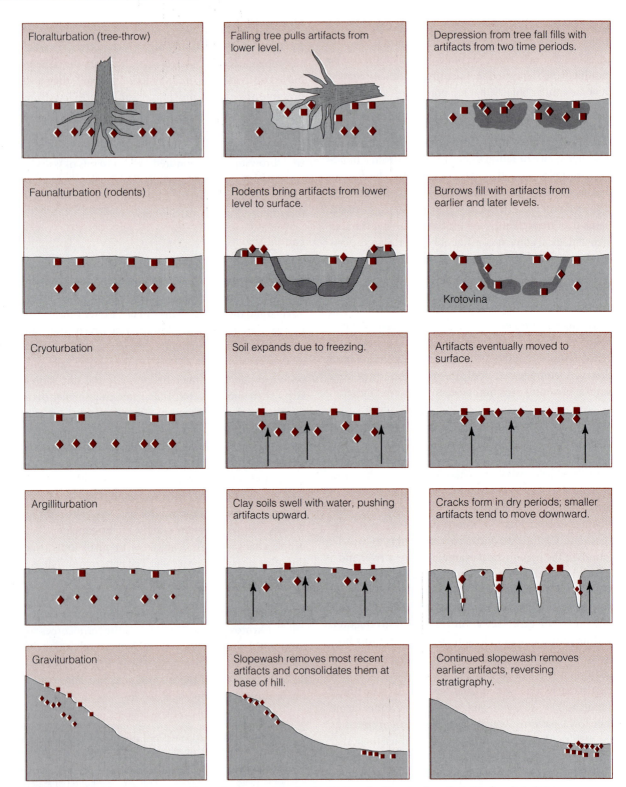

Figure 7-9 The effects of some natural formation processes on the distribution of artifacts in a hypothetical archaeological site.

And burrowing animals are only one factor. Even the humble earthworm can obliterate the edges of features like burials, pits, and hearths, making them more difficult for the archaeologist to see and record.

Cryoturbation

In northern climates, freeze/thaw processes can move artifacts up in a stratigraphic sequence. As the soil freezes, it expands, pushing artifacts upward. As the soil thaws, soil particles move down first, partially or completely filling the void below artifacts, ensuring that the artifacts cannot move back down. Thus, freeze/thaw cycles move large artifacts upward (sometimes at a rate of several centimeters per year). This can create a site in which artifacts are vertically size-sorted, with the smallest artifacts at the bottom of the sediment and larger ones near the top (the opposite effect of burrowing animals). Cryoturbation also tends to orient buried artifacts vertically—that is, with their long axis pointing up and down.

Argilliturbation

A similar process happens in clay-rich soils that undergo wet/dry cycles. As these soils become wet, they expand and push larger artifacts upward for the same reason as cryoturbation. But as these soils dry, they form cracks—sometimes several meters in depth—down which artifacts can fall. Run this process over and over for hundreds or thousands of years, and a site's stratigraphy can become thoroughly churned.

Graviturbation

Archaeological materials deposited on hillsides eventually move downslope. This is accomplished through precipitation (slopewash), gravity (soil creep), or the slow movement of water-saturated sediments (solifluction). In any case, the result is that archaeological materials originally deposited on a hillside move downslope and eventually come to rest in a context completely different from the one where they were originally lost, discarded, cached, or ritually interred. This can also result in reverse stratigraphy, because the material closest to the surface will be the first to slide or tumble down the slope.

Some sites (like Gatecliff) have a high degree of stratigraphic integrity—meaning that artifacts are found where they were lost, discarded, cached, or ritually interred. Other sites are complex, with little stratigraphic integrity. In these sites, a range of cultural and natural formation processes have moved artifacts from their initial archaeological context. But these processes do *not*

Figure 7-10 The site of Cagny-l'Epinette, showing the distribution of artifacts and rock on a portion of Stratum I1.

make archaeology impossible. It does mean, though, that one of our first tasks is to establish just how the artifacts got to where the archaeologists found them. Although how we do this is different for each site, the following case study shows how understanding a site's geologic context is essential to knowing what the site can, or cannot, tell us about ancient human behavior.

An Ancient Living Floor at Cagny-l'Epinette?

The site of Cagny-l'Epinette sits on a gently sloping terrace in a broad river valley in northern France (Figure 7-10). French archaeologist Alain Tuffreau and his team had slowly and carefully excavated its 3 meters of sediments for many years. In the lower levels, in sediments that were some 200,000 to 300,000 years old, Tuffreau found artifacts as well as the bones of various large game animals. He interpreted Stratum I1 as a living floor, a surface like those sandwiched between the thick silt layers at Gatecliff Shelter, where our ancient human ancestors lived, made tools, and butchered animals. Tuffreau carefully mapped the locations of artifacts across Stratum I1 to look for clusters that could reconstruct where different activities took place and create a fuller picture of the past.

cryoturbation A natural formation process in which freeze/thaw activity in a soil selectively pushes larger artifacts to the surface of a site.

argilliturbation A natural formation process in which wet/dry cycles in clay-rich soils push artifacts upward as the sediment swells and then moves them down as cracks form during dry cycles.

graviturbation A natural formation process in which artifacts are moved downslope through gravity, sometimes assisted by precipitation runoff.

Archaeological Ethics
Should Antiquities Be Returned to the Country of Origin?

Many of the world's major museums contain artifacts that come from many different countries. The majority of these were acquired through legal channels. But some pieces have more checkered pasts. The Rosetta Stone, for example, is a large basalt tablet inscribed in three scripts, which allowed French linguist Jean-François Champollion to decipher Egyptian hieroglyphics. It was found by a French soldier in 1799 during Napoleon's conquest of Egypt. Fortunes change quickly in war, however, and by 1801 the Rosetta Stone was in the British Museum, where it is today.

Britain scored another "victory" in nearly the same year in Greece, one that has caused considerable consternation between these two countries.

The Acropolis is a limestone plateau that stands above modern downtown Athens. Temples and shrines adorn the plateau, and among them is the Parthenon, built between 447 and 438 BC and dedicated to the goddess Athena. It has been a sacred place in Greek culture for more than 2500 years and has served as a Catholic church and, during Turkish rule, as a mosque. A portion of the Parthenon was destroyed in 1687 when the Venetians bombed it; the damage might not have been so great had the Turks not been using the temple to store gunpowder.

The current problem began about 1800, when Thomas Bruce (better known as Lord Elgin) was British ambassador to Turkey. At that time, Turkey ruled Greece as part of the Ottoman Empire. Elgin removed statues and portions of the 75-meter marble frieze from the Parthenon, sending them to England aboard British military vessels. Elgin was later captured by the French and spent 2 years in prison, during which time the marbles were kept at his home, sometimes in the coal shed.

Elgin had spent most of his fortune removing the marbles and many other Greek art treasures. By 1816, he had lost his wife, contracted syphilis, and was deeply in debt. He sold the marbles to the British Museum for a fraction of what they cost him, and he died penniless in 1841.

Greece has been demanding the return of the marbles ever since. The late Greek minister of culture, Melina Mercouri, argued that they symbolize Greece itself, and many Greeks feel that the sculptures belong in Greece.

However, when he was director of the British Museum, Sir David Wilson countered that the museum acquired the marbles legally, had done nothing wrong, and that *any* such return—and most particularly that of the marbles—smacks of "cultural fascism." It is true that the museum purchased the sculptures legally; and Lord Elgin always claimed he had permission from the Turkish government to remove them.

But Greece points out that the Turks, as occupiers of Greece, did not have the right to give Greek patrimony away. And, in fact, the surviving paperwork shows that

But there were a few troubling aspects to Level I1 at Cagny-l'Epinette. Unlike Gatecliff, where the living floors were only a few centimeters thick, the artifacts found in Stratum I1 were separated by 11 to 64 centimeters of sediments. This could mean that (1) instead of one living floor, Cagny-l'Epinette preserved multiple floors, or perhaps (2) the artifacts had been deposited on one living floor, but had later been moved up and down by burrowing rodents. But it could also mean that the artifacts were deposited at widely different times through different formation processes.

Also troubling was the fact that the sediments of Stratum I1 were fluvial sands, deposited by a river. The fact that the deposit was mostly sand suggested that the river was usually slow moving, but the presence of some larger rocks pointed to periods of higher river energy. This could mean nothing more than that the river occasionally flowed over the terrace and created a pleasant sandy surface on which people later camped, made tools, and ate the game they killed along the river's banks. But many of the stone tools bore breaks that suggested they had been treated roughly, as if they had

Elgin had permission from the Turks only to draw, make casts, and do some small excavations. Some people claim that Elgin abused his political position and used bribes to remove the marbles from Greece. But the British Museum points out that Elgin probably saved these priceless treasures from the decay that political violence and pollution has visited upon the statues that remain on the Acropolis.

Britain argues that the marbles are now part of the world's, not just Greek, patrimony, and that they deserve to be in the British Museum, where many more people from around the world can enjoy them. The British Museum also points out that it is legally prevented from disposing of its holdings unless they are duplicates or worthless.

Finally, the British Museum claims that, if it returned the marbles to Greece, the floodgates would open, myriad countries would demand the return of art objects, major museums would be empty, and the world would have far less access to these cultural treasures.

Greece points out that it would be simple for England to pass a law to return the marbles, that pollution is now under control in Athens, and that conservation measures protect the sculptures (and that, in fact, the British Museum itself damaged them decades ago by using harsh cleaning solutions and chisels on them). The marbles themselves would be housed in a proposed museum at the base of the Acropolis, although construction of that museum is on hold since archaeological remains were discovered on its site.

Should treasures like the Parthenon's marbles be returned to their country of origin? Or should they be housed someplace where more of the world's people can enjoy them? Should we take into account the (often-nefarious) ways in which artifacts were acquired when making this decision, or are we opening up a tidal wave of litigation that will ultimately serve no one well? Do we consider whether the country of origin is capable of caring for artifacts by itself? Do we consider current national borders or those that existed at the time of the taking (do the sculptures go to Greece or Turkey?) On the one hand, returning treasures to the country of origin would seem to encourage a balkanization of the ancient world that will not serve archaeology or humanity well. But on the other hand, consider this: Seeking to defend the British Museum's claim to the marbles, the Parliamentary Assembly of the Council of Europe passed a resolution stressing "the unity of the European cultural heritage." Does keeping the marbles in Britain achieve this goal better than keeping them in Greece?

---

rolled along in a stream bed and been struck by other cobbles. Could the artifacts have been left by the same river that deposited the sand, and not by people?

The animal bones presented a third problem. As you will learn in Chapter 11, one way we know that animals were hunted is by the presence of distinctive breaks that form when fresh limb bones are broken open for their calorie-rich marrow. Another way is by the presence of cut-marks, where stone knives nicked bone as an animal was butchered. Oddly, the bones recovered at Cagny-l'Epinette bore very few such telltale characteristics. Perhaps they were the remains of animal carcasses that had floated downstream, and not the remains of game hunted by people. How could the excavators know for certain?

Determining the Effect of Formation Processes

All archaeologists dream of finding an undisturbed site. By this, they usually mean a site that Mother Nature has not thoroughly mixed up or that looters have not destroyed. But deep down, archaeologists know that *there is no such thing as an undisturbed site*. Even sites

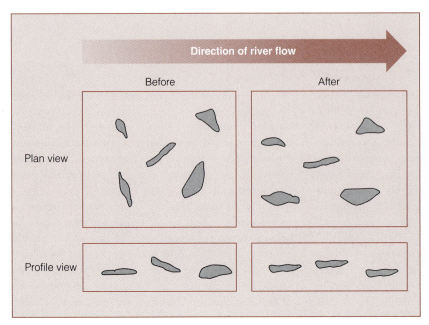

Figure 7-11 How artifacts become oriented to the direction of river flow.

such as Cerén and Pompeii are not as pristine as they may first seem. As you learned in this chapter, a lot can happen between the time an artifact is deposited in the ground and when an archaeologist excavates it. Formation processes affect all archaeological sites to one extent or another. Our task is to figure out how these processes have affected a site in order to know what analytical use the site has.

Late in the excavation of Cagny-l'Epinette, Tuffreau was joined by Harold Dibble, Philip Chase (University of Pennsylvania), and Shannon McPherron (Max Planck Institute). The recovery strategy changed somewhat in order to collect data relevant to determining the kind and effect of formation processes on the site.

Recall from Chapter 6 that two observations we can make on artifacts found in situ are their inclination (the angle at which they are lying in the ground) and their orientation (the compass bearing of their long axis). The archaeologists at Cagny-l'Epinette collected this information in the later seasons from not only the artifacts and bones, but also from all unmodified stones found in situ. This information is important to under-

standing the site as a geological deposit, and that information, in turn, is essential to understanding the site as an archaeological deposit. What did it tell the archaeologists?

After compiling the data, Dibble and his colleagues discovered that the artifacts were oriented largely along two axes, perpendicular to one another. One of these axes was the same as the ancient stream that ran over the site. The other followed the slope of the terrace. And it was not only the artifacts that fit this pattern; unmodified rock and bone did, too. The inclination data were also intriguing. Artifacts, bone, and unmodified rock lay nearly, but not quite, flat—those that pointed in the same direction as the ancient stream had their "downstream" ends raised slightly above their "upstream" ends. What do these patterns mean?

First, the fact that the artifacts, bones, and unmodified rock all fit the same orientation and inclination patterns suggested that the same process was responsible for their deposition. Second, experimental studies show that when a river washes an object along, those objects eventually come to rest with their long axis pointing along the direction of the river's flow (Figure 7-11). This was true at Cagny-l'Epinette. At this site, a river probably deposited the rocks, bones, and artifacts. Some of these artifacts were apparently left exposed on the terrace's surface as the river's channel shifted. While they were exposed, rainfall washed over them and, as a result of slopewash, they came to point downslope—perpendicular to the direction of the river's previous flow. By the time the river shifted to flow over the terrace again, these artifacts were sufficiently buried that their orientations were preserved and not affected by the river.

Fluvial geologists also know that stones on river bottoms tend to lie nearly, but not entirely, flat. The river removes sediment from the upstream ends of stones and then redeposits it beneath the downstream end. This is known as **imbrication**, and it results in stones lying with their upstream ends slightly lower than their

imbrication A fluvial process through which stones in a stream- or riverbed come to rest overlapping like shingles on a roof, with their upstream ends lying slightly lower in elevation than their downstream ends.

downstream ends, or with the downstream end of one stone overlapping the upstream end of another.

These patterns strongly suggested that the artifacts in Stratum I1 were probably washed out of a site located farther upstream and then redeposited some unknown distance downstream. So, Level I1 of Cagny-l'Epinette is not the pristine living floor that archaeologists originally thought it was.

But neither is it completely useless. Cagny-l'Epinette still contains a record of what ancient humans did in northern France more than 200,000 years ago. That record is not as detailed as originally thought, but we now know what analytical utility this stratum in the site has. For example, the distribution of artifacts within the site is probably meaningless, for it does not reflect activity areas but only fluvial action and slopewash. But the site is still useful for making comparisons between the I1 artifact assemblage as a whole and those from other strata at the site, or from other sites. Likewise, the data from Stratum I1 could serve as a control, a background against which to compare data from other strata at the site to demonstrate that those other strata do indeed contain a living floor.

Conclusion

The important point of this discussion—and, in fact, this entire chapter—is that understanding the effects of site formation processes is the first step in knowing what an archaeologist can realistically accomplish with the information from a site. Archaeologists need to keep in mind all the processes that affect how artifacts and ecofacts enter the ground—and everything that can happen to them once they are there. In so doing, the archaeologist has to think of the site not only as a record of human behavior, but as a record of natural processes also. He or she must think of the site as a geological record, as well as an archaeological record. Increasingly, archaeologists find that extremely careful and meticulous data, such as the orientation and inclination of plain old rocks as well as of artifacts, are needed to accomplish this goal. Thus, this realization of the importance of formation processes affects the way we go about excavating archaeological sites.

Summary

- Geoarchaeology applies the concepts and methods of the geosciences to archaeological research.

- Geoarchaeology uses stratigraphic principles to place sites in a chronological framework and studies the processes of site formation, which includes all the human and natural processes that work together to create an archaeological site.

- When dealing with stratigraphy, archaeologists rely on the law of superposition, which holds that (all else being equal) older geological strata tend to be buried beneath younger strata.

- But the law of superposition is only an organizing principle; in some instances, reverse stratigraphy can form in which the law of superposition is literally turned on its head.

- The stratigraphic record in some sites, such as burial mounds or pueblos, results from deliberate human activities: People systematically deposited strata as cultural features. But in many other sites, stratigraphy results from a complex interplay between natural and cultural deposition.

- You must understand the difference between an artifact's systemic and archaeological contexts in order to know how an artifact in the ground relates to the complex chain of human behavior and natural processes that brought it there.

- Artifacts can enter the archaeological record through a variety of cultural depositional processes, including loss, discard, caching, and ritual interment.

- Once in the archaeological context, artifacts can continue to be moved and altered by a variety of natural site formation processes, including landslides, burrowing animals, earthworms, tree throw, and the actions of water and climate.

- Geoarchaeologists use an understanding of site formation processes to determine how much artifact movement occurred during or after sedimentation. A range of methods and tests are used to accomplish this task.

Additional Reading

Courty, M. A., P. Goldberg, and R. Macphail. 1989. *Soils and Micromorphology in Archaeology*. Cambridge: Cambridge University Press.

Davidson, D. A., and I. A. Simpson. 2001. Archaeology and Soil Micromorphology. In D. Brothwell and A. Pollard (Eds.), *Handbook of Archaeological Sciences*, pp. 167–178. Chichester, England: John Wiley and Sons.

Rapp, George, and Christopher Hill. 1996. *Geoarchaeology: The Earth Science Approach to Archaeological Interpretation*. New Haven, CT: Yale University Press.

Schiffer, Michael B. 1987. *Formation Processes of the Archaeological Record*. Albuquerque: University of New Mexico Press.

Stein, Julie, and William Farrand (Eds.). 1999. *Sediments in Archaeological Context*. Salt Lake City: University of Utah Press.

Waters, Michael R. 1992. *Principles of Geoarchaeology: A North American Perspective*. Tucson: University of Arizona Press.

Online Resources

COMPANION WEB SITE
Visit **http://anthropology.wadsworth.com** and click on the Student Companion Web Site for Thomas/Kelly *Archaeology*, 4th edition, to access a wide range of material to help you succeed in your introductory archaeology course. These include flashcards, Internet exercises, Web links, and practice quizzes.

RESEARCH ONLINE WITH INFOTRAC COLLEGE EDITION
From the Student Companion Web Site, you can access the InfoTrac College Edition database, which offers thousands of full-length articles for your research.

8

Chronology Building: How to Get a Date

© Jeffrey S. Dean and the Laboratory of Tree-Ring Research/University of Arizona

Betatakin, a cliff dwelling in Tsegi Canyon (Arizona).

Preview

THIS CHAPTER IS ABOUT dating archaeological sites—how archaeologists get a grasp on time. Here, you'll find a broad range of dating techniques: tree-ring dating, radiocarbon dating, thermoluminescence dating, and others that allow us to date organic material, rocks—even dirt itself. The chemical and physical underpinnings of these techniques can be mind-boggling, but you need to have at least a basic understanding of them in order to understand when you can and cannot use a particular technique.

You also need to understand the basis of these techniques in order to know just what the "date" is actually telling you, because dates in and of themselves mean nothing. Demonstrating the *validity of associations* between dates and human behavior is the key issue in archaeological dating.

INTRODUCTION

The Fourth Egyptian Dynasty lasted from 2680 to 2565 BC. The Roman Coliseum was constructed between AD 70 and 82. The Battle of the Little Big Horn took place on June 25, 1876. Each date represents the most familiar way of expressing chronological control—the **absolute date.** Such dates are expressed as specific units of scientific measurement—days, years, centuries, or millennia—but no matter what the measure, all such absolute determinations attempt to pinpoint a specific year or a specific range of years (the latter are sometimes referred to as chronometric, rather than absolute, dates). The advent of absolute dating was part of what revolutionized archaeology in the 1960s.

Absolute dating methods were not available in the early days of archaeology. Prior to the 1950s, most dates were instead **relative dates.** As the name implies, relative dates are not specific segments of absolute time but, rather, express relationships or comparisons: The stepped pyramid at Saqqara in Egypt is *earlier* than Khufu's pyramid; the historic settlement of Williamsburg is *later* than the pueblos of Chaco Canyon; Folsom spear points are *earlier* than Chupadero Black-on-white pottery. Relative dates are obviously not as precise as absolute dates, but prior to the 1950s, they were the best that archaeology had.

absolute date A date expressed as specific units of scientific measurement, such as days, years, centuries, or millennia; absolute determinations attempting to pinpoint a discrete, known interval in time.

relative dates Dates expressed relative to one another (for instance, earlier, later, more recent, and so forth) instead of in absolute terms.

index fossil concept The idea that strata containing similar fossil assemblages are of similar age. This concept enables archaeologists to characterize and date strata within sites using distinctive artifact forms that research shows to be diagnostic of a particular period of time.

RELATIVE DATING

The keys to relative dating are (1) the law of superposition introduced in Chapter 7 and (2) the **index fossil concept.**

Developed in the early nineteenth century, the index fossil concept is often attributed to British geologist William "Strata" Smith (1769–1839), although it was in circulation throughout Europe at the time. Geologists of Smith's day wrestled with the problem of how to correlate the ages of widely separated exposures of rock. Smith observed that forms of life changed over time, and so different fossils characterize different rock strata. Thus, widely separated strata could be correlated and assigned to the same time period if they contained the same fossils. It seems like a simple idea, but it allowed Smith and others to make the first geological maps, and these radically altered the way that geologists conceived of the landscape. Now they could see broad patterns that told a story of ancient seas, mountain building, and ice ages.

The Index Fossil Concept in Archaeology

Archaeology faced a similar problem. The law of superposition could indicate which artifact types or styles were older than other forms in particular sites, but how could the individual site chronologies be chronologically related to one another? The index fossil concept provided the answer. In archaeology, however, artifacts replace fossils, and strata in widely separated sites that contain the same distinctive artifact forms—called **time-markers** in archaeology—are assumed to be of similar age.

The index fossil concept was introduced to archaeology by Swedish archaeologist Oscar Montelius (1843–1921). Trained in the natural sciences, Montelius switched to archaeology and became interested in Europe's Neolithic, Bronze, and Iron Ages. Working for the State Historical Museum in Stockholm, he traveled over Europe examining collections from various sites, paying special attention to objects in unmixed contexts, such as those from burials, hoards, and individual rooms.

Using hundreds of cases, Montelius divided the Bronze, Neolithic, and Iron Ages into chronological subdivisions, each with its own set of distinctive artifacts or artifact styles, such as particular kinds of axe heads, swords, or brooches. In some cases, Montelius had stratigraphic controls to help decide which artifact styles were earlier or later, and sometimes the artifacts appeared in contexts, such as Egyptian tombs, where documentary sources could provide the age. But he also employed assumptions about how styles change over

time and arranged objects in sequences such that they formed, in his opinion, a "logical" progression from, say, small simple brooches to large, complex ones. This simple-to-complex assumption might work in paleontology because animal forms are linked through biological reproduction. But it is tenuous in archaeology, because artifacts don't reproduce; their shapes come from their makers' minds and not directly from "ancestral" artifacts.

Nonetheless, Montelius advanced archaeology by developing a way to create a chronology of artifact time-markers for Europe.

Time-Markers in the American Southwest

What Montelius could have really used, however, was a master sequence—a site with a deep stratigraphic profile that would permit the law of superposition to demonstrate the changing sequence of artifact types and styles. Nels Nelson, who was aware of European archaeology (and even helped excavate a cave in Spain), searched for just such a master sequence for the American Southwest during his excavation at Pueblo San Cristobal (New Mexico). Nelson knew that there were deep deposits at San Cristobal, and he hoped that a carefully controlled excavation into them would show whether certain artifacts could act as time-markers (Figure 8-1).

Selecting an area with minimal disturbance, Nelson isolated a block of debris measuring 3 feet by 6 feet wide and nearly 10 feet deep. Clearly, the midden had accumulated over a long interval, and several distinctive kinds of pottery were buried there. Because the dusty black midden lacked sharp stratigraphic divisions, Nelson personally excavated the block in 1-foot arbitrary levels, cataloging the potsherds recovered by level. Imposing arbitrary levels on an undifferentiated stratigraphy seems almost pedestrian today but, in 1914, Nelson's stratigraphic method was revolutionary and immediately seized upon by New World archaeologists as a fundamental of excavation (for the record, however, Nelson got the idea of stratigraphic excavation from his European colleagues).

Nelson then applied the law of superposition to look for culture change within the midden column. All else being equal, the oldest trash should lie at the bottom,

time-markers Similar to index fossils in geology; artifact forms that research shows to be diagnostic of a particular period of time.

© American Museum of Natural History

Figure 8-1 General view across Nels Nelson's excavations at San Cristobal (New Mexico). The 700-year-old walls of this huge pueblo are clearly evident. Note also that no screens appear anywhere; sifting of archaeological deposits did not become standard practice until almost 50 years after this picture was taken.

prehistoric ceramics of San Cristobal. Just as geologists learned to distinguish certain extinct life forms as characteristic of various rock strata, so too could archaeologists use distinctive artifact forms to characterize and correlate strata between archaeological sites. Pottery was a natural choice given that potsherds were common cultural debris and Nelson knew that ceramic styles varied considerably across the American Southwest.

More than 2000 potsherds turned up in the 10-foot test section at San Cristobal. Nelson first grouped the potsherds into obvious types and then plotted their distribution according to depth below the surface (we'll discuss the principles of creating types in Chapter 9). Table

capped by more recent accumulations. Even though the dense midden lacked tangible stratigraphy, Nelson searched for time-markers in the form of distinctive pottery types.

Nelson thus applied the index fossil concept to the

8-1 summarizes his results: Column 1 contains the frequency of corrugated pottery, the most common everyday cooking ware. Because the relative frequency of corrugated potsherds remained more or less constant throughout the occupation of San Cristobal, Nelson

TABLE 8-1 Potsherd Frequencies from Pueblo San Cristobal, New Mexico

DEPTH BELOW SURFACE	CORRUGATED WARE	BISCUIT WARE	TYPE I: BLACK-ON-WHITE WARE	TYPE II: TWO-COLOR GLAZE	TYPE III: THREE-COLOR GLAZE	TOTAL
Column number	1	2	3	4	5	
1st foot	57 (36.7)	10 (6.5)	2 (1.3)	81 (52.2)	5 (3.2)	155
2nd foot	116 (31.3)	17 (4.6)	2 (.01)	230 (62)	6 (1.6)	371
3rd foot	27 (15.3)	2 (1.1)	10 (5.7)	134 (76.1)	3 (1.7)	176
4th foot	28 (21.3)	4 (3)	6 (4.5)	93 (70.9)	0 (0)	131
5th foot	60 (17.3)	15 (4.3)	2 (.01)	268 (77.6)	0 (0)	345
6th foot	75 (18.6)	21 (5.2)	8 (1.9)	297 (73.8)	1? (.01)	402
7th foot	53 (23.1)	10 (4.3)	40 (17.5)	126 (55)	0 (0)	229
8th foot	56 (24.6)	2 (.01)	118 (51.9)	51 (22.4)	0 (0)	227
9th foot	93 (45.4)	1? (.01)	107 (52.5)	3 (1.4)	0 (0)	204
10th foot	84 (54.4)	1? (.01)	69 (44.8)	0 (0)	0 (0)	154
Total	649	83	364	1,283	15	2,394

SOURCE: Nelson 1916.

Figures in parentheses are row-wise percentages.

rejected Column 1 as a potential time-marker. Column 2 tabulates the frequencies of biscuit ware, a dull whitish-yellow pottery that Nelson thought was traded into San Cristobal from elsewhere. But these frequencies did not change markedly throughout the stratigraphic column either, and he also rejected biscuit ware as a potential time-marker.

Nelson then turned to the three remaining kinds of pottery—which he termed Types I, II, and III—and discovered, just as the Europeans had with their fossils, that certain forms were associated with specific stratigraphic levels (Figure 8-2). The most ancient levels at San Cristobal contained a predominance of Type I painted pottery, black designs on a white background. Type I potsherds were most numerous at and below the 8-foot mark and only rarely recovered above 7 feet. Type II pottery—red, yellow, and gray potsherds ornamented with a dark glaze—occurred most commonly at and above the 7-foot mark. In other words, Type I potsherds characterized the lower strata, and the Type II potsherds characterized the upper deposits.

The Type III pottery, three-colored glazed ware, was rare at San Cristobal and appeared only in the uppermost levels of Nelson's column. This made sense, given that Pueblo peoples were making three-colored wares when the Spaniards arrived in New Mexico in the sixteenth century.

Nelson's arbitrary levels made possible the definition of three important ceramic time-markers. Not only did he document the specific ceramic changes at San Cristobal, but more important, his controlled stratigraphic excavation provided a master sequence with which to place other sites, strata, or features in the region into a relative chronological sequence. Alfred Kidder later applied Nelson's observations to Pecos Pueblo, using the presence of black-on-white ware to locate the original settlement.

The Next Step: Seriation

The index fossil concept was essential to the archaeology of the early twentieth century. The law of superposition permitted archaeologists to produce a chronology of cultural change at a particular site, and the index fossil concept allowed archaeologists to date sites *relative* to one another. Given this discovery, archaeologists could date other Southwestern Pueblo sites based on the type of pottery found in them. A site with predominantly black-on-white pottery would be older than one that contained red glazed pottery. The archaeologist did not know *how much* older the first site was than the second, but he or she could nonetheless still place sites into a relative chronological sequence based on their ceramics. This was a tremendous advance for the time.

And this advance became the basis of **seriation,** a relative dating technique that was crucial to archaeology

Figure 8-2
Examples of Nels Nelson's Types I (bottom), II (middle), and III (top) pottery from San Cristobal Pueblo.

seriation A relative dating method that orders artifacts based on the assumption that one cultural style slowly replaces an earlier style over time; with a master seriation diagram, sites can be dated based on their frequency of several artifact (for instance, ceramic) styles.

in the mid-twentieth century. First developed by European archaeologists in the late nineteenth century, the technique was introduced to the New World by Alfred Kroeber (1876–1960). Seriation is grounded in the same commonsense observation that guided Oscar Montelius: Styles change and new technologies arise over time. In ancient times just as now, most new ideas are slow to catch on, with only a few pioneers participating in the fad. Eventually, a new idea may become chic and replace earlier vogues, only to fall gradually into disuse and be replaced by the next "new thing."

The index fossil concept relied primarily on the presence or absence of distinctive kinds of artifacts. Seriation refined this by using changes in the *frequencies* of artifacts or styles to date sites relative to one another (paleontologists, by the way, do the same thing with fossils).

To get a sense of how seriation works, look at Figure 8-3, which shows changes in lighting technologies in late nineteenth-century Pennsylvania. At mid-century, most houses were illuminated by candles and oil lamps; only a few households had gas lamps. But over the next 50 years, more and more families switched to gaslights. Those who could not afford such installations used kerosene lamps (made possible by the growing petroleum industry in Pennsylvania and elsewhere). By 1900, however, electric lights were replacing gaslights and, by 1940, gaslights had all but disappeared. By that year, virtually everyone used incandescent light bulbs—which by 1950 were already being replaced by fluorescent lamps.

The shape of such popularity curves, which James Ford termed "battleship curves" because they often look like a battleship's silhouette from above, is the basis for seriation. By arranging the proportions of temporal types into lozenge-shaped curves, one can determine a relative chronological sequence.

This phenomenon is evident in Nelson's potsherd counts from San Cristobal Pueblo (Figure 8-4 translates the frequencies from Table 8-1 into a seriation diagram). As we've already noted, when San Cristobal was first built, ceramics were most commonly decorated with black designs painted on a white background; corrugated ware was also fairly common. Moving up Nelson's stratigraphic column, however, two-color glaze rapidly takes over in popularity, with black-on-white pottery fading out. In the top half of the column, three-color pottery comes into use. The town dump at San Cristobal faithfully preserved these changes in ceramic "fashion."

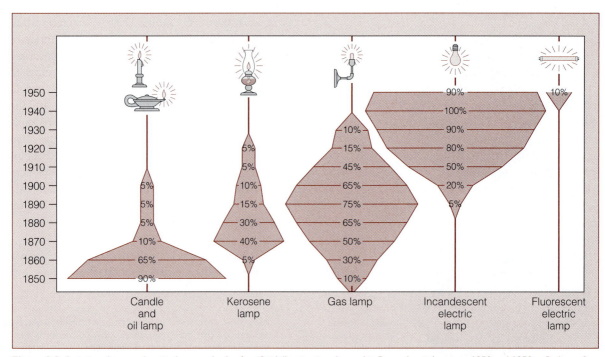

Figure 8-3 Seriation diagram showing how methods of artificial illumination changed in Pennsylvania between 1850 and 1950. *Redrawn from Mayer-Oakes 1955, figure 15.*

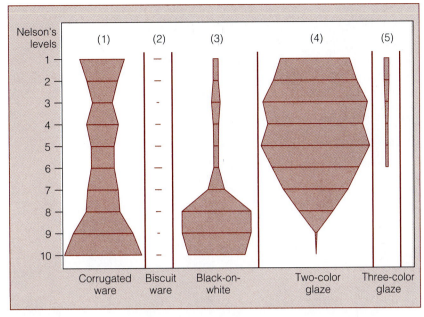

Figure 8-4 Seriation diagram based on Nelson's San Cristobal potsherd frequencies.

not sufficiently specific. And archaeologists still use the index fossil concept, but only as a rough guide. For example, excavations have shown that Folsom spear points, like those found at the Folsom site mentioned in Chapter 6, date to around 10,300 to 10,900 years ago. If we excavated a site with Folsom points in it, we would gleefully tell our colleagues that "we had a Folsom site," and they would know that the site probably dated between 10,300 and 10,900 years. But we would *always* try to refine that estimate by using one of the absolute dating techniques mentioned below.

Dating Sites with Seriation

This sequence can help archaeologists date other archaeological sites in the American Southwest. Instead of just using the presence or absence of a particular artifact type, we use frequencies of those different artifacts to place sites into a finer chronological sequence. For example, sites with high percentages of black-on-white ceramics would be older than sites with high percentages of two-color glaze and small percentages of black-on-white pottery. These sites, in turn, would be older than sites with high percentages of two-color glaze, small percentages of corrugated ware, and only trace amounts of black-on-white pottery. And these sites would be older than sites dominated by two-color glaze with trace amounts of three-color glaze.

We can use the seriation method based on a single master stratigraphy, or we can compile one analytically by linking several overlapping stratigraphies at different stratified sites. Thus, seriation takes the index fossil concept and refines it to permit a more fine-grained relative sequence. Nonetheless, seriation still cannot tell us *how old* a site or stratum is, only whether it is older or younger than another.

Seriation was a common technique in the mid-twentieth century, but today it is used mostly where absolute dating methods cannot be employed or are

ABSOLUTE DATING

Absolute dating gave archaeology an incredibly powerful tool and helped shape it into the science that it is today. In this chapter, we will only highlight the most commonly used methods among the many techniques available. And we will give special attention to radiocarbon dating as a way to demonstrate the issues that archaeologists must consider when determining what a date actually means.

Tree-Ring Dating

Tree-ring dating, also called **dendrochronology,** was developed by Andrew E. Douglass (1867–1962), an astronomer interested in the effect of sunspots on the earth's climate. Douglass knew that trees growing in temperate and arctic areas remain dormant during the winter and then burst into activity in the spring. This results in the formation of the familiar concentric growth rings. Because each ring represents a single year,

tree-ring dating (dendrochronology) The use of annual growth rings in trees to assign calendar ages to ancient wood samples.

it's a simple matter to determine the age of a newly felled tree: just count the rings. Trees have alternating dark and light rings (Figure 8-5). The light rings are a year's spring/summer growth, and the dark rings are that year's late summer/fall growth (the darkness comes from the cell walls; when they do not grow quickly, the cell walls crowd together and take up a greater proportion of the ring's space).

For many tree species, the widths of the rings vary, and Douglass reasoned that the rings might preserve information about past climatic change. Because environmental patterning affects all the trees maturing in a given region, Douglass reasoned, year-by-year patterns of tree growth manifested as variable ring widths should fit into a long-term chronological sequence.

Douglass began his research on living trees, mostly yellow pines in central Arizona. He examined recent stumps and cores taken from still-living trees, counted the rings, and recorded the pattern of light and dark ring widths. He then extended this chronology backward in time by searching for an overlap between the early portion of young trees with the final years of growth of an old tree or stump. In doing so, he created a master sequence of tree rings extending back in time. But, altogether, the stumps and living trees went back only about 500 years.

Douglass worked in the American Southwest, where arid conditions enhance preservation. Sampling ancient beams in pueblo sites, he slowly constructed a prehistoric "floating chronology," which spanned

© American Museum of Natural History

Figure 8-5 Cross section of a ponderosa pine showing a detailed record of the tree's 108-year life span. Each year is represented by a light (summer) and a dark (winter) ring; evidence of fire scars is also preserved.

several centuries but was not tied into the sequence based on modern samples (Figure 8-6). Eventually, Douglass bridged this gap between the sequences of ancient and modern trees and gave Southwestern archaeology a reliable, year-by-year dating tool.

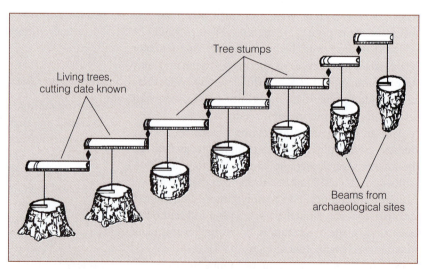

Figure 8-6 How a tree-ring chronology is built up by matching portions of tree-ring sequences from known-age living trees (lower left) to older archaeological samples; the diamonds indicate the portions of the sequences that overlap.

Year-by-Year Chronology Becomes a Reality

In August 1927, Douglass traveled to Betatakin, an impressive cliff dwelling in northeastern Arizona (see this chapter's opening photo). He collected two dozen samples that placed the construction of Betatakin within a decade of AD 1270. Accuracy to this degree was stunning back then—and still is, compared with every other technique.

But we can be even more accurate with tree-ring dating. Jeffrey Dean of the University of Arizona's Laboratory of Tree-Ring Research collected further samples from Betatakin in the 1960s. The total collection grew to 292 individual beams, allowing Dean to document the growth of Betatakin literally room by room—his findings are summarized in Figure 8-7. (The samples, by the way, from both living trees and prehistoric beams are taken using a hand or power drill equipped with a special bit that removes only a quarter-inch diameter cylinder of wood, so the technique does not harm living trees and is minimally destructive of archaeological materials.)

Dean found that Betatakin was first occupied about AD 1250 by a small group who built a few structures that were soon destroyed. This occupation was probably transient, the rockshelter serving as a seasonal camping spot for people traveling to plant fields at some distance from their home.

The actual village at Betatakin was founded in AD 1267, when three room clusters were constructed; a fourth cluster was added in AD 1268. The next year, a group of maybe 20 to 25 people felled several trees, cut them to standardized length, and stockpiled the lumber, presumably for future immigrants to the village. Inhabitants stockpiled additional beams in AD 1272, but they did not use them until AD 1275, which signaled the beginning of a 3-year immigration period during which more than ten room clusters and a kiva were added. Population growth at Betatakin slowed after AD 1277, reaching a peak of about 125 people in the mid-1280s. The village was abandoned sometime between AD 1286 and AD 1300 for unknown reasons.

Methodology of Tree-Ring Dating

In practice, tree-ring dating works like this: The archaeologist digs up a sample of charcoal or wood of the appropriate species and that bears at least 20 rings. He or she then sends it to the appropriate lab—there are several around the world (such as the University of Arizona's Laboratory of Tree-Ring Research)—with appropriate contextual data. There, an analyst will cut or sand the sample down so that the rings are easily visible, and the widths are then measured individually.

Now the hard work begins. Normally, the archaeologist will have some idea of how old the site is—perhaps less than 500 years old, or between 750 and 1000 years old. A lab analyst will try to match the sample to the appropriate portion of the regional sequence. This can be a slow, laborious process, because the analyst is looking for a segment of the master sequence that has the same order of variable-width rings as the archaeological sample—say, a pattern of four thick summer rings, followed by three thin ones, then three thick rings, two thin ones, and finally four not-quite-so-thick rings. Computer programs can assist in this task, but the matching often requires visual comparison because some samples have oddities, such as missing rings or partial rings, that only a trained technician can detect.

For tree-ring dating to work, the analyst has to make several adjustments and consider several factors. For example, trees grow more quickly when they are young than when they are old. Thus, absolute tree-ring width

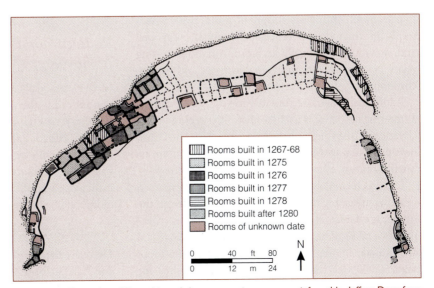

Figure 8-7 Floor plan of Betatakin and the construction sequence inferred by Jeffrey Dean from the tree-ring evidence. *Redrawn from Dean 1970, figure 13.*

is a function of climate and a tree's age. But by using the estimated curvature of the ring on a sample, dendrochronologists solve this problem through a mathematical function that converts a tree's rings into a standardized index that takes the tree's age into account.

Additionally, a sample's age is the age of the last (outermost) ring present on the piece. But if that ring is not present—if the outer portion of the sample was adzed off or burnt away—we still won't know what year the tree died. However, by looking for markings that are diagnostic of the outer edge of a tree—such as signs of bark or beetle activity—a trained analyst can determine whether the outermost ring on the sample was the tree's final ring. If so, then you have what is known as a *cutting date*; if not, then your date is only a maximum age (that is, we could say that a specimen was cut down after, say, AD 1225 but we would not be able to say *how many* years after).

Finally, the sample sent to the lab must also have at least 20 rings visible on it in order to increase the chance that the sample will match one and only one segment of the master sequence. A sample with few rings might match to several segments, leaving the archaeologist guessing which match is the correct one.

We can apply tree-ring dating to many species of trees as long as the species reflects climatic change. The most commonly used are piñon pine, ponderosa pine, Douglas fir, juniper, and white fir. Limber pine, bristlecone pine, oak, red cedar, and the giant sequoia are also useful. But some species are not suitable. Cottonwood, for example, grows only near water sources and taps into a more continuous supply of groundwater. As a result, its rings do not reflect local climate very well and, without climatically induced variation in ring width, we cannot link individual samples and build a chronology.

Additionally, because climate varies between regions, a tree-ring sequence is useful only for the region whose climate the tree rings reflect. A tree-ring sequence from northern New Mexico, for example, is not useful in the Mediterranean, or even in southern New Mexico.

Dendrochronological sequences have been developed in many areas, including the American Southwest, the Arctic, the Great Plains, the American Midwest, Germany, Great Britain, Ireland, New Zealand, Turkey, Japan, and Russia. In the American Southwest alone, more than 60,000 tree-ring dates have been established for some 5000 sites. Here the logs used to make pueblo rooms and pithouses allow the tree-ring sequence to extend back to 322 BC; using oaks preserved in ancient bogs, one sequence in Germany extends back to 8000 BC.

Tree-ring dating has tremendous potential to provide absolute dates—to the year, in many cases—for archaeological sites, subject to the one important limitation of all dating methods: There must always be a clear-cut association between the datable specimen (the tree) and cultural behavior (say, the construction of the building). At Betatakin, for example, Dean found that beams were scavenged from old rooms and incorporated into new rooms. In Alaska, archaeologists found that the driftwood used in some structures had apparently lain on the shore for a century before being used. In both cases, the tree-ring dates would be older (perhaps much older) than the cultural behavior of interest.

Tree Rings and Climate

Dendrochronology also provides climatic data. Because tree-ring width is controlled by precipitation as well as temperature, trees preserve a record of past environmental conditions. Although tree metabolism is complex, analysts have made great progress in such ecological reconstructions. In the American Southwest, for instance, detailed models can tell us how much rain fell in, say, northwestern New Mexico, year by year, even season by season. For example, these data demonstrate that catastrophic floods occurred there in AD 1358. These detailed climatic reconstructions can provide archaeologists with fine-grained paleoenvironmental chronologies—provided the research focuses on an area with a dendrochronological sequence.

Radiocarbon Dating: Archaeology's Workhorse

In 1949, physical chemist Willard F. Libby (1908–1980) announced to the world that he had discovered a revolutionary new dating technique: radiocarbon dating. For his efforts, Libby deservedly received the Nobel Prize in chemistry in 1960. Although dendrochronology is a more precise technique, radiocarbon dating is more widely applicable and is the workhorse in archaeology's stable of dating methods.

How It Works

There are three principal isotopes of carbon—^{12}C, ^{13}C, and ^{14}C. The isotope ^{14}C (read this as "carbon-14") is of interest here, even though it is the rarest: only one ^{14}C atom exists for every trillion atoms of ^{12}C in living material. ^{14}C is produced in the upper atmosphere, where cosmic radiation creates neutrons that replace one of nitrogen's (^{14}N) protons to create ^{14}C. This ^{14}C is oxidated to form carbon dioxide, which is dispersed throughout the atmosphere by stratospheric winds. About 98 percent of all ^{14}C enters the oceans; plants take up much of the rest through photosynthesis. From plants, it enters herbivores, and then carnivores. So all organic life contains radioactive carbon (including you).

All radioactive isotopes are unstable and break down, or "decay," over time. ^{14}C breaks down through beta emissions (the emission of a negatively charged electron) back into ^{14}N. The amount a living organism loses through decay is replaced from the environment, so as long as an organism is alive, the amount of ^{14}C in it remains in equilibrium with the atmosphere. But once the organism dies, it ceases to take ^{14}C in, and hence the amount of ^{14}C in its body begins to decrease through decay.

But not very quickly. Libby calculated that after 5568 years, half of the ^{14}C available in a sample will have converted to ^{14}N; this is termed the **Libby half-life** of ^{14}C. (We have since learned that the actual half-life of ^{14}C is 5730 years—the so-called Cambridge half-life. To convert a date using the Libby half-life to one using the Cambridge half-life, simply multiply the Libby date by 1.03.)

What do we mean by "half-life"? Imagine a sample of charcoal that contains 100 atoms of ^{14}C (actually, it would contain much more, but let's keep it simple). After 5730 years, 50 of these atoms would have decayed into ^{14}N. After another 5730 years, half of the remaining 50 ^{14}C atoms (that is, 25 atoms) would have converted to ^{14}N, leaving us with only 25 ^{14}C atoms. After another 5730 years (a total of 17,190 years), this amount would be halved again to about 12 ^{14}C atoms. As you can see, after a long time very few ^{14}C atoms remain. Theoretically, radiocarbon dating should extend far back in time, but current technology places a practical limit on it: Radiocarbon dating is good only for organic remains that are no more than about 45,000 years old.

Radiocarbon dating can be used on any organic material, although some are better sources of dates than others. Carbon, or charcoal, is perhaps the most common material dated in archaeology. After being collected in the field, the sample is sent to one of the world's 130 radiocarbon labs with appropriate contextual data. The archaeologist first examines the sample microscopically for intruding root hairs or other organic contaminants, and he or she will try to identify the wood species (see "Are All Organics Created Equal?" below).

The lab pretreats the carbon with one of several protocols, depending on its characteristics. The sample might, for instance, be physically crushed and dispersed in de-ionized water, then washed with hot hydrochloric acid to remove carbonates and then with an alkali wash (NaOH) to remove organic acids (these could make the date younger or older if not removed). Such pretreatment is important because even a small amount of contamination can greatly alter the measured date of a sample.

Once the sample has been pretreated, the lab counts the amount of ^{14}C in the sample by using a scintillation or ionization detector (devices akin to very sophisticated Geiger counters), which counts the number of beta emissions over a measured interval of time. The rate of emissions will be high if the sample is young and low if the sample is very old. By using an established equation, the lab converts the measured rate of beta emissions to an age.

What the Lab Can Tell You

The archaeologist who submits a sample will eventually receive a detailed report from the radiocarbon lab. Here's one date we received on a carbon sample from the Pine Spring site in southwestern Wyoming:

Beta-122584 6510 +/– 70 BP

The alphanumeric string records the laboratory and sample number: Beta Analytic (a radiocarbon lab in Florida) and sample number 122584 (in our reports, we always publish this number with the date so that another archaeologist could consult data in the lab's sample logbook). The second part estimates the age of the sample in radiocarbon years BP (before present— "present" being defined as 1950). Therefore, the radiocarbon lab told us this about the Pine Spring sample: A plant died and burned about 6510 radiocarbon years before AD 1950.

Why 1950? In radiocarbon dating, the present is defined as the year AD 1950—the year Libby invented

> **Libby half-life** The time required for half of the carbon-14 available in an organic sample to decay; the standard is 5568 years, although it is known that the half-life is closer to 5730 years.

the method. The reason for this is that "the present" keeps becoming the past, so we need a standard that keeps still. This means that a date of, say, 1000 BP obtained in the year 1960 is actually about 1054 years old in the year 2004 (add 54 years because 2004 is 54 years after AD 1950).

Why "radiocarbon years"? Labs measure samples in radiocarbon years, not calendar years. As we will see, radiocarbon dating has certain biases, and the laboratory date must be corrected to reflect actual calendar years. We'll return to this below.

Can You Handle the Uncertainty?

So far, so good. But remember that the lab report attached "+/− 70" to the age estimate. The decay process of ^{14}C is a statistical process, and the number of beta emissions is not constant over short periods (but the rate does average out over the half-life). For this reason, the lab measures the amount of beta emissions over several lengths of time and then averages those emissions to get an age. In Beta-122584, the number 6510 estimates the actual age of the sample; it is the mean of a number of measurements made by the lab.

That counting process also produces a standard deviation, read as "plus or minus," which estimates the degree of consistency among the counting runs. The standard deviation expresses the range within which the true date falls. We know from statistical theory that there is a 68 percent chance that the true date falls within one standard deviation on either side of the mean date. By both adding and subtracting 70 years from the age estimate, we know that there is a 68 percent chance that the true age of the carbon falls between 6440 (6510 − 70) and 6580 (6510 + 70) radiocarbon years BP. If you want to be even more certain, statistical theory tells us that there is a 95 percent chance that the actual age falls within *two* standard deviations of the mean date, which in this case means between 6370 and 6650 radiocarbon years BP.

The standard deviation must never be omitted from the radiocarbon date, because without it one has no idea how precise a date is. When archaeologists get a date back from a lab, they will first look at the mean date, but they will evaluate that date's utility by looking at the standard deviation. If it is very large, the date may be worthless (although it depends on the specific research question).

Are All Organics Created Equal?

The simple answer is no.

Bone, for example—and especially very old bone (>5000 years)—can create problems. Bone is very complex chemically and contains non-organic as well as organic components. In addition, it can be easily contaminated by younger carbon percolating in from the surrounding sediments. For these reasons, bones can give dates that are quite a bit older or younger than their actual ages. One way around this problem is to extract the amino acids chemically and date the carbon that is part of those organic molecules.

We also have to take care with plant remains. All plants take in carbon through the process of photosynthesis, but different plant species do it through one of three **photosynthetic pathways.** The first such pathway (discovered in experiments with algae, spinach, and barley) converts atmospheric carbon dioxide into a compound with three carbon atoms. This so-called C_3 pathway is characteristic of sugar beets, radishes, peas, wheat, and many hardwood trees. A second pathway converts carbon dioxide from the air into a complex compound with four carbon atoms. This C_4 pathway is used by plants from arid and semiarid regions, such as maize, sorghum, millet, yucca, and prickly pear. A third, the CAM pathway ("crassulacean acid metabolism"), is found in succulents, such as cactus.

The importance of these different photosynthetic pathways is that C_4 plants end up taking in *more* ^{14}C relative to the other isotopes of carbon than do C_3 and CAM plants. Because Libby developed radiocarbon dating before this diversity in photosynthesis was known, his system uses the photosynthetic process of C_3 plants as the standard. This can create problems.

Imagine a maize plant growing next to an oak; the maize, being a C_4 plant, will take in more ^{14}C than the oak, a C_3 plant. If both die at the same time, and both are later dated by an archaeologist, the maize sample will appear to be *younger* than the oak tree by 200 to 300 years, because the maize began the decay process with more radiocarbon than did the oak.

Fortunately, radiocarbon labs can correct this problem by measuring the ratio of ^{13}C to ^{12}C and using that value to normalize the resulting date on the sample.

photosynthetic pathways The specific chemical process through which plants metabolize carbon; the three major pathways discriminate against carbon-13 in different ways, therefore similarly aged plants that use different pathways can produce different radiocarbon ages.

And this is why archaeologists should always try to identify the kind of plant that they are dating.

The Reservoir Effect

A second problem concerns the **reservoir effect.** Libby's method was based on the abundance of ^{14}C in the atmosphere, but some organisms obtain their carbon from sources whose carbon content may be significantly different from that of the atmosphere. Snails that live in lakes in areas of limestone will incorporate "dead" carbon (meaning that the carbon source is so old that no discernible ^{14}C remains) by incorporating the limestone's carbonate into their shells. If dated, a snail that died yesterday in such a situation can appear to be hundreds, or even thousands, of years old.

Similarly, this affects dating the remains of marine organisms that archaeologists find in coastal sites. Fish and shellfish take in carbon from the water, not the atmosphere. The ocean is another reservoir of carbon containing more "old" carbon than the atmosphere at any given time. Given that the radiocarbon method is based on an atmospheric standard, marine organisms also tend to date somewhat older than they actually are—by about 400 years, although the exact amount varies throughout the oceans. This creates an ancillary problem in dating skeletal remains of humans or animals who relied heavily on seafood, for their skeletons will reflect the isotopic composition of the foods they consumed—and hence they also would appear to be older than they actually are. Again, labs can correct this problem if they have background information on the sample.

Tree Rings Refine Radiocarbon Dating

In order to test the radiocarbon method, Libby had to calculate radiocarbon dates on material of known ages. He chose wood from the tombs of Egyptian pharaohs, because those burials were dated through documents. Although Egyptologists warned that the radiocarbon dates did not quite square with the historically derived dynastic chronology, Libby attributed this disparity to experimental error. But we now know that the effect is due to differential production of atmospheric ^{14}C over time.

The first investigator to find fault with the atmospheric assumption was Hessel de Vries of the Netherlands. In the 1950s, de Vries cut several beams from historic buildings and determined the age of the wood by counting the rings. When he dated the known-age specimens by radiocarbon assay, he found the ^{14}C dates to be 2 percent older than expected for the known-age wood. Scientists at the time generally dismissed the work, because the errors de Vries discovered were relatively small—just barely outside the limits of expected error.

But the specter of larger errors finally inspired several radiocarbon labs to look more closely into the problem. In one landmark study, Hans Suess (University of California, San Diego) analyzed wood from bristlecone pine trees. Native to the western United States, bristlecones are the world's oldest living organisms (some living specimens are 4600 years old). Working from live trees to ancient stumps, investigators had already extended the bristlecone tree-ring sequence back nearly 8200 years (by the tree-ring technique discussed above). Suess radiocarbon-dated dozens of known-age samples and compared the results obtained by each method. When he did so, it became clear that significant fluctuations, now known as **de Vries effects,** occurred in the atmospheric ^{14}C concentrations. There were at least 17 such fluctuations over the past 10,000 years, produced, we believe, by pulses in sunspot activity.

This tree-ring research led to the discovery that the production of ^{14}C has not remained constant over time as Libby assumed. This is generally not a big problem for dates younger than about 3500 years; but it becomes progressively worse as we move farther back in time. In fact, a piece of carbon that gives a radiocarbon date of around 10,000 years is actually closer to 12,000 years old.

So the bad news is that *radiocarbon years are not the same as calendar years.* The good news is that we can fix the problem.

The fluctuations in ^{14}C are worldwide because the earth's atmosphere is so well mixed; studies made during aboveground testing of atomic bombs show that material released into the atmosphere is more or less evenly distributed throughout the atmosphere in a few years. We say "more or less" because southern hemisphere radiocarbon dates are 24 to 40 years too old compared with northern hemisphere dates (that is, a

reservoir effect When organisms take in carbon from a source that is depleted of or enriched in ^{14}C relative to the atmosphere; such samples may return ages that are considerably older or younger than they actually are.

de Vries effects Fluctuations in the calibration curve produced by variations in the atmosphere's carbon-14 content; these can cause radiocarbon dates to calibrate to more than one calendar age.

sample of carbon from South Africa will give a radiocarbon age that is 24 to 40 years older than a sample from Germany that is the same age). The land-to-ocean ratio is smaller in the southern than in the northern hemisphere, and this means that the oceans deplete the southern hemisphere's atmosphere of ^{14}C relative to the northern hemisphere. But 24 to 40 years is minor, and we can correct for it before calibration.

Using tree-ring chronologies from several places in the world, researchers have extended the calibration curve to 11,800 calendar years. Other methods push the calibration curve back even farther, but they are still controversial. We can now convert radiocarbon dates into calendar dates through easy-to-use programs available on-line (by the way, this also takes care of the Cambridge/Libby half-life discrepancy mentioned above). And radiocarbon labs routinely provide the calibrated date along with the conventional radiocarbon age (see "Looking Closer: How to Calibrate Radiocarbon Dates").

In the Old World, calibration had an enormous effect. In areas where writing was invented quite early, historical records provide a firm chronology over some 5000 years. Radiocarbon dates for the Near East and Egypt were corrected and supplemented by independent historical records. Western European chronologies, however, lacked historical evidence and were therefore arranged according to radiocarbon determinations alone. Over the years, archaeologists interpreted these data as indicating that the early traits of civilization, such as metallurgy and monumental funerary architecture, were originally developed in the Near East and later diffused into Europe, first appearing in the Mediterranean region. Near Eastern peoples appeared to be the inventors, and the barbaric Europeans the recipients. This, in fact, was the conclusion that Oscar Montelius reached after he used the index fossil concept to construct European chronologies. In his day, the Near East was considered the "cradle of civilization."

Radiocarbon calibration changed much of that. Colin Renfrew (Cambridge University) showed that calibration shifted most European chronologies several centuries *earlier*, altering the temporal relationships between developments in Europe and those of the Mediterranean and Near East. Stonehenge, for example, formerly considered to be the work of Greek craftsmen who traveled to the British Isles in 1500 BC, was under construction in 2750 BC and therefore predates even the Mycenaean civilization. Monumental temples were built on Malta before the pyramids of Egypt, and the elaborate British megalithic tombs are a full millennium older than those in the eastern Mediterranean. These "corrected" radiocarbon dates suggested that western Europe was not simply a passive recipient of cultural advances from the Mediterranean, and that the Near East was not the sole cradle of civilization.

Accelerator Dating: Taking Radiocarbon to the Limit

Some scholars see archaeology as an odd science because it progresses through unique and unrepeatable experiments. Digging remains our primary "experimental" method, and all archaeologists know that, as they dig, they are destroying data that no one has even yet thought of collecting. Before 1950, for example, archaeologists rarely saved charcoal—how could they have anticipated radiocarbon dating? This is why, today, we slowly excavate only that portion of a site necessary to answer a question, and it's why we compulsively save at least a sample of everything we find. We know that future technologies will allow us to learn things that we cannot even imagine now. New methods of radiocarbon dating demonstrate this fact.

Recall that labs obtain conventional radiocarbon dates by counting beta emissions. To do this effectively, you need to submit a fairly large sample of carbon (see Table 8-2). Back in the 1970s, in fact, archaeologists sometimes said you needed a good "double handful" of carbon for a decent date. But often all we find are small, isolated bits of carbon; we can't simply combine them

TABLE 8-2 Recommended Sample Sizes for Radiocarbon and AMS Dating		
	CONVENTIONAL (grams)	AMS (milligrams)
Charcoal	10–30	20–50
Wood	15–100	20–100
Dung	10–30	20–100
Peat	10–30	30–100
Seeds	n/a	20–50
Organic sediments	200–2000	2–10 grams
Bone/antler	200	2–10 grams
Shell	20–100	50–100
Pollen	n/a	15
Water	n/a	1 liter

SOURCE: Beta Analytic Laboratory

Looking Closer
How to Calibrate Radiocarbon Dates

Let's calibrate the 6510 +/– 70 BP radiocarbon date mentioned in the text. We could calculate the calendar age simply by subtracting AD 1950 from 6510, given that BP in radiocarbon dating means "before AD 1950." This gives an answer of 4560 BC. But recall that radiocarbon years are not the same as calendar years.

The first calibration curve used tree rings of known age that were removed one by one and then radiocarbon-dated. A curve was then statistically created to fit the resulting data points. From this curve, one can calculate a calendar age from a radiocarbon age. The figure shows a portion of the calibration curve and Beta Analytic's calibration of 6510 +/– 70 BP. The radiocarbon age is on the y-axis, and the corresponding calendar age is on the x-axis. The black bar is one standard deviation on either side of the mean date; the clear bar is two standard deviations. To find the calibrated calendar age, draw a line from the mean date on the y-axis horizontally to the calibration curve, then drop down and intersect the

x-axis. The radiocarbon date of 6510 BP converts to a calendar age of 5435 BC, a difference of *875 years* from the straightforward conversion. (We can convert the BC date to a calibrated BP date by adding 1950 to 5435, meaning that the tree that was burned to make our carbon sample died 7385 years ago.) By following the same procedure for the standard deviation, we can say that there is a **68 percent chance** that the actual date lies between 5465 and 5345 BC—a span of some 120 years. That may not seem terribly precise, but for something that's over 7000 years old, it's about as good as it gets.

Some dates are more difficult to calibrate. The de Vries effects—those annoying "blips" in the curve—can cause a radiocarbon date to calibrate to more than one calendar date. Nonetheless, these dates are still "absolute" in that they point to *a particular age range at a known level of probability*. Sometimes those age ranges are large, sometimes they are small. Whether they are useful depends on your research question.

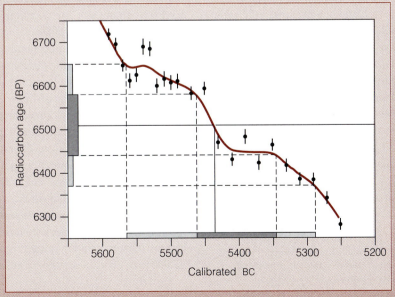

A portion of the calibration curve, showing how the radiocarbon date of 6510 +/– 70 BP is calibrated to a calendar age.

because we'd then risk combining carbon of vastly different ages—which will produce a standard deviation so large that the date may be useless.

The development of **accelerator mass spectrometry (AMS)** for radiocarbon dating in the 1980s changed this by drastically reducing the quantity of datable material required. Accelerator technology does not count beta emissions as conventional technology does. Instead, it uses an electrostatic tandem accelerator and a technique known as mass spectrometry to count the *proportion* of carbon isotopes in a sample. Given that a single gram of modern organic material contains some 59 *billion* atoms of ^{14}C, a much smaller amount of material is required. In fact, AMS requires only a few milligrams of carbon—a sample about the size of a sesame seed.

This new radiocarbon method allows archaeologists to test old ideas by allowing sites or objects to be dated that previously defied adequate dating. In some cases, AMS dating has corrected some significant errors. Following is one example.

How Old Is Egyptian Agriculture?

In 1978, Fred Wendorf (Southern Methodist University) and his research team made a remarkable discovery in southern Egypt, just west of the Nile River, in a series of small sites in Wadi Kubbaniya (a *wadi* is a dry stream drainage). The sites contained many stone tools (mostly blades fashioned from flint) and some large grinding stones. They also found the bones of fish, especially catfish and eel, and of waterfowl, wild cattle, hartebeest, and gazelle. They also found several hearths, from which they took some 30 charcoal samples that dated the site to between 17,000 and 18,300 years old.

None of the food remains were surprising in a site of this age. The evidence pointed to a hunting-and-gathering population that fished, hunted, and gathered plants along what was then a sluggish stream.

What was surprising, however, were four small grains of domesticated barley and one grain of wheat. In 1978, all evidence suggested that agriculture had begun about 10,000 years ago, far to the east in places such as Iran and Iraq. The evidence from Wadi Kubbaniya, however, suggested that agriculture in the Near East was 7000 to 8000 years *older*. This was indeed an important find.

But note that the few grains of wheat and barley were not themselves dated; instead, their age was based on their *association* with hearths that contained charcoal that was dated. In Chapter 7, you learned that objects, especially small objects like seeds, can move around quite a bit in archaeological sites. So the question was: Were the seeds deposited at the same time that the hearths were used?

Wendorf saw no obvious evidence that the seeds had been moved from a later level. But he knew that such evidence is often hard to see and that the best thing would be to date the wheat and barley themselves. But these small seeds, even if lumped together, would be too small a sample for the conventional radiocarbon method.

Wendorf is a cautious archaeologist, and he knew that his claim needed further testing. In 1978, AMS dating was just under development, but Wendorf knew that it could provide a test of the conventional radiocarbon dates. And so he submitted four barley seeds for analysis along with some charcoal from the hearths as a control (in fact, these were among some of the first archaeological samples dated with the new technique). As before, the charcoal yielded dates from 17,500 to 19,000 years old, but all the barley seeds were *less than 5000 years old*. The barley seeds (and presumably the lone wheat seed as well) were contaminants—seeds that had somehow worked their way down from a later level into an ancient site. Admirably, Wendorf quickly published a retraction of his earlier claim. Were it not for AMS dating, our understanding of the origins of agriculture might be quite different—and wrong.

By permitting archaeology to obtain reliable dates on extremely small samples, AMS dating also allows us to date objects that ethical considerations would otherwise prevent us from dating (see "Looking Closer: Is the Shroud of Turin the Burial Cloth of Christ?"). AMS dating fulfilled the wishes of many archaeologists.

One wish, however, was not fulfilled. Archaeologists initially thought that AMS would push the radiocarbon barrier back to 100,000 or more years. But that wish has not come true: Researchers keep trying, but for now AMS cannot reliably date anything that is older than about 45,000 years. For these sites, we need other methods.

Trapped Charge Dating

Those other methods are jointly known as **trapped charge dating,** which consists of three basic processes:

accelerator mass spectrometry (AMS) A method of radiocarbon dating that counts the proportion of carbon isotopes directly (rather than using the indirect Geiger counter method), thereby dramatically reducing the quantity of datable material required.

trapped charge dating Forms of dating that rely upon the fact that electrons become trapped in minerals' crystal lattices as a function of background radiation; the age of the specimen is the total radiation received divided by the annual dose of radiation.

Looking Closer
Is the Shroud of Turin the Burial Cloth of Christ?

Accelerator dating is finding uses beyond its original realm. Antiquarians and musicians, for instance, are turning to AMS technology to detect fakes, such as fraudulent Stradivarius violins.

AMS dating grabbed headlines when it was applied to the Shroud of Turin, thought by many to be the cloth in which Christ's crucified body had been wrapped. Although the Roman Catholic Church never officially proclaimed the shroud to be Christ's burial cloth, 3 million of the faithful filed past the shroud when it was displayed in the Cathedral of St. John the Baptist in 1978. Many believed they had looked into the face of Christ. What did they see?

The shroud itself is a simple linen cloth, slightly more than 14 feet long and a yard wide. On it appears a pale sepia-tone image of the front and back of a naked man about 6 feet tall. Pale carmine stains of presumed blood mark wounds to the head, side, hands, and feet. Believers take the shroud to be a true relic of Christ's Passion. But critics since the fourteenth century have been convinced that the shroud is a cruel, if clever, hoax.

The mystery deepened when scientists from various research centers examined the shroud in detail, photographing it under ultraviolet and infrared light, bombarding it with x-rays, peering at it microscopically. But the scientists could not come up with a clear conclusion either way. Creationists immediately asked why the United States government should support places like the Smithsonian Institution when scientists cannot even explain how such an "obvious fraud" was perpetrated.

For nearly 40 years, scientists had argued that radiocarbon dating could definitively determine if the shroud was *not* Christ's burial cloth, because, for the shroud to even possibly be Jesus' burial cloth, it had to be about 2000 years old. If it were a fourteenth-century hoax, then it would only be some 600 years old. Unfortunately, conventional radiocarbon methods would have destroyed a handkerchief-sized piece of the shroud, and church authorities rejected all such requests. But because AMS

© David Lees / CORBIS

Shroud of Turin.

necessitates only a minuscule sample of linen—easily removed from unobtrusive parts of the shroud—the Pontifical Academy of Sciences agreed in 1984 to such dating.

After years of squabbling about the ground rules, each of three laboratories (at the University of Arizona in Tucson, the British Museum in London, and the Swiss Federal Institute in Zurich) finally received a postage stamp–size piece of the shroud plus control specimens of various known ages. Only British Museum officials, who coordinated the research, knew which specimen was which. When the owner of the shroud, Pope John Paul II, was informed of the outcome, his response was simple: "Publish it."

And so they did. In October 1988, a gathering of ecclesiastical and technological specialists hosted a news conference at which Anastasio Cardinal Ballestrero, archbishop of Turin, solemnly announced that all three laboratories agreed that the flax plants from which the linen in the shroud was made had been grown in medieval times—between AD 1260 and 1390—long after the death of Jesus.

Although a certain degree of mystery still surrounds the shroud, particularly since nobody can explain how such an image was created using medieval technology, one thing is clear: Radiocarbon dating unambiguously resolved a controversy that spanned five centuries. The Shroud of Turin could not possibly be the authentic burial cloth of Jesus.

thermoluminescence, optically stimulated luminescence, and electron spin resonance. Rare a decade ago, these techniques are increasingly common in archaeology today. Their age ranges are unknown, but they extend back to at least 300,000 years.

Their geochemical basis is complex, but we will keep the explanations simple. Working archaeologists need to understand both the potential and the limitations of these dating tools.

The same principle underlies all three techniques: Over time, background gamma radiation (generated primarily by uranium, thorium, and a radioactive isotope of potassium) in sediment causes some electrons of the atoms of certain minerals, notably quartz and feldspar, to move to a different energy state. When this happens, some electrons are "trapped" in atomic imperfections in the minerals' crystal lattices (Figure 8-8). As time passes, an increasing number of electrons are trapped in this way.

Assuming that the radiation dose is constant over time, electrons become trapped at a constant rate. If we could somehow measure the number of electrons trapped in the crystal lattice, we would have an estimate of the *total* radiation dose the specimen has received over time. If we then knew the *annual* background radiation dose, we could calculate a specimen's age simply by dividing the first measure by the second. How might we calculate these values?

We figure the annual dose by burying a radiation-measuring device, called a **dosimeter**, in an archaeological site and retrieving it a year later. The device records how much radiation it was exposed to in a year's time.

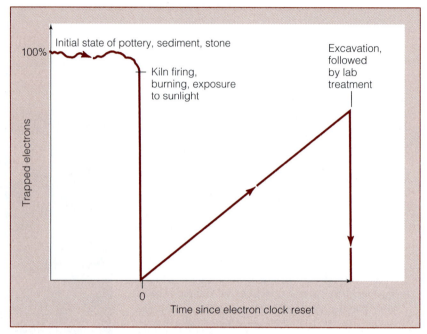

Figure 8-8 The process of setting an object's clock to zero in trapped charge dating. An object begins with some number of trapped electrons that are "reset" when the object is heated or exposed to sunlight. The object then slowly gathers more trapped electrons through time due to background radiation; its clock is again reset in the lab, where the number of trapped electrons are estimated to calculate the object's age.

To determine a specimen's total radiation dose, we need to measure the number of trapped electrons in that specimen. Obviously, you can't just count them. But several methods accomplish this task, and the three techniques are partially distinguished by the methods used to determine the total radiation dose, as well as the kinds of material that they date. To understand *how* we can measure the total radiation dose, you must first understand *what* it is that trapped charge techniques measure.

The important thing to know is that electrons that are moved *out* of their orbits (that is, trapped) by background radiation are *returned* to their orbits by sufficient heat (500° C) or by exposure to even a few minutes of sunlight. Through the application of heat or light, the specimen has its clock reset to zero, so to speak, and the slow trapping process will begin again. So, strictly speaking, *trapped charge dating identifies the last time a specimen had its electron traps emptied.* Knowing this tells us how to apply the different techniques.

dosimeter   A device to measure the amount of gamma radiation emitted by sediments. It is normally buried in a stratum for a year to record the annual dose of radiation. Dosimeters are often a short length of pure copper tubing filled with calcium sulfate.

Thermoluminescence

Thermoluminescence (TL) measures the total radiation dose by heating a specimen rapidly to 500° C. Trapped electrons in quartz and feldspar crystals slip free and move back to their orbits. When they do, they release energy in the form of light. Using special equipment, the lab measures the amount of light released as the specimen is heated; this gives us the needed measure of the total radiation dose. Like radiocarbon dating, trapped charge dating produces a mean date with a standard deviation.

Archaeologists have used TL to date ceramics. Imagine a ceramic pot, consisting of clay with some sand added to give the pot strength. The sand contains quartz and feldspar that have been slowly accumulating trapped electrons. When that pot is fired, however, those traps are emptied, and the pot's clock is reset. Eventually, the pot breaks and its sherds discarded. Once those sherds become buried, the quartz and feldspars are exposed to gamma radiation and begin to collect trapped charges again. When the sample is reheated under laboratory conditions (a small portion of the specimen has to be destroyed for analysis), the intensity of the light emission measures the number of electrons that were trapped between the two episodes of heating—in the original fire and in the lab. The time between when a pot was fired and its burial is usually unimportant. (Museums use the method to detect ceramic forgeries, because TL can quickly distinguish between an ancient clay figurine and a twentieth-century fake.) The method is also used to date burned stone artifacts, because heat resets the TL clock of the minerals in the stone. After the stone cools and is buried, its minerals are subjected to background radiation and electrons begin to be trapped again.

The artifact's context is therefore especially important, because what interests the archaeologist is the age of the artifact, which may or may not coincide with the events that trapped charge methods date. For instance, if a stone tool was accidentally burned 1000 years after its manufacture, TL will date the age of the burning, not the age of the artifact's manufacture—and it is usually the latter that interests archaeologists. Nonetheless, by paying attention to context, trapped charge dating has the potential to rewrite prehistory, because it can date objects that radiocarbon cannot and because it can date objects that are beyond the range of radiocarbon.

For example, archaeologists Ofer Bar-Yosef (Harvard University) and Bernard Vandermeersch (University of

© Ofer Bar-Yosef

Figure 8-9 The cave site of Qafzeh (Israel).

Bordeaux) employed this technique to challenge our understanding of human evolution. The transition between **Neanderthals** and modern *Homo sapiens* was for many years based on the chronology of western Europe. There, *Homo sapiens* replaced Neanderthals about 40,000 years ago. But for various reasons, Bar-Yosef suspected that "archaic *Homo sapiens*" (called such because their skulls appear to be transitional between earlier hominids and biologically modern humans) appeared earlier in the Near East. Excavating the site of Qafzeh in Israel (Figure 8-9), Bar-Yosef and Vandermeersch found strata containing skeletal remains of archaic *Homo sapiens* along with stone tools, some of which had burned in hearths. Tests showed that these strata were beyond the range of radiocarbon dating and

thermoluminescence A trapped charge dating technique used on ceramics and burnt stone artifacts—anything mineral that has been heated to more than 500° C.

Neanderthals (or Neandertals) An early form of humans who lived in Europe and the Near East about 300,000 to 30,000 years ago; biological anthropologists debate whether Neanderthals were in the direct evolutionary line leading to *Homo sapiens*.

hence must be at least 45,000 years old—older than the western European counterparts.

But how much older? TL dating provided the answer. Dating a series of the burnt stone tools, Bar-Yosef found that the artifacts had burned some 92,000 +/– 5000 years ago, much earlier than the European chronology. The date's standard deviation might seem large, but note that it is only 5 percent of the mean date and, assuming that the tools were made by archaic *Homo sapiens*, it suggests that modern humans might be earlier in the Near East than in Europe.

Optically Stimulated Luminescence

Another trapped charge dating technique, **optically stimulated luminescence,** is finding many uses in archaeology because it can date the most common material in archaeological sites: dirt. This technique relies on the fact that some of the trapped electrons are sensitive to sunlight as well as to heat.

Sand grains of quartz and feldspar have their clocks reset (referred to as bleaching) in a matter of minutes as they blow through the air and are exposed to sunlight; once buried, they begin accumulating trapped electrons again. *OSL therefore dates the time when the sands were buried.* Although OSL can be used on a variety of sediments, eolian sands are the best because they are more likely to have been sufficiently bleached by sunlight (and thus have their clocks reset) than alluvial sands.

Instead of measuring luminescence through the application of heat, OSL measures it by passing light of a particular wavelength over the specimen. This causes light-sensitive electrons to emit their own light as they return to orbit; the intensity of that light is a measure of the total radiation dose. This technique, by the way, requires some special handling, because the archaeologist must take soil samples in such a way that the samples are not exposed to sunlight—either by hammering a steel tube into sediments and capping it or by taking the sample in the dark under red light.

OSL offers enormous potential to archaeologists because it dates dirt itself, but we still have to be careful about contamination. Archaeology learned this lesson at Jinmium Rockshelter in Australia.

optically stimulated luminescence A trapped charge dating technique used to date sediments; the age is the time elapsed between the last time a few moments exposure to sunlight reset the clock to zero and the present.

Named after a female character in an Aboriginal Dreamtime myth (who turned herself into stone to evade a lover), Jinmium Rockshelter is a lone block of sandstone that Native Australians used as a temporary shelter for thousands of years. While there, they painted its ceiling with pictures of kangaroos and other animals.

For years, all evidence suggested that people first occupied Australia about 40,000 years ago. And so the archaeological community was shocked when thermoluminescence dates on Jinmium's sediments dated them to as early as 175,000 years. What's more, red ocher, a stone commonly used to make red pigment, appeared in Jinmium sediments that TL dated to 75,000 years. If this date was true, Jinmium was the site of the world's oldest art!

But many archaeologists were skeptical, including Richard Fullagar (Australian Museum), who first dated the sediments. A new team, headed by Richard Roberts (La Trobe University), decided to try the then-new method of OSL on the shelter's sediments. Why? Simply put, some electrons have their clocks set quickly, after only a few minutes exposure to sunlight. Others, however, require hours or even days of exposure. OSL measures the signal from the quick-bleaching electrons, and TL measures the signal from slow-bleaching electrons. This means that TL dates on sediments could be too old, because they might measure the signal from electrons that were not fully bleached—whose clocks were not fully reset—before they were slowly buried by the winds that carried sands into the shelter.

This turned out to be a problem at Jinmium Rockshelter. As the wind blew, the sandstone block eroded, grain by grain. Those grains had had their clocks reset millions of years ago. Deposited in the shelter's shade, the slow-bleaching electrons were not exposed to sufficient sunlight to have their clocks fully reset, and these contaminated the samples that the first team of archaeologists dated with TL. The problem is identical to combining carbon samples of different ages. Let's say that a hearth is really 1000 years old. And suppose that a burrowing rodent causes a 10,000-year-old piece of carbon to enter that hearth. If we dated a sample of the hearth's charcoal that contained both 1,000-year-old and 10,000-year-old pieces of carbon, the resulting date would be somewhere in between—and it would make the hearth appear to be much older than it actually is. The same is true with trapped charge dates on sediments: Even if only 1 or 2 percent of the grains in a sample were from the sandstone block, TL would produce misleadingly early dates.

So Roberts's team redated the sediments *grain-by-grain* using OSL. The OSL technique guaranteed that they were dating the last time the grain had its clock fully reset, and dating each individual quartz grain allowed them to discover some anomalously early dates. Grain-by-grain dating is the standard today, with a single OSL date actually being the result of 1000 dates on quartz grains from a single sample. Their redating, backed up by AMS radiocarbon dates as well, showed that human occupation at Jinmium was less than 10,000 years old, and the site's claim to fame in Australian prehistory fell by the wayside.

Electron Spin Resonance

Our final trapped charge dating method is **electron spin resonance,** whose primary archaeological application is the dating of tooth enamel.

Ninety-six percent of tooth enamel consists of the mineral hydroxyapatite, which contains no trapped charges when formed. Once the tooth is deposited in the ground, however, it accumulates charges from the background radiation. To measure those trapped charges, a portion of the specimen is exposed to electromagnetic radiation, which resets the electrons. In this case, the total radiation dose is proportional to the amount of microwave energy absorbed by the specimen.

ESR dating has also challenged our understanding of human evolution. As we noted above, the European chronology showed that modern humans rapidly replaced Neanderthals about 40,000 years ago. But when ESR was applied to tooth enamel of animals found in strata containing evidence of *Homo sapiens* and Neanderthals at Qafzeh in Israel, as well as at three nearby cave sites (Tabun, Skhul, and Kebara), the dates showed that *Homo sapiens* existed as early as 120,000 years ago, and Neanderthals as late as 60,000 years ago. This means that for a long period of time, perhaps as much as 60,000 years, modern humans and Neanderthals existed side by side—a different scenario than in western Europe, where they may have overlapped for much less time.

Trapped charge dating techniques can date objects that are beyond the range of radiocarbon dating. But we must remember that what we are dating is *the last time that the clock was reset*—by light in the case of OSL and by heat in the case of TL (neither seem to affect ESR measurements). Like radiocarbon dating, these techniques date accurately to a range of years, not a single year.

Potassium-Argon and Argon-Argon

Archaeologists have a variety of other radiometric dating techniques that, like radiocarbon dating, are based on the fact that radioactive isotopes decay at known rates. These include **potassium-argon dating,** and its variant, **argon-argon dating.** *These techniques are useful for dating the age of the formation of a particular layer of rock itself.*

Because these radioactive isotopes have extremely long half-lives, they are useful only for dating materials that are hundreds of thousands or millions of years old—they cannot be used on rock that is less than 200,000 years old. For this reason, these are important dating methods for archaeologists who work in Africa and other places where early human remains are found. We will examine the particular method of potassium-argon dating, the technique used to establish the age of the Laetoli footprints (see Chapter 7) and its new variant, argon-argon dating.

Many rocks, including volcanic minerals, contain traces of potassium, which, like carbon, occurs naturally in several isotopic forms. One of these, potassium-40 or ^{40}K, decays slowly, with a half-life of 1.31 *billion* years, into argon-40 (^{40}Ar), an inert, stable gas—hence the name potassium-argon dating. By comparing the relative proportions of these potassium and argon isotopes in a sample, we can determine its age. As with radiocarbon dating, the principle is simple: The more ^{40}Ar in a sample relative to ^{40}K, the older that sample is.

For potassium-argon dating to work, there must have been no argon trapped at the time of rock formation. Like trapped charge dating methods, a rock's argon-accumulating clock must have been reset to zero such that all argon is the result of potassium decay. Fortunately, volcanic rock provides a comparable method for

electron spin resonance A trapped charge technique used to date tooth enamel and burned stone tools; it can date teeth that are beyond the range of radiocarbon dating.

potassium-argon dating An absolute dating technique that monitors the decay of potassium (K-40) into argon gas (Ar-40).

argon-argon dating A high-precision method for estimating the relative quantities of argon-39 to argon-40 gas; used to date volcanic ashes that are between 500,000 and several million years old.

"zeroing out" the potassium-argon clock. During all major volcanic eruptions, high temperatures drive all gases—including ^{40}Ar—out of the microscopic rock crystals. Such episodes set the potassium-argon clock to zero, and all ^{40}Ar present in the ash today therefore accumulated since the ash was ejected from the volcano. In addition, all argon must be retained in the rock structure without loss to the atmosphere. Some rocks "leak" argon, and so care must be exercised in deciding which rock types to subject to potassium-argon dating.

This is why volcanic ash deposits are so useful. If an archaeologist finds human fossils or stone tools just *below* a layer of volcanic ash, the law of superposition tells us that the potassium-argon method will provide a *minimum* age estimate for the tools and fossils contained in the archaeological stratum below. Find fossils between two layers of volcanic ash deposits, and you bracket the age of the archaeological material (although you can't date the archaeological material itself). This is how the Laetoli footprints were dated.

The maximum age range of potassium-argon dating is theoretically the age of the earth. Although this method is not as precise as radiocarbon dating, its results are close enough, and it provides dates for some critically important early sites in Africa and elsewhere.

For example, potassium-argon dating was used to estimate the age of **Homo erectus,** an early hominid, in Asia. For decades, investigators believed that *Homo erectus* evolved exclusively in Africa, the earliest fossils being slightly less than 2 million years old (Figure 8-10). Then, sometime after 1.5 million years ago, *Homo erectus* expanded out of Africa, colonizing other parts of the Old World.

Thus, human paleontologists were shocked in 1971, when Garniss Curtis (then of the University of California, Berkeley) used potassium-argon to date the sediments associated with an infant *Homo erectus* skull from Mojokerto, Java. Because Java is a long way from Africa, most investigators thought that the Mojokerto skull should be much younger than a million years. But Curtis estimated that it was nearly twice that age—1.9 million years old. Most paleontologists rejected this extraordinarily ancient age because they were con-

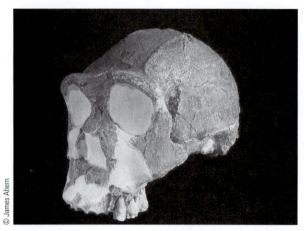

Figure 8-10 A 1.8 million-year-old *Homo erectus* skull (KNM-ER 3733, from Koobi Fora, Kenya).

vinced that the only hominids in the world prior to 1 million years ago lived in Africa.

Both these early dates and the technique itself came under criticism. Although potassium-argon dating had been around for decades, the laboratory methods were cumbersome, and the process required a large sample that increased the chance for contamination (in a manner analogous to Jinmium's TL dates).

So Curtis teamed up with Carl Swisher (Institute of Human Origins, Arizona State University) to develop a new dating method. The argon-argon method simplifies the lab process and avoids the contamination problem by using small samples. The method works by irradiating the volcanic crystals. When a neutron penetrates the potassium nucleus, it displaces a proton, converting the potassium into ^{39}Ar, an "artificial" isotope not found in nature. The minute quantities of artificially created argon and naturally occurring ^{40}Ar are then measured to estimate the ratio of potassium to ^{40}Ar. This high-precision method also allows investigators to focus on single volcanic crystals, which can be dated one by one; thus any older contaminants can be discarded.

In 1992, Curtis and Swisher used the argon-argon method to date some white volcanic pumice obtained from the matrix inside the braincase of the Mojokerto fossil. The result was virtually the same as the "old fashioned" potassium-argon date: 1.8 million +/− 40,000 years. These dates remain controversial, but received some support with the discovery of 1.75 million-year-old *Homo erectus* (some classify it as *Homo ergaster*) at the site of Dmanisi, in the country of Georgia. More to

Homo erectus A hominid who lived in Africa, Asia, and Europe between 2 million and 500,000 years ago. These hominids walked upright, made simple stone tools, and may have used fire.

TABLE 8-3 Summary of Absolute Dating Methods

TECHNIQUE	TARGET MATERIAL	RANGE OF ACCURACY	COMMENTS
Carbon-14	Any organic material; carbon is the most common.	To 45,000 BP	Requires calibration; calibration curve only reliable to about 11,000 years. Accelerator mass spectrometry permits dating of minute samples.
Thermoluminescence	Ceramics, burnt stone	Unknown, but perhaps back to 300,000 years	Dates the last time an object was heated to 500° C.
OSL	Quartz, feldspars in eolian sands	Unknown, but perhaps back to 300,000 years	Dates the last time sand was exposed to sunlight sufficient to empty the electron traps. Samples must avoid sunlight; lab must date individual grains.
Electronic spin resonance	Tooth enamel, burned stone tools, corals, shells	10,000 to 300,000 or more years	Dates when a tooth was buried. Electron traps reset by exposure to electromagnetic radiation in the lab.
Potassium-argon	Volcanic ash	200,000 to several million years	Dates the eruption that produced the ash. Needs large sample.
Argon-argon	Volcanic ash	200,000 to several million years	Dates the eruption that produced the ash. Needs smaller sample.

the point, dating techniques such as the argon-argon method will be increasingly important in evaluating fossil evidence in the years to come.

What Do Dates Mean?

These are just some of the ways that archaeologists can date sites—there are many others. It is important to keep in mind what materials the different techniques date, how far back in time they can extend, and what events the techniques actually date (summarized in Table 8-3), because these factors are necessary to answering the most important question of all: What do the dates mean?

We can never date archaeological sites by simple equivalences. The radiocarbon lab, for instance, takes a chunk of charcoal and tells you how long ago that tree died. By itself, this date says nothing important about your site. However, if we can show that the charcoal came from a tree used as a roof beam in a pueblo, then we have a date that matters.

In every case, you have to show that the dated event is contemporaneous with a behavioral event of interest—

such as building a house, cooking a meal, killing a deer, or making a pot. We can drive this point home by examining a common issue of radiocarbon dating: the **old wood problem.**

How Old Are the Pyramids?

When most people hear the word "archaeology," they think about Egypt's pyramids (Figure 8-11). And with good reason: They are impressive structures, especially the three that stand watch over modern Cairo on the Giza plateau. One of these, the pyramid of Khnum-khuf ("the god Khnum is his protection"; often abbreviated to Khufu, or, in Greek, Cheops) is the largest in Egypt. Khufu began building his tomb soon after his reign began in 2551 BC. Made of some 2,300,000 blocks of stone, each weighing an average of 2½ tons, the pyramid measures 230 meters (756 feet) on a side and is

old wood problem A potential problem with radiocarbon (or tree-ring) dating in which old wood has been scavenged and reused in a later archaeological site; the resulting date is not a true age of the associated human activity.

Figure 8-11 The pyramids at Giza.

© Charles & Josette Lenars/CORBIS

oriented only 3 minutes and 6 seconds off true north. It contains several interior passageways and three chambers—one at the end of a tunnel cut into the bedrock deep below the structure. The burial chamber, in the center of the pyramid, has several roofs above it; the Egyptians specifically engineered this roof to distribute the weight of the overlying rock outward and prevent the chamber from being crushed. The pyramid's exterior was originally covered in polished white limestone—making it a landmark that would have shone above the horizon for miles around (the limestone was scavenged by later pharaohs). At 146 meters (481 feet), Khufu's pyramid remained the world's tallest building for 4440 years—until the Eiffel Tower was built in 1889! It is a remarkable piece of architectural engineering.

How old is it? The ages of the pyramids are based on historical documents—the hieroglyphs that cover the insides of tombs and temples (and that are found on papyrus used to stuff the bulls, crocodiles, ibexes, and other animals that were mummified and buried in the pyramids and other structures). The hieroglyphs give us the dates of the reigns of kings and document their

accomplishments. The Egyptian civilization is probably one of the best dated in the world, and the pyramids on the Giza Plateau outside Cairo are among the oldest in Egypt.

But some speculate that the pyramids are actually thousands of years older, built by a civilization some 10,000 years ago. To check the ages based on historical documents, a consortium of archaeologists in 1984, led by Shawki Nakhla and Zahi Hawass (The Egyptian Supreme Council of Antiquities), decided to date the pyramids through radiocarbon dating. But what could they date? The pyramids are made of stone, and the organic remains buried in them were often treated with tar and chemicals that make them unreliable for radiocarbon dates.

But Nakhla and Hawass knew of another source of carbon. Contrary to popular belief, the pyramids were put together with mortar. Workmen made this mortar by burning gypsum, apparently on the work platforms that were erected around the pyramid as it was being constructed. They mixed the resulting ash with water and sand and then slopped the mortar into the cracks between the massive blocks of stone. Inadvertently, pieces of carbon from the fires were caught in the mortar, trapped there for eternity.

In 1984 and 1985, the Egyptian's archaeological teams scrambled over the pyramids like ants on an anthill, looking for fingernail-sized bits of carbon. They found quite a few pieces, dated them using the AMS method, and then calibrated the dates.

They found not a shred of evidence that the pyramids were thousands of years older than the documentary sources indicate. But what they found still surprised them.

The radiocarbon dates on Old Kingdom (2575–2134 BC) pyramids were from 100 to 400 years *older* than the documentary dates suggested. And yet dates on later Middle Kingdom pyramids (2040–1640 BC) were not far off from their accepted ages. Why were the Old Kingdom dates "too old"?

The first explanation was the "old wood" problem: In desert (or high-altitude or arctic) environments, wood can lie around without decaying for a long time. In California's White Mountains, you can make a fire today from bristlecone wood, send a piece of the charcoal to a lab, and be told that your fire was 2000 years old. The wood is 2000 years old—but the fire that made the charcoal is not.

Egyptian archaeologists thought this "old wood" problem was unlikely. By Old Kingdom times, the Nile River valley had been occupied for millennia, and by a large population. Excavations near the pyramids reveal a community of stoneworkers, builders of the pyramids, that housed 20,000 people. All the Nile's people cooked over wood and used wood in house construction. And there is not much wood to begin with along the Nile; the floodplain is rich, but it's a narrow strip of green in a vast, treeless desert. For these reasons, the archaeologists postulated that there could have been no old wood lying along the Nile.

But perhaps Egyptians found another source of old wood. The Old Kingdom's construction projects at Giza were massive: three huge and several small pyramids, associated temples, boat docks on the Nile, the Sphinx, and the workers' quarters. These projects required massive amounts of wood—for construction; for ovens to bake bread for the workers; for levers, wedges, and sledges to move the stone blocks; for scaffolding; and for firewood to produce the mortar.

To get all the wood needed, it is likely that Khufu and other pharaohs raided older settlements or looted their predecessor's temples and tombs for wood—which Egypt's dry climate would preserve for hundreds, even thousands, of years. We know that pharaohs raided earlier temples and tombs for construction material and jewelry. Perhaps for these Old Kingdom projects, they also sought out firewood. This may account for the early dates on Old Kingdom pyramids.

But then, why were the Middle Kingdom radiocarbon dates not "too old"? By Middle Kingdom times, Nakhla and Hawass reasoned, earlier construction projects had depleted the sources of old wood, and Middle Kingdom builders had to make do with the wood at hand—which would not have been very old.

The point here is that every absolute dating technique dates a particular event, but it is up to the archaeologist to decide how the age of that particular event is meaningful in terms of human behavior.

THE CHECK, PLEASE

How an archaeologist excavates a site depends on several factors, one of these being cost. None of these dating methods is cheap. Right now, a standard radiocarbon date runs about $300 (including the $^{13}C/^{12}C$ calculation); an AMS date costs about $600. Bone dates can run as high as $850 per sample. Tree-ring dates are cheaper—the University of Arizona's Tree-Ring Lab charges about $25 per sample. TL and OSL dates may cost $800 a shot. There are no commercial rates for the other trapped charge and radiometric dating methods, but they have hidden costs. Because so much background data is required for their successful implementation, it is often necessary to finance a visit to the site by the specialist and cover additional sediment and dosimetry studies.

Archaeologists try to get as many dates as they can for a site, but they always have to do so within budget limitations.

DATING IN HISTORICAL ARCHAEOLOGY

As we pointed out in Chapter 1, historical archaeology is a rapidly growing subfield of archaeology. Sometimes, historical archaeologists work on sites whose ages are well known; for example, there is no question about when Jefferson's home at Monticello was built

Archaeological Ethics
What's Wrong with Buying Antiquities? (Part I)

There is, unfortunately, a lively market in ancient artifacts, and it is the greatest threat to archaeology today. Across the country, folks get together at artifact "fairs" to swap stories and buy and sell artifacts. Often, these are things that Grandpa found on the farm when he was a little boy and that were passed down through the family. Sometimes, they are objects that people find while out walking. They picked them up out of curiosity and placed them on their mantle or mounted them in a picture frame in the den. It seems harmless enough.

Sometimes these artifacts appear on e-Bay or other online sales venues. Some of these auction houses have policies that prohibit the sale of unethically or illegally obtained materials. For example, e-Bay's policy states:

Native American human remains, gravesite-related items, and burial items may not be listed on e-Bay. Native American masks and "prayer sticks" from all Southwestern tribes are also prohibited. This prohibition includes Native Hawaiian human remains, gravesite-related items and burial items.

E-Bay's policy also states:

Artifacts taken from any federal, state, public Department of Interior Agencies (NPS, BLM, USFWS) and Department of Agriculture Agencies (USFS), Native American land, or battlefield are prohibited for sale.

Nonetheless, on the day we wrote this, e-Bay was auctioning 11 Mimbres black-on-white pots. The total value of these pots was estimated at about $78,000.

Mimbres pottery is special. It was manufactured only between AD 1000 to 1150 in southern New Mexico's Mimbres Valley. The bowls are especially noteworthy because they contain naturalistic designs that are rare in Southwestern pottery: depictions of rabbits, bighorn sheep, birds, and people. Even more important, these bowls are disproportionately found in graves. They usually were ritually "killed" by punching a small hole in the bowl's center and then were placed over the deceased's head. Of the 11 bowls on auction at e-Bay, 8 were ritually killed. Most if not all of these bowls had probably been taken from graves—a violation of e-Bay's policy.

The selling of artifacts promotes their unauthorized and destructive collection. *There is not a single Mimbres pueblo that has not been looted;* some were flattened by bulldozers in a search for the graves that lie beneath the pueblos' floors. Others were scooped up at night by a front loader and dumped into trucks, the dirt later sorted in secret. Looters are arrested when they can be caught—two men were convicted in 2001 of looting a

and occupied. But often they work on sites that are not documented, and these sites need to be dated.

Dendrochronology is sometimes used, but radiometric and trapped charge techniques are not. Even with small standard deviations, these methods are not sufficiently precise to be useful to historical archaeology. If we already know that a Spanish settlement in Florida was occupied sometime in the sixteenth century, a radiocarbon date on the site of AD 1550 +/− 25 would tell us that there is a 96 percent chance that the site was occupied sometime between AD 1500 and AD 1600—and that's what we already knew.

For this reason, historical archaeology employs its own dating methods. These use documented changes in technology and styles of material culture to make fine-grained use of the index fossil concept and seri-

ation. For example, before 1830, the metal fibers in nails ran crosswise to the nail's axis; after that, the fibers ran lengthwise. Examine the nails in a site, and you can tell if it dates to before or after 1830. Likewise, nineteenth-century glass often had a purplish cast, caused by sunlight reacting with magnesium oxide, but after World War I, manufacturers stopped adding magnesium to glass. Purple glass is always older than AD 1917.

Often, this information is contained in industrial and other written documents. But sometimes, the archaeologist has to get creative. Kathleen Deagan knew that green and clear glass bottle fragments littered sixteenth-century Hispanic sites in Florida and the Caribbean and that these artifacts could be used as time-markers. The problem was that not a single complete bottle from this period survived anywhere. But

Mimbres site, sentenced to a year in prison, and ordered to pay almost $20,000 in restitution. But no amount of money can replace what they destroyed. And for every looter arrested, a dozen evade the law.

And Mimbres sites are not the only ones hit hard: Dry caves that preserve organic remains such as baskets are targets, as are Maya, Inka, and Egyptian sites—almost any site, in fact.

You can be sure that in gathering Mimbres bowls, plenty of other artifacts were disturbed and destroyed, to say nothing of the human remains. We will never know what information was lost from looted sites, but we can be sure that it was volumes, because not only does the artifact disappear into the marketplace, but its contextual information is also obliterated.

Buying artifacts is like buying drugs: The buyer is the only reason the business exists. And the business is the reason that we are losing irreplaceable artifacts and information about the past every day.

And that's what's wrong with buying artifacts.

A Classic Mimbres bowl.

rather than give up, Deagan turned to paintings, because bottles, it turns out, are frequently depicted in sixteenth-century Spanish art. By studying these dated paintings, Deagan constructed a chronological sequence of bottle forms. By reconstructing bottle forms from the glass fragments present on sites, she could use this chronological sequence to date the sites.

Pipe Stem Dating

One clever way to date Colonial-period American sites was developed in the mid-twentieth century by J. C. "Pinky" Harrington (1901–1998). Clay tobacco pipes and broken fragments turn up by the hundreds on many Colonial-era archaeological sites. These clay pipes held great potential as time-markers, because

they generally broke within a year or so of their manufacture. And their shapes, decorations, stem lengths, and thicknesses changed markedly in the seventeenth and eighteenth centuries.

The difficulty in applying any of these observations to archaeological sites was that the fragile clay pipes rarely survived in a condition sufficiently complete to allow fruitful analysis. However, while working with the pipe collection from Jamestown, including some 50,000 small chunks of broken stems, Harrington observed that the early pipe stems had relatively large bores, which became smaller in the later specimens.

Measuring the stem hole diameters for 330 pipes of known age from Jamestown, Colonial Williamsburg (Virginia), and Fort Frederica (St. Simons Island, Georgia), Harrington found that the inside diameter changed through time. His resulting pipe stem chronology ran from AD 1620 to1800 and was divided into five cultural periods. Fifteen years later, Lewis Binford reworked the original data to derive a statistical regression formula for estimating age from the size of pipe stem holes: $y = 1931.85 - 38.26x$, where x is the mean stem bore for a sample of pipe fragments and y is the projected mean date. By calculating the mean bore diameters of the pipe stems found in a site and plugging that value into the equation, we can come up with a pretty good estimate of the site's age.

Terminus Post Quem *Dating*

Dates in historical archaeology are generally of two types: They either define a temporal cutoff point (the site cannot be any older than a particular year) or they estimate a central temporal tendency (the site's "average" age). Let us explain how each works.

Kathleen Deagan and Joan Koch excavated an important cemetery named Nuestra Señora de la Soledad in downtown St. Augustine. They first classified the sherds into the various ceramic types commonly found on Spanish American sites. One such type, Ichtucknee Blue on White (Figure 8-12), is named for the surface decoration (blue designs on white background) and the Ichtucknee River in north central Florida (where the type was first recognized). The estimated age of Ichtucknee Blue on White ceramics ranges between AD 1600 to 1650.

Deagan and Koch could date each grave pit according to the concept of *terminus post quem* (**TPQ**), the date *after* which the object must have found its way into the ground. At Soledad, the TPQ indicates the first possible date that the latest-occurring artifact could have been deposited in that grave pit. So when a sherd of Ichtucknee Blue on White turned up in the grave fill at Soledad, excavators knew that this grave could not have been dug before AD 1600 (because Ichtucknee Blue on White did not exist before that date). Had the same grave pit contained a sherd of, say, San Luís Polychrome (with an associated age range from 1650 to 1750), then the TPQ date would be revised to 1650.

terminus post quem (TPQ) The date after which a stratum or feature must have been deposited or created.

© American Museum of Natural History

Figure 8-12 Ichtucknee Blue on White plate: AD 1600–1650.

TPQ estimates the earliest possible date for the grave, based on the accuracy of the known date range for a particular artifact. When combined with the excavation data and documentary evidence about site usage, the TPQ estimates enabled Deagan and Koch to group the Soledad burials into three culture periods: seventeenth-century Spanish (TPQ: pre-1700), eighteenth-century Spanish (TPQ: pre-1762), and eighteenth-century British (TPQ: post-1762). Once this classification was established, they could look for cultural differences and similarities among burial assemblages: The Spanish-period burials, for example, were mostly shroud wrapped, whereas the British used coffins. The Spanish crossed the arms over the chest, whereas the British were interred with arms along the sides. Spanish burials were oriented toward the east, British toward the west, and so forth.

Mean Ceramic Dates

There is some disagreement about the utility of *terminus post quem* ceramic dating in historical archaeology. Many find the concept useful in providing a baseline for site chronology, but other archaeologists are less enthusiastic. They point to several complicating factors: For example, less is known about seventeenth-century Anglo-American ceramics, and status differences influence relative ceramic frequencies. In addition, there may be a considerable time lag between an artifact's date of manufacture and its date of deposition, making TPQ dating subject to gross error.

TABLE 8-4 Applying the Mean Ceramic Date Formula to the Brunswick Hepburn–Reonalds Ruin

CERAMIC TYPE	MEDIAN YEAR OF MANUFACTURE	X	SHERD COUNT	=	PRODUCT
22	1791		483		865,053
33	1767		25		44,175
34	1760		32		56,320
36	1755		55		96,525
37	1733		40		69,320
43	1758		327		574,866
49	1750		583		1,020,250
44	1738		40		69,520
47	1748		28		48,944
53, 54	1733		52		90,116
56	1733		286		495,638
29	1760		9		15,840
Totals			1960		3,446,567

$3,446,567 \div 1960 = 1758.4$

SOURCE: South 1977a, table 32. Used by permission of the author and Academic Press.

Stanley South (University of South Carolina) derived a provocative method to minimize these perceived problems. South's **mean ceramic date** approach emphasizes the mid-range or median age, rather than beginning and end dates for ceramic wares. Using Noël Hume's *A Guide to Artifacts in Colonial America*, South constructed a model based on selected ceramic types defined by attributes of form, decoration, surface finish, and hardness plus the temporal dates assigned by Noël Hume for each type.

Seventy-eight ceramic types were included in South's formulation. Canton porcelain, for instance, was manufactured between 1800 and 1830. The median date for this type is thus $(1800 + 1830)/2 = 1815$. Bellarmine Brown, a salt-glazed stoneware decorated with a well-molded human face, ranges from 1550 through 1625; the median date is thus 1587. The mean ceramic date pools this information across a feature (such as a grave pit or house) or site to determine the median date of manufacture for each time-sensitive sherd and then averages these dates to arrive at the mean occupation date implied by the entire collection. Table 8-4 shows how South calculated the mean ceramic date for sediments filling the cellar of the Hepburn-Reonalds Ruin (North Carolina). The median date of each ceramic type is then weighted by multiplying each type's median date by the number of sherds found of that type. These products are then added and divided by the total number of sherds. Available historic records revealed that the building was probably still standing in 1734 and burned in 1776; the median historic date is thus $(1734 + 1776)/2 = 1755$. South's mean ceramic date came out to be 1758.4, only 3½ years later than the median historic date. Moreover, the pipe stem date for this site is 1756, so substantial agreement exists among all three sources. In fact, South has found that the mean ceramic dates seldom deviate beyond a range of +/− 4 years from the known median historic date. Such agreement is nothing short of remarkable.

The mean ceramic date relies on two central assumptions: (1) that ceramic types are roughly contemporary at all sites where they occur, and (2) that the mid-range date of manufacture approximates the modal date of popularity. These are, of course, some fairly large

mean ceramic date A statistical technique for combining the median age of manufacture for temporally significant pottery types to estimate the average age of a feature or site.

assumptions, but the method still seems to produce useful age estimates on historic-era sites.

CONCLUSION

In Chapter 1 we pointed out that archaeology underwent a revolution of sorts in the 1960s. Walter Taylor's generation began that revolution in the 1940s and 1950s, but it was Lewis Binford's generation who brought about the transformation of archaeology. Binford, however, claimed that the widespread availability of absolute dating methods in the 1960s, notably radiocarbon dating, brought a huge change in how we do archaeology.

As you have seen, relative dating techniques helped to lift the fog of time that obscures the past. They were a significant advance because they helped to place objects and cultures into a historical sequence. Absolute dating techniques were an even more significant advance, because they could assign artifacts to a particular year or a specific range of years. Absolute dating techniques allow us to see not only the order of events, but the rate of change as well. Why did this permit Binford's generation to change archaeology?

One reason is that absolute dating techniques freed archaeologists to do other things with their data. Instead of spending time on seriation diagrams, an archaeologist could simply send a piece of carbon to a lab for a radiocarbon date.

But a more significant reason is that absolute dating techniques allowed archaeologists to control a major dimension of their data—age—in a more rigorous and absolute manner. Seriation was grounded in an often-unspoken theory of culture change—material items appear, grow in popularity, then disappear. No one knew, or really seemed to care, why this happened; all that mattered was that the technique provided a way to build a chronology. But for archaeologists to transcend chronology, they needed to know more. They needed to know how rapidly an item became prevalent, or how rapidly another replaced it. They needed to know how long a piece of material culture was used—50 years, 500 years, 5000 years? They needed to know whether an item first appeared in a particular region and then spread to others, or whether it had multiple centers of origin at the same time.

Relative dating methods could not answer these questions very precisely, and, in fact, relative dating methods tended to carry their own answers to them. Archaeologists relying on seriation, for instance, tended to see innovations as having only one center and then spreading from there. They saw cultural change as gradual, rather than abrupt. Absolute dating methods permitted archaeologists to know when styles appeared, how quickly they spread, and whether there were multiple centers of innovation. These methods opened the door to questions about past lifeways instead of focusing simply on chronology. This is why absolute dating techniques had a large effect on archaeological paradigms.

In recent years, technology has afforded us increasingly sophisticated ways to date artifacts, sites, and strata, and they show no sign of stopping. We can expect, then, that continual advances in dating methods will not only permit a greater understanding of the chronology of the past, but will also help create new paradigms, new ways of understanding the past.

Summary

- Contemporary archaeologists have a battery of techniques that can date objects of the past; these are divided into relative and absolute methods.

- Relative dating methods include use of index fossils and seriation. Called time-markers in archaeology, index fossils are artifacts with known dating orders that allow strata in different sites to be correlated; seriation refines this approach, placing sites or strata into a relative sequence based on changing frequen-

cies of material culture. These techniques help understand the chronological order of culture change, but not the actual age.

- The advent of absolute dating methods helped usher in a new age of archaeology.

- Tree-ring dating (dendrochronology) enables archaeologists to establish the precise year of death for many species of trees commonly found in archaeological sites. This technique is limited to relatively small regions and, in the American Southwest, where it is an important technique, only dates sites of the last 2000 years.

- Radiocarbon dating is a major radiometric technique that uses the known rate of decay of carbon-14 to determine the age of organics. It is useful for archaeological sites that are less than 45,000 years old.

- The atmospheric level of radiocarbon has changed over (at least) the last 20,000 years. Using correlations between tree rings and radiocarbon levels, archaeologists can calibrate dates—that is, convert radiocarbon years into calendar years—of the past 10,000 years.

- The accelerator (AMS) technique allows us to radiocarbon-date minute amounts of carbon.

- Trapped charge dating methods—thermoluminescence, optically stimulated luminescence, and electron spin resonance—date ceramics or burnt stone tools, eolian sediments, and tooth enamel, respectively. They date an object by calculating the amount of radiation an object was subjected to since the object's electron "clock" was last reset by heat (TL) or sunlight (OSL). These techniques date items tens of thousands of years old—beyond the range of radiocarbon dating.

- Potassium-argon dating and argon-argon dating are radiometric techniques used to date volcanic rock, especially ashes. These techniques are useful in places where archaeological sites are too old to use radiocarbon and trapped charge dating.

- Keep in mind that, by themselves, dating techniques tell us nothing about cultural activities. Radiocarbon dating, for example, tells us only when a plant or an animal died. In each case, the event being dated must be related to a behavioral (cultural) event of interest.

- Documentary evidence usually provides dates for historical sites. When such evidence is not available, known ages of particular artifact types can be used in various ways to create age-range or median ages for historical features or sites; these include TPQ and mean ceramic age dates.

Additional Reading

Nash, Stephen E. 1999. *Time, Trees, and Prehistory: Tree Ring Dating and the Development of North American Archaeology, 1914–1950.* Salt Lake City: University of Utah Press.

Nash, Stephen E. 2000. *It's About Time: A History of Archaeological Dating in North America.* Salt Lake City: University of Utah Press.

Taylor, R. E., and M. J. Aitken (Eds.). 1997. *Chronometric Dating in Archaeology.* New York: Plenum Press.

Online Resources

COMPANION WEB SITE
Visit **http://anthropology.wadsworth.com** and click on the Student Companion Web Site for Thomas/Kelly *Archaeology*, 4th edition, to access a wide range of material to help you succeed in your introductory archaeology course. These include flashcards, Internet exercises, Web links, and practice quizzes.

RESEARCH ONLINE WITH INFOTRAC COLLEGE EDITION
From the Student Companion Web Site, you can access the InfoTrac College Edition database, which offers thousands of full-length articles for your research.

9

The Dimensions of Archaeology: Time, Space, and Form

Preview

I N THE NINETEENTH CENTURY, archaeological sites were viewed as little more than mines in which to prospect for artifacts. But trained archaeologists, such as Nelson and Kidder, shifted their objectives to focus more on understanding the person behind the artifact rather than the artifact itself. And in the 1960s, archaeology further refined that focus, wishing not only to reconstruct what happened in the past, but to explain that past as well.

To achieve these objectives, archaeology analyzes how artifacts and features fall into changing patterns over space and time; this chapter shows how archaeologists identify those patterns. We first consider classification—the ways that archaeologists divide the many kinds of objects found into reasonable and useful artifact types. We then discuss the concepts of archaeological cultures, periods, phases, assemblages, and components—all of which are used to organize archaeological data into space-time systematics.

INTRODUCTION

The title of this chapter comes from an article by archaeologist Albert Spaulding (1914–1990), who pointed out that archaeology is about patterns in artifacts and features through time and across space. For example, the kinds of houses found in much of the American Southwest in 200 BC were semi-subterranean pithouses, usually round, and covered with heavy log roofs and a layer of sod. They were warm in the winter and cool in the summer. At the same time (200 BC), but in a different place—farther north toward the Great Basin—houses were more ephemeral, consisting of simple windbreaks or shade structures for summer houses and conical log structures for the winter. Returning to the Southwest, we see a dramatic change in house form around AD 700. At that time, many people made and lived in square, aboveground masonry homes—the familiar pueblos—rather than pithouses. Back in the Great Basin, however, people continued to live in the same sort of houses that they occupied in 200 BC. Archaeologists have spent the greater part of the last century documenting such patterns in how material culture changes through time and across space; these patterns are what archaeologists seek to explain. How we go about organizing data into meaningful spatial and temporal patterns is the subject of this chapter.

This organization is vital to the field, because archaeology's major strength is its access to tremendous quantities of time and space. Although many ethnologists study cultural evolution and culture change, they are restricted to short-term study if they deal exclusively with ethnographic evidence. And even if they include oral history or historical documents, ethnologists cannot go back in time more than a century or two. Archaeology, on the other hand, can address the entire complex history of humanity based on the things that people left behind, from 2.5 million-year-old stone tools in Africa to World War II destroyers on the bottom of Pacific lagoons. No other social science has so much time at its disposal.

A collection of artifacts that can provide key time-markers in archaeology.

Archaeologists also deal with worlds of "space." Many ethnologists study entire societies for years on end, but none can realistically employ the tools of ethnography to study an entire region such as the American Southwest, to say nothing of continents or hemispheres. So what archaeology loses in detail it makes up for by recording what the ethnologist cannot: patterns of human behavior as they were manifested over vast reaches of space, far beyond the confines of a single community.

The goal of archaeology is to reconstruct and explain the past: What did people do, and why did they do it? But to reach this goal, we must first gain a firm grasp on artifact patterning in time and space. You must know the when and the where in broader terms before contemplating the how, the who, the what, and especially the why. Defining a spatial and temporal framework requires that archaeologists date the physical remains, classify archaeological objects into useful categories, and explore their distribution across time and space. In

Looking Closer
Preserving the *Hunley*

In 1864, the Confederacy was losing the Civil War and it took desperate measures to destroy the Union Navy whose blockades were strangling the south. The Confederacy thought they had the trick in a secret weapon: a small submarine (shown in Figure 9-1) designed to destroy Union vessels from beneath the waves.

The South had planned submarine warfare from the war's beginning. Funded by Horace Hunley, whose name would grace the third design, submarines were built and tested by steam engineers James McClintock and Baxter Watson. The subs were bold and ingenious designs, but the early versions had leakage and control problems (the *Pioneer* was intentionally destroyed to prevent it from falling into Union hands, and the *American Diver* sank somewhere off Alabama's coast on a test run). Even the first attempts to use the *Hunley* were catastrophes. It capsized on its first and second runs, losing nearly half the first crew and the entire second crew, including Hunley himself. Nonetheless, the submarine was recovered, and a third crew stepped forward.

Crammed into a space 18 feet long and 4 feet wide, seven men propelled the *Hunley* by manually turning a crankshaft while the captain guided the sub and worked the ballast tanks that controlled depth. Two manholes fore and aft, only 15 inches in diameter, were the only escape routes; a single candle lit the captain's depth gauge.

The tactic was to approach a Union ship, dive, and then ram a long, barbed spar with a 90-pound explosive charge attached to it into the enemy's hull. As the sub backed away, a rope played out. At 150 feet, the rope tightened and detonated the charge.

This design worked perfectly on February 17, 1864, when the *Hunley* met the *U.S.S. Housatonic*. Although Union sailors fired at the *Hunley*, their shots were futile. The Union's largest ship sank within minutes.

The *Hunley* surfaced, signaled shore, and started home. But she never made it. For reasons still unknown, she sank before reaching port, trapping and killing all eight men aboard. This time, the *Hunley* was not retrieved, and a submarine did not sink a ship again until World War I.

Her location remained a mystery until persistent efforts by author Clive Cussler and archaeologists Ralph Wilbanks, Wes Hall, and Harry Pecorelli located her in 1995 (using a magnetometer towed behind a research vessel) only 30 feet below the surface. The submarine's hatches were unopened (only one viewport was broken) and the hull unbreached. Buried beneath 3 feet of silt, the sub was protected from the saltwater currents that normally destroy iron ships.

Once removed from the water, however, the iron ship, filled with the remains of the crew members and their personal effects, would have quickly corroded. The vessel itself was a special problem, because it was made of different sorts of metals and was so large. Chlorides

previous chapters we've discussed the fieldwork of archaeology. In this and succeeding chapters, we move into the other half of archaeology: the part that goes on after the excavation.

AFTER THE EXCAVATION: CONSERVATION AND CATALOGING

Suppose that you've just completed a regional survey and have excavated a sample of the sites discovered. You did the survey and excavations by the book, dated the

sites, studied the sites' formation processes, and so on. You've returned home with many, many carefully labeled bags full of bones, stone tools, ceramics, beads, and figurines. What happens to all the stuff now that the fieldwork is over?

The first step is to conserve the recovered materials. Once this meant little more than washing the artifacts off with water (but not things that water would obviously damage, such as basketry). But today, many archaeologists hesitate to wash some artifacts because even this simple operation might destroy some information. Stone and ceramic artifacts, for example, can contain pollen or residues of blood, plants, or other materials that can be identified and used to reconstruct

---

in seawater had infiltrated the iron hull. If the chlorides were to dry out, they would form crystals that would expand and destroy the metal. To prevent this, the hull was sprayed with water from the moment it was raised until it was placed into a specially designed water-filled tank. A lab now keeps the tank's fresh water at 10° C to prevent the growth of fungus and algae and to reduce the rate of corrosion. The lab also monitors the tank for pH, temperature, chlorides, conductivity, and oxygen.

The entire inside of the vessel, which had filled with silt, has been excavated, and the human remains and personal effects removed (the human remains were reburied in April 2004 in Charleston, South Carolina).

The sea itself is partly responsible for the sub's preservation. Through microbial and electrochemical reactions, the ship developed a carbonate coating that reduced the amount of oxygen that reached the actual metallic surface. By preventing oxygen from reaching the outside of the sub, the carbonate coating still protects it; without it, the sub would see more corrosion in 6 months than in the last 136 years. Keeping this carbonate layer intact is thus critical to preservation of the vessel. But no one really knows how to preserve the *Hunley* indefinitely.

Metal artifacts are normally preserved through electrolysis—that is, by running an electric current through the water, which then removes oxygen. But this technique may not work on a long-term basis, and it may be ineffec-

Courtesy of the Navy Art Collection, Washington, DC

Figure 9-1 Drawing of the *Hunley* by R. G. Skerrett, 1902, after a painting in the Confederate Memorial Library Society Museum, Richmond, Virginia.

tive for large objects, especially where many surfaces are welded, bolted, or riveted together. One solution would be to dismantle the entire sub; but this option, understandably, does not excite the *Hunley*'s conservators.

An alternative is to anneal the sub through hydrogen reduction. This means baking the sub in a hydrogen furnace over a week or more, slowly raising the temperature to 1060° C. This, too, has its problems, the first being locating a furnace that is large enough and that can withstand the hydrochloric acid that is a by-product of this process. Clearly, the preservation of this important piece of American history will puzzle conservators for years to come.

tool use and diet (see Chapter 11)—but not if a scrupulous lab worker has thoroughly scrubbed the piece. In general, though, a simple cleaning is in order.

Other artifacts may require more attention, especially organic or metal artifacts recovered from wet deposits. Conservation on wooden artifacts recovered from the Ozette site (see Chapter 6) began as soon as excavators removed them from the muddy matrix, because wet wooden artifacts quickly crumble as they dry out. Richard Daugherty preserved Ozette's wooden artifacts by soaking them in vats of Carbowax—polyethylene glycol—melted and diluted with water. He needed huge vats to soak the houses' cedar timbers. Some of the artifacts, especially those made of hardwoods (which have small pores and soak up liquid slowly), had to soak for years.

And during an excavation near New York's Wall Street, archaeologists found several Revolutionary War–era cannons lying on the bottom of what was once the East River. The first task in preserving these artifacts was to replace the brackish water that had impregnated the metal with fresh water. Looking for watertight containers large enough to hold the bulky cannons, project directors Roselle Henn (U.S. Army Corps of Engineers) and Diana diZerega Wall (City College of New York) finally settled on metal coffins! The conservation of artifacts has become a significant specialty within archaeology (see "Looking Closer: Preserving the *Hunley*").

It may also be necessary to reconstruct broken pieces. This is frequently done with pottery because ceramics are often found in pieces, and reconstruction obviously tells us more about vessel shape, size, and decoration. Piecing together a broken pot is like trying to put together a three-dimensional jigsaw puzzle where every piece is a different shape and there is no picture on the box. It requires a particular personality—somebody who can stay put for long hours—and a sculptor's eye. Some people can do this with ease, others are lucky if they get two pieces to fit.

The cataloging procedure that actually starts at the excavation (and that we discussed in Chapter 6) continues in the lab after the field season is over. Every single item must be accounted for and its provenience retained through a catalog. And the novice's first job in a lab is almost guaranteed to be cataloging: writing all those minute numbers on artifacts or labels and entering the information into a database. This can take a great deal of time. In fact, as a rule of thumb, for every week spent excavating, archaeologists spend 3 to 5 weeks or more cleaning, conserving, and cataloging the finds. Sometimes it seems mindless, but cataloging is essential because, without the catalog, provenience is lost, and without provenience an artifact's value to future researchers is greatly reduced.

ARCHAEOLOGICAL CLASSIFICATION

Cataloging and conservation are just the beginning because, at the end of those tasks, you are faced with thousands of artifacts that differ in terms of function, style, raw material, provenience, and condition. This is where the really time-consuming part of archaeology begins. Archaeologists spend far more time analyzing their finds than they do excavating them.

Archaeologists begin to get a handle on variability in artifacts through **typology,** the classification of artifacts into types. Even before cataloging and conservation begins, an archaeologist will have begun to classify the objects. When things turn up in the sifter, the screener will sort the finds into simple categories of stone, bone, shell, ceramic, organic, brick, cloth, wood, metal, or some other category depending on the nature of the site. Sometimes, objects can't be identified and sorted in the field, so the on-site rule is always "When in doubt, sent it to the lab."

In the lab, the cataloged artifacts are usually then further separated into even finer categories. The stone tool analyst might sort the stone artifacts into waste flakes and retouched pieces (flakes that have been chipped into tools) and then sort each of those into even narrower categories. Ceramics may be sorted into decorated and undecorated sherds, or into rim sherds (those that preserve a bit of the vessel's rim or mouth) and body sherds. And so forth.

But then what? How should you deal with all this stuff?

Here's a clue: The archaeologist's first responsibility is to simplify. Generations of archaeologists have found it unrealistic, even preposterous, to cope simultaneously with all the variability that turns up in even the simplest batch of archaeological objects. You could write a detailed paragraph on each artifact that you found. But although that might produce a wonderful

typology The systematic arrangement of material culture into types.

descriptive catalog, it would teach us little. Meaning lies not in endless data, but in patterns *within* those data. And patterns appear only when you isolate some aspect of the variation and ignore the rest (for the time being).

So you simplify to reveal meaningful patterns. Because archaeology's twin strengths are time and space, we first develop the categories necessary to reveal patterns in material culture through time and space. Such patterning is known in archaeology as **space-time systematics.** And our first step in that direction is identifying types of artifacts.

Types of Types

Archaeology's basic unit of classification is termed a **type.** Be careful here because "type," like "culture," is an everyday word appropriated by anthropology and reassigned a very specific, nonintuitive meaning.

Archaeologists can classify the same object in many different ways. Think about a familiar set of modern artifacts, say, a workshop of woodworking tools. Carpenters classify their tools by function—hammers, saws, planes, files, drills, and spokeshaves. But when insuring a carpenter's workshop, the insurance agent uses another classification, sorting these same tools into new categories, such as flammable and nonflammable, or perhaps according to replacement value: "under $10," "between $10 and $25," and so on. Should the carpenter relocate, the furniture movers will group these same tools into another set of divisions such as heavy or light, bulky or compact, or perhaps fragile or unbreakable. While storing the tools, the carpenter may classify them into "things my kids can touch" and "things my kids should not touch."

This discussion serves to make two important points. First, *types are abstractions* imposed by the archaeologist on a variable batch of artifacts. We saw in Chapter 2 how cultures classify the world differently. Dogs are considered food in some cultures, pets in others. There is nothing inherent in dogs that makes them "really" food or "really" pets. And there is nothing inherent in an artifact that makes it belong to one and only one type.

As we've said before, your analysis (and the types you create) will depend on your research question. Suppose, for instance, we wanted to learn whether everyone in an ancient society made pots, or if pots were made only by specialized potters. To do this, we might develop a way to classify pots into those made by novices and those made by experts, maybe by classifying pots

according to the quality of their construction or painting. On the other hand, if we were interested in the household functions carried on in different rooms, then we might classify a site's ceramics into cooking vessels, water jars, serving vessels, and storage containers. We can classify the same object in many different ways.

Do *not* think that our goal is always to classify things the way ancient peoples would have classified them. Archaeologists may divide stone scrapers into many different types based on their shape (to see if any could be useful time-markers), but ancient peoples may have recognized only two kinds: ones that were still useful and ones that were used up. Both classifications have their purpose, and both are valid.

And this brings us to our second point: We formulate a classification with a specific purpose in mind. Archaeology has no general, all-purpose classification. As Irving Rouse (Yale University) puts it, "Classification—for what?"

In Chapter 8, you saw one answer to this question: to create time-markers. At San Cristobal, Nelson sought distinctive types of pottery that he could use to assign strata or sites to a relative chronology. We began that discussion with some pottery types, such as biscuit ware and three-color glaze pottery. Nelson was not concerned with the pots' functions, or quality, or anything else; he simply wanted to know if some types were earlier or later than other types. Another researcher might have a different purpose and create a different typology.

But where do such types come from? To answer this question, let's first consider three major types of types.

Morphological Types

Modern observers exploring the range of material remains left by an extinct group will encounter many unfamiliar artifacts. To make sense of the past using these remains, the first analytical step is to describe the artifacts carefully and accurately by grouping them into **morphological types.**

---

space-time systematics The delineation of patterns in material culture through time and over space. These patterns are what the archaeologist will eventually try to explain or account for.

type A class of archaeological artifacts defined by a consistent clustering of attributes.

morphological type A descriptive and abstract grouping of individual artifacts whose focus is on *overall* similarity rather than function or chronological significance.

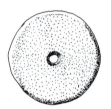

Figure 9-2 Two prehistoric stone disks excavated from Ventana Cave (Arizona). *After Haury (1950:29)/American Museum of National History.*

facts. This means that every morphological type must encompass a certain range of variability: several colors may have been applied; the quality of manufacture might vary; absolute size may fluctuate; and so forth.

Morphological types are purely descriptive. We ascribe no function to them at this point, and they don't necessarily have any chronological significance. No set rules exist for creating morphological types, although basic raw material (pottery, stone, shell, bone, and so on) is normally the first criterion, followed by shape. Morphological types help communicate what the archaeologist found without describing every single specimen.

Temporal Types

Temporal types are morphological types that have specific chronological meaning for a particular region. In other words, they are time-markers. If morphological Type B, for instance, occurs only in strata dating between AD 500 and 1000, then it can be elevated to the status of a temporal type. This promotion is important because, when artifacts belonging to temporal Type B turn up in undated contexts, the time span from AD 500 to 1000 becomes the most plausible hypothesis for their age.

Functional Types

Functional types reflect how objects were used in the past. Functional types can crosscut morphological types. A set of stone scrapers, for instance, might have all been used to prepare hides (that is, they all had the same function), so they are a functional type. But some are big and others are small; some are thin and others are thick; some are made of chert, but others are of quartzite and obsidian; some are sharpened on the ends of stone flakes, others along their sides. But all these objects are the same with regard to their function. The remaining variability is (for now) irrelevant.

Functional types can also crosscut temporal types. Sometimes, pots are painted with distinctive designs for a limited period (like some of the pottery types that Nelson defined at San Cristobal). These distinctive styles of finish make the ceramics a temporal type. But all the differently decorated pots may be of the same functional type—they may all be cooking vessels, water jars, or seed storage pots.

Emil Haury (1904–1992), an eminent Southwestern archaeologist, drafted one such description of some enigmatic stone disks (Figure 9-2) he recovered while digging at Ventana Cave, in Arizona:

> Discs—Of the twenty-four stone discs, twenty-two are centrally perforated. They were all made of schist, from 36 to 75 mm. in diameter and averaging 8 mm. in thickness. The customary way of producing them was by breaking and then smoothing the rough corners by abrasion.... Only one was well made.... Drill holes are bi-conical and not always centrally placed. Two were painted red. Next to nothing is known about these discs.

Note that Haury did not speculate on how people used the discs; he simply illustrated and described the discs in enough detail so that other archaeologists could visualize the artifacts without having to view them first-hand. Such bald description is the primary function of a morphological type (sometimes termed a class in archaeological literature).

Morphological types have a second, basic property: They are abstract. Types are not the artifacts per se; they are the composite descriptions of many similar arti-

Doing Typology

A good typology possesses two crucial characteristics:

> First, regardless of its final purpose, *a typology must minimize the differences within each created*

temporal type A morphological type that has temporal significance; also known as a time-marker or index fossil.

functional type A class of artifacts that performed the same function; these may or may not be temporal and/or morphological types.

type and maximize the differences between each type. If a lot of overlap and ambiguity occurs in the types, then they will not reveal any significant or meaningful patterning.

Second, the typology must be *objective and explicit*. This means that the result should be replicable by any trained observer. If it is not replicable, then your methods cannot be duplicated (and your work is therefore not scientific).

Once you've created your typology, you can focus on placing it in time and across space. Here's an example.

Projectile Point Typology at Gatecliff

To show you how typology works, we're going to take you step-by-step through Thomas's classification of the Gatecliff projectile points. And by now, you know that the first question to ask is this: What was the goal of Thomas's classification?

When Thomas began excavating Gatecliff Shelter, he was searching for a useful way to classify projectile points to create temporal types (time-markers) that could be tested against the radiocarbon dates available at Gatecliff. Once defined, these temporal types could estimate the age of surface assemblages (where radiocarbon dates could not be processed). That was the goal—the research question—of the Gatecliff typology.

Choosing Criteria

Great Basin archaeologists knew that projectile points were made out of different types of stone, such as chert, quartzite, obsidian, or rhyolite. But experience showed that raw material did not change over time in a systematic way; in fact, it mostly told archaeologists what kind of material was locally available. A typology based on raw material would not help construct temporal types.

But archaeologists who worked in the Great Basin also knew that projectile point *shape* changed over time. Small points, for example, tended to occur in upper (later) strata; larger points occurred in lower (earlier) strata. And small points that were notched from the side seemed to occur stratigraphically above small points notched from the corners. These observations suggested that a typology based on shape and size could be used to construct temporal types.

The first step in applying your criteria can be informal, sometimes just separating superficially similar

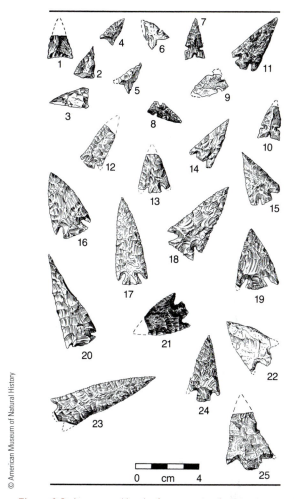

Figure 9-3 An unsorted batch of stone projectile points recovered at Gatecliff Shelter (Nevada).

artifacts into piles on the laboratory table. We can ignore variables like stratigraphy, time depth, cultural affiliation, and even provenience because (for now) the primary concern is to reduce the complexity to our primary criteria—shape and size.

Look at the projectile points in Figure 9-3. These are just a few of the 400 points recovered from Gatecliff Shelter. If you are any kind of observer at all, you will distinguish some important similarities and differences among them. The points at the top of the figure, for instance, are smaller than those at the bottom. Another difference is in how the points are notched for hafting. Some are notched from the side (for example, 7, 8, and 9), and others from the base (for instance, 14 and 15); some are notched from the corner (16 and 24), and some are not notched at all (1 and 3).

Defining Attributes

Differences like size and notch position are **attributes,** which are measurable or observable qualities of an object. We could make an infinite number of observations and take an infinite number of measurements on a projectile point, a few of which are shown in Figure 9-4. There are no rules governing the number of attributes to record; in general, we try to use as few as seem necessary to accomplish the purpose of the typology.

The two attributes of size and notching are sufficient to create workable morphological types. But it is insufficient simply to say "size" and "notch position." To define adequate attributes, we must explain precisely what we mean by the terms, so that another observer could make identical observations.

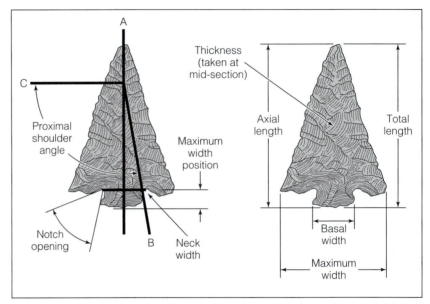

Figure 9-4 A Great Basin projectile point and some of the data that can be recorded from it. These observations are only a few of all that could be made on a projectile point.

Take size. We all know what size means, but it can be recorded in several ways. Measure the length of a projectile point and you know something about its size. The width also reflects size. Or you can weigh something to find its size. So, what size are we talking about?

Weight provides a good way to measure the size of a projectile point (although it is necessary to estimate the original weight of broken specimens). Other attributes that measure size (such as length, width, and thickness) all correlate with weight: As a point gets longer, wider, and/or thicker, it also becomes heavier. But weight is the easiest to measure, and so it was one of the first attributes Thomas used to define morphological types. The lightest point in the Gatecliff sample weighs only 0.4 gram (about the weight of a common paper clip) and the heaviest, more than 5 grams (about the same as a nickel). The weights for the 25 Gatecliff points in Figure 9-3 are presented in Table 9-1.

Notice that the weights are patterned, with certain natural breaks in the distributions, defining three projectile point sizes in this collection (this is even clearer when you look at the data on all 400-plus points):

Small points: Weight less than 1.0 gram

Medium points: Weight between 1.0 and 2.5 grams

Large points: Weight over 2.5 grams

Some variability arises naturally among projectile points because flintknappers cannot fix their mistakes; they must work around errors, creating some variability in the finished product. In addition, points break when they are used. If they are not too severely broken, they can be reshaped into usable points—but this too makes them smaller than the maker initially intended (this can have an effect on typology; see "Looking Closer: The Frison Effect"). But for each of the three weight categories, the point's maker had a mental template of what the "proper" point's size should be. By and large, the three size categories reflect natural breaks in the distribution of weights.

The second attribute is notch position. Among the small points (Points 1 to 10 in Figure 9-3), some have notches and others do not. Two categories are hence apparent: small, unnotched points and small, side-notched points. Thomas was hardly the first archaeologist to note this distinction, and the literature of Great Basin archaeology refers to these two morphological types in this way:

attribute An individual characteristic that distinguishes one artifact from another on the basis of its size, surface texture, form, material, method of manufacture, and design pattern.

TABLE 9-1 Attributes for Gatecliff Shelter Projectile Points

SPECIMEN NUMBER	WEIGHT IN GRAMS	PROXIMAL SHOULDER ANGLE
1	(0.9)	—
2	0.8	—
3	0.9	—
4	0.4	—
5	(0.9)	—
6	(0.4)	200
7	0.8	180
8	(0.6)	180
9	0.7	180
10	(0.8)	190
11	2.3	100
12	(1.5)	100
13	(1.4)	95
14	1.5	85
15	2.5	80
16	4.1	110
17	3.5	120
18	3.9	130
19	3.5	120
20	(4.2)	150
21	(2.8)	80
22	(3.4)	85
23	(5.5)	80
24	2.7	100
25	(5.5)	60

Note: Weights in parentheses are estimates on broken points.

Cottonwood Triangular (Points 1–5)

Weight: less than 1.0 gram

Notching: absent

Desert Side-notched (Points 6–10)

Weight: less than 1.0 gram

Notching: present (from the side)

So the smallest points—Points 1 through 10—belong to already-recognized morphological types.

Points 11 through 15 are medium sized (weighing between 1.0 and 2.5 grams) and have notches creating a small base (or stem). Thomas described them as follows:

Rosegate series (Points 11–15)

Weight: between 1.0 and 2.5 grams

Notching: present

Point types are named by the archaeologists who create them. The first name generally refers to the site or region where they were first distinguished. The last name describes some morphological characteristic. Thomas's term "Rosegate" is a combination of "Rose Spring," a site in southeastern California, and "Eastgate," a small overhang near Eastgate, Nevada. Originally, two different point types were defined, one named after each site, but Thomas could find no significant difference between the two, and so he combined them. (In this case, he modified the naming convention somewhat: The first term still denotes the places of discovery, but because "Rosegate" combines two former types, it is termed a series—a higher-order category.) Points 11 through 15 have now been "typed."

The larger points are more complicated. Numbers 16 through 25 weigh more than 2.5 grams. Some have expanding bases (that is, the neck is narrower than the base), and others have contracting bases. But "expanding" and "contracting" are ambiguous terms, and on given points, archaeologists often disagree about just which stems expand and which contract. Look at Point 24: We call this stem contracting, but you might think that it is expanding. Who's right? Neither, because we have yet to define the attribute—a necessary step toward replicability.

The stem is created by the notches—the two slits added so that the point can be tied more securely to a shaft. The lower edge of this notch forms an angle with the major longitudinal axis of the point, and angles are useful because they can be measured.

To measure the angle, draw an imaginary line along the long axis of the point (Line A in Figure 9-4). Now draw another line (Line B) along the bottom of the point's notch, extending it to where it intersects the line you drew down the axis. Finally, draw a line perpendicular to that point of intersection on the opposite side of the point (Line C) and measure the angle between Line C and Line B.

Thomas called this attribute the proximal shoulder angle (PSA), because this side of the notch is nearest ("proximal to") the point shaft. Table 9-1 lists the proximal shoulder angles for the ten large points (Points 16 through 25) from Gatecliff Shelter. Now the difference between expanding and contracting stems is apparent: Points 16 through 20 have PSAs greater than 110°, and Points 21 through 25 have PSAs smaller than that. On this basis, Thomas separated them into the following morphological types:

Looking Closer
The Frison Effect

Stone tools are important temporal types because they are ubiquitous in prehistoric archaeological sites. But stone tools are resharpened and, through resharpening, they not only become smaller, they also change shape. This can have an effect on tool typologies.

François Bordes (1919–1981) was a well-known French archaeologist whose groundbreaking research on stone tools influenced many archaeologists. (Bordes, a member of the French underground during World War II, also wrote several science fiction novels under the pen name of Francis Carsac.)

The stone tools found in Neanderthal cave sites especially intrigued Bordes. These assemblages, dating from 130,000 to 35,000 years ago, are referred to as **Mousterian,** after Le Moustier, the site where they were first found. Through experimentation, Bordes figured out how the tools were produced; using this information, as well as shape and inferred function, he divided Mousterian tools into 63 types, including a variety of points, scrapers, knives, handaxes, and denticulates (flakes with crenulated edges). He created this typology simply by laying assemblages out and then sorting them into morphological categories. This seat-of-the-pants typology was common in Bordes's day, though statistical analysis later supported his findings.

Bordes then looked at Mousterian sites and found something interesting: The 63 tool types co-occurred in set frequencies, creating four fundamental patterns. For example, the Mousterian of Acheulean Tradition contained many handaxes, denticulates, and backed knives, but only moderate numbers of scrapers; the Typical Mousterian contained few handaxes and backed knives.

Bordes found that none of the four assemblages was restricted in time; instead, they often seemed to alternate with one another throughout a site's strata. Bordes argued that the four assemblages reflected four different cultural groups of Nean-

derthals, just as different car and architecture styles reflected different groups of Europeans.

Bordes's typology did what a typology is supposed to do: It allowed Bordes to see a higher level of patterning that demanded explanation. Bordes's interpretation of the patterning assumed that the stone tools were in their final intended form. Different scrapers, for example, had different shapes because their makers had different ideas about what a "proper" scraper should look like.

But scrapers wear out, often quite quickly, and are rejuvenated by removing a few flakes along their edges. In the 1960s, George Frison (University of Wyoming) pointed out that stone artifacts can change their shape considerably over the course of their useful lives through such resharpening. Harold Dibble (University of Pennsylvania) decided to investigate whether the "Frison effect," rather than different mental templates, was responsible for at least some of the variation in Mousterian scraper types. Undertaking some experimental and archaeological studies, he eventually concluded that resharpening could account for some of Bordes's scraper types. For example, single edge scrapers turn into "transverse scrapers" simply by resharpening.

Does this mean that Bordes's typology was wrong? Absolutely not. He saw and categorized morphological variation, and that process allowed him to see a higher level of patterning. Only his interpretation of the patterning may be wrong or at least incomplete, because some differences in tool form reflect not cultural differences, but simply how heavily some tools were used. Strata with many transverse scrapers, for example, probably saw heavier use by Neanderthals than strata dominated by single edge scrapers. Archaeologists proceed in exactly this way—they sort through variability, removing those parts that are explained by humdrum factors so that they can determine what are the more intriguing parts. Classification is an important first step in that process.

Elko Corner-notched
(Points 16–20)

Weight: Greater than 2.5
grams

PSA: ≥110° and ≤150°

Gatecliff Contracting Stem
(Points 21–25)

Weight: Greater than 2.5
grams

PSA: <100°

Elko points were initially recognized at sites in Elko County, Nevada, and Thomas first defined Gatecliff points from data recovered at Gatecliff Shelter. As morphological types, they differ only in basal form, as described by the PSA measurements.

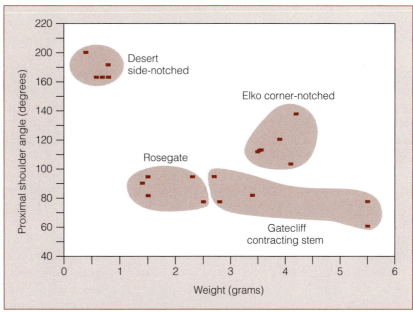

Figure 9-5 The relationship between the attributes of weight and proximal shoulder angle for the 25 Great Basin projectile points in Figure 9-3.

We have now classified all 25 points. This example is purposely simplified, but it demonstrates the first step in projectile point classification. Although a number of additional attributes were necessary to deal with the more than 400 points found at Gatecliff, the fundamental procedures are the same.

Memorizing endless type names may seem meaningless, but dealing with these five descriptive names is many times better than coping with 25 individual artifacts—to say nothing of the 400 individual points at Gatecliff, or the thousands found throughout the Great Basin. And that is the function of morphological types.

What Did the Typology Do?

Our typology has now organized the jumble of projectile points into groups based on measurable characteristics. But before we use the typology to think in broader terms—those crucial dimensions of time and space—we must first ask if it has fulfilled the two necessary characteristics of a typology.

Consider the first characteristic: *minimize the differences within and maximize the differences between each type.*

In the past, archaeologists accomplished this goal simply by placing artifacts on a table and sorting them into piles. However, most typologies today make use of statistical analyses (with names like cluster and dis-

criminant analysis) that are designed to take a set of attributes and provide an objective measure of how well a typology accomplishes this goal. We've avoided statistical detail of the Gatecliff typology because it is beyond the scope of this book, but you can get a sense of where such an analysis might go by looking at Figure 9-5. In this figure, we plotted the 20 notched points in terms of their weight and PSA. The Desert Side-notched, Elko Corner-notched, and Rosegate points are clearly different from the others in terms of both weight and notching—the differences within each group are minimized and the differences between them maximized. Rosegate and Gatecliff Contracting Stem points are less easily distinguished. They are similar in terms of PSA, and their difference in weight is less clear. However, Gatecliff points are more frequently resharpened than are Rosegate points—making them smaller than they were originally. The difference is subtle here, but a larger sample would separate these two point types more clearly in terms of weight. Therefore, the typology

Mousterian A culture from the Middle Paleolithic ("Middle Old Stone Age") period that appeared throughout Europe after 250,000 and before 30,000 years ago. Mousterian artifacts are frequently associated with Neanderthal human remains.

meets the first criterion: It minimizes the differences within groups and maximizes the differences between groups.

The second characteristic was that *the typology must be objective and explicit.* Thomas's typology actually made use of many more attributes than simply weight and proximal shoulder angle, and he defined more than the four projectile point types we've discussed here. By examining patterning in attributes, Thomas was able to organize the resulting Great Basic projectile point types into a flowchart, shown in Figure 9-6. To see how this typology is objective and explicit, let's take an "unknown" projectile point and classify it according to the Gatecliff criteria. Figure 9-4 (page 214) illustrates Artifact 20.4/2010, a projectile point recovered during Kelly's survey of the Carson Desert.

Projectile point 20.4/2010 has the following attributes:

Total length: 37.5 mm
Axial length: 37.5 mm
Basal indentation ratio: 1
Maximum width: 18 mm
Length to maximum width position: 4 mm
Basal width: 7 mm
Neck width: 7 mm
Proximal shoulder angle: 100°
Notch opening: 40°
Weight: 1.6 grams

To type this point, a few definitions of Thomas's other attributes are needed.

Total length is obvious; axial length, however, is the length from the point's tip to the basal concavity. For Artifact 20.4/2010, there is no basal concavity and so the axial length equals the total length. (If this point had a concave base, the axial length would be somewhat shorter than the total length.) The utility of this measurement is that, by dividing the axial length by the total length, we have a measure of how concave is the base, what Thomas called the basal indentation ratio. A high ratio means a relatively shallow concavity; a low ratio means a relatively deep concavity.

The maximum width position is simply the distance from the point's base to the point's greatest width. By dividing the maximum width position by the total length, we have one measure of a point's shape. A high ratio indicates a more triangular point (like 20.4/2010); a lower ratio indicates a more leaf-shaped point.

With these attributes, we can now classify Artifact 20.4/2010 using the flowchart. We begin with the question: Is the point notched? The answer is yes, and so we follow the arrow down to the next box. Is the point side-notched? No, so we move on to the corner-notched box. We are now faced with a set of three questions: Is its basal width (BW) less than or equal to 10 mm? Yes, it is. Is its PSA between 90° and 130°? Also, yes. Is the neck width (NW) less than the basal width plus .5 mm? Yes.

If the answer to any of these three questions were no, then we would have moved to the box below. But the answer to all these questions is yes, so the point is typed as a Rosegate. With this key, any trained student would classify this point as accurately as the most seasoned archaeologist. By using an explicit and objective typology, archaeologists know that, when they talk about a "Desert side-notched" or "Rosegate" or some other type of point, each of them are talking about the same thing. We have created attributes that are objective and explicit. And that is what "replicability" is all about.

Therefore, the typology fulfills both of the essential characteristics: It sorts things using objective and explicit criteria into categories that minimize the differences within them, and maximize the differences between them.

So far, we've only been talking about morphological types, but remember that the goal of this typology was to create temporal types, time-markers. Now that we've identified the types occurring at Gatecliff, we can determine whether they have any temporal significance.

Gatecliff Projectile Points as Temporal Types

As the name implies, temporal types help archaeologists monitor time; they provide us with index fossils that allow archaeologists to date surface sites and strata within buried sites.

In Chapter 7, we compared the stratigraphy of Gatecliff Shelter to a giant layer cake stacked 40 feet high. Geology's law of superposition tells us that, all else being equal, the oldest artifacts lie at the bottom, with later artifacts showing up in progressively higher strata. The Gatecliff deposits thus provide extraordinary temporal control over the past 7000 years, so when we plot the vertical distribution of the more than 400 classifiable projectile points from Gatecliff Shelter, we arrive at

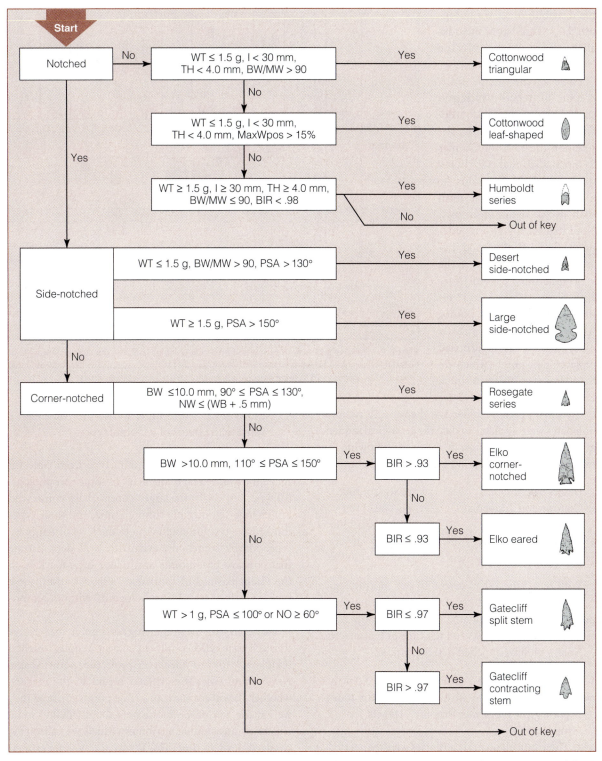

Figure 9-6 The Central Great Basin projectile point key.   *From Thomas, 1981,* Journal of California and Great Basin Anthropology *3:7–43, p. 25, a Malki Museum Press Publication. Used by permission. The Journal is available by subscription. Malki Museum, 11–795 Fields Road, P.O. Box 578, Banning, CA 92220, www.malkimuseum.org.*

the distribution shown in Figure 9-7. (This figure includes all the types used to classify the entire Gatecliff collection.)

Look at the sharp stratigraphic differences (which, you should note, exhibit the battleship curves like those in the seriation diagrams of Chapter 8; note also that the living floors are labeled "horizons"— a different use of that term than as we define it below). Note that all the Desert Side-notched and Cottonwood Triangular points occurred in the very uppermost part of Gatecliff Shelter. These had replaced Rosegate series points, which are confined to slightly older strata. These, in turn, had replaced Elko points, which are found lower, in still-older strata. Elko points had replaced Gatecliff points, which are older still. Because 47 radiocarbon dates were available to date the geological sequence at Gatecliff, it was possible to assign the following time ranges to the projectile point types discussed above:

Desert Side-notched	post–AD 1300
Cottonwood Triangular	post–AD 1300
Rosegate series	AD 500–AD 1300
Elko Corner-notched	1500 BC–AD 500
Gatecliff Contracting Stem	2500 BC–1500 BC

With this critical step, several of our morphological types have become temporal types. Each time similar points are found in undated contexts, we now have a clue (a hypothesis, really) to their time of manufacture.

Note what has happened in this example:

1. Individual artifacts were initially grouped strictly on formal criteria; all that mattered for morphological types was that the artifacts looked alike.
2. These morphological categories were then tested against independent evidence—specifically, the layer-cake stratigraphy and the chain of 47 radiocarbon dates available from Gatecliff Shelter.
3. All five morphological categories were significantly restricted in time, and so they were elevated to the status of temporal types.

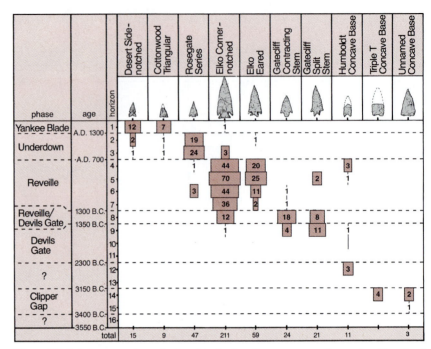

Figure 9-7 Relative proportions of selected projectile point types across the stratigraphic units of Gatecliff Shelter. Note how one or two extremely abundant temporal types seem to dominate most strata. *After Thomas (1983b: figure 66); Courtesy American Museum of Natural History.*

cantly restricted in time, and so they were elevated to the status of temporal types.

Not every morphological point type from Gatecliff made the grade. The frequencies of some morphological types (especially the larger, concave base points) did not change significantly through time, and these types flunked the test for graduating to the level of temporal type. Maybe somebody, eventually, will demonstrate that concave base points are indeed time-markers in the Great Basin; but until that demonstration, these types remain merely "morphological," without temporal significance.

We began with the simplifying assumption that change through time reflects shifts in ancient peoples' "mental templates" for an idealized projectile point shape. Never mind what the artifacts meant to the makers, whether they were spear or arrow points, or how they were made. For now, we care only about whether some cluster of measurable attributes (which we call types) changed through time. This is why and how we created some projectile point time-markers at Gatecliff Shelter.

This is also why we must recognize that time-markers have distinct limitations. The seriation-like diagram for Gatecliff projectile points shows us what changes over time and what does not, which permits us to pose more interesting questions. For instance, although we now know that Desert Side-notched and Cottonwood Triangular points post-date AD 1300, we do not know *why* two morphological types existed simultaneously. Are two social groups living at Gatecliff after AD 1300? Are Desert Side-notched points designed for hunting bighorn, whereas Cottonwood points are for rabbits? Are Cottonwood points for "war arrows"— left unnotched so that they remain embedded in a body even if the shaft is pulled out? Or perhaps the difference is technological: Could the Cottonwood Triangular points be unfinished, intended to be later notched (and thereby becoming Desert Side-notched points)? Notching is often the last thing done to a point, and if done incorrectly, it can ruin hours of work. Were Cottonwood Triangular points made by novices who were not adept at notching points? All these guesses are hypotheses at present untested—and they would have been impossible without first creating projectile point temporal types.

SPACE-TIME SYSTEMATICS

So far we have been talking only about the temporal dimension of archaeology, change in artifacts over time. We now shift and consider the spatial dimension of these temporal changes.

Americanist archaeology has adopted a relatively standardized framework for integrating the kind of chronological information just discussed into a regional framework. Gordon Willey (1913–2002) and Philip Phillips (1900–1993) initially set out this regional infrastructure in their influential book *Method and Theory in American Archaeology* (1958). Since then, the nomenclature has varied somewhat from region to region, some terms have been discarded because they reflect out-dated theoretical paradigms, and others do not have quite the significance that they once carried. Nonetheless, the 50-year-old Willey–Phillips framework remains the most generally accepted system in the Americas.

Archaeological Cultures: Dividing Space

To begin, however, we must go back to before Willey and Phillips's day, to the early twentieth-century concept of *culture areas*. Long before anthropology existed as a discipline in America, scholars recognized that not

Figure 9-8 North American culture areas. Such areas were important to nineteenth-century anthropology, but are less so today.

all Native American societies were alike. Some people were nomadic, others lived in large pueblos. Some hunted bison, others were maize farmers. Those in California relied heavily on acorns for their food; Northwest Coast peoples fished and hunted sea mammals. By the late nineteenth century, American anthropology had formalized these observations into culture areas (Figure 9-8), large regions defined primarily in terms of what people ate (which of course had a lot to do with the environment). The theory that attempted to explain these geographic patterns is no longer important to anthropology, but the culture areas left a legacy in that archaeologists who study the prehistory of North America tend to focus on one of these culture areas. They work on the Plains, or in the southeastern United States, California, or the Southwest.

Working with the prehistory of one of these regions, archaeologists quickly saw "sub-culture areas"—regions within a culture area whose material culture (such as house styles, settlement patterns, ceramics, or subsistence) differed from one another. These subdivisions of

Profile of an Archaeologist
A Cultural Resource Management Archaeologist

William Doelle is the President of Desert Archaeology, Inc., a cultural resource management firm in Tucson, Arizona, and the Center for Desert Archaeology, a nonprofit corporation that promotes the study and preservation of archaeological sites in the American Southwest.

© William Doelle

"Holy <expletive deleted>!" It was the only appropriate response to the cream-colored stone tool that had just caught my eye.

I was walking the centerline of a half-built road. It had been under construction, but representatives from the Tohono O'odham Nation in southern Arizona had protested when they observed road machinery cutting through a buried Hohokam village ("Hohokam" means "those who have gone" in the O'odham language and refers to village sites dating after AD 700). Work was halted, and the slow legal process of compliance begun.

A competitive bid process awarded an archaeological contract to my young firm. We were in our second week of fieldwork when the cream-colored tool—a Clovis point—was found. Unable to identify any intact Clovis-age deposits, however, we concluded that Hohokam farmers who lived at what we called the Valencia site had encountered this spearpoint in their fields and brought it back to their village.

This first work on the Valencia Site on Tucson's south side took place in 1983. Despite the construction, our excavations yielded some 25 intact Hohokam pithouses. In the last 20 years, I have conducted six additional projects at this site, each one expanding our knowledge of the Valencia community between AD 400 and 1200. An overview of that work provides a cross-section of the diversity in modern cultural resource management, or CRM—the professional area where I have made a living since 1974.

Our 1983 fieldwork was constrained to a narrow strip less than 20 meters wide and some 500 meters long. While we were in the field, we focused on that limited space because we had a great deal to accomplish in a very brief time—the bulldozers were waiting for us to finish. After the fieldwork, three of us volunteered to complete a map that put the site in a fuller context. I had been aware that there was a prehistoric ballcourt just 50 meters from our excavation, but only with the complete map did the full settlement plan make sense. There was

culture areas are called "traditions" or *archaeological cultures.* Figure 9-9 shows the location of the three major archaeological cultures of the Southwest culture area: the Hohokam, Mogollon (*muh*-gee-own), and Anasazi. These three regions are distinguished from one another in terms of pottery and architectural styles.

However, these archaeological cultures are *not* the same as ethnographic cultures. If we could go back in

time in, say, the Mogollon region and travel around, we would probably encounter several different languages, as well as different customs in different villages. In all likelihood, people in a village at the southern end of the Mogollon region considered themselves different from those who lived at the northern end. By drawing lines around areas on a map and labeling them archaeological cultures, we are simply drawing attention to spatial

an open, central plaza, surrounded by low trash mounds that were the surface indications of residential areas.

It wasn't long before we conducted an intensive surface collection of the entire site, refined our initial map, and did further excavations to define the site's southern boundary. Archaeologists had improved the ceramic typology, and we used it to plot distributions of ceramics by time periods as short as 50 years. It was clear that initial settlement had clustered around the ballcourt and plaza, but around AD 1000 the community became more dispersed, with houses scattered along a mile of the Santa Cruz river. Two decades later, there is still debate about the reasons for this change. Were ballcourts abandoned around AD 1000 or did they last for another century? Regardless, the pattern at the Valencia Site has since been shown to hold at all other ballcourt villages in Tucson.

The next big research opportunity came along in 1991. The local community college planned a new campus in an area that we thought was outside the Valencia Site, but reexamination showed that to be wrong. So, we carried out a surface collection and testing program to provide information for the college. As it turned out, this area held an earlier, more subtle pithouse site, almost certainly the ancestral village for Valencia. Our work in 1991 helped planners to place high-impact features like new two-story buildings off the main occupation area. In the winter of 1997–98, when we conducted preconstruction excavations, we documented over 100 early pithouses and projected a total of around 400. The arrangement of houses around a large central plaza provided the excavators with information to develop a refined model of early Hohokam villages.

My company had grown from one fulltime employee in 1983 to 35 in 1997. Thus, I was largely an observer in the research process. I work on management issues like an open house for the community college, tours by the cultural committees from the Tohono O'odham Nation, and writing grant proposals so that things like storm sewers do not destroy archaeological sites. I keep watch over the rapid development of Tucson and work with various groups—such as the community college, the city, the Tohono O'odham, the archaeological community, park planners, and landscape architects—to develop plans to preserve archaeological sites.

I have found that the opportunities to be creative are tremendous in CRM, and I plan to pursue at least another decade as head of my CRM firm before retiring. These opportunities are further enhanced through the nonprofit Center for Desert Archaeology. Through grants, endowment building, and a membership program, this institution pursues a mission of preservation archaeology. We balance research, public outreach, and stewardship in our programs in the American Southwest and Mexican Northwest. Archaeology in the private sector presents unique challenges, but I have found it to offer great rewards.

differences in the kinds of artifacts that are found in those regions. The *meaning* of these differences is another matter.

Periods: Dividing Time

As archaeologists began to investigate the prehistory of regions, they also discovered that the Native American culture that ethnographers documented (and that formed the basis for maps of culture areas) had not always been there. The people who lived in the American Southwest some 5000 years ago, for example, were nomadic hunter-gatherers who never knew maize or built pueblos. As the chronologies of different culture areas were worked out, prehistory was organized into slices of time that were given different names.

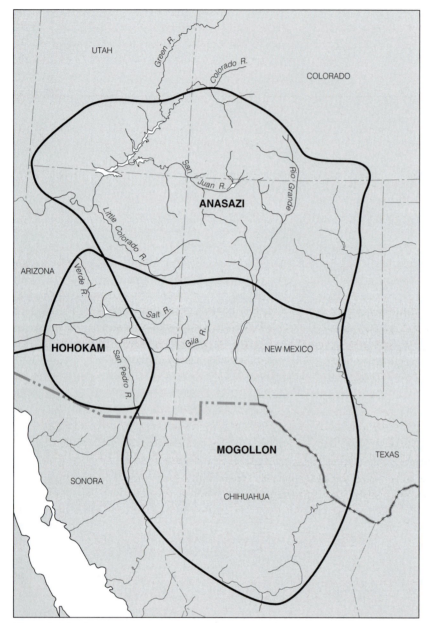

Figure 9-9 Southwestern archaeological cultures, or traditions. The theory that lay behind these areas is also outdated today, but the patterns that stand behind these traditions still demand explanation. *From L. Cordell, Prehistory of the Southwest, p. 15, 1984. Reprinted by permission of Elsevier.*

Archaeologists divided prehistory into **periods** based on gross changes in easily observable archaeological remains, such as subsistence or house forms. These were sometimes labeled "stages," although that term is rarely used today (see Chapter 15). But the concept of periods is still used to organize archaeological thinking about time. For example, pick up a text on Southwestern archaeology and an early chapter will be on the "Paleo-Indian Period" (from 9000 to 5500 BC), a period of time in which the distinctive Pueblo archaeological cultures, such as the Mogollon, did not exist, and people were nomadic hunters of large game and gatherers of some plant foods.

The next chapter might be on the "Archaic Period" (from 5500 BC to AD 100). This is a time when people made heavier use of plant resources, began to develop distinctive region traditions in material culture, and experimented with agricultural crops, most notably maize. This may be followed by chapters that describe "Early Village" and "Pueblo" periods.

Major cultural transitions, such as the appearance of ceramics, settled life, or agriculture, were labeled *horizons*. These are analogous to (but should not be confused with) soil horizons and marker beds in that they form cultural "fault lines" that can crosscut archaeological cultures and culture areas. This kind of cultural horizon might have different ages in different regions. Maize, for example, was first domesticated in southern Mexico; over time people farther to the north adopted it, and it gradually spread to other people living still farther to the north. Thus, the agriculture horizon appears progressively later in time as we move from southern Mexico to the Great Lakes region (the northern limit of maize horticulture). This concept is not heavily used in archaeology today because of its association with an outdated

period A length of time distinguished by particular items of material culture, such as house form, pottery, or subsistence.

evolutionary paradigm and because we now know that many transitions, including that from hunting and gathering to agriculture, were not as quick as the horizon concept assumed (see Chapter 15).

Nonetheless, like archaeological cultures, the concepts of periods and horizons helped to map out major spatial and temporal patterns in material culture. Periods and horizons record change over time, archaeological cultures record change over space. Knowing *how* and *when* material culture changed over time and space is an obvious first step toward explaining *why* those changes occurred.

Phases: Combining Space and Time

As archaeologists became increasingly familiar with the time markers of a region, they observed that different regions in a culture area did not all change in lockstep with one another. Pottery, for example, may first appear at different times in different areas (forming a ceramic horizon that crosscuts different culture areas); likewise, from a common base, pottery styles may differentiate over time at different rates and in different ways in different regions. In other words, there are temporal and spatial changes in material culture of which periods and horizons were just first approximations.

A **phase** is a block of time that is characterized by one or more distinctive artifact types, a particular kind of pottery, housing style, and/or projectile point, for example. The phase has become the practicable and intelligible unit of archaeological study, defined by Willey and Phillips as "an archaeological unit possessing traits sufficiently characteristic to distinguish it from all other units similarly conceived…[and] spatially limited to the order of magnitude of a locality or region and chronologically limited to a relatively brief interval of time."

How do we construct phases?

Phases are defined by temporal types (like our Gatecliff points), items of material culture that show patterned changes over time. We have already seen how to derive temporal types: You group individual artifacts into morphological types, then test them against independent data (such as site stratigraphy, correlation with other known sites, or direct dating of the artifacts themselves). We recognize those types of artifacts that change systematically and observably through time as time-markers.

The next analytical step is to see how the time-markers themselves cluster to reflect site chronology. Here we have to define a few other terms that archaeologists commonly use.

Archaeological sites consist of **assemblages,** collections of artifacts recovered from some unit of provenience. We could talk about a site's stone tool or ceramic or projectile point assemblage. In this case, the provenience might be the site itself. We could also talk about the assemblage of a particular stratum, say, the stone tool assemblage of Stratum 22 at Gatecliff. In a well-stratified and carefully excavated site like Gatecliff, there could be many assemblages.

We might then analytically cluster these assemblages into **components.** A component is considered a culturally homogeneous unit within a single site. By "culturally homogeneous" we mean that, although the assemblages that go into a component might have been deposited during different years and by different individuals, they were deposited by people who were the same culturally. Some small archaeological sites may contain only one assemblage representing a single component; some could contain multiple assemblages that nonetheless still represent one component. Others may contain multiple assemblages representing several components. And some sites may be too badly mixed to sort out assemblages and define components at all.

Because defining archaeological components rests on the intangible factor of cultural homogeneity, there can be no firm rules for their construction, but it helps if the strata are obvious from the stratigraphic profile, as at Gatecliff. Gatecliff's numerous strata of non-artifact-bearing silts separated the deposits into discrete living floors. During analysis, we could keep the floors distinct (as individual assemblages) or group them together on the basis of shared similarities. Although Gatecliff contained many living surfaces, Thomas decided that it contained only five distinct cultural components, each incorporating the assemblages from one to six living surfaces. Components are thus site-specific—a given component is, by definition, from a single site.

phase An archaeological construct possessing traits sufficiently characteristic to distinguish it from other units similarly conceived; spatially limited to roughly a locality or region and chronologically limited to the briefest interval of time possible.

assemblage A collection of artifacts of one or several classes of materials (stone tools, ceramics, bones) that comes from a defined context, such as a site, feature, or stratum.

component An archaeological construct consisting of a stratum or set of strata that are presumed to be culturally homogeneous; a set of components from various sites in a region will make up a phase.

Each component at Gatecliff is defined by its associated array of dates and its particular set of characteristic artifacts, including our much-analyzed projectile points and artifacts such as incised slates and carved wooden pegs (used to construct snares to trap small mammals).

How do these observations help create phases? By comparing Gatecliff's components with those of other nearby sites, we define the spatial and temporal range of particular artifact types and from this comparison a regional chronology of phases is constructed. Briefly, assemblages (all items of one kind from one stratum or location) are grouped into site-specific components (differentiated in culture and in time). Components from nearby sites are grouped into phases. These building blocks therefore identify similarities across space and time.

To see how this works, consider the three hypothetical archaeological sites in Figure 9-10. These three hypothetical sites are located in the same geographic region—say, Montana. They have been carefully excavated and analyzed and, as is often the case, no single site contains the complete cultural sequence. The first site has Components A and B; the second site contains Component B plus a new component called C; and the third site has Components A and C but lacks Component B. By analyzing the temporal types shared among the components and comparing the absolute dates, a regional sequence of phases can be constructed from evidence at these three sites.

To give a more concrete example, archaeologists working in the central Great Basin divide the post-3550 BC era into five phases, each defined by one or more temporal projectile point types. You can see these in Figure 9-7 (page 220), which showed how different morphological point types at Gatecliff sort out in time. These phases were defined on the basis of the analysis of assemblages from many stratified sites and the consistent association of particular morphological artifact types with particular spans of time.

For instance, the latest of these, the Yankee Blade Phase (named after a nineteenth-century silver mine in the nearby town of Austin) is typified by Desert Side-notched and Cottonwood Triangular points, as well as simple pottery. This phase began about AD 1300 and lasted until Euroamerican contact, about 1850 in central Nevada. The other phases were similarly defined, each composed of different kinds of artifacts (primarily projectile points) and spanning other episodes of time.

Phases: The Basic Units of Space-Time Systematics

The phase is archaeology's basic unit of time-space systematics, combining both spatial and temporal patterns in the material culture we dig up. Phases are defined by time, but also by space. There is no Yankee Blade Phase in Georgia, or New Mexico, or even Utah because the nature and tempo of change in material culture in these areas was not the same as in the central Great Basin. Even within the Great Basin, phases are not synchronous. Figure 9-11 shows some of the phase names used in the western and central Great Basin. Time and periods appear at left, along the vertical axis; space appears along the horizontal axis. This diagram is one result of archaeologists' efforts to create space-time systematics. Each phase, or block, in this figure—Cowhorn, Early Lovelock, Grass Valley—is defined by particular artifact types that have particular temporal ranges in their particular regions.

We can see what the temporal boundaries are of say, the Yankee Blade Phase, but you might be wondering where the geographic "edge" of the central Great Basin chronology is. At the town of Austin, in central Nevada? Or 100 miles east at Fallon in the Carson Desert? It's hard to say. Think of phases as analogous to pieces of a three-dimensional puzzle with

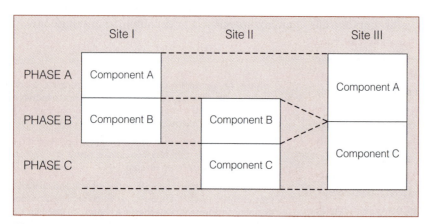

Figure 9-10 Relationship of archaeological sites to the analytical concepts of component and phase.

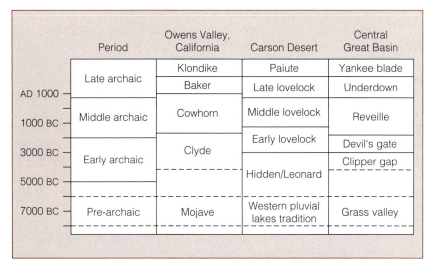

Period		Owens Valley, California	Carson Desert	Central Great Basin
Late archaic		Klondike	Paiute	Yankee blade
		Baker	Late lovelock	Underdown
Middle archaic		Cowhorn	Middle lovelock	Reveille
Early archaic		Clyde	Early lovelock	Devil's gate
				Clipper gap
			Hidden/Leonard	
Pre-archaic		Mojave	Western pluvial lakes tradition	Grass valley

y-axis labels: AD 1000, 1000 BC, 3000 BC, 5000 BC, 7000 BC

Figure 9-11 Time-space systematics: some of the phases used in three regions of the Great Basin, with period names. Dashed lines indicate phase boundaries that are not well dated.

very fuzzy edges. Neighboring regions do not necessarily have the same phases, because they did not see the same progression of change in material culture.

The construction of phases allows archaeologists to synthesize reams of data into a series of (admittedly simplistic) time-slices which, in turn, can be compared and contrasted with similar schemes from neighboring areas. They allow us to see, in a rough way, differences and similarities in the spatial and temporal scale of artifact change over time. Because we presume that artifacts reflect behavior, phases are ultimately ways to track spatial and temporal change in human cultural behavior. Phases are the first step toward developing ideas about regional patterns and trends—ideas that can be tested, refined, and expanded.

Phases can be as short as a few generations or thousands of years long. The length depends in part on the kind of archaeological remains involved and upon our contemporary knowledge of those remains. If pottery styles changed rapidly, then we can, with sufficient study of tightly controlled and well-dated stratigraphic excavations, develop short phases using seriation. Chronological control tends to be better for younger material, and so young phases tend to be shorter than old phases. One of the phases preceding the 550-year-long Yankee Blade Phase is the Reveille Phase, from 1300 BC to AD 700—some 2000 years. The Reveille phase is longer simply because the material remains used for its definition (including Elko series projectile points) continued to appear over a longer span of time than the remains used to define the Yankee Blade Phase (Desert Side-

notched points, Cottonwood Triangular points, and pottery). Phases covering the most recent prehistory of the American Southwest may be only 25 to 50 years long.

The phase concept is vague, and deliberately so. Archaeology needs to impose a set of minimal units on time. The phase is that minimal unit. They allow archaeologists provisionally to define time, which is actually a continuous variable, as if it were a discrete set of temporally ordered points. When we discuss the Yankee Blade phase, we are treating the time span from AD 1300 to AD 1850 as if it were an instant. By definition, two components of the Yankee Blade phase are simultaneous, provided that "simultaneous" is understood to last 550 years.

But bear in mind that phases are always defined *provisionally*. As knowledge of the Yankee Blade phase expands, we may be able to recognize divisions within the phase—for instance, to distinguish an early Yankee Blade component from a late Yankee Blade component. When this happens, the initial phase is divided into *subphases*. This increasing subdivision reflects the amount of research accomplished on each phase and underscores the degree to which our knowledge of the archaeological record is a contemporary phenomenon. This is why we leave the concept of phase vague, so that it can accommodate new findings and help us learn more, rather than place blinders on our ability to see new patterns in prehistory.

CONCLUSION: SPACE-TIME SYSTEMATICS AND ARCHAEOLOGICAL OBJECTIVES

We began this chapter by pointing out that this search for patterning falls along three dimensions: space, time, and form (of artifacts). And this search leads to the

Archaeological Ethics
What's Wrong with Buying Antiquities (Part II)?

In Chapter 8, we argued that the buying and selling of artifacts promotes the destruction of archaeological sites. Like most archaeologists, we don't have a problem with the weekend collector who picks up arrowheads. Frankly, we'd rather they didn't do it, but we know that most of these people are well intentioned and not responsible for the massive loss of data that professional looting causes. We also understand that professional archaeologists don't "own" the past.

But there is another side to this. The serious collectors, the ones willing to shell out thousands of dollars for Mimbres pots or Etruscan statues, argue that if it were not for them, many of the world's treasures would never be recovered at all. Should we, they ask, let wonderful pieces of ancient art lie beneath the ground, not to be excavated until archaeologists get the time and funding? Given that archaeologists have to dig so slowly, that will take centuries! And in the meantime, aren't those pieces in harm's way, from the ravages of time and other countries' lax antiquities laws?

Wouldn't it be preferable, some collectors ask, to recover artifacts now, quickly, so that they do not deteriorate any more than they already have, and get them out where they can be enjoyed by people? The latter rings hollow if those precious objects are only displayed in a person's home or locked away in a private vault. But collectors counter that many private collections eventually end up in public museums. Indeed, they point out that the world's major museums own objects that were originally gathered by private collectors, at a collector's own expense. And they are right (look at the Parthenon marbles). Thus, collectors argue that any archaeologist who is proud of a museum but who criticizes collecting is a hypocrite.

We disagree. Had there been professional archaeologists around when Lord Elgin was removing the Parthenon's marbles, we'd like to think they would have raised hell about it. In addition, the needs of archaeology today are different than those of the past. Remember that for archaeologists today an artifact's provenience is as important as, if not more important than, the artifact itself. Looters don't record context, and so there is a big difference between nineteenth-century collecting and twenty-first–century looting.

This point was driven home on April 11, 2003, a few days after the U.S. military entered Baghdad. Although the Pentagon had assured several professional organizations that Iraqi cultural institutions would be protected, they left the Baghdad Museum unguarded, and it was looted. Some artifacts were wantonly smashed, and the computer and paper records were partially destroyed. Initially, the media reported that some 170,000 artifacts were stolen, but it turns out that museum personnel moved many of the museum's more significant items to safer locations in anticipation of the war. They moved gold artifacts, for example, to a bank vault.

construction of space-time systematics, a simplification of the enormous variation in material culture over time and space into some meaningful patterns. You now have some sense of how we go about doing that. But the construction of space-time systematics is not the goal of archaeology, it is the means to an end. The goals of archaeology are to reconstruct and explain the past. How do space-time systematics help accomplish these goals?

Let us look at the case of Shoshone pottery to answer this question (Figure 9-12). Shoshone ceramics appear suddenly in many parts of the Desert West about AD 1300 (forming a ceramic horizon), and the Shoshone people made similar pottery until about 1860. Shoshone pottery thus implies certain limits: time (AD 1300–1860, the Yankee Blade Phase in the central Great Basin) and space (the Desert West).

With its temporal parameters estimated, Shoshone pottery becomes a useful time-marker. Sites containing these potsherds in the Desert West can be provisionally assigned to the AD 1300–1860 interval.

But we are nowhere near finished. In fact, we have just begun, for Shoshone pottery, taken as a time-

An investigation headed by Colonel Matthew Bogdanos, USMC, concluded that 40 items were stolen from the main galleries, including the 4300-year-old Bassetki statue and the heads of Roman era statues, as well as 3138 items from the old storage rooms and 10,337 items from a basement storage room. As of January, 2004, 4302 items had been returned, most through an amnesty program, but others were recovered through raids or customs inspections in Iraq, Jordan, Italy, Great Britain, and the United States. Some of these items were outside of Iraq within days of their theft.

Bogdanos's investigation found that some of the thieves did not know what they were doing. For example, the thieves took an entire shelf of fakes but overlooked some nearby genuine artifacts. Perhaps military personnel who, Bogdanos's evidence showed, used the museum as a firing position did some of this looting.

But the investigation also showed the presence of thieves with intimate knowledge of the museum. And they had inside help, given that some locked storage areas were opened with keys. These thieves were selective in what they took from the galleries, forgoing beautiful replicas for the most valuable genuine pieces. In the looted basement storage room, for example, the only room entered was that containing a huge collection of ancient gold and silver coins. Fortunately for Iraq, the thieves apparently dropped the keys to the cabinets and lost them in the unlit room (the electricity was off by this time; Bogdanos found the keys after hours of searching). The looters lit a fire in a desperate effort to find the keys, but they apparently only had time to abscond with the contents of 103 small plastic boxes that contained nearly 10,000 cylinder seals, pins, beads, pendants and necklaces. The artifacts taken were so selective that many believe that, although the looting was carried out by Iraqis, it was orchestrated by wealthy, unscrupulous buyers in Europe, Japan, or the United States.

Other Iraqi museums were also hit, and archaeological sites were attacked by armed looters. Although some called for a "shoot first, ask questions later" approach to looters, one can hardly blame a poverty-stricken Iraqi farmer for exploiting an opportunity to make 10 years worth of wages in a night of digging. Instead, it's the wealthy buyers in developed nations who are to blame. They are the ones that drive this destruction, who encourage a country to rob itself of its cultural patrimony and to destroy irreplaceable records of human history.

Iraq is a stark reminder of what is wrong with buying antiquities. If collectors truly wish to see the world's heritage protected (and do not simply want to add to their personal collections), then they should turn their financial resources to aiding those countries that need assistance in discovering, protecting, and displaying their cultural heritage.

marker, leaves many more questions unanswered. Was this pottery introduced by migrating Shoshone-speaking peoples? Or did the idea of pottery simply spread across the Desert West? Did the various peoples of the Desert West independently invent the idea of pottery? Or were the vessels traded in from neighboring ceramic-manufacturing areas?

Each is a research question that could inspire years of investigation: Is it possible to document a population movement across the Desert West at AD 1300? If so, where did these newcomers come from? And what happened to the pre-AD 1300 inhabitants of the Desert West? Are there signs of trading activity or warfare in AD 1300?

Questions like this can pile up without end. Although we cannot reconstruct what happened in the past by looking only at time-markers, we also don't even know the relevant questions to ask or hypotheses to test until we know something about the when and the where of the past.

And reconstructing *what* happened in the past is itself but one step in the process. As we pointed out in

© Donald R. Tuohy/ Nevada State Museum

Figure 9-12 Shoshone ceramic vessel.

Chapter 1, archaeologists today are equally interested in *why* prehistory took the particular courses that it did; we are interested in explaining the past as well as in reconstructing it. The time-marker Shoshone pottery tells us that distinctive potsherds occur in archaeological deposits dating from AD 1300 to 1860 across the Desert West. But viewed as a time-marker, Shoshone pottery tells us nothing about *why* pottery was introduced in 1300. For some reason, one segment of the Desert West cultural system changed, and people began manufacturing pottery. This complex issue can be studied only by pursuing related shifts in the lifeway, drawing evidence from the settlement pattern and demography, cultural ecology, social organization, and religion.

For example, let's say that we eventually conclude through research that the pottery was introduced through a migrating Shoshone population. The next question would be: Why did this population migrate in? What gave it the ability to replace the existing (pre-AD 1300) population? Did climate change to render the pre-AD 1300 adaptation untenable, thereby enabling the Shoshone to invade the Desert West? Did the ecological adaptation change to make ceramic vessels more efficient after AD 1300? Could it be that a ceramic-using population moved into the Desert West and intermarried with the previous inhabitants? Did population growth drive the migration, or was it warfare, or some environmental calamity?

By definition, we base our time-markers on selected aspects of shared culture; time-markers deliberately ignore much cultural behavior. Obviously, questions such as diffusion, migration, invention, and adaptation are complex, reflecting changes in the underlying cultural systems. Time-markers, grounded only in shared behavior, are patently inadequate for unraveling the mechanics of cultural systems.

In many respects, the space-time systematics of archaeology have been worked out, especially for North American archaeology, and they no longer preoccupy archaeology the way they did in the first half of the twentieth century. Nonetheless, space-time systematics were and are a crucial first step in the archaeological process. It is only after documenting temporal and spatial change in selected artifacts that we can set about reconstructing what people actually did in the past. And in the following chapters, we will discuss how archaeologists go about doing exactly that.

Summary

- Archaeology's major contribution to anthropological knowledge is found in large-scale patterns in space and time. Although archaeology cannot recover the detail that ethnography can, it contributes to anthropology by studying the long-term temporal processes and vast spatial patterning that ethnology cannot record.

- After the excavation, archaeologists catalog and conserve the artifacts recovered. This can be time-consuming and can require the help of trained specialists.

- The next task is to classify the artifacts in order to construct space-time systematics. This involves typology, the construction of a process to place artifacts into types. This process begins during the excavation, where artifacts may be sorted according to their raw material for the sake of convenience. Classification becomes more rigorous in the lab.

- Archaeologists create morphological types by relying on the shared aspect of culture. We assume that people made an item of material culture in a particular way because they shared a common idea of what a tool or object "ought" to look like. At this point, whether the final form was important to the maker or meaningful in any way is not significant to our analysis.

- The type is the basic unit of artifact analysis. It is an idealized construct that allows archaeologists to transcend individual artifacts so they can consider more generalized categories.

- Morphological types are descriptive and emphasize broad similarities. Temporal types monitor how artifacts change through time. And functional types group artifacts in terms of their function, regardless of their morphology.

- A typology groups artifacts in such a way that the differences within groups are minimized and the differences between groups are maximized.

- Types are based on criteria that are objective, explicit, and replicable.

- Spatial patterning in material culture helps define archaeological cultures or traditions, but these are not the same as ethnographic cultures.

- By seeking out clusters of temporal types we construct site components, which are culturally homogeneous units within a single site and can be synthesized into phases—archaeological units of cultural homogeneity that are limited in both time and space. Phases are the basic archaeological building blocks for regional synthesis.

- Space-time systematics is but one step toward the larger goals of reconstructing and explaining the past.

Additional Reading

Dunnell, Robert C. 1971. *Systematics in Prehistory*. New York: Free Press.

Lyman, R. Lee, and Michael O'Brien. 2003. *W. C. McKern and the Midwestern Taxonomic Method*. Tuscaloosa: University of Alabama Press.

Lyman, R. Lee, Michael O'Brien, and Robert C. Dunnell (Eds.). 1997. *Americanist Culture History: Fundamentals of Time, Space, and Form*. New York: Plenum Press.

Whallon, Robert E., Jr., and James A. Brown (Eds.). 1982. *Essays on Archaeological Typology*. Evanston, IL: Center for American Archaeology Press.

Online Resources

COMPANION WEB SITE
Visit **http://anthropology.wadsworth.com** and click on the Student Companion Web Site for Thomas/Kelly *Archaeology*, 4th edition, to access a wide range of material to help you succeed in your introductory archaeology course. These include flashcards, Internet exercises, Web links, and practice quizzes.

RESEARCH ONLINE
WITH INFOTRAC COLLEGE EDITION
From the Student Companion Web Site, you can access the InfoTrac College Edition database, which offers thousands of full-length articles for your research.

10 Taphonomy, Experimental Archaeology, and Ethnoarchaeology

OUTLINE

© Robert Kelly

Mikea women pounding maize in southwestern Madagascar (and watching the anthropologists).

Preview

WE HAVE NOW EXPLORED how archaeologists locate and excavate sites, how they date those sites, and how they construct cultural chronologies. Now it is time to move a step up the theoretical ladder and examine the role of middle-range research in modern archaeology.

We have already discussed the various natural and cultural processes that combine to create the archaeological record. Low-level theory enables us to generate data from this record. Now, we can apply theory developed in middle-range research to relate these data to past human behaviors. If you flip back to the model of archaeological inquiry in Figure 3-10 (page 74), you'll recall that archaeologists sometimes put down their trowels, climb out of their trenches, and conduct research designed to give them the tools they need to interpret the data they have generated. That is what this chapter is about.

Here, we concentrate on three areas of middle-range research that we introduced in Chapter 3:

- Taphonomy studies the role that natural processes play in creating the archaeological record.
- Experimental archaeology uses controlled experiments to replicate the past under different conditions to look for links between human behavior and its archaeological consequences.
- Ethnoarchaeology studies living societies to see how behavior is translated into the archaeological record.

INTRODUCTION

Archaeologists are often compared to detectives, and this comparison is both appropriate and instructive. Both are concerned with what happened in the past, and both make inferences about the past based on recovered material remains. But, ideally, detectives deal with crime scenes that are found and sealed off as soon after the crime as possible. Imagine detectives confronted by a crime scene that is several thousand years old, in which nothing organic survives and burrowing rodents have jumbled the evidence. Even Sherlock Holmes would have a hard time making his conclusions stand up in court. And yet, this is what archaeologists deal with all the time.

Archaeologists also deal with the complication that, unlike detectives, they often recover objects whose function and meaning are unknown. Imagine if our detectives first had to figure out that the metallic cylinder lying on the floor was a spent cartridge (and not a piece of jewelry, child's toy, or the ever-popular ritual object). Detectives routinely use "common sense"—knowledge of their own culture, actually—to decide if something "doesn't look right" at a crime scene. Imagine how much more slowly investigations would proceed if those detectives first had to decide if the distribution of furniture in the room—a chair lying on its side, dishes strewn about the floor—was culturally normal or an aberration.

A complex suite of natural and cultural processes interacts to create archaeological sites, and they make each site unique. And this means that archaeological interpretation is *never* straightforward; the low-level facts of archaeology cannot explain themselves. Middle-range research aims to provide archaeology with the tools needed to infer behavior from the contemporary archaeological record.

MIDDLE-RANGE RESEARCH: WHAT IS IT?

To develop such tools, archaeologists must observe behavior and its material correlates simultaneously, but independent of one another. In an archaeological site, we have only the material remains. Behavior must be inferred from those remains and thus it cannot be observed independent of them. Where, then, do archaeologists get the means to make these inferences?

Let's consider how archaeology's sibling discipline, geology, solved this problem. Like the archaeological record, the geological record consists of two things: objects and the relationships among them. A "geological fact" is a contemporary observation made by a geologist on objects from the geological record. Rocks do not speak, so how do geologists go from contemporary observations to meaningful inferences of the remote geological past?

Geologists addressed this question in the eighteenth century. A Scottish doctor and farmer, James Hutton (1726–1797), was also intrigued by geology. He formulated a simple principle that provides one of the cornerstones of modern geology. What became known as the **principle of uniformitarianism** asserts that the processes now operating to modify the earth's surface are the same as those of the geological past. It's that simple: Geological processes in the past and the present are assumed to be *identical.*

We know from modern observations, for instance, that as glaciers move, their massive weight leaves striations—that is, scratches—on bedrock deposits. They also deposit rock and earth at their fronts and sides, often in distinctive formations called moraines. Study of modern glaciers shows that moraines and striations are formed only through glacial action.

Now suppose a geologist finds moraines and striated rocks in New England, where no glaciers exist today. Armed with knowledge of contemporary glacial processes, a geologist can confidently interpret those features as evidence of past glaciers.

The same logic applies to archaeology. Archaeologists recover the material remains of past human behavior. And, like geologists, archaeologists must also look to the contemporary world to provide them with hypotheses that account for the formation and deposition of these physical remains. This is an important point: Observation of the contemporary world provides the information necessary to infer past human behavior and natural processes from observations on archaeological objects.

Some Bones of Contention

Perhaps you are thinking that, sure, this makes sense—but shouldn't the meaning of remains still be relatively obvious?

To address this question, consider a simple problem in the interpretation of animal bones (also known as **faunal** remains) from archaeological sites. As we will discuss in Chapter 11, archaeologists study animal bones to learn about past diets, hunting and butchering practices, how animals were domesticated, the season in which the hunt occurred, and other related issues.

Most of these faunal studies begin by considering the relative frequencies of animal bones in a site. When analyzing the bones from Suberde, a seventh-millennium BC Neolithic village in Turkey, Dexter Perkins and Patricia Daly observed that the upper limb bones of wild oxen were usually missing. Perkins and Daly suggested that the frequencies of the different bones resulted from how people had butchered the oxen. They must have first skinned the animals, then stripped the meat from the forequarters and hindquarters, and then thrown away the defleshed upper limb bones. Perkins and Daly presumed that the meat was piled on the skin and that the lower limb bones were used to drag the hide bearing the meat back home. Calling this the "schlepp effect," they believed their interpretation explained why only lower limb bones were discarded at the habitation site.

Now jump across Europe to England, where R. E. Chaplin analyzed the bones recovered from a late ninth-century AD Saxon farm. The facts in this case also included a shortage of the limb bones of sheep and cattle, but Chaplin suggested that these bones disappeared because the carcasses were dressed and exported to market.

Across the Atlantic, archaeologists working on American Plains Indian sites also discovered that the upper limb bones of food animals were often missing. Theodore White decided that the bones were destroyed during the manufacture of bone grease. Relying on

---

principle of uniformitarianism The principle asserting that the processes now operating to modify the earth's surface are the same processes that operated long ago in the geological past.

faunal In archaeology, animal bones in archaeological sites.

ethnographies of Plains Indians, White argued that the limb bones were pulverized and boiled to render their grease to make pemmican (a mixture of dried meat, fat, and berries), which was stored for the winter.

We could cite other examples, but the point should be clear: Three different teams made three different inferences from exactly the same archaeological facts—the lack of upper limb bones in habitation sites.

Archaeologists face such problems daily: several competing hypotheses accounting for the same body of facts. And all the hypotheses are reasonable.

Scientific protocol stipulates how to select among the competing hypotheses (and for the present, we will restrict our attention to the three target hypotheses). Each one is a generalized statement about human behavior. But a contemporary archaeologist can never observe a Neolithic villager butchering a wild ox, and none of us will ever watch nineteenth-century American Plains Indians making bone grease. Archaeologists must therefore concentrate on finding the material *consequences* of activities like butchering Neolithic oxen or making bison bone grease.

We do this by constructing a series of logical if... then statements: *If* bone grease were manufactured from bison bones, *then* we should find artifacts X, Y, and Z and physical residues M, N, and O; bones should be distributed in patterns C, D, and E; and bone elements J, K, and L should be missing. Similarly, to test the second hypothesis, we must generate some if... then statements regarding the trading of meat and bones. Before we can do that, we need answers to some very specific questions: Which are the best cuts to trade? How far can meat be transported before it spoils? Is meat marketed only in the winter months? Are carcasses butchered in special ways so that certain cuts can be traded? Then we can create arguments like "*If* these carcasses were being dressed for market, *then* we should see marks A and B on bones X and Y, and the site should include features G or H and implements K and L."

These if... then statements become *bridging arguments*, a concept we first mentioned in Chapter 2 (page 41) that translate hypotheses into specific expectations that can be tested using archaeological evidence. These

bridging arguments are essential to testing ideas with archaeological evidence, and their construction is one of the most difficult things that archaeologists do.

But—we hope you are wondering—how do we know these things? Why do archaeologists surmise that making bone grease requires artifacts X, Y, and Z? And how do we know which bone elements are destroyed in the process? Hypothesis testing is only as robust as these if... then bridging arguments. If we generate incorrect implications, then our hypothesis testing will be worse than useless, because it will lead us to specious or erroneous conclusions. For instance, if we assume that the lack of limb bones *always* means that people were rendering grease from bones, we would make a completely incorrect inference if the lack of limb bones in a particular site was really the result of the schlepp effect.

Here is where the notion of middle-range research comes into play. Because the facts cannot speak for themselves, archaeologists must provide bridging arguments that breathe behavioral life into the objects of the past. Properly formulated, middle-range theory links human behavior to empirical data that are archaeologically observable. Although it has been an important aspect of archaeological inquiry for more than a century, Lewis Binford's call for middle-range research served to focus additional attention on this neglected area of archaeology.

To create relevant bridging arguments, archaeologists must observe the workings of a culture in its systemic context, much as geologists defined their processes through observation of the contemporary world—such as streams carrying silt to a delta or the wind blowing sand across dunes. Geologists interested in glacial processes cannot study firsthand the massive continental glaciers that once covered portions of the Northern Hemisphere. But they can examine the effects that mountain glaciers today have on the landscape and use those observations to infer the past from geological traces.

Archaeologists do the same: They study modern analogies in order to understand the processes that created the archaeological record.

Analogy versus Middle-Range Theory

We used the term "analogy" in the previous paragraph, and you may be asking yourself if there is a difference between it and middle-range theory. The answer is that *middle-range theory is a particularly rigorous analogy.*

To see what we mean by this, let's first consider what a simple analogy is. An **analogy** notes similarities

analogy Noting similarities between two entities and inferring from that similarity that an *additional* attribute of one (the ethnographic case) is also true of the other (the archaeological case).

between two entities—for example, an archaeological feature and an ethnographic description of a similar feature—and infers from those facts that an *additional* attribute of one (the ethnographic feature) is also true of the other (the archaeological feature). Following Nicholas David (University of Calgary) and Carol Kramer (1943–2002), simple analogies take the following form:

- An archaeological object is characterized by attributes A, B, C, and D.
- The ethnographic analogy is characterized by A, B, C, and D and has the function or property E.
- Therefore, the archaeological object also has the function or property E.

For example, the first archaeologists to excavate ancient pueblo ruins in the American Southwest discovered many **kivas** in the settlements. Kivas are religious structures where native peoples of the American Southwest held various rituals. They are usually round and semi-subterranean, with massive log roofs that were covered by dirt. They were entered via a ladder placed in a central opening in the roof that also served as a smokehole.

Many kivas share certain features: an exterior, stone-lined vertical shaft that opens near the kiva floor, a central fireplace, and an upright stone slab (or a small masonry wall) between the fireplace and the shaft's opening. These features (shown in Figure 10-1) are probably functional. The fireplace provided light and warmth. The shaft provided ventilation, and the upright stone deflected wind blowing down the shaft and prevented smoke and embers from annoying the ritual's participants.

Along the wall opposite the ventilator shaft, archaeologists usually find a very small pit or simply a depression called the **sipapu** (a Hopi term meaning "place of emergence"). Unlike the fireplace, ventilator shaft, and deflector stone, the sipapu has no apparent material function. To interpret this recurrent feature, archaeologists turned to living Pueblo societies, such as the Hopi, who use kivas today for rituals.

Hopi kivas also contain this small, innocuous pit, and its size belies its cultural significance, for the sipapu symbolizes the place where the Hopi emerged from the underworld. In traditional Pueblo theology, the world consists of several levels, and oral histories recount stories of people moving from one level to the next by crawling through a small opening. The current world,

the Hopi say, is the fourth world, with more worlds above it. The kiva's sipapu is a reminder of these stories, a portal through which the natural and supernatural worlds communicate. Archaeologists infer that sipapus in archaeological kivas had the same function as they do in modern kivas.

Does this inference fit the definition of an analogy? Let's put it into the David and Kramer definition:

- Archaeological kivas are semi-subterranean with entry through the smokehole; they have a central fireplace, a ventilator shaft, a deflector stone, and a small pit opposite the ventilator shaft.
- Hopi kivas are semi-subterranean with entry through the smokehole; they have a central fireplace, a ventilator shaft, a deflector stone, and a small pit (the sipapu) opposite the ventilator shaft. The sipapu represents the hole where the Hopi emerged into the current world; it allows communication between the natural and supernatural worlds.
- Therefore, the sipapus in archaeological kivas also represented the place where ancient peoples say they emerged from a previous underworld, and they also allowed communication between the natural and supernatural worlds.

Such analogies must be used cautiously. Why? Because just as we enumerated the similarities between the Hopi and the archaeological kivas, we can also list the *differences* between them: Hopi kivas are often square, not round; they are often placed in open plazas or streets between room blocks, rather than incorporated into blocks of residential rooms as they were at many prehistoric pueblos. We could list the similarities between Hopi and archaeological kivas and stack those up against the differences. But how similar do ethnographic and archaeological cases have to be for the analogy to hold true?

kiva A Pueblo ceremonial structure that is usually round (but may be square or rectangular) and semi-subterranean. They appear in early Pueblo sites and perhaps even in the earlier (pre-AD 700) pithouse villages.

sipapu A Hopi word that loosely translates as "place of emergence." The original sipapu is the place where the Hopi are said to have emerged into this world from the underworld. Sipapus are also small pits in kivas through which communication with the supernatural world takes place.

Figure 10-1 Looking down into an unroofed kiva at Mesa Verde National Park; note the square opening for the ventilation shaft (at the top of the photo), the upright stone between the ventilation shaft and the central hearth, and the sipapu—the small hole near the bottom of the photo.

Formal and Relational Analogies

To answer this question, we must introduce you to two major kinds of analogy, which Alison Wylie (Barnard College) terms **formal** and **relational analogies.** Formal analogies rely on similarities in *form*—hence "formal" attributes—between the archaeological and ethnographic cases, regardless of whether the analogies come from the same culture. For example, we infer that stone projectile points, such as those you saw in Chapter 9, are in fact projectile points because they are so similar to the stone tips found on the projectiles of many ethnographically known peoples the world over. Formal analogies are, of course, strengthened (1) if many ethnographic cases demonstrate the same pattern and (2) if the archaeological and ethnographic cases have many attributes in common. But no rules exist to tell us *how many* ethnographic cases make a strong analogy, or *how many* similarities between the archaeological and ethnographic cases are needed to justify the analogy.

Relational analogies entail formal similarities, but the archaeological and ethnographic cases are related in some fashion. By "related," we mean that they both come from societies with similar settlement systems, economies, or environments—for instance, they may both be desert-adapted hunting-and-gathering societies or the ethnographic society that serves as an analogy may be a cultural descendant of the archaeological case.

In addition, relational analogies may entail "natural" relations, that is, a causal and hence *necessary* link

© Robert Kelly

between the attributes of an object or a feature and their interpretation. We'll come back to this aspect of relational analogies in a moment.

Our kiva example entails elements of both formal and relational analogies. There are formal similarities between the archaeological and Hopi kivas, and modern Hopi culture is clearly related to ancient Puebloan culture. Analogies such as this have been and always will be important to archaeological inference.

However, analogy entails certain risks. Suppose, for instance, you are studying a prehistoric horticultural and pastoral society in the deserts of Kenya. In the site you've excavated are many stone scrapers. You are interested in inferring who used these tools, men or women. As we will see in Chapter 13, inferring the activities of different genders from archaeological data is an extremely difficult task. Analogy is one option for making the inference.

Knowing that analogies are safer, the closer they are in time and space to the archaeological case, you look around Africa for a contemporary society that is roughly comparable to the archaeological one—one that lives in a similar environment with a similar economy and a similar culture. Doing so, you encounter the ethnographic research of Steven Brandt and Kathryn Weedman (University of Florida) with several Ethiopian peoples. Among these people today are individuals who work cattle skins to manufacture bedding and bags. About a third of those who work hides use stone tools.

These seem to be wonderful sources for building an analogy, but which Ethiopian group should you use? If you pick the Gamo, you'll find that men do all the hide-working and tool manufacture. The Gamo-based analogy would imply that men also did all the hide-working in your archaeological society. But among the Konso, *women* do virtually all the stone-tool manufacture and hide-working (Figure 10-2), so the Konso analogy would obviously lead to a very different conclusion.

Like dynamite and backhoes,

analogies are part of the archaeologist's toolkit, but they must be used with caution.

One way out of this problem is to determine the relative strength of the analogy. By increasing the number of formal similarities between an ethnographic and archaeological case, we increase the probability that the formal analogy is correct. Still, though, we wouldn't know if an analogy that relies on ten attributes is twice as good as one with only five. Even the best analogy is no more than a probability—and retains the chance that it could be wrong.

Drawing the analogy from an ethnographic case that is culturally related to the archaeological one improves the analogy, but what if recent events caused cultural discontinuity between the past and the present? And what happens with archaeological cases that have no clear ethnographic referent, such as the 10,000-year-old Folsom site we mentioned in Chapter 6?

Middle-Range Theory as Powerful Analogy

As we noted above, relational analogies can rely not just on cultural continuity but also on "natural" relationships, by which Wylie means causal linkages between attributes of a thing and the inference to be made from it.

© Steven Brandt / Kathryn Weedman

Figure 10-2 Sokati Chirayo, a Konso woman in Ethiopia, working a hide with a stone scraper mounted in a wooden handle.

Archaeological Ethics
The Ethics of Doing Ethnoarchaeology

Ethnoarchaeology does not come naturally to most archaeologists, who are more accustomed to dealing with the dead than with the living. We are used to thinking about whether our crews are well fed, happy, and satisfied—but not about whether the site feels the same way.

But doing ethnoarchaeology means thinking about the ethics of working with members of another culture. Cultural anthropologists have thought about this quite a bit—in fact, the first line of the American Anthropological Association's Statement on Ethics reads: "Anthropologists' paramount responsibility is to those they study."

Anthropologists involve the host population in the project, seek the approval of those who participate, and avoid harm. For every house he measured, every settlement that he mapped, every photo that he took in Madagascar, Kelly explained his goals and asked permission. If the individual declined, he moved on.

Often, however, conflict arises between research goals and human decency. One cannot stand idly by while people are harmed, but an anthropologist also has a responsibility to the research and to the organization that sponsored it. Bram Tucker (Ohio State University) confronted such a problem during his research with the Mikea:

In July 1998, I was living in Behisatse, a hamlet of six houses in the Mikea Forest. I was studying how the Mikea make a living in an unpredictable environment. Rainfall, the main source of water for wild and domestic plants and animals, varies unpredictably from 100 mm to 1500 mm each year. Mikea deal with this unpredictability by diversifying their economy, combining foraging with farming, herding, and producing hard goods for market. They forage in different microenvironments. They plant a mix of crops that do well in rainy years and those that do well in dry years.

Some years, even the best economic strategies are ineffective, and the food supply is inadequate. This was the case in 1998. The maize crop germinated late because of insufficient rainfall, and then in February grasshoppers ate the withered stalks. Thieves ransacked manioc fields in the night. By March, the families at Behisatse were relying almost entirely on wild ovy tubers (*Dioscorea acuminata*). Ovy is an excellent food, but is prone to overharvesting. As the ovy patches near camp were depleted, foragers traveled increasing distances to find food, returning to camp each evening with barely enough to see them through the night.

I was faced with an ethical dilemma. The curious scientist in me wanted to know how Mikea households cope with food shortage. But as their friend and honorary kinsman, I couldn't just watch them go hungry!

My field assistant and I informed the camp elder that we planned to do something to help. The next day we visited a farmer friend in a distant village. I purchased 100 Kg of manioc, enough to feed everyone in Behisatse for a month and a half, for 40,000 Malagasy francs, about $7. The farmer said it would take a week to finish drying the manioc. During the following week at Behisatse, the adults continued to forage for ovy all day, leaving the children back at camp hungry. So, at each meal we prepared twice as much food as normal and invited the children to join us. Eventually our manioc gift arrived. Our friends continued to work hard and forage frequently, but they could now afford to rest a little without worry.

I still learned a lot about how Mikea cope with food shortage. By the time our gift arrived, people were starting several alternative strategies, including planned movements to other locations and recalling debts from more prosperous acquaintances. But as field researchers, we become part of the communities we study. As such, we have a responsibility to help out when we can.

We refer to analogies based on such causal linkages as middle-range theory. Middle-range theory is a special kind of analogy simply because it *is* theory. As you will recall from Chapter 3, theories explain things; they answer why questions. Middle-range theory tries to make an analogy more certain by explaining *why* there is a *necessary* relationship between an object's or feature's attributes and an inference made from those attributes. Relying on the principle of uniformitarianism, middle-range theory attempts to explain *why* an inference should necessarily be true.

This is hardly an easy task. In fact, this may be an archaeologist's most difficult chore. Consider the hypothetical example above in which the archaeologist wished to know if men or women used stone scrapers. What theory would *necessarily* link some observable attribute of a scraper—such as length, width, thickness, raw material, or context—to the gender of its user? It's hard to imagine.

Certainty may forever elude archaeological inference, but archaeologists have been able to make new and more secure inferences from archaeological remains by constructing their middle-range theories through taphonomy, experimental archaeology, and ethnoarchaeology.

Taphonomy

The word "taphonomy" (from the Greek term *tapho*, meaning "death" or "tomb") was coined by the Russian paleontologist I. A. Efremov; it refers to the study of how organisms become part of the fossil record. Archaeologists use the term to refer to the study of how natural processes contribute to the formation of archaeological sites. In Chapter 7, we discussed site formation processes—how human behavior and natural processes affect the creation of the archaeological record. Taphonomy is an important aspect of the study of site formation processes because it considers how human behavior and natural processes incorporate bones and plants into sites.

Taphonomists study some bizarre stuff. One might record how large animal carcasses decompose on an African savanna (Figure 10-3). How long does it take the carcass to disarticulate? Which bones separate first? Which ones are carried away by carnivores? And how far? Is decomposition in the rainy season the same as in the dry season? Others might examine lion kills and ask what telltale markings lions leave behind. How do these differ from the evidence that human hunters leave behind?

Another might find raptor nests along a cliff and collect their feces or vomit (many raptors eat prey whole and then regurgitate the bones and hair). What do rodent bones look like after they have passed through a raptor? Or what do fish bones look like that have passed through a dog? How about through a human? Depending on your perspective, taphonomic research is either gross or really cool.

In archaeology, taphonomy has expanded from paleontology's traditional concern with bones to include plant remains. What are the various ways that seeds, leaves, twigs, and pollen enter archaeological sites? Here you might study the feces of various herbivores, the plant-collecting behavior of packrats (more on them in Chapter 11), or the way that wind or water carries leaves, pollen, and sediments.

Recall that taphonomy aims primarily at understanding how natural processes contribute to a site's formation. Although it's not easy, it's easier to infer natural processes from artifacts and ecofacts rather than human behavior because natural processes are more mechanistic and hence more predictable than human behavior. This observation is useful to archaeology for two reasons: First, recall that data are *observations* on objects, and that archaeologists seek *patterns* in their data. Therefore, one strategy for understanding an archaeological site is first to *remove all the patterns that are the result of natural processes*. Once we do this, we know that the remaining patterns are the ones that need to be explained in terms of human behavior. We saw this approach at the site of Cagny-l'Epinette (discussed in Chapter 7).

Second, understanding how a site formed is crucial to understanding not only the human behavior that occurred at the site but also the *environmental context* of that behavior. It can tell us if the climate was temperate or tropical, if a landscape was eroding away or aggrading, if streams were running or were dry, if forest fires were prevalent, and so on.

In taphonomic research, archaeologists develop bridging arguments by simultaneously yet independently observing natural processes in action and their material results. By trying to explain *why* those natural processes produce the particular material results that they do, you move from simple analogies into middle-range theory.

© Diane Gifford-Gonzalez, photo by Michael J. Mehlman

Figure 10-3 Diane Gifford-Gonzales collecting data for a taphonomic study in Africa.

The Hudson-Meng bison **bonebed** provides an example of what taphonomic research can do for archaeology.

Taphonomy at the Hudson-Meng Bison Bonebed

The Hudson-Meng site lies in a low swale in windswept northwest Nebraska, where the remains of at least 500 bison are crowded into an area of about 1000 meters square (Figure 10-4). Twenty-one spear points (or point fragments) were found among the remains. AMS dates indicate that the site is about 9500 radiocarbon years old.

Paleontologist Larry Agenbroad (Northern Arizona

University) was the first to dig at Hudson-Meng, in the 1970s. Using the standard conventions of the day, he inferred human behavior from *patterns* he observed in the faunal remains. One clear pattern was that the tops of the crania were missing. Mandibles were present along with some cranial fragments, but the top of nearly every single skull was missing. Agenbroad knew that modern Plains Indians often broke bison skulls open to remove the brains and use them in tanning hides. Using this as an analogy, he reasoned that the skull tops at Hudson-Meng were missing for the same reason and therefore that humans must have killed the animals.

Agenbroad then made several more inferences. How could people on foot, armed only with spears, have killed 500 bison? People without horses, Agenbroad decided, could not control a herd of 500 bison. So he inferred that there must be a low cliff nearby that is now buried beneath the sand that blows daily across western Nebraska. The hunters drove the bison over the cliff

bonebed Archaeological and paleontological sites consisting of the remains of a large number of animals, often of the same species, and often representing a single moment in time—a mass kill or mass death.

© Lawrence C. Todd

Figure 10-4 Students excavating a small portion of the Hudson-Meng site, Nebraska. A weatherport covers this excavation.

and then dragged some 500 of them to a processing area. And, calculating that 500 bison could produce nearly 10,000 kilograms of dried meat, Agenbroad inferred that the ancient hunters were a large group and that they had a sophisticated storage system.

So Agenbroad made inferences about (1) the presence of humans, (2) hunting strategy, (3) group size, and (4) food storage, all based on the patterning—the missing skull tops—evident in the skeletal assemblage. These inferences were all based on an analogy with historically known Plains Indians, one that had elements of both formal and relational analogies:

It was a formal analogy because it relied on the similarity in bison skull form (the missing top of the cranium), and similarities between the site and ethnographically documented butchering practices.

It was a relational analogy because it took a known practice of Plains Indians and extrapolated back in time to the ancestors of Plains Indians.

However, this is not middle-range theory because Agenbroad did not try to explain the character of the skulls he found in light of what might happen to bison

craniums butchered by known Plains Indian practices. The necessary bridging argument we mentioned above was assumed, not demonstrated.

From a taphonomic perspective, modern archaeologists look at the foundation of Agenbroad's inferences (the missing crania) and wonder: Could a natural process create the same pattern?

Hudson-Meng has always presented some troubling facts. For example, comparing it with similar bison kill sites, we might expect something closer to 150 points and point fragments, not just 21.

And why are there no cut marks on the bones? In the process of butchering 500 bison, it seems likely that a stone knife would occasionally have cut to bone as it sliced through tendons and meat. Archaeologists have encountered thousands of such telltale nicks at other kill/butchery sites, but only carnivore tooth marks appear on the bones at Hudson-Meng.

Finally, many of the skeletal remains are in anatomical position, lying in the ground as if the bison had simply died there and were buried undisturbed. If ancient hunters had butchered these animals, we'd expect them to have removed at least some of the meaty portions of the body, such as the upper rear leg (containing the femur).

Lawrence Todd (Colorado State University) and David Rapson (University of Wyoming) were bothered by these facts, and so they excavated a portion of the Hudson-Meng site using a battery of high-precision excavation techniques. They also applied the perspective of taphonomy, and began by asking this simple question:

How Do Bison Fall Apart?

For years, taphonomists had studied the carcasses of large animals as they lay decomposing on North America's high plains, Africa's Serengeti, and elsewhere. Some of these animals had been shot; others had frozen to death or simply died of old age. Some were ravaged by carnivores, others were undisturbed. Some died on hillsides, others in gullies. Some died in the winter or wet season, others in the summer or dry season. Sometimes the hide dried to form an armor-like case, holding the bones together years after death, sometimes the rotting carcass burst from the maggots within. In other words, taphonomists had documented what actually happens to a large animal carcass under a variety of natural circumstances.

Are there any patterns in how these large animal skeletons fall apart? Absolutely. Andrew Hill (Yale University) and Anna Behrensmeyer (Smithsonian Institution) found that the first joint to disarticulate is where the scapula attaches to the vertebral column, allowing the entire front limb to drop away. Then the caudal (tail) vertebrae-to-sacrum joint goes, followed by the scapula-humerus joint, and then the "elbow," where the humerus articulates with the radius and ulna. The last joints to disarticulate tend to be those of the vertebrae. Such documented sequences of natural disarticulation provide a baseline against which to judge the distinctiveness of human butchering practices.

Through time, the decomposing bison carcass eventually collapses into a flat pile of bones (Figure 10-5). The skull often ends up resting on its mandibles (the lower jaw). Carni-vores may drag some limb bones away and, eventually, the entire skeleton lies flat on the ground—with the skull poking up above all the other bones.

Then what happens? The bones become a sediment trap, catching the blowing dust and sand. It takes 10 to 15 centimeters of sediment to cover the now-collapsed limb bones and rib cage, but 30 to 40 centimeters to cover the skull. This means that much of the skull is left sticking up above the ground surface after the rest of the bones are buried. And once leg bones, vertebrae, and ribs are buried—thus covering most of the irregular surface that trapped blowing sand—sediment accumulates less quickly, leaving the top of the skull exposed for a longer period of time than the rest of the skeleton.

Then the sun does its work. Sunlight is quite destructive of bone, and the exposed top of the skull quickly flakes away. Eventually, the top of the skull is destroyed and the rest is buried.

Taphonomy and Uniformitarianism

So the incomplete crania, the basis of Agenbroad's analogy, are readily explained by natural processes, not human behavior. This is more than simple analogy—it is middle-range theory because we understand *why* bison bones disarticulate, become buried, and weather the way that they do. But this understanding is based on observations of modern animals. Can we trust these observations to explain archaeological remains?

The principle of uniformitarianism applies here, because ancient animals, like the bison that died at

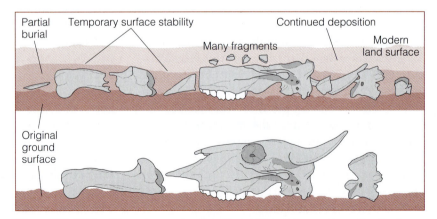

Figure 10-5 Todd and Rapson's reconstruction of how taphonomic processes, rather than human butchering, created the pattern of incomplete crania at the Hudson-Meng site. The animal dies and decomposes; as the body collapses into a pile of bone (bottom), it continues to trap sediment until it is mostly buried, although the skull's top remains exposed. The cranium weathers (top), and the small bone fragments that flake off are blown away by the wind.

Hudson-Meng, had the same anatomy as the animals observed in taphonomic studies. Bison disarticulation is governed by the amount of cartilage and tendons holding bones together and the amount of muscle tissue around them. The more cartilage, tendon, and muscle in a joint, the more resistant that joint is to disarticulation. If skeletal disarticulation is largely a product of anatomy, and if bison anatomy has not changed over the past 10,000 years (and it hasn't), then modern observations are relevant to the interpretation of archaeological data.

Likewise, the effects of sunlight on bone are a product of the nature of bone and the nature of sunlight. And given that neither sunlight nor bone composition has changed over time, we have gone beyond analogy to explain *why* particular natural factors have particular predictable effects on bone. This is what qualifies the work as middle-range theory.

And, it suggests that humans played little role, if any, in the deaths of the 500 bison at Hudson-Meng. But if humans did not dispatch the 500 bison at Hudson-Meng—what happened? Todd and Rapson hypothesize that a summer storm sparked a massive prairie fire that drove the bison herd into the swale for protection (many of the bison lie with their heads to the southeast, which, using analogy with modern bison behavior, suggests that they were responding to a northwest wind). None of the bones are burned, so these animals were not burned to death. But the fire could have jumped the swale and asphyxiated the bison by sucking up all the oxygen for a few critical minutes. This hypothesis remains to be tested.

And what of the 21 projectile points found there? As you have seen in previous chapters, archaeological sites are often reoccupied. In their careful excavations, Todd and Rapson found several thin soils containing a few archaeological remains *above* the bison. In fact, Agenbroad found fewer than 10 points *among* the bones. The spear points, then, were probably discarded or lost long after the bison had died, decomposed, and become buried, and a few points moved downward through rodent burrowing and sediment processes into the bonebed.

EXPERIMENTAL ARCHAEOLOGY

Taphonomy uses observations of modern processes to help make inferences from archaeological data. But what if this is impossible? What if we want to know the material effects of behaviors *that no longer exist*? This is especially relevant to human behaviors, because people did things in the past that they no longer do today. Understanding the material remains of these behaviors requires experimental archaeology.

Experimental archaeology is by no means new. Nearly 100 years ago, for example, Saxton Pope, a surgeon at the University of California Medical Center (San Francisco) began experimenting with archery methods. The poignant story began in 1911, when a starving, defeated Indian was found crouching in a slaughterhouse corral near Oroville, California. His family may have been murdered, or perhaps they starved to death. Ishi (circa 1860–1916) himself may have lost his will to live. He could neither speak nor understand English. The local sheriff locked him in the jail, because "wild" Indians were not allowed to roam about freely in those days.

Alfred Kroeber, a young anthropologist at the University of California, heard the story and recognized the Indian's language as Yahi, a native language of California. Kroeber named the man Ishi ("human" in Yahi) and brought him to San Francisco, where he stayed at the university museum, worked as an assistant janitor, and demonstrated arrow-making and fire-starting for museum visitors. Kroeber and his staff taught Ishi their culture, and the Indian revealed many secrets of his survival.

But Ishi soon developed a tubercular cough—which later cost him his life—and he was treated daily by Dr. Pope. Over their short association, Pope and Ishi found a common interest in archery. An odd combination: Pope, the urbane scholar paired with the Yahi Indian, hair singed in tribal custom, together shooting arrows through the parks of downtown San Francisco. Pope was a good student and, after Ishi's death (see "Looking Closer: What Happened to Ishi?"), the doctor continued his research, studying bows and arrows in museum collections and often test-shooting the ancient specimens.

Pope wrote *Hunting With the Bow and Arrow* in 1923, describing his experiments in archery. The book provided baseline information for interpreting ancient finds and quickly became the bible of the bow-hunting fraternity (in fact, it is credited with reviving the sport of bow hunting in America).

From early studies such as Pope's, experimental archaeology expanded dramatically and has become an important way for archaeologists to reconstruct the past.

Looking Closer
What Happened to Ishi?

By all accounts, Ishi was well cared for in his modest quarters at the University of California's museum in San Francisco. At the time, however, the museum was located next to the university's medical center, where physicians performed autopsies on the bodies of the poor and kept the skeletal remains for study. Ishi always expressed trepidation about these remains, and he made clear to Kroeber that no autopsy should be performed on him when his time came.

Unfortunately, his time came when Kroeber was on sabbatical leave on the East Coast. When Kroeber left, he suspected that Ishi was ill, and he kept in close contact via letters with museum authorities. When Pope informed Kroeber of Ishi's impending death, Kroeber demanded that Ishi not be autopsied and that his remains be cremated, in accordance with Yahi custom (or, at least, with what Kroeber believed to be Yahi custom). Kroeber must have feared that the museum would autopsy Ishi, for he wrote to a colleague in 1916, "If there is any talk about the interests of science, say for me that science can go to hell."

But Kroeber's directions arrived too late, and the hospital staff autopsied Ishi. Eventually, Ishi's remains were cremated and his ashes placed in a Pueblo Indian jar at Mount Olive Cemetery, near San Francisco.

But not all his remains were cremated; Ishi's brain was preserved in a jar of formaldehyde and presented to Kroeber on his return to Berkeley.

Given Kroeber's passionate feelings toward Ishi, it is odd that just a few months after his passing, Kroeber wrote to renowned biological anthropologist Alés Hrdlička at the Smithsonian Institution, asking him if the institution wished to have Ishi's brain, given that "There is no one here who can put it to scientific use." Hrdlička agreed, and Ishi's brain was sent to a Smithsonian warehouse in Maryland. And there it sat for nearly 85 years (alongside the brain of John Wesley Powell [whose career is summarized in Chapter 2]).

In 1997, some members of the Maidu tribe requested that the University of California turn over Ishi's remains for proper burial. The ashes were located, but the university denied that the brain had been removed, and the Smithsonian denied that it had it. But these denials were impossible once Orin Starn (Duke University) found Kroeber's correspondence and tracked down Ishi's brain at the warehouse.

On August 8, 2000, Ishi's ashes and his brain were returned to California's Pit River tribe, who buried the remains in a secret place.

Why did Kroeber do it? Why did he send Ishi's brain away rather than cremate or bury it? We don't really

How Were Stone Tools Made?

Many prehistoric techniques died with their practitioners, and experimental archaeologists have been forced to rediscover them. Making stone tools is one such technique, and many archaeologists have experimented by manufacturing their own stone tools.

To make a stone tool, you must first locate and collect the appropriate raw materials—rocks that break with a glassy fracture such as obsidian, quartzite, or chert. This may require excavating into bedrock, because frost-fracturing and sunlight can ruin surface specimens. Some ancient peoples excavated major quarries into bedrock using only fire and wooden wedges.

If the stone is chert or quartzite, you might improve it by **heat-treatment**—burying large **flakes** or small

heat-treatment A process whereby the flintknapping properties of stone tool raw material are improved by subjecting the material to heat.

flake A thin, sharp sliver of stone removed from a core during the knapping process.

know, because Kroeber never talked publicly about Ishi. Perhaps Kroeber simply saw the autopsy as a *fait accompli* and decided that some good might as well come out of it (although the Smithsonian never used Ishi's brain for any scientific study). Others might see in Kroeber's actions a fundamental, if unconscious, racism toward Native Americans. With a century of hindsight, it is easy to criticize the past actions of scientists.

But anthropologist Nancy Scheper-Hughes (University of California, Berkeley) suggests another interpretation. Scheper-Hughes studies violence—physical and psychological—and she understands the myriad ways that people respond to the grief that comes with the loss of loved ones. She interprets Kroeber's actions as evidence of "disordered mourning." Kroeber had lost his first wife—also to tuberculosis—only 2 years before Ishi's death. Indeed, Kroeber was depressed and melancholic from 1915 to 1922 (because of these losses and the effects of Ménière's disease); he even briefly left anthropology to enter psychoanalytic therapy and training as an analyst. Scheper-Hughes sees Kroeber's actions as a way to conceal deep feelings of loss—over Ishi and over the loss of his first wife—that were too difficult to confront. So perhaps we should not be so quick to pass judgment on Kroeber.

Ishi, a Yana-Yahi man.

cores in about 5 centimeters of sand, then burning a fire on top for a day or so. Ancient flintknappers learned that they could more easily chip and shape stone treated in this way. The problem is that, over the millennia, plenty has been forgotten about the detailed technology required to make good stone tools from a pile of rocks.

Fortunately, a school of experimentalists—many of them dedicated amateur archaeologists—has rediscovered some of this technology. One of the best known, Don Crabtree (1912–1980) spent a lifetime experi-menting with stone tool manufacturing methods (Figure 10-6). One of his projects was to rediscover the techniques used to fabricate Folsom spear points.

Remember from Chapter 6 that Folsom points, such as those found at the Folsom site in New Mexico, date to 10,200–10,900 radiocarbon years ago. These

core A piece of stone that is worked ("knapped"). Cores sometimes serve merely as sources for raw materials; they also can serve as functional tools.

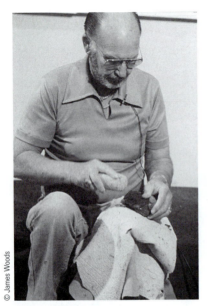

© James Woods

Figure 10-6 Accomplished flintknapper Don Crabtree uses a hammerstone to percussion-flake a block of obsidian.

© American Museum of Natural History

Figure 10-7 Folsom-style spear points manufactured by Don Crabtree. Note the two large "fluting" flakes that were removed from the points at the bottom of the photograph.

exquisite points turn up in many sites on the Great Plains and in the Rocky Mountains where, mounted on spears or darts, they brought down game, including bison. Although the points are often only about 6 to 8 centimeters (2½ to 3 inches) long, Crabtree counted over 150 minute sharpening flakes removed from their surface.

The most distinctive property of Folsom artifacts are the **flutes**—wide, shallow, longitudinal grooves on each face of the point (Figure 10-7). Flutes are made by removing **channel flakes** from the point's base on both sides. Nobody is sure why these artifacts were thinned in this fashion, but everybody agrees that fluting is an extraordinary feat of flintknapping.

The technical quality of Folsom points intrigued Crabtree. With enough practice, one can learn to quickly fashion many projectile points. But making Folsom

flute Distinctive channel on the faces of Folsom and Clovis projectile points formed by removal of one or more flakes from the point's base.

channel flake The longitudinal flake removed from the faces of Folsom and Clovis projectile points to create the flute.

points must have required hours, assuming that one understood how to do it in the first place. And in the twentieth century, nobody did.

Archaeologists speculated for years how ancient peoples removed the channel flakes. And for 40 years, Crabtree tried every way he could think of to manufacture Folsom replicas. He eventually described 11 different methods he had tried to remove channel flakes. Most simply didn't work: Either the method was impossible with primitive tools or the resulting flute was different from those on the Folsom points. One method succeeded only in driving a copper punch through his left hand.

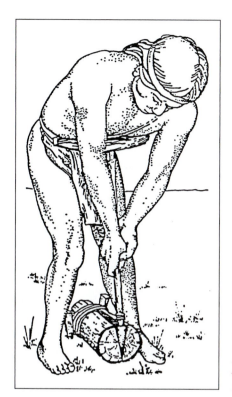

Figure 10-8 Conjectural reconstruction of the use of a chest crutch to drive off the central flute from a Folsom point.

Crabtree eventually concluded that channel flakes could be removed in only two ways. In one experiment, he placed an antler shaft, known as a "punch," on the bottom of the unfinished artifact and then struck the punch with a sharp upward blow. Because placement of the antler punch was critical, this technique required two workers. A second technique was based on the seventeenth-century observations of Juan de Torquemada, a Spanish Franciscan friar who traveled through the Central American jungles in 1615. This method used a chest crutch to drive flakes off a core, and Crabtree wondered if it could also remove channel flakes off a Folsom point.

So Crabtree manufactured a chest crutch following Torquemada's description, padding one end and equipping the other with the end of an antler (Figure 10-8). He tied an unfinished experimental Folsom point into a wood-and-thong vise, which he gripped between his feet. Bracing the crutch against his chest and pressing downward, he successfully detached perfect channel flakes, time after time. The resulting artifacts were almost identical to prehistoric Folsom points.

Crabtree's research unleashed an avalanche of experimentation in the fluting problem (it also had some

unintended practical consequences; see "Looking Closer: Obsidian Blade Technology: Modern Surgery's Newest Ancient Frontier"). These efforts show that some ten different methods can successfully remove channel flakes and produce the distinctive flutes of Folsom points.

Experimental Archaeology and Uniformitarianism

Archaeologists have used replicative experiments in many different areas of archaeology. They have experimented with ways of moving enormous blocks of stone, such as the huge statues on Easter Island in the Pacific Ocean. They have experimented with ways to manufacture just about everything that is found in archaeological sites—stone tools, pottery, basketry, metal tools, houses, and so on. They've even built structures and then burned them down to see how destruction translates into archaeology.

But what do these experiments prove? Researchers found many ways to remove channel flakes from Folsom points, but which method was actually used in Folsom times? Where's the element of uniformitarianism?

Obviously, a variety of methods work. Crabtree demonstrated that it was *not impossible* to use a chest crutch to replicate Folsom points. But experiments show that other methods were also possible. None of the experimental flintknappers demonstrated conclusively how Folsom points were *actually made*. Replicative experiments often only demonstrate that a given technique could have been used in the past—that it was *not impossible*.

To determine which method or methods were used by Folsom flintknappers, further research is required to compare the characteristics of ancient Folsom points and the waste flakes from their manufacture with experimentally produced Folsom points and waste flakes. Because we know that stone breaks according to certain principles of fracture mechanics, we know that the characteristics of flakes produced today in experiments can help us infer what techniques were used in the past.

But even lacking this element, experimental archaeology can still teach us something about the past. For example, experimental archaeology has taught us three important things about Folsom spear point

Looking Closer
Obsidian Blade Technology: Modern Surgery's Newest Ancient Frontier

 Should you try your hand at flintknapping, it won't be long until you've sliced your fingers. In his 50 years of flintknapping, Don Crabtree slashed himself in every conceivable way—across his fingers, through his palm, through a fingernail; one flake zipped right through his shoe.

Examining his cuts one day, Crabtree noticed that, although he still had scars from jagged-edged flint flakes, the wounds caused by obsidian had healed quickly and were almost invisible. He wondered about that.

Then Crabtree saw a friend slice himself while handling some newly made obsidian artifacts. The gash bled profusely, and a physician was summoned. But by the time the doctor arrived, some 20 minutes later, the wound had already begun to heal.

Curious, Crabtree used an electron microscope to compare some fresh obsidian flakes with new razor blades. Interestingly, he found that the fresh flakes were many times sharper than the best razor blades.

Recognizing the potential of such super sharp instruments for surgical applications, Crabtree worried that "the surgeon who pioneers the use of such blades may be accused of reverting to caveman tactics." But in 1975, when Crabtree himself faced major surgery, he managed to cajole his surgeon, Dr. Bruce A. Buck, into using obsidian blades Crabtree himself had fashioned:

The first surgery was when I had a rib removed and a lung section. The cut goes from right under the breast there, clear around back under the shoulder blade. So it's about an 18" cut. And you know I hardly have a scar....And then I've had abdominal surgery four times, from my sternum down to the pelvis....Then I had bilateral femur arteries of woven dacron tubing put in....And there was no problem with sterilization. A fresh blade comes off sterile.

Not long thereafter, more assessments cropped up in medical journals reporting on successful experimental surgeries and speculating about additional applications. Everyone was impressed with the "exquisitely sharp" obsidian edge. It turns out that obsidian blades are as sharp as the newest diamond scalpels, were 100 to 300 times sharper than steel scalpels, and left a smaller cut with much clearer edges—meaning that obsidian blade incisions were quicker to heal and less likely to leave a scar than incisions made with a steel blade.

Several archaeologists now produce obsidian blades commercially for surgery, and these have been used in eye surgery, breast biopsies, bilateral vasectomies, facial plastic surgery, and nerve microsurgery.

manufacture. First, regardless of which technique is used, it's difficult to flute points; it takes years of practice. Second, fluting results in a rather high breakage rate near the end of the manufacturing sequence, regardless of the technique. And third, fluting appears to have no specific function. In fact, after Folsom times, similar but unfluted spear points were made for another thousand years. Presumably, these were as effective as Folsom points.

This last point adds a new dimension to our understanding of Folsom spear points. Bruce Bradley, one of the world's premier flintknappers, suggests that fluting was part of a pre-hunt ritual. We don't know if Bradley is right, but the fluting experiments tell us that we need to consider other hypotheses to not only explain *how* people fluted their points, but also *why*.

Furthermore, the uniformitarian element of experimental archaeology often comes in the guise of telling us what *could* or *could not* have happened in the past. Although this may not pinpoint the precise technique that was actually used, it can provide powerful tests of hypotheses.

Here's another example.

Building the Pyramids

Swiss author Eric von Däniken has long argued that aliens from outer space built the world's prehistoric wonders, including the pyramids. Von Däniken looked at those engineering marvels (see Chapter 8) and asked, How is it possible that a primitive people working with the simplest of tools could have built structures of such astounding size and architectural sophistication? In fact, he asked, how could the Egyptians have even moved the large stones and statues without the aid of advanced technology?

This hypothesis can be tested using experimental archaeology: Can stones weighing several tons be moved using only the tools and materials that the ancient Egyptians had available to them? If not, then perhaps von Däniken's hypothesis has some merit. But if such stones *can* be moved with Egyptian technology, then his hypothesis is undermined.

Had von Däniken actually bothered to learn anything about Egyptian archaeology, he would have quickly discovered paintings within tombs that depict men hauling stones and statues. One shows 172 men pulling a statue of Djehutihotep (a Middle Kingdom noble) estimated to weigh some 58 tons (thus, each man is pulling about 650 pounds). The statue rides on a wooden sledge accompanied by a man who pours a liquid onto the runway in front of the sledge—no doubt to ease the workmen's burden.

But does this method really work? Can it haul stone up ramps hundreds of feet long? Maybe the Egyptian tomb painters just made it up.

More than a decade ago, experimental archaeology answered this question. Archaeologist Mark Lehner (Oriental Institute of the University of Chicago and Harvard Semetic Museum) and stonemason Roger Hopkins staged an experiment to see whether they could really move large blocks of stone in this manner. Working with Egyptian quarrymen and masons, they built a pyramid 20 feet high using ancient Egyptian technology. A TV crew from the series *NOVA* filmed the experiment, and so they had to complete the pyramid on a tight schedule—3 weeks.

Lehner experimented with several possible techniques to move and lift stone. One entailed the method depicted in Djehutihotep's tomb, but with the loaded sledge resting on wooden rollers. As the sledge was pulled, the workmen would pick up the rollers behind the sledge and move them to the front. Although this idea seemed sound, Lehner's experiment showed that, if the rollers were not placed perfectly, the sledge would veer off course. The same error happened if the rollers were not perfectly lathed. Lehner concluded that moving large stones over long distances with this method might have been more trouble than it was worth.

Another idea was that wooden levers helped to lift the stones up high. In this method, one side of the block is levered up, and planks are placed beneath it. Then the block's opposite side is levered up, and planks are placed below that side. The workers then repeated the process until they raised the stone to the desired height. This idea worked for small rises but, as the block rose higher, levering became difficult and the stone's balance became precarious.

Lehner then turned to ramps. Archaeologists have found remnants of ramps at several Egyptian sites, including the stone quarry beside the Giza Plateau. These ramps consist of two parallel retaining walls, the area between them filled with rubble and topped with a coat of sand or crushed gypsum. In this top layer, the Egyptians set planed logs, perpendicular to the retaining wall, about 50 centimeters apart.

Egyptologists speculate on the kinds of ramps used by the ancient Egyptians. Some suggest a straight ramp—although, by the time the pyramid reached its peak, the ramp would have been hundreds of meters long. Other suggestions include ramps that formed a spiral up the sides of the pyramid or multiple ramps built at different levels during construction.

Lehner built his ramp with an incline of about 7 percent. He found that a 2-ton stone resting on a sledge could easily be hauled up by 20 men. Once the stone was on top of the pyramid, 4 or 5 men using levers could roll it. With this method, Lehner built his pyramid within the 3 weeks allotted for the task.

As in the Folsom fluting experiments, researchers found many ways to build a ramp, and perhaps the Egyptians used all of them. But the precise technique does not matter in this case. The principles involved in simple machines like levers and wedges have not changed from the days of the pharaohs; their capabilities today are the same as they were in the past. This is the important element of uniformitarianism that allows Lehner's experiments to test von Däniken's outlandish hypothesis. With no more than dirt ramps, wooden sledges, rope, and plenty of strong backs, the ancient Egyptians were well equipped to move the stones necessary to build their pyramids and temples. Aliens from outer space were not required.

What Were Stone Tools Used For?

In some cases, experimental archaeology can do more than show us what might or might not have been possible. Experiments can also help establish the unambiguous signatures of past human activities and contribute to archaeology's bridging arguments. Returning to stone tools, one promising direction of experimental study is determining the function of prehistoric stone implements.

As stone tools are used, the edges become damaged and dulled. Compare the edges of used and unused stone tools under a microscope, and you will see **microwear** consisting of minute striations, polish, pitting, and/or microflaking—all of which can reveal something about how the tool was used and what it was used on.

Given that few people use stone tools in their daily lives today, we must turn to experimental research. Microwear research was begun by the late Russian archaeologist Sergei Semenov, whose major work, *Prehistoric Technology*, was published in the Soviet Union in 1957. Many archaeologists followed his lead and have conducted hundreds of experiments to find out what kinds of microwear result from a specific use. Some of the variables include the type of motion (cutting, scraping, boring), the length of time a tool is used, the material being worked (for example, meat, antler, bone, wood, hide), and the stone tool's raw material (chert, basalt, obsidian, and so on).

Ruth Tringham (University of California, Berkeley) studied with Semenov and was one of the first to follow up his research. She reproduced tools from British flint and used each in different ways on antler, bone, wood, skin, flesh, and plant fiber, carefully maintaining constant direction of force and counting the number of strokes. Some of the tools were hand-held, others were hafted to handles.

Tringham then examined and photographed the experimental tools under a low-power (40X to 60X) stereoscopic microscope. Tringham concentrated on the microflaking that occurs as stone tools are used and found that different kinds of use produce different kinds of microflakes on different parts of the tools. Cutting, for instance, produced a series of tiny uneven flake scars along both sides of the working edge. Scraping, however, produced flake scars only on the surface opposite that in direct contact with the worked material. Boring produced distinct trapezoidal flake scars, especially on the sides of the tool.

In addition, Tringham found that edge damage varied with the type of materials being worked. Soft materials such as skin and flesh produced only scalar-shaped scars, whereas hard materials such as antler and bone slowly crushed the edges, eventually dulling the tool so that it would no longer cut at all.

Tringham's experiments established the value of functional analysis with low-power microscopy, and numerous investigators have followed her, taking advantage of the relatively inexpensive equipment and rapid rate of analysis.

Lawrence Keeley (University of Illinois) pioneered an alternative approach. He used high-powered microscopy (up to 400X) and focused on micropolishes rather than microflaking. He found that different worked materials produce different kinds of polish. Some polishes were pitted, some were not; some were extensive, others were present only on the high points of a tool's microtopography (Figure 10-9). Keeley's approach is now the most commonly used one in the analysis of stone tool wear patterns.

But M. H. Newcomer (University of London) was skeptical of Keeley's ability to determine tool use from microwear analysis, and so Keeley agreed to a series of blind experiments to test his method's accuracy. Newcomer manufactured 15 tools of fine-grained black English flint. He then worked on a series of materials, such as pine wood, ox hide, and lamb meat, and replicated a range of simple activities, such as scraping, slicing, and boring.

Newcomer then turned the artifacts over to Keeley. The implements were cleaned using detergent, warm water, some chemicals, and an ultrasonic cleaning tank

microwear Minute, often microscopic evidence of use damage on the surface and working edge of a flake or artifact; it can include striations, pitting, microflaking, and polish.

THIS IS NOT USED

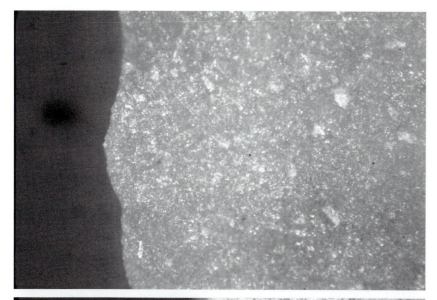

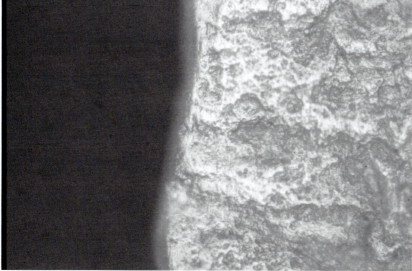

Figure 10-9 Comparison of tool use wear polishes. On the top is a photo taken of a tool's edge before use; on the bottom, the same tool edge after using it to scrape the inside of a hide (both photos taken at 200X).

identified the business end of the tool. Keeley contends that the only mistake should not be held against him. He admits to "simple human error" in the case of Tool 10: There is no doubt in Keeley's mind that, had he looked at the right area of the implement's edge, he would have made the correct interpretation of its function. And Tool 5, used to scrape pig hide for 31 minutes, had no apparent wear, as fat will not damage flint.

Keeley's success fell off slightly when he reconstructed tool use (12 of 16 correct), but it is still not bad. His accuracy fell more when identifying the material being worked (10 of 16 correct), but look at some of the "misses": In conducting his butchering experiments, Newcomer had used a wooden cutting board, and Keeley felt that the wood and meat polishes confounded the interpretation of Tool 12. Similarly, Keeley misread the polish on Tool 7 as bone polish and that on Tool 11 as antler polish. But as it turned out, Newcomer had used extremely well-seasoned wood in both cases, at least 10 years old. Such hard wood would mimic the effects of antler.

All in all, these results are not bad, and they established the validity of Keeley's high-power microwear method, which has become an important method in the analysis of ancient stone tools.

Others have followed Keeley's example and conducted more experiments to refine his method. For example, experimental research shows that tools used for only a few minutes do not develop distinctive microwear (this may be why Keeley got the material worked by Tool 15 wrong—11 minutes was not enough time to develop the polish distinctive of bone). So, only

(this is now fairly standard in microwear studies because it removes even fingerprints and organic deposits from tool surfaces). Keeley then used his high-power method to study each piece, looking at (1) general tool size and shape, (2) type and placement of damage, (3) distribution and orientation of microscopic scratches, and (4) location and extent of polish.

How well did Keeley's method do? Table 10-1 shows some remarkable results. In 14 of 16 interpretations (because the right and left edges of Tool 14 seemed different, they were scored independently), he correctly

TABLE 10-1 Results of Blind Testing in High-Power Microwear Analysis

TOOL NUMBER	USE BY NEWCOMER	INTERPRETATION BY KEELEY	CORRECT INTERPRETATIONS		
			Area used	Activity	Material worked
1	Whittling seasoned ash sapling (2 cm dia.) for 18 min.	Cutting (slicing, rather than whittling) wood (branch less than 4 cm dia.)	C		C
2	Chopping ash sapling (3 cm) on pine cutting board for 21 min.	Chopping wood	C	C	C
3	Sawing ash sapling (2.5) cm for 12 min.	Sawing, possibly wood	C	C	C
4	Cutting raw lamb meat on cutting board for 44 min.	Cutting unknown material, possibly vegetable matter or meat	C	C	½C
5	Scraping fat from raw pig hide for 31 min.	Unused			
6	Whittling seasoned pine for 14 min.	(1) Whittling wood (2) graving wood or bone (secondary use)	C	C	C
7	Drilling seasoned pine for 14 min.	Graving, planing, and scraping bone	C		
8	Cutting raw lamb meat on cutting board for 28 min.	Cutting meat	C	C	C
9	Unused	Unused	C	C	C
10	Cutting ox hide on cutting board for 23 min.	Cutting meat (guess)—wrong area of edge thought to have been used (counts as wrong interpretation)			
11	Scraping ash sapling (1.5 cm) for 13 min.	Scraping antler (or possibly wood)	C	C	½C
12	Cutting frozen lamb meat on cutting board for 23 min.	Cutting or sawing wood	C	C	
13	Cutting bracken fern for 26 min.	Slicing unknown material, but probably vegetable matter	C	C	C
14a	Right edge used to skin off rabbit then cut skin into strips	Cutting meat	C	C	C
14b	Left edge used to cut forefeet off rabbit at joint	Cutting meat, cartilage, bone (i.e., breaking joint)	C	C	C
15	Scraping ox bone for 11 min.	Scraping possibly hide, less likely antler	C	C	

SOURCE: From Newcomer and Keeley 1979, table 1. Reprinted by permission of Elsevier.

microwear on heavily used tools can be fruitfully studied. Others have found that some microwears are difficult to distinguish, such as those produced by working hard wood versus bone (as Keeley found). And different kinds of stone—chert, quartzite, and so on—produce different kinds of polishes. In addition, archaeological objects may have seen multiple uses, with the latest form of wear masking an earlier form. Ancient peoples also resharpened stone tools when they became dull—an act that removes the microwear-bearing edges. Thus, only the tool's last use is available for the analyst. Tools were also dropped, trampled, and affected by geological processes—all of which can mask microwear traces. Because archaeological tools almost certainly go through more confusing life histories than Newcomer's experimental tools, Keeley's success rate is probably the best that the archaeologist should expect.

This experimental research is important, but it is still not quite middle-range theory because it does not tell us *why* microchipping and polish develop in the ways that they do. For example, what is it about chert that results in one type of polish when working meat and another when working antler? The answer to this question would allow archaeologists to implement the principle of uniformitarianism and assume that processes observed in the present can be expected to be true of the past as well. Fortunately, some researchers, such as mechanical engineer Brian Cotterell (University of Sydney) and archaeologist Johan Kamminga (Australian National University), have investigated the micromechanics of stone tool wear. As research of this kind develops, experimental studies of use-wear will have an even more secure footing and play an even more important role in archaeological inference.

Taphonomy is good for understanding the role that natural processes play in creating patterns in data at archaeological sites. And experimental archaeology is useful for establishing how things might have been made in the past or for discovering "mechanical" relationships between behavior and material remains, such as tool use and microwear. But how do we develop middle-range theory to study larger behavioral patterns of human behavior?

ETHNOARCHAEOLOGY

What if we wanted to know about ancient kinship, social, or political organizations that no longer exist? These questions were the sort that archaeology in the 1960s sought to answer, and they required the sorts of behavioral inferences that Walter Taylor and Lewis Binford sought.

Binford Takes Off for Points North

In the 1960s, the ways to infer social behavior from archaeological remains were little more than simple rules of thumb that were often culturally biased. Archaeologists began to test them through ethnoarchaeology, with the understanding that if generalizations cannot cover *contemporary* behavior, then they cannot be used to interpret the evidence of *ancient* behavior.

Binford was concerned with this inferential problem and, to help solve it, he conducted significant ethnoarchaeological research in the 1970s among the Nunamiut Eskimo of Alaska. Binford's real interest lay in the Middle Paleolithic archaeology of Europe, especially France (see "In His Own Words: Why I Began Doing Ethnoarchaeology" by Lewis R. Binford). Why would he study living Eskimos in Alaska if he were interested in the Middle Paleolithic archaeology of France?

Recall from Chapter 9 (see "The Frison Effect" on page 216) that the French archaeologist François Bordes argued that different stone tool Mousterian assemblages were a product of different Neanderthal cultures. These assemblages often alternated throughout the strata of some key French sites, and Bordes argued that this meant that the caves were used alternately by different "tribes" of Neanderthals.

Binford saw things differently. He suspected that the different assemblages were the by-products of different activities, not different tribes. He argued that Bordes's inference (different tool assemblages = different Neanderthal tribes) needed to be evaluated. But we cannot evaluate an inferential argument using archaeological data, because the systemic context (the behavior) cannot be observed independently of the archaeological data. Binford had to find a place where he could observe living hunting peoples and see what remains their activities left behind. The Nunamiut's Arctic environment was somewhat analogous to the French Middle Paleolithic environment, and the Nunamiut hunted large game (caribou and sheep), as had the Neanderthals. But Binford was not as interested in animal bones or the Nunamiut as he was in evaluating the concepts that archaeologists of the time employed to understand the past.

Binford accompanied Nunamiut hunters on their hunting trips, recording what they did at each locality and what debris was left behind. In so doing, he demonstrated that the same people—the same individuals, in fact—leave different kinds of tools and bones at different locations on a landscape. What Nunamiut hunters left behind was not just a product of their culture, but also of the season of the year, the distance back to camp, the availability of transportation, the amount of food already in camp, the weather, and other factors. Although culture plays a significant role in determining what kinds of artifacts are left behind, Binford demonstrated that archaeologists couldn't uncritically *assume* that a difference in artifacts reflects *only* a difference in culture. Other hypotheses, such as site function, have to be tested and discarded before inferring that different tool assemblages in a site's strata indicate use of the site by different cultures.

Ethnoarchaeology has frequently provided such cautionary tales. But ethnoarchaeology can also be a powerful tool for creating middle-range theory. It can do so (1) if it focuses on aspects of ethnographic data that are archaeologically observable, and (2) if it attempts to

In His Own Words
Why I Began Doing Ethnoarchaeology

by Lewis R. Binford

In 1967 I received funds to go to Europe for a year to work more closely with François Bordes in Bordeaux. My program for research was the following. If we could not study the chipped stone directly, perhaps we could study faunal remains and the horizontal distributions, on excavated archaeological floors, of both fauna and chipped stone. Then it might be possible to relate variability in the lithics to these other properties of the archaeological sites in question. I worked for a year in France, identifying and plotting all the stone tools and animal bones by anatomical part and by breakage pattern.

Thus began a series of disillusionments. I performed one correlation study after another—so many, in fact, that I needed a great steel trunk in order to carry all the papers back to the United States. I could tell you cross-correlations between any pair of Mousterian tool-types, between tools and bones, between bones and the drip-lines in cave sites, between almost any type of data you care to name. What I found, of course, was many new facts that nobody had seen before. But none of these new facts spoke for themselves.

My metal trunk was so big and heavy that I decided to return home by boat and that 5-day trip from Le Havre to New York gave me an opportunity for some disconsolate self-reflection. The whole project was obviously a total failure. What had I done wrong? What had I not done that I should have done? Could it really be that archaeologists simply cannot learn anything about the past? Where was I missing the real problem?

By the time we steamed into New York City, just before the New Year of 1969, some of the answers to these problems were suggested, at least in my thoughts. I prepared a research proposal to go to the Arctic in the spring of 1969 to live with a group of Eskimo hunters. My reasons for going there were little more specific at that stage than that it could hardly fail to be a good educational experience. If I was ever to be able to make accurate inferences from archaeological facts, I was convinced that I had to understand the dynamics of living systems and study their static consequences.

explain why a relationship between behavior and archaeologically observable remains should necessarily hold true. As we will see, however, the principle of uniformitarianism is harder to implement in ethnoarchaeology than in taphonomy or experimental archaeology.

Ethnoarchaeologists have researched pottery and stone tool production, hunting and butchering, plant gathering, architecture, trash disposal, trade, and burial rituals in many kinds of societies all over the world. All these studies help archaeologists create better ways of inferring human behavior from archaeological remains. Here we describe one such project conducted by Kelly in Madagascar.

Ethnoarchaeology in Madagascar

Kelly was trained as an archaeologist, with interests in the archaeology of western North America. He was particularly interested in how nomadism factored into peoples' lives. In some cultures, especially hunting-and-gathering societies, people are highly nomadic, moving as often as every week. In others, especially part-time farming cultures, people change their residence less frequently, perhaps only once or twice a year. Some people return seasonally to a settlement for several years in a row, and some stay year-round in sedentary villages.

Kelly was concerned with archaeology's ability to discern different levels of nomadism archaeologically, and

Figure 10-10 Mikea habitations. Clockwise from upper left: A family sits around a hearth outside a lean-to in a temporary forest camp; a wattle-and-daub house in a permanent village (note the lack of trash); a house with shade structure in a forest hamlet; and a set of houses lacking shade structures in a seasonal hamlet.

so he looked for an ethnographic situation where he could see variation in nomadism and study its material consequences. He finally learned of the Mikea, a little-known society in the forest of southwestern Madagascar who grow maize and manioc, raise cattle, and do some hunting and gathering.

If you know anything about Madagascar, it probably has to do with lemurs leaping through a tropical forest, but such forests actually make up only a small part of Madagascar. The southwest part of the island, where the Mikea live, is drier and more open. It has distinct wet and dry seasons, and the wet season is blisteringly hot. The forest contains dense vine-covered thickets, stands of 5-meter-high cacti, and baobab trees. There are no rivers in the Mikea Forest and only a few wells. Bordering the forest on one side is the Mozambique Channel and on the other, a vast savanna.

Mikea live in four major kinds of settlements that differ in how long they are occupied (Figure 10-10). Many have houses in large, permanent villages of 1000 people or more located on the edge of the forest. Here they grow manioc and other crops and raise cattle, pigs, and chickens. These villages frequently host weekly markets that people attend from many miles around.

Some Mikea live most of the year in forest hamlets, in kin-related groups of about 40 people. Most people who live in these hamlets also maintain a house in the larger villages. Around these forest hamlets are **slash-and-burn** maize fields. As the arable land around the settlement becomes exhausted, the hamlet is moved, about every 3 to 10 years.

Some Mikea who live in the villages also occupy seasonal hamlets in the forest during the growing season so that they can tend to their maize fields. These are much like forest hamlets, but they differ in that they are mostly occupied for a much shorter period of time—during the growing season.

Finally, Mikea in the forest hamlets and some who live in the villages, move away from their homes and into the forest during the dry season. These foraging camps are smaller and are occupied for up to 2 weeks. While in these camps, people collect tubers and honey and search tree hollows for estivating hedgehogs.

Kelly focused on the question "Are the different lengths of stay reflected in the material remains left behind at these sites?"

Mikea Settlements from an Archaeological Perspective

Recall that ethnoarchaeology's first objective is to relate behavior to archaeologically observable phenomena. Over time, the only thing that might remain of the Mikea settlements are features, such as postholes, hearths, and pits, as well as scattered trash, such as burnt maize, bone fragments, and broken tools.

Accordingly, Kelly and his associates collected data on houses, features, and the distribution of trash in

slash-and-burn A horticultural method used frequently in the tropics wherein a section of forest is cut, dried, and then burned, thus returning nutrients to the ground. This permits a plot of land to be farmed for a limited number of years.

Looking Closer
Doing Ethnoarchaeology in Madagascar (by Robert Kelly)

I conducted ethnographic work in Madagascar with my wife, Lin Poyer, a cultural anthropologist. On our first trip we flew to Washington, DC, then to Paris, Cairo, Nairobi, and finally to the capital of Madagascar, Antananarivo. The entire trip took nearly 48 hours. Once in the capital, we introduced ourselves to the necessary officials and ensured that our permits were in order. We then flew to the provincial capital of Toliara, where we met our Malagasy colleagues, Jean-François Rabedimy and Jaovola Tombo.

You do archaeology with a trowel and ethnography with a pencil and notebook, but that is just the beginning of the differences between the two. Because Madagascar was a French colony, all educated people speak French, and few speak English. And the Mikea spoke only their dialect of Malagasy. So for weeks, our daily language was a mixture of French, Malagasy (as we learned the dialect), and English.

There's also no schedule—an ethnographer is always "on the job." One time we arranged to leave for another village "early in the morning." Our guide arrived at 3 AM, and so we got up, packed, and left. Another time, the men in the village, armed with spears, went off to catch cattle rustlers—at midnight. So, we stayed up all night to learn the result.

We spent several weeks, on and off, in the bush, living in Mikea hamlets and foraging camps. We were there in the dry season, and so we either walked many kilometers to the nearest well or we did what the Mikea do: dig up *babo* (a wonderful water-engorged tuber) and eat it. Meals were tubers, white rice with a dollop of peanut butter, and the occasional scrawny chicken or dried fish.

The Mikea asked us for virtually everything that we owned, especially clothing (which is hard for them to come by). We avoided such dunning by carrying no spare clothing. We freely handed out tobacco, however (a standard gift among the Mikea); occasionally we gave gifts of food, money, and clothing; and, when possible, provided medical assistance.

The Mikea were both curious and suspicious about why we were there. They couldn't believe that foreigners would come such a long way just to measure house posts, draw maps, and weigh tubers. They were remarkably patient with us.

An ethnographer tries to immerse him- or herself in another culture and to participate in it as much as possible. We witnessed trance dances, spirit possession ceremonies, and a sheep sacrifice. Like the Mikea, we traveled on foot or by oxcart, often in the cool of the night. We dug tubers, hunted hedgehogs, ate honey from a hive while bees buzzed about, and slept on the ground around a fire.

But I found that the largest difference between archaeology and ethnography is that, although you return from an archaeological excavation pretty much the same person you were when you left, that is never the case with ethnography. It's an extreme growth experience; you learn as much about your limits and prejudices as you do about another culture. It's also a special growth experience for an archaeologist, because you quickly learn the difficulty of interpreting human behavior from static material remains.

some 30 settlements; for some they recorded data over a 3-year period (see "Looking Closer: Doing Ethnoarchaeology in Madagascar"). They also counted the number of posts in houses and measured their diameters—an activity that amused their Mikea hosts (and once sparked an accusation of witchcraft). They mapped the settlements, showing the locations of houses and features, as well as the placement of trash deposits. Through interviews, Mikea told the history of each settlement, how they were used, why they were abandoned, as well as other information. What did Kelly find out?

Trash Disposal

Ethnoarchaeologists often begin by observing what people do with their trash. In foraging camps, people unceremoniously toss ash from fires and other trash into bushes, only 1 to 2 meters away from the family hearth. In the forest and seasonal hamlets, trash is disposed in an arc some 3 to 9 meters in front of the house door. Unlike the foraging camps, hamlets were periodically swept clean. This meant that larger items would end up in the trash arc, whereas smaller pieces missed by the broom were trampled into the sand.

And as people occupied their hamlets for longer periods of time, they deposit their trash farther away from their house's door. For example, Kelly visited one settlement the year it was established and found that trash was deposited some 3 to 4 meters from the house. A year later, trash was deposited some 8 meters away. Why? Early in a settlement's life, bushes grow near the house, and they are a convenient place to toss trash. Eventually, however, the bushes are destroyed (for firewood, by children playing, and by goats and cattle foraging). As bushes disappear, trash is swept into bushes farther from the house. In hamlets occupied for several years, in fact, periodic cleanings create a second trash deposit, this time as a ring around the entire settlement.

The permanent villages exhibit a major change in the disposal of trash. Here one cannot simply sweep trash to the side of one's household, because this would mean sweeping trash into a neighbor's space. Consequently, people throw trash into pits next to the houses (the pits were excavated to make mud for the wattle-and-daub house) or they collect trash in baskets inside the houses and periodically dump it at the edge of the settlement, as much as 30 or 40 meters away.

By the way, this doesn't imply that Mikea settlements are filthy or reeking of rotting garbage. Much of the trash, in fact, is maize husks and other dry plant material. Any wet garbage—including almost all bones—is eaten by ever-hungry dogs and pigs.

House Posts

After trash, the next thing an ethnoarchaeologist might notice are houses. Other ethnoarchaeological studies have found, not surprisingly, that people invest more labor and care in houses that they expect to inhabit for a long time, and the Mikea were no different. But how is that investment reflected archaeologically?

In the villages, Mikea often build wattle-and-daub houses about 10 square meters in size. They first set posts upright in the ground, 75 centimeters deep (the length of an adult's arm), and then weave smaller saplings horizontally between these posts. They pack this lattice with coarse mud, smoothing the surface. The house has a door made of planks, usually with a lock, and one or two windows, with wooden shutters. The floors are packed clay. Most of these houses have thatch roofs that extend beyond the walls, forming a narrow veranda around the house. A wattle-and-daub house takes a month or more to build but, if the owner maintains the roof, the house will last 25 years or more.

In the forest hamlets, Mikea have more modest homes. About half the size of village houses, they are made of thinner posts not so deeply set and have roofs of baobab bark slabs and walls of bark, grass, or reeds. A cold wind blows nightly in the dry season, so the door is on the north wall, and the south wall is woven tightly. There is a hearth just inside and to one side of the door. Two to three meters outside the door is another hearth, covered by a shade structure, the top of which serves to store dried corn and tools. These forest hamlet houses can be built in a week and need repair every year or so. Some are used for only a year.

The houses in seasonal hamlets look similar to those in forest hamlets, but they appear to a westerner's eye to be shabbier. They are often shorter and have fewer shade structures outside the front door.

Because foraging camps are used in the dry season and it rarely rains at that time of the year, houses are rare in foraging camps; when they are present, they are no more than lean-tos or simple box-like structures, fashioned from whatever wood is handy and built in an hour or two.

As you might expect, the longer people intend to live in a house, the more time they invest in it. Foraging camps are the most transient of the four settlement types and contain the most ephemeral of shelters (when present at all—some families simply sleep by the fire), whereas the permanent villages contain the largest houses with the most substantial walls and roofs.

The amount of labor involved in each of these houses is reflected in a house's roof and walls, but these things disappear. However, the amount of labor is also reflected in the postholes. And these features are familiar to most archaeologists, because they are often all that remain of ancient houses. What can they tell us?

Plenty, and all of it is pretty commonsense. Although some of the wattle-and-daub houses are large, many of the reed or grass houses are about the same size. Nonetheless, the long wall of village houses contained *twice* as many posts as did the same wall in houses in seasonal hamlets; houses in forest hamlets fell between these two. In addition, the posts used in seasonal hamlets (those settlements used the least amount of time) had more variable diameters than the posts used in the more permanent settlements—especially the wattle-and-daub houses. In seasonal hamlets, people used whatever wood was handy, often scavenging poles from abandoned houses. Post diameters as well as consistency in post diameters reflect the fact that people are more selective about the wood they use when building houses that are more permanent.

Features Outside Houses

Recall from Chapter 3 that features are artifacts that can't be removed from a site—things like hearths, houses, pits, and postholes. In Mikea settlements, these outdoor features include different kinds of houses, fenced compounds, animal corrals, wash areas, cook houses, public troughs, drying racks, stores, wells, ceremonial enclosures, maize threshers, bellows, and storage bins and racks. The particular kinds of features found in a settlement are linked to the particular kinds of activities that take place in Mikea settlements and are not so useful to the development of universal middle-range theory. But differences in the range of diversity of features among the different settlement types are useful.

The more permanent a Mikea settlement is, the greater the range of features it contains. When people intend to stay in one place for years or plan to return to a settlement seasonally for several years, they invest more time in features that have a single purpose, rather than "making do" with temporary facilities. Washhouses, for example, are never found in foraging camps or seasonal hamlets: People are basically "camping" at both, and water is a rare commodity in dry season forest camps. People bathe back at the forest hamlet or village. Washhouses are also rarely found in forest hamlets—where the small, related community means that people can expect privacy without bothering to build a separate facility. However, washhouses are common in the densely populated villages, where privacy is more difficult, and where investment in a facility is worthwhile.

Table 10-2 summarizes these differences among Mikea settlements. In this table we related some archaeologically recoverable variables (trash distribution, postholes, features) to human behavior (the length of occupation). Simply by recording the way trash is distributed, the range of features present, the number of postholes per house, and the variation in posthole diameter, we could place a new settlement into one of the four categories with a high degree of accuracy. This fulfills the first criterion of a middle-range study—it focuses on aspects of ethnographic data that are archaeologically observable. But does it explain why the relationship between behavior and archaeologically observable remains is necessarily true? What do such ethnoarchaeological studies do for archaeology?

Ethnoarchaeology and Uniformitarianism

As we have pointed out, middle-range theory tries to *explain* patterning between behavior and material remains. Such explanations depend on the principle of uniformitarianism. It is relatively easy to see how this

TABLE 10-2 Summary of Differences in Mikea Settlements

SETTLEMENT TYPE	HOUSE SIZE	POST VARIABILITY	SECONDARY POSTS	DISTANCE TO TRASH (meters)	FEATURE DIVERSITY
Villages	Various, but can be large	Low	Many, closely spaced	10–40+	High
Forest hamlets	Small	Low–Medium	Fewer, farther apart	4–9	Medium
Seasonal hamlets	Small	High	Fewer, farther apart	3–4	Medium–Low
Foraging camps	Lean-tos or "boxes," if present at all	n/a	n/a	1–2	Low

n/a = not applicable

principle applies in both taphonomy and experimental archaeology, because both study natural processes and mechanical relationships.

But the principle of uniformitarianism is tougher to apply in ethnoarchaeology, because human behavior is anything but mechanical. We conducted our study of the Mikea within the materialist paradigm (explained in Chapter 3); more specifically, it relied upon a theoretical framework known as human behavioral ecology. One of the tenets of this framework is that, because people have many demands on their time, they make choices that maximize the utility of their decisions. Choices about what kind of house to build reflect this fact. Why would someone in a forest hamlet invest more than a month in building a wattle-and-daub house when one built in less than a week will suffice for the time that the hamlet will be occupied? The "extra" 3 weeks can then be put toward clearing another maize field, building a ceremonial enclosure, or some other task more important than house-building. Similarly, why take time to select just the right poles for a house in a seasonal hamlet that will be occupied for only a few months of the year? From a materialist perspective, the time would be better spent in clearing more fields, planting, weeding, or preparing for a celebration. In fact, the Mikea themselves said that the longer they intended to remain in a settlement, the more care they put into constructing houses and facilities such as maize-threshing bins and outhouses. They also said they would be more selective in their building material, choosing poles of a particular diameter for posts and even searching out certain species of wood, such as ones known for their ability to resist destruction by insects.

These seem like logical choices, and several ethnoarchaeological studies have found similar patterns in trash disposal, house form, and feature diversity in other societies in the world. Combined with these other studies, the Mikea research helps form a strong formal analogy; combined with the theoretical framework of human behavior ecology, it also contains elements that make it middle-range theory.

What about Culture?

But the issue of culture can make ethnographic analogies, even ones strong enough to qualify as middle-range theory, problematic. We have discussed, for instance, the disposal of trash among the Mikea as being simply a function of how long a settlement is occupied. The longer it is occupied, the farther away

from a house trash is removed. But cultural ideas about trash may come into play.

Ian Hodder, a postprocessual archaeologist, conducted ethnoarchaeological research with the Moro and Mesakin in Sudan. Both groups raise various grains, as well as pigs, cattle, and goats. In both, families live in household compounds. But the Moro's compounds are relatively free of trash, whereas the Mesakin's are messier; in particular, the Moro keep pig bones out of the compounds.

Hodder argues that some of the difference between the two societies and the way they deal with trash lies in different ideas about women. Moro men see contact with women as potentially "polluting" their strength and authority. And, because Moro women take care of pigs, they are associated with these animals; men are associated with cattle. As a result, Moro men consider pig remains to be foul, and Moro women take care to remove pig bones from the trash and dispose of them separately. The Mesakin do not share the Moro's beliefs about women, and they treat pig bones the same as any other animal remains. Thus, Hodder argues that archaeologists need to consider the symbolic meanings of material culture in order to appreciate how it will be treated as trash.

But the "cultural" component is very difficult to study archaeologically. And this means that the principle of uniformitarianism will remain difficult to implement in ethnoarchaeology. For some archaeologists, this means that ethnoarchaeology can provide us only with strong analogies, not middle-range theory.

For others, ethnoarchaeological studies conducted across a spectrum of societies provide archaeology with analogies that, taken together, suggest some important principles of human behavior. These principles could *provisionally* be taken as uniform for the purpose of creating and testing hypotheses and allow ethnoarchaeology to act as middle-range theory to support archaeological inferences. Let's see how this might work.

Settlement Pattern Change in the Mimbres Valley

Specifics aside, the Mikea case suggests that more labor is invested in more-permanent rather than in more-transient houses. This could be reflected archaeologically in the use of more substantial building materials (such as wattle-and-daub or stone masonry rather than poles and grass), a larger number of posts, and more standardized posts. This information can be used to make archaeological interpretations.

Margaret Nelson and Michelle Hegmon (Arizona

State University) have surveyed and excavated in the eastern Mimbres region of southern New Mexico for a number of years. (This is the region where we find the Mimbres pottery that we mentioned in Chapter 8.) The Mimbres region is far removed from Madagascar, but exhibits some similarities: Both regions are arid, and both are or were occupied by maize horticulturalists.

Nelson and Hegmon's survey found sites that contained two components, one dated to the Classic Mimbres Phase (AD 1000–1150), and the other to the Post Classic Phase (AD 1150–1300).

Nelson and Hegmon were interested in understanding the abandonment of regions. Although many archaeologists previously argued that people abandoned the Mimbres region after AD 1150, Nelson and Hegmon believed that the region was still occupied but that the settlement pattern had changed in such a way that it gave the region the *appearance* of having been abandoned.

Nelson and Hegmon found that during the Classic Mimbres Phase, people lived in large, pueblo villages. The houses were built of stone masonry, with roofs of heavy beams (Figure 10-11). Radiocarbon and tree-ring dating indicated that many of these villages were, indeed, no longer occupied after AD 1150.

But another kind of settlement was also in use during the Classic Mimbres Phase. Although people lived in large pueblo villages, they also used what Nelson and Hegmon term "farmsteads." These were small sites, consisting of only one or a few structures, usually open on one side and lightly constructed of a few, small posts, with few interior features. Nelson and Hegmon argue that a few members of the family occupied these sites during the growing season to care for the young maize plants. Located some distance from the villages, the field houses contained only minimal shelter requirements.

Nelson and Hegmon's careful excavation and extensive dating showed that, on some of these sites, someone modified the flimsy Classic Phase structures in farmsteads during the following Post Classic Phase. Added to the lightly constructed buildings were larger and more numerous posts, masonry walls, and more substantial roofs. Eventually, they formed small pueblos of some 6 to 12 rooms. Inside these small pueblo structures was also a greater diversity of features than was found in the Classic Phase field houses. From these data, Nelson and Hegmon argue that the Mimbres region had not been abandoned. Instead, during the Post Classic phase, people moved out of the large pueblos into smaller, dispersed communities and turned their field houses into permanent residences.

Nelson and Hegmon's Classic Phase field houses are analogous to Mikea seasonal hamlets, and their Post Classic Phase modifications are analogous to Mikea village house construction. Taken by itself, the Mikea case is only analogy—and a weak one at that, given that no cultural link exists between the Mikea and the prehistoric peoples of the American Southwest.

However, the Mikea study does highlight some necessary links between house size and construction elements—for example, large houses require larger support posts. Coupled with other ethnoarchaeological studies that reach similar conclusions, the Mikea data help form a strong formal analogy with elements of middle-range theory that provide a solid warrant for treating Nelson and Hegmon's interpretation as a viable hypothesis for further testing.

In this way, ethnoarchaeology will continue to play an important role in future archaeological inference.

Figure 10-11 Margaret Nelson (right) standing inside a Mimbres pueblo room; some postholes are visible on the floor.

CONCLUSION

Archaeology is all about making inferences from artifacts, ecofacts, features, and their contexts. Middle-range theory is what allows archaeologists to know that they really do know something about the past. It lies at the heart of archaeology, because archaeology is the study of the past based on material remains. As you have seen in this chapter, archaeologists go about constructing all-important middle-range theory through taphonomy, experimental archaeology, and ethnoarchaeology. It requires that archaeologists step out of their excavation trenches and conduct a different kind of research. Some archaeologists, in fact, have permanently hung up their trowels and devoted their careers to the development of middle-range theory. And this is good, because without middle-range theory, our inferences from archaeology would be little more than just-so stories, with no more credence behind them than silly ideas like aliens building pyramids. In the following chapters, we will see how archaeologists have put studies in taphonomy, experimental archaeology, and ethnoarchaeology to use in reconstructing the past.

Summary

- Because the "facts" of archaeology are incapable of speaking for themselves, archaeologists must follow geology's principle of uniformitarianism and study ongoing processes and their material remains.

- Analogy is one way to reconstruct the past but is limited in its utility to societies that have very close geographic and cultural counterparts (preferably ones with a historical connection) or to fairly low-level inferences.

- Middle-range research allows archaeologists to make better inferences from archaeological data by clarifying the basis for the inference; it is research designed to create bridging arguments that link human behavior and/or natural processes to their material remains.

- The principle of uniformitarianism is critical in the development of middle-range theory because it is what allows confidence in a middle-range theory's ability to infer human behavior or natural processes from archaeological remains.

- Analogies can be formal, relational, or a mixture of both. Formal analogies rely on similarities in form, and relational analogies rely on cultural continuity or causal linkages to justify their use in archaeological inference.

- Middle-range theory is a particular kind of analogy in that it attempts to demonstrate *why* a particular pattern in archaeological data can be unambiguously interpreted in a particular way.

- Taphonomy studies how natural processes help create the archaeological record; it helps weed out patterns that result from natural processes and thus helps define patterns that need to be interpreted in human behavioral terms. It also helps the archaeologist understand the environmental context of past human behavior.

- Experimental archaeology studies things that can no longer be observed in action today, such as ancient technologies that are no longer practiced.

- Replicative experiments are one class of experimental archaeology. They can help show what techniques could or could not have been used in the past.

- Experimental archaeology, such as stone tool use-wear studies, can also link human behavior and material signatures.

- Ethnoarchaeologists study living societies, observing artifacts, features, and material remains while they still exist in their systemic, behavioral contexts. Ethnoarchaeology links human behavior with archaeologically observable material remains.

- Of the three ways to develop middle-range theory, the principle of uniformitarianism is most difficult to implement in ethnoarchaeology.

Additional Reading

Andrefsky, William. 1998. *Lithics: Macroscopic Approaches to Analysis*. Cambridge: Cambridge University Press.

Binford, Lewis R. 1978. *Nunamiut Ethnoarchaeology*. New York: Academic Press.

David, Nicholas, and Carol Kramer. 2001. *Ethnoarchaeology in Action*. Cambridge: Cambridge University Press.

Longacre, William A., and James M. Skibo (Eds.). 1994. *Kalinga Ethnoarchaeology: Expanding Archaeological Method and Theory*. Washington, DC: Smithsonian Institution Press.

Schick, Kathy, and Nicholas Toth. 1993. *Making Silent Stones Speak: Human Evolution and the Dawn of Technology*. New York: Touchstone.

Online Resources

COMPANION WEB SITE
Visit **http://anthropology.wadsworth.com** and click on the Student Companion Web Site for Thomas/Kelly *Archaeology*, 4th edition, to access a wide range of material to help you succeed in your introductory archaeology course. These include flashcards, Internet exercises, Web links, and practice quizzes.

RESEARCH ONLINE WITH INFOTRAC COLLEGE EDITION
From the Student Companion Web Site, you can access the InfoTrac College Edition database, which offers thousands of full-length articles for your research.

11 People, Plants, and Animals in the Past

Outline

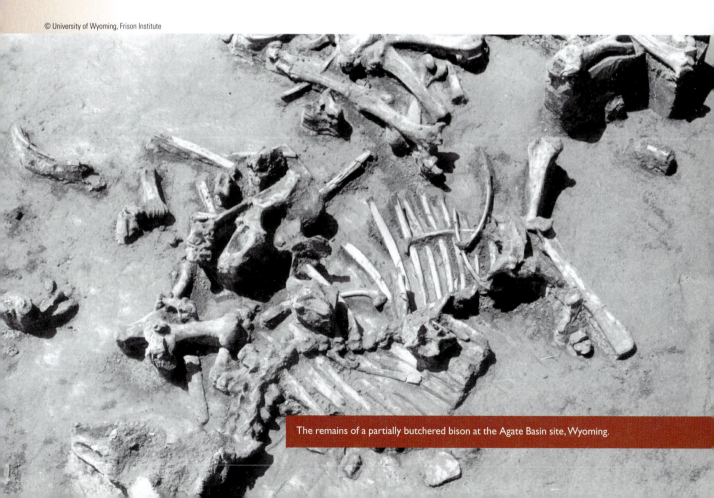

The remains of a partially butchered bison at the Agate Basin site, Wyoming.

Preview

ARCHAEOLOGISTS HAVE PLENTY of methods and techniques for reconstructing how people made a living in the past, and in this chapter, we discuss a few of them.

We begin with faunal analysis, the identification and interpretation of animal remains recovered in an archaeological context. Animal bones not only enable the archaeologist to study ancient hunting methods and diet, but they also assist in reconstructing past environments. Of course, getting at the meaning behind the bones is neither easy nor straightforward. This chapter will provide you with the basics for understanding what we can do with a bunch of animal bones.

Plant remains are also valuable to archaeology. We have already seen how the study of tree rings provides archaeologists with a trustworthy way of dating specific events of the past—when a certain Pueblo dwelling was built, for example. We learned also that tree-ring analysis indicates something about past climates, environments, and the local history of forest fires. Archaeological plant remains—pollen, seeds, charcoal, and phytoliths—also tell us about what wild plants people collected, the crops they grew, the fuels they burned, and even the roles played by plants in rituals. Plant and animal remains can also tell us in what season of the year people occupied a site.

INTRODUCTION

So far, we have talked mostly about artifacts and features—objects created by humans and left behind. Archaeological sites also contain ecofacts—plant and animal remains; some of these are food refuse, left by humans, but sometimes, similar remains enter sites through natural processes (as when plants and animals die on a site). As you'll recall, taphonomic studies figure out how plant and animal remains accumulate in archaeological sites. In this chapter, we are more concerned with what plant parts and animal bones tell us about human behavior.

Formation processes are critical to inferences based on plant and animal remains. In fact, as you read this and later chapters, keep asking yourself: How do archaeologists know to interpret their data in one way rather than another? What middle-range research stands

behind the inferences that archaeologists make? Could there be other interpretations? If so, how can we test those alternatives?

Archaeologists use many methods to recover and interpret animal and plant remains. So many, in fact, that we can present only a few here. Rather than blanket the field, we will introduce some of the major categories of data and provide a sense of how archaeologists go about interpreting them. We begin with archaeofaunas.

WHAT'S AN ARCHAEOFAUNA?

An **archaeofauna** consists of the animal bones recovered from an archaeological site. Archaeofaunas differ from paleontological assemblages because humans *may* have had a hand in their formation. Animal bones turn up in two major archaeological contexts:

archaeofauna The animal bones found in an archaeological site.

- At a **kill** or butchering **site,** bones may lie more or less the way they were when the hunters left, affected by carnivore scavenging, weathering, and other natural factors.
- In camps and villages, we find bones where hunted animals were brought back or domesticated animals were butchered.

Sometimes a site's faunal remains number in the tens of thousands and include some animals killed on the site, some that were transported from kill sites elsewhere, and many noncultural remains (these are bones of animals that simply died in the site or that carnivores or raptors brought in after people abandoned the site).

After recovering an archaeofauna, archaeologists commonly perform a **faunal analysis;** the person who does this is a **zooarchaeologist** (also known as a **faunal analyst**). To show you how this is done, let's look at how one zooarchaeologist went about analyzing the archaeofauna of the Folsom component at Wyoming's Agate Basin site.

The Agate Basin Site

Sometime around 1916, rancher William Spencer was riding across the broken terrain of his ranch in eastern Wyoming. Visiting a spring, he noticed some large bones protruding from the edge of an arroyo (just as George McJunkin did at the Folsom site in New Mexico). His curiosity piqued, he returned to the spring several times, eventually collecting a number of large, beautiful spear points as well as bison bones from the site.

Years later, in 1941, Spencer met Robert Frison, a state game warden, at an informal gathering of history buffs under some cottonwood trees on the Cheyenne River, a short distance north of the Agate Basin site. Frison's job took him outdoors a lot, and he had visited many sites and developed quite an interest in Paleoindian artifacts. The following year, the men visited the site together and found more bison bones and spear points. Frison thought the points could be old, so he sent one to Frank H. H. Roberts at the Smithsonian Institution (Frison knew Roberts because Frison knew the man who had discovered the Lindenmeier Folsom site in Colorado, which Roberts had excavated).

The points intrigued Roberts, and so he conducted excavations at Agate Basin that summer and in the following years. Later, William Bass (then at the University of Kansas) excavated there, and then, in the 1970s, Robert Frison's nephew, archaeologist George Frison (see Chapter 9) and Dennis Stanford (Smithsonian Institution) worked there together. (See Figure 11-1).

Frison and Stanford published a thorough report on their research, but there is always more that we can do with archaeological collections. For this reason, Matt Hill (Iowa State University) decided to take another look at Agate Basin's Folsom component archaeofaunas.

Let's begin with Hill's conclusions. About 10,780 radiocarbon years ago, a small group of Folsom hunters camped by the Agate Basin site in late March or early April. They killed at least 11 bison (*Bison antiquus*) and five pronghorn antelope (*Antilocapra americana*), probably not too far away from their camp. They partially butchered the bison at the kill site and, for the most part, brought entire limbs back to camp. The antelope were field-dressed at the kill site, and the nearly intact carcasses were carried back to the Agate Basin camp. Despite their success, the hunters may have had a hard time making ends meet. Unlike later hunter-gatherers on the Plains, these Folsom hunters seem not to have relied heavily on meat storage.

How did Hill extract all this information from a bunch of broken bones?

Identifying Bones

Hill began by identifying the bones from the Folsom component, working through the cataloged collection, piece by piece, and assigning each bone or bone fragment to a species, if possible.

"Identifying the bones" is more complicated than it might sound. Field archaeologists know, at least in a rough way, what mammal, bird, reptile, and fish bones look like, but far more detailed information is needed in faunal analysis. The first step is to assign each specimen to **element** (the anatomical part of the body). Is this bone a rib splinter, part of the pelvis, or a skull

kill sites Places where animals were killed in the past.

faunal analysis Identification and interpretation of animal remains from an archaeological site.

zooarchaeologist (also faunal analyst) An individual who studies the faunal (animal) remains recovered from archaeological sites.

element In faunal analysis, a specific skeletal part of the body—for example, humerus or sternum.

© University of Wyoming, Frison Institute

Figure 11-1 The Agate Basin site, showing the Folsom level under excavation in 1978.

fragment? A femur, tibia, or calcaneus (the heel bone)? Identifying elements requires a solid working knowledge of comparative anatomy (Figure 11-2).

But conventional comparative anatomy classes are insufficient because they deal with whole bones—not the dirty fragments that archaeologists confront. Classroom experience helps, but you really learn faunal analysis by handling a lot of bones yourself.

The next step is to identify the specimens to **taxon** (kind of animal). One's success here depends on the condition of the specimen and the expertise of the analyst. The aim is to identify each bone to species, but sometimes the bones are so fragmentary that you can only identify them to higher-order groups, such as family or class. For instance, one can rarely determine whether a long bone fragment (that is, a small piece

of one of the long limb bones, such as a femur shaft) came from a deer or a bighorn sheep—but anyone can tell that it's not a mouse bone. In this case, the analyst might only be able to identify the fragment to the order Artiodactyla (because deer and sheep are in different families, the next-broader level of classification is used). Identification to taxon, therefore, often means "narrowing down the possibilities," rather than identifying the exact species—although that is always preferred.

In other cases, the specimen might be so difficult to identify that you can only assign it to one of five standard animal **size classes.** Rodent- and rabbit-size animals are in size class 1; wolf- and pronghorn antelope–size animals are class 2; animals the size of mule deer and bighorn sheep are in class 3; bison- and elk-size animals are in class 4; and in class 5 are large animals such as giraffes, hippos, and elephants.

So, how did Hill know whether a scrap of bone was a piece of a bison femur, a pronghorn radius, a flat-headed peccary tibia, or a striped skunk skull? The zooarchaeologist makes these identifications through a

taxon In faunal analysis, the classification of a skeletal element to a taxonomic category—species, genus, family, or order.

size classes A categorization of faunal remains, not to taxon, but to one of five categories based on body size.

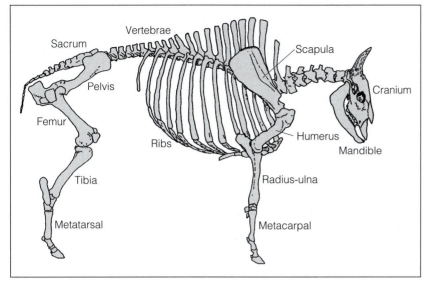

Figure 11-2 Bison skeleton showing major elements.

comparative collection. The standard zooarchaeology lab commonly contains box after box of modern animal skeletons—everything from elephants to deer mice. Each box is labeled with the species, the individual's approximate age at death, its sex, and where and when it was collected. A comparative collection contains examples of young and old, as well as male and female, members of a species. These collections are put together by hunting or trapping the animals, picking up road kills (you need a license to do these things in most states), or acquiring carcasses from a state fish and game office (sometimes confiscated from poachers).

Once collected, the specimens are manually defleshed and cleaned. Sometimes the remains are buried and nature is allowed to take its course. Other methods include simmering the bones in a solution of detergent or placing the greasy bones in a colony of dermestid beetles, which, over a few weeks' time, will literally pick the bones clean of all tissue.

Using a comparative collection, Hill identified the archaeological bones to taxon. Measurements taken on some adult bones helped determine if the bone was from a male or female.

Hill eventually assigned all the Agate Basin bones to element and taxon (or size class). Most bones were bison or pronghorn, but other species included wolf, striped skunk, and frogs. But because there were only a

few bones from most of these species, Hill focused on the bison and pronghorn.

Natural or Cultural?

Recalling the discussion of taphonomy in Chapter 10, you should be wondering how Hill could be certain (1) that the bison and pronghorn remains were deposited by humans and (2) that they were deposited during the same occupation of the site.

For one thing, the bones bore some stone tool cut marks (which we know how to distinguish from carnivore tooth marks), some were burned, and some of the larger ones had impact fractures—distinctive breaks that resulted when the Folsom people smashed the bones open to retrieve the fatty, calorie-rich marrow. Frison and Stanford also found a cluster of antelope bones, some of them burned, around a hearth.

A few of the bones did show evidence of carnivore gnawing. But tooth marks appeared on only a few bison humeri and femora, and on only three antelope specimens. So, the evidence pointed to humans as the agents responsible for the antelope and bison bones at Agate Basin.

Hill also thinks that the antelope and bison bones were deposited during the same occupation of the site. The Folsom assemblage is not large, nor is it widely dispersed; some of the remains, in fact, still lie in anatomical position. This is what we would expect to see in a one-shot use of the site. In addition, we might expect all the bones to be equally weathered, just as we saw at the Hudson-Meng site—an "instantaneous" herd death, where nearly all the skulls were weathered in the same way.

To reach this conclusion, Hill took bone size into account. Because antelope bones are smaller than bison

comparative collection A skeletal collection of modern fauna of both sexes and different ages used to make identifications of archaeofaunas.

bones, they are more easily broken (by carnivores and also by hunters, who broke the bones for their marrow). Because they're smaller, sediment will cover antelope bones more quickly than the larger bison bones. So, even if all the faunal remains were deposited at about the same time, the bison bones should be slightly more weathered than the antelope bones. This was the case at Agate Basin, and Hill concluded that the bison and antelope bones in the Folsom component were animals killed by the same people during the same occupation.

What to Count?

To reconstruct human behavior at Agate Basin, Hill needed to search for meaningful patterns in the bone data, and this required that he count the bones.

Zooarchaeologists count bones in two ways, depending upon their objectives. One method involves the **number of identified specimens,** or **NISP.** This count is simply the total number of bone specimens that are identified to a particular taxon. Table 11-1 shows the NISP for the Folsom component at the Agate Basin site. NISP is useful for comparing large numbers of collections from different sites, but it has a severe limitation in reconstructing human behavior at a single site.

Table 11-1 suggests that bison were more important than pronghorn at Agate Basin. But what if the 1033 bison specimens came from a single highly fragmented skeleton, whereas each of the 297 antelope bones came from 297 different individuals? If this were the case, then antelope would be many times more important than bison at this site. Or, maybe the species were butchered in different ways, with certain bones becoming highly fragmented (and hence disappearing from the archaeological record altogether or turning into unidentifiable elements that are not included in the NISP counts).

Problems like this have led archaeologists to another way of comparing bone frequencies, called the **minimum number of individuals,** or **MNI.** Developed by paleontologists, MNI is the minimum number of individuals that are necessary to account for all the skeletal

TABLE 11-1 NISP Counts for the Folsom Component at the Agate Basin Site

COMMON NAME	SCIENTIFIC NAME	NISP
Bison	Bison antiquus	1,033
Pronghorn antelope	Antilocapra americana	297
Wolf	Canis lupus	7
Coyote	Canis latrans	3
Red fox	Vulpes vulpes	1
Striped skunk	Mephitis mephitis	1
Flat-headed peccary	Platygonus compressus	1
Dog	Canis sp. (possibly domesticated)	5
Jackrabbit	Lepus cf. townsendii or californicus	10
Rabbit	Sylvilagus cf. nutallii or audubonii	4
Grouse	Centrocercus urophasianus	2
Frog	Rana pipiens	Few
Elk	Cervus elaphus (antler only)	2
Camel	Camelops sp. (possible tool)	1

SOURCE: Hill 2001.

The "sp." in some scientific names means that the genus is certain, but the species is not. The "cf." in other cases means that the specimen compares very well with one or two species within a genus, but that the researcher is not certain of the species identification. Camel became extinct about 11,200 radiocarbon years ago, and there is no good evidence that humans ever hunted them; the specimen here might be a piece that a Folsom hunter picked up someplace or evidence of an animal that died at the site long before the hunters camped there.

elements of a particular species found in the site. Suppose, for instance, that you excavated 100 fragments of bison bone from a site. The NISP equals 100, but what is the MNI? That is, what is the minimum number of individual bison required to account for those 100 bone fragments?

To figure this out, you must tabulate bone frequency by element (left femur, right tibia, hyoid, and so on) to determine the most *abundant* skeletal element. This process requires that you not only assign the specimens their correct *element*, but for those bones that come in pairs, to their correct *side* as well. If four right femurs show up in the 100 bone fragments, then you know that *at least* four bison account for the fragments.

But MNI has some limitations as well. When bones are fragmented, it is possible that the "four right femurs" are really fragments from the same upper leg bone. To eliminate this problem, you must compare the bone fragments, one by one, to see whether two fragments could have come from the same bone. In our hypothetical example, if we found that two of the four right femur fragments could have come from the same femur, then the MNI would only be three.

number of identified specimens (NISP) The raw number of identified bones (specimens) per species; a largely outmoded way of comparing archaeological bone frequencies.

minimum number of individuals (MNI) The smallest number of individuals necessary to account for all identified bones.

Calculating MNI also depends on how you divide your site. Agate Basin was probably occupied once by Folsom hunters for a few weeks. It is what archaeologists call a *fine-grained* assemblage, meaning that it hasn't become complicated by additional, overlapping occupations. But what if the site were *coarse-grained*? What if it had been repeatedly occupied over a long period of time such that the resulting assemblage is the result of many periods of use over decades—or even thousands of years? We could compute the minimum number of individuals for a coarse-grained assemblage, but this might have the unfortunate consequence of reducing hundreds of bone fragments to a very few MNI, perhaps just one or two individuals. This would obviously be a poor choice. Sometimes investigators calculate their minimum numbers based on stratigraphic breaks observed during excavation. Once again, however, the MNI per species depends on how fine one wishes to draw the stratigraphic boundaries.

Ultimately, the decision depends on the site's specific characteristics. In general, MNI is most useful and accurate when fine stratigraphic divisions are used and when bones are not overly fragmented. The Folsom component at Agate Basin meets these criteria.

Where did Hill go from here? Of the 1033 bison bones, Hill could identify 843 to element; likewise, he could identify 198 of the 297 antelope bone fragments to element. Although the antelope specimens were fragmented, Hill identified four right and one left humeri (upper arm bones). This might suggest an MNI of four (given that the single left humerus could be a match to one of the right humeri). But the single left humerus was not the same size as any of the right humeri, and so Hill concluded that *at least* five antelope were brought to the site.

Because they are larger and heavier, the bison long bones were more intact. Taking the humeri, radii, femora, and tibiae, Hill assigned each to a side and then decided, using a comparative collection, whether they were male or female (or indeterminate, because young, less-developed animals don't yet exhibit characteristics that allow assigning to a sex). He then compared their sizes to see if the rights and lefts of each sex could possibly have come from the same animal, or whether the femora and tibiae, and the humeri and radii could anatomically refit (that is, would they fit together in their usual anatomical positions; femora and tibiae, for example, articulate at the patella, the knee cap). If they did refit, then they could have come from the same animal (Figure 11-3).

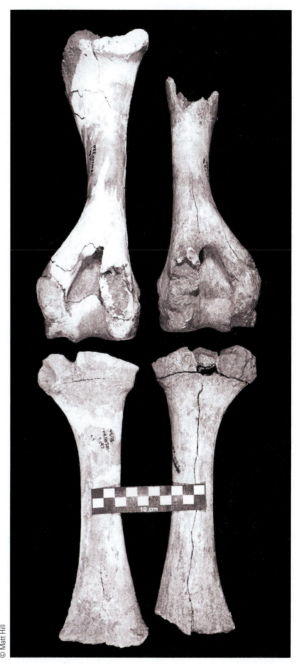

Figure 11-3 Anatomically refit calf bison humeri (top) and radii (bottom). Carnivore gnawing has removed the proximal (upper) end of the humerus on the right.

From this comparison, Hill determined that there were *at least* four males, four females, and three immature bison brought to the site.

So now we know the minimum number of animals that Folsom hunters killed at the Agate Basin site: eleven bison and five pronghorn antelope.

Reconstructing Human Behavior at Agate Basin

By looking at which specific elements were present, Hill found that elements of the **axial skeleton** (the head, mandibles, vertebrae, ribs, sacrum, tail) for both bison and pronghorn were rare compared with bones from the **appendicular skeleton** (everything else). Bison limb bones were also more common relative to the other bison bones, and antelope lower leg bones (especially for the front legs) and toes were rare.

What accounts for these patterns?

Viewed as food, bones function two ways—as a support for meat and as a container of marrow. Experimental research can quantify how much food value a bone represents in terms of these two entities. Bison long bones, for instance, rank high in both meat and marrow content, suggesting that hunters brought back only the high-utility portions of the bison and left the axial skeleton at the kill site.

The pronghorn skeletons at the Agate Basin site were more complete than the bison skeletons. Apparently, the antelope were gutted and then field-dressed by removing the feet and lower limb bones, which contain little marrow and have little meat wrapped about them. The hunters then carried the rest of the antelope back to camp as more or less complete carcasses. The ribs and vertebrae may have been crushed for bone grease or consumed whole by dogs and carnivores, as suggested by taphonomic research.

Ethnoarchaeological studies suggest some other possibilities. Hunters consider several factors when deciding which parts of an animal to transport home: the distance back to camp, the number of hunters present, weather, terrain, and food needs of the household. If the animal is killed near camp, women and children might come out to help carry the entire carcass of a large animal back. If so, then the entire skeleton might end up in the camp, rather than at the kill site. If an animal is killed far from camp, the hunters might eat some of it immediately and then butcher the animal, bringing only meat and a very few bones back to camp. In this case, most of the skeleton would remain at the kill site.

Based on these ethnoarchaeological observations, Hill suggested that hunters at Agate Basin killed most of the animals individually, relatively close to camp. The smaller antelope were carried back with minimal field butchery. However, because the bison could not be carried whole, it is likely that the Agate Basin hunters (and perhaps their wives and children) ate some of the meat attached to the vertebrae and ribs at the kill site and then transported the legs—with their large meat packages and high marrow content—to camp using the lower limbs as convenient handles.

What Do Broken Toes Mean?

Although relatively rare at this site, some bison metapodials (portions of the foot), as well as bison and antelope phalanges (toe bones) had been broken open, presumably to extract the marrow. But foot bones do not contain much marrow, and they have no meat attached to them. Why did the hunters bother with toes, when they apparently had bison haunches and antelope tenderloin roasting on the fire?

Hill interprets the processing of the foot bones as evidence that, despite the eleven bison and five antelope, the Agate Basin Folsom hunters were experiencing some hard times. From paleoclimatic data, we know that the average annual temperature was some 11° C colder during Folsom times; perhaps late winter or early spring storms—which can strike with a vengeance on the high plains—made that day's hunt impossible. Or perhaps the meat stored in camp was frozen, leaving the camp's inhabitants with no choice but to extract marrow from low-utility elements, such as metapodials and phalanges.

Hill also concluded that these Folsom hunters were living more hand-to-mouth than did later hunter-gatherers on the high plains. The late winter and early spring is a tough season for hunter-gatherers, because game animals are lean (and lean meat is difficult to digest) and plants are not yet ripe. Many foragers survive the spring by relying on food stored from a previous fall hunt. But the data from Agate Basin suggest that these Folsom hunters lacked stored food, because they were hunting on a weekly or even daily basis during the spring that they occupied the site.

This interpretation depends on knowing that the Folsom hunters camped at Agate Basin in the spring. How did Hill know this?

In What Season Was Agate Basin Occupied?

Recall from the discussion of seasonal rounds in Chapter 4 that hunter-gatherers do not spend the entire year

axial skeleton The head, mandibles, vertebrae, ribs, sacrum, and tail of an animal skeleton.

appendicular skeleton All parts of an animal excluding the axial skeleton.

in a single camp or village. Folsom hunters moved across the landscape; so did the nineteenth-century Shoshone in Nevada and so do Mikea forager-horticulturalists. To understand what life was like in the past, we must pay attention to **seasonality,** the time of year that a site was used. This is important because only after we have identified the range of seasonal activities can we understand the entire seasonal round.

Hill determined the seasonality of Agate Basin by beginning with the knowledge that modern bison give birth during the last two weeks of April and the first two weeks of May. Hill assumed that bison in the past did likewise. This uniformitarian assumption seems justified because giving birth in the early spring is adaptive, allowing calves the maximum time to mature sufficiently to survive the next winter. Even considering the likelihood of climate change, it is highly likely that the birthing season of modern bison approximates that of their ancient cousins.

Bone development and tooth eruption in modern bison also follow quite predictable schedules (as they do for all animals, including humans). Young animals are most useful to archaeologists—indeed, once all their teeth have erupted, adults lose their value as seasonal indicators. The Agate Basin collection contained only a few young animals, but they were important in assessing the season of occupation. The teeth of the youngest bison showed that it was about 11 months old when it died. A second young bison had teeth that suggested an age of about 23 months. In other words, these two animals were just one month shy of their first and second birthdays, respectively. Assuming that these two bison were born in late April–early May, then they probably died in late March or early April. The presence of some fetal bison bones (either a late-term fetus or a newborn) supports this inference. With this information, Hill concluded that Folsom hunters occupied Agate Basin at the tail end of winter or the beginning of spring.

The Zooarchaeology of a Peruvian Civilization

Now that we know something about the basics of faunal analysis, let's jump to Peru, to see how these techniques work in a very different context (see also "Looking Closer: What Did Sixteenth-Century Colonists Eat in Spanish Florida?").

The site of Chavín de Huántar (cha-*veen* day *whan*-tar) is one of the most celebrated ceremonial centers in the Andes. It flourished from about 850 to 200 BC, making it one of the earliest civilizations in South America. Located at an elevation of nearly 3150 meters (10,000 feet) above sea level, Chavín de Huántar is ringed by snow-covered mountains (with peaks rising over 5500 meters [18,000 feet]).

The initial settlement was a small ceremonial center surrounded by numerous domestic structures that made up a vigorous highland community. Its location on a key trade route midway between the Peruvian coast and the lowland tropical forest to the east made Chavín de Huántar a natural trade center.

The site has given its name to the famous Chavín art style, which some claim is the pinnacle of Andean artistry. Chavín art contains a range of fantastical and representational figures, usually combining the features of humans, snakes, jaguars, caymans (alligators), and birds with intricate geometrical and curvilinear motifs. The most elegant expression of the Chavín style is in the 150 stone carvings of the huge Chavín de Huántar temple complex (we will discuss these images in Chapter 14).

The site's ceremonial buildings are honeycombed with rooms, passageways, stairways, vents, and drains (Figure 11-4). Inside the largest structure is a knife-shaped monolith 15 feet tall, set into a narrow, interior gallery. The top of the elaborately carved sculpture reached through the ceiling, into a gallery above, where the priests of Chavín de Huántar, acting as the voice of an oracle, may have spoken to the worshipers below.

Chavín's art and temple architecture attracts the attention of Andean archaeologists, but we also need to know something about the more mundane aspects of the Chavín lifeway.

What, for instance, did the Chavín people eat? We could look to the stone iconography expressed in their sculpture, but it is unlikely that people living at 10,000 feet in the Andes dined on alligator and jaguar. Religious iconography is not a very accurate reflection of everyday diet.

George Miller (California State University, Hayward) and Richard Burger (Yale University) took a more direct approach to the problem by looking at the trash of the center's several thousand inhabitants.

seasonality An estimate of what part of the year a particular archaeological site was occupied.

Looking Closer
What Did Sixteenth-Century Colonists Eat in Spanish Florida?

Elizabeth Reitz (University of Georgia) and C. Margaret Scarry (University of North Carolina) have used historical documentation to chronicle subsistence practices in sixteenth-century Spanish Florida. Accounts from St. Augustine and elsewhere emphasize the chronic shortages of traditional Iberian foods and the substitution of less-valued New World resources. Why, then, would faunal analysis be useful to historical archaeology if documentary sources are available?

One reason is that significant biases and gaps often exist in documentary sources (see Chapter 16). Many important records were lost; letters often exaggerated (or falsified) the situation to elicit greater support from the Spanish crown. Contradictions in eyewitness accounts are common.

The main problem, however, is that the historic record for Spanish Florida rarely contains the mundane details that archaeologists need. Even though the contemporary accounts show that the Spanish were displeased with their new diet, there is no substitute for the physical evidence obtained through archaeological excavation. Reitz and Scarry synthesized the subsistence data recovered in excavations at St. Augustine and Santa Elena (South Carolina). Their results demonstrate the importance of dietary reconstruction in historical archaeology.

Many colonists found that their traditional Old World subsistence practices did not work in the New World. Key Iberian food crops failed miserably in coastal Florida, and the Spanish were forced to alter their husbandry techniques.

Lacking any sophisticated ecological knowledge, the settlers had to pass through a period of adjustment and experimentation. The earliest shipments of livestock to St. Augustine and Santa Elena reflected Iberian food preferences. The Spanish tried to cater to the traditional preference for mutton, but sheep could not defend themselves against wild dogs and wolves and would not reproduce freely. Several species, especially marine fishes, first filled the gap left by mutton; however, the meat supply of Spanish Florida eventually shifted to beef and especially pork.

The colonists of Spanish Florida tried to raise their favorite Old World crops, particularly wheat and grapes. But they noted how successfully the Native Americans grew their own indigenous crops, and soon the Spaniards were supplementing their harvests with maize, beans, and squash (the native peoples, in turn, adopted the Spanish peach).

In effect, the Spanish strategy shifted toward an essentially aboriginal subsistence pattern, complemented by those European domesticates that could survive and prosper. Considerably more than half of the meat consumed in St. Augustine and Santa Elena by both Spanish settlers and aborigines derived from wild species, especially deer, shark, sea catfish, drum, and mullet. Spaniards also ate small mammals—such as opossums, squirrels, and raccoons—which they disparagingly termed "the scum and vermin."

The subsistence pattern that emerged at St. Augustine was a fusion of the various elements available to the Spanish colonists. Although they continued to use Old World livestock, the dietary importance of the various animals shifted significantly. And although they still raised some Old World cultigens, these were mostly fruits and vegetables that supplemented a diet based on domesticated New World plants. Thus, despite adopting many aboriginal items, the St. Augustine diet remained distinctly Spanish, processed through the unmistakably Spanish institutions of the slaughterhouse and the marketplace. Occasionally, the rare supply ship from home would provide European delicacies, such as olives, walnuts, and hazelnuts.

St. Augustine was established 70 years after the Spaniards began colonizing the New World, and some valuable lessons had been learned in this interval. Nevertheless, Reitz and Scarry found that significant dietary adaptations were still necessary to cope with the conditions of coastal Florida. These important dietary adjustments took place within the first 40 years of the colonization of Spanish Florida. But once established, the balance remained virtually unchanged for the next two centuries.

Figure 11-4 The main temple at Chavín de Huántar.

When Burger first went to Chavín de Huántar, there was no reliable chronological sequence (except for sculptural style), so he conducted basic excavations to bring temporal order to the sites. Subsistence remains were, of course, encountered in the domestic structures, and refuse heaps were excavated around the ceremonial center. For our purposes, we will restrict our attention to the recovered faunal remains—more than 12,000 fragments of discarded food bone.

The bones were identified, first to body part and then to taxon. Next, the investigators computed the MNI for each of the three major cultural phases. They then estimated the "usable meat values" for each phase by multiplying the MNI figures per phase by the average animal's butchered weight for each taxon.

Early Patterns at Chavín de Huántar

Four kinds of camelids (animals of the family *Camelidae*) live today in the Andes. The llama was used mostly as a pack animal, and secondarily for its coarse hair. The alpaca was valued mostly for its fine and abundant fleece. Both of these domesticated species played important

roles in religious rituals. Guanacos, wild llamas, were hunted as a source of meat. Finally, the vicuña, also a wild species, was hunted mostly for its extremely fine hair.

During the earliest or Urabarriu phase (900–500 BC), more than half the meat came from camelids (see Figure 11-5). Using measurements taken on the archaeological bones and comparing them to those taken on a comparative collection, Miller and Burger concluded that most of the larger camelids from the Urabarriu phase were llamas. And stable isotope analysis (a technique we will discuss in Chapter 12) of their bones suggests that these early llama herds may have consumed considerable quantities of maize and therefore were probably domesticated. The smaller camelids seem to be mostly vicuña.

White-tailed deer came in second (31 percent of the available meat). Skunk, large cats (either jaguar or puma), fox (or dog), and guinea pig bones also turned up in small numbers. The bones of some of these rarer animals may have been used for tools, rather than for food (although guinea pigs are today considered a delicacy in

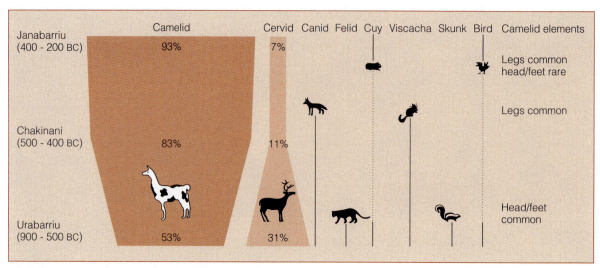

Figure 11-5 Changing relative abundance of the major animal groups in faunal remains at Chavín de Huántar.   *After Miller and Burger (1995: figure 4); courtesy of the authors and the Society for American Archaeology.*

highland Peru). In other words, the Urabarriu phase bones strongly suggest a transitional pattern of mixed hunting and herding.

The Later Fauna at Chavín de Huántar

Things changed markedly during the subsequent Chakinani phase (500–400 BC). Deer frequencies drop off dramatically, and camelid frequencies jump to 83 percent, with llama bones becoming considerably more common than those of vicuña.

The large faunal sample from the terminal Janabarriu phase (400–200 BC) continues this trend: camelid bones constitute 93 percent of the assemblage. During this phase, the rapidly expanding population had virtually abandoned hunting in favor of domesticated llamas. This much seems clear.

But recall that Miller and Burger identified the bones from Chavín de Huántar to both taxon and element. The taxonomic changes through time indicated that subsistence activities changed markedly at Chavín de Huántar. But by looking at differential representation of elements (that is, body parts), Miller and Burger explored the way in which the various animal products were distributed throughout the community.

They found a curious pattern: The early Urabarriu camelid assemblage consisted mostly of head and foot

bones. During the two subsequent phases, however, leg bones become considerably more frequent, with cranial and foot bones becoming rare. What does this intriguing pattern mean?

Camelid Taphonomy

As we pointed out in Chapter 10, interpretation requires middle-range theory, and one source of such theory is ethnoarchaeology. George Miller had conducted ethnoarchaeological research on contemporary South American pastoralists in the **puna,** the high grassy plateau of southern Peru. This experience helped him to analyze the remains excavated by Burger. Interestingly, Miller found that the bone refuse in modern herding communities mirrored almost exactly the early pattern from Chavín de Huántar: plenty of head and foot bones, and not many leg bones. Why?

Miller first considered the matter of bone survival. He conducted a variety of experiments on camelid bones to see which ones tend to survive and which ones disappear. Not surprisingly, he found that the extremely dense foot bones and enamel-covered teeth lasted much longer than the long, hollow leg bones and the relatively porous vertebrae.

Miller then looked at the way in which butchering patterns might create a different representation of skeletal parts. Put simply, the process of modern camelid butchering accelerates the skewing effects already suggested from the bone density studies. Because people commonly break up the leg bones to get at the marrow

puna Native American (Quechua) term for the treeless, windswept tablelands and basins of the higher Andes.

inside, such long bones commonly enter the archaeo-logical record fragmented (and hence are more difficult to identify to element and taxon). Like other taphono-mists, Miller discovered that when dogs gnaw on camelid remains, they consume spongy bones (such as vertebrae) almost entirely, but even repeated gnawing leaves dense teeth and foot bones marked, but intact. In other words, the processes involved in differential preservation—bone density, butchering patterns, and carnivore gnawing—all operated to bias the modern faunal assemblage in precisely the manner observed from the early deposits at Chavín de Huántar.

But another factor is at work here, what Miller calls the *ch'arki* effect. Today, herders of the puna preserve llama and alpaca meat by alternately drying it out in the intense Andean sun, then freezing it during the cold, high-altitude nights. (The product of this freeze-drying process—called **ch'arki** in the native Quechua lan-guage—has made its way into English as "jerky.")

But unlike the overpriced beef jerky peddled in bars and gas stations throughout the United States, Peruvian ch'arki consists of meat dried on the bone. In general, the bones of the head and feet are cut off in the ch'arki-making process and eaten at home by the local herding communities. Ch'arki is a major trade item between the highland puna herders and those living in the inter-montane valleys and along the Pacific coast today.

So, what does ch'arki production look like if all you have are bones? That is, what is the archaeological evi-dence of ch'arki-making?

The pattern depends entirely on whether you are making or receiving the ch'arki. If you're in the puna, where llama are herded and ch'arki is made, you will find lots of cranial and foot bones. These are the heavy, dense bones (without much meat attached) that nobody wants to drag around the Andes. So they are cut off and discarded, entering the archaeological record of the puna. But if you are on the receiving end of the ch'arki trade network—in the downhill intermontane valleys and along the coast—then the pattern is the opposite. The camelid bones you receive from the uplands are those still left adhering to the ch'arki chunks. So, your garbage will contain lots of leg bones and vertebrae, but not many skull parts or foot bones.

Given this simple taphonomic patterning based on behavior of modern camelid-herding communities, we can return to the bone assemblages from Chavín de Huántar and look at the bones in a more informed manner.

The Behavior behind the Bones

Remember that the faunal remains from the Chakinani (500–400 BC) and Janabarriu (400–200 BC) phases con-tained mostly camelid bones—mostly llama and some vicuña, with deer frequencies dropping off markedly from earlier times. The rapidly expanding population at Chavín de Huántar had forsaken hunting in favor of camelid herding. Miller and Burger also found that, whereas the camelid assemblage from earlier deposits consisted mostly of head and foot bones, leg bones dominated the later archaeological record, with cranial and foot elements rare.

Middle-range studies also tell us that three of the major taphonomic factors—differential bone densities, fracturing of long bones, and carnivore gnawing—all *decrease* survival of leg bones. Although these fac-tors influenced the composition of this assemblage, the observed superabundance of leg bones suggests that taphonomy alone cannot account for the faunal distributions.

Instead, we must look to the ch'arki effect. The eth-noarchaeological findings indicated that the observed late phase pattern at Chavín de Huántar is almost exactly the *opposite* of what we see among contem-porary alpaca herders living on the puna. Obviously, there are some important differences between modern communities and that of late Chavín times. What are they?

Then and now, the valley floor surrounding Chavín de Huántar is well suited for maize agriculture but pro-vides poor pasturage. It also lacks the cold, dry weather needed to produce ch'arki. Because llama herding is most effective in the puna, it seems likely that the ch'arki was prepared there. Thus, it appears that high-altitude herding communities traded ch'arki to the val-ley residents of Chavín de Huántar. In return, the valley communities may have sent agricultural products (such as maize) into the mountains, where few crops can grow.

Translated into bones, this means that discarded fau-nal elements (cranial and foot bones) should turn up at sites in the puna; downhill, the imported ch'arki should result in mostly upper limb bones and vertebrae enter-ing the archaeological record of domestic dwellings along the valley floors. And this is precisely the pattern

ch'arki Native South American (Quechua) term for freeze-dried llama and alpaca meat.

observed in the archaeological record of Chavín de Huántar and inferred for the surrounding puna sites.

From this evidence, Miller and Burger concluded that the earliest occupants of Chavín de Huántar used llamas mostly as pack animals, camelid meat being a by-product of culling the herds. Meat was also obtained by hunting vicuña and white-tailed deer. People living on the valley floor were basically self-sufficient in the Urabarriu phase, acquiring their own meat as needed.

Then, the ritual importance of Chavín de Huántar increased through time, and the local community grew in size. The associated increase in agricultural production on the valley floor made hunting of local wild species less productive, and thereafter meat was derived almost exclusively from domesticated llamas. Because the valley floor was poorly suited for llama herding, there was an increased need for long-distance trade with the high-altitude regions. Ch'arki was traded in, and agricultural products (among other commodities) were traded out during the later Janabarriu phase.

The differential distribution of camelid bones thus reflects important economic and social relationships between Chavín de Huántar and surrounding communities. These exchange relationships were probably also reinforced by a shared participation in the Chavín religious cult, both at the massive valley-floor temple and at small shrines located in the various high-altitude villages. With time, the residents of Chavín de Huántar shifted from a generalized economic system with only loose ties to the upland neighbors to a more specialized subsistence pattern that depended heavily on long-distance exchange with the upland herders in the puna.

Recall that this interpretation of Chavín de Huántar's faunal assemblage is based partially on ethnographic analogy. Lidio Valdez (Trent University) points out that the analogy employed for ch'arki production is only one of several that could be drawn from the Andes. Ch'arki is made in other ways throughout the Andes, and each leaves a different faunal signature. Did Miller and Burger pick the right analogy? And Peter Stahl (State University of New York, Binghamton) suggests Chavín de Huántar's local environment could have per-mitted ch'arki production. But even if Miller and Burger's hypothesis is eventually modified or even rejected, their work illustrates the utility of combining ethnoarchaeological and taphonomic research to understand patterning in archaeological faunal data.

These two examples, a Folsom camp in Wyoming and the sequence at Chavín de Huántar in Peru, show some of the ways archaeologists pursue faunal analysis and what it can contribute to our understanding of the past. Bones, however, are only half the story.

STUDYING PLANT REMAINS FROM ARCHAEOLOGICAL SITES

A **paleoethnobotanist** is an archaeologist who specializes in recovering and identifying plant remains from ancient contexts, focusing on the world of plant–people interactions.

Plant remains are particularly vulnerable to the biases of archaeological preservation. Some archaeological sites sometimes contain well-preserved concentrations of **macrobotanical remains** (readily recognizable plant parts): caches of corncobs, pine nuts, a hearth's charcoal, or acorn mush adhering to the inside wall of a food bowl. For years, much of what we knew about ancient plants came from archaeological sites in arid climates, which had a far better chance of preserving them for study. The archaeological deposits inside Danger and Hogup caves (in Utah), for instance, consisted almost entirely of plant seeds, hulls, and chaff. In places, virtually no dirt was present, even though the deposits were more than 10 feet deep. From column samples of the fill, investigators reconstructed the vegetational history near both sites. Such studies can highlight the degree to which modern plant distributions can mislead the archaeologist studying the cultural ecology of even the fairly recent past.

In more humid climates, plant remains generally are preserved only when they have been burned and carbonized. For this reason, the most common method of recovering plant remains is flotation (as we discussed in Chapter 6). But plant remains are also sometimes preserved in waterlogged contexts (shipwrecks, mudslides, and wells), sun-dried adobe bricks, wattle-and-daub walls, and ceramics.

paleoethnobotanist An archaeologist who analyzes and interprets plant remains from archaeological sites in order to understand the past interactions between human populations and plants.

macrobotanical remains Nonmicroscopic plant remains recovered from an archaeological site.

Archaeologists also find plant remains in curious places, such as inside ancient human stomachs (preserved through mummification) and in human **coprolites** (desiccated feces); this evidence of past diets is about as direct as one could hope for. Evidence of past plant consumption is also preserved in the chemistry of human bone (but we'll discuss this in Chapter 12). And it comes in a microscopic form too, as pollen and phytoliths.

Palynology

Palynology, the analysis of ancient plant pollen and spores, has long been useful to the study of prehistoric ecological adaptations by helping to reconstruct past environments. The basics of palynology are easy to understand.

Most plants shed their pollen into the atmosphere, where the wind rapidly disperses it. Pollen grains—microscopic male gametes—are present in most of the earth's atmosphere; a single pine branch can produce as many as 350 million pollen grains. Pollen grains are tenacious and under the right conditions can preserve for tens of thousands of years, or even longer.

Determining what these pollen concentrations mean can be quite challenging, but the initial steps in extracting and identifying pollen are rather straightforward. Sometimes pollen is recovered by core sampling, in which a circular tube is forced downward by a mechanical drilling rig into a sediment record. Lake bottoms are often good places to prospect for pollen.

We can also take pollen samples manually from archaeological stratigraphic profiles. The surface of the excavation profile is first scraped with a trowel (that has been cleaned with distilled water), and 0.2 to 0.3 liter of material is then extracted from the sediment with a clean trowel and placed in a sterile, sealable container. Samples are often taken at 5- or 10-centimeter intervals to provide a continuous record of the pollen rain throughout the period of deposition. The archaeologist takes the samples from the bottom of the profile to the top (rather than from the top to the bottom) so that the samples are not contaminated by falling dirt. The proveniences of the pollen samples are recorded in the same way that the archaeologists record the proveniences of artifacts and ecofacts. Pollen samples can also be taken from sealed deposits within architectural features (such as ancient floors or the fill found in pits), and they can be retrieved from artifacts such as grinding stones by washing the surfaces in distilled water.

Occasionally, we find pollen in human burials, on the inside of ceramic vessels, trapped inside the weave of ancient baskets, or even adhering to the working surface of a stone tool. The analyst must always be certain that he or she has collected the sample from a recently exposed surface so that the modern pollen rain does not contaminate it.

In the laboratory, pollen grains are isolated from the soil matrix with repeated hydrofluoric acid baths and centrifuging (pollen survives the acids baths that destroy most everything else in the sample). A sample of the solution is then placed on a microscope slide, which is scanned at magnifications between 400X and 1000X.

Palynology is possible only because different plants produce pollen that look very different under a microscope. Pine pollen, for example, has two "wings" on it that carry it long distances on the wind. Elm pollen, on the other hand, is a lumpy round ball. This difference means that the individual grains can be identified, sometimes to species, and tabulated until the analyst records a statistically significant number, say about 400 to 500 grains per slide. (A skilled analyst can tabulate this number of pollen grains in 2 to 3 hours). The palynologist then converts the counts to percentages and creates a **pollen diagram** that shows the proportional shift in pollen frequencies between stratigraphic levels within a site.

Fluctuations in pollen percentages reflect changes in plant densities, and a primary application of palynology is to reconstruct past environments. Peter Mehringer's (Washington State University) research at the Lehner Ranch Site shows how this works.

Reconstructing Past Environments at the Lehner Ranch Site

The question of when people first arrived in North America is still hotly debated. The people who made Folsom points were among the earliest peoples in the New World, but earlier still were people who made a different kind of fluted point, known to archaeologists

coprolite Desiccated feces, often containing macrobotanical remains, pollen, and the remains of small animals.

palynology The technique through which the fossil pollen grains and spores from archaeological sites are studied.

pollen diagram A chart showing the changing frequencies of different identified pollens through time from samples taken from archaeological or other sites.

Figure 11-6 Pollen diagram from the Lehner Ranch site (Arizona).   *After Mehringer and Haynes (1966: figure 8).*

as **Clovis** points. The name Clovis comes from an important site near Clovis, New Mexico where, a few years after the discoveries at the Folsom site, these distinctive spear points were found lying stratigraphically beneath diagnostic Folsom artifacts. Clovis artifacts date to about 10,900 to 11,200 BC and, at about a dozen sites, they are associated with the bones of extinct mammoths and mastodons.

One of those sites is the Lehner Ranch site in southern Arizona's San Pedro Valley, excavated by C. Vance

Clovis The earliest well-established Native American culture, distributed throughout much of North America and dating 10,900 to 11,200 BC.

Haynes (University of Arizona), among others. Here, Haynes found several distinctive Clovis fluted points and stone butchering tools in association with mammoth remains. It is hard to imagine mammoths plodding among the creosote and ocotillo of the southern Arizona landscape today. Clovis hunters clearly lived in an environment that was different from today's, and Peter Mehringer turned to the fossil pollen record to help Haynes reconstruct what that environment was like.

Figure 11-6 shows the pollen diagram from the Lehner Ranch site. Lehner has a complex stratigraphy, and Haynes could not find a single locality that contained a continuous and unbroken pollen record. So, this diagram is a composite, showing the results of three separate but overlapping pollen profiles.

Pollen diagrams can look daunting, but don't let them put you off. Along the left edge is the sample number and, in the next column to the right, the stratigraphic unit, accompanied by the sample's depth. In this case, samples were taken at 10 cm intervals. Because this pollen diagram is a composite of three different profiles (shown at right), some of the stratigraphic units appear more than once. For instance, Unit K appeared at 260–270 cm in Profile I, 170–180 cm in Profile VIII, and 180–190 cm in Profile II.

Figure 11-7 C. Vance Haynes (right) examines the "black mat" marker bed at the Lehner Ranch site as archaeologists Nicole Waguespack and Todd Surovell look on.

Running along the top of the chart are the plant taxa—*Pinus* is pine pollen, *Juniperus* is juniper pollen, *Quercus* is oak, and so on. The horizontal scales below these are simply the percentages of the different kinds of plant pollen—for instance, artemisia constituted about 16 percent of the plants found at 160 cm in Profile I. The shaded areas show the changing frequencies of different pollen. For example, pollen of cheno-ams (chenopodiaceae and amaranthaceae, closely related plants of the goosefoot family and amaranth) is most common at the lowest levels of the site (look at Samples 13 and 14 in stratigraphic Units g and i). It becomes less common through time, until stratigraphic Unit m (Samples 23 through 28), where it begins to pick up. The assumption is that pollen roughly mirrors the local abundance of the plant species producing it; thus, goosefoot and amaranth were common early in the sequence, then became less common and, later in time, returned.

To go further, you must recognize the difference between *local* and *regional* environments. Look around at any landscape, and you will see microenvironments that do *not* reflect the regional environment. A flowing spring in a desert, for example, might support a dense stand of spruce, aspen, and mountain mahogany. Analysis of pollen from sediments near such a spring would suggest that the environment was a dense forest, when in fact the regional environment is a vast sage-

brush steppe. We need to understand what both local and regional environments looked like and, even more, we need to avoid confusing the two.

Mehringer had to cope with this potential difference between local and regional environments at Lehner Ranch. A distinctive "black mat" marker bed in the stratigraphy at Lehner Ranch suggests that the immediate area was a wet bog during late Clovis times (Figure 11-7). Was that a local condition, or was it true for the larger regional environment? Pollen from composites (herbs such as ragweed and sagebrush) and cheno-ams (plants that prefer wetter conditions) dominates the pollen diagram, suggesting that the region was wetter. This pattern characterizes many post-Pleistocene pollen profiles from southwestern deserts, but it creates a problem because it could mask the presence of less-common yet ecologically sensitive indicators. Although the dominant cheno-am and composite pollen undoubtedly represent *locally* occurring species, they are insufficient for interpreting *regional* vegetation or climate.

To offset the high frequency of composite and cheno-am pollen, Mehringer applied a technique known as the *double fixed sum*. The dark profiles in the diagram are based on a standard summary for all pollen types identified, with the percentages based on the first 200 pollen grains encountered in each sample. A total of 25 such 200-grain sample counts are represented (for various reasons, some samples could not be run; note, for example, there is no Sample 4 in the diagram).

Mehringer then made a second, 100-grain count (represented by the lighter areas). He computed the percentages for the second count by ignoring cheno-am and composite pollen, counting only the other, rarer pollen types. By comparing the results of both counts, one can study the gross frequencies of the dominants as well as fluctuations in the densities of the rarer but more environmentally sensitive species.

The pollen from stratigraphic Units i, j, and k at the Lehner Ranch reflect the climatic conditions that prevailed during Clovis times. Look carefully at the pollen frequencies of Samples 15 and 16 in Profile I, Samples 1, 2, and 3 in Profile VII, and Samples 13 and 14 in Pro-

file II. The environment of the time these samples represent is "read" by moving across the diagram. Notice that the normal pollen count—the dark portions of the figure—show a significant jump in short-spine *compositae* pollen in stratigraphic Unit k. The double fixed sum count shows slightly greater abundances of pine, oak, and juniper pollen. For trees such as pine, oak, and juniper to grow on the valley floor, the regional environment must have been slightly moister and/or cooler before and during the deposition of the lower part of Unit k. Somewhat later, during the deposition of upper stratigraphic Unit k and Unit l, a sharp increase in the *compositae* categories and a decline in tree pollen signal a shift to fully modern conditions.

Overall, the vegetation represented by the pollen

Looking Closer
Palynology of Shanidar Cave: Why Formation Processes Matter

Shanidar Cave (Iraq) was occupied sporadically over the past 100,000 years. In several seasons of excavation, Ralph Solecki (then of Columbia University) discovered several Neanderthal skeletons (one of which served as the inspiration for the shaman in Jean Auel's novel *The Clan of the Cave Bear*). One burial, Shanidar IV, was very fragile, and the entire block was removed in a plaster jacket, earth and all. The block was transported to an Iraqi museum, where it remained unopened for 2 years. Later, it was discovered that the Shanidar IV grave actually contained four individuals: three adults and an infant.

Whether Neanderthals intentionally buried their dead is a hotly contested issue. Some argue that they did not and hence lacked burial ritual—a key trait of modern humans. The palynology of Shanidar Cave played an important role in this debate.

Solecki took soil samples from the cave's strata as well as from within Shanidar IV. French palynologist Arlette Leroi-Gourhan (Musée de l'Homme, Paris) tested the Shanidar IV samples for pollen and—to everyone's surprise—found it preserved in surprising quantities; she found especially high amounts near the feet, the shoulders, and the base of the spine. Micro-

scopic examination indicated that these three samples contained dense concentrations of at least seven species of brightly colored wildflowers, including grape hyacinth, bachelor's button, and hollyhock.

Leroi-Gourhan suggested that the flowers had been woven into the branches of a pine-like shrub, which apparently grew nearby on the Ice Age hillside. She also concluded that the individuals found in the Shanidar IV grave were laid to rest between late May and early July, the time when the flowers would have been in bloom. These pollen data suggested that this Neanderthal burial took place as a formal interment, with a degree of planning and "humanness" that few were willing to grant Neanderthals at the time.

But scientists always ask themselves, "Do we really know what we think we know?" And in this case, the answer to that question focused on formation processes. Pollen is light, and it could have blown into the cave from the outside. Perhaps the pollen in the burial fill was simply what we call "background pollen rain."

But if the flower pollen was background rain, then it should have been present throughout the cave's deposits, not just the grave. Yet, it was not; the sediments outside the grave contained far *less* flower pollen than

spectra from Lehner Ranch suggests a desert grassland, which today occupies slightly wetter sites nearby. Mehringer and Haynes concluded that the climate at the Lehner site 11,000 years ago was only slightly wetter and cooler than today, followed by a rapid shift toward drier conditions. As many palynology studies have found, only a small shift in temperature and/or precipitation was required to produce dramatic differences in the environment at the Lehner Ranch site. And with only slight changes in rainfall and temperature, mammoths, horses, tapirs, and a range of other animals disappeared from the southern Arizona landscape forever.

The main contribution of pollen analysis to archaeology is the reconstruction of environmental change. Pollen studies, properly applied, can also help archaeologists understand past human behavior (see "Looking Closer: Palynology of Shanidar Cave: Why Formation Processes Matter"). And pollen also can play a role in figuring out what plants were important in prehistoric diet. An example from Nevada's Stillwater Marsh shows how and introduces other sources of paleoethnobotanical information.

What Plants Did People Eat in the Stillwater Marsh?

You will recall from Chapter 4 that after our survey of the Carson Desert (Nevada), high precipitation flooded the marsh and exposed dozens of archaeological sites and human burials. We discuss the burials in Chapter

the burial pit. In addition, the pollen grains in the burial samples were clumped, which is how they would be deposited if the pollen had fallen from flowers that had been laid in the grave, rather than blown into the cave. And some pollen even lay in the form of the flowers' anthers, suggesting that the entire flower was once present. None of these patterns are what we'd expect if the pollen had simply blown into the cave.

But nothing is ever simple in archaeology. Perhaps the pollen came into the site as flowers, but does this mean that the flowers were laid in the grave by the hands of a grieving Neanderthal?

Jeffrey Sommer (University of Michigan) suggests another possibility: rodents. Solecki noted that Shanidar IV and, in fact, all the site's burials were riddled with rodent burrows. In fact, Solecki thought he could locate burials by tracing rodent burrows through the deposits.

Many of those burrowing rodents died in the cave, and their skeletons tell us that they were *Meriones persicus*, the Persian jird. These interesting creatures apparently store large numbers of entire flower heads, neatly clipped from their stems—including those of the species that Leroi-Gourhan had identified—in the side tunnels of their burrows. Sommers points out that the number of flower heads

© Ralph Solecki

Neanderthal skull as it was being exposed at Shanidar Cave (Iraq). This person was probably killed by rooffall inside the cave.

that this rodent routinely stores is more than enough to account for the amount of pollen that Leroi-Gourhan found.

Although it is not conclusive, an alternative explanation for the Shanidar burial "bouquets" is that they were placed there by the humble jird. And the search for convincing evidence of ritual and religion among Neanderthals must continue.

12, and here we focus on the plant remains that were recovered from one site that we excavated in the wake of the flood.

Site 26CH1062 is not a particularly glamorous site (refer to Figure 4-9, page 97). It sits on a low clay dune and consists of several pits, postholes, and at least two shallow houses that were perhaps little more than windbreaks. Radiocarbon dates show that the site was occupied at least twice, once about 1400 radiocarbon years ago and again about 1000 years ago. We water-screened all the deposits and recovered a large number of stone tools, manufacturing waste flakes, shells, and faunal remains. We floated soil samples from several of the features and retrieved many carbonized macrobotanical remains.

The macrobotanical remains were sent to paleoethnobotanist David Rhode, at Nevada's Desert Research Institute. Looking at the samples under a microscope at 15–40X, Rhode identified the various carbonized seeds and bits of burnt wood (using a comparative collection, much like those that faunal analysts use). Most of the charcoal was reed (*Phragmites australis*), greasewood (*Sarcobatus* sp.), and some willow (*Salix* sp.). Because these plants can be found today in the Carson Desert, we were not surprised that they turned up in the samples. They could have been used as firewood, in housing, or as tools.

The seeds were more interesting. Rhode found the carbonized seeds of several plants, including cattail, dock, seepweed, chenopods, pickleweed, silverscale, heliotrope, saltbush, and goosefoot. The inhabitants of the site could have gathered any of these as food, and all occur in the area today.

One of the most abundant seeds was that of bulrush (*Scirpus* sp.). The indigenous peoples of the Carson Desert, the Paiute, used bulrush (and many other wetland plants) as food. This makes sense, because experimental data show that bulrush seeds are an efficiently gathered and nutritious resource (we'll return to these kinds of foraging experiments in Chapter 15).

But *did* people collect bulrush seeds for food? And, if so, did they collect it in the Stillwater Marsh? It is possible that the bulrush seeds came in attached to bulrush plants that were used to build the temporary houses on

the site or as material to make temporary containers. Any accidental burning of these artifacts could have toasted the seeds and left them behind for us to recover. Were bulrush plants, and not just their seeds, present on the site? To answer this question, we looked at another source of plant data in archaeological sites.

Phytoliths

One important method of learning about plants in ancient sites is the analysis of microscopic plant opal **phytoliths,** literally, "plant stones." As plants take in water through their roots, they also take in silica, which is then deposited in mineral form between cells, within cell walls, or sometimes in the cells themselves (Figure 11-8). Phytoliths occur in members of the grass family, as well as in rushes, sedges, palms, conifers, and deciduous trees. When dead plant material decays, the almost-indestructible opal phytoliths—they can last for millions of years—are deposited in the ground.

Importantly, phytoliths take the shape of the cells in which they were deposited. Because different grasses have different cell shapes, their phytoliths also have different shapes. This means that we can identify the presence of certain kinds of plants long after those plants have decayed and disappeared.

Phytolith analysis is similar to pollen analysis: Both deal with plant remains at a microscopic level; samples for each are collected in the same way; and the same laboratory can be used for both analyses (although separate samples are needed for each, because the acid baths used to reduce a sample for pollen destroys phytoliths).

But there is an important difference. Although a plant produces a single form of pollen, phytoliths can vary within a single species, and not all plants produce phytoliths. Phytoliths are most useful for identifying the abundance of different kinds of grasses, although research continues to refine this ability and extend it to other plants.

Phytolith analysis was extremely useful in the Stillwater Marsh. We sent soil samples to Linda Scott Cummings (Paleo Research Labs, Colorado) and, as expected, she found that phytoliths were well preserved. Phragmites, a common marsh grass, probably accounted for most of the phytoliths, along with several other marsh grasses. What was most intriguing, however, was the complete *lack* of sedge phytoliths, which are produced by plants such as bulrush. This suggests that no bulrush plants decayed on the site. If they had,

phytoliths Tiny silica particles contained in plants. Sometimes these fragments can be recovered from archaeological sites, even after the plants themselves have decayed.

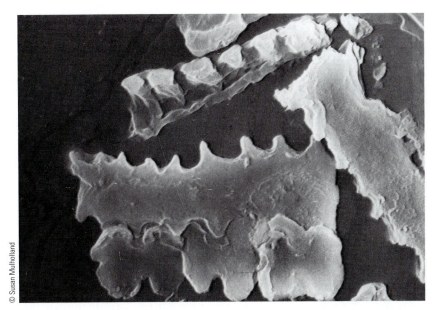

Figure 11-8 What a phytolith looks like under the microscope.

© Susan Mulholland

Cummings would have found their phytoliths in the soil samples.

Perhaps, then, there was no bulrush in the Stillwater Marsh 1000 years ago. But where did all those bulrush seeds come from? Perhaps a visiting Paiute brought some bulrush seed cakes from another wetland, such as Walker Lake to the south or Winnemucca Lake to the west. This is a question about the regional environment. Although phytoliths can tell which plants were present on a specific site, pollen data are better for looking at regional patterns.

So, in addition to flotation and phytolith samples, we also took pollen samples from several of the features. These were sent to Peter Wigand, then at the Desert Research Institute, where he analyzed them using the protocols we described above. He found that the pollen in the samples was little different from the modern pollen rain of today; in fact, he found that sedge pollen was somewhat overrepresented in the samples: bulrush might even have been somewhat *more* abundant in the Stillwater Marsh of the past than it is today.

So, now we know (a) that burnt bulrush seeds were present on the site, (b) that bulrush plants were not on the site, but that (c) bulrush was abundant in the wetland at the time the site was occupied. Given that ethnographic data show that bulrush seeds were eaten by the Paiute, and experimental data indicate that bulrush is an efficiently gathered and nutritious food, we concluded that bulrush seeds were brought to the site to be eaten.

The macrobotanical remains were also interesting in what was *not* present. Completely missing were the seeds of upland plants such as ricegrass (*Oryzopsis hymenoides*) or piñon (*Pinus monophylla*) pine nut hulls—both important food sources to the nineteenth-century Shoshone and Paiute in the Great Basin. This suggests that, when people lived in the Carson Desert, they got their plant food exclusively from the wetland and did not travel even a few kilometers into the low foothills to gather ricegrass, nor did they hike another 20 kilometers into the hills to gather piñon.

Site Seasonality

The seasonality of the Agate Basin site was determined using faunal remains, but at 26CH1062 we used the macrobotanical remains. Recall that we found bulrush seeds, along with cattail, seepweed, dock, chenopods, pickleweed, heliotrope, silverscale, saltbush, and goosefoot seeds. We know from ethnographic and experimental data that most of these seeds ripen in the mid- to late summer and into the early winter. Dock and heliotrope are gathered throughout the summer only. Late summer is therefore the only time when all of these are available, and that is probably the best estimate of when the site was occupied (although an occupation through the fall cannot be ruled out).

Wood Rat Nests

One important, if somewhat surprising, source of plant macrofossils is the ancient nests of **wood rats** (*Neotoma* sp.) that are found throughout the arid desert west

---

wood rats (also pack rats) Rodents that build nests of organic materials and thus preserve a record, often for thousands of years, of changing plant species within the local area of the nest.

© Steve Jackson

Figure 11-9 Wood rat midden in the Bighorn Mountains, Wyoming. The upper midden is a meter high.

(Figure 11-9). (Most people call these rodents pack rats, but the accepted scientific name is wood rats; they're the same critter.)

Wood rats are fascinating animals. They bring home extensive quantities of food and nest material, including wood, rock, bone, paper—anything that they can drag into a crevice or rockshelter. Archaeologists in the western United States know that wood rat nests are good places to look for organic artifacts—arrows, atlatl pieces, and basketry fragments are all incorporated into wood rat nests (as well as small tools or notepaper that a forgetful archaeologist might leave out overnight!).

Field studies demonstrate that pack rats do not travel more than 100 meters from their nests to collect mate-

rials. In contrast to pollen studies, wood rat nests reflect the *immediate* environment around their nests.

After collecting material, the rats build their nests in protected locations, such as crevices in cliffs or in cave mouths or rockshelters. This certainly helps to preserve the collected twigs and branches, but they do something else to the nests that guarantees their preservation: The rats urinate all over them. Their urine forms a lacquer-like covering on the nest that also promotes the preservation of organic materials—for thousands of years. As a result, researchers throughout arid North America use wood rat assemblages to reconstruct late Pleistocene and **Holocene** vegetational change.

Wood rat nests are often as hard as rock, and so you use hammers, chisels, saws, and pry bars to excavate them. (By the way, the nests have a strong smell. Some people hate it and others, oddly enough, like it.) After samples are taken from different levels in the nest, they are soaked in distilled water if they are covered with urine lacquer. After samples are dry, the analyst then sorts and identifies the materials. Specimens from each sample are radiocarbon-dated, and the resulting data help to reconstruct past environments.

Wood Rat Nests and Piñon in the Stillwater Mountains

We noted earlier that neither piñon pine nuts nor their hulls appear in sites in the Stillwater Marsh, and we suggested this meant that people did not travel to the mountains to collect them. But did people not collect piñon nuts because they did not need them, or because there was no piñon pine in the mountains 1000 or more years ago?

To answer this question, Peter Wigand and his colleague Cheryl Nowak studied a number of wood rat middens from several locations in western Nevada, including the Stillwater Range, which borders the Carson Desert. They found that evidence for piñon pine—in the form of branches, needles, and cones—did not appear in wood rat nests until about 1200 years ago in the Stillwater Mountains and considerably later in ranges farther west. So perhaps piñon was not present in the Stillwater Mountains, only 20–30 kilometers distant, in sufficient density to make a trip worthwhile at the time people occupied the marsh sites.

You will recall from Chapter 4 that research in the Carson Desert was aimed at understanding whether

Holocene The post-Pleistocene geological epoch that began about 10,000 radiocarbon years ago and continues today.

wetland food resources provided better returns and were preferred over those of the mountains. If we assume that the past environments of the Carson Desert and Stillwater Mountains were similar to the modern ones, then the data from 26CH1062 suggest that Native Americans eschewed piñon in favor of marsh plants. But the wood rat nest data suggest that the specific reason may be that piñon was not present in sufficient abundance to make a trip to the mountains worth the effort. This example shows that *it is essential that archaeologists make economic interpretations of subsistence data in light of paleoenvironmental reconstructions.* The former without the latter is almost useless.

Coprolites of Hidden Cave

Human coprolites are another source of information on prehistoric diet. Paleontologists first used the term "coprolite" (from the Greek *kopros* "dung" and *lithikos* "stone") about 1830 to describe fossilized dinosaur feces. Archaeologists use the term, but the feces we analyze are just desiccated, not fossilized. Coprolites are not common in the archaeological record, but they are, for obvious reasons, an excellent source of information on human diet.

Archaeologists find coprolites of many different kinds of animals, including humans, in dry archaeological sites. The archaeologist's first task is to identify which are human, and which belong to other species such as deer or mountain sheep. Believe it or not, some archaeologists have devoted time to identifying the criteria that distinguish human feces from, say, that of a coyote.

David Rhode, the same paleoethnobotanist who studied the macrobotanical remains from 26CH1062, also looked at human coprolites from Hidden Cave, a site that overlooks the Stillwater Marsh (see Chapter 4; Figure 4-4 on page 85). The cave's original opening was very small, barely large enough to crawl into; and even though the cave opens into a large chamber, it was a lousy place to live or even to spend the night. It is dark and dusty and, if you made a fire for warmth or light, the chamber would soon fill with smoke. Thus, we were not surprised when we found no hearths, stone tool waste flakes, or bones left over from meals. People did not live in Hidden Cave; instead, they used it as a place to cache various kinds of gear—in pits between 3800 and 1500 years ago.

But there were also many quids—expectorated pieces of plants (such as cattail and bulrush) that people had chewed for their juices. And found nearby were bits of cordage, made from strips of bark rolled together. This suggests that people also used the cave as a place where they could escape the summer afternoon's heat, passing the afternoon by chewing succulent stalks of bulrush and cattail in the cave's cool interior while rolling bark together to make cords to tie together bundles, repair sagebrush bark sandals, or repair torn baskets.

Many of the artifacts found in Hidden Cave were projectile points; these might suggest that men were the primary visitors to the cave (we'll deal with such gender assumptions in Chapter 13). Many coprolites were also found. Rhode decided to investigate the coprolites to see what the men who used the shelter were eating. He was surprised by what he found.

Rhode prepared the 19 coprolites by first soaking them in a solution of trisodium phosphate to reconstitute them (yes, really!). He then washed each specimen through fine mesh screens and dried the residue. Next, he examined and sorted this material under a microscope.

A small macrobotanical remain from each coprolite was AMS radiocarbon-dated. In so doing, Rhode found that the coprolites fell into two time periods: One batch dated between 3800 and 3400 BP, the other from 1900 to 1500 BP. All of the coprolites contained abundant evidence of plants, fish, and bird remains (people may also have eaten large mammals, but obviously their bones would not appear in coprolites).

Bulrush seeds were the most common seeds, some showing evidence of burning and milling (striations left from the action of grinding stones). Cattail pollen was also common. Rhode also found small feathers of waterfowl, as well as the bones of tui chub, a species of minnow that lives in the Stillwater Marsh. In fact, fish cranial (head) and caudal (tail) bones tell us that these small fish were eaten whole. Insects showed up too, as well as snails.

Curiously, only one coprolite contained a piñon pine nut hull. This coprolite, Number 167, also contained cattail seeds and pollen. This is interesting, because piñon nuts ripen in late September or early October, whereas cattail pollen is collected in July. Clearly, one of these resources must have been stored, and it was most likely the piñon. (By the way, this coprolite dated to 1740 BP, again indicating that piñon was not present in the region until later in the region's history; but we don't know if it came from the Stillwater Mountains.)

All this was interesting, but then came the surprise. We can determine if a man or woman voided a

Archaeological Ethics
Are Archaeologists Responsible for Media Reports?

Like all scientists, archaeologists are obliged to be as careful as possible in their research, to publish it in such a way that it might be critiqued by others, and to be honest about what hypotheses the research does or does not support.

But the wider public is also interested in the past, so archaeology gets pretty good coverage in the media, especially when a story breaks that appears to overturn previous knowledge.

There are, of course, huge differences between the media and professional reports. Read a professional archaeological publication, and it will be full of hedges and caveats about small sample size, inadequacy of middle-range theory, other interpretations, and conflicting evidence. We hedge our conclusions because we know that archaeological inference is difficult. We make things complicated. We have to, because it's hard to know what happened in the past.

The media, on the other hand, simplifies things. And it has to; it's the media's job to take complex issues and make them intelligible to a public that probably knows little about the subject. But this can create problems.

In the 1990s, several archaeologists reported evidence of cannibalism in the American Southwest. The evidence came in the form of human bones that bore cut marks, suggesting that flesh was stripped from them. Some of the long bones and vertebrae were also smashed open, in the same way that deer and bison bones are broken open to extract the marrow. Still other bones were burned, and some broken ends bore evidence of "pot polish"—abraded surfaces that have been experimentally reproduced by stirring boiling deer bones in a ceramic pot.

One proponent of the cannibalism hypothesis is Christy Turner (Arizona State University). In his book, *Man Corn,* he and his late wife, Jacqueline, document nearly 300 individuals that, Turner argues, bear evidence of cannibalism. These come from 76 archaeological sites—most are Chacoan sites in the Four Corners region of the Southwest and date from AD 900 to 1250. Most of the remains concentrate in the late twelfth century—the time of the demise of the Chacoan system, with its large pueblos and vast road network (see Chapters 4 and 5). Turner argues that Toltec religious cult members, migrants from Mesoamerica, used cannibalism as a way to terrify and control the local population.

The basic data can't really be denied: Some people's bodies were dismembered and boiled and, in all likelihood, this means that they were eaten. But some archaeologists take exception to the Turners' *interpretation,* pointing out that broken, cut-marked bones could be evidence of a burial ritual, a reverent dismemberment that is part of a number of cultures around the world today and not evidence of cannibalism. Others suggest that the violence could have been inflicted on "witches" only, an effort to thoroughly destroy any trace of a social miscreant. In either case, no one need have eaten anyone else.

There is, however, one direct case of cannibalism. In a kiva's central fireplace in a site in Cowboy Wash in southwestern Colorado, researchers found a human coprolite that contained the protein myoglobin, which exists only in human muscle tissue. The most parsimonious explanation is that one individual consumed the coprolite depending on the abundance of the sex hormones estradiol, progesterone, and testosterone. This is done using a complex technique known as high-pressure liquid chromatographic analysis. After applying this technique, Rhode found that the coprolites' levels of sex hormones clearly indicated that women had voided the coprolites. We don't know if it was also women who cached the projectile points, spit out the quids, and spun cordage. But coprolite analysis clearly opens up new approaches to diet as well as new approaches to reconstructing the lives of men and women in the past.

flesh of another and, some hours later, defecated in the center of a very sacred place.

It is not so much the evidence for or against cannibalism that concerns us here. Instead, we are concerned with what the media did with this topic and the responsibilities of the archaeologist in dealing with the media.

The press tends to seek stories that seem to dramatically overturn everything that we thought we knew; and some journalists especially like stories that make researchers look as though they are trying to hide "the truth." In this case, the evidence for cannibalism caught the attention of media all over the world—American, European, and Japanese news services picked up the story, with titles like "American Cannibalism?" "Anasazi Cannibalism," "Researchers Divided over whether Anasazi Were Cannibals," and "Did Cannibalism Kill Anasazi Civilization?" PBS produced a documentary in 2000 entitled "Cannibals of the Canyon" (referring to Chaco Canyon). Even the television program *King of the Hill* (co-created by the son of an archaeologist) used "Anasazi cannibalism" as a story line.

The media loved the story because it was gruesome and because it overturned previously held images of Native Americans as peaceful peoples living in harmony with nature and their neighbors.

Such claims and such casual treatment of cannibalism upset many Puebloan peoples. They point out that their oral histories contain no stories of cannibalism and, therefore, archaeologists were probably wrong. (Actually, there are published accounts of cannibalism in Pueblo traditions.) And do 300 cases (not all of which are accepted by other researchers) spread out over a vast area and some 350 years make the Puebloan people "cannibals"? Cases of can-

nibalism certainly occur in Euroamerican history. Most notable among them is the Donner Party, the group of 87 emigrants who, in 1846, were stranded for 5 months in the Sierra Nevada and were forced to feed off those who had already succumbed to starvation. But nobody asks whether Euroamericans are cannibals. It seems that, despite the horrible things that some *individuals* might resort to, Euroamericans *as a people* could not be cannibals.

Indians are understandably upset, because they know that even asking the question about them implies that Indians *could be* cannibals. And that's as damaging as actually having done the deed.

The archaeologists who research this subject have, for the most part, done so responsibly. Their reports are written in measured tones. They make no extravagant claims. They know that cannibalism is hard to prove. In fact, many think that whether cannibalism occurred or not is unimportant. What does matter, and what research by the Turners and others makes clear, is that the Puebloan world saw a period of intense intervillage conflict, including warfare, in the twelfth and thirteenth centuries. For most archaeologists, the more interesting and archaeologically testable subject lies not in cannibalism but in understanding cycles of violence.

Can archaeologists be held responsible for media reports? To a large extent, the answer is no. The media will print what they think will sell (and cannibalism in the headline certainly outsells intervillage violence). Does this mean that archaeologists should censor themselves? Should they try to steer a journalist in the "right" direction? Should they withhold information that they suspect will be spun in the wrong way?

Lipid Analysis: Squeezing Fat from Ceramics

The analysis of faunal and macrobotanical remains, phytoliths, pollen, and coprolite analysis are fairly standard in archaeology's effort to reconstruct the past. But archaeologists and their associates in allied fields are always developing new techniques that extract even more information from archaeological remains and increase our ability to reconstruct the past. For example, some analysts are attempting to extract ancient blood from the microcracks in stone tools and identify it to species. Another technique allows us to extract identifiable food residues from pottery.

The reconstruction of the plant component of ancient diets is more elusive than determining the role of meat. This is largely because of a substantial bias in preservation: Bone preserves better than plant remains. Macrobotanical remains are also more difficult to retrieve from archaeological sites. Flotation increases the recovery rate, but plant remains are still hard to come by: Water-screening allowed us to retrieve some 300,000 animal bones from 26CH1062 (mostly small fish bones, so the number is a bit exaggerated), but we collected only a few handfuls of macrobotanical remains. So archaeologists are always looking for new ways to retrieve information on plants from archaeological sites.

One promising way is to extract **lipids** from artifacts and even from sediments themselves. Lipids are those organic substances that resist mixing with water. This includes the fats, oils, and waxes that are found in both plant and animal tissues. Because they resist mixing with water, lipids have a tendency to remain where they were deposited (and even washing in the laboratory may not remove them).

Cooking vessels are a particularly good place to look for lipids, because the lipids are released from the plant or meat when heated and are absorbed into the fabric of the pottery. Cooking vessels often have a thick carbon residue inside, the result of many simmering stews, but the best place to look for lipids is actually in the walls of the pottery itself.

How do we identify lipids? Recall from our discussion of radiocarbon dating in Chapter 8 that there are three major kinds of carbon in the atmosphere—^{14}C, ^{13}C, and ^{12}C. Recall also that plants of different photosynthetic pathways take in these carbons in different amounts. Thus different classes of plants have different ratios of ^{13}C to ^{12}C, and the plant's fatty acids register this ratio.

The archaeological sample comes from a piece of the interior of a pot. The sherd is ground up and subjected to a laboratory process that separates the fatty acids in the lipid fraction. This extract is then subjected to gas chromatography and mass spectrometry. Without going into the details, these devices measure the ratio of ^{13}C to ^{12}C. Different ratios distinguish the fatty acids in

the lipids of plants from those of animals; ongoing research shows that different plant taxa (and, to a lesser extent, different animal species) can be identified using this technique.

One of this method's pioneers, Richard Evershed (University of Bristol, England), has identified the lipids of leafy vegetables (perhaps cabbage) from pottery in Europe. He has also identified residues of milk and of meat. Looking at medieval pots from England, he found that the amount of lipids increased from the bottom to the top of the pot. This makes sense, because fats and oil rise to the top of a stew or soup as it cools, and upper portions of pots would therefore absorb more than the lower portions. In fact, on the inside bottom of some pots he found the fatty acid signature of beeswax. This was not part of a meal, but part of the manufacture of the pot: Ethnoarchaeological research has found that many potters smear beeswax on the inside of a pot that is still warm from the kiln in order to season it.

Mary Malainey (Brandon University, Canada), along with colleagues Roman Przybylski and Barbara Sherriff, enhanced this technique by creating a comparative fatty acid "collection"—similar to a faunal analyst's or paleoethnobotanist's comparative collective—of some 130 plants, mammals, fish, and birds native to southwestern Canada. Malainey used lipid analysis to find evidence of meat, maize, plants (excluding maize), fish, and beaver residues on 200 potsherds from sites in southern Canada.

This technique works only with cooking pots, which could record a variety of different kinds of meals. The method holds great promise for reconstructing some elements of the diet that have otherwise proved elusive. There is even the possibility that lipids could be extracted from soil samples and help recover more information on plant foods, such as tubers and roots, that do not preserve well and are rarely found carbonized.

THE SYMBOLIC MEANING OF PLANTS: THE UPPER MANTARO VALLEY PROJECT

So far, we have been talking about plants, animals, and people from a strictly economic perspective: What did people eat in the past, and when did they eat it? But more can be done with plant and animal remains in

lipids Organic substances—including fats, oils, and waxes—that resist mixing with water; found in both plant and animal tissues.

archaeological sites. As discussed in Chapter 3, processual archaeology emphasizes the analysis of natural resources—such as plant remains—as a key to understanding how people coped with ecological issues of the past. But postprocessual archaeology encourages us to seek other things about the past, including not only how people interacted materially with their environment, but how they interacted with it symbolically as well. The Upper Mantaro Valley Project in Peru is one example.

The upper Mantaro Valley sits at 3300 meters (about 10,800 feet) above sea level in the central Andes of Peru. The intensively settled and cultivated valley floors are surrounded by rocky hillsides, supporting a few rocky fields, but mostly grasses, a few shrubs, and small trees (Figure 11-10). Thousands of years of intensive cultivation and herding have undoubtedly changed the character of these upland valleys, but nobody is certain just how. Although some investigators believe that the landscape was originally forested, pollen analysis suggests that this area has been relatively treeless since humans first moved in, several thousand years ago.

The Upper Mantaro Archaeological Project excavated numerous house compounds from six archaeological sites spanning the period AD 500–1500 (divided into six phases: Pancán 1 through Pancán 4 and Wanka II and III). During the Wanka II phase, the population of the Upper Mantaro area aggregated into large, walled towns located on protected knolls just above the rolling upland zone. The archaeological evidence suggests that this was a time of fights between villages, with land use probably restricted to areas close to the walled settlements. After the Inka conquest during Wanka III times, the population was relocated into small villages on the valley floor. (The Inka often relocated conquered peoples as a way to control them.)

The researchers collected 6-liter soil samples from the floors, middens, pits, and hearths encountered in each excavation unit. The more than 900 samples contained thousands of pieces of charcoal and plant

Figure 11-10 Peaks in the Andes Mountains overlooking a homestead (lower right) on the *puna* in central Peru.

fragments, recovered by both dry screening and flotation of the sediments. The recovered plant remains were classified into three simple categories: grass, stem (small-diameter twig fragments), and wood (pieces of mature wood). The wood category was further subdivided if the tree species could be identified.

Paleoethnobotanists Christine Hastorf (University of California, Berkeley) and Sissel Johannessen (U.S. Army Corps of Engineers) examined these flotation samples to analyze the changing patterns of fuel use in the central Andes of Peru. People can burn a number of different things in fires to cook food and to heat their homes. Grass, tied in tight bundles, small twigs, dung from herbivores, and, of course, mature wood can all be used. What does it mean if people use one source rather than another?

Hastorf and Johannessen found that grass, twigs, and mature wood were all used for fuel, and that mature wood was always the dominant fuel source. But it is the relative frequencies, rather than the absolute figures, that matter. Figure 11-11 graphs the ratio of wood to stems and wood to other (stems and grass) fuel sources for the six phases that cover the 1000-year-long sequence of the Upper Mantaro Valley. Prior to AD 1300 (during the Pancán phases), the relative proportion of mature wood fragments dropped; this means that over time, people used more grass and stems as fuel, rather than mature wood. Then, during Wanka II and Wanka III times, this trend reversed, with stem and grass remains decreasing again.

Hastorf and Johannessen also noted that the species composition of the mature wood shifted through time. Up to 40 different kinds of wood are present in the Upper Mantaro Valley samples, with no particular taxa being especially dominant. But the most common taxa did change in relative frequency through time. The five most popular wood types during the early Pancán phases (from yet-unidentified trees) dropped out entirely by Wanka II times. And beginning around AD 1300, new wood types appeared. One notable example is *Buddleia* sp. (known as *quishuar* in Quechua), a high-elevation tree that became the most popular fuel source during Inka (Wanka III) times.

What Explains Wood Use?

Let's work through the analysis step by step, following the arguments developed by Hastorf and Johannessen. First, we must consider whether the charcoal distributions on the diagram can be attributed to factors other than fuel use. Is it possible, for instance, that we are looking at changing patterns in the use of house construction materials, changing subsistence practices, or perhaps differential plant preservation through time?

Hastorf and Johannessen rejected all these possibilities. They noted that most of the charcoal comes from fire refuse accumulated over a span of several months or years. Although the possibility exists that some of the charcoal resulted from inadvertent fires (such as accidental burning of thatch roofs and roof beams), the investigators assume that the majority of the charcoal reflects intentional fuel use for heating and cooking. They also note that the composition of the house compounds (mud and stone), the general subsistence remains, and the depositional contents are basically constant throughout the 1000-year sequence. And there is little reason to believe that rates of preservation changed significantly through time.

Hastorf and Johannessen then moved to interpret the charcoal distributions strictly in terms of changing fuel use patterns. Beginning their paleo-

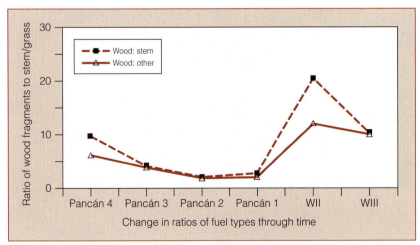

Figure 11-11 The changing ratios of wood to other fuel types through time in the Upper Mantaro area of Peru. *After Hastorf and Johannessen (1991) courtesy Christine Hastorf*

ethnobotanical analysis in standard fashion, they first determined whether the archaeological patterning of fuel use revealed long-term shifts in the relationship between these highland people and their environment.

From this strictly economic perspective, the increased reliance through time on twigs and grasses during the Pancán sequence is just what one might expect in a relatively treeless landscape. Through time, the growing human population and more intensive agricultural land-use patterns made fuel wood scarce. It makes sense that, as people denuded their landscape of trees, they turned to less-desirable fuels, such as small shrubby plants, twigs, and grasses.

But if this is so, then why would this trend reverse during later Wanka times? Contrary to strictly ecological expectations, the archaeologically recovered plant remains show that the use of high-quality fuels actually *increased* after AD 1300.

Perhaps the evidence from settlement pattern archaeology provides a clue. Beginning in Wanka II times, an elite class began social and political consolidation of the area. Maybe this elite class mandated some sort of fuel management program, perhaps in the form of tree cultivating, resulting in a greater availability of mature wood sources. This scenario is certainly possible, because we know that tree cultivation was practiced during Inka times.

Fuel, of course, has an important economic role in Andean life, especially at an elevation in excess of 3300 meters where the days, to say nothing of the nights, are cold. The increased fuel management/tree cultivation explanation provides a workable, rational answer in economic terms, but leaves several questions unanswered:

Why does the change take place in Wanka II times? Why not earlier (when the population first increased) or later (when the Inka took over and restructured the location of the production system)?

Why would cultivation be chosen to alleviate the fuel shortage? Why not simply go farther afield to gather fuel? Or why not just shift to lower-quality fuels?

And why do certain tree taxa show up during Inka times, when they were absent before?

At this point, Hastorf and Johannessen decided to explore explanations that went beyond conventional economic and ecological factors. They delved into the ethnographic and ethnohistoric records to document the relationships among Andean people, the upland forest, and traditional fuel sources. In so doing, Hastorf and Johannessen found that wood is more than simply fuel in the Andes. It also has an important symbolic dimension.

Collecting fuel was an important aspect of Inkan life, consuming up to 4 hours each day for some segments of the population. We know from documentary accounts that logs, kindling, and straw were also important tribute items in the Inka state.

But trees also had important, symbolic connotations in Andean cosmology. Certain sacred trees were planted at administrative sites. Others were symbolically linked with deities. In fact, the Inka burned *quishuar,* the wood that appeared during Wanka III times, in large quantities at festivals and ritually burned human figures carved of *quishuar* as sacrifices to the divine ancestor of the Inka dynasty. Trees were also symbolically associated with water, as well as with women, clouds, winter, and the moon.

From these and other ethnohistoric and ethnographic examples, Hastorf and Johannessen concluded that wood had strong symbolic as well as economic roles in Inka life, being used to cement social relations (perhaps because it was so important and so rare). Brothers-in-law, for instance, sometimes provided wood and straw to relatives at a wake (Figure 11-12).

Relating Ideology to the Past

Hastorf and Johannessen supplemented their ecological perspective with a new appreciation of the cultural

© Christine Hastorf

Figure 11-12
Ethnohistoric sketch of an Inka man linking himself to his in-laws by presenting them with wood and straw fuel at a wake.

relationship between ancient Andean people and their environment. But why did the change take place in Wanka II times?

Hastorf and Johannessen argue that the ideology associated with the planting of certain trees could have been a factor in establishing the local political consolidation occurring at that time: The tree symbolized family continuity on the land, with the roots symbolizing ancestors and the fruits, the children. In fact, a ritual step in contemporary marriage ceremonies is termed "to bring the branch" and involves the bringing forth of ritual offspring. The dramatic increase in the use of *quishuar* might thus be attributed to its ritual significance of bringing social groups together into larger entities, rather than simply its mundane use as firewood.

These investigators believe that the act of planting trees—which could be interpreted as a purely economic response to a fuel shortage—was chosen from the other available alternatives because of cultural values concerning the ways in which cultivation and trees func-

tioned as symbols of life and lineage, socially and politically.

CONCLUSION

This chapter has illustrated how archaeologists go about investigating the relationships among people, plants, and animals. From these remains we can determine what plants and animals people ate, what seasons of the year they were taken, and what sorts of tactics were used to hunt or gather them. They can help reconstruct trade relations. Often, archaeologists view information from plant and animal remains as evidence of ancient peoples' purely materialistic and mundane relations with their environment. And often, that is correct. But the final example from Peru suggests that our interpretations of the past may often be layered, and that material interactions with the environment may have symbolic importance as well.

Summary

- Plant and animal remains aid in the reconstruction of past diet and environments. Dietary reconstructions mean little without their environmental context.

- Faunal analysis—the study of animal remains in archaeological sites—can provide direct evidence of which species were hunted (or collected) for food, how many animals were killed, how they were captured, and what butchering methods were employed.

- Faunal remains can help establish the season of the year when a site was occupied using animal birthing and tooth eruption schedules.

- Plant remains are also powerful sources of data regarding ancient life. Flotation is the most commonly used method for recovering plant macrofossils from archaeological sites.

- Palynology—the study of pollen—is most useful in reconstructing past *regional* environments. Pollen diagrams enable us to document how local and regional vegetation has changed through time.

- The nests of wood rats can preserve millennia-long records of *local* environmental change.

- Macrofossils (intact plant parts) are important to paleoenvironmental reconstruction but are also direct evidence of which plant species were exploited, the season of site occupation, and plant processing technology.

- Phytoliths, small grains of silica that form inside plant stems, are less sensitive indicators of plants on a site, but can demonstrate which plant stems (as opposed to seeds) were present on a site.

- Coprolites (desiccated feces) provide evidence of what people ate. They are especially useful indicators of plants (because some seeds pass through undigested) and small animals (because their bones, feathers, or fur may also pass through). Coprolites also tell us what people ate in a single day and hence can point to food storage practices.

- New methods, such as the analysis of lipids on the insides of ceramic cooking vessels, provide information on plant use and on the roles of meat and cooking techniques.

- People's interaction with the environment has an economic basis, but culture may frequently place layers of symbolic meaning on top of that interaction.

Additional Reading

Brothwell, D., and A. Pollard (Eds.). 2001. *Handbook of Archaeological Sciences.* Chichester, UK: John Wiley and Sons.

Grayson, Donald K. 1984. *Quantitative Zooarchaeology: Topics in the Analysis of Archaeological Faunas.* Orlando, FL: Academic Press.

Pearsall, Deborah M. 2000. *Paleoethnobotany: A Handbook of Procedures.* New York: Academic Press.

Reitz, Elizabeth, and Elizabeth Wing. 1999. *Zooarchaeology.* Cambridge: Cambridge University Press.

Sobolik, Kristin. 2003. *The Archaeologist's Toolkit, Volume 5: Archaeobiology.* Walnut Creek, CA: Altamira Press.

Online Resources

COMPANION WEB SITE
Visit **http://anthropology.wadsworth.com** and click on the Student Companion Web Site for Thomas/Kelly *Archaeology*, 4th edition, to access a wide range of material to help you succeed in your introductory archaeology course. These include flashcards, Internet exercises, Web links, and practice quizzes.

RESEARCH ONLINE WITH INFOTRAC COLLEGE EDITION
From the Student Companion Web Site, you can access the InfoTrac College Edition database, which offers thousands of full-length articles for your research.

12 | Bioarchaeological Approaches to the Past

OUTLINE

© George Gill

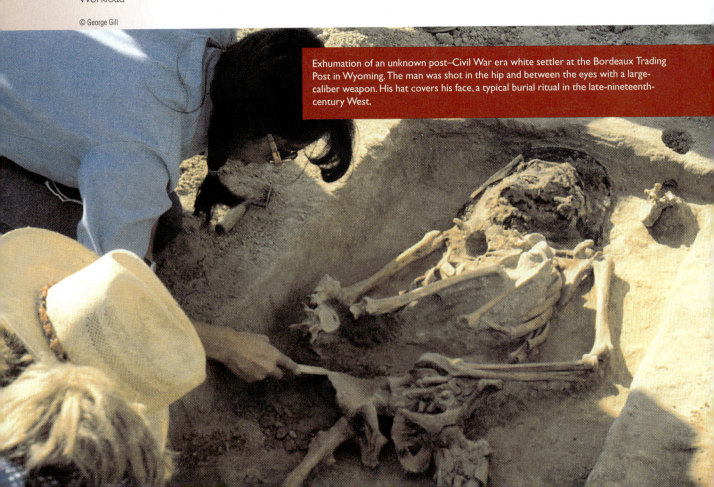

Exhumation of an unknown post–Civil War era white settler at the Bordeaux Trading Post in Wyoming. The man was shot in the hip and between the eyes with a large-caliber weapon. His hat covers his face, a typical burial ritual in the late-nineteenth-century West.

Preview

THIS CHAPTER EXAMINES bioarchaeology, a specialty that straddles the fields of archaeology and biological anthropology. Bioarchaeologists study the human biological component of the archaeological record. Some bioarchaeologists study the origin and distribution of ancient diseases; others reconstruct human diets, analyze the evidence for biological stress in archaeological populations, and reconstruct past demographic patterns—all of this by exploring human bone, bone chemistry, and the DNA preserved in human tissues. Although this chapter is a bit heavy on chemistry and biology, the archaeological payoff is worth the effort.

The analysis of human remains today is a sensitive subject in many parts of the world. Handling, photographing, and sampling the physical remains of a once-living, breathing human being is upsetting to many Native Americans (and, actually, to plenty of other Americans as well). These concerns surfaced in the Kennewick case that we introduced in Chapter 1. Here, we discuss the astonishing amount of information that science can learn from human skeletal remains (and this chapter merely scratches the surface). In the process, we will demonstrate how scientists can conduct such studies in a respectful and sensitive manner. No skeletal remains of Native Americans are portrayed in this or any other chapter.

INTRODUCTION

In Chapter 4, we described Kelly's archaeological survey project in the Carson Desert of western Nevada. We mentioned that the survey had failed to find many archaeological sites in the marsh because they were obscured by sand and vegetation. However, in the mid-1980s, the greatest floods the Carson Desert had witnessed in a millennium exposed many sites in the marsh.

But more was exposed than arrowheads and faunal remains. Kelly visited the marsh in the summer of 1986, while the Nevada State Museum was recording the new archaeological sites for the U.S. Fish and Wildlife Service (on whose lands most of the new sites were located). Many of the newly exposed sites were accessible only by airboat. Jetting up to the shore of one site, Kelly saw several human skulls rolling about in the wake. The flood had not only exposed many new sites, but dozens and dozens of human burials as well.

In 1987, after the floodwaters had receded, Kelly returned to the Stillwater Marsh to excavate one of the habitation sites (Site 26CH1062, which we mentioned in Chapter 11) and to survey the marsh for burials and human bone. By this point, Clark Spencer Larsen (Ohio State University), a noted **bioarchaeologist,** had joined the team. Bioarchaeologists like Larsen study the human biological component of the archaeological record. Larsen received graduate training in biological anthropology, with a focus on the human skeleton as a record of past human activity. But because he worked with skeletal remains recovered from archaeological sites, Larsen was fully aware of the complex nature of archaeological data as well.

A well-trained field archaeologist can tell the difference between human and animal bones. But few archaeologists are trained to go beyond such simple identification. When modern archaeologists expect to

bioarchaeology The study of the human biological component evident in the archaeological record.

Looking Closer
Native Americans and the Stillwater Burials

The first people to find the Stillwater burials were looters, people searching for skulls to place on their fireplace mantels. Anthropologists hesitate to call any cultural practice gruesome, but that is the first word that comes to mind.

Fortunately, several dedicated amateur and professional archaeologists raised a cry, and soon the Fallon Paiute-Shoshone Tribe, located next door to the Stillwater Marsh, asked that the U.S. Fish and Wildlife Service (USFWS) protect their heritage. The USFWS enlisted the support of the tribe for collection and analysis of human remains in the marsh and did so with the assistance of the Nevada State Museum. In the meantime, the USFWS increased patrols of the marsh and began a public education campaign aimed at reducing looting. By September of 1986, over 4000 human remains had been professionally collected and 144 intact human burials recorded.

What was to be done with these remains? At the time, no legislation specifically protected American Indian burials. But in the 1980s, archaeologists understood this was a sensitive issue for American Indians, and everyone involved at Stillwater felt the need to do something "right."

But what was the right thing?

The first right thing was to involve the local Indian community, the Fallon Paiute and Shoshone. Local solutions always work better than those imposed by a distant government. And things work better if the people involved are genuinely respectful of the other side. Fortunately, the USFWS archaeologist, Anan Raymond, was the right person for this task, and he began consulting with the tribe shortly after the first human remains turned up. Eventually, a Memorandum of Understanding detailed precisely how the remains would be collected, analyzed, and reburied.

At first, the tribe wished for the remains to stay where they were found. But knowing that looters would disturb the burials, they agreed that burials should be excavated if they were in danger of being disturbed; the others would be covered over and their location plotted on a USFWS map so that they could be periodically checked. The chair of the Fallon tribe inspected every burial located during our archaeological survey, and we excavated only those for which he gave permission.

Analyzing the remains was next. Although the tribe consented to non-destructive analysis, they were hesitant to allow radiocarbon dating, stable isotope analysis, or the cutting of long bones to obtain cross sections. Still, the tribe was interested in what these analyses could tell them and eventually permitted destructive analyses provided that (1) the tribe approve the studies, (2) destructive analysis be kept to a minimum, and (3) we use already-broken bones. Although this limited the number of radiocarbon dates, it permitted the stable isotope analysis. We also used CAT scans to obtain long bone cross sections rather than cut intact humeri and femura.

The tribe then requested that the remains be reburied. Raymond, however, wished to see the remains preserved for the future. Working in a spirit of cooperation, the consulting parties eventually decided on a novel approach: a subterranean concrete crypt. This satisfied the tribe's desire to see the remains reinterred, and yet it allowed the remains to be safely stored for future analyses.

Today, the Stillwater burials rest in small, individual redwood coffins in a 12' x 10' x 30' ventilated concrete vault buried on USFWS land. The door has two locks on it: The USFWS holds the key to one, the tribe holds the key to the other.

In the end, good scientific research resulted and, although the tribe retained the power to deny any analysis, it chose not to. We are convinced that the reason for this is that the tribe was consulted from the beginning, rather than as an afterthought, and the importance of the scientific data was described in layman's terms. Most importantly, the tribe was given a seat at the table—one of genuine authority, respect, and power.

encounter human remains—as did Kelly when he approached the Stillwater Marsh—they involve a bioarchaeologist from day one. And if those remains are Native American, as they were at Stillwater Marsh, archaeologists likewise involve the appropriate American Indian community (or communities). And so, before proceeding further, we'd like you to know that all the data collection discussed in this chapter was approved beforehand by the local Native American community (see "Looking Closer: Native Americans and the Stillwater Burials").

In 1987, we surveyed the previously flooded portions of the wetland, looking for new archaeological sites and keeping an eye open for all human remains. Along with the Nevada State Museum, we recovered the remains of over 500 individuals. This was significant because the Stillwater finds *tripled* the number of human burials known from the entire state of Nevada. These remains were studied by Larsen and a team of bioarchaeologists he assembled to handle specific analyses.

SKELETAL ANALYSIS: THE BASICS

Larsen first had to confirm that all the bones collected by the survey team were in fact human. After all, the flood had washed out plenty of archaeological midden, scattering ancient and recent animal bone among the human remains. Although human bone is distinctive, archaeological skeletal remains are often fragmented and weathered, making them difficult to identify. We have seen surgeons who were unable to identify a bone scrap as a piece of a human femur. But archaeologists are accustomed to seeing things in their broken, dirty, smashed forms. Larsen learned how to identify bone through classes in human anatomy and **osteology,** but his real skill was acquired simply by handling thousands of human bone fragments. Figure 12-1 shows some of the major bones of the human skeleton, including ones mentioned in this chapter.

Bioarchaeologists working with bones from grave sites are accustomed to working with well-defined sets of remains, each from a single individual; this is why, unlike zooarchaeologists, bioarchaeologists are rarely concerned with issues of MNI or NISP.

Instead, bioarchaeologists are concerned with whether the human remains constitute a **burial population,** individuals who came from a specific area and

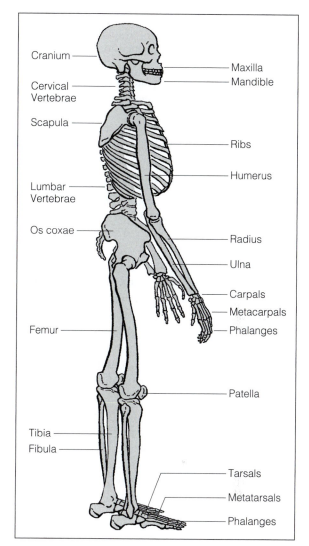

Figure 12-1 Some major bones of the human skeleton.

who died over a relatively short period of time (as might be found in a historic-period cemetery). The Stillwater burials, however, derived from a 16-square-kilometer area of marsh, not a single, well-defined cemetery. Few of the burials contained any grave goods (meaning that we could not use temporal types to place the burials within archaeological phases). And only a

osteology The study of bone.

burial population A set of human burials that come from a limited region and a limited time period. The more limited the region and the time period, the more accurate will be inferences drawn from analysis of the burials.

few of the burials could be dated by AMS radiocarbon determinations. Most of the projectile points found in the nearby sites could be assigned to temporal types; but these time spans were quite large (600 years for the Underdown phase and 1500 years for the Reveille phase). Although hardly ideal, these temporal types provided at least some rough parameters for the living population that this skeletal sample represented.

Good preservation conditions will provide the bioarchaeologist with a nearly complete human skeleton. But sometimes, only the hardest bones survive—parts of the skull, the central portions of the limb bones, and—the hardest portion of the human skeleton—the teeth. We've seen burials where nothing remained except for an eerie smile in the sand.

Ancient cultural practices can also mix human skeletal remains together and make it difficult to group skeletal remains by individual. Many eastern Native American tribes, for example, laid bodies out in a **charnel house,** where the body was allowed to decompose in the open. Eventually, the bones were cleaned of remaining flesh, bundled together, and ritually placed into a communal grave (these are known as **bundle burials**). Over time, the bones of various individuals would commingle. Careful excavation might be able to re-group bones by individual, but sometimes this is impossible. In other cases, as at the Stillwater Marsh, post-depositional processes scatter the once-intact burials. In fact, of the 500 individuals recovered, only 54 were encountered as intact primary burials. In this chapter, we focus on the analysis of those remains.

Determining Sex

After removing any nonhuman bones from the collection, Larsen assigned sex and age to the intact burials. How can we determine sex from bones? One obvious place where men and women differ is the pelvic area. Evolution designed women's hips (the hips are techni-

cally composed of two halves, the right and left os coxae or innominates) to birth children; as a result, the **sciatic** (sy-*a*-tik) **notch,** a U-shaped indentation in each os coxae's posterior (rear) portion, is wider in women than in men. There is variation among the world's population in *how much* wider, but within a burial population, one can usually see a clear difference between those os coxae with wide and those with narrow sciatic notches.

Unfortunately, the os coxae are quite porous, making them some of the first bones to decompose. So if preservation is not excellent, the bioarchaeologist must look elsewhere.

The human skull also provides clues to a deceased individual's sex. Adult male skulls tend to be more robust than female skulls, with heavier brow ridges over the eyes, larger mastoid processes (two protrusions of bone on the bottom of the skull, one beneath each ear), and more rugged muscle attachments. Male skulls also tend to have squarer chins and eye orbits. A skilled bioarchaeologist can often "sex" a skull simply by its feel. Again, the world's populations vary in how robust or how gracile male and female skulls are; but within a burial population, bioarchaeologists can usually detect discernible differences between *adult* male and female skulls. The sex of a child, however, is difficult to determine because the sexually distinctive characteristics of bone do not develop until young adulthood.

Larsen found that the Stillwater collection contained almost twice as many males as females, but sex could not be assigned to a large number of the burials (because some of the adult burials were poorly preserved or were missing key elements; others were the skeletons of children).

Determining Age

Age at death is next. Here, like a zooarchaeologist, Larsen used osteological standards based on comparative collections. Because the pattern and timing of crown formation and tooth eruption is consistent among human populations, teeth are extremely useful for telling the age of younger individuals. Larsen determined age by recording which teeth had formed their crowns and/or erupted through the mandible or maxilla (the lower and upper jaw bones, respectively).

Patterns of bone fusion are also useful for determining age in skeletons of youths and young adults. At birth, many bones are actually several different pieces. The long bones, such as the femora or humeri, are

charnel house A structure used by eastern North Americans to lay out the dead where the body would decompose. The bones would later be gathered and buried or cremated.

bundle burial Burial of a person's bones, bundled together, after the flesh has been removed or allowed to decay off the bones.

sciatic notch The angled edge of both halves of the posterior (rear) side of the pelvis; measurement of this angle is used to determine sex in human skeletons. Although its width varies among populations, narrow notches indicate a male and wider notches indicate a female.

made up of the central shaft and the two **epiphyses**—the ends that articulate with other bones. The epiphyses fuse to the shaft at known rates. For example, the proximal epiphysis of the radius ("proximal" refers to the end of a long bone that is closest to the body's center, in this case, the end of the radius closest to the elbow; "distal" refers to the end of the long bone farthest from the body) completely fuses by about age 19, whereas portions of the scapula do not fuse until age 23. Noting to what extent various bones are fused can estimate an individual's age at the time of their death.

But most bones are fully fused by age 25 and, by that same age, most teeth have erupted. Therefore, other methods are required to age the skeletons of mature adults, and these are more difficult to implement. The first of these is bone wear. After age 30, bones begin to wear down. Much of the wear is related to a person's activity level (as well as diet). But some bones tend to wear no matter what. One particularly sensitive area is the **pubic symphysis,** the place where the right and left os coxae meet in a person's groin area. As the cartilage between the two halves erodes with age, the symphysis undergoes distinct changes. At age 20, for example, the symphysis has a distinct set of surface ridges that look like ocean waves. By age 35, these ridges have disappeared, and a rim has formed along the edge of the symphysis. By age 50, the rim has disappeared, and the symphysis looks like a shriveled prune. But because the os coxae are among the first bones to decay, this useful method of determining skeletal age is not applicable to many archaeological skeletons.

Another method to age a skeleton uses the degree of tooth wear and loss. Because teeth wear down continually with age, bioarchaeologists have generated standardized tables (from non-industrial populations) to estimate age from the extent of tooth wear. But caution is required here too, because the rate of tooth wear and loss is strongly related to diet. People dependent on food processed on grinding stones will have higher rates of wear because of all the grit in their diet. And if their food is high in carbohydrates, people may also experience a higher rate of tooth loss from cavities (see "Cavities" later in the chapter).

Using these methods, Larsen determined that the Stillwater burials ranged in age from fetuses to individuals of more than 50 years old—but these age estimates have some limitations. Rarely can bioarchaeologists assign a specific age estimate to a skeleton; instead, because of the different indicators of age and slight error

factors in the various methods, skeletons are placed into five-year age classes (0–5 years, 6–10 years, 11–15 years, and so on). It's also difficult to pin down the age of individuals older than about 50 years.

How Well Did the Stillwater People Live?

Eventually, Larsen derived the basics of the Stillwater population: He knew how many men, women, infants, and adolescents there were, and he knew these individuals' approximate ages. Now he could turn to questions he wanted to ask of this population. One of these was: How well did the people of Stillwater Marsh people live? He did not ask this question out of idle curiosity. Instead, he wanted to use the Stillwater population to shed light on a major dilemma of anthropology.

Prior to the 1960s, many anthropologists assumed that the lives of ancient hunter-gatherers were, to use the words of seventeenth-century philosopher Thomas Hobbes (1588–1679), "nasty, brutish, and short." In this view, hunter-gatherers had to work excessively hard, lived hand-to-mouth with barely enough food, suffered from high rates of infant mortality, and lived short lives.

But research with the Ju/'hoansi (see "Looking Closer: Bushmen, !Kung, San, Basarwa, Ju/'hoansi") of southern Africa's Kalahari Desert and other foragers in the 1960s suggested that hunter-gatherers actually had plenty of leisure time, an adequate diet, and low levels of disease. Anthropologist Marshall Sahlins (University of Chicago) went so far as to label hunter-gatherers the "original affluent society." In the 1960s, this image of prehistoric peoples resonated with those seeking an alternative to the perceived excesses of modern industrial life.

Is one of these characterizations more accurate than the other? Both were based on ethnographic data, but the observers might have been predisposed to see

---

epiphyses The ends of bones that fuse to the main shaft or portion of bone at various ages; most bones are fused by age 25. This fact can be used to age skeletons of younger individuals.

pubic symphysis Where the two halves of the pelvis meet in the groin area; the appearance of its articulating surface can be used to age skeletons.

Looking Closer
Bushmen, !Kung, San, Basarwa, Ju/'hoansi

The "Bushmen," former hunter-gatherers of southern Africa, are certainly one of the best-known peoples in the world of anthropology. Open any standard anthropological textbook, and you will probably find mention of them. For a time, they were the stereotypical hunter-gatherers, and the film *The Gods Must Be Crazy* brought them (or rather, a biased image of them) fully into the industrial world's consciousness.

With all this notoriety, you'd think that we'd know what to call them. But the names for people change with changing times. There are actually many different groups of Bushmen. The most well-known is the !Kung. The word "!Kung" is said to mean "they," but no one really knows. And these people prefer to call themselves "Ju/'hoansi" (pronounced Zhu-oo-an-zi, with a click of your tongue off the roof of your mouth just behind your front teeth about the time you pronounce the "oo").

There is, in fact, no indigenous term for the "Bushmen" as a whole, because the people labeled as such did not see themselves as a single group. They acquired their name from the Dutch, who called them *Bossiesman*—literally, Bushmen—a term that connoted wild, savage people. But they are also known as "San," having acquired this name from Dutch settlers, who had asked the pastoral Khoi-Khoi people (a.k.a. the Hottentots—there's a long story there, too) to identify the peoples of the interior desert. The Khoi-Khoi replied "San" (or "Sonqua" or "Soaqua"), meaning "other" people (also with negative connotations).

Anthropologists eventually rejected these terms, because the people themselves disliked them. But they still had to be called something. One suggestion was the made-up word "Basarwa," which comes from the word "Masarwa," meaning "people of the west." Changing the "ma" to "ba" puts the word on equal linguistic footing with the names of other peoples in the region (for example, the "Bakwena"). But this ploy does not seem to have caught on.

In fact, because the different groups today see themselves as politically united, they have taken to calling themselves Bushmen, turning a former derogatory name into a term of empowerment.

Confusing, yes—but the power to name is important, and as power relationships change, who gets to name things also changes.

hunter-gatherers in one way rather than the other. Larsen thought that the skeletal data of an archaeological population could provide a more objective assessment of the nature of the foraging lifeway. Larsen wanted to see whether the Stillwater foragers of 1000 years ago were closer to the "nasty, brutish, and short" or the "original affluent society" image of hunter-gatherers.

To do this, Larsen turned to **paleopathology,** the study of ancient disease. This specialization includes the identification of specific diseases, but few specific diseases can be identified from bones (syphilis [venereal and nonvenereal], tuberculosis, and leprosy are the major ones that leave distinctive lesions and other characteristics on bone). Broken bones, even if healed, are also easy to identify; unhealed breaks are usually evidence of trauma that was the immediate cause of death.

But bioarchaeologists can glean more from human skeletons if they look at human bone as being formed by complex interrelationships among the environment, behavior, physiology, and cultural behavior (see Figure 12-2). Larsen used this perspective to look for *nonspecific* indicators of stress, particularly those caused by nutritional deficiencies and/or nonspecific infectious disease in the Stillwater burial population. Though

paleopathology The study of ancient patterns of disease and disorders.

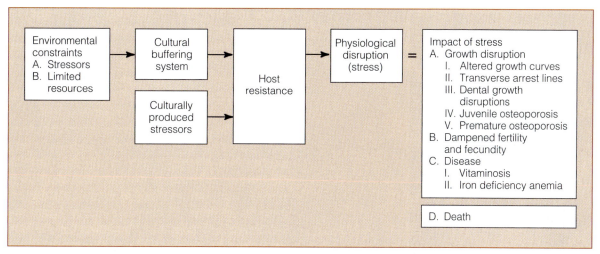

Figure 12-2 Environmental factors operate through and in conjunction with cultural behavior to produce disease or malnutrition, which results in physiological disruption—some of which leaves material imprints on human bone.

challenging, the study of biological stress has become an important area of bioarchaeology.

Disease and Trauma at Stillwater

Larsen found little trace of specific diseases among the skeletal remains from Stillwater Marsh—no evidence of syphilis, tuberculosis, or leprosy. He did, however, find some telltale signs of iron deficiency anemia.

Iron is essential for adequate transport of oxygen by red blood cells. But sometimes iron is limited, perhaps by the lack of red meat in the diet (a primary source of easily absorbed iron), chronic diarrhea, or parasites (such as hookworm, which can cause internal bleeding and the loss of a body's iron stores). Regardless of the specific cause, whenever iron is limited, the body produces more red blood cells. Because red blood cells are produced in the marrow cavities of bone, these cavities enlarge. When this happens in the cranium, the surface of the skull takes on a spongy appearance, a characteristic known as **porotic hyperostosis**. The same phenomenon can happen to bone in the eye sockets (where it is known as **cribra orbitalia**). Larson documented evidence of iron deficiency in only 4 of the 54 burials from the Stillwater Marsh.

The Stillwater group showed little evidence of physical trauma. Sheilagh Brooks (retired, University of Nevada, Las Vegas), who also studied the Stillwater materials, found only 18 individuals with bone breaks (all healed); 6 of these (5 males and 1 female) had broken noses. In general, then, the Stillwater population seemed to have been relatively healthy, suffering from a few broken bones (and perhaps the occasional fistfight).

These observations were made largely on adult skeletons, but many anthropologists will tell you that, to understand overall quality of life, you must look at the children. Because they are fragile, children's skeletons (especially those of the very young) are rarely well preserved, making it more difficult to find appropriate samples to study. But human bone has a "memory," and some childhood events leave a telltale record on the adolescent and adult skeleton.

Growth Arrest Features

Childhood growth may be periodically arrested because of disease, trauma, or malnutrition. Whenever this happens, the bones record the cessation of growth. In long bones, such as the tibia and femur, this growth arrest appears as a thin line of bone perpendicular to the bone's long axis. These lines are not visible on the outside of the bone, but they do appear in x-rays and are known as **Harris lines.** These lines form in childhood,

porotic hyperostosis A symptom of iron deficiency anemia in which the skull takes on a porous appearance.

cribra orbitalia A symptom of iron deficiency anemia in which the bone of the upper eye sockets takes on a spongy appearance.

Harris lines Horizontal lines near the ends of long bones indicating episodes of physiological stress.

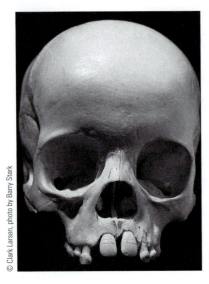

© Clark Larsen, photo by Barry Stark

Figure 12-3
Enamel hypoplasias.

plasias, and that most of these occurred between the ages of 3 and 4. But the number of hypoplasias per tooth, and the average width of the grooves, was less than for other Native American populations. Larsen and Hutchinson concluded that the children of Stillwater Marsh had seen some hard times, but conditions were by no means as bad as they might have been.

The specific cause of the Stillwater hypoplasias, however, is more difficult to determine. They could have resulted from physical trauma to the face, parasitic infection, or malnutrition. We know that trauma was relatively rare (and restricted to adults), and the evidence for extensive infections was limited. Larsen and Hutchinson concluded that fluctuations in the food supply from the marsh—subject to the vagaries of local climate—most likely caused periods of malnutrition for young children.

In fact, the young population might be especially hard hit by a fluctuating food supply. Among hunter-gatherers, children are often not fully weaned until they are 3, 4, or even 5 or 6 years old. This means that, if the 3- or 4-year-olds at Stillwater Marsh were in the process of being weaned during a severe winter or a lean spring, the child might very well suffer a limited period of malnutrition. That the individual survived to adulthood, however, demonstrates that this hard time was not insurmountable.

Workload

To this point, Larsen had discovered that the people who lived in the Stillwater Marsh enjoyed a relatively healthy life. But other skeletal data show that this life came at a cost.

As we said before, bones have a memory—they are a lifetime diary that records whether you lived life as a hotshot fighting forest fires or as a couch potato. Bones can be hard to read, but they do not lie.

Bioarchaeologists use a variety of ways to determine how much physical labor a person saw in his or her lifetime. When working with the Stillwater collection, Larsen relied on patterns of osteoarthritis and the study of bone biomechanics.

Osteoarthritis

Osteoarthritis is a joint disorder created by the loss of cartilage, often caused by mechanical stress. This condition appears as a bony growth (known as an **osteophyte**) that forms a lip around the edge of an articular surface of a long bone's epiphysis (for example, at the

but disappear later in life, as the bone is remodeled as it grows.

Teeth likewise register the cessation of growth. Adult teeth form, of course, in the mandible and maxilla when children are quite young. When a child becomes severely ill or is malnourished, tooth growth stops. If the child recovers, growth starts up again, but the episode of growth arrest is forever encoded as shallow grooves, known as **enamel hypoplasias,** across the front of the teeth (Figure 12-3). Because teeth grow at known rates, bioarchaeologists can measure the distance from the hypoplasia to the tip of the root to estimate how old a child was when the growth arrest event took place. Likewise, the width of a hypoplasia indicates the duration of the period of stress.

Enamel hypoplasias are permanent and therefore are more useful measures of stress than are Harris lines. For this reason, Larsen focused on enamel hypoplasias. (He could also analyze them without the cost of x-rays and with minimal disturbance to the bone.) Working with Dale Hutchinson (University of North Carolina), Larsen found that two-thirds of the individuals had hypo-

enamel hypoplasias Horizontal linear defects in tooth enamel indicating episodes of physiological stress.

osteoarthritis A disorder in which the cartilage between joints wears away, often because of overuse of the joint, resulting in osteophytes and eburnation.

osteophyte A sign of osteoarthritis in which bones develop a distinct "lipping" of bone at the point of articulation.

© Clark Larsen

Figure 12-4 A vertebra with osteoarthritis.

elbow or knee) or between vertebrae, as shown in Figure 12-4. When the cartilage disappears completely, the articular surfaces rub against one another, creating a polish known as **eburnation.** Eburnated joints are extremely painful to move.

Larsen found that *every single adult* skeleton in the Stillwater collection had osteoarthritis in at least one joint. In fact, this was the most severe osteoarthritis that Larsen had ever seen in any skeletal population. The people of Stillwater marsh may have lived a healthy life, but they apparently had to work—and suffer aches and pains—for it.

Males were slightly more osteoarthritic than females, and not in all the same places. Men suffered from osteoarthritis more in the hip, ankle, and foot; women, more in their lumbar vertebrae—their lower back. Larsen suggested that the males in the Stillwater population probably did more walking—and more difficult walking—than did women. This makes sense, because women probably foraged for plants, fish, and small game within a short distance of camps within the marsh itself, while the men probably traveled farther, into the rougher terrain of the Stillwater Mountains, in search of large game. The women were hardly taking it easy, though. They, too, had osteoarthritis that indicated they did a great deal of difficult walking, no doubt carrying children and gear when they moved camp. But men evidently did even more walking.

Why the high incidence of osteoarthritis in the lower backs of women? Larsen pointed to two likely factors: child rearing and food processing. Because hunter-gatherer children breastfeed until they are several years old, children must stay with their mothers. And if the Stillwater women were to complete their daily foraging tasks, they probably had to carry the children with them (just as Ju/'hoansi women do). If so, then the Stillwater women probably carried children throughout most of their adult lives—with resulting strain on the lower back.

In addition, the seeds and tubers that women collected in the marsh were ground on metates. A lifetime of such seed grinding could have led women to overuse their lower vertebrae and given them a higher incidence of osteoarthritis there.

Biomechanics

Larsen also worked with Christopher Ruff (Johns Hopkins University) to transfer knowledge from civil engineering to the analysis of **long bone cross sections.** Civil engineers know that the type of supports used in a building is a function of how much stress the building will place on the beams (which is largely a function of the building's height). Bones are the same, except that, unlike a building's support beams, bones change their cross section over time as they respond to stress. Although the specifics are complex, the principle is simple: When femora are placed under heavy mechanical stress (for example, by routine walking over difficult terrain while carrying a heavy load), they tend to develop a more oval cross section. The cross sections of the femora of a couch potato, on the other hand, are more rounded.

Larsen and Ruff obtained cross sections of the femora through CAT scans at the Veteran's Administration hospital in Reno, Nevada. Although the overall bone mass was relatively low in the Stillwater femora, bone strength was among the highest that Larsen and Ruff had ever seen. And, as was true for osteoarthritis, the femur cross sections indicated that men did more—and more-strenuous—walking than did women. This could be because the Stillwater folk, especially the men, were generally robust, with large, heavy bones. But when Larsen and Ruff looked at the cross sections of

eburnation A sign of osteoarthritis in which the epiphyses of long bones are worn smooth, causing them to take on a varnish-like appearance.

long bone cross sections Cross sections of the body's long bones (arms and legs) used to analyze bone shape and reconstruct the mechanical stresses placed on that bone—and hence activity patterns.

the humeri (the upper arm), they found no difference between men and women, and no real difference between the Stillwater and other populations of native North Americans. This suggests that the difference in men's and women's femoral cross sections was produced by a difference in men's and women's behavior and not simply by differences in the size of men and women.

In sum, the femur cross sections and the patterns in osteoarthritis indicated that the people living at Stillwater Marsh walked a great deal to make a successful living. And men did more walking than women. Neither of these conclusions was particularly striking, but it was conclusive proof that the people who lived at Stillwater were nomadic and gave Larsen clearer ideas about differences in men's and women's lives.

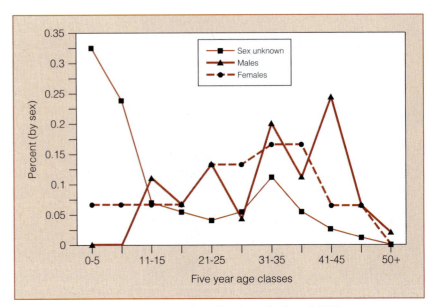

Figure 12-5 The Stillwater mortality profile. *From data in Brooks et al., 1988.*

Paleodemography

Still another way to judge quality of life is to examine patterns of mortality. **Paleodemography** reconstructs parameters such as life expectancy at birth, the age profile of a population, and patterns in the ages of death. Bioarchaeologists do this by constructing various sorts of **mortality profiles** for a prehistoric population based on the age and sex data of burials. Mortality profiles show at what age adult males, adult females, and children died.

Paleodemography works best with well-defined cemetery populations (that is, for a skeletal sample derived from the same biological population over a few years or decades). Available radiocarbon dates showed that most of the Stillwater burials dated to the Underdown phase, but this phase covers 600 years. This means that

paleodemography The study of ancient demographic patterns and trends.

mortality profiles Charts that depict the various ages at death of a burial population.

the Stillwater population is not an ideal candidate for a paleodemographic study.

Still, bioarchaeologist Sheilagh Brooks was able to derive some useful data from mortality profiles for the Stillwater burials. One of these profiles (Figure 12-5) shows the burial data sorted into 5-year age classes by sex. Note first that the 0–5 age category is composed entirely of "unknowns"; as we mentioned earlier, it is almost impossible to determine the sex of very young children.

Why did so many children die so young? Ethnographic data show that the mortality of newborns and toddlers is very high among hunting and gathering populations—50 to 60 percent of all children born in a foraging population do not survive to 5 years of age. The Stillwater mortality profile reflects this sad fact.

Notice also that there are no strong peaks in female age at death. Girls may have had a slightly higher chance of dying at a young age compared with boys, and men may have had a slightly greater chance of surviving into their 40s than women. The female mortality profile shows an increase in deaths beginning at age 21, the early child-bearing years; this is also similar to other foraging populations. The male profile has several peaks and no distinctive pattern. Finally, notice that few individuals are assigned to the 46–50 and 50+ age categories; this reflects a shorter overall life expectancy. Although we might regard the late 40s as the prime of life, a 47-year-old person in Stillwater was an elder.

Stature

Measuring stature is yet another way to assess quality of life. Bioarchaeologists estimate stature with equations that relate the length of certain long bones to an individual's height. These equations were created, incidentally, from huge cadaver populations (composed of individuals who donated their bodies to science).

The femur is the best bone for computing stature (because tall people tend to have long femora and shorter people tend to have shorter femora). But because the relationship between height and femur length varies from population to population, it is important that the bioarchaeologist apply the appropriate equation. Here, for instance, is the stature formula, which has an error factor of +/− 3.5 centimeters, for ancient populations in central Mexico:

$$\text{living height} = (2.26 \times \text{femur length}) + 66.38$$

This equation tells us that, if a femur excavated in central Mexico measures 40 centimeters in length, it likely belonged to an individual who stood about 157 centimeters tall (5 feet 2 inches) give or take 3.5 centimeters. Different formulae are available for skeletons recovered from other parts of the world.

Height provides a useful measure of overall health, because it is closely related to diet. However, because different populations have different genetic capacities for height, it is best to use this variable as a measure of health when looking at data for one burial population across time. Larsen did not use height estimates for the Stillwater burials, because most of the burials dated to the same phase, and no good comparative population data were available.

However, Larsen did use height estimates to track health changes in another project that examined individuals who lived on St. Catherines Island and elsewhere along the coast of Georgia. Here he was interested in testing hypotheses about the effect of maize agriculture on a human population's health. He estimated the heights from skeletons of the hunting-and-gathering population (pre-AD 1150) and those of the agricultural population (post-AD 1150). Contrary to what you might expect, he found that the average agricultural male was 1 percent, and the average female agriculturalist 3 percent, *shorter* than their foraging ancestors. In this case, agriculture was a poorer diet than the previous hunting-and-gathering one, and it hit women harder than men. (If this makes you wonder why people switched from hunting and gathering to agriculture, turn to Chapter 15).

RECONSTRUCTING DIET FROM HUMAN BONE

The people who lived at Stillwater were hunter-gatherers. But can we go beyond this general statement to talk more specifically about what people ate? Following the old adage "You are what you eat," diet can be reconstructed from human bone in several ways. We discuss how two of these methods were used on the Stillwater burial population below.

Cavities

Dental **caries** (cavities) can help differentiate between agriculturalists and hunter-gatherer populations. You might think that cavities happen to those who do not brush their teeth regularly or properly, but this is not strictly true. Caries result when simple carbohydrates, especially refined sugar but also including starchy foods like maize or tubers, remain on your teeth. Bacteria that feed on the carbohydrates produce an acid as a by-product that dissolves tooth enamel. If you ate mostly meat, you would have few caries—regardless of whether you brushed your teeth.

The prevalence of caries, then, serves as an indicator of starchy diets (which, in ancient North America, generally means the consumption of maize). A skilled bioarchaeologist, in fact, can glance at a subject's teeth and make a good guess as to whether the person was an agriculturalist or hunter-gatherer—just by looking for caries.

The people at Stillwater Marsh were strictly hunter-gatherers; they did not grow or eat maize. Because their diet was low in simple carbohydrates (and obviously did not include refined sugar at all), only 3 percent of the Stillwater skeletons had dental caries—a remarkably low figure.

This is not to say that they were free of dental problems. The Stillwater folks lost many of their teeth by middle age, generally due to excessive tooth wear—a product of the grit in their diet from seeds and tubers ground on metates. They also suffered from abscesses,

caries Cavities.

Profile of an Archaeologist
A Native American Archaeologist

Dorothy Lippert is an archaeologist with the Smithsonian Institution.

Deciding to become an archaeologist was the easy part. I had no fixed ideas about what such a career would consist of other than that I would be participating in the scientific process of understanding our human past. I was unaware of the extent to which my own Native American heritage would play; in the beginning, I didn't realize that this part of my identity would so closely focus both my career and my beliefs about what we are meant to do as archaeologists. My reasons for choosing this discipline initially centered around a love of history

and science, although I had little patience for understanding history as a simple series of dates and even less for reducing science to sterile sets of data. Archaeology, for me, has always been a humanistic endeavor, one in which we come to know and respect people of the past in the same way we should people of the present day.

I find that archaeologists who are also Native American seem to have similar views of the discipline, particularly when talking about prehistoric archaeological work in North America. This is most likely because we know these people as our ancestors and in the course of practicing archaeology it becomes our privilege and our responsibility to care for them and to speak about their lives. A common thread within indigenous cultures is a respect for our elders and this permeates archaeology as it is practiced by Native Americans.

In 2003, there were 11 Native Americans with doctorates in archaeology. It is my suspicion that this number reflects both the small numbers of Native Americans who hold doctorates in any subject as well as the emotional and scholarly hazards that archaeology holds for us. The impression that many tribal people have had up to now of archaeology is that it is something that is done to Native peoples by outsiders. Those of us who try to practice archaeology from a Native perspective are still caught by this impression and in some people's eyes, have become outsiders ourselves. Tribal people

which appear as large voids in the mandibles and maxillas. In fact, some teeth had shallow grooves worn into their sides, where a person had habitually twirled a toothpick-sized twig to overstimulate the nerves and alleviate the pain of an abscess.

Bone and Stable Isotopes

Ancient diets can also be reconstructed by analyzing the carbon and nitrogen stable isotopes preserved in human bone.

We already encountered the concept of isotopes when discussing radiocarbon dating (in Chapter 8). Carbon, you will remember, has both stable and unstable isotopes. One stable form, ^{12}C, makes up about 99 percent of the world's carbon; ^{13}C is also stable but accounts for only about 1 percent. The unstable isotope, ^{14}C, most familiar to archaeologists because of its importance for dating, is extremely rare.

As we pointed out in Chapter 8, plants take carbon in through one of three photosynthetic pathways: C_3, C_4, and CAM. You will recall that the C_4 plants (such as

have insinuated to me that I must not be truly Native if I can bring myself to practice archaeology. I also have the added burden of having studied human osteology. Frequently, when I meet other Native people, I don't mention that I'm an archaeologist until late in the conversation, in hopes of forestalling a negative response.

Other Natives are more supportive, saying that it's about time that we (indigenous people) have started doing this work. Many understand just how difficult a career this can be and encourage me to continue. In their minds, as in my own, archaeology is a way to work for Native Americans, both the ancestors and present-day communities.

I think that many non-Native archaeologists are unaware of these kinds of reactions. Some seem convinced that archaeology done with a Native perspective will somehow be less scientific, as if their cultural heritage plays no role in their own studies. While I am a firm believer in maintaining scientific rigor in our analyses, I see no reason not to illuminate these studies with the cultural legacy that was maintained, sometimes at horrendous cost, by our ancestors. As Natives begin to participate fully in archaeology, I think the discipline will become broader in its approach and more open to combinations of different knowledge bases in order to understand a more human past.

When I speak with other Native Americans about the practice of archaeology, I find that we all tend to use this discipline to answer questions that are influenced by our cultural background. For instance, in my own studies of health and medical theory, I was interested in the ways that these were experienced by a small community whose inhabitants lived and died some 400 years ago. I could never quite see my research as the simple practice of collecting data, rather I felt myself to be engaged in communication with these ancient ones. Their cold, white bones used my breath and mind to tell this world their long forgotten story. Through the practice of this science, I became their voice.

Even when reading archaeological reports and looking through pages of dry, scholarly text, I find that I am searching for the humanity of the people whose remains or material objects are being studied. I have also realized that this perspective is not limited only to indigenous archaeologists. There are a number of non-Natives who seem to intuitively approach our science with a very humanistic flair. I believe that in the years to come, more and more archaeologists will begin to appreciate just how much more fun it is if we see our discipline as dealing with fellow beings. Shakespeare summed it up well. "You are not stones, nor bones, but men." While archaeology frequently encounters both stones and bones, it is best if we keep in mind that what we are really meeting up with are human beings.

maize) take in more ^{13}C and ^{14}C isotopes than do C_3 and CAM plants. Because human bones reflect the isotopic ratios of plants ingested during life, bioarchaeologists can reconstruct the dietary importance of certain classes of plants by measuring the ratio of carbon isotopes contained in **bone collagen,** the organic component of bone. A diet rich in C_4 plants (such as maize), for example, can produce bones with a significantly higher ratio of ^{13}C to ^{12}C than diets low in C_4 plants.

Nitrogen also has two stable isotopes, ^{14}N and ^{15}N. Some plants obtain their nitrogen from the air and others absorb nitrogen from the soil. These diverse mechanisms result in different ratios of ^{15}N to ^{14}N in various plants. Using this information, bioarchaeologists analyze a bone's stable isotope composition to determine which plants were eaten and which were not. In addition, we know that carnivores tend to lose ^{14}N through their urine, but they retain ^{15}N. This means that humans who consume large amounts of meat have a

bone collagen   The organic component of bone.

higher ratio of ^{15}N to ^{14}N than those who eat mostly plants. To complicate things further, marine plants tend to have ^{15}N to ^{14}N ratios that are 4 percent higher than terrestrial plants. These differences are passed up the food chain, and so marine mammals also tend to have higher ratios of ^{15}N to ^{14}N than terrestrial mammals. You can't interpret the values blindly, however, because of environmental differences. For example, hot desert soils tend to have higher nitrogen ratios than cool forest soils; so much so, in fact, that bones of desert-dwelling individuals with purely terrestrial diets can produce nitrogen values that, in another part of the world, would suggest a marine diet.

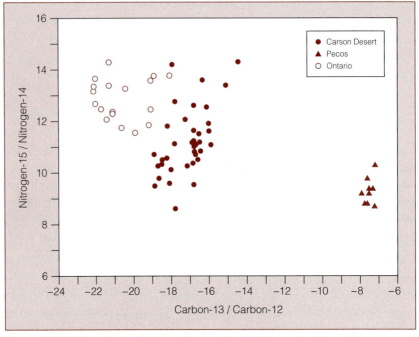

Figure 12-6 Stable carbon and nitrogen isotopes for the Stillwater burial population compared with those of Archaic Ontario hunter-gatherers and of Pecos Pueblo maize horticulturalists.

Control for these environmental factors, however, and differences in nitrogen values tell us whether people relied more heavily on marine than terrestrial foods or had more or less meat in their diets. Carbon and nitrogen values are measured relative to a known international standard.

Larsen submitted samples of human bone from 39 of the individuals recovered at Stillwater Marsh to Margaret Schoeninger (University of California, San Diego), one of the world's premier analysts of bone chemistry. With the human bone samples, Larsen also submitted several modern plant specimens and animal bones (identified to species) to act as controls.

The actual measurement of a bone's carbon and nitrogen isotope ratios is a complex process involving a mass spectrometer and need not concern us here. But Schoeninger's findings are not difficult to understand. To make her point, Schoeninger compared the results of the analysis of the Stillwater materials to two very different populations (Figure 12-6): the skeletal remains from Pecos Pueblo in New Mexico, a maize-dependent population, and the skeletal remains of a foraging population from Ontario, Canada, which was heavily dependent on meat. In Figure 12-6, the horizontal axis plots the ratio of ^{13}C to ^{12}C—higher ratios are farther to the right (indicating more C_4 plants like maize in the diet), and lower ratios to the left (meaning fewer C_4

plants in the diet). Don't let the negative numbers confuse you. To make measurements comparable, Schoeninger reports the stable isotope values calibrated as deviations from an agreed-upon standard (the fossil *belemnitella*, in the Pee Dee limestone formation of South Carolina). The vertical axis plots the ratio of ^{15}N to ^{14}N, higher ratios are at the top (more carnivorous diet) and lower ratios are at the bottom (less carnivorous diet).

As Figure 12-6 shows, the Pecos population has a high ratio of ^{13}C to ^{12}C and a low ratio of ^{15}N to ^{14}N. This means that the Pecos population ate plenty of maize and very little meat. At the upper left part of the graph, the Ontario hunting population has a high ratio of ^{15}N to ^{14}N, with virtually no C_4 plants in its diet; this makes sense, because the Ontario foragers lived in an environment unsuitable for horticulture and relied primarily on fish, moose, and caribou (rather than plants) for food. The Stillwater ("Carson Desert") population lies between these two extremes, with very few C_4 plants in its diet, but a diet that was a mixture of plant and animal foods.

Schoeninger took her results even further. Remember that she also analyzed some modern plant samples, one of which was piñon pine. It turns out that piñon has a very low ratio of ^{15}N to ^{14}N. Schoeninger figured that if piñon was important to the Stillwater diet, then their bones should have a much lower nitrogen ratio than the graph indicates. Because they do not, Schoeninger concluded that piñon could not have been an important component of the diet. Instead, by looking at the values for the other plant and animal control samples, Schoeninger concluded that a strictly marsh-based diet (that is, including no food plants from mountain environments) could readily account for the observed carbon and nitrogen isotope ratios in the Stillwater remains.

Note in Figure 12-6 that the Stillwater population has a greater *range* of nitrogen values than either the Ontario or Pecos populations. Schoeninger looked to see if this range was associated with an individual's age or sex. For example, if men spent time hunting large game then perhaps they ate more meat than women; or maybe children ate less meat than adults. However, there was no association between nitrogen values and age or sex.

Perhaps, then there was a change through time, with the importance of meat increasing or decreasing through time. But, again, Schoeninger found no clear association between nitrogen values and the radiocarbon ages on the burials.

Consequently, Schoeninger suggested that the range of nitrogen values might be a product of dietary variability. Although bone chemistry is a lifelong average of one's diet, the period of youth and adolescence is particularly important because this is when bone collagen forms. If the foods available in the wetlands varied from decade to decade because of flooding, fires, climate change, or other factors, then perhaps people ate different suites of food over the years. In some years, perhaps jackrabbits were commonly roasted over the fire; in other years, bulrush seed cakes might have been the daily fare. If this dietary variability accounts for the differential nitrogen ratios, then it suggests that the Pecos farmers and Ontario foragers had far more monotonous diets than did the people living at Stillwater Marsh.

LIVES OF AFFLUENCE? OR NASTY, BRUTISH, AND SHORT?

We can now return to Larsen's original research question: Does the Stillwater burial population reflect human lives that were "nasty, brutish, and short" or those of an "affluent society"?

The answer, evident from these various analyses, is "Both" and "Neither." The people of Stillwater Marsh consumed a varied diet that probably went beyond their minimal nutritional needs. They were relatively healthy, generally free of serious disease, disorders, broken bones, and infections. This part seems to fit the "original affluent society" image.

But the Stillwater people also worked hard, and some had good reason to complain about aching knees and backs. Some youngsters suffered from periods of malnutrition, and a large proportion of the Stillwater children did not live to their fifth birthday. Nobody lived much beyond 50 years. These data conform more to the "nasty, brutish, and short" model.

Our objective, of course, is not to pigeonhole the Stillwater burial population; it is to learn what life was like for people in the past. We seek to understand the various factors that influenced their diet, their rates of infection and bone breakage, their workloads and their dental health. In some ways, the Stillwater population had a good life; in other ways, it was not so easy. The past can almost never be characterized in simple black-and-white terms.

Most of the time, bioarchaeologists analyze human skeletons to answer questions about human behavior and quality of life. But recently developed technology now allows us to analyze the biology of ancient human populations in order to answer some old questions in new ways. The rest of this chapter explores the developing frontiers of archaeology at the molecular level.

ARCHAEOLOGY AND DNA: TRACING HUMAN MIGRATION

How was the world colonized? Are modern humans related to Neanderthals? When did Native Americans arrive in the New World?

In the past, archaeologists used artifacts alone to talk about ancient migrations and the historical relationships among the world's populations. But modern genetic technology provides another avenue to begin reconstructing the past. By using genetic material—DNA from human skeletal remains and living peoples—geneticists and archaeologists have joined forces to create a new approach to reconstructing the past known as

Archaeological Ethics
Should We Excavate and Analyze Human Remains?

In many places in the world, archaeologists have no qualms about excavating human skeletal remains. But in the United States, conducting research on American Indian remains is a sensitive issue indeed. In fact, archaeologists who do field research in the United States today generally excavate human remains only if they are in the way of a construction project that cannot be re-routed. And no archaeologist would excavate a burial without consulting at least the nearest tribe (in fact, such consultation is mandated by law if the excavation is on federal land). Sometimes this consultation works out well, as it did in Stillwater. But tribal attitudes change, and if the Stillwater remains were exposed today instead of nearly 20 years ago, it's possible that their excavation and analysis would be blocked. It has become increasingly difficult for bioarchaeologists to work with extant collections; those involved with the Kennewick case had to file a lawsuit to get access to that skeleton.

All of this raises major ethical questions. Some modern archaeologists believe that we should simply forgo the analysis of human skeletons and accept that as the price to be paid for showing respect and sensitivity to modern Native Americans who find the excavation and analysis of ancestral remains disrespectful. Many other Americans would agree with them.

Although many museums curate both Indian and non-Indian skeletal remains, the proportion of Native American skeletons often outweighs the non-Indian remains—reflecting, in large measure, the historical interest of American archaeology in excavating American Indian burial sites. And reburying non–Native American remains often seems to be the obvious, and respectful, thing to do. Those Civil War dead who are discovered today are sometimes studied, but always reburied. From the outset, archaeologists agreed to rebury the remains of those who died in the *Hunley,* the Confederate submarine that sank on its first mission (see "Looking Closer: Preserving the *Hunley*," page 208).

Archaeologists have long curated Native American remains in museum collections, in case new techniques enable us to learn more about the past. And such breakthroughs do occur: Who, in 1965, would have thought that within two decades we would be extracting genetic material from 7000-year-old human skeletons? We've only given you a glimpse of what we can learn from human skeletons; and each year there are new techniques. There is so much more to learn.

The scientists wish to learn more about the past in order to increase our understanding of the history of humanity. This is a good thing. But Native Americans wish to see their ancestors, and themselves, treated with respect. This is also a good thing. Which should we choose?

Does science trump every other concern? Answer yes, and you appear ethnocentric.

Does one group of people have the right to shut the door on an area of knowledge? Answer yes, and you would seem to condone book burning.

What is knowledge worth? What is knowledge *for?* Every archaeologist, especially those who study human skeletal remains, must carefully consider these questions today.

molecular archaeology The use of genetic information in ancient human remains to reconstruct the past.

molecular archaeology. As is so often true, this new approach raises as many questions as it attempts to answer.

A Little Background on DNA

Most of our genetic information exists as 46 chromosomes inside the nucleus of each cell in our bodies; this stuff, called **nuclear DNA** (deoxyribonucleic acid), makes each human being unique, and it's inherited from both of your biological parents. Your DNA contains the recipe for your biological composition, telling your body to create blue or green eyes, to be short or tall, to have straight or curly hair. A **gene** is a segment of a chromosome, one small piece of the recipe that codes for particular biological attributes; your body has about 50,000 genes.

Nuclear DNA is extraordinarily useful to the genetics of living populations, but it is not so useful to archaeology. Nuclear DNA degrades fairly quickly, and, by the time the human body decomposes, nuclear DNA is no longer intact (although sections of about 200 nucleotide base pairs can survive for thousands of years).

But another form of DNA, known as **mitochondrial DNA (mtDNA),** is found in the cells' mitochondria (organelles responsible for the cell's energy metabolism)—outside the nucleus. mtDNA contains only about 0.0006 percent of the genetic material of nuclear DNA, which would seem to limit its use, but mtDNA has three interesting properties. First, although it contains only a limited segment of the total genetic recipe, each cell contains thousands of copies of it (in contrast to just the two in the nucleus). This translates to a greater probability of retrieving mtDNA than nuclear DNA. But don't think that there are gobs of mtDNA just lying in archaeological sites: Its recovery is made possible through the technique of polymerase chain reaction (PCR), which enables researchers to create billions of copies of a very small sample of mtDNA, so that this genetic material can be more readily studied.

The second intriguing property of mtDNA is that you inherit yours *only* from your mother. Although mtDNA is present in the tail of sperm, after fertilization occurs the tail breaks off. This means that your mtDNA comes entirely from the ovum. If you are female, you pass along the same mtDNA to all your children. If you are male, none of the mtDNA that you inherited from your mother is passed on to your biological offspring. This makes it possible to define molecular "family trees" and to trace the movement of female lineages.

Finally, mtDNA seems to change in a particular way and at a particular rate that makes it potentially useful to archaeology. Briefly, although mtDNA is probably not completely free from the pressures of natural selection, it appears to be under less selective pressure than nuclear DNA. And because it is transferred from mother to offspring as a chunk, it does not recombine (as does nuclear DNA). Instead, mtDNA appears to change over time largely as a result of random mutations. Nuclear DNA can also change as a result of random mutation (this is, in fact, one of the main ways that new genetic material appears in a species). But compared with nuclear DNA, mtDNA mutates rapidly, about 2 to 4 percent every million years. Although this may seem awfully slow, it is *nearly 10 times* faster than nuclear DNA's mutation rate. *If* one is willing to assume that this rate of change has been constant through time, then differences in the mutations between related mtDNA samples can be used to estimate how much time has elapsed since the branches of the family tree diverged. For this reason, mtDNA is sometimes used as a "clock" to date the timing of human population movements in the remote past.

Prospecting for Ancient DNA

In 1984, Allan Wilson (1943–1991) and his student Vince Sarich (University of California, Berkeley) were the first to identify genetic materials from old tissue. When they cloned DNA from the 140-year-old skin of quagga—a recently extinct, zebra-like African beast—the Berkeley team showed the world that DNA could indeed survive after the death of an organism.

The next year, Swedish researcher Svante Pääbo (Max Planck Institute of Evolutionary Anthropology, Germany) cloned DNA from a 4400-year-old Egyptian mummy. This was the first time that anyone had applied PCR techniques to ancient humans. Not long after, Pääbo pushed the barrier back another 2600 years into the past by extracting ancient DNA from human brains preserved at the Windover site in Florida.

nuclear DNA Genetic material found in a cell's nuclei; this material is primarily responsible for an individual's inherited traits.

gene A unit of the chromosomes that controls inheritance of particular traits.

mitochondrial DNA (mtDNA) Genetic material found in the mitochondria of cells; it is inherited only from the mother and appears to mutate at a rate of 2–4 percent per 1 million years.

Some 7000 to 8000 years ago, ancient Native Americans at Windover buried their dead in a spring that flowed through an ancient limestone sinkhole. Water levels fluctuated seasonally, with a maximum depth of less than 4 feet. At the bottom were several strata of peat—compact, dark brown organic material built up from the partial decay and carbonization of vegetation. The team of archaeologists, headed by Glen Doran (Florida State University), dug into these peat levels while pumps bailed out the encroaching water. Because peat deposits are anaerobic, Doran found many well-preserved skeletons, some still held in place by large stakes, probably placed there at the time of burial to keep the bodies from floating to the surface.

The low oxygen level and neutral pH of the peat bog were also perfect for preserving soft tissue. More than 60 well-preserved human brains turned up at Windover, including the one used by Pääbo in his pioneering extraction of ancient DNA. Geneticists were particularly excited about the number of burials, because it provided the first chance to examine gene frequencies across a prehistoric burial population.

Microbiologists were surprised to find how little the genetic makeup of the Windover population had changed during the thousand years that the burial ground was used, possibly a sign of ancient inbreeding. If this trend held for other early Native American populations, it would suggest that early Indian groups tended to stay put, perhaps explaining the remarkable linguistic diversity among the New World's indigenous peoples.

An African Eve?

The work at Windover signaled the birth of molecular archaeology as a viable way to explore the human past. However, as spectacular as the 8000-year-old brains from Windover might be, Wilson's research team at Berkeley had only begun to examine the possibilities in studying ancient DNA.

Wilson and his team collected mtDNA samples from around the world and compared the human data with that of chimpanzee (as a control). The most striking fact about mtDNA is how much of it we all share. At the molecular level, all living human groups share all but about 0.6 percent mtDNA. As you might expect, humans and chimpanzees share somewhat less; humans and horses share even less, and so forth. The 0.6 percent figure is important because it suggests a way to determine the relatedness among all living individuals and groups.

By examining the mtDNA from various modern human populations, Wilson could see what a close-knit species we really are. This was a surprise, because mtDNA is supposed to evolve fairly rapidly. Components of the modern global sample turned out to be remarkably alike—both within geographical populations and between continental groups. The result was a family tree for all of (surviving) humanity. Africa provided the longest branch on the tree, suggesting this is where human mtDNA began to differentiate. Those of African descent also showed the most variability among themselves and were the most distinct from other populations of the world. Wilson argued that this pattern is precisely what one would expect *if all modern humans had descended from a single population in Africa.*

These investigators went a step further, suggesting that all the genetic composition evident in living human populations could be traced to a single ancient African ancestor. Because mtDNA is passed down strictly through the maternal line, this fictive ancestor must have been female. She was quickly nicknamed Eve, after the biblical first woman and wife of Adam.

Even more controversial than Eve's African origin was the molecular clock that Wilson and his group derived. Because geneticists assume that mtDNA changes at a constant rate, the 0.6 percent figure is important for another reason: It provides a relatively precise way to gauge the first appearance of *Homo sapiens* (modern humans). Although this so-called **molecular clock** does not keep perfect time, it does suggest some genetic limits within which human evolution may have taken place.

Wilson's molecular clock suggested that Eve must have lived about 200,000 years ago. If so, then the first descendants of Eve (early modern humans) must have fanned out of Africa to supplant other hominids about this time. This theory, which has come to be known as the "out of Africa" hypothesis, had, it turned out, also been framed independently on the basis of the fossil evidence alone.

To call the Eve hypothesis controversial is an understatement. Some biological anthropologists, such as

molecular clock Calculations of the time since divergence of two related populations using the presumed rate of mutation in mtDNA and the genetic differences between the two populations.

Milford Wolpoff (University of Michigan), see strong continuity between pre-200,000 and post-200,000 year old skulls from various parts of the Old World. To these anthropologists, the skeletal data argue for continuity in various parts of the Old World (humans had not yet colonized the New World by this date) rather than recent replacement by a migrating population from Africa. (Although Africa is still the homeland of humanity, as we saw in Chapter 7, the question here is whether *all* modern humans derive from a later African expansion.)

Others charged that the Eve hypothesis was based on modern genetic distributions and that it needed to be tested by using DNA extracted from ancient bone. One particularly controversial area is whether the Neanderthals of Europe and the Near East are related to modern humans or if they are an evolutionary dead end. Looking at the skeletal biology, those biological anthropologists who see continuity between the Neanderthals and modern Europeans argue that Neanderthals are part of the human line. Others see skeletal differences too large to place Neanderthals in the ancestry of modern humans. Mitochondrial DNA has now been successfully extracted from three different sets of Neanderthal remains (and more efforts are underway), and *none* of these fall within the observed range of living human variation (but we have no mtDNA yet from Upper Paleolithic modern human skeletons with which to compare the Neanderthal data). This has not satisfied critics, who point to potential sources of error in the mtDNA extraction process and insist that, if Neanderthal maternal lineages are rare in modern humans, the relatively small number of samples could have missed them.

DNA will probably never replace human skeletal remains as the primary source of information about the human biological component of the archaeological record. But in conjunction with more traditional skeletal analyses, it will add new dimensions, questions, and knowledge to the complex story of human history. Research into the first colonization of the New World provides one example.

Skulls and DNA: Tracking the First Americans

The most consequential, if least dramatic, event in the history of the Americas came when that first human footprint appeared in the New World. Nobody knows exactly when this happened, or where. We do not know what these initial colonists of the New World wore, spoke, looked like, or thought. We do not know when they left their Asian homeland or what conditions they experienced along the way.

And yet there remains no reasonable doubt that the first Americans did indeed travel across a land bridge from Asia during the late Pleistocene; it is the timing and conditions surrounding their arrival (or arrivals) that remain incompletely known.

Clovis points, which we mentioned in Chapter 11, appeared in North America about 13,500 calendar years ago (about 11,500 radiocarbon years). Not so long ago the standard textbook account was that Clovis was the first and only migration and from this all native peoples of the New World descended. In this account, small numbers of people migrated from Asia via the Bering land bridge that formed between Russia and Alaska sometime during the height of the last glacial age, between 25,000 and 10,000 years ago. The standard account had these hunters walking from Asia into Alaska, migrating down the so-called ice-free corridor between the continental ice sheets that covered the Canadian Rockies on the west and much of Canada to the east.

A number of problems have risen with this scenario. First, it doesn't appear that the ice-free corridor was open until about 13,000 years ago—a little too late to allow Clovis through in order to be in the continental United States by 13,500 years ago. In addition, current studies suggest that, even when the corridor was open, it may have been uninhabitable—a vast wasteland of rock, sand, and lakes so laden with silt washing out from glaciers that they could support no fish or plant life.

Even more important, South America contains a number of sites that appear to be as old as, if not older than, Clovis. The best-known and -documented of these is the site of Monte Verde, in southern Chile (Figure 12-7). Like the Windover sites, Monte Verde is located in a wet peat bog, and so the preservation was remarkable. The excavator, Tom Dillehay (Vanderbilt University), found the remains of wooden structures, stone projectile points, hearths, pegs driven into the ground with leather straps still tied on, slabs of organic material identified as mammoth (or mastodon) meat, footprints, and other definitive evidence of human occupation.

Although the site's preservation is phenomenal, what makes it really special is that it appears to be 1000 years

Figure 12-7 Monte Verde (Chile); note the level of preservation in this wet site.

older than Clovis. If people came to the New World from Asia via Alaska and reached southern Chile by 14,500 years ago, then they had to pass through North America prior to this date. A handful of sites exist that *might* provide evidence of a pre-Clovis occupation of North America—sites such as Meadowcroft Rockshelter in Pennsylvania and some mammoth kill sites in Wisconsin. But none of these are as well demonstrated as Monte Verde, and some archaeologists still wonder why it is that, although Clovis appears in virtually all 48 contiguous states, evidence for a pre-Clovis occupation is almost impossible to find—despite the dogged efforts of many archaeologists.

Possibly the first migrants bypassed the interior of North America by migrating along the western coast. At first, this may have been to avoid the massive glaciers that covered much of northern North America. Once south of the ice sheets, however, they may have simply kept their maritime economy and continued to move along the coast all the way to Tierra del Fuego. Clovis

people may have been a later migration from Asia or a population that eventually left the western coast and adapted to terrestrial hunting.

Testing the early coastal migration hypothesis means looking for early sites along the western coast. But this is harder than it sounds, for when the Pleistocene ended about 10,000 years ago, the massive continental glaciers melted, and sea levels rose, flooding the existing coastlines. Any sites deposited on the New World's western coast 14,000 or more years ago are now under water—150 meters deep in places—and thick layers of silt. Some archaeologists have tried dredging likely places on the sea bottom for artifacts, but they are looking for the proverbial needle in a haystack, and most have come up empty-handed.

Bioarchaeology and the Colonization

Frustrated with the difficulties of finding early archaeological sites, some have turned to bioarchaeological evidence. Christy Turner (Arizona State University) has

Looking Closer
Tracking Native Americans' Ancestors through Historical Linguistics

One controversial line of evidence used to track Native Americans' ancestry came from Joseph Greenberg (1915–2001), who reanalyzed the available data from every known American Indian language—a gargantuan task. Like many archaeologists at the time, Greenberg believed that Native Americans arrived in the New World in three separate migratory pulses, leaving behind three large linguistic groups—Amerind, Na-Dene, and Eskimo-Aleut.

This reconstruction suggests that the earliest wave of immigrants—the large "Amerind" language family—must have arrived about 12,000 years ago; they were the people of the Clovis complex. These ancestral American Indians spread throughout most of North, Central, and South America. According to Greenberg, virtually all the indigenous languages spoken throughout the Americas derived from this single ancestral language. Na-Dene and Eskimo-Aleut populations arrived some time later, forming the peoples of large portions of Canada's and Alaska's forests, and the Eskimo and Aleut peoples of the Arctic coast respectively.

But Greenberg's reconstruction has come under heavy fire from his linguistic colleagues, many of whom are concerned about the accuracy of the methods employed. One linguist, for example, showed that Greenberg's method shows a close relationship between Native American languages and Finnish!

Lingering questions such as these make many archaeologists wary of accepting the reconstructions of historical linguistics without solid archaeological support.

---

conducted extensive studies of variability in human teeth. He knows what he is talking about: He's looked at some 200,000 teeth from 9000 individuals.

Focusing on the crown and root areas, Turner discovered that modern and pre-contact American Indian teeth are most similar to those of northern Asians. For example, individuals in both groups tend to have shovel-shaped incisors (incisors whose lateral edges curve to give the incisors a shovel shape) and three-rooted lower first molars. Examining geographic patterns in the frequency of different dental traits, Turner found three major groups: one that included all Native Americans from southern Canada to Tierra del Fuego (a group sometimes labeled "Amerind," for American Indians), another that included the Na-Dene (Athapaskan) speakers of northern Canada and central Alaska, and a third that included the Eskimo and Aleut. At the time, this grouping seemed to correlate with Native American language families (see "Looking Closer: Tracking Native Americans' Ancestors through Historical Linguistics").

Turner postulates an initial migration out of northeast Asia at the end of the Ice Age followed by two later migrations (oddly, he sees the Na-Dene arriving after the Eskimo-Aleut). Turner could not, however, place a date on these migrations.

The Skulls' Story

Recently, a new twist has been added to the story, this time using skulls rather than teeth. We have very few human remains that date to the New World's colonization era. In fact, for the entire New World, we only have about 40 skeletons that are 10,000 or more calendar years old; only a handful of these are Clovis-aged skeletons. Given two spacious continents and a period of 2000–3000 years, these 40 burials are not a good burial population. But some archaeologists and biological anthropologists still find it curious that a large number of these early skeletons have skulls whose shapes are distinctly different from those of later Native Americans. Kennewick, the case study that began this book

© Smithsonian Institution, photo by Chip Clark

Figure 12-8 Facial reconstruction of Spirit Cave man by Sharon Long.

(see Chapter 1), is one of those skeletons; another comes from Spirit Cave, a site in the Carson Desert, in Nevada (Figure 12-8).

The early skulls, such as those of Kennewick and Spirit Cave, are different from other Native American skulls because they are long and narrow, rather than round; they have a high-bridged nose and a gracile mandible, but prominent and square chins. Several studies conclude that, in a biological sense, the earliest Native Americans (including Kennewick) are more closely related to groups such as the Ainu, the native peoples of northern Japan, than to living Native Americans. (Some skulls from South America, in fact, appear to be more like those of Africans or Australians than later Native Americans.) Because skull shape largely

haplogroup Genetic lineages defined by similar genes at a locus on a chromosome.

reflects genes, the implication is that the earliest colonists of the New World came from a different Asian population than later migrants (who must have then genetically "swamped" the people who were already here).

mtDNA's Story

So, teeth and skull shape suggest that more than one migration occurred—perhaps even three or more. But when did these migrations begin? Here the geneticists jump in. They argue that the initial population moving out of northeastern Asia ran into a severe geographic bottleneck as they passed across the Bering Strait into the New World, limiting the genetic diversity in the newly arrived population. This explains why Native Americans from Canada to southern South America are genetically similar. It also means that the differences between Asian and Native American populations must generally *postdate* the time when they separated at the Bering Strait. Thus measurement of the genetic distance between New World and Asian populations should estimate the time elapsed since these two groups separated, the age when someone first set foot in the New World.

Now we return to mtDNA. Recall that you inherit your mtDNA only from your mother. Using blood samples of living Native Americans from all over the New World, several studies have found that there are only five mtDNA lineages in the Americas, referred to as **haplogroups**. These are labeled A, B, C, D, and X. Three of these—A, C, and D—are found in northern Asia. Along with other evidence, such as Turner's dental records, this fact points to an Asian origin for Native Americans. And the fact that so few haplogroups are present among Native Americans suggests that the migration(s) entailed only small groups who brought a limited sample of their original population's genetic diversity with them. In fact, it is possible that 95 percent of all Native Americans came from a small number of Asian founding families.

What about the other two haplogroups? Haplogroup B appears today in south central China and coastal southern Asia. It is possible that it has simply disappeared in northern Asia. It's also possible, as some geneticists argue, that it points to a separate migratory wave from Asia. This could support the argument from the skulls—an early migration from southern China—but geneticists think that Haplogroup B came in a later, not earlier, migration.

Haplogroup X is more enigmatic. It is very rare

among living Native Americans as well as Native American skeletal remains; it is most common among speakers of Algonkian languages, in northeastern North America, but it is also found in the 8000-year-old Windover burials. It's present in Asia (though very rare), as well as in Europe (where it is only slightly more common).

Some geneticists and archaeologists suggest that haplogroup X points to an ancient migration from *Europe*, in addition to ones from Asia. This seems implausible, because it would require a transatlantic voyage more than 8000 years ago; no land bridge ever connected North America and Europe. On the other hand, some geneticists ask: If haplogroup X points to an ancient migration from Europe, then shouldn't the more-common European haplogroups (such as H) be at least present among modern Native Americans? Because the European haplogroups do not appear among Native Americans, these geneticists suggest that haplogroup X is indicative of an extremely ancient (tens of thousands of years) shared genetic heritage between Native Americans and Europeans—perhaps dating back to the time of the African Eve. We simply don't know.

Can mtDNA Tell Us When the Colonization Occurred?

Recall that the molecular clock uses the number of differences due to random mutations between two geographically separated haplogroups to determine when they split apart. Using this principle, one study suggests that differences in the mtDNA of Native Americans and Asians point to a migration somewhere between 21,000 and 42,000 BP. Another study at Emory University arrived at a migration time of between 22,000 to 29,000 years ago.

Archaeological data cannot support even the more conservative of these claims; possible pre-Clovis sites in North America range in age from 14,000 to 18,000 years old; and Monte Verde is at most 14,500 years old.

Could the geneticists be wrong? Can the mtDNA clock be used to date human migrations? Much can happen between the time one population splits off from another and goes its merry way.

Some critics, fellow geneticists among them, point out that the mtDNA studies depend on the critical, but unconfirmed, assumption that all the observed genetic diversity among New World populations began after these tribes crossed the Bering land bridge into the New World. But suppose the tribes had split up someplace in Asia, prior to arriving in America. If that happened, then the biological clock would have begun ticking

before, and perhaps long before, colonization of the New World. Perhaps the population split between those people (or rather, their descendants) who would migrate to the New World and those who would remain in Asia did occur 21,000 or 29,000 or 42,000 years ago—but the actual migration occurred much, much later. In sum, mtDNA differences may record when populations diverged, but not necessarily when populations migrated.

On the other hand, maybe mtDNA cannot even record when populations split. Some researchers suggest that we really don't know the rate at which mtDNA mutates. Wilson's original research calculated the molecular clock's rate by dividing the difference between human and chimpanzee mtDNA by 5 million years, the assumed date of separation between the human and chimpanzee lines. But we now suspect that the split between the human and chimpanzee lines is older—that it occurred perhaps as much as 7 million years ago. If so, then the mtDNA clock might run *slower* than Wilson originally thought.

On the other hand, a recent study in Europe used the standard mtDNA clock to predict that haplogroup V (a haplogroup that appears in Europe but not in the New World) should appear in the Basque region of Spain about 10,000 years ago. However, analysis of nearly 100 human skeletal remains could not find that haplogroup in any individual that was more than 4000 years old. So, perhaps the clock runs *faster* than we think.

Maybe we've got the mtDNA molecular clock ticking too slowly or too quickly, or maybe the clock can speed up and slow down—given that we really don't know, it's best if mtDNA studies are verified by other methods.

The Guys Have Their Say

Recently, molecular archaeological studies have turned to the Y chromosome—genetic material that, unlike mtDNA, is inherited only through the male line. Like mtDNA, the Y chromosome also carries DNA that we don't think is under much pressure from natural selection and that mutates at a constant rate (at least, that's the assumption). Only a few Y chromosome haplogroups are known for Native Americans. One of these, haplogroup 10, also occurs in northern Asia. Both Asian and New World Y chromosomes contain a particular mutation (known as M242), suggesting that the mutation occurred before the migration. But the Native American haplogroup also contains another mutation, called M3, which does not appear in Asia. Using the hypothesized rate of mutation in the DNA of the Y chromosome, Mark Seielstad (Harvard School of Public Health) and his team propose that the split between the Asian and what would become the New World population occurred *no more* than 18,000 years ago. The colonization of the New World, then, had to occur sometime *after* this date.

Although this date is more consistent with the available archaeological data, we cannot accept an estimate simply because it fits existing knowledge. If we did that, we would never learn anything new. As was the case with African Eve, we presently lack any kind of final, definitive word about the peopling of the New World based on genetic data. But the preliminary results are sufficiently intriguing to suggest that, whatever the answer may be, molecular archaeology provides a major new source of data regarding the first Americans, as well as ancient migrations and population movements in general. If nothing else, these data will force archaeologists to reconsider whether they really do know what they think they know. And that, as we have said before, is what science is all about.

CONCLUSION

The study of human skeletal remains is about as close as archaeologists can get to studying the people of the past. Where burial populations are available, our knowledge of the past can grow by leaps and bounds. Through analyses of skeletal morphology and bone chemistry, we can learn a great deal about men's and women's workloads, diets, patterns of disease, trauma, and quality of life. And the field of bioarchaeology is really in its infancy: The field is producing new ways of analyzing bone every year and promises to expand our knowledge of the past considerably.

One of these areas is molecular archaeology, which promises to help reconstruct human migrations, if we can figure out how genes can be used as clocks. This is an area of middle-range theory that will require considerable attention in the future.

Bioarchaeology deals with the material effects of people's lives on their bones and genes. Although the links between behavior and bones are by no means direct or simple, in the following two chapters we move into elements of past human lives that are even more difficult to reconstruct: the realms of social and political behavior and the meaning of symbols.

Summary

- Bioarchaeology is the study of the human biological component evident in the archaeological record; it examines the health and workload of ancient populations. This specialty requires expertise in the method and theory of both biological anthropology and field archaeology.

- We use characteristics of several bones, notably the pelvis and skull, to determine an individual's sex.

- An individual's age can be determined by tooth eruption; patterns of bone fusion, tooth wear, and bone wear are used to age individuals over the age of 25.

- Paleopathology is the study of those ancient diseases that leave skeletal traces. Iron deficiency, for example, leaves a distinctive spongy appearance on the skull and the interior of the eye orbits. In addition, growth arrest features, such as Harris lines and enamel hypoplasias, indicate childhood periods of severe disease or malnutrition.

- Bones respond to the routine mechanical stresses placed upon them; patterns of osteoarthritis and long bone cross sections can point to different patterns of workload between the sexes or to changes through time.

- Paleodemography looks at patterns of death in a population, determining life expectancy, child mortality, and peaks in the age of death for men and women.

- Stature estimates can track changes in the quality of diet.

- Bioarchaeologists can also reconstruct diet: High frequency of dental caries indicates a diet high in simple carbohydrates and sugars. The ratios of carbon and nitrogen isotopes in bone can reconstruct the dietary importance of various kinds of plants and animals.

■ Molecular archaeology uses data from living and ancient peoples to reconstruct population migra-

tions. Especially useful is mtDNA and the genetic material in Y chromosomes. Although we still have much to learn about the rates at which DNA mutates, current studies suggest that DNA studies will someday be important to reconstructing the past.

Additional Reading

Jones, Martin. 2001. *The Molecule Hunt: Archaeology and the Search for Ancient DNA.* New York: Arcade Publishing.

Larsen, Clark Spencer. 1997. *Bioarchaeology: Interpreting Behavior from the Human Skeleton.* Cambridge: Cambridge University Press.

Larsen, Clark Spencer. 2000. *Skeletons in Our Closet: Revealing Our Past Through Bioarchaeology.* Princeton: Princeton University Press.

Larsen, Clark Spencer, and Robert L. Kelly (editors and contributors). 1995. *Bioarchaeology of the Stillwater Marsh: Prehistoric Human Adaptation in the Western Great Basin.* Anthropological Papers of the American Museum of Natural History 77. New York.

White, Tim D. 2000. *Human Osteology.* 2nd ed. San Diego: Academic Press.

Online Resources

COMPANION WEB SITE
Visit **http://anthropology.wadsworth.com** and click on the Student Companion Web Site for Thomas/Kelly *Archaeology*, 4th edition, to access a wide range of material to help you succeed in your introductory archaeology course. These include flashcards, Internet exercises, Web links, and practice quizzes.

RESEARCH ONLINE WITH INFOTRAC COLLEGE EDITION
From the Student Companion Web Site, you can access the InfoTrac College Edition database, which offers thousands of full-length articles for your research.

13 Reconstructing Social and Political Systems of the Past

OUTLINE

Preview

W E NOW TURN to some aspects of past human society that are more difficult to infer from archaeological data than the diet, activities, seasonality, and settlement patterns already discussed. In this chapter, we explore ancient social and political organizations—what they were and how archaeologists find out about them.

This chapter explores three key components of human society—gender, kinship, and social status—each of which entails its own interpretive problems and middle-range difficulties. What men and women did in the past is essential to understanding how a society operates, yet assigning specific artifacts to men and women is difficult. Kinship is a major structuring principle of human social organization, but it leaves ambiguous traces. The archaeological record reflects social status a bit more clearly, but many ancient societies may have been organized politically in ways that have no straightforward ethnographic analogies today. We also discuss trade—its role in political and social systems and how archaeologists track trade relations. Although we are entering a more difficult realm of archaeology, we will show that reconstructing past social and political systems is not impossible.

INTRODUCTION

Recall from Chapter 2 that Americanist archaeology is firmly situated within the broader field of anthropology. Right now, we must return to archaeology's roots in anthropology to define some terms and concepts.

Social Vocabulary

Social organization refers to the rules and structures that govern relationships between individuals within a group of interacting people. These relationships are never simple, because people belong to groups on many different levels; some of these crosscut one another, and others are hierarchically organized.

You, for example, simultaneously belong to one or more families (as a son or daughter, husband or wife, brother or sister) and to a town, a state, and a country. You are biologically male or female, and you may be a

member of a sports club, political party, or community organization. Perhaps you hold a formal position in some of these groups. In other words, you play various roles in a variety of social groups. Which identity is currently operating depends upon the situation.

Some social groups are residential, consisting of domestic families or households, territorial bands, or community-level villages. Residential groups tend to be physical agglomerations of people; they are face-to-face associations. Residential groups appear in the archaeological record as households and villages.

Other groups are nonresidential—associations of people that regulate some aspect of society. Nonresidential groups are groups in the abstract sense; in fact,

> **social organization** The rules and structures that govern relations within a group of interacting people. Societies are divided into social units (groups) within which are recognized social positions (statuses), with appropriate behavior patterns prescribed for these positions (roles).

some may never convene. Nonresidential groups are usually manifested archaeologically through the use of symbols, ceremonies, mythologies, or insignias of membership that appear as particular styles of material culture, such as ceramics, architecture, rock art, or burials. In a sense, the residential group functions to regulate discrete spatial matters, whereas the nonresidential group binds these territorial units together.

A related concept is **political organization,** the formal and informal institutions that regulate a society's collective acts. Sometimes, control will rest primarily at the level of the residential group, but in other cases, the nonresidential group exerts a powerful influence. The nineteenth-century Great Basin Shoshone and Paiute, for example, lived in nuclear families, three or four of which lived together in a residential group called a band. Such groups were ephemeral, and families would come and go in an ever-changing set of associations. Clusters of families would sometimes come together for a communal jackrabbit or antelope drive. When they did, one individual, recognized for his hunting ability, would take charge, but his authority would disappear when the drive was over. Shoshone families did not "do as they pleased," but neither did they participate in a formalized, permanent level of political integration above the family. This means that although behaviors such as murder and theft were considered antisocial, punishment varied depending on the particular circumstances and families involved.

Contrast this with nineteenth-century Tahitian society. At the time of European contact, Tahiti—an island in the South Pacific with a population of some 100,000—had a horticultural economy of taro, breadfruit, yams, and coconuts. People also raised pigs and chickens, caught fish, and collected shellfish. Families lived in small villages along the coast and in the island's interior.

Unlike Shoshone bands, the membership of Tahitian villages was more or less permanent, with several strong and overarching levels of control. Tahitian villages were organized into about 20 competing **chiefdoms.** A sacred chief (*arii rahi*) ruled each of these chiefdoms.

political organization A society's formal and informal institutions that regulate a population's collective acts.

chiefdom A regional polity in which two or more local groups are organized under a single chief (who is the head of a ranked social hierarchy). Unlike autonomous bands and villages, chiefdoms consist of several more or less permanently aligned communities or settlements.

Below the sacred chiefs were "small chiefs" (*arii rii*), and under the small chiefs were sub-chiefs (*raatira*). Below the sub-chiefs were the commoners (*manahune*). Sacred chiefs claimed to be descended directly from the gods, whereas commoners were said to exist only to provide for the needs of chiefs. A person from one of these four classes could not marry someone from a different class. Chiefs owned the land in their respective villages, and they had larger houses and canoes than commoners, as well as distinctive clothing. Some chiefs had craft specialists in their employ, and chiefs controlled communal fishing gear and village production.

The sacred chief also controlled the distribution of food and goods between villages. Periodically, he demanded tribute for special feasts and demonstrated his authority by redistributing food and goods to all who attended. The chief always retained some portion of the tribute for use by his household; chiefs also handed out punishments for social transgressions.

Clearly, the Great Basin and Tahiti provide extreme examples of social and political organizations. To understand such differences, we will restrict the present discussion to three broad areas of human social and political behavior: gender, kinship, and social status.

From Artifact to Symbol

Before doing so, however, we must emphasize an important issue in middle-range theory. As you have seen, archaeologists use the physical residues of human behavior to reconstruct past human activities. People butcher an animal and leave behind stone tools and some of the bones. They make, use, and break a pot, leaving the sherds behind in a trash midden. Natural processes then act on those remains. Discarded artifacts are sometimes reclaimed or recycled, meaning that they remain part of the cultural system long after fulfilling their original function. Archaeologists consider all these dimensions of artifact use and reuse when interpreting the archaeological record.

Now we add another dimension to our consideration of artifacts, an aspect that is especially important to understanding social and political organization. It may seem that archaeologists act as though artifacts only reflect human behavior. But it is important to remember that artifacts are not just things, they are also *symbols.* Important life transitions, for instance, are often marked by material culture. In American society of the 1950s and 1960s, getting your first car was not simply acquiring a mode of transportation; the car you drove carried a symbolic meaning—it said something about your position in life. Similarly, thousands of years ago, a bow was a weapon for hunting, and it may also have been a powerful symbol of adulthood.

How an artifact enters the archaeological record is a product of how it was used. But because material culture carries symbolic meanings, people sometimes actively manipulate material culture to send culturally specific symbolic messages. Bringing flowers or a bottle of wine to dinner is a standard American way to thank a host. But such a gesture would be meaningless to the Mikea (the forager-horticulturalists we discussed in Chapter 10), who instead expect guests to bring tobacco.

This fact—*that material culture reflects symbolic meanings as well as functional behaviors*—means that artifacts can be exceedingly difficult to understand. But archaeologists are making progress in using artifacts to infer ancient social and political organization, and this chapter provides several examples of how this works. We will return to this dimension of artifacts again in Chapter 14.

ARCHAEOLOGY AND GENDER

Anthropologists distinguish between sex and gender, and between gender roles and gender ideology. Sex refers to inherited, biological differences between males and females. Gender, on the other hand, refers to culturally constructed ideas about sex differences. Humans have only two sexes, male and female—but there can be more than two genders. Some societies recognize men who choose to live as women or women who choose to live as men as a third gender. In some Plains Indian tribes, for example, **berdaches** (also known as "two-spirits") were men who chose to live as women, performing women's traditional roles, and even marrying men (although marriage in this case did not imply a sexual relationship).

This leads us to the difference between gender *role* and gender *ideology*. **Gender role** refers to the different participation of males and females in the various social, economic, political, and religious institutions of a cultural group. These roles describe culturally appropriate behavior for men and women. In some societies, women can play very public roles, for example, in politics; in others, women's public participation may be limited (though their private participation may still be influential). **Gender ideology** refers to the culturally specific meaning assigned to terms such as "male," "female," "sex," and "reproduction." In some societies, men and women have a generally equal footing; in others, men are considered of greater importance; and in others, the activities of men and women are so differently valued that adult men and women interact very little. In traditional New Guinean societies, for example, men spend much of their leisure time in a communal men's house, rather than in their separate family homes.

These facts are important to understanding other societies, and they are important to understanding archaeological inference. Some years ago, recognition of gender ideology led Margaret Conkey (University of California, Berkeley) and Janet Spector (whom you met in Chapter 2) to argue that archaeology had a strong **androcentric** bias. Archaeologists at the time were mostly male, and they viewed the world largely in terms of men's activities and perceptions (and, in fact, in terms of white, middle-class, European male understandings of the world). Conkey and Spector saw this as a product of the reigning American gender ideology, in which women's contributions were downplayed and women were supposed to stay home and not participate in the "important" activities of the public sphere. They documented several cases in which this gender ideology was projected onto the past, with males portrayed as stronger, more active, and more important than women, who were portrayed as weak, passive, and dependent. According to the archaeological interpretations of the day, men made things happen and women went along for the ride.

Conkey and Spector argued that archaeologists saw specific artifact forms as associated with one gender or the other: Hunting weaponry was always male, plant-collecting gear was always female. Men made projectile points and stone tools; women made pottery and baskets. Archaeologists blithely assumed that a woman

berdaches Among Plains Indian societies, men who elected to live life as women; they were recognized by their group as a third gender.

gender role The culturally prescribed behavior associated with men and women; roles can vary from society to society.

gender ideology The culturally prescribed values assigned to the task and status of men and women; values can vary from society to society.

androcentric A perspective that focuses on what men do in a society, to the exclusion of women.

© William S. Webb Museum of Anthropology

Figure 13-1 The site of Indian Knoll (Kentucky). In the days of WPA archaeology, a huge portion of the site was excavated, and hundreds of human burials uncovered.

buried with a grinding stone *used* this artifact in life. But they assumed that a man buried with the same grinding stone had *manufactured* it.

Conkey and Spector found that most archaeologists failed to identify the sources for their assumptions and rarely tried to confirm or validate them. In other words, *the only middle-range theory operating here was the archaeologists' culturally biased view of gender roles.*

As an example, consider the site of Indian Knoll in western Kentucky, a 2-acre, 8-foot-deep shell midden along the Green River (Figure 13-1). This midden accumulated over a long period, from about 6100 to 4500 years ago. Indian Knoll was first excavated in 1916 by C. B. Moore and then in the 1930s and 1940s by William Webb (1882–1964). (Formally trained as a

physicist, Webb was almost certainly the only archaeologist to help develop the atomic bomb.)

Indian Knoll is a **shell midden**—the remains of tens of thousands of shellfish meals are preserved there—but it was also a burial place. Between the two of them, Moore and Webb excavated some 1200 burials at the site. Men were generally buried with axes, fishhooks, and other tools; women were buried with beads, mortars, and pestles.

Also in some burials were beautifully polished stones, a few inches long, and somewhat triangular in cross-section, with the sides slightly convex. A hole was drilled neatly lengthwise down the middle of the stone. With these stones were often found pieces of whittled, slightly curved antler, with a neat hook at one end.

Moore was puzzled by these enigmatic objects. He thought the stones might have served to hold cords the appropriate distance apart when weaving fishing nets; the antlers he thought might be netting needles.

shell midden   The remnants of shellfish collecting; some shellfish middens can become many meters thick.

But having seen well-preserved examples from dry caves in Texas and Arizona, Webb recognized these artifacts as parts of atlatls, or spearthrowers. A wooden atlatl arm, perhaps 2 feet long, fit into one end of the drilled stone and the antler hook into the other; both were held in place by pitch or tree resin. The hook on the tapered end of the antler held the atlatl dart in place as the hunter took aim, and the stone weight increased the centrifugal force of the weapon as the hunter swung the atlatl overhead, launching the dart. The wooden atlatl arm and accompanying darts would have long since decayed in the Indian Knoll midden, but the stone and antler remained.

Webb was curious about the distribution of these atlatls. Of the 76 burials that held atlatl weights, 31 were adult males, 13 were adult females, and 18 were those of children (sex could not be identified on the remaining 14 individuals). Why, Webb wondered, did people place hunting weapons in the graves of women and children? In 1946, he wrote "it is hardly to be supposed that infants, children, *and women* would have any practical use in life for an atlatl" (emphasis added).

Trying to explain this apparent conundrum, Webb noted that the people of Indian Knoll often buried these beautifully made atlatls intact; but they also sometimes intentionally broke the spearthrowers at the time of burial, as evidenced by the presence of all the fragments of an atlatl weight in grave fill. Adding this to the fact that the atlatls were buried with children and women, Webb argued that the artifacts reflected an intentional burial ritual, rather than grave goods for use in the afterlife. We know that in some Native American societies, people cut their hair as a symbol of mourning. Perhaps thousands of years ago at Indian Knoll, the destruction and burial of atlatls carried a similar symbolic meaning—a way for men to express their grief for a deceased child, wife, sister, or mother in a culturally appropriate way.

Notice how Webb's argument is grounded in the assumption—by no means illogical—that atlatls were interred with adult males because they were tools used by men during their lifetime (hence they would need them in the afterlife). By this reasoning, of course, one must likewise assume that some of the women at Indian Knoll also hunted. But because Webb could not conceive of women as hunters, he searched for another explanation for the inclusion of atlatls in women's graves. Although his final explanation could still be right— why, otherwise, did people bury atlatls with children?—

Webb's underlying logic demonstrates the importance of using caution to detect our own cultural biases, especially when it comes to matters of gender roles.

Before we look at how archaeologists reconstruct what men and women did in the past, let us pause to consider whether this difficult task is even necessary. Do we really need to know whether men or women did the hunting, or plant gathering, or other tasks? Isn't this concern with gender simply an imposition of the *current* American culture of political correctness? We don't think so; and the following ethnographic example demonstrates the importance of knowing what men and women did in the past.

Hunting in Africa's Rain Forest

Popularly known as "Pygmies," the BaMbuti are hunter-gatherers who live in the Ituri Rain Forest of central Africa. There, a number of different cultural groups such as the Efe, Aka, and Mbuti live in small temporary camps. They hunt a variety of animals and gather wild plants and honey in the forest. Nearly all these groups exchange meat for agricultural produce with their neighbors, Bantu horticulturalists. They also sometimes work for them in their fields.

Years ago, Colin Turnbull (1924–1994) initiated a long-running debate in anthropology when he observed that some BaMbuti hunt individually with bows and arrows whereas other groups hunt communally with nets (Figure 13-2). Among net-hunters, women and children drive game (such as the duiker, a small antelope) through the forest into nets, where men club the animals (though in some groups women kill the netted game). Archers shoot monkeys and other prey that seek refuge in treetops, but they, too, hunt the duiker. Archers sometimes hunt communally, but they also hunt alone.

From an archaeological perspective, these two kinds of BaMbuti societies would differ in their hunting technology—one would leave behind nets and evidence of their manufacture; the other, projectile points, bows, and arrows. Such differences in technology are precisely the sort of patterning that archaeologists seek to document and explain.

Why do the BaMbuti use different hunting methods? Turnbull attributed the difference to simple cultural preference; some groups, Turnbull argued, chose to use nets and other groups preferred the bow. But other anthropologists saw it differently. Some argued that

© Barry Hewlett

Figure 13-2 A young Aka girl removes a blue duiker caught in a net.

archers, (2) net hunting is no more or less efficient than bow hunting, and (3) bow hunters did not live nearer to or trade more with Bantu peoples than net hunters. In other words, the evidence contradicted every available hypothesis.

Then Bailey and Aunger observed that whereas women participate in net hunts, they rarely hunt in the archer groups. So the question, perhaps, is not why some BaMbuti hunt with nets and others with bows and arrows, but rather *how women decide whether to participate in hunts.*

Recall that many BaMbuti trade meat with Bantu horticulturalists for produce; in fact, they can acquire up to 3 calories worth of agricultural food for every calorie of meat they trade. Some women also work as laborers for horticulturalists, and they receive some of the produce as payment. Bailey and Aunger argued that women decide to hunt or to work in fields depending on which activity gives them the greatest return for their effort. Testing this hypothesis, Bailey and Aunger found that net hunters live near Bantu with *small* gardens whereas bow hunters live near Bantu with *large* gardens.

In areas where gardens are small, Bantu women do not need BaMbuti women as laborers and, because they cannot work for produce, BaMbuti women help with the hunting. Presumably, as long as many people are available, net hunting is a better way to utilize this extra labor. Where gardens are large, Bantu women need assistance. They hire BaMbuti women, who apparently make a greater return as workers than as hunters. Without the extra labor, men hunt individually, with bows and arrows. The key to BaMbuti hunting technology, then, depended not on the hunting technology or environment alone, but also on women's choices.

This example demonstrates that options, decisions, and activities by both men and women condition the larger patterns in material culture that archaeology excels in revealing.

Reconstructing Male and Female Activities from Archaeology

One reason for archaeology's androcentric bias was the fact that for decades, the field was male-dominated. Another was that archaeologists were simply unaware of the extent to which their own culture affected the way they viewed and understood the world. We believed that, as true scientists, we could be objective about the past.

Bantu horticulturalists introduced net hunting to the forest and that it had spread because it was more efficient than bow hunting; those who lived close to the Bantu had already benefited from this technology, whereas those living farther away had yet to acquire it. Others suggested that net hunting was a response to the crowding created by Bantu emigration; nets were a way to extract more food from limited portions of the forest. The bow hunters, on the other hand, worked in Bantu fields, receiving produce through their labor rather than by trading meat, and so they eschewed net hunting.

Others argued the inverse: that net hunting was less efficient than bow hunting and net hunters sacrificed efficiency for volume, using nets to harvest a surplus of meat for trade. Another explanation was that the thick undergrowth of the net hunters' environment made archery an impractical hunting technique there.

Anthropologists Robert Bailey (University of Illinois, Chicago) and Robert Aunger (University College, London) decided to test these competing hypotheses. Drawing upon ethnographic and environmental records, they found that (1) no significant differences exist between the environments of net hunters and those of

This attitude has changed significantly in recent years. Half of all professional archaeologists in the United States today are women, and few modern archaeologists would blithely make such simplistic correlations as atlatl = male or pottery = female. We recognize the biases of past archaeological research and understand that knowing what men and women did in the past is not just politically correct; it is important to understanding prehistory.

Some feminist archaeologists believe that it is unnecessary to ascribe particular tasks to men or women in order to take a gendered perspective on prehistory. But others argue that we can't answer important anthropological questions unless we know, for a particular archaeological case, whether men or women used this or that artifact.

Can we reconstruct what men and women did in the past? If so, how?

These questions raise some difficult problems of middle-range theory. In Chapter 12, we explored one approach. Skeletal analysis can tell us something about the different mechanical stresses placed on men and women, but the cause of these stresses still requires some guesswork.

Stable isotope analysis can also point to differences in men's and women's diets. Following up Christine Hastorf's and Sissel Johannessen's research in the Upper Mantaro Valley (see Chapter 11), Michael DeNiro (University of California, Santa Barbara) analyzed bone samples from human skeletons dating to the different phases for carbon and nitrogen stable isotopes. He found no significant differences between men and women during the Wanka II phase, during which men and women apparently ate much the same foods. But analysis of human remains from the Wanka III phase (after the Inka had expanded into the Mantaro Valley) showed that half of the men had a considerably higher maize intake. DeNiro sees this as evidence that men participated in rituals (where maize beer was consumed) more often. If so, then not only did men participate in the public sphere of life more than women, but some men participated more than other men. This interpretation thus points out differences between men and women, as well as among men.

But human skeletal evidence can take us only so far. What about everything else found in archaeological sites? How would we know if a man or woman made or used a particular stone tool, pot, or basket? Because archaeologists lack an established method for objectively deriving this sort of information from material remains, most investigators are forced to rely on ethnographic analogy, with all its inherent limitations.

Were Ceramics Made by Men or Women?

Ceramic technology provides a case in point. There are two basic ways to make a pot. In the first method the potter constructs the vessel by hand, either by molding the clay or by rolling it into a long "snake" and then coiling it up to build the pot's base and walls; the pot's walls are then smoothed by hand.

The other technique is to throw a lump of clay onto a wheel that is rotated manually by the potter (and today by a powered device). The potter then uses the spinning clay's centrifugal force to shape it by hand. The method used on a given pot is relatively easy to determine from characteristics of potsherds.

Working from this simple baseline, Prudence Rice (Southern Illinois University) surveyed ethnographic data from a variety of societies around the world and discovered that, when pottery is fashioned by hand, it is usually manufactured by women. By contrast, men usually manufacture pottery made on a wheel. Archaeologists can draw on this kind of strong analogy to infer past behavior with a high (but not absolute) degree of certainty: If archaeological evidence shows that pottery was made by hand, then we infer that the pottery was *probably* made by women. By contrast, if we find evidence that pottery was made on the wheel, then we say that the potter was *probably* male.

As we cautioned in Chapter 10, this sort of analogy can be made stronger if we can actually *explain* the inferred pattern; but in this case, this explanation is not easy. There is, of course, no inherent reason why women could not have used the wheel to produce pottery (and, indeed, many female potters do so today). The uniformitarian assumption that we discussed in Chapter 10 fails in this case.

Perhaps the reason lies in the *purpose* of pottery made on the wheel versus that made by hand. Archaeologists know that the wheel is associated with craft specialization and the marketing of pottery. Thus, it appears that when pottery moves from production for the residential group to production for the nonresidential group, the task shifts from women to men. *Why* this should happen, however, is much harder to say.

An alternative approach is to use an ethnographic analogy that is historically linked to the archaeological population being studied. Rosemary Joyce used this approach to create some deeper understanding of Maya men and women.

Gender in Maya Iconography

In previous chapters, we have mentioned the Maya civilization of southern Mexico and Central America (and we'll talk still more about the Maya in Chapter 15).

The Maya developed a remarkable art style and often depicted themselves on stone stelae, on polychrome (multicolored) pottery, in paintings and carvings on lintels inside temples and tombs, and in books called **codices,** which were long strips of paper, many meters in length when unfolded, made of pounded inner tree bark. (The Spanish considered them heretical and destroyed all they could find; only four survive today.)

The images commonly depict Maya wearing intricate, complex costumes (Figure 13-3). To the Western eye, these costumes appear flamboyant, even outlandish. But to the Maya, ways of dressing encoded immense amounts of cultural information. These figures rarely have overt sexual characteristics, in large part because of the elaborate costuming. Women are sometimes identified with a particular glyph, but not always.

Because we can read Maya hieroglyphic writing, we know much of what is going on in these images. And the images themselves tell us something about Maya sex roles. For example, women are often portrayed (especially on polychrome pottery) weaving, preparing maize for meals, and serving food to others. Joyce and others, notably Tatiana Proskouriakoff (1909–1985), used these images to discover that Maya iconography displays

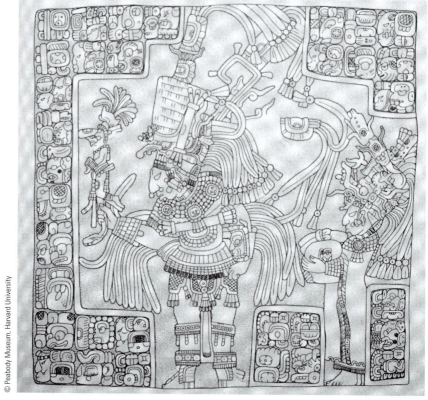

© Peabody Museum, Harvard University

Figure 13-3 A Mayan drawing from the site of Yachilan, Lintel 32. The figure at the right wears a huipil and carries a textile bundle.

women wearing three distinctive dress styles: a simple wrapped garment that covers the breasts, body, and legs, but leaves the arms bare; a woven *huipil,* a housecoat-like garment that covers the entire body; and, more rarely, a jade-bead skirt, often with a fish-monster-and-shell belt. Some interpret the latter to be individuals who are impersonating the male maize god, who is always depicted with such costuming.

Joyce used these clothing styles to identify women on the carved stelae, despite the lack of overt sexual characteristics. Women are seen holding and offering ceramic vessels, bundles of cloth, or paper and bloodletting instruments (the Maya believed that rulers had to sacrifice their blood, often by cutting their tongues, to communicate with the gods and renew the world). The remaining figures, the male ones, often hold weapons, shields, or scepters that represent double-headed axes—the instruments of war.

Although one might interpret the women in the images simply as servants, Joyce wondered if there was a deeper interpretation, and so she turned to ethno-

codices Maya texts, long strips of paper, many meters in length when unfolded, made of the pounded inner bark of certain trees; these texts helped analysts interpret Maya hieroglyphics on stelae.

graphic data gleaned from the codices, early Spanish observations, and modern ethnography.

The modern Maya participate in what anthropologists call a **cargo system,** in which a responsible, married man is selected annually to direct the ceremonial system (today this system is a combination of Catholicism and the indigenous religion). This individual is responsible for holding a number of feasts that accompany rituals; his wife, who acts as an assistant, takes on the title of "Mother of" the man's named position. Other elderly women are responsible for preparing food, tending to incense for purification ceremonies, and ensuring that everyone observes appropriate manners and protocol during the feasts. In this way, men and women occupy complementary roles in the important feasts of the cargo system.

Joyce argues that women depicted in the Classic Maya stelae may have occupied similar complementary, rather than subservient, roles. She points out that Maya ethnographers discuss the complementarity of men and women, and the need for rulers to "assert claims to represent in themselves the split and complementary totality that they would like to control." Joyce suggests that the pairing of male and female figures on stelae in culturally appropriate ways could symbolize a ruler's need to combine male and female elements to acquire and maintain political power. This could include not only a claim to male/female prerogatives and powers, but might also extend to the right of male rulers to claim the products of female labor, such as weaving.

Interpretations such as this are impossible without adequate ethnographic analogy, and therefore they are subject to both the potentials and the pitfalls of such analogies (as we discussed in Chapter 10). For example, other archaeologists might point out that the cargo system is a poor analogy for interpreting Maya stelae because many of the women shown on stelae are often partners in marriages between royal families—marriages that created key military alliances, as they did in Europe. Thus, the purpose of women in these images is starkly different from that entailed in the cargo system.

One way to probe the strength of an analogy is to look for additional formal similarities between the analogy and the archaeological case, and there is at least one in this instance. Joyce found that women are often paired with men on stelae—sometimes on the "backs" of stelae (that is, the stelae's side that faces away from the largest public area), whereas male figures occupy the more public sides. Sometimes, the women are depicted in a lower position than their male counterparts.

Joyce points out that, when viewed from prominent vantage points in a ceremonial center, women depicted on the stelae are more frequently to the left of the male images. Ethnographic data show an association between Maya women and left-hand and lower elevations, whereas men are associated with the right-hand and upper elevations. This ethnographic pattern may hold true for Maya stelae as well and, if it does, might strengthen the analogy.

Nonetheless, modern archaeologists still find it difficult to say much with certainty about gender roles in the past, let alone move beyond such relatively mundane activities to an understanding of gender ideology. Doing so may be limited to those instances where a close, historically linked analogy is available.

ARCHAEOLOGY AND KINSHIP

Kinship refers to the socially recognized network of relationships through which individuals are related to one another by ties of descent (real or imagined) and marriage. A kinship system blends the facts of biological descent and relatedness with cultural rules that define some people as close kin and others as distant kin, or not kin at all. These groupings are important because they strongly condition, and sometimes dictate, the nature of relationships between individuals.

Kinship may not seem very significant to you. We don't mean that you don't care about your family, but on a day-to-day basis, most of the people you interact with are not kin. Instead, they are friends, teachers, representatives of the government, bosses, subordinates, and so on. But in the non-industrial world, most people interact on a daily basis with people who are kin. The same was true of much of the ancient world.

So, if you fail to understand a society's kinship pattern, you might misread a lot of their behavior. For

---

cargo system Part of the social organization found in many Central American communities in which a wealthy individual is named to carry out and bear the cost of important religious ceremonies throughout the year.

kinship Socially recognized network of relationships through which individuals are related to one another by ties of descent (real or imagined) and marriage.

example, a woman from the island of Pingelap in Micronesia once casually listed the members of her household to Kelly: "That child there is my son, and that girl is my daughter. The young woman over there is my sister and the man next to her is her husband. Of course, my father over there [pointing to a man splitting open coconuts] is my mother's brother." If her last statement brings images of incest to mind, we assure you that you are wrong, and understanding the kinship system shows why.

Forms of Kinship

The world of kinship is incredibly complex; we will simplify matters here by concentrating on three basic forms of kinship. In Figure 13-4, the triangles stand for males and the circles for females. The equal sign (=) stands for marriage, the solid horizontal lines connect siblings, and the vertical lines indicate offspring. The square (indicating either sex) places you within the kinship diagram.

Bilateral descent should be familiar because it is the standard kinship in North America, as well as in many other industrialized nations. In bilateral descent, an individual traces his or her relatives *equally* on the mother's and father's sides. Although you might be closer to your mother's or father's side (because of geography, divorce, or personalities), neither side of the family is *a priori* more important than the other. Evidence of this is the fact that names applied to relatives on either side of the family are the same. Father's brother and mother's brother, for example, are both "uncles" (in English).

Kinship in cultures with bilateral descent tend to lack "depth"—meaning that few individuals know who their great or great-great grandparents are, much less their great-great grandparents' siblings' offspring's offspring. This is because *in bilateral descent, the nuclear family is the important economic unit.*

The next two kinds of kinship systems are strikingly different from bilateral descent because they privilege one side of the family over the other; these are *unilineal* descent systems. In **patrilineal descent,** the nuclear

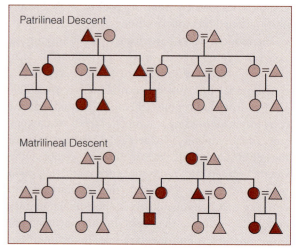

Figure 13-4 Patrilineal and matrilineal descent. The dark colored circles (females) and triangles (males) show who belongs to one patrilineage (top) and matrilineage (bottom).

family may constitute the residential unit, but the most important group is the **patrilineage,** people to whom you are related *through the male line*. Figure 13-4 shows two hypothetical kin diagrams, one of which represents patrilineal descent, in which the shaded individuals belong to "your" patrilineage. These are all the people that are biologically related to you through a male—your father and his siblings, your father's father and his siblings, your father's brothers' children, and your father's father's brothers' children; we could extend the same to your great grandfather's and great-great grandfather's generation, and so on. These individuals are members of one patrilineage.

In patrilineal descent, you acquire your patrilineage from your father. The other people in the diagram belong to other patrilineages (societies with unilineal descent commonly forbid marriage between men and women of the same lineage). So, your mother belongs to a different patrilineage than your father and, consequently, a different patrilineage than you.

Patrilineal societies make up about 60 percent of the world's known societies. They are associated with a wide range of conditions, including hunting-and-gathering, agricultural, and pastoral societies. They are also associated with internal warfare—that is, war with close neighbors.

Keep in mind that patrilineages contain both males and females—because anyone biologically linked to you through a male is a member of your lineage (such as your father's brother's daughters). Your father's sister

---

bilateral descent A kinship system in which relatives are traced equally on both the mother's and father's side.

patrilineal descent A unilineal descent system in which ancestry is traced through the male line.

patrilineage Individuals who share a line of patrilineal descent.

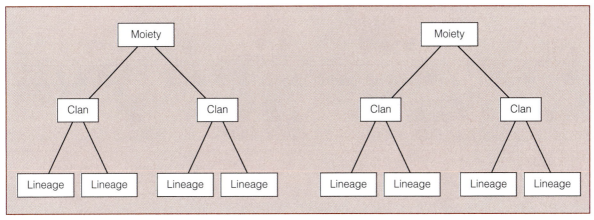

Figure 13-5 The relationships among lineages, clans, and moieties.

is included, but not her offspring. And don't think that members of patrilineal societies are confused about matters of human reproduction. They understand the biological facts of life completely, and they do not ignore "kin" on their mother's side. But in patrilineal descent, your mother's side is simply less important. This is because the lineage normally owns or controls land and other resources, not the nuclear family. The lineage makes decisions about whether to move a village, go to war, or dig irrigation ditches. Thus, although the nuclear family matters, it is secondary to the interests and concerns of the patrilineage.

This difference is reflected in kin terms. Men call their biological father by a term meaning "father," but they may also call their father's brother "father," and consequently, they may call their father's brother's offspring "brother" and "sister," rather than "cousins." In patrilineal descent your mother's brother's children belong to another lineage (*their* father's lineage), and so they are called by a term that we might translate as "cousin," but not "brother" or "sister." Your father's and mother's siblings are the same *kind* of relative in a bilateral descent system, but not in a patrilineal descent system.

The bottom chart in Figure 13-4 contains the same biological facts as the top one, but they are now organized into a **matrilineal descent.** Here, you trace relatives through the female line, forming **matrilineages.** In matrilineal societies you get your lineage from your mother. Your lineage includes you, your mother, her siblings and her sisters' offspring, your mother's mother, her siblings and her sisters' offspring, and so on. As in patrilineal societies, nuclear families exist, but the primary unit is the matrilineage.

By now, you can probably guess why the Pingelapese woman said that her mother's brother was her father: In matrilineal societies, the mother's brother is a "fictive" father. The biological father, in fact, may have little to do with his biological offspring. Instead, he spends his time with his sister's children—because they are members of his lineage, and so it is they, not his biological offspring, who will inherit whatever resources, knowledge, or privileges he possesses.

Matrilineal societies are rare, composing only about 10 percent of the world's societies. They appear to be associated with horticulture, long distance hunting, and/or warfare with distant enemies.

Finally, to complicate things even more, we need to note that lineages are sometimes clustered into **clans,** which is a set of lineages that claim to share a distant, often-mythical, ancestor (Figure 13-5). Clans, in turn, may be clustered into **moieties** (*moy*-i-tees; from the French word meaning "half"; in any society with moieties, there are only two). Moieties often perform reciprocal ceremonial obligations for each other, such as burying the dead of the other or holding feasts for one another. We come back to these terms below, but first

matrilineal descent   A unilineal descent system in which ancestry is traced through the female line.

matrilineage   Individuals who share a line of matrilineal descent.

clans   A group of matri- or patrilineages who see themselves as descended from a (sometimes-mythical) common ancestor.

moieties   Two groups of clans that perform reciprocal ceremonial obligations for one another; moieties often intermarry.

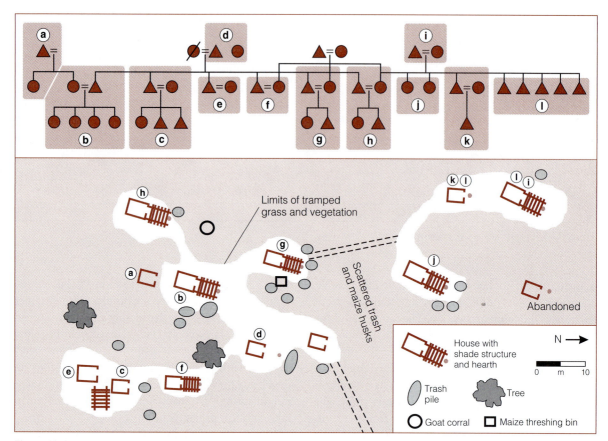

Figure 13-6 Mikea hamlet map with kinship chart; notice how the patrilineages are linked by marriage and yet are separated on the ground.

we must consider the visibility of such abstract groupings in the archaeological record.

Do Descent Systems Appear Archaeologically?

We return to Madagascar's Mikea (already discussed in Chapter 10), a patrilineal society who also practice **patrilocal residence**—a cultural "rule," commonly associated with patrilineal descent, in which a wife lives with her husband in his original village.

Recall that some Mikea live in forest hamlets of about 40 people. Figure 13-6 is a map of one Mikea hamlet, accompanied by the kinship chart of the families who lived there (the lines drawn through some of the symbols indicate deceased individuals). The dia-

gram also indicates which families lived in which house. In some cases, young children (over the age of 10) and single, elderly individuals lived in small, separate houses.

This figure demonstrates several facets of Mikea hamlets. First, the houses are arranged in a linear, north-to-south scatter, their doors facing north (recall from Chapter 10 that they are placed thus to avoid a cold southern wind at night). Second, the hamlet contains two clusters of houses, marked by trampled areas of vegetation around the houses, and an untrampled belt of vegetation and trash (mostly maize husks) between the two. A path (shown with dotted lines) connects the two clusters.

The kin diagram shows the presence of two patrilineages at this hamlet. On each side of the kin diagram is an older man and his wife, with their sons and their wives, and their unmarried children and grandchildren. Furthermore, these two patrilineages are linked by virtue of several marriages between the sons of one of the elder couples and the daughters of the other.

patrilocal residence A cultural practice in which a newly married couple live in the groom's village of origin; it is often associated with patrilineal descent.

This is typical of Mikea forest hamlets. Members of two patrilineages live together, somewhat united by marriage ties or a link through a woman. We say "somewhat" because there was always a palpable tension between these residential groups. For example, when Kelly gifted clothing to the hamlet depicted in the figure, one of the elder man's sons from the southern group insisted on taking charge of the distribution. And for the next 2 days, the northern group repeated accusations of stinginess and complained of an inappropriate distribution. Sharing (of tools and labor) occurred *within* each of these clusters, but was rarer *between* the two (see "Looking Closer: Did People Share Food at Pincevent?").

Finally, and most important, notice that the patrilineages map onto the ground: The northern cluster of houses contains men (and unmarried sisters) who belong to the same lineage along with their wives and children. Likewise, the southern cluster contains brothers who belonged to another lineage, with their wives and offspring. The same social relationships mapped out in virtually every settlement we visited. Another ethnoarchaeological study conducted by Rob Gargett (San Jose State University) and Brian Hayden (Simon Fraser University) found a similar pattern in Australian Aboriginal communities: The closer a social relationship is between two people or two groups, the closer they live to one another.

The difficulty, of course, is that archaeologically the Mikea hamlets appear simply as two clusters of houses. Although we might infer that each cluster represents a social grouping, we'd be hard pressed to say whether it was a patrilineage, matrilineage, or some other grouping, such as a clan or moiety. As with gender, we might have to fall back on a strong ethnographic analogy. Let's explore how this course of action might work in archaeology.

Looking for Matrilineal Descent

Anthropologists Melvin Ember and Carol Ember (Yale University, Human Relation Area Files) have devoted their careers to compiling and analyzing worldwide ethnographic data to find underlying patterns and correlations. Some of these relate human social organization to material culture and are useful to archaeologists.

We noted above that patrilineal societies may practice patrilocal residence. Likewise, matrilineal societies often practice **matrilocal residence,** in which the groom lives in the wife's village. The Embers found that people practicing patrilocal residence tend to live in houses less than 60 square meters in size. Mikea houses fall comfortably within this range. The Embers also found that houses in matrilocal societies are larger, generally over 100 square meters in size. The reason for this difference appears to be that, in patrilocal societies, the residential group is the nuclear family (as among the Mikea), but in matrilocal societies, clusters of sisters often inhabit one large house, dividing it into interior spaces for each nuclear family. Iroquois longhouses are one example. The Iroquois often built enormous houses with dividing walls separating the interior space into units, each occupied by a sister, her husband, and their unmarried children.

So, where is the uniformitarianism here? For these observations to serve as middle-range theory to reconstruct the past, we must explain *why* residential units differ between matrilocal and patrilocal societies. Anthropologists don't have a good answer to this question (yet). But recall that matrilineal societies are often associated with long-distance hunting or external warfare. Warfare with distant neighbors takes men away for long periods of time and, obviously, the men might not come back. The houses of matrilocal societies may reflect (and help create) bonds of assistance and cooperation between sisters while their husbands are away.

Can these observations help us infer kinship from archaeological remains?

Kinship at Chaco Canyon

To answer this question, we return to Chaco Canyon in northwest New Mexico. As you will recall from previous chapters, Chaco Canyon contains a number of large pueblos, or Great Houses, constructed between AD 900 and 1130. The Great Houses were connected to one another and to a vast network of pueblos outside the canyon by the road system that we described in Chapter 5. But Chaco Canyon also contains many smaller pueblos—these first appear about AD 700 (Figure 13-9)—and even older semi-subterranean pithouses.

---

matrilocal residence A cultural practice in which a newly married couple live in the bride's village of origin; it is often associated with matrilineal descent.

Looking Closer
Did People Share Food at Pincevent?

Among hunter-gatherers, plant foods and small game animals are not widely shared; large game, however, is often shared throughout a community, and its distribution tells us something about social relationships. The remarkable site of Pincevent provides an example.

Pincevent lies about 60 kilometers south of Paris, on the bank of the Seine. Here, hunter-gatherers stayed in the autumn, about 12,000 years ago, ambushing caribou as they migrated south and crossed the river. The hunters took their kills back to camp, where they butchered, shared, and ate them.

At Pincevent, spring floods gently covered each fall's midden with a thin layer of silt, preserving the spatial distribution of artifacts and faunal remains. The layers contain several hearths, each surrounded by an arc of flintknapping debris and caribou bones (shown in Figure 13-7) that probably represent different nuclear families. And the distribution of reindeer bones point to how meat was shared among these families. How so?

When a butchered animal is shared, pieces of bone go along with the meat. James Enloe (University of Iowa) and Francine David (Centre National de la Recherche Scientifique) used this assumption to trace shared caribou meat from one of Pincevent's strata, IV-20, by refitting the bones. You refit bones by laying them out on a table and comparing each bone to the others to see which fragments fit back together, which joints articulate, or which are "bilateral matches" (the left and right limb bones of the same animal). It's incredibly time-consuming but, if you have the patience of Job, it can be quite rewarding.

Figure 13-7 Hearth O123 at Pincevent with scattered flint chips and caribou bone.

Figure 13-8 shows the mapped debris clusters for Level IV-20, with each hearth numbered (for example, M89). The lines connect refitted broken bones, anatomical refits, or bilateral matches (lefts and rights of the same animal) for the humeri and radiocubitus units (the radius-ulna) of several reindeer. The first thing Enloe and David learned was that individual reindeer were shared between at least two households. Those hearths with no refits, such as R143 and G64, were either not contemporaneous with the others or they were not included in the social network. Notice that the most refits for a hearth are with the next closest hearth; there is only one "long-distance" refit, between E74 and O123.

The upper leg is a meaty portion of a reindeer, and those elements circulate widely. Less-meaty portions, such as metacarpals (bones of the forefeet) and the

---

Arguing from the Embers' cross-cultural patterns, Peter Peregrine (Lawrence University) suggests that Chacoan pueblo society practiced matrilocal residence. Why? The pithouses, the earliest of the Chaco dwellings, average about 15 square meters in size, placing them well below the ethnographic range of matrilocal houses. The early small pueblos are not isolated

houses, but clusters of rooms that abut one another. Although individual rooms were small, collectively they covered from 70 to over 300 square meters. Using the Embers' cross-cultural data, Peregrine suggests that these pueblos may represent matrilocal residence. However, instead of a single large house divided into interior subdivisions, Peregrine argues the Chacoans

radiocubitus, remain closer to home. This makes sense: Low-utility portions of animals are not worth sharing. But this points to some potential kinship relations. Enloe and David suggest that hearths with both meaty and not very meaty body parts were probably the homes of the hunters—Hearths M89, T112, and V105. These are also hearths with substantial scatters of debris, evidence of a lot of activity. But there are two smaller, less-dense debris scatters, Hearths L115 and E74. Metacarpals refit between L115 and both T112 and V105, suggesting that Hearth L115 was occupied by children or an elderly relative of those living at T115 and V105.

Hearth E74 also had a small debris scatter, with few and poor quality tools. The limb bones here are mostly the radiocubitus, the less-meaty portion of the forelimb. Enloe and David suggest that this hearth might be that of a grandparent of one or more of the hunters' households.

Thus, Enloe and David draw some tentative inferences about kin relations at a 12,000-year-old

site, based on the distribution of reindeer bone elements and on the nutritional properties of the food represented by those bones.

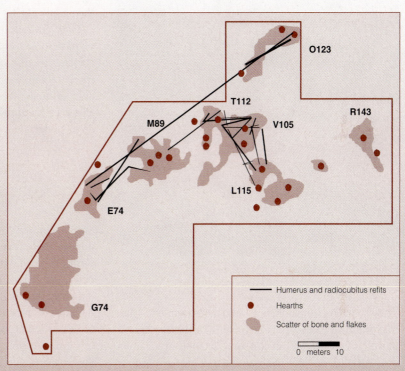

Figure 13-8 Placement of Pincevent hearths and the scatters of flint chips and bone around the hearths; the lines connect caribou humeri or radiocubitus bones that refit within and between the hearths.

built separate rooms, their side-by-side spatial arrangement reflecting a degree of social solidarity not seen in the earlier pithouse villages.

Not everyone agrees with Peregrine's inference, and contradictory data come from burials recovered from Pueblo Bonito in the early twentieth century. Recall that women remain in their own village under a matrilocal

residential pattern, with men coming from other villages. This means that women in such a village should genetically be more *similar* to one another than the men. Conversely, with patrilocal residence, the women should be genetically more *diverse* than the men.

In Chapter 12, we discussed how bioarchaeologists can use skeletal data to track population movements.

© Robert Kelly

Figure 13-9 A small pueblo in Chaco Canyon.

These data can include not only measurements (like maximum cranial length and breadth or the height and breadth of eye orbits), but also some 200 nonmetric traits of the skull. The latter include the presence or absence of foramina (holes where blood vessels pass through bone), which, in certain places (for example, above the eye orbits) also provide clues to genetic affinity.

Michael Schillaci and Christopher Stojanowski (University of New Mexico) analyzed the genetic traits of

bilocal residence A cultural practice in which a newly married couple may live in either the village of the groom or the village of the bride.

status The rights, duties, privileges, powers, liabilities, and immunities that accrue to a recognized and named social position.

ascribed status Rights, duties, and obligations that accrue to a person by virtue of their parentage; ascribed status is inherited.

achieved status Rights, duties, and obligations that accrue to a person by virtue of what they accomplished in their life.

the Pueblo Bonito burial population specifically to determine post-marital residence patterns. Although the sample size was small, the female sample showed *greater* variation than did the male sample. Schillaci and Stojanowski suggested that, instead of matrilocal residence, the people of Pueblo Bonito practiced patrilocal or **bilocal residence** (where the married couple resides either with the husband's or the wife's family). Bilocal residence, in fact, was common at the time of European contact among the eastern Pueblos who live along the upper Rio Grande and who might be descended from the people of Chaco Canyon.

Like gender roles and ideology, kinship is an element of past social organizations that is difficult to reconstruct. But our increasing ability to use genetic data and markers coupled with strong ethnographic analogies and ethnoarchaeological studies should eventually allow us to draw some secure inferences from the archaeological record.

ARCHAEOLOGY AND SOCIAL STATUS

Status consists of the rights, duties, privileges, and powers that accrue to a recognized and named social position. In our own society, the status of "mother" is determined both by the duties she owes to her son or daughter and the responsibilities she can legitimately demand of her children. Similarly, a child owes certain obligations to a parent and can expect certain privileges in return. As you will see, gender and age play important roles in status.

Two major ways of assigning status are through *ascription* and *achievement*. An **ascribed status** is assigned to individuals at birth, without regard to innate differences or abilities. Prince Charles, for example, has high status and expects to become king of England—not because of anything he has done, but simply because his mother is Queen Elizabeth II. His status and rights were ensured at birth.

Alternatively, many statuses are **achieved** and require that an individual possess certain admirable qualities or have accomplished certain tasks (the importance of these qualities and tasks being culturally defined). Rather than being assigned at birth, achieved statuses are earned through individual effort. A Shoshone man who proved to be a good hunter might achieve status as a leader in hunts but, upon his death, no one would automatically fill his former position.

Egalitarian Societies

The concept of status allows us to bridge from the level of the individual to that of the entire society. A society is termed **egalitarian** when there is no fixed number of positions of status; instead, the number of valued statuses is equal to the number of persons with the ability to fill them. No one individual wields complete authority over another. The important feature, then, is that *members of egalitarian societies generally have equal access to critical, life-sustaining resources.*

The social system of the nineteenth-century Great Basin Shoshone people was generally egalitarian, with leadership by those individuals believed to be the most capable of supervising others. Anthropologists call such small-scale egalitarian societies **bands**. Authority was restricted to particular, short-term circumstances. A good hunter, for instance, might assume a temporary position of leadership when a group decided to hunt bighorn. An accomplished dancer might take charge of communal gatherings. Or the opinion of a gifted naturalist might convince others of the medicinal attributes of particular plants. But these individuals would have no authority outside their area of expertise. The key to leadership here is experience and social standing; such a social position is *not* inherited in an egalitarian society. Gender and age are the primary dimensions of status in egalitarian communities.

Ranked Societies

Ranked societies limit the positions of valued status so that not everyone of sufficient talent can actually achieve them. Such a social structure entails a hierarchy in which relatively permanent social stations are maintained, *with people having unequal access to life-sustaining resources.* Gender and age still play a role in the division of labor in ranked societies. But ranked societies tend to have economies that redistribute goods and services throughout the community, with those doing the redistributing keeping some portion for themselves. This creates one or more ranked social tiers to the society. Many tribes of the American Northwest Coast (see Chapter 2) were ranked societies, as was Tahitian society (mentioned above). Localized residential kin groups (such as a patrilineage) control resources, and major economic goods flow in and out of a regional center.

Death and Social Status

The categories "egalitarian" and "ranked" define a social spectrum of statuses that can be inferred from analyses of material culture. Mortuary remains are one important source of information on extinct political systems. For the past three decades, many archaeologists have used ethnographic data to show that *societies that have important social distinctions among living individuals will have material distinctions among the dead.*

Death, in a sense, is a period of separation and reintegration for both the deceased and those they leave behind. The deceased are separated from the living and must be properly integrated into the world of the dead. Social ties existed between the living and the once-living, and the ceremonial connections at death reflect these social relations. Mortuary rituals reflect who people were and the relationships they had with others when they were alive. Therefore, they should reflect the person's degree of social status in a society.

Rank and Status at Moundville

We can examine the ranking of social status at Moundville, one of the best-known and most intensively investigated ceremonial centers in the United States. Sprawling across 300 acres, Moundville overlooks Alabama's Black Warrior River. Three thousand people once lived here, and for centuries, Moundville was the largest center in the American Southeast (Figure 13-10).

This complex of about 30 earthen mounds was a bustling ritual center between about AD 1050 and 1450.

egalitarian societies Social systems that contain roughly as many valued positions as there are persons capable of filling them; in egalitarian societies, all people have nearly equal access to the critical resources needed to live.

band A residential group composed of a few nuclear families, but whose membership is neither permanent nor binding.

ranked societies Social systems in which a hierarchy of social status has been established, with a restricted number of valued positions available; in ranked societies, not everyone has the same access to the critical resources of life.

© The University of Alabama, Moundville Archaeological Park

Figure 13-10 Moundville (Alabama), looking southwest over Mound E; Mound A is in the center of the clearing.

The ubiquitous C. B. Moore conducted archaeological investigations at Moundville in 1905 and 1906, digging into both platform mounds and village areas. The Alabama Museum of Natural History then excavated at Moundville from 1930 through 1941. Over a half-million square feet of the village areas at Moundville were uncovered during this 11-year period, in part by workers in the Civilian Conservation Corps. The more than 3000 excavated burials from Moundville provide a unique database for studying Mississippian social structure.

Like most **Mississippian** political units, this maize-based society engaged in extensive trade, and their skilled artists worked in stone, ceramics, bone, and copper. Moundville contains 20 major ceremonial mounds—large flat-topped earthen structures designed to function both as artificial mountains (elevating elite residences and possibly temples above the landscape) and as mortuary areas. A stout bastioned palisade protected Moundville's large central plaza. This suggests that warfare was probably a recurring feature of life at Moundville (Figure 13-11).

Moundville was a major participant in the "Mississippian tradition," a term referring to the hundreds of societies that thrived between about AD 800 and 1500 throughout the southeastern United States. In their heyday, the Mississippian elite presided over breathtaking ceremonial centers (as at Moundville) that were invested with power by the thousands of people who lived in smaller nearby farmsteads.

Mississippian A widespread cultural tradition across much of the eastern United States from AD 800–1500. Mississippian societies engaged in intensive village-based maize horticulture and constructed large, earthen platform mounds that served as substructures for temples, residences, and council buildings.

Southeastern Ceremonial Complex An assortment of ceremonial objects that occurs in the graves of high-status Mississippian individuals. Ritual exchange of these artifacts crosscut the boundaries of many distinctive local cultures.

The Symbolism of Grave Goods at Moundville

Christopher Peebles (Indiana University) and Susan Kus (Rhodes College) took advantage of this database and analyzed Moundville's burials with an eye toward reconstructing Moundville's political organization. They began with the grave goods, many of which display the distinctive symbols characteristic of what archaeologists call the **Southeastern Ceremonial Complex.**

During the Mississippian period, artifacts that bore striking stylistic similarities appear in a number of sites and several large centers, including Moundville, across the southeastern United States from Oklahoma to Florida. These artifacts include conch shell gorgets and cups, copper plates, ceremonial axes and batons, effigy pipes, and flint knives—many decorated with one or more of a set of symbols, such as the "forked eye," the cross, the sun circle, the hand and eye, and the bi-lobed arrow (Figure 13-12). The distribution of these items parallels a trade network of exotic items, as well as basics such as food and salt. But the similarities in the motifs imply more than simple trade; a higher degree of social interaction was at work.

Whatever the Southeastern Ceremonial Complex really was—and archaeologists still debate it—it crosscut the boundaries of many widely separate residential groups. At each major site are artifacts that bear local symbols. At Moundville, these artifacts are specially constructed animal effigy vessels or parts of animals (such as canine teeth, claws, and shells). The local sym-

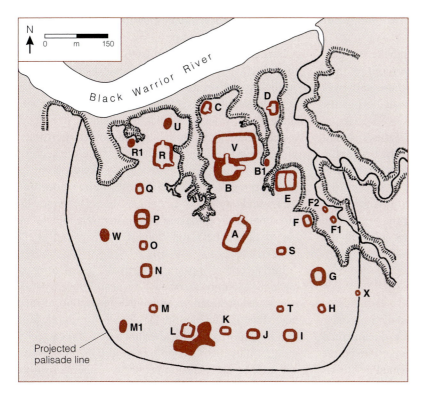

Figure 13-11 A map of the site of Moundville; the letters designate mounds mentioned in the text. *From* Archaeology of the Moundville Chiefdom, *edited by Vernon James Knight, Jr. and Vincas P. Steponaitis, published by the Smithsonian Institute Press, Washington, D.C.; copyright © 1998 by the Smithsonian Institution. Used by permission of the publisher.*

bols probably functioned as status items within Moundville whereas the ceremonial complex symbols designated the rank of individuals in the overall region.

Each burial mound at Moundville contained a few high-status adults as indicated by their grave goods. These included copper axes, copper gorgets, stone disks, various paints, and assorted exotic minerals—such as galena (cubes of natural lead), mica (paper-thin sheets of translucent silicate minerals), and sheet copper. Copper and mica items often depict scalloped circles, swastikas, and the "hand-eye" motif (an open hand with an eye in the palm). Presumably, individuals buried with these artifacts had statuses and reputations recognized throughout the entire Moundville cultural system. Each mound also contained some presumably lower-status individuals who were buried with only a few ceramic vessels. Other commoners were buried in cemeteries away from the mounds with no burial goods (or, at least, none that preserved).

By correlating the presence of higher- and lower-status symbols, Peebles and Kus could infer that social

status was ascribed at Moundville. Some infants and children—clearly too young to have accomplished anything noteworthy in life—were buried with lavish grave goods. These children must have been important because of who they were at birth, not because of what they had done in their short lives. This is clear evidence of a ranked society.

Two Axes of Social Patterning

On the basis of ethnographic evidence, Peebles and Kus predicted that the Moundville population may have been subdivided along two major social axes, which they termed the superordinate and subordinate.

The subordinate division recognizes that certain symbols and the energy expended on mortuary ritual reflect the statuses of age and sex. With respect to age, the older the individual, the greater the opportunity for lifetime achievement, and hence the higher the deathbed rank can be. This means that at Moundville (along the subordinate axis, at least), adult burials should be more lavish than those of children, and children should be accompanied by more grave goods than infants. And because the subordinate division is also graded by gender, men and

Figure 13-12 An image in the Southeastern Ceremonial Complex style, pounded in copper. Note particularly the forked eye motif around the eye, which probably represents a symbolic association with peregrine falcons, known for their keen vision and skill as hunters (from Spiro, Oklahoma).

© American Museum of Natural History

women should not be expected to have equivalent grave goods.

The superordinate division at Moundville is a partially hereditary ordering based on criteria other than age and sex. Among the elite—people whose status was assigned at birth—some individuals will be infants, some children, and the rest adults.

Peebles and Kus predicted that the statuses should form a pyramid-shaped distribution. At the base of the pyramid are the commoners, whose statuses are determined strictly by sex and age. The next step up the social ladder, the next rank, consists of those few individuals with ascribed status. Finally, at the top will be the paramount individuals, those who enjoy all the emblems of status and rank available in the society.

Quantitative Distribution of Moundville Grave Goods

This model was tested by performing a statistical analysis of the grave goods of 2053 of the best-documented burials from Moundville. This analysis uncovered three distinct clusters and subclusters, represented by burials that contained similar kinds of grave goods (and diagrammed in Figure 13-13). The seven burials of Cluster IA—the supreme division—are presumably chiefs, those individuals enjoying the highest of statuses and the ultimate political authority. All males (we think; these are based on Moore's field assessments), the elite were buried in Mounds C and D, small mortuary mounds in a secluded area to the north of the plaza, and were accompanied by a lavish array of material culture, including numerous ceremonial complex–adorned artifacts. Infants and human skulls (of individuals presumably sacrificed for the occasion) were buried as part of the Cluster IA ritual. Distinctive artifacts in these graves were large axes of copper—a metal too soft to have allowed the implements to function as chopping tools. These, then, must have served primarily as symbols, a culturally meaningful way to communicate an individual's high status and a visual reminder of the reasons for differences in people's ranks.

Cluster IB burials, both children and adult males, were interred in the mounds surrounding the plaza and in cemeteries near mounds. They also had a number of ceremonial complex artifacts plus mineral-based paints included in their grave goods. Cluster II, the final cluster of the superordinate division, included adults and children buried in cemeteries near the mounds and beneath what were charnel houses near the main plaza;

their grave goods included chest beads, copper gorgets, and galena cubes.

Hierarchically below the Level A elite are those of subordinate Levels B and C (who enjoyed status largely on the basis of sex and age differences). In Cluster III, for instance, stone ceremonial axes are found only with adult males, whereas infants and children have "toy" vessels, clay "playthings," and unworked freshwater shells. Unworked bird claws and deer and turtle bones were found only with adults. The individuals in the lowest segment, Level C, were mostly buried away from the mounds and major ceremonial areas at Moundville. But some of the burials in this cluster were individuals buried as retainers and isolated skulls placed at the bases of large posts.

Burial context appears to clarify the nature of ranking in the Moundville society. The most elite were buried in a sacred area and accompanied by symbols of their exalted status. The Moundville elite also apparently lived in larger, more complex dwellings than did the commoners. Elite membership was conditioned by genealogy and, because social position was inherited within the elite, even children occupied such social positions.

Farther down the ladder, the villagers' graves also reflected their social status in life at this level, positions conditioned largely by sex and age distinctions rather than by inheritance. Their less glamorous grave goods were distributed in a different way. Graves contained pottery vessels, bone awls, flint projectile points, and stone pipes, all of which were distributed mostly to older adults. Peebles and Kus infer that these individuals were required to achieve—rather than inherit—their social status. Over half of the Moundville graves contained commoners buried with no grave goods at all.

Peebles and Kus suggested that Moundville conformed to a chiefdom model, a society similar to that of Tahiti and characterized by a status framework with fewer valued positions, although they saw no direct evidence for a redistributive economy.

How Well Did the Elite Eat?

Similar forms of social organization have been recognized at other Mississippian sites in Tennessee, Georgia, Oklahoma, and the lower Illinois Valley. In all cases, burial populations served as the source of inference. The burial goods reflect some clear status differences between men and women and among classes. Some individuals clearly had different access to exotics. Did this difference also extend to some of the more basic

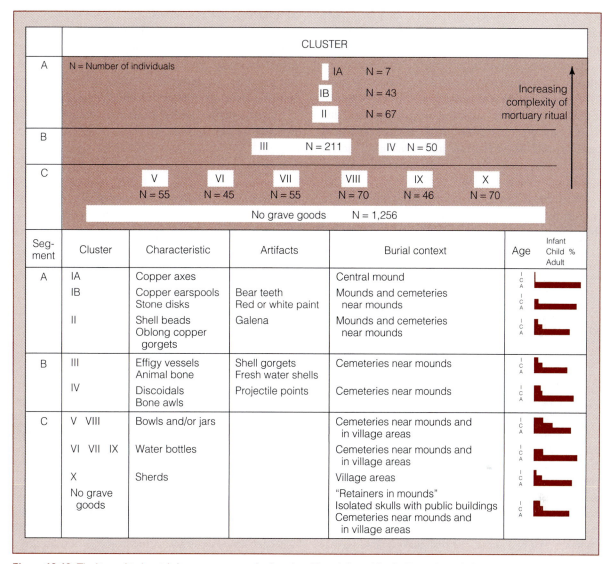

Figure 13-13 The hierarchical social clusters represented in burials at Moundville. *After Peebles and Kus (1977: figure 3)*

necessities of life? For example, did the elite eat better than the commoners?

If the elite were better off than commoners, then we would expect that they had more nutritious diets, which might include eating more meat. In fact, through a faunal analysis of the trash associated with elite residences on Mounds G and Q (on opposite sides of the plaza, as shown in Figure 13-11), Ed Jackson and Susan Scott (University of Southern Mississippi) found evidence of many animals, including deer, turkey, bobcat, cougar, fox, bear, falcon, bison, and shark. The faunal remains indicated that those living on the top of the mounds ate the choicest cuts of meat from a wide vari-

ety of game—including imported items, such as bison and shark. The elite did indeed have access to resources that the commoners did not.

Bone chemistry, as you now know, can also tell us something about what people ate at Moundville. Margaret Schoeninger, the analyst who examined the Stillwater skeletal remains, also studied a sample of male and female remains from both low- and high-status burials. Her analysis suggested that there was little difference in the amount of maize and fish that people ate, but that men ate more meat than women, and that high-status men ate more meat than low-status men. These differences did fit the predictions, but they were not large and, although high-status men may have eaten the most meat, it does not seem that women and low-status men ate inadequate amounts of meat.

Did these differences in diet create significant differences in the quality of life? Mary Lucas Powell (University of Kentucky) hypothesized that, if the elites limited commoners' access to critical resources, then the elite should be taller, live longer, and show less evidence of caries, growth arrest features, iron deficiency (such as cribra orbitalia—see Chapter 12), infectious disease, and trauma than commoners.

In a nutshell, Powell could find no significant differences between the elite and the commoners. It appears that, although differences in social status allowed the Moundville elite to live well, the commoners did not lead lives of want. However, both of these analyses are hampered by the fact that some of the highest-status burials were excavated by Moore in the early twentieth century. We have his notes and the grave goods, but Moore did not save the human skeletal remains, and so the highest stratum of the Moundville hierarchy is not available for biological study.

Kinship at Moundville

Despite the differences in rank, Moundville was still an integrated society. And it may have been bonds of kinship that provided the integrating factor and that pre-

Archaeological Ethics
Development and Archaeology

Sites that provide us with much of what we know about the social and political organizations of past civilizations often have spectacular architecture and dramatic landscapes. Of these, Machu Picchu is perhaps the most dramatic (see this chapter's opening photo). Perched on a knife-like ridge at 2300 meters (7546 feet) elevation, Machu Picchu overlooks the Urubamba River more than 1000 feet below. Beside it rises a sugarloaf mountain that is daily shrouded in fog. Many people claim the site has special spiritual qualities; one woman claims she encountered an alien spaceship there.

Such gibberish masks the truth about Machu Picchu— "old mountain" in Quechua, one of the native languages of Peru. Built in the fifteenth century, it was a retreat for Inka rulers who otherwise lived in the capital of Cuzco, 100 kilometers away. Massive stone structures, plazas, terraces, and canals cover every inch of the ridge's 13 square kilometers and are made with typical Inka precision and a lack of mortar. The ridge's sides are covered with stone terraces where maize and other crops were grown.

An innkeeper in the nearby town of Aguas Calientes led explorer Hiram Bingham (1875–1956) to the site in 1911. Since that time, the site has become a tourist mecca, drawing more than 300,000 visitors each year. You can get there by walking several days from Cuzco along the old Inka road or by taking a four-hour train ride from Cuzco. From the valley floor, you ride a bus up the winding switchbacks to the site. Today, there is a small hotel at the base of the mountain and a few others in Aguas Calientes.

Though well worth the effort, the trip to Machu Picchu is not easy. And Peru would like to make it easier.

Peru is a poor nation. Two-thirds of the population live in poverty, and the country's foreign debt in 2003 exceeded US$30 million. It needs tourists' cash, and the Cuzco–Machu Picchu area is the country's best bet. Peru wants to build new hotels near Machu Picchu, a new high-speed railroad to bring day-tourists from Cuzco, and two cable cars to haul tourists up the mountain.

But more tourists means more hands and feet on the ancient walls and steps, more trash, and more decline in the ruins' magnificence.

What's more, geologists have determined that the site's dramatic location places it at risk of landslides— two have temporarily closed the road up to the site in the past. The proposed cable car towers will be in particularly sensitive areas and could create vibrations that could destabilize Machu Picchu's stone walls. The towers would also mar the vista that is one of the site's most attractive qualities. UNESCO, which made Machu Picchu a World Heritage Site in 1983, opposes the cable

vented extreme differences between the elite and the commoners. Indeed, although chiefdoms are internally ranked, their members commonly understand that everyone is ultimately, albeit sometimes distantly, a relative of the chief, who might even use kinship terms to refer to his followers.

To help reconstruct Moundville's social organization, Vernon Knight (University of Alabama) employed an ethnographic analogy with the nineteenth-century Chickasaw, the Native Americans who lived in the vicinity of Moundville at the time of European contact. Knight noted that there are two major classes of mounds at Moundville. Some of the mounds contain burials; others were residential mounds, with evidence for

wattle-and-daub or thatch structures on their flat tops.

These mounds alternate around the square Moundville plaza so that each residential mound is paired with one and sometimes two burial mounds, forming eight burial/residential mound groups. Knight saw in this pattern a parallel to Chickasaw society.

The ethnographic data are limited, and Chickasaw society had undergone profound changes because of European contact, but Knight found that the ideal Chickasaw village had sets of houses arranged around a square plaza, just as the mounds at Moundville form a square plaza. In Chickasaw society, each set of houses belonged to a matrilocal clan that was the political and

---

cars. Although Peru dropped the proposal, it has suggested that it might revive it.

Peru's government is obliged to increase the welfare of their nation. If tourist dollars are a source of income, why should Peru suffer just so that the rest of the world knows that Machu Picchu will remain pristine for their viewing pleasure? On the other hand, if tourism destroys the site, Peru loses what should have been a renewable tourist resource. Archaeologists want people to know about the past, but we obviously don't want to see sites destroyed or their value and beauty compromised. How do we balance the need for development with the need to protect precious archaeological resources?

Many nations face this question. In some cases, sites have simply been placed off-limits. Today, you must view Stonehenge in England from a distance, and two nearby highways mar the site's serenity. Likewise, France's famous Paleolithic cave site of Lascaux (see Chapter 14) is off-limits to the public to protect its 17,000-year-old paintings from the damaging effects of humidity caused by tourists' breath.

Solutions to these problems are not cheap. France spent millions to clean Lascaux and to build an incredibly

accurate duplicate of its central chamber. Britain has proposed building tunnels over the highways near Stonehenge.

But many important sites are in poor nations that cannot afford such luxuries. If their sites are indeed "world" heritage resources, then does it behoove the international community to pony up and make tourism viable in such a way that a site's integrity and scientific value are maintained? But if the international community has a financial interest in archaeological sites, can it also assert a proprietary interest? In early 2001, the Afghani Taliban used cannons and explosives to destroy the 175-foot-tall, 1500-year-old Bamiyan Buddhas, huge statues carved into a mountainside, because the Taliban's brand of Islam prohibited idols. The world reacted with shock and disgust, and many countries condemned the act (and some are now trying to rebuild the statues). At what point does the world's interest in its global heritage override national sovereignty? Does the "world" have the authority to tell Peru what it can or cannot do at Machu Picchu, what the British can do with Stonehenge, or what the Taliban can do to statues in their own country?

land-owning unit. In addition, the clans were grouped into moieties, and each moiety lived on opposite sides of the square village layout. The highest ranking clan of each moiety was located on opposite sides of the north end of the square plan, with lower ranking clans to the south. Thus, Chickasaw villages spatially mirrored the kinship structure.

Knight wondered if this kinship pattern extended back to the inhabitants of Moundville. Perhaps, he suggested, each of the eight residential/burial mound units represents the high-ranking home of the leader of eight clans. Knight pointed out that the Moundville plaza can be neatly bifurcated by a line passing through Mound B at the north end of the plaza, through the central Mound A, and then between smaller burial mounds K and J (refer to Figure 13-11). Extrapolating from the Chickasaw analogy, the resulting halves might represent two moieties, each comprising four clans. Note also that the most elite burials were recovered in Mounds C and D; although these are not the largest mounds, they are located at either side of the north edge of the plaza.

But Moundville and Chickasaw villages exhibit crucial differences:

- In the Chickasaw camp layout, a large fire hearth in the center of the village structurally and symbolically united the two moieties. There was, however, no central mound or ceremonial structure.
- Knight points out that nineteenth-century Chickasaw society was not a chiefdom and did not possess a central individual who was the uniting focus of the social and political organization. In Moundville, the large Mound B, at the north end of the site, might have been the home of the chief—the highest ranking individual—and evidence of a tier in the social organization that was not present among the Chickasaw.

In sum, Knight's analysis of the layout of Moundville's mounds, along with bioarchaeological and faunal analyses, supports a conclusion that Moundville was a chiefdom.

exotics Material culture that was not produced locally and/or whose raw material is not found locally.

TRADE AND POLITICAL ORGANIZATION

In our discussion of Moundville, we mentioned the Southeastern Ceremonial Complex, a social phenomenon that included an extensive trade network. All societies—from egalitarian bands to chiefdoms to modern states—exchange goods, ideas, and services. The geographic scale of trade tells us something about the nature of the nonresidential group that a population participated in and about how far-flung were their political, economic, and kinship connections.

In archaeological sites in the Great Basin, for example, archaeologists frequently find beads made of the shells of *Olivella*, *Haliotis*, and *Dentalia*—marine organisms that live along the coasts of California and Oregon. Obviously, they point to some sort of interaction between people on either side of California's Sierra Nevada.

The California shell beads in Great Basin sites are not numerous. They appear as personal ornaments in some burials, but they are not exclusively associated with men or women, the old or the young. Many are found in residential sites where, because they are small, they were probably lost as they fell off clothing or a necklace. It is more difficult to say if the beads indicate exchange of goods between the peoples of the Great Basin and California or were simply the personal belongings of people (wives or husbands? emigrants?) who moved from California to the Great Basin.

Anthropologists have found that, as societies change from egalitarian bands (like the Great Basin Shoshone) to ranked societies (such as those of Tahiti or Moundville), the formal trade of **exotics** becomes an integral part of the economy. Exotics are artifacts made of raw material or in a style that indicates contact with the people of a distant region. Members of the elite trade or give away exotics at competitive feasts (such as the potlatch; see Chapter 2) as a way to communicate and maintain the social order. Exotic artifacts, therefore, are symbols of status and prestige—visual reminders of an individual's social, political, or religious connections to a larger world. As such, they are signs of power and, consequently, of social and political organization as well.

Tracing Exotics

Archaeologists have several methods to determine which objects are locally produced and which are non-local. In some cases, it is fairly easy to determine which objects are *not* locally produced or acquired. Recall that at Moundville, for example, some of the elite burials contained copper axes. This copper is not smelted, for smelting technology did not exist in North America prior to European contact. Instead, the copper was extracted in its raw form. We know that this kind of copper deposit, known as native copper, is not found around Moundville. In fact, native copper occurs only in the southern Appalachian Mountains and near the Great Lakes. The copper artifacts at Moundville have been traced to a geological deposit in the southern Appalachian source. Likewise, the galena cubes have been traced to geological sources in Missouri and Wisconsin.

Human societies create many different kinds of trade systems, but they tend to be of two major types. The first is **direct acquisition,** wherein you go to the natural source of a raw material and extract the material yourself, exchange goods or services for it or for a finished artifact, or receive an artifact or raw material as a gift. Direct acquisition might entail a special trip or it may be embedded into a foraging excursion or a visit to relatives.

The second major type is **down-the-line trade,** in which people acquire a particular raw material or an artifact fashioned from that raw material from their neighbors, who have immediate access to the raw material. These people then trade it to others who live still farther away from the source, who may in turn trade it to people living still farther away. Down-the-line trade usually exhibits a steady decline in the frequency of artifacts made of a particular material in sites farther and farther away from the raw material's source. Occasionally, an unexpectedly high density of the raw material at a site distant from the source may signal that the site is a secondary trading center.

Down-the-line trade can move raw materials long distances. For example, archaeologists have found incised Gulf Coast shells in sites along the Missouri River in Montana.

Nobody knows how the copper axes made their way to Moundville—perhaps they were gifts sent between ranking elites—but they clearly signal that only a few people had the authority and power to acquire them or to merit receiving them as gifts. Although the copper axes had no material function—they would have made poor cutting implements—they were powerful symbols of the "connections" an elite individual had and per-

haps of his ability to draw upon social, economic, military or religious sanctions should anyone contest his hold on power.

Above we mentioned that the copper axes at Moundville were traced to geological sources in the southern Appalachian Mountains. Archaeologists do this primarily by "fingerprinting" an object and comparing it with similar fingerprints of known geologic sources of the raw material. Several different methods can do this; we'll focus on three here—one used to trace obsidian and two used to trace ceramics to their sources.

Fingerprinting Obsidian

Obsidian—the volcanic glass that makes such impressively sharp implements—occurs naturally only in geologic deposits of the western United States. So, why do obsidian artifacts appear in **Hopewell** burial mounds and sites in Ohio and Illinois?

You will recall from Chapter 2 that Squier and Davis mapped and studied the earthworks of the eastern United States, especially along the Ohio River Valley and its tributaries. We now know that some of the flat-topped pyramid mounds—such as those at Moundville—belong to the Mississippian period. But other mounds—geometric earthworks and some effigy mounds—are earlier, belonging to the Hopewell culture. "Hopewell" refers to a particular archaeological culture found in the Midwest, especially the Ohio River Valley, between 200 BC and AD 400. Hopewell peoples were predominately hunter-gatherers, although they also cultivated indigenous plants and small amounts of maize. They lived in small, sedentary villages.

Hopewell culture is best known for its elaborate mortuary rituals, which suggest the beginnings of a ranked society. Many goods appear in elite Hopewell

direct acquisition A form of trade in which a person/group goes to the source area of an item to procure the raw material directly or to trade for it or finished products.

down-the-line trade An exchange system in which goods are traded outward from a source area from group to group, resulting in a steady decline in the item's abundance in archaeological sites farther from the source.

Hopewell A cultural tradition found primarily in the Ohio River Valley and its tributaries, dating from 200 BC–AD 400. Hopewell societies engaged in hunting and gathering and in some horticulture of indigenous plants. They are known for their mortuary rituals, which included charnel houses and burial mounds; some central tombs contained exotics. They also constructed geometric earthworks as ceremonial enclosures and effigy mounds.

graves, including copper ornaments, incised pottery, carved mica, ceramics, and obsidian. The fact that obsidian is found almost exclusively in burials of Ohio Hopewell sites, rather than in middens, suggests that obsidian played something other than a purely functional role in Hopewell society. (We'll talk more about Hopewell in Chapter 14.)

Squier and Davis recorded small numbers of obsidian spear points in five Hopewell mounds, and more have since turned up in Tennessee, Illinois, and elsewhere. At the time, Squier and Davis thought that the obsidian probably came from Mexico or perhaps the American Southwest. But this was simply a guess. Early in the twentieth century, several archaeologists proposed the Rocky Mountains as the source—specifically the obsidian outcrops in Yellowstone National Park. More than a century after Squier and Davis first reported on the obsidian, James Griffin (1905–1997) used the then-new technique of neutron activation analysis to source the obsidian in the Ohio Hopewell mounds to Obsidian Cliff in Yellowstone National Park, some 2400 kilometers away. Because some questions have been raised about the accuracy of Griffin's method, Richard Hughes (Geochemical Research Laboratory, California)—one of the world's leading authorities on obsidian sourcing—used the current sourcing method, **energy dispersive x-ray fluorescence (XRF),** to test Griffin's findings.

How can XRF trace obsidian artifacts to their geologic source? Many geological deposits form slowly—over years, decades, thousands, or even tens of thousands of years. But obsidian deposits are produced during a single lava flow, and hence they are created in a geologic instant. A volcano could produce multiple flows, but because each flow forms quickly, it usually has a unique chemical "fingerprint." This fingerprint appears as particular amounts of trace elements—like zinc, rubidium, strontium, and barium. Different flows contain different amounts of these elements. If we can fingerprint samples from all geologic sources of obsidian—a formidable but not impossible task—and then fingerprint obsidian artifacts, we should be able to match up an artifact with its source.

XRF allows us to accomplish this goal. The analyst shoots an x-ray beam onto a piece of obsidian, causing the electrons to become excited and emit fluorescent x-ray energies. Because different trace elements emit different levels of energy; the analyst can measure the spectra of energy emitted from the piece of obsidian and, from this, determine the proportion of each trace element present—defining the sample's distinctive trace element fingerprint. Comparing the sample's trace element composition statistically with all known sources allows the analyst to find the best match and, presumably, the geologic source of an artifact. XRF is a very useful technique because it is non destructive, works well on very small samples (down to 1 millimeter in diameter), takes only minutes to complete, and is relatively inexpensive.

Hughes's analysis confirmed that most Hopewell obsidian came from Obsidian Cliff in Yellowstone National Park. But he also discovered that some obsidian, especially that found in Illinois and Indiana Hopewell sites, came from Bear Gulch in southeast Idaho.

Griffin had assumed that all the obsidian in Hopewell sites had come from one place and that there was no obsidian in sites between the Hopewell culture area and the Rocky Mountains. For these reasons, he suggested that the Midwest obsidian was obtained in a "one-shot" visit by Hopewell people to the source itself—in other words, through direct acquisition. But we now know that obsidian from the Yellowstone region appears in small quantities on other Hopewell-age sites in Wisconsin, Iowa, Illinois, and Indiana. Instead of direct acquisition, high-ranking Hopewell individuals might have used down-the-line trade to acquire obsidian—its shiny black surfaces serving to remind people not of vacations to Yellowstone, but of the important social ties some individuals had to other high-ranking persons in distant Hopewell communities.

Fingerprinting Ceramics

To understand how archaeologists can fingerprint ceramics and trace them to their point of origin, we must first expand upon our earlier discussion of pottery manufacture.

The first step in making a pot, of course, is to acquire the clay. Clays occur as geologic deposits, usually water-laid, and different sources have different grain sizes and mineral composition. The mineral composition of the clay determines to some extent the kind of pottery that you can make from it. Potters use clay that is nearly pure kaolinite, for example, to manufacture fine porcelains.

energy dispersive x-ray fluorescence (XRF) An analytical technique that uses obsidian's trace elements to "fingerprint" an artifact and trace it to its geologic source.

After it is acquired, the clay is dried and pounded to remove any impurities. The potter then mixes in water and kneads the mixture to remove air bubbles. Clay's most important characteristic is that it is plastic; it can be modeled into shape. But as clay dries, it shrinks and then, when fired, it expands. Both processes can potentially crack the vessel.

Thousands of years ago, potters found that these problems could be alleviated by adding **temper** to the clay. Temper can be one of many kinds of materials: plant fiber, seed chaff, ash, ground-up shell or rock, sand, or even ground-up bits of old broken pots (sometimes called grog). The temper acts to hold the clay in place, gives the vessel strength, and prevents excessive shrinkage or expansion. After the temper is added, the potter shapes the pot and then fires it in an oven or an open-air fire, at temperatures in excess of 1000° C if possible.

If we could characterize the mineral composition of clays and tempers for both pots and likely geologic sources—as XRF does for obsidian artifacts and geologic sources—then we could fingerprint a pot (and, if sand or crushed rock were used, its temper) and trace both to their geologic sources. Archaeologists do this with several techniques, including **instrumental neutron activation analysis** (or **INAA,** an improvement over the technique Griffin used on the Hopewell obsidians).

Likewise, minerals in the clay and in the pot's temper can also be identified through **petrographic analysis** (explained below).

Archaeologists have used these techniques to determine the sources of pottery in many different places in the world, and we draw upon a case from the islands in Micronesia to show how this is done.

Tracing Pottery in Micronesia

Micronesia comprises some 2500 islands in the western Pacific. Some of these are "high" islands—the tops of extinct, partially subsided volcanoes. These can reach elevations of several hundred feet and are primarily made of basalt and related volcanic stone. The others are "low" islands—atolls that form as coral grows up around the rim of an extinct, submerged volcano. As the coral breaks the surface of the sea, it catches sand, which eventually allows plant life to take hold. The habitable portions of some atolls are only a quarter-mile long and 200 yards wide. People inhabited most Micronesian high islands and atolls at least 2000 years ago.

None of these islands is very large. Although Micronesia's islands are spread over an oceanscape the size of the continental United States, the total landmass of the islands is only about the size of the state of Rhode Island. But Micronesians were expert mariners who used detailed knowledge of the wind, sun, currents, waves, swells, birds, and fish to sail across hundreds of miles of open ocean in outrigger canoes. A lively trade existed between many of the islands, especially between high islands and atolls.

The high islands have sources of clay for ceramic vessels. But, being only coral and sand, atolls have no clays suitable for pottery. Because pottery is found in archaeological sites on the atolls, it must have been imported from one of the high islands. If we knew which ones, then we could begin to reconstruct Micronesia's trade networks.

Micronesians fashioned their pottery by hand, and they used shell, sand, and (more rarely) grog temper. Because the high islands formed through separate geologic events, the bedrock geology of each is unique. And, given that the clays and some of the sands are derived from the bedrock, their mineral compositions should also be distinctive of each high island. This can be tested through petrographic analysis of the temper and neutron activation analysis of the clays.

The first step is to show that each high island's sands and clays are unique. If they are, then a fingerprint of the clay and temper of an atoll's pottery should indicate on which high island that atoll's pottery was made. If two or more islands' clays are the same, however, then it won't be possible to assign one atoll's pottery to a particular high island.

William Dickinson (University of Arizona) studied the sand tempers of several of the high islands as well as the temper found in pottery on several atolls, including Ulithi and Fais, located near the high island of Yap. To conduct petrographic analysis, you cut a thin section of the pottery and grind it to about 30 microns in thickness so that the minerals are translucent. This section is

temper Material added to clay to give a ceramic item strength.

instrumental neutron activation analysis (INAA) An analytical technique that determines the trace element composition of the clay used to make a pot to identify the clay's geologic source.

petrographic analysis An analytical technique that identifies the mineral composition of a pot's temper and clay through microscopic observation of thin sections.

mounted on a slide, and the various minerals identified beneath a polarizing microscope at 25–400X. To make source identifications, the analyst must also take samples of the temper and identify its mineral composition. Sometimes a temper is distinguished by the presence or absence of key minerals, but normally the fingerprint consists of a particular combination of a standard range of minerals (feldspars, hornblendes, and so on) and different kinds of sand (for example, calcareous beach or volcanic sands).

Dickinson discovered that the sand tempers of different high islands have different mineral compositions (in addition, people on the high islands of Yap and Palau made grog-tempered ceramics). Comparing the tempers of ceramics on various high islands with those recovered from potsherds of Ulithi, Fais, and other atolls, Dickinson found that the ceramics on the atolls were all made using temper from the high island of Yap. Although it's possible that the temper was imported, the lack of clays on atolls suggests that people on Yap most likely made the pottery and traded it to those folks living on the atolls.

Christophe Descantes (University of California, Berkeley), Hector Neff (California State University, Long Beach), and Michael Glascock (University of Missouri) followed up on Dickinson's analysis by using INAA to study sherds from several high islands and atolls. Neutron activation analysis identifies a sherd's trace elements, those in the temper and the clay combined, by bombarding a potsherd with neutrons generated by a nuclear reactor. This produces radioactive isotopes of the elements. These isotopes immediately begin to decay (some have *very* short half-lives) and emit gamma radiation of different energy levels. By measuring the spectrum of gamma radiation, an analyst can identify the concentrations of 30 or more isotopes. This provides the trace element fingerprint of a sherd. (This technique is destructive, and it leaves the tested sherd radioactive. But where people made ceramics, potsherds are usually abundant and the archaeologist can afford to sacrifice some.)

Although the high islands have different geologic histories, it is possible that two widely separate islands could produce similar clays and tempers. But a statistical analysis of the trace element compositions of the various islands' sherds showed that most of the high islands—Yap, Palau, Chuuk, Kosrae, and Pohnpei—can be distinguished from one another.

The archaeologists then used INAA to analyze sherds from the atolls of Fais, Satawal, and Ulithi. What did they find out? In a nutshell, the trace element compositions of sherds from the atolls were all similar to pottery from Yap; none were similar to pottery of Palau, Chuuk, Pohnpei, or Kosrae. In other words, they reached the same conclusion that Dickinson had, based on analysis of the sherds' tempers alone.

What do these analyses tell us about the relationship between the high island of Yap and the surrounding atolls?

Around the year AD 1400, Yap had extended its influence and political control to many outer atolls, as well as to Palau. A system of ranking on Yap was mediated in part by *rai*, large perforated limestone disks. Many of these are less than a meter in diameter but, during the early nineteenth century, some *rai* were quite large, up to 2 meters in diameter (Figure 13-14). These were transferred as part of competitive feasts similar to those held on the American Northwest Coast (see Chapter 2; *rai* are sometimes referred to as "stone money," but they are not directly comparable to currency). Interestingly, these stone disks were not produced on Yap, but were imported from Palau, some 245 kilometers to the southwest.

Yap also obtained exotic goods through a trade network, called *sawei*, between Yap and its outlying atolls (Ulithi is fairly close to Yap, but Satawal lies hundreds of miles to the east). This exchange system reflects a political organization that included Yap, Palau, and several atolls. The smaller atolls sent woven fiber mats, sennit rope, and shell valuables to Ulithi, which then sent the goods to Yap. In return, Yap sent taro, yams, sweet potatoes, and bananas to Ulithi, where they were distributed to the smaller atolls. Yap also sent timber for building the oceangoing canoes necessary for this trade to continue.

Some describe this exchange network as a tribute system, but specialists disagree over the equality of the trade. Indeed, if an atoll expressed reservations about sending goods to Yap, Yapese sorcerers would threaten to bring typhoons down upon it (a considerable threat to an island whose highest point is only a few feet above sea level). But such threats were probably not necessary, because the atolls seem to have received more material support from Yap than vice versa. And they could seek refuge on Yap should a storm or drought strike their atoll. The petrographic and INAA analyses of the ceramics confirm that the *sawei* system is ancient and it both reflects and helped construct a political system that tied Yap with outlying atolls.

CONCLUSION

In reconstructing social and political organizations, archaeologists remember that artifacts were not just utilitarian items, but also carried symbolic meanings—meanings that could be manipulated and that played a role in how those artifacts eventually ended up in an archaeological context. Sometimes these symbolic meanings reflect elements of social and political organization—such as gender roles, kinship systems, trade networks, and political connections. However, it's hard to construct middle-range theory that allows us to infer social and political organization from archaeological remains, and it may forever require well-supported ethnographic analogy. However, new techniques—analysis of physical and chemical properties of artifacts and the use of genetic markers in human skeletal remains—give archaeology ways to test various hypotheses and continue to improve its reconstruction of the past.

In the following chapter, we go into an even more difficult area of archaeology: the analysis of symbols, concepts, and abstract thought. As you will see, reconstructing social and political organization is a walk in the park compared with trying to draw inferences from symbolic systems.

© Robert Kelly

Figure 13-14 *Rai* displayed before a ceremonial structure on the island of Yap in Micronesia.

Summary

- This chapter dealt with social and political systems of the human past, defining what they were and how archaeologists study them.

- The basic social unit is the *group* (both residential and nonresidential); how that group operates is a matter of gender, kinship and status.

- We separated sex, which is a matter of biology, from gender, which is culturally based interpretations of biology.

- Ethnographic research demonstrates that the sorts of patterns archaeologists are best at finding—large temporal and spatial differences in material goods, especially technology—can be related to different

divisions of labor, which are a product of male and female decision making. Thus, knowing what men and women did is important to understanding larger social and economic patterns.

- But inferring what men and women did is difficult. Bioarchaeological analyses provide some clues as to differences in workload and diet, but strong empirical generalizations or historically linked ethnographic analogies are often needed.

- Kinship refers to the socially recognized network of relationships through which individuals are related to one another by ties of descent (real or imagined) and marriage. Like gender, kinship too plays a role in understanding the choices that people made in the distant past.

■ Social groupings are reflected "on the ground" in terms of house spacing and placement. Genetic distance studies of human skeletal remains provide clues to post-marital residence.

■ Status refers to the rights, duties, and privileges that define the nature of interpersonal relations. Social statuses are apportioned according to culturally determined criteria.

■ A key element in political organizations is the difference between *ascribed statuses*, which are parceled out to individuals at birth without regard to the characteristics of those receiving status, and *achieved* status, which comes from what one accomplishes in life.

■ A society is *egalitarian* if achieved status is the common (or only) means whereby an individual acquires a high position; people in egalitarian societies have equal access to important resources.

■ In a *ranked* society, ascribed status places people at birth into a ranked order of privilege; ranked societies exhibit a hierarchy, and its members have unequal access to basic resources.

■ Egalitarian and ranked societies are often studied through patterning in mortuary remains on the assumption that treatment in death reflects status in life.

■ Trade networks reflect the geographic scale of non-residential groups, economic patterns, and political authority. Trade is established by determining whether artifacts were made or obtained locally and by determining the source of raw materials for artifact manufacture.

■ Obsidian, clay, and temper sourcing studies can demonstrate the geographic scale of an economic and/or political organization.

Additional Reading

Ember, Melvin, and Carol Ember. 1995. Worldwide Cross-Cultural Studies and Their Relevance for Archaeology. *Journal of Archaeological Research* 30: 69–94.

Galloway, Patricia (Ed.). 1989. *The Southeastern Ceremonial Complex: Artifacts and Analysis.* Lincoln: University of Nebraska Press.

Nelson, Sarah M. 1995. *Gender in Archaeology: Analyzing Power and Prestige.* Walnut Creek, CA: Altamira Press.

Parker Pearson, Michael. 1982. Mortuary Practices, Society and Ideology: An Ethnoarchaeological Study. In Ian Hodder (Ed.), *Symbolic and Structural Archaeology* (pp. 99–113). Cambridge: Cambridge University Press.

Sinopoli, Carla. 1991. *Approaches to Archaeological Ceramics.* New York: Plenum Press.

Smith, Bruce D. (Ed.). 1990. *The Mississippian Emergence.* Washington, DC: Smithsonian Institution Press.

Steponaitis, Vincas P. 1983. *Ceramics, Chronology, and Community Patterns: An Archaeological Study at Moundville.* New York: Academic Press.

Online Resources

COMPANION WEB SITE
Visit **http://anthropology.wadsworth.com** and click on the Student Companion Web Site for Thomas/Kelly *Archaeology*, 4th edition, to access a wide range of material to help you succeed in your introductory archaeology course. These include flashcards, Internet exercises, Web links, and practice quizzes.

RESEARCH ONLINE
WITH INFOTRAC COLLEGE EDITION
From the Student Companion Web Site, you can access the InfoTrac College Edition database, which offers thousands of full-length articles for your research.

14

The Archaeology of the Mind

OUTLINE

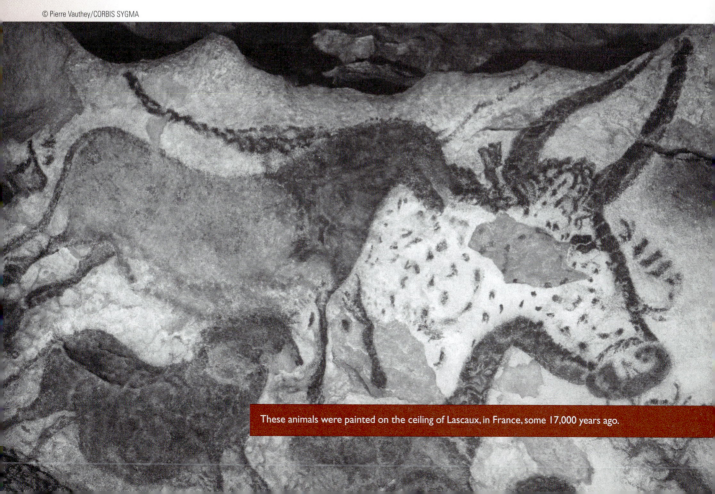

These animals were painted on the ceiling of Lascaux, in France, some 17,000 years ago.

Preview

*A*S CULTURAL BEINGS, humans construct the world in which they live. By "construct" we mean that they physically alter the world—through farming, construction, trash disposal, logging, mining, and so forth. In addition, human cultures interpret their world symbolically, which leads to different approaches to the physical world. In this chapter, we will concentrate on these symbolic meanings. Some archaeologists have attempted to infer the symbolic meanings of specific artifact forms, and others have tried to reconstruct concepts and perceptions about how the ancients viewed the world and the place of humans in it.

As you might guess, symbolic approaches in archaeology raise some difficult issues, with both scientific and humanistic perspectives being applied. Although a huge range of human behavior falls under the category of "symbolic," we will concentrate on investigations of ritual and religion, iconography, and the interpretation of prehistoric rock art.

INTRODUCTION

When processual archaeology gained prominence in the 1960s, it generated numerous studies of prehistoric demography, settlement patterns, subsistence, technology, and the human use of landscapes, plants, and animals. These important approaches relied heavily on rigorous scientific methods. The focus was heavily materialistic, because processual archaeologists believed that subsistence behavior provided the infrastructure for the rest of the cultural system (see Chapter 3).

At the outset, processual archaeologists were optimistic that they could study *all aspects* of the human condition from archaeological data. But most proces-

> **cognitive archaeology** The study of all those aspects of ancient culture that are the product of the human mind: the perception, description, and classification of the universe; the nature of the supernatural; the principles, philosophies, ethics, and values by which human societies are governed; and the ways in which aspects of the world, the supernatural, or human values are conveyed in art.

sual archaeologists remained lukewarm toward **cognitive archaeology** throughout the 1970s and 1980s. For many, the archaeological record relating to "ideas" seemed too shaky and ambiguous to be approached in an explicitly scientific, objective manner. And cultural materialists assumed that the cognitive aspects of culture—including religion—were "epiphenomena," mere dependent variables deriving from the more critical technological and economic basics; as such, they were unimportant to understanding the past.

The appeal of cultural materialism to Americanist archaeology is fairly easy to understand. This is a research strategy that places priority on just those things that archaeologists are most confident in recovering from their sites—evidence about past environments, technologies, and economies.

But some archaeologists felt that such heavy-handed materialism dehumanized the past. They argued for an "archaeology of the mind" that emphasizes the values, ideas, and beliefs that make us all human. To be sure, any archaeology of the mind will have a more post-processual than processual flavor, because such an approach will necessarily be concerned with recovering *meanings* (rather than law-like statements or general-izations about human behavior). Today, much of cog-nitive archaeology remains interpretive, but as we will demonstrate, such symbolic approaches can indeed lend themselves to scientific testing as well—if appro-priate linkages can be made between the interpretations of ancient symbols and those human behaviors that can be more directly inferred from the archaeological record.

All humans interact with their world through their cultural perception of it, and modern archaeologists can ill afford to overlook the power of symbols. Take food, for example. Economic decisions might appear to be rather straightforward: Eat this food because it is nutritious and efficiently gathered, harvested, or hunted, and avoid that food because it is not. Although such decisions do heavily condition subsistence practices, we also face an ever-changing background of cultural information about what is/is not edible. As we pointed out in Chapter 2, some societies consider dogs to be food, even prestigious feast foods. Yet people in other cultures are repulsed by the idea of eating their "pets." And some animals may be highly valued in particular cultures, not because of their nutritional content, but because of their symbolic meaning. Native peoples of New Guinea hunted cassowary birds not for food, but because their feathers were highly valued gifts that were given away at feasts (see "Looking Closer: Food Taboos in the Near East").

Symbolism goes beyond food to permeate all arenas of human life. We saw in Chapter 11, for example, that even something as apparently mundane and utilitarian as firewood was symbolically loaded for the Inka. And Chapter 13 explained how kinship involves the differ-ential imposition of symbolic ideas about kin onto bio-logical relationships. Male and female tasks also differ among societies, depending on what symbolic value a culture gives to different tasks. In industrial societies, advertising tells us that clothing, houses, cars, hair-styles, tattoos, beer—virtually everything, in fact—car-ries symbolic meaning.

Humans live in a material world, and nobody can avoid the realities of survival. But people also live in a culturally constructed world, and material decisions are always made against a backdrop of symbolic meanings.

This is why a number of archaeologists have turned to an ideational emphasis in their research, examining the active role of symbols in shaping the economic, social, and even technological structure of societies.

WHAT'S A SYMBOL?

The ability to use symbols goes to the essence of what it means to be human. Language is made possible by sym-bols; so are stories, art, and poetry. For anthropologists such as Clifford Geertz (Princeton University) and David Schneider (1918–1995), symbols shape the way that people see, understand and feel about the world. We discussed the symbolic element of human culture in Chapter 2; now we consider symbols in more detail.

To most anthropologists, a **symbol** is an object or act (verbal or nonverbal) that by cultural convention stands for something else *with which it has no necessary connection*. Consider a simple symbol that is familiar to many Americans: a red circle with a red line running diagonally through it. With a capital "P" in the center of the circle, the symbol tells us "no parking"; with a ciga-rette in the middle, it means "no smoking." (The "P" and the cigarette, by the way, are not symbols but signs, because they do have a connection to what they sig-nify—the word "parking" itself and the visual image of a cigarette). Virtually all Americans understand that a red circle with a diagonal line through it forbids what-ever is in the circle.

But is there is any *necessary* connection between a red circle with a line through it and prohibition of a certain behavior? No. In fact, this symbol might just as easily mean the opposite: Parking *is* allowed here, smoking *is* permitted here. If you were not enculturated into the meaning of the symbol, you would have no way of de-ducing the symbol's meaning merely from the symbol itself—*because there is no necessary connection between a symbol and the thing it stands for*. Some anthropolo-gists suggest that a few basic symbols might have an inherent meaning genetically programmed into our consciousness; the color red, for example, might carry the meaning of danger. But the vast majority of the

---

symbol An object or act (verbal or nonverbal) that, by cultural convention, stands for something else *with which it has no necessary connection*.

Looking Closer
Food Taboos in the Near East

Many members of the Jewish and Islamic faiths eschew pork. The prohibition against the eating of pork is very ancient, dating back to the Near Eastern roots of both religions. Many other peoples eat pork; it's a perfectly nutritious food, and pigs can be raised quite efficiently. Why did Near Easterners not eat it? Here we contrast two different explanations for this food taboo—one materialist, the other symbolic.

Marvin Harris, the pre-eminent cultural materialist (see Chapter 3) argued that pigs were prohibited in the ancient Near East because they are poorly suited for life in the desert. Pigs are forest dwellers, and they do well in such wet environments. Harris suggested that any food, even a formerly useful food, will be tabooed when the cost of producing it outweighs its value (in calories or nutrients). In the desert, the cost of trying to keep pigs alive would indeed be high.

But Harris's materialist explanation has two problems. For one thing, why would a taboo with supernatural sanctions be necessary if the food was clearly inefficient to produce or procure? Certainly, people are rational enough to see when raising or harvesting a particular food is not worth the effort. Second, the prohibition against pork is only one of a lengthy list of tabooed foods. This list first appears in the book of Leviticus in the Old Testament, and later in Deuteronomy. In those passages, God prohibited the followers of Moses from eating shellfish, pigs, rabbits, camels, insects, and a variety of birds. Many of these, such as camels, are perfectly suited for life in the desert.

Mary Douglas (University College, London), a symbolic anthropologist, argues that you cannot explain one of these tabooed foods without explaining all of them. She proposes a different explanation based on Near Eastern cultural ideas about animals. The prohibited animals in Leviticus were said to be "unclean," and Douglas focused on the meaning of that term. She pointed out that unclean often means "disorderly." You might say that your house is "not clean" when in fact what you mean is that clothing is lying on the floor and you haven't put the furniture back from last week's party. You might say that dishes sitting beside the sink are "dirty" when in fact you were just eating off of them moments earlier. They are not dirty, they are simply not "in their place" (cleaned, dried, and in the cupboard).

Taking this approach to the complete list of food prohibitions, Douglas found that virtually all the prohibited animals are ones that ancient Near Easterners saw as violating their cultural ideas about the order of creation. Animals were supposed to be those that walk, hop, or jump on all four feet. Thus, insects that "swarm upon the land" are unclean because they are outside the cultural order of life. Likewise, edible animals were supposed to be those that have cloven hooves and that chew the cud. The herd animals of the Near East—cattle, sheep, and goats—have cloven hooves and chew the cud. The pig has a cloven hoof, but it does not chew the cud. Consequently, it is unclean because it is an anomaly in the natural order of animals. Avoiding certain animals, then, had little to do with food itself, but with a continual cultural affirmation of what constitutes God's order in the world.

Which explanation is right? Douglas's argument is appealing because it provides an explanation for all the forbidden animals. But archaeologists are continually confronted with trying to test competing hypotheses drawn from different paradigms. Often, the truth lies somewhere in between. And, usually one answer raises a new question: If pork was prohibited because it fell outside the natural order, what gave rise to that particular view of the world?

symbols we use have no such "natural" meaning. (And if you think they do, rent a car in Paris and figure out the "natural" meaning of French road signs.)

This is why symbols are so powerful. A simple symbolic act can be made to carry enormous amounts of information. And, in fact, the same symbol can carry different meanings under different situations. Consider a simple wink of the eye. In one situation, it can signal a playful conspiracy between two people against a third; in another, the same gesture is flirting (or harassment). But in another culture, a wink might mean nothing more than that a person has something irritating his or her eye.

Because symbols have no necessary connection to their culturally assigned meaning, they can be used in different ways. Much of the humor, pathos, and poignancy in literature and the arts come from the playful or artful use of symbols (such as the use of the red prohibition circle in the film *Ghostbusters*). This is another way in which symbols are powerful.

But their essential qualities make symbols difficult to study archaeologically. If there is no necessary connection between a symbol and what it stands for, then how can an outsider know the meaning of a particular symbol? How would you know that a red circle with a line through it *prohibits* rather than *permits* a behavior? Deciphering these messages is difficult enough in an ethnographic context, where one has ready access to language, informants, and observable behavior. But it is manifestly more difficult—and some would say impossible—to understand symbolic behavior in an archaeological context, where the physical symbol survives, but its meaning does not.

Consider, for example, the rock art shown in Figure 14-1. This is one of the thousands of images found at La María, a complex of rockshelters in Patagonia (a region of southern Argentina). The central figure is a guanaco, a wild camelid once hunted by native peoples of the region. Along the guanaco's back and haunches is a series of white dots, and other white dots are on the

© Robert Kelly

Figure 14-1 A panel of art from a rockshelter at La María, in southern Patagonia. The central figure is a guanaco, a wild camelid.

body. In the upper right is a hand silhouette, created when the artisan placed his or her right hand on the wall and then blew paint over it. Between the hand and the guanaco runs a red, white, and black line, immediately below which is a line of red dots.

What do these images mean? Was the hand painted as part of ritual? Or is it little more than graffiti "tagging"? What do the lines and dots represent? Are they representations of a hunting fence or drive line? Is it a map? Does the guanaco "mean" guanaco? Or is it a symbol that stands for something else, like a lineage? What about the dots on the guanaco? Is this hunting or fertility magic or an appeal to a supernatural being represented by the figure? We have no easy answers to these questions.

To interpret symbols, anthropologists might look at the various ways a particular symbol is used and its (possibly varied) contexts. They might see which symbols are consciously manipulated and which are not; which can be used for humor (and who finds them funny). They might see if some symbols are exclusively used by or associated with women or men. By viewing a symbol's use in a variety of circumstances, we can construct an understanding of what the symbol means. This approach, however, requires the living context of the symbol, which archaeologists do not have.

This means that ancient symbolic systems may remain forever silent as to their specific, detailed meanings.

But many contemporary archaeologists think it's worthwhile to examine human behavior as a system of meanings rather than simply as acts that meet material needs. Recall, for example, our discussion in Chapter 10 of the different treatment of pig bones in African societies. In the following two examples, we will explore some of the potential and limitations involved with attempting an archaeology of the mind.

THE PEACE PIPE AS RITUAL WEAPON

Writing in the late 1970s, archaeologist Robert L. Hall (University of Illinois, Chicago) used the calumet—the peace pipe—to demonstrate how a cognitive approach could broaden the horizons of archaeological investigations.

Hall focused on the Hopewell culture (mentioned in Chapter 13). Hopewell "culture" probably included many different peoples speaking different languages and living various ways, from the lower Mississippi to Minnesota, and from Nebraska to Virginia. But during Hopewell times (between 200 BC and AD 400) these diverse people apparently shared a unifying set of symbols that may indicate a common set of religious beliefs. Archaeologists referred to this common set of symbols found over a wide area as the **Hopewell Interaction Sphere.**

To understand what was going on, let's first consider whether the Hopewell people shared a common religion. Broadly speaking, anthropologists consider **religion** to be a specific set of beliefs about one's relation to the supernatural. Religion is a society's mechanism for relating supernatural phenomena to the everyday world—a set of rituals that enlists supernatural powers for the purpose of achieving or preventing transformations of state in humans and nature—in other words, to make sure that good things happen and bad things do not. In some religions, individuals use rituals to influence the course of events; in others, they help novices find their path in a world that they see as beyond their control. All living cultures have some form of religion, and we suppose that was true of past societies as well.

Religious beliefs are manifested in everyday life as **ritual,** a succession of discrete behaviors that must be performed in a particular order under particular circumstances—such as saying prayers at certain times of the day accompanied by particular acts or gestures. Rituals are fundamentally religious acts because they are the mechanisms by which individuals attempt to intercede with the supernatural.

This particular definition of religion is especially relevant to archaeology because of archaeology's emphasis on ritual. Rituals are behavioral acts that often entail material culture and therefore can be represented in the archaeological record. The analysis of past ritual behavior is thus archaeology's major contribution to the study of religion.

Some of the highly standardized Hopewell artifacts are perhaps indicative of rituals. One particularly intriguing artifact is the stone platform pipe, some examples of which are shown in Figure 14-2. Hopewell artists fashioned these from pipestone, often ornamenting them with carved mammals, birds, or reptiles that rest on a straight or curved base. The pipes were probably used to smoke tobacco (which is indigenous to the New World; the earliest evidence of tobacco in the eastern United States dates to about AD 100).

The effort taken to carve these pipes suggests that whatever rituals the pipes were involved in were a critical aspect of Hopewell ceremonial life. Hundreds of pipes were found in the so-called Mound of the Pipes at Mound City, near Chillicothe, Ohio. Some think that this mound was a monument to a master carver of sacred pipes.

What were the pipes used for? What did they signal to their users?

To try to explain these pipes, Hall looked to historical and ethnographic data. He was especially intrigued by the fact that the "peace pipe" used historically to establish friendly contact almost always took the form of a weapon. He then reasoned that all cultures engage in certain culturally dictated customs whose exact meaning and origin may be lost in time. For example, the rite of toasting with drinks in Western culture originally was the sloshing and spilling together of two persons' drinks to reduce the possibility that one planned to poison the other. But how many of us who have toasted

---

Hopewell Interaction Sphere The common set of symbols found in the midwestern United States between 200 BC and AD 400.

religion A specific set of beliefs about one's relation to the supernatural; a society's mechanism for relating supernatural phenomena to the everyday world.

ritual A succession of discrete behaviors that must be performed in a particular order under particular circumstances.

Figure 14-2 Hopewell effigy pipes. The bowl for tobacco is on the animals' backs. These would have been placed on the end of a wooden stem and may represent the hook on the end of an atlatl.

© American Museum of Natural History

rated with an effigy spur. Hall observed that the animal on the bowl was almost always carved precisely where an atlatl spur would be. And the curvature of the platform seemed to correspond to the curvature of the atlatl.

These correspondences led Hall to conclude: "I see the Hopewell platform pipe as the archaeologically visible part of a transformed ritual atlatl, a symbolic weapon which in Middle Woodland times probably had some of the same functions as the calumet of historic times, itself a ritual arrow."

friends realize the origin of the custom? Or saluting, a custom that stems from the act of raising visors on armored helmets in order to expose the faces of the two persons encountering each other? Hall suggested that, although the original functions of the gestures lost their practical significance, the acts survive as elements of etiquette or protocol.

Hall applied similar reasoning to the Hopewell platform pipes by calling upon ethnographic data. Throughout historic times in the eastern United States, Indian tribes observed the custom of smoking a sacred tribal pipe. When the pipe was present, violence was ruled out. Moreover, the peace pipe usually was made in the shape of an atlatl (like those that appear in Figure 14-3)—a weapon that was a forerunner to the bow and arrow used in historic times. The Pawnee peace pipe, for instance, looked like an arrow, and the Osage word for calumet translated as "arrowshaft." Hall suggested that the weaponlike appearance resulted from a specific ceremonial custom. Could it be that, at least during the period of European contact, the peace pipe symbolized a ritual weapon?

Hall then projected his idea back into ancient Hopewell times. Suppose that the distinctive Hopewell platform pipes were also ritual weapons—but made before these people knew of the bow and arrow. At the time, the most common Hopewell weapon was the atlatl (the spearthrower—discussed in Chapter 13).

Hall suggested that the distinctive Hopewell platform pipe symbolically represented a flat atlatl, deco-

Hall went on to propose that the importance of the Hopewell pipe might well extend beyond mere symbolism—that the platform pipe was not merely one of many items exchanged between groups, but that "it may have been part of the very mechanism of exchange." Adaptively oriented research on eastern United States prehistory has conventionally defined the Hopewell Interaction Sphere primarily in economic and environmental terms. Perhaps, by maintaining relationships between large-scale networks of ritual trading partners, far-flung Hopewell communities joined economic forces, looking to one another for support in lean years.

Hall suggested that a shift away from strictly materialistic thinking—toward a more cognitive approach—could generate a broader understanding of the Hopewell lifeway. Reasoning from Native American ethnographic analogies, Hall contended that peace pipe rituals served to mediate interaction over a vast area of eastern North America. By promoting a common set of symbols—perhaps linked to some common religious ideas—the Hopewell Interaction Sphere tended to reduce regional differences and promote contact and communication between discrete groups.

We pointed out that interpretations of the symbolic meanings of artifacts are difficult to test *directly*. But it would be possible to test the *implications* of Hall's conclusions by assessing whether the archaeology of the Hopewell Interaction Sphere supports the social and political ramifications of Hall's interpretation of the

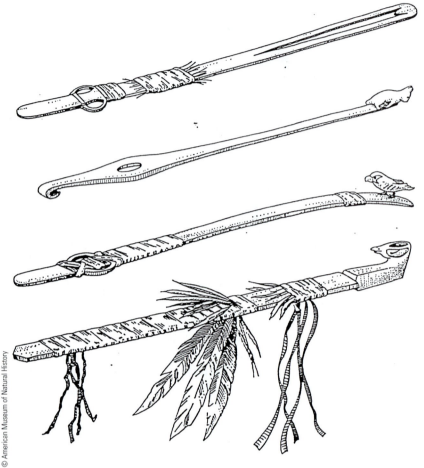

© American Museum of Natural History

Figure 14-3 Some representations of atlatls in aboriginal North American art.

stone pipes. For example, is there evidence of conflict in Hopewell sites? If it is present, how does it relate to the distribution of stone pipes and their source areas? Or how does the distribution of pipes across the Hopewell Interaction Sphere relate to evidence for subsistence stress (from faunal, macrobotanical, and human skeletal remains)? In other words, *if we treat symbolic interpretations as hypotheses, it is possible to test them by linking them to phenomena that are more archaeologically accessible.* To see how this might work, let's return to an example that we have used before, the Chavín culture of Peru.

EXPLORING ANCIENT CHAVÍN COSMOLOGY

In Chapter 11, we discussed the Chavín culture of the central Andes. Specifically, we looked at the faunal remains recovered from Chavín de Huántar and learned what these finds could tell us about subsistence and trade.

But to most archaeologists, the term "Chavín" conjures up much more than llama bones. Archaeologists commonly consider Chavín to be Peru's first highland civilization because of its stratified social and political organization and its achievements in metallurgy, weaving, monumental architecture, irrigation systems, and stone sculpture. Chavín was the first Andean civilization.

Chavín also left a lasting legacy in Andean **cosmology.** By cosmology we mean a culture's understanding of how the world works, how it originated and developed, how the various parts fit together, what laws they obey, and, especially, the place of humans in the natural and supernatural worlds. A glimpse of a culture's cosmology can often be found in its **iconography**—its art forms or writing systems (such as Egyptian or Maya hieroglyphics) that symbolically represent ideas about religion or cosmology.

The iconography at Chavín de Huántar established the tone of subsequent central Andean cosmology. All deities of the succeeding generations in the central Andes looked more or less like the gods in the temple at Chavín de Huántar. Archaeologists Richard Burger and George Miller (whose faunal analysis of Chavín de Huántar we discussed in Chapter 11) have explored the

cosmology The study of the origin, large-scale structure, and future of the universe. A cosmological explanation demonstrates how the universe developed—both the totality and its constituent parts—and also describes what principles keep it together.

iconography Art forms or writing systems (such as Egyptian or Maya hieroglyphics) that symbolically represent ideas about religion or cosmology.

Figure 14-4 One of the carved stone heads on the temple at Chavín de Huántar which represent a shaman's transition from human to jaguar.

But the local highland animals of Chavín de Huántar are conspicuously absent from the thousands of known temple sculptures, ceramics, and textiles that display the widespread Chavín style. Instead, the Chavín style drew inspiration for its stylized fangs and talons, feathers and scales from the jaguar, crested eagle, monkey, serpent, and cayman (alligator). These creatures are native to the cloud forests and rain forests of the *eastern* Andean slope, if not the floodplains of Amazonia itself—located several hundred miles to the east, on the other side of the Andes. These same animals play a prominent role in the mythology and religious symbolism of modern people of Amazonia, but they were utterly foreign to the inhabitants of Chavín de Huántar.

Why were the major animals of Chavín religious art drawn from outside the local highland environment?

nature of Chavín cosmology, looking in particular at the distinctive Chavín iconography that appeared over a wide area of the central Andes nearly 2500 years ago.

Animal Symbolism in Chavín Iconography

Chavín de Huántar has given its name to one of the Americas' most famous art styles—Chavín. Chavín iconography is derived from stone sculptures at Chavín de Huántar, some examples of which appear in Figures 14-4 and 14-5. This art style was reproduced in many villages in the central Andes on locally made ceramics, textiles, goldwork, and stone.

You will recall from Chapter 11 that the community of Chavín de Huántar depended on a range of animals for food, including wild deer, vicuña, llama, and guinea pigs. These were local beasts, probably encountered by local residents on a daily basis.

Figure 14-5 A stone carving of a jaguar outside the temple at Chavín de Huántar.

Where Did Chavín Cosmology Come From?

Archaeologists have proposed several hypotheses to explain this puzzling aspect of Chavín cosmology. The first is that the climate was radically warmer and more humid during Chavín times. If so, then maybe the lowland complex of animals—the jaguar, the cayman, the crested eagle, and so forth—could have once lived in the highlands around Chavín de Huántar.

But this hypothesis is not correct. Several lines of evidence demonstrate that the climate was similar to the modern pattern during the Chavín time period (900–200 BC) and remember from Chapter 11 that the animal bones recovered from Chavín de Huántar belong to the same species as modern highland animals—camelids, deer, and so forth. Paleoenvironmental change cannot explain the nature of Chavín iconography.

Another hypothesis was championed by Peruvian archaeologist Julio Tello (1880–1947), discoverer of Chavín civilization and first excavator at Chavín de Huántar (in the 1930s), and later by American archaeologist Donald Lathrap (1927–1990). Plants indigenous to Amazonia—including manioc, bottle gourd, hot peppers, and possibly peanuts—all appear at Chavín de Huántar. Tello suggested that immigrants from the tropical forest introduced the lowland plants and animals to Chavín de Huántar. Lathrap attributed the migration to population pressure in the lowland Amazonian or Orinoco basins that forced the early Chavín folk into the Andean highlands. According to Lathrap, the heavy Amazonian component of Chavín religious art displayed homage and deference to the ancient homeland and subsistence regime that was responsible for the initial success of the Chavín elite.

But this hypothesis also seems to be incorrect. In the first place, the lowland crops are impossible to grow in the Andean environment. Their presence suggests trade or some other kind of contact between Chavín de Huántar and Amazonia, but they could not have been plants brought with and grown by an immigrant population. Burger also hypothesizes that, if a tropical forest people had moved wholesale into the Andes, their ceramic traditions should show a direct relationship to the Amazonian homeland. But the earliest ceramics at Chavín de Huántar show a conspicuous lack of Amazonian characteristics; the pottery looks local rather than imported. It also is clear that the basic high-altitude mixed agricultural subsistence pattern prac-

ticed by the pioneer population at Chavín de Huántar was not Amazonian at all; it had developed in place—in the highlands—at least a thousand years earlier. The ceramic and subsistence evidence make it unlikely that a tropical forest group was responsible for the lowland iconography evident on the earliest buildings at Chavín de Huántar.

For these reasons, Burger advocates a third hypothesis to explain the Amazonian elements of Chavín cosmology. Chavín de Huántar occupies a strategic gateway position, in a corridor that extends from the Pacific coast, to the highland Andes, and down to the lowland rain forest to the east. Burger argues that Chavín's religious leaders deliberately imported Amazonian symbolism, perhaps in the belief that the exotic lowland people had especially powerful esoteric knowledge. This interpretation, supported by ethnographic and ethnohistoric documentation, suggests that shamans and healers may have made pilgrimages to the distant lowlands—viewed as the powerful source of sacred knowledge, medicinal plants, and other ritual necessities. In fact, in many parts of the world anthropologists have found that people who live outside dense forests often ascribe magical powers or sacred knowledge to their neighbors who live in the forests. Burger argues that the Chavín people imported religious knowledge from the remote, exotic tropics to the Andean highlands.

Analysis of Chavín iconography provides some of the details, explaining the cult's remarkable success. Early sculptural evidence suggests that Chavín ideology held that priests had the ability to turn themselves into mythical beasts, in order to intervene with supernatural forces. Temple sculptures clearly demonstrate that, employing hallucinogenic snuff and beverages, Chavín shamans could transform themselves into jaguars or crested eagles. Specially designed drug paraphernalia—stone mortars, bone trays, spatulas, miniature spoons, and tubes—all seem to be part of the Chavín ritual toolkit. Use of similar artifacts can be documented among modern South American people.

Burger believes that this analogy—based on sixteenth-century ethnohistoric sources—may explain the singular success of the Chavín cult in uniting previously unrelated cultures throughout the Andean highlands and along the Peruvian coast.

The historical documents also provide a hypothesis for how this religious network might have operated 2000 years earlier. At the center of the religion was a large ritual complex featuring an **oracle,** accessible only to certain cult specialists. Based on the oracle's secret projections, cult members were able to provide "insider information," offering favorable intervention with the natural elements, protection against disease, and specialized knowledge concerning auspicious times for planting and harvesting.

Under this regional religious system, local communities could establish "branch shrines" by pledging support for the religion. If the pledge was accepted, a local priest was assigned, but in return, local communities allotted agricultural lands to produce tribute and promised public labor for farming and herding. In effect, these local branches supported the religion's headquarters with large quantities of cotton, corn, dried fish, llamas, guinea pigs, raw materials (such as gold and obsidian), and manufactured goods (such as fine cloth).

Burger suggests that this ethnohistoric cult provides a workable model of the distinctive regional organization that characterized Chavín civilization. He hypothesizes that the oracle cult center was located at the archaeological site of Karwa, which unfortunately was looted during the 1970s. Iconographic elements—particularly stylized felines and raptorial birds—woven into textile fragments recovered from tombs at Karwa show unmistakable ties to the sculptures at Chavín de Huántar. Despite the nearly 400 miles separating the two sites, the complex elements of Chavín cosmology seem to have been transported intact, without simplification or misrepresentation.

The Role of Cosmology in Andean Civilization

This model suggests that Chavín iconography was a widespread religion subdivided into a number of localized branches, each sharing in the major elements of Chavín iconography—probably reflecting major deities—but complemented by distinctive localized elements. According to this view, the Chavín religion maintained its characteristic regional flavor, but also demonstrated a willingness to incorporate motifs and symbols significant to local constituencies.

Burger emphasizes that the long-standing interest of archaeologists in Chavín iconography has led to a deep understanding of how this distinctive civilization came to be. Had this research taken place within a strictly materialistic framework, Burger suggests, the direction would have been much different and considerably more restricted. He stresses that interregional exchange and tribute in the form of gifts to the religious center, rather than local agricultural production, contributed to the development of Chavín civilization.

The spread of Chavín elements (500–250 BC) across the central Andes happened at a turbulent time, following the collapse of many early coastal political systems. An unprecedented amount of contact occurred between distant and unrelated groups, producing a previously unknown degree of sharing of ideology and technology, reinforced by the actual movement of goods and people. For Burger, Chavín culture was a forerunner of the many later attempts in Andean history to create single social entities out of a diversity of local cultures.

So, why did Chavín succeed where earlier attempts failed?

Relying on historical evidence from the sixteenth-century regional ceremonial complex, Burger argues that Chavín was a large-scale religion, transcending political and ethnic boundaries. Chavín ideology and rituals were sufficiently powerful to support a hierarchical organization, with officials overseeing local cult activities and monitoring deviation among local congregations. Although regional diversity was evident throughout the reach of the Chavín cult, a central authority exerted its power and extracted tribute from smaller communities. Thus, Chavín religion spread not because of political expansion, but because of the extension of a powerful shared cosmology, rendered visible in ritual objects and manifested through the growth of complex interregional exchange networks.

Civilization (a term we discuss in Chapter 15) had appeared in the central Andes by about 400 BC. According to Burger, the centers of the Chavín horizon rivaled the classic Greek cities in size and beauty, with massive public structures of finely cut and polished masonry, and the settlements were home to a complex society, differentiated by both social status and economic activities.

Burger argues that this power came from the original priests of Chavín de Huántar, who focused the growing Chavín mythology on the mysterious rather than the mundane. It was these mysterious animals of the lowlands that ultimately determined the long-term success of Chavín society and economy.

oracle A shrine in which a deity reveals hidden knowledge or divine purpose.

Archaeological Ethics
What Role Do Oral Traditions Play in Archaeology?

 We pointed out in this chapter that ethnographic and ethnohistoric information is often crucial to reconstructing the past. Part of this information might consist of oral traditions—accounts of the past that are passed down by word of mouth from generation to generation.

Oral traditions are part of an ongoing culture and, for this reason, they can raise some ethical concerns if oral traditions conflict with archaeological data. Is one of these an inherently better source of information about the past? Archaeologists may privilege the archaeology, but Native Americans may favor the oral traditions. Who's right?

Many American archaeologists ignored or even denigrated oral traditions in the past, but that has changed dramatically in the past two decades. This has partly been a response to recognition of the colonialist nature of archaeology in North America (and elsewhere, for example, Australia). Desiring to return "control" of the past to descendants, many archaeologists place oral traditions on an equal footing with "scientific" archaeology. Many Native Americans (and even some archaeologists) ask: Who should know their past better than the descendants themselves?

But other archaeologists will point out that oral traditions are often selective in what they remember or alter the nature or sequence of events over time to suit particular political needs. This is not a matter of lying. Oral traditions are a product of current events and sensibilities, and whereas they can contain accounts of past events, they are not always straightforward accounts of what "really happened" in the past.

For example, the image that many white Americans have of the mid-nineteenth century settlement of the West is of the small, lonely caravan of Conestoga wagons forming a circle to repel the Plains Indians' "wheel of death" attacks. We get this image from Western "oral" tradition—movies and novels. However, John Unruh (1937–1976), a historian who carefully read all surviving emigrant diaries of the years 1840–1860, found virtually no mention of such encounters. Most wagon trains were large, and far more people died of cholera and accidents than from Indian attacks (in fact, more Indians died at the hands of the emigrants than vice versa). Most attacks occurred along the Snake and Humboldt Rivers in Idaho and Nevada, not on the Plains. And many immigrants traveled not on wagons, but by pushing a cart carrying their belongings across the prairies and mountains. The popular image was created by the media (as early as 1850) to justify the taking of Native American land; in so doing, they created America's own "origin myth." Oral histories are a product of the time and culture in which they are produced; they are not necessarily purely factual accounts of the past.

Oral histories can also change over time, and the older the events described, the greater the likelihood that some elements have been dropped and others added. Northern Plains Indians' oral traditions contain many stories that incorporate horses. But horses were not present on the Plains until the Spanish introduced them after AD 1530. In fact, people such as the Lakota did not have horses until after AD 1740. Thus, horses were added to Plains traditions fairly recently.

For these reasons, many archaeologists feel that oral traditions are not a source of information on par with archaeology. Instead, they see them as a source of hypotheses that must be corroborated by archaeological data. In this way, archaeology becomes an arbiter of the "truthfulness" of oral traditions (including those of white America).

One message of Chavín art may have been that the prosperity and well-being of the community depended on maintaining the favor of forces alien to the local habitat and daily experience—forces redolent of the powers of the distant and mysterious tropical forest. The mediation of this relationship required the services of ritual specialists. This explanation suggests that Chavín ideology—heavily emphasizing the exotic trop-

But to some native peoples this is insulting and tantamount to heresy, because testing oral traditions is in fact questioning them. Many Christian fundamentalists feel the same way. If biblical archaeology corroborates the Bible, fine. But if it does not, some might argue, it is because archaeology, not the Bible, is imperfect.

And, in fact, we acknowledge that archaeology will always be imperfect. There is still much that it cannot retrieve about the past, and archaeologists can make mistakes. In addition, archaeologists conduct research from the point of view of a particular paradigm—which, in turn, is couched within a particular culture. Thus, some say, archaeology is just another "story" of the past. If archaeology is not perfect, then how can it be the final arbiter of oral traditions?

Some would answer that archaeology has standards of evidence, evaluation, and self-criticism, but so does the study of oral traditions. Peter Whiteley (American Museum of Natural History), for example, points out that oral histories can be evaluated in terms of their *consistency*—do different people give the same account, and does the same person give the same account over time? And if some elements of an account are validated by independent sources (for instance, historical documents or archaeology), then this lends some credibility to the account's other elements.

Many archaeologists today argue that neither archaeology nor oral traditions have the final say; one can test the other. But it is important to remember that there is an important difference between the two.

Archaeology and oral history are fundamentally about different kinds of information. Archaeology is about things rooted in time and space. Oral history encodes cultural and religious knowledge, things that are timeless and spaceless. A scientific archaeology deals only with claims about the material world, not the non-material world. When oral history makes claims about events rooted in time and space, then it can be tested, including corroboration by a scientific archaeology. With such verification, an oral tradition's claim to describe historical events becomes stronger.

But disproving an oral history's material or historical claims does not negate the tradition's ability to carry interesting and culturally important information. Many Native Americans, for instance, claim that their ancestors did not migrate to North America from Asia, contrary to all scientific data (see Chapter 12). Instead, they say that they have "always" been here. They point to oral traditions that describe a journey to this world from a previous one via a hole or cave (see the discussion of Hopi kivas in Chapter 10). One response to this discrepancy is for archaeologists to simply say, "You're wrong," and leave it at that. Others, however, might look deeper.

Pawnee historian Roger Echo-Hawk (Denver Art Museum) did just that, suggesting that Native American origin myths actually do talk about a migration from Asia. He points out that oral traditions must have an element of memorability to them, so that bland historical details are translated into more memorable stories. Accordingly, he argues that caves or holes are metaphors and mnemonic devices for describing the cold and seasonal darkness of the Arctic. Taking this approach to various Native American origin tales, he finds evidence for the large lakes that covered portions of the western United States some 12,000 years ago (Utah's Great Salt Lake, for example, is a mere remnant of the massive Lake Bonneville) and also for the Rocky Mountains and the Grand Canyon. If he is correct, then some Native American oral traditions encode 12,000-year-old information. And this would make them an additional—and valuable—source of information about the past.

ical forest fauna—ritually reinforced the wealth and power of Chavín de Huántar society.

Current evidence suggests that social stratification may have first appeared in the highlands in association with long-distance exchange—offering local leaders an unparalleled opportunity to control and manipulate the existing socioeconomic system. Burger argues that tribute supplied to regional ceremonial centers by travelers and pilgrims could have been a major source of wealth and power for newly emerging elites.

Religious ideology seems to have played a central role in promoting and legitimizing these profound sociopolitical transformations, suggesting that many of the key ingredients for social complexity existed in the central Andes prior to the Chavín horizon. Although it remains a hypothesis to be tested, it was perhaps the power of Chavín's symbols—rather than a change in food resources, climate, or population density—that played a key role in the development of the Andes' first civilization.

BLUEPRINTS FOR AN ARCHAEOLOGY OF THE MIND

Note that the two examples we have discussed so far share a couple of things. First, neither tries to interpret the exact meaning of the various symbols involved. Hall does not tell us what the raptors or other animals carved in stone on Hopewell pipes "mean." Neither do Burger and Miller attempt to explain what the jaguars, caymans, or crested eagles symbolized to those who participated in the religion and iconography of the central Andes of some 2500 years ago.

Archaeologists simply cannot make the inferential leap from an ancient symbol to its past meaning based strictly on the symbol itself. Instead, we can only speak in general terms about what the symbols imply about a level of human interaction that is different from a purely material interaction with their environment.

Second, both examples rely upon solid ethnographic and ethnohistoric data. Hall's idea that Hopewell pipes were part of a peace pipe ritual was based on copious ethnographic data on such rituals among many eastern North American peoples. Likewise, Burger and Miller would have been hard pressed to generate a viable hypothesis to account for Chavín iconography without access to a rich historical and ethnographic record of the Andes Mountains.

Upper Paleolithic The last major division of the Old World Paleolithic, beginning about 40,000 years ago and lasting until the end of the Pleistocene (ca. 10,000 BC).

Good researchers will always need to draw upon imagination to propose testable hypotheses. But ancient symbolic systems always pose the danger that imaginations can run amuck. Without some solid means to check the results of symbolic studies, archaeologists will always be in danger of what Kent Flannery and Joyce Marcus (University of Michigan) call "a bungee jump into the Land of Fantasy."

Likewise, Colin Renfrew (Cambridge University) warns of the pitfalls inherent in "new-age archaeology," insisting that cognitive archaeology proceed within the framework of acceptable scientific method. One must recognize that, at best, archaeology can capture only certain, limited aspects of ancient ideas. Renfrew discourages attempts to reconstruct "worldviews" or "totalities of thought"—emphasizing the notable lack of success among ethnographers who have tried to do this (and they work with living people, whose totality of thought is very much intact).

Marcus and Flannery also suggest that cognitive archaeology can follow relatively rigorous methods, *provided ample historical and ethnographic documentation is available.* In fact, they warn that if such data are lacking, "far less success should be anticipated."

So, what do we do with truly ancient symbolic systems that have no such historically linked ethnographic data? Do we simply shrug our shoulders and turn to some other problem? To answer this question, let's examine how archaeologists have studied one of the earliest symbolic systems, the Upper Paleolithic cave art of western Europe.

UPPER PALEOLITHIC CAVE ART

You will recall from Chapter 12 that the lineage that would eventually become *Homo sapiens* split from the rest of the primate lineage more than 5 million years ago. But the earliest evidence for artistic expression appears only in the last 90,000 years and does not become widespread until the last 40,000 years.

The **Upper Paleolithic** (40,000–10,000 BC) in Europe is distinguished by the appearance of a complex technology of stone, bone, and antler as well as wall art, portable art objects, and decorated tools—an example of which appears in Figure 14-6. Archaeologists sometimes call this an artistic "explosion," and the metaphor is appropriate. Only a handful of objects from the pre-

© American Museum of Natural History

Figure 14-6 Carved from reindeer antler, this bison probably served as the end of an atlatl and is an example of the artistic work that typifies the European Upper Paleolithic.

example, two bulls appear to be running toward and to either side of you—a trick made possible by clever use of the cave's contours.

Upper Paleolithic paintings sometimes turn up in the most obscure of places, difficult to locate even with modern equipment. The art is often found in the deepest recesses of caves, some at the very ends of passages, showing that a cave's entire passable extent was explored. Imagine entering one of these caves with only a reed torch or stone lamp burning tallow as your source of light. There are pits, pools, and rivers to avoid, narrow passageways to crawl through, and jutting rocks to duck under; and, remember, you have to find your way outside again. At Lascaux, cave art even appears at the base of a deep pit. Not only does the descent into the darkness require a rope, but carbon dioxide also accumulates at the pit's base, making breathing difficult.

Upper Paleolithic artisans clearly intended to place their art in difficult places to access. And this remoteness strongly suggests a connection between the art and religious ritual, a suggestion supported by the occasional finds of bear teeth or ocher-covered flint blades stuffed into cracks in the cave walls; perhaps these were offerings of some sort.

The content of the art is also intriguing. Human beings rarely appear and, when they do, they are poorly executed in comparison with the marvelous animal figures. Also, Upper Paleolithic art contains no actual "scenes." Although images often overlap, no one has identified a "story" or landscape. And whereas the cave art provides vivid evidence documenting the range of animals living in Ice Age Europe, certain animals are

ceding 5 million years can be called art (and many of these may not be artifacts at all). But many, many Upper Paleolithic sites contain engraved, carved, or sculpted objects, and caves occupied by Upper Paleolithic peoples often contain wall paintings.

Cave paintings occur in 200 French caves, and still more are found in Spain. Much of the painting dates to the **Magdalenian** phase (16,000–10,000 BC). However, a new site, Grotte Chauvet, was discovered in France in 1994, and AMS radiocarbon dates on the paintings themselves (the black paint is charcoal, and fat or blood is sometimes used as a binder) and some torch marks on the walls date to 24,000–30,000 BC.

Upper Paleolithic wall paintings have intrigued archaeologists for more than a century. More than simple line drawings, these are masterworks created by talented artisans who knew animal anatomy and behavior well. Careful shading shows the contours of animals' shoulders and haunches. Stags lower their heads to bugle in the rutting season. Some animals may be pregnant. Many of the images were painted with brushes, and hand silhouettes by the hundreds cover some cave walls.

The paintings are deliberately dramatic. The artists understood the principles of perspective, and they sometimes employed the natural topography of cave walls to bring the animals to life. As you walk down one dark, narrow passage in the French cave of Lascaux, for

Magdalenian The last major culture of the European Upper Paleolithic period (ca. 16,000–10,000 BC); named after the rockshelter La Madeleine, in southwestern France. Magdalenian artisans crafted intricately carved tools of reindeer bone and antler; this was also the period during which Upper Paleolithic cave art in France and Spain reached its zenith.

emphasized, especially horses, aurochs (wild cattle), bison, ibex, stags, and reindeer, with occasional mammoths, bears, rhinoceros, and large cats. The ancient artists sometimes painted some images on top of (or partially overlapping) previous paintings, suggesting that the act of making the art was more important than the final product itself.

What accounts for the particular forms that the art takes and the locations where these forms were painted?

Art or Magic?

Various nineteenth-century scholars viewed Upper Paleolithic cave art romantically, as an early expression of a growing human sense of beauty and perfection. This "art-for-art's-sake" perspective stressed what humans could accomplish in the leisure time that technology could bring. So viewed, the animals had no particular meaning; they were simply artistic expressions of the things that people saw around them. The lack of scenes or stories in the art was taken to be evidence that the artistic sense was in a rudimentary stage of development.

David Lewis-Williams (University of Witwatersrand, South Africa) points out the circularity in this approach: An innate aesthetic sense is inferred from beautiful art, and the presence of beautiful art is evidence of this innate sense. The art-for-art's-sake approach likewise fails to explain why the artists chose such remote locations. If art was something done in leisure time for public enjoyment, why decorate remote, dangerous reaches of caves?

Other anthropologists suggested that the cave art involves **sympathetic magic,** grounded in the principle that "like controls like." In the late nineteenth century, Salomon Reinach (1858–1932) proposed that the images were intended to promote the fertility of game animals, thus ensuring an abundant food supply for Upper Paleolithic hunters: If you draw pregnant animals, then the real animals will become pregnant and the food supply will be ensured. Abbé Henri Breuil subsequently developed a similar line of thought, suggesting that the images were a form of sympathetic magic designed to guarantee the success of a hunt: If you kill the stylized animal on the wall, you will also kill the real animal out in the valley.

It is true that the artists drew some animals with spears thrust into them (although only a few may represent pregnant animals). But whereas bison and horse are the most frequently depicted animals, most of the bones recovered from Upper Paleolithic caves in Europe are red deer and reindeer. If this art represents sympathetic magic, then it was not very successful.

The sympathetic magic interpretation assumes that the animals are literal and that they have no symbolic meaning. But other scholars view the Upper Paleolithic cave paintings as a structured code, drawing upon a theoretical paradigm known as **structuralism.** Briefly, structuralism argues that humans understand reality as paired oppositions. The concept of "life," for example, is meaningless without the opposite concept of "death." Likewise, the concept of "male" means nothing without the opposing concept of "female." From a structuralist perspective, culture—and its material expressions, such as art—is played out in terms of such paired oppositions. So viewed, the task of the archaeologist becomes discerning and interpreting these pairs of oppositions.

Following this paradigm, French archaeologists André Leroi-Gourhan (1911–1986) and Annette Laming-Emperaire (1917–1978) argued that Upper Paleolithic cave imagery contained binary oppositions that "stand for" male and female (although Laming-Emperaire backed away from this interpretation later in her life). Criticizing what she saw as simplistic, off-the-cuff interpretations, Laming-Emperaire advocated a more systematic approach to cave art. She sought to identify not merely the animals represented in the images, but also where in a cave particular images were found (the entrance, middle chambers, the rear), their positions (ceiling, wall, and so on), signs of use, archaeological remains, and associations among images. In other words, Laming-Emperaire did what a good archaeologist should do: She systematically analyzed both the contents and the contexts of the images.

It remained for Leroi-Gourhan to complete the work begun by Laming-Emperaire. Rejecting previous ethnographic analogies and earlier models of cognitive evolution, Leroi-Gourhan instead assumed that the minds of Upper Paleolithic people were every bit as complex as those of modern people. Collecting systematic, quantitative data from 66 French caves, Leroi-Gourhan's

sympathetic magic Rituals in which doing something to an image of an object produces the desired effect in the real object.

structuralism A paradigm holding that human culture is the expression of unconscious modes of thought and reasoning, notably binary oppositions. Structuralism is most closely associated with the work of the French anthropologist Claude Levi-Strauss.

maps suggested that the various cave elements clustered into four major set of images:

- Small herbivores (horse, ibex, stag, reindeer, and hind)
- Large herbivores (bison, auroch)
- Rare species (mammoth, deer, ibex)
- Dangerous animals (cat, bear, rhinoceros)

Working in the structuralist paradigm, Leroi-Gourhan associated the small herbivores with "maleness" and the large herbivores with "femaleness." He also defined two major groupings of abstract signs—a set of "narrow" symbols (such as rows of dots, arrow-like representations, and straight lines) that he believed were "male," and a second set of "wide" symbols (rectangles, upside-down Vs, and some curvilinear symbols) that he associated with "female." In this way, the abstract symbols and the animal portrayals were viewed as complementary.

Leroi-Gourhan then looked for patterning in the placement of images within cave settings. Dividing the caves into entrances, central areas, peripheral areas, and back areas, he discovered that stags (a male sign) tended to appear in cave entrances. Male signs and images (stags, horses, and ibex) were also in the peripheral areas, whereas dangerous animals and carnivores appeared mostly in the backs of the caves. The central areas contained both male and female signs (along with horses, bison, and aurochs).

To some, the presence of a male sign at the entrance might suggest that the caves were regarded as "male" places, a stag being the equivalent of an ancient "No women allowed" sign. But Leroi-Gourhan reversed the argument, suggesting instead that the caves were considered female (whether this means that only women or men entered the caves is unknown). Keep in mind that structuralism arrays the world into oppositions: If there is a male, there must be a female. Leroi-Gourhan pointed out that central areas contain male elements placed around female elements (with male elements also found in peripheral areas and at the entrance). Where is the female to balance the male? It must be the cave itself.

Armed with these inferences, Leroi-Gourhan could now interpret the "meaning" of the caves: This is where Upper Paleolithic people dealt with the oppositions and contradictions that, according to structuralist thinking, are the inevitable consequence of thinking as a human. Inside the caves, they used symbols drawn from the world of nature to create and communicate a cosmol-

ogy that explained life's fundamental oppositions: Male and female, nature and culture, human and supernatural, life and death.

But some empirical problems plague Leroi-Gourhan's analysis. Sometimes he used an image to determine whether a portion of a cave was "central" or "peripheral," and in others he reversed the process, assigning an indistinct painting to a particular species depending on where it was located. Both are instances of circular reasoning. And the associations that formed the baseline of his analysis have not held up as more caves are investigated. Eventually, his ideas collapsed under the very empirical standards that he had constructed; that's often how science progresses.

Of greater interest (at least today) are the ways in which Leroi-Gourhan interpreted the symbols. To pursue his structuralist paradigm, Leroi-Gourhan needed to define binary oppositions, the most prominent of which were male and female symbols. In so doing, he was required to jump from the symbol to its meaning. Because symbols take on meaning only from culture, there is always the danger that archaeologists will draw upon their own culture, rather than that of the ancient people to whom these symbols meant something. This was clearly a problem with Leroi-Gourhan's interpretation of abstract symbols of the Upper Paleolithic. Living in a world where Freudian psychology was popular, Leroi-Gourhan interpreted "narrow" and "wide" symbols as representing male and female genitalia. We see here how a paradigm affects the way that we understand the world. It is unlikely that, in a pre-Freudian world, Leroi-Gourhan would have proposed that lines = penises and rectangles = vaginas.

How did Leroi-Gourhan attribute different animal species to men and women? Like most symbolic anthropologists, he looked for associations in the symbols, focusing on bison and horses. In a limited number of cave paintings and engravings, he found women depicted next to bison and men painted next to horses (although the interpretation of some figures as men or women is dubious, as is the contemporaneity of the juxtaposed images). There were also opposite associations—men with bison and women with horses—or ambiguous ones, such as men *and* women with bison *and* horses.

Recall that the same symbol can be employed in many different ways even in the same culture. Do the opposite or ambiguous associations suggest that Leroi-Gourhan is simply wrong—that bison do not really "stand for" female and horses do not "stand for" male—or are they plays on the symbolic meanings of bison and horses? Maybe the men with bison are berdaches (see Chapter 13), and the women with horses are what the Lakota called "manly-hearted women."

Or maybe all of this is just a product of Leroi-Gourhan's imagination and culture. Maybe the bison and horses and other animals had different meanings in different caves at different times in the past. Maybe the images are **totems,** symbols of different clans (as Laming-Emperaire eventually concluded).

That Leroi-Gourhan was influenced by Freud and structuralism does not automatically mean that his interpretation of the symbols in the paintings is wrong. *The problem is that we cannot assess whether he was right.*

The most secure way to go from symbols to their meanings is by using some historical or ethnographic information, as Burger and Miller did with Chavín art and Hall did with Hopewell platform pipes. But given that we lack any associated ethnographic data for the Upper Paleolithic, we must ask if there is anything we can do with this art other than admire its beauty and mystery.

Shamanism?

David Lewis-Williams offers an alternative explanation of Upper Paleolithic cave art that, although still speculative, is more firmly grounded in middle-range theory. In brief, Lewis-Williams argues that Upper Paleolithic cave art is evidence of shamanic trances. His explanation does not rely on an interpretation of the images' symbols, and he tries to explain multiple aspects of the art, including the particular abstract elements, as well as the locations of images in caves and their association with animal images.

Lewis-Williams begins by pointing out that virtually all hunting and gathering societies known to anthro-

pology practice a form of religion that involves shamanism. **Shamans** are individuals (often men, but including women in some societies) who claim to be able to access supernatural powers, spirits, or deceased individuals and tap into the power and influence that they offer to the world of the living. They often do this through trances, brought on by the use of psychotropic drugs or by fasting, dehydration, and sensory deprivation. Shamans culturally interpret the visions seen while in an altered state of consciousness as communication with the supernatural world.

The Lakota, for example, performed **vision quests** in which men would lie for days on a mountaintop until starvation, dehydration, and exposure brought about visions. These visions were a way for men to communicate with the supernatural world and locate their source of power. Africa's Ju/'hoansi used trances, sometimes brought on by hours of physically and emotionally draining dancing, as a way to contact the ghosts of deceased individuals and perform healing rituals on gravely ill members of the band.

After several decades of study, Lewis-Williams argues that much (though by no means all) of the world's rock art is the result of shamanism. The art is a record of what a shaman saw while in a trance, a way to understand and interpret the meaning of the vision. How can Lewis-Williams say this? If anything is archaeologically inaccessible, it would seem to be what somebody saw in a trance thousands of years ago!

Lewis-Williams relies on cross-cultural psychological and neurological research to bolster his argument. According to this research, when individuals go into a trance, they go through three levels of consciousness, each with distinctive "visual" aspects. In the first stage, a person sees dots, grids, zigzags, nested curves (like rainbows), and meandering lines. These may flicker, vibrate, merge, and break apart. Known as entoptic (from the Greek word meaning "within vision") phenomena, these images appear even with your eyes closed, because they are a product of the optical nervous system. Because they are a function of the brain's hard-wiring, and given that all people everywhere (and we assume in the past, too) have the same neurology, all people should see the same entoptic images. Lewis-Williams thus injects the important element of uniformitarianism, which you will recall is essential to middle-range theory.

In the second, deeper stage of trance, a person's mind tries to make sense of the entoptic images by converting them into forms that are culturally meaningful (mean-

totem A natural object, often an animal, from which a lineage or clan believes itself to be descended and/or with which lineage or clan members have special relations.

shaman One who has the power to contact the spirit world through trance, possession, or visions. On the basis of this ability, the shaman invokes, manipulates, or coerces the power of the spirits for socially recognized ends—both good and ill.

vision quest A ritual in which an individual seeks visions through starvation, dehydration, and exposure; considered in some cultures to be a way to communicate with the supernatural world.

ing that the particular images become culturally biased). Just as a nineteenth-century Lakota might see horses with riders on them, teepees, mountains, and bison, the mind of an Upper Paleolithic shaman would convert abstract images into things familiar to them, including animals such as aurochs and reindeer.

Those slipping into the third and final stage of trance will sense that they are moving through a tunnel or a vortex, with entoptic images swirling around them and merging into culturally intelligible ones. Again, this experience seems to be universal, generated by human neurology.

Shamans in many hunting and gathering cultures talk about reaching the "other side" by moving through a hole or cave, an experience sometimes described as "dying." Upon reaching the third stage, a person is often unable to recognize any stimulus outside the visions. The images become more vivid and, although they may merge with one another and with abstract images, a person senses that they are nonetheless real. At this point, the person has entered an altered state of consciousness, and he or she no longer understands that they are viewing images. Instead, they see themselves as having become part of the image.

But does an understanding of the neurological basis of trance (and dreams) help us understand Upper Paleolithic rock art? Let's look at one especially well-known

site that Lewis-Williams has studied: the French cave of Lascaux.

The Cave of Lascaux

Found by schoolboys in 1940, Lascaux is perhaps the most famous of all the European caves (see "Looking Closer: The Discovery of Lascaux"). The Paleolithic artists who painted the images inside Lascaux some 17,000 years ago would not recognize the outside of the cave today. The schoolboys entered the cave through a sinkhole, then crawled down a long rubble-filled tunnel. Today, however, those lucky few who can enter Lascaux (it is closed to regular public visitations) walk through two airlock doors, then step into an antibacterial footbath (to remove any microbes brought from the outside), all the time listening to the hum of an expensive ventilation system designed to maintain the cave's humidity and preserve the paintings inside.

But the inside of the cave remains much as the Paleolithic artists left it. You first enter the Hall of the Bulls, whose ceiling sparkles with calcite (see the chapter's opening photo and Figure 14-7). You are struck immediately by the immense aurochs and horses, painted in red and black, that circle the roof; at 5 meters long, the bulls are the largest in all of European cave art. Smaller stags are present, some with many-tined antlers, as well

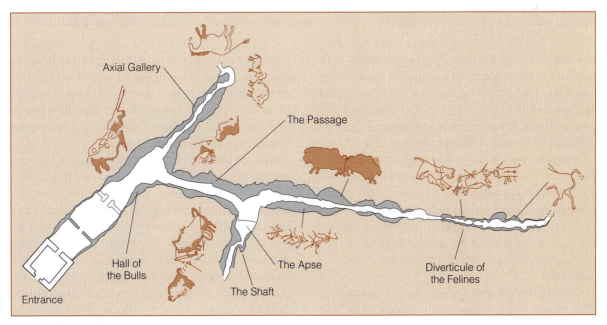

Figure 14-7 Map of Lascaux

Looking Closer
The Discovery of Lascaux

Like so many major archaeological discoveries, Lascaux was found by accident. And it wasn't even a person who found it, but a dog.

Lascaux is located in the beautiful Dordogne region of southern France, a limestone karst topography rich in caves and rockshelters, many of which our human ancestors inhabited. In the 1940s, however, this region saw many refugees, people who were fleeing from the advancing German army. Life was hard and dangerous, but boys still found time to explore the hillsides and look for buried treasure.

In early September, several boys were hiking through the hills around Lascaux. The eldest was 18-year-old Marcel Ravidat (nicknamed "Jailbird" after a character in the novel *Les Miserables*). His dog, Robot, became lost, but the boys eventually found him in a shallow pit. Farmers once dumped animal carcasses there, and the dog was no doubt intrigued by lingering odors. Bending down to scoop up his dog, Ravidat also became intrigued when he felt cold air rising from a small hole in the pit's bottom.

The boys had heard rumors of a tunnel that connected a sixteenth-century manor house to the Montignac castle, a tunnel that locals said contained treasure (of course). Ravidat decided that the hole was an entrance to the tunnel and, on September 12, 1940, he returned with three other boys—Simon Coencas, Georges Agniel, and Jacques Marsal—to explore it. Using improvised tools, they dug down, eventually breaking into a cavern. As their homemade paraffin lanterns lit the way, the boys crawled down a long pile of rubble. At the bottom, they found a pool of water surrounded by low gleaming white walls. They explored farther.

The boys thought they were in a tunnel, and so they were stunned when they saw a vividly painted horse in the flickering lights. Holding their lights higher, they could see that the entire ceiling was painted. Reindeer, horses, a bear, and abstract markings covered the walls; bulls circled the ceiling. The boys just stood and stared. It was better than treasure.

They explored the cave over the next few days, finding more passages and images. Ravidat undertook the dangerous climb down into the Well, where he found the now-famous bird-man image. The boys guessed that the images were old, but they had no idea that they were looking at some of the world's oldest art.

The boys informed a local schoolteacher, who brought

as a bear. Many of the paintings take advantage of the cave's natural topography to accentuate a raised head or shoulders. One peculiar animal has two horns sprouting, unicorn-like, from its head. This painting is well executed, and Lewis-Williams suggests that the artist intended to create an ambivalent species.

A narrow, natural ledge 5 to 6 feet above the floor seems to form a ground line for the animals (something rarely seen in Paleolithic art). But because the ledge is too narrow to stand on, the ancient artisans must have constructed platforms to reach the ceiling. Beneath these paintings is room for groups of people to have participated in rituals; whether they did so, however, is unknown.

Moving straight ahead, you enter the narrow Axial Gallery, which slopes more deeply into the earth. Many horses are on the walls here, with some aurochs and stags. Two of the horses have what appear to be spears or darts shooting toward them. A long line of black dots appear beneath a large stag in a bellowing posture; a horse faces the stag. Lewis-Williams sees these dots as evidence of the merging of abstract and representational images that occurs in trance.

Near the end of the Axial Gallery is one of the most intriguing images in Lascaux. Painted on a jutting piece of rock is a life-size image of a horse, upside-down and apparently falling through the air. This image is not entirely visible until you walk around the bulge in the wall, single file. Several flint blades, covered in ochre and jammed into a crack, were found near this horse image. Walking around the "falling" horse, you encounter another horse, this one upright, and then the end of the passage.

Retracing your steps, you move back through the

word to Abbé Henri Breuil (1877–1961). Breuil was a priest, but he was also a scholar of Upper Paleolithic cave art (he taught for a while at the Collège de France). He had found and explored several caves, and professionals acknowledged his expertise with the title "the Pope of Prehistory." He would later explore and document the art in Lascaux, which he called the "Sistine Chapel of Prehistory."

But with a war on, there was little to be done immediately. Breuil advised the boys to pitch camp near the mouth of the cave and protect it. To their credit, the boys did exactly that. They faithfully guarded the cave, leading visitors through to prevent destruction and living in a conical log hut (after their tent burned down) heated by a wood stove through the winter of 1940–41.

But the war intensified. In the summer of 1942, Ravidat joined a resistance group, and Marsal was captured by the German army and sent to a labor camp. Coencas lost his parents, though he himself was saved by the French Red Cross. Agniel returned home to help support his parents.

And so Lascaux, the greatest of the French caves, sat until 1947, when work finally began again at the site. In 1948, it was opened to visitors, and Marsal became a guide. A ventilation system was installed in 1958 but, by 1963, the steady stream of visitors had brought in more humidity and microorganisms than the system could handle, and a green fungus began to cover the paintings. The cave was closed to the public and remains closed to this day, although the fungus has been removed. Only a few people are allowed to visit the site each week, and the waiting list is several years long.

Fortunately, the French government constructed an astonishingly precise replica of the Hall of the Bulls only 200 meters from the real cave. Lascaux II opened to the public in 1983, and a reunion meeting there in 1986 brought the four friends together at the cave again.

Lascaux continues to figure prominently in analyses of Upper Paleolithic cave art, and its magnificence is enjoyed by the tens of thousands who visit Lascaux II each year. And it all began with a lost dog.

Hall of the Bulls and to the left. Passing through a low opening, you enter the Passage—this one longer than the Axial Gallery. The original opening was even smaller than it is today, and Upper Paleolithic artisans had to crawl through it.

In the Passage, the walls bear no calcite and the stone is softer. More horses and bulls are painted and engraved on the walls, although they are not as well preserved as in other parts of the cave. Images are piled up on top of one another, and the art here seems to be less "composed" than in the Axial Gallery and the Hall of the Bulls.

About 15 meters down the Passage, you encounter the Apse on your right, a small domed chamber with walls covered in engravings and a few paintings. Many different species are present—horses, bison, aurochs, ibex, deer, and perhaps even a wolf and lion. These images also overlay one another, producing a confusing jumble. Many engraved lines cut through the images.

Behind the Apse is the "Shaft" or "Well," a 5 meter-deep pit. Stone lamps were found at the bottom—turned upside down, as if the users meant to extinguish them. At the bottom of the pit is one of the oddest images of Upper Paleolithic art, which we show in Figure 14-8: A bison, his head lowered in defensive posture, appears to have a spear through the body. Some interpret the lines emanating from its belly to be entrails. In front of the bison is a stick figure of a man, his penis apparently erect, who appears to be falling backward from the bison's blow. The figure only has four fingers, however, and his head looks more like that of a bird. Beneath the man is a long vertical line, with what appears to be a bird perched on its top. The meaning of this image is the source of endless speculation.

© Charles & Josette Lenars/CORBIS

Figure 14-8 Bison and "falling man" in Lascaux. It is not known if these images were painted at the same time (as a "scene") or at different times.

Climbing out of the Shaft (which today is covered by a grid and accessed by a ladder), you return to the Passage and continue moving down its length. The walls contain more images for the next 15 meters or so, and then the images cease as the passage narrows and the ceiling drops. You encounter the two charging bison that we mentioned above—the ones that appear to be running toward and around you. After dropping to your knees and crawling along the cave floor, you encounter the Diverticule of the Felines, with its soft clay walls. If you are a small person, you are crouching; a larger person might be lying on his stomach.

Here there are aurochs and horses and bison, but also large cats—panthers or cave lions. Spears appear to pierce some of them, others are cut by lines or geometric markings or have lines emanating from their mouths and anuses. The images are well composed but seem to have been more hastily engraved than others in the cave. This section of the cave was perhaps rarely visited, because otherwise its soft clay walls would not have survived so well.

What Does All This Mean?

Leaving Lascaux, you might turn to look at the Hall of the Bulls one last time, trying to imagine how the scene would appear in the flickering light of a stone lamp. Something significant obviously transpired in these dark places. The aurochs, bison, and horses painted on

Lascaux's walls and ceilings were not the fleeting whimsy of a Paleolithic artist. The same images appear in many caves and were used over thousands of years.

We do not know the specific meanings of these world-famous images (and, in truth, we probably never will). Lewis-Williams thinks that this art is somehow related to altered states of consciousness, but the images themselves could not, of course, have been produced while the artist was in a trance state, because one would need to be fully conscious to mix the paints, negotiate the cave's twists and turns with a stone lamp, and build scaffolding where needed. But Lewis-Williams thinks that the paintings at Lascaux and elsewhere provide firm evidence of Upper Paleolithic people trying to come to terms with understanding the meaning of altered states of consciousness—dreams and trances.

He sees the larger chambers, like the Hall of the Bulls, as places where communal rituals may have taken place, with people seeking assistance from a spirit world that existed belowground. Although the floor of Lascaux was damaged before it was investigated, the floors at Grotte Chauvet contain many human footprints, some 25,000 or more years old. Some of the prints are big and some are small, telling us that people of all ages visited even more remote portions of this cave.

Lewis-Williams also suggests that the distribution of art within a cave may parallel the stages of trances. In the front chamber are animals that figured in the lives of Upper Paleolithic people. Here, too, we find some abstract signs—the rectangles, wavy lines, and rows of dots that are apparent in early stages of trance. Deeper inside the cave, the narrowing passageway mimics the movement into the deeper states of trance. Lewis-Williams suggests that the falling horse at the end of the Axial Gallery is not falling at all, but it is instead an artist's representation of the vortex that one senses in the deeper stages of trance.

Farther into the cave, we see "confused" images, such as those in the Apse and the Diverticule of the Felines.

These, Lewis-Williams suggests, may represent the merging of abstract and natural images in the deeper stages of trance or efforts by one shaman to bond with the power of another by drawing an image over that drawn by another shaman. Although rare in Upper Paleolithic art (and absent at Lascaux), occasional animal images take on human characteristics. They walk on two feet, sometimes hold their front legs in a human way, or turn to stare at the observer with an eerily human gaze. These might record instances where observers entered the deepest stages of trance and were unable to see the difference between themselves and animals.

Lewis-Williams suggests that vision quests may have been held in the deepest cave recesses. Without food or water, the total darkness and silence of a cave is a perfect medium for the production of visions. Perhaps people of the Upper Paleolithic saw caves as one place to access the spirit world.

Recall that some images make use of the bumps and contours of a cave's wall; Lewis-Williams believes this is more than a clever artistic trick. Shamans in hunting-and-gathering cultures often speak of a strong yet permeable membrane between themselves and the spirit world. Lewis-Williams suggests that the nature of trance would have suggested that portions of the spirit world lie belowground. By mimicking the vortex of trance, caves are the closest a person could come to the spirit world; the rest of the journey had to be made through trance. If the cave wall is the membrane between this world and the spirit world, then paintings and engravings were perhaps ways to access that spirit world. By using the cave's contours, the artist makes the painting more a part of the cave wall itself and, in so doing, in-creases its power. The flints, teeth, and bones left shoved into cracks may also have been similar efforts to break through the membrane and contact the spirit world.

In sum, Lewis-Williams argues that Upper Paleolithic art is not art for art's sake; nor is it fertility or hunting magic. Instead, he argues that the art reflects humanity's effort to come to grips with the perception that their quotidian life was not all that made up existence, to answer the question "What is the meaning of life?" And that fact gives us, the denizens of the twenty-first century, a strong link to the artisans who painted bulls on the ceilings of caves by torch light thousands of years ago.

CONCLUSION

An archaeology of the mind attempts to move beyond the more easily accessible matters of diet and settlement patterns to religion, ritual, and cosmology. People respond to their world through culture, an integrated set of symbolic meanings that are communicated through material culture. But given that there is no necessary link between symbols and their meanings, the development of reliable middle-range theory is almost impossible, and so this crucial area of human behavior often eludes archaeologists. Successful efforts rely upon historically linked ethnographic analogies, but these are limited to the more recent prehistory of regions with good ethnographic data. More ancient symbolic systems must be studied in ways that make use of uniformitarian elements of human neurology or perhaps a few symbolic universals (though these remain to be demonstrated).

Summary

- Although processual archaeology was initially optimistic that all aspects of the human condition were available for archaeological investigation, the proponents of processual approaches during the 1970s and 1980s were lukewarm, if not outright hostile, toward efforts to interpret symbols and construct an "archaeology of the mind."

- Modern cognitive archaeology aims to study the perception, description, and classification of the universe; the nature of the supernatural; the principles, philosophies, and values by which human societies are governed; and the ways in which aspects of the world, the supernatural, or human values are conveyed in art.

- Studying these ancient modes of thought requires the interpretation of symbols, objects, or acts (verbal and nonverbal) that by cultural convention stands for something else *with which it has no necessary connection.* This means that, without some ethnographic context, there is no obvious way to connect a symbol to its meaning.

- Archaeologists attempt to understand past religions—the specific set of beliefs based on one's ultimate relation to the supernatural. Such religious beliefs are manifested in everyday life through rituals—behaviors such as prayer, music, feasting, sacrifice, and taboos. As such, ritual is a material manifestation of the abstract idea of religion and archaeology's easiest portal to the study of ancient religions.

- Archaeologists also attempt to understand cosmology. This encompasses how past cultures explain their universe—how it originated and developed; how the various parts fit together and what laws they obey—and express their concern with what the future of the universe holds.

- Where archaeologists have some ethnographic data available that are closely related to the archaeological

case, they may be able to extrapolate backward from the present to the past. Even these cases, however, harbor the chance that a symbol meant something different in the past than it does in the present.

- Iconography, a culture's expression of abstract ideas in art and writing systems, can also be used to reconstruct the religious and other ideas that stand behind the art.

- The study of ancient symbols runs the risk of becoming a free-for-all, with any interpretation being as valid as another. It is perhaps especially important, then, that the study of ancient iconography and other manifestations of a culture's cosmology and religion adhere to the canons of scientific analysis.

- In instances where ethnographic data are not available, the archaeologist must be more restrained in his or her interpretations and focus not on the specific meaning of particular symbols, but look to the more general character of thought itself.

Additional Reading

Bahn, Paul. 1998. *The Cambridge Illustrated History of Prehistoric Art.* Cambridge: University of Cambridge Press.

Hall, Robert L. 1997. *An Archaeology of the Soul: North*

American Indian Belief and Ritual. Urbana: University of Illinois Press.

Von Hagen, Adriana, and Craig Morris. 1998. *The Cities of the Ancient Andes.* London: Thames and Hudson.

Online Resources

COMPANION WEB SITE
Visit **http://anthropology.wadsworth.com** and click on the Student Companion Web Site for Thomas/Kelly *Archaeology,* 4th edition, to access a wide range of material to help you succeed in your introductory archaeology course. These include flashcards, Internet exercises, Web links, and practice quizzes.

RESEARCH ONLINE WITH INFOTRAC COLLEGE EDITION
From the Student Companion Web Site, you can access the InfoTrac College Edition database, which offers thousands of full-length articles for your research.

15 Understanding Key Transitions in World Prehistory

OUTLINE

Pyramids at the Maya site of Tikal. How do societies develop from egalitarian hunting-and-gathering bands into stratified societies with elite leadership?

Preview

THIS CHAPTER WILL INTRODUCE two milestones in the long-term evolution of human culture and, simultaneously, examine the role that paradigms play in interpreting the past.

Before considering these milestones, we will consider unilineal evolution, a now-defunct paradigm through which early anthropologists attempted to explain cultural evolution. We then concentrate on how archaeologists have tried to explain the origins of agriculture and the origins of civilization (and the "state"), each a major transition in long-term human history. As we examine the paradigms and explanatory theories used by archaeologists to understand these transitions, we emphasize two points. First, whereas each paradigm or theory contributes something to our understanding of these transitions, no single paradigm appears to give a complete accounting. Second, we emphasize the importance of differentiating between the *specific processes* at work, which can vary tremendously from case to case, and the *general conditions* that engender cultural change, which may be more universal.

INTRODUCTION

Archaeologists consider many kinds of questions, from small ones such as "Is this a potsherd?" to big ones, such as "What is human nature?" Answering the broader questions of cultural evolution is one of archaeology's most significant contributions to anthropology. In this chapter, we illustrate the different ways that archaeologists approach two of archaeology's perennial "big" questions: the origins of agriculture and the origins of a form of political organization that anthropologists call the "state."

Earlier, we emphasized that archaeologists approach their research from both scientific and humanistic points of view. This is more than a simple difference in taste, because the study of human history requires its own particular blend of methods and theories. Laboratory scientists can always repeat their experiments, changing one variable while holding others constant, to determine what effect a particular variable has on the outcome. But archaeology (and the other historical sciences) cannot do this. The Inka civilization of the high Andes Mountains, for example, existed only once and will never happen again. One cannot rewind history and replay it with one different variable—say, by changing the Andean Mountains to a desert—to see what happens.

Humanistic research directs us to the "when," "how," and "what" questions of prehistory. This research defines the particular processes and events at work in a given case. But to answer "why" questions, archaeologists benefit from a more comparative approach, one that looks for patterns among specific historical sequences that point to the general *conditions* of cultural change. To understand, for example, why civilizations and states evolved (terms we will define below), we can compare what happened in Egypt, China, Mexico, and other places where such forms of human organization first appeared. Doing this helps define how sequences of development were similar or different, leading us to suggest hypotheses that might explain general patterns in human cultural evolution.

Throughout this exercise, you should keep in mind a distinction between "necessary" and "sufficient" conditions of change. "Necessary conditions" must exist for a particular change to occur; "sufficient conditions" are the minimal ones needed for a change to occur. A basic knowledge of plant reproduction, for instance, is *necessary* for an agriculturalist (because you can't farm unless you know that plants come from seeds). But, as we demonstrate below, such knowledge is apparently not *sufficient* to inspire all foragers to transform themselves into agriculturalists. Other conditions must be in place for this economic change to occur.

Evolutionary Studies

Why did agriculture begin where it did? Why did farming not appear in other places? Why did large states—with their magnificent architecture, artwork, writing, and calendars—appear in some places and not in others?

A century ago, Western scholars answered these questions with a paradigm known today as **unilineal cultural evolution.** Before going any further, you must understand that *anthropology discarded unilineal cultural evolution a long ago.* So, why bring it up at all? Evolutionary frameworks have been around since before the days of Charles Darwin, some with strong racist overtones. So, at the outset, we want to be clear about which evolutionary paradigms we are endorsing, and which we believe must be avoided.

Unilineal Cultural Evolution

The nineteenth century was an exciting time for European intellectuals. Recall from Chapter 1 that Boucher de Perthes was retrieving stone artifacts from France's river gravels and claiming a great antiquity for them. By the second half of the century, it was clear that Europe, as well as the New World, had an ancient history. What, European scholars asked themselves, had the past been like?

At the same time, several European countries had established themselves as major colonial powers. In their colonies in Africa, Asia, and the Americas, west Europeans encountered people who were strikingly different from themselves. Why, Europeans asked, were the peoples of the world so diverse?

They found answers to both questions in the paradigm of unilineal cultural evolution. To understand why, we must remember the degree to which nineteenth-century scholarship in the West depended on Enlightenment philosophy (see Chapter 3)—especially the

notion of progress. Recall that Enlightenment thinking held that progress resulted from increasingly "rational" thought, which allowed people to acquire the wealth and leisure time necessary to control nature and improve themselves morally. "Progress," in the Enlightenment sense, meant not only moving toward material perfection, but toward moral and spiritual perfection as well.

Enlightenment philosophy viewed the human past as a record of the march toward perfection. By the mid-nineteenth century, archaeology had demonstrated that Europeans had passed through several stages in their progress to modernity (enshrined in the now-famous Stone, Bronze, and Iron Ages). But archaeology was a fledgling science, lacking adequate methods to reconstruct the details of the past. Stratified sites showed technological change but, without the necessary middle-range theory, the archaeological record remained silent on matters such as kinship, politics, or social organization.

But this hardly stopped Western scholars, who attempted to reconstruct the past using an Enlightenment-era version of the **comparative method.** Today, this term refers to the testing of hypotheses against a range of human societies, but in the nineteenth century, the "comparative method" translated cultural diversity into a neat, evolutionary sequence, in which *different living peoples represented different stages in humanity's march of progress.* The comparative method argued that people were different because some had made more progress than others, and that consequently the world's different peoples provided living snapshots of the past.

Although Enlightenment philosophy held that all people shared the same capacity for progress, it seemed clear that some had done better than others. Why?

Darwin and the Origin of Species

With the Bible to guide them, many nineteenth-century scholars believed that the diversity of animal life arose in the biblical act of Creation. But just as the archaeological record showed that human societies had changed through time, the paleontological record likewise

unilineal cultural evolution The belief that human societies have evolved culturally along a single developmental trajectory. Typically, such schemes depict Western civilization as the most advanced evolutionary stage; anthropology rejects this idea.

comparative method In Enlightenment philosophy, the idea that the world's existing peoples reflect different stages of human cultural evolution.

reflected multiple significant changes in animal life through the ages. Initially, scholars attributed this diversity to the biblical flood, but growing evidence suggested that many changes were gradual, not catastrophic. Was species diversity really a product of a one-time act of creation, or was something else involved?

With the publication of *On the Origin of Species* in 1859, Charles Darwin (1809–1882) provided a new way to understand biological diversity. Darwin's revolutionary volume suggested that, because the world's food supply is inherently inadequate, the young of any species must struggle to survive. Most don't make it. The survivors who live to foster the next generation do so because of fortuitously favored characteristics. Consequently, through the process of **natural selection,** some physical characteristics are passed along to the next generation, and others are not. (Exactly how this happened was mysterious because genetics was all but unknown at the time.) The evolutionary process, being gradual and continuous, eventually gives rise to new species as individuals appear with characteristics that permit them to inhabit a new environment or a new niche. Darwin's ingenious argument thus introduced the notion that organisms descend from a common ancestor, and it provided evidence that the earth and its various life forms are dynamic and ever-changing.

Although the word "evolution" will always be associated with Darwin, he used the word "evolved" only once in the first edition of *Origin.* And although Darwin would later write about humans (in *The Descent of Man*), in *Origin* he mentioned humans only once—on nearly the last page (see Chapter 1). Nevertheless, the far-reaching implications of his work were hardly lost on scholars of ancient human history.

Lubbock's *Pre-historic Times* and Social Darwinism

Darwin's neighbor in Kent, England was the banker and statesman John Lubbock (1834–1913), later known as

Lord Avebury. He was also an armchair anthropologist and, in 1865, he published the nineteenth century's most influential archaeology textbook, *Pre-historic Times, as Illustrated by Ancient Remains, and the Manners and Customs of Modern Savages.* In it, Lubbock married the Enlightenment's comparative approach with a rudimentary (and not entirely correct) understanding of natural selection.

Lubbock used the Enlightenment's comparative method to illustrate the life of the "paleolithic" (Old Stone Age) and "neolithic" (New Stone Age) people by reference to contemporary "primitives"—meaning the native peoples of Africa, Asia, and Australia. Lubbock argued that modern primitives were to archaeology as modern pachyderms were to paleontology. Although Lubbock made no specific analogies between particular living peoples and archaeological cultures, the implication was clear: Contemporary "primitives" were living approximations of what Europeans used to be.

Although not the only (or even the first) scholar to suggest this, Lubbock was highly influential. In fact, others soon expanded his argument, suggesting that living "primitives" were not merely "like" the past— they were in fact *living relics of prehistory.* Australian Aborigines were said to be lineal descendants of Neanderthals, and Eskimos were the descendants of the Magdalenians (the people who produced the Upper Paleolithic rock art of Europe). Using the comparative approach, these scholars barely needed archaeology. If you wanted to know what the past was, just find a living people who approximated the archaeological culture and describe them. There was no need to infer anything from archaeology, because the past still existed!

So, why did some people *appear* to be "back in the past" while others had apparently made so much progress?

Remember that scientific paradigms exist within a social context; for the nineteenth century, this meant colonialism. European scholars were unable to escape the belief in racial inequality that colonialism fostered. In nineteenth-century **social Darwinism,** cultural evolution became an extension of biological evolution by suggesting that both people and social forms compete for survival, with the richest and most powerful becoming the "fittest." Lower socioeconomic classes were seen as "the least fit" of industrial European society, and "primitive" peoples were the "least fit" people of the nineteenth-century world.

Social Darwinists argued that human societies varied in their "evolutionary" status from highly evolved

natural selection The process through which some individuals survive and reproduce at higher rates than others because of their genetic heritage; leads to the perpetuation of certain genetic qualities at the expense of others.

social Darwinism The extension of the principles of Darwinian evolution to social phenomena; it implies that conflict between societies and between classes of the same society benefits humanity in the long run by removing "unfit" individuals and social forms. Social Darwinism assumed that unfettered economic competition and warfare were primary ways to determine which societies were "fittest."

TABLE 15-1 Morgan's Three Phases of Human Cultural Evolution

PHASE	SUBPHASE	HALLMARK	EXAMPLE
Savagery	Lower	Subsistence on fruit and nuts	None survived into historical period.
	Middle	Fish, fire	Australian aborigines, Polynesians
	Upper	Bow and arrow	Athapaskan tribes of Hudson's Bay Territory
Barbarism	Lower	Pottery	Eastern Native American tribes
	Middle	Animal domestication; construction with adobe, brick, and mortar; irrigation	Pueblos
	Upper	Iron smelting	Grecian tribes of the Homeric Age and Germanic tribes of the time of Caesar
Civilization		Phonetic alphabet; literary records	Ancient civilization: Greece and Rome Modern civilization: Britain

groups (the Europeans) to those who differed only slightly from the advanced apes. Cultural differences, they believed, were grounded in biological differences. Today, of course, we know that culture has nothing to do with biology, because any person can be enculturated into any culture.

Lubbock, however, argued that through the process of natural selection, humanity was improving biologically, culturally, intellectually, and spiritually. Left alone, capitalist societies would prosper and improve. In fact, Lubbock concluded on an upbeat note: "The future happiness of our race, which poets hardly ventured to hope for, science boldly predicts."

The downside, of course, is that the world's "primitives" were doomed. In Lubbock's view, these people had not evolved sufficiently, and no degree of remedial education could repair the damage done by millennia of natural selection. Although neither Darwin nor Lubbock advocated exploitation of these populations, both believed that "primitive" peoples were condemned to extinction. Thus, the paradigm of unilineal evolution provided "scientific" justification for British colonization of the world.

Lewis Henry Morgan's *Ancient Society*

Across the Atlantic, one of the best known of the unilineal theorists was Lewis Henry Morgan (1818–1881), a Rochester lawyer-turned-ethnologist. He lived at a time when Americans saw United States history as all about progress and destiny, when they considered its westward expansion both inevitable and laudable.

In *Ancient Society* (1877), Morgan divided the progress of human achievement into three major phases— savagery, barbarism, and civilization (Table 15-1), a unilineal scheme that defined a kind of evolutionary

ladder. The bottom rung was for the primeval, rudimentary, and primitive; the top rung belonged to Western civilization (particularly that of western Europe), with other groups and cultural practices arrayed between these two extremes. In this view of unilineal evolution, all peoples were thought to pass through the same stages—the ascending rungs of the evolutionary ladder—if they were intellectually capable of doing so. As the author of anthropology's first textbook, Edward Tylor (see Chapter 2), wrote, "The institutions of man are as distinctly stratified as the earth on which he lives. They succeed each other in series substantially uniform over the globe, independent of what seem the comparatively superficial differences of race and language."

But even top-rung Western civilization was not the evolutionary peak. Recall that Enlightenment thought was grounded in progress—technological, cultural, moral, *and* spiritual. Above the elite classes of Europe on the evolutionary scale stood the angels, and above the angels was God Himself. Viewed this way, the British aristocracy was closer to God than, say, the Australian Aborigines were. By today's standards, the hubris of colonialism is simply shocking.

How "Evolution" Became a Dirty Word

In the early twentieth century, the nascent field of anthropology turned against this **ethnocentric** notion of progress. Franz Boas (1858–1942), often called the "father of American anthropology," and his students rejected unilineal evolution as a valid way of studying

ethnocentric (also ethnocentrism) The attitude or belief that one's own cultural ways are superior to any other.

the human condition. In large measure, this was be-cause of the paradigm's racist overtones and the colo-nial excesses that it supported. A Jewish immigrant from Germany, Boas was quite familiar with exclusion and ethnocentrism.

Boas argued that each culture is unique and should be valued as such. He argued that cultures change in ways unique to themselves and that current evidence did not warrant sweeping generalizations. Instead, Boas argued in favor of **historical particularism.** He pointed out that, because cultural evolution was so complex and had taken so many diverse paths, there was no single line of progressive evolution and, consequently, cultures cannot be placed into a unilineal evolutionary scheme. Human institutions such as matrilineal descent, slavery, private property, or formal courts are associated with an array of other sociocultural features. Complex forms of kinship, for example, can accompany the simplest kinds of technology (as among Australian Aborigines).

Although Boas admitted to some degree of regularity in history, he believed that earlier researchers had exag-gerated the patterns. And even if patterns did exist, Boas believed that the patient accumulation of ethno-graphic detail and historical facts must precede the construction of any generalities concerning human cul-tural evolution.

The Return of Evolution

Unilineal cultural evolution collapsed under the assault from Boas and his students. But research conducted under the paradigm of historical particularism eventu-ally amassed sufficient data from ethnography and archaeology to show strong regularities in cultural evolution.

Within a decade after Boas's death—he died at lunch after presenting an anti-racism lecture at Columbia University—evolution paid another visit to the halls of anthropology. Although evolutionary thinking does not today dominate anthropological explanation, it does play a significant role in archaeology. Evolutionary thought has changed markedly over time, and several current paradigms compete for Darwin's mantle.

A complete description of those paradigms is beyond our scope, but before we consider explanations of world prehistory, we wish to point out three key differ-ences between unilineal and modern evolutionism.

First, modern evolutionism contains none of the racist or moral overtones of nineteenth-century unilin-eal evolutionism. Contemporary evolutionism does not believe that differences between cultures are a product of differences in intellect or morality. Instead, as part of a larger materialist paradigm, modern evolutionism accentuates the role of ecological, demographic, and/or technological factors in conditioning how cultures change.

Second, contemporary evolutionary thinking recog-nizes that, if natural selection is at work on cultural phenomena, it operates in a far subtler manner than it does among animals. Natural selection depends on dif-ferential reproductive success for particular traits to become more prevalent. This means that plants or ani-mals with a favored trait survive and reproduce at a higher rate than those who lack the trait—among ani-mals, by either attracting more mates or by providing more resources to their young. But whereas animals pass most behavioral traits on genetically, humans pass critical behaviors on through culture. Individual hu-mans can also adapt to change, alter their behavior, and adopt new technologies. Their genetic composition does not determine what "tools" they have to be suc-cessful in life. Although anthropology today is marked by considerable debate over the role of natural selection in cultural behavior, anthropologists agree that (1) cul-tural behavior is not genetic and therefore (2) the trans-mission of cultural information from generation to generation does not depend directly on biological reproduction (although one may affect the other).

Third, although unilineal evolutionists argued over the details of the evolutionary sequence, they united in believing in a single immutable sequence. Modern evo-lutionism is not concerned with the evolutionary se-quence of particular cultural behaviors like matrilineal kinship or monotheistic religions. The human past is vastly more complex than nineteenth-century scholars imagined it to be.

More than a century of archaeological research has amply demonstrated the intricate details that make up a particular historical sequence; this is the *specific* evo-lution of particular cultures. But modern evolutionary theory looks at prehistory to extract the "big picture," the *general* evolutionary pattern that characterized the

historical particularism The view that each culture is the product of a unique sequence of developments in which chance plays a major role in bringing about change.

TABLE 15-2 Summary of Differences among Bands, Tribes, Chiefdoms, and States

CHARACTERISTIC	BAND	TRIBE	CHIEFDOM	STATE
Subsistence	Foraging	Foraging, horticulture, pastoralism (herding)	Agriculture; pastoralists often incorporated within society.	Agriculture, industrial, pastoral separated as specialists.
Economic organization	Equal access to strategic resources through sharing and reciprocity	Reciprocity; limited redistribution of goods by charismatic leaders	Chief redistributes goods collected from lower-ranking people; society includes some non-food producers.	Elites control access to strategic resources like land and labor; includes many non-food producers such as craft specialists.
Political organization	Egalitarian; no permanent positions of authority	Egalitarian; temporary and limited roles of authority; competitive feasting to establish rank	Differences in status based on genealogical closeness to chief, who holds a permanent, inherited office.	State controlled by elites and run by administrative specialists; includes military and fiscal specialists.
Social organization	Based on actual and fictive kinship; major units are nuclear family and bands of flexible membership.	Kinship-based, egalitarian descent groups; less flexibility	Kinship important in determining rank; lineages are ranked in clans.	Class membership (elite or commoner) is most important; kinship and descent important within class.
Settlement pattern	Temporary camps; some seasonal settlements reoccupied.	Sedentary villages (temporary camps among pastoralists)	Sedentary villages of different sizes; ranked (chief's village has highest rank).	Hierarchy of settlements reflects administrative functions; may be cities.
Population density	Low	Low to medium	Medium to high	High

deep human past. It is this long-term patterning that concerns us here.

An Evolutionary Sequence

In the rest of this chapter, we examine two major transitions in human cultural evolution—the origins of agriculture and the origins of the state. We begin by situating these transitions into a generalized historical sequence that illustrates some patterns in human cultural evolution (Table 15-2).

Prior to about 12,000 years ago, all our ancestors lived in hunting-and-gathering bands. Although few hunter-gatherer bands survive today, they were common in many parts of the world during the nineteenth century, surviving on wild plants and animals and often changing their camps several times throughout the year. Most settlements housed less than three dozen people, although larger aggregations occurred when resources were particularly abundant.

Hunting-and-gathering bands are *usually* egalitarian (refer to Chapter 13). They lack hereditary differences in social rank and are integrated on the basis of age and gender. Leadership is informal and temporary, based mostly on age, competence, and personal magnetism. The Great Basin Shoshone of the nineteenth century are a frequently cited example of bands, as are the Inuit (Eskimo), South African Bushmen, and Australian Aborigines.

Were it not for the domestication of plants and animals, the entire world would still be living a hunting-and-gathering lifestyle. But we know that agriculture came into being at several places over the past 10,000 years. Archaeologists often refer to agricultural crops as domesticated plants, because the plants are genetically manipulated versions of wild species that came to require human intervention for their continued survival. Modern maize, for example, would have a hard time propagating itself if humans stopped planting it.

It was largely with the advent of domesticated plants that **tribal societies** appeared. Characterized by larger and more sedentary settlements, tribal societies occur throughout the world and vary considerably in appearance. Although community size is generally larger than that of hunters and gatherers, autonomous village societies still lack hereditary differences in rank, and larger villages maintain no authority over smaller neighboring communities. Although everyone in tribal society is

tribal societies A wide range of social formations that lie between egalitarian foragers and ranked societies (such as chiefdoms); tribal societies are normally horticultural and sedentary, with a higher level of competition than seen among nomadic hunter-gatherers.

equal at birth, considerable disparities in prestige can accrue during one's lifetime, and ritual privileges are often differentially distributed along gender lines. Early twentieth-century examples include the Pueblo Indians of the American Southwest, communities in highland New Guinea, and many peoples of the Amazon Basin. Some hunting-and-gathering societies—ones that lived in environments that supported high population densities without recourse to agriculture—are classified as "tribal" as well (such as those along the Northwest Coast of North America, or the Hopewell culture of the midwestern United States; see Chapters 2, 13, and 14).

A third social form, ranked society (discussed in Chapter 13), sometimes evolved when the egalitarian ethic (which downplays success and prestige) gave way to the belief that individuals are inherently unequal at birth. Commonly, certain family groups are considered to have descended from esteemed ancestors, supernatural beings, or gods. The closer this relationship, the greater one's hereditary rank and power. Marrying wisely becomes a way to enhance the rank of your children.

In some societies, such as the Natchez (who lived along the lower Mississippi River at the time of European contact) and many African societies, smaller villages were subject to the powerful, hereditary leadership of the larger, stronger neighboring communities. These societies—large-scale ranked societies with loss of village autonomy—are called chiefdoms. An example includes the prehistoric society of Moundville, which we discussed in Chapter 13.

Under certain conditions, **archaic states** evolved from competing chiefdoms. We use the term "archaic" to distinguish this ancient social form from modern industrial states, which are commonly governed by elected presidents or prime ministers. The term "state" refers to a form of political organization—not to be confused with its modern meaning as an entity within a nation.

Most archaic states operated as kingdoms, characterized by a strong and centralized government with a professional bureaucratic ruling class. The appearance of archaic states marks a major shift in human social organization, because these societies devalued the kinship bonds evident in chiefdoms, tribes, and bands. States maintained their authority through an established legal system and the power to wage war, levy taxes, and draft soldiers. Generally, states had populations numbering (at least) in the tens of thousands, and urban centers exhibited a high level of artistic and architectural achievement. A state religion was usually practiced, even in areas of linguistic and ethnic diversity. The Classic Maya, Aztec, Inka, and ancient Egyptian societies are examples of archaic states.

One final term needs some attention: **civilization.** In common usage, "civilization" refers to behaviors that are ethnocentrically associated with proper behavior and some definition of high culture. But in anthropological terms, no such value judgment is implied. Instead, "civilization" refers to characteristics often associated with the archaic state, such as writing and bureaucratic records, calendrical systems, and the construction of monumental architecture.

Patterns in the Evolutionary Sequence

This sequence tells us several things. First, we know that agriculture is a relatively recent phenomenon, developing only after the end of the Pleistocene period (about 10,000 years ago). But once it appeared, agriculture spread rapidly throughout much of the world. The domestication of plants and animals was hardly a single event; instead, the process happened several times, in several different areas of the world. Figure 15-1 shows the major hearths of plant and animal domestication. These regions are all independent centers of domestication, unconnected to one another, although in many cases the plants and animals they produced eventually spread over much of the globe.

Note also that the shift from egalitarian to ranked society is associated with agriculture. Egalitarian societies are associated with hunting and gathering and **horticulture.** Chiefdoms and states tend to be associated with **intensive agriculture.**

Finally, we have learned that chiefdoms and archaic states appear even later in prehistory than agriculture, only in the past 5000 years or so, and they are always

archaic state A centralized political system found in complex societies, characterized by having a virtual monopoly on the power to coerce.

civilization A complex urban society with a high level of cultural achievement in the arts and sciences, craft specialization, a surplus of food and/or labor, and a hierarchically stratified social organization.

horticulture Cultivation using hand tools only and in which plots of land are used for a few years and then allowed to lie fallow.

intensive agriculture Cultivation using draft animals, machinery, or hand cultivation in which plots are used annually; often entails irrigation, land reclamation, and fertilizers.

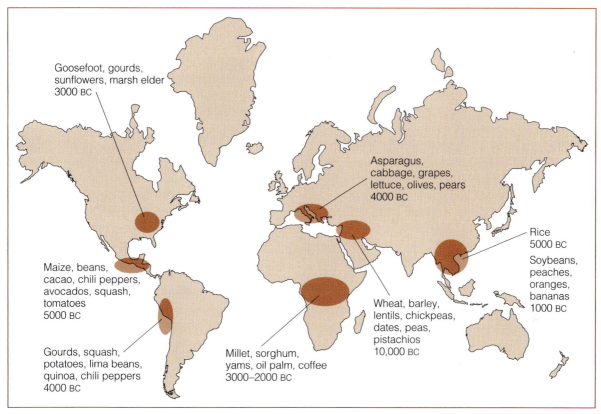

Goosefoot, gourds,
sunflowers, marsh elder
3000 BC

Asparagus,
cabbage, grapes,
lettuce, olives, pears
4000 BC

Rice
5000 BC

Soybeans,
peaches,
oranges,
bananas
1000 BC

Maize, beans,
cacao, chili peppers,
avocados, squash,
tomatoes
5000 BC

Wheat, barley,
lentils, chickpeas,
dates, peas,
pistachios
10,000 BC

Gourds, squash,
potatoes, lima beans,
quinoa, chili peppers
4000 BC

Millet, sorghum,
yams, oil palm, coffee
3000–2000 BC

Figure 15-1 The major hearths of agriculture—places where various wild plants were independently domesticated—and the approximate dates that domestication occurred.

associated with high population densities. No hunter-gatherers live or lived in archaic states; no states are dependent on hunting and gathering for food.

In sum, a century of global archaeological research discerned some links among economy, social and political organization, and population density—links that will be well demonstrated as we explore the origins of agriculture and the origins of the archaic state.

WHY WERE PLANTS DOMESTICATED?

Scholars of the eighteenth and nineteenth centuries were largely unconcerned with explaining the *process* of plant and animal domestication. They focused instead on historical questions, such as when did plant domestication begin, and did it come before or after the domestication of animals? This was, of course, a necessary step, because one cannot ask *why* something happened until you know roughly *when* and *how* it

happened. But once archaeological data began to accumulate, archaeologists shifted their attention from the "what" and the "when" of plant and animal domestication to the "why."

The Unilineal Paradigm: Childe and Braidwood

The **oasis theory** was made popular in the 1940s by Australian-British archaeologist V. Gordon Childe (1892–1957). A prolific author, Childe was one of the first modern archaeologists to synthesize the archaeology of Europe and the Near East.

Childe knew that, as the Ice Age ended, the world's climate became warmer and drier. In desert areas,

oasis theory Proposed by V. Gordon Childe, it argues that animal domestication arose as people, plants, and animals congregated around water sources during the arid years that followed the Pleistocene. In this scenario, agriculture arose because of "some genius" and preceded animal domestication.

Childe argued, people and animals flocked to oases, such as the Nile River, in search of water and food. This association eventually produced a symbiotic relationship between animals and people. People drove away predators and fed animals their surplus grain. Animals became accustomed to humans and were gradually domesticated.

Childe thus assumed that people grew crops before they domesticated animals, but he was unclear about why they became agriculturalists. He simply suggested that people became familiar with the "nobler grasses"— ancient ancestors of modern wheat and barley—that grew on the banks of the Nile, where they thrived on alluvial soil enriched by annual flooding. Childe felt that it remained only for "some genius" to produce similar artificial conditions elsewhere through irrigation and begin to grow wheat and barley.

Although Childe's explanation seemed plausible, the chronology for the Near East was sketchy, and no solid archaeological evidence for early food production was available. Shortly after World War II, Robert Braidwood (1907–2003) set out to search for that evidence. The hilly flanks of the mountains of southwestern Asia seemed a logical place to search because wild wheat, barley, and legumes grew there and wild cattle, sheep, and goats lived there.

So Braidwood set off for the foothills of Iraq and Turkey, directing excavations designed to test explanations regarding the origins of domestication. He obtained some of the first radiocarbon dates on early agriculture and, after learning that climate had been essentially stable during the period of animal and plant domestication, Braidwood rejected Childe's oasis theory.

In its place, Braidwood proposed a **hilly flanks theory,** which saw agriculture developing as a "logical outcome" of the evolutionary tendency to specialize. As foragers "settled in" after the Pleistocene, they became familiar with their plant and animal neighbors; eventually, this accumulated knowledge permitted them to cultivate rather than simply gather plants.

---

hilly flanks theory Proposed by Robert Braidwood, it claims that agriculture arose in the areas where wild ancestors of domesticated wheat and barley grow, attributing agriculture's appearance to human efforts to continue to increase the productivity and stability of their food base, coupled with culture being "ready" to accept an agricultural lifeway.

population pressure The effects of a population reaching carrying capacity.

Although Childe and Braidwood disagreed about the "where" and "how" of plant domestication, both assumed that humanity continually seeks to improve its technology and subsistence. And, because they thought that plant domestication provided a more abundant and reliable economic base than foraging, they also assumed that all it took for agriculture to appear was the *idea* and the *capacity* (the necessary plants). Anyone, they thought, with the idea and capacity would switch from foraging to agriculture. In this regard, Childe and Braidwood still subscribed to a portion of the paradigm of unilineal evolution.

But their explanations ran afoul of both archaeological and ethnographic data. If the idea of agriculture is sufficient, then the transition from foraging to agriculture should be quick (at least in archaeological time). And yet nearly everywhere, that transition was slow. In the eastern woodlands of the United States, for example, native peoples grew squash, sunflower, marsh elder, and chenopods some 4000 years ago. Maize (known in North America as corn), an import from Mexico, appeared in the woodlands about 2000 years ago. But it was only 1100 years ago that a full-fledged agricultural economy based on maize appeared. Because they obviously had the idea of agriculture 4500 years ago and maize 2000 years ago, why didn't these people become fulltime agriculturalists sooner?

Ethnographic research also turned up hunter-gatherers who knew about and understood agriculture, but who continued to hunt animals and gather. Ethnographer Richard Lee (University of Toronto) once asked /Xashe, a Ju/'hoansi man of Africa's Kalahari Desert, why he did not plant food. /Xashe's memorable response was, "Why should we plant when there are so many mongongos [edible nuts] in the world?"

The Materialist Paradigm: Population Pressure

Childe and Braidwood assumed that the idea for agriculture would be picked up by anyone who had it, but /Xashe reminds us that agriculture takes hard work. The forager who wants seeds simply picks and processes them; but the farmer must till the soil, plant the seeds, and later harvest, process, and probably store the seeds. Why would anybody take on the additional labor of agriculture?

In the 1960s, several archaeologists argued that agriculture was related to **population pressure** brought about by slow population growth. Lewis Binford (see Chapter 1) argued that people adopt domesticated plants *only when forced to do so.* In his **density-equilibrium model,** Binford rejected Braidwood's notion that agriculture developed simply because of the accumulation of knowledge. Rather than viewing agriculture as a chance to "move up the evolutionary scale," Binford proposed that agriculture happened when population growth outstrips an environment's **carrying capacity.** Population growth requires that some people move to more marginal environments, and it is these people who turn to agriculture to make up for the lack of high-ranked resources.

In framing this argument, Binford turned unilineal evolutionism on its head. Instead of agriculture being a step up in progress, it became the strategy implemented by the "losers," people who had to make marginal land productive—and who, in the end, needed to work harder. The unilineal evolutionists saw hunting and gathering as an onerous lifeway, with agricultural productivity providing a breakthrough. Binford's hypothesis suggested just the opposite. Who is right?

Is It Better to Farm or Forage?

Binford assumed that some resources were collected more efficiently than others, but he lacked the data to back up this assumption. Bear in mind that the plants we know as the major agricultural plants—such as maize, wheat, millet, and rice—*did not exist* at the end of the Pleistocene. What did exist were their wild forerunners, but these were often substantially different from the domesticated plants of today.

The wild form of maize, for example, is southern Mexico's **teosinte,** a tall tropical grass with a small head of grains on it that is no bigger than your pinky. It looks nothing like the sweet corn you buy at the supermarket. Of all the wild plants that foragers in southern Mexico harvested, why did teosinte become a domesticated one?

The reason is that maize, and other plants that were eventually domesticated, have the latent genetic capacity to be modified. Human use of these plants over many generations—which included the intentional sowing of seeds with favorable characteristics (such as size)—constitutes natural selection. The result of this process is the vast maize fields of Iowa, the extensive rice terraces of Asia, the millet fields of Africa, and so on.

But in the beginning, these domesticated plants were far more modest and one wonders: Why would hunter-gatherers have bothered with them at all? To answer this

question, we must consider a resource's **return rate:** the relationship between the amount of energy a resource provides measured against the amount of time it takes to procure and process (see "Looking Closer: Hunter-Gatherers as Optimal Foragers").

Return rates can be complicated by many factors, but experimental data show that large game generally have high return rates, whereas seeds (including those of wild wheat, barley, and teosinte) have much lower rates. **Optimal foraging theory** predicts that, as high return rate resources (such as large game animals) become scarce, foragers add lower return rate resources (such as seeds) to their diet. Higher return rate resources can become scarce because of environmental change or because a human population has overexploited them. Ethnographic and experimental data suggest that people may have turned to the seeds of those plants that eventually became agricultural plants when high ranked resources, such as large game, became scarce.

But many hunter-gatherers around the world expanded their diets to include a variety of plant resources—including native peoples of California and the Great Basin—yet they did not become agriculturalists (even though California is today one of the world's major agricultural regions). And when Steve Simms (Utah State University) and Ken Russell (1950–1992) conducted ethnoarchaeological research with Bedouins in Jordan, they found the return rate from cultivated wheat (which includes the cost of tilling the soil and sowing the seeds) was little different from the return rate of gathering wild wheat. So, what's the advantage of agriculture?

A Selectionist Perspective

The answer to this question may come from a third paradigm, one that focuses on the underlying process of natural selection.

density-equilibrium model Proposed by Binford, it attributes the origins of agriculture to population pressure in favorable environments that resulted in emigration to marginal lands, where agriculture was needed to increase productivity.

carrying capacity The number of people that a unit of land can support under a particular technology.

teosinte A plant native to southern Mexico; believed to be the wild ancestor of maize.

return rate The amount of energy acquired by a forager per unit of harvesting/processing time.

optimal foraging theory The idea that foragers select foods that maximize the overall return rate.

Looking Closer
Hunter-Gatherers as Optimal Foragers

Optimal foraging theory belongs to the more general paradigm of human behavioral ecology, a framework that studies human behavior by applying the principles of natural selection within an ecological context.

Optimal foraging models assume that foragers try to maximize their *rate* of food intake. Its most widely applied version, the diet-breadth model, asks: Which foods should an efficient forager harvest from all those available? The model assumes that foragers take those food resources that give them, on average, the highest *rate* of energy intake. This requires that we know the return rates of the potential food resources. We obtain these values through ethnoarchaeological and experimental research.

Steven Simms (Utah State University), for instance, was interested in the return rates of the Great Basin's plant resources, such as Indian ricegrass (*Oryzopsis hymenoides*). No one collects these resources today, so he did it himself. After some practice, Simms collected ricegrass seeds the way Shoshone women had done it a century before: He walked through a field, hitting the tops of the plants with a woven "seed beater"—which was shaped like a ping-pong paddle—and knocked the seeds into a basket held in his other hand. After collect-

Figure 15-2   An Aché man hunting.

ing the seeds, Simms ground them into flour using a stone mano and metate.

Timing these activities in one experiment, Simms found that after 41 minutes he had 98 grams worth of ricegrass seed flour. Knowing that ricegrass contains 2.74 calories per gram, he calculated the return rate as follows:

$$(2.74 \text{ calories/gram} \times 98 \text{ grams})/$$
$$41 \text{ minutes} = 6.55 \text{ calories/minute, or}$$
$$393 \text{ calories/hour}$$

David Rindos (1949–1996) argued that plant domestication is an example of **coevolution,** the result of natural selection operating simultaneously on both plants and the people using them. He argued that, because of some plants' genetic composition and because of how they must be harvested, the very act of harvesting them results in unintentional selection in such a way that the plants become dependent on humans for survival. And it is this side of the coevolutionary process that makes

the plant species more productive, such that humans will in turn become more dependent on it: The humans and plants *coevolve.* This may happen, for example, when people plant seeds outside a plant's normal range. Eventually, the people and plants become mutually dependent: The people need the plants for food and the plants need the people to survive outside their normal range. So, whether humans become agriculturalists depends a lot on the genetic capacity of the plants at hand. Eventually, those agricultural plants may provide better return rates than the available wild plants. When that happens, people eschew the gathering of wild plants for domesticated ones.

Rindos ignored the impact of population growth or

coevolution An evolutionary theory that changes in social systems are best understood as mutual natural selection among components rather than as a linear cause-and-effect sequence.

Using such return rate data and information on the time it takes to search for foods, the diet-breadth model predicts which resources a forager should use. Why shouldn't a forager take any food that he or she encounters? Because time spent harvesting and processing one resource is time *not* spent searching for another. Large game, for example, generally take a long time to find, but they have high return rates. Plant foods are easier to find, but they generally have low return rates (some require a lot of processing: Acorns, for example, require repeated leaching to remove tannic acid).

The diet-breadth model predicts which resources a forager should take upon encountering them, and which they should ignore. It therefore predicts whether the diet should be broad and generalized or narrow and focused on a few select foods. The model predicts that, as high return rate resources become rare, the diet should expand and include low return rate resources.

Kim Hill (University of New Mexico) and Kristen Hawkes (University of Utah) demonstrated this principle among the Aché, seasonal hunter-gatherers in the tropical forest of Paraguay. Aché hunters take a range of animals while hunting with bows and arrows, including peccaries (65,000 calories/hour), deer (27,300 calories/hour), birds (4700 calories/hour), and monkeys (1200 calories/hour). When the Aché used shotguns, however, their diet changed. Because shotguns don't require the line of sight necessary for bow hunting, the Aché could forgo lengthy periods of stalking and shoot animals more quickly after sighting them. The optimal foraging model predicted the effect: When shotguns were used, the diet breadth contracted, and small birds and monkeys were ignored. When the Aché went back to using bows and arrows, the diet expanded to include the smaller game.

Optimal foraging models cannot account for foods that are eaten because of their symbolic value nor can it predict which foods will be tabooed for cultural reasons, because the model predicts which foods should be taken *if maximization of the return rate is the only foraging goal*. But with such predictions as a backdrop to an analysis of archaeofaunas and botanical remains, optimal foraging models can help determine which foods were or were not eaten for purely cultural reasons. For example, if the model predicts a food should be eaten, but the archaeological data suggests it was not, then this allows the archaeologist to hypothesize that the particular food was tabooed.

climate change. And he claimed that human intent doesn't matter, that humans "intended" to become agriculturalists as much as certain ant species "intended" to develop symbiotic relationships with fungi. As a Darwinian paradigm, the coevolutionary approach holds that if a particular behavior, such as agriculture, increased the rate of survival of the young, then that behavior would become more prevalent.

Another Look at the Environment

But humans foraged for hundreds of thousands of years before agriculture appeared in the early Holocene period. If Rindos is right, why didn't agriculture appear sooner?

Braidwood would have said that human culture was "not ready for it," but Peter Richerson (University of California, Davis), Robert Boyd (University of California, Los Angeles), and Robert Bettinger (University of California, Davis) argue that it was the environment that was not ready for it.

These scholars point out that the Pleistocene (the 2 million years preceding the Holocene) was an odd time in earth's climatic history. Thick glaciers covered vast parts of the globe and tied up a lot of the world's water supply. As you probably know, this means that sea level dropped. But sea level dropped because there was less water running into the ocean. And there was less water because the Pleistocene was not only colder than today, in many places it was also drier.

Additionally, the Pleistocene atmosphere contained less carbon dioxide (this is why, you will recall from Chapter 8, late Pleistocene radiocarbon dates are so far off from their calibrated calendar ages). Plants take in carbon dioxide through photosynthesis and release oxygen. Less carbon dioxide means that plants were "asphyxiating" in the Pleistocene; consequently, plant productivity was lower. And, to make matters worse, climate was more variable during the Pleistocene than during the Holocene, making plants a less reliable source of food than animals before 10,000 years ago.

For these reasons, Richerson and his colleagues argue that agriculture *could not* have appeared before the Holocene. Rindos's process of coevolution could not have arisen until the Holocene, when plant exploitation could provide a sufficiently abundant and reliable food source. But Richerson adds that, by providing a reliable food source, agriculture caused human population to grow, and the ensuing population pressure forced neighbors to adopt agriculture as a way to increase food productivity (as Binford argued). As a result, agriculture quickly spread during the Holocene to most parts of the globe that could support it and where foraging did not provide higher return rates.

A Social Perspective

So far, each of the paradigms offered to explain the origins of agriculture has privileged the power of human intent and the conditions of environment, demography, and selection. But looking at what we know about agriculture around the world, we see another possibility. In some places, agriculture is indeed *preceded* by population growth—for example, in large sedentary communities. But in other places, such as southern Mexico (where maize was domesticated), sedentary villages appear a thousand or more years *after* plant domestication. And some regions that are suitable for agriculture, such as California, were occupied by hunting-and-gathering peoples until European contact, even though they were densely populated. Population and environment may not be the only relevant variables here.

Some archaeologists, such as Brian Hayden (Simon Fraser University), suggest that agriculture arose as a way to increase productivity so that certain individuals could garner prestige and power through competitive feasts and ostentatious displays of wealth in the form of exotic items obtained through trade (like the potlatch we described in Chapter 2). This increase in productivity, Hayden argues, was possible because new technologies such as nets, baskets, and grinding stones allowed hunter-gatherers to harvest resources such as fish and seeds efficiently, allowing people to create the food surpluses needed for competitive feasts. Hayden argues that efforts to increase productivity for these feasts led people to agriculture.

To support this explanation, Hayden points to another post-Pleistocene trend: the trade of exotic goods, such as carved shells, rare stones, and beads. These trade goods (along with exotic domesticated foods) may have figured in competitive feasts or other social displays of power. And Hayden suggests that this "food-fight" theory explains why some of the earliest domesticates were not essential to subsistence, such as chili peppers, bottle gourds, and avocados.

The Origins of Agriculture in the Near East

Different paradigms clearly offer different explanations for the origins of agriculture, and each one makes some sense. To evaluate these alternatives, let's turn to the archaeology of the Near East, one of the world's major hearths of plant domestication.

In the Near East, agriculture originated in a broad arc of mountains in Israel, Jordan, Syria, Iraq, and Iran—sometimes called the **Fertile Crescent**—where wild wheat and barley still grow today. Although Braidwood saw no evidence for it, significant climate change occurred at the end of the Pleistocene. Based on data from palynology and other studies, we know that around 18,000 years ago, the Near East was cooler and drier than it is today. Annual precipitation and temperature increased until about 13,500 BP but, between 13,000 and 11,600 BP, the world saw a rapid return to cooler and drier but highly variable conditions during a climatic interval known as the **Younger Dryas.** After this time, climate returned to wetter and warmer conditions. And after 9000 BP, the Near East became considerably more arid.

We can't tell exactly when intentional agriculture began, because it's difficult for paleoethnobotanists to distinguish wild wheat and barley from their early

Fertile Crescent A broad arc of mountains in Israel, Jordan, Syria, Iraq, and Iran where wild wheat, barley, and other domesticated plants are found today.

Younger Dryas A climatic interval, 13,000 to 11,600 BP, characterized by a rapid return to cooler and drier, but highly variable, climatic conditions.

domesticated forms. The best evidence suggests that a full-time agricultural economy began about 10,000 to 9000 BP. Less intensive, but nonetheless intentional, cultivation may have begun much earlier. Following is what the evidence seems to show.

Prior to 15,500 BP, nomadic foragers occupied the southwest Fertile Crescent, an area known as the Levant (in Israel, Jordan, and Syria). They lived primarily along major waterways and the Mediterranean coast, hunting gazelle and taking a variety of plant foods. Soon, however, these nomadic folks became sedentary. The **Natufian** culture (ca. 14,500–

Figure 15-3 A portion of a large house at the Natufian site of Ain Mallaha, Israel (in Hebrew, the site is called Eynan). Note the substantial postholes that suggest the house was covered by a large, heavy roof.

11,600 BP) built round, semi-subterranean structures, 3 to 6 meters in diameter, with stone foundations and probably wood-and-brush upper walls and roof; an excavated example appears in Figure 15-3. Abundant remains of house mice suggest a continual source of fresh garbage at these sites, which, in turn, suggests that people were there year-round (this conclusion is supported by seasonality studies of gazelle teeth).

Natufian settlements were located in places where natural stands of wheat and barley were readily available. People harvested these wild cereals, as demonstrated by the plant macrofossils, grinding and pounding stones, and sickle sheen on flint blades. But the plant foods appear to be wild, not domesticated, forms.

The Younger Dryas climatic interval interrupted the Natufian lifeway about 13,000 BP. Some villages were abandoned, and people returned to a more nomadic lifeway as plant foods became less abundant. Ofer Bar-Yosef (Harvard University) suggests that the Younger Dryas may have encouraged the now-large Natufian population to make land more productive by husbanding and later intentionally planting "wild" cereals. The extreme climatic variability of the Younger Dryas interval, however, probably made reliance on agriculture a risky venture.

After the Younger Dryas (ca. 11,600 BP), climate returned to the wetter, warmer, and more stable conditions that are conducive to the growth of cereals. Foragers returned to village life; but this time the villages

were considerably larger, signaling a growth in population. We find these **Neolithic** sites in the mountains, within the natural range of wild wheat and barley. Away from the mountains, nomadic hunter-gatherers living in small, temporary settlements occupied the deserts.

Neolithic sites contain many large, oval dwellings, some containing two rooms. There were storage structures in each site as well, including large stone silos and bins. Flotation has recovered copious amounts of carbonized seeds of barley, wheat, and other plants. We cannot be certain if these plants were cultivated, but they were an important part of Neolithic subsistence. Neolithic peoples still hunted gazelle, and they gathered various fruits and wild seeds.

With the return of a more benevolent climate about 11,600 years ago, habitats opened up that were conducive to agriculture. Bar-Yosef estimates that human population exploded at this time by more than 1000 percent. During the Younger Dryas, people developed the techniques that gave agriculture at least the return

Natufian A cultural manifestation in the Levant (the southwest Fertile Crescent) dating from 14,500 to 11,600 BP and consisting of the first appearance of settled villages, trade goods, and possibly early cultivation of domesticated wheat, but lacking pottery.

Neolithic The ancient period during which people began using ground stone tools, manufacturing ceramics, and relying on domesticated plants and animals—literally, the "New Stone Age"—coined by Sir John Lubbock (in 1865).

Archaeological Ethics
Who Should Control and Own Sacred Sites?

Many places around the United States, as well as in other countries, are considered sacred sites. The Wailing Wall in Jerusalem is sacred to members of the Jewish faith. The Kabbah in Mecca is sacred to Moslems, and Mount Calvary is sacred to Christians. Devil's Tower in Wyoming is sacred to about 30 tribes, and South Dakota's Black Hills are sacred to the Lakota.

Sacred sites are sensitive because they embody religious ideas and history. And (particularly important for this discussion) sacred sites often include archaeological remains. Who should own and control these places?

This issue arose when the Church of Jesus Christ and Latter-Day Saints sought to purchase about 900 acres of land in Wyoming that belonged to the federal Bureau of Land Management (BLM).

The LDS Church originated in upstate New York in 1830, but followers were persecuted in town after town, and they eventually migrated to a new home in the open land of the West. They founded Salt Lake City, the religion's world center today, and many of the faithful moved there in the nineteenth century. Some moved in wagons; others put their belongings in handcarts that

they bravely pushed across the prairies. In 1856, an early winter blizzard trapped one of these handcart parties along Wyoming's Sweetwater River, in a place now known as Martin's Cove. Before rescuers could reach them, 150 members of the party perished.

The LDS Church considers Martin's Cove, located on BLM land, to be sacred, and for this reason it leased the land from the BLM and built an interpretive trail there. In 2001, the church sought to obtain the land permanently. Unable to find suitable land to swap for Martin's Cove (the usual way that the government deaccessions land), the church sought legislative action, and Representative James Hansen (R-Utah) introduced a bill that would require the BLM to sell the land to the LDS Church.

But many organizations opposed the sale. Some pointed out that the church was not the only group with a stake in this land. Although this is the alleged site of the handcart party's suffering (some historians place Martin's Cove at another place on the river), it also contains Native American archaeological sites and portions of the California trail, which many non-church members traveled. Should these groups surrender their interests in the land?

---

rate of gathering wild plants. By 9000 years ago, a growing population now required that the full productivity of agriculture be harnessed, and agricultural communities appeared.

Comparing the Paradigms

So, which explanation is right?

As we pointed out in Chapter 3, paradigms reflect particular perspectives on the world—elevating some variables and downplaying the importance of others. The paradigm channels researchers toward certain explanations and guides them away from others. But because human behavior is complex, it is unlikely that

any single paradigm will adequately capture the entire picture; each just sees one portion of the puzzle. A complete explanation for the origins of agriculture, or any aspect of human evolutionary history, probably requires input from several different paradigms. We can see how this works in the various explanations for the origins of agriculture.

Clearly, agriculture requires a working knowledge of plant foods. But the plants that would eventually be domesticated were being used at least 18,000 years ago; surely, foragers did not require *thousands* of years to understand that seeds produce plants. Unilineal evolutionists might have argued that these ancient hunters lacked the intelligence to understand plants sufficiently

Another concern was that Hansen's bill would set a dangerous precedent. If the church was allowed to buy Martin's Cove, then shouldn't any organization be allowed to buy any piece of federal land that the organization considered sacred? Jack Trope, executive director of the Association of American Indian Affairs, said that there is inadequate protection of Native American sacred lands on federal property and that the Martin's Cove bill could remedy this by opening the door to the purchase of sacred sites by tribes—places such as Devil's Tower and the Black Hills.

Should sacred sites on public land be sold or transferred to the organization or group that considers them sacred? Many such sites are sacred to more than one group (such as Devil's Tower). Who gets to own them? And what about stewardship? Although one might assume that those who consider a site sacred will take good care of it, how could we guarantee that the views and opinions of other stakeholders will be considered?

And if we sell public lands that one group considers sacred, are we only furthering the balkanization of cultures within the United States? At present, sacred lands that are public property are the subject of ongoing discussions about the relations between people. Take

Devil's Tower, for example. This nearly 1300 foot-tall basalt tower (made famous in Steven Spielberg's movie *Close Encounters of the Third Kind*) is climbed by some 5000 people each year. Some tribes wish the climbing to cease, because climbing Bear's Lodge (as Devil's Tower is known to some tribes) is akin to scaling a cathedral or mosque for recreation. The monument currently has only a voluntary ban in effect for June, when Sun Dances are held nearby. Many climbers obey the ban out of respect for the tribes, although some professional guides disregard it. Should Devil's Tower be owned and controlled by the tribes? What's the right thing to do?

On the one hand, it might seem appropriate for those who consider land sacred to control it. But if we balkanize the landscape into "your" sacred land and "my" sacred land, don't we lose the continuing conversation between the peoples of different religions and cultures that is so vital to a democracy?

This concern is reflected in the position taken by the United States government with respect to Martin's Cove. In the fall of 2003, after legislative efforts failed, the LDS Church agreed to an offer of a 25-year extension to its current lease and, for the time being, has dropped efforts to purchase the property.

to be agriculturalists. But these were the same people who were capable of fine artistry and tool manufacture (as evidenced by Upper Paleolithic art and stone technology), and their hunting strategies required detailed understandings of animal behavior. Certainly, these late Pleistocene foragers were every bit as intelligent as people today. Knowledge is necessary *but not sufficient* to explain the origins of agriculture.

As Childe suggested, climatic change also clearly has something to do with agriculture, although not in the way he thought. Foragers could not become agriculturalists until the environment was capable of supporting agriculture, and this may not have happened until the early Holocene. And the Younger Dryas clearly altered

the Natufian lifeway, requiring that a former sedentary foraging population make the land more productive, through the cultivation of wild wheat and barley.

Did population pressure play a role? The earliest evidence for agriculture does not come from marginal areas (contrary to Binford's expectations), but from the homeland of wild wheat and barley. Evidence from Natufian settlements also suggests that population growth had caused some groups to become sedentary on choice localities that included stands of wild wheat and barley. By the beginning of the Neolithic, this expanded population may have congregated around these localities and created local population pressure on resources, requiring people to expand their diets and rely more heavily on plants. Because wheat and barley respond genetically (through selection) to human harvesting by becoming more abundant, their domestication was perhaps inevitable.

What about social processes? Did competitive feasting have anything to do with agriculture? Natufian settlements do provide archaeological evidence for trade—sea shells, some from as far away as the Atlantic Ocean, beads made of rare stone, and figurines carved in bone and stone. Many burials contain elaborate personal ornaments, including necklaces, belts, bracelets, and headdresses. It is possible that these ornaments indicate trade relations that, in turn, reflect the building of social alliances. But Natufian sites lack storage structures (which appear only in Neolithic sites). And wheat and barley were important to the diets of both, not peripheral "luxury" items. Natufian and Neolithic communities were probably self-sufficient, and the need for alliances probably arose much later. However, it is likely that feasting and trade created alliances that were critical to survival when crops failed or animals migrated in the climatically uncertain world of the Younger Dryas. Agriculture may have helped make possible the feasts that, in turn, helped to form those social alliances.

Finally, what about human intentionality? Rindos claimed that human intentionality had nothing to do with agriculture and, at one level, this must be true: It's unlikely that a forager in the Levant woke up one morning 10,000 years ago and decided to become a farmer. But human intention must have played *some* role. The changes that occurred in the wild cereals suggest that humans *intended* to increase harvest productivity and efficiency, for example, by saving the largest seeds for the next planting, by transporting plants to favored localities, or by irrigating natural stands. They *intended* to forage as well as possible, and these intentions led them to agriculture.

Processes and conditions similar to those we've described for the Near East were also at work in Asia, Africa, and the Americas. We still have much to learn about the origins of agriculture. In this brief overview, we have tried to provide a feel for the paradigms archaeologists use to understand this research problem, how archaeological data can be used to evaluate

affinal Relatives that one is related to by marriage, rather than blood.

hypotheses, and how most paradigms contribute some pieces to a research puzzle.

WHY DID THE ARCHAIC STATE ARISE?

We now turn to a second major transition in human cultural evolution, the origins of the archaic state. Some instances where archaic states arose are shown in Figure 15-4. Nearly every student of anthropology today lives in a state society, and some probably consider the state to be the "natural" form of human social and political organization. But not so long ago (in archaeological time), nobody lived in a state society. Evolutionarily speaking, states are simply the latest form of human organization (and probably not the last). How did they arise?

We first need to define what we mean by the archaic state. There are many definitions; we follow one proposed by Kent Flannery:

> The state is a type of very strong, usually highly centralized government, with a professional ruling class, largely divorced from the bonds of kinship which characterize simpler societies. It is highly stratified and extremely diversified internally, with residential patterns often based on occupational specialization rather than blood or **affinal** relationships. The state attempts to maintain a monopoly of force, and is characterized by true law.

Not all archaic states fit this definition exactly, but it points out the salient aspects of most such political formations.

The archaic state is a complex form of sociopolitical organization. States generally have powerful economic structures and often a market system. An elite controls the state economy and maintains authority by laws and by privileged access to key goods, services, and ideology. Archaic states generally have populations numbering at least in the hundreds of thousands, and this population is often concentrated in large cities. Some people were specialists—potters, weavers, stone masons, and so on—who depended on the labor of others for subsistence (that is, they did not grow their own food). Archaic states are also known for a high level of artistic achievement, monumental architecture, and an "official" state religion.

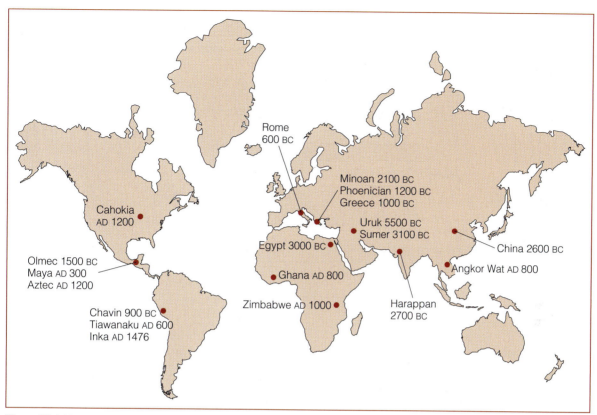

Figure 15-4 Major primary archaic states; these are places where state forms of political organization developed independently.

Theories about the origin of the archaic state date from the nineteenth-century evolutionists. As with agriculture, unilineal evolutionists argued that "civilization" appeared when people were intellectually and morally prepared to enter into a social contract and to give up some of their liberties in exchange for benefits, such as protection in time of war. As with agriculture, this approach fails to explain why states originated where and when they did.

We know that the formation of archaic states did not depend on domesticated animals, metal tools, or wheeled transportation, because states appeared in places such as Mesoamerica where none of these existed prior to European contact. The first three explanations we'll present—which privilege irrigation, warfare, population growth, and environment—fall within the materialist paradigm. A fourth explanation focuses on the role of ideology and falls more within the postprocessual paradigm. As with the origins of agriculture, we believe that it's possible to reconcile these different views.

The Irrigation Hypothesis

In his influential book *Oriental Despotism* (1957), Karl Wittfogel (1896–1988) asserted that the mechanisms of large-scale irrigation were directly responsible for creating the archaic state. His **irrigation hypothesis** argued that irrigation systems require an extraordinary level of coordination above the individual farmer. How this works is shown in Figure 15-5. First, someone must construct the system, dig the channels, and build the dams and headgates. This requires organization above the household, because portions of the system benefit everyone, but not all portions benefit each individual household (for instance, the ones downstream from your home). Irrigation systems are inherently problematic, because people living upstream could take all the water, leaving nothing for those downstream. Wittfogel

irrigation hypothesis Proposed by Karl Wittfogel, it attributes the origin of the state to the administrative demands of irrigation.

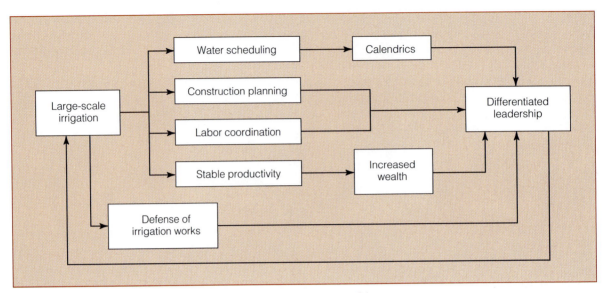

Figure 15-5 Schematic diagram of Wittfogel's irrigation hypothesis for the origin of the state.

pointed out that this means that irrigation systems inherently require a level of continuing control above that of the individual farmers who benefit from it.

Wittfogel argued that the great Asian societies of China, India, and Mesopotamia followed a radically different evolutionary course than did the societies of western Europe and elsewhere. The particular forms of archaic states in the Orient evolved because of the conditions required by large-scale irrigation—the imposition of inordinately strong political controls to maintain the hydraulic works, the tendency for the ruling class to merge with the ruling bureaucracy, the close identification of the dominant religion with governmental offices, and the diminution of private property and economic initiative.

Wittfogel contended that, after a creative period in which the bureaucracy began, stagnation set in, corrupting power and creating a despotic and feudal system. He also saw the hydraulic society as an initial step toward totalitarianism (a German intellectual who spent time in a concentration camp for speaking out against the Nazis, Wittfogel was vehemently antifascist).

According to Wittfogel's theory, the state evolved in direct response to the demands of large-scale irrigation. The need for coordinated labor, massive construction, and so forth led to increased wealth and military strength and eventually to the powerful ruling bureaucracy that characterized state development.

The Warfare and Circumscription Hypothesis

Ethnologist Robert Carneiro (American Museum of Natural History) terms Wittfogel's irrigation hypothesis a "voluntaristic" theory, one requiring that "at some point in their history, certain peoples spontaneously, rationally, and voluntarily gave up their individual sovereignties and united with other communities to form a larger political unit deserving to be called a state." In this respect, Wittfogel's explanation is more in line with unilineal evolutionism—that is, people give up individual freedoms when they are ready to take the next "step" in cultural development. But by studying modern tribal societies and chiefdoms, Carneiro knew that autonomous political units never willingly surrender their sovereignty, and he saw no reason why they should have done so in the past.

Carneiro argues, instead, that egalitarian settlements transform into chiefdoms, and chiefdoms into states, only when coercive force is involved; warfare thus plays an especially pertinent role in the early stages of state development, as shown in Figure 15-6. Of course, some tribes might agree to cooperate in times of stress, but such federations are temporary and voluntarily dissolved once the crisis has passed. Carneiro's initial premise stipulates that political change of lasting significance arises only from coercive pressure. And warfare, he suggested, is the only mechanism powerful enough to impose bureaucratic authority on a large scale.

© Robert Kelly

Figure 15-6 A carving of a decapitated head from the 3500-year-old site of Cerro Sechín in Peru. The carving is one of 400 decorating a stone facade that forms the base of a platform mound. The facade is covered by images of warriors and the jumbled body parts of their victims. Some archaeologists believe this frieze commemorates a mythical or historical battle.

It is clear from the archaeological record, however, that warfare is considerably older and more widespread than the state. Because warfare does not invariably lead to archaic state formation, Carneiro adds that, though *necessary*, warfare is not *sufficient* in itself to account for the state. According to Carneiro, only in areas where agricultural land is at a premium—areas that are environmentally "circumscribed"—will warfare lead to state formation. Competition over land arose first where natural barriers—such as mountains, deserts, or seas—restricted the availability of arable land. The vanquished peoples had no place to flee and thus were required to submit to the expanding political units of the victors. A centralized political authority was needed to maintain a standing army as well as to control conquered populations.

In Carneiro's **warfare and circumscription hypothesis**, shown in Figure 15-7, the combination of population growth and circumscribed agricultural resources leads to increased warfare, which in turn fosters the centralized political organization characteristic of state-level complexity. He musters support for his hypothesis from the archaeology of initial archaic states near the Nile, the Tigris-Euphrates (Mesopotamia), the Indus Valley, and the valleys of Mexico and Peru—all of which evolved in areas of circumscribed agricultural land. Conversely, in areas where agricultural land was plenti-

ful and not tightly bounded—such as in northern Europe, central Africa, and the eastern woodlands of North America—states were quite late in developing, if they did at all.

A Multicausal Theory

Scientists often propose ideas before the data to evaluate them are available. This was certainly the case with Wittfogel's and Carneiro's explanations for the rise of the state. But over the past few decades, archaeologists have studied the origins of the state all over the world, in places such as Mesopotamia, the Indus Valley, Mesoamerica, China, and the Andes. From these studies we can see that neither irrigation nor circumscription and warfare alone account for all the archaeological data. In some places, irrigation exists without states; in others, states exist without irrigation agriculture. In some, warfare precedes state formation, but in others, it follows. As with agriculture, it is impossible to specify a single "prime mover" for states. No *single* condition is both *necessary* and *sufficient* to create an archaic state.

As we pointed out above, in studying the origins of any social institution it is important to differentiate between the *conditions* that generate cultural change and the *process* that actually creates the change. Drawing on three case studies—France, Japan (both during the Middle Ages), and the Inka—ethnologist Allen Johnson (UCLA) and archaeologist Timothy Earle (Northwestern University) searched for more general conditions rather than specific factors. They concluded that three general *conditions* are necessary and sufficient for archaic states to form:

1. High population density that strains the food production system

warfare and circumscription hypothesis Proposed by Robert Carneiro, it attributes the origin of the state to the administrative burden of warfare conducted for conquest as a request of geographic limits on arable land in the face of a rising population.

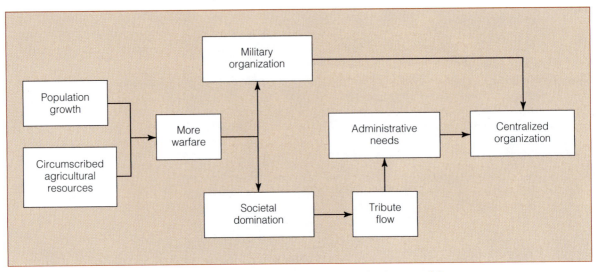

Figure 15-7 Schematic diagram of Carneiro's circumscription and warfare hypothesis for the origin of the state.

2. A need for a system of integration (such as trade or irrigation)
3. The possibility that the economy could be controlled to permit the financing of regional institutions (such as a state religion) and to support a ruling class

Given these *conditions*, however, any number of specific *processes* can result in a state.

Figure 15-8 shows how these conditions might result in social change as population grows after agriculture. A growing population demands that land become more productive. Horticulturalists, such as Madagascar's Mikea (see Chapter 10), may use slash-and-burn farming, where a plot of land supports one to three harvests and is allowed to lie fallow for some time. As population grows, however, a family cannot switch their land because all available land is occupied. If there are no new fields, people must artificially fertilize land. The native peoples of northeastern North America did this with fish remains. In the Near East, people used manure from domesticated animals. Lacking domesticated animals, the Aztec collected the "night soil" from residents of large villages for use as fertilizer.

As the best arable land is used, some people are pushed to marginal lands (as Binford argued). Here they must develop intensive agriculture, using labor-intensive ways to make land more productive. This can entail canals that must be maintained as they fill with silt and debris. In mountainous regions, people build terraces along hillsides (as they did at Machu Picchu) to create flat, arable land where there had been only a steep hillside. The Aztec created **chinampas**—long, low islands in shallow lakes—by dredging soil from the lake bottom and piling it up. All of these require labor and, at some point, the system simply cannot produce more at a given level of technology.

So, what happens during an environmental calamity, when a severe drought, flood, or insect plague strikes?

Today, farmers in developed nations have insurance to buffer against disasters. In the past, horticulturalists also tried to buffer environmental fluctuations. The Hopi and Zuni Indians in the American Southwest, for example, plant fields of maize in different environmental locations. They plant some on south-facing hillsides, others on hilltops, and still others on the valley floor. They know that, by putting their fields in different microenvironments, they increase the probability that at least one of those fields will survive. If one field is lost to drought, another might prosper; if insects attack one field, the others might be spared.

As population grows, the need for such buffering strategies increases. These include family-level decisions, such as field placement and long-term household

chinampas A form of intensive agriculture; low mounds the Aztec built by piling up sediments from the bottoms of shallow lakes and marshes to form islands of arable land.

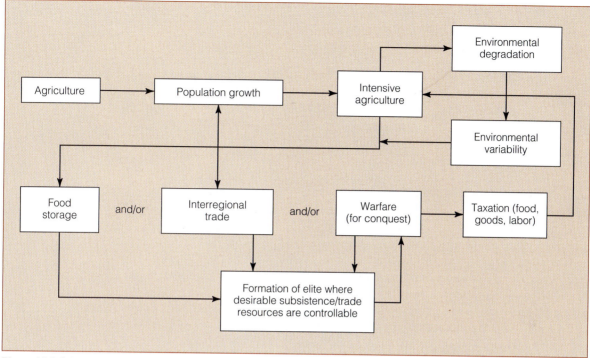

Figure 15-8 Schematic diagram of multicausal origins of the archaic state.

food storage, but they also include group-level responses, such as interregional trade, conquest, or some sort of cooperative system of exchange, perhaps based on religious obligations. These group responses require a system of social integration. This is also the point at which the specific *processes* of state development can differ. States will have different histories and will take on different characters depending on whether trade, warfare, or religion is the primary "system of integration" (the theory's second condition).

At some point, the individuals who negotiate the relations between groups take on a special importance. These middlemen could manipulate and exploit social ties—marriages and trade relations, primarily—between villages and centers in times of stress. They are individuals who, for whatever specific reason, hold sway over a productive resource by controlling territory and/or labor. A system of social integration therefore might create Johnson and Earle's third condition: the possibility that an individual or group could control the economy to permit the financing of regional institutions and to support a ruling class.

In times of stress, people living under high population densities compete for land and resources. Some unfortunates may petition those who control produc-

tive land for some of their stores, land, or protection. If those who control productive land do not share, they themselves could be attacked. By allowing others to migrate to their territory or share in their long-term stores, those on productive land buy security. And it appears that they did this by exacting tribute or taxation from the petitioners, which they then used to support an army as well as their entourage or court. By controlling key resources, some individuals become the "elite."

Such social systems, however, require an "explanation" that provides an account of why some people are elite and some are peasants. What role does ideology play in the origin of archaic states?

The Role of Ideology in State Formation

To this point, we have explored the *material conditions* that create archaic states. This is because processual research provided an understanding of how significant cultural change takes place when the technology and economic base changes. Subsistence-level change produces population growth that eventually requires new mechanisms to buffer fluctuations in the food base. This, in turn, cause shifts in social organization.

Ideological changes develop as a means to validate the new social organization—to explain why some people live in luxurious houses with servants and the best food, while others toil in the fields and inhabit more humble abodes.

By **ideology,** we mean the cultural, religious, or cosmological ideas that provide group members with a rationale for their existence. *Ideology masks the fact that one group is exploiting another.* Unilineal evolutionism, for example, was an ideology in the sense that it provided a justification for the domination of colonized lands by Western nations.

In archaic states, ideologies are often linked to religion, and here we see how the kinship links that tie the elite in chiefdoms to the population often become severed in states. In early states, the elite claimed that they were different from everyone else and that they deserved their lofty position, because they were descended from the gods. If they considered themselves kin to the peasants, then this would mean that the peasants, too, were kin to the gods. Such a situation could undermine the elites' control of the region's resources. That archaic states often suffered internal warfare is evidence that people can sometimes see through the ideology.

Ideologies have a tendency to take on a life of their own, and here is where they can play a causal role in the development of states. As we pointed out in Chapter 14, humans see the world through their own cultural logic, a logic that is expressed as a particular symbolic system. This "cultural" world can provide its own engine of change. If kings are descended from the gods, then they should be all-powerful. If they are all-powerful, then shouldn't the entire world be under their rule? Possibly for this reason, states tend to be expansionist, eventually collapsing when they reach beyond their physical limits of control. Sometimes this expansion is militaristic, and sometimes it is based on religion (we saw a possible example of this in Chapter 14's discussion of the expansion of the Chavín culture in central Peru).

The Maya: A Case Study in State Formation

As we did with agriculture, let's take these abstract ideas and see how they help us understand a particular case, the lowland Maya of Central America. Figure 15-9

Figure 15-9 A map of the lowland Maya region, with sites discussed in the text. Many other Maya sites exist in the lowlands, the Yucatan Peninsula, and the highlands to the east in Mexico, Guatemala, Honduras, and El Salvador.

shows the location of some of the sites we mention below.

We have visited the Maya in previous chapters. Here we focus on the lowland Maya, who lived (and still live) in Mexico's Yucatan Peninsula, Belize, and portions of Guatemala and Honduras. Some occupied the Petén rain forest, and others lived on the more arid Yucatan Peninsula.

By 5000 BP, agriculture had begun in the highlands to the west of the lowland Maya region. Here the Maya grew maize, beans, squashes, pumpkins, chili peppers, amaranth, and cotton. As expected, population grew after a shift to full-time agriculture, and some people apparently moved into the lowland regions.

Evidence for human settlement of the lowland Maya region pre-agricultural is limited. This is partly due to the difficulty of finding small, ephemeral sites in a forest that is dense enough to hide large stone temples and partly due to the fact that Maya settlements destroyed earlier occupations. But current evidence suggests that few people lived in the area until maize horticulturalists moved there about 4000 years ago. Settlements from this time period lack any large public

ideology A set of beliefs—often political, religious, or cosmological in nature—that rationalizes exploitative relations between classes or social groups.

buildings, elaborate burials, or exotic trade items, suggesting that the early farmers were egalitarian.

The Middle Preclassic Period: Population Growth

During the Middle Preclassic Period (900–300 BC) population grew, emigrants arrived from other areas, and a lively trade developed in colorful feathers of tropical birds and animal skins. Archaeological surveys show that all major regions of the lowlands were occupied by sedentary, slash-and-burn horticulturalists by 500 BC. This growth apparently approached the region's carrying capacity, for farmers were finding ways to make the land produce more food. In the swamps of Belize, for example, farmers built raised fields, much like the Aztec *chinampas* we described above. They also grew a greater variety of crops, including maize, but also beans, squash, tomatoes, chilies, ramon and cashew nuts, avocado, papaya, guava, and cacao (chocolate). Still, analyses of skeletal isotope data suggests that maize sometimes constituted only about 30 percent of the diet, and faunal data show that white-tailed deer, turtles, fish, and dogs were eaten.

The increase in population precipitated a change from more or less egalitarian communities to small chiefdoms. Some of these late Middle Preclassic period centers were quite large; Nakbé, for example, covered some 50 hectares (125 acres). These centers contained large buildings and stone platforms, built with public labor. Previously, people were interred beneath the floors of houses but, during the Middle Preclassic, some individuals were buried within the stone platforms or the buildings themselves. Patricia McAnany (Boston University) suggests that these burials signal a shift to **ancestor worship,** a religion in which one's deceased ancestors serve as important intermediaries between the natural and supernatural. From ethnographic data, anthropologists know that ancestor worship tends to occur with restrictive claims on land, and the burials within the public structures may have served to justify a kin group's claim to territory. Thus, by the end of the Middle Preclassic period, groups exerted control over land just, as we might expect, at the time when all land was occupied.

The Late Preclassic Period: Formation of Chiefdoms

By the beginning of the Late Preclassic Period (300 BC– AD 250) a few sites, such as Altar de Sacrificios and Seibal, developed into towns of several thousand people, but no single center emerged. The Maya built public buildings in these centers, some including the corbelled arch. (Arches with a keystone did not exist in the pre-contact New World; corbelled arches were made by piling stone blocks up, moving each layer in a little closer until the walls could be bridged with a lintel stone.) They also erected stelae using local hieroglyphic styles, and they participated in a lively trade in exotic goods, including polychrome pottery, jade, and obsidian.

Survey data suggest that the regional population grew again by some 350 percent during the Late Preclassic Period, and people aggregated into a few large settlements. El Mirador, for example, covered some 15 square kilometers and contained more than 200 stone structures. One was a pyramid some 182 feet high; another was built atop a hill, with multiple tiers cut into the hillside. Others were large public buildings decorated with plaster and stone masks of deities. And at Nakbé and El Mirador, extensive stone causeways were built to traverse the swamps. These rose 4 meters high in places and were filled with crushed white stone.

Nonetheless, during most of the Late Preclassic, Maya political organization had no single center. Instead, many small centers controlled the territory around themselves.

The Classic Period: State Formation

But this changed near the end of the Preclassic Period and during the Classic Period (AD 250–700), when the lowland Maya took on the characteristics of the archaic state. There is evidence for warfare in earlier times, but now it seems that Maya leaders wrestled for control over centers, as attested to by burned buildings, fortifications such as palisades and moats, and mass burials of males with fractured bones—all of which first appear in the Late Preclassic. The causeways connected sites, suggesting alliances between the centers. Such evidence of supra-village control and coordination is a hallmark of the state.

During the Classic period these centers became solidified, albeit temporarily, as states. The sites of Tikal (tee-*call*) and Uaxactún (wah-shock-*toon*) became major centers, and others soon followed. Tikal, shown in Figure 15-10, would grow to cover 16 square kilometers and house some 80,000 people (larger than sixteenth-century London). It contained numerous

---

ancestor worship A religion in which one's deceased ancestors serve as important intermediaries between the natural and supernatural.

© San Diego Museum of Man, photo by Peter D. Harrison, Ca. 1993

Figure 15-10 A painting by Carlos Vierra (1915) of Tikal based on his imagining the site's appearance soon after its abandonment.

stone public buildings, causeways, and pyramids with remarkably steep stairways leading to ceremonial chambers and astronomical observatories on their tops (see this chapter's opening photo). Hieroglyphs became standardized across the southern Maya lowlands, suggesting the development of a common political culture and some kind of political interaction and coordination.

Survey data indicate that population continued to grow throughout the Classic Period. As many as 10 million people lived in the lowland Maya area—more than live there today. Moreover, this population was more concentrated. Many Preclassic centers were abandoned during the early Classic period, and their inhabitants moved into the large centers, such as Tikal. So, not only does the overall population increase, there is also an *aggregation* of population during the Classic period in large centers.

Population growth and aggregation created new problems for the Maya as they exacerbated the local effects of drought and conquest. Stable isotope, macrobotanical, and faunal data suggest that the commoners had an increasingly more monotonous diet of maize, while the elite continued to enjoy a more varied diet. And skeletal data show that males decreased in average height during the Classic period.

Producing enough food to feed the growing and aggregated population may have been difficult. Many of the centers were located next to *bajos*—low-lying areas that today are little more than swampy ground. Research by Vernon Scarborough and Nicholas Dunning (University of Cincinnati) suggests that in the past, the *bajos* were shallow lakes that could have provided the Maya with freshwater. By 100 BC, these *bajos* had filled with silt that washed in as slash-and-burn horticulture denuded the surrounding land of forest. As the *bajos* filled up, Late Preclassic centers relocated.

In Classic centers, and even in some Preclassic sites, Scarborough and Dunning found extensive water collection and control devices. The Maya modified natural gullies, runnels, and basins to channel runoff into small artificial reservoirs. Causeways and plazas were not just a way to keep one's feet out of the mud, but were also part of a system of water catchment and dams. At Tikal, the paved areas could capture some 900,000 cubic meters of water in a single season. Some of the catchment basins are positioned to provide water for fields surrounding the *bajos*, but direct evidence for irrigation is still lacking.

The large centers contained rectangular ballcourts, sunken stone-walled courtyards, sometimes with stone rings mounted high on the two long side walls; one is shown in Figure 15-11. The ballgame first appears in Preclassic sites and, although nobody knows exactly how the game was played, it likely involved driving a rubber ball through the stone rings without using hands or feet. This was more than just entertainment, because ballgame images depicted on polychrome pots and stone carvings clearly depict human sacrifice as part of the ritual "game." By the time of the Spanish conquest, the game was played throughout Mesoamerica with a new twist: The winning team and their supporters pursued the losers and their boosters to take their clothing and jewelry.

Commoners lived in compounds of stone-walled, thatch-roofed houses with above- and belowground storage structures. In the arid north, the belowground storage structures, called *chultuns*, probably were used to store water. Status differences are reflected in house compounds of different sizes and the presence of exotic goods such as jade and obsidian. Elite burials became more elaborate and contained exotics and labor-intensive items such as polychrome pottery.

Figure 15-11 A ballcourt at the Maya site of Copán, Honduras. The stone rings are visible above the sloping left wall.

ate the gods. Without these rituals, the Maya believed, chaos would reign and the universe would collapse. Kings and their power were essential to the world's continuity. Power flowed from father to son or from brother to brother, and royal families were ranked in terms of their kinship distance from the king.

Seeing themselves as descended from the gods, these kings competed with one another to determine who was the greatest among them. In fact, David Webster (Pennsylvania State University) suggests that the Maya might have seen war as a way for Maya kings to not only subdue unruly neighbors but also to demonstrate their ability to quell the potential for chaos in the world. Warfare, the need to control subdued centers, and the need to reward those who supported the king in these endeavors produced the political hierarchy of the Maya in the Classic period. The stelae and other evidence on monumental architecture record the exploits of the elites. It is this hierarchy of power that makes Maya Classic centers archaic states.

We know that Maya courts were places of intrigue and backroom deals, perhaps like those in Medieval and Renaissance Europe, with lords and sublords plotting coups and competing for power. Iconography between AD 250 and 600 is replete with images of warfare; some sites show evidence of violent destruction, such as the toppling of stelae, and subsequent rebuilding.

This hieroglyphic evidence also tells us that, by AD 700, the internecine competition among the many small centers had reduced itself to a single rivalry between Tikal and Calakmul (kah-lock-*mool*). Each of these centers was allied with several smaller centers. These alliances were the result of centuries of warfare, with one center eclipsing another only to be conquered by a former rival. Tikal and Caracol, for example, fought for 250 years. Caracol eventually eclipsed Tikal in AD 562 only to become an ally of Calakmul later (along with the centers of Naranjo and Dos Pilas). Tikal

The Maya also had an elaborate calendar (in fact, they had three; see "Looking Closer: How the Maya Reckoned Time"), and they marked the dates of events on the stelae that we have discussed in previous chapters. After years of hard work, Tatiana Proskouriakoff (1909–1985) and Yuri Knorosov (1922–1999) figured out how to read the glyphs. Using the stelae and other archaeological sources of information, we can piece together the shifting rivalries of Maya political life.

During much of the late Classic Period, the lowlands were divided into numerous centers that alternately competed and allied with one another to control stretches of land and to garner prestige. The glyphs carved on stelae and painted on pottery tell us the names of the *K'uhul Ajaw*, or "divine lord," who ruled over a Maya capital. For instance, the royal name of a seventh-century ruler of Palenque was K'inich Kan B'alam ("Great Sun-Snake Jaguar"); a fourth-century ruler of Tikal was Yax Nuun Ayiin ("First Crocodile"). Maya kings had some of the coolest names in prehistory.

But the Maya were not trying to be cool. The names were intended to reflect a king's divine status. Maya kings claimed to be descended from the gods; the stelae portrayed their lives and succession to the throne as repeating mythical events of the past. To reinforce Mayan ideology, the kings conducted rituals at auspicious times according to the ritual calendar to propiti-

Looking Closer
How the Maya Reckoned Time

The Maya were keen observers of astronomical events, and their rituals were governed by three precise calendars. The Maya did not invent these calendars, but they appear to have perfected them.

The first of these calendars was the Long Count. Figure 15-12 shows the two sides of a jade plaque that commemorates the ascent to the throne of one of Tikal's rulers, Zero-Moon-Bird (his name appears as one of the glyphs). On one side, Zero-Moon-Bird wears a jaguar headdress and tramples a captive underfoot. On the other is a series of glyphs. Look at them closely, and you will see that five of them have bars and/or dots to their left. These are calendar glyphs, and they date Zero-Moon-Bird's coronation.

The Maya used bars to symbolize five and dots to symbolize one (a stylized shell stood for zero). The Long Count dates an event by counting the number of days that have passed since "the beginning of time." The date is given in a series of units: *Baktun* are units of 144,000 days; *katun*, units of 7200 days; *tun*, 360 days; *uinal*, 20 days; and *kin*, 1 day. The number of each unit is denoted by the bars and dots. Looking at the figure, we see that the second glyph from the top—the baktun glyph—has one bar (indicating 5) and three dots (3) next to it for a total of 1,152,000 days (144,000 × 8). The next glyph down (the katun glyph) has 2 bars (10) and 4 dots (4), for a total of 100,800 days (7200 × 14); likewise there are 3 tun (1080 days), 1 uinal (20 days), and 12 kin (12 days). Archaeologists write Long Count dates as the

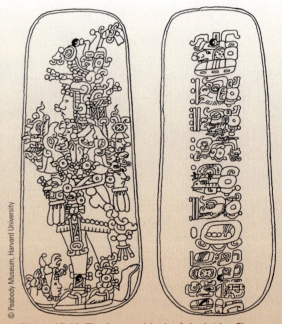

© Peabody Museum, Harvard University

Figure 15-12 The front and back of the Leiden Plaque; on the back are glyphs that indicate the age of the event depicted on the front.

series of units; in this case, 8.14.3.1.12. The total number of days is their sum: The event depicted occurred 1,253,912 days since the beginning of the calendar.

Although epigraphers debate it, many place the beginning of the Maya calendar at August 13, 3114 BC. So the date in the Gregorian calendar is approximately

returned to power, allying itself with Palenque and other centers. Eventually, around AD 695, Tikal defeated Calakmul, captured its war effigy (a large jaguar carving), and may have killed its ruler, Jaguar Paw. These shifting alliances and changing centers of power were no different from those of Europe in the sixteenth through nineteenth centuries.

Conquered populations sent annual tribute to the royal court of the victor in the form of cotton, feathers, shells, jade, cacao, and possibly maize and labor. Much of the warfare was status-related. By dominating powerful neighbors, a king communicated his authority to his people. And by assisting that king, lesser nobles could earn privileges and acquire control over conquered resources that might permit them to move up in status.

No single Maya center was ever able to maintain control over the entire lowlands; nor did any center main-

$$1,253,912/365 = 3435.37$$
$$3435.37 - 3114 = 321.37 \text{ AD}$$

We then subtract a year, because the Gregorian calendar implies a "0" year BC. Count the days from the calendar's start date, and the glyph gives a date for Zero-Moon-Bird's coronation as September 17, AD 320.

The second calendar is called the *tzolk'in*, or Sacred Almanac (shown in Figure 15-13). It is best envisioned as two cogged wheels, one with the numbers 1 through 13 on it, the other with 20 named days (such as "flint knife," "monkey," and "lizard"). This defines a sacred year of 260 days (13 × 20) with each day having a unique number-name combination.

The third calendar was the *haab*, or Vague Year, which consisted of 18 months of 20 days each, with 5 extra days added at the end. (The Maya were aware that the year was 365.25 days in length, but they did not use a leap year.) The Vague Year and the Sacred Almanac worked together to produce a cycle of 18,980 days. The exact same day—with the same number-name combination and Vague Year day—occurs only once every 52 years. The days when the 52-year cycle began over were critical to the Maya and required world renewal ceremonies.

The Maya recognized cycles of time, and a return to the beginning of time (or the end of time, some say), according to the Maya calendar, will occur on December 23, 2012.

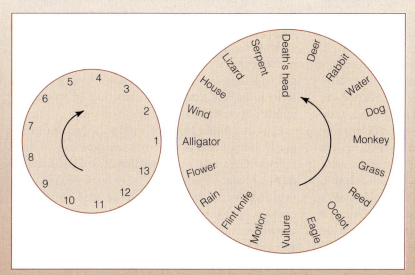

Figure 15-13 The Sacred Almanac. Each day has a name and a number. Envision the two wheels turning opposite to one another, and you can see that the current day is "1 alligator," tomorrow will be "2 wind," the day after tomorrow "3 house," and so on.

tain control for many generations. Still, it appears that some tried. And in the act of trying, the Maya meet the definition of an archaic state.

So, What Explains the Origin of the Maya State?

All archaeologists who try to explain the origins of a *particular* state find it nearly impossible to put their finger on the single factor without which the state would not have formed. Instead, each explanation points to one or more important conditions. Carneiro's explanation focused on competition over land generated initially by population pressure, and some evidence supports this idea in the Maya case. Raised-field agriculture, occupation of virtually all land, the control of water, high population estimates, and human skeletal analyses all suggest that the Maya had reached the land's carrying capacity. And, in one sense, Maya land was circumscribed—by the ocean to the east, the dry Yucatan Peninsula to the north, and the highlands to the east and south (which witnessed their own population growth).

But the archaeological evidence also shows that the control of water played a role in determining where the centers were erected. Although it is unclear whether the water was used to irrigate fields, this is less important than the level of organization and authority needed to construct the reservoirs and to apportion the water. So, in one sense, Wittfogel's "irrigation hypothesis" also plays a role here.

But both explanations can be subsumed under the more general scenario of Johnson and Earle. Recall that their explanation required three conditions: (1) stress on food resources created by high population density, (2) the need for an overarching system of integration, and (3) opportunities for economic control. All of these characteristics are found among the Maya of the late Preclassic and Classic periods. The high population density places pressure on the agricultural economy and, in dry years, this pressure can be so severe that it leads to outright conflict. Warfare, as well as efforts to prevent it, requires a system of social integration, as do efforts to ensure the flow of trade goods, information, and rituals between allied centers. The large centers, however, had the ability to control labor and, hence, agricultural productivity and warfare. It is possible that, as one large center gained the edge in authority, families moved to it and smaller centers gave their allegiance (and their labor) in return for protection. To maintain their positions of power, leaders of the large centers controlled the religion and calendrical rituals that provided a powerful integrating ideology for the Maya.

So when we examine the material and ideological fundamentals of Maya culture, we see that they satisfy each of Johnson and Earle's three conditions. As with the origins of agriculture, there is no single "prime mover" to account for the development of a particular archaic state, and various paradigms each contribute something to a final explanation.

Conclusion

We have only briefly discussed the origins of agriculture and the archaic state. The specific developmental sequences for each differ widely throughout the world, but the variables of population, environment, warfare, trade, and ideology all seem to play key roles in one or both of these cultural changes. The specific *processes* that gave rise to the transition differ from case to case, but the general *conditions* appear to be similar. Explanations that seek to attribute these major changes in human cultural evolution using single variables—such as knowledge, environment, irrigation, or warfare—seem to be less useful than ones that incorporate a number of variables and perspectives.

Human cultural behavior and large-scale change in social and political organization are products of multiple variables that work in different combinations in different parts of the world. One of archaeology's tasks is to reconstruct these different, specific historical sequences. Another is to use these sequences to discover conditions that are both sufficient *and* necessary to account for major transitions in cultural evolution. In this chapter, we have recounted two instances in which archaeologists have tried to do precisely this.

Summary

- The nineteenth-century idea of unilineal evolution claimed that the differences among modern peoples resulted from differential progress various peoples had made toward "modernity"—which was defined as an upper-class, western European lifestyle.

- Living "primitives" were seen as providing evidence of the stages of human cultural evolution; for some scholars, "primitive" peoples were still "back in the Stone Age."

- Darwin did not actually use the term "evolution" in his revolutionary work *On the Origin of Species,* but he provided social Darwinists with a scientific explanation for why some peoples had not made progress, as well as the expectation that primitive peoples would all become extinct.

- Social Darwinism suggested that human progress depends on competition and, in the nineteenth century, this theory was used to justify global imperialism, racism, and the excesses of capitalism.

- American anthropology rejected unilineal cultural evolution, replacing it with historical particularism that sought to understand each culture within itself, not as a stage in human evolution.

- Archaeology's processual agenda, with its emphasis on adaptive processes, brought back an interest in evolutionary processes by focusing on the degree of regularity in human behavior. Archaeological research does show some patterns in human cultural evolution; in particular, increasing population density is associated with major changes in economy and social/political organization.

- The origins of agriculture appear to have resulted from (1) climate changes at the end of the Pleistocene that were favorable for plant domestication,

(2) population growth that caused foragers to take less efficient resources, including small seeds, and (3) the existence in some places of plants that responded to human foraging by becoming more

- Archaic states appear to be a response to (1) population growth and the resultant need to intensify agriculture, (2) coordination of mechanisms of social integration, such as trade and ideology, and (3) the potential to control productive resources. The specific character and history of an archaic state, however, depends on the particular environmental situation, the importance of warfare versus trade, and the kind of ideology that supports the elite rulers.

- Archaeology uses specific historical sequences, constructed through a more humanistic approach to prehistory, to determine what conditions are necessary and sufficient to explain major cultural evolutionary transitions.

Additional Reading

Coe, Michael, and Mark Van Stone. 2001. *Reading the Maya Glyphs.* London: Thames and Hudson.

Harrison, Peter. 1999. *The Lords of Tikal: Rulers of an Ancient Maya City.* London: Thames and Hudson.

Price, T. Douglas (Ed.). 2000. *Europe's First Farmers.* Cambridge: Cambridge University Press.

Price, T. Douglas, and Anne Birgitte Gebauer (Eds.). 1995. *Last Hunters—First Farmers: New Perspectives on the Prehistoric Transition to Agriculture.* Santa Fe: School of American Research Press.

Sabloff, Jeremy. 1989. *The Cities of Ancient Mexico: Reconstructing a Lost World.* London: Thames and Hudson.

Schele, Linda, and David Freidel. 1990. *A Forest of Kings: The Untold Story of the Ancient Maya.* New York: William Morrow.

Smith, Bruce. 1995. *The Emergence of Agriculture.* New York: Scientific American Library.

Toby, Susan. 2004. *Ancient Mexico and Central America.* London: Thames and Hudson.

Online Resources

COMPANION WEB SITE
Visit **http://anthropology.wadsworth.com** and click on the Student Companion Web Site for Thomas/Kelly *Archaeology,* 4th edition, to access a wide range of material to help you succeed in your introductory archaeology course. These include flashcards, Internet exercises, Web links, and practice quizzes.

RESEARCH ONLINE
WITH INFOTRAC COLLEGE EDITION
From the Student Companion Web Site, you can access the InfoTrac College Edition database, which offers thousands of full-length articles for your research.

16 Historical Archaeology: Insights on American History

Outline

Preview

HISTORICAL ARCHAEOLOGY is currently one of the most important directions in Americanist archaeology, but to this point, we have only briefly glimpsed what historical archaeologists actually do (for example, in discussing Thomas's excavations at Santa Catalina on St. Catherine's Island, Georgia). In this chapter, we look at historical archaeology in more depth.

Historical archaeology is fundamentally similar to the prehistoric archaeology that we've discussed. Both fields maintain high standards of excavation, dating, and interpretation but, because of its close relationship with the discipline of history, historical archaeology has its own distinctive flavor. Commonly less concerned with grand explanation, historical archaeologists can often shed light on those lesser-known aspects of the historical past (such as the daily life of slaves), correct mistaken assumptions about history, and use the archaeological record to derive views of the past that sometimes contrast with the picture derived from documentary evidence alone.

INTRODUCTION

Archaeologists have been investigating historic-period sites for a very long time. In fact, the first bona fide historical archaeology in America took place about 150 years ago. James Hall, a trained civil engineer, was a direct descendant of Miles Standish, who arrived with the Pilgrims aboard the *Mayflower* in 1620 and eventually became a leader in Plimouth Colony. Wanting to learn more about his celebrated ancestor, Hall located the foundations of the Standish homestead in Duxbury, Massachusetts and, in 1853, he conducted detailed excavations there.

For more than a century, Hall's field notes and artifact collection from the Standish house remained unknown to anybody but immediate family members. In the 1960s, however, they surfaced in Mexico and were brought to the attention of James Deetz (1930–2000), a historical archaeologist working at Plimouth Plantation. As he looked over the surviving materials,

Deetz was impressed at the high quality of Hall's 1853 excavation.

After carefully gridding the site and establishing datum points to maintain vertical control, Hall made a meticulous site map. He tried to recover artifacts *in situ*, plotting their locations onto this master site map. He even recorded stratigraphic relationships within the house ruin. After the excavation, Hall cataloged each artifact, carefully numbering each find. In short, Hall's 1853 excavation technique comports nicely with today's standards of acceptable archaeological practice.

Almost simultaneously, a second pioneering exploration in historical archaeology took place in Canada, under very different circumstances. In 1855, the Canadian government commissioned Father Félix Martin, a Jesuit priest from Montreal, to explore and excavate the site of Sainte Marie, Georgian Bay (near Midland, Ontario).

Custer's Last Stand (1899) by Edgar Samuel Paxson (1852–1919). Historical archaeology asks: Is this how it happened?

Sainte Marie was a tiny mission outpost founded in 1639 to bring Christianity to the local Huron Indians. Although they were 800 miles west of their supply base in Quebec, the missionaries enjoyed some success and several left the mission proper to work with surrounding Huron communities. But during the winter of 1648–49, the Huron villages in this area came under attack from raiding Iroquois war parties. The resident Jesuit priests refused to flee, and several died martyrs' deaths. In March, the surviving priests abandoned Mission Sainte Marie. Although it had lasted only a decade, Sainte Marie became a sacred place in Christian history, what archaeologist Kenneth Kidd would later describe as "the pulsating heart of French missionary effort in America."

Father Martin had this heritage in mind when he went to Sainte Marie in 1855. Seeking to establish a personal link to his own Jesuit past, Martin identified the site's location, mapped and described the ruins, painted several watercolors, and conducted limited excavations. Years later, the Jesuit Order purchased the site to encourage its preservation and make it available for religious pilgrimages. Today, the Martyrs Shrine Church stands nearby, honoring both the Jesuit missionaries and the Christian Huron people who once lived there.

These two mid-nineteenth-century digs illustrate two important themes that eventually came to distinguish the field of historical archaeology. For one thing, both excavators were motivated by a dynamic and personal connection to their own past—Hall to his Pilgrim heritage and Father Martin to the legacy of his martyred Jesuit brothers. For both men, the past had a special relevance to the present.

Both excavators also were familiar with the documentary sources relating to their excavations. This meant that, before looking to the archaeology of their respective sites, they had some knowledge of what to expect: where to dig, what to look for, and generally what kind of material record they should encounter—expectations derived from basic historical sources. By themselves, however, these historical sources were incomplete and not entirely satisfying. Encountering the archaeological record itself—the physical remains of the past—induced Martin and Hall to undertake their own excavations.

So, what constitutes modern **historical archaeology**? Kathleen Deagan, the historical archaeologist profiled

in Chapter 1, defines the field as "the study of human behavior through material remains, for which written history in some way affects its interpretation." Although this simple definition certainly captures the field, others point out that, because historical archaeology encompasses the last 500 years, historical archaeology also inherently must address the history of colonialism and capitalism. Below we will show you how historical archaeology takes on different flavors depending on which of these definitions you choose.

Why Do Historical Archaeology?

At this point, you might be asking yourself, why bother with the archaeology of historical sites if they are already described in documentary sources? Won't archaeology, with its problems of context, preservation, and interpretation, always prove inferior to the written sources?

Documentary sources can indeed be superior to archaeology. But they can also be quite selective and biased. Slave owners wrote little about the day-to-day life of slaves because they did not think it important, and slaves only rarely wrote letters or diaries, because most were illiterate (and often forbidden from learning). Most authors of documentary sources were biased toward the interests of their particular cultural, political, or ethnic group, and sometimes the documentary sources are simply wrong. Today, archaeologists look at archaeological and documentary records *as equally valid yet independent* lines of evidence. Rather than discard differences between the two as "exceptions" or "noise," we sometimes look for "ambiguities" between the historical and archaeological evidence, recognizing that *differences between the two are as important as each piece of information alone.* We will demonstrate in this chapter that historical archaeology is an essential component to our understanding of the relatively recent past.

HISTORICAL ARCHAEOLOGY: JUST A "HANDMAIDEN TO HISTORY"?

In the early days, excavations in historic period sites merely supplemented the "known," documentary view of the past. In the words of Ivor Noël Hume (former director of the archaeological program at Colonial

---

historical archaeology The study of human behavior through material remains, for which written history in some way affects its interpretation.

Williamsburg, Virginia), the proper role of historical archaeology was to serve as a "handmaiden to history"; the historical archaeologist was effectively "a historian with a pen in one hand and a trowel in the other."

This perspective was particularly evident in projects closely linked to historical reconstruction and restoration. Archaeologists, for instance, recovered most of the architectural detail necessary to restore and interpret public sites such as Plimouth Plantation (Massachusetts), Jamestown and Colonial Williamsburg (Virginia), and Fort Michilimackinac (Michigan). Such projects in historical archaeology began in America in the 1940s and 1950s, concentrating on a very few selected sites—particularly houses of the rich and famous, forts, and other military sites.

Colonial Williamsburg served as a model for this early-stage historical archaeology. Architectural historians concentrated most of their early excavations at Williamsburg, their goal being little more than exposing historic-period building foundations. They did not dig very carefully and showed little interest in the trash middens and smaller structures that would eventually captivate archaeological interest. Only later did historical archaeologists follow the example of their colleagues in prehistoric archaeology and develop independent, artifact-based methods for dating sites and components.

Historical Archaeology Comes of Age

Things changed markedly in the 1960s, partly because of the growing impact of cultural resource management. Federal legislation from the 1960s requires that archaeology be done in advance of construction projects (we will discuss this further in Chapter 17). This "applied" version of archaeology proved to be a boon for both prehistoric and historical archaeology. In the beginning, most historical archaeologists received their training on prehistoric sites. But today, the field of historical archaeology is highly specialized, with its own journals and professional societies—and not just in the United States, but around the globe. Historical archaeologists today study everything from the earliest colonial settlements to early nineteenth-century mining camps to World War II battlefields (Figure 16-1).

© Lin Poyer

Figure 16-1 A World War II plane in the Marshall Islands. Today, historical archaeologists study everything from the colonial past to World War II–related sites.

Early on, Lewis Binford clearly saw that historical archaeology readily fit beneath the umbrella of processual archaeology. Binford himself excavated at Fort Michilimackinac, an eighteenth-century French-British frontier site on Mackinac Island, Michigan. Binford believed that archaeologists could pursue processual objectives on historic-period sites only if historical archaeologists would recognize the importance of transcending their own particularistic objectives.

Stanley South (University of South Carolina) helped the transition along. In his influential book *Method and Theory in Historical Archeology* (1977), South argued that historical archaeologists should work within an explicitly evolutionary framework, employ logically grounded scientific methods, apply quantitative methods to data analysis, and formulate the findings of historical archaeology as timeless, spaceless generalizations about the human condition.

Characteristics of Historical Archaeology

Contemporary historical archaeology is every bit as diverse as the rest of Americanist archaeology, but three key factors provide historical archaeology with a slightly different flavor from its prehistoric counterpart.

For one thing, modern historical archaeology often has a *postprocessual* slant to it. Because historical archaeologists commonly have access to texts, ethnohistoric data, and oral traditions, they can often learn something about the meanings of symbols, ethnic affiliation, income, religion, occupation, family composition, economic network, and political restrictions—even before putting a trowel into the ground. It is not surprising, then, that a preeminent historian of archaeology, Bruce Trigger (McGill University), has argued that the most successful symbolic studies lie in the field of historical rather than prehistoric archaeology. The availability of textual information has also made possible many humanistic inquiries, such as Janet Spector's study of gender relations among the nineteenth-century Eastern Dakota people (Chapter 2). Spector's analysis would have been considerably less convincing had she worked on the archaeology of Paleoindian people living 12,000 years ago, without benefit of ethnographic or ethnohistoric documentation or the rich oral traditions of living descendants. Historical archaeologists are hardly wed to a postprocessual agenda, but the field is certainly amenable to it.

In addition, it is true that historical archaeology, especially as practiced in the United States, deals with time periods that are considerably shorter than are those of prehistoric archaeology. Documentary sources can often provide the precise years that a structure (or site) was used, along with detailed information on how its use changed over time. Prehistoric archaeologists may consider themselves lucky if they date an assemblage to a span of a few hundred years. Historical archaeology tends not to study large-scale processes, such as those we discussed in Chapter 15. Instead, the high degree of temporal resolution of historical archaeology leads historical archaeologists to focus on the specific individuals and events that were part of those larger processes—for example, how a nineteenth-century frontier fort's trash reflects the development of the world trade system.

Finally, we must recognize that historical archaeology is often very close to us—not just temporally (the last 500 years in the United States), but also emotionally—whether one is of European, Hispanic, African, Native American, or Asian descent. The archaeology of the last five centuries records the time that all these different peoples came together and created the modern world. And discussion of this recent history is embedded in the continuing discussion of the modern world, with all its cultural, political, and ethical challenges. Because relatively few members of minority groups are professional archaeologists today, such discussions of the recent past can sometimes become emotionally charged (see "In Her Own Words: Why Are So Few African-Americans Doing African-American Archaeology?" by Theresa A. Singleton).

Remember from Chapter 3 that many postprocessual archaeologists argue that archaeology should be more politically aware and proactive. For historical archaeologists working in this paradigm, this can mean using archaeological evidence to expose the ideologies that mask the social contradictions within society and to "emancipate" people by allowing them to evaluate history for themselves.

Themes in Historical Archaeology

These characteristics suggest three major themes of research in historical archaeology today. Although these directions hardly capture all of historical archaeology—and each theme exists within prehistoric archaeology as well—they seem to define the dominant research domains within historical archaeology today.

In Her Own Words
Why Are So Few African-Americans Doing African-American Archaeology?

Theresa A. Singleton is professor of anthropology at Syracuse University.

By concentrating on ethnic minorities that are both culturally and physically distinct from the white majority in the United States, archaeologists inadvertently created an ethnic archaeology of the Other. The results, combined with the fact that the archaeological profession in this country is almost totally white, have produced a study of ethnicity that more often reflects the perspectives of its investigators than the perspectives of those being investigated—an outcome that is the exact opposite of what this research was intended to do. Such realities are difficult to face and when raised are highly controversial, but archaeologists are beginning to address these concerns....

The fact that too few of the archaeologists engaged in this research are African-Americans is only part of the problem. A far more serious problem is that African-Americans are rarely involved in this research in any substantive way. Most discussions concerning the involvement of blacks in African-American archaeology consider blacks only as consumers of this research, rather than as part of the research process. Input from African-Americans should also be considered in generating questions to be investigated and in the interpretation of the results.

The development of an African-American archaeology that is informed by African-American perspectives should involve the following: First, it should expand on the existing African-American resources used in archaeological studies. Many archaeologists use WPA [Depression-era] narratives, but other comparable material such as the antebellum autobiographies of African-Americans or other scholarly creative writings of African-Americans are rarely used. Second, it should establish stronger alliances between archaeologists and African-Americanists. This research interest began isolated from the work of African-Americanists, but there is no reason that it should continue within this vacuum. Although individual archaeologists work with African-Americanists, these collaborations have not resulted in formal research and training programs. Finally, it should include as part of the project the particular black community in which the research is being undertaken. These communities should not be viewed only as activists for or consumers of an archaeological product; they are contributors to an ongoing dialogue that maximizes the interpretive potential of the archaeological record. Only when archaeologists begin to realize that the inclusion of African-Americans is an asset to this research will African-American archaeology cease to be just another anthropological discourse of an Other.

First, modern historical archaeology has shied away from a focus on the "oldest," "largest," and "most historically significant" sites, favoring instead the study of historically disenfranchised groups. Many historical archaeologists are working to uncover the history of African-American and Asian-American cultures, Native Americans during the historic period, and Hispanic-Americans—peoples whose histories are still sometimes ignored, only partially recorded, or related in a biased manner. There is a distinct parallel here to W. W. Taylor's call of a half-century ago, when he urged archaeologists to transcend the grandiose and to get on with the anthropology of "real" people (see Chapter 1).

Second, historical archaeology commonly tackles questions about the recent past that history books answer unsatisfactorily. In this regard, some historical archaeologists are more like forensic archaeologists (which we will discuss in Chapter 18), collecting data like crime scene detectives to resolve disputes over the nature of key historical events.

Third, we see many historical archaeologists researching the nature of European colonialism (the developing capitalism of that time) and its effects on indigenous peoples. The postprocessual emphasis on power, for instance, meshes easily with historical archaeology's ample record of developing capitalist society of the last several centuries. Some use this research to challenge standard public presentations of mainstream history, calling into question, for example, the melting pot interpretation of America's past. This approach challenges citizens to think more critically of their history.

Let's look at some examples of each of these themes in historical archaeology.

Hidden History: The Archaeology of African Americans

African-American history is inextricably linked to slavery, and especially slavery on plantations. Plantation archaeology began in 1931 at Mount Vernon (Virginia), George Washington's home. In his role as director of research and restoration at Mount Vernon, Morley Jeffers Williams—a landscape architect—wanted to locate the various structural remains on the property, so he conducted extensive and systematic archaeological testing. Although hardly up to contemporary standards, these excavations did permit the reconstruction of the first president's garden and outbuildings and kicked off the study of plantation archaeology, as we now know it.

Most early plantation archaeology was aimed at architectural reconstruction and, prior to the 1980s, few restored plantations addressed the issue of slavery explicitly. Instead, the restorations usually emphasized the "big house" and the grandeur of the elite who lived there; guides commonly referred to slaves as "servants." This often-melancholy, *Gone with the Wind* perspective focused on the passing of an antebellum way of life (one that many white people saw as genteel, although descendants of slaves hold a different opinion).

Slave archaeology began in earnest in the late 1960s—doubtless connected to, or inspired by, the social upheavals of the time—when Charles Fairbanks (1913–1984) began exploring coastal plantations in Georgia and Florida. Fairbanks was the first to study the institution of slavery from the archaeological record and, when he emphasized the richness and diversity of the Southern heritage, he was clearly departing from the traditional "melting pot" theme in America. Fairbanks and his students set out to dispel myths concerning the biological and cultural inferiority of African-Americans—myths that were being used to legitimize continued segregation and discrimination (an example of the political use of archaeology).

Today, the field of African-American archaeology is a growth industry, helping to uncover information about aspects of slave life on which the documentary sources are often silent. We can demonstrate this by looking at the slave archaeology of Monticello, the home of Thomas Jefferson.

Slave Archaeology at Monticello

Visitors motoring up the serpentine driveway to Thomas Jefferson's Monticello, shown in Figure 16-2,

© William Kelso and the Thomas Jefferson Memorial Foundation

Figure 16-2 Low-level aerial photograph showing Monticello (at the upper right) and Mulberry Row (the line of trees running horizontally through the middle of the photo).

are first struck by the world-famous architecture, the vast gardens, and glimpses of mountains in the sprawling Virginia countryside. Walking through Monticello, polite guides provide the visitor with ample details about the life of Thomas Jefferson—the third president, architect, inventor, scholar, diplomat—and archaeologist.

But only recently have we heard much about Thomas Jefferson the slave owner. In the days when Jefferson lived at Monticello, the approach to the main house was called Mulberry Row, and it was lined by 19 buildings—the houses and workshops of Jefferson's slaves, hired laborers, artisans, and indentured servants. The mansion at Monticello still stands, attracting tourists by the thousands, yet today aboveground traces of all but four of the structures along Mulberry Row have vanished.

Historical archaeologists working at Monticello have brought Mulberry Row back to life. Work here was begun by William Kelso (currently director of archaeology for the Association for the Preservation of Virginia Antiquities "Jamestown Rediscovery" project), and it continues under Monticello's archaeology program, directed by Fraser Neiman.

Jefferson had mixed feelings about slavery. He had a slave force numbering 200 people at times and knew that, without slave labor, the agrarian economy of the day would collapse. Yet he regarded the institution of slavery as preeminently brutal and immoral—and he personally favored its abolition. Recognizing this dilemma, Jefferson once said that slavery is like holding a wolf by the ears: "We can neither hold him nor safely let him go. Justice is in one scale, self-preservation in the other."

Jefferson reportedly did not mistreat his slaves, but he doubted whether Caucasians and Africans could successfully create a biracial society (despite the fact that he probably fathered six children with Sally Hemings [1773–1835], one of

his house slaves). Instead, he favored a plan to transport free blacks back to Africa or elsewhere.

How Well Did Jefferson's Slaves Live?

Research at Mulberry Row is aimed at learning more about the living and working conditions of Jefferson's slaves. Although few ruins were visible, Kelso soon found by exploratory excavation that the subsurface record of Mulberry Row was relatively undisturbed (Figure 16-3). The residents of Mulberry Row were probably the house servants and artisans who may have enjoyed a better standard of living than the field hands, who lived in settlements farther down the mountain.

Homes along Mulberry Row contained pig, cow, and deer bones; some of these bones were ground up, suggesting the use of meat in stews. Houses also contained ceramic assemblages, dating to AD 1770–1800, that were probably the remnants of table settings from Jefferson's home. No longer usable in the mansion (perhaps having lost a few key pieces), they were given to slave families. These hand-me-downs reflect the growing

Figure 16-3 Excavating slave dwellings built during Jefferson's lifetime at Monticello. Evident in this picture are the remains of Building l, the storehouse (foreground); Building m, the smokehouse-dairy (center); and the rebuilt walls of an 1809 stone slave house (background).

consumer revolution of the late eighteenth century and the availability of houseware replacements.

Social Life in Slave Houses

Neiman points out that the archaeology of Mulberry Row helps to answer a question posed by the historical documents. About 1776, Jefferson mapped his plan for buildings along Mulberry Row and included a building, some 17 × 34 feet in dimension, which he labeled the "Negro Quarter." By 1790, this building had burned and, in 1792–1793, Jefferson built several smaller homes on the site; these he labeled structures r, s, and t on a map made in 1796. He intended these structures to be slave homes; they were only 12 × 14 feet in dimension and were made of split logs, with dirt floors and chimneys of wood and mud.

In 1793, Jefferson served as President Washington's secretary of state, but he still minded the details of his plantation. Jefferson wrote to his overseer, instructing him to move Critta Hemings (the sister of Sally Hemings) and her family to the new House r. Hemings had been living in Building e—a stone house still standing today along Mulberry Row—and she was part of the house staff. According to Jefferson's description, Building e had two rooms, each about 290 square feet in size. It had a brick floor, a stone fireplace, and a single entry door decorated with a pedimented portico supported by columns.

Taken at face value, Hemings appears to have been demoted—she had to move to a smaller house with dirt floors and no architectural embellishments. Yet, she continued as a house servant—normally a favored status. In fact, Jefferson instructed the overseer to place her and her family in House r because "she is wanted around the house." How do we explain this apparent paradox?

The answer comes from the archaeology. The excavations at Monticello retrieved data on nine of the slave houses located on Mulberry Row (Figure 16-4). Three of the houses date to the 1770s (based on documentary evidence and ceramic dates; see Chapter 8). According to Jefferson's maps, the "Negro Quarter" house contained two large rooms, but only a single entryway. The two rooms had separate fireplaces that shared a single flue. A second building originally had a plan similar to that of the "Negro Quarter." A third structure was a single large room, some 250 square feet in size, with a single entryway and a wood and clay fireplace.

These houses contained what historical archaeologists call "sub-floor pits," or cellars. These are rectangular holes, some 3½ × 4 feet, and 1 to 3 feet deep. The early houses at Monticello contain up to four of these pits.

These early houses at Monticello are fairly typical of slave dwellings throughout the Chesapeake Bay area in the eighteenth century (although at other plantations, early slave houses usually contain four to ten sub-floor pits). The function of the sub-floor pits is not clear, but they probably served as places for families to store important belongings. If so, then they suggest that multiple families occupied the early slave dwellings. Neiman points out that theft is a real concern in situations where you have little choice over your housemates. The sub-floor pits may have helped maintain a semblance of privacy and security in an otherwise open structure, because it would have been difficult to steal something if first it had to be exhumed from a pit.

Beginning about 1790, however, a transition in housing occurs at Monticello and at other plantations in the region (Figure 16-5). Houses became smaller—about 140 square feet (although they then became larger in

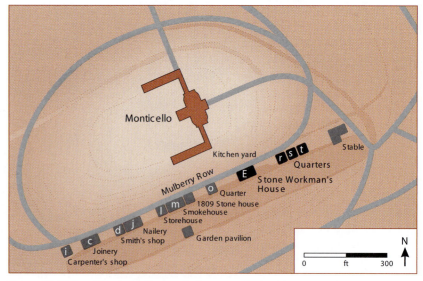

Figure 16-4 Map of Monticello showing the locations of buildings excavated along Mulberry Row. *Used by permission of the Monticello Department of Archaeology.*

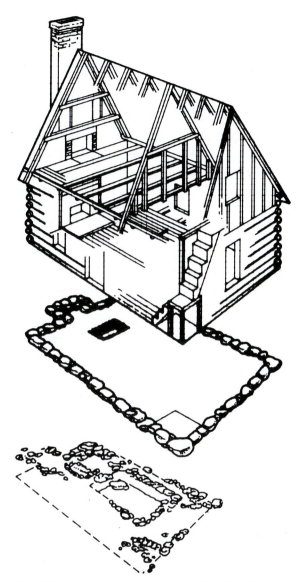

Figure 16-5 Artist's reconstruction of post-1790 slave housing at Monticello. This figure shows a view of a typical slave cabin and its foundation (with a single sub-floor pit in front of the fireplace) superimposed over the archaeological plan (servant's House o) at Monticello.

the early nineteenth century)—and were extremely modest, consisting usually of a single room. But they had only one sub-floor pit, not multiple pits, and these pits are smaller. This suggests that only one family lived there, and they did not have much need to stash possessions out of sight. And even where structures had two rooms, the rooms were separated by a solid wall, and a separate door opened into each room, permitting privacy. In fact, no sub-floor pits have been found in slave houses that date after AD 1800 at Monticello.

So, when Jefferson asked that Critta Hemings and her family be moved to House r, perhaps this was not a demotion. Instead, Hemings would now live in her own house, with her immediate family, where she could control her own household. A home of her own must have seemed quite a step up in her world.

But it must have been a small consolation. After all, she and her family were still slaves.

Beyond Plantation Archaeology: New York City's African Burial Ground

When most people think of slavery, they think of the Old South and a cotton-based economy. How many people know that slavery was deeply ingrained in the economy north of the Mason-Dixon Line as well?

But we were all reminded of this forgotten past when, in 1991, the bones of 427 enslaved Africans, interred by their own community and forgotten for centuries, were discovered beneath a parking lot in downtown New York City at a place now known as the African Burial Ground.

Slavery in Old New York?

The story begins in 1626, when the Dutch West India Company unloaded its first shipment of enslaved Africans in New Amsterdam (today's New York City): 11 young men from what today is the Congo-Angola region of southwestern Africa (Figure 16-6). Two years later, the Dutch imported three African women "for the comfort of the company's Negro men." The Dutch at the time were experiencing a labor shortage in their colonies, and they found slave labor to be the answer to building and maintaining the colony.

Some scholars argue that the Dutch treated slaves better. They point out that some slaves had more rights than New Amsterdam's Jews, who were forbidden from owning land or serving in the militia. Under the Dutch, the Africans were permitted to intermarry with whites, attend white churches, own property, and enjoy the same status as whites in court.

According to this view, the Dutch practiced half-freedom; true slavery was introduced in 1664, when the Dutch ceded Manhattan to the British. At that time, enslaved Africans made up about *40 percent* of New Amsterdam's total population. Everywhere one looked in colonial New York, there were toiling slaves—loading and unloading ships on the waterfront, building the streets, and erecting the buildings to house the people

Figure 16-6 Nineteenth-century engraving depicting an African being auctioned into slavery in Dutch New Amsterdam.

© The Granger Collection, N.Y.

and businesses of this bustling port city crowded onto the southern tip of Manhattan Island. And the British continued to import slaves throughout the first half of the eighteenth century.

On the eve of the American Revolution, New York City had the largest number of enslaved Africans of any English colonial city except for Charleston, South Carolina. In fact, New York City had the highest proportion of slaves to Europeans of any northern settlement. Despite what is found in most American history books, it is clear that the African population had a significant hand in the building of colonial New York.

Eighteenth-century New York law prohibited the burial of Africans in Manhattan's churchyards. Left without a place to bury their dead, New York's African population eventually established a cemetery on a deserted tract of land lying just outside the city's protective wooden palisade (the "wall" of modern "Wall Street" fame). There, from roughly 1712 to 1790, the community buried somewhere between 10,000 and 20,000 people (mostly black, but also a few lower-class whites). A 1755 map of downtown New York clearly shows the "Negro Burial Ground" covering perhaps five city blocks.

In 1827, New York abolished slavery altogether. In the meantime, African-American populations abandoned the downtown area, moving northward in New York City. Over the subsequent decades, the Negro Burial Ground was slowly swallowed up by urban expansion. By the late twentieth century, Manhattan's forgotten cemetery lay buried beneath 20 feet of fill, a scant two blocks north of New York's City Hall.

Archaeology Can Be Contentious

But the Negro Burial Ground was not destined to lie undisturbed. In 1990, the city of New York sold the property to the General Services Administration (GSA), the arm of the federal government responsible for constructing and maintaining federal buildings. The GSA planned to build a 34-story office tower at 290 Broadway, with a 4-story pavilion on the parking lot area to house the United States attorney's office, a regional office of the Environmental Protection Agency, and a district office of the Internal Revenue Service. Although administrators knew that the pavilion was slated to rise directly above a colonial cemetery, they seriously underestimated its extent and the extraordinary degree of preservation.

As we will discuss in Chapter 17, the United States has a legal framework to protect its archaeological resources—particularly those on public land. Part of this legislation requires that an environmental impact statement be filed before any construction can begin. Archaeologists and historians routinely participate in preparing such impact statements. The archaeological firm retained for the 290 Broadway historical inventory correctly noted that the "Negro Burial Ground" appeared on historical maps of the area and probably lay nearby. But, recognizing the long-standing construction history of the site, the impact statement concluded that the digging of nineteenth- and twentieth-century basements had probably obliterated any human remains within the historical boundaries of the cemetery. Although the researchers did note that a portion of the old cemetery might have survived beneath an old alleyway, nobody expected much in the way of human remains to surface when construction began at 290 Broadway.

Still, because there remained a possibility of finding significant archaeological deposits in the construction zone, federal law required that exploratory archaeological excavations be undertaken. Those excavations began in September of 1991 and, right away, human bone was found—and not just a few scattered remains, but dozens (then hundreds) of intact human burials (Figure 16-7).

insisted that the archaeologists work faster, excavating skeletons 10 and 12 hours a day, 7 days a week. Laboratory crew members were reassigned to field excavation duty—anything to speed things up. The cost of the excavation skyrocketed, and the African-American community was upset about the way the project was being handled.

Eventually, a working consensus was forged. A 5-year research program was planned, headed by Dr. Michael L. Blakey, a bioarchaeologist and, at the time, director of the Cobb Biological Anthropology Laboratory at Howard University, the nation's premier black research university (he is now at the College of William and Mary). Blakey had already conducted research at the First African Baptist Cemetery in Philadelphia, and so he was more than qualified to conduct the scientific research at the African Burial Ground (see "In His Own Words: Balancing Interests at the African Burial Ground" by Michael L. Blakey).

Blakey's analysis of some 400 individuals from the burial ground is a chilling statement on human brutality. Blakey found that half of the population died before reaching the age of 12, with another peak in mortality occurring between the ages of 15 and 20. Some of this was probably due to diseases for which Africans had not developed immunity, complicated by the cold weather. But some people were clearly worked to death. Both men and women had enlarged muscle attachments, demonstrating continual demands on their physical labor, and some had lesions from torn muscle attachments. The bones also showed cranial and spinal fractures—a result of carrying excessive loads on the head and shoulders.

This hard life must have contrasted dramatically with their lives in Africa, for the teeth show little evidence of hypoplasias (see Chapter 12), showing that as children these African men and women had lives relatively free of malnutrition and severe disease. It also contrasted sharply with the life of the other citizens of New York. For example, Blakey found that English settlers were eight times more likely to live past the age of 55 than African slaves.

The African Burial Ground Today

Visitors flock to the African Burial Ground center from around the world, and it has become a point of connection for Africans and Americans, white or black. Guided tours and videotapes of the African Burial Ground project are available through the Office of Public Education

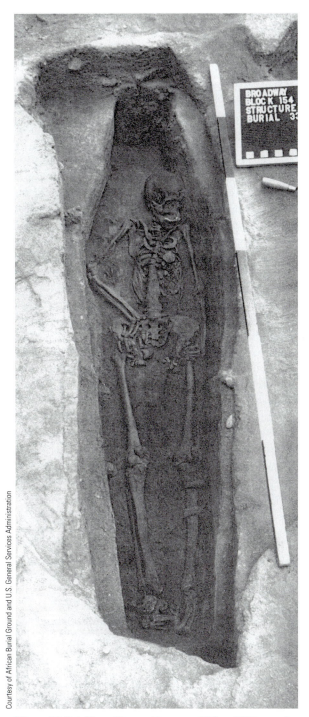

Figure 16-7 A 35- to 40-year-old woman with her child, interred at the African Burial Ground. Both probably died during childbirth or shortly thereafter.

Courtesy of African Burial Ground and U.S. General Services Administration

The excavations at 290 Broadway began interfering with construction schedules. Worried that the archaeology might delay the $276 million project, the GSA

In His Own Words
Balancing Interests at the African Burial Ground

Michael L. Blakey is professor at the College of William and Mary.

The African Burial Ground in New York City is the earliest and largest African cemetery in North America. Originally located just outside the walls of the colonial city, enslaved and free Africans used the cemetery beginning sometime in the seventeenth century and continuing until 1794.

Public and scientific controversy began when part of the site was uncovered in 1991. African-Americans sought to stop archaeological excavation and building construction. They wanted to establish a fitting memorial and to determine for themselves whether research should be conducted. Rising protests, town meetings, and lobbying efforts were mounted by the African-American "descendant community" in order to assure proper treatment of their ancestors.

One set of concerns that involved the African Burial Ground had to do with the politics of the past. Eurocentric distortions and omissions of African and African-American anthropology and history have been persistently cited by black scholars and activists as far as the mid-nineteenth century.

The very existence of an African Burial Ground in colonial New York raised the issue of false historical representation. The vast majority of educated Americans had learned that there was little if any African presence in New York during the colonial period, and that the northern American colonies had not engaged in the practice of slavery. The Burial Ground helped show that these notions comprised a kind of national myth. Africans arrived in New York and its Dutch predecessor, New Amsterdam, from the beginning; they had represented 15 to 40 percent of these colonies and had labored in most aspects of the building of the city and its economy. The majority of these people had been enslaved until Emancipation Day in 1827. In an attempt to ensure a fair and empowering interpretation of the past, African-Americans were determined to include scholars from their own communities prominently in any research that might be done on the site. This site constituted one of the few means of restoring lost pages of American history that might reveal untold dimensions of African-American identity.

I organized a research team consisting of anthropologists, historians, geneticists, and other scientists who had previous experience in the study of both African-American and African archaeology and biology. Based at Howard University, the research group prominently includes African-American and African scholars who shared many of the descendant community's concerns. Following partly from the African-American tradition of "scholar activism" and partly from anthropological approaches to "public engagement," Howard anthropologists and their consultants involved the community in discussions of their proposed research design. They assumed that descendant or culturally affiliated persons should have the right to determine whether research was sufficiently worthwhile as to amount to something more than desecration of the cemetery.

and Interpretation of the African Burial Ground, which is actively engaged in bringing the findings to a broader public through newsletters, workshops, and lectures. Finally, all the human remains were reburied in October 2003.

The African Burial Ground is a prime example of how archaeology can recover "lost" history. But the African Burial Ground is also a story about how a descendant community can be empowered through archaeology.

A final note: The artifacts and excavation documents from the African Burial Ground were stored in a basement of one of the buildings at the World Trade Center, along with those from the Five Points Project, another large historical archaeology dig in downtown New York. Most of the African Burial Ground material was recovered after the building's collapse on September 11, 2001; fortunately, the human remains were still stored in laboratories at Howard University. But virtually everything from the Five Points Project (the neighbor-

Through public meetings, researchers described their methods for restoring the lost history of the enslaved Africans who were buried there. The community introduced their own research questions and thoughts about how the site should be interpreted. This community feedback was incorporated in the research design, so long as the integrity of the scientific method remained intact. The result was a better and more meaningful research project that was not only acceptable to the descendant community, but which they had become part of.

There were now two types of client: An ethical client (descendant or culturally affiliated communities) and a business client (the federal government, responsible for funding the project's research). While responsible for satisfying the legal requirements of its business client, the research team took on responsibility for seeing that agreements made with its ethical client were carried out. One such agreement was the return of skeletons for reburial and memorialization once the important data had been gathered. Thus, scientific, cultural, spiritual, or religious treatments of the cemetery would complement its significance rather than compete.

Although few artifacts remain, one woman was found wearing a string of glass and cowrie shell beads around her waist. In what is today Ghana and Benin, such beads would have been given as a wedding present. The coffin lid of one man's burial had an elaborate heart-shaped design made of brass tacks. One likely possibility being

explored is the Asanti adinkra symbol "Sankofa," which means, "look to the past to inform decisions about the future."

The New York African Burial Ground tells us that archaeology, physical anthropology, and history are often important in the minds of everyday people. Whether as a basis for defining national and group identity, the elucidation of processes leading to current social conditions, or as a guide to the future, disciplines that construct the past do so within the context of broader cultural and political meanings.

It is important for a community to be empowered to evaluate its own past, for better or worse, and to honor that past in ways that are meaningful for it. African-Americans are certainly not singular in these respects. Indigenous people in many parts of the world are advocating control of their cultural patrimony, including sacred archaeological sites and skeletal remains curated by museums. National legislation has begun to protect those rights for Native Americans.

Working with the remains of the dead also means having an impact on living communities that are affiliated with the dead. Archaeologists and skeletal biologists who work with archaeological populations are well served when they have had "holistic" training in the history, ethnography, ethics, and even the political issues of living communities. These issues mark the terrain often entered when digging for the past.

hood that was the setting for Martin Scorsese's film *Gangs of New York*) was lost.

Beyond Slavery

We have focused on slavery—on and off plantations—because it was a dramatic and key element of African-American history whose full impact is often not communicated in standard documentary sources. But African-American history is much more than slave his-

tory, and a number of historical archaeologists have turned their attention to the archaeology of early free black communities (see "Looking Closer: Fort Mose: Colonial America's Black Fortress of Freedom") in the South and African-American settlements in the West. Still other American historical archaeologists work to recover the history of other peoples by excavating the immigrant communities of early nineteenth-century mining towns, Chinese railroad labor camps, and early Mormon communities.

Looking Closer
Fort Mose: Colonial America's Black Fortress of Freedom

African-American archaeology is not exclusively focused on slavery. Yet another perspective on African-American history was achieved through the discovery of Fort Mose, 50 miles south of the Georgia-Florida border. Here, archaeologist Kathleen Deagan and her colleagues at the University of Florida found concrete evidence of the first legally sanctioned, free African-American community in the country.

Beginning with the founding of Charles Towne by the British in 1670, Spain employed free Africans to further its colonial objectives by having them populate and hold territories vulnerable to foreign encroachment. Both free and slave Africans were also used in military operations, a black militia having been established in St. Augustine. By 1673, the Spanish crown declared that all escaped fugitives from British plantations were to be granted sanctuary and, eventually, freedom in Spanish Florida "so that by their example and by my liberality, others will do the same." Like so many episodes in African-American history, the story of Fort Mose is incompletely known, a forgotten footnote to mainstream American history.

Deagan found the lost site of Fort Mose in 1986, and her excavations have provided an opportunity to re-examine the role of African-Americans in colonial history. She is particularly interested in the

effect of freedom on the blacks of Fort Mose. How much did they adapt to Spanish ways? Did they attempt to revive their African heritage?

Recognizing the relevance of the Fort Mose research, the state of Florida was quick to help out. State Representative Bill Clark, who sponsored the bill helping to finance the archaeology, has called Deagan's discovery of Fort Mose "a major historical find for black people." To Clark, himself an African-American, the excavations demonstrate that "blacks were never content to be slaves.... These are America's first freedom fighters."

Figure 16-8 Kathleen Deagan (center) and Florida State Representative Bill Clark (left) work with the excavation team to recover archaeological evidence at Fort Mose, Florida.

CORRECTING INACCURACIES

Historical archaeologists also attempt to correct inaccuracies in the public view of history. Sometimes these inaccuracies are simple mistakes or unintentional omissions and are often innocuous. For example, recall the *Hunley*, the Confederate submarine mentioned in Chapter 9. Historians believed that the sub's explosive charge was mounted on a 22-foot yellow pine boom that projected forward from the top of the hull. But

physical inspection of the *Hunley* shows that the boom was a 17-foot hollow iron pipe that jutted forward from the bottom of the hull.

This is a somewhat trivial detail, but other historical inaccuracies are vastly more significant.

What Happened at the Battle of the Little Bighorn?

In the 1850s, American settlers were moving west through land that was the traditional territory of several tribes, including, on the northern high plains, the Lakota. When the settlers were simply moving through, relations were not so violent, but once settlers opted to remain and forts were constructed, hostilities ensued. By the late 1860s, the Lakota had gained the upper hand, and so they were prepared to discuss terms of peace.

By signing the Laramie Treaty of 1868, Red Cloud and other Lakota leaders agreed to cease hostilities, and the United States created the Great Sioux Reservation, which included the Black Hills in eastern South Dakota; the treaty agreed that whites would make no settlements or unauthorized incursions into this territory. Still, some Indian leaders refused to sign (among them Gall, Sitting Bull, and Crazy Horse), and they were granted permanent hunting rights in the Powder River region of Wyoming and Montana.

But the legal details of the treaty were difficult to understand (and some are still in dispute). Apparently, the treaty allowed for railroad surveys in the Black Hills, which were conducted in 1872 and 1873. But an 1874 military expedition to the Black Hills to locate a military post may not have been allowed in the treaty. Regardless, what matters is that this expedition discovered gold, and the federal government only half-heartedly tried to stop the ensuing rush of miners. By 1875, the government was trying to reduce the size of the Sioux reservation and also ordered that the non-treaty bands relocate to the reservation. In 1876, the government sent General George Armstrong Custer to find these Lakota and move them to the reservation.

On June 25, with the aid of Crow and Arikara scouts, Custer tracked a large band of Lakota, Northern Cheyenne, and Arapaho to the Little Bighorn River in Montana. Despite his scouts' warnings, he decided to attack. He broke his men into three battalions. One, headed by Captain Frederick Benteen, went to the south to cut off an escape route. Major Marcus Reno led another into the valley to attack the village from the southeast. Custer himself led the third over the river bluffs, eventually reaching a position north of the village. Reno encountered heavy resistance that brought him to a standstill, but his efforts did succeed in creating an exodus from the village. Custer apparently then moved through the low hills northeast of the river, pursuing the women, children, and elderly as they fled down the valley.

Images of the Battle

No United States soldier survived to describe what happened or what Custer's final moments were like, and so,

except for the final result, what happened was murky. Nonetheless, sensationalist newspaper accounts quickly formed an image of the battle and Custer's gallant "last stand." Years later, that vivid image was immortalized in several paintings. In 1895, Adolphus Busch (the brewery magnate) commissioned Otto Becker to paint *Custer's Last Fight*. The image shows Custer, his men bravely circled around him, almost calmly fighting a huge band of Lakota and Cheyenne. Busch then sent lithographs of the image to 150,000 saloons around the country. In 1900, Frederic Remington also painted an image of the battle's final moments where, again, a cool and collected Custer commands the men clustered around him.

Perhaps the most famous image is that by Edgar Samuel Paxson (see the chapter's opening photo), completed in 1899, which includes 200 individuals (some are recognizable individuals, as Paxson studied all the available photographs of Custer's men as well as those of Cheyenne and Lakota warriors). Here we see Custer calmly standing in a whirlwind of activity, revolvers at the ready, his chest thrust out defiantly. The men of the Seventh Cavalry are gathered around him, disciplined to the end.

Images like these helped to create a fatalistic attitude toward the country's push to the west: Some would have to die in expanding the country westward, but they would die proud, knowing that what they were doing—bringing civilization to the wilderness (or massacring Indians and dispossessing them of their land, depending on your perspective)—was their god-given destiny. And Indians who stood in the way of this destiny should be punished.

But there were other images of the battle. Although none of Custer's battalion survived, many of the 1200 or so Indian warriors did, including such notables as Sitting Bull, Gall, Crazy Horse, and Black Elk (then 13 years old). Many of the Indian survivors were interviewed in the following years, and their accounts were used to draw Indian images of the battle.

The Indian images tell a different story, as shown in Figure 16-9. In the first place, they are far more bloody than the paintings by Paxson and others, who sanitized the gruesome hand-to-hand combat. The Indians' images are filled with blood and entrails, decapitation and dismemberment. More importantly, they show groups of men spread over the battlefield—some firing, others running for their lives. Unlike the images created by white artists, the Indians' images show no grand last

Figure 16-9 *Battle of the Little Bighorn* (circa 1898) by Kicking Bear (1846?–1904). Kicking Bear made this painting at the request of Frederic Remington; Custer appears in yellow buckskins at the left.

stand. In fact, there is nothing glorious in their pictures at all; there is only confusion and carnage. Which image is accurate?

An Archaeological Perspective on the Battle

Today, the battlefield is a national monument, but it still remains a lonely and windswept place. In 1983, a brush fire burned the area, which led Douglas Scott (National Park Service) and Richard Fox (University of South Dakota) to conduct a survey of the entire battlefield. They checked a sample of the grave markers (individual gravestones marked where bodies were found some time after the battle) and systematically surveyed the battlefield using metal detectors for battle-related artifacts. They found plenty: gun parts, belt buckles, buttons, bridle pieces, human remains, and lots of spent cartridges and bullets. Each item was recorded and its location carefully mapped.

The cartridges and bullets were especially interesting, because they are amenable to forensic analyses. Scott and Fox knew that the cavalry was armed only with .45 caliber single-shot Springfield carbines and .45 caliber Colt pistols. The Indians had these, too, but forensic studies showed they were also equipped with

some 40 other types of weapons, from obsolete muzzle-loaders to repeating rifles (acquired through the illegal arms trade of the day). Careful mapping allowed Scott and Fox to ascertain combatant positions (Indian and soldier alike) using cartridge case locations and bullet orientations (which revealed the direction from which the bullet was fired). Most important, in many instances they could use discharged cartridges to trace individual combatant movements by matching the distinctive "fingerprint" that a gun's firing pin makes on the cartridge. What did they learn?

Where Was Custer?

We know that Custer's body was found on the hilltop that bears his name, surrounded by most of his headquarters staff. But where was he during the battle? We know that Custer's battalion had broken into two wings. Previous scholars argued that Custer was with the right wing because brass cartridges had been found along the path taken by the right wing, and Custer's .50-caliber Remington rifle was thought to be the only weapon on the battlefield that used brass cartridges. But Scott and Fox found many brass cartridges at the site, with firing pin fingerprints indicating that brass cartridges were fired from several different .50 caliber guns (by both soldiers and Indians). The brass cartridges, therefore, can't be used to pinpoint Custer's personal movements. We don't know where Custer himself fought; we only know where his body eventually came to rest.

Where Were the Indians and the Soldiers?

Scott and Fox also found cavalry cartridge cases on Custer Hill, on the low ridges running to the east and south, and on Calhoun Hill (to the south of Custer Hill). Many more *Indian* cartridges are found in these same places (as well as on the rise coming up from the river—the direction from which the Indians would have attacked). In addition, in some places expended government bullets were found next to government-issue cartridges. A cartridge drops to the ground as a rifle is reloaded, but obviously the corresponding bullet should appear at the target. Some of the bullets may have resulted from men shooting their horses to use them as shields. But others were probably fired by Indians, using guns they had claimed from Reno's unsuccessful attack or weapons taken from the bodies of Custer's men.

Also odd is the lack of evidence for formal skirmish lines. Army tactics at the time called for companies to form skirmish lines as a defensive measure. To form a skirmish line, a company's men stood about 5 yards apart, with about 15 yards between companies. Such a tactical maneuver leaves a distinctive trace: piles of government-issue cartridges spaced about 5 yards apart. Scott and Fox found only tentative evidence for one skirmish line, on Calhoun Hill. Otherwise, the archaeological evidence fit the Indian accounts of chaos and hand-to-hand fighting.

Eventually, about 100 soldiers made it to Custer Hill, where order was apparently restored, albeit briefly. More Indians slowly arrived. Eventually, about 45 men, 5 of them mounted, made a break down a ridge to the east of Custer Hill. But Scott and Fox found no evidence of a skirmish line there. Instead, the men were perhaps trying to distract the Indians from the mounted soldiers, who were probably trying to reach Benteen. But these men, even the riders, were quickly pursued.

Eventually, Custer Hill was overrun, and more men ran down the hill to the ravine. Indians recalled that some fired into the air, but others failed even to draw their revolvers. And many did what soldiers before (and after) have done when confronted with death: They froze, with little choice but to accept the inevitable.

The battle lasted less than 90 minutes, and the final part took place not on Custer Hill, as the paintings suggest, but in the ravine, where terrified soldiers who "shot like drunken men," according to Iron Hawk, were hunted down and killed in a terrifying game of hide-and-seek.

Fox argues that Custer was moving confidently in an offensive tactical maneuver when he was caught completely off-guard, forcing a rapid transition from an offensive to a defensive posture. But Custer and his men were so rapidly surrounded that they had no time to regroup and carry out formal tactical maneuvers. The coordination of Custer's offensive attack rapidly gave way to confusion, chaos, and death. Near the top of Custer Hill, in fact, there is no sign of formal tactics. Instead, the distribution of Springfield cases suggests that men clustered together tightly in a non-tactical maneuver—something that Indian eyewitnesses recalled years later—firing against the Indians who surrounded them.

To the Last Bullet?

The romantic image of the battle has the soldiers holding off the Indians until their last bullet was fired. In fact, less than a month after the battle, the Helena *Herald* reported the tragedy with the headline "Not Until Their Ammunition Was Gone Were Our Troops Butchered."

But there were almost no Colt .45 cartridge cases found on the battlefield—none, in fact, on Custer Hill. A soldier could fire a revolver six times before he had to reload (unlike the single-shot carbines, from which a soldier had to remove the empty cartridge before reloading). But with their limited accuracy, handguns were only good for close combat. The Indians recalled soldiers using their sidearms, but they said that the soldiers had no time to reload. The distribution of .45 caliber Colt cartridges confirms this account. Close combat came so quickly and with such overwhelming force that soldiers either had no time to use their revolvers or, more likely, no time to reload them (and the Indians collected the revolvers, still filled with empty or usable cartridges, after the battle).

The romantic images of the battle suggest that Custer and his men were in calm control until the very end. But the archaeology agrees with the Indians' accounts: Custer was caught off-guard. Perhaps he didn't expect the warriors to be so motivated to protect their women and children. Perhaps he expected Reno and Benteen to cut through and assist them. We don't know. We do know, however, that the popular images of the battle are

Archaeological Ethics
Archaeology and the Values of Descendant Communities

The African Burial Ground is one of many cases in which archaeologists try to take into account the opinions, values, and perspectives of descendant communities. Although admirable, such a stance does raise some ethical questions.

When word of the burials reached African-American leaders in Harlem, they expressed concern over the lack of community involvement in the project. As one citizen put it, "If it was an African find, we wanted to make sure that it was interpreted from an African point of view." The Government Services Administration (GSA) countered that it had made appropriate notification as mandated by law: "We didn't include the Harlem community board because the project isn't in Harlem, it's in lower Manhattan."

The situation reached a flashpoint when a backhoe operator accidentally destroyed several of the burials. Large-scale protests ensued, culminating in a one-day blockade that shut down construction. To some, the debate surrounding the African Burial Ground became a "microcosm of the issues of racism and economic exploitation confronting New York City." Archaeology never proceeds in a social vacuum.

The GSA eventually commissioned an advisory committee—comprising historians, anthropologists, museum professionals, architects, attorneys, clergy, government officials, and concerned community members—to represent the interests of the African descendant community at large.

Supported by then-Mayor David N. Dinkins (New York City's first African-American mayor), the African descendant community became actively involved in the preservation, dedication, and management of the cemetery site. Blakey's active participation became an overt symbol that the city was considering the African descendant community's wishes. But there were differences of opinion about how the remains should be treated. Some in the descendant community felt that archaeological investigations were disrespectful, adding the insult

of grave robbing to the injury of slavery. Others believed that a thorough scientific study was not only a way of honoring the dead, but also of restoring them to their rightful place in American history.

Eventually, the government scrubbed all plans to erect the four-story pavilion. Instead, this piece of prime New York real estate was set aside as a permanent memorial. On February 25, 1993, the New York City Landmarks Commission designated the site the African Burial Ground and the Commons Historical District. Later that year, the African Burial Ground achieved National Historic Landmark status. Sherrill D. Wilson, an African-American anthropologist, noted that the sudden involvement of black scholars was "very revolutionary.... [Such scholarship] is going to set a precedent for what happens to African burial grounds in the future and how African heritage will be viewed by the public."

The African Burial Ground appears to have worked out to the satisfaction of most people. But it raises some questions. First, what defines a descendant community? To our knowledge, no living person demonstrated a lineal relationship to anyone in the African Burial Ground. Who decides who belongs to the descendant community?

And, once that decision is made, what is the appropriate role of descendant communities? Can anyone, with appropriate training, work on any type of site, or is the only valid work on a site done by a member of a descendant community? Can only Native Americans work on Native American sites; African-Americans on African-American sites, Euro-Americans on European sites? We have asked this question before, and we will ask it now in a different way: Do we want a world in which there is "my" history and "your" history? Is there a line between empowerment of a descendent community and the balkanization of the world of knowledge about the past? If so, how would we know where that line is? And, assuming that the balkanization of knowledge is undesirable, how do we keep from crossing that line?

inaccurate. The Battle of the Little Bighorn did not end in a "glorious" last stand. Instead, it ended like most battles: in chaos, panic, horror, and carnage.

The Monument Today

A pillar was erected on Custer's Hill in 1881 as a tribute to the Seventh Cavalry. One hundred and ten years later, Congress recognized the more complex nature of the site's history and changed the name from Custer Battlefield to Little Bighorn Battlefield National Monument. At the same time, it authorized a memorial to honor the fallen Cheyenne, Lakota, and Arapaho warriors. The new memorial, dedicated in June 2003, consists of a low, circular, granite-lined earthwork and contains bronze silhouettes of mounted warriors. Its name: Peace Through Unity.

RE-EXAMINING AMERICA'S HISTORY

We now come to perhaps the most divisive aspect of historical archaeology—re-examining history. A national narrative can be contentious, because a nation's history defines who its citizens are and, in no small way, creates their identity. No one wishes to identify with a history of dishonorable acts. This is why slavery was long ignored at reconstructed plantation sites and why revisionist histories of western settlement remain controversial. Going back in time, it seems, is like going deeper into a people's identity and soul. There are many, for example, who do not welcome reinterpretations of Custer's Last Stand, because the myth has become "their" history, right or wrong. Everyone wants their history to be uplifting; scholars also want it to be honest. Here's one example from Annapolis, Maryland.

Historical Archaeology in Annapolis

Working with the Historic Annapolis Foundation, Mark Leone (University of Maryland) has conducted "backyard archaeology" for decades, excavating in basements and backyards, beneath parking lots and pavements throughout Annapolis. By looking at floor plans, dishes, facades, architecture, silverware, furniture, and gardens, Leone is trying to demonstrate the degree to which our history is "constructed"—that is, written and presented for contemporary purposes. And in doing that, Leone has established the relevance of eighteenth-century Annapolis to ourselves and the way we understand not only our past, but also the present and the future.

Because of the explicit political agenda behind Leone's work, it is important to understand his theoretical perspective. Leone works within a postprocessual paradigm called **critical theory.** As applied to archaeology, critical theory emphasizes the importance of archaeologists' understanding of the specific contexts within which they work and of the notion that knowledge is situated within a cultural framework (as we pointed out in Chapter 3) and that it consequently can serve special interests. Critical theory assumes that domination in some form is a central element of modern capitalist society.

"Critical" in this sense means that the relationship between the assumptions and discoveries of a scholarly discipline on the one hand and its ties to modern life on the other are a central concern and subject to examination. Such an approach relates the questions, methods, and discoveries of a science like anthropology to those of the anthropologist's own culture. Critical theorists seek simultaneously to explain the social world, to criticize it, and to empower their audience to deal with it more productively by advocating change.

Pre-1760 Colonial America: The Georgian Order

Before continuing, we must situate Leone's work in a larger context. Folklorist Henry Glassie (Indiana University) and archaeologist James Deetz (1930–2000) both explored the way in which changing cultural ideas were reflected in the material record of the American colonies. As such, they took a decidedly ideational (rather than materialist) approach to the past. Glassie examined early colonial houses in Virginia, while Deetz looked at the overall pattern of material culture in New England. Deetz argued that early British colonists in New England had a **medieval mind-set** that encouraged a group-oriented, corporate, and relatively undifferentiated lifestyle. He found that by 1660, however, the culture of American colonies had changed. This particular culture is sometimes known as the **Georgian order.**

medieval mind-set The culture of the early (pre-AD 1660) British colonies that emphasized the group rather than the individual and in which the line between culture and nature was blurred; people were seen as conforming to nature.

Georgian order A worldview (ca. 1660/1680–1820) arising in the European Age of Reason and implying that the world has a single, basic immutable order. Using the powers of reason, people can discover what that order is and can thereby control the environment as they wish. The Georgian order is informed by the rise of scientific thought and by the balance and order in Renaissance architecture and art.

Glassie and Deetz found that material remains of the late seventeenth century reflect a culture of increasing individualism and control. It this regard, American colonial culture reflected elements of the Enlightenment. You will recall from Chapter 15 that the Enlightenment focused on progress and on the ability of rational thought to control nature and improve human morality and spirituality. During the late seventeenth century, Deetz argued, Georgian attitudes created material culture patterns that emphasized control, often by partitioning space, and reflected a focus on the individual. These patterns in material culture were strikingly different from the previous "medieval" culture of the colonies. Here is how Deetz saw the differences:

- **Architecture** Medieval houses had only one or two rooms, with asymmetrical floor plans. All domestic activity took place in these rooms, from sleeping and eating to working and socializing. But with the Georgian worldview, houses became functionally structured and compartmentalized, with more balanced floor plans.
- **Ceramics** The medieval mind-set was characterized by plain, utilitarian earthenware. Food was served directly from the cooking pot and consumed from "trenchers," wooden trays that were shared with one or more "trencher mates." During this period, ceramics played a small role in food consumption. Georgian culture entailed ceramics that were purchased as matched sets of plates and teacups. Serving vessels appeared, and one plate was allotted to each individual around the family table. And whereas medieval ceramics were natural-colored earthenwares, Georgian ceramics became progressively whiter as technology improved.
- **Mortuary art** Gravestones also became white, replacing earlier green, black, blue, and red markers, and the backs were sculpted smooth, "denying their origin in the native stone." The messages engraved on the medieval tombstones reminded the living of their mortality with engraved death's heads and simple epitaphs such as "Here lies buried…". But in Georgian culture, the typical inscription changed to "In memory of…," and the urn and willow motif was used as a "symbol of commemoration." Georgian epitaphs praised the worldly achievements of individuals.

- **Food preparation** Medieval diners usually attacked a portion of meat still articulated in joints, "showing in part at least the vestiges of the anatomy of the beast from which they came." But Georgian food was dominated by segmented cuts of meat that were more difficult to identify to anatomical part. Archaeologically, this change is seen as a shift from chopping bones to sawing them.
- **Refuse disposal** During early medieval days, trash was simply tossed out of doors and windows, creating a sheet of refuse that domestic animals scavenged. By the mid-eighteenth century, however, trash was deposited in an orderly manner, in square pits up to 7 feet deep. Chamber pots also came into use, reflecting a desire for increased privacy.

These changes in material culture signal a shift to a culture that focused on the individual, rather than the group, and on the control of nature. Glassie and Deetz believe these patterns point to a simple cultural idea: Culture was to nature as order was to chaos. This reflects a general Enlightenment theme: For nature to be controlled, it had to be ordered, and for it to be ordered, it had to be brought into the world of culture.

Capitalism and Power in Historic Annapolis

Leone was interested not just in the operation of the Georgian worldview, but also in how and why it came to exist. He chose to examine these questions in the community of Annapolis.

Annapolis has been a small community since it was founded about 1650. It became the capital of Maryland in 1695, later experiencing a "golden age" of wealth and fame that peaked between about 1760 and the end of the American Revolution. In a move designed to symbolically subordinate the military to civil authority, George Washington came to Annapolis to resign his command of the Continental Army. The Treaty of Paris, which officially ended the American Revolution, was also signed there. During the early days of the United States, even though Annapolis remained the state capital, the international, commercial, and industrial potential of nearby Baltimore attracted many of the area's wealthiest residents. Although the United States Naval Academy moved to Annapolis in 1845, the nineteenth century signaled an era of "gentle eclipse" for Annapolis. The 1950s saw the beginning of a commercial revival based on yachting, tourism, and new highways that defined Annapolis as a suburb of Washington, DC, and Baltimore, less than 30 miles away.

Leone and his team consciously deconstructed the ideology behind the historical development of Annapolis and its environs: Why did some people become rich? Why were some poor? What was the relationship between the two? How did the American Revolution affect these inequalities?

Eventually, Leone developed a "theory of power" to explain the growth of Chesapeake society under the European and American systems. By 1720, a class structure had developed in which a few families of the gentry controlled most of the wealth. The social position of the rest of the population—poorer whites, Native and African-Americans—remained the same before and after the American Revolution.

The Power Garden: Landscape Archaeology as Ideology

Leone paid special attention to the formal landscapes of Annapolis. Recognizing that formal gardens were a new addition to wealthy households, Leone wanted to understand what this piece of material culture had to say about the formation of the Georgian order.

Shown in Figure 16-10, the best known of Annapolis' formal gardens in the late eighteenth century was that of William Paca—a signer of the Declaration of Independence. If we could ask him, Paca would probably say that he built his garden in the style that he did because he "enjoyed" it or because it was fashionable. But this only raises the question of *why* this particular garden style was fashionable.

Paca's garden, once described as "the most elegant in Annapolis," was originally built in the 1760s, behind a large, five-part Georgian mansion—which sported a facade and a floor plan exhibiting bilateral symmetry.

The garden is likewise Georgian, with a central axis, and a straight, broad path that descends through several sets of steps as one leaves the house, dividing the space into two parts. These steps lead down over a series of small terraces, creating the same visual effect of bilateral symmetry as that of Georgian architecture.

The garden survived into the early twentieth century, when it was destroyed to make room for a 200-room hotel. When the hotel was torn down in 1968, Stanley South excavated in and around the standing house. Historical archaeologists then moved into the garden area, first testing and then excavating large areas. Original wall footings, documenting the terraces (which could be seen in stratigraphic profile), were found; thus, the garden's basic topography was reconstructed. Trenching and examination of the profiles showed a canal and pond at the bottom of the garden, surrounded by a natural garden (in the terminology of the time, a "wilderness") in the lowest third of the garden. Foundations of a central pavilion and springhouse and of footings for a bridge over the ponds were discovered; 125 paleobotanical samples were recovered from the wet fill. These archaeological data were combined with

© Maryland Historical Society, Baltimore

Figure 16-10 The William Paca garden (Annapolis).

a few period descriptions and with a contemporary portrait of William Paca that showed the garden as background. The pavilion, bathhouse, springhouse, and Chinese Chippendale bridge all have been restored. Today, the Paca garden is open to the public as both an archaeologically based reconstruction and a horticultural experiment.

Leone first visited the restored garden in the early 1980s, and his impressions remained the touchstone for his subsequent archaeological analyses. He later wrote, "As I began to walk through the garden from the top, which is 16 feet higher than the bottom, which is 270 feet away, I found it difficult to tell distances; I felt I was being controlled, as paths, precise borders, openings, stairs, and objects that had to be stepped over operated everywhere to control me. This sensation was especially true regarding sight."

This effect is not simply the impact of fastidious design. Paca's sensibilities were affected by larger cultural ideas, and his garden expresses the Enlightenment idea of the power of Reason over Nature. By putting trees and shrubs into their "proper" places, Paca's landscape architect was demonstrating that nature controlled by culture was more lovely and desirable than wilderness—that is, than nature uncontrolled by culture.

After studying two other large gardens in Annapolis, Leone synthesized what he believed to be the rules behind the design. The Paca garden was constructed following the laws of perspective and used Baroque rules for creating optical illusions. Convergent or divergent lines of sight (to make distances appear shorter or longer, depending on the specific need in each garden) were created, and rows of beds or shrubs were formed into trapezoids and focal points (rather than strictly parallel lines) to manipulate the view. "The gardens are three-dimensional spaces," he wrote, "built consciously using rules which were well understood to create illusions for those who walked through them."

But why the illusion? Leone asked. And why would such Anglo-American gardens proliferate just before the American Revolution and then slowly disappear—like the rest of Georgian material culture—in the decades leading up to the Civil War?

For answers, Leone turned to the general body of materialist theory and formulated a hypothesis to explain governance through ostentatious displays. When money forms the only power base, Leone argued, those governing have little need to demonstrate their right or power to govern; they are in control and intend to stay

that way. But ostentatious displays become important when factors other than simple wealth come into play, when it is necessary to convince the governed that those in power deserve to stay there. *Show* becomes important when those in authority do not necessarily control the purse strings or when the wealthy do not control the power structure.

The William Paca garden was built by a wealthy man who lived in a time of contradictions. Although not born to particular affluence, he married into plenty of it. Although a slave owner, he argued for the Bill of Rights. Although descended from planters and tied to merchants, he grew up and lived in economic circumstances in which he and everyone around him was facing serious economic and political change.

Paca could have built his garden anytime during his lifetime, but he chose to do so when his power to protect his wealth was being diminished by Britain. Parliamentary restrictions on trade and local office-holding compromised profits and power in the 1760s. Paca was isolated socially and economically by a large and difficult-to-control slave population as well as by poor white farmers and day laborers who were anxious to learn who their future allies would be in the coming war with Britain.

Leone argues that the formal Anglo-American gardens were built deliberately to demonstrate a knowledge of—and control over—the laws of nature. Paca was trying to create the illusion that either (1) he still retained power over his own wealth or (2) he should be granted the political clout to do so. In this perspective, the garden was not a statement of what existed. Paca's garden both reflected and helped create an ideology (see Chapter 15), at a time when the wealth and prestige of his class were being undermined and diminished.

Leone points out that the Paca garden illustrates the principles that defined the layout of Annapolis as a whole. The early street patterns and building placements still dominate life in the city. This archaeological study of Paca's garden reveals that perspective and its power to invite attention are still actively used to manage relations of power in the city today. The relations among the prominence of the state capitol, the isolation of the Naval Academy, and the invisibility of the African-American community are all managed using the same spatial principles exhibited in Paca's garden. Together, Leone argues, historical archaeological and critical theory illustrate the origins of modern—and exploitative—social relations that continue to the present.

Taking Critical Theory Public

As discussed in Chapter 3, archaeology's postprocessual critique calls attention to the important role played by local politics in archaeological interpretation—and particularly to interpretation within the field of historical archaeology.

Critical theorists argue that the proper role of the historian is to unearth the beginnings of contemporary class-based ideologies—distortions that rationalize forms of exploitation, such as slavery, sexism, and racism. Applied to historical archaeology, critical theory suggests that, once a repressed people can be shown a past in which things were different, they can use this knowledge to challenge and attempt to change the inequities of the present. From this position, the responsible historian (and historical archaeologist) should form alliances with members of oppressed classes and work toward social change to better the workers' condition. To the critical theorist, capitalism has negative social elements that should be confronted.

Leone grounded his research at Annapolis in the belief that archaeologists and historians should "stand up" against the oppressive excesses of capitalism. In other words, it was not enough for archaeologists simply to learn about abuse of power in the past; it was essential that this knowledge be brought forward into the present.

The call for historical archaeology to become more political comes from two directions. As archaeology becomes more public, individual archaeologists are increasingly called upon to interpret their findings for the public. Such interpretation takes many forms— traditional museum exhibits, outdoor history museums, site-specific tourist facilities, and television and other media interpretations of "the past." But the problem immediately surfaces—which and whose past?

Consider the case of Annapo-

lis, where historical preservation has played a major role in the commercial renaissance of the city. Annually, more than 1 million people visit Annapolis, a city of only about 32,000 people. As in many other small, historical towns, local residents work hard to protect those things that attract visitors.

The encapsulated history of Annapolis has been peddled to generations of tourists who buy guidebooks, listen to tour guides, and saunter through the historic-house museums (Figure 16-11). Prominent are references to the ultimate first tourist, none other than George Washington himself. Discussing his many visits, conventional Annapolis history plays up the social and domestic aspects of Washington's jaunts into the city— going to the racetrack, attending social events and plays, and visiting a host of friends and family members. In effect, the image of Washington-in-Annapolis largely mirrored the profile of just the sort of visitor that Annapolis wanted to attract—the high-end tourist with some money to spend, but without an attitude.

Through the lens of critical theory, however, Leone and his colleagues noticed something interesting about

© Parker Potter

Figure 16-11 Tourists learning about the archaeology of Annapolis.

the tourism process. As the tourists poured through, they were presented the history of Annapolis as a collection of disconnected units from different time periods and institutions. History-for-the-tourist was left in the hands of diverse groups and institutions, some overlapping, some in competition. Annapolis had no unified history to connect the different parts of the city. Black and white populations were presented as unconnected, as were the histories of the city of Annapolis and the Naval Academy.

As written and presented by whites, black history (viewed from the nineteenth-century perspective) was separated from white history (presented from the eighteenth-century perspective). Slavery was not seen as an antecedent to relationships between contemporary groups.

Leone and his associates—notably an archaeologist-cum-lawyer, Parker Potter—designed an on-site program for the 5,000 to 10,000 visitors who stopped by each year. Tourists visiting Historic Annapolis often have a chance to walk through the ongoing archaeological excavations. Well-prepared guides explain what the archaeologists are doing and why they are doing it.

Did Critical Theory Succeed at Annapolis?

The site excursions were enormously popular with tourists and residents in Annapolis, and they seemed to rally the city's support to protect the archaeological sites of Annapolis. But in regard to social change, Leone and Potter were frustrated with the results. Potter believed that the Archaeology in Annapolis tour program failed to effect any significant change in Annapolis. "As far as I can tell," Leone has written, "[the tours] changed consciousness not at all.... We were speaking to the wrong audience."

For a historical archaeology of capitalism to be fruitful, Leone realized, "there would have to be a dialogue with those who see knowledge about themselves as a way of dealing with their own oppression or victimization." This was disappointing in a sense because it suggested that critical theory—as a strategy for effecting social change (its avowed goal)—might not work as intended (at least not by itself).

On reflection, Leone still believed that the Archaeology in Annapolis program had successfully explored the histories of the white residents who lived there (even if the white tourists to Annapolis did not seem to pick up on the message to "stand up against capital-

ism"). But he also realized that, in its early stages, the archaeology program had overlooked a major portion of the city by not explicitly addressing the African-American experience through archaeology.

This realization led Leone and the public programming effort at Annapolis in another direction—into the contemporary African-American community of Annapolis.

The dialog between Annapolis archaeologists and the African-American community immediately raised three related questions:

- Was there, indeed, any way to tell whether archaeological material was associated with African-Americans?
- Does the African-American community care about that record? (Some important questions: Can you tell us about freedom, not just about slavery? Is there anything left from Africa?
- What would an African-American historical archaeology look like?

Faced with this entirely new direction, Leone realized, "We ourselves had to admit we did not know the answers."

So began a new interchange at Annapolis, between white archaeologists and African-Americans. No longer was the archaeologist the "teacher," with the community serving only as "listener." In this dialog, all participants defined themselves as professionals, informants, scholars, students, and fund-raisers. Everyone involved, according to Leone, admitted ignorance on some topics, but also expressed a willingness to learn. This experiment in historical archaeology is still ongoing.

CONCLUSION: HISTORICAL ARCHAEOLOGY'S FUTURE

Historical archaeology is the growth industry of Americanist archaeology in the twenty-first century. In part, cultural resource management and the large number of historical sites that are uncovered by the construction activities of a growing population drive this. But it is also driven by a desire to understand the colonial and post-colonial history of the United States and the roles played by all the peoples who have found a home in

America. For this reason, historical archaeology will continue to occupy a prominent place in Americanist archaeology for years to come. We expect that the processual paradigm will continue to be important, but that postprocessual approaches will play a large and significant role as issues such as power, domination, class, and resistance figure prominently in the world's recent (colonial) history.

For this reason also, historical archaeology will continue to be the source of some heated disputes. Some of these disputes will focus on who has the right to study and interpret the material remains that document the history of those other groups—African-, Asian-, Native, Hispanic-, and Euro-Americans. We predict that these debates will be less contentious and more productive if archaeologists maintain a dialog with the public and descendant communities and yet do not withdraw from their scientific standards of excavation and interpretation.

Other disputes will focus on the proper place of politically motivated interpretations of the past. Leone, for example, suggests that capitalism creates its own view of the past, which masks the formation of inequities that are essential to the operation of capitalism today—a bourgeois class of consumers and an economically and politically repressed group of workers. But some might legitimately argue that any archaeology pursuing a political position is biased from the start, and hence all its interpretations of the past are suspect. Those in historical archaeology who pursue the paradigm of critical theory will have to meet this challenge in the future by combining a passionate desire to use archaeology to effect social change with a dispassionate and thorough scientific analysis of archaeology's data.

Summary

- Historical archaeology looks at material remains from past societies that also left behind some form of written documentation ("history") about themselves. So defined, the first bona fide historical archaeology in America took place about 150 years ago.

- During the first half of the twentieth century, historical archaeologists labored mostly to supplement historical records, serving as a kind of "handmaiden to history." This perspective is evident in public interpretive projects, such as Plimouth Plantation, Colonial Williamsburg, and the Little Bighorn battlefield. Such projects tended to concentrate on a very few selected sites, particularly houses of the rich and famous, forts, and other military sites.

- Things changed in the 1960s, when some processual archaeologists realized that they could refine their archaeological methods and theories by working in the contexts of verifiable historical controls. Mainstream historical archaeology distanced itself from an emphasis on the "most historically significant" sites—looking instead at the larger social contexts.

- In the 1960s, historical archaeology began to focus on historically disenfranchised groups in our own culture, seeking to uncover the history of African-Americans, Asian-Americans, Native Americans during the historic period, and Hispanic-Americans.

- Historical archaeology has also been fertile ground for postprocessual interests because texts can provide data with which to place archaeological remains in context.

- The study of the symbolic meaning of material remains also proceeds more comfortably in historical archaeology, where documents can provide interpretations of material culture.

- Historical archaeology is today one of the most rapidly expanding and exciting directions in Americanist archaeology; current trends—challenges to existing histories and the recovery of the history of disenfranchised groups—will generate debates and dialog for years to come.

Additional Reading

Deagan, Kathleen, and Darcie MacMahon. 1995. *Fort Mose: Colonial America's Black Fortress of Freedom.* Gainesville: University Press of Florida/Florida Museum of Natural History.

Deetz, James. 1977. *In Small Things Forgotten: The Archaeology of Early American Life.* Garden City, NY: Anchor Books.

Ferguson, Leland B. 1992. *Uncommon Ground: Archaeology and Early African America, 1650–1800.* Washington, DC: Smithsonian Institution Press.

Fox, Richard. 1993. *Archaeology, History, and Custer's Last Battle: The Little Big Horn Re-examined.* Norman: University of Oklahoma Press.

Orser, Charles E., Jr. 1995. *A Historical Archaeology of the Modern World.* New York: Plenum.

Singleton, Theresa A. (Ed.). 1985. *The Archaeology of Slavery and Plantation Life.* Orlando, FL: Academic Press.

Online Resources

COMPANION WEB SITE
Visit   http://anthropology.wadsworth.com and click on the Student Companion Web Site for Thomas/Kelly *Archaeology,* 4th edition, to access a wide range of material to help you succeed in your introductory archaeology course. These include flashcards, Internet exercises, Web links, and practice quizzes.

RESEARCH ONLINE WITH INFOTRAC COLLEGE EDITION
From the Student Companion Web Site, you can access the InfoTrac College Edition database, which offers thousands of full-length articles for your research.

17 Caring for America's Cultural Heritage

Outline

© Charles Reher

Archaeologists in Wyoming excavate a site in the path of a railroad trestle, the other side of which is under construction in the background.

Preview

T HIS CHAPTER DESCRIBES the role that archaeology plays in conserving America's cultural heritage. Threats to this heritage come from those who loot archaeological sites for personal gain and from relentless development across the country. Over the years, the federal government has passed various laws to protect the nation's cultural heritage in archaeological sites, historic buildings, and landscapes.

These laws have created an important new direction for applied archaeology, generally known as cultural resource management (or CRM). Linked with construction, development, and federal agency activities, CRM requires new ways of thinking about archaeological standards, principles, ethics, and training. The CRM framework today dominates the practice of archaeology in America.

Another body of law safeguards the rights of indigenous peoples and regulates the repatriation of human skeletal remains and certain cultural objects to Indian tribes and Native Hawaiian organizations. Still more laws attempt to stop the flow of illegally acquired antiquities. Although this chapter focuses on the United States, many other countries have similar laws that try to preserve their cultural heritage, stop looting, and protect the rights of indigenous peoples.

INTRODUCTION

Commercial development is going on all around us. Nearly everywhere you look, you see bridges, dams, roads, and buildings under construction. Pipelines, power lines, highways, and fiber optic cables increasingly slice across our landscape. Such development destroys as much as it constructs. As transportation systems improve, they pave over the American past. As new houses and hospitals spring up, we see archaeological remains carted away in dump trucks. As power lines go up, construction teams bulldoze archaeological sites into rubble.

We should all be concerned about the trade-offs that arise from such development. Most people benefit from improved transportation, better hospitals, and more efficient communication services but, at the same time, these projects destroy important parts of America's cultural heritage. Developers are not evil people, and neither are those who care about preserving our past. So this leaves us with a critical question: What part of our past must we save, and what part can we do without?

This question is hardly unique to the United States. Most modern nations try to balance economic development and heritage preservation through laws and regulations. In this country, **cultural resource management** is the field that conducts activities related to compliance with legislation that protects cultural resources.

It is difficult to emphasize the importance of CRM to contemporary archaeology. Prior to the 1960s, nearly all American archaeologists worked for universities and museums. Today, the number of archaeologists in the United States not only vastly exceeds those working in the 1960s, but well over half of them make their living working in the framework of cultural resource management. In fact, CRM projects account for about 90 per-

cultural resource management (CRM) A professional field that conducts activities, including archaeology, related to compliance with legislation aimed at conserving cultural resources.

cent of the field archaeology conducted today in the United States.

How did this change come about?

THE DEVELOPMENT OF CULTURAL RESOURCE MANAGEMENT

The impact of development did not begin affecting America's cultural heritage with the onset of strip malls and interstate highways. In fact, a concern with historic preservation extends to the earliest days of the United States. In 1789, for example, wealthy Bostonians formed the Massachusetts Historical Society in response to the destruction of John Hancock's house. The society became a watchdog to ensure that other historically significant properties were not lost. And, in 1813, the federal government ordered the preservation of Independence Hall in Philadelphia.

These isolated instances demonstrate that historic preservation has been an issue in the past. But in truth, a systematic concern for preserving America's cultural heritage developed rather slowly, coincident with the more broadly based environmental preservation movement. Both movements flourished in the 1960s and 1970s, but their roots extend back another century.

America's environmental movement can be traced to such late nineteenth-century writers as Henry David Thoreau, John Muir, and Ernest Thompson Seton, each of whom inspired generations to take notice of the natural world around them and to respond to increasing human impact on that landscape. Some, appalled at the needless slaughter of the Great Plains bison in the late nineteenth century, began working to save the continent's indigenous wildlife. Others, called to action by George Perkins Marsh's widely read *Man and Nature* (1864), worked to stave off the wholesale environmental degradation evident around the world.

President Theodore Roosevelt was particularly concerned with Marsh's plea that disturbed environments should be allowed to heal naturally or be restored by specific conservation management plans. Roosevelt insisted that large areas of forest and grazing land be set aside in the United States, to protect timber supplies *for future use and development.* About the same time, John Muir (founder of the Sierra Club) argued for leaving large tracts of western lands untouched *for their long-term aes-*

thetic values. These two often-conflicting philosophies remain with us today and have profound effects on modern historic preservation.

Early Efforts to Preserve America's Heritage

Archaeology and the preservation of cultural and historic properties were swept along with the conservation movement nearly from its beginning. In 1880, the Archaeological Institute of America (formed in 1879 and still a major international archaeological organization today) sent Adolph Bandelier to New Mexico to explore the pueblo ruins there (you will remember Bandelier, author of *The Delight Makers,* from Chapter 3). Bandelier discovered that a local rancher had dismantled the roof of the Spanish church at Pecos Pueblo in 1858, recovering adobe and timber to construct outhouses. "Treasure hunters" had ripped out the mission's carved lintel beams and made boxes of them; they also looted graves inside the mission compound. The destruction of America's national heritage—which subsumed all Native American history—was well underway by the mid-nineteenth century.

Reports of this destruction aroused concern among the wealthy patrons of the Archaeological Institute and, in 1882, several influential members tried to pass legislation in Congress that would allow the government to withdraw some lands containing important sites from public sale. But the bill went nowhere.

Fortunately, where Congress refused to act, private citizens stepped in. One of the first sites to be protected was Ohio's Serpent Mound, a remarkable 1400 foot-long snake effigy mound (see Figure 2-3 on page 35). Treasure hunters had heavily damaged the site by the 1870s, and it was probably not pristine even when Squier and Davis (the Moundbuilder investigators whom you met in Chapter 2) mapped it some 40 years earlier. Frederic Putnam (1838–1945), of Harvard University's Peabody Museum, realized that the nation would soon lose this unique site. So, he decided to save it the old-fashioned way: He bought it. Working with wealthy Bostonians, Putnam raised $6000 and purchased the 65-acre property. Harvard University owned the site until 1900, when it transferred title to the Ohio Historical Society, which owns and maintains the site today. (Incidentally, this "old-fashioned" approach to saving sites by buying them continues today through the Archaeological Conservancy, which has preserved nearly 250 sites in 37 states.)

Profile of an Archaeologist
A Federal Archaeologist

*Terry Fifield is the archaeologist for the Prince of Wales Island Districts,
Tongass National Forest, Alaska.*

Terry Fifield

Prince of Wales Island, in the southern portion of southeast Alaska's Alexander Archipelago, is an archaeological frontier. Anthropologist Fredericka DeLaguna stayed north of here when she did her southeast Alaskan fieldwork. Cultural anthropologists have studied the totem poles of Kasaan (on eastern Prince of Wales Island). Linguists have studied the Tlingit and Haida languages of the island. And today a few researchers work at select sites. The Forest Service, responding to passage of the NHPA, began to consider the island's archaeological resources in its planning efforts in the early 1970s. Through the 1980s, a Forest Service archaeologist was stationed in the city of Ketchikan, 45 miles to the east. Crews worked on Prince of Wales Island during the summer to survey planned timber harvest units and roads for historic and archaeological sites. I was one of those seasonal archaeologists in the early 1990s; I also worked for the National Park Service and Bureau of Indian Affairs in northern Alaska.

In 1994, I moved my family to the Craig/Klawock area on the west coast of Prince of Wales Island. I was the first Forest Service archaeologist to live there, and the first to have the opportunity to get to know the residents and become familiar with the land and seascape. As luck would have it, during my first summer, Dave Putnam, a quaternary geologist/archaeologist working with me, spotted a scrap of spruce root basketry eroding from a muddy riverbed in the estuary of the Thorne River. Dave and I worked closely with the state of Alaska (on whose land the discovery was located), other Forest Service resource groups, the Alaska State Museum, and local tribal people. Within a few days, having assembled a small team and having received a lot of advice, we excavated a pedestal of mud containing the oldest example of spruce root basketry known from North America's Northwest Coast.

In 1888, as secretary of the American Association for the Advancement of Science, Putnam formed the Committee on the Preservation of Archaeological Remains on Public Lands and appointed prominent ethnologists Alice Fletcher (1838–1923) and Matilda Coxe Stevenson (1849–1915) to it. Their report detailed the vandalism and destruction of archaeological sites, especially those of the American Southwest, and documented an extreme need to protect sites across the country. But Fletcher, Stevenson, and Putnam were not naive: Knowing that Congress would be reluctant to set aside so much land, they recommended that the AAAS concentrate on establishing a precedent by setting aside one important tract of land—Frijoles Canyon, near Santa Fe, New Mexico (which today survives as Bandelier National Monument; see Figure 3-7 on page 67).

But the Boston Brahmins beat them to the punch. In 1889, a group of wealthy Bostonians petitioned the federal government to save Casa Grande, an important pueblo site that contains a massive (but slowly decaying) four-story adobe structure in southern Arizona. Their efforts paid off—first when Congress appropri-

I made mistakes in that situation, especially in the area of consulting with Native Americans. Being new to the island, I was unfamiliar with clan and tribal boundaries and failed to locate the correct clan leaders for advice. But, I did try to make the contacts and we did one thing right. To preserve it, we immersed the basket in isopropyl alcohol-laced water for a few days and then invited local weavers to come view it. We did not know the basket's age then, but the site's stratigraphy suggested it was several thousand years old. The scene that played out in the Forest Service conference room over the next few days was a powerful one. Weavers from Klawock, Craig, and Hydaburg came by to study the 11 × 13-inch swatch of woven fabric. Haida and Tlingit alike saw the similarities between this ancient basket and the craft they had learned from their aunts and grandmothers. Before the basket was hand-carried to the Alaska State Museum in Juneau for curation, the Forest Service conference room was host to a small but moving ceremony affirming the importance of this artifact to its people and place of origin.

Study of the Thorne River basket eventually revealed it to be a collecting basket woven of spruce root almost 6000 years ago. In 1998, the basket and its discovery were the subject of the Alaska Archaeology Week

poster. The poster, featuring Margaret Davidson's technical drawing and watercolor reconstruction, was popular with Native American weavers all over southeast Alaska. People again imagined the chain of knowledge linking 300 generations of women over nearly six millennia. This important discovery provided tangible proof to today's subsistence-oriented residents that the lifeways and traditions of the island's native people extend deeply into the past.

The excitement and celebration of science and tradition surrounding the Thorne River Basket discovery has colored my approach to handling archaeological information. Here on Prince of Wales Island, where many people are of Native American ancestry, there is widespread interest in studying and understanding the past. But there is also some apprehension about where archaeological specimens go, and perhaps more importantly, what happens to the knowledge that scientists draw from research. I believe an essential part of what we do as archaeologists must be to communicate what we have learned to the people most affected, to the public at large, and to our professional colleagues. As with most situations involving people, it's all about communication, in this case sharing information and the excitement of learning about the past.

ated $2000 for the site's repair in 1889, and again 3 years later, when President Benjamin Harrison withdrew the site (and 480 acres of land around it) from future sale, thus creating the nation's first archaeological "reservation."

The Antiquities Act of 1906

Although the concern for preserving the past was sincere, the late nineteenth-century approach was piecemeal, and the looting and destruction of archaeological sites proceeded at an alarming pace. The cliff dwellings in the Mesa Verde area of southwestern Colorado were especially hard-hit by pothunters. Tucked beneath massive arches in sandstone cliffs, the large pueblos of the Mesa Verde region—and the tens of thousands of well-preserved artifacts they contained—had been protected from the elements since the dwellings were abandoned in the late thirteenth century.

This fact did not escape the notice of skilled pothunters working the area. They tore the roofs off structures, and blasted holes through the stone and adobe walls to let sunlight in. Six-hundred-year-old roof beams disappeared in the looters' campfires, hundreds of purloined pots appeared on an expanding curios market, and long-sacred kivas were damaged beyond repair.

One digger aroused special concern, even though his excavations were more careful than most—and directed at acquiring knowledge rather than curiosities for sale. Swedish scientist Gustaf Erik Adolf Nordenskiöld (1868–1895) was especially attracted to the new finds at Mesa Verde. Traveling to the Southwest in 1891, Nordenskiöld worked with Richard and Alfred Wetherill, local ranchers and archaeological "guides" (who had excavated innumerable sites and supervised excavations at Pueblo Bonito in Chaco Canyon; Southwestern archaeologists still debate their legacy). Nordenskiöld dug extensively at Cliff Palace (shown in Figure 17-1), the largest of the Mesa Verde pueblos. From this site, he excavated a huge artifact collection that he exported to Sweden (specimens that eventually landed in Finland's National Museum, where they remain today).

Although archaeologists admired his lavishly illustrated publication *The Cliff Dwellers of the Mesa Verde* (1893), many were angry that lax American laws could not stop such an important collection from leaving the country.

Public concern over looting reached a boiling point in the late nineteenth century. In 1902, the newly formed American Anthropological Association (AAA) made a priority of establishing adequate antiquities legislation. The Colorado Cliff-Dwellings Association, an early nineteenth-century women's organization based in Denver, raised funds to rent portions of the Ute reservation that contained pueblo ruins. This sort of action by wealthy citizens who had some clout with their congressional representatives was particularly important in encouraging Congress to protect sites. In 1900, portions of Frijoles Canyon, the place that Stevenson and Fletcher suggested be protected, were finally withdrawn by Congress; Mesa Verde was similarly protected in 1904, as were portions of Chaco

Figure 17-1 The site known as Cliff Palace, in Mesa Verde National Park, was occupied in the late 1200s; it was among the first archaeological sites in the United States to be protected by the government.

Canyon a year later. The time had come for formal protection of archaeological sites.

Between 1900 and 1906, several organizations pressed to pass antiquities legislation. But these well-meaning efforts failed for several reasons. Those sponsoring the various bills were unwilling to compromise, congressmen of western states feared that large portions of public lands would disappear, and agency heads would not accept legislation that granted jurisdiction over sites on various agency lands to the Secretary of the Interior. But eventually, Edgar Lee Hewett (1865–1946) successfully championed the necessary compromising legislation.

Born in Illinois, Hewett moved west as a young man to become superintendent of schools in Colorado. He became fascinated by pueblo ruins and began excavating in 1896. Eventually, he earned a doctoral degree from the University of Geneva in Switzerland and became president of the School of American Research (then known as the School of American Archaeology) in Santa Fe, New Mexico. Hewett was a fair archaeologist, but he was a brilliant administrator and an effective lobbyist. And so, in 1905, the AAA made him secretary of a committee charged with working toward antiquities legislation.

Hewett helped hammer out the first draft of the **Antiquities Act,** which, after considerable lobbying and rewriting, was signed into law by Theodore Roosevelt in 1906. The Antiquities Act contained three important provisions:

- The act made it illegal to excavate or collect remains from archaeological sites on public lands without a permit from the relevant government agency;
- The act stipulated that permits would be granted only to museums, universities, and other scientific or education institutions "with a view to increasing knowledge" and that objects gathered would only be "for permanent preservation in public museums."
- The act invested the president with the authority to create national monuments on federal lands containing "historic landmarks, historic and prehistoric structures, and other objects of historic or scientific interest" and to "reserve as a part thereof parcels of land, the limits of which in all cases shall be confined to the smallest area compatible with the proper care and management of the objects to be protected."

Roosevelt made use of the act immediately, naming Devil's Tower in Wyoming and Montezuma's Castle in Arizona (a pueblo cliff dwelling inaccurately named after the famed Aztec leader) national monuments in 1906 (and that same year, Mesa Verde became a national park, the first park created explicitly for its archaeological rather than environmental significance).

The Antiquities Act became the foundation of all future archaeological legislation. Note, however, that the act is not limited to archaeological sites, but includes historic landmarks and "other objects of historic or scientific interest." In fact, the first monument, Devil's Tower, falls into this category.

Legislation is always a compromise or amalgam of various interests. Key congressional sponsors of the Antiquities Act were eager to create legislation that would allow protection of "natural wonders," such as Arizona's petrified forest (which became the fourth national monument)—hence the expansion of the Antiquities Act to include more than archaeological sites.

The River Basin Surveys

The Antiquities Act was a compromise in another way as well. Hewett knew that Congress preferred not to proclaim policies (no matter how well intentioned). Instead, legislators like to begin by "solving" problems, later affirming the policies necessary to implement the solution—if it seemed to work and appealed to the electorate. Knowing this, Hewett shrewdly refrained from suggesting the federal government was *responsible* for the protection of archaeological sites. Hewett instead highlighted the problems of looting and crafted the Antiquities Act to address this problem by (1) creating a permit process and (2) establishing a mechanism for setting aside protected land. The resulting Antiquities Act thus *implied* that the government had a responsibility toward sites on federal land. While this was progress, without solid affirmation of that policy, archaeological sites remained vulnerable from development.

Beginning in the 1930s, archaeologists became increasingly involved with site preservation as the federal government began constructing dams around the country

Antiquities Act Passed in 1906, this act (1) requires federal permits before excavating or collecting artifacts on federal land, (2) established a permitting process, and (3) gave the president the authority to create national monuments.

to generate electricity and irrigate land. As noted in Chapter 1, many sites were excavated during the Depression as part of the Civil Works Administration and Works Progress Administration. One particularly well-run project was the TVA (Tennessee Valley Authority), which created a number of large dams on the Tennessee River and its tributaries. Many sites were excavated in advance of the construction and flooding.

All of this ended when the United States entered World War II in 1941 (and the government-sponsored work parties were disbanded). But dam construction continued to threaten sites. Largely due to the unrelenting efforts of a small group of archaeologists called the Committee for the Recovery of Archaeological Remains (initially consisting of Frederick Johnson, John Brew, Alfred Kidder, and William Webb), the National Park Service worked with the Smithsonian Institution to create and fund a river basin survey program. Although archaeologists often had to cobble together funding, river basins were surveyed prior to inundation, and many archaeological sites that would have disappeared beneath the waters were recorded and excavated.

HISTORIC PRESERVATION COMES OF AGE

The river basin survey program was important because the federal government recognized responsibilities beyond merely protecting sites from theft. This program was tacit admission that the federal government was responsible for any and all effects of its projects on archaeological sites. This statement of policy became codified during the turbulent years of the 1960s and 1970s, when concern for resource conservation reached a critical point.

In the 1960s, a large portion of the American public—many aroused by Rachel Carson's *Silent Spring*

(1962)—recognized that wilderness and wildlife refuges alone could not stem the effects of pollution. Numerous demonstrations were held in the 1960s (Earth Day among them) and, by the early 1970s, an environmental movement was in full swing. The voter appeal of these popular movements was not lost on legislators, and many of them became "conservationists" as well. In fact, sufficient power came down on the side of the ecologists for laws to be drafted protecting the *nonrenewable resources* of the nation.

When most people think of nonrenewable resources, they think of redwoods, whooping cranes, and baby seals. Others think of energy-related assets, such as oil, coal, and uranium. But most legislators have a legal background, and in the course of legally defining national resources, they realized that properties of historic value must be included. After all, they reasoned, how many Monticellos do we have? Shouldn't archaeological and historic sites be considered nonrenewable resources?

The concern with historic preservation was largely about the destruction of historic buildings through urban renewal programs and the construction of national highways in the 1950s and 1960s. Nonetheless, archaeological sites were included in historic preservation legislation and are now considered **cultural resources,** to be legally protected just like redwoods, whooping cranes, and shale oil fields. That legal protection came through various laws and established the framework within which archaeology in the United States must operate today. The most important of these is the National Historic Preservation Act of 1966.

THE NATIONAL HISTORIC PRESERVATION ACT

The Antiquities Act is a short, one-page piece of legislation, intelligible to just about anyone. The **National Historic Preservation Act (WHPA)** on the other hand, is lengthy, tedious, and shot through with bureaucratic jargon. But every archaeologist working in the United States must be intimately familiar with its details.

The NHPA formally stated the policy that lay behind the 1906 Antiquities Act: "It shall be the policy of the Federal Government...to foster conditions under which our modern society and our prehistoric and historic resources can exist in productive harmony...." Three years later, Congress made this policy even more explicit in the National Environmental Policy Act

---

cultural resources Physical features, both natural and artificial, associated with human activity, including sites, structures, and objects possessing significance in history, architecture, or human development. Cultural properties are unique and nonrenewable resources.

National Historic Preservation Act (WHPA) Passed in 1966, this act created (1) the National Register of Historic Places, (2) the Advisory Council on Historic Preservation, (3) State Historic Preservation Offices, as well as (4) a process to mitigate the impact of development; it also requires that government agencies provide good stewardship of their cultural resources.

Archaeological Ethics
The Preservation Dilemma: Should We Not Dig at All?

As we have pointed out before, archaeologists frequently leave a portion of a site behind so that a future archaeologist with better techniques and different questions can learn more from the site. The federal legislation we discussed in this chapter is designed to preserve sites wherever possible.

Many federal land-managing agencies take this legislation to mean that it is *always* preferable to preserve sites rather than excavate them because we will have better techniques in the future. In fact, the regulations governing the NHPA define archaeological excavation itself as an adverse effect, placing it in the same category as erosion, neglect, and looting! As a result, some archaeologists have been denied research permits for sites on federal lands because the sites were *not* threatened by construction or looting.

William Lipe (Washington State University), a noted Southwestern archaeologist and past president of the Society for American Archaeology, points out that this position contains a serious paradox. Because we assume that our methods will always improve, we should always postpone excavation. As a result, we preserve sites for a future that is always just over the horizon, and we never excavate and we never learn anything. What, then, is the point of preserving sites at all?

Under the extreme preservationist position, the only reason for excavation is if looting, construction, or erosion threatens a site. Lipe points out that this assumes that a well-reasoned research question, backed up by solid field methodology, is not as important a reason to investigate a site as these threats.

But all archaeologists try to answer a question with as little excavation as possible. This is partly because they want to preserve as much as possible for the future, and it is partly because it is expensive to excavate, analyze, and curate archaeological materials; we can rarely secure enough funds to do more than small, well-targeted excavations. "Let's face it," Lipe observes, "modern archaeological research is one of the smallest current and future threats to the integrity of the archaeological resource."

In fact, Lipe reminds us: "Under the NHPA, if sites are preserved on the grounds that this makes it possible for them to be studied in the future, one measure of a preservation program's success is whether anything...has been learned by the subsequent study of those sites." If we fail to learn from sites because we have preserved them but locked them away from researchers, then the NHPA has failed.

This does not mean, of course, that we should run out and excavate every site preserved on public lands. It does mean that figuring out how to balance the need to preserve archaeological sites with the desire to learn from them is an ethical challenge facing archaeology today.

(NEPA): "...it is the continuing policy of the Federal Government" to "preserve important historic, cultural, and natural aspects of our national heritage...."

Whereas previous legislation approached historic preservation in a piecemeal fashion and was largely reactive, the National Historic Preservation Act created a systematic, nationwide program of historic preservation. It has therefore had far-reaching effects on American archaeology. The act created State Historic Preservation Offices, headed by State Historic Preservation Officers (SHPO, or "shippo" in archaeological slang). Subsequent amendments created Tribal Historic Preservation Offices on Indian reservations as well; many tribes, such as the Cherokee, Hopi, Zuni, and Navajo, now have large and successful historic preservation programs.

Historic preservation offices are tasked with creating state (or reservation) inventories of archaeological and historic properties, assisting federal agencies in complying with the State Historic Preservation Act, evaluating national register nominations (we'll discuss these below), and serving as repositories for resource information, such as state site files.

The NHPA also created the national Advisory Council on Historic Preservation. This council consists of 20 members, including heads of various federal agencies, representatives of tribes, the National Trust for Historic Preservation, and the National Conference of State Historic Preservation Officers; the president also appoints a few members. The council's mission is "to promote the preservation, enhancement, and productive use of our Nation's historic resources, and advise the President and Congress on national historic preservation policy." It also ensures that government agencies comply with the act, helps resolve disputes, and assists SHPOs.

Sections 106 and 110 of the act are perhaps the two most relevant portions for archaeologists because, in one way or another, these sections provide most American archaeologists with their livelihoods.

Section 110: The Government Must Inventory Lands

As part of its proactive stance, Section 110 of the act requires that all government agencies be good stewards of their cultural resources. This is partially accomplished through the development of historic preservation programs and through the inventory of public lands for archaeological and historic sites. Such an inventory is only an agency's first step in ensuring that actions on federal lands consider the effects of those actions on archaeological and historic sites.

As a result of Section 110, many archaeologists now work for federal agencies—in Bureau of Land Management field offices, for instance, or the National Park Service. But few agencies have been able to enumerate all of their holdings, because such inventories commonly require a 100 percent pedestrian survey (of the kind that we described in Chapter 4), and the federal government manages hundreds of millions of acres of land. By the late 1990s, less than 10 percent of all federal lands had been surveyed. But because Section 110 mandates an inventory, federal agencies continue to whittle away at it, often by working jointly with local college and university research programs.

Section 106: The Government Must Consider the Effects of Its Actions on Historic Properties

Section 106 is very short, but it has had far-reaching effects. Here is what it says in its entirety:

> The head of any Federal agency having direct or indirect jurisdiction over a proposed Federal or Federally assisted undertaking in any State and the head of any Federal department or independent agency having authority to license any undertaking shall, prior to the approval of the expenditure of any Federal funds on the undertaking or prior to the issuance of any license, as the case may be, take into account the effect of the undertaking on any district, site, building, structure, or object that is included in or eligible for inclusion in the National Register. The head of any such Federal agency shall afford the Advisory Council on Historic Preservation established under Title II of this Act a reasonable opportunity to comment with regard to such undertaking.

In other words: If you want to build something on federal property or modify that landscape, or if you want to construct something that requires federal funding, licenses, or permits, regardless of whose property you will build it on (all of these are what is meant by the term "undertaking"), then you must determine whether the project will adversely affect any sites "included in or eligible for" the National Register (we'll get to this later). If it will, you must *mitigate* the impact of the project. What does all this mean?

In the worst case, a project's "effect" might mean "destroy"—but it might also mean altering a site in a way that detracts from what made it significant in the first place. For example, constructing an addition to a historic building that is not compatible with the building's style could be an adverse effect, even if the original building remains intact. But note that Section 106 does not imply we must protect sites at any cost, it just means that the government must understand and consider the value of prehistoric and historic sites in agency planning and activities.

If a site is deemed significant, then the contractor is obligated to mitigate the project's impact on it. Mitigating the impact of a highway, for example, might mean scientifically excavating the sites along the right-of-way. Or perhaps moving the road a little to one side. Which solution is chosen depends largely on the cost of the excavation versus the cost of moving the road.

The National Register and Archaeological Significance

Section 106 applies to sites that are "included in or eligible for inclusion in the National Register," which is a list of significant sites and places that are historically important. If an archaeological site is not "significant," the law says it does not get studied or sampled, excavated or protected. In other words, when the bulldozers come through, the site is history. Thus, the concept of significance is crucial to the protection of sites. What does it mean?

Archaeologists use the term "significant" in two very different ways. Usually, they follow common English usage: "Blackwater Draw might be the most significant Paleoindian site in North America." "Significant" in this case is equivalent to "important," "intriguing," or "consequential." But many contemporary archaeologists use the term in a specialized, legalistic way that requires some explanation.

The National Historic Preservation Act authorized creation of the **National Register of Historic Places,** a listing of districts, sites, buildings, structures, and objects that are significant in American history, architecture, archaeology, engineering, and culture. There are now over 70,000 properties listed on the National Register. They are eligible for certain tax benefits and federal financial assistance for rehabilitation. Just because a site is on the register or eligible for it, however, does not mean that it can't be altered or destroyed (although it makes it more difficult). It does mean that the federal government must *consider the impact* of undertakings on sites that are on or eligible for the register. (The disposition of National Register sites on private property is up to the owner.)

According to NHPA's regulations, an archaeological site is significant if it meets one or more of the following four criteria:

- Association with events that made important contributions to broad patterns of history, prehistory, or culture

- Association with important people in the past

- Possession of distinctive characteristics of a school of architecture, construction method, or characteristics of high artistic value

- Known to contain or likely to contain data important in history or prehistory

Legal significance is based strictly on these four criteria. They can be applied not only to individual sites, but also to multiple properties whose sum total is more significant than any one property. For example, there may be nothing particularly significant about a single nineteenth-century townhouse, but an entire district of such houses could be significant. It is the neighborhood, rather than any single house, that is significant in this case. Such neighborhoods can be named historic districts, and their integrity and significance would be compromised if one townhouse were torn down to put in a fast-food restaurant.

If getting something listed on the National Register sounds difficult, it is. It's not just the archaeologist who decides, but also the responsible federal agency, the SHPO, the state review board, and the Keeper of the National Register. But note that Section 106 of NHPA does not say that a site must be on the register to be protected, but only that it must be *eligible* for inclusion.

Archaeologists involved with cultural resource management are responsible for helping to determine which sites are eligible for the National Register and which are not. Exactly what standards archaeologists follow in determining significance is often a matter of heated debate. Some tribes argue that many sites are significant under the first criteria, but in the past most archaeologists sought eligibility under the fourth criterion ("known to contain or likely to contain data *important* in history or prehistory"). In this case, the archaeologist must clearly define which research questions a site will help answer. And the nature of those questions will determine which sites are eligible and which are not—therefore, which sites are studied and which are destroyed.

As you might imagine, archaeologists often feel conflicted in making such judgments. Suppose that a proposed interstate highway route will obliterate a particular archaeological site. It is your duty as the consulting archaeologist to figure out whether this site is significant, according to the criteria spelled out in the NHPA's

National Register of Historic Places A list of significant historic and prehistoric properties, including districts, sites, buildings, structures, and objects.

regulations. Does it contain unique artifacts or rare contexts (such as pithouses)? Will it contribute to our understanding of prehistoric subsistence, settlement, and trade? We'll return to this matter below.

Compliance Archaeology

Before a site can be judged to be significant, however, you have to find it. We learned about finding sites through sample survey in Chapter 4. CRM surveys are a little bit different.

In general, compliance with Section 106 begins with a review of the available literature and SHPO site files to see what is already known about the proposed project area. This is followed by a systematic survey, conducted according to state standards, following procedures we described in Chapter 4 (often using 100 percent surveys). In the parlance of CRM, the area surveyed is called the **area of potential effect** (or APE). This includes the "area of direct effect," the area directly affected by the construction project and areas that are *anticipated* to be affected by the project after its completion as well. For example, a reservoir project might include not only the inundation zone and dam construction site in the APE, but also areas that will be developed for recreation, such as campgrounds, boat launches, or associated hiking trails (which may extend far beyond the area of direct impact).

In research survey projects, the research question determines what the survey area will be. But in CRM, the size and nature of the development project determines the survey area. As a result, APEs can take on odd shapes. The APE of a fiber optic cable or gas pipeline, for example, might be 100 feet wide and hundreds of miles long. In other cases, "viewsheds," the areas that can be seen from a significant site, are also considered part of the APE. The preservation of historic trails, such as the Oregon and California Trails, might require that an energy company place oil-drilling rigs far enough away or tuck them behind hills so that a hiker's enjoyment of a historic trail is not compromised.

If sites are located during the survey, then the archaeologists might conduct test excavations of those sites to assess their significance. Those that are determined to be eligible for the register and that cannot be avoided by the project might be slated for "data recovery." This can entail large-scale excavations and associated analyses of the artifacts, ecofacts, and sediments. However, mitigation might also require, on the one hand, that a project be moved (for example, shift the oil well), or, on the other hand, that a building or site be recorded in detail before destruction.

At each step in this process, a report is filed with the federal agency providing oversight of the project and with the SHPO. The construction project will have the necessary clearance and permits only when the SHPO and agency have decided on how to resolve a project's adverse effects on significant sites.

Private cultural resource management firms carry out most of these compliance projects (some firms are housed in universities or state agencies). Prior to 1966, most archaeologists were employed in colleges, universities, and museums. But today, because of legislation like the National Historical Preservation Act, the majority of archaeologists are employed in federal agencies or CRM firms. And if you are wondering who pays for all this, it is the highway construction company, the mining company, the fiber optic cable company, or the government—whoever is doing the construction. Ultimately, of course, we all pay when we use the new facility—through tolls, Internet costs, and telephone charges—or higher taxes. But put this into perspective: Although millions of dollars are spent each year on compliance archaeology, the sum is a fraction of total construction costs. The archaeology for the average pipeline, for example, is less than 1 percent of the total construction cost. In return, you are assured that irreplaceable cultural resources will be there for your grandchildren and that those significant sites that have to be destroyed to permit development will first be studied as intensively as current methods allow.

THE ARCHAEOLOGICAL RESOURCES PROTECTION ACT

The Antiquities Act made it illegal to collect and/or excavate a site on federal property without a permit, and the penalties for violators were pretty stiff for 1906:

area of potential effect (APE) The area that will be directly and indirectly affected by a construction project; in some cases it might encompass not only areas that are affected by construction but also areas seen from it.

Looking Closer
Help Find Moundville's Stolen Ceramics

The site of Moundville, discussed in Chapter 13, is now a state archaeological park managed by the University of Alabama. In 1939, the Jones Archaeological Museum opened there, built by the Civilian Conservation Corps. The museum long displayed human burials, but out of deference to Native American sensibilities, all remains were removed from public display in 1989.

There is something else that is not on display either: The 264 ceramic vessels and artifacts stolen from Moundville's archaeological repository in 1980. So far, the FBI has been unable to recover a single pot. These vessels amounted to one-fifth of the entire Moundville collection and were some of the finest specimens. The thieves knew exactly what they were looking for, and given that the pots have not turned up on the art market, it is likely that the theft was carried out on behalf of a well-heeled and unscrupulous collector.

You might be able to help recover these priceless pieces of Native American heritage. The Moundville Web site (*http://moundville.ua.edu/home.html*) contains photos of all the stolen vessels. If you see any of these for sale on the Web, in auctions, art houses, or flea markets, report it to the contacts listed on the Web site.

"a sum of not more than five hundred dollars" and/or imprisonment "for a period of not more than ninety days." But these sanctions mean little in today's world, where a single Mimbres painted bowl or Mississippian vessel can fetch thousands or even tens of thousands of dollars on the illegal antiquities market (see "Looking Closer: Help Find Moundville's Stolen Ceramics"). Under the Antiquities Act alone, looters saw the penalties as nothing more than a small cost of "doing business." In fact, prior to 1979 there were only 18 convictions under the Antiquities Act.

Despite the Antiquities Act's intentions, looting and site vandalism continue to destroy America's cultural heritage. The federal government estimates that of the 2 million archaeological sites presently recorded in the American Southwest, between 50 and 90 percent have already been looted to some degree. And as off-road sports become more popular and open access to remote regions of federal land, looting is accelerating. As shown in Figure 17-2, large-scale looting of archaeological sites is a major threat to the preservation of America's cultural heritage.

The **Archaeological Resources Protection Act** of 1979 (**ARPA**) tried to change this, making it a felony "to excavate, remove, damage, or otherwise alter or deface or attempt to excavate, remove, damage or otherwise alter or deface any archaeological resources located on public lands or Indian lands" without a permit. ARPA also made it illegal to sell, receive, or transport artifacts illegally removed from federal lands. The penalty for violating ARPA is a fine of up to $250,000 and/or up to 5 years in prison. (Collecting arrowheads from the surface, however, was specifically exempted and is not a punishable activity in the act.) The government can also confiscate any equipment used to loot the sites, including vehicles.

ARPA also allows judges to assess civil penalties that can take into account the archaeological or commercial value of the artifacts as well as the cost of restoration and repair of the site. The commercial value is pretty straightforward; the archaeological is less so, because it requires calculating what it would have cost to excavate and analyze professionally the portion of a site that was

Archaeological Resources Protection Act (ARPA) Passed in 1979, this act (1) prohibits the excavation or removal of artifacts from federal property without a permit, (2) prohibits the sale, exchange, or transport of artifacts acquired illegally from federal property, and (3) increased the penalties for violations of the act over those of the Antiquities Act.

Figure 17-2 A Mimbres pueblo site in the process of being looted by bulldozer; the operator plows away the pueblo walls to expose burial pits beneath the rooms. These burials often contain Mimbres bowls that fetch a high price on the antiquities black market.

disturbed. Looters move more dirt in a weekend than an archaeologist would move in an entire season, or two or three, of excavation. Considering the cost of chronometric dates and of faunal, macrobotanical, and geoarchaeological analyses, the "archaeological value" can be extremely high.

These penalties may seem stiff to some people (looters, mostly). But looted sites are lost forever; they cannot be replaced, and it is difficult to put a value on such a loss. Consider also that many looters are often involved in other illegal activities as well—fencing stolen goods, drugs, burglary, and so on. Some have been videotaped looting sites with automatic rifles slung over one shoulder. ARPA, in fact, has proven to be a way to track down some serious criminals (see "Looking Closer: ARPA and Elephant Mountain Cave").

Even with the added protection of ARPA, it is difficult to police millions of acres of federal land, and so looting continues to destroy the nation's cultural heritage. Numerous federal and private agencies have taken aggressive anti-looting measures, such as site monitoring (using motion-sensitive cameras in some cases), substantial fencing, and more diligent law enforcement. The successful "Adopt a Site" program pairs motivated avocational archaeologists with particularly vulnerable sites that benefit from continued monitoring. And still, vandalism and looting are probably the major threats to American archaeology today.

What about State and Private Land?

The above laws apply to federal land (and, in the case of Section 106 compliance, projects on private, state or other lands that entail federal funding, licenses, or permits). Some states have laws that cover cultural resources on state land; in some cases, these laws are as stringent as federal ones, and in others they are quite lax.

But these laws do not generally apply to private land. Many private landowners are wary of archaeologists because they believe that, if they find something significant on their property, the government can confiscate the artifacts or even take their land. In some countries, this is true. In England or Mexico, for example, "treasure laws" give the government ownership of all subsurface historical resources. But this is not true in the United States. No matter how significant or remarkable a site may be, if it is on private property, it belongs to the landowner. The government cannot take it away. The only exception concerns human burials. In many states (but not all), the *intentional* destruction of a burial, regardless of its age, is a violation of state law—even if that burial is on your property.

The sanctity of private land in the United States can be frustrating, however, because the lack of legislation means that the commercial mining of terrestrial (and underwater) sites for artifacts is often completely legal

Looking Closer
ARPA and Elephant Mountain Cave

The police didn't know what to make of the mummified remains of two headless Indian children. But there they were, buried in Jack Lee Harelson's backyard.

In the 1980s, Jack Lee Harelson had a day job as an insurance agent, but his real passion was looting archaeological sites. For years, he looted a cave on Elephant Mountain, in an isolated region of Nevada's Black Rock Desert, on land managed by the Bureau of Land Management. Here he devastated a 10,000-year record of human occupation, stealing a range of artifacts including 10,000-year-old sandals (among the oldest dated footwear in the world). Harelson also unearthed two large baskets, later radiocarbon-dated to 2000 years old, that contained the bodies of two young children, mummified in the dry desert cave. He looted the burial bundles of rabbit nets, coiled baskets, large ceremonial obsidian blades, and deer-hoof rattles. Although it's not clear why, Harelson decapitated the two children, saved the skulls, and buried the remains in plastic bags in his backyard.

Harelson's ex-business partner and his ex-wife tipped the police off to the grisly scene. In 1996, an Oregon court found Harelson guilty under ARPA and assessed him with a civil penalty. In that assessment, the BLM argued that, "Of the 36,000 archaeological sites recorded in Nevada, only four contain 10,000-year stratified records, Elephant Mountain Cave would have been the fifth and the only one in Western Nevada. Harelson destroyed all of this potential and should be liable for the full civil penalty." In 2002, a federal administrative law judge agreed and decided to use the archaeological value of the resources—that is, the cost to professionally excavate and analyze what Harelson had ripped from the cave's fragile sediments—as the basis for the assessment. The judge's decision: $2.5 million. When the assessment was upheld, Pat Barker, the BLM State Archaeologist in Nevada, said, "The loss to the American people from the destruction of the Cave, and the insult to Native Americans from the desecration of the burials in the Cave, far outweighs the economic value of the illegal collection. Unfortunately we cannot recover the dignity of the Native Americans and the record of our shared humanity."

But the story doesn't end here. Having lost his license as an insurance agent because of the conviction, Harelson turned to other activities, including illegal gun sales and the continued illegal excavation of sites in Nevada and Oregon. Undercover agents moved in and learned that Harelson was also planning to kill four people: his ex-wife, a former business partner, an Oregon police sergeant, and the judge of his 1996 trial. In 2002, an Oregon trooper posed as a hitman, and Harelson offered him $10,000 to kill one of his ex-business partners. Harelson wanted proof, however, and so the trooper doctored a photo to look like the corpse. After Harelson paid the "hitman" $10,000 in opals, the SWAT team moved in.

Harelson is being held without bail in Oregon, charged with ARPA violations and also with conspiracy to commit murder. This is the sort of person who loots archaeological sites.

---

or subject to only a minor penalty. As a result, important archaeological sites on private land can be rapidly destroyed. Archaeologists in Kentucky learned this lesson the hard way.

The Slack Farm Incident

Slack Farm sits on a pleasant stretch of rich bottomland along the Ohio River in northern Kentucky. In the fifteenth century, the Ohio River Valley was the center of a thriving chiefdom society, supported by maize agriculture. Several large sites, complete with flat-topped temple mounds such as those we described at Moundville (see Chapter 13), were the centers of large populations. Some of these Mississippian communities may have been even larger than the small towns that lie along the river today.

Prior to 1987, the Slack family knew of and protected a large fifteenth-century Mississippian site on their property. But when they sold the farm, the new owner was uninterested in protecting the site and, in fact, he leased the property for 6 months to two men for $10,000. These two individuals, in turn, subleased portions of the land to eight others. The leasers' intent was not to grow tobacco or maize, but to mine artifacts.

Using everything from shovels to bulldozers, the ten men mined their shares and paraded the skulls and pots they recovered from the 500-year-old cemetery around town. Within a few weeks, the field looked like a war zone—just look at Figure 17-3—pockmarked with craters. Human skeletal remains were strewn about alongside beer cans as the looters made a mad rush for valuable artifacts.

Someone in town finally alerted the police, but they could only charge the men with "desecration of a venerated object," which at the time carried a penalty of $500 and a maximum of 6 months in prison. Some of the pots they had found were probably sold on the black market

for thousands of dollars, so the fine was a mere annoyance. Archaeologists later determined that, although only about 10 to 15 percent of the cemetery had been disturbed, more than 600 graves had been disinterred.

Outrage in the Native American community and the public at large brought a halt to the looting, and archaeologists tried to assess the damage and retrieve some information (all the skeletal remains were reburied in 1988). But because the crime was merely a misdemeanor, no one would prosecute, and all ten men walked away. As a result, Kentucky revised its burial laws, upgrading the penalty for desecrating a grave (including those on private property) from a misdemeanor to a felony.

Still, the looting of archaeological sites on private land will continue unabated until the market for artifacts disappears. Given that this is unlikely, the alternative is that an educated public must simply refuse to accept it, as at Slack Farm.

CHALLENGES FACING CRM ARCHAEOLOGY

CRM legislation has defined a new philosophy of governmental decision-making which requires that environmental and cultural variables be considered side by side with technological and economic benefits when planning future construction. These new requirements have created a market for thousands of archaeological contracts, which produce reports detailing the nature of the archaeological resources endangered and how a project's impact should be mitigated. All things considered, legislation has been a tremendous boon for archaeology, but many still see some serious problems. One of these revolves around the idea of significance as enshrined in the National Register.

Significance: Yours or Mine?

It will always be impossible to save everything, and so CRM

Figure 17-3 Several hundred burials at the Slack Farm site, a fifteenth-century Mississippian burial ground, were looted and destroyed in the 1980s.

© David Pollack/Kentucky Heritage Council

archaeologists must make judgments about what to protect and what to lose. In fact, all archaeologists have to make such decisions when weighing the costs of curating everything brought back from the field. For example, what is the cost of keeping a metric ton of soil samples in storage versus what we think the future benefit might be? Archaeologists take this responsibility very seriously.

In this context, some archaeologists are bothered because the substantive and legal meanings of "significant" are commonly at odds. Some archaeologists feel that every single site is eligible under the register's fourth category of significance ("known or likely to contain data important in history or prehistory"). But consider the case of a small scatter of stone waste flakes or ceramic fragments that contains no stratigraphy, no temporal types, and nothing that can be chronometrically dated. Rather than record one of these small, potentially uninformative sites, many archaeologists would rather focus on those that can provide dates and information on subsistence, social organization, cultural change over time, and the like. To them, it's a matter of where precious time and money are best spent.

On the other hand, as you will recall from Chapter 4, survey projects can squeeze information from undated surface sites—information that is useful for placing the larger and seemingly more significant excavated sites into a regional context. Additionally, our techniques become better with each passing year, and we can be certain that in the future we will be able to extract more and more information from sites that today do not appear to be significant. For example, in the future, we may be able to date scatters of stone waste flakes that today cannot be dated. What is insignificant today may be quite significant tomorrow. To what degree are the compliance requirements of CRM—the identification and preservation of "significant" archaeological data—skewing the archaeological record for future researchers?

Still another problem exists. CRM legislation was framed by a consortium of professional archaeologists, historians, architects, and lawmakers who hammered out the current definition of "significance" in the National Register sense. But critics believe that the current approach to significance falls flat in the real world, because the National Register definition assumes that significance is *inherent* in historic properties. And yet to some degree, significance lies in the eye of the beholder and can run up against some serious roadblocks when the views of indigenous peoples and descendant com-

munities are considered (see "In Their Own Words: Contrasting Views of 'Significance' at Zuni Pueblo" by Roger Anyon and T. J. Ferguson).

What Happens to All the Data?

Many of the challenges facing CRM archaeology echo problems that affect all of archaeology (such as how can we extract more information from the archaeological record more quickly and efficiently?). But a larger problem lies in the accessibility of the basic data being generated.

CRM projects generate reports that are often thousands of pages long with multiple appendices (or a CD) containing data tables. These are expensive to publish and so most become "gray literature"—photocopied reports that sit in SHPO files, unseen by anyone but the relevant agencies, clients, and a few other archaeologists. They take up so much room that many SHPOs now require that reports be filed electronically.

A few decades ago, a person could easily keep up with everything published in their geographic area of research. But now it is almost impossible to even know of, let alone read, everything that is produced. Millions of dollars are spent annually on CRM projects, but the information—and acquiring information is what CRM is all about—is not very accessible. Many states are trying to rectify this problem by making electronic reports available on-line and by compiling site information into large GIS databases. This is extremely time-consuming, and many states simply cannot afford the cost. Making data accessible in a timely manner and a reasonable format is a challenge facing not only CRM, but all of archaeology as well.

The Need for Professional Standards

Yet another challenge concerns professional standards. Americanist archaeology has rapidly evolved from a relatively small "academic" discipline to one with a major daily impact on the public. As economic development proceeds, archaeologists assume the responsibility for representing the public interest in mitigating the adverse effects of such development on the archaeological record. CRM archaeologists realize that they have an obligation to the scientific community, as well as to the companies who hire them, the public, and federal agencies.

This has made many archaeologists, especially those involved in CRM, realize the need for a code of

In Their Own Words

Contrasting Views of "Significance" at Zuni Pueblo

Roger Anyon is cultural resources coordinator for Pima County, Arizona, and T. J. Ferguson is proprietor of Anthropological Research, LLC, and an adjunct professor of anthropology, University of Arizona.

Cultural resource management in the US is conducted under a patchwork of legal and regulatory mandates promulgated by people educated, working, and living in a Euroamerican cultural milieu—rather than being informed by Zuni values. The differing cultural views of archaeological sites and of human burials are instructive.

As viewed by archaeologists, and enshrined in federal regulatory language, archaeological sites are valued for their potential to inform about the past: sites are abandoned inanimate things from which information can be extracted.

As viewed by Zunis, archaeological sites are an essential link to the land, their ancestors, their culture and traditions: sites embody life forces. Religious offerings made when sites were established and lived in, and when they were left during the tribe's migrations, still have power and significance in present day Zuni religion. Zunis have no concept of sites having been abandoned. Ancestral spirits continue to reside in these places, the stewards of the land that provide a temporal link to present day Zuni.

Archaeologists view human remains as they do sites: things holding information about population structure, diet, disease, genetics, burial practices, and so forth. To Zunis, human burials are on a journey: each person passes through four stages during their journey of existence, of which the life that we know is only the first. Each human burial is at some point along the latter three stages of that life journey, completed only when the skeletal remains have finally disintegrated into the earth. No human burial should be disturbed; disrupting the journey that each individual must complete has unimagined consequences for both the deceased and the living.

In general, the Euroamerican view of cultural resources is restrictive, limiting them to archaeological remains and to those places actively used today in a cultural tradition. These small "cultural islands" within the larger landscape have a fixed significance. For Zunis cultural resources are any tangible or intangible aspect of the world that has meaning, regardless of when it was last active in any cere-

Figure 17-4 Faron Nastacio, a Zuni tribal member, takes a tree-ring sample from a historic structure at Ojo Caliente as part of a large dendrochronology project on the Zuni Indian Reservation.

mony. Cessation of ritual activities at a shrine or disused trail for hundreds of years does not diminish its present cultural significance. Nor are cultural resources bounded for Zunis. How can one bound and separate a spring at which a deer drinks from the ancestral archaeological sites this deer visits to pay its respect to the spirits inhabiting that site?

In the Zuni view the entire landscape is a cultural resource, with no fixed boundaries and no fixed significance. Temporal and spatial contexts define meaning and significance, and these may change—for example, by time of year, by virtue of the conduct of a particular ceremony, or depending upon the landscape scale within which it is viewed.

archaeological ethics and standards of performance, backed up by an effective method of policing transgressors. Archaeologists have responded to this challenge in several ways, most recently through the **Register of Professional Archaeologists,** or **RPA.**

The register was established in 1998 with backing from the Society for American Archaeology, the Society for Historical Archaeology, the American Anthropological Association, and the Archaeological Institute of America. According to its Web site, RPA is "a listing of archaeologists who have agreed to abide by an explicit code of conduct and standards of research performance." Its goal is the "establishment and acceptance of universal standards in archaeology." In 2004, there were about 1500 registered professional archaeologists. Compare this with the Society for American Archaeology's membership of about 6700, at least half of whom work in CRM.

Why haven't more archaeologists become RPAs? The drawback, to be honest, is the lack of incentive to register. No one can get a plum contract *because* he or she is an RPA. Only one state, Mississippi, required that archaeologists submitting reports to the SHPO for approval be RPAs; however, the legality of this requirement was questioned and it was soon rescinded (RPA is just a registry, not a certification program; states cannot require that someone belong to a private organization for certification).

The culture of archaeology is such that archaeologists have generally resisted registration and certification efforts. But even barbers have to be certified—and hair grows back, but archaeological sites do not. Perhaps for this reason, several states are considering using RPA standards, and the day may come when archaeologists will have to be certified in some fashion in order to practice their profession. Time will tell.

CRM and Education

Within a period of two decades or so, CRM has radically transformed the practice of Americanist archaeology, particularly with respect to career opportunities, funding sources, and guiding philosophy. Today, CRM provides archaeologists with several hundred million dollars in funding, and several thousand people make their living doing CRM archaeology. Many archaeologists employed in colleges, universities, and museums who wish to pursue "pure" research projects now find that they have to fit themselves into the CRM mold and speak the language of compliance archaeology.

Statistics suggest that any student considering archaeology as a profession will probably pursue that career in CRM. It can be extremely rewarding, if you are adequately prepared for it. However, in the past, many CRM archaeologists claimed that American universities and colleges do not prepare their archaeology graduates with the tools they need to be effective in the world of CRM. This is rapidly changing, as most younger college faculty cut their teeth on CRM archaeology. Any student considering archaeology as a career should think about acquiring skills relevant to CRM in his or her program of study (see "Looking Closer: What Courses Prepare You for a Career in Archaeology?")

INTERNATIONAL EFFORTS TO PROTECT CULTURAL RESOURCES

Although we move from domestic to international perspective, the problem is the same: illegal trafficking in artifacts obtained by theft or by the pillaging of archaeological sites.

In several of the "Archaeological Ethics" boxes (scattered throughout this book), we have mentioned the subject of looting. We have already pointed out that looting within the United States has reached epidemic proportions and, sadly, the international problem is even worse. Some would say that Lord Elgin looted the Parthenon marbles from Greece. Napoleon took the **Rosetta Stone** from Egypt as part of the spoils of war. Archaeological sites in Iraq were looted in the aftermath of the second Gulf War.

Responsible museums today refuse to accept artifacts illegally imported from the country of origin, and many also decline to display illegitimate artifacts already in their collections. The Trustees of the American Museum of Natural History, for instance, forbid curators from authenticating or appraising any artifacts, its Museum Shop refuses to sell antiquities in any form, and the museum's *Natural History* magazine will

Register of Professional Archaeologists (RPA) A listing of archaeologists who have agreed to abide by an explicit code of conduct and standards of research performance; created in 1998.

Rosetta stone A black basalt stone tablet found in 1799 that bears an inscription in two forms of ancient Greek and ancient Egyptian. By working from the Greek texts, scholars were able to decipher the ancient Egyptian hieroglyphs.

Looking Closer
What Courses Prepare You for a Career in Archaeology?

The modern archaeologist is the last of the Renaissance scholars: a jack-of-all-trades and master of one. As you near the end of this text, you might be thinking of what courses would best prepare you for a career in archaeology. First, we suggest you major in anthropology and take courses in biological, linguistic, and cultural anthropology. Thereafter, consider the following:

- Introductory courses in geology, biology, and chemistry
- Geomorphology and soils (pedology) courses
- Advanced chemistry (if things such as stable isotope analysis interest you)
- Vertebrate anatomy (if zooarchaeology appeals to you)
- Ecology and paleoecology (for instance, palynology)
- An introductory business course (this will come in handy if you go into CRM)

- Math—all you can handle, but at least through calculus II
- Statistics (an introductory course plus one that covers multivariate statistics)
- Computer modeling and geographic information systems
- A technical writing course (although a creative writing course is also useful)
- Humanities courses (philosophy of science, historiography, ethnohistory, American Indian studies courses, history)
- At least three semesters of foreign language, especially if you wish to work overseas

Other useful skills to acquire: familiarity with database, statistics, graphics, digital image, word processing and Web construction software; digital photography; use of total stations; basic map reading. Also, spend as much time as possible working on archaeological projects in the summer; look into internships with local CRM outfits.

not accept advertising for antiquities, regardless of how they were acquired.

One might think that, because the conservation of archaeology has been linked to the environmental movement, a public who is daily made aware of issues such as global warming, forest conservation, and biodiversity would also be aware of the international trade in looted artifacts. But this is not the case. The sound of chain saws in distant rain forests have been successfully linked to the personal lives of millions of Americans, but the looting of foreign archaeological sites has not. But make no mistake about the scale of the problem. A few years ago, in fact, Charles S. Koczka, former senior special agent for the U.S. Customs Service, estimated that illegal trafficking in antiquities *may be second only to the drug trade* in international crime. In many

instances, in fact, the people involved in the drug trade are also looting archaeological sites.

Viewed globally, the problem is simply astounding. Thousands of graves are looted in China each year (despite the fact that the Chinese government has stiff penalties against looting). Maya stelae are cut apart with rock saws, and the glyphs sold individually. Thieves cut or chip rock art off caves and cliffs in North and South America, Australia, and Africa and hustle them away to waiting buyers. Armed looters ransack Peruvian tombs for gold; Spanish shipwrecks are plundered for silver; graves of World War I dead are robbed of medals and military paraphernalia. There is literally no place in the world free of looting. At the present rate, there will be precious little left by the end of the twenty-first century, or even by mid-century. And it is no consolation, as some have proposed, that many of these artifacts may eventually end up in museums, because the information that their all-important provenience could have given us is lost forever.

Like the drug trade, the illegal trade in antiquities is hard to stop as long as there is a market. It is difficult to stem the flow of looted antiquities when wealthy, unscrupulous buyers are willing to pay top dollar for artifacts. Many of the plundered sites are in poor or developing nations where, on the one hand, a single jade carving is worth several years' salary and where, on the other, the government lacks the necessary funds to protect their sites. The buyers, however, are in wealthy countries, especially the United States, Japan, and Germany.

To stop the global traffic in illegally acquired antiquities, many nations (including the United States) signed the **UNESCO Convention of 1970** with the unwieldy but accurate name of "Means of Prohibiting and Preventing the Illicit Import, Export, and Transfer of Ownership of Cultural Property." The 100 countries that have signed this convention agree, among other things, to put into place the legislation and administration to do the following:

- Regulate the import and export of cultural objects;
- Forbid their nations' museums from acquiring illegally exported cultural objects;
- Establish ways to inform other nations when illegally exported objects are found within a country's borders;
- Return or otherwise provide restitution of cultural objects stolen from public institutions; and
- Establish a register of art dealers and require them to register.

In keeping with the convention, the United States passed laws such as the 1983 Cultural Property Implementation Act and signed treaties with several countries that specifically prohibit the importing of artifacts without established "pedigrees" into the country. Some of these treaties "grandfather in" artifacts excavated before the treaty's date; this means that an importer must now prove that artifacts were excavated prior to a treaty's date or were otherwise obtained in ways not prohibited by the treaty. As more and more countries establish such treaties, it will become increasingly difficult for someone to import illegally acquired antiquities. Wartime presents special difficulties for the protection of cultural resources, but even here, the world has worked out some

agreements—most notably the 1954 Hague Convention (see "Looking Closer: Archaeology and War").

These treaties and legislative mechanisms do work. In 2003, an appeals court upheld the conviction of Frederick Schultz, an art dealer who had been convicted under the National Stolen Property Act, of conspiring to sell artifacts acquired illegally from Egypt, including the head of a statue of Amenhotep III, which he had sold for $1.2 million. But, as anyone familiar with the drug trade knows, as long as someone is willing to pay high prices for merchandise—whether it's heroin or Maya jades—someone will smuggle it across borders. The only way to stop the trade is to stop the desire for the objects. And that task, sadly, seems almost insurmountable. Archaeologists hope that by continuing to educate the public and by strengthening laws, we will eventually reduce the population of buyers to the point where the market will collapse.

THE NATIVE AMERICAN GRAVES PROTECTION AND REPATRIATION ACT OF 1990

So far, we have discussed government responses to the need to conserve cultural resources. But in 1990, a piece of legislation was passed whose purpose was to actually *rebury* some of those cultural resources that other legislation protects and preserves. The **Native American Graves Protection and Repatriation Act** (**NAGPRA**) moves cultural resource law away from the area of preservation

UNESCO Convention of 1970 Requires that signers create legislation and the administration to (1) regulate the import and export of cultural objects, (2) forbid their nations' museums from acquiring illegally exported cultural objects, (3) establish ways to inform other nations when illegally exported objects are found within a country's borders, (4) return or otherwise provide restitution of cultural objects stolen from public institutions, and (5) establish a register of art dealers and require them to register.

Native American Graves Protection and Repatriation Act (NAGPRA) Passed in 1990, this act (1) protects Indian graves on federal and tribal lands, (2) recognizes tribal authority over treatment of unmarked graves, (3) prohibits the commercial selling of native dead bodies, (4) requires an inventory and repatriation of human remains held by the federal government and institutions that receive federal funding, (5) requires these same institutions to return inappropriately acquired sacred objects and other important communally owned property to native owners, and (6) set up a process to determine ownership of human remains found on federal and tribal property after November 16, 1990.

Looking Closer
Archaeology and War

In early 2003, when a second war with Iraq appeared inevitable, archaeologists feared that bombing might cause irreparable damage to Iraq's archaeological sites, museums, and cultural institutions. This was more than mere worry because in 1991, during the first Gulf War, Saddam Hussein positioned weapons in museums and on top of archaeological sites. As a result, some sites were bombed; for example, 400 artillery shells hit the 4000-year-old Ziggurat at Ur, in southern Iraq. And, after the war, sites were looted and artifacts sold on the black market. (And these fears were justified: The U.S. team that investigated the Baghdad Museum looting found rocket-propelled grenades and other evidence that Iraq's army used the museum as a military installation.)

So, in the months leading up to the second Iraq war, the Society for American Archaeology (SAA), one of the world's premier organizations of professional archaeologists, decided to act. SAA did not want a repeat of 1991's events, but it faced an ethical dilemma. If it asked the Pentagon not to bomb sites or museums, was it tacitly supporting the targeting of other places, such as schools and residences, where innocent civilians could be harmed? (And was it realistic to ask the military *not* to target an anti-aircraft gun located on a site or museum?) Yet, if SAA said nothing, it would be turning its back on a critical part of its own mission: protection of the world's archaeological heritage.

So SAA decided to look to the war's aftermath, the inevitable occupation of Iraq. To do so, it turned to UNESCO's 1954 Hague Convention for the Protection of Cultural Property in the Event of Armed Conflict.

This treaty lays out wartime behaviors toward heritage resources such as museums and sites. In plain language, the Hague Convention states that an occupying force will do everything it can to prevent the looting and destruction of sites that often occurs in the chaos of war and its aftermath. Although Congress never ratified this treaty, the U.S. military has abided by it.

In a letter to Secretary of Defense Donald Rumsfeld, SAA asked the Pentagon to continue this tradition. SAA explained why it thought this mattered:

> . . . when human lives are at stake [why] should we care about archaeological artifacts? Certainly, attending to medical, security, and health concerns should be the top priorities of an occupying force. But eventually, hostilities will end and people will return to their daily lives. The artifacts held in museums and that remain to be found in archaeological sites are the documents of a people's history. Those documents connect people to the past and in so doing connect them to the future.

Eventually, the Pentagon drew up a "no-strike" list that contained more than 4000 archaeological sites and cultural institutions and abided by it. And, although sites and museums were looted, the damage might have been even greater had the military ignored the Hague Convention.

into the field of human rights legislation. Because NAGPRA has had a huge impact on American archaeology, we devote the remainder of this chapter to it.

In 1988, the Senate Select Committee on Indian Affairs was told by the American Association of Museums that 43,306 individual Native American skeletons were held in 163 museums in the United States. Some of these were skulls removed from battlefields—including heads taken from the 1864 Sand Creek Massacre in Colorado, where soldiers and militiamen massacred some 150 Cheyenne and Arapaho, mostly women and children. Native Americans pointed out that, although Indian people represent less than 1 percent of the U.S. population, their bones constitute more than 50 percent of the skeletal collection in the Smithsonian Institution. Many senators were shocked.

And they should have been. Although archaeologists obviously had nothing to do with decapitating fallen Indian warriors, they had been aware for 20 years that many Native Americans were upset by the excavation, analysis, and display of their ancestors' skeletal remains. Walter Echo-Hawk (Pawnee) said "We don't expect everyone to share our beliefs; but it doesn't take the wisdom of Solomon to understand that our dead deserve to rest in peace.... All we're asking for is a little common decency.... We're not asking for anything but to bury our dead." Such statements spurred the Senate into action and brought an end to decades of wrangling that pitted museums, universities, and federal agencies against Native American tribes. In 1990, Congress passed NAGPRA and on November 16 of that year, President George H. W. Bush signed it into law.

NAGPRA explicitly provides for the protection of Indian graves on federal and tribal lands and prohibits the commercial sale or interstate transport of Native American bodies or body parts.

It also required that all institutions that receive federal funds complete an inventory of all human skeletal remains held in their collections prior to passage of the act and present that inventory to the federal government. Those inventories showed that American institutions held more than 117,000 sets of human remains, most of which are from Native American burials. This inventory covered skeletal remains as well as three special classes of objects:

- **Funerary objects** Objects placed with a human body as part of a death rite or ceremony or made to contain human remains at the time of burial (regardless of whether they are known to have been associated with a deceased individual);
- **Sacred objects** Specific ceremonial objects necessary for current practice of traditional Native American religions by present-day adherents;
- **Objects of cultural patrimony** Objects that have ongoing historical, traditional, or cultural importance central to a Native American group or culture (rather than to an individual) and that were "inalienable" at the time they left the tribe's possession (that is, no one person had the right to give them away).

If these human remains and objects are Native American, then the museum community must consult with appropriate Native American representatives of tribes determined to be "culturally affiliated" with the remains and objects regarding their repatriation. We'll return to the concept of cultural affiliation below.

Human Remains Discovered after NAGPRA

So far, we've only discussed human remains, funerary and sacred objects, and objects of cultural patrimony found *before* the passage of NAGPRA. NAGPRA also dictates how archaeologists are to treat human remains and objects found on federal or tribal land *after* the law's passage. In brief, NAGPRA states that ownership of the covered items are determined as follows:

- First, ownership resides with any lineal descendants.
- If lineal descendants cannot be determined, and in the case of unassociated funerary objects, sacred objects, and objects of cultural patrimony, the ownership resides with (in this order):
  1. The tribe (or Native Hawaiian organization) on whose land the remains or objects were found; or
  2. The tribe (or Native Hawaiian organization) who has the closest cultural affiliation with the remains (following the definition above) and who stakes a claim to the remains or objects; or, if cultural affiliation cannot be determined,
  3. The tribe who is recognized as aboriginally occupying land that was determined to be traditionally theirs by a final judgment of the Indian Claims Commission (a commission established in the 1950s to adjudicate Indian land claims); unless,

funerary objects Any items placed with a human body or made to contain human remains at the time of burial (regardless of whether they are known to have been associated with a deceased individual).

sacred objects Specific ceremonial items necessary for current practice of traditional Native American religions.

objects of cultural patrimony Any items with ongoing historical, traditional, or cultural importance that were once owned by the entire tribe (rather than by an individual) and were "inalienable" at the time they left the tribe's possession (that is, no one person had the right to give them away).

4. The preponderance of the evidence shows that another tribe has a stronger cultural affiliation than the tribe specified by the Indian Claims Commission's final judgment.

As of October 2003, 27,777 sets of human remains had been determined to be culturally affiliated and offered to the relevant tribes for repatriation, along with about 636,386 funerary objects, 1185 sacred objects, and 267 objects of cultural patrimony. Critical to the disposition of these remains and those found in the future is the definition of "Native American" and the concept of "cultural affiliation" in the law.

Native Americans and Cultural Affiliation

NAGPRA recognizes the possibility, however slim, that European peoples visited North America before AD 1500, when Columbus' voyages opened the New World to European colonization. We know, for example, that the Vikings had a short-lived settlement in Newfoundland around the year AD 1000 (archaeologists have found and excavated the site of L'anse aux Meadows, which is mentioned in Viking sagas). Neither tribes nor archaeologists wanted non-Indian remains repatriated to Indian tribes. Thus, NAGPRA explicitly defined "Native American" for the purposes of the law: "Native American means of, or relating to, a tribe, people, or culture that is indigenous to the United States."

Once an institution determines that remains and covered objects are Native American, they then have to decide if they are to be repatriated. But to which tribe? Many tribes expressed a desire to have only *their* specific tribal ancestors returned to them. The Eastern Shoshone on the Wind River Reservation in Wyoming do not wish their ancestral remains repatriated because they question the accuracy of museum records. The Blackfeet do not want remains returned unless the museum is *absolutely positive* the remains are Blackfeet, because they don't want responsibility for the remains of a traditional enemy.

And tribes have different ideas about what should be done with the remains. The Zuni asked that skeletons identified as Zuni remain under museum curation. California's Chumash, after having reclaimed their ancestral remains through repatriation, elected to preserve them in their own repository. Many other tribes rebury or cremate repatriated remains. These differences of opinion meant that the government needed a proce-

dure to decide which tribes have control over which remains.

That decision rests on the concept of **cultural affiliation.** Tribes that are determined to be culturally affiliated with particular burials, funerary and sacred objects, and objects of cultural patrimony are entitled to have those burials and objects repatriated to them.

How do we determine cultural affiliation? NAGPRA was quite explicit: Cultural affiliation

> means that there is a relationship of shared group identity which can be reasonably traced historically or prehistorically between a present day Indian tribe or Native Hawaiian organization and an identifiable earlier group.

Cultural affiliation is determined by the "preponderance of the evidence based upon geographical, kinship, biological, archaeological, anthropological, linguistic, folklore, oral traditional, historical, or other relevant information or expert opinion." If remains or objects cannot be culturally affiliated under the law, then they are classed as "unaffiliated" (or "unclaimed" if found after 1990). NAGPRA does not say what happens to those remains; for the time being, they are in limbo and they remain in the museums.

Determining cultural affiliation is not impossible, and it has been done in many instances. But it is also not easy. In fact, it is often very hard to reasonably trace a shared group identity from an identifiable earlier group to an extant tribe.

There are several reasons why this is so. The archaeological and historical record shows that many Native American tribes have migrated, often from distant places. The Navajo and Apache, for example, are the only speakers of Athapaskan in the American Southwest. Given that most speakers of Athapaskan live in northwestern Canada and central Alaska, archaeologists are confident that the Navajo and Apache migrated into the Southwest (although no one is sure exactly when, it was probably not before AD 1000). So, are human skeletal remains from Chaco Canyon culturally affiliated with the Navajo, on whose traditional lands the site sits, or with Puebloan peoples? And if the latter, which? Zuni? Hopi? Taos? San Lorenzo? Acoma? All of these peoples have moved around the landscape and developed into the people they are today over time.

We also know that some tribes formed as a result of colonialism. The Spanish introduction of horses to the Great Plains after AD 1530, for example, helped create the complex mosaic of horse-mounted bison-hunting tribes like the Lakota, Crow, Cheyenne, Comanche, and Arapaho. In the face of such radical changes in lifestyle, archaeologists often find it difficult to "reasonably trace a shared group identity" from an identifiable earlier group to an extant tribe for remains that are more than a few hundred years old.

In discussions of NAGPRA, in fact, a time limit of 500 or 1000 years was proposed; remains older than this would automatically fall into the "culturally unaffiliated" category. But, recognizing that our methods get better all the time, the final decision was to let our methods and ingenuity, rather than an arbitrary age limit, determine what could or could not be culturally affiliated.

Finally, another source of contention is that NAGPRA only provides for affiliation to federally-recognized tribes. Numerous Indian tribes are recognized by a state, but not by the federal government. And still other tribes exist but are recognized by neither the federal or a state government. Members of these organizations feel excluded (though some states now have their own NAGPRA-like laws that include state-recognized tribes).

Although some archaeologists remain flatly opposed to NAGPRA, the vast majority recognize that the statute has forced a dialog that was long overdue. But this does not mean that answers come easily. We introduced this text with a description of the discovery of "Kennewick Man," a 9400-year-old human skeleton in Washington. In that case, a judge eventually decided that the individual was *not* Native American as defined in the law, and that even if he were, he could *not* be culturally affiliated with the tribes who claimed him. This ruling could have a far-reaching impact on American archaeology, so let's look more closely at how the judge arrived at his decision.

Is Kennewick Native American?

Most people would probably assume that a 9400-year-old skeleton was Native American. In fact, the Department of Interior concluded that Kennewick Man is Native American simply because he pre-dates the European colonization of the New World.

But recall NAGPRA's definition of Native American: "of, or relating to, a tribe, people, or culture that is indigenous to the United States." This definition, the judge said, means that age is not *sufficient* evidence to

determine that a burial is Native American under NAGPRA. Consequently, the judge ruled that the Department of the Interior was wrong to use age alone to establish that Kennewick was Native American.

The judge did not have to determine whether Kennewick Man is or is not Native American under NAGPRA, but he still offered an opinion that has implications for determining the status of similarly ancient burials.

The key word in the definition, believe it or not, is the word "is" in the phrase "that is indigenous." Although acknowledging that "the requirements for establishing 'Native American' status under NAGPRA are not onerous," the judge also argued that the phrase requires showing a "general relationship to a *present-day* tribe, people, or culture" (emphasis added). Kennewick, he pointed out, had no artifacts associated with it; and, because it had eroded from a riverbank, the nature of any burial ritual, which is a cultural act, is gone. Thus, the judge concluded that the culture of Kennewick Man "is unknown and apparently unknowable."

This leaves Kennewick's skeletal remains. As we pointed out in Chapter 1, Kennewick's cranial morphology—the shape of his skull—is different from that of later Native Americans. No matter how you measure it, the Kennewick skull looks more like southeast Asians, Polynesians, or Japan's Ainu, not other Native Americans. For this reason, the judge declared that Kennewick was not Native American. In February 2004, the Ninth Circuit Court of Appeals upheld this ruling.

Some archaeologists might disagree with these rulings. Although the authors of NAGPRA used the present tense in the definition of NAGPRA, they certainly did not intend to exclude Native American groups that, for reasons of tragedies or warfare, left no descendants (cultural or biological). The judge even acknowledged this fact. Perhaps the key term in the definition then, should not be the word "is," but the word "indigenous." And by any standard definition of that term, Kennewick is indigenous because it is highly likely that he was born and lived in the United States before another colonizing population arrived.

Others could point out that the cranial attributes that set Kennewick apart—a steep nasal bone, projecting cheekbones, a long and narrow skull—are found individually among later Native Americans, suggesting some gene flow between Kennewick's population and later Native Americans. Recently discovered human burials in Baja California also suggest that Kennewick's biological population survived into the late Holocene. NAGPRA doesn't apply in Mexico, of course, but these studies show that Kennewick's population did not go extinct and did contribute, in places, to the larger Native American population. And this means that Kennewick meets NAGPRA's definition of Native American: "of, or relating to, a tribe, *people,* or culture that is indigenous to the United States."

Can Kennewick Be Culturally Affiliated with Modern Tribes?

Assuming that Kennewick is Native American, the next question is whether he can be culturally affiliated with the tribes who claim such affiliation. Recall NAGPRA's definition of cultural affiliation: "a relationship of shared group identity which can be reasonably traced historically or prehistorically between a present day tribe or Native Hawaiian organization and an identifiable earlier group." This is a far more rigorous definition than the definition of "Native American."

Cultural affiliation requires that we establish an identifiable earlier group. With only one burial and no grave goods, it is impossible for archaeologists to identify Kennewick's social group. That alone means that Kennewick cannot meet the requirement of cultural affiliation under the law.

In addition, the law stipulates that we must show shared group identity and reasonably trace that identity over time. As we have said, this becomes more difficult, the older a burial is, because we have to trace the "shared group" relationship over a longer timespan. The secretary of the interior originally decided that Kennewick was affiliated with the tribes who requested him—the Umatilla, Colville, Yakama, Nez Perce, and the Wanapum Band—based largely on the continuity of the archaeological record in the region where Kennewick was found and on oral traditions.

It is true that people have lived in the Columbia Plateau for the past 13,000 years. The law, however, does not state that cultural affiliation is based on evidence of continuity. It instead specifies a "shared group identity which can be reasonably traced" over the period of occupation. The archaeological record of the Columbia Plateau shows tremendous cultural changes over time—in the style of projectile points and houses that were used, in burial rituals, in economy and trade

patterns. In fact, evidence of sedentary occupation of the region doesn't appear until 3000 years ago—6000 years after Kennewick died. In other words, in this particular case, archaeology cannot reasonably trace shared group identity over time.

But if archaeology can't, can oral history? We discussed the difficulty of using oral history as a way to reconstruct ancient events in Chapter 14. It is not possible to decide beforehand whether oral traditions are more or less reliable than archaeology. Each case must be decided on its own merits.

In Kennewick's case, the oral traditions of the Umatilla and other plateau peoples describe three periods of time. During the earliest time period, monsters roamed the world, and animals acted like humans. In the second time period, Coyote transformed the landscape and created people.

The third time period includes humans. Traditions associated with this period describe a lifeway that is similar to the ethnographic present; it includes hunting and gathering, salmon fishing, pithouses, and food storage. But that lifeway did not begin until well after 6000 years ago. The lifeways described in the oral traditions do not include what we know, from archaeology, of pre-6000 BP lifeways.

In some cases, the oral traditions describe natural events that could refer to the early Holocene, that is, to Kennewick Man's day. For example, there is a story of a battle between the "warmweathers" and the "coldweathers," set in a time when people died from the cold and the Columbia River froze. This might refer to the late Pleistocene environment. But it could also refer to the Little Ice Age, a global cold period from about AD 1500–1800. The same can be said of accounts of volcanic eruptions, floods, and other events or animals. Their presence in oral traditions does not *unambiguously* mean that the tradition encodes 9400-year-old observations.

As Roger Echo-Hawk pointed out in Chapter 14, it is possible that some oral traditions preserve eyewitness accounts through the use of metaphors that add power to stories of the past and make them a memorable storehouse of moral laws. For example, oral traditions among Columbia Plateau tribes include tales in which bison turn to stone or mythical beings create valleys and hills by dragging huge fish across the landscape. But this property of oral traditions makes them difficult to use to trace "shared group identity" across time.

Clearly, the tales do not relate eyewitness accounts, and thus they could be explanations of how a landscape came to be using observations made on that landscape long after the natural events that formed it actually took place.

Taking all these data into account, the judge decided that, under the requirements of NAGPRA, Kennewick cannot be culturally affiliated with the tribes who claimed affiliation.

What Does NAGPRA Mean by "Identity"?

Some archaeologists point out that NAGPRA is problematic because it employs the Western notion that "identity" is fixed at birth (and hence immutable). In Western culture, one is Irish or English, Spanish or Basque, French or German—implying that ethnicity has hard boundaries, both spatially and temporally. Assuming that such boundaries were "natural," the American government created them among Indians through the treaty and reservation process.

Those hard boundaries are now codified in NAGPRA. It was not the judge's place to decide whether NAGPRA was right or wrong in its definition, but only to determine how that definition ought to be implemented in the Kennewick case. Given the law's definition and the available evidence, there is no "preponderance of evidence" to argue in favor of a cultural affiliation between Kennewick and the tribes who claimed identity with him.

But NAGPRA does not define what is meant by "identity," and this creates some discordance between conclusions reached under NAGPRA and Native American sensibilities.

NAGPRA assumes that human groups have a distinct point of formation, and yet, few actually do. Cultures change over time, even if we ignore the effect of migrations. NAGPRA further assumes that, as one moves back in time, we will encounter some point at which shared group identity is lost. And it is lost not because the archaeological record is too poor to trace it (although that is often the case). Instead, it is lost because the differences between the modern tribe and the past group are so numerous or large that members of the modern and ancient groups would not share an identity—that the ancient and modern peoples, if they could somehow meet one another in time, would not see each other as being the same.

But what is enough cultural change for the archaeologist to cut the tie of cultural affiliation between the past and the present may not be enough for Indians. Many Native Americans feel affiliated with *any* burial in their traditional territory, no matter the burial's age. In these cases, Indians feel betrayed—given that the purpose of NAGPRA was to allow tribes to bury "their" dead. In a legal sense, feelings of betrayal don't matter; the law is what it is. But such feelings do matter if we see NAGPRA as a way to do the right thing ethically. For this reason alone, Kennewick, and other cases like it, will continue to challenge archaeology and Native Americans alike.

CONCLUSION

Archaeology is a nonrenewable resource. Once we excavate a site, we can't dig it again. Once a site is looted, we can never get it back. For these reasons, archaeologists today excavate only what they must in order to answer a research question and work to protect archaeological sites from development on the one hand, and theft on the other. Archaeologists are willing to make some concessions to development; they will make no concessions to looting, within or outside the United States. From these twin concerns has grown the large field of cultural resource management and the many legislative acts designed to protect archaeological sites.

But these efforts are not enough. Without strong public support for archaeology, we will fight a losing battle against development and looting. We hope that through this textbook you have seen how much archaeology can learn from mere scraps of rock, bone, charcoal, pottery, and dirt. Archaeology needs *your* support if it is to succeed in saving the past for the future. Report looting to local authorities. Raise a cry if someone is looting burials. Speak out against the sale of artifacts on the Web and in flea markets. Stand up and be counted if a developer plans to destroy a site to put in a mall. If it seems like a daunting task, just remember the words of anthropologist Margaret Mead:

Never underestimate the power of a small group of committed people to change the world. Indeed, it's the only thing that ever has.

Summary

- America has been concerned with preserving its cultural heritage for as long as it has existed as a country. Although individual sites were protected through specific pieces of legislation or by the actions of concerned citizens, the first legislation to protect all sites on public lands was the 1906 Antiquities Act.

- A truly systematic effort to preserve cultural resources did not come about until the 1966 National Historic Preservation Act (NHPA), which required that the government inventory all cultural resources (historic structures and archaeological sites) on its properties and that it ensure that development projects consider their effects on significant archaeological sites. The act established the National Register of Historic Places and State Historic Preservation Offices.

- The NHPA and National Environmental Protection Act (NEPA) gave rise to the field of cultural resource management (CRM), which provides archaeological services to those organizations that need to comply with the provisions of the NHPA.

- CRM archaeologists are involved in the governmental decision-making that requires environmental and cultural variables be considered side by side with technological and economic benefits when planning future construction.

- CRM is today the most influential force in Americanist archaeology. The bulk of archaeological work being done has shifted from the academic side to the private and government sectors.

- The 1979 Archaeological Resources Protection Act provided further safeguards against the destruction of archaeological sites on federal and tribal land by increasing the penalties for excavating without a permit; but looting still continues to be the major threat to the nation's cultural resources.

- The United States and many nations around the world are working to stop the flow of illegally acquired antiquities. Although many measures have been put into place, most countries still find it difficult to stop antiquities from entering a country where buyers are willing to pay high prices for them.

- The 1990 Native American Graves Protection and Repatriation Act, often seen as human rights rather than archaeological legislation, ensures that human remains, funerary objects, sacred objects, and objects of cultural patrimony are offered for repatriation to culturally affiliated tribes and Native Hawaiian organizations. This process is still underway for most of the nation's museums and universities.

Additional Reading

Brodie, Neil, and Kathryn Walker Tubb (Eds.). 2002. *Illicit Antiquities: The Theft of Culture and the Extinction of Archaeology.* London: Routledge.

Cleere, Henry (Ed.). 1989. *Archaeological Heritage Management in the Modern World.* London: Unwin Hyman.

King, Thomas F. 2003. *Places That Count: Traditional Cultural Properties in Cultural Resource Management.* Walnut Creek, CA: Altamira Press.

Neumann, Thomas W., and Robert Sanford. 2001. *Cultural Resources Archaeology.* Walnut Creek, CA: Altamira Press.

Online Resources

COMPANION WEB SITE

Visit **http://anthropology.wadsworth.com** and click on the Student Companion Web Site for Thomas/Kelly *Archaeology,* 4th edition, to access a wide range of material to help you succeed in your introductory archaeology course. These include flashcards, Internet exercises, Web links, and practice quizzes.

RESEARCH ONLINE
WITH INFOTRAC COLLEGE EDITION

From the Student Companion Web Site, you can access the InfoTrac College Edition database, which offers thousands of full-length articles for your research.

18

Archaeology's Future

Outline

Courtesy Alutiig Museum, photo by Richard Lee

Preview

Throughout this book, we have tried to paint a realistic picture of what Americanist archaeology is all about. We have often reached into the past to demonstrate how today's archaeology has evolved over the last 150 years. Now we will look forward to address two of the key challenges facing Americanist archaeology in the twenty-first century:

- How is archaeology relevant to the modern world?
- How should archaeologists share control over knowledge of the past?

As we explore these related issues, we will probably find more questions than answers.

INTRODUCTION

We began this book by describing Kennewick Man, an important archaeological find that fostered an equally important legal case. The legalities of the Kennewick case highlight even larger issues surrounding the role of archaeology in modern society. But before we consider those issues, we must first recap some key concepts from earlier chapters.

We have emphasized throughout this text the "big picture" of archaeology: the place of archaeological objects in the modern world. We discussed archaeology's contribution to the larger field of anthropology and the different ways that archaeologists think—the different paradigms that we use to reconstruct and explain the past.

We then focused on the particulars of archaeological fieldwork and analysis: how to find and excavate sites; how to date and analyze artifacts and dirt; and how to interpret the remains of plants, animals, and people themselves. You have seen how archaeologists can extract an enormous amount of information from broken, dirty bits of ancient objects to reconstruct ancient cultural behavior—and archaeology is still a relatively young science, making progress each year. The future promises *even greater* knowledge and understanding—achieved by methods that will be even more remarkable than those described in this text.

We then examined two major transitions in the human past: the beginnings of agricultural economies and the origins of the archaic state. Both transitions triggered major changes in world history, each with lasting repercussions—and both processes can be known only through archaeology. These examples served to show what archaeology can learn about the past and the contribution that archaeology makes to an understanding of world history. These two examples likewise demonstrated that the different paradigms of archaeology need *not* compete, but can provide complementary tools for reconstructing the past.

Shawn Dickson (Sioux), mapping artifacts at a Russian workstation on Afognak Island (Alaska).

465

We examined historical archaeology, the particular methods available to understand the more recent past. Here we saw archaeology's special power to correct historical inaccuracies, to recover portions of history unrecorded in documents, and to bring new meaning to the present by re-evaluating the past.

Finally, we looked at the "business" of archaeology—cultural resource management—and its link to laws that govern the preservation of cultural resources, which accounts for most of modern archaeology. We revisited the Kennewick case and discussed NAGPRA, a law that, instead of protecting the *objects* of the past, is intended to protect the various *interests* in the past. This law explicitly recognizes that archaeologists are not the only ones interested in antiquity and that the past holds different meanings for different people.

And through the "Archaeological Ethics" boxes, we discussed issues that reiterated a point first made in Chapter 1: Americanist archaeology is not just about the dead; it's also about the living. We will devote part of this final chapter to exploring the implications of that statement.

Virtually everyone cares about the past, to one degree or another. But people care about history for different reasons. We will always face important issues regarding (1) what is done with our knowledge of the past, (2) who gets to "tell the story," and (3) who controls access to data. We believe that archaeology plays several roles in the modern world and, although each of these functions can be beneficial, some soul-searching is required for professional archaeologists to understand and fulfill their responsibilities. We discuss some of these different roles below.

ARCHAEOLOGICAL SCIENCE: PURE OR APPLIED?

Anthropology is conventionally perceived as a **pure science,** as the systematic pursuit of knowledge for its own

pure (basic) science Systematic research directed toward acquisition of knowledge for its own sake.

applied science Research to acquire the knowledge necessary to solve a specific, recognized problem.

sake. And it is true that anthropologists, like many other scientists, are commonly motivated more by intellectual curiosity than by the practical applications of what they learn. Anthropologists have traditionally looked for answers to the larger, holistic questions regarding the human condition: How, where, and when did humanity arise? What is the relative importance of nature versus nurture? How (and why) did the major social institutions evolve? These are large-scale questions about the basic nature of the human condition, issues without immediate practical application or "relevance."

But anthropologists have long attempted to apply their findings to practical ends—that is, to do **applied science.** During World War II, for instance, some American anthropologists volunteered their services in the war effort. Several collaborated on "national character" studies—detailed memoranda on European and Asian countries that tried to characterize peoples who were either allies or enemies, or who lived in enemy-occupied territory. Working with knowledgeable people in the United States, these anthropologists eventually evolved their own research methods—the "cultures at a distance" approach—to generalize about countries inaccessible because of wartime conditions.

One of the best known of these studies was conducted by Ruth Benedict (1887–1948). At the time a recognized authority on American Indians, Benedict temporarily left her professorship at Columbia to join the Bureau of Overseas Intelligence of the U.S. War Department (1943–1946). She eventually took on a study of Japanese national character, providing information that would ultimately prove critical for the Allied forces occupying Japan during the post-war period.

Applied anthropology is now a huge field. Applied anthropologists evaluate domestic social programs, improve corporate working conditions, develop culturally appropriate methods of delivering health care or agricultural assistance programs, and devise and implement international development programs, to mention only a few areas. Some CRM archaeologists also see themselves as applied anthropologists.

Modern archaeology likewise attempts to apply its knowledge and insights to the modern world. In this chapter, we will present multiple examples of how applied archaeology (1) brings the *techniques* of archaeology to non-traditional venues and (2) applies our knowledge of the human past to concrete economic or social problems.

THE GARBAGE PROJECT

Emil Haury (1904–1992) was the senior archaeologist at the University of Arizona for decades. A specialist in Southwestern prehistory, Haury continually taught his students that "if you want to know what is really going on in a community, look at its garbage."

Haury's earthy advice was not lost on his students and colleagues. In 1971, the University of Arizona launched a long-term, in-depth study of a community's garbage. But it must have surprised Haury when the Garbage Project decided to focus on the garbage of contemporary Tucson.

The Garbage Project was begun by William Rathje (then at the University of Arizona, now at Stanford University), a Harvard-trained archaeologist who had previously specialized in Maya archaeology. Through the Garbage Project, Rathje applied archaeological methods to the analysis of modern American society.

Rathje was dissatisfied with available research techniques for dealing with contemporary society, particularly the dependence on interviews and questionnaires because, like many anthropologists, Rathje realized that they can be problematic. Respondents on questionnaires might lie or give answers that they think are truthful, but actually are not.

Archaeologists, of course, have methods designed to reconstruct human behavior from trash. Rathje reasoned, "Why can't we use these methods to study modern human behavior?"

How Do Archaeologists Collect Trash?

Although it would eventually investigate community trash and landfills around the country (Figure 18-1), Rathje's Garbage Project began in Tucson, Arizona in

Figure 18-1 At California's Sunnyvale landfill, garbage project coordinators Bill Rathje (center) and Wilson Hughes (to Rathje's left) search for newspapers to date a landfill sample.

1973. Garbage was picked up from randomly selected households, and a sampling design ensured that different socioeconomic neighborhoods were included. Student volunteers from the University of Arizona sorted the garbage on special tables provided by Tucson's sanitation department. Student workers had appropriate inoculations and wore laboratory coats, surgical masks, and gloves. Students sorted garbage items into about 150 categories—under the larger headings of food, drugs, sanitation products, amusement and educational items, communication, and pet-related products—and recorded the data on forms for computer processing. The principles of archaeological classification provided objective, repeatable categories of data retrieval. The Garbage Project has involved hundreds of students and 60 participating organizations, recording more than 2 million items from 15,000 household refuse samples from some 250,000 pounds of garbage.

In case you're wondering, courts have ruled that garbage is "abandoned property," meaning that rummaging through someone's trash is not a crime. Nonetheless, the Garbage Project uses various procedures to ensure the anonymity of individuals and households. Volunteers do not record information such as names or addresses, and nothing is saved (although aluminum is recycled); ultimately, the garbage goes to the landfill it was originally headed for.

The Archaeology of Us

The Garbage Project has studied a number of contemporary social issues, including alcohol consumption. Years ago, the Pima County Health Department conducted interviews with a sample of Tucson households to discover how much beer people drank in a week. The sample was carefully chosen using conventional sociological procedures, and informant anonymity was assured. Many took the health department's information as accurate measures of the rate of alcohol consumption in Tucson.

How did the questionnaires stack up against the material evidence—the beer bottles and cans that Rathje's volunteers recorded? It turned out that a large discrepancy existed between front-door answers given to interviewers and back-door behavior reflected in the contents of the trash. Garbage cans don't lie, and the difference from the health department questionnaire's results were striking: The Garbage Project found significantly heavier beer consumption—in the form of more drinkers and higher rates of drinking—than was reported to the interviewers.

This should astound nobody. People drink more beer than they own up to. But the degree of distortion is noteworthy. The skewing, it turns out, correlates with socioeconomic factors. Low-income households typically distorted their interviews by reporting no beer consumption at all (low-income households may receive food stamps and, fearing the loss of support, they might lie on surveys). By contrast, middle-income respondents did admit to drinking beer, but they significantly underreported the amount they actually consumed. These individuals probably gave an honest, though inaccurate, estimate because they don't perceive themselves to be "beer drinkers." These findings actually provided future studies with a way to correct for this inevitable skewing in the data of health questionnaires.

The Garbage Project also analyzed trends in food discard. In 1918, the War Food Administration (one of the few precursors to Rathje's Garbage Project) collected food discard data for U.S. households. At the end of World War I, households discarded 25 to 30 percent of the total amount of solid food brought into the household. But the Garbage Project found a rate of only 10 to 15 percent. Refrigeration as well as food preservatives are probably the major causes of the decline in waste.

In the mid-1980s, Rathje found that, after the National Academy of Sciences published a report linking cancer and heart disease to a diet high in red meat, people in Tucson ate less red meat. And they also discarded twice as much fat from the red meat they did buy. Consumers were obviously trying to cut down on their fat intake. But at the same time, Rathje found an increase in consumers' use of processed meats, such as lunch meats, that contain non-separable fat. Even with a decline in red meat consumption, people's intake of fat actually *increased* because of the use of processed meat products—the exact opposite of the report's intended effect.

Myths about America's Landfills

Everyone knows that we produce a lot of trash. But it's hard to say how much we're producing and whether it's increasing or decreasing. Studies suggest that we create between 2 and 8 pounds of trash per person per day. Surprisingly, although the kinds of trash have changed—no one throws out bucketloads of ash and clinkers from coal-burning furnaces anymore—the amount generated per person has remained about the same over the last 80 years. The overall volume has increased, of course, because there are more people today (four times as many as in 1890).

Prior to the 1940s, many rural households disposed of trash in their own dumps—in a gully or along a river. In cities, garbage was used to create new land. The southern tip of Manhattan, for example, has been growing since the seventeenth century. Speculators would purchase the rights to a stretch of the East River, build piers, and then dump garbage between them. One enterprising builder acquired a ship, filled it with garbage and then sank it between the piers (CRM archaeologists found it later). Eventually, the speculators created land that they then sold.

Formal landfills, however, did not appear on the landscape until the early twentieth century. In fact, it was not until after 1945, when the country's rural population shifted to the industrial cities, that landfills became a significant feature on the American landscape. As in previous centuries, cities used these landfills to create usable space for development; New York's La Guardia airport, for example, sits on one.

Six decades later, more than 70 percent of our garbage—180 million tons annually—goes into some 5,500 active landfills across the country. Landfills are the largest human-made structures in the world; some are many times the size of such massive prehistoric structures as Khufu's Pyramid near Cairo or the Temple of the Sun at Teotihuacan outside Mexico City. The twentieth century's lasting monuments for posterity will be places like Staten Island's Fresh Kills landfill. Even before rubble from the World Trade Center was deposited there, the landfill covered 3000 acres and rose to more than 150 feet in places—3 billion cubic feet of trash.

But space for landfills around large cities is rapidly dwindling; New York City, for example, trucks some of its garbage as far away as New Mexico. One reason is that old landfills were simply holes in the ground, while new landfills are complex places governed by a host of regulations and technologies designed to control toxic substances and methane gas. As a result, the national cost of garbage disposal is skyrocketing—$15 billion a year and rising. This means that we need to know as much about landfills as possible.

But surprisingly, prior to Rathje's studies, little was known about what is actually in landfills and what actually happens there. Rathje argues that "if we are making such a large contribution to future generations, we should know exactly what we are bequeathing them. The only way to unlock these entombed secrets is to excavate." And so Rathje dug, and his research exposed a number of myths about landfills.

The Garbage Project used systematic archaeological methods to explore nine landfills across the United States, recovering about 12 metric tons of debris deposited between 1952 and 1989.

Landfills are generally covered with layers of earth on a set schedule, so they are conveniently stratified. And these strata can be chronologically ordered using newspapers and magazines. But the size of modern landfills did not allow Rathje to sample them with a trowel and dustpan. Instead, he used backhoe trenches (up to 25 feet deep) and a 3 foot-diameter auger equipped with steel teeth that can cut through anything, including a car chassis. Each auger load was hand-sorted, allowing the Garbage Project personnel to calculate what's in America's landfills.

Let's first consider what Americans *think* is in their landfills. The Garbage Project conducted several surveys, with startling results. Many people think disposable diapers, plastic bottles, and large appliances take up most space in landfills. But Rathje's excavations show that these three items *together* take up *less than 5*

percent of a landfill's volume. All kinds of plastics take up less than 15 percent of landfills. And the percent volume of plastic is going down as manufacturers continually "lightweight" packaging—making milk jugs, for example, out of less and less plastic. The volume of plastic is going up because the population is rising but, as a percentage of our trash, the much-maligned plastic container appears to be decreasing.

So, something else must be taking up the space. A survey conducted at an Audubon Society meeting concluded that fast-food containers, polystyrene foam cups and packaging, and disposable diapers constituted 70 to (an impossible) 115 percent of landfills, but Rathje shows that these products together take up *less than 3 percent* of a landfill's volume.

So, what's in landfills? What fills up the 3000 acres at Fresh Kills?

The largest component, it turns out, is *paper*—packaging, newspapers, telephone books, magazines, and mail order catalogs. Paper takes up *40 to 50 percent* of the volume in American landfills. Despite the growing commitment to local recycling programs, the amount of paper is steadily rising—up from 35 percent in 1970. The rest of a landfill consists of, in descending order of volume, construction/demolition debris, metals, plastics, other materials, food and yard waste, and glass.

And, here's the really bad news: Contrary to popular opinion, paper doesn't biodegrade in landfills. The Garbage Project has found 40-year-old newspapers, still fully readable (and some with 40-year-old hot dogs wrapped in them). Our landfills are constructed on the belief that the nasty stuff inside will decompose on its own, like some kind of monumental compost heap.

But very little in our landfills actually biodegrades. Compost heaps work only when we chop up the organics, add fluids, and regularly churn the whole batch. This doesn't happen in landfills: Nothing is chopped up, fluids are often prohibited, and debris is compacted, not churned. Methane production, a by-product of decomposition, ceases 15 to 20 years after a landfill is closed, indicating that decomposition has stopped. But Rathje's excavations show that after 20 years, from one-third to one-half of all organic materials are still recognizable. These remaining organics may eventually break down, but only after many more decades, if not longer.

Most of our knowledge about solid waste disposal and landfill design comes from laboratory experiments, but the inside workings of landfills—what actually happens—have remained almost entirely unknown. Plenty of federal policies regulate landfills, but usually government planners work with "logical assumptions" about what landfills "should" contain.

Rathje doesn't assume, he digs. If we are interested in finding sensible ways to dispose of our trash, we need to know *exactly* what is being thrown away and what happens to it after it enters a landfill. By applying some archaeological approaches, Rathje has learned that many of the long-held assumptions about America's garbage are just that—rubbish.

FORENSIC ARCHAEOLOGY

When Thomas was a first-year curator at the American Museum of Natural History (in the early 1970s), he received a telephone call from a Sergeant McTigue of the New York City bomb squad. At the time, McTigue was working a series of New York City subway bombings. Nearly a dozen such attacks had occurred, killing one person and injuring several others. McTigue suspected that a political protest group was behind the bombings, and he had even identified a prime suspect ("I know the creep who's doin' it.").

Before he could make an arrest, however, McTigue had to establish that, in fact, a crime had been committed. Otherwise, "the perp's lawyer will claim that it was a natural gas explosion, and we can't prove otherwise." To clinch his case, McTigue needed to produce parts of the actual detonating device that had triggered the explosion. Knowing this, McTigue kept sorting through the debris left by each underground explosion. But he never could find what he was looking for. So "the perps" remained free to bomb again, which they did with alarming regularity.

As he was investigating yet another ruined subway station, McTigue finally admitted to himself that he was a cop—trained in standard law enforcement techniques—and not an expert in sorting through trash and debris. But if he wasn't, who was? That's what archaeologists do, right?

That insight brought McTigue to Thomas's office. He explained the problem in simple terms: Suppose that he were to treat each crime scene as if it were an ancient archaeological site. What are the systematic, standardized techniques that archaeologists use to recover their data?

So McTigue and Thomas spent 3 hours working through Archaeology 101: how to establish a three-dimensional grid system and datum point, map surface finds, remove archaeological strata, and use sifters and flotation devices. They went over note taking, photography, and cataloging. Armed with this new investigative strategy, McTigue said "Thanks" and took off.

A few days later, there was the sergeant with his bomb squad on the 6 o'clock news. They were quickly yet efficiently digging and measuring, photographing and sifting the ruins of the latest subway bombing. Except for being a little older (and also heavily armed), the police looked no different from other novices on their first "dig class." After a week or two, Thomas got another call from Sergeant McTigue and, sure enough, they'd found the detonating device they were looking for. An arrest was quickly made, and New York's subway bombings came to an end.

This is an example of **forensic archaeology**—using established archaeological techniques to assist law enforcement agencies. This has become increasingly common in the past 20 years—although, as you will see, for some tragic reasons.

Archaeologists as Crime Busters

Today, several archaeological organizations regularly conduct seminars and workshops for law enforcement personnel. For 20 years, the Oklahoma City Police Academy has sent trainees to an archaeological field program, now taught by Kent Buehler of the Oklahoma Archeological Survey. There, police trainees learn how to read a soil profile, probe the ground to find subsurface pits, read topographic maps and soil reports, as well as how to find and map surface evidence. Through the use of mock crime scenes, trainees acquire basic identification skills, such as distinguishing human from animal bones, and they learn basic mapping and evidence-collection skills.

Protecting the Rights of the Dead

Archaeologists also work directly with investigative teams on crime scenes. In Louisville, Kentucky, for example, Phil DiBlasi (University of Louisville) has worked on several cases involving violations of cemetery laws.

forensic archaeology The application of archaeological and bioarchaeological knowledge for legal purposes.

Louisville's Eastern Cemetery was established in 1843, although it was probably used for burials before then. The wealthy of Louisville were buried there along with slaves and the indigent. In the 1980s, the cemetery's backhoe operator routinely encountered bones when digging a grave, and he was just as routinely told to "get rid of them" when he brought them to the cemetery owners.

But the reuse of graves, even ones that are more than a century old, is illegal in Kentucky, where your grave is yours forever. The backhoe operator's conscience began to bother him, and he finally blew the whistle.

Kentucky's attorney general at the time was Fred Cowan, whose brother was an archaeologist. Cowan quickly saw that archaeological documentation was needed to create evidence for prosecution and, for assistance, he called upon the University of Louisville's Archaeology Program, run by DiBlasi.

Grave plots in the cemetery were roughly 40 square feet in size. By taking the total cemetery area, subtracting the square footage allotted to roads and buildings, and dividing by 40, DiBlasi calculated the maximum number of burials the cemetery could hold. Comparing that figure with the cemetery's records, he found that the cemetery had exceeded its capacity many years ago.

To confirm this, DiBlasi used shallow backhoe trenches, such as those shown in Figure 18-2, to show that virtually all areas of the cemetery, even those lacking headstones, contained rectangular east-west oriented pits that were most likely graves. Grave plots that still-living people had purchased were opened to see if someone were already occupying the gravesite. In every single case, DiBlasi found at least one person (and sometimes as many as three people) already in a grave. Using coffin hardware as time-markers, DiBlasi showed that grave reuse had begun by at least 1858. His standard archaeological information—plan views, stratigraphies, photographs, and artifact dating—were important in the effort to prosecute the cemetery's operators.

DiBlasi has since worked on a number of other historic cemeteries, collecting crime scene evidence and showing that graves allegedly removed during previous construction projects were never actually moved. In one case, DiBlasi found unmarked grave pits in the African-American section of a cemetery, and, at their bottoms, coffin nails and fragments of delicate burial cloths lying in situ, but no sign of a body. This, DiBlasi argued, corroborated local oral histories that describe how this section of the cemetery was routinely robbed

© Robert Kelly

Figure 18-2 University of Louisville archaeologist Phil DiBlasi (in trench) uses a backhoe trench to expose unmarked grave pits at a paupers' cemetery.

of cadavers in the nineteenth and early twentieth centuries—most likely by local medical students and faculty.

The Archaeology of Mass Disasters

As archaeologists become increasingly involved with criminal investigations domestically, they are also increasingly involved with international investigations. These are sad cases as they involve people who were lost in war, massacres, and assassinations. Professional archaeologists have joined investigatory teams to recover MIAs in Vietnam, excavate mass graves of missing persons in South and Central America, and work with United Nations investigatory teams to collect data for tribunals and courts from massacre sites in Croatia, El Salvador, and Rwanda. We'll just look at the last of these.

The violence in Rwanda began in April 1994, shortly after Rwandan president Juvenal Habyarimana was killed in an airline crash (allegedly caused by a missile). An ethnic war broke out between the Hutus and Tutsis and, within months, more than 500,000 people were slaughtered. Many were rumored to be civilians, including women and children who were mercilessly clubbed, burned, or macheted to death. Seeking to determine whether the deaths resulted from civil war or genocide, United Nations investigators authorized archaeological investigations at key sites in central Rwanda.

One such excavation took place at Home St. Jean, where an estimated 4000 to 6000 people were killed. The Midwest Archeological Center, a branch of the National Park Service, assisted in the investigations at the massacre site. Working with forensic specialists, the archaeological team first mapped and photographed the site. They mapped the locations of surface skeletal materials, numbering each item and collecting it for analysis. Through this process, the team discovered six potential mass graves and began working on the largest.

In Her Own Words
The Journey of a Forensic Anthropologist

Clea Koff earned her MA in anthropology from the University of Nebraska-Lincoln in 1999; she is the author of The Bone Woman: A Forensic Anthropologist's Search for Truth in the Mass Graves of Rwanda, Bosnia, Croatia, and Kosovo.

Figure 18-3 Clea Koff excavating a mass grave in Yugoslavia.

My first experience with archaeology was at the age of 10, digging around in my backyard to find the dead bird I had buried the previous winter. I found the bird and an old hairpin. Years later, on a college-level archaeological dig in the Greek countryside, we found Athenian coins, stone foundations, and one human skeleton.

This was my first exposure to human bones and it was a profound experience. I became curious about what the bones could tell us about people, about how they lived and died.

About this time, I read a book describing how forensic anthropologists were helping investigate human rights abuses in Latin America, not only helping to return the remains of missing persons to their families, but also providing evidence to prosecute criminals. I desperately wanted to become a part of this effort and so took more classes in anthropology, archaeology, and human osteology at the University of Arizona. As part of my training, I helped the county medical examiner identify human remains and completed the Armed Forces Institute of Pathology/National Museum of Health and Medicine course in Forensic Anthropology.

In 1996, I joined a team of forensic experts brought together by Physicians for Human Rights to work on behalf of the United Nations International Criminal Tribunals for Rwanda and the former Yugoslavia, the international bodies prosecuting war criminals for genocide and crimes against humanity in those two countries. Our job was to locate, exhume, and analyze human remains from mass graves to provide evidence of the decedents' age, sex, and cause of death. For 6 months, I helped analyze five mass graves, each holding from 30 to over 400 remains.

Once the stratigraphy was determined through hand excavation of several test trenches, the overburden was removed with a backhoe. The archaeologists then exposed human remains by standard archaeological procedures and photographed, mapped, and removed them from the grave.

The archaeologists recovered several hundred sets of remains using these procedures, making this one of the largest exhumations ever conducted in the investigation of human rights violations. Autopsies were conducted to determine sex, age, kind of trauma, and cause of death. Decomposition is rapid in tropical environments, and many of the identifications were made using the techniques discussed in Chapter 12.

Cut marks on bones showed that many individuals were killed by machetes from behind, as if they were fleeing their attackers; cut marks on the bones of hands and forearms showed that some people were unmercifully macheted to death, their arms raised in a desperate effort to ward off the blows. These were clearly unarmed

We worked long hours under the protection of military guards, and often lived in military compounds.

However, working at mass grave sites has a legacy that goes beyond the mandate of the tribunals to hold accountable those responsible for these crimes. For example, after the exhumation and analysis at the first site in Rwanda, Kibuye, was completed, a "Clothing Day" was convened. It was publicized on the radio that our team would be displaying clothing from the grave, and we asked survivors to view the clothing in the hopes of providing leads to probable identifications. This day was important as it was our first opportunity to interact with survivors of this particular massacre.

I shall never forget one woman. She looked as though she was in her fifties, wearing a traditional kanga (a large, printed piece of cloth worn wrapped around the body) over a knit shirt. She was a dignified woman who held her head high, as though not wanting to be involved in this sordid business, but having no choice.

She recognized one of the jackets on display and assented to an interview about the clothing. I asked her for her name and to whom she thought the jacket belonged. She gave a man's name, adding that he could still be alive, having removed his jacket at some point and lent it to someone who was subsequently killed at Kibuye.

I then asked her if she knew if this man had any surviving relatives. Yes, she replied, he'd had a sister. I asked for the sister's name and she gave one, pointedly not looking at me. The name sounded familiar, so I flipped back to the first page of the witness statement and there was that name. It was her name. She was talking about her brother.

As this dawned on me, my eyes shifted to that dirty, empty jacket baking in the sun. I thought of her brother and of my brother, and what I would feel if that thing that had come out of a mass grave looked like my brother's jacket. I couldn't look her in the eye at first, so I looked at her hands—one hand on her purse and one hand grasping her other arm, holding herself together.

I finally looked at her face, unable to talk. Her eyes brimmed ever-so-slightly with tears as she looked out into the distance. I looked where she was looking and saw nothing. I wanted to apologize, to hug her, but I had no protocol. So I just capped my pen, and put my hand on her forearm. She said nothing, I said nothing, but she held her head high. As I held that woman's arm I had a true sensation of being on the continuum of history for the Rwandans affected by the genocide.

We are irretrievably part of their process of healing. I continue to try to understand and articulate this phenomenon.

civilians, murdered as part of a program of genocide. The meticulous archaeological documentation provided critical evidence for the United Nations tribunal, which quickly handed down numerous indictments.

Archaeologists are playing an increasingly important role in the investigation and documentation of human rights abuses (see "In Her Own Words: The Journey of a Young Forensic Anthropologist" by Clea Koff). In fact, as we write this, teams are at work uncovering mass graves in Iraq that could contain over 300,000 bodies of people whose deaths were allegedly ordered by Saddam Hussein.

Archaeology and the World Trade Center

The story is all too well known: On September 11, 2001, two airplanes piloted by al-Qaeda terrorists slammed into the 110-story World Trade Center towers. Within hours, the towers and neighboring buildings collapsed into a massive pile of concrete and twisted steel. Rescue efforts, which had begun even before the towers collapsed, continued for days afterward.

Emotionally taxing as the attack was, clean-up efforts had to begin immediately, and they continued, round-the-clock, for the next 7 months. The steel girders were

In His Own Words
Disaster Archaeology

Richard A. Gould is professor of anthropology at Brown University.

Archaeologists use their skills only to study past human cultures, or so it seemed to me until October 6, 2001. That was the day I first saw the World Trade Center disaster scene. What I found there that day and on subsequent visits to the site and its surroundings changed my outlook toward archaeology and many other things.

As I walked the streets and alleys east of Ground Zero, I encountered fragmented human remains scattered in the gritty, gray matrix of ash and pulverized building materials that covered the fire escapes, sidewalks, and dumpster tops of lower Manhattan. This initial encounter was followed by repeated visits to the area, reports to the authorities, and a rooftop survey with Brooklyn College archaeologist Sophia Perdikaris. The aftermath of this appalling disaster was initially marked by feelings of inadequacy, followed by a realization that archaeological skills could help the healing process for the victims' families and friends. By locating, recording, and recovering human remains and personal effects using archaeological methods and entering this evidence in a chain of custody, we could help victims' families and friends cope with their terrible loss.

Following a workshop at Brown University that brought together archaeologists and police, fire, and emergency-services professionals, we began recruiting and training volunteers. Our team was eventually invited by the New York City Office of the Chief Medical Examiner to perform forensic recoveries at a location next to Ground Zero, in March of 2002. By then, few remains were left undisturbed by the city's clean-up efforts, so our results were disappointing. But later, the NYC Fire Department's "Phoenix Unit" found human remains across lower Manhattan—including the specific localities I had reported earlier and at the location where we performed our trial excavations.

The lessons from this experience guided further training. Eventually, we created a volunteer unit that included safety, medical, and public affairs experts, which we dubbed Forensic Archaeology Recover (FAR). We trained and prepared in a variety of ways based on advice from different agencies in Rhode Island. But we never expected what happened next.

Shortly after 11 PM on February 20, 2003, a fast-moving fire devastated The Station Nightclub in West Warwick, Rhode Island, killing 100 people and leaving others horribly burned. Almost exactly one year after our deployment to the WTC, our volunteer team was activated by

recycled, but the rest of the debris—over 1.7 million tons—was hauled off in a continuous stream of trucks to the Hudson River. Here the debris was loaded onto barges and taken to the Fresh Kills landfill on Staten Island (the same landfill that Rathje had sampled years before).

This was no ordinary clean-up operation. Besides the sheer enormity of the task, the massive rubble pile was the world's largest crime scene. The debris had to be manually searched for the remains of victims, as well as for personal effects that could help identify people whose bodily remains might have simply vanished. The

debris was run through sorters to remove large objects, then it was spread out on the ground and manually searched with rakes. Later, a conveyor belt operation sped up the search.

Within days of the disaster, Brooklyn College archaeologist Sophia Perdikaris put out an informal call to archaeologists for assistance. She recognized that although archaeologists usually deal with ancient artifacts, they are also skilled at finding small things in a vast matrix of dirt and rock, at recognizing and identifying fragments of human bone, and at recognizing broken fragments of objects for what they used to be.

the Rhode Island State Fire Marshall's Office and was at the disaster scene by February 26.

Although it was a much smaller scale than the WTC disaster, the West Warwick nightclub fire presented FAR with technical and emotional challenges that went beyond anything we experienced in New York. Twenty-two FAR volunteers responded.

The medical examiner's staff had already recovered and identified the fire's victims. Our initial task was to recover, record, and enter as evidence hundreds of personal items for the R. I. State Medical Examiner's Office to repatriate to the victims' families. The winter conditions required that we dry-sieve the frozen remains. At the request of the fire marshal, we also watched for specific items related to the investigation. While maintaining its primary humanitarian activities, FAR also came to play an increasingly investigative role.

The work took place within a limited area surrounded by a chain-link fence covered with flowers, photographs, and messages. Hundreds of mourners, survivors, and the media viewed our activities through the fence. It was like working in a fish bowl, but the FAR team remained focused on the archaeological tasks. This

in itself did much to comfort and reassure those watching, as I learned by speaking with my own friends, several of whom lost relatives or close friends in the fire. It was trying at times, for myself and other members of the team, but it taught us that victims' families and friends find it reassuring to know that there are people willing to engage in this kind of recovery effort on their behalf.

Disaster scenes are always complex and chaotic. Archaeology can bring a degree of order out of chaos to comfort the people affected and to help to understand the circumstances of the disaster.

FAR is continuing to train and to recruit new team members—hoping, of course, that nothing like these disasters happens again. This sort of work is not for everyone. We have found, however, that with people who combine their skills and dedication in the way that FAR has done, it is possible. As I watched the FAR volunteers at work, I experienced pride and elation at their efforts while sharing the sense of loss that comes with these kinds of disasters. Perhaps we, as archaeologists and as members of our respective communities, need closure, too. Now I think we know how to find it.

Overwhelmed by the response, she asked the Society for American Archaeology for help. The society set up an online registrar and within a week had over 300 individuals and organizations prepared to volunteer at the landfill. The FBI declined to take advantage of this resource, because they were already overwhelmed with police and fire personnel who had the appropriate clearance and hazardous materials training.

Nonetheless, this effort, and his personal experience with the World Trade Center disaster, inspired archaeologist Richard Gould (Brown University) to develop a volunteer archaeological unit designed to assist at disaster scenes (see "In His Own Words: Disaster Archaeology" by Richard Gould). Most archaeological excavations are pretty happy affairs, with plenty of banter and good-natured ribbing. Gould shows us that the archaeology of disasters is quite different.

REDISCOVERING ANCIENT TECHNOLOGY

There are also more cheerful applications of archaeology. So far, we've been looking at the utility of archaeological methods to modern problems. But the more traditional goal of archaeology—knowledge about the past—can also be applied to current problems.

For example, some archaeologists have found ways to harness ancient technologies to benefit modern populations. Ancient techniques for growing and storing foodstuffs have often fallen into disuse and been forgotten. Yet some of these techniques were developed in places ill-suited for agriculture and might be of value to modern populations coping with strained agricultural systems.

Throughout the world, peasant populations use increasingly marginal land as populations expand and as wealthier farmers and corporations claim exclusive use of prime farmland. In addition, intensive agricul-

tural practices sometimes lead to severe degradation of soil and water, making even highly desirable farmland less productive.

Throughout Peru and Bolivia we find ample evidence of vast expanses of former croplands during pre-Hispanic times that are all but abandoned today. Between 50 and 75 percent of the ancient Inka agricultural terraces are no longer in use. Some archaeologists suggest that, along the Peruvian coastline, up to 40 percent more farmland was irrigated in pre-conquest times than today.

Some pre-Hispanic technologies have been completely forgotten; in other places, practices such as sunken gardens in dry coastal areas of high groundwater and systems of raised fields in waterlogged areas in the Amazon Basin (similar to the *chinampas* we discussed in Chapter 15) are used today only on a limited basis.

Several teams of archaeologists have been studying these ancient Andean agricultural systems with an eye toward reintroducing selected aspects of these technologies, as shown in Figure 18-4. Working from aerial photographs of the Lake Titicaca area along the Peru–Bolivia border, Clark Erickson (University of Pennsylvania) identified a series of ancient raised fields along the lake's margin.

Figure 18-4 Quechua farmers from the Andean community of Huatta reconstructing raised-field patterns in the seasonally flooded plain around Lake Titicaca (Peru). This reconstructed agricultural system is based on both indigenous knowledge systems and intensive archaeological research on ancient field patterns. The retaining wall and platform (at left) are made of sod blocks, and the archaeologically excavated canal appears on the right.

Subsequent archaeological excavations revealed that, starting about 3000 years ago, farmers dug a series of parallel canals and piled the earth between them to form long, low mounds roughly 3 feet high, 15 to 30 feet wide, and up to 300 feet long. These artificial canals provided moisture during drought periods, and the organic-rich muck periodically dredged from the canals fertilized the fields (reducing the need for fallow periods between plantings). Pollen analysis showed that ancient farmers grew potatoes and quinoa (a high-altitude, protein-rich grain) on these fields. We now know, in fact, that these farmers had created more than 200,000 acres of these raised agricultural platforms on the low-lying land near Lake Titicaca.

Experiments based on the archaeological findings show that the water in the canals running between the raised surfaces also served as heat sinks. Collecting warmth during the day and slowly releasing it at night, the canals kept temperatures around the crops about 2° higher than in the surrounding area, both reducing frost damage and extending the length of the growing season—an important attribute at Titicaca's elevation of 3800 meters (12,500 feet).

Modern agricultural technology has damaged the delicate highland environment. Although Erickson does not advocate a naïve "turning back of the clock," he does believe that ancient methods of agriculture provide viable alternatives for rural development. For instance, experimental raised-field farming provides twice the potato yield versus plots using conventional (modern) techniques.

The ancient technology also appears to be cost effective. Several agribusiness experiments in this area, often directed at producing cash rather than subsistence crops, required huge investments in capital. In contrast, projects involving ancient technologies used human labor to produce subsistence products and eliminated the need to import seed, chemicals, and machinery.

Erickson is cautiously optimistic when evaluating the results of these experiments. Some communities participate freely, others do not. Some began the experiment but then abandoned it. The reintroduced technology seems to work best for family-based agricultural fields, with more resistance turning up in community-owned fields. And, of course, the modern sociopolitical situation is different from that of the past, when agricultural technology and productivity were controlled by the Andean state. Today, the failure to adopt or continue raised-field agriculture may not be due to problems in technology, but rather to sociopolitical constraints.

Some argue that, if we do not make archaeology relevant to the modern world, then the modern world will find itself able to get along without archaeology. In this section, we have discussed some examples of how archaeological techniques and knowledge can shed light on modern problems and improve the lives of living peoples. These are cases of archaeologists trying to meet one of its challenges in the twenty-first century (see also "In Her Own Words: Zooarchaeology and Biological Conservation" by Virginia Butler).

Another use of archaeology is perhaps less directly, but no less significantly, pragmatic. Increasingly, archaeologists are incorporating the public into research programs through the active participation of interested members and through public education programs. We examine this facet of modern archaeology in the next section.

PUBLIC EDUCATION

In 1979 and 1980, when we excavated Hidden Cave in western Nevada, we explicitly combined the scientific research project with a public education campaign.

Located outside of Fallon, Nevada, and away from public view, Hidden Cave had been ransacked by vandals for decades. The Bureau of Land Management put a locked gate across the cave's small opening, but looters simply cut or blasted their way through it. Some dragged tires in and burned them just to watch the black smoke pour out of the cave's small opening. BLM archaeologist Brian Hatoff figured that the only way to save the site was to stabilize the remains through judicious excavation. And, instead of doing the work quietly, he suggested that the excavation be turned into a public education campaign in the hopes that it would encourage the local community to "take possession" of the site and protect it themselves.

And so, twice daily on every weekend of the excavation, dozens of people made the trek up the hot, dusty, barren hillside. On each tour, the tour guide introduced visitors to the region's paleoecology and archaeology, pointing out old lake shorelines and rock art along the path. Inside the cave, as Figure 18-5 shows, tourists welcomed the cave's cool relief from the summer sun as they watched the excavation in process and learned

In Her Own Words
Zooarchaeology and Biological Conservation

Virginia Butler is associate professor of anthropology at Portland State University.

Habitats and species around the world are being lost with increasing speed in the face of human population growth and habitat destruction. Under legislation such as the Endangered Species Act (1973), recovery plans are being developed to save or re-establish species and environments. Drawing from recent records, decisions are made on which species should be targeted for recovery, and which should be disregarded. In stark terms, these decisions determine which organisms "belong on the ark." But with access to faunal records dating back hundreds and thousands of years, zooarchaeology brings a much-needed historical perspective to wildlife management policy.

Zooarchaeological research demonstrates the ways past human predation and landscape alteration affected animal populations, and this has important implications for wildlife management. Environments that early European explorers encountered were not free of human influence—they were occupied by Native Americans. Contemporary policy that creates preserves without considering past human actions is trying to recreate environments that never existed. Management of wapiti (elk) in Yellowstone National Park provides a case in point. In the 1990s, over 60,000 wapiti lived in the greater Yellowstone area, yet wapiti remains are rare in archaeological sites. The rarity of wapiti remains suggests that humans kept this animal's populations low through hunting. Charles Kay (Utah State University) argues that this means the "hands off" management policy in Yellowstone, which allows wapiti populations to increase unchecked, does not duplicate pre-AD 1900 conditions, and has led to serious overgrazing of the park.

My own research in California's Owens Valley helps understand the effects of habitat loss and exotic (introduced) species on the loss of native fish species in the American west. Owens Valley contains four indigenous species of fish: pupfish, chub, a minnow, and the Owens sucker, the first three of which are in severe decline. Analyzing an 8000-year zooarchaeological record, Michael Delacourt (California State University, Sacramento) and I found that both the size and abundance of the different species changed over time in response to changes in climate that affected the size of the valley's lakes. But none of them were in danger of extinction. The only thing that changed in the last 100 years was the introduction of exotic species, predatory fish against which the indigenous species cannot compete. With this information, managers can make informed decisions about how to save the indigenous species from extinction.

Zooarchaeological research is aiding conservation measures in many other ways. For example, when wildlife biologists re-establish a species, they try to do so with animals from a source population that is closely related to the original native stock. Since new techniques allow genetic data to be extracted from skeletal remains, genetic analysis of zooarchaeological remains can provide the genetic signature of the locally extinct native stock. In Oregon, for example, biologists wanting to re-introduce the sea otter turned to archaeological remains to determine whether Alaskan or southern California sea otters are the closest genetic match to the population that formerly inhabited Oregon's waters.

Through these and other approaches, zooarchaeology promises to help us understand long-term animal population dynamics so we can take the necessary steps to stop the loss of species diversity and conserve environments for future generations to enjoy.

© David H. Thomas

Figure 18-5 Archaeologist Brian Hatoff explains Hidden Cave's stratigraphy to a school group.

about excavation strategy and recent findings. We also actively solicited coverage of the excavation by the media.

After the fieldwork was over, Thomas published a standard scientific monograph on the site. But in addition, he created a permanent display in the Churchill County Museum in the nearby town of Fallon, and interpretive displays were erected inside Hidden Cave and along the trail (the museum also now maintains a Web site for the cave). Tours are still run, twice a month, to the site. And over the past 20 years, tens of thousands of visitors and school children have visited the site, learning to appreciate archaeology.

Several graduate programs in the United States, Canada, and Great Britain focus on the public education component of archaeology. The Society for American Archaeology maintains an online *Archaeology for the public* Web site and produces educational materials for primary and secondary schools. Most state governments sponsor an "Archaeology Month," with public

lectures, tours, workshops, and educational displays. Bureau of Land Management archaeologist Jeanne Moe runs Project Archaeology, a national education program that sponsors workshops to train teachers how to teach students about the importance of stewardship of the nation's archaeological sites. And an ever-increasing number of federal, state, and local archaeological parks are a focus of educational opportunities.

It is entirely proper for archaeologists to devote some attention to public education, because, after all, it is ultimately the public that financially supports the research. In addition, archaeologists know that members of an educated public are far less likely to vandalize or loot archaeological sites—and more likely to report such activities and publicly denounce them (as they did in the Slack Farm case we discussed in Chapter 17).

But taking archaeology public is not always easy. There are many different "publics," and some are less anxious than others to hear what archaeologists have to say (and a few are downright hostile). This is especially

© David H. Thomas

Figure 18-6 The Alamo.

commonly praised as a strategic move that successfully delayed Mexican forces and ultimately set up a victory for Texas at the subsequent Battle of San Jacinto, where Santa Anna was roundly defeated.

Enshrined in folklore, the Alamo remains one of America's most cherished cultural icons. According to frontier ideology, Americans arrived in Texas to transform the wilderness into a productive part of the United States. And the birth of Texas, it is written, was made possible by the death of the Alamo defenders. Many a Texan ranks the Alamo alongside Lexington and Concord in terms of historical significance.

But for many Texans of Hispanic descent (see "Looking Closer: Hispanic, Latino, Chicano, or Anglo?"), the Alamo is a recurring bad dream, excluding them from an honorable role in Texas history. More than half of San Antonio's current population is Hispanic, and many challenge the traditional heroic image of the Alamo.

The Alamo, they point out, began as a small-scale Spanish mission long before it became an Anglo-Texan shrine. Known as Mission San Antonio de Valero, it was established by a handful of brave and unarmed friars who were trying to bring Christianity to the untamed Texas wilderness. They were men of peace whose goal was saving souls.

What does this have to do with archaeology?

Some members of San Antonio's Hispanic community believe that additional research should be conducted at the Alamo—archaeological research that emphasizes *not* the short-lived 1836 battle, but rather the eighteenth-century mission period. Archaeologist Anne Fox (University of Texas, San Antonio) agrees, and she believes that further excavations at the Alamo would shed new light on this little-known chapter of San Antonio history.

But there is a problem. The Daughters of the Repub-

true when dealing with sites that figure prominently in American history, places such as the Little Bighorn battlefield (Chapter 16) or the Alamo.

Refighting the Battle of the Alamo

In 1836, a Mexican force of perhaps 4000 soldiers commanded by General Antonio López de Santa Anna reached the outskirts of San Antonio, Texas. The Anglo-American garrison, numbering 187 men under the command of Colonel William Travis, withdrew to the Alamo (Figure 18-6). For 13 days, the Texans withstood siege until Mexican troops breached the walls and killed the Alamo defenders.

Today's textbooks commonly pay homage to this heroic episode in the Texan war of independence against Mexico. As one historian put it, the courageous trio—Travis, Bowie, and Crockett—shed their blood upon "a holy altar." Their martyrs' deaths are commemorated in the battle cry "Remember the Alamo!" and

Looking Closer
Hispanic, Latino, Chicano, or Anglo?

Numerous pejoratives have been applied to people of Latin American descent living north of Mexico. Largely to avoid such negative connotations, the terms "Hispanic" and "Latino" have come into common usage (as in the U.S. census).

But disagreement persists about terminology. In places such as Texas, people use "Hispanic" to distinguish themselves as people related in some way to Mexico, Spain, Cuba, or another Spanish-speaking country; "Anglo" distinguishes white, English-speaking people from those of Hispanic descent. We used "Hispanic" in our discussion of the Alamo because it conforms with local usage. But others prefer the term "Latino" (and the feminine "Latina") to emphasize Latin American origins. In other parts of the American West, people call themselves "Chicano" with a sense of pride, and for some it implies Native American as well as Hispanic ancestry. Other Latino and Hispanic people prefer that they simply be called "Americans."

lic of Texas (DRT) are the state-appointed custodians of the Alamo, its archaeological record, and its extensive archives on Texas history. For years, the DRT discouraged research into the Alamo-as-mission because they believed that mission-period research detracted from the "true" historical significance of the Alamo as the cradle of Texas liberty.

That attitude has softened in recent years, but in the eyes of the DRT, it is still those "13 days to glory" that constitute the Alamo's primary significance. Anthropologist Holly Breachley Brear analyzed the social and political situation of the modern Alamo. She argues that, if the DRT were to recognize the earlier mission period or to honor the Mexican soldiers who fought in the Battle of the Alamo, they would be empowering an ethnic group directly descended from the "enemy"; in so doing, they would threaten the sociopolitical power balance in modern San Antonio. But many politically active Hispanics encourage broader archaeological research and public interpretation of the Alamo-as-mission to highlight peaceful Hispanic origins within the state of Texas.

Fox finds the apprehensiveness of the DRT toward mission research troublesome, because it seems to perpetuate the animosity between the current Texan and Mexican populations. Nonetheless, Fox believes that archaeologists should just provide the historical facts and maintain a reputation of not taking sides.

But such "historical facts" can threaten prevailing ideology and can place archaeologists on one side even if they don't intend to be there. During one field season, an Austin newspaper reporter complained that the archaeologists working on mission-period remains outside the Alamo "seemed to be drawing as much reverent attention from the tourists as the indoor exhibits on David Crockett, William Travis, and the other heroes of 1836." The problem is clear: Archaeologists allowed to dig at the Alamo are supposed to find the concrete evidence of the "relevant" past—the 1836 past.

Fortunately, a new generation of DRT members shows an increasing interest in telling a more complete story of the Alamo. Although they still emphasize the 1836 battle, today they present a more evenhanded view. For example, they highlight the local Hispanic populace, some of whom stayed at the Alamo, and others who refused to choose sides. As time passes, the various extreme positions are moderating, downplaying fractious dichotomies such as "heroes" and "enemies."

Such are the tensions surrounding America's sacred sites. When archaeologists excavate and interpret their findings, they are increasingly faced with pressure and conflict from the various public constituencies. The world of archaeology is only beginning to appreciate the ramifications and conflicts involved when we take multiple versions of reality to the American public.

WHO HAS THE AUTHORITY TO STUDY THE PAST?

These examples imply that archaeology has unfettered access to the past. But the authority of archaeology is increasingly being questioned. Who has the right to acquire the data of the past? Who gets to analyze it? Who gets to use the remains of the past? We have already considered how these challenges to archaeology arise over the analysis of human skeletal remains; they are also seen in the study of Native American spiritual sites.

Figure 18-7 An aerial view of the Bighorn Medicine Wheel (1974), when it was surrounded by a wire fence. Today it is protected by a log fence.

© U.S. Forest Service

A Spiritual Site: The Bighorn Medicine Wheel

Look at Figure 18-7 and you will see the Bighorn Medicine Wheel, an ancient stone arrangement perched atop a 9640-foot windswept peak in Wyoming's Bighorn Mountains. There are actually quite a few medicine wheels in the mountains of the high plains, but the Bighorn Mountains site is by far the largest. Today, you reach it by driving up a gravel road to a parking lot and then walking 1½ miles up the ridge. If you arrive in July or August, you might avoid trudging through snowdrifts.

The modern visitor is first struck by the simplicity of the structure: A stone circle, or "wheel," nearly 90 feet in diameter; in the background stretches the vast Bighorn Basin. Inside the stone circle, 28 stone "spokes" radiate out from a central "hub," which is marked by a stone **cairn** about 4½ meters across. Five smaller cairns lie along the Wheel's periphery.

The Western world first took notice of the Medicine Wheel in 1903, when an article in *Forest and Stream* magazine pointed out similarities between the Wheel and the celebrated Aztec calendar stone. Many archaeologists trekked to the site in the following decades; most concluded that the Wheel was constructed in several stages over a long period. Cultural materials recovered in association with the Wheel date to the Late Prehistoric and early historic periods. And there is no evidence that the Wheel has anything to do with the Aztecs. On these matters, archaeologists agree.

But who built it (and why) is more controversial. Some suggest that the rock cairns were graves, each marking where a powerful person was buried. The lines of rocks (the spokes) show the different directions in which the departed ranged "on the warpath," recording the deeds of each dead chief. The rock piles at the ends of the lines may represent enemies killed in battle.

Drawing upon the ethnohistoric record, others suggested the site was for vision quests (see Chapter 14), the Plains Indian ritual where an individual sought communication with the spirit world. For example, the Crow gave an account of the Bighorn Medicine Wheel based on the experience of Red Plume (also known as Long Hair), a famous Crow chief who visited the wheel in the late 1700s:

Red Plume . . . obtained his inspiration and received his medicine and the token which resulted in the application of that name by him at the Medicine Wheel. As a

cairn An artificial mound of stones. May be deliberately constructed as an aid to navigation, as a memorial, or to mark the location of a grave.

young man, Red Plume visited the wheel in the hope of receiving a strong medicine which would make of him a great warrior and chief. Without food, water, or clothing, he remained for four days and nights awaiting recognition from the spirits. On the fourth night he was approached by the three little men and one woman who inhabited the underground passage to the wheel and was conducted by them to the underground chamber. He remained there for three days and three nights and was instructed in the arts of warfare and in leading his people. He was told that the Red Eagle would be his powerful medicine and would guide him and be his protector through life. He was told to wear always upon his person as an emblem of his medicine, the soft little feather which grows upon the back above the tail of the eagle. This little red plume gave him his name. Upon his death, after many years of successful warfare and leadership, he instructed his people that his spirit would occupy the shrine at the medicine wheel which is not connected with the rim, except by an extended spoke, and that they might at all times communicate with him there.

From its lofty perch, the Medicine Wheel is well suited for vision questing. Several contemporary Native American people say they have used it this way. Up-slope winds whistle through countless crevices, creating a babel of moaning and shrieking voices. Some archaeological evidence suggests the rock cairns were protected by small enclosures during the early historic period, perhaps providing a modicum of shelter for those fasting, waiting, and seeking supernatural advice.

But there are other explanations. Astronomer John Eddy suggested that Native Americans constructed the Medicine Wheel as an astronomical observatory. Noting that selected stone cairns might once have held wooden poles, Eddy argued that these posts could have served as foresight and backsight, defining the azimuth of the rising or setting of some important celestial object (probably the sun).

By predicting significant celestial events such as the summer and winter solstices, the Medicine Wheel could have imparted powerful knowledge, useful for calendrical or ritual purposes. Because of its elevation—the site is buried beneath deep snow drifts throughout the winter—Eddy focused on the summer solstice. And in a dramatic, televised recreation, Eddy showed that two of the cairns pointed directly at the rising sun on the summer solstice of 1972. He suggested that the other cairns

mark rising spots of the brightest stars in the summer dawn (stars that appear a few days before the solstice).

But there are problems with this argument. For one thing, the Medicine Wheel lacks convincing evidence for such sighting poles. In addition, the cairns are so large that precise sighting (even with a pole) would not be possible. And even allowing for poles and precision, Eddy's astronomical argument still leaves one cairn unaccounted for. Finally, the numerous collective seasonal movements of the sun, moon, and stars provide so many celestial sightings that we might expect the cairns to point to *something* significant in the heavens simply by pure chance.

Other investigators suggest that the Medicine Wheel was built to aid travel, the rock piles left as directional aids to newcomers. Still others believe that the floor plan of the Medicine Wheel was a two-dimensional imitation of the 28-raftered lodge built as part of the Sun Dance ceremony. Other hypotheses hold that the Medicine Wheel may have been a boundary marker, a depiction of a mythical turtle, or an enduring stone marker demonstrating geometrical expertise.

In brief, we don't know what the Medicine Wheel was in the past. But we do know what it is today.

The Medicine Wheel as a Modern Sacred Site

After taking in the simple majesty of the stone structure and the breathtaking view, the modern visitor is soon struck by the number of offerings left at the site, a scene reminiscent of the Vietnam memorial in Washington, DC. Scattered among the cairns and stone spokes are medicine bundles, antlers, coins, beadwork, photographs, bundles of sage or sweetgrass, and strips of cloth tied to the heavy wooden fence that now surrounds the site. The prehistoric use of the Medicine Wheel may forever remain an enigma but, to many contemporary Indian people, the Medicine Wheel remains a holy place, one of many sacred sites where ceremonies are performed to this day.

And yet many of the most important sacred sites—places like the Bighorn Medicine Wheel—are being overrun each year by thousands of non-Indians: well-meaning tourists, scientific teams, and New Agers seeking a spiritual experience. Indians are greatly concerned that the plants, paths, shrines, rocks, and other aspects of their sacred sites are being destroyed by the curious, and their power diffused by the insensitive.

North American archaeologists agree that the Bighorn Medicine Wheel is one of America's more intriguing ancient sites—and with its stunning setting and puzzling past, the Medicine Wheel is a natural for the heritage tourist. Or is it? Should tourists be encouraged to visit the Bighorn Medicine Wheel?

How do archaeologists balance the dual concerns of bringing American archaeology to the interested public while respecting the wishes of the descendant populations still involved with many of those sites? Some Native Americans claim that all prehistoric sites are sacred. Should they be closed to the public? Should only Indians get to visit these places? Should only Indians study and interpret them?

In the case of the Medicine Wheel, a coalition representing varied interests—tribal, scientific, ecological, and governmental—is trying to protect, preserve, and respect the site. One mutual decision was to close the last mile and a half of the road to the site (allowance is made for the disabled). This solution minimizes the negative impact of tourism, respects the religious freedom of native people, and yet keeps this place accessible to those who wish to see firsthand the structure that has drawn people here for centuries.

William Tallbull (1921–1996), a Northern Cheyenne elder who had a deep and long-lasting personal relationship to the Medicine Wheel, felt it important to keep the site accessible. He believed it inappropriate to exclude anybody (see "In His Own Words: Archaeological Sites or Sacred Places? A Native American Perspective" by William Tallbull). In his perspective, if the educational and contemplative potential of sacred sites can be maintained, then they can offer an important opportunity for teaching tolerance and respect.

Who Owns the Past?

Whether we consider the Medicine Wheel, the Alamo, Hidden Cave, or any other site, it is impossible for archaeologists to escape a central issue: Who owns the past? This is not a question of who owns a site—that's a simple matter of property law—but who has the authority to uncover, interpret, and present knowledge gained from the past?

The past can be a powerful place to visit and, for many, archaeological sites like the Medicine Wheel are strong symbolic reminders of identity and continuity. But is it appropriate that only "descendants" should be "owners" of their past? Is the ancestral perspective the only admissible one?

Leave aside the sticky issue of defining who is a "descendant," and just consider the extreme case—giving complete power to one group of people, be they white, black, Hispanic, or Indian; rich or poor; urban or rural. Our point is a familiar one: Power corrupts, and absolute power corrupts absolutely. It's true in politics, and it's true in archaeology. The Nazis provide a vivid example of this.

Nazi Archaeology: The Danger of Owning the Past

Gustav Kossinna (1858–1931) did not live to see Hitler's ascension to power in 1933, but his work was inspirational to the Nazi elite. A linguist-turned-prehistorian, Kossinna sought to link Germanic culture to particular types of artifacts. Bettina Arnold (University of Wisconsin, Milwaukee) notes that Kossinna's work was intended to help the Germans rebuild their country after the First World War. In fact, his book on German prehistory was dedicated "To the German people, as a building block in the reconstruction of the externally as well as internally disintegrated fatherland."

Kossinna wrote that the presence of allegedly "Germanic" artifacts was archaeological proof demonstrating Germany's prior claim to vast stretches of territory, including large parts of Poland. Kossinna and his acolytes argued that waves of Germanic people had emanated from a northern European core area, carrying with them major cultural achievements such as agriculture, pottery, and metallurgy (none of which fit with the archaeological evidence as we know it). In one of his dinnertime monologues, Arnold notes, Hitler even claimed that the ancient Greeks were Germans who had migrated south.

Prehistory was largely ignored in Germany prior to Hitler's rise to power, and Arnold suggests that it was therefore easy for the Nazis to appropriate the past for their own purposes. From the time Hitler rose to power in 1933 through the end of World War II, eight new chairs of archaeology were established at German universities, and considerable funding became available for excavation. Of course, these new archaeologists were appointed and funded only if they were enthusiastic Nazi party members.

The interest in prehistory went to the highest levels of Nazi political power. Heinrich Himmler—the leader of the SS, Hitler's terrifying personal army—formed a wing of the SS called the *Ahnenerbe* ("Ancestor Heritage"). He looked to prehistory to establish an identity

In His Own Words
Archaeological Sites or Sacred Places? A Native American Perspective

The late William Tallbull was an elder of the Northern Cheyenne tribe.

To the Indigenous Peoples of North America, the archaeological sites found on North American soil are not "archaeological" sites. They are sites where our relatives lived and carried out their lives.

Sacred Sites such as the Medicine Wheel and Medicine Mountain are no different. To Native Americans they are living cultural sites from which help comes when "The People" needed or need help. They were/are places where tribal peoples went in times of famine and sickness, in periods of long drought when animals would leave, or in more current times when tribes are being torn apart by politics, alcohol, or other abuses.

The men make a pledge to go and vision quest at these places, seeking help. As we leave to go to these sites, our every breath is a prayer. We follow the path to the sites; observing a protocol that has been in place for thousands of years. The Native American approaching these sites must stop four times from the beginning of his or her journey to arrival at the site. A trip to a Sacred Site was/is not done just for curiosity, but only after much preparation and seeking.

Many blessings have come to "The Peoples" in this way. Many tribes have received covenants (bundles) from these sites. Some Tribes still carry the bundles that were received from a certain mountain or site. These are considered no different than the covenants given Moses or the traditional law that went with it.

When Native Peoples have been blessed by a site or area, they go back to give thanks and leave offerings whenever they get a chance. These should be left undisturbed and not handled or tampered with.

Today many of our people are reconnecting with these sites after many years of being denied the privilege of practicing our own religion at these very sacred areas. In the past, trips were made in secret and hidden from curious eyes.

If you go to see a Sacred Site, remember you are walking on "holy ground," and we ask that you respect our culture and traditions. If you come to a site that is being used for a religious purpose, we hope you will understand.

for the SS, using a Germanic-like rune as the source of the unit's double lightning-strike insignia. His archaeologists ventured as far as Tibet and Iceland searching for Atlantis, the Holy Grail, and Aryan kings (and providing the inspiration for Steven Spielberg's *Raiders of the Lost Ark*).

During the war, archaeologists were part of the *Sonderkommando Jankuhn*, a military organization led by SS-archaeologist Herbert Jankuhn, which looted museums and libraries in conquered lands in the search for artifacts that would demonstrate Germany's ancestral claim on virtually all of Europe. Posters exhorted Ger-

mans to preserve and report all archaeological finds to authorities because every potsherd was "a document of our ancestors." (This attitude was not motivated by a love of prehistory, for although allegedly Germanic artifacts were preserved, unrelated archaeological sites in places such as Poland and Czechoslovakia were destroyed.)

Archaeological excavations in Germany were wildly misinterpreted to support claims for Aryan superiority, and contrary evidence was suppressed. Open-air theaters, known as *Thingstätten*, where Nazi propaganda plays were performed, were built only in places where the community could demonstrate prehistoric Germanic occupation. For many of these, Arnold points out, the archaeological data were grossly misinterpreted, if not outright fabricated.

Not all German scholars, however, were complacent; and even Hitler recognized that Himmler sometimes went too far with his archaeological fantasizing. Opposition was nonetheless squashed, books outside the party line were banned, and scientists who would not toe the party line were ostracized. There were no open debates, and the Nazi party controlled all discussion of the past.

Nazi archaeology is, to be sure, an extreme case. No form of modern archaeology is in the same pigeonhole. But even extreme cases have value because they warn what can happen when a single group appropriates complete control over the past.

It is precisely the issue of power and control—who determines exclusive access to the past—that created the conflict over Kennewick Man. In Chapter 1, we used the Kennewick case to raise some tough questions: *What gives archaeologists the right to poke into the past, to study the dead? Who owns the past, anyway? And who gets to decide?* We can now return to those questions and consider them in a broader context.

Kennewick Man and Repatriation

In Chapter 17, we discussed how NAGPRA (the Native American Graves Protection and Repatriation Act of 1990) provides control over some (and perhaps eventually, all) Native American burials in the United States.

This is, to put it mildly, a divisive issue. Many archaeologists in the past, and some today, are incensed that human burials and grave goods are being reburied. To these archaeologists, the Kennewick case demonstrates what happens when communities that claim descent from an ancient person are provided exclusive control over ancient remains and objects: How does this differ, some ask, from Nazi book-burnings?

A long-standing social policy in America emphasizes the common heritage of the citizenry. So viewed, the scientific community is responsible for understanding the human condition of all, including Indian people, ancient and living. By removing cultural materials from museums and reburying skeletal remains, selected elements of the common heritage are removed from the public domain. A vocal minority views NAGPRA (and other repatriation efforts) as blatant destruction of archaeological collections and the common American heritage. They urge archaeologists to stand up for their rights and duties as scientists. Repatriation and reburial efforts, in this sense, are viewed as censorship, undermining the ability of scientists to inspect the work of others for errors and misinterpretations (a procedure basic to all modern, ethical science). How is it, some archaeologists ask, that we argue for laws to protect cultural heritage, yet simultaneously condone repatriation? If the objects of the past are so important that the government must protect them, then why do we willingly lose some of the most important ones, forever?

Some archaeologists warn that, decades downstream, we will look back at NAGPRA and condemn the archaeological and museum communities for shortsightedness, for caving in to political demands and allowing the destruction of irreplaceable scientific materials.

These archaeologists make some valid points. Given the far-reaching concern over the Kennewick case—in tribal, scientific, and mainstream venues—it seems clear that Americans are indeed interested in what ancient human remains have to say. And it is true that, once a skeleton is reburied, it is probably gone forever. Down the road of reburial, scientists claim, lies a balkanization of knowledge, a "tyranny of the minority" that ultimately will serve nobody.

Many American Indians and many archaeologists take a different view. The human body is a powerful symbol, especially the human skeleton—the last vestige of what was once a living, breathing person. When federal troops forced Cherokee and Choctaw people to move from their homes in the southeastern United States to Oklahoma in 1838, some families dug up the bones of their relatives and took them along on the bitter Trail of Tears, burying them after their arrival in Oklahoma.

For other Native Americans, skeletons are powerful symbols of colonialism. My God, some Indians say, they killed us, they took away our land, they tried to take away our language and traditions (and succeeded in many cases)—and now they've come for our dead! Some see science as yet another act of colonialism, another way to deny Indians their basic humanity and rights.

This side also makes some valid points. How do we decide who is right? Should science trump all other concerns? In the specific case of human remains, the question has to be solved legally, through the balance that NAGPRA sought to establish. Ethical questions are irrelevant to the implementation of NAGPRA, which only cares about the proper legal course of action.

But these ethical concerns led to the passage of NAGPRA, and the question of who controls the dead is more than a simple question of law: It clearly involves ethical and moral standards as well. Although we can provide no simple, pat answers, we can offer some observations.

Why *We Do Archaeology Affects How We Do Archaeology*

Henry Ford once said that "history is bunk" and, as practicing archaeologists, we obviously disagree. History tells us how we became the people we are today. History contains important lessons about the nature of humans and cultural change—lessons that have practical applications, lessons that help us frame and understand the challenges facing the world today. If we didn't believe strongly that we can learn from, and not just about the past, then we would not be archaeologists.

Hardcore scientists tend to think that people should be united by a passionate belief in pure science, a passionate curiosity about the world around us. This is a laudable desire, and perhaps the day will come when we can all metaphorically climb aboard the starship *Enterprise* and "seek out new worlds and new civilizations"—just for the sheer thrill of it.

But that day is not today. We live in a world partitioned by walls of our own social construction—barriers of race, nationality, ethnicity, wealth, and culture. Listen to the news on any day, and you'll see that this is the greatest challenge facing the world.

And in that world, archaeology can ill afford to stick its head in the sand, claim the high moral ground of pure science, and ignore the ways that other people understand or give meaning to the past. Archaeologists often claim that we do archaeology because understanding the past will help us construct a better tomorrow. But if in doing so we tell a group of people that their interests and concerns do not matter, that scientists will tell them what is best, haven't we contributed to the major problem facing the world today—and substantially undermined any reason for doing archaeology in the first place?

For this reason, archaeologists will continue to debate and discuss the past with various groups outside archaeology, and the discussion will not be easy. Passing

judgment on anybody's values or beliefs is tricky business. Should we take seriously the Asatru Folk Assembly, a group of Euroamericans who claim to maintain an ancient Celtic religion, when they argue that Kennewick Man is their ancestor? And what about actress Shirley MacLaine, who claims (quite sincerely from all accounts) that she's a reincarnated Inka princess? Should we negotiate with Ms. MacLaine if she were to launch a repatriation claim for Inka gold held by museums? Should we give equal time in textbooks to Erick von Däniken, who claims that the pyramids and other architectural wonders of the prehistoric world were built by travelers from other planets?

We don't champion any of these causes. But just because some *individuals* make frivolous claims does not justify setting aside the voices of other *groups*. Shirley MacLaine may have no rights to Inka gold, but the Peruvian government or the Quechua (the indigenous people of the highland Andes) might have very valid claims indeed. Participating in a continual dialog will take effort, and it will sometimes result in the loss of objects, such as human skeletal remains and funerary objects, and the data that those objects represent.

But a "dialog" implies at least two partners, participating as equals. It does *not* mean that archaeologists should abdicate their responsibility as trained observers and interpreters of the data of archaeology. In fact, it is essential that archaeologists and other interested communities work jointly, because when control rests in the hands of one exclusive group—be it scientists or descendants—we run the risk of approaching a Nazi-style archaeology. Professional archaeologists should continue to do archaeology, because if we quit, someone else will surely step in to fill the void, to make their own claims about the past. We worry that the vacuum would be filled by groups like the Asatru Folk Assembly or the followers of von Däniken—people who do not criticize their own ideas, who fail to adhere to high standards of evidence, and who don't make their data and arguments explicit and public.

Archaeologists can sometimes get lost in the myriad details of archaeological investigations—the intricacies of radiocarbon dating, ceramic petrography, and so on. A considered dialog is beneficial because it continually reminds us about why we do archaeology. Many archaeologists, in fact, have already found that there are enormous advantages, both political *and* scientific, to bringing in rather than shutting out other groups.

Seeking Common Ground

A growing number of American archaeologists have developed research programs that incorporate the perspectives of Indian and other descendant communities. Each year, we see more examples of archaeologists using archaeology to help communities reconnect to their past, to establish ties broken by past sociopolitical forces. Many archaeologists have worked hard to make participation in field projects financially possible for members of descendant communities. The Society for American Archaeology, for example, annually awards field school scholarships to Native American students.

More archaeologists are tackling projects in close consultation with tribal councils and descendant communities at the beginning, rather than the end, of a project, devising research in such a way that it is useful to the tribe or community. These projects often incorporate public education programs specifically designed for the descendant community. Here's an example from Alaska that demonstrates both the advantages of seeking community involvement and the pitfalls when this is not done.

Digging Kodiak: Native American Archaeologists at Work

Kodiak Island lies along the southern coast of Alaska, a land of windswept mountains and craggy shorelines. In the winter, violent storms hit once a week; even in the summer it is cool and wet. Aboriginally, it was the home of voles and ermines, red foxes, otters, and the fearsome Kodiak brown bear.

Kodiak Island is also the aboriginal home of the Alutiiq, an Eskimo people (see "Looking Closer: Inuit, Eskimo, Yup'ik, Iñupiaq?"), who today run their own archaeological programs through the Alutiiq Museum and Archaeological Repository.

Looking Closer
Inuit, Eskimo, Yup'ik, Iñupiaq?

The native peoples of the far north divide indigenous peoples there into two groups: Indians and Eskimo/Inuit. Indians speak an Athapaskan or Algonquian language; the Eskimo/Inuit speak one of the (related) Aleut, Yup'ik, or Inuit-Iñupiaq languages. Indians tend to live in interior areas; Eskimo/Inuit live on the Aleutian Islands (where the related language of Aleut is spoken) and on the coasts of Alaska, Canada, and Greenland. There are also cultural differences between the two groupings in, for example, traditions, clothing, rituals, and religion.

In Greenland and Canada, most "Eskimo" people call themselves "Inuit" (meaning "person" or "people"); the Canadian government, in fact, recognizes "Inuit" as the official term. "Eskimo" is commonly heard in Alaska, but even there, native people of the north coast may call themselves "Iñupiaq," and those along the western and southern coasts may prefer "Yup'ik" (these also are the local dialects' terms for "person"). In addition, native peoples have other terms for their specific geographic/linguistic group. The specific term "Alutiiq," for example, is widely used to refer to both the native people of Kodiak Island and their language.

The Canadian government banned the word "Eskimo" because it was said to have a pejorative meaning, "eaters of raw meat." However, linguists don't know what it means. It first appears in English as "Esquimawes" in 1584. But this may have come from a Basque word, which Basque whalers (who hunted off Canada's eastern shores) got from a Montagnais word, *ayassime·w* (the Montagnais are an Indian nation of southeastern Canada). No one knows the meaning of the Montagnais word, but linguistic analysis suggests that it was probably not "eaters of raw meat."

Archaeology began on Kodiak Island in the 1930s, when a famed Smithsonian Institution anthropologist—Alés Hrdlička (1869–1943; his last name is pronounced hair-*lich*-ka—although some Alutiiqs called him "hard liquor")—dug up one of their ancient burial grounds, which had been used for about 3000 years until about AD 1500.

Hrdlička excavated several hundred graves and removed thousands of associated artifacts. This collection alone constituted more than 5 percent of the Smithsonian's holdings in physical anthropology.

From Hrdlička's strictly scientific perspective, the Kodiak Island bones and artifacts were an important cultural resource from which anthropologists could reconstruct millennia of the cultural and biological history of Alaska's Native peoples.

But the descendants of those buried in the cemetery remember Hrdlička as a man who did not respect the living of Kodiak Island. It was a different time, and Hrdlička saw no need to consult with the Alutiiq people. Had he done so, he might have discovered that Alutiiqs did not share Hrdlička's commitment to science, and they deeply resented the fact that he had dug up hundreds of their ancestors and shipped them to a museum more than 7000 miles away.

Returning the Dead

This resentment simmered for decades until the late 1980s (prior to the passage of NAGPRA or the special law that governs Smithsonian repatriations), when the people of Larsen Bay, one of Kodiak's native communities, requested that the bones and funerary objects be returned to the community for reburial.

This simple request for repatriation forced curators and archaeologists to confront the knotty ethical and moral problems inherent in their treatment of Native American burial grounds.

The Smithsonian Institution immediately refused the request, pointing to the scientific importance of the collection and questioning the relationship between the modern people of Kodiak Island and those buried in the ancient cemetery. The Larsen Bay Tribal Council took offense at this knee-jerk response and continued to press for return of the collection.

After several years of controversy, the Smithsonian Institution eventually agreed to return several hundred human skeletons and funerary objects to the Kodiak Island peoples. In the fall of 1991, priests from the

Russian Orthodox Church officiated at the reburial ceremony. Village elders sang hymns in the Alutiiq, Russian, and English languages. Leaders from the tribal council and Smithsonian Institution spoke as the remains were returned to Kodiak's soil.

As it turns out, this was a curious situation. For although the native community had argued for the return of archaeological and skeletal materials, at the same time it was encouraging and supporting archaeological research.

A New, New Archaeology in Kodiak

Archaeology went through an important transition in the 1960s, when processual archaeology, the *new* archaeology, came on the scene. It now appears that another new archaeology is underway, one that recognizes multiple interests in the past. Kodiak Island again provides an example.

While the Kodiak repatriation struggle was going on, Amy Steffian (then a graduate student at the University of Michigan) requested permission to dig further at Hrdlička's site. She and her colleagues argued that archaeological research could provide important clues about modern Alutiiq identity. Native community leaders not only granted her permission to excavate, but they also helped with a research grant from the Kodiak Area Native Association's bingo fund and provided student interns for the project. It's not that the Alutiiq hated archaeology; they just hated an archaeology that implied that they could not be full partners, that said their participation was not needed.

Today, Steffian serves as deputy director of the Alutiiq Museum, an outgrowth of the Kodiak Area Native Association's Culture and Heritage division. Recognizing that they were losing a record of their heritage to winter storms, vandalism, and time, the Alutiiq founded the Culture and Heritage program in 1987 to create an island-wide strategy of archaeological research and to promote educational programs on Alutiiq culture, language, and arts. Eight native corporations today fund and govern the Alutiiq Museum; they also oversee their own archaeological research projects, employing professional archaeologists to work with crews of native people (as shown in this chapter's opening photograph) and community volunteers. The Alutiiq Museum curates the resulting collections and displays artifacts in a native-governed repository. In fact, the artifacts repatriated from Hrdlička's excavation are today stored and available for study in the Alutiiq Museum.

The museum also provides professional and technical support to the "Dig Afognak" archaeological program, which is organized and staffed through the Afognak Native Corporation. Dig Afognak offers the opportunity to live and work with native people in the remote wilderness of the Kodiak archipelago, a 20-minute floatplane ride from the city of Kodiak. Participants live in heated platform tents, dine in a large field kitchen, and bathe in a native-style sauna. Dig Afognak's purpose is "to regain, restore, and carry forward the light of our culture" and "to make the circle complete" by inviting the interested public to join the effort.

The founding of the museum and the growth of archaeological programs produced new career opportunities for Native people. Alutiiq people have long participated in local excavations and are employed in various capacities in the museum. Many of the Alutiiq students involved in the archaeology program are now pursuing college degrees in history and anthropology. One of these, Sven Haakanson, Jr., became director of the museum after completing a PhD in anthropology at Harvard. Several other Alutiiq women who were once interns on field projects now form one-third of the museum's staff.

Other archaeologists who conduct research on Kodiak today follow this example. Ben Fitzhugh (University of Washington), for example, excavated a 135-year-old Alutiiq-Russian site on the south shore of Kodiak with local junior high and high school students. The project discovered a 5000-year-old site beneath the Russian colonial-era one, providing an opportunity to explore changes in Alutiiq heritage unknown without the aid of archaeology. The students later presented the project's findings to the community in a series of conference-style papers. The students left the project not only with knowledge of archaeological methods and strategies, but also with bragging rights: They knew more about Kodiak's deep past than most of their parents.

Later, Fitzhugh and local high school students combined archaeological data on floor plans with the accounts of elders who had grown up in traditional earthen structures to build a replica *ciqlluaq*, or sod house, that today is an educational resource (see Figure 18-8). Through projects such as these, communities take ownership of their heritage and work to promote its protection.

Figure 18-8 Helena Tunohun, an Alutiiq high school student, helps with the construction of a *ciqlluaq*, a traditional sod house, as part of an educational experience in archaeology on Kodiak Island in 1997.

The beginning of this new brand of archaeology on Kodiak Island was NAGPRA. This legislation forced archaeologists to consult with local communities over their research and to do some soul-searching. Although NAGPRA calls for the repatriation of many archaeological collections, in some cases the result has been increased protection of the unexcavated archaeological record. And, ironically, NAGPRA may have engendered changes within archaeology and the Native American community whose end result will be the acquisition of more, not less, information about the past.

CONCLUSION

In this chapter, we have looked at the role of archaeology in the future. We examined some ways in which archaeology can be of pragmatic value—by using archaeological techniques to understand modern garbage and to gather the data needed to bring criminals to justice.

Perhaps even more important, however, will be archaeology's role in knocking down the walls that so often divide people of the world. Archaeology can do this in part by the information that it gathers. Archaeology can show, for example, how different environmental and historical circumstances work together to create the diversity of human societies. In so doing, archaeology proves that unilineal evolution and the racist assumptions that stand behind it are wrong. But archaeology also contributes not only by *what* it learns about the past, but *how* it goes about learning it—the way in which it incorporates different perspectives, attitudes, and concerns of descendant communities and other stakeholders in the past.

Archaeology, as we have said, is not just about the dead; it's also about the living. And, it turns out, archaeology is not just about the past; it's also about the future.

Summary

- One way or another, virtually all archaeological research depends on public support. Particularly within the last two decades, responsible archaeologists have recognized the importance of returning to the public some of the benefits and insights—that is, the archaeological knowledge.

- Although archaeology is conventionally perceived as a "pure" science, many archaeologists are finding ways to apply the techniques of archaeology to new problems, such as the analysis of contemporary garbage and landfills to help solve the nation's trash problem.

- Others are involved in forensic archaeology, working with law enforcement officials, providing training in the recovery and analysis of material remains, and generating firsthand evidence to be presented in courts of law; and others use archaeology to recover ancient technologies that benefit developing nations.

- Many other archaeologists are involved in public education, adding educational components to "pure" research projects.

- In the past 20 years, archaeology has become increasingly concerned with incorporating multiple voices into their research and educational efforts. In some cases, this has created problems, as the various stakeholders in archaeology contest who "owns" the past; this is especially prevalent on what are perceived by some communities to be sacred sites.

- Yet in a growing number of cases, archaeologists have created vibrant research and educational programs that create a better understanding of the past with the input of descendant communities' perspectives. In addition, such archaeological programs bring people of different backgrounds together and further break down social, ethnic, racial, and cultural walls that divide the world.

Additional Reading

Brown, Michael F. 2003. *Who Owns Native Culture?* Cambridge: Harvard University Press.

Koff, Clea. 2004. *The Bone Woman: A Forensic Anthropologist's Search for Truth in the Mass Graves of Rwanda, Bosnia, Croatia, and Kosovo.* New York: Random House.

Layton, Robert (Ed.). 1989. *Who Needs the Past? Indigenous Values and Archaeology.* One World Archaeology Series. London: Unwin Hyman.

Lynott, Mark J., and Alison Wylie. 2000. *Ethics in American Archaeology: Challenges for the 1990s.* 2d ed. Washington, DC: Society for American Archaeology.

Watkins, Joe. 2000. *Indigenous Archaeology: American Indian Values and Scientific Practice.* Walnut Creek, CA: Altamira Press.

Zimmerman, Larry. 2003. *Presenting the Past.* Walnut Creek, CA: Altamira Press.

Zimmerman, Larry J., Karen D. Vitelli, and Julie Hollowell-Zimmer (Eds.). 2003. *Ethical Issues in Archaeology.* Walnut Creek, CA: Altamira Press.

Online Resources

COMPANION WEB SITE
Visit **http://anthropology.wadsworth.com** and click on the Student Companion Web Site for Thomas/Kelly *Archaeology,* 4th edition, to access a wide range of material to help you succeed in your introductory archaeology course. These include flashcards, Internet exercises, Web links, and practice quizzes.

RESEARCH ONLINE WITH INFOTRAC COLLEGE EDITION
From the Student Companion Web Site, you can access the InfoTrac College Edition database, which offers thousands of full-length articles for your research.

Glossary

A horizon The upper part of a soil where active organic and mechanical decomposition of geological and organic material occurs.

absolute date A date expressed as a specific unit of scientific measurement, such as days, years, centuries, or millennia; an absolute determination attempting to pinpoint a discrete, known interval in time.

accelerator mass spectrometry (AMS) A method of radiocarbon dating that counts the proportion of carbon isotopes directly (rather than using the indirect Geiger counter method), thereby dramatically reducing the quantity of datable material required.

achieved status Rights, duties, and obligations that accrue to a person by virtue of what they accomplished in their life.

adaptive perspective A research perspective that emphasizes technology, ecology, demography, and economics in the definition of human behavior.

affinal Relatives that one is related to by marriage, rather than blood.

alluvial sediments Sediments transported by flowing water.

Americanist archaeology The brand of archaeology that evolved in close association with anthropology in the Americas; it is practiced throughout the world.

analogy Noting similarities between two entities and inferring from that similarity that an *additional* attribute of one (the ethnographic case) is also true of the other (the archaeological case).

ancestor worship A religion in which one's deceased ancestors serve as important intermediaries between the natural and supernatural.

androcentric A perspective that focuses on what men do in a society, to the exclusion of women.

anthropology The study of all aspects of humankind—biological, cultural, and linguistic; extant and extinct—employing an all-encompassing holistic approach.

antiquarian Originally, someone who studied antiquities (that is, ancient objects) largely for the sake of the objects themselves—not to understand the people or culture that produced them.

Antiquities Act Passed in 1906, this act (1) requires federal permits before excavating or collecting artifacts on federal land, (2) established a permitting process, and (3) gave the president the authority to create national monuments.

appendicular skeleton All parts of an animal excluding the axial skeleton.

applied science Research to acquire the knowledge necessary to solve a specific, recognized problem.

arbitrary level The basic vertical subdivision of an excavation square; used only when easily recognizable "natural" strata are lacking and when natural strata are more than 10 centimeters thick.

archaeofauna The animal bones found in an archaeological site.

archaeological context Once artifacts enter the ground, they are part of the archaeological context, where they can continue to be affected by human action, but where they also are affected by natural processes.

archaeological record The documentation of artifacts and other material remains, along with their contexts recovered from archaeological sites.

Archaeological Resources Protection Act (ARPA) Passed in 1979, this act (1) prohibits the excavation or removal of artifacts from federal property without a permit, (2) prohibits the sale, exchange, or transport of artifacts acquired illegally from federal property, and (3) increased the penalties for violations of the act over those of the Antiquities Act.

archaeological site Any place where material evidence exists about the human past. Usually, "site" refers to a concentration of such evidence.

archaeology The study of the past through the systematic recovery and analysis of material remains.

archaic state A centralized political system found in complex societies, characterized by having a virtual monopoly on the power to coerce.

area of potential effect (APE) The area that will be directly and indirectly affected by a construction project; in some cases it might encompass not only areas that are affected by construction but also areas seen from it.

argilliturbation A natural formation process in which wet/dry cycles in clay-rich soils push artifacts upward as the sediment swells and then moves them down as cracks form during dry cycles.

argon-argon dating A high-precision method for estimating the relative quantities of argon-39 to argon-40 gas; used to date volcanic ashes that are between 500,000 and several million years old.

artifact Any movable object that has been used, modified, or manufactured by humans; artifacts include stone, bone, and metal tools; beads and other ornaments; pottery; artwork; religious and sacred items.

ascribed status Rights, duties, and obligations that accrue to a person by virtue of their parentage; ascribed status is inherited.

assemblage A collection of artifacts of one or several classes of materials (stone tools, ceramics, bones) that comes from a defined context, such as a site, feature, or stratum.

attribute An individual characteristic that distinguishes one artifact from another on the basis of its size, surface texture, form, material, method of manufacture, and design pattern.

axial skeleton The head, mandibles, vertebrae, ribs, sacrum, and tail of an animal skeleton.

B horizon A layer found below the A horizon where clays accumulate that are transported downward by water.

band A residential group composed of a few nuclear families, but whose membership is neither permanent nor binding.

berdaches Among Plains Indian societies, men who elected to live life as women; they were recognized by their group as a third gender.

bilateral descent A kinship system in which relatives are traced equally on both the mother's and father's side.

bilocal residence A cultural practice in which a newly married couple may live in either the village of the groom or the village of the bride.

bioarchaeology The study of the human biological component evident in the archaeological record.

biological anthropology A subdiscipline of anthropology that views humans as biological organisms; also known as physical anthropology.

bone collagen The organic component of bone.

bonebed Archaeological and paleontological sites consisting of the remains of a large number of animals, often of the same species, and often representing a single moment in time—a mass kill or mass death.

bridging arguments Logical statements linking observations on the static archaeological record to the dynamic behavior or natural processes that produced it.

bundle burial Burial of a person's bones, bundled together, after the flesh has been removed or allowed to decay off the bones.

burial population A set of human burials that come from a limited region and a limited time period. The more limited the region and the time period, the more accurate will be inferences drawn from analysis of the burials.

C horizon A layer found below the B horizon that consists of the unaltered or slightly altered parent material; bedrock lies below the C horizon.

cairn An artificial mound of stones. May be deliberately constructed as an aid to navigation, as a memorial, or to mark the location of a grave.

cargo system Part of the social organization found in many Central American communities in which a wealthy individual is named to carry out and bear the cost of important religious ceremonies throughout the year.

caries Cavities.

carrying capacity The number of people that a unit of land can support under a particular technology.

ch'arki Native South American (Quechua) term for freeze-dried llama and alpaca meat.

channel flake The longitudinal flake removed from the faces of Folsom and Clovis projectile points to create the flute.

charnel house A structure used by eastern North Americans to lay out the dead where the body would decompose. The bones would later be gathered and buried or cremated.

chiefdom A regional polity in which two or more local groups are organized under a single chief (who is the head of a ranked social hierarchy). Unlike autonomous bands and villages, chiefdoms consist of several more or less permanently aligned communities or settlements.

chinampas A form of intensive agriculture; low mounds the Aztec built by piling up sediments from the bottoms of shallow lakes and marshes to form islands of arable land.

civilization A complex urban society with a high level of cultural achievement in the arts and sciences, craft specialization, a surplus of food and/or labor, and a hierarchically stratified social organization.

clans A group of matri- or patrilineages who see themselves as descended from a (sometimes-mythical) common ancestor.

classical archaeology The branch of archaeology that studies the "classical" civilizations of the Mediterranean, such as Greece and Rome, and the Near East.

Clovis The earliest well-established Native American culture, distributed throughout much of North America and dating 10,900 to 11,200 BC.

codices Maya texts, long strips of paper, many meters in length when unfolded, made of the pounded inner bark of certain trees; these texts helped analysts interpret Maya hieroglyphics on stelae.

coevolution An evolutionary theory that changes in social systems are best understood as mutual natural selection among components rather than as a linear cause-and-effect sequence.

cognitive archaeology The study of all those aspects of ancient culture that are the product of the human mind: the perception, description, and classification of the universe; the nature of the supernatural; the principles, philosophies, ethics, and values by which human societies are governed; and the ways in which aspects of the world, the supernatural, or human values are conveyed in art.

colluvial sediments Sediments deposited primarily through the action of gravity on geological material lying on hillsides.

comparative collection A skeletal collection of modern fauna of both sexes and different ages used to make identifications of archaeofaunas.

comparative method In Enlightenment philosophy, the idea that the world's existing peoples reflect different stages of human cultural evolution.

component An archaeological construct consisting of a stratum or set of strata that are presumed to be culturally homogeneous; a set of components from various sites in a region will make up a phase.

conjunctive approach As defined by Walter W. Taylor, using functional interpretations of artifacts and their contexts to reconstruct daily life of the past.

coprolite Desiccated feces, often containing macrobotanical remains, pollen, and the remains of small animals.

core A piece of stone that is worked ("knapped"). Cores sometimes serve merely as sources for raw materials; they also can serve as functional tools.

cosmology The study of the origin, large-scale structure, and future of the universe. A cosmological explanation demonstrates how the universe developed—both the totality and its constituent parts—and also describes what principles keep it together.

cribra orbitalia A symptom of iron deficiency anemia in which the bone of the upper eye sockets takes on a spongy appearance.

cryoturbation A natural formation process in which freeze/thaw activity in a soil selectively pushes larger artifacts to the surface of a site.

cultural anthropology A subdiscipline of anthropology that emphasizes nonbiological aspects; the learned social, linguistic, technological, and familial behaviors of humans.

cultural disturbance processes Human behaviors that modify artifacts in their archaeological context, for instance, digging pits, hearths, canals, and houses.

cultural materialism A research paradigm that takes a scientific approach and that emphasizes the importance of material factors—such as environment, population density, subsistence, and technology—in understanding change and diversity in human societies.

cultural resource management (CRM) A professional field that conducts activities, including archaeology, related to compliance with legislation aimed at conserving cultural resources.

cultural resources Physical features, both natural and artificial, associated with human activity, including sites, structures, and objects possessing significance in history, architecture, or human development. Cultural properties are unique and nonrenewable resources.

culture An integrated system of beliefs, traditions, and customs that govern or influence a person's behavior. Culture is learned, shared by members of a group, and based on the ability to think in terms of symbols.

culture history The kind of archaeology practiced mainly in the early to mid-twentieth century; it "explains" differences or changes over time in artifact frequencies by positing the diffusion of ideas between neighboring cultures or the migration of a people who had different mental templates for artifact styles.

data Relevant observations made on objects that then serve as the basis for study and discussion.

datum point The zero point, a fixed reference used to keep control on a dig; usually controls both the vertical and horizontal dimensions of provenience.

de Vries effects Fluctuations in the calibration curve produced by variations in the atmosphere's carbon-14 content; these cause radiocarbon dates to calibrate to more than one calendar age.

deconstruction Efforts to expose the assumptions behind the alleged objective and systematic search for knowledge. A primary tool of postmodernism.

deductive reasoning Reasoning from theory to account for specific observational or experimental results.

deflation A geologic process whereby fine sediment is blown away by the wind and larger items—including artifacts—are lowered onto a common surface and thus become recognizable sites.

density-equilibrium model Proposed by Binford, it attributes the origins of agriculture to population pressure in favorable environments that resulted in emigration to marginal lands, where agriculture was needed to increase productivity.

direct acquisition A form of trade in which a person/group goes to the source area of an item to procure the raw material directly or to trade for it or finished products.

domestic economy The organization of reproduction and basic production, exchange, and consumption within camps, houses, apartments, or other domestic settings.

dosimeter A device to measure the amount of gamma radiation emitted by sediments. It is normally buried in a stratum for a year to record the annual dose of radiation. Dosimeters are often a short length of pure copper tubing filled with calcium sulfate.

down-the-line trade An exchange system in which goods are traded outward from a source area from group to group, resulting in a steady decline in the item's abundance in archaeological sites farther from the source.

eburnation A sign of osteoarthritis in which the epiphyses of long bones are worn smooth, causing them to take on a varnish-like appearance.

ecofact Plant or animal remains found in an archaeological site.

egalitarian societies Social systems that contain roughly as many valued positions as there are persons capable of filling them; in egalitarian societies, all people have nearly equal access to the critical resources needed to live.

electron spin resonance A trapped charge technique used to date tooth enamel and burned stone tools; it can date teeth that are beyond the range of radiocarbon dating.

element In faunal analysis, a specific skeletal part of the body—for example, humerus or sternum.

enamel hypoplasias Horizontal linear defects in tooth enamel indicating episodes of physiological stress.

enculturation The process whereby individuals learn their culture.

energy dispersive x-ray fluorescence (XRF) An analytical technique that uses obsidian's trace elements to "fingerprint" an artifact and trace it to its geologic source.

Enlightenment A shift in Western philosophy that advocated ideas of linear progress, absolute truth, science, rational planning of ideal social orders, and the standardization of knowledge. It held that rational thought was the key to progress; that science and technology would free people from the oppression of historical traditions of myth, religion, and superstition; and that the control of nature through technology would permit the development of moral and spiritual virtues.

eolian sediments Materials transported and accumulated by wind (for example, dunes).

epiphyses The ends of bones that fuse to the main shaft or portion of bone at various ages; most bones are fused by age 25. This fact can be used to age skeletons of younger individuals.

ethnoarchaeology The study of contemporary peoples to determine how human behavior is translated into the archaeological record.

ethnocentric (also ethnocentrism) The attitude or belief that one's own cultural ways are superior to any other.

ethnographers Anthropologists who study one culture and write detailed descriptions of that culture's traditions, customs, religion, social and political organization, and so on.

ethnographies The descriptions of cultures written by ethnographers.

ethnology That branch of anthropology dealing chiefly with the comparative study of cultures.

exotics Material culture that was not produced locally and/or whose raw material is not found locally.

experimental archaeology Experiments designed to determine the archaeological correlates of ancient behavior; may overlap with both ethnoarchaeology and taphonomy.

faunal In archaeology, animal bones in archaeological sites.

faunal analysis Identification and interpretation of animal remains from an archaeological site.

faunalturbation A natural formation process in which animals, from large game to earthworms, affect the distribution of material within an archaeological site.

feature The nonportable evidence of technology; usually fire hearths, architectural elements, artifact clusters, garbage pits, soil stains, and so on.

Fertile Crescent A broad arc of mountains in Israel, Jordan, Syria, Iraq, and Iran where wild wheat, barley, and other domesticated plants are found today.

flake A thin, sharp sliver of stone removed from a core during the knapping process.

floralturbation A natural formation process in which trees and other plants affect the distribution of artifacts within an archaeological site.

flotation The use of fluid suspension to recover tiny burned plant remains and bone fragments from archaeological sites.

flute Distinctive channel on the faces of Folsom and Clovis projectile points formed by removal of one or more flakes from the point's base.

forensic archaeology The application of archaeological and bioarchaeological knowledge for legal purposes.

formal analogies Analogies justified by similarities in the formal attributes of archaeological and ethnographic objects and features.

formation processes The ways in which human behaviors and natural actions operate to produce the archaeological record.

full-coverage survey Performing 100 percent coverage of a large region; used where topography and archaeological remains make it feasible and where the relationships between specific sites (as opposed to types of sites) are the subject of interest.

functional type A class of artifacts that performed the same function; these may or may not be temporal and/or morphological types.

funerary objects Any items placed with a human body or made to contain human remains at the time of burial (regardless of whether they are known to have been associated with a deceased individual).

gender ideology The culturally prescribed values assigned to the task and status of men and women; values can vary from society to society.

gender role The culturally prescribed behavior associated with men and women; roles can vary from society to society.

gene A unit of the chromosomes that controls inheritance of particular traits.

general systems theory An effort to describe the properties by which all systems, including human societies, allegedly operated. Popular in processual archaeology of the late 1960s and 1970s.

geoarchaeology The field of study that applies the concepts and methods of the geosciences to archaeological research.

geographic information system (GIS) A computer program for storing, retrieving, analyzing, and displaying cartographic data.

geomorphology The geological study of landforms and landscapes, for instance, soils, rivers, hills, sand dunes, deltas, glacial deposits, and marshes.

georeferenced Data that are input to a GIS database using a common mapping reference—for example, the UTM grid—so that all data can be spatially analyzed.

Georgian order A worldview (ca. 1660/1680–1820) arising in the European Age of Reason and implying that the world has a single, basic immutable order. Using the powers of reason, people can discover what that order is and can thereby control the environment as they wish. The Georgian order is informed by the rise of scientific thought and by the balance and order in Renaissance architecture and art.

glacial till The mixture of rock and earth pushed along the front and sides of a glacier.

global positioning system Hand-held devices that use triangulation from radio waves received from satellites to determine your current position in terms of either the UTM grid or latitude and longitude.

graviturbation A natural formation process in which artifacts are moved downslope through gravity, sometimes assisted by precipitation runoff.

ground-penetrating radar A remote sensing technique in which radar pulses directed into the ground reflect back to the surface when they strike features or interfaces within the ground, showing the presence and depth of possible buried features.

haplogroup Genetic lineages defined by similar genes at a locus on a chromosome.

Harris lines Horizontal lines near the ends of long bones indicating episodes of physiological stress.

heat-treatment A process whereby stone tool raw material (usually flakes or unfinished tools) are heated beneath a fire to improve their flintknapping qualities.

high-level (or general) theory Theory that seeks to answer large "why" questions.

hilly flanks theory Proposed by Robert Braidwood, it claims that agriculture arose in the areas where wild ancestors of domesticated wheat and barley grow, attributing agriculture's appearance to human efforts to continue to increase the productivity and stability of their food base, coupled with culture being "ready" to accept an agricultural lifeway.

historical archaeology The study of human behavior through material remains, for which written history in some way affects its interpretation.

historical particularism The view that each culture is the product of a unique sequence of developments in which chance plays a major role in bringing about change.

Holocene The post-Pleistocene geological epoch that began about 10,000 radiocarbon years ago and continues today.

hominids Members of the evolutionary line that contains humans and our early bipedal ancestors.

Homo erectus A hominid who lived in Africa, Asia, and Europe between 2 million and 500,000 years ago. These hominids walked upright, made simple stone tools, and may have used fire.

Hopewell A cultural tradition found primarily in the Ohio River Valley and its tributaries, dating from 200 BC–AD 400. Hopewell societies engaged in hunting and gathering and in some horticulture of indigenous plants. They are known for their mortuary rituals, which included charnel houses and burial mounds; some central tombs contained exotics. They also constructed geometric earthworks as ceremonial enclosures and effigy mounds.

Hopewell Interaction Sphere The common set of symbols found in the midwestern United States between 200 BC and AD 400.

horticulture Cultivation using hand tools only and in which plots of land are used for a few years and then allowed to lie fallow.

humanism A doctrine, attitude, or way of life that focuses on human interests and values. In general, a humanistic approach tends to reject a search for universals and stress instead the importance of the individual's lived experience.

hypothesis A proposition proposed as an explanation of some phenomena.

iconography Art forms or writing systems (such as Egyptian or Maya hieroglyphics) that symbolically represent ideas about religion or cosmology.

ideational perspective The research perspective that defines ideas, symbols, and mental structures as driving forces in shaping human behavior.

ideology A set of beliefs—often political, religious, or cosmological in nature—that rationalizes exploitative relations between classes or social groups.

imbrication A fluvial process through which stones in a stream- or riverbed come to rest overlapping like shingles on a roof, with their upstream ends lying slightly lower in elevation than their downstream ends.

in situ From Latin, meaning "in position"; the place where an artifact, ecofact, or feature was found during excavation or survey.

index fossil concept The idea that strata containing similar fossil assemblages are of similar age. This concept enables archaeologists to characterize and date strata within sites using distinctive artifact forms that research shows to be diagnostic of a particular period of time.

inductive reasoning Working from specific observations to more general hypotheses.

infrastructure In cultural materialism, the elements most important to satisfying basic human survival and well-being—food, shelter, reproduction, health—which are assumed to lie at the causal heart of every sociocultural system.

instrumental neutron activation analysis (INAA) An analytical technique that determines the trace element composition of the clay used to make a pot to help identify the clay's geologic source.

intensive agriculture Cultivation using draft animals, machinery, or hand cultivation in which plots are used annually; often entails irrigation, land reclamation, and fertilizers.

irrigation hypothesis Proposed by Karl Wittfogel, it attributes the origin of the state to the administrative demands of irrigation.

kill sites Places where animals were killed in the past.

kinship Socially recognized network of relationships through which individuals are related to one another by ties of descent (real or imagined) and marriage.

kiva A Pueblo ceremonial structure that is usually round (but may be square or rectangular) and semi-subterranean. They appear in early Pueblo sites and perhaps even in the earlier (pre-AD 700) pithouse villages.

Koshare An English rendering of a word from Keresan (one of the Pueblo Indian languages) that refers to ritual clowns in Rio Grande Pueblo society.

krotovina A filled-in animal burrow.

landscape archaeology The study of ancient human modification of the environment.

law of superposition The geological principle stating that, in any pile of sedimentary rocks that have not been disturbed by folding or overturning, each bed is older than the layers above and younger than the layers below; also known as Steno's law.

Libby half-life The time required for half of the carbon-14 available in an organic sample to decay; the standard is 5568 years, although it is known that the half-life is closer to 5730 years.

linguistic anthropology A subdiscipline of anthropology that focuses on human language; its diversity in grammar, syntax, and lexicon; its historical development; and its relation to a culture's perception of the world.

lipids Organic substances—including fats, oils, and waxes—that resist mixing with water; found in both plant and animal tissues.

living floors A distinct buried surface on which people lived.

long bone cross sections Cross sections of the body's long bones (arms and legs) used to analyze bone shape and reconstruct the mechanical stresses placed on that bone—and hence activity patterns.

low-level theories The observations and interpretations that emerge from hands-on archaeological field and lab work.

macrobotanical remains Nonmicroscopic plant remains recovered from an archaeological site.

Magdalenian The last major culture of the European Upper Paleolithic period (ca. 16,000–10,000 BC); named after the rockshelter La Madeleine, in southwestern France. Magdalenian artisans crafted intricately carved tools of reindeer bone and antler; this was also the period during which Upper Paleolithic cave art in France and Spain reached its zenith.

mano A fist-sized, round, flat, hand-held stone used with a metate for grinding foods.

marker bed An easily identified geologic layer whose age has been independently confirmed at numerous locations and whose presence can therefore be used to date archaeological and geological sediments.

matrilineage Individuals who share a line of matrilineal descent.

matrilineal descent A unilineal descent system in which ancestry is traced through the female line.

matrilocal residence A cultural practice in which a newly married couple live in the bride's village of origin; it is often associated with matrilineal descent.

matrix-sorting The hand-sorting of processed bulk soil samples for minute artifacts and ecofacts.

mean ceramic date A statistical technique for combining the median age of manufacture for temporally significant pottery types to estimate the average age of a feature or site.

medieval mind-set The culture of the early (pre-AD 1660) British colonies that emphasized the group rather than the individual and in which the line between culture and nature was blurred; people were seen as conforming to nature.

mestizos Spanish term referring to people of mixed European and Native American ancestry.

metate A large, flat stone used as a stationary surface upon which seeds, tubers, and nuts are ground with a mano.

microwear Minute, often microscopic evidence of use damage on the surface and working edge of a flake or artifact; it can include striations, pitting, microflaking, and polish.

midden Refuse deposit resulting from human activities, generally consisting of sediment; food remains such as charred seeds, animal bone, and shell; and discarded artifacts.

middle-level (or middle-range) theory Hypothesis that links archaeological observations with the human behavior or natural processes that produced them.

minimum number of individuals (MNI) The smallest number of individuals necessary to account for all identified bones.

Mississippian A widespread cultural tradition across much of the eastern United States from AD 800–1500. Mississippian societies engaged in intensive village-based maize horticulture and constructed large, earthen platform mounds that served as substructures for temples, residences, and council buildings.

mitochondrial DNA (mtDNA) Genetic material found in the mitochondria of cells; it is inherited only from the mother and appears to mutate at a rate of 2–4 percent per 1 million years.

moieties Two groups of clans that perform reciprocal ceremonial obligations for one another; moieties often intermarry.

molecular clock Calculations of the time since divergence of two related populations using the presumed rate of mutation in mtDNA and the genetic differences between the two populations.

morphological type A descriptive and abstract grouping of individual artifacts whose focus is on *overall* similarity rather than function or chronological significance.

mortality profiles Charts that depict the various ages at death of a burial population.

Mousterian A culture from the Middle Paleolithic ("Middle Old Stone Age") period that appeared throughout Europe after 250,000 and before 30,000 years ago. Mousterian artifacts are frequently associated with Neanderthal human remains.

multiple working hypotheses A set of hypotheses that are tested against the empirical record from the simplest to the most complex.

National Historic Preservation Act (NHPA) Passed in 1966, this act created (1) the National Register of Historic Places, (2) the Advisory Council on Historic Preservation, (3) State Historic Preservation Offices, as well as (4) a process to mitigate the impact of development; it also requires that government agencies provide good stewardship of their cultural resources.

National Register of Historic Places A list of significant historic and prehistoric properties, including districts, sites, buildings, structures, and objects.

Native American Graves Protection and Repatriation Act (NAGPRA) Passed in 1990, this act (1) protects Indian graves on federal and tribal lands, (2) recognizes tribal authority over treatment of unmarked graves, (3) prohibits the commercial selling of native dead bodies, (4) requires an inventory and repatriation of human remains held by the federal government and institutions that receive federal funding, (5) requires these same institutions to return inappropriately acquired sacred objects and other important communally owned property to native owners, and (6) set up a process to determine ownership of human remains found on federal and tribal property after November 16, 1990.

Natufian A cultural manifestation in the Levant (the southwest Fertile Crescent) dating from 14,500 to 11,600 BP and consisting of the first appearance of settled villages, trade goods, and possibly early cultivation of domesticated wheat, but lacking pottery.

natural level A vertical subdivision of an excavation square that is based on natural breaks in the sediments (in terms of color, grain size, texture, hardness, or other characteristics).

natural selection The process through which some individuals survive and reproduce at higher rates than others because of their genetic heritage; leads to the perpetuation of certain genetic qualities at the expense of others.

Neanderthals (or Neandertals) An early form of humans who lived in Europe and the Near East about 300,000 to 30,000 years ago; biological anthropologists debate whether Neanderthals were in the direct evolutionary line leading to *Homo sapiens*.

Neolithic The ancient period during which people began using ground stone tools, manufacturing ceramics, and relying on domesticated plants and animals—literally, the "New Stone Age"—coined by Sir John Lubbock (in 1865).

new archaeology An approach to archaeology that arose in the 1960s emphasizing the understanding of underlying cultural processes and the use of the scientific method; today's version of the "new archaeology" is sometimes called processual archaeology.

non-site archaeology Analysis of archaeological patterns manifested on a scale of kilometers or hectares, rather than of patterns within a single site.

nuclear DNA Genetic material found in a cell's nuclei; this material is primarily responsible for an individual's inherited traits.

number of identified specimens (NISP) The raw number of identified bones (specimens) per species; a largely outmoded way of comparing archaeological bone frequencies.

oasis theory Proposed by V. Gordon Childe, it argues that animal domestication arose as people, plants, and animals congregated around water sources during the arid years that followed the Pleistocene. In this scenario, agriculture arose because of "some genius" and preceded animal domestication.

objectivity The attempt to observe things as they actually are, without prejudging or falsifying observations in light of some preconceived view of the world—reducing subjective factors to a minimum.

objects of cultural patrimony Any items with ongoing historical, traditional, or cultural importance that were once owned by the entire tribe (rather than by an individual) and were "inalienable" at the time they left the tribe's possession (that is, no one person had the right to give them away).

old wood problem A potential problem with radiocarbon (or tree-ring) dating in which old wood has been scavenged and reused in a later archaeological site; the resulting date is not a true age of the associated human activity.

optically stimulated luminescence A trapped charge dating technique used to date sediments; the age is the time elapsed between the last time a few moments exposure to sunlight reset the clock to zero and the present.

optimal foraging theory The idea that foragers select foods that maximize the overall return rate.

oracle A shrine in which a deity reveals hidden knowledge or divine purpose.

osteoarthritis A disorder in which the cartilage between joints wears away, often because of overuse of the join, resulting in osteophytes and eburnation.

osteology The study of bone.

osteophytes A sign of osteoarthritis in which bones develop a distinct "lipping" of bone at the point of articulation.

paleodemography The study of ancient demographic patterns and trends.

paleoethnobotanist An archaeologist who analyzes and interprets plant remains from archaeological sites in order to understand the past interactions between human populations and plants.

paleopathology The study of ancient patterns of disease and disorders.

palynology The technique through which the fossil pollen grains and spores from archaeological sites are studied.

paradigm The overarching framework, often unstated, for understanding a research problem. It is a researcher's "culture."

participant observation The primary strategy of cultural anthropology in which data are gathered by questioning and observing people while the observer lives in their society.

patrilineage Individuals who share a line of patrilineal descent.

patrilineal descent A unilineal descent system in which ancestry is traced through the male line.

patrilocal residence A cultural practice in which a newly married couple live in the groom's village of origin; it is often associated with patrilineal descent.

petrographic analysis An analytical technique that identifies the mineral composition of a pot's temper and clay through microscopic observation of thin sections.

phase An archaeological construct possessing traits sufficiently characteristic to distinguish it from other units similarly conceived; spatially limited to roughly a locality or region and chronologically limited to the briefest interval of time possible.

photosynthetic pathways The specific chemical process through which plants metabolize carbon; the three major pathways discriminate against carbon-13 in different ways, therefore similarly aged plants that use different pathways can produce different radiocarbon ages.

phytoliths Tiny silica particles contained in plants. Sometimes these fragments can be recovered from archaeological sites, even after the plants themselves have decayed.

pithouse A semi-subterranean structure with heavy log roof, covered with sod.

Pleistocene A geologic period from 2 million to 10 thousand years ago, which was characterized by multiple periods of extensive glaciation.

plow zone The upper portion of a soil profile that has been disturbed by repeated plowing or other agricultural activity.

political economy The organization of reproduction, production, exchange, and consumption within and between bands, villages, chiefdoms, states, and empires.

political organization A society's formal and informal institutions that regulate a population's collective acts.

pollen diagram A chart showing the changing frequencies of different identified pollens through time from samples taken from archaeological or other sites.

population pressure The effects of a population reaching carrying capacity.

porotic hyperostosis A symptom of iron deficiency anemia in which the skull takes on a porous appearance.

postmodernism A paradigm that rejects grand historical schemes in favor of humanistic approaches that appreciate the multiple voices of history. It seeks to see how colonialism created our vision of the world we occupy today; it eschews science and argues against the existence of objective truth.

postprocessual paradigm A paradigm that focuses on humanistic approaches and rejects scientific objectivity; it sees archaeology as inherently political and is more concerned with interpreting the past than with testing hypotheses. It sees change as arising largely from interactions between individuals operating within a symbolic and/or competitive system.

potassium-argon dating An absolute dating technique that monitors the decay of potassium (K-40) into argon gas (Ar-40).

potlatch Among nineteenth-century Northwest Coast Native Americans, a ceremony involving the giving away or destruction of property in order to acquire prestige.

potsherd Fragment of pottery.

principle of infrastructural determinism Argument that the infrastructure lies at the causal heart of every sociocultural system, that human society responds to factors that directly affect survival and well-being, and that such responses determine the rest of the sociocultural system.

principle of uniformitarianism The principle asserting that the processes now operating to modify the earth's surface are the same processes that operated long ago in the geological past.

processual paradigm The paradigm that explains social, economic, and cultural change as primarily the result of adaptation to material conditions; external conditions (for example, the environment) are assumed to take causal priority over ideational factors in explaining change.

projectile points Arrowheads, dart points, or spear points.

proton precession magnetometer A remote sensing technique that measures the strength of magnetism between the earth's magnetic core and a sensor controlled by the archaeologist. Magnetic anomalies can indicate the presence of buried walls or features.

provenience An artifact's location relative to a system of spatial data collection.

pubic symphysis Where the two halves of the pelvis meet in the groin area; the appearance of its articulating surface can be used to age skeletons.

puna Native American (Quechua) term for the treeless, windswept tablelands and basins of the higher Andes.

pure (basic) science Systematic research directed toward acquisition of knowledge for its own sake.

ranked societies Social systems in which a hierarchy of social status has been established, with a restricted number of valued positions available; in ranked societies, not everyone has the same access to the critical resources of life.

reclamation processes Human behaviors that result in artifacts moving from the archaeological context back to the systemic context, for example, scavenging beams from an abandoned structure to use them in a new one.

Register of Professional Archaeologists (RPA) A listing of archaeologists who have agreed to abide by an explicit code of conduct and standards of research performance; created in 1998.

relational analogies Analogies justified on the basis of close cultural continuity between the archaeological and ethnographic cases or similarity in general cultural form.

relative dating Dates expressed relative to one another (for instance, earlier, later, more recent, and so forth) instead of in absolute terms.

religion A specific set of beliefs about one's relation to the supernatural; a society's mechanism for relating supernatural phenomena to the everyday world.

remote sensing The application of methods that employ some form of electromagnetic energy to detect and measure characteristics of an archaeological target.

reservoir effect When organisms take in carbon from a source that is depleted of or enriched in ^{14}C relative to the atmosphere; such samples may return ages that are considerably older or younger than they actually are.

return rate The amount of energy acquired by a forager per unit of harvesting/processing time.

reuse processes Human behaviors that recycle and reuse artifacts for some purpose other than the one for which they were created, but before the artifact enters an archaeological context.

reverse stratigraphy The result when one sediment is unearthed by human or natural actions and moved elsewhere, whereby the latest material will be deposited on the bottom of the new sediment, and progressively earlier material will be deposited higher and higher in the stratigraphy.

ritual A succession of discrete behaviors that must be performed in a particular order under particular circumstances.

rockshelter A common type of archaeological site, consisting of a rock overhang that is deep enough to provide shelter but not deep enough to be called a cave (technically speaking, a cave must have an area of perpetual darkness).

Rosetta stone A black basalt stone tablet found in 1799 that bears an inscription in two forms of ancient Greek and ancient Egyptian. By working from the Greek texts, scholars were able to decipher the ancient Egyptian hieroglyphs.

sacred objects Specific ceremonial items necessary for current practice of traditional Native American religions.

sample fraction The percentage of the sample universe that is surveyed. Areas with a lot of variability in archaeological remains require larger sample fractions than do areas of low variability.

sample units Survey units of a standard size and shape, determined by the research question and practical considerations, used to obtain the sample.

sample universe The region that contains the statistical population and that will be sampled. Its size and shape are determined by the research question and practical considerations.

sciatic notch The angled edge of both halves of the posterior (rear) side of the pelvis; measurement of this angle is used to determine sex in human skeletons. Although its width varies among populations, narrow notches indicate a male and wider notches indicate a female.

science The search for universals by means of established scientific methods of inquiry.

scientific method Accepted principles and procedures for the systematic pursuit of secure knowledge. Established scientific procedures involve the following steps: define a relevant problem; establish one or more hypotheses; determine the empirical implications of the hypotheses; collect appropriate data through observation and/or experimentation; compare these data with the expected implications; and revise and/or retest hypotheses as necessary.

seasonal round Hunter-gatherers' pattern of movement between different places on the landscape timed to the seasonal availability of food and other resources.

seasonality An estimate of what part of the year a particular archaeological site was occupied.

sedimentary rock Rock formed when the weathered products of pre-existing rocks have been transported by and deposited in water and are turned once again to stone.

seriation A relative dating method that orders artifacts based on the assumption that one cultural style slowly replaces an earlier style over time; with a master seriation diagram, sites can be dated based on their frequency of several artifact (for instance, ceramic) styles.

settlement pattern The distribution of archaeological sites across a region.

settlement system The movements and activities reconstructed from a settlement pattern.

shaman One who has the power to contact the spirit world through trance, possession, or visions. On the basis of this ability, the shaman invokes, manipulates, or coerces the power of the spirits for socially recognized ends—both good and ill.

shell midden The remnants of shellfish collecting; some shellfish middens can become many meters thick.

shovel-testing A sample survey method used in regions where rapid soil buildup obscures buried archaeological remains; it entails digging shallow, systematic pits across the survey unit.

sipapu A Hopi word that loosely translates as "place of emergence." The original sipapu is the place where the Hopi are said to have emerged into this world from the underworld. Sipapus are also small pits in kivas through which communication with the supernatural world takes place.

site formation The human and natural actions that work together to create an archaeological site.

size classes A categorization of faunal remains, not to taxon, but to one of five categories based on body size.

slash-and-burn A horticultural method used frequently in the topics wherein a section of forest is cut, dried, and then burned, thus returning nutrients to the ground. This permits a plot of land to be farmed for a limited number of years.

Smithsonian number A unique catalog number given to sites; it consists of a number (the state's position alphabetically), a letter abbreviation of the county, and the site's sequential number within the county.

social Darwinism The extension of the principles of Darwinian evolution to social phenomena; it implies that conflict between societies and between classes of the same society benefits humanity in the long run by removing "unfit" individuals and social forms. Social Darwinism assumed that unfettered economic competition and warfare were primary ways to determine which societies were "fittest."

social organization The rules and structures that govern relations within a group of interacting people. Societies are divided into social units (groups) within which are recognized social positions (statuses), with appropriate behavior patterns prescribed for these positions (roles).

soil Sediments that have undergone in situ chemical and mechanical alteration.

soil resistivity survey A remote sensing technique that monitors the electrical resistance of soils in a restricted volume near the surface of an archaeological site; buried walls or features can be detected by changes in the amount of resistance registered by the resistivity meter.

Southeastern Ceremonial Complex A specific assortment of ceremonial objects that occurs in the graves of high-status Mississippian individuals. Ritual exchange of these artifacts crosscut the boundaries of many distinctive local cultures.

space-time systematics The delineation of patterns in material culture through time and over space. These patterns are what the archaeologist will eventually try to explain or account for.

statistical population A set of counts, measurements, or characteristics about which relevant inquiries are to be made. Scientists use the term "statistical population" in a specialized way (quite different from "population" in the ordinary sense).

statistical sampling The principles that underlie sampling strategies that provide accurate measures of a statistical population.

status The rights, duties, privileges, powers, liabilities, and immunities that accrue to a recognized and named social position.

stelae Stone monuments erected by Maya rulers to record their history in rich images and hieroglyphic symbols. These symbols can be read and dated.

strata (singular, "stratum") More or less homogeneous or gradational material, visually separable from other levels by a discrete change in the character of the material—texture, compactness, color, rock, organic content—and/or by a sharp break in the nature of deposition.

stratified random sample A survey universe divided into several sub-universes that are then sampled at potentially different sample fractions.

stratigraphy A site's physical structure produced by the deposition of geological and/or cultural sediments into layers, or strata.

structuralism A paradigm holding that human culture is the expression of unconscious modes of thought and reasoning, notably binary oppositions. Structuralism is most closely associated with the work of the French anthropologist Claude Levi-Strauss.

structure The behavior that supports choices made at the level of the infrastructure, including the organization of reproduction, production, exchange, family structure, division of labor, age and sex roles, political units, social organization, and warfare.

superstructure A group's values, aesthetics, rules, beliefs, religions, and symbols, which can be behaviorally manifested as art, music, dance, literature, advertising, religious rituals, sports, games, hobbies, and even science.

symbol An object or act (verbal and nonverbal) that, by cultural convention, stands for something else *with which it has no necessary connection.*

sympathetic magic Rituals in which doing something to an image of an object produces the desired effect in the real object.

systematic regional survey A set of strategies for arriving at accurate descriptions of the range of archaeological material across a landscape.

systemic context A living behavioral system wherein artifacts are part of the ongoing system of manufacture, use, reuse, and discard.

taphonomy The study of how organisms become part of the fossil record; in archaeology it primarily refers to the study of how natural processes produce patterning in archaeological data.

taxon In faunal analysis, the classification of a skeletal element to a taxonomic category—species, genus, family, or order.

temper Material added to clay to give a ceramic item strength through the firing process.

temporal type A morphological type that has temporal significance; also known as a time-marker or index fossil.

teosinte A plant native to southern Mexico; believed to be the wild ancestor of maize.

terminus post quem (TPQ) The date after which a stratum or feature must have been deposited or created.

test excavation A small initial excavation to determine a site's potential for answering a research question.

testability The degree to which one's observations and experiments can be reproduced.

theory An explanation for observed, empirical phenomena. It is empirical and seeks to explain the relationships between variables; it is an answer to a "why" question.

thermal infrared multispectral scanner (TIMS) A remote sensing technique that uses equipment mounted in aircraft or satellite to measure infrared thermal radiation given off by the ground. Sensitive to differences as little as 0.1 degree centigrade, it can locate subsurface structures by tracking how they affect surface thermal radiation.

thermoluminescence A trapped charge dating technique used on ceramics and burnt stone artifacts—anything mineral that has been heated to more than 500° C.

time-markers Similar to index fossils in geology; artifact forms that research shows to be diagnostic of a particular period of time.

total station A device that uses a beam of light bounced off a prism to determine an artifact's provenience; it is accurate to +/– 3 millimeters.

totem A natural object, often an animal, from which a lineage or clan believes itself to be descended and/or with which lineage or clan members have special relations.

trade language A language that develops among speakers of different languages to permit economic exchanges.

trait list A simple listing of a culture's material and behavioral characteristics, for example, house and pottery styles, foods, degree of nomadism, particular rituals, or ornaments. Trait lists were used primarily to trace the movement of cultures across a landscape and through time.

trapped charge dating Forms of dating that rely upon the fact that electrons become trapped in minerals' crystal lattices as a function of background radiation; the age of the specimen is the total radiation received divided by the annual dose of radiation.

tree-ring dating (dendrochronology) The use of annual growth rings in trees to assign calendar ages to ancient wood samples.

tribal societies A wide range of social formations that lie between egalitarian foragers and ranked societies (such as chiefdoms); tribal societies are normally horticultural and sedentary, with a higher level of competition than seen among nomadic hunter-gatherers.

type A class of archaeological artifacts defined by a consistent clustering of attributes.

typology The systematic arrangement of material culture into types.

UNESCO Convention of 1970 Requires that signers create legislation and the administration to (1) regulate the import and export of cultural objects, (2) forbid their nations' museums from acquiring illegally exported cultural objects, (3) establish ways to inform other nations when illegally exported objects are found within a country's borders, (4) return or otherwise provide restitution of cultural objects stolen from public institutions, and (5) establish a register of art dealers and require them to register.

unilineal cultural evolution The belief that human societies have evolved culturally along a single developmental trajectory. Typically, such schemes depict Western civilization as the most advanced evolutionary stage; anthropology rejects this idea.

Upper Paleolithic The last major division of the Old World Paleolithic, beginning about 40,000 years ago and lasting until the end of the Pleistocene (ca. 10,000 BC); period during which modern humans replaced Neanderthals.

UTM Universal transverse Mercator, a grid system whereby north and east coordinates provide a location anywhere in the world, precise to 1 meter.

vision quest A ritual in which an individual seeks visions through starvation, dehydration, and exposure; considered in some cultures to be a way to communicate with the supernatural world.

warfare and circumscription hypothesis Proposed by Robert Carneiro, it attributes the origin of the state to the administrative burden of warfare conducted for conquest as a request of geographic limits on arable land in the face of a rising population.

water-screening A sieving process in which deposit is placed in a screen and the matrix washed away with hoses; essential where artifacts are expected to be small and/or difficult to find without washing.

wickiup A conical structure made of poles or logs laid against one another that served as fall and winter homes among the prehistoric Shoshone and Paiute.

wood rats (also pack rats) Rodents that build nests of organic materials and thus preserve a record, often for thousands of years, of changing plant species within the local area of the nest.

Younger Dryas A climatic interval, 13,000–11,600 BP, characterized by a rapid return to cooler and drier, but highly variable, climatic conditions.

zooarchaeologist (also faunal analyst) An individual who studies the faunal (animal) remains recovered from archaeological sites.

Bibliography

The following chapter-by-chapter bibliography contains the specific references used in each chapter as well as some additional references that can provide the student with more in-depth reading on particular subjects. We've arranged this bibliography by chapter specifically so that the student would be able to more easily locate additional readings on a particular subject. Where direct quotes have been used, their source is indicated here at the end of the appropriate entry.

Chapter 1

Babcock, Barbara A., and Nancy J. Parezo. 1988. *Daughters of the Desert: Women Anthropologists and the Native American Southwest 1880–1980.* Albuquerque: University of New Mexico Press.

Benedict, Jeff. 2002. *No Bone Unturned: The Adventures of a Top Smithsonian Forensic Scientist and The Legal Battle for America's Oldest Skeletons.* New York: HarperCollins.

Binford, Lewis R. 1962. Archeology as anthropology. *American Antiquity* 28: 217–225.

———. 1964. A consideration of archaeological research design. *American Antiquity* 29: 425–441.

———. 1965. Archaeological systematics and the study of cultural process. *American Antiquity* 31: 203–210.

———. 1968. Archeological perspectives. In Sally R. Binford and Lewis R. Binford (Eds.), *New Perspectives in Archeology* (pp. 5–32). Chicago: Aldine.

———. 1972. *An Archaeological Perspective.* New York: Seminar Press.

——— (Ed.). 1977. *For Theory Building in Archaeology.* New York: Academic Press.

———. 1983a. *In Pursuit of the Past: Decoding the Archaeological Record.* London: Thames and Hudson ("In His Own Words" text quoted from pp. 19, 23).

——— (Ed.). 1983b. *Working at Archaeology.* New York: Academic Press.

———. 1989. *Debating Archaeology.* San Diego: Academic Press.

———. 2001. *Constructing Frames of Reference: An Analytical Method for Archaeological Theory Building Using Ethnographic and Environmental Data Sets.* Berkeley: University of California Press.

Binford, Sally R., and Lewis R. Binford (Eds.). 1968. *New Perspectives in Archeology.* Chicago: Aldine.

Brigham, Clarence S. 1937. Clarence Bloomfield Moore. *Proceedings of the American Antiquarian Society* (1936) 46: 13–14.

Brown, Ian W. 1978. James Alfred Ford: The man and his works. Southeastern Archaeological Conference, Special Publication no. 4.

Caldwell, Joseph. 1959. The new American archaeology. *Science* 129(3345): 303–307.

Chatters, James C. 2001. *Ancient Encounters: Kennewick Man and the First Americans.* New York: Simon and Schuster.

Claassen, Cheryl (Ed.). 1994. *Women in Archaeology.* Philadelphia: University of Pennsylvania Press.

Daniel, Glyn. 1976. *A Hundred and Fifty Years of Archaeology.* Cambridge: Harvard University Press.

——— (Ed.). 1981. *Towards a History of Archaeology.* New York: Thames and Hudson.

Davis, Mary B. (Comp.). 1987. *Field Notes of Clarence B. Moore's Southeastern Archaeological Expeditions, 1891–1918: A Guide to the Microfilm Edition.* Bronx, NY: Huntington Free Library, Museum of the American Indian.

Deagan, Kathleen. 1973. Mestizaje in colonial St. Augustine. *Ethnohistory* 20: 55–65.

———. 1978a. Cultures in transition: Fusion and assimilation among the Eastern Timucua. In Jerald Milanich and Samuel Proctor (Eds.), *Tacachale: Essays on the Indians of Florida and Southeastern Georgia During the Historic Period* (pp. 89–119). Gainesville: University Press of Florida.

———. 1978b. The material assemblage of 16th century Spanish Florida. *Historical Archaeology* 12: 25–50.

———. 1980. Spanish St. Augustine: America's first "melting pot." *Archaeology* 33(5): 22–30.

———. 1981. Downtown survey: The discovery of 16th century St. Augustine in an urban area. *American Antiquity* 46: 626–634.

———. 1982. Avenues of inquiry in historical archaeology. In Michael B. Schiffer (Ed.), *Advances in Archaeological Method and Theory*. Vol. 5 (pp. 151–177). New York: Academic Press ("In Her Own Words" text quoted from pp. 170–171).

———. 1983. *Spanish St. Augustine: The Archaeology of a Colonial Creole Community*. New York: Academic Press.

———. 1987. *Artifacts of the Spanish Colonies of Florida and the Caribbean, 1500–1800*, vol. 1, *Ceramics, Glassware, and Beads*. Washington, DC: Smithsonian Institution Press.

———. 1988. Neither history nor prehistory: The questions that count in historical archaeology. *Historical Archaeology* 22: 7–12.

———. 1991. Historical archaeology's contributions to our understanding of early America. In Lisa Falk (Ed.), *Historical Archaeology in Global Perspective* (pp. 97–112). Washington, DC: Smithsonian Institution Press.

——— (Ed.). 1995. *Puerto Real: The Archaeology of a Sixteenth-Century Spanish Town in Hispaniola*. Gainesville: University Press of Florida.

———. 1996. Colonial transformation: Euro-American cultural genesis in the early Spanish-American colonies. *Journal of Anthropological Research* 52: 135–160.

Deagan, Kathleen, and José María Cruxent. 2002a. *Archaeology at La Isabela: America's First European Town*. New Haven: Yale University Press.

———. 2002b. *Columbus's Outpost Among the Tainos*. New Haven: Yale University Press.

Dunnell, Robert C. 1979. Trends in current Americanist archaeology. *American Journal of Archaeology* 83: 437–449.

———. 1986. Five decades of American archaeology. In David J. Meltzer, Don D. Fowler, and Jeremy A. Sabloff (Eds.), *American Archaeology Past and Future: A Celebration of the Society for American Archaeology 1935–1985* (pp. 23–49). Washington, DC: Smithsonian Institution Press.

Ford, James Alfred. 1949. Cultural dating of prehistoric sites in the Virú Valley, Peru. Pt. 2 of "Surface survey of the Virú Valley, Peru" by James Alfred Ford and Gordon R. Willey. *Anthropological Papers of the American Museum of Natural History* 43(1). New York.

———. 1952. Measurements of some prehistoric design developments in the southeastern states. *Anthropological Papers of the American Museum of Natural History* 44(3). New York ("In His Own Words" text quoted from pp. 317–318).

———. 1954. The type concept revisited. *American Anthropologist* 56: 42–54.

———. 1957. A quantitative method for deriving cultural chronology. Pan American Union, Technical Manual, I. (Reprinted as University of Missouri, Museum of Anthropology, Museum Brief, no. 9.)

———. 1962. A quantitative method for deriving cultural chronology. Washington, DC: Pan American Union, Technical Manual, I.

———. 1969. A comparison of formative cultures in the Americas: Diffusion or the psychic unity of man? *Smithsonian Contributions to Anthropology*, Vol. 2. Washington, DC.

Ford, James Alfred, and Clarence H. Webb. 1956. Poverty Point, a late Archaic site in Louisiana. *Anthropological Papers of the American Museum of Natural History* 46(1): 1–140. New York.

Ford, James Alfred, and Gordon R. Willey. 1941. An interpretation of the prehistory of the eastern United States. *American Anthropologist* 43: 325–363.

Grayson, Donald K. 1983. *The Establishment of Human Antiquity*. New York: Academic Press.

Irwin-Williams, Cynthia. 1990. Women in the field: The role of women in archaeology before 1960. In G. Kass-Simon and Patricia Farnes (Eds.), *Women of Science: Righting the Record* (pp. 1–41). Bloomington: Indiana University Press.

Kidder, Alfred V. 1924. *An Introduction to the Study of Southwestern Archaeology*. New Haven: Yale University Press.

———. 1928. The present state of knowledge of American history and civilization prior to 1492 (pp. 749–753). Paris: International Congress of History, Oslo ("In His Own Words" text quoted from p. 753).

———. 1960. Reminiscences in Southwest archaeology, I. *Kiva* 25: 1–32.

Kidder, Alfred V., and Samuel J. Guernsey. 1921. Basketmaker caves of northeastern Arizona. *Papers of the Peabody Museum of American Archaeology and Ethnology* 8(2). Cambridge, MA.

Kidder, Alfred V., Jesse D. Jennings, and Edwin M. Shook. 1946. Excavations at Kaminaljuyu, Guatemala. Washington, DC: Carnegie Institution of Washington Publication no. 561. Washington, DC.

Lamberg-Karlovsky, C. C. (Ed.). 1989. *Archaeological Thought in America.* Cambridge: Cambridge University Press.

Levine, Mary Ann. 1994. Creating their own niches: Career styles among women in Americanist archaeology between the wars. In Cheryl Claassen (Ed.), *Women in Archaeology* (pp. 9–40). Philadelphia: University of Pennsylvania Press.

Moore, Clarence B. 1905. Certain aboriginal remains of the Black Warrior River. *Journal of the Academy of Natural Sciences of Philadelphia.* Second Series, 13: 123–244.

———. 1907. Moundville revisited. *Journal of the Academy of Natural Sciences of Philadelphia.* Second Series, 13: 337–405.

Nelson, Nels C. 1909. Shellmounds of the San Francisco Bay region. *University of California Publications in American Archaeology and Ethnology* 7(4): 310–356.

———. 1914. Pueblo ruins of the Galisteo Basin, New Mexico. *Anthropological Papers of the American Museum of Natural History* 15(1). New York.

Parezo, Nancy J. (Ed.). 1993. *Hidden Scholars: Women Anthropologists and the Native American Southwest.* Albuquerque: University of New Mexico Press.

Taylor, Walter W. 1948. A study of archeology. *American Anthropological Association, Memoir,* 69.

———. 1954. Southwestern archaeology, its history and theory. *American Anthropologist* 56: 561–570.

———. 1972. Old wine and new skins: A contemporary parable. In Mark P. Leone (Ed.), *Contemporary Archaeology* (pp. 28–33). Carbondale: Southern Illinois University Press.

Trigger, Bruce G. 1980. Archaeology and the image of the American Indian. *American Antiquity* 45: 662–676.

———. 1999. *A History of Archaeological Thought.* 2d ed. Cambridge: Cambridge University Press.

Victor, Katharine L., and Mary C. Beaudry. 1992. Women's participation in American prehistoric and historical archaeology: A comparative look at the journals *American Antiquity* and *Historical Archaeology.* In Cheryl Claassen (Ed.), Exploring Gender Through Archaeology: Selected Papers From the 1991 Boone Conference. *Monographs in World Archaeology,* no. 11 (pp. 11–21). Madison, WI: Prehistory Press.

Wardle, H. Newell. 1956. Clarence Bloomfield Moore (1852–1936). *Bulletin of the Philadelphia Anthropological Society* 9(2): 9–11.

Watson, Patty Jo. 1973. The future of archeology in anthropology: Cultural history and social science. In Charles L. Redman (Ed.), *Research and Theory in Current Archeology* (pp. 113–124). New York: Wiley.

Wauchope, Robert. 1965. (Obituary of) Alfred Vincent Kidder, 1885–1963. *American Antiquity* 31(2, pt. 1): 149–171.

Webb, Clarence H. 1968. (Obituary of) James Alfred Ford, 1911–1968. *Texas Archaeological Society Bulletin* 38: 135–146.

White, Nancy M., Lynne P. Sullivan, and Rochelle A. Marrinan. 1999. *Grit-Tempered: Early Women Archaeologists in the Southeastern United States.* Knoxville: University of Tennessee Press.

Willey, Gordon R. 1967. (Obituary of) Alfred Vincent Kidder. *National Academy of Sciences Biographical Memoirs.* Vol. 39 (pp. 292–322). New York: Columbia University Press.

———. 1969. (Obituary of) James Alfred Ford, 1911–1968. *American Antiquity* 34: 62–71.

Willey, Gordon R., and Jeremy A. Sabloff. 1993. *A History of American Archaeology.* 3d ed. New York: Freeman.

Williams, Barbara. 1981. *Breakthrough: Women in Archaeology.* New York: Walter.

Wissler, Clark. 1914. A pioneer student of Ancient America (Bandelier obituary). *El Palacio* 1(6, 7): 8.

———. 1917. The new archaeology. *The American Museum Journal* 17(2): 100–101.

Woodbury, Richard B. 1954. Review of *A Study of Archeology* by Walter W. Taylor. *American Antiquity* 19: 292–296.

———. 1960. Nels C. Nelson and chronological archaeology. *American Antiquity* 25: 400–401.

———. 1973. *Alfred V. Kidder.* New York: Columbia University Press.

———. 1993. *Sixty Years of Southwestern Archaeology: A History of the Pecos Conference.* Albuquerque: University of New Mexico Press.

Chapter 2

Atwater, Caleb. 1820. Description of the antiquities discovered in the state of Ohio and other western states. *Archaeologia Americana: Transactions and Collections of the American Antiquarian Society* 1: 105–267.

Baldwin, J. D. 1872. *Ancient America.* New York: Harper.

Bell, James A. 1994. *Reconstructing Prehistory: Scientific Method in Archaeology.* Philadelphia: Temple University Press.

Benedict, Ruth. 1948. Anthropology and the humanities. *American Anthropologist* 50: 585–593.

Boas, Franz. [1888] 1940. *Race, Language and Culture.* New York: Macmillan.

Carrithers, Michael. 1990. Is anthropology art or science? *Current Anthropology* 31: 263–282.

———. 1992. *Why Humans Have Culture: Explaining Anthropology and Social Diversity.* Oxford: Oxford University Press.

Cerroni-Long, E. L. 1996. Human science. *Anthropology Newsletter* 37(1): 50, 52.

Deetz, James. 1983. Scientific humanism and humanistic science: A plea for paradigmatic pluralism in historical archaeology. *Geoscience and Man* 23: 27–34.

de Laguna, Frederica. 1957. Some problems of objectivity in ethnology. *Man* 57: 179–182.

Esber, George S. 1987. Designing Apache homes with Apaches. In Robert W. Wulff and Shirley J. Fiske (Eds.), *Anthropological Praxis: Translating Knowledge into Action* (pp. 187–196). Boulder: Westview Press.

Feder, Kenneth L. 1995. *Frauds, Myths, and Mysteries: Science and Pseudoscience in Archaeology.* 2d ed. Mountain View, CA: Mayfield.

Flannery, Kent V. 1967. Culture history vs. cultural process: A debate in American archaeology. *Scientific American* 217(2): 119–121.

———. 1973. Archeology with a capital S. In Charles L. Redman (Ed.), *Research and Theory in Current Archeology* (pp. 47–53). New York: Wiley and Sons.

Fotiadis, M. 1994. What is archaeology's "mitigated objectivism" mitigated by? Comments on Wylie. *American Antiquity* 59: 545–555.

Fox, Richard G. (Ed.). 1991. *Recapturing Anthropology: Working in the Present.* Santa Fe: School of American Research Press.

Geertz, Clifford. 1973. *The Interpretation of Cultures.* New York: Basic Books.

———. 1983. *Local Knowledge: Further Essays in Interpretive Anthropology.* New York: Basic Books.

Harris, Marvin. 1968. *The Rise of Anthropological Theory.* New York: Thomas Y. Crowell.

———. 1985. *Good to Eat: Riddles of Food and Culture.* New York: Simon and Schuster.

———. 1991. Anthropology: Ships that crash in the night. In Richard Jessor (Ed.), *Perspectives on Social Science: The Colorado Lectures* (pp. 70–114). Boulder: Westview Press.

Hill, Jane. 1995. Science in anthropology: A perspective from linguistic anthropology. *Anthropology Newsletter* 36(7): 20.

Horgan, John. 1996. *The End of Science: Facing the Limits of Knowledge in the Twilight of the Scientific Age.* Reading, MA: Addison-Wesley.

Jefferson, Thomas. 1787. *Notes on the state of Virginia.* London: John Stockdale (reprinted Chapel Hill: University of North Carolina Press, 1954).

Keesing, Roger. 1981. *Cultural Anthropology: A Contemporary Perspective.* New York: Holt, Rinehart, and Winston.

Kelley, Jane Holden, and Marsha P. Hanen. 1988. *Archaeology and the Methodology of Science.* Albuquerque: University of New Mexico Press.

Kemeny, John G. 1959. *A Philosopher Looks at Science.* New York: Van Nostrand Reinhold.

Kroeber, Alfred, and Clyde Kluckhohn. 1952. Culture: A critical review of concepts and definitions. *Papers of the Peabody Museum of American Archaeology and Ethnology* 47(1). Cambridge, MA.

Kuznar, Lawrence. 1997. *Reclaiming a Scientific Anthropology.* Walnut Creek, CA: Altamira.

Lamberg-Karlovsky, C. C. (Ed.). 1989. *Archaeological Thought in America.* Cambridge: Cambridge University Press.

Mcgee, R. Jon, and Richard L. Williams. 2004. *Anthropological Theory: An Introductory History.* 3d ed. New York: McGraw Hill.

Meltzer, David J. 1998. Introduction. In *Ancient Monuments of the Mississippi Valley* [reprint of 1848 publication] (pp. 1–95). Washington, DC: Smithsonian Institution Press.

Morell, Virginia. 1993. Anthropology: Nature-culture battleground. *Science* 261: 1798–1802.

———. 1994. An anthropological culture shift. *Science* 264: 20–22.

Peacock, James. 1994. Challenges facing the discipline. *Anthropology Newsletter* 35(9): 1, 5.

Phillips, Philip. 1955. American archaeology and general anthropological theory. *Southwestern Journal of Anthropology* 11: 246–250 (quote from p. 246).

Rowe, John Howland. 1965. The renaissance foundations of anthropology. *American Anthropologist* 67: 1–20.

Salmon, Merrilee H. 1982. *Philosophy and Archaeology.* New York: Academic Press.

Salmon, Merrilee H., and Wesley C. Salmon. 1979. Alternative models of scientific explanation. *American Anthropologist* 81: 61–74.

Spector, Janet. 1993. *What This Awl Means: Feminist Archaeology at a Wahpeton Dakota Village.* St. Paul, MN: Minnesota Historical Society Press (quotes from pp. 15, 65, 89, 121; "In Her Own Words" text quoted from pp. 19–29).

Squier, Ephraim G., and Edwin H. Davis. 1998 [1848]. *Ancient Monuments of the Mississippi Valley,* edited and with an introduction by David J. Meltzer. Washington: Smithsonian Institution Press.

Thomas, Cyrus. 1894. *Report on the Mound Explorations of the Bureau of Ethnology.* Washington, DC: Smithsonian Institution.

Tylor, Edward Burnett. 1871. *Primitive Culture.* Vols. 1 and 2. London: Murray (quote from p. 1).

U'mista Culture Centre. 1983. *Box of Treasures.* Film. Directed by Dennis Wheeler, narrated by Gloria Cranmer Webster. Alert Bay, Canada: U'mista Cultural Centre.

Walens, Stanley. 1981. *Feasting with Cannibals: An Essay on Kwakiutl Cosmology.* Princeton: Princeton University Press.

Watson, Patty Jo. 1995. Archaeology, anthropology, and the culture concept. *American Anthropologist* 97: 683–694.

Webster, Gloria Cranmer. 1991. The contemporary potlatch. In Aldona Jonaitis (Ed.), *Chiefly Feasts: The Enduring Kwakiutl Potlatch* (pp. 227–250). Seattle: University of Washington Press; New York: American Museum of Natural History.

White, Leslie A. 1949. *The Science of Culture.* New York: Grove Press.

———. 1959. *The Evolution of Culture.* New York: McGraw-Hill.

———. 1975. *The Concept of Cultural Systems.* New York: Columbia University Press.

Willey, Gordon R., and Philip Phillips. 1958. *Method and Theory in American Archaeology.* Chicago: University of Chicago Press.

Chapter 3

Babcock, Barbara A. 1982. Ritual undress and the comedy of self and other: Bandelier's *The Delight Makers.* In Jay Ruby (Ed.), *A Crack in the Mirror: Reflexive Perspectives in Anthropology* (pp. 187–203). Philadelphia: University of Pennsylvania Press.

Bamforth, Douglas B., and Albert C. Spaulding. 1982. Human behavior, explanation, archaeology, history, and science. *Journal of Anthropological Archaeology* 1: 179–195.

Bandelier, Adolph. 1883. A visit to the aboriginal ruins in the Valley of the Rio Pecos. *Papers of the Archaeological Institute of America* (American Series) 1(2): 34–133.

———. 1890. Final report of investigations among the Indians of the Southwestern United States, carried on mainly in the years from 1880 to 1885, Part I. *Papers of the Archaeological Institute of America* (American Series III). Cambridge, MA.

———. 1892. Final report of investigations among the Indians of the Southwestern United States, carried on mainly in the years from 1880 to 1885, Part II. *Papers of the Archaeological Institute of America* (American Series IV). Cambridge, MA.

———. 1966. *The Southwestern Journals of Adolph F. Bandelier, 1880–1882.* Edited and annotated by Charles H. Lange and Carroll Riley. Albuquerque: University of New Mexico Press.

———. 1971 [1890]. *The Delight Makers: A Novel of Prehistoric Pueblo Indians.* San Diego: Harcourt Brace Jovanovich ("Looking Closer" text quoted from pp. 3–4, 485–489).

———. 1975. *The Southwestern Journals of Adolph F. Bandelier, 1885–1888.* Edited and annotated by Charles H. Lange, Carroll Riley, and Elisabeth M. Lange. Albuquerque: University of New Mexico Press.

Bandelier, Adolph, and Edgar L. Hewett. 1937. *Indians of the Rio Grande Valley.* Albuquerque: University of New Mexico Press.

Bapty, Ian, and Tim Yates (Eds.). 1990. *Archaeology After Structuralism: Post-Structuralism and the Practice of Archaeology.* London: Routledge.

Binford, Lewis R. 1983. *In Pursuit of the Past: Decoding the Archaeological Record.* London: Thames and Hudson.

———. 1989a. Science to seance, or processual to "post-processual" archaeology. In *Debating Archaeology* (pp. 27–40). San Diego: Academic Press.

———. 1989b. Review of Hodder, *Reading the Past: Current Approaches to Interpretation in Archaeology.* In *Debating Archaeology* (pp. 69–71). San Diego: Academic Press.

Bingham, Hiram. 1914. Bandelier. *The Nation* 98(2543, March 26): 328–329.

Bintliff, John. 1991. Post-modernism, rhetoric, and scholasticism at TAG: The current state of British archaeological theory. *Antiquity* 65: 274–278.

Clarke, David L. 1968. *Analytical Archaeology.* London: Methuen.

———. 1972. Archaeology: The loss of innocence. *Antiquity* 47: 6–18.

Clifford, James. 1988. *The Predicament of Culture: Twentieth Century Ethnography, Literature, and Art.* Cambridge: Harvard University Press.

Clifford, James, and George E. Marcus (Eds.). 1986. *Writing Culture: The Poetics and Politics of Ethnography.* Berkeley: University of California Press.

Daniel, Glyn. 1991. Post-processual developments in Anglo-American archaeology. *Norwegian Archaeological Review* 24: 65–76.

———. 1995. Expanding middle-range theory. *Antiquity* 69: 449–458.

Dark, K. R. 1995. *Theoretical Archaeology.* Ithaca: Cornell University Press.

Gibbon, Guy. 1989. *Explanation in Archaeology.* Oxford: Basil Blackwell.

Habermas, J. 1987. *The Philosophical Discourse of Modernity.* Oxford: Oxford University Press.

Hagelberg, Erika. 1993, August/September. DNA from archaeological bone. *The Biochemist*, pp. 17–22.

Hammond, George P., and Edgar F. Goad. 1949. *A Scientist on the Trail: Travel Letters of A. F. Bandelier, 1880–1881.* Berkeley, CA: Quivira Society.

Harris, Marvin. 1979. *Cultural Materialism: The Struggle for a Science of Culture.* New York: Random House.

———. 1985. *Good to Eat: Riddles of Food and Culture.* New York: Simon and Schuster.

———. 1994. Cultural materialism is alive and well and won't go away until something better comes along. In R. Borofsky (Ed.), *Assessing Cultural Anthropology* (pp. 62–76). New York: McGraw-Hill.

Harris, Marvin, and Eric B. Ross (Eds.). 1987. *Food and Evolution: Toward a Theory of Human Food Habits.* Philadelphia: Temple University Press.

Harvey, David. 1989. *The Condition of Postmodernity: An Enquiry into the Origins of Cultural Change.* Cambridge, MA: Blackwell.

Harvey, Oliver. 2000. Ghouls dig up war heroes. *The Sun* [London], 11 November, 2000.

Hassan, I. 1985. The culture of postmodernism. *Theory, Culture and Society* 2: 119–132.

Hegmon, Michelle. 2003. Setting theoretical egos aside: Issues and theory in North American archaeology. *American Antiquity* 68: 213–244.

Henderson, Julian (Ed.). 1989. *Scientific Analysis in Archaeology and Its Interpretation.* Los Angeles: UCLA Institute of Archaeology.

Hill, James N. 1991. Archaeology and the accumulation of knowledge. In Robert W. Preucel (Ed.), Processual and Postprocessual Archaeologies: Multiple Ways of Knowing the Past (pp. 42–53). *Center for Archaeological Investigations, Occasional Paper*, no. 10. Carbondale: Southern Illinois University.

Hobbs, Hulda R. 1940, June. Bandelier in the Southwest. *El Palacio* 47: 121–136.

Hodder, Ian. 1982a. *Symbols in Action: Ethnoarchaeological Studies of Material Culture.* Cambridge: Cambridge University Press.

——— (Ed.). 1982b. *Symbolic and Structural Archaeology.* Cambridge: Cambridge University Press.

———. 1985. Postprocessual archaeology. In Michael B. Schiffer (Ed.), *Advances in Archaeological Method and Theory.* Vol. 8 (pp. 1–26). Orlando, FL: Academic Press.

———. 1986. *Reading the Past: Current Approaches to Interpretation in Archaeology.* Cambridge: Cambridge University Press.

———. 1989a. Post-modernism, post-structuralism and post-processual archaeology. In Ian Hodder (Ed.), *The Meaning of Things.* One World Archaeology, no. 6 (pp. 64–78). London: Unwin Hyman.

———. 1989b. Writing archaeology: Site reports in context. *Antiquity* 63: 268–274.

———. 1990. Archaeology and the post-modern. *Anthropology Today* 6(5): 13–15.

———. 1991a. Postprocessual archaeology and the current debate. In Robert W. Preucel (Ed.), Processual and Postprocessual Archaeologies: Multiple Ways of Knowing the Past (pp. 30–41). *Center for Archaeological Investigations, Occasional Paper*, no. 10. Carbondale: Southern Illinois University.

———. 1991b. Interpretive archaeology and its role. *American Antiquity* 56: 7–18.

———. 1995. *Theory and Practice in Archaeology.* London: Routledge.

———. 1999. *The Archaeological Process: An Introduction.* Oxford: Blackwell.

———. (Ed.). 2001. *Archaeological Theory Today.* Oxford: Blackwell.

Hodge, Frederick Webb. 1914. Bandelier obituary. *American Anthropologist* 16: 349–358.

———. 1932. Biographical sketch and bibliography of Adolphe Francis Alphonse Bandelier. *New Mexico Historical Review* 7: 353–370.

Johnson, Matthew. 1999. *Archaeological Theory: An Introduction.* Oxford: Blackwell.

Knapp, A. Bernard. 1996. Archaeology without gravity: Postmodernism and the past. *Journal of Archaeological Method and Theory* 3: 127–158.

Lange, Charles H., and Carroll L. Riley. 1996. *Bandelier: The Life and Adventures of Adolph Bandelier.* Salt Lake City: University of Utah Press.

Lyotard, Jean François. 1984. *The Postmodern Condition: A Report on Knowledge.* Translated by G. Bennington and B. Massumi. Minneapolis: University of Minnesota Press.

Marcus, George E., and Michael M. J. Fischer. 1986. *Anthropology as Cultural Critique: An Experimental Moment in the Human Sciences.* Chicago: University of Chicago Press.

Miller, Daniel, and Christopher Tilley (Eds.). 1984. *Ideology, Power and Prehistory.* Cambridge: Cambridge University Press.

Mithen, Steven. 1989. Evolutionary theory and postprocessual archaeology. *Antiquity* 63: 483–494.

Pinsky, Valerie, and Alison Wylie (Eds.). 1995. *Critical Traditions in Contemporary Archaeology: Essays in the Philosophy, History and Socio-Politics of Archaeology.* Albuquerque: University of New Mexico Press.

Preucel, R. W. (Ed.). 1991. Processual and Postprocessual Archaeologies: Multiple Ways of Knowing the Past. *Center for Archaeological Investigations, Occasional Paper,* no. 10. Carbondale: Southern Illinois University.

———. 1995. The postprocessual condition. *Journal of Archaeological Research* 3: 147–175.

Price, Barbara J. 1982. Cultural materialism: A theoretical review. *American Antiquity* 47: 709–741.

Radin, Paul. 1942. *The Unpublished Letters of Adolphe F. Bandelier Concerning the Writing and Publication of* The Delight Makers. El Paso: Carl Hertzog.

Rosenau, Pauline Marie. 1992. *Post-Modernism and the Social Sciences: Insights, Inroads, and Intrusions.* Princeton: Princeton University Press.

Sabloff, Jeremy A., Lewis R. Binford, and Patricia A. McAnany. 1987. Understanding the archaeological record. *Antiquity* 61: 203–209.

Saunders, Nicholas. 2002. Excavating memories: Archaeology and the Great War, 1914–2001. *Antiquity* 76: 101–108.

———. 2003. *Trench Art: Materialities and Memories of War.* Oxford: Berg Press.

Shanks, Michael, and Christopher Tilley. 1987a. *Reconstructing Archaeology: Theory and Practice.* Cambridge: Cambridge University Press.

———. 1987b. *Social Theory and Archaeology.* Albuquerque: University of New Mexico Press.

———. 1992. *Re-Constructing Archaeology: Theory and Practice.* 2d ed. London: Routledge.

Sherratt, Andrew. 1993. The relativity of theory. In Norman Yoffee and Andrew Sherratt (Eds.), *Archaeological Theory: Who Sets the Agenda?* (pp. 119–130). Cambridge: Cambridge University Press.

Skibo, James M., William H. Walker, and Axel E. Nielsen (Eds.). 1995. *Expanding Archaeology.* Salt Lake City: University of Utah Press.

Spaulding, Albert C. 1968. Explanation in archeology. In Sally R. Binford and Lewis R. Binford (Eds.), *New Perspectives in Archeology* (pp. 33–39). Chicago: Aldine.

———. 1985. Fifty years of theory. *American Antiquity* 50: 301–308.

Tilley, Christopher. 1990. *Reading Material Culture.* Oxford: Blackwell.

Watson, Patty Jo. 1973. The future of archeology in anthropology: Cultural history and social science. In Charles L. Redman (Ed.), *Research and Theory in Current Archeology* (pp. 113–124). New York: Wiley.

———. 1986. Archaeological interpretation, 1985. In David J. Meltzer, Don D. Fowler, and Jeremy A. Sabloff (Eds.), *American Archaeology Past and Future: A Celebration of the Society for American Archaeology 1935–1985* (pp. 439–457). Washington, DC: Smithsonian Institution Press.

White, Leslie (Ed.). 1940. *Pioneers in American Anthropology: The Bandelier-Morgan Letters, 1873–1883.* Albuquerque: Coronado Cuarto Centennial Publ., 1540–1940 (quotes from pp. 212–213).

Wilk, Richard. 1985. The ancient Maya and the political present. *Journal of Anthropological Research* 41: 307–326.

Wissler, Clark. 1914. A pioneer student of Ancient America (Bandelier obituary). *El Palacio* 1 (6, 7): 8.

Wolf, Eric R. 1982. *Europe and the People Without History.* Berkeley: University of California Press.

Wylie, Alison. 1992. The interplay of evidential constraints and political interests: Recent archaeological research on gender. *American Antiquity* 57: 15–35.

———. 1994. On "capturing facts alive in the past" (or present): Response to Fotiadis and to Little. *American Antiquity* 59: 556–560.

Yoffee, Norman, and Andrew Sherratt (Eds.). 1993a. *Archaeological Theory: Who Sets the Agenda?* Cambridge: Cambridge University Press.

———. 1993b. Introduction: The sources of archaeological theory. In Norman Yoffee and Andrew Sherratt (Eds.), *Archaeological Theory: Who Sets the Agenda?* (pp. 1–9). Cambridge: Cambridge University Press.

Chapter 4

Ammerman, A. J. 1981. Surveys and archaeological research. *Annual Review of Anthropology* 10: 63–88.

Binford, Lewis R. 1964. A consideration of archaeological research design. *American Antiquity* 29: 425–441.

Blanton, Richard E. 1978. *Monte Albán: Settlement Patterns at the Ancient Zapotec Capital.* New York: Academic Press.

Davis, Hester A. 1991. Avocational archaeology groups: A secret weapon for site protection. In George S. Smith and John E. Ehrenhard (Eds.), *Protecting the Past* (pp. 175–180). Boca Raton, FL: CRC Press. ("Archaeological Ethics" text quoted from this work.)

Dillon, Brian D. (Ed.). 1989. *Practical Archaeology: Field and Laboratory Techniques and Archaeological Logistics.* Archaeological Research Tools 2. Los Angeles: Institute of Archaeology, UCLA.

Dunnell, Robert C., and William S. Dancey. 1983. The siteless survey: A regional scale data collection strategy. In Michael B. Schiffer (Ed.), *Advances in Archeological Method and Theory.* Vol. 6 (pp. 267–287). New York: Academic Press.

Ebert, James. 1992. *Distributional Archaeology.* Albuquerque: University of New Mexico Press.

Fish, Suzanne K., and Stephen A. Kowalewski (Eds.). 1990. *The Archaeology of Regions: A Case for Full-Coverage Survey.* Washington, DC: Smithsonian Institution Press.

Fletcher, Roland. 1977. Settlement studies. In David L. Clarke (Ed.), *Spatial Archaeology* (pp. 47–162). New York: Academic Press.

Foley, Robert. 1981. Off-site archaeology: An alternative approach for the short-sited. In Ian Hodder, Glynn Isaac, and Norman Hammond (Eds.), *Pattern of the Past: Studies in Honour of David Clarke* (pp. 157–183). Cambridge: Cambridge University Press.

Frison, George C. 1984. Avocational archaeology: Its past, present, and future. In E. L. Green (Ed.), *Ethics and Values in Archaeology* (pp. 184–193). New York: Free Press.

Hester, Thomas R., Harry J. Shafer, and Kenneth L. Feder. 1997. *Field Methods in Archaeology.* 7th ed. Mountain View, CA: Mayfield.

Hyslop, John. 1984. *The Inka Road System.* Orlando: Academic Press.

Judge, W. James, James I. Ebert, and Robert K. Hitchcock. 1975. Sampling in regional archaeological survey. In James W. Mueller (Ed.), *Sampling in Archaeology* (pp. 82–123). Tucson: University of Arizona Press.

Kelly, Robert. 2001. Prehistory of the Carson Desert and Stillwater Mountains, Nevada: Environment, Mobility, and Subsistence. *University of Utah Anthropological Papers* 123. Salt Lake City.

Kowalewski, Stephen A. 1990a. Merits of full-coverage survey: Examples from the Valley of Oaxaca, Mexico. In Suzanne K. Fish and Stephen A. Kowalewski (Eds.), *The Archaeology of Regions: A Case for Full-Coverage Survey* (pp. 33–85). Washington, DC: Smithsonian Institution Press.

———. 1990b. Scale and complexity: Issues in the archaeology of the Valley of Oaxaca. In Joyce Marcus (Ed.), Debating Oaxaca Archaeology. *Museum of Anthropology, University of Michigan Anthropological Papers* 84: 207–270. Ann Arbor.

Lekson, Stephen H. 1986. *Great Pueblo Architecture of Chaco Canyon.* Albuquerque: University of New Mexico Press.

Lewarch, Dennis E., and Michael J. O'Brien. 1981. The expanding role of surface assemblages in archaeological research. In Michael B. Schiffer (Ed.), *Advances in Archaeological Method and Theory.* Vol. 4 (pp. 297–342). New York: Academic Press.

McManamon, Francis P. 1984. Discovering sites unseen. In Michael B. Schiffer (Ed.), *Advances in*

Archaeological Method and Theory. Vol. 7 (pp. 223–292). New York: Academic Press.

Morris, Craig, and Adriana von Hagen. 1993. *The Inka Empire and Its Andean Origins.* New York: Abbeville Press.

Mueller, James W. 1974. The use of sampling in archaeological survey. *Society for American Archaeology Memoir* 28.

——— (Ed.). 1975. *Sampling in Archaeology.* Tucson: University of Arizona Press.

Murra, John V. 1994. John Hyslop, 1945–1993. *Andean Past* 4: 1–7.

Noble, David Grant (Ed.). 1984. *New Light on Chaco Canyon.* Santa Fe: School of American Research Press.

Parsons, Jeffrey R. 1990. Critical reflections on a decade of full-coverage regional survey in the Valley of Mexico. In Suzanne K. Fish and Stephen A. Kowalewski (Eds.), *The Archaeology of Regions: A Case for Full-Coverage Survey* (pp. 7–31). Washington, DC: Smithsonian Institution Press.

Peck, Mary. 1994. *Chaco Canyon: A Center and Its World.* Santa Fe: Museum of New Mexico Press.

Plog, Stephen, Fred Plog, and Walter Wait. 1978. Decision making in modern surveys. In Michael B. Schiffer (Ed.), *Advances in Archaeological Method and Theory.* Vol. 1 (pp. 383–421). New York: Academic Press.

Rossignol, Jacqueline, and LuAnn Wandsnider (Eds.). 1992. *Space, Time, and Archaeological Landscapes.* New York: Plenum Press.

Sebastian, Lynne. 1992. *The Chaco Anasazi: Sociopolitical Evolution in the Prehistoric Southwest.* Cambridge: Cambridge University Press.

Steward, Julian H. 1938. Basin-plateau aboriginal sociopolitical groups. Washington, DC: *Bureau of American Ethnology Bulletin* 120.

Tainter, Joseph A. 1983. Settlement behavior and the archaeological record: Concepts for the definition of "archaeological site." *Contract Abstracts and CRM Archaeology* 3(2): 130–132.

Thomas, David Hurst. 1969. Great Basin hunting patterns: A quantitative method for treating faunal remains. *American Antiquity* 34(4): 392–401.

———. 1972a. A computer simulation model of Great Basin Shoshonean subsistence and settlement patterns. In David L. Clarke (Ed.), *Models in Archaeology* (pp. 671–704). London: Methuen.

———. 1972b. Western Shoshone ecology: Settlement patterns and beyond. In Don D. Fowler (Ed.), Great Basin Cultural Ecology, a Symposium. *Desert Research Institute Publications in the Social Sciences* 8: 135–153.

———. 1973. An empirical test for Steward's model of Great Basin settlement patterns. *American Antiquity* 38(2): 155–176.

———. 1978. The awful truth about statistics in archaeology. *American Antiquity* 43(2): 231–244.

———. 1983a. The archaeology of Monitor Valley: 1. Epistemology. *Anthropological Papers of the American Museum of Natural History* 58(1): 1–194.

———. 1983b. The archaeology of Monitor Valley: 2. Gatecliff Shelter. *Anthropological Papers of the American Museum of Natural History* 59(1): 1–552.

———. 1987. The archaeology of Mission Santa Catalina de Guale: 1. Search and discovery. *Anthropological Papers of the American Museum of Natural History* 63(2): 47–161.

———. 1988. The archaeology of Monitor Valley: 3. Survey and additional excavation. *Anthropological Papers of the American Museum of Natural History* 66(2): 131–633.

Thomas, David Hurst, and Robert L. Bettinger. 1976. Prehistoric piñon ecotone settlements of the upper Reese River Valley, central Nevada. *Anthropological Papers of the American Museum of Natural History* 53(3): 263–366.

Vivian, R. Gwinn. 1990. *The Chacoan Prehistory of the San Juan Basin.* San Diego: Academic Press.

Williams, Leonard, David Hurst Thomas, and Robert Bettinger. 1973. Notions to numbers: Great Basin settlements as polythetic sets. In Charles L. Redman (Ed.), *Research and Theory in Current Archeology* (pp. 215–237). New York: Wiley.

Chapter 5

Abbott, James T., and Charles D. Frederick. 1990. Proton magnetometer investigations of burned rock middens in West-Central Texas: Clues to formation processes. *Journal of Archaeological Science* 17: 535–545.

Aldenderfer, Mark, and Herbert Maschner (Eds.). 1996. *Anthropology, Space, and Geographic Information Systems.* New York: Oxford University Press.

Allen, K. M. S., S. W. Green, and E. B. W. Zubrow (Eds.). 1990. *Interpreting Space: GIS and Archaeology*. London: Taylor and Francis.

Ambler, J. Richard. 1989. *The Anasazi: Prehistoric People of the Four Corners Region*. 4th ed. Flagstaff: Museum of Northern Arizona Press.

Avery, T. E., and T. R. Lyons. 1981. *Remote Sensing: Aerial and Terrestrial Photography for Archaeologists*. Washington, DC: National Park Service, Supplement 7.

Bevan, Bruce W. 1983. Electromagnetics for mapping buried earth features. *Journal of Field Archaeology* 10: 47–54.

Bevan, Bruce W., and J. Kenyon. 1975. Ground-penetrating radar for historical archaeology. *MASCA Newsletter* 11(2): 2–7.

Boyd, Mark, F., Hale G. Smith, and John W. Griffin. 1951. *Here They Once Stood: The Tragic End of the Apalachee Missions*. Gainesville: University of Florida Press.

Brody, J. J. 1990. *The Anasazi: Ancient Indian People of the American Southwest*. New York: Rizzoli.

Carr, Christopher. 1977. A new role and analytical design for the use of resistivity surveying in archaeology. *Mid-Continental Journal of Archaeology* 2: 161–193.

———. 1982. *Handbook on Soil Resistivity Surveying: Interpretation of Data from Earthen Archaeological Sites*. Evanston, IL: Center for American Archeology Press.

Clark, Anthony. 1990. *Seeing Beneath the Soil: Prospecting Methods in Archaeology*. London: Batsford.

Conyers, Lawrence B. 1995. The use of ground-penetrating radar to map the buried structures and landscape of the Cerén site, El Salvador. *Geoarchaeology* 10: 275–299.

Cordell, Linda S. 1984. *Prehistory of the Southwest*. Orlando, FL: Academic Press.

Crown, Patricia L., and W. James Judge (Eds.). 1991. *Chaco and Hohokam: Prehistoric Regional Systems in the American Southwest*. Santa Fe: School of American Research Press.

Crumley, Carole. 1994. Historical ecology: A multidimensional ecological orientation. In C. Crumley (Ed.), *Historical Ecology: Cultural Knowledge and Changing Landscapes*. (pp. 1–16). Santa Fe: School of American Research Press (quote from p. 6).

Deuel, Leo. 1969. *Flights into Yesterday: The Story of Aerial Archaeology*. New York: St. Martin's Press.

Donoghue, D. N. M. 2001. Remote sensing. In D. Brothwell and A. Pollard (Eds.), *Handbook of Archaeological Sciences*. (pp. 555–564). Chichester, England: John Wiley and Sons.

Ebert, James I. 1984. Remote sensing applications in archaeology. In Michael B. Schiffer (Ed.), *Advances in Archaeological Method and Theory*. Vol. 7 (pp. 293–362). New York: Academic Press.

Eddy, Frank, Dale R. Lightfoot, Eden A. Welker, Layne L. Wright, and Dolores C. Torres. 1996. Air photographic mapping of San Marcos Pueblo. *Journal of Field Archaeology* 23: 1–13.

Ehrenberg, Ralph E. 1987. *Scholars' Guide to Washington, DC for Cartography and Remote Sensing Imagery*. Washington, DC: Smithsonian Institution Press.

Gabriel, Kathryn. 1991. *Roads to Center Place: A Cultural Atlas of Chaco Canyon and the Anasazi*. Boulder: Johnson Books.

Garrison, Ervan G., James G. Baker, and David Hurst Thomas. 1985. Magnetic prospection and the discovery of Mission Santa Catalina de Guale, Georgia. *Journal of Field Archaeology* 12: 299–313.

Good, Diane L. 1989. Birds, beads and bells: Remote sensing of a Pawnee sacred bundle. *Kansas State Historical Society, Anthropological Series*, no. 15.

Goodman, Dean. 1994. Ground-penetrating radar simulation in engineering and archaeology. *Geophysics* 59: 224–232.

Harp, Elmer, Jr. 1975. *Photography in Archaeological Research*. Albuquerque: University of New Mexico Press.

Johnston, R. B. 1961. Archaeological application of the proton magnetometer in Indiana (U.S.A.). *Archaeometry* 4: 71–72.

Kantner, John. 1997. Ancient roads, modern mapping: Evaluating prehistoric Chaco Anasazi roadways using GIS technology. *Expedition Magazine* 39: 4962.

———. 2004. Geographical approaches for reconstructing past human behavior from prehistoric roadways. In M. F. Goodchild and D. G. Janelle (Eds.), *Spatially Integrated Social Sciences: Examples in Best Practice* (pp. 323–344). Oxford: Oxford University Press.

Kvamme, Kenneth L. 1989. Geographic information systems in regional archaeological research and data management. In M. B. Schiffer (Ed.), *Archaeological Method and Theory*. Vol. 1 (pp. 139–204). Tucson: University of Arizona Press.

Lister, Robert H., and Florence C. Lister. 1981. *Chaco Canyon: Archaeology and Archaeologists*. Albuquerque: University of New Mexico Press.

Lyons, T. R., and T. E. Avery. 1984. *Remote Sensing: A Handbook for Archaeologists and Cultural Resource Managers*. Washington, DC: National Park Service.

Martin, William A., James E. Bruseth, and Robert J. Huggins. 1991. Assessing feature function and spatial patterning of artifacts with geophysical remote-sensing data. *American Antiquity* 56: 701–720.

Morris, Craig. 1995. Airborne archeology. *Natural History* 104(12): 70–72.

Parrington, Michael. 1983. Remote sensing. *Annual Review of Anthropology* 12: 105–124.

Riley, D. N. 1987. *Air Photography and Archaeology*. London: Duckworth.

Sabins, Floyd F., Jr. 1996. *Remote Sensing: Principles and Interpretation*. 3d ed. New York: W. H. Freeman.

Sanders, John, and Peggy Sanders. 1986. Archaeological Graphic Services remote mapping system. *Advances in Computer Archaeology* 3: 40–55.

Scollar, Irwin, A. Tabbagh, A. Hesse, and I. Herzog (Eds.). 1990. *Archaeological Prospecting and Remote Sensing*. Cambridge: Cambridge University Press.

Shapiro, Gary. 1984. A soil resistivity survey of 16th-century Puerto Real, Haiti. *Journal of Field Archaeology* 11: 101–110.

———. 1987. Archaeology at San Luis: Broad-scale testing, 1984–1985. *Florida Archaeology*, no. 3.

Sheets, Payson D. 2002. *Before the Volcano Erupted: The Ancient Cerén Village in Central America*. Austin: University of Texas Press.

Sheets, Payson D., and Donald K. Grayson (Eds.). 1979. *Volcanic Activity and Human Ecology*. New York: Academic Press.

Sheets, Payson D., and Brian R. McKee (Eds.). 1994. *Archaeology, Volcanism, and Remote Sensing in the Arenal Region, Costa Rica*. Austin: University of Texas Press.

Sheets, Payson D., and Tom Sever. 1988, November/December. High-tech wizardry. *Archaeology* 41(6): 28–35.

Snead, J., and Preucel, R. 1999. The ideology of settlement: Ancestral Keres landscapes in the northern Rio Grande. In W. Ashmore and A. B. Knapp (Eds.), *Archaeologies of Landscape: Contemporary Perspectives* (pp. 169–197). Oxford: Blackwell Publishers.

Steponaitis, Vincas P., and J. P. Brain. 1976. A portable differential proton magnetometer. *Journal of Field Archaeology* 3: 455–463.

Thomas, David Hurst. 1993. The archaeology of Mission Santa Catalina de Guale: Our first 15 years. In Bonnie G. McEwan (Ed.), *The Missions of La Florida* (pp. 1–34). Gainesville: University Press of Florida.

Ubelaker, Douglas. 1990. Review of "Birds, beads and bells: Remote sensing of Pawnee sacred bundle" by Diane L. Good. *Plains Anthropologist* 35: 213–214.

von Frese, R. R. B., and V. E. Noble. 1984. Magnetometry for archaeological exploration of historical sites. *Historical Archaeology* 18(2): 38–53.

Wescott, Konnie L., and R. Joe Brandon (Eds.). 1999. *Practical Applications of GIS for Archaeologists: A Predictive Modeling Kit*. London: Taylor and Francis.

Wescott, Konnie L., and James A. Kuiper. 1999. Using a GIS to model prehistoric site distributions in the Upper Chesapeake Bay. In Konnie Wescott and R. Joe Brandon (Eds.), *Practical Applications of GIS for Archaeologists: A Predictive Modeling Kit*, (pp. 59–72). London: Taylor and Francis.

Weymouth, John W. 1986. Geophysical methods of archaeological site surveying. In Michael B. Schiffer (Ed.), *Advances in Archaeological Method and Theory*. Vol. 9 (pp. 311–395). Orlando, FL: Academic Press.

Weymouth, John W., and Robert Huggins. 1985. Geophysical surveying of archaeological sites. In George R. Rapp, Jr., and J. Gifford (Eds.), *Archaeological Geology* (pp. 191–235). New Haven: Yale University Press.

Wheatley, David, and Mark Gillings. 2002. *Spatial Technology and Archaeology: The Archaeological Applications of GIS*. London: Taylor and Francis.

Willey, Gordon R. 1953. Prehistoric Settlement Patterns in the Virú Valley, Peru. *Bureau of American Ethnology, Bulletin* 155. Washington, DC.

Wynn, J. C. (Ed.). 1986. Special issue: Geophysics in archaeology. *Geophysics* 51: 533–639.

Zeanah, David. 2004. Sexual division of labor and central place foraging: a model for the Carson Desert of western Nevada. *Journal of Anthropological Archaeology* 23: 1–12.

Zeanah, D. W., J. A. Carter, D. P. Dugas, R. G. Elston, and J. E. Hammett. 1995. *An Optimal Foraging Model of Hunter-Gatherer Land Use in the Carson Desert*. Report in partial fulfillment of U.S. Fish and Wildlife Service Contract # 14-48-0001-93015(DB) prepared for U.S. Fish and Wildlife Service and U.S. Department of the Navy.

Chapter 6

Bird, Junius. 1980. Comments on sifters, sifting, and sorting procedures. In Martha Joukowsky, *A Complete Manual of Field Archaeology* (pp. 165–170). Englewood Cliffs, NJ: Prentice Hall.

Collis, John. 2001. *Digging Up the Past: An Introduction to Archaeological Excavation.* Phoenix Mills, UK: Sutton Publishing.

Dancey, William S. 1981. *Archaeological Field Methods: An Introduction.* Minneapolis: Burgess.

Daugherty, Richard, and Ruth Kirk. 1976. Ancient Indian village where time stood still. *Smithsonian* 7(2): 68–75.

Dibble, Harold L. 1987. Measurement of artifact provenience with an electronic theodolite. *Journal of Field Archaeology* 14: 249–254.

Fladmark, Knud R. 1978. *A Guide to Basic Archaeological Field Procedures.* Burnaby, British Columbia: Department of Archaeology, Simon Fraser University.

Folsom, Franklin. 1992. *The Black Cowboy.* Niwot, CO: Roberts Rinehart.

Fowler, Brenda. 2001. *Iceman: Uncovering the Life and Times of a Prehistoric Man Found in an Alpine Glacier.* Chicago: University of Chicago Press.

Joukowsky, Martha. 1980. *A Complete Manual of Field Archaeology: Tools and Techniques of Field Work for Archaeologists.* Englewood Cliffs, NJ: Prentice Hall.

Kirk, Ruth, and Richard Daugherty. 1974. *Hunters of the Whale.* New York: William Morrow.

Lock, Gary. 2003. *Using Computers in Archaeology: Towards Virtual Pasts.* London: Routledge.

Loud, Lewellyn L., and Mark R. Harrington. 1929. Lovelock Cave. *University of California Publications in American Archaeology and Ethnology* 25: 1–183.

McMillon, Bill. 1991. *The Archaeology Handbook: A Field Manual and Resource Guide.* New York: John Wiley and Sons.

Meltzer, David. 1993. *Search for the First Americans.* Washington, DC: Smithsonian Institution Press.

Pendleton, Michael W. 1983. A comment concerning testing flotation recovery rates. *American Antiquity* 48: 615–616.

Percy, George. 1976. The use of a mechanical earth auger at the Torreya Site, Liberty County, Florida. *Florida Anthropologist* 29(1): 24–32.

Purdy, Barbara A. 1996. *How to Do Archaeology the Right Way.* Gainesville: University Press of Florida.

Rick, John W. 1996. Total stations in archaeology. *Bulletin of the Society for American Archaeology* 14(4): 24–27.

Samuels, Steven. (Ed.). 1991a. *Ozette Archaeological Research Reports*, vol. 1, *House Structure and Floor Midden.* Pullman, WA: Washington State University and National Park Service, Pacific Northwest Regional Office.

———. (Ed.) 1991b. *Ozette Archaeological Research Reports*, vol. 2, *Fauna.* Pullman, WA: Washington State University and National Park Service, Pacific Northwest Regional Office.

South, Stanley. 1994. The archaeologist and the crew: From the mountains to the sea. In Stanley South (Ed.), *Pioneers in Historical Archaeology: Breaking New Ground* (pp. 165–187). New York: Plenum Press.

Struever, Stuart. 1968. Flotation techniques for the recovery of small-scale archaeological remains. *American Antiquity* 33: 353–362.

Wagner, Gail E. 1982. Testing flotation recovery rates. *American Antiquity* 47: 127–132.

Watson, Patty Jo. 1974. Flotation procedures used on Salts Cave sediments. In Patty Jo Watson (Ed.), *Archeology of the Mammoth Cave Area* (pp. 107–108). New York: Academic Press.

———. 1976. In pursuit of prehistoric subsistence: A comparative account of some contemporary flotation techniques. *Midcontinental Journal of Archaeology* 1: 77–100.

Yarnell, Richard A. 1974. Intestinal contents of the Salts Cave mummy and analysis of the initial Salts Cave flotation series. In Patty Jo Watson (Ed.), *Archaeology of the Mammoth Cave Area* (pp. 109–112). New York: Academic Press.

———. 1982. Problems of interpretation of archaeological plant remains of the Eastern Woodlands. *Southeastern Archaeology* 1(1): 1–7.

Chapter 7

Browman, David L., and Douglas R. Givens. 1996. Stratigraphic excavation: The first "new archaeology." *American Anthropologist* 98: 1–17.

Davis, Jonathan O. 1978. Quaternary tephrochronology of the Lake Lahontan area. *Nevada Archaeological Survey Research Paper*, no. 7.

Davis, Jonathan. 1983. Geology of Gatecliff Shelter: Sedimentary facies and Holocene climate. In "The archaeology of Monitor Valley: 2. Gatecliff Shelter" by David Hurst Thomas. *Anthropological Papers of the American Museum of Natural History* 59(1): 64–87.

Dibble, Harold, Philip Chase, Shannon McPherron, and Alain Tuffreau. 1992. Testing the reality of a "living floor" with archaeological data. *American Antiquity* 62: 629–651.

Ellis, Florence Hawley. 1983. Foreword to Stephen H. Lekson (Ed.), The Architecture and Dendrochronology of Chetro Ketl, Chaco Canyon, New Mexico. *Reports of the Chaco Center*, no. 6. Albuquerque: Division of Cultural Research, National Park Service. ("In Her Own Words" text quoted from this work.)

Feibel, C. S., N. Agnew, B. Latimer, M. Demas, F. Marshall, S. A. C. Waane, and P. Schmid, 1996. A new look at the Laetoli hominid footprints: A preliminary report on the conservation and scientific restudy. *Evolutionary Anthropology* 4: 149–154.

Frisbie, Theodore R. 1975. A biography of Florence Hawley Ellis and bibliography of Florence Hawley Ellis. In Theodore R. Frisbie (Ed.), Collected Papers in Honor of Florence Hawley Ellis. *Papers of the Archaeological Society of New Mexico* 2: 1–11, 12–21.

———. 1991. Florence Hawley Ellis, 1906–1991. *Kiva* 57(1): 93–97.

Greenfield, Jeanette. 1989. *The Return of Cultural Treasures.* Cambridge: Cambridge University Press.

Harris, E. 1989. *Principles of Archaeological Stratigraphy.* 2d ed. New York: Academic Press.

Hawley, Florence M. 1934. The significance of the dated prehistory of Chetro Ketl, Chaco Canyon, New Mexico. *University of New Mexico Bulletin*, Monograph Series 1(1). Albuquerque: University of New Mexico Press.

———. 1937. Reversed stratigraphy. *American Antiquity* 4: 297–299.

Hay, Richard I., and Mary D. Leakey. 1982. The fossil footprints of Laetoli. *Scientific American* 246(2): 50–57.

Herz, Norman, and Ervan Garrison. 1998. *Geological Methods for Archaeology.* Oxford: Oxford University Press.

Holliday, Vance T. (Ed.). 1992. *Soils in Archaeology: Landscape Evolution and Human Occupation.* Washington, DC: Smithsonian Institution Press.

Leakey, Mary, and J. M. Harris (Eds.). 1987. *Laetoli: A Pliocene Site in Northern Tanzania.* Oxford: Clarendon Press.

Rapp, George, and John A. Gifford (Eds.). 1985. *Archaeological Geology.* New Haven: Yale University Press.

Schiffer, Michael B. 1972. Archaeological context and systemic context. *American Antiquity* 37: 156–165.

———. 1976. *Behavioral Archeology.* New York: Academic Press.

———. 1987. *Formation Processes of the Archaeological Record.* Albuquerque: University of New Mexico Press.

Steen-McIntyre, Virginia. 1985. Tephrochronology and its application to archaeology. In George Rapp, Jr., and John A. Gifford (Eds.), *Archaeological Geology* (pp. 265–302). New Haven: Yale University Press.

Stein, Julie K. 1987. Deposits for archaeologists. In Michael B. Schiffer (Ed.), *Advances in Archaeological Method and Theory.* Vol. 11 (pp. 337–395). New York: Academic Press.

——— (Ed.). 1992. *Deciphering a Shell Midden.* San Diego: Academic Press.

Straus, Lawrence G. 1990. Underground archaeology: Perspectives on caves and rockshelters. In M. B. Schiffer (Ed.), *Archaeological Method and Theory.* Vol. 2 (pp. 255–304). Tucson: University of Arizona Press.

Thomas, David Hurst. 1983. The archaeology of Monitor Valley: 2. Gatecliff Shelter. *Anthropological Papers of the American Museum of Natural History* 59 (part 1). New York (quote is from pp. 55–56).

Tuttle, Russell, D. Webb, E. Weidl, and M. Baksh. 1990. Further progress on the Laeotoli trails. *Journal of Archaeological Science* 17: 347–362.

Waters, Michael R. 1992. *Principles of Geoarchaeology: A North American Perspective.* Tucson: University of Arizona Press (quotes from pp. 3, 7, 11).

Chapter 8

Aitken, M. J. 1989. Luminescence dating: A guide for non-specialists. *Archaeometry* 31: 147–159.

———. 1990. *Science-Based Dating in Archaeology.* London: Longman.

Baillie, M. G. L. 1995. *A Slice Through Time: Dendrochronology and Precision Dating.* London: Batsford.

Banning, E. B., and L. A. Pavlish. 1978. Direct detection in radiocarbon dating. *Journal of Field Archaeology.* 5: 480–483.

Bannister, Bryant. 1962. The interpretation of tree-ring dates. *American Antiquity* 27: 508–514.

———. 1970. Dendrochronology. In Don Brothwell and Eric Higgs (Eds.), *Science in Archaeology: A Survey of Progress and Research.* 2d ed. (pp. 191–205). New York: Praeger.

Bannister, Bryant, and William J. Robinson. 1975. Tree-ring dating in archaeology. *World Archaeology* 7: 210–225.

Beck, Charlotte (Ed.). 1994. *Dating in Exposed and Surface Contexts.* Albuquerque: University of New Mexico Press.

Bennett, C. L., R. P. Beukens, M. R. Clover, H. E. Gove, R. B. Liebert, A. E. Litherland, K. H. Purser, and W. E. Sondheim. 1977. Radiocarbon dating using electrostatic accelerators: Negative ions provide the key. *Science* 198: 508–510.

Berger, R. 1979. Radiocarbon dating with accelerators. *Journal of Archaeological Science* 6: 101–104.

Binford, Lewis R. 1962. A new method of calculating dates from kaolin pipe stem samples. *Southeastern Archaeological Conference Newsletter* 9(2): 19–21.

———. 1972. The "Binford" pipe stem formula: A return from the grave. *The Conference on Historic Site Archaeology Papers* 6: 230–253.

Bowman, Sheridan. 1990. *Radiocarbon Dating.* Berkeley: University of California Press.

———. 1994. Using radiocarbon: An update. *Antiquity* 68: 838–843.

Braun, David P. 1985. Absolute seriation: A time-series approach. In Christopher Carr (Ed.), *For Concordance in Archaeological Analysis: Bridging Data Structure, Quantitative Technique, and Theory* (pp. 509–539). Kansas City, MO: Westport.

Browman, David L. 1981. Isotopic discrimination and correction factors in radiocarbon dating. In Michael B. Schiffer (Ed.), *Advances in Archaeological Method and Theory.* Vol. 6 (pp. 241–295). New York: Academic Press.

Chaffee, Scott D., Marian Hyman, Marvin W. Rowe, Nancy J. Coulam, Alan Schroedl, and Kathleen Hogue. 1994. Radiocarbon dates on the All American Man pictograph. *American Antiquity* 59: 769–781.

Chase, A. F., D. Z. Chase, and H. W. Topsey. 1988. Archaeology and the ethics of collecting. *Archaeology* 41(1): 56–60, 87.

Creel, Darrell, and Austin Long. 1986. Radiocarbon dating of corn. *American Antiquity* 51: 826–837.

Dale, W. S. A. 1987. The shroud of Turin: Relic or icon? In H. H. Andersen and S. T. Picraux (Eds.), Nuclear Instruments and Methods in Physics Research: Section B, Beam Interactions with Materials and Atoms. *Proceedings of the Fourth International Symposium on Accelerator Mass Spectrometry* B29: 187–192.

Deagan, Kathleen. 1983. *Spanish St. Augustine: The Archaeology of a Colonial Creole Community.* New York: Academic Press.

Dean, Jeffery S. 1978. Independent dating in archaeological analysis. In Michael B. Schiffer (Ed.), *Advances in Archaeological Theory and Method.* Vol. 1 (pp. 223–255). New York: Academic Press.

de Vries, Hessel L. 1958. Variation in concentration of radiocarbon with time and location on earth. *Proceedings Koninklijke Nederlandse Akademie Wetenschappen* B, 61: 94–102.

Douglass, Andrew Ellicott. 1929. The secret of the Southwest solved by talkative tree rings. *National Geographic* 56(6): 736–770.

Drennan, Robert D. 1976. A refinement of chronological seriation using nonmetric multidimensional scaling. *American Antiquity* 41: 290–302.

Dunnell, Robert C. 1970. Seriation method and its evaluation. *American Antiquity* 35: 305–319.

Feathers, James. 2003. Use of luminescence dating in archaeology. *Measurement Science and Technology* 14: 1493–1509.

Fleming, Stuart. 1977. *Dating Techniques in Archaeology.* New York: St. Martin's Press.

———. 1979. *Thermoluminescence Techniques in Archaeology.* New York: Oxford University Press.

Fritts, H. C. 1976. *Tree Rings and Climate.* New York: Academic Press.

Fullagar, R. L. K., D. M. Price, and L. M. Head. 1996. Early human occupation of northern Australia: Archaeology and thermoluminescence dating of Jinmium rockshelter, Northern Territory. *Antiquity* 70: 751–773.

Gove, H. E. 1987. Turin workshop on radiocarbon dating the Turin shroud. *Nuclear Instruments and Methods in Physics Research* B29(1, 2): 193–195.

Grün, R. 1999. Trapped charge dating (ESR, TL, OSL). In D. Brothwell and A. Pollard (Eds.), *Handbook of Archaeological Sciences* (pp. 47–62). Chichester, England: John Wiley and Sons.

Haas, Herbert, James Devine, Robert Wenke, Mark Lehner, Willy Wolfli, and George Bonani. 1987.

Radiocarbon chronology and the historical calendar in Egypt. In Oliver Aurenche, Jacques Evin, and Francis Hours (Eds.), Chronologies in the Near East: Relative Chronologies and Absolute Chronology 16,000–4,000 BP. (pp. 585–606). *British Archaeology Reports International Series* 379. Oxford, England.

Harrington, Jean C. 1954. Dating stem fragments of seventeenth and eighteenth century clay tobacco pipes. *Quarterly Bulletin: Archaeological Society of Virginia* 9(1).

Hedges, R. E. M., and J. A. J. Gowlett. 1986. Radiocarbon dating by accelerator mass spectrometry. *Scientific American* 254(1): 100–107.

Heighton, Robert F., and Kathleen A. Deagan. 1972. A new formula for dating kaolin clay pipestems. *The Conference on Historic Site Archaeology Papers* 6(2): 220–229.

Hu, Q., P. E. Smith, N. M. Evensen, and D. York. 1994. Lasing in the Holocene: Extending the 40Ar-39Ar laser probe method into the 14C age range. *Earth and Planetary Science Letters* 123: 331–336.

Jull, A. J. T., D. J. Donahue, and P. E. Damon. 1996. Factors affecting the apparent radiocarbon age of textiles: A comment on "Effects of fires and biofractionation of carbon isotopes on results of radiocarbon dating of old textiles: The shroud of Turin" by D. A. Kouznetsov et al. *Journal of Archaeological Science* 23: 157–160.

Kouznetsov, Dmitri A., Andrey A. Ivanov, and Pavel R. Veletsky. 1996. Effects of fires and biofractionation of carbon isotopes on results of radiocarbon dating of old textiles: The shroud of Turin. *Journal of Archaeological Science* 23: 109–121.

Long, A., and Bruce Rippeteau. 1974. Testing contemporaneity and averaging radiocarbon dates. *American Antiquity* 39: 205–215.

Loy, Thomas H., Rhys Jones, D. E. Nelson, Betty Meehan, John Vogel, John Southon, and Richard Cosgrove. 1990. Accelerator radiocarbon dating of human blood proteins in pigments from Late Pleistocene art sites in Australia. *Antiquity* 64: 110–116.

Marquardt, William H. 1978. Advances in archaeological seriation. In Michael B. Schiffer (Ed.), *Advances in Archaeological Method and Theory*. Vol. 1 (pp. 257–314). New York: Academic Press.

Mazess, Richard B., and D. W. Zimmermann. 1966. Pottery dating from thermoluminescence. *Science* 152(3720): 347–348.

McDougall, I. 1990. Potassium-argon dating in archaeology. *Science Progress* 74: 15–30.

McNutt, Charles H. 1973. On the methodological validity of frequency seriation. *American Antiquity* 38: 45–60.

Messenger, Phyllis (Ed.). 1989. *The Ethics of Collecting Cultural Property: Whose Culture? Whose Property?* Albuquerque: University of New Mexico Press.

Michels, Joseph W. 1973. *Dating Methods in Archaeology*. New York: Seminar Press.

Nelson, Nels. 1916. Chronology of the Tano Ruins, New Mexico. *American Anthropologist* 18: 159–180 (Table 8-1 is from p. 166).

Orser, Charles E., Jr., and Brian M. Fagan. 1995. *Historical Archaeology*. New York: HarperCollins.

Ralph, Elizabeth K., and Mark C. Han. 1966. Dating of pottery by thermoluminescence. *Nature* 210(5033): 245–247.

———. 1969. Potential of thermoluminescence in supplementing radiocarbon dating. *World Archaeology* 1: 157–169.

Renfrew, Colin. 1979. *Problems in European Prehistory*. Edinburgh: Edinburgh University Press.

Roberts, R. G., M. Bird, J. Olley, R. Galbraith, E. Lawson, G. Laslett, H. Yoshida, R. Jones, R. L. K. Fullagar, G. Jacobsen, and Q. Hua. 1998. Optical and radiocarbon dating at Jinmium rock shelter in northern Australia. *Nature* 393: 358–362.

Rouse, Irving. 1967. Seriation in archaeology. In Carrol L. Riley and Walter W. Taylor (Eds.), *American Historical Anthropology: Essays in Honor of Leslie Spier* (pp. 153–195). Carbondale: Southern Illinois University Press.

South, David B. 1972. Mean ceramic dates, median occupation dates, red ant hills and bumble bees: Statistical confidence and correlation. *The Conference on Historic Site Archaeology Papers* 6: 164–174.

South, Stanley A. 1977. *Method and Theory in Historical Archeology*. New York: Academic Press (Table 8-4 is from p. 220).

Stafford, T. W., Jr., A. J. T. Jull, T. H. Zabel, D. J. Donahue, R. C. Duhamel, K. Brendel, C. V. Haynes, Jr., J. L. Bischoff, L. A. Payen, and R. E. Taylor. 1984. Holocene age of the Yuha burial: Direct radiocarbon determinations by accelerator mass spectrometry. *Nature* 308: 446–447.

Stahle, David W., and Daniel Wolfman. 1985. The potential for archaeological tree-ring dating in eastern North America. In Michael B. Schiffer (Ed.),

Advances in Archaeological Method and Theory. Vol. 8 (pp. 279–302). New York: Academic Press.

Staley, David P. 1993. The antiquities market. *Journal of Field Archaeology* 20: 347–355.

Stallings, W. S., Jr. 1939. Dating Prehistoric Ruins by Tree-Rings. *Laboratory of Anthropology Bulletin* no. 8. Santa Fe, NM.

Stuckenrath, R. 1977. Radiocarbon: Some notes from Merlin's diary. *Annals of the New York Academy of Science* 288: 181–188.

Stuiver, Minze, and Paula J. Reimer. 1993. Extended 14C database and revised CALIB 3.0 14C age calibration program. *Radiocarbon* 35: 215–230.

Stuiver, Minze, and Hans E. Suess. 1966. On the relationship between radiocarbon dates and true sample ages. *Radiocarbon* 8: 534–540.

Suess, Hans E. 1955. Radiocarbon concentration in modern wood. *Science* 122: 415–417.

Swisher, C. C., III, G. H. Curtis, T. Jacob, A. G. Getty, and A. Suprijo Widasmoro. 1994. Age of the earliest known hominids in Java, Indonesia. *Science* 263: 1118–1121.

Taylor, R. E. 1985. The beginnings of radiocarbon dating in American antiquity: A historical perspective. *American Antiquity* 50: 309–325.

———. 1987a. AMS 14-C dating of critical bone samples: Proposed protocol and criteria for evaluation. In H. H. Andersen and S. T. Picraux (Eds.), Nuclear Instruments and Methods in Physics Research: Section B, Beam Interactions With Materials and Atoms. *Proceedings of the Fourth International Symposium on Accelerator Mass Spectrometry*, B29: 159–163. Ontario, Canada.

———. 1987b. *Radiocarbon Dating: An Archaeological Perspective.* New York: Academic Press.

Taylor, R. E., and M. J. Aitken (Eds.). 1997. *Chronometric Dating in Archaeology.* New York: Plenum Press.

Taylor, R. E., Austin Long, and Renee S. Kra (Eds.). 1992. *Radiocarbon After Four Decades: An Interdisciplinary Perspective.* New York: Springer-Verlag.

Turnbaugh, William, and Sarah Peabody Turnbaugh. 1977. Alternative applications of the mean ceramic date concept for interpreting human behavior. *Historical Archaeology* 11: 90–104.

Valladas, H., H. Cachier, P. Maurice, F. Bernaldo de Quiro, J. Clottes, V. Cabrera Valdés, P. Uzquiano, and M. Arnold. 1992. Direct radiocarbon dates for prehistoric paintings at the Altamira, El Castillo and Niaux caves. *Nature* 357: 68–70.

van der Merwe, Nikolaas J. 1982. Carbon isotopes, photosynthesis, and archaelogy. *American Scientist* 70: 596–606.

van der Plicht, Johannes. 1993. The Groningen radiocarbon calibration program. *Radiocarbon* 35(1): 231–237.

Wendorf, Fred, R. Schild, A. E. Close, D. J. Donahue, A. J. T. Jull, T. H. Zabel, H. Wieçlowska, M. Kobusiewicz, B. Issawi, N. el Hadidi, and H. Haas. 1984. New radiocarbon dates on the cereals from Wadi Kubbaniua. *Science* 225: 645–646.

Wendorf, Fred, R. Schild, N. el Hadidi, A. E. Close, M. Kobusiewicz, H. Wieçlowska, B. Issawi, and H. Haas. 1979. The use of barley in the Egyptian late Paleolithic. *Science* 205: 1341–1347.

Willis, E. H. 1969. Radiocarbon dating. In Don Brothwell and Eric Higgs (Eds.), *Science in Archaeology* (pp. 46–57). London: Thames and Hudson.

Wintle, Ann G. 1996. Archaeologically relevant dating techniques for the next century. *Journal of Archaeological Science* 23: 123–138.

Chapter 9

Adams, William Y. 1988. Archaeological classification: Theory versus practice. *Antiquity* 62: 40–56.

Adams, William Y., and Ernest W. Adams. 1991. *Archaeological Typology and Practical Reality: A Dialectical Approach to Artifact Classification and Sorting.* Cambridge: Cambridge University Press.

Binford, Lewis R. 1973. Interassemblage variability— The Mousterian and the "functional" argument. In Colin Renfrew (Ed.), *The Explanation of Culture Change: Models in Prehistory* (pp. 227–254). London: Duckworth.

Cordell, Linda. 1984. *Prehistory of the Southwest.* New York: Academic Press.

Cronyn, J. M. 1990. *The Elements of Archaeological Conservation.* London: Routledge.

Dunnell, Robert C. 1971. *Systematics in Prehistory.* New York: Free Press.

———. 1986. Methodological issues in Americanist artifact classification. In Michael B. Schiffer (Ed.), *Advances in Archaeological Method and Theory.* Vol. 9 (pp. 149–207). New York: Academic Press.

Ford, James. 1954. The type concept revisited. *American Anthropologist* 56: 42–54.

Griset, Suzanne (Ed.). 1986. Pottery of the Great Basin and adjacent areas. *University of Utah Anthropological Papers*, no. 111.

Haury, Emil W. 1950. The Stratigraphy and Archaeology of Ventana Cave, Arizona. Albuquerque: University of New Mexico Press; Tucson: University of Arizona Press (quote from p. 329).

Klejn, L. S. 1982. Archaeological typology. Translated by P. Dole. British Archaeological Reports, International Series, no. 153. Oxford, England.

Krieger, Alex D. 1944. The typological concept. *American Antiquity* 9: 271–288.

Lyman, R. Lee, and Michael O'Brien. 2003. *W. C. McKern and the Midwestern Taxonomic Method.* Tuscaloosa: University of Alabama Press.

Lyman, R. Lee, Michael O'Brien, and Robert C. Dunnell (Eds.). 1997. *Americanist Culture History: Fundamentals of Time, Space, and Form.* New York: Plenum Press.

Rouse, Irving. 1960. The classification of artifacts in archaeology. *American Antiquity* 25: 313–323.

Spaulding, Albert C. 1953. Statistical techniques for the discovery of artifact types. *American Antiquity* 18: 305–313.

———. 1960. The dimensions of archaeology. In G. E. Dole and R. L. Carneiro (Eds.), *Essays in the Science of Culture in Honor of Leslie A. White* (pp. 437–456). New York: Thomas Y. Crowell.

———. 1977. On growth and form in archaeology: Multivariate analysis. *Journal of Anthropological Research* 33: 1–15.

Spier, Leslie. 1917. An outline for a chronology of Zuñi ruins. *Anthropological Papers of the American Museum of Natural History* 18(3): 207–331.

———. 1931. N. C. Nelson's stratigraphic technique in the reconstruction of prehistoric sequences in southwestern America. In S. A. Rice (Ed.), *Methods in Social Science* (pp. 275–283). Chicago: University of Chicago Press.

Steward, Julian H. 1954. Types of types. *American Anthropologist* 56: 54–57.

Sutton, Mark Q., and Brooke S. Arkush. 1996. *Archaeological Laboratory Methods: An Introduction.* Dubuque, IA: Kendall/Hunt Publishing.

Thomas, David Hurst. 1981. How to classify the projectile points from Monitor Valley, Nevada. *Journal of California and Great Basin Anthropology* 3: 7–43.

Whallon, Robert E., Jr., and James A. Brown (Eds.). 1982. *Essays on Archaeological Typology.* Evanston, IL: Center for American Archaeology Press.

Willey, Gordon R., and Philip Phillips. 1958. *Method and Theory in American Archaeology.* Chicago: University of Chicago Press (quote is from p. 22).

Wissler, Clark. 1926. *The Relation of Nature to Man in Aboriginal America.* New York: Oxford University Press.

Chapter 10

Agenbroad, Larry. 1978. *The Hudson-Meng Site: An Alberta Bison Kill in the Nebraska High Plains.* Washington, DC: University Press of America.

Andrefsky, William. 1998. *Lithics: Macroscopic Approaches to Analysis.* Cambridge: Cambridge University Press.

Behrensmeyer, Anna K., and Susan M. Kidwell. 1985. Taphonomy's contributions to paleobiology. *Paleobiology* 1: 105–119.

Binford, Lewis R. 1967. Smudge pits and hide smoking: The use of analogy in archaeological reasoning. *American Antiquity* 32: 1–12.

——— (Ed.). 1977. *For Theory Building in Archaeology.* New York: Academic Press.

———. 1978a. Dimensional analysis of behavior and site structure: Learning from an Eskimo hunting stand. *American Antiquity* 43: 330–361.

———. 1978b. *Nunamiut Ethnoarchaeology.* New York: Academic Press.

———. 1980. Willow smoke and dogs' tails: Hunter-gatherer settlement systems and archaeological site formation. *American Antiquity* 45: 4–20.

———. 1982. The archaeology of place. *Journal of Anthropological Archaeology* 1: 5–31.

———. 1983. *In Pursuit of the Past: Decoding the Archaeological Record.* London: Thames and Hudson ("In His Own Words" text quoted from pp. 98, 100–101).

———. 1986. An Alyawara day: Making men's knives and beyond. *American Antiquity* 51: 547–562.

Binford, Lewis R., and James F. O'Connell. 1984. An Alyawara day: The stone quarry. *Journal of Anthropological Research* 40: 406–432.

Brandt, Steve A., and Kathryn Weedman. 1997. The ethnoarchaeology of hideworking and flaked stone-tool use in southern Ethiopia. In K. Fukui, E. Kuimoto, and M. Shigeta (Eds.), *Ethiopia in Broader Perspective: Papers of the XIIth International Conference of Ethiopian Studies* (pp. 351–361). Kyoto: Shokado Book Sellers.

Buck, Bruce A. 1982. Ancient technology in contemporary surgery. *The Western Journal of Medicine* 136: 265–269.

Chaplin, R. E. 1971. *The Study of Animal Bones from Archaeological Sites.* New York: Seminar Press.

Coles, John M. 1973. *Archaeology by Experiment.* New York: Scribner's.

Cotterell, Brian, and Johan Kamminga. 1990. *Mechanics of Pre-Industrial Technology.* Cambridge: Cambridge University Press.

Crabtree, Don E. 1966. A stoneworker's approach to analyzing and replicating the Lindenmeier Folsom. *Tebiwa* 9: 3–39.

———. 1968. Mesoamerican polyhedral cores and prismatic blades. *American Antiquity* 33: 446–478.

———. 1979. Interview. *Flintknappers' Exchange* 2(1): 29–33 ("Looking Closer" text quoted from p. 30).

David, Nicholas, and Carol Kramer. 2001. *Ethnoarchaeology in Action.* Cambridge: Cambridge University Press.

Efremov, I. A. 1940. Taphonomy: A new branch of paleontology. *Pan-American Geologist* 74(2): 81–93.

Flenniken, J. Jeffrey. 1978. Reevaluation of the Lindenmeier Folsom: A replication experiment in lithic technology. *American Antiquity* 43: 473–480.

———. 1981. Replicative systems analysis: A model applied to the vein quartz artifacts from the Hoko River site. *Laboratory of Anthropology Reports of Investigations*, no. 59. Pullman: Washington State University.

———. 1984. The past, present, and future of flintknapping: An anthropological perspective. *Annual Review of Anthropology* 13: 187–203.

Frison, George C. 1989. Experimental use of Clovis weaponry and tools on African elephants. *American Antiquity* 54: 766–784.

Gamble, C. S., and W. A. Boismier (Eds.). 1991. Ethnoarchaeological Approaches to Mobile Campsites. *International Monographs in Prehistory.* Ann Arbor.

Gifford, Diane P. 1981. Taphonomy and paleoecology: A critical review of archaeology's sister disciplines. In Michael B. Schiffer (Ed.), *Advances in Archaeological Method and Theory.* Vol. 4 (pp. 365–438). New York: Academic Press.

Graham, Martha. 1994. *Mobile Farmers: An Ethnoarchaeological Approach to Settlement Organization Among the Rarámuri of Northwestern Mexico.* International Monographs in Prehistory, Ethnoarchaeological Series 3. Ann Arbor, Michigan.

Grayson, Donald K. 1986. Eoliths, archaeological ambiguity, and the generation of "middle-range" research. In David J. Meltzer, Don D. Fowler, and Jeremy A. Sabloff (Eds.), *American Archaeology Past and Future: A Celebration of the Society of American Archaeology 1935–1985* (pp. 77–133). Washington, DC: Smithsonian Institution Press.

Gryba, Eugene M. 1988. A Stone Age pressure method of Folsom fluting. *Plains Anthropologist* 33: 53–66.

Hayden, Brian. 1979. *Palaeolithic Reflections: Lithic Technology and Ethnographic Excavation Among Australian Aborigines.* Atlantic Highlands, NJ: Humanities Press.

———. 1987. *Lithic Studies Among the Contemporary Highland Maya.* Tucson: University of Arizona Press.

Hayden, Brian, and Aubrey Cannon. 1984. The structure of material systems: Ethnoarchaeology in the Maya highlands. *Society for American Archaeology Papers*, no. 3.

Henry, Donald O., and George H. Odell (Eds.). 1989. Alternative Approaches to Lithic Analysis. *Archaeological Papers of the American Anthropological Association*, no. 1. Washington, DC: American Anthropological Association.

Hill, Andrew. 1979a. Butchery and natural disarticulation: An investigatory technique. *American Antiquity* 44: 739–744.

———. 1979b. Disarticulation and scattering of mammal skeletons. *Paleobiology* 5: 261–274.

Hill, Andrew, and Anna Kay Behrensmeyer. 1984. Disarticulation patterns of some modern East African mammals. *Paleobiology* 10: 366–376.

Hodder, Ian. 1982. *Symbols in Action.* Cambridge: Cambridge University Press.

———. 1987. The meaning of discard: Ash and domestic space in Baringo. In S. Kent (Ed.), *Method and Theory in Activity Area Research* (pp. 424–448). New York: Columbia University Press.

Holly, Gerald A., and Terry A. Del Bene. 1981. An evaluation of Keeley's "Microwear approach." *Journal of Archaeological Science* 8: 337–352.

Keeley, Lawrence H. 1974. Technique and methodology in microwear studies: A critical review. *World Archaeology* 5: 323–336.

———. 1980. *Experimental Determination of Stone Tool Uses: A Microwear Analysis.* Chicago: University of Chicago Press.

Keeley, Lawrence H., and M. H. Newcomer. 1977. Microwear analysis of experimental flint tools: A test case. *Journal of Archaeological Science* 4: 29–62.

Kelly, Robert, Lin Poyer, and Bram Tucker. 2004. Mobility and houses in southwestern Madagascar: Ethnoarchaeology among the Mikea and their neighbors. In F. R. Sellet, R. Greaves, and P. L. Yu (Eds.), *Archaeology and Ethnoarchaeology of Mobility*. Gainesville: University Press of Florida (forthcoming).

Kelly, Robert, Jean-François Rabedimy, and Lin A. Poyer. 1999. The Mikea of southwestern Madagascar. In R. B. Lee and R. Daly (Eds.), *The Cambridge Encyclopedia of Hunter-Gatherers* (pp. 215–219). Cambridge: Cambridge University Press.

Koch, Christopher P. (Ed.). 1989. *Taphonomy: A Bibliographic Guide to the Literature*. Orono, ME: Center for the Study of the First Americans.

Kosso, P. 1991. Method in archaeology: Middle-range theory as hermeneutics. *American Antiquity* 56: 621–627.

Kramer, Carol.1997. *Pottery in Rajasthan: Ethnoarchaeology in Two Indian Cities*. Washington, DC: Smithsonian Institution Press.

Kroeber, Theodora. 1961. *Ishi in Two Worlds: A Biography of the Last Wild Indian in North America*. Berkeley: University of California Press.

Lehner, Mark. 1997. *The Complete Pyramids: Solving the Ancient Mysteries*. London: Thames and Hudson.

Longacre, William A. (Ed.). 1991. *Ceramic Ethnoarchaeology*. Tucson: University of Arizona Press.

Longacre, William A., and James M. Skibo (Eds.). 1994. *Kalinga Ethnoarchaeology: Expanding Archaeological Method and Theory*. Washington, DC: Smithsonian Institution Press.

Moss, Emily. 1983. *The Functional Analysis of Flint Implements—Pincevent and Pont d'Ambon: Two Case Studies From the French Final Palaeolithic*. British Archaeological Reports, International Series, no. 177.

Nelson, Margaret. 1999. *Mimbres During the Twelfth Century: Abandonment, Continuity, and Reorganization*. Tucson: University of Arizona Press.

Newcomer, M. H., and L. H. Keeley. 1979. Testing a method of microwear analysis with experimental flint tools. In Brian Hayden (Ed.), *Lithic Use-Wear Analysis* (pp. 195–205). New York: Academic Press. (Data for Table 10-1 from this publication's Table 1.)

O'Connell, James F. 1995. Ethnoarchaeology needs a general theory of behavior. *Journal of Archaeological Research* 3: 205–255.

Odell, George Hanley (Ed.). 1996. *Stone Tools: Theoretical Insights Into Human Prehistory*. New York: Plenum Press.

Odell, George Hanley, and F. Odell-Vereecken. 1980. Verifying the reliability of lithic use-wear assessments by "blind tests": The low power approach. *Journal of Field Archaeology* 7: 87–120.

Perkins, D., Jr., and P. Daly. 1968. A hunter's village in Neolithic Turkey. *Scientific American* 219(5): 96–106.

Pope, Saxton T. 1974. Hunting with Ishi—the last Yana Indian. *Journal of California Anthropology* 1: 152–173.

Poyer, Lin, and Robert Kelly. 2000. Mystification of the Mikea: Constructions of foraging identity in southwest Madagascar. *Journal of Anthropological Research* 56: 163–185.

Raab, L. Mark, and Albert C. Goodyear. 1984. Middle-range theory in archaeology: A critical review of origins and applications. *American Antiquity* 49: 255–268.

Saitta, Dean J. 1992. Radical archaeology and middle-range methodology. *Antiquity* 66: 886–897.

Scheper-Hughes, Nancy. 2002. Ishi's brain, Ishi's ashes: Anthropolology and genocide. *Anthropology Today* 17(1): 12–18.

———. 2003. "Ishi's Ashes: Anthropology and Genocide." In K. Kroeber (Ed.), *Ishi in Three Centuries* (pp. 99–131). Lincoln: University of Nebraska Press.

Schick, Kathy, and Nicholas Toth. 1993. *Making Silent Stones Speak: Human Evolution and the Dawn of Technology*. New York: Touchstone.

Schiffer, Michael B., James M. Skibo, Tamara C. Boelke, Mark A. Neupert, and Meredith Aronson. 1994. New perspectives on experimental archaeology: Surface treatments and thermal response of the clay cooking pot. *American Antiquity* 59: 197–217.

Semenov, Sergei, 1964. *Prehistoric Technology*. Translated by M. W. Thompson. London: Cory, Adams, and MacKay.

Shea, John J. 1987. On accuracy and relevance in lithic use-wear analysis. *Lithic Technology* 16(2–3): 44–50.

Sheets, Payson D. 1987. Dawn of a new Stone Age in eye surgery. In Robert J. Sharer and Wendy Ashmore (Eds.), *Archaeology: Discovering Our Past* (pp. 230–231). Mountain View, CA: Mayfield Publishing.

Stahl, Ann B. 1995. Has ethnoarchaeology come of age? *Antiquity* 69: 404–407.

Starn, Orin. 2003. *Ishi's Brain: In Search of the Last "Wild" Indian*. San Francisco: W. W. Norton and Company.

Tindale, Norman B. 1985. Australian aboriginal techniques of pressure-flaking stone implements: Some personal observations. In Mark G. Plew, James C. Woods, and Max G. Pavesic (Eds.), *Stone Tool Analysis: Essays in Honor of Don E. Crabtree* (pp. 1–33). Albuquerque: University of New Mexico Press.

Todd, Lawrence C., and David Rapson. 1999. Formational analysis of bison bonebeds and interpretation of Paleoindian subsistence. In J-P. Brugal, F. David, J. G. Enloe, and J. Jaubert (Eds.), *Le Bison: Gibier et Moyen de Subsistance des hommes du Paléolithique aux Paléoindiens des Grandes Plains* (pp. 479–499). Antibes, France: Association pour la promotion et la diffusion des Connaissance Archéologiques.

Trigger, Bruce G. 1981. Archaeology and the ethnographic present. *Anthropologica* 23: 3–17.

———. 1995. Expanding middle-range theory. *Antiquity* 69: 449–458.

Tringham, Ruth, G. Cooper, G. Odell, R. Voiytek, and A. Whitman. 1974. Experimentation in the formation of edge damage: A new approach to lithic analysis. *Journal of Field Archaeology* 1: 171–196.

Tunnell, C. 1977. Fluted projectile point production as revealed by lithic specimens from the Adair-Steadman site in northwest Texas. In Eileen Johnson (Ed.), Paleoindian Lifeways. Lubbock: West Texas Museum Association, Texas Tech University. *The Museum Journal* 17: 140–168.

Vaughan, Patrick C. 1985. *Use-Wear Analysis of Flaked Stone Tools.* Tucson: University of Arizona Press.

Weedman, Kathryn. 2002. On the spur of the moment: Effects of age and experience on hafted stone scraper morphology. *American Antiquity* 67: 731–744.

White, Theodore E. 1953. A method of calculating the dietary percentage of various food animals utilized by aboriginal peoples. *American Antiquity* 18: 396–398.

———. 1954. Observations on the butchering technique of some aboriginal peoples, nos. 3, 4, 5, and 6. *American Antiquity* 19: 254–264.

Whittaker, John C. 1994. *Flintknapping: Making and Understanding Stone Tools.* Austin: University of Texas Press.

Wilshusen, Richard H., and Glenn D. Stone. 1990. An ethnoarchaeological perspective on soils. *World Archaeology* 22: 104–114.

Wylie, Alison. 1985. The reaction against analogy. In M. B. Schiffer (Ed.), *Advances in Archaeological Method and Theory.* Vol. 8 (pp. 63–112). New York: Academic Press.

Yellen, John E. 1976. Settlement patterns of the !Kung: An archaeological perspective. In R. B. Lee and I. DeVore (Eds.), *Kalahari Hunter-Gatherers* (pp. 47–72). Cambridge: Harvard University Press.

———. 1977. *Archaeological Approaches to the Present: Models for Reconstructing the Past.* New York: Academic Press.

Chapter 11

Adams, Karen R., and Robert E. Gasser. 1980. Plant microfossils from archaeological sites: Research considerations and sampling techniques and approaches. *The Kiva* 45: 293–300.

Betancourt, Julio L., Thomas R. Van Devender, and Paul S. Martin (Eds.). 1990. *Packrat Middens: The Last 40,000 Years of Biotic Change.* Tucson: University of Arizona Press.

Billman, B. R., P. M. Lambert, and B. L. Leonard. 2000. Cannibalism, warfare, and drought in the Mesa Verde region during the twelfth century AD. *American Antiquity* 65: 145–178.

Binford, Lewis R. 1978. *Nunamiut Ethnoarchaeology.* New York: Academic Press.

———. 1981. *Bones: Ancient Men and Modern Myths.* New York: Academic Press.

Brewer, Douglas J. 1992. Zooarchaeology: Method, theory, and goals. In M. B. Schiffer (Ed.), *Archaeological Method and Theory.* Vol. 4 (pp. 195–244). Tucson: University of Arizona Press.

Brothwell, D., and A. Pollard (Eds.). 2001. *Handbook of Archaeological Sciences.* Chichester, England: John Wiley and Sons.

Bryant, Vaughn M., Jr., and Stephen A. Hall. 1993. Archaeological palynology in the United States: A critique. *American Antiquity* 58: 277–286.

Bryant, Vaughn M., Jr., and Richard G. Holloway. 1983. The role of palynology in archaeology. In Michael B. Schiffer (Ed.), *Advances in Archaeological Method and Theory.* Vol. 6 (pp. 191–224). New York: Academic Press.

Crabtree, Pam J. 1990. Zooarchaeology and complex societies: Some uses of faunal analysis for the study of trade, social status, and ethnicity. In M. B. Schiffer (Ed.), *Archaeological Method and Theory.*

Vol. 2 (pp. 155–205). Tucson: University of Arizona Press.

Cummings, Linda Scott. 2001. Phytolith analysis. In R. L. Kelly (Ed.), Prehistory of the Carson Desert and Stillwater Mountains: Environment, Mobility, and Subsistence in a Great Basin Wetland (pp. 251–252). *University of Utah Anthropological Papers* 123. Salt Lake City.

Dincauze, Dena. 2000. *Environmental Archaeology: Principles and Practice*. Cambridge: Cambridge University Press.

Dongoske, K. E., D. L. Martin, and T. J. Ferguson. 1999. Critique of the claim of cannibalism at Cowboy Wash. *American Antiquity* 65: 179–190.

Evershed, R. P., S. N. Dudd, M. J. Collins, O. E. Craig, and R. J. Sokal. 2001. Lipids in archaeology. In D. Brothwell and A. Pollard (Eds.), *Handbook of Archaeological Sciences* (pp. 331–350). Chichester, England: John Wiley and Sons.

Faegri, K., P. E. Kaland, and K. Krzywinski. 1989. *Textbook of Pollen Analysis*. 4th ed. New York: Wiley.

Frison, George C., and Dennis Stanford. 1982. *The Agate Basin Site: A Record of the Paleoindian Occupation of the Northwestern High Plains*. New York: Academic Press.

Gilbert, B. Miles. 1980. *Mammalian Osteology*. Laramie, WY: Modern Printing.

Gilbert, Robert I., Jr., and James H. Mielke (Eds.). 1985. *The Analysis of Prehistoric Diets*. Orlando, FL: Academic Press.

Grayson, Donald K. 1984. *Quantitative Zooarchaeology: Topics in the Analysis of Archaeological Faunas*. Orlando, FL: Academic Press.

Harper, K. T., and G. M. Alder. 1970. Appendix I: The macroscopic plant remains of the deposits of Hogup Cave, Utah, and their paleoclimatic implications. In C. Melvin Aikens, Hogup Cave. *University of Utah Anthropological Papers* 93: 215–240.

Hastorf, Christine A., and Sissel Johannessen. 1991. Understanding changing people/plant relationships in the prehispanic Andes. In Robert W. Preucel (Ed.), Processual and Postprocessual Archaeologies: Multiple Ways of Knowing the Past (pp. 140–155). *Center for Archaeological Investigations, Occasional Paper, no. 10*. Southern Illinois University at Carbondale

Hastorf, Christine A., and Virginia S. Popper (Eds.). 1988. *Current Paleoethnobotany: Analytical Methods and Cultural Interpretations of Archaeological Plant Remains*. Chicago: University of Chicago Press.

Hather, Jon G. (Ed.). 1994. *Tropical Archaeobotany: Applications and New Developments*. London: Routledge.

Haury, Emil W., E. B. Sayles, and William W. Wasley. 1959. The Lehner mammoth site, southeastern Arizona. *American Antiquity* 25: 2–30.

Hill, Matthew G. 2001. *Paleoindian Diet and Subsistence Behavior on the Northwestern Great Plains of North America*. PhD dissertation, University of Wisconsin, Madison. (Table 11-1 is from p. 55.)

———. 2005. *Paleoindian Diet and Subsistence Behavior on the Northwestern Great Plains*. Boulder: University Press of Colorado.

Holden, T. G. 2001. Dietary evidence from the coprolites and the intestinal contents of ancient humans. In D. Brothwell and A. Pollard (Eds.), *Handbook of Archaeological Sciences* (pp. 403–414). Chichester, England: John Wiley and Sons.

Kantner, J. 1999a. Anasazi mutilation and cannibalism in the American southwest. In L. R. Goldman (Ed.), *The Anthropology of Cannibalism* (pp. 75–104). Westport: Bergin and Garvey.

———. 1999b. Survival cannibalism or sociopolitical intimidation? Explaining perimortem mutilation in the American southwest. *Human Nature* 10: 1–50.

Kuckelman, K. A., R. R. Lightfoot, and D. L. Martin. 2002. The bioarchaeology and taphonomy of violence at Castle Rock and Sand Creek Pueblos, southwestern Colorado. *American Antiquity* 67: 486–511.

Lambert, P. M., B. L. Leonard, B. R. Billman, R. A. Marlar, M. E. Newman, and K. J. Reinhard. 2000. Response to critique of the claim of cannibalism at Cowboy Wash. *American Antiquity* 65: 397–403.

Leroi-Gourhan, Arlette. 1975. The flowers found with Shanidar IV, a Neanderthal burial in Iraq. *Science* 190: 562–564.

Lyman, R. Lee. 1994. *Vertebrate Taphonomy*. Cambridge: Cambridge University Press.

Malainey, Mary E., R. Przybylski, and B. L. Sherriff. 1999a. Identifying the former contents of late precontact period pottery vessels from western Canada using gas chromatography. *Journal of Archaeological Science* 26: 425–438.

———. 1999b. The fatty acid composition of native food plants and animals of western Canada. *Journal of Archaeological Science* 26: 83–94.

———. 1999c. The effects of thermal and oxidative decomposition on the fatty acids composition of food plants and animals of western Canada: Implications for the identification of archaeological vessel residues. *Journal of Archaeological Science* 26: 95–103.

Marlar, R. A., B. L. Leonard, B. R. Billman, P. M. Lambert, and J. E. Marlar. 2000. Biochemical evidence of cannibalism at a prehistoric site in southwestern Colorado. *Nature* 7 September: 74–78.

Mehringer, Peter J., and Vance Haynes. 1965. The pollen evidence for the environment of early man and extinct mammals at the Lehner mammoth site, southeastern Arizona. *American Antiquity* 31: 17–23.

Miksicek, Charles H. 1987. Formation processes of the archaeobotanical record. In Michael B. Schiffer (Ed.), *Advances in Archaeological Method and Theory.* Vol. 10 (pp. 211–247). New York: Academic Press.

Miller, George. 1979. An Introduction to the Ethnoarchaeology of the Andean Camelids. PhD diss., University of California, Berkeley.

Miller, George, and Richard Burger. 1995. Our father the cayman, our dinner the llama: Animal utilization at Chavín de Huántar, Peru. *American Antiquity* 60: 421–458.

———. 2000. Ch'arki at Chavín: Ethnographic models and archaeological data. *American Antiquity* 65: 573–576.

Minnis, Paul E. 1981. Seeds in archaeological sites: Sources and some interpretive problems. *American Antiquity* 46: 143–152.

Monks, Gregory G. 1981. Seasonality studies. In Michael B. Schiffer (Ed.), *Advances in Archaeological Method and Theory.* Vol. 4 (pp. 177–240). New York: Academic Press.

Moore, P. D., J. A. Webb, and M. E. Collinson. 1991. *Pollen Analysis.* Oxford: Blackwell Scientific.

Olsen, Stanley J. 1960. Post-cranial skeletal characters of Bison and Bos. *Papers of the Peabody Museum of American Archaeology and Ethnology* 35(4).

———. 1964. Mammal remains from archaeological sites, part 1: Southeastern and southwestern United States. *Papers of the Peabody Museum of American Archaeology and Ethnology* 61(1).

———. 1968. Fish, amphibian, and reptile remains from archaeological sites, part 1: Southeastern and southwestern United States. *Papers of the Peabody Museum of American Archaeology and Ethnology* 61(2).

———. 1973. Mammal remains from archaeological sites, part 1: Southeastern and southwestern United States. *Papers of the Peabody Museum of Archaeology and Ethnology* 56(1).

Pearsall, Deborah M. 2000. *Paleoethnobotany: A Handbook of Procedures.* New York: Academic Press.

Piperno, Dolores R. 1987. *Phytolith Analysis: An Archaeological and Geological Perspective.* San Diego: Academic Press.

Rapp, George, and Susan C. Mulholland (Eds.). 1992. *Phytolith Systematics: Emerging Issues.* New York: Plenum Press.

Reitz, Elizabeth J., and C. Margaret Scarry. 1985. Reconstructing historic subsistence with an example from sixteenth-century Spanish Florida. *Society of Historical Archaeology, Special Publication Series,* no. 3.

Reitz, Elizabeth, and Elizabeth Wing. 1999. *Zooarchaeology.* Cambridge: Cambridge University Press.

Rhode, David. 2001. Macrobotanical remains. In R. L. Kelly (Ed.), Prehistory of the Carson Desert and Stillwater Mountains: Environment, Mobility, and Subsistence in a Great Basin Wetland (pp. 254–262). *University of Utah Anthropological Papers* 123. Salt Lake City.

———. 2004. Coprolites from Hidden Cave, revisited: Evidence for occupation history, diet, and gender. *Journal of Archaeological Science* 30: 909–922.

Rovner, Irwin. 1983. Plant opal phytolith analysis: Major advances in archaeobotanical research. In Michael B. Schiffer (Ed.), *Advances in Archaeological Method and Theory.* Vol. 6 (pp. 225–266). New York: Academic Press.

Smith, P., and M. Wilson. 2001. Blood residues in archaeology. In D. Brothwell and A. Pollard (Eds.), *Handbook of Archaeological Sciences* (pp. 313–322). Chichester, England: John Wiley and Sons.

Sobolik, Kristin. 2003. *The Archaeologist's Toolkit,* vol. 5, *Archaeobiology.* Walnut Creek, CA: Altamira Press.

Solecki, Ralph S. 1971. *Shanidar: The First Flower People.* New York: Knopf.

Sommer, Jeffrey. 1999. The Shanidar IV 'Flower Burial': A Reevaluation of Neanderthal Burial Ritual. *Cambridge Archaeological Journal* 9: 127–137.

Stahl, Peter. 1999. Structural density of domesticated South American camelid skeletal elements and the archaeological investigation of prehistoric Andean ch'arki. *Journal of Archaeological Science* 26: 1347–1368.

Sutton, Mark Q., Minnie Malik, and Andrew Ogram. 1996. Experiments on the determination of gender from coprolites by DNA analysis. *Journal of Archaeological Science* 23: 263–267.

Turner, C. G., II, and J. A. Turner. 1999. *Man Corn: Cannibalism and Violence in the Prehistoric American Southwest.* Salt Lake City: University of Utah Press.

Valdez, Lidio. 2000. Ch'arki consumption in the ancient central Andes: A cautionary note. *American Antiquity* 65: 567–572.

White, T. D. 1992. *Prehistoric Cannibalism at Mancos 5MTUMR-2346.* Princeton: Princeton University Press.

Wigand, Peter. 2001. Pollen. In R. L. Kelly (Ed.), *Prehistory of the Carson Desert and Stillwater Mountains: Environment, Mobility, and Subsistence in a Great Basin Wetland* (pp. 252–254). *University of Utah Anthropological Papers* 123. Salt Lake City.

Wigand, Peter, and Cheryl Nowak. 1992. Dynamics of northwest Nevada plant communities during the last 30,000 years. In C. A. Hall, V. Doyle-Jones, and B. Widawski (Eds.), *The History of Water: Eastern Sierra Nevada, Owens Valley, White-Inyo Mountains* (pp. 40–62). White Mountain Research Station Symposium 4.

Chapter 12

Benditt, J. 1989. Molecular archaeology: DNA from a 7,000-year-old brain opens new vistas in prehistory. *Scientific American* 261: 25–26.

Brooks, Sheilagh, Michele Haldeman, and Richard Brooks. 1988. *Osteological Analyses of the Stillwater Skeletal Series, Stillwater Marsh, Churchill County, Nevada.* U.S. Fish and Wildlife Service Cultural Resource Series Number 2.

Brown, Terence A., and Keri A. Brown. 1992. Ancient DNA and the archaeologist. *Antiquity* 66: 10–23.

Buikstra, Jane E., and Della C. Cook. 1980. Paleopathology: An American account. *Annual Review of Anthropology* 9: 433–470.

Buikstra, Jane E., and L. Konigsberg. 1985. Paleodemography: Critiques and controversies. *American Anthropologist* 87: 316–333.

Cann, Rebecca, Mark Stoneking, and Alan C. Wilson. 1987. Mitochrondrial DNA and human evolution. *Nature* 325: 31–36.

DeNiro, Michael J. 1987. Stable isotopy and archeology. *American Scientist* 75: 182–191.

DeNiro, Michael J., and S. Epstein. 1981. Influence of diet on the distribution of nitrogen isotopes in animals. *Geochimica de Cosmochimica Acta* 45: 341–351.

Dillehay, Tom D. 1989. *Monte Verde: A Late Pleistocene Settlement in Chile,* Vol. 1, *Paleoenvironment and Site Context.* Washington, DC: Smithsonian Institution Press.

———. 1997. *Monte Verde: A Late Pleistocene Settlement in Chile,* Vol. 2, *The Archaeological Context and Interpretation.* Washington, DC: Smithsonian Institution Press.

Doran, Glen H., David N. Dickel, William E. Ballinger, Jr., O. Frank Agee, Philip J. Laipis, and William W. Hauswirth. 1986. Anatomical, cellular and molecular analysis of 8,000-yr-old human brain tissue from the Windover archaeological site. *Nature* 323: 803–806.

Eshleman, Jason A., Ripan S. Mahli, and David Glenn Smith. 2003. Mitochondrial DNA studies of Native Americans: Conceptions and misconceptions of the population prehistory of the Americas. *Evolutionary Anthropology* 12: 7–18.

Ezzo, Joseph A., Clark Spencer Larsen, and James H. Burton. 1995. Elemental signatures of human diets from the Georgia Bight. *American Journal of Physical Anthropology* 98: 471–481.

Goodman, Alan, and George Armelagos. 1988. Infant and childhood morbidity and mortality risks in archaeological populations. *World Archaeology* 21: 225–243.

Herrmann, Bernd, and Susanne Hummell (Eds.). 1994. *Ancient DNA: Recovery and Analysis of Genetic Material from Paleontological, Archaeological, Museum, Medical, and Forensic Specimens.* New York: Springer-Verlag.

Horai, Satoshi, Rumi Kondo, Yuko Nakagawa-Hattori, Seiji Hayashi, Shunro Sonoda, and Kazuo Tajima. 1993. Peopling of the Americas, founded by four major lineages of mitochondrial DNA. *Molecular Biological Evolution* 10(1): 23–47.

Huss-Ashmore, Rebecca, Alan H. Goodman, and George J. Armelagos. 1982. Nutritional inference from paleopathology. In Michael B. Schiffer (Ed.), *Advances in Archaeological Method and Theory.* Vol. 5 (pp. 395–474). New York: Academic Press.

Hutchinson, Dale, and Clark Spencer Larsen. 1988. Determination of stress episode duration from linear enamel hypoplasias: A case study from St. Catherines Island, Georgia. *Human Biology* 60: 93–110.

———. 1995. Physiological stress in the prehistoric Stillwater Marsh: Evidence of enamel defects. In C. S. Larsen and R. L. Kelly (Eds.), Bioarchaeology of the Stillwater Marsh: Prehistoric Human Adaptation in the Western Great Basin (pp. 81–95). *Anthropological Papers of the American Museum of Natural History,* Number 77. New York.

Katzenberg, M. Anne, Henry P. Schwarcz, Martin Knyf, and F. Jerome Melbye. 1995. Stable isotope evidence for maize horticulture and paleodiet in southern Ontario, Canada. *American Antiquity* 60: 335–350.

Kelly, Robert. 2003. Maybe we do know when people came to North America; and what does it mean if we do? *Quaternary International,* 109–110: 133–145.

Konigsberg, Lyle W., and Jane E. Buikstra. 1995. Regional approaches to the investigation of past human biocultural structure. In Lane Anderson Beck (Ed.), *Regional Approaches to Mortuary Analysis* (pp. 191–219). New York: Plenum Press.

Larsen, Clark Spencer. 1987. Bioarchaeological interpretations of subsistence economy and behavior from human skeletal remains. In Michael B. Schiffer (Ed.), *Advances in Archaeological Method and Theory.* Vol. 10 (pp. 339–445). Orlando, FL: Academic Press.

———. 1995. Biological changes in human populations with agriculture. *Annual Review of Anthropology* 24: 185–213.

Larsen, Clark Spencer, and Robert L. Kelly (Eds.). 1995. Bioarchaeology of the Stillwater Marsh: Prehistoric Human Adaptation in the Western Great Basin. *Anthropological Papers of the American Museum of Natural History,* Number 77.

Larsen, Clark Spencer, Christopher B. Ruff, and Robert L. Kelly. 1995. Structural analysis of the Stillwater postcranial human remains: behavioral implications of articular joint pathology and long bone diaphyseal morphology. In C. S. Larsen and R. L. Kelly (Eds.), Bioarchaeology of the Stillwater Marsh: Prehistoric Human Adaptation in the Western Great Basin (pp. 107–133). *Anthropological Papers of the American Museum of Natural History,* Number 77. New York.

Martin, Debra L., Alan H. Goodman, and George J. Armelagos. 1985. Skeletal pathologies as indicators of quality and quantity of diet. In Robert I. Gilbert and James H. Mielke (Eds.), *The Analysis of Prehistoric Diets* (pp. 227–279). Orlando: Academic Press.

Meltzer, David J. 1989. Why don't we know when the first people came to North America? *American Antiquity* 54(3): 471–490.

———. 1995. Clocking the First Americans. *Annual Review of Anthropology* 24: 21–45.

Nei, Masatoshi. 1992. Age of the common ancestor of human mitochondrial DNA. *Molecular Biology and Evolution* 9(6): 1176–1178.

Ortner, Donald J., and Walter G. J. Putschar. 1985. *Identification of Pathological Conditions in Human Skeletal Remains.* Washington, DC: Smithsonian Institution Press.

Pääbo, Svante. 1993, November. Ancient DNA: Genetic information that had seemed lost forever turns out to linger in the remains of long-dead plants and animals. *Scientific American,* pp. 87–92.

Powell, J., and W. A. Neves. 1999. Craniofacial morphology of the first Americans: Pattern and process in the peopling of the new world. *Yearbook of Physical Anthropology* 42: 153–188.

Powell, Mary Lucas. 1985. The analysis of dental wear and caries for dietary reconstructions. In R. I. Gilbert, Jr., and J. H. Mielke (Eds.), *The Analysis of Prehistoric Diets* (pp. 307–338). Orlando: Academic Press.

Price, T. Douglas (Ed.). 1989. *The Chemistry of Prehistoric Human Bone.* Cambridge: Cambridge University Press.

Rogers, Juliet, and Tony Waldron. 1989. Infections in paleopathology: The basis of classification according to most probable cause. *Journal of Archaeological Science* 16: 611–625.

Rothschild, Bruce M., and Larry D. Martin. 1993. *Palaeopathology: Disease in the Fossil Record.* Boca Raton, FL: CRC Press.

Sahlins, Marshall. 1968. Notes on the original affluent society. In Richard Lee and Irven DeVore (Eds.), *Man the Hunter* (pp. 85–89). Chicago: Aldine.

Schoeninger, Margaret. 1995. Dietary reconstruction in the prehistoric Carson Desert: Stable carbon and nitrogen isotopic analysis. In C. S. Larsen and R. L. Kelly (Eds.), Bioarchaeology of the Stillwater Marsh: Prehistoric Human Adaptation in the Western Great Basin (pp. 96–106). *Anthropological Papers of the American Museum of Natural History,* Number 77. New York.

Seielstad, Mark, Nadira Yuldasheva, Nadia Singh, Peter Underhill, Peter Oefner, Peidong Shen, and R. Spencer Wells. 2003. A novel Y-chromosome variant puts an upper limit on the timing of first entry into the Americas. *American Journal of Human Genetics* 73: 700–705.

Stone, Anne C., and Mark Stoneking. 1993. Ancient DNA from a Pre-Columbian Amerindian population. *American Journal of Physical Anthropology* 92: 463–471.

Stoneking, Mark. 1994. In defense of "Eve": A response to Templeton's critique. *American Anthropologist* 96(1): 131–141.

Szathmary, Emöke J. E. 1993. Genetics of aboriginal North Americans. *Evolutionary Anthropology* 1(6): 202–220.

Templeton, Alan R. 1993. The "Eve" hypotheses: A genetic critique and reanalysis. *American Anthropologist* 95: 51–72.

———. 1994. "Eve": Hypothesis compatibility versus hypothesis testing. *American Anthropologist* 96: 141–147.

Torroni, Antonio, Theodore G. Schurr, Chi-Chuan Yang, Emöke J. E. Szathmary, Robert C. Williams, Moses S. Schanfield, Gary A. Troup, William C. Knowler, Dale N. Lawrence, Kenneth M. Weiss, and Douglas C. Wallace. 1991. Native American mitochondrial DNA analysis indicates that the Amerind and the Nadene populations were founded by two independent migrations. *Genetics* 130: 153–162.

Turner, Christy G., II. 1979. Dental anthropological indications of agriculture among the Jomon people of central Japan, pt. 10: Peopling of the Pacific. *American Journal of Physical Anthropology* 51: 619–636.

Verano, John W., and Douglas H. Ubelaker (Eds.). 1992. *Disease and Demography in the Americas.* Washington, DC: Smithsonian Institution Press.

Walker, Phillip L. 1986. Porotic hyperostosis in a marine-dependent California Indian population. *American Journal of Physical Anthropology* 69: 345–354.

Chapter 13

Alkire, William. 1977. *An Introduction to the Peoples and Cultures of Micronesia.* 2d ed. Menlo Park, CA: Cummings.

Bacus, Elisabeth A., Alex W. Barker, Jeffrey D. Bonevich, Sandra L. Dunavan, J. Benjamin Fitzhugh, Debra L. Gold, Nurit S. Goldman-Finn, William Griffin, and Karen M. Mudar (Eds.). 1993. *A Gendered Past: A Critical Bibliography of Gender in Archaeology.* Technical Report 25. Ann Arbor: University of Michigan, Museum of Anthropology.

Bailey, Robert C., and Robert Aunger. 1989. Hunters vs. archers: Variation in women's subsistence strategies in the Ituri Forest. *Human Ecology* 17: 273–297.

Beck, Lane Anderson (Ed.). 1995. *Regional Approaches to Mortuary Analysis.* New York: Plenum Press.

Claassen, Cheryl (Ed.). 1992. Exploring Gender Through Archaeology: Selected Papers from the 1991 Boone Conference. *Monographs in World Archaeology,* no. 11. Madison, WI: Prehistory Press.

Cobb, Charles R. 1993. Archaeological approaches to the political economy of nonstratified societies. In M. B. Schiffer (Ed.), *Archaeological Method and Theory.* Vol. 5 (pp. 43–100). Tucson: University of Arizona Press.

Conkey, Margaret W., and Janet Spector. 1984. Archaeology and the study of gender. In Michael B. Schiffer (Ed.), *Advances in Archaeological Method and Theory.* Vol. 7 (pp. 1–38). Orlando, FL: Academic Press.

Costin, Cathy Lynne, and Timothy Earle. 1989. Status distinction and legitimation of power as reflected in changing patterns of consumption in late prehispanic Peru. *American Antiquity* 54: 691–714.

DeNiro, Michael J., and Margaret J. Schoeniger. 1983. Stable carbon and nitrogen isotope ratios of bone collagen: Variations within individuals, between sexes, and within populations raised on monotonous diets. *Journal of Archaeological Science* 10: 199–203.

Descantes, Christophe, Hector Neff, Michael D. Glascock, and William R. Dickinson. 2001. Chemical characterization of Micronesian ceramics through instrumental neutron activation analysis: A preliminary provenance study. *Journal of Archaeological Science* 28: 1185–1190.

Dickinson, W. R., and R. Shutler, Jr. 2000. Implications of petrographic temper analysis for Oceanic prehistory. *Journal of World Prehistory* 14: 203–266.

Ember, Melvin. 1973. An archaeological indicator of matrilocal versus patrilocal residence. *American Antiquity* 38: 177–182.

Ember, Melvin, and Carol Ember. 1995. Worldwide cross-cultural studies and their relevance for archaeology. *Journal of Archaeological Research* 30: 69–94.

Enloe, James. 2003. Food sharing past and present: Archaeological evidence for economic and social interactions. *Before Farming* 2003/1: 1–23.

Enloe, James, and Francine David. 1992. Food sharing in the Paleolithic: Carcass refitting at Pincevent. In J. L. Hofman and J. G. Enloe (Eds.), *Piecing Together the Past: Applications of Refitting Studies in Archaeology* (pp. 296–315). British Archaeological Reports International Series 578. Oxford.

Fitzpatrick, Scott M., William R. Dickinson, and Geoffrey Clark. 2003. Ceramic petrography and cultural interaction in Palau, Micronesia. *Journal of Archaeological Science* 30: 1175–1184.

Galloway, Patricia (Ed.). 1989. *The Southeastern Ceremonial Complex: Artifacts and Analysis*. Lincoln: University of Nebraska Press.

Gargett, R., and B. Hayden. 1991. Site structure, kinship, and sharing in Aboriginal Australia: Implications for archaeology. In E. M. Kroll and T. D. Price (Eds.), *The Interpretation of Archaeological Spatial Patterning* (pp. 11–32). New York: Plenum Press.

Gero, Joan M. 1985. Socio-politics and the woman-at-home ideology. *American Antiquity* 50: 342–350.

———. 1991. Genderlithics: Women's roles in stone tool production. In Joan M. Gero and Margaret W. Conkey (Eds.), *Engendering Archaeology: Women and Prehistory* (pp. 163–193). Oxford: Basil Blackwell.

Gero, Joan M., and Margaret W. Conkey (Eds.). 1991. *Engendering Archaeology: Women and Prehistory*. Oxford: Basil Blackwell.

Gibson, Alex M., and Ann Woods. 1990. *Prehistoric Pottery for the Archaeologist*. Leicester, England: Leicester University Press.

Goodenough, Ward H. 1965. Rethinking "status" and "role": Toward a general model of the cultural organization of social relationships. In Michael Banton (Ed.), *The Relevance of Models for Social Anthropology* (pp. 1–24). *Association for Social Anthropology Monographs*, no. 1. New York: Praeger.

Griffin, James B., A. A. Gordus, and G. A. Wright. 1969. Identification of the sources of Hopewellian obsidian in the middle west. *American Antiquity* 34: 1–14.

Hastorf, Christine. 1991. Gender, space and food in prehistory. In Joan Gero and Margaret Conkey (Eds.), *Engendering Archeology: Women and Prehistory* (pp. 132–158). Oxford: Basil Blackwell.

Hatch, James W., Joseph W. Michels, Christopher M. Stevenson, Barry E. Scheeta, and Richard A. Geidel. 1988. Hopewell obsidian studies: Behavioral implications of recent sourcing and dating research. *American Antiquity* 55: 461–479.

Houston, S. D., and P. A. McAnany. 2003. Bodies and blood: Critiquing social construction in Maya archaeology. *Journal of Anthropological Archaeology* 22: 26–41.

Hughes, Richard E. 2005. The sources of Hopewell obsidian: Thirty years after Griffin. In Douglas K. Charles and Jane E. Buikstra (Eds.), *Recreating Hopewell*. Gainesville: University Press of Florida (forthcoming).

Jackson, Ed, and Susan Scott. 2003. Patterns of elite faunal utilization at Moundville, Alabama. *American Antiquity* 69: 552–572.

Joyce, Rosemary. 1995. The construction of gender in Classic Maya monuments. In Rita Wright (Ed.), *Gender and Archaeology* (pp. 167–195). Philadelphia: University of Pennsylvania Press.

Knight, Vernon, J., Jr. 1998. Moundville as a diagrammatic ceremonial center. In V. J. Knight, Jr., and V. Steponaitis (Eds.), *Archaeology of the Moundville Chiefdom* (pp. 44–62). Washington, DC: Smithsonian Institution Press.

Knight, Vernon, J., Jr., and Vincas Steponaitis. 1998. *Archaeology of the Moundville Chiefdom*. Washington, DC: Smithsonian Institution Press.

Mills, Barbara. 1999. Recent research on Chaco: Changing views on economy, ritual, and society. *Journal of Archaeological Research* 10: 65–117.

Nelson, Sarah M. 1995. *Gender in Archaeology: Analyzing Power and Prestige*. Walnut Creek, CA: Altamira Press.

Orton, Clive, Paul Tyers, and Alan Vince. 1993. *Pottery in Archaeology*. Cambridge: Cambridge University Press.

O'Shea, John M. 1984. *Mortuary Variability: An Archaeological Investigation*. Orlando: Academic Press.

Parker Pearson, Michael. 1982. Mortuary practices, society and ideology: An ethnoarchaeological study. In Ian Hodder (Ed.), *Symbolic and Structural Archaeology* (pp. 99–113). Cambridge: Cambridge University Press.

———. 1995. Return of the living dead: Mortuary analysis and the new archaeology revisited. *Antiquity* 69: 1046–1048.

Peebles, Christopher S. 1971. Moundville and surrounding sites: Some structural considerations of mortuary practices II. In James A. Brown (Ed.), Approaches to the Social Dimensions of Mortuary Practices. *Society for American Archaeology Memoir* 25: 68–91.

———. 1977. Biocultural adaptation in prehistoric America: An archeologist's perspective. In Robert L. Blakely (Ed.), Biocultural Adaptation in Prehistoric America (pp. 115–130). *Southern Anthropological Society Proceedings*, no. 11. Athens: University of Georgia Press.

———. 1981. Archaeological research at Moundville: 1840–1980. *Southeastern Archaeological Conference Bulletin* 24: 77–81.

———. 1987. Moundville from 1000 to 1500 AD as seen from 1840 to 1985 AD. In Robert D. Drennan and Carlos A. Uribe (Eds.), *Chiefdoms in the Americas* (pp. 21–41). Lanham, MD: University Press of America.

Peebles, Christopher S., and Susan M. Kus. 1977. Some archaeological correlates of ranked societies. *American Antiquity* 42: 421–448.

Peregrine, Peter. 2000. Matrilocality, corporate strategy, and the organization of production in the Chacoan world. *American Antiquity* 66: 36–46.

Powell, Mary L. 1988. *Status and Health in Prehistory: A Case Study of the Moundville Chiefdom.* Washington, DC: Smithsonian Institution Press.

———. 1991. Rank, status and health in the Mississippian chiefdom at Moundville. In Mary L. Powell, Patricia S. Bridges, and Ann Marie Wagner Mires (Eds.), *What Mean These Bones? Studies in Southeastern Bioarchaeology* (pp. 22–51). Tuscaloosa: University of Alabama Press.

Price, T. Douglas, and Gary M. Feinman (Eds.). 1995. *Foundations of Social Inequality.* New York: Plenum Press.

Renfrew, Colin, and Stephen Shennan (Eds.). 1982. *Ranking, Resource and Exchange.* Cambridge: Cambridge University Press.

Rice, Prudence M. 1987. *Pottery Analysis: A Sourcebook.* Chicago: University of Chicago Press.

———. 1991. Women and prehistoric pottery production. In D. Walde and N. Willows (Eds.), *The Archaeology of Gender* (pp. 436–443). Calgary, Archaeological Association of the University of Calgary.

———. 1996a. Recent ceramic analysis: 1. Function, style, and origins. *Journal of Archaeological Research* 4: 133–163.

———. 1996b. Recent ceramic analysis: 2. Composition, production, and theory. *Journal of Archaeological Research* 4: 165–202.

Schillaci, Michael, and Christopher Stojanowski. 2000. Postmarital residence and population structure at Pueblo Bonito. *American Journal of Physical Anthropology* supplement 30: 271.

———. 2002. A reassessment of matrilocality in Chacoan culture. *American Antiquity* 67: 343–356.

Schoeninger, Margaret J., and Christopher Peebles. 1981. Notes on the relationship between social status and diet at Moundville. *Southeastern Archaeological Conference Bulletin* 24: 96–97.

Schoeninger, Margaret J., and Mark Schurr. 1999. Human subsistence at Moundville: The stable isotope data. In V. J. Knight, Jr., and V. Steponaitis (Eds.), *Archaeology of the Moundville Chiefdom* (pp. 120–132). Washington, DC: Smithsonian Institution Press.

Sinopoli, Carla. 1991. *Approaches to Archaeological Ceramics.* New York: Plenum Press.

Smith, Bruce D. (Ed.). 1990. *The Mississippian Emergence.* Washington, DC: Smithsonian Institution Press.

Steponaitis, Vincas P. 1983. *Ceramics, Chronology, and Community Patterns: An Archaeological Study at Moundville.* New York: Academic Press.

Waring, A. J., Jr., and Preston Holder. 1945. A prehistoric ceremonial complex in the southeastern United States. *American Anthropologist* 47: 1–34.

Wason, Paul K. 1994. *The Archaeology of Rank.* Cambridge: Cambridge University Press.

Webb, William S. 1974 [1946]. *Indian Knoll.* Knoxville: University of Tennesse Press (quote from p. 330).

Welch, Paul D., and C. Margaret Scarry. 1995. Status-related variation in foodways in the Moundville chiefdom. *American Antiquity* 60: 397–419.

Wright, Rita (Ed.) 1996. *Gender and Archaeology.* Philadelphia: University of Pennsylvania Press.

Wylie, Alison. 1992. The interplay of evidential constraints and political interests: Recent archaeological research on gender. *American Antiquity* 57: 15–35.

Chapter 14

Anyon, Roger, T. J. Ferguson, Loretta Jackson, Lillie Lane, and Philip Vicenti. 1997. Native American oral tradition and archaeology: Issues of structure, relevance, and respect. In Nina Swidler, Kurt E. Dongoske, Roger Anyon, and Alan S. Downer (Eds.), *Native Americans and Archaeologists: Stepping Stones to Common Ground* (pp. 77–87). Walnut Grove, CA: Altamira.

Bahn, Paul. 1998. *The Cambridge Illustrated History of Prehistoric Art.* Cambridge: University of Cambridge Press.

Bender, Barbara. 1993. Cognitive archaeology and cultural materialism. *Cambridge Archaeological Journal* 3: 257–260.

Burger, Richard L. 1992. *Chavín and the Origins of Andean Civilization.* London: Thames and Hudson.

Conrad, Geoffrey W. 1981. Cultural materialism, split inheritance, and the expansion of ancient Peruvian empires. *American Antiquity* 46: 3–26.

Conrad, Geoffrey W., and Arthur A. Demarest. 1984. *Religion and Empire: The Dynamics of Aztec and Inca Expansionism.* Cambridge: Cambridge University Press.

D'Altroy, Terence N. 1992. *Provincial Power in the Inka Empire.* Washington, DC: Smithsonian Institution Press.

D'Andrade, Roy G. 1995. *The Development of Cognitive Anthropology.* Cambridge: Cambridge University Press.

Echo-Hawk, Roger. 2000. Ancient history in the New World: Integrating oral traditions and the archaeological record in deep time. *American Antiquity* 65: 267–290.

Flannery, Kent V., and Joyce Marcus. 1993. Cognitive archaeology. *Cambridge Archaeological Journal* 3: 260–270.

Hall, Robert L. 1977. An anthropocentric perspective for eastern United States prehistory. *American Antiquity* 42: 499–518.

———. 1997. *An Archaeology of the Soul: North American Indian Belief and Ritual.* Urbana: University of Illinois Press.

Kehoe, Alice B., and Thomas F. Kehoe. 1973. Cognitive models for archaeological interpretation. *American Antiquity* 38: 150–154.

Laming-Emperaire, Annette. 1962. *La signification de l'art rupestre Paléolithique.* Paris: Picard.

Lathrap, Donald W. 1973. Gifts of the cayman: Some thoughts on the subsistence basis of Chavín. In Donald W. Lathrap and Jody Douglas (Eds.), *Variation in Anthropology* (pp. 91–105). Urbana: Illinois Archaeological Survey.

———. 1977. Our father the cayman, our mother the gourd: Spinden revisited, or a unitary model for the emergence of agriculture in the New World. In Charles A. Reed (Ed.), *Origins of Agriculture* (pp. 713–751). The Hague: Mouton.

———. 1985. Jaws: The control of power in the early nuclear American ceremonial center. In C. B. Donnan (Ed.), *Early Ceremonial Architecture in the Andes* (pp. 241–267). Washington, DC: Dumbarton Oaks Research Library and Collection.

Leroi-Gourhan, André. 1968. *The Art of Prehistoric Man in Western Europe.* London: Thames and Hudson.

———. 1980. *Treasures of Prehistoric Art.* Translated from the French by Norbert Guterman. New York: Harry H. Abrams.

———. 1982. *The Dawn of European Art: An Introduction to Palaeolithic Cave Painting.* Cambridge: Cambridge University Press.

Lewis-Williams, David. 2002. *The Mind in the Cave.* London: Thames and Hudson.

Marcus, Joyce, and Kent Flannery. 1996. *Zapotec Civilization.* London: Thames and Hudson.

Mason, Ronald. 2000. Archaeology and Native North American oral traditions. *American Antiquity* 65: 239–266.

Mithen, Steven. 1995. Palaeolithic archaeology and the evolution of mind. *Journal of Archaeological Research* 3: 305–332.

Renfrew, Colin. 1982. *Towards an Archaeology of the Mind: An Inaugural Lecture Delivered Before the University of Cambridge on 30 November 1982.* Cambridge: Cambridge University Press.

———. 1993. Cognitive archaeology: Some thoughts on the archaeology of thought. *Cambridge Archaeological Journal* 3: 248–250.

Renfrew, Colin, and Ezra B. W. Zubrow (Eds.). 1994. *The Ancient Mind: Elements of Cognitive Archaeology.* Cambridge: Cambridge University Press.

Valladas, Hélène. 2003. Direct radiocarbon dating of prehistoric cave paintings by accelerator mass spectrometry. *Measurement Science and Technology* 14: 1487–1492.

Von Hagen, Adriana, and Craig Morris. 1998. *The Cities of the Ancient Andes.* London: Thames and Hudson.

Whiteley, Peter. 2002. Archaeology and oral tradition: The scientific importance of dialogue. *American Antiquity* 67: 405–415.

Chapter 15

Bar-Yosef, Ofer. 1998. The Natufian Culture in the Levant, threshold to the origins of agriculture. *Evolutionary Anthropology* 6: 159–177.

Bar-Yosef, Ofer, and R. H. Meadow. 1995. The origins of agriculture in the Near East. In T. Douglas Price and Anne B. Gebauer (Eds), *Last Hunters, First Farmers: New Perspectives on the Prehistoric Transition to Agriculture* (pp. 39–94). Santa Fe: School of American Research Press.

Bender, Barbara. 1978. Gatherer-hunter to farmer: A social perspective. *World Archaeology* 10: 204–222.

Bettinger, Robert L. 1991. *Hunter-Gatherers: Archaeological and Evolutionary Theory.* New York: Plenum Press.

Binford, Lewis R. 1968. Post-Pleistocene adaptations. In Sally R. Binford and Lewis R. Binford (Eds.), *New Perspectives in Archeology* (pp. 313–341). Chicago: Aldine.

Blanton, Richard E., Stephen A. Kowalewski, Gary Feinman, and Jill Appel. 1981. *Ancient Mesoamerica: A Comparison of Change in Three Regions.* Cambridge: Cambridge University Press.

Boserup, Ester. 1965. *Conditions of Agricultural Growth: The Economics of Agrarian Change Under Population Pressure.* Chicago: Aldine.

Boyd, Robert, and Peter J. Richerson. 1985. *Culture and the Evolutionary Process.* Chicago: University of Chicago Press.

Braidwood, Robert J. 1959. Archeology and the evolutionary theory. In B. J. Meggers (Ed.), *Evolution and Anthropology: A Centennial Appraisal* (pp. 76–89). Washington, DC: Anthropological Society of Washington.

Carmichael, David L., Jane Hubert, Brian Reeves, and Audhild Schanche (Eds.). 1994. *Sacred Sites, Sacred Places.* One World Archaeology, Vol. 23. London: Routledge.

Carneiro, Robert L. 1970. A theory of the origin of the state. *Science* 169: 733–738 (quote is from p. 734).

———. 1988. The circumscription theory: Challenge and response. *American Behavioral Scientist* 31: 497–511.

Childe, V. Gordon. 1951. *Man Makes Himself.* New York: New American Library.

Coe, Michael. 1996. *The Maya.* 6th ed. London: Thames and Hudson.

Cohen, Mark Nathan. 1977. *The Food Crisis in Prehistory: Overpopulation and the Origins of Agriculture.* New Haven: Yale University Press.

———. 1981. The ecological basis of new world state formation: General and local model building. In Grant D. Jones and Robert R. Kautz (Eds.), *The Transition to Statehood in the New World* (pp. 105–122). Cambridge: Cambridge University Press.

Cowan, C. Wesley, and Patty Jo Watson (Eds.). 1992. *The Origins of Agriculture: An International Perspective.* Washington, DC: Smithsonian Institution Press.

Cowgill, George L. 1975a. On the causes and consequences of ancient and modern population changes. *American Anthropologist* 77: 505–525.

———. 1975b. Population pressure as a non-explanation. In A. Swelund (Ed.), Population Studies in Archaeology and Biological Anthropology: A Symposium (pp. 127–131). *Society for American Archaeology Memoir,* no. 33. Washington, DC.

———. 1988. Comment on "Ecological theory and cultural evolution in the Valley of Oaxaca" by William T. Sanders and Deborah L. Nichols. *Current Anthropology* 29: 54–55.

Darwin, Charles. 1958 [1859]. *The Origin of Species.* New York: The New American Library.

Demarest, Arthur A. 1989. Ideology and evolutionism in American archaeology: Looking beyond the economic base. In C. C. Lamberg-Karlovsky (Ed.), *Archaeological Thought in America* (pp. 89–102). Cambridge: Cambridge University Press.

Demarest, Arthur A., and Geoffrey W. Conrad (Eds.). 1992. *Ideology and Pre-Columbian Civilizations.* Santa Fe: School of American Research Press.

Diamond, Jared. 1988. The golden age that never was. *Discover* 9(12): 70–79.

Dunnell, Robert C. 1980. Evolutionary theory and archaeology. In Michael B. Schiffer (Ed.), *Advances in Archaeological Method and Theory.* Vol. 3 (pp. 35–99). New York: Academic Press.

———. 1989. Aspects of the application of evolutionary theory in archaeology. In C. C. Lamberg-Karlovsky (Ed.), *Archaeological Thought in America* (pp. 35–49). Cambridge: Cambridge University Press.

Durham, William. 1981. Overview: Optimal foraging analysis in human ecology. In Bruce Winterhalder and Eric Alden Smith (Eds.), *Hunter-Gatherer*

Foraging Strategies: Ethnographic and Archaeological Analyses (pp. 218–232). Chicago: University of Chicago Press.

———. 1990. Advances in evolutionary culture theory. *Annual Review of Anthropology* 19: 187–210.

———. 1992. Applications of evolutionary culture theory. *Annual Review of Anthropology* 21: 331–355.

Earle, Timothy K. (Ed.). 1991. *Chiefdoms: Power, Economy, and Ideology*. Cambridge: Cambridge University Press.

Earle, Timothy K., Terence D'Altroy, Cathy LeBlanc, Christine Hastorf, and Terry Levine. 1980. Changing settlement patterns in the Yanamarca Valley, Peru. Los Angeles: Institute of Archaeology, University of California, *Journal of New World Archaeology* 4(1).

Ehrenreich, Robert M., Carole L. Crumley, and Janet E. Levy (Eds.). 1995. Heterarchy and the analysis of complex societies. *Archeological Papers of the American Anthropological Association*, no. 6. Washington, DC.

Fedick, Scott L. 1995. Indigenous agriculture in the Americas. *Journal of Archaeological Research* 3: 257–303.

Flannery, Kent V. 1965. The ecology of early food production in Mesopotamia. *Science* 147: 1247–1255.

———. 1966. The postglacial "readaptation" as viewed from Mesoamerica. *American Antiquity* 31: 800–805.

———. 1969. Origins and ecological effects of early domestication in Iran and the Near East. In P. J. Ucko and G. W. Dimbleby (Eds.), *The Domestication and Exploitation of Plants and Animals* (pp. 73–100). Chicago: Aldine.

———. 1972. The cultural evolution of civilizations. *Annual Review of Ecology and Systematics* 3: 399–426. (Quote is from pp. 403–404).

———. 1973. The origins of agriculture. *Annual Review of Anthropology* 2: 271–310.

Fried, Morton H. 1967. *The Evolution of Political Society*. New York: Random House.

Fritz, Gayle J. 1990. Multiple pathways to farming in precontact eastern North America. *Journal of World Prehistory* 4: 387–435.

Harner, Michael J. 1970. Population pressure and the social evolution of agriculturalists. *Southwestern Journal of Anthropology* 26: 67–86.

Harris, David R. 1972. The origins of agriculture in the tropics. *American Scientist* 60: 180–193.

———. 1994. Agricultural origins, beginnings and transitions: The quest continues. *Antiquity* 69: 873–877.

Harris, David R., and Gordon C. Hillman (Eds.). 1989. *Foraging and Farming: The Evolution of Plant Exploitation*. London: Unwin Hyman

Harrison, Peter D. 1981. Some aspects of preconquest settlement in southern Quintana Roo, Mexico. In Wendy Ashmore (Ed.), *Lowland Maya Settlement Patterns* (pp. 259–286). Albuquerque: University of New Mexico Press.

Hawkes, Kristen, and James F. O'Connell. 1985. Optimal foraging models and the case of the !Kung. *American Anthropologist* 87: 401–405.

Hawkes, Kristen, James F. O'Connell, and N. Blurton Jones. 1987. Hardworking Hadza grandmothers. In R. Foley and V. Standen (Eds.), *Comparative Socioecology of Mammals and Man* (pp. 341–366). London: Basil Blackwell.

Hayden, Brian. 1990. Nimrods, piscators, pluckers, and planters: The emergence of food production. *Journal of Anthropological Archaeology* 9: 31–69.

———. 1995. A new overview of domestication. In T. Douglas Price and Anne B. Gebauer (Eds.), *Last Hunters, First Farmers: New Perspectives on the Prehistoric Transition to Agriculture* (pp. 273–300). Santa Fe: School of American Research Press.

Hill, Kim, and Kristen Hawkes. 1983. Neotropical hunting among the Aché of eastern Paraguay. In R. Hames and W. Vickers (Eds.), *Adaptive Responses of Native Amazonians* (pp. 139–188). New York: Academic Press.

Houston, S. D. 2000. Into the minds of ancients: Advances in Maya glyph studies. *Journal of World Prehistory* 14: 121–201.

Houston, S. D., and Patricia McAnany. 2003. Bodies and blood: Critiquing social construction in Maya archaeology. *Journal of Anthropological Archaeology* 22: 26–41.

Johnson, Allen W., and Timothy Earle. 1987. *The Evolution of Human Societies: From Foraging Group to Agrarian State*. Stanford: Stanford University Press.

Keegan, William F. 1986. The optimal foraging analysis of horticultural production. *American Anthropologist* 88: 92–107.

Kelly, Robert L. 1995. *The Foraging Spectrum*. Washington, DC: Smithsonian Institution Press.

Lee, Richard B. 1979. *The !Kung San: Men, Women and Work in a Foraging Society*. Cambridge: Cambridge University Press (quote is from the frontispiece).

Lee, Richard B., and Irven DeVore (Eds.). 1968. *Man the Hunter*. Chicago: Aldine.

Lees, Susan H. 1994. Irrigation and society. *Journal of Archaeological Research* 2: 361–378.

Lubbock, Sir John. 1865. *Pre-historic Times, As Illustrated by Ancient Remains, and the Manners and Customs of Modern Savages*. London: Williams and Norgate.

Manzanilla, Linda. 2001. State formation in the New World. In Gary Feinman and T. Douglas Price (Eds.), *Archaeology at the Millennium: A Sourcebook* (pp. 381–414). New York: Kluwer Academic/Plenum.

Marcus, Joyce. 1992. *Mesoamerican Writing Systems: Propaganda, Myth, and History in Four Ancient Civilizations*. Princeton: Princeton University Press.

———. 2003. Recent Advances in Maya Archaeology. *Journal of Archaeological Research* 11: 71–148.

McAnany, Patricia. 1995. *Living with the Ancestors: Kinship and Kingship in Ancient Maya Society*. Austin: University of Texas Press.

Morgan, Lewis Henry. 1974 [1877]. *Ancient Society*. Edited with an introduction and annotations by Eleanor Leacock. Gloucester, MA: Peter Smith.

O'Connell, James F., and Kristen Hawkes. 1981. Alyawara plant use and optimal foraging theory. In Bruce Winterhalder and Eric Alden Smith (Eds.), *Hunter-Gatherer Foraging Strategies: Ethnographic and Archaeological Analyses* (pp. 99–125). Chicago: University of Chicago Press.

Richerson, Peter J., Robert Boyd, and Robert Bettinger. 2001. Was agriculture impossible during the Pleistocene but mandatory during the Holocene? A climate change hypothesis. *American Antiquity* 66: 387–411.

Rindos, David. 1984. *The Origins of Agriculture: An Evolutionary Perspective*. Orlando, FL: Academic Press.

Sahlins, Marshall D., and Elman R. Service. 1960. *Evolution and Culture*. Ann Arbor: University of Michigan Press.

Scarborough, Vernon. 1994. Maya water management. *National Geographic Research and Exploration* 10(2): 184–199.

Service, Elman. 1971. *Primitive Social Organization: An Evolutionary Perspective*. 2d ed. New York: Random House.

———. 1975. *Origins of the State and Civilization: The Process of Cultural Evolution*. New York: Norton.

Simms, Steven, and Kenneth Russell. 1997. Bedouin hand harvesting of wheat and barley: Implications for early cultivation in southwestern Asia. *Current Anthropology* 38: 696–702.

Smith, Bruce D. 1992. *Rivers of Change: Essays on Early Agriculture in Eastern North America*. Washington, DC: Smithsonian Institution Press.

———. 2001. The transition to food production. In Gary Feinman and T. Douglas Price (Eds.), *Archaeology at the Millennium: A Sourcebook* (pp. 199–230). New York: Kluwer Academic/Plenum.

Smith, Eric Alden. 1991. *Inujjuamiut Foraging Strategies: Evolutionary Ecology of an Arctic Hunting Economy*. New York: Aldine de Gruyter.

Smith, Eric Alden, and Bruce Winterhalder (Eds.). 1992. *Evolutionary Ecology and Human Behavior*. New York: Aldine de Gruyter.

Spencer, Charles. 1990. On the tempo and mode of state formation: Neoevolutionism reconsidered. *Journal of Anthropological Archaeology* 9: 1–30.

Tallbull, William. 1994. Archaeological sites or sacred places? Native American perspective. In David Hurst Thomas, *Exploring Ancient Native America* (pp. 238–239). New York: Macmillan.

Tylor, Edward Burnett. 1889. On a method of investigating the development of institutions, applied to laws of marriage and descent. *Journal of the Royal Anthropological Institute* 18: 245–272 (quote is from p. 269).

Upham, Steadman (Ed.). 1990. *The Evolution of Political Systems: Sociopolitics in Small-Scale Sedentary Societies*. Cambridge: Cambridge University Press.

Webster, D. 2000. The not so peaceful civilization: A review of Maya war. *Journal of World Prehistory* 14: 65–119.

Winterhalder, Bruce, and Eric Alden Smith (Eds.). 1981. *Hunter-Gatherer Foraging Strategies: Ethnographic and Archaeological Analyses*. Chicago: University of Chicago Press.

Wittfogel, Karl A. 1957. *Oriental Despotism: A Comparative Study of Total Power*. New Haven: Yale University Press.

Wright, Henry T. 1986. The evolution of civilizations. In David J. Meltzer, Don D. Fowler, and Jeremy A. Sabloff (Eds.), *American Archaeology Past and Future: A Celebration of the Society for American Archaeology*

1935–1985 (pp. 323–365). Washington, DC: Smithsonian Institution Press.

Chapter 16

Ascher, Robert, and Charles H. Fairbanks. 1971. Excavation of a slave cabin: Georgia, U.S.A. *Historical Archaeology* 5: 3–17.

Beaudry, Mary C. (Ed.). 1988. *Documentary Archaeology in the New World*. Cambridge: Cambridge University Press.

Binford, Lewis R. 1968. Some comments on historical versus processual archaeology. *Southwestern Journal of Anthropology* 24: 267–275.

Blakey, Michael L. 1995. Race, nationalism, and the Afrocentric past. In P. R. Schmidt and T. Patterson (Eds.), *Making Alternative Histories: The Practice of Archaeology and History in Non-Western Settings* (pp. 213–228). Santa Fe: School of American Research Press.

Boakyewa, Ama Badu. 1995, January 1. African Burial Ground and Five Points Archaeological Projects. Press release. Office of Public Education and Information, African Burial Ground.

Brear, Holly Breachley. 1995. *Inherit the Alamo: Myth and Ritual at an American Shrine*. Austin: University of Texas Press.

Cotter, John L. 1994. Beginnings. In Stanley South (Ed.), *Pioneers in Historical Archaeology: Breaking New Ground* (pp. 15–25). New York: Plenum Press.

Crader, Diana C. 1990. Slave diet at Monticello. *American Antiquity* 55: 690–717.

Deagan, Kathleen. 1982. Avenues of inquiry in historical archaeology. In Michael B. Schiffer (Ed.), *Advances in Archaeological Method and Theory*. Vol. 5 (pp. 151–177). New York: Academic Press (quote from p. 153).

Deagan, Kathleen, and Darcie MacMahon. 1995. *Fort Mose: Colonial America's Black Fortress of Freedom*. Gainesville: University Press of Florida/Florida Museum of Natural History.

Deetz, James. 1977. *In Small Things Forgotten: The Archaeology of Early American Life*. Garden City, NY: Anchor Books.

———. 1988. Material culture and worldview in colonial Anglo-America. In Mark Leone and Parker Potter (Eds.), *The Recovery of Meaning: Historical Archaeology in the Eastern United States* (pp.

219–233). Washington, DC: Smithsonian Institution Press.

———. 1991. Introduction: Archaeological evidence of sixteenth- and seventeenth-century encounters. In Lisa Falk (Ed.), *Historical Archaeology in Global Perspective* (pp. 1–9). Washington, DC: Smithsonian Institution Press.

Fairbanks, Charles H. 1984. Plantation archaeology of the southeastern coast. *Historical Archaeology* 18: 1–14.

Falk, Lisa (Ed.). 1991. *Historical Archaeology in Global Perspective*. Washington, DC: Smithsonian Institution Press.

Fehrenbach, T. R. 1968. *Lone Star: A History of Texas and the Texans*. New York: Macmillan.

Ferguson, Leland B. 1992. *Uncommon Ground: Archaeology and Early African America, 1650–1800*. Washington, DC: Smithsonian Institution Press.

Fox, Richard. 1993. *Archaeology, History, and Custer's Last Battle: The Little Big Horn Re-examined*. Norman: University of Oklahoma Press.

Glassie, Henry. 1975. *Folk Housing in Middle Virginia*. Knoxville: University of Tennessee Press.

Handler, Jerome, and Frederick Lange. 1978. *Plantation Slavery in Barbados: An Archaeological and Historical Investigation*. Cambridge: Harvard University Press.

Handsman, Russell G., and Mark P. Leone. 1989. Living history and critical archaeology in the reconstruction of the past. In Valerie Pinsky and Alison Wylie (Eds.), *Critical Traditions in Contemporary Archaeology: Essays in the Philosophy, History and Socio-Politics of Archaeology* (pp. 117–135). Cambridge: Cambridge University Press.

Hume, Noël. 1964. Handmaiden to history. *North Carolina Historical Review* 41(2): 215–225 (quote is from p. 215).

Kelso, William M. 1986. Mulberry Row: Slave life at Thomas Jefferson's Monticello. *Archaeology* 39(5): 28–35.

Kidd, Kenneth E. 1949. *The Excavation of Ste Marie I*. Toronto: University of Toronto Press.

———. 1994. The phoenix of the north. In Stanley South (Ed.), *Pioneers in Historical Archaeology: Breaking New Ground* (pp. 49–65). New York: Plenum Press (quote is from p. 49).

Leone, Mark P. 1984. Interpreting ideology in historical archaeology: Using the rules of perspective in the

William Paca garden in Annapolis, Maryland. In Daniel Miller and Christopher Tilley (Eds.), *Ideology, Power, and Prehistory* (pp. 25–36). Cambridge: Cambridge University Press.

———. 1986. Symbolic, structural, and critical archaeology. In David J. Meltzer, Don D. Fowler, and Jeremy A. Sabloff (Eds.), *American Archaeology Past and Future: A Celebration of the Society for American Archaeology 1935–1985* (pp. 415–438). Washington, DC: Smithsonian Institution Press.

———. 1987. Rule by ostentation: The relationship between space and sight in eighteenth-century landscape architecture in the Chesapeake region of Maryland. In Susan Kent (Ed.), *Method and Theory for Activity Area Research: An Ethnoarchaeological Approach* (pp. 604–633). New York: Columbia University Press.

———. 1988a. The Georgian order as the order of merchant capitalism in Annapolis, Maryland. In Mark P. Leone and Parker B. Potter (Eds.), *The Recovery of Meaning: Historical Archaeology in the Eastern United States* (pp. 235–261). Washington, DC: Smithsonian Institution Press.

———. 1988b. The relationship between archaeological data and the documentary record: Eighteenth century gardens in Annapolis, Maryland. *Historical Archaeology* 22(1): 29–35 (quotes are from p. 32).

———. 1995. A historical archaeology of capitalism. *American Anthropologist* 97: 251–268 (quotes from p. 261, 262)

Leone, Mark P., Paul R. Mullins, Marian C. Creveling, Laurence Hurst, Barbara Jackson-Nash, Lynn D. Jones, Hannah Jopling Kaiser, George C. Logan, and Mark S. Warner. 1995. Can an African-American historical archaeology be an alternative voice? In Ian Hodder, Michael Shanks, Alexandra Alexandri, Victor Buchli, John Carman, Jonathan Last, and Gavin Lucas (Eds.), *Interpreting Archaeology: Finding Meaning in the Past* (pp. 110–124). London: Routledge.

Leone, Mark P., Parker B. Potter, Jr., and Paul A. Shackel. 1987. Toward a critical archaeology. *Current Anthropology* 28: 283–302.

Leone, Mark P., and Neil Asher Silberman. 1995. *Invisible America: Unearthing Our Hidden History.* New York: Henry Holt.

Little, Barbara J. (Ed.). 1992. *Text-Aided Archaeology.* Boca Raton, FL: CRC Press.

Ofori-Ansa, Kwaku. 1995. Identification and validation of the Sankofa symbol. *Update: Newsletter of the African Burial Ground and Five Points Archaeological Projects* 1(8): 3.

Orser, Charles E., Jr. 1984. The past ten years of plantation archaeology in the southeastern United States. *Southeastern Archaeology* 3: 1–12.

———. 1995. *A Historical Archaeology of the Modern World.* New York: Plenum.

Potter, Parker B., Jr. 1994. *Public Archaeology in Annapolis: A Critical Approach to History in Maryland's Ancient City.* Washington, DC: Smithsonian Institution Press.

Rothschild, Nan A. 1990. *New York City Neighborhoods: The 18th Century.* San Diego: Academic Press.

Schoelwer, Susan P. 1985. *Alamo Images: Changing Perceptions of a Texas Experience.* Dallas: DeGolyer Library and Southern Methodist University Press.

Schofield, John, William Gray Johnson, and Colleen M. Beck. 2002. *Matériel Culture: The Archaeology of Twentieth Century Conflict.* London: Routledge.

Schuyler, Robert. 1976. Images of America: The contribution of historical archaeology to national identity. *Southwestern Lore* 42(4): 27–39.

Scott, Douglas D., Richard A. Fox, Melissa A. Connor, and Dick Harmon. 1989. *Archaeological Perspectives on the Battle of the Little Big Horn.* Norman: University of Oklahoma Press.

Scott, Elizabeth M. (Ed.). 1994. *Those of Little Note: Gender, Race, and Class in Historical Archaeology.* Tucson: University of Arizona Press.

Shackel, Paul A. 1993. *Personal Discipline and Material Culture: An Archaeology of Annapolis, Maryland, 1695–1870.* Knoxville: University of Tennessee Press.

———. 1996. *Culture Change and the New Technology: An Archaeology of the Early American Industrial Era.* New York: Plenum Press.

Shackel, Paul A., Paul R. Mullins, and Mark S. Warner. 1998. *Annapolis Pasts: Historical Archaeology in Annapolis, Maryland.* Knoxville: University of Tennesee Press.

Singleton, Theresa A. (Ed.). 1985. *The Archaeology of Slavery and Plantation Life.* Orlando, FL: Academic Press.

———. 1995. The archaeology of slavery in North America. *Annual Review of Anthropology* 24: 119–140. ("In Her Own Words" text quoted from pp. 121–2, 134–5)

Sobel, Mechal. 1987. *The World They Made Together: Black and White Values in Eighteenth-Century Virginia.* Princeton: Princeton University Press.

South, Stanley. 1977a. *Method and Theory in Historical Archeology.* New York: Academic Press.

——— (Ed.). 1977b. *Research Strategies in Historical Archaeology.* New York: Academic Press.

——— (Ed.). 1994. *Pioneers in Historical Archaeology: Breaking New Ground.* New York: Plenum Press.

Thomas, David Hurst. 1988. Saints and soldiers at Santa Catalina: Hispanic designs for colonial America. In Mark P. Leone and Parker B. Potter (Eds.), *The Recovery of Meaning in Historic Archaeology* (pp. 73–140). Washington, DC: Smithsonian Institution Press.

———. 1995. Spanish missions: Ideology and space at Santa Catalina. In Mark P. Leone and Neil Asher Silberman (Eds.), *Invisible America: Unearthing Our Hidden History* (pp. 66–67). New York: Henry Holt.

Wall, Diane diZerega. 1994. *The Archaeology of Gender: Separating the Spheres in Urban America.* New York: Plenum Press.

Weber, David J. 1988. Refighting the Alamo: Mythmaking and the Texas revolution. In *Myth and the History of the Hispanic Southwest: Essays by David J. Weber* (pp. 133–151). Albuquerque: University of New Mexico Press.

Chapter 17

Adovasio, J. M., and Ronald C. Carlisle. 1988. Some thoughts on cultural resource management archaeology in the United States. *Antiquity* 62: 72–87.

Anonymous. 1989. Archeology and the Oklahoma City Police Training Academy. *Newsletter, Oklahoma Archeological Survey* 8(4): 1.

Anyon, Roger, and T. J. Ferguson. 1995. Cultural resources management at the Pueblo of Zuni, New Mexico, USA. *Antiquity* 69: 913–930. ("In Their Own Words" text quoted from pp. 913–915.)

Blanton, Dennis B. 1995. The case for CRM training in academic institutions: The many faces of CRM. *Bulletin of the Society for American Archaeology* 13(4): 40–41.

Brodie, Neil, Jennifer Doole, and Colin Renfrew. 2001. *Trade in Illicit Antiquities: The Destruction of the World's Archaeological Heritage.* Cambridge: McDonald Institute of Archaeology.

Carpenter, Edmund. 1991. Repatriation policy and the Heye collection. *Museum Anthropology* 15(3): 15–18.

Cleere, Henry (Ed.). 1993. Managing the archaeological heritage. *Antiquity* 67: 400–402.

Cook, Karen. 1993. Bones of contention. *The Village Voice* 38(18): 23–27.

Domenici, Pete V. 1991. Preface B. In George S. Smith and John E. Ehrenhard (Eds.), *Protecting the Past* (pp. v–vi). Boca Raton, FL: CRC Press.

Echo-Hawk, Roger C., and Walter R. Echo-Hawk. 1994. *Battlefields and Burial Grounds: The Indian Struggle to Protect Ancestral Graves in the United States.* Minneapolis: Lerner.

Echo-Hawk, Walter (Ed.). 1992. Special Issue: Repatriation of American Indian remains. *American Indian Culture and Research Journal* 16(2): 1–200.

Elia, Ricardo J. 1993. U.S. cultural resource management and the ICAHM charter. *Antiquity* 67: 426–438.

Elston, Robert G. 1992. Archaeological research in the context of cultural resource management: Pushing back in the 1990s. *Journal of California and Great Basin Anthropology* 14: 37–48.

Fowler, Don D. 1982. Cultural resources management. In Michael B. Schiffer (Ed.), *Advances in Archaeological Method and Theory.* Vol. 5 (pp. 1–50). New York: Academic Press.

———. 1986. Conserving American archaeological resources. In David J. Meltzer, Don D. Fowler, and Jeremy A. Sabloff (Eds.), *American Archaeology: Past and Future: A Celebration of the Society for American Archaeology 1935–1985* (pp. 135–162). Washington, DC: Smithsonian Institution Press.

Gathercole, Peter, and David Lowenthal (Eds.). 1990. *The Politics of the Past.* London: Unwin Hyman.

Goldstein, Lynn, and Keith Kintigh. 1990. Ethics and the reburial controversy. *American Antiquity* 55: 585–591.

González-José, Rolando, Antonio González-Martín, Miguel Hernández, Héctor M. Pucciarelli, Marina Sardi, Alfonso Rosales, and Silvina Van der Molen. 2003. Craniometric evidence for palaeoamerican survival in Baja California. *Nature* 425: 62–65.

Harrington, Spencer P. M. 1991, May/June. The looting of Arkansas. *Archaeology* 44(3): 22–30.

———. 1993, March/April. Bones and bureaucrats. *Archaeology* 46(2): 28–38.

Hoffman, Ellen. 1993, December. Saving our world's heritage. *Omni,* pp. 52–54, 58, 60–61.

Holloway, Marguerite. 1995. The preservation of the past. *Scientific American* 272(5): 98–101.

King, Thomas F. 1991. Some dimensions of the pothunting problem. In George S. Smith and John E. Ehrenhard (Eds.), *Protecting the Past* (pp. 83–92). Boca Raton, FL: CRC Press.

Lipe, William. 2002. In defense of digging: Archaeological preservation as a means, not an end. In Mark J. Lynott and Alison Wylie (Eds.), *Ethics in American Archaeology*. 2d ed. (pp. 113–117). Washington, DC: Society for American Archaeology.

Lovvorn, Marjorie B., George W. Gill, Gayle F. Carlson, John R. Bozell, and Terry L. Steinacher. 1999. Microevolution and the skeletal traits of a Middle Archaic burial: Metric and multivariate comparison to paleoindians and modern Amerindians. *American Antiquity* 64: 527–545.

McGimsey, C. R., III, and H. A. Davis. 1977. *The Management of Archaeological Resources: The Airlie House Report*. Washington DC: Society for American Archaeology.

McManamon, Francis P. 1991. The many publics for archaeology. *American Antiquity* 56: 121–130.

———. 1992. Managing America's archaeological resources. In LuAnn Wandsnider (Ed.), Quandaries and Quests: Visions of Archaeology's Future (pp. 25–40). *Center for Archaeological Investigations, Occasional Paper*, no. 20. Carbondale: Southern Illinois University.

———. 1994. Changing relationships between Native Americans and archaeologists. *Historic Preservation Forum* 8(2): 15–20.

McManamon, Francis P., and Alf Hatton. 2000. *Cultural Resource Management in Contemporary Society*. London: Routledge.

McManamon, Francis P., Patricia C. Knoll, Ruthann Knudson, George S. Smith, and Richard C. Waldbauer (Comps.). 1993. *The Secretary of the Interior's Report to Congress: Federal Archeological Programs and Activities*. Washington, DC: Departmental Consulting Archeologist Archeological Assistance Program, National Park Service, Dept. of the Interior.

Messenger, Phyllis (Ed.). 1989. *The Ethics of Collecting Cultural Property: Whose Culture? Whose Property?* Albuquerque: University of New Mexico Press.

Murray, Tim. 1996. Coming to terms with the living: Some aspects of repatriation for the archaeologist. *Antiquity* 70: 217–220.

National Park Service. 1995, Fall/Winter. Special Report: The Native American Graves Protection and Repatriation Act. *Federal Archeology*.

Neary, John. 1993, September/October. Project sting. *Archaeology*, pp. 52–59.

Preston, Douglas J. 1989. Skeletons in our museums' closets. *Harper's Magazine* (February) 278(1665): 66–75 (quote by Walter Echo-Hawk from p. 75).

Richman, Jennifer R., and Marion P. Forsyth (Eds.). 2003. *Legal Perspectives on Cultural Resources*. Walnut Creek, CA: Altamira Press.

Rose, Jerome C., Thomas J. Green, and Victoria D. Green. 1996. NAGPRA is forever: Osteology and the repatriation of skeletons. *Annual Review of Anthropology* 25: 81–103.

Russell, Steve. 1995. The legacy of ethnic cleansing: Implementation of NAGPRA in Texas. *American Indian Culture and Research Journal* 19(4): 193–211.

Shackley, Steven. 1995, March. Relics, rights and regulations. *Scientific American*, p. 115.

Smith, George S., and John E. Ehrenhard (Eds.). 1991. *Protecting the Past*. Boca Raton, FL: CRC Press.

Smith, Laurajane. 1994. Heritage management as postprocessual archaeology? *Antiquity* 68: 300–309.

Staley, David P. 1993. The antiquities market. *Journal of Field Archaeology* 20: 347–355.

Thompson, Raymond H. 2000. Edgar Lee Hewett and the political process. *Journal of the Southwest* 42: 273–318.

Wendorf, Fred, and Raymond H. Thompson. 2002. The Committee for the Recovery of Archaeological Remains: Three decades of service to the archaeological profession. *American Antiquity* 67: 317–330.

Woodbury, Nathalie F. S. 1992, March. When my grandmother is your database: Reactions to repatriation. *Anthropology Newsletter*, pp. 6, 22.

Chapter 18

Arden, H. 1989. Who owns our past? *National Geographic Magazine* 175(3): 376–392.

Arnold, Bettina. 1992, July/August. The past as propaganda. *Archaeology* 45(4): 30–37.

Bray, Tamara L., and Thomas W. Killion (Eds.). 1994. *Reckoning With the Dead: The Larsen Bay Repatriation and the Smithsonian Institution*. Washington, DC: Smithsonian Institution Press.

Brear, Holly. 1995. *Inherit the Alamo: Myth and Ritual at an American Shrine.* Austin: University of Texas Press (quote is from p. 146).

Butler, V. L. and M. G. Delacorte. 2004. Doing zooarchaeology as if it mattered: Use of faunal data to address current issues in fish conservation biology in Owens Valley, California. In R. L. Lyman and K. Cannon (Eds.), *Zooarchaeology and Conservation Biology.* Salt Lake City: University of Utah Press (forthcoming).

Carney, Heath J., Michael W. Binford, Alan L. Kolata, Ruben R. Marin, and Charles R. Goldman. 1993. Nutrient and sediment retention in Andean raised-field agriculture. *Nature* 364: 131–133.

Connor, Melissa. 1996. The archaeology of contemporary mass graves. *Bulletin of the Society for American Archaeology* 14(4): 6, 31.

Crowell, Aron L., Amy F. Steffian, and Gordon L. Pullar (Eds.). 2001. *Looking Both Ways: Heritage and Identity of the Alutiiq People.* Fairbanks: University of Alaska Press.

Deloria, Vine, Jr. 1992a. Indians, archaeologists, and the future. *American Antiquity* 57: 595–598.

———. 1992b. Afterword. In Alvin M. Josephy, Jr. (Ed.), *America in 1492: The World of the Indian Peoples Before the Arrival of Columbus* (pp. 429–443). New York: Knopf.

———. 1993. Sacred lands. *Winds of Change* 8(4): 30–37.

———. 1995. *Red Earth, White Lies: Native Americans and the Myth of Scientific Fact.* New York: Scribner's.

Eddy, John A. 1974. Astronomical alignment of the Big Horn medicine wheel. *Science* 184: 1035–1043.

———. 1977. Medicine wheels and Plains Indian astronomy. In Anthony F. Aveni (Ed.), *Native American Astronomy* (pp. 147–169). Austin: University of Texas Press.

Erickson, Clark L. 1988. Raised field agriculture in the Lake Titicaca Basin: Putting ancient agriculture back to work. *Expedition* 30(3): 8–16.

———. 1992a. Applied archaeology and rural development: Archaeology's potential contribution to the future. *Journal of the Steward Anthropological Society* 20(1, 2): 1–16.

———. 1992b. Prehistoric landscape management in the Andean highlands: Raised field agriculture and its environmental impact. *Population and Environment* 13(4): 285–300.

———. 1993. The social organization of prehispanic raised field agriculture in the Lake Titicaca Basin. In

V. L. Scarborough and B. L. Isaac (Eds.), *Research in Economic Anthropology: Economic Aspects of Water Management in the Prehistoric New World.* Supplement 7: 369–426. Greenwich, CT: JAI Press.

———. 1995. Archaeological methods for the study of ancient landscapes of the Llanos de Mojos in the Bolivian Amazon. In Peter W. Stahl (Ed.), *Archaeology in the Lowland American Tropics: Current Analytical Methods and Applications* (pp. 66–95). Cambridge: Cambridge University Press.

———. 2003. Agricultural landscapes as world heritage: Raised field agriculture in Bolivia and Peru. In Jeanne-Marie Teutonico and Frank Matero (Eds.), *Managing Change: Sustainable Approaches to the Conservation of the Built Environment* (pp. 181–204). Oxford: Getty Conservation Institute and Oxford University Press.

Ferguson, T. J. 1996. Native Americans and the practice of archaeology. *Annual Review of Anthropology* 25: 63–79.

Ford, Richard I. 1973. Archeology serving humanity. In Charles L. Redman (Ed.), *Research and Theory in Current Archeology* (pp. 83–93). New York: Wiley.

Fowler, Don. 1987. Uses of the past: Archaeology in the service of the state. *American Antiquity* 52: 229–248.

Green, Ernestine L. (Ed.). 1984. *Ethics and Values in Archaeology.* New York: Free Press.

Greenbuerg, D. W. 1929. Sheridan's historic settings. *The Midwest Review* 7(10): 50–69ff, 71, 90 (quote describing Red Plume's vision from p. 66).

Greenlee, Bob. 1995. *Life Among the Ancient Ones: Two Accounts of an Anasazi Archaeological Research Project.* Boulder: Hardscrabble Press.

Grey, Don. 1963. Big Horn medicine wheel site, 48BH302. *Plains Anthropologist* 8: 27–40.

Kay, C. E. and R. T. Simmons (Eds.). 2002. *Wilderness and Political Ecology: Aboriginal Influences and the Original State of Nature.* Salt Lake City: University of Utah Press.

Klesert, Anthony L. 1992. A view from Navajoland on the reconciliation of anthropologists and Native Americans. *Human Organization* 51: 17–22.

Klesert, Anthony L., and Alan S. Downer (Eds.). 1990. Preservation on the reservation: Native Americans, Native American lands and archaeology. *Navajo Nation Papers in Anthropology*, no. 26.

Klesert, Anthony L., and Shirley Powell. 1993. A perspective on ethics and the reburial controversy. *American Antiquity* 58: 348–354.

Kolata, Alan L., and Charles Ortloff. 1989. Thermal analysis of Tiwanaku raised field systems in the Lake Titicaca Basin of Bolivia. *Journal of Archaeological Science* 16: 233–263.

Lauwerier, R. C. G. M., and I. Plug (Eds.). 2004. *The Future from the Past: Archaeozoology in Wildlife Conservation and Heritage Management.* Oxford: Oxbow Books.

Lipe, William D. 1995. The archeology of ecology. *Federal Archaeology* 8(1): 8–13.

Long, William R. 1993, August 24. Old canals carry hope to Andes. *Los Angeles Times.*

Mansfield, Victor N. 1980. The Bighorn Medicine Wheel as a site for the vision quest. *Archaeoastronomy Bulletin* 3(2): 26–29.

Meighan, Clement.1992. Some scholars' views on reburial. *American Antiquity* 57: 704–710.

Nicholas, Lynn H. 1994. *The Rape of Europe: The Fate of Europe's Treasures in the Third Reich and the Second World War.* New York: Knopf.

Ovenden, Michael W., and David A. Rodger. 1981. Megaliths and medicine wheels. In Michael Wilson, Kathie L. Road, and Kenneth J. Hardy (Eds.), *Megaliths to medicine wheels: Boulder structures in archaeology. Proceedings of the Eleventh Annual Chacmool Conference* (pp. 371–386). Calgary: The Archaeological Association of the University of Calgary.

Powell, Shirley, Christiana Elnora Garza, and Aubrey Hendricks. 1993. Ethics and ownership of the past: The reburial and repatriation controversy. In Michael B. Schiffer (Ed.), *Archaeological Method and Theory.* Vol. 5 (pp. 1–42). Tucson: University of Arizona Press.

Rathje, William L. 1984. The garbage decade. *American Behavioral Scientist* 28(1): 9–29.

———. 1991. Once and future landfills. *National Geographic* 25(May): 116–134 (quote from p. 120).

Rathje, William, and Cullen Murphy. 2001. *Rubbish! The Archaeology of Garbage.* Tucson: University of Arizona Press.

Rathje, William L., W. W. Hughes, D. C. Wilson, M. K. Tani, G. H. Archer, R. G. Hunt, and T. W. Jones. 1992. The archaeology of contemporary landfills. *American Antiquity* 57: 437–447.

Riding In, James. 1992. With ethics and morality: A historical overview of imperial archaeology and American Indians. *Arizona State Law Journal* 24(1): 11–34.

Swidler, Nina, Kurt E. Dongoske, Roger Anyon, and Alan S. Downer (Eds.). 1997. *Native Americans and Archaeologists: Stepping Stones to Common Ground.* Walnut Creek, CA: Altamira Press.

Photo Credits

This page constitutes an extension of the copyright page. We have made every effort to trace the ownership of all copyrighted material and to secure permission from copyright holders. In the event of any question arising as to the use of any material, we will be pleased to make the necessary corrections in future printings. Thanks are due to the following authors, publishers, and agents for permission to use the material indicated.

Chapter 1 **1:** © Faith Kidder Fuller/School of American Research **5:** © David H. Thomas **7:** © American Museum of Natural History **9:** © Robert Neuman/Harvard University **10:** © American Museum of Natural History **11:** © Faith Kidder Fuller **13:** © American Museum of Natural History and Junius Bird **15:** © Denver Museum of Nature and Science **16:** Courtesy of Walter W. Taylor **17:** Courtesy of Lewis R. Binford, photo by Grant Spearman **20:** © Kathleen Deagan

Chapter 2 **24:** Courtesy of the Southeast Archaeological Center, National Park Service, photo by David G. Anderson **31:** © American Museum of Natural History **35 (top):** © Ohio Historical Society **35 (bottom):** © Peabody Museum, Harvard University **44:** © American Museum of Natural History **45:** © American Museum of Natural History, drawing by Diana Salles

Chapter 3 **50:** © Ofer Bar-Yosef **53:** © American Museum of Natural History, photo by Dennis O'Brien **55:** © University of Wyoming, Frison Institute **56:** © Robert Kelly, photo by Jim Yount **63:** © Charles & Josette Lenars/CORBIS **65:** © Stuart Rome, Drexel University **67:** © David H. Thomas **70:** © Charles E. Lord, Museum of New Mexico **72:** © Michelle Hegmon

Chapter 4 **77:** © Dewitt Jones/CORBIS **81:** © American Museum of Natural History **84:** © Robert Kelly **85:** © American Museum of Natural History, photo by Dennis O'Brien **92:** © Charles A. Lindbergh; Courtesy of the School of American Research **97:** © Robert Kelly **100:** © American Museum of Natural History, photo by Dennis O'Brien **102:** © David H. Thomas

Chapter 5 **107:** © American Museum of Natural History, photo by Samantha Williams **113:** After Boyd et al. (1951); courtesy of the University Press of Florida **114:** © American Museum of Natural History, photo by Dennis O'Brien **117:** © Payson Sheets **118 (top):** © Payson Sheets **118 (bottom):** © Payson Sheets **122:** © Wescott and Kuiper and Taylor & Francis Publishing **123:** © David Zeanah

Chapter 6 **128:** © American Museum of Natural History, photo by Deborah Mayer O'Brien **131:** © Robert Kelly **132:** © Denver Museum of Nature and Science **133 (top left):** © National Museum of the American Indian **133 (top right):** © Ruth Kirk **134 (top):** © AP/Wide World Photos **134 (bottom):** © South Tyrol Museum of Archaeology/www.iceman.it **143:** © Robert Kelly **146 (top):** © Robert Kelly **146 (bottom):** © Patty Jo Watson **148:** © Chap Kusimba

Chapter 7 **151:** © American Museum of Natural History, photo by Susan Bierwirth **154:** © American Museum of Natural History **155:** © American Museum of Natural History **160:** © American Museum of Natural History, photo by Susan Bierwirth **164:** Courtesy Museum of New Mexico **169:** © Shannon McPherron

Chapter 8 **175:** © Jeffrey S. Dean and the Laboratory of Tree Ring Research/University of Arizona **178:** © American Museum of Natural History **179:** © American Museum of Natural History, photo by Craig Chesek **182:** © American Museum of Natural History **191:** © David Lees/CORBIS **193:** © Ofer Bar-Yosef **196:** © James Ahern **198:** © Charles & Josette Lenars/CORBIS **201:** © Steven LeBlanc and the Mimbres Foundation **202:** © American Museum of Natural History

Chapter 9   206: From left © Archivo Iconografico, S.A./CORBIS; Bettmann/CORBIS; George H. H. Huey/ CORBIS **209:** Courtesy of the Navy Art Collection, Washington, DC **213:** © American Museum of Natural History **222:** © William Doelle **230:** © Donald Tuohy/ Nevada State Museum

Chapter 10   233: © Robert Kelly **238:** © Robert Kelly **239:** © Steven Brandt/Kathryn Weedman **242:** © Diana Gifford-Gonzales, photo by Michael J. Mehlman **243:** © Lawrence C. Todd **247:** © American Museum of Natural History **248 (left):** © James Woods **248 (right):** © American Museum of Natural History **253:** © Doug Damforth **257:** © Robert Kelly **262:** © Margaret Nelson

Chapter 11   265: © University of Wyoming, Frison Institute **268:** © University of Wyoming, Frison Institute **271:** © Matt Hill **275:** © Robert Kelly **281:** © Robert Kelly **283:** © Ralph Solecki **285:** © Susan Mulholland **286:** © Steve Jackson **291:** © Robert Kelly **293:** © Christine Hastorf

Chapter 12   296: © George Gill **304:** © Clark Larsen, photo by Barry Stark **305:** © Clark Larsen **308:** © Dorothy Lippert **316:** © Tom Dillehay **318:** © Smithsonian Institution, photo by Chip Clark

Chapter 13   322: © Wolfgang Kaehler/CORBIS **326:** © William S. Webb Museum of Anthropology **328:** © Barry Hewlett **330:** © Peabody Museum, Harvard University **336:** © James Enloe **338:** © Robert Kelly **340:** © The University of Alabama, Moundville Archaeological Park **341:** © American Museum of Natural History **351:** © Robert Kelly

Chapter 14   353: © Pierre Vauthey/CORBIS SYGMA **357:** © Robert Kelly **359:** © American Museum of Natural History **360:** © American Museum of Natural History **361 (top left):** © Robert Kelly **361 (bottom):** © Robert Kelly **367:** © American Museum of Natural History **374:** © Charles & Josette Lenars/CORBIS

Chapter 15   377: © Charles & Josette Lenars/CORBIS **388:** © Kim Hill **391:** © Ofer Bar-Yosef **397:** © Robert Kelly **402:** © San Diego Museum of Man, photo by Peter D. Harrison, ca. 1993 **403:** © American Museum of Natural History **404:** © Peabody Museum, Harvard University

Chapter 16   408: © Buffalo Bill Historical Center, Cody, Wyoming **411:** © Lin Poyer **414:** © William Keslo and the Thomas Jefferson Memorial Foundation **415:** © William Kelso and the Archaeological Institute of America **418:** © The Granger Collection, N.Y. **419:** Courtesy of African Burial Ground and U.S. General Services Administration **422:** © Kathleen Deagan **424:** Courtesy of the Autry National Center/Southwest Museum, Los Angeles **429:** © Maryland Historical Society **431:** © Parker Potter

Chapter 17   435: © Charles Reher **438:** © Terry Fifield **440:** © Robert Kelly **448:** © Paul Minnis/Mimbres Foundation **450:** © David Pollack/Kentucky Heritage Council **452:** © Barbara Mills

Chapter 18   464: Courtesy Alutiiq Museum, photo by Richard Lee **467:** Courtesy Bill Rathje, photo by Jim Sugar **471:** © Robert Kelly **472:** © Clea Koff/Physicians for Human Rights **476:** © Clark Erikson **479:** © David H. Thomas **480:** © David H. Thomas **482:** © U.S. Forest Service **490:** © Ben Fitzhugh

Index

Iñupiaq people, 488
Iraqi museums, 228–229
Iron deficiency anemia, 303
Iroquois people, 335
Irrigation hypothesis, 395–396, 406
Ishi, 245, 246–247
Isotopes
    carbon, 184–185, 308
    nitrogen, 309–311
Ituri Rain Forest, 327–328

James, King of England, 6
Jankuhn, Herbert, 485
Jefferson, Thomas, 35–36, 40, 62, 414–417
Jennings, Jesse, 80
Jinmium Rockshelter, 194
Johannessen, Sissel, 292–294, 329
Johanson, Don, 26
Johnson, Allen, 397
Johnson, Frederick, 442
Joyce, Rosemary, 329–331
Judge, James, 91

Kafka, Franz, 62
Kamminga, Johan, 255
Kant, Immanuel, 62
Kantner, John, 125
Karwa site, 363
Keeley, Lawrence, 252–253, 254
Keesing, Roger, 30
Kelly, Robert, 258
Kelso, William, 415
Kennewick Man
    cultural affiliation of, 460–461
    discovery and analysis of, 2–3
    NAGPRA legislation and, 3, 459–461, 486–487
    skull shape of, 317–318, 459
Keres people, 124
Khufu's pyramid, 197–199
Kidd, Kenneth, 410
Kidder, Alfred V. "Ted," 1, 11–12, 15, 16, 66, 109, 131, 179, 442
Kill sites, 267
Kinship, 331–338
    bilateral descent, 332
    Chaco Canyon example, 335–338
    clans and moieties, 333
    food sharing and, 336–337
    forms of, 332–334
    matrilineal descent, 333, 335
    Moundville example, 344–346
    patrilineal descent, 332–333
    residence patterns, 334–335
    social status and, 344–346
Kivas, 237, 238, 239
Kluckhohn, Clyde, 28

Kneberg, Madeline, 14
Knight, Vernon, 345
Knorosov, Yuri, 403
Koch, Joan, 202
Koczka, Charles S., 454
Kodiak Island, 488–490
Koff, Clea, 472–473
Koshares, 68, 70
Kossinna, Gustav, 484
Kowalewski, Stephen, 102, 103
Kramer, Carol, 237
Kroeber, Alfred, 28, 132, 180, 245, 246–247
Krotovina, 167
Kuiper, James, 121, 122
Kus, Susan, 340–342
Kusimba, Chapurukha (Chap), 148–149
Kusimba, Sibel Barut, 149
Kuznar, Lawrence, 33
Kwakwak'awakw potlatch, 30–33

Laetoli footprints, 153–156
    age of, 155–156
    current status of, 157
    discovery of, 153–154
    geologic profile of, 154–155, 156
Laetolil Beds, 154–155
La Isabela, 20, 21
Lakota people, 423
La María site, 357
Laming-Emperaire, Annette, 368, 370
Lamus, Blair, 80
La Navidad, 20
Landfills, 468–470
Landsat satellite images, 111
Landscape archaeology, 122–125
    Carson Desert and, 123–124
    Chacoan roads and, 124–125
Language
    historical linguistics and, 317
    linguistic anthropology and, 27–28
Laramie Treaty (1868), 423
Larsen, Clark Spencer, 297, 299–307
Larsen Bay Tribal Council, 489
Lascaux cave site, 345, 367, 371–375
    description of, 371–374
    discovery of, 372–373
    map of, 371
    meaning of images in, 374–375
Last of the Mohicans, The (Cooper), 68
Late Preclassic Period, 401
Lathrap, Donald, 362
Latinos, 481
Law of superposition, 153–156
    example of, 153–156
    formulation of, 153